Freedom on My Mind

A HISTORY OF AFRICAN AMERICANS

with Documents for the AP® COURSE

Alysha Butler
McKinley Technology High School, Washington, D.C.

Rachel Williams-Giordano
Cambridge Rindge and Latin School, Massachusetts

Deborah Gray White
Rutgers University

Mia Bay
University of Pennsylvania

Waldo E. Martin Jr.
University of California, Berkeley

bedford, freeman & worth publishers
Boston | New York

Updated Third Edition

Program Director, High School: Yolanda Cossio
Program Manager, High School Humanities and U.S. History: Caitlin Kaufman
Executive Development Editor for High School Media: Lisa Samols
Development Editors: Amber Jones, Mark Leidner, Sophie Dora Tulchin
Senior Media Editor for Assessment: Justin Perry
Associate Media Editor: Michael Emig
Associate Project Manager, Content Development: Sophie Dora Tulchin
Director of Marketing, High School: Janie Pierce-Bratcher
Marketing Manager, High School: Tiffani Tang
Marketing Coordinator, High School: Brianna DiGeronimo
Senior Director, Content Management Enhancement: Tracey Kuehn
Executive Managing Editor: Michael Granger
Content Project Managers: Christina Horn, Edward Dionne
Senior Workflow Project Manager: Lisa McDowell
Production Supervisor: Brianna Lester
Director of Design, Content Management: Diana Blume
Interior Design: Jerilyn DiCarlo
Cover Design: William Boardman
Art Manager: Matthew McAdams
Senior Director, Rights and Permissions: Hilary Newman
Associate Director, Research and Permissions, Text Assets: Elaine Kosta, Lumina Datamatics, Inc.
Senior Executive Permissions Editor, Art Permissions: Cecilia Varas
Photo Researcher: Krystyna Borgen, Lumina Datamatics, Inc.
Project Management: Nagalakshmi Karunanithi, Project Manager, Lumina Datamatics, Inc.
Copyeditor: Matthew Van Atta
Composition: Lumina Datamatics, Inc.
Printing and Binding: Lakeside Book Company

ISBN 978-1-319-57982-1 (Student Edition)

Printed in the United States of America.

1 2 3 4 5 6 30 29 28 27 26 25

Acknowledgments

Text acknowledgments and copyrights appear at the back of the book on page N-22, which constitutes an extension of the copyright page. Art acknowledgments and copyrights appear on the same page as the art selections they cover.

Bedford, Freeman & Worth Publishers
120 Broadway, New York, NY 10271
bfwpub.com/catalog

For the ancestors whose wings were clipped but who still taught us how to fly: Bernice Moltimore Butler, Cecil Butler, and Joseph Williams especially

For our children: Miles Edward Arnold, Anthony J. Giordano III, Alexios J. Giordano, and Angelo J. Giordano

And for the students learning to spread their wings in your classrooms today

About the Cover Image

Night Bird ▸ **Delita Martin, 2020**

Much like the AP® African American Studies Course, *Night Bird* by Delita Martin is a work of art that draws from several different mediums. A relief printing made from charcoal, acrylic, liquid gold leaf, decorative papers, and hand stitching, this image conveys a multifaceted interpretation of the African American experience, even as it features a singular subject.

Delita Martin is an artist currently based in Huffman, Texas, whose work has been exhibited both nationally and internationally. Her current work deals with reconstructing the identity of Black women by piecing together the signs, symbols, and language found in what could be called everyday life from slavery through modern times. Martin's goal is to create images as a visual language to tell the story of women who have often been marginalized, offering a different perspective of the lives of Black women.

About the Authors of the AP® Edition

Alysha Butler

Alysha Butler is a 24-year veteran social studies teacher who currently teaches AP® African American Studies and U.S. History for District of Columbia Public Schools. She has also served on the Development Committee for the AP® African American Studies course. As a Senior Program Manager for Inclusive Social Studies Curriculum for the Digital Team at GBH, she has developed and written online resources for PBS LearningMedia's History and Civics Collections. She graduated from Florida Atlantic University with a B.A. and M.A. in History with a special focus on African American women during Reconstruction. She was awarded the 2024 Margaret Sue Copenhaver Contribution to Education Award, recognized as the 2019 History Teacher of the Year by the Daughters of the American Revolution for the District of Columbia, and was 2019 Gilder Lehrman National History Teacher of the Year for her innovative lessons and civics-based student projects. In 2019 she was a D.C. Community Cornerstone Awardee, and in 2020 she became the first teacher ever appointed to the Gilder Lehrman Board of Trustees. She has presented at the National Council for Social Studies Convention, the CCSSO Social Studies Collaborative, and the Middle States Council of Social Studies Convention. Her most recent published essays include "Why My Students Were Not Surprised on January 6th" and "Avoiding the Trap of Whitewashing the Founding Era: Teaching Black Liberation during the American Revolution." She is also author of the chapter "Giving Honor and Teaching History in Life and Death: Teaching History and Civic Duty with the Preservation of Black Cemeteries" in *Bringing Teachers to the History Museum: A Guide to Facilitating Teacher Professional Development* (Rowman & Littlefield) and "Insurrection Nation" in *Hot Button: Teaching Sensitive Social Studies Content* (The Book House).

Photo by Debi Milligan

Rachel Williams-Giordano is a high school social science teacher at Cambridge Rindge and Latin in Cambridge, Massachusetts. She holds M.A.T. and M.Ed. degrees from Emmanuel College and a B.S. in Political Science from Georgia Southern University. Rachel has over 15 years of experience in the classroom and was a Massachusetts History Teacher of the Year finalist in 2023. She currently teaches AP® United States History, AP® United States Government and Politics, and AP® African American Studies, which she launched at Cambridge Rindge Latin School during its pilot phase. She has also served as a Reader and Question Leader for the AP® African American Studies Exam as well as a Reader for the AP® United States Government and Politics Exam. In addition to her work in the classroom, Rachel has mentored student teachers from Harvard University and Brandeis University, served as co-chair for the Faculty Advisory Committee at her school, and currently serves as a union representative. In her previous teaching roles at Boston Collegiate Charter School, Rachel developed a new curriculum for her ninth-grade Global Studies course and led the ninth-grade teaching team at Boston Collegiate Charter School. After five years at Boston Collegiate, Rachel was offered a principal fellowship with UP Education, which led to her accepting a role as Principal of Match Charter School, where she led instructional programming and supervised staff and students. As the lead APSI consultant nationally for the AP® African American Studies course since 2022, she facilitates the training of both new and experienced teachers nationwide.

About the Authors of *Freedom on My Mind*

Bill Cardoni

Deborah Gray White (Ph.D., University of Illinois at Chicago) is Emeritus Board of Governors Distinguished Professor of History at Rutgers University. She is the author of many works including *Lost in the USA: American Identity from the Promise Keepers to the Million Mom March*; *Too Heavy a Load: Black Women in Defense of Themselves, 1894–1994*; *Let My People Go: African-Americans, 1804–1860*; *Ar'n't I a Woman? Female Slaves in the Plantation South*; and the edited volume *Telling Histories: Black Women Historians in the Ivory Tower*. She is a recipient of the John Simon Guggenheim Fellowship and the Woodrow Wilson International Center Fellowship. She holds the Carter G. Woodson Medallion and the Frederick Douglass Medal for excellence in African American history. She is a recipient of the Stephen A. Ambrose Oral History Award, and the Association for the Study of African American Life and History Living Legacy Award. As coeditor of the three-volume *Scarlet and Black* series, White led the investigation of the three-century history of Native Americans and African Americans at Rutgers University.

Trustees of the University of Pennsylvania

Mia Bay (Ph.D., Yale University) is the Paul A. Mellon Professor of American History at the University of Cambridge. Her publications include the Bancroft Prize-winning *Traveling Black: A Story of Race and Resistance*; *To Tell the Truth Freely: The Life of Ida B. Wells*; *The White Image in the Black Mind: African-American Ideas about White People, 1830–1925*; and the edited volume *Ida B. Wells, The Light of Truth: Writings of an Anti-Lynching Crusader*. She is a recipient of the Alphonse Fletcher Sr. Fellowship and the National Humanities Center Fellowship. An Organization of American Historians Distinguished Lecturer, Bay is a member of the executive board of the Society of American Historians, serves on the editorial boards of the *Journal of African American History*, *Modern Intellectual History*, and the African American Intellectual History Society's *Black Perspectives* blog, and is on the Scholarly Advisory Board of the Gilder Lehrman Institute. Currently, she is at work on a study of African American views on Thomas Jefferson.

Coral Martin

Waldo E. Martin Jr. is the Alexander F. and May T. Morrison Professor of American History and Citizenship at the University of California, Berkeley. The principal focus of his scholarship and teaching is the Modern African American Freedom Struggle. With Joshua Bloom, he co-authored *Black Against Empire: The History and Politics of the Black Panther Party* (2013, rev. 2016). With Jetta Grace Martin and Joshua Bloom, he coauthored a Young Adult history of the party: *Freedom! The Story of the Black Panther Party* (Levine Querido, 2022). The second edition of his *Brown v. Board of Education: A Brief History with Documents* was published in 2020. His first book, *The Mind of Frederick Douglass*, was published in 1985. His book of essays *No Coward Soldiers: Black Cultural Politics in Postwar America* came out in 2005. With Deborah Gray White and Mia Bay, he is the coauthor of *Freedom on My Mind: A History of African Americans with Documents* (2017). With Patricia A. Sullivan, he is the coeditor of *Civil Rights in the US: An Encyclopedia* (2 vols., 2000). His current book project is *A Change Is Gonna Come*, an analysis of the cultural politics of the modern African American freedom struggle.

Dear Future AP® African American Studies Students:

Riley Ferrell

As you embark on this journey into the rich and complex history of African American life, culture, and contributions, I want to extend a warm welcome. This course is not just another history class, it is an exploration of the deep, enduring impact that African Americans have had on the fabric of the United States and the world. It challenges the conventional narratives and invites you to engage with history, literature, politics, and culture in ways that will transform your understanding of the past and present.

What to Expect

AP® African American Studies is a rigorous and deeply enriching course that will push you intellectually and emotionally. You will encounter stories of resilience, struggle, and triumph that have shaped the African American experience. Expect to engage with a wide array of primary sources — speeches, letters, autobiographies, and artistic works — that bring history to life in a vivid and personal way. You'll discuss pivotal events like the transatlantic slave trade, the Harlem Renaissance, the Civil Rights movement, and contemporary issues that continue to shape the African American experience.

This class requires an open mind and a willingness to critically engage with material that may be both challenging and enlightening. It will also demand a high level of commitment, not just in terms of workload but in the depth of thought and reflection you bring to your studies. You will need to be prepared for vigorous discussions, complex readings, and thought-provoking assignments that encourage you to think critically about the world around you.

Why This Class Is Exceptional

What makes this course truly extraordinary is the way it connects the dots between history and contemporary issues. It provides a lens through which you can better understand current social justice movements, the importance of cultural expression, and the ongoing quest for equality and human dignity. This course is not just about learning history; it's about understanding how history lives within us, influences us, and drives us forward.

For me, this class has been nothing short of transformative. It has given me a deeper appreciation for the creativity of African Americans, and it has sharpened my critical thinking skills. I've gained a richer understanding of how history is constructed and the importance of diverse voices in shaping our collective memory. The knowledge and perspectives I've acquired here will stay with me long after I've left the classroom.

I encourage you to approach this course with an open heart and a curious mind. Let it challenge you, inspire you, and perhaps even change you. The stories you will learn are not just those of the past; they are the stories of today, and they will guide us into the future.

Best wishes,

Riley Ferrell

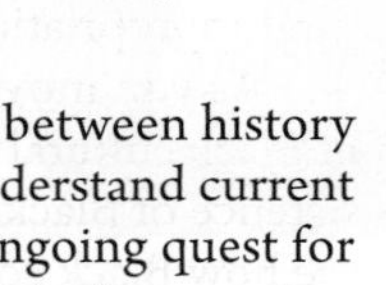

AP® African American Studies student in Rachel Williams-Giordano's class,
Cambridge-Rindge and Latin School

Courtesy Tyrone Lee

This course off ers an immersive exploration of Black history and culture, designed to reshape the way you view the world and your place within it. Throughout this journey, you will discover how deeply connected modern Black culture is to centuries of rich traditions, innovations, and struggles. From the clothes we wear to the music we listen to, every aspect of contemporary Black culture can be traced back to our ancestors and their lived experiences, spanning from the African continent to the diaspora. The rhythms and melodies of African drumbeats echo in today's hip-hop, jazz, and gospel. The colors, styles, and patt erns of modern fashion are infused wiThsymbolism, telling stories of heritage and resistance. Every chapter of Black history, whether marked by triumph or challenge, has left an indelible mark on the present.

This course goes far beyond simply memorizing dates, names, and events. It invites you to engage critically wiThthe past, to understand how Black culture has continually evolved and adapted through the centuries, all while shaping global societies. You will explore the complex intersections of race, identity, and power, learning how Black communities have created spaces for themselves in a world that oft en marginalized them. Through an in-depThstudy of historical movements like the Harlem Renaissance, the Civil Rights Movement, and the rise of Afrofuturism, you will see how art, literature, and activism have been powerful tools of expression and resistance.

What sets this course apart is its commitment to not only deepening your knowledge of Black history but also fostering a sense of connection and responsibility. You will be challenged to rethink common narratives, question what you know about Black culture, and appreciate the nuances and diversity within it. By examining the historical context of today's cultural phenomena, you'll see how issues like systemic racism, economic inequality, and cultural appropriation have their roots in the past and still aff ect modern Black communities.

As you move through the course, you'll develop a profound respect for the continuity of Black cultural expression and its infl uence on global trends. You'll also recognize the persistence of Black innovation, resistance, and resilience in the face of systemic barriers. You'll see how Black communities have continually found ways to thrive and contribute, infl uencing not just American society, but the entire world. From pioneering technology to shaping social movements and leading artistic revolutions, the contributions of Black people are vast and far-reaching.

By the end of this course, you won't simply be prepared for the AP exam. You will walk away wiTha whole new understanding of of Black history and its critical role in shaping our present and future. You'll be equipped wiThthe tools to analyze culture wiTha more critical eye, to see the connections between past and present, and to appreciate the deep-rooted infl uences that defi ne modern Black culture. Most importantly, you will leave wiTha heightened sense of pride, appreciation, and responsibility to carry forward the knowledge and legacies of those who have come before you.

Tyrone Lee

AP® African American Studies student in Alysha Butler's class,
McKinley Technology High School

Why This Book This Way

"Freedom is never voluntarily given by the oppressor; it must be demanded by the oppressed," wrote Martin Luther King Jr. in his "Letter from Birmingham City Jail." Written in April 1963 while he was incarcerated for participating in a nonviolent protest against racial segregation, King's letter was a rebuttal to white religious leaders who condemned such protests as unwise and untimely. King's understanding of freedom also summarizes the remarkable history of the many generations of African Americans whose experiences are chronicled in this book. Involuntary migrants to America, the Africans who became African Americans achieved freedom from slavery only after centuries of struggle, protest, and outright revolt. Prior to the Civil War, most were unfree inhabitants of a democratic republic that took shape around the ideals of "life, liberty, and the pursuit of happiness." Although largely exempted from these ideals, African Americans fought for them.

Writing of these enslaved noncitizens in the first chapter of *The Souls of Black Folk* (1903), Black historian W. E. B. Du Bois proclaimed, "Few men ever worshipped Freedom with half such unquestioning faith as did the American Negro." Du Bois saw a similar spirit among his contemporaries: he was certain that "there are to-day no truer exponents of the pure human spirit of the Declaration of Independence than the American Negroes." Yet Du Bois lived in an era when freedom was still the "unattained ideal." Segregated and disfranchised in the South, and subject to racial exploitation and discrimination throughout the nation, Black people still sought "the freedom of life and limb, the freedom to work and think, the freedom to love and aspire." Moreover, as long as Black people were not free, America could not be the world's beacon of liberty. The Black freedom struggle would continue, remaking the nation as a whole.

Our Approach

Like Du Bois, we, the authors of *Freedom on My Mind*, take African Americans' quest for freedom as the central theme of African American history and explore all dimensions of that quest, situated as it must be in the context of American history. Our perspective is that African American history complicates American history rather than diverges from it. This idea is woven into our narrative, which records the paradoxical experiences of a group of people at once the most American of Americans — in terms of their long history in America, their vital role in the American economy, and their enormous impact on American culture — and at the same time the Americans most consistently excluded from the American dream. Juxtaposed against American history as a whole, this is a study of a group of Americans who have had to fight too hard for freedom yet have been systematically excluded from many of the opportunities that allowed other groups to experience the United States as a land of opportunity. This text encourages students to think critically and analytically about African American history and the historical realities behind the American dream.

The following themes and emphases are central to our approach:

The principal role of the Black freedom struggle in the development of the American state. Our approach necessitates a study of the troubled relationship between African Americans and the American democratic state. *Freedom on My Mind* underscores the disturbing fact that our democracy arose within the context of a society structured around enslavement, though it ultimately gave way to the democratic forces unleashed by the Revolution that founded the new nation and the Civil War that reaffirmed federal sovereignty. Exempt from the universalist language of the Declaration of Independence — "all men are created equal" — African Americans have been, as Du Bois insightfully noted, "a concrete test of the underlying principles of the great republic." Most vividly illustrated during the political upheavals of Reconstruction and the Civil Rights movement — which is often called America's second Reconstruction — African American activism has been crucial to the evolution of American democratic institutions.

The diversity of African Americans and the African American experience. Any study of the African American freedom struggle must recognize the wide diversity of African Americans who participated in it, whether they did so through open rebellion and visible social protest; through more covert means of defiance, disobedience, and dissent; or simply by surviving and persevering in the face of overwhelming odds. Complicating any conceptions students might have of a single-minded, monolithic African American collective, *Freedom on My Mind* is mindful of Black diversity and the ways and means that gender, class, and ethnicity — as well as region, culture, and politics — shaped the Black experience and the struggle for freedom. The book explores African Americans' search for freedom in slave rebellions, everyday resistance to slavery, the abolitionist movement, Reconstruction politics, post-emancipation labor struggles, the Great Migration, military service, civil rights activism, Black Power, and the Black Lives Matter movement. It shows how American democracy was shaped by African Americans' search for, as Du Bois put it, "human opportunity."

An emphasis on culture as a vital force in Black history. *Freedom on My Mind* also illuminates the rich and self-affirming culture Blacks established in response to their exclusion from and often adversarial relationship with American institutions — the life Du Bois metaphorically characterized as "behind the veil." The rhythms and structure of Black social and religious life, the contours of Black educational struggles, the music Du Bois described as the "greatest gift of the Negro people" to the American nation, the parallel institutions built as a means of self-affirmation and self-defense — all of these are examined in the context of African Americans' quest for freedom, escape from degradation, and inclusion in the nation's body politic.

A synthesis that makes Black history's texture and complexity clear. While culture is central to *Freedom on My Mind*, we offer an analytical approach to African American culture that enables students to see it as a central force that both shaped and reflected other historical developments, rather than as a phenomenon in a vacuum. How do we process Black art — poetry, music, paintings, novels, sculptures, quilts — without understanding the political, economic, and social conditions that these pieces express?

When spirituals, jazz, the blues, and rap flow from the economic and social conditions experienced by multitudes of Blacks, how can we not understand Black music as political? Indeed, African American culture, politics, and identity are inextricably entwined in ways that call for an approach to this subject that blends social, political, economic, religious, and cultural history. Such distinctions often seem arbitrary in American history as a whole and are impossible in chronicling the experiences of African Americans. How can we separate the religious and political history of people whose church leaders have often led their communities from the pulpit and the political stump? Therefore, *Freedom on My Mind* sidesteps such divisions in favor of a synthesis that privileges the sustained interplay among culture, politics, economics, religion, and social forces in the African American experience.

Twenty-first-century scholarship for today's classroom. Each chapter offers a synthesis of the most up-to-date historiography and historiographical debates in a clear narrative style. So much has changed since Du Bois pioneered the field of African American history. Once relegated to Black historians and the oral tradition, African American history as a scholarly endeavor flowered with the social history revolt of the 1960s, when the events of the Civil Rights movement drew new attention to the African American past and the social upheaval of the 1960s inspired historians to recover the voices of the voiceless. Women's history also became a subject of serious study during this era, and as a result of all these changes, we now survey an American history that has been reconstituted by nearly a half century of sustained attention to race, class, and gender. Yet, although the scholarship has evolved since Du Bois wrote *Souls*, we have tried to remain true to the spirit of that text and write, with "loving emphasis," the history of African Americans.

Freedom on My Mind

What's Inside This AP® Edition

Written by three leading scholars of African American history and newly adapted to align with the AP® course by two leaders in AP® African American Studies, *Freedom on My Mind* empowers students to think critically and analytically about the diversity of African American experiences. This book examines African Americans' quest for freedom as a central theme, situating that quest in the context of American history.

In this updated AP® edition, supports for developing and practicing the core skills of the AP® course are threaded throughout the book, from Unit Openers aligned to the AP® course units to plenty of AP® Exam practice right where you need it. AP® Working with Sources document collections and AP® Skill Workshops at the end of each chapter build the source analysis and argumentation skills that are key to success in the course, on the exam, and in the course project.

Units aligned to the AP® course put key content in context.

Illustrated introductions align to each of the AP® course units, offering key context for historical and cultural developments. Unit Thematic Timelines place these developments in relationship to each of the AP® course themes. Unit Warmups provide practice with visual analysis and activate preexisting knowledge to engage students right off the bat.

AP® Working with Sources collections hone source analysis and argumentation skills.

Designed to build AP® source analysis and argumentation skills, these document collections feature primary textual and visual sources from all genres, with scaffolded analysis questions to help students analyze each document individually before tackling a practice Document-Based Question that accompanies each set.

AP® Skill Workshops provide consistent, scaffolded instruction and support.

These essential workshops are the ultimate reading and writing coaches, walking step-by-step through each of the course skills across multiple genres and how to apply them to the tasks they'll encounter on the AP® Exam and in the Individual Student Project.

AP® Exam Practice builds skills and confidence throughout the school year.

Completely new and exclusive to this edition, AP® Exam Practice appears at the end of every chapter and unit, plus there's a full-length Practice Exam at the back of the book, offering ample opportunity to practice new AP® skills.

Read on to learn more!

Unit openers aligned to the AP® course highlight and contextualize important content.

Short, informative **unit openers** introduce each unit, giving everyone a frame of reference for the unit content and a foundational understanding of context before moving into the chapters.

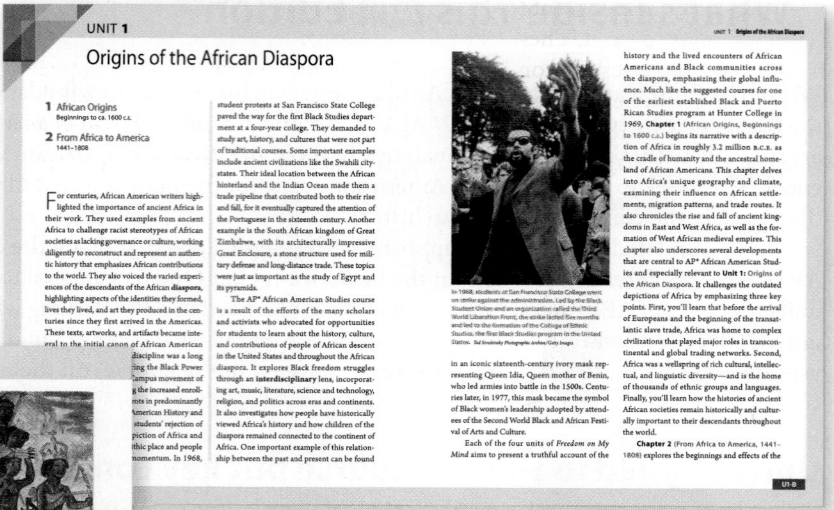
UNIT 1

Origins of the African Diaspora

1 African Origins
Beginnings to ca. 1600 C.E.

2 From Africa to America
1441–1808

For centuries, African American writers highlighted the importance of ancient Africa in their work. They used examples from ancient Africa to challenge racist stereotypes of African societies as lacking governance or culture, working diligently to reconstruct and represent an authentic history that emphasizes African contributions to the world. They also voiced the varied experiences of the descendants of the African **diaspora**, highlighting aspects of the identities they formed, lives they lived, and art they produced in the centuries since they first arrived in the Americas. These texts, artworks, and artifacts became integral to the initial canon of African American ... discipline was a long ... ing the Black Power ... ampus movement of ... g the increased enroll... nts in predominantly ... merican History and ... students' rejection of ... piction of Africa and ... thic place and people ... momentum. In 1968, student protests at San Francisco State College paved the way for the first Black Studies department at a four-year college. They demanded to study art, history, and cultures that were not part of traditional courses. Some important examples include ancient civilizations like the Swahili city-states. Their ideal location between the African hinterland and the Indian Ocean made them a trade pipeline that contributed both to their rise and fall, for it eventually captured the attention of the Portuguese in the sixteenth century. Another example is the South African kingdom of Great Zimbabwe, with its architecturally impressive Great Enclosure, a stone structure used for military defense and long-distance trade. These topics were just as important as the study of Egypt and its pyramids.

The AP® African American Studies course is a result of the efforts of the many scholars and activists who advocated for opportunities for students to learn about the history, culture, and contributions of people of African descent in the United States and throughout the African diaspora. It explores Black freedom struggles through an **interdisciplinary** lens, incorporating art, music, literature, science and technology, religion, and politics across eras and continents. It also investigates how people have historically viewed Africa's history and how children of the diaspora remained connected to the continent of Africa. One important example of this relationship between the past and present can be found in an iconic sixteenth-century ivory mask representing Queen Idia, Queen mother of Benin, who led armies into battle in the 1500s. Centuries later, in 1977, this mask became the symbol of Black women's leadership adopted by attendees of the Second World Black and African Festival of Arts and Culture.

Each of the four units of *Freedom on My Mind* aims to present a truthful account of the history and the lived encounters of African Americans and Black communities across the diaspora, emphasizing their global influence. Much like the suggested courses for one of the earliest established Black and Puerto Rican Studies program at Hunter College in 1969, **Chapter 1** (African Origins, Beginnings to 1600 C.E.) begins its narrative with a description of Africa in roughly 3.2 million B.C.E. as the cradle of humanity and the ancestral homeland of African Americans. This chapter delves into Africa's unique geography and climate, examining their influence on African settlements, migration patterns, and trade routes. It also chronicles the rise and fall of ancient kingdoms in East and West Africa, as well as the formation of West African medieval empires. This chapter also underscores several developments that are central to AP® African American Studies and especially relevant to **Unit 1:** Origins of the African Diaspora. It challenges the outdated depictions of Africa by emphasizing three key points. First, you'll learn that before the arrival of Europeans and the beginning of the transatlantic slave trade, Africa was home to complex civilizations that played major roles in transcontinental and global trading networks. Second, Africa was a wellspring of rich cultural, intellectual, and linguistic diversity—and is the home of thousands of ethnic groups and languages. Finally, you'll learn how the histories of ancient African societies remain historically and culturally important to their descendants throughout the world.

Chapter 2 (From Africa to America, 1441–1808) explores the beginnings and effects of the

In 1968, students at San Francisco State College went on strike against the administration. Led by the Black Student Union and an organization called the Third World Liberation Front, the strike lasted five months and led to the formation of the College of Ethnic Studies, the first Black Studies program in the United States. Ted Streshinsky Photographic Archive/Getty Images

U1-B

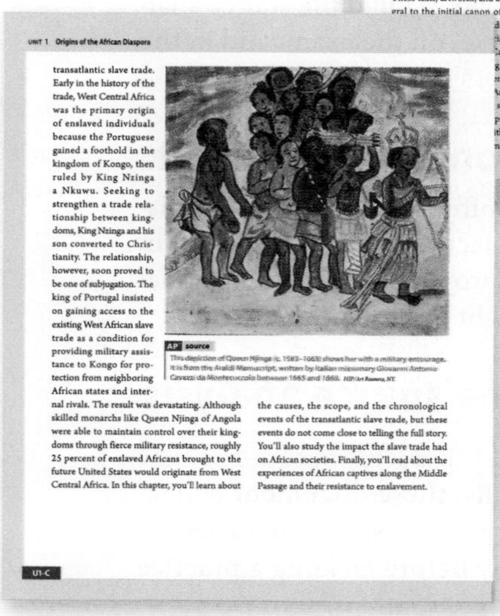
UNIT 1 Origins of the African Diaspora

transatlantic slave trade. Early in the history of the trade, West Central Africa was the primary origin of enslaved individuals because the Portuguese gained a foothold in the kingdom of Kongo, then ruled by King Nzinga a Nkuwu. Seeking to strengthen a trade relationship between kingdoms, King Nzinga and his son converted to Christianity. The relationship, however, soon proved to be one of subjugation. The king of Portugal insisted on gaining access to the existing West African slave trade as a condition for providing military assistance to Kongo for protection from neighboring African states and internal rivals. The result was devastating. Although skilled monarchs like Queen Njinga of Angola were able to maintain control over their kingdoms through fierce military resistance, roughly 25 percent of enslaved Africans brought to the future United States would originate from West Central Africa. In this chapter, you'll learn about the causes, the scope, and the chronological events of the transatlantic slave trade, but these events do not come close to telling the full story. You'll also study the impact the slave trade had on African societies. Finally, you'll read about the experiences of African captives along the Middle Passage and their resistance to enslavement.

AP source

This depiction of Queen Njinga (c. 1583–1663) shows her with a military entourage. It is from the Araldi Manuscript, written by Italian missionary Giovanni Antonio Cavazzi da Montecuccolo between 1665 and 1668. HIP/Art Resource, NY.

U1-C

◂ Illustrated unit introductions offer an overview of each unit's content.

These brief, accessible sections walk through key developments and processes covered in the chapters of a given unit. Here, you'll also find additional coverage of content in the AP® course and Exam Description that is not covered in any other textbook for this course.

▸ Thematic Unit Timelines tie history to the AP® course themes.

Unit introductions are followed by a **thematic unit timeline** contextualizing the chronology of key concepts, developments, and processes from the AP® African American Studies Course and Exam Description in relationship to the four AP® course themes: **Migration and the African Diaspora; Intersections of Identity; Creativity, Expression, and the Arts; and Resistance** and **Resilience.**

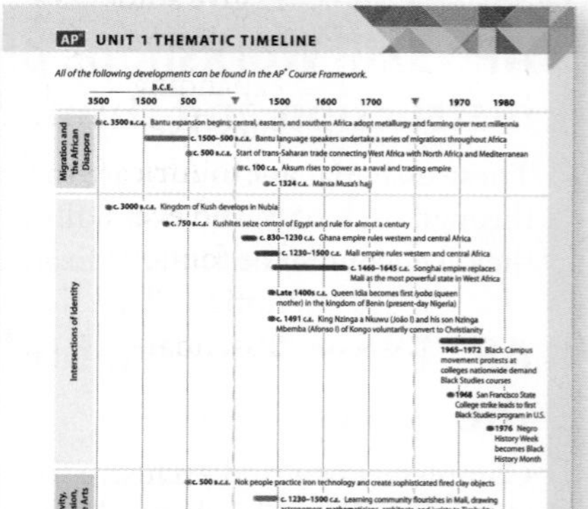

AP UNIT 1 THEMATIC TIMELINE
All of the following developments can be found in the AP® Course Framework.
B.C.E.
3500
1500
500
1500
1600
1700
1970
1980
Migration and the African Diaspora
c. 3500 B.C.E. Bantu expansion begins; central, eastern, and southern Africa adopt metallurgy and farming over next millennia
c. 1500–500 B.C.E. Bantu language speakers undertake a series of migrations throughout Africa
c. 500 B.C.E. Start of trans-Saharan trade connecting West Africa with North Africa and Mediterranean
c. 100 C.E. Aksum rises to power as a naval and trading empire
c. 1324 C.E. Mansa Musa's hajj
Intersections of Identity
c. 3000 B.C.E. Kingdom of Kush develops in Nubia
c. 750 B.C.E. Kushites seize control of Egypt and rule for almost a century
c. 830–1230 C.E. Ghana empire rules western and central Africa
c. 1230–1500 C.E. Mali empire rules western and central Africa
c. 1460–1645 C.E. Songhai empire replaces Mali as the most powerful state in West Africa
Late 1400s C.E. Queen Idia becomes first iyoba (queen mother) in the kingdom of Benin (present-day Nigeria)
c. 1491 C.E. King Nzinga a Nkuwu (João I) and his son Nzinga Mbemba (Afonso I) of Kongo voluntarily convert to Christianity
1965–1972 Black Campus movement protests at colleges nationwide demand Black Studies courses
1968 San Francisco State College strike leads to first Black Studies program in U.S.
1976 Negro History Week becomes Black History Month
Creativity, Expression, and the Arts
c. 500 B.C.E. Nok people practice iron technology and create sophisticated fired clay objects
c. 1230–1500 C.E. Learning community flourishes in Mali, drawing astronomers, mathematicians, architects, and jurists to Timbuktu
1977 Ivory mask of Queen Idia adopted as symbol for Second World Black Festival of Arts and Culture
Resistance and Resilience
1526 Transatlantic slave trade begins
1526 Africans enslaved in Santo Domingo lead the earliest known slave revolt in North America
1965 Black college students enter predominately white institutions in large numbers for the first time
U1-D

▼ Unit Warmups offer fun, engaging source analysis practice.

Unit Warmups provide visual analysis practice and invite students to use any preexisting knowledge of course content to predict key concepts and developments they will encounter in the chapters for the unit. These get students engaged and thinking about what they're about to learn via preview questions on images in the chapters. Taken from the chapters in the unit, these images come with helpful **Key Context notes** to help students tackle the **Prediction Questions**, which are tied directly to **AP® course skills.** Later, students will revisit their predictions and analyses of these images when they encounter them in the chapters' visual activities.

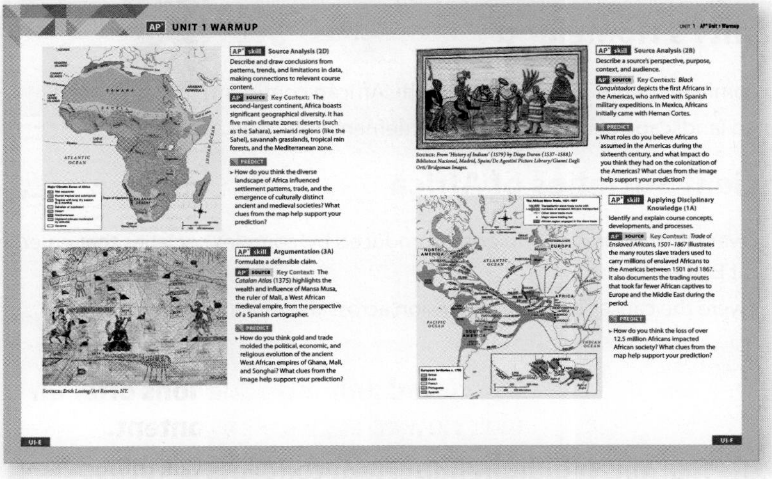

Chapter-opening features contextualize important AP® course content.

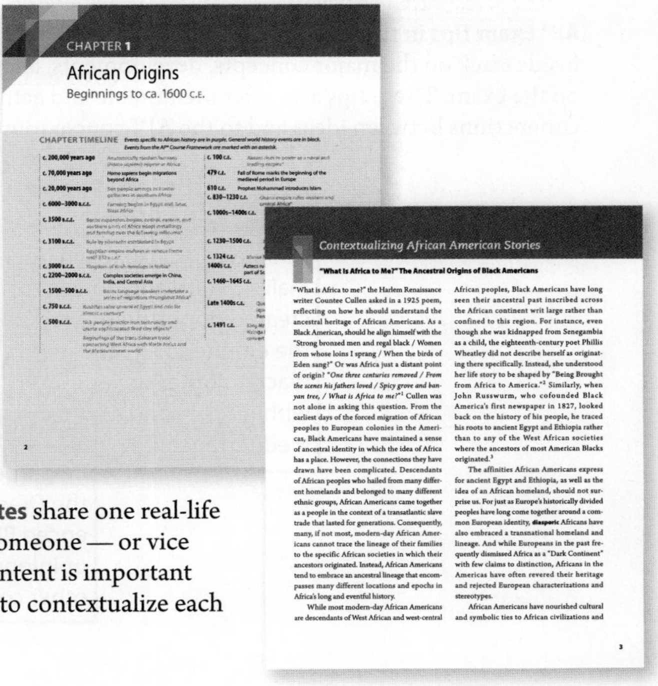

- ► **Chapter Timelines** give students a sense of chronology broken down for each chapter, reinforcing and expanding on the AP® Unit Thematic Timelines. Events in purple are especially relevant to African and/or African American history, and events marked with an asterisk can also be found in the AP® course and Exam Description's Topics, Learning Objectives, and Essential Knowledge statements.

- ► **Contextualizing African American Stories vignettes** share one real-life example of how the chapter's content affected someone — or vice versa. These stories reaffirm why the chapter content is important while working hand-in-hand with the timelines to contextualize each chapter for students.

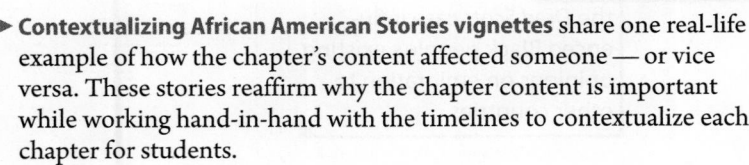

Support for AP® skills and content in the margins of the chapter narrative ensures every student is prepared.

▾ Chapter headings include questions aligned to the AP® course Learning Objectives.

These **questions** help students read actively and engage with the AP® course objectives as they read the chapter content.

Africa: Humanity's Homeland

What are the most prominent geographic features of the African continent?

How did Africa's varied landscape affect patterns of settlement and trade between diverse cul

Ancient Societies of Africa

What were the features of, and goods produced by, complex societies that emerged in ancient East and West Africa?

What were the causes of Bantu expansion across the African continent?

▾ AP® Exam Tips in the margins highlight important concepts to focus on for the AP® Exam.

AP® Exam Tips in the margins of the book offer a boost where it matters most, with the inside track on the major concepts, developments, and processes you can expect to see on the exam. These tips also offer memorable and active on-the-spot advice for making connections between ideas and to the AP® course sources.

AP® exam tip

Be sure you can explain how Mali's wealth and power created opportunities for the empire to expand its reach to other societies within Africa and a Mediterranean.

AP® exam tip

Be prepared to explain how the *Dred Scott* case influenced Black people's existing opinions on emigration to other countries.

▾ AP® Skills: Applying Disciplinary Knowledge notes help students apply the skills of the course to the content of the chapter.

The **AP® Skills: Applying Disciplinary Knowledge** questions identify places to apply key disciplinary practices, reasoning processes, and skills students will need to perform well on the AP® Exam. Designed to help students read actively and think critically about the African American experience, these marginal notes assess students' understanding of the key concepts, developments, and processes described in the chapter narrative.

AP® skills

Applying Disciplinary Knowledge: How does Harriet Jacobs's recounting of her experience on this page illustrate the unique vulnerabilities and injustices faced by en

AP® skills

Applying Disciplinary Knowledge: Why did the admission of Missouri threaten to upset the balance of free and slave states?

AP® skills

Applying Disciplinary Knowledge: Can you identify the connection between the abolitionist movement and the woman suffrage movement?

▾ A running glossary keeps track of important concepts and events.

The **running glossary** is also unique to this AP® edition. Extending across the entire book, this helpful reference tool calls out the most important concepts and events in each chapter, with definitions visible at a glance. Even more terms are defined in a full **Glossary/Glosario** at the back of the book.

free Black **uplift**: the idea, especially popular among the elite, that Black self-help, leadership, and autonomy were necessary to elevate the race as a whole. Like Forten, other free Blacks who prospered usually came from families that had been free for more than one generation.

Ironically, the very success of Black entrepreneurs attracted the animosity of whites, and successful communities were often victims of violence. Seneca

uplift
The idea that racial progress demands autonomous Black efforts; especially seen as the responsibility of the more fortunate of the race to help lift up the less fortunate.

griot
Prestigious historians, storytellers, and musicians who maintained and shared a community's history, traditions, and cultural practices.

From the small Malinke kingdom of Kangaba, near the present Mali–Guinea border, came Sundiata, a legendary figure whose name means "lion prince." The story of his exploits was passed down by generations of **griots**, or storytellers, whose stories also may have served as inspiration for Disney's *The Lion King*. Many of the details are impossible to confirm, but the account of his early life in the *Epic of Sundiata* describes him as the twelfth son and sole survivor of Kangaba ruler Nare Maghan.

An art program designed to develop AP® skills and support work with AP® course sources.

▸ Critical thinking questions promote visual source analysis.

AP® African American Studies is an interdisciplinary course that requires students to examine the diversity of African American experiences through direct encounters with varied sources, including visual sources. From stimulus-based multiple-choice questions to Short-Answer and Document-Based Questions, visual sources are also an important part of the AP® Exam, and a major challenge for students to analyze. That's why this AP® edition of *Freedom on My Mind* provides a robust **caption and critical analysis question** for every image in the book, asking students to analyze multiple perspectives and develop well-supported responses.

A Plantation Burial
Enslaved people gather at sunset in a secluded forest for a funeral on the plantation of Mississippi governor Tilghman Tucker. A Black preacher, at center, delivers an emotional address to the mourners; before him is the casket, and in the foreground is the dug grave. In the distance on the right, a white couple — presumably the governor and his wife — is hidden among the trees. **How does this painting portray the significance of religious practices for enslaved people?** *GL Archive/Alamy Stock Photo.*

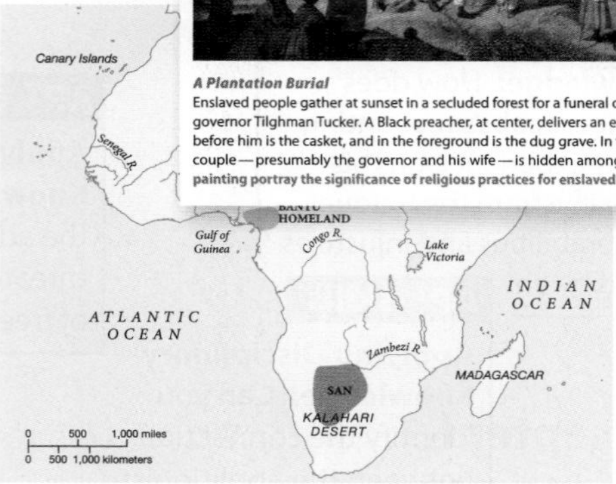

MAP 1.2 Ancient Societies of Africa
During the ancient period, Africa was home to some of the world's first large-scale states, as well as societies that pioneered new ones. This map locates some of the earliest world societies that emerged in Africa during the ancient period. **What geographic features do Egypt, Nubia, and Aksum have in common? How do these commonalities help explain the development of each society?**

AP® source ***Harriet Tubman***
Harriet Tubman, born Araminta "Minty" Ross, endured a brutal childhood and young adulthood in slavery. Following her final, permanent escape in 1849, she helped many more enslaved people — including members of her own family — escape to freedom and spoke out against the horrors of slavery. During the Civil War, she served the Union as a cook, nurse, teacher, scout, and spy. **What is the significance of visual depictions of African American leaders in photography and art — as with Harriet Tubman's portrait — during this time?** *Library of Congress, Prints and Photographs Division, Washington, D.C., LC-USZ62-7816.*

◂ AP® course sources are visible at a glance.

The art in this textbook often overlaps with the required and optional AP® course sources. Throughout the book, you'll be able to see where the art program aligns to the AP® course framework at a glance, thanks to a helpful **AP® Source icon**. These reference points also emphasize for students that some visual sources are especially important to know.

AP® source ***Katherine Dunham on Broadway***
Katherine Dunham, center, performs in the all-Black musical *Cabin in the Sky*, which she co-choreographed with George Balanchine. Dunham integrated her research on dance traditions brought by enslaved Africans to the Caribbean into her work as a choreographer and performer. **Explain how Dunham's work helped advance the cultural renaissance and place African American dance in a global context.** *George Karger/Getty Images.*

▸ Revisit Your Prediction Activities help students make connections and practice source analysis.

Revisit Your Prediction Activities appear in situ with all of the images in the Unit Warmups. These are designed to support students in the AP® skill of making connections between concepts as they use evidence from the chapter narrative to support their arguments as they revisit their predictions and revise their responses.

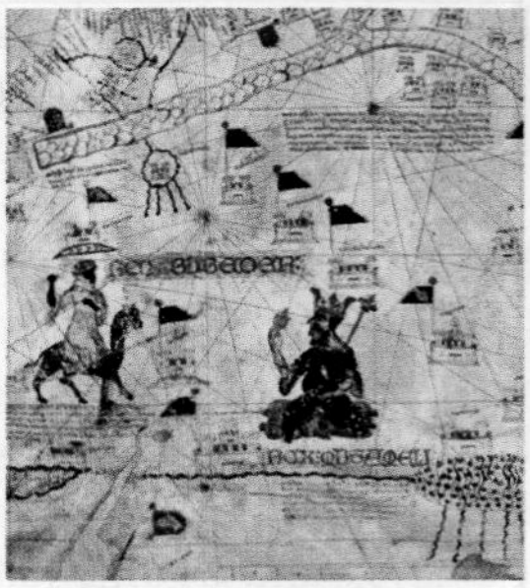

AP® source ***Facsimile of the Catalan Atlas Showing the Nugget, 1375***

Largely devoid of geographic detail, this Spanish nautical map c with pictures, including sketches of camels, as well as a large an ruler identified as "Muse Melley," "lord of the Negroes of Guinea." T Mansa Musa, who ruled the Mali empire between 1312 and 133 on the map is closer to North Africa than to West Africa. A devo attention of the Islamic and European worlds in 1324, when he caravan included twelve hundred servants and eighty camels ca he distributed to the needy along his route. Not soon forgotten, fourteenth-century maps of the world. **What does the map c Islam?** *Erich Lessing/Art Resource, NY.*

ACTIVITY ▸ Revisit Your Prediction

In the AP® Unit Warmup (p. U1-E), you made a prediction about this image. **How do you think gold and trade molded the political, economic, and religious evolution of the ancient West African empires of Ghana, Mali, and Songhai? What clues from the image help support your prediction? Support or revise your original prediction using evidence from this chapter.**

The Creation of an African American Culture

This late-eighteenth-century painting, *The Old Plantation*, depicts a group of enslaved people on a South Carolina plantation. Their activities strongly suggest the persistence of West African cultural traditions and practices in the Lower South. This painting may depict a wedding, which sometimes featured the tradition of "jumping the broom," or it may depict a dance. Many of the participants' accoutrements — the women's head ties and the players' instruments, for example — are West African in origin. But the other garments shown are typical of American working-class attire during this period, and the slave cabins and other plantation buildings remind us of the setting in which this distinctly African American culture was taking shape. **What does this painting reveal about how the forced labor systems affected the formation of African American musical and linguistic practices?** *The Old Plantation, attributed to John Rose, Beaufort County, South Carolina, c. 1785–1790/The Colonial Williamsburg Foundation, Gift of Abby Aldrich Rockefeller.*

ACTIVITY ▸ Revisit Your Prediction

In the AP® Unit Warmup (p. U2-E), you made a prediction about this image. **How do you think African American forms of self-expression in art, music, and language combined influences from diverse African cultures with local sources? What details in this painting help support your prediction? How can self-expression be considered a form of resistance and a demonstration of resilience? Support or revise your original prediction using evidence from this chapter.**

End-of-chapter features make reviewing course content and applying new skills a breeze.

CHAPTER **6** REVIEW ▸ **PRACTICING AP® SKILLS**

AP® ESSENTIAL VOCABULARY AND SOURCES

**Essential terms and required sources from the AP® Course are marked with an asterisk.*

Missouri Compromise (1820) p. 212
Indian Removal Act (1830) p. 213
Black Seminoles* (*Gopher John*, a Black Seminole leader and interpreter, 1863) p. 214
Second Great Awakening p. 223
gag rule p. 224
Amistad* case p. 224
Creole* insurrection p. 225
truant p. 226
lying out p. 226
Harriet Tubman* (Photographs of Harriet Tubman Throughout Her Life: Matte Collodion Print of Harriet Tubman, 1871–1876) p. 226
North Star p. 228
Underground Railroad* p. 229
invisible church p. 231
ring shout* p. 231
abroad marriages p. 236
fictive kin p. 238

APPLYING DISCIPLINARY KNOWLEDGE: ESSENTIAL QUESTIONS

1. Discuss the deepening political, economic, social, and slavery-related divisions between the North and South in the years 1820 to 1860. How was each region becoming more distinctive, and how were the two regions becoming more opposed to each other? In what ways did the two regions remain linked despite the growing divide between them?
2. How did the actions of Denmark Vesey, Nat Turner, David Walker, and the enslaved people aboard the *Amistad* and the *Creole* resonate throughout the country? Compare the effects of their actions in the North and in the South and discuss the implications for enslaved and free Blacks. What do these effects and implications tell you about the state of the nation during this period?
3. Discuss the various types of enslaved resistance. How did individual enslaved people's circumstances — their age, gender, location, or skill level, for example — make it more or less difficult to defy their enslavers or escape permanently?
4. How did gender affect enslaved people's experiences? In what ways were enslaved women's hardships different from enslaved men's? In what ways were enslaved women and men arguably more equal than white women and men of this period?

Applying Disciplinary Knowledge: Essential Questions serve as checkpoints that allow students to demonstrate their understanding of key concepts, developments, and processes covered in the chapter narrative.

SUGGESTED REFERENCES

The Expansion and Consolidation of Slavery

Baptist, Edward E. *The Half Has Never Been Told: Slavery and the Making of American Capitalism.* New York: Basic Books, 2014.
Berry, Daina Ramey. *The Price for Their Pound of Flesh: The Value of the Enslaved, from Womb to Grave, in the Building of a Nation.* Boston: Beacon Press, 2017.
Campbell, Randolph B. *An Empire for Slavery: The Peculiar Institution in Texas, 1821–1865.* Baton Rouge: LSU Press, 1991.
Deyle, Steven. *Carry Me Back: The Domestic Slave Trade in American Life.* New York: Oxford University Press, 2006.
Follett, Richard. *The Sugar Masters: Planters and Slaves in Louisiana's Cane World, 1820–1860.* Baton Rouge: LSU Press, 2007.
Johnson, Walter. *Soul by Soul: Life Inside the Antebellum Slave Market.* Cambridge: Harvard University Press, 1999.
Franklin, John Hope, and Loren Schweninger. *Runaway Slaves: Rebels on the Plantation.* New York: Oxford University Press, 1999.
Glymph, Thavolia. *Out of the House of Bondage: The Transformation of the Plantation Household.* Cambridge: Cambridge University Press, 2008.
Jones, Norrece T., Jr. *Born a Child of Freedom, Yet a Slave: Mechanisms of Control and Strategies of Resistance in Antebellum South Carolina.* Hanover: University Press of New England/Wesleyan University Press, 1990.
McLaurin, Melton A. *Celia, a Slave.* New York: Avon, 1999.
Rivers, Larry Eugene. *Rebels and Runaways: Slave Resistance in Nineteenth-Century Florida.* Urbana: University of Illinois Press, 2012.
Schermerhorn, Calvin. *Money over Mastery, Family over Freedom: Slavery in the Antebellum Upper South.* Baltimore: Johns Hopkins University Press, 2011.

Suggested References lists arranged by topic are designed to support students' own research as they embark on their Individual Student Projects.

Key terms and AP® course sources are gathered in a list of **AP® Essential Vocabulary and Sources** that serves as an easy-to-find reference point. All of the terms and sources found in the AP® course framework are also marked with an asterisk to help focus students' review of the chapters in preparation for the AP® Exam.

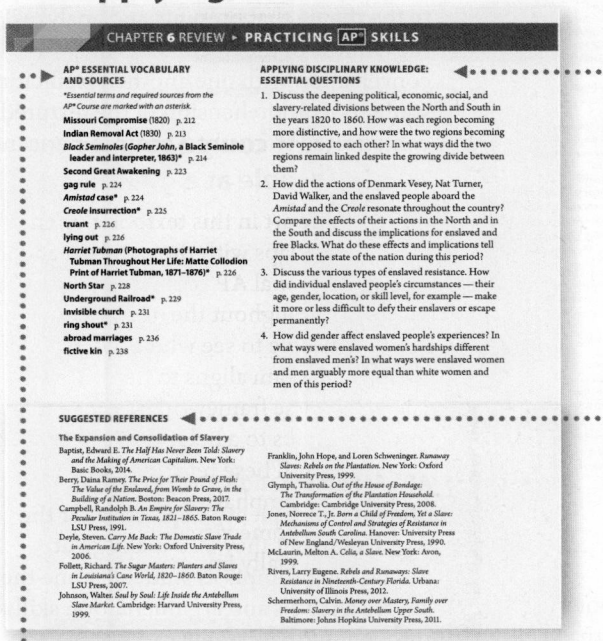

AP® Working with Sources collections hone source analysis and argumentation skills.

We believe that the primary goals of our book — to highlight the deep connections between Black history and the development of American democracy, illustrate the diversity of Black experience, emphasize the centrality of Black culture, and document the inextricable connections among Black culture, politics, economics, and social and religious life — could not be realized to their fullest extent through narrative alone. That's why each chapter in *Freedom on My Mind* includes an **AP® Working with Sources collection** — a rich, themed set of textual and visual primary sources.

Each collection focuses on a particular chapter topic, from firsthand accounts of the slave trade to perspectives on the Black Lives Matter movement. With built-in supports to build and practice AP® source analysis and argumentation skills, these document collections feature primary textual and visual sources from all genres, including personal letters, memoirs, poetry, public petitions, newspaper accounts, photographs, visual arts, cartoons, propaganda, and more. By placing the texts of these historical actors in conversation with one another, we enable students to witness the myriad variations of and nuances within Black experiences.

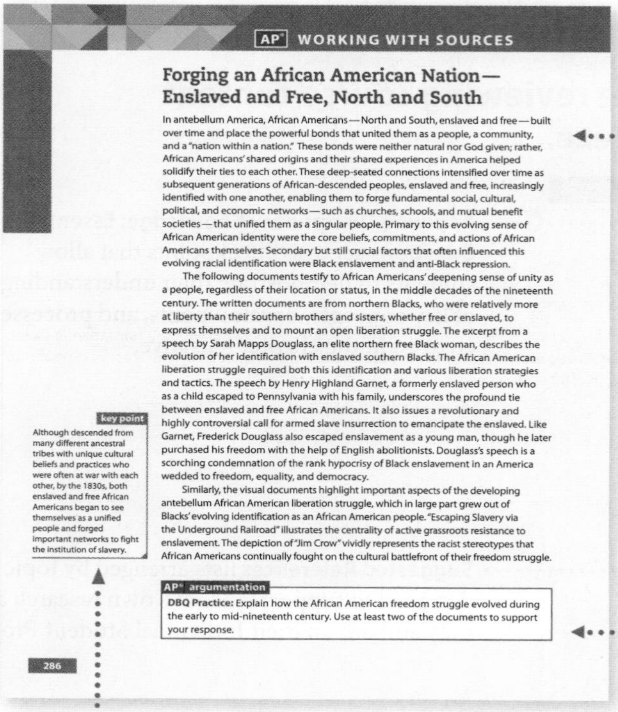
AP® WORKING WITH SOURCES

Forging an African American Nation — Enslaved and Free, North and South

In antebellum America, African Americans — North and South, enslaved and free — built over time and place the powerful bonds that united them as a people, a community, and a "nation within a nation." These bonds were neither natural nor God given; rather, African Americans' shared origins and their shared experiences in America helped solidify their ties to each other. These deep-seated connections intensified over time as subsequent generations of African-descended peoples, enslaved and free, increasingly identified with one another, enabling them to forge fundamental social, cultural, political, and economic networks — such as churches, schools, and mutual benefit societies — that unified them as a singular people. Primary to this evolving sense of African American identity were the core beliefs, commitments, and actions of African Americans themselves. Secondary but still crucial factors that often influenced this evolving racial identification were Black enslavement and anti-Black repression.

The following documents testify to African Americans' deepening sense of unity as a people, regardless of their location or status, in the middle decades of the nineteenth century. The written documents are from northern Blacks, who were relatively more at liberty than their southern brothers and sisters, whether free or enslaved, to express themselves and to mount an open liberation struggle. The excerpt from a speech by Sarah Mapps Douglass, an elite northern free Black woman, describes the evolution of her identification with enslaved southern Blacks. The African American liberation struggle required both this identification and various liberation strategies and tactics. The speech by Henry Highland Garnet, a formerly enslaved person who as a child escaped to Pennsylvania with his family, underscores the profound tie between enslaved and free African Americans. It also issues a revolutionary and highly controversial call for armed slave insurrection to emancipate the enslaved. Like Garnet, Frederick Douglass also escaped enslavement as a young man, though he later purchased his freedom with the help of English abolitionists. Douglass's speech is a scorching condemnation of the rank hypocrisy of Black enslavement in an America wedded to freedom, equality, and democracy.

Similarly, the visual documents highlight important aspects of the developing antebellum African American liberation struggle, which in large part grew out of Blacks' evolving identification as an African American people. "Escaping Slavery via the Underground Railroad" illustrates the centrality of active grassroots resistance to enslavement. The depiction of "Jim Crow" vividly represents the racist stereotypes that African Americans continually fought on the cultural battlefront of their freedom struggle.

key point
Although descended from many different ancestral tribes with unique cultural beliefs and practices who were often at war with each other, by the 1830s, both enslaved and free African Americans began to see themselves as a unified people and forged important networks to fight the institution of slavery.

AP® argumentation
DBQ Practice: Explain how the African American freedom struggle evolved during the early to mid-nineteenth century. Use at least two of the documents to support your response.

286

Each collection begins with an **introduction to the theme** that presents and analyzes the context of the documents in conversation with one another, facilitating students' comprehension of the textured, complicated stories of African Americans.

AP® Argumentation: DBQ Practice prompts offer plenty of practice for the AP® Exam, but they also make great discussion prompts as students hone their source analysis and argumentation skills throughout the school year.

Key Point notes in the margin of the introductions help students digest the most important contextual information and provide a foundation for actively reading the sources that follow.

As with the art program, several documents in these collections overlap with the required and optional AP® course sources. Throughout the book, you'll be able to see that alignment to the AP® course framework at a glance thanks to a helpful **AP® Source icon**. These reference points also emphasize for students that some textual sources are especially important to know.

DOCUMENT 1 **AP® source** Phillis Wheatley | *On Being Brought from Africa to America, 1773*

DOCUMENT 6 *Private Hubbard Pryor, before and after Enlisting in the U.S. Colored Troops, 1864*

The following side-by-side photographs show PRIVATE HUBBARD PRYOR (c. 1842–1890) literally transformed by his enlistment in the U.S. Colored Troops. Compare the two images, especially taking note of Pryor's dress, facial expression, and posture in each photo. Keep in mind that it was not yet a convention to smile for the camera.

Breaking it Down These images were consciously staged. What point do you think the photographer was trying to make with the clothing, objects, countenance, and positioning of Private Pryor? Use what you have learned in this chapter to evaluate the picture on the left. What do you see, think, wonder, and predict about his experience as a soldier in the war? What effect might both of these photos have had on those who viewed them?

Breaking It Down notes follow the headnotes, providing students with a specific task or key questions with which to focus their reading of the source.

Headnotes for each document offer students key context for the author, subject, audience, and purpose of the source.

Finally, a set of five **Practicing AP® Skills questions** invite students to apply the skills and reasoning processes of the course.

PRACTICING AP® SKILLS

1. **AP® Comparison.** Compare Equiano and Hall's details about the transatlantic slave journey and the transatlantic slave trade. To what extent do their accounts support or counter each other?
2. **AP® Causation.** Describe and analyze the various roles Europeans and Africans played in the slave trade. What details from the documents support your analysis?
3. **AP® Causation.** Explain how these documents reveal the effects of the transatlantic slave trade on West African communities.
4. **Connecting to AP® Themes.** Explain how the documents collectively provide insight into both the commodification of enslaved Africans during the transatlantic journey as well as the resilience and resistance of enslaved Africans.
5. **Class Discussion.** What are the benefits and limitations in using firsthand accounts of the transatlantic slave journey to better understand the transatlantic slave trade?

A Connecting to AP® Themes question offers an opportunity to connect the documents to one of the four AP® course themes.

A **discussion-based question** rounds out the set — perfect practice for skills needed to ace the presentation and oral defense of the Individual Student Projects that serve as the capstone of the AP® African American Studies course.

AP® Skills Workshops build essential skills in context.

AP® Skills Workshops at the end of every chapter walk students step-by-step through how to build, refine, and apply the skills and reasoning processes of the AP® African American Studies course. From sourcing a primary document, to developing a continuity and change argument, to putting the Individual Student Project together, these workshops introduce, and help develop, essential AP® skills in context.

Recap boxes throughout the workshops serve as comprehension checks and reference points for student review.

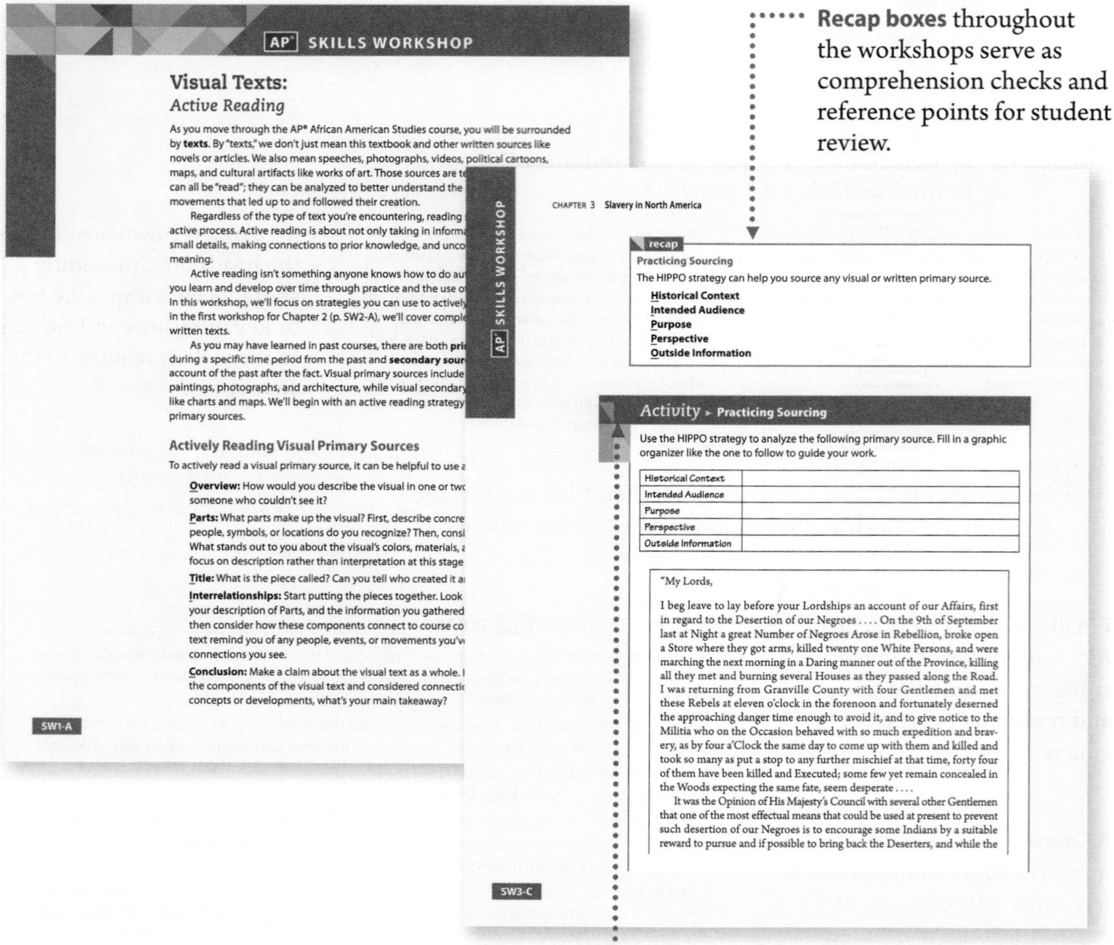

AP® SKILLS WORKSHOP

Visual Texts:
Active Reading

As you move through the AP® African American Studies course, you will be surrounded by **texts.** By "texts," we don't just mean this textbook and other written sources like novels or articles. We also mean speeches, photographs, videos, political cartoons, maps, and cultural artifacts like works of art. Those sources are t[...] can all be "read"; they can be analyzed to better understand the [...] movements that led up to and followed their creation.

Regardless of the type of text you're encountering, reading [...] active process. Active reading is about not only taking in inform[...] small details, making connections to prior knowledge, and unco[...] meaning.

Active reading isn't something anyone knows how to do au[...] you learn and develop over time through practice and the use o[...] In this workshop, we'll focus on strategies you can use to actively[...] in the first workshop for Chapter 2 (p. SW2-A), we'll cover compl[...] written texts.

As you may have learned in past courses, there are both **pri[...]** during a specific time period from the past and **secondary sour[...]** account of the past after the fact. Visual primary sources include[...] paintings, photographs, and architecture, while visual secondary[...] like charts and maps. We'll begin with an active reading strategy[...] primary sources.

Actively Reading Visual Primary Sources

To actively read a visual primary source, it can be helpful to use a[...]

Overview: How would you describe the visual in one or tw[...] someone who couldn't see it?

Parts: What parts make up the visual? First, describe concre[...] people, symbols, or locations do you recognize? Then, consi[...] What stands out to you about the visual's colors, materials, [...] focus on description rather than interpretation at this stage[...]

Title: What is the piece called? Can you tell who created it a[...]

Interrelationships: Start putting the pieces together. Look [...] your description of Parts, and the information you gathered [...] then consider how these components connect to course co[...] text remind you of any people, events, or movements you'v[...] connections you see.

Conclusion: Make a claim about the visual text as a whole. [...] the components of the visual text and considered connecti[...] concepts or developments, what's your main takeaway?

SW1-A

AP® SKILLS WORKSHOP

CHAPTER 3 Slavery in North America

recap

Practicing Sourcing

The HIPPO strategy can help you source any visual or written primary source.

Historical Context
Intended Audience
Purpose
Perspective
Outside Information

Activity ▸ Practicing Sourcing

Use the HIPPO strategy to analyze the following primary source. Fill in a graphic organizer like the one to follow to guide your work.

Historical Context	
Intended Audience	
Purpose	
Perspective	
Outside Information	

"My Lords,

I beg leave to lay before your Lordships an account of our Affairs, first in regard to the Desertion of our Negroes . . . . On the 9th of September last at Night a great Number of Negroes Arose in Rebellion, broke open a Store where they got arms, killed twenty one White Persons, and were marching the next morning in a Daring manner out of the Province, killing all they met and burning several Houses as they passed along the Road. I was returning from Granville County with four Gentlemen and met these Rebels at eleven o'clock in the forenoon and fortunately deserned the approaching danger time enough to avoid it, and to give notice to the Militia who on the Occasion behaved with so much expedition and bravery, as by four a'Clock the same day to come up with them and killed and took so many as put a stop to any further mischief at that time, forty four of them have been killed and Executed; some few yet remain concealed in the Woods expecting the same fate, seem desperate . . . .

It was the Opinion of His Majesty's Council with several other Gentlemen that one of the most effectual means that could be used at present to prevent such desertion of our Negroes is to encourage some Indians by a suitable reward to pursue and if possible to bring back the Deserters, and while the

SW3-C

Each workshop culminates in an **activity** that allows students to practice the skills they have just learned.

Plenty of AP® Exam practice throughout the book gets every student AP® ready.

With frequent practice opportunities, every student will be prepared to take the AP® Exam at the end of the course.

AP® EXAM PRACTICE

Multiple-Choice Questions

Questions 1–2 refer to the following.

Chisholm: I stand before you today as a candidate for the D
tion for the presidency of the United States of America. I an
of black America, although I am black and proud. I am not t
women's movement of this country, although I am a wom
proud of that. I am not the candidate of any political polici
cial interests. I stand here now, without endorsements fro
politicians or celebrities or any other kind of prop, I do not
the tired clichés that have too long been an accepted part
I am the candidate of the people of America. . . .

Reporter: You represent a trend for more women and
women to get involved with politics and go after elected offi

Chisholm: Yes I specifically recommend, do I recommen
women and specifically black women to enter into politics.
am feeling and recognizing that as a result of over 20 yea
only emerging 8 years ago publicly, there is a great need f
the political arena. I happen to believe that there's certain as
that probably would be given much more attention if we l
voices in the halls of the legislatures on the city, state, and
I will — legislation that pertains to daycare centers, educati
mental services — the kind of legislation that has to do wit
and preservation of the most important resources that any r
is its human resources.

Source: Shirley Chisholm, *Presidential Announcement Speech*, 1972

1. Which of the following broader contextual trends best explains Chisholm's political ambition and perspective on Black political participation in the 1970s?
   (A) By 1971, the disparity between Black and white federal political representation had been eliminated.
   (B) Throughout the nineteenth century, Black women became increasingly disillusioned with politics and community leadership after being silenced or sidelined when bringing up the need for both racial and gender equality.
   (C) At the time of Chisholm's campaign, the majority of Black Americans in the South were still unable to vote due to the prevalence of racial violence and discriminatory local voting requirements.
   (D) Between 1970 and 2006, the number of Black elected officials in the United States would increase by sixfold.

2. Chisholm's organizational efforts most directly led to which of the following?
   (A) The acceptance of Black Republicans and other Black Independents
   (B) The establishment of the Congressional Black Caucus
   (C) The ratification of the Equal Rights Amendment
   (D) The election of the first Black president of the United States

EP16-A

Short-Answer Question

Short-Answer Question

1. **Answer A, B, C, and D.**
   (A) Describe the broader context that led to the ratification of the Reconstruction Amendments.
   (B) Explain how one of the Reconstruction Amendments fulfilled the postwar hopes of African Americans who supported Black enlistment in the Union army.
   (C) Explain how one of the Reconstruction Amendments was undermined by state or local laws during Reconstruction.
   (D) Using one specific example, explain how the Thirteenth Amendment impacted Black political participation in politics.

AP® EXAM PRACTICE

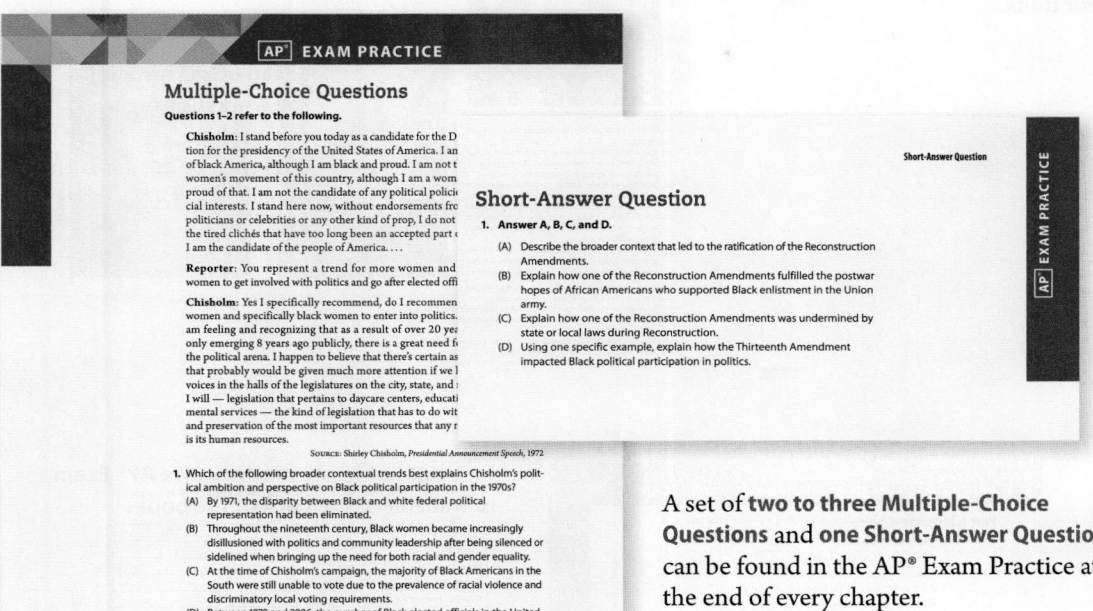

A set of **two to three Multiple-Choice Questions** and **one Short-Answer Question** can be found in the AP® Exam Practice at the end of every chapter.

A set of **15 Multiple-Choice Questions, three Short-Answer Questions,** and **one Document-Based Question** appear at the end of each of the four units.

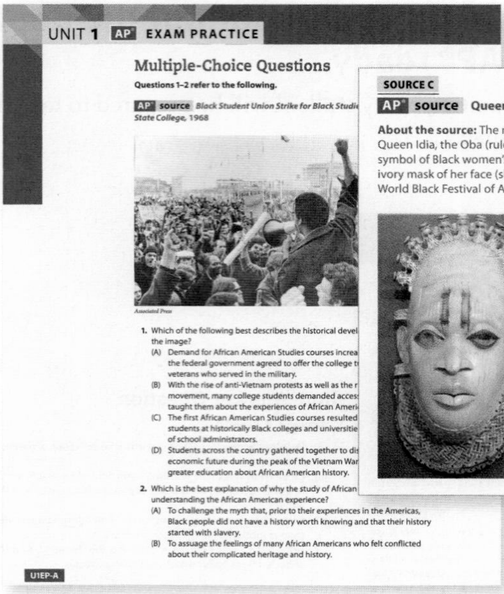
UNIT 1 AP® EXAM PRACTICE

Multiple-Choice Questions

Questions 1–2 refer to the following.

AP® source *Black Student Union Strike for Black Studi… State College, 1968*

Associated Press

1. Which of the following best describes the historical devel… the image?
(A) Demand for African American Studies courses increa… the federal government agreed to offer the college t… veterans who served in the military.
(B) With the rise of anti-Vietnam protests as well as the r… movement, many college students demanded acces… taught them about the experiences of African Ameri…
(C) The first African American Studies courses resulted… students at historically Black colleges and universitie… of school administrators.
(D) Students across the country gathered together to di… economic future during the peak of the Vietnam War… greater education about African American history.

2. Which is the best explanation of why the study of African… understanding the African American experience?
(A) To challenge the myth that, prior to their experiences in the Americas, Black people did not have a history worth knowing and that their history started with slavery.
(B) To assuage the feelings of many African Americans who felt conflicted about their complicated heritage and history.

U1EP-A

SOURCE C

AP® source Queen Idia Masks, Sixteenth Century and 1977

About the source: The mask on the left was created in the sixteenth century and depicts Queen Idia, the Oba (ruler) of Benin from circa 1504 to 1550. Queen Idia became an iconic symbol of Black women's leadership throughout the African diaspora in 1977, when an ivory mask of her face (shown at right) was adopted as the symbol for FESTAC (Second World Black Festival of Arts and Culture).

Universal History Archive/Getty Images

PIUS UTOMI EKPEI/Getty Images

Last but not least, a **full practice AP® Exam** is available at the back of the book.

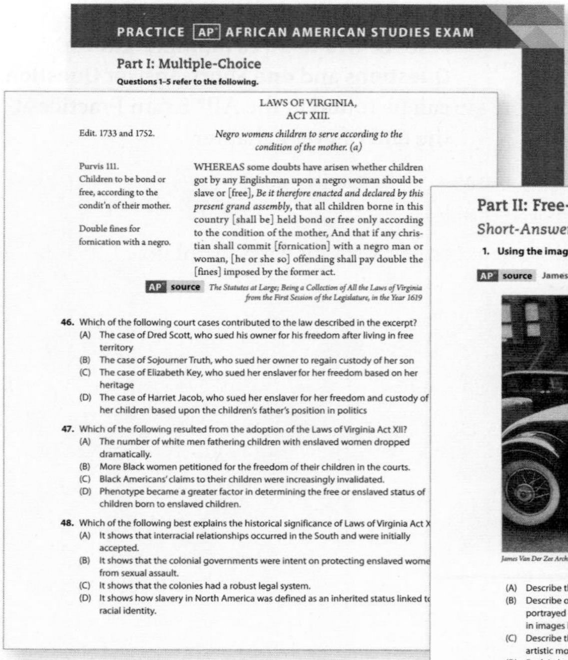
PRACTICE AP® AFRICAN AMERICAN STUDIES EXAM

Part I: Multiple-Choice

Questions 1–5 refer to the following.

LAWS OF VIRGINIA,
ACT XIII.

Edit. 1733 and 1752. — *Negro womens children to serve according to the condition of the mother. (a)*

Purvis 111. Children to be bond or free, according to the condit'n of their mother. Double fines for fornication with a negro.

WHEREAS some doubts have arisen whether children got by any Englishman upon a negro woman should be slave or [free], *Be it therefore enacted and declared by this present grand assembly*, that all children borne in this country [shall be] held bond or free only according to the condition of the mother, And that if any christian shall commit [fornication] with a negro man or woman, [he or she so] offending shall pay double the [fines] imposed by the former act.

AP® source *The Statutes at Large; Being a Collection of All the Laws of Virginia from the First Session of the Legislature, in the Year 1619*

46. Which of the following court cases contributed to the law described in the excerpt?
(A) The case of Dred Scott, who sued his owner for his freedom after living in free territory
(B) The case of Sojourner Truth, who sued her owner to regain custody of her son
(C) The case of Elizabeth Key, who sued her enslaver for her freedom based on her heritage
(D) The case of Harriet Jacob, who sued her enslaver for her freedom and custody of her children based upon the children's father's position in politics

47. Which of the following resulted from the adoption of the Laws of Virginia Act XII?
(A) The number of white men fathering children with enslaved women dropped dramatically.
(B) More Black women petitioned for the freedom of their children in the courts.
(C) Black Americans' claims to their children were increasingly invalidated.
(D) Phenotype became a greater factor in determining the free or enslaved status of children born to enslaved children.

48. Which of the following best explains the historical significance of Laws of Virginia Act X…
(A) It shows that interracial relationships occurred in the South and were initially accepted.
(B) It shows that the colonial governments were intent on protecting enslaved wome… from sexual assault.
(C) It shows that the colonies had a robust legal system.
(D) It shows how slavery in North America was defined as an inherited status linked t… racial identity.

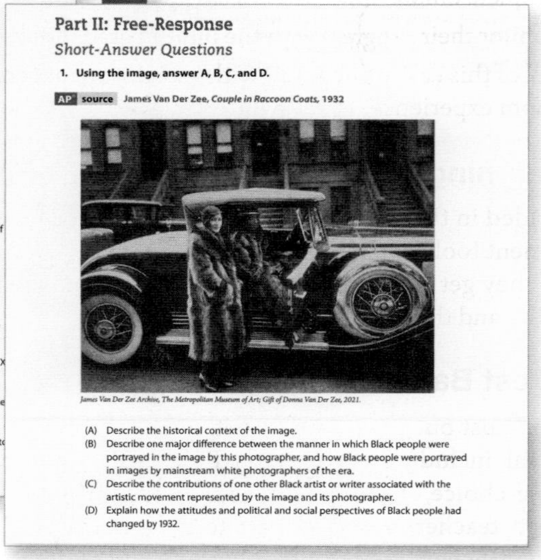
Part II: Free-Response

Short-Answer Questions

1. Using the image, answer A, B, C, and D.

AP® source James Van Der Zee, *Couple in Raccoon Coats*, 1932

James Van Der Zee Archive, The Metropolitan Museum of Art; Gift of Donna Van Der Zee, 2021.

(A) Describe the historical context of the image.
(B) Describe one major difference between the manner in which Black people were portrayed in the image by this photographer, and how Black people were portrayed in images by mainstream white photographers of the era.
(C) Describe the contributions of one other Black artist or writer associated with the artistic movement represented by the image and its photographer.
(D) Explain how the attitudes and political and social perspectives of Black people had changed by 1932.

A Complete Package to Support AP® Teachers and Students.

Teacher's Edition | Written *by* Teachers *for* Teachers

The wraparound Teacher's Edition for *Freedom on My Mind* for the AP® course is an invaluable resource for both experienced and new AP® African American Studies teachers. Written by seasoned AP® instructors and workshop presenters, the Teacher's Edition includes thoughtful instruction for planning, pacing, differentiating, and enlivening your AP® African American Studies course.

Teacher's Resource Materials | Lesson Planning Made Easy

The Teacher's Resource Materials accompany the Teacher's Edition and contain materials to effectively plan the course, including a detailed suggested pacing guide, handouts, suggested responses to questions, videos, and so much more.

Achieve bfw publishers | More than Just an e-Book

Achieve is our new online courseware, offering flexible assessment tools and content to support students of all levels. In Achieve, you have everything you need for a successful course at your fingertips. Teachers can access all of the Teacher's Resource Materials and the Teacher's Edition e-book. Students can stay organized and on schedule with a user-friendly interface that is as powerful as it is intuitive. This is a one-stop shop where students can easily:

- find their mobile-friendly and fully accessible e-book;
- increase their understanding with ready-made quizzes;
- complete online homework or assessments; and
- monitor their progress with the built-in gradebook.

Plus, all of this easily integrates with learning management systems for a seamless classroom experience.

LearningCurve | Game-Like Adaptive Quizzing

Embedded in the book's digital platform is the LearningCurve, an adaptive game-like assessment tool that helps students focus on the material they need the most help with. When they get a question wrong, feedback tells them why and links them to content review — and then they get a chance to try again.

Test Bank | Your Home for AP® Exam Prep

Get the most out of the course with ample practice for success on the AP® Exam! The Test Bank includes a full-length AP® African American Studies-style practice test with multiple-choice, short-answer, and document-based questions for each unit. The Test Bank lets teachers quickly create tests in minutes. The platform is fully customizable, allowing teachers to enter their own questions, edit existing questions, set time limits, incorporate multimedia, and scramble answers and change the order of questions to prevent academic dishonesty. Detailed result reports feed into a gradebook or can be exported to Microsoft Excel.

Acknowledgements

In completing this book, we owe thanks to the many talented and generous friends, colleagues, and editors who have provided us with suggestions, critiques, and much careful reading along the way.

Foremost among them is the hardworking group of scholar-teachers who reviewed the second edition for us. We are deeply grateful to them for their insights and suggestions, and we hope we do them justice in the third edition. We thank Marcus Anthony Allen, *North Carolina A&T State University*; Eva Semien Baham, *Dillard University*; Travis D. Boyce, *University of Northern Colorado*; Richard A. Buckelew, *Bethune-Cookman University*; Heather Cooper, *University of Iowa*; Valerie Grim, *Indiana University-Bloomington*; Carmen Harris, *University of South Carolina Upstate*; Worth Kamili Hayes, *Tuskegee University*; Dr. Marilyn K. Howard, *Columbus State Community College*; Karen Sotiropoulos, *Cleveland State University*; Cornelius St. Mark, *Savannah State University*; Robert D. Taber, *Fayetteville State University*; Eric M. Washington, *Calvin College.*

We remain grateful to reviewers of the first edition, whose advice is still reflected in the narrative and Document Projects: Luther Adams, *University of Washington Tacoma*; Ezrah Aharone, *Delaware State University*; Jacqueline Akins, *Community College of Philadelphia*; Okey P. Akubeze, *University of Wisconsin–Milwaukee*; Lauren K. Anderson, *Luther College*; Scott Barton, *East Central University*; Diane L. Beers, *Holyoke Community College*; Dan Berger, *University of Washington Bothell*; Christopher Bonner, *University of Maryland*; Susan Bragg, *Georgia Southwestern State University*; Lester Brooks, *Anne Arundel Community College*; E. Tsekani Browne, *Montgomery College*; Monica L. Butler, *Seminole State College of Florida*; Thomas L. Bynum, *Middle Tennessee State University*; Erin D. Chapman, *George Washington University*; Meredith Clark-Wiltz, *Franklin College*; Alexandra Cornelius, *Florida International University*; Julie Davis, *Cerritos College*; John Kyle Day, *University of Arkansas at Monticello*; Dorothy Drinkard-Hawkshawe, *East Tennessee State University*; Nancy J. Duke, *Daytona State College, Daytona Beach*; Reginald K. Ellis, *Florida A&M University*; Keona K. Ervin, *University of Missouri–Columbia*; Joshua David Farrington, *Eastern Kentucky University*; Marvin Fletcher, *Ohio University*; Amy Forss, *Metropolitan Community College*; Delia C. Gillis, *University of Central Missouri*; Kevin D. Greene, *The University of Southern Mississippi*; LaVerne Gyant, *Northern Illinois University*; Timothy Hack, *Middlesex County College*; Kenneth M. Hamilton, *Southern Methodist University*; Martin Hardeman, *Eastern Illinois University*; Jarvis Hargrove, *North Carolina Central University*; Jim C. Harper II, *North Carolina Central University*; Margaret Harris, *Southern New Hampshire University*; Patricia Herb, *North Central State College*; Elizabeth Herbin-Triant, *University of Massachusetts Lowell*; Pippa Holloway, *Middle Tennessee State University*; Marilyn Howard, *Columbus State Community College*; Carol Sue Humphrey, *Oklahoma Baptist University*; Bryan Jack, *Southern Illinois University Edwardsville*; Jerry Rafiki Jenkins, *Palomar College*; Karen J. Johns, *University of Nebraska at Omaha*; Winifred M. Johnson, *Bethune-Cookman University*; Gary Jones, *American International College*; Ishmael Kimbrough III, *Bakersfield College*; Michelle Kuhl, *University of Wisconsin Oshkosh*; Lynda Lamarre, *Georgia Military College*; Renee Lansley, *Framingham State University*; Talitha LeFlouria, *University of Virginia*; Monroe Little, *Indiana University–Purdue University Indianapolis*; Margaret A. Lowe, *Bridgewater State University*; Vince Lowery, *University of Wisconsin–Green Bay*; Robert Luckett, *Jackson State University*; Steven Lurenz, *Mesa*

Community College; Peggy Macdonald, *Florida Polytechnic University*; Bruce Mactavish, *Washburn University*; Gerald McCarthy, *St. Thomas Aquinas College*; Suzanne McCormack, *Community College of Rhode Island*; Anthony Merritt, *San Diego State University*; Karen K. Miller, *Boston College*; Steven Millner, *San Jose State University*; Billie J. Moore, *El Camino Compton Center*; Maggi M. Morehouse, *Coastal Carolina University*; Lynda Morgan, *Mount Holyoke College*; Earl Mulderink, *Southern Utah University*; Cassandra Newby-Alexander, *Norfolk State University*; Victor D. Padilla Jr., *Wright College*; N. Josiah Pamoja, *Georgia Military College, Fairburn*; Leslie Patrick, *Bucknell University*; Abigail Perkiss, *Kean University*; Alex Peshkoff, *Cosumnes River College*; Melvin Pritchard, *West Valley College*; Margaret Reed, *Northern Virginia Community College, Annandale Campus*; Stephanie Richmond, *Norfolk State University*; John Riedl, *Montgomery College*; Natalie J. Ring, *University of Texas at Dallas*; Maria Teresa Romero, *Saddleback College*; Tara Ross, *Onondaga Community College*; Selena Sanderfer, *Western Kentucky University*; Jonathan D. Sassi, *CUNY–College of Staten Island*; Gerald Schumacher, *Nunez Community College*; Gary Shea, *Center for Advanced Studies and the Arts*; Tobin Shearer, *University of Montana*; John Howard Smith, *Texas A&M University–Commerce*; Solomon Smith, *Georgia Southern University*; Pamela A. Smoot, *Southern Illinois University Carbondale*; Karen Sotiropoulos, *Cleveland State University*; Melissa M. Soto-Schwartz, *Cuyahoga Community College*; Idris Kabir Syed, *Kent State University*; Linda D. Tomlinson, *Fayetteville State University*; Felicia A. Viator, *University of California, Berkeley*; Eric M. Washington, *Calvin College*; and Joanne G. Woodard, *University of North Texas*.

Our debt to the many brilliant editors at Bedford/St. Martin's and Bedford, Freeman & Worth is equally immeasurable. We are grateful to the team at Bedford/St. Martin's (Macmillan Learning): Michael Rosenberg, William J. Lombardo, and Cynthia Ward, who guided us through the revision process and suggested many improvements. Matt Glazer did a masterful job seeing the book through the production process. Melissa Rodriguez in the marketing department understood how to communicate our vision to teachers; they and the members of college sales forces did wonderful work in helping this book reach the classroom. We also thank the rest of our editorial and production team for their dedicated efforts: Media Editor Mollie Chandler; Assistant Editor Carly Lewis; copyeditor Kitty Wilson; proofreaders Jon Preimesberger and Jananee Sekar; indexer Michael Ferreira; art researchers Bruce Carson and Cecilia Varas; and text permissions researcher Michael McCarty.

In writing this book, we have also relied on a large number of talented scholars and friends within the academy to supply us with guidance, editorial expertise, bright ideas, research assistance, and many other forms of support, and we would like to thank them here. The enormous — but by no means comprehensive — list of colleagues, friends, students, and former students to whom we are indebted includes Isra Ali, Marsha Barrett, Rachel Bernard, Melissa Cooper, John Day, Jeff Dowd, Joseph L. Duong, Ann Fabian, Jared Farmer, Larissa Fergeson, Krystal Frazier, Raymond Gavins, Sharon Harley, Nancy Hewitt, Martha Jones, Stephanie Jones-Rogers, Mia Kissil, Christopher Lehman, Thomas Lekan, Emily Lieb, Leon F. Litwack, Julie Livingston, David Lucander, Catherine L. Macklin, Jaime Martinez, Story Matkin-Rawn, Gregory Mixon, Donna Murch, Kimberly Phillips, Alicia Rodriguez, David Schoebun, Karcheik Sims-Alvarado, Jason Sokol, Melissa Stein, Ellen Stroud, Melissa Stuckey, Anantha Sudakar, Patricia Sullivan, Keith Wailoo, Dara Walker, and Wendy Wright. Deborah would especially like to thank Maya White Pascual for her invaluable assistance with many of the documents in the last third of the book. Her insight, skill, and talent were absolutely indispensable. Finally, all three of us are grateful to our families and loved ones for the support and forbearance that they showed us during our work on this book.

Deborah Gray White
Mia Bay
Waldo E. Martin Jr.

I would like to thank my parents Allen E. Butler and Ernestine Gissendanner Butler for planting the initial seed of love for Black Studies and my grandparents Cecil Butler and Bernice Moltimore Butler for watering it with their rich personal stories of the Black experience that I could not find in my history books in grade school. I would like to thank my sister Shannon Butler and my husband, Meshaun Arnold for your support and words of encouragement along the way. I would also like to express my gratitude to Caitlin Kaufman for giving me the opportunity to work on this project. I would like to thank the students and teachers who have the courage and dedication to continue the work of telling our ancestors' stories despite the current political climate so that we may face the future with confidence and purpose. Lastly, I would like to acknowledge all the ancestors whose names I may never know but who I recognize had a direct hand in getting me where I am today.

Alysha Butler

My heartfelt thanks to my mother for her unwavering belief in my potential, always holding me to high standards and reminding me that I have the ability to achieve the goals I set for myself.

I would also like to express my deepest gratitude to my mother and grandparents, who instilled in me the importance of education. I will always remember the summers spent engaging with our family's encyclopedia collection to expand my understanding of the United States. Though I may have complained at the time, I recognize the importance of researching various aspects of how events have unfolded.

To my aunts, uncles, and cousins, thank you for encouraging me to be my best self and for celebrating my passion for history.

A special thank you to my husband, Anthony James Giordano Jr., for his constant support and for being my biggest champion throughout this journey. I am deeply grateful to Bella Sandoval, Dionne Campbell, and Laura Embriano for their invaluable words of encouragement while I engaged in the development of both the AP® African American Studies curriculum for our students and this book.

Additionally, I would like to extend my gratitude to Tanya Milner and Damon Smith for offering me the opportunity to launch AP® African American Studies at our school.

To the BFW editors, thank you for your support and guidance throughout this process. A special thank you to Caitlin for this amazing opportunity to work on this book.

Finally, I must thank my students. Your intellectual curiosity and willingness to engage with the course materials have inspired me and many others to continue to teach the truth.

Rachel Williams-Giordano

Brief Contents

UNIT 1 ▸ Origins of the African Diaspora *U1-A*

1 African Origins Beginnings to ca. 1600 C.E. *2*

2 From Africa to America 1441–1808 *36*

UNIT 2 ▸ Freedom, Enslavement, and Resistance *U2-A*

3 Slavery in North America 1619–1740 *74*

4 African Americans in the Age of Revolution 1741–1783 *118*

5 Slavery and Freedom in the New Republic 1775–1820 *162*

6 Black Life in the Slave South 1820–1860 *206*

7 The Northern Black Freedom Struggle and the Coming of the Civil War 1830–1860 *250*

8 Freedom Rising: The Civil War 1861–1865 *294*

UNIT 3 ▸ The Practice of Freedom *U3-A*

9 Reconstruction: The Making and Unmaking of a Revolution 1865–1877 *336*

10 Black Life and Culture during the Nadir 1877–1915 *380*

11 The New Negro Comes of Age 1915–1930 *428*

UNIT 4 ▸ Movements and Debates *U4-A*

12 Catastrophe, Recovery, and Renewal 1930–1942 *470*

13 Fighting for a Double Victory in the World War II Era 1938–1950 *502*

14 The Early Civil Rights Movement 1945–1963 *544*

15 Multiple Meanings of Freedom: The Movement Broadens 1961–1976 *588*

16 Racial Progress in an Era of Backlash and Change 1965–2000 *634*

17 African Americans in the Twenty-First Century 2000–Present *676*

Contents

About the Cover Image *v*

About the Authors of the AP® Edition *vi*

About the Authors of *Freedom on My Mind* *vii*

Dear Future AP® African American Studies Students *viii*

Why This Book This Way *x*

What's Inside This AP® Edition *xiii*

Maps and Figures *xlv*

Introduction: The Study of African American History *xlvi*

UNIT 1 ▸ Origins of the African Diaspora *U1-A*

CHAPTER 1 African Origins, Beginnings to ca. 1600 C.E. 2

Museum of Fine Arts, Houston, Texas/Museum purchase funded by Brown Foundation Accessions Endowment Fund/Bridgeman Images.

Contextualizing African American Stories: **"What Is Africa to Me?" The Ancestral Origins of Black Americans** *3*

Africa: Humanity's Homeland *4*

- A Varied Landscape *4*
- The African Origins of Humankind *6*
- Peopling a Continent *6*

Ancient Societies of Africa *8*

- Egypt *10*
- Nubia, Kush, and Aksum *12*
- The Nok and the Bantu *13*

West Africa's Medieval Empires *15*

- Ghana *15*
- Mali *18*
- The Songhai *22*

West Africa in the Sixteenth Century *23*

- Religious Beliefs and Practices *23*
- Kinship Ties and Political Alliances *24*
- Benin, Wealth, and Power *25*
- Slavery in West Africa *27*

Conclusion: Transatlantic Ties *29*

Chapter 1 Review ▸ Practicing AP® Skills *29*

AP® WORKING WITH SOURCES ▸ Imagining Africa *31*

PHILLIS WHEATLEY, *On Being Brought from Africa to America*, 1773 • BELINDA, *The Petition of Belinda*, 1782 • JOHN RUSSWURM, *On the Egyptians as Africans*, 1827 • GEORGE H. JOHNSON, *The Sphinx Builder Speaks*, 1919 • CLAUDE MCKAY, *Outcast*, 1922 • *Honoring African American History with a Kente Cloth Stole*

AP® SKILLS WORKSHOP ▸ Visual Texts: *Active Reading* *SW1-A*

AP® SKILLS WORKSHOP ▸ Visual Texts: *Multiple-Choice Questions* *SW1-F*

AP® EXAM PRACTICE *EP1-A*

CHAPTER 2 From Africa to America, 1441–1808 *36*

Bibliotheque de L'Arsenal, Paris, France/Archives Charmet/Bridgeman Images.

***Contextualizing African American Stories:* Enslaved Africans and the Portuguese Prince** *37*

The Rise of the Transatlantic Slave Trade *38*

- Europe on the Eve of the Slave Trade *39*
- Maritime Expeditions and First Contacts *39*
- The Enslavement of Indigenous Peoples *41*
- The First Africans in the Americas *43*
- The Business of Slave Trading *45*

The Middle Passage *49*

- Capture and Confinement *49*
- On the Slave Coast *53*
- Inside the Slave Ship *55*
- Hardship and Misery on Board *58*

Conclusion: The Slave Trade's Diaspora *60*

Chapter 2 Review ▸ Practicing AP® Skills *61*

AP® WORKING WITH SOURCES ▸ Firsthand Accounts of the Slave Trade *63*

OLAUDAH EQUIANO, *The Interesting Narrative of the Life of Olaudah Equiano, or Gustavus Vassa, the African*, 1789 • FLORENCE HALL, *Memoirs of the Life of Florence Hall*, 1810 • JAMES BARBOT JR., *General Observations on the Management of Slaves*, 1700 • ALEXANDER FALCONBRIDGE, *An Account of the Slave Trade on the Coast of Africa*, 1788 • *The Brig Sally's Log*, 1765

AP® SKILLS WORKSHOP ▸ Written Texts: *Active Reading* *SW2-A*

AP® SKILLS WORKSHOP ▸ Written Texts: *Multiple-Choice Questions* *SW2-F*

AP® EXAM PRACTICE *EP2-A*

UNIT 1 AP® EXAM PRACTICE *U1EP-A*

UNIT 2 ▸ Freedom, Enslavement, and Resistance *U2-A*

CHAPTER 3 Slavery in North America, 1619–1740 *74*

TO BE SOLD on board the Ship *Bance-Yland*, on tuesday the 6th of *May* next, at *Ashley-Ferry*; a choice cargo of about 250 fine healthy NEGROES, just arrived from the Windward & Rice Coast. —The utmost care has already been taken, and shall be continued, to keep them free from the least danger of being infected with the SMALL-POX, no boat having been on board, and all other communication with people from *Charles-Town* prevented.

Austin, Laurens, & Appleby.

N. B. Full one Half of the above Negroes have had the SMALL-POX in their own Country.

Sarin Images/Granger —

***Contextualizing African American Stories:* "20. and Odd Negroes": The Story of Virginia's First African Americans** *75*

Slavery and Freedom in Early English North America *76*

- Settlers, Servants, and the Enslaved in the Chesapeake *77*
- The Expansion of Slavery in the Chesapeake *83*
- The Creation of the Carolinas *85*
- Africans in New England *89*

Slavery in the Middle Atlantic Colonies *93*

- Slavery and Half-Freedom in New Netherland *93*
- Slavery in England's Middle Colonies *96*

Frontiers and Forced Labor *98*

- Slavery in French Louisiana *99*
- Black Society in Spanish Florida *101*
- Slavery and Servitude in Early Georgia *103*
- The Stono Rebellion *104*

Conclusion: Regional Variations of Early American Slavery *105*

Chapter 3 Review ▸ Practicing AP® Skills *106*

AP® WORKING WITH SOURCES ▸ Making Slaves *108*

The Codification of Slavery and Race in Seventeenth-Century Virginia, 1630–1680 • *The Massachusetts Body of Liberties, 1641* • *An Act for Regulating of Slaves in New Jersey, 1713–1714* • *The South Carolina Slave Code, 1740* • *The Black Code of Louisiana, 1724*

AP® SKILLS WORKSHOP ▸ Sourcing *SW3-A*

AP® EXAM PRACTICE *EP3-A*

CHAPTER 4 African Americans in the Age of Revolution, 1741–1783 *118*

© Massachusetts Historical Society, Boston, MA/Bridgeman Images.

Contextualizing African American Stories: **The New York Slave Plot of 1741** *119*

African American Life in Eighteenth-Century North America *121*
- Enslaved and Free Blacks across the Colonies *121*
- Shaping an African American Culture *123*
- The Great Awakening and Slavery *126*

The African American Revolution *131*
- The Road to Independence *131*
- Black Patriots *134*
- Black Loyalists *138*

Slavery, Soldiers, and the Outcome of the Revolution *142*
- American Victory, British Defeat *143*
- The Fate of Black Loyalists *144*
- Closer to Freedom *147*

Conclusion: The American Revolution's Mixed Results for Blacks *150*

Chapter 4 Review ▸ Practicing AP® Skills *151*

AP® WORKING WITH SOURCES ▸ Black Freedom Fighters *153*

PHILLIS WHEATLEY, *A Poem to the Earl of Dartmouth*, 1772 • PHILLIS WHEATLEY, *Letter to the Reverend Samson Occom*, 1774 • LEMUEL HAYNES, *Liberty Further Extended*, 1776 • JEAN BAPTISTE ANTOINE DE VERGER, *Soldiers in Uniform*, 1781 • BOSTON KING, *Memoirs of a Black Loyalist*, 1798 • JOHN SINGLETON COPLEY, *The Death of Major Peirson*, 1782–1784

AP® SKILLS WORKSHOP ▸ Short-Answer Questions *SW4-A*

AP® EXAM PRACTICE *EP4-A*

CHAPTER 5 Slavery and Freedom in the New Republic, 1775–1820 *162*

Absalom Jones, 1810, by Raphaelle Peale (1774–1825)/Delaware Art Museum, Wilmington, Delaware/ Gift of Absalom Jones School/ Bridgeman Images.

Contextualizing African American Stories: **Benjamin Banneker Questions Thomas Jefferson about Slavery in the New Republic** *163*

The Limits of Democracy *165*
- The Status of Slavery in the New Nation *166*
- Slavery's Cotton Frontiers *168*
- Slavery and Empire *172*

Slavery and Freedom outside the Plantation South *175*
- Urban Slavery and Southern Free Blacks *175*
- Gabriel's Rebellion *177*
- Achieving Emancipation in the North *180*

Free Black Life in the New Republic *183*
Free Black Organizations *184*
Free Black Education and Employment *187*
Rising White Hostility *190*
Black Soldiers and Civilians in the War of 1812 *191*
The Colonization Debate *192*
Conclusion: African American Freedom *194*
Chapter 5 Review ▸ Practicing AP® Skills *195*
AP® WORKING WITH SOURCES ▸ Free Black Activism *197*
JANE COGGESHALL, *Petition for Freedom,* 1785 • ABSALOM JONES AND OTHERS, *Petition to Congress on the Fugitive Slave Act,* 1799 • JAMES FORTEN, *Letters from a Man of Colour,* 1813 • *Sentiments of the People of Color,* 1817 • ONA JUDGE, *Washington's Runaway Slave,* 1845 • EDWARD WILLIAMS CLAY, *Bobalition,* 1833
AP® SKILLS WORKSHOP ▸ Document-Based Questions: *Prompts* *SW5-A*
AP® EXAM PRACTICE *EP5-A*

CHAPTER 6 Black Life in the Slave South, 1820–1860 *206*

GL Archive/Alamy Stock Photo.

Contextualizing African American Stories: **William Wells Brown and Growing Up in the Slave South** *207*
The Expansion and Consolidation of Slavery *208*
Slavery, Cotton, and American Industrialization *209*
The Missouri Compromise Crisis *211*
Slavery Expands into Indian Territory *212*
The Domestic Slave Trade *215*
Black Challenges to Slavery *217*
Denmark Vesey's Plot *218*
David Walker's Exile *221*
Nat Turner's Rebellion, the *Amistad* Case, and the *Creole* Insurrection *223*
Everyday Resistance to Slavery *225*
Disobedience and Defiance *225*
Escaping Slavery *227*
Survival, Community, and Culture *230*
Religion *230*
Gender, Age, and Work *232*
Marriage and Family *234*
Conclusion: Surviving Slavery *238*
Chapter 6 Review ▸ Practicing AP® Skills *240*

AP® WORKING WITH SOURCES ▸ Testimony of Enslaved People *242*
Slave Punishment • Lewis Clarke, *Questions and Answers about Slavery*, 1845 • Bethany Veney, *Narrative of Bethany Veney, a Slave Woman*, 1889 • Mary Reynolds, *The Days of Slavery*, 1937

AP® SKILLS WORKSHOP ▸ Document-Based Questions: *Skillful Skimming* *SW6-A*

AP® EXAM PRACTICE *EP6-A*

CHAPTER 7 The Northern Black Freedom Struggle and the Coming of the Civil War, 1830–1860 *250*

The Art Archive at Shutterstock.

***Contextualizing African American Stories:* Mary Ann Shadd and the Black Liberation Struggle before the Civil War** *251*

The Boundaries of Freedom *252*
- Racial Discrimination in the Era of the Common Man *252*
- The Growth of Free Black Communities in the North *256*
- Black Self-Help in an Era of Moral Reform *259*

Forging a Black Freedom Struggle *262*
- Building a National Black Community: The Black Convention Movement and the Black Press *263*
- Growing Black Activism in Literature, Politics, and the Justice System *265*
- Abolitionism: Moral Suasion, Political Action, Race, and Gender *269*

Slavery and the Coming of the Civil War *272*
- Westward Expansion and Slavery in the Territories *272*
- The Fugitive Slave Law Crisis and Civil Disobedience *274*
- Confrontations in "Bleeding Kansas" and the Courts *278*
- Emigration and John Brown's Raid on Harpers Ferry *281*

Conclusion: Whose Country Is It? *283*

Chapter 7 Review ▸ Practicing AP® Skills *284*

AP® WORKING WITH SOURCES ▸ Forging an African American Nation—Enslaved and Free, North and South *286*
Sarah Mapps Douglass, *To Make the Slaves' Cause Our Own*, 1832 • Henry Highland Garnet, *An Address to the Slaves of the United States of America*, 1843 • Frederick Douglass, *What to the Slave Is the Fourth of July?*, 1852 • *Escaping Slavery via the Underground Railroad* • *Jim Crow*

AP® SKILLS WORKSHOP ▸ Document-Based Questions: Thesis Statements *SW7-A*

AP® EXAM PRACTICE *EP7-A*

CHAPTER 8

Freedom Rising: The Civil War, 1861–1865 *294*

The Hour of Emancipation, 1863, by William Tolman Carlton (1816–1888)/Private Collection/ Photo © Christie's Images/ Bridgeman Images.

Contextualizing African American Stories: **Robert Smalls and the African American Freedom Struggle during the Civil War** *295*

The Coming of War and the Seizing of Freedom, 1861–1862 *296*

War Aims and Battlefield Realities *296*
Union Policy on Black Soldiers and Black Freedom *298*
Freedom Seekers and Freedpeople *301*

Turning Points, 1862–1863 *305*

The Emancipation Proclamation *305*
The U.S. Colored Troops *307*
African Americans in the Major Battles of 1863 *310*

Home Fronts and War's End, 1863–1865 *312*

Riots and Restoration of the Union *313*
Black Civilians at Work for the War *314*
Union Victory, Emancipation from Slavery, and the Renewed Struggle for Equality *317*

Conclusion: Emancipation and Equality *322*

Chapter 8 Review ▸ Practicing AP® Skills *323*

AP® WORKING WITH SOURCES ▸ Wartime and Emancipation *325*

ALFRED M. GREEN, *Let Us . . . Take Up the Sword*, 1861 • ISAIAH C. WEARS, *The Evil Injustice of Colonization*, 1862 • SUSIE KING TAYLOR, *Reminiscences of My Life in Camp*, 1902 • *The Emancipation Proclamation*, 1863 • WILLIAM TOLMAN CARLTON, *Watch Meeting — Dec. 31st — Waiting for the Hour*, 1863 • *Private Hubbard Pryor, before and after Enlisting in the U.S. Colored Troops*, 1864 • *Freedmen's Memorial*, 1876

AP® SKILLS WORKSHOP ▸ Document-Based Questions: *Introductions* *SW8-A*

AP® EXAM PRACTICE *EP8-A*

UNIT **2** AP® EXAM PRACTICE *U2EP-A*

UNIT 3 ▸ The Practice of Freedom *U3-A*

CHAPTER 9 **Reconstruction: The Making and Unmaking of a Revolution, 1865–1877** *336*

Library of Congress, Prints and Photographs Division, Washington, D.C., LC-DIG-ppmsca-17564.

***Contextualizing African American Stories:* Jourdon and Mandy Anderson Find Security in Freedom after Slavery** *337*

A Social Revolution *338*

- Freedom and Family *339*
- Church and Community *341*
- Land and Labor *344*
- The Hope of Education *346*

A Short-Lived Political Revolution *350*

- The Political Contest over Reconstruction *351*
- Black Reconstruction *354*
- The Defeat of Reconstruction *358*

Opportunities and Limits outside the South *360*

- Autonomy in the West *361*
- The Right to Work for Fair Wages *363*
- The Struggle for Equal Rights *365*

Conclusion: Revolutions and Reversals *367*

Chapter 9 Review ▸ Practicing AP® Skills *368*

AP® WORKING WITH SOURCES ▸ The Vote *370*

SOJOURNER TRUTH, *Equal Voting Rights*, 1867 • PROCEEDINGS OF THE AMERICAN EQUAL RIGHTS ASSOCIATION, *A Debate: Negro Male Suffrage vs. Woman Suffrage*, 1869 • MARY ANN SHADD CARY, *Woman's Right to Vote*, Early 1870s • A. R. WAUD, *The First Vote*, 1867 • A. CLARK, *Address of the Colored State Convention to the People of Iowa on Behalf of Their Enfranchisement*, 1868 • THOMAS NAST, *Colored Rule in a Reconstructed(?) State*, 1874

AP® SKILLS WORKSHOP ▸ Document-Based Questions: Evidence *SW9-A*

AP® EXAM PRACTICE *EP9-A*

CHAPTER 10 **Black Life and Culture during the Nadir, 1877–1915** *380*

Granger/Granger – All rights reserved.

***Contextualizing African American Stories:* Ida B. Wells: Creating Hope and Community amid Extreme Repression** *381*

Racism and Black Challenges *382*

- Racial Segregation *383*
- Ideologies of White Supremacy *386*

Disfranchisement and Political Activism 388
Lynching and the Campaign against It 390

Freedom's First Generation 393
Black Women and Men in the Era of Jim Crow 393
Black Communities in the Cities of the New South 397
New Cultural Expressions 401

Migration, Accommodation, and Protest 405
Migration Hopes and Disappointments 405
International Migrations 407
The Age of Booker T. Washington 408
The Emergence of W. E. B. Du Bois 410

Conclusion: Racial Uplift in the Nadir 416

Chapter 10 Review ▸ Practicing AP® Skills 417

AP® WORKING WITH SOURCES ▸ Agency and Constraint 419
The Lynching of Charles Mitchell, 1897 • The Executive Committee of the State Convention of Colored Citizens of Kentucky, *Call for a Convention*, 1885 • A Georgia Negro Peon, *The New Slavery in the South*, 1904 • W. E. B. Du Bois, *Along the Color Line*, 1910 • Letter to the Editor, *From the South*, 1911 • *Chain Gang*

AP® SKILLS WORKSHOP ▸ Document-Based Questions: *Commentary* SW10-A

AP® EXAM PRACTICE EP10-A

CHAPTER 11 The New Negro Comes of Age, 1915–1930 428

Gilder Lehrman Collection, New York/Bridgeman Images.

***Contextualizing African American Stories:* Zora Neale Hurston and the Advancement of the Black Freedom Struggle** 429

The Great Migration 430
Origins and Patterns of Migration 430
West Indian Migrants 434
Black Community Aid Societies 435
Changes in Church Membership and Worship 436
Segregation, Self-Sufficiency, and Political Power 437

War Abroad, Violence at Home 439
African Americans in the Great War 440
Race Riots and Red Summer 441
The Rebirth of the KKK 444

The New Negro Arrives 445
Institutional Bases for Social Science and Historical Studies 446
The Universal Negro Improvement Association 449
The Harlem Renaissance 453

Conclusion: The New Negro Comes of Age 457

Chapter 11 Review ▸ Practicing AP® Skills 458

AP® WORKING WITH SOURCES ▸ The Harlem/New Negro Renaissance *460*

ALAIN LOCKE, *Foreword to* The New Negro, 1925 • JAMES WELDON JOHNSON AND JOHN ROSAMOND JOHNSON, *Lift Every Voice and Sing*, 1900 • MA RAINEY, *Prove It on Me Blues*, 1928 • LANGSTON HUGHES, *I, Too*, 1926 • GWENDOLYN BENNETT, *To a Dark Girl*, 1927 • AUGUSTA SAVAGE, *Gamin*, c. 1930 • JAMES VAN DER ZEE, *Couple in Raccoon Coats*, 1932 • ARCHIBALD MOTLEY, *Tongues (Holy Rollers)*, 1929

AP® SKILLS WORKSHOP ▸ Document-Based Questions: *Conclusions* *SW11-A*

AP® EXAM PRACTICE *EP11-A*

UNIT **3** AP® EXAM PRACTICE *U3EP-A*

UNIT **4** ▸ Movements and Debates *U4-A*

CHAPTER 12 Catastrophe, Recovery, and Renewal, 1930–1942 *470*

Margaret Bourke-White/Time Life Pictures/Getty Images.

Contextualizing African American Stories: The Campaign to Free "the Scottsboro Boys" *471*

The Great Depression and the New Deal *472*
- Economic Crisis and Joblessness *472*
- Inequality in the New Deal *475*
- Black Voters in the Democratic Party *477*

Coming Together to Battle Hardship *478*
- Surviving through Church and Community *479*
- Black Collective Action and Interracial Unionism *480*
- The Communist Party's Appeal *481*
- Organizing for Civil Rights *483*

Black Culture in Hard Times *485*
- The Chicago Renaissance *486*
- African American Art within a Global Context *488*
- Cultural Activism and the Arts *489*
- Fighting Racial Stereotypes in Popular Culture *490*

Conclusion: Freedom Struggle, Mass Movements, and Mass Culture *493*

Chapter 12 Review ▸ Practicing AP® Skills *494*

AP® WORKING WITH SOURCES ▸ Communist Radicalism and Everyday Realities *495*

W. E. B. Du Bois, *Negro Editors on Communism: A Symposium of the American Negro Press,* 1932 • Angelo Herndon, *You Cannot Kill the Working Class,* 1934 • Russell Lee, *Negro Drinking at "Colored" Water Cooler in Streetcar Terminal, Oklahoma City, Oklahoma,* 1939 • Margaret Bourke-White, *The Louisville Flood,* 1937 • Marion Post Wolcott, *Negroes Jitterbugging in a Juke Joint on Saturday Afternoon, Clarksdale, Mississippi Delta,* 1939

AP® SKILLS WORKSHOP ▸ Multiple-Choice Questions with Paired Stimuli *SW12-A*

AP® EXAM PRACTICE *EP12-A*

CHAPTER 13 Fighting for a Double Victory in the World War II Era, 1938–1950 *502*

Schomberg Center, NYPL/Art Resource, NY.

Contextualizing African American Stories: **James Tillman and Evelyn Bates Mobilize for War** *503*

The Crisis of World War II *505*
- America Enters the War and States Its Goals *505*
- African Americans Respond to the War *506*
- Racial Violence and Discrimination in the Military *509*

African Americans on the Home Front *513*
- New Jobs and Wartime Migration *513*
- Race Riots during the War Years *516*
- Organizing for Economic Opportunity *517*

The Struggle for Citizenship Rights *520*
- Fighting and Dying for the Right to Vote *521*
- New Beginnings in Political Life *525*
- Social and Cultural Changes *526*
- Desegregating the Military and the GI Bill *528*

Conclusion: A Partial Victory *531*

Chapter 13 Review ▸ Practicing AP® Skills *532*

AP® WORKING WITH SOURCES ▸ African Americans and the Tuskegee Experiments *534*

Interview with a Tuskegee Syphilis Study Participant, 1972 • *Tuskegee Study Participants* • *Letter from U.S. Public Health Service to Surgeon General* • Alexander Jefferson, *Interview with a Tuskegee Airman,* 2006 • *Tuskegee Airmen* • William H. Hastie and George E. Stratemeyer, *Resignation Memo and Response,* 1943

AP® SKILLS WORKSHOP ▸ Responding to Short-Answer Questions without Stimuli *SW13-A*

AP® EXAM PRACTICE *EP13-A*

Hulton-Deutsch Collection/ Corbis/Getty Images.

CHAPTER 14 The Early Civil Rights Movement, 1945–1963 544

Contextualizing African American Stories: **Paul Robeson: A Cold War Civil Rights Warrior** *545*

Anticommunism and the Postwar Black Freedom Struggle *547*

African Americans, the Cold War, and President Truman's Loyalty Program *547*
Loyalty Programs Force New Strategies *551*

The Transformation of the Southern Civil Rights Movement *553*

Triumphs and Tragedies in the Early Years, 1951–1956 *553*
New Leadership for a New Movement *557*
The Watershed Years of the Southern Movement *558*
White Resistance and Presidential Sluggishness *564*

Civil Rights: A National Movement *567*

Racism and Inequality in the North and West *568*
Fighting Back: The Snail's Pace of Change *571*
The March on Washington and the Aftermath *574*

Conclusion: The Evolution of the Black American Freedom Struggle *578*

Chapter 14 Review ▸ Practicing AP® Skills *579*

AP® WORKING WITH SOURCES ▸ We Are Not Afraid *581*

ANNE MOODY, *Coming of Age in Mississippi*, 1968 • CLEVELAND SELLERS, *The River of No Return*, 1973 • ELIZABETH ECKFORD, *The First Day: Little Rock*, 1957 • *Images of Protest and Terror*

AP® SKILLS WORKSHOP ▸ Individual Student Project: Topic Selection *SW14-A*

AP® EXAM PRACTICE *EP14-A*

Associated Press/AP Images.

CHAPTER 15 Multiple Meanings of Freedom: The Movement Broadens, 1961–1976 588

Contextualizing African American Stories: **Stokely Carmichael and the Meaning of Black Power** *589*

The Emergence of Black Power *591*

Expanding the Struggle beyond Civil Rights *591*
Early Black Power Organizations *593*
Malcolm X *596*

The Struggle Transforms *598*

Black Power and Mississippi Politics *598*
Bloody Encounters *602*
Black Power Ascends *604*

Economic Justice and Affirmative Action *607*

Politics and the Fight for Jobs 607
Urban Dilemmas: Deindustrialization, Globalization, and White Flight 608
Tackling Economic Injustice 611

War, Radicalism, and Turbulence 613
The Vietnam War and Black Opposition 613
Urban Radicalism 617

Conclusion: Progress, Challenges, and Change 620

Chapter 15 Review ▸ Practicing AP® Skills 621

AP® WORKING WITH SOURCES ▸ Black Power: Expression and Repression 623

NINA SIMONE, *Mississippi Goddam*, 1963 • LOÏS MAILOU JONES, *Ubi Girl from Tai Region*, 1972 • FAITH RINGGOLD, *The Flag Is Bleeding*, 1967 • *COINTELPRO Targets Black Organizations*, 1967 • *FBI Uses Fake Letters to Divide the Chicago Black Panthers and the Blackstone Rangers*, 1969 • *"Special Payment" Request and Floor Plan of Fred Hampton's Apartment*, 1969 • *Tangible Results*, 1969 • *Church Committee Report*, 1976

AP® SKILLS WORKSHOP ▸ Individual Student Project: Source Selection SW15-A

AP® EXAM PRACTICE EP15-A

CHAPTER 16 Racial Progress in an Era of Backlash and Change, 1965–2000 634

Don Hogan Charles/Archive Photos/Getty Images.

Contextualizing African American Stories: **Shirley Chisholm: The First of Many Firsts** 635

Opposition to the Black Freedom Movement 637
The Emergence of the New Right 638
Law and Order, the Southern Strategy, and Anti–Affirmative Action 638
The Reagan Era 641

The Persistence of the Black Freedom Struggle 644
The Transformation of the Black Panthers 645
Black Women Find Their Voice 647
The Fight for Education 649
Community Control and Urban Ethnic Conflict 650
Black Political Gains 652
The Expansion of the Black Middle Class 654

The Different Faces of Black America 657
The Class Divide 657
Hip-Hop, Violence, and the Emergence of a New Generation 660
Gender and Sexuality 662
Ethnic Diversity 664

Conclusion: Black Americans on the Eve of the New Millennium 666

Chapter 16 Review ▸ Practicing AP® Skills 667

AP® WORKING WITH SOURCES ▸ All Africa's Children *669*

A Statistical Look at Foreign-Born Blacks in the United States, 1980–2016 • *Can We All Get Along? Interviews with Immigrants and Native-Born Blacks* • DOUGLASS S. MASSEY, MARGARITA MOONEY, KIMBERLY C. TORRES, AND CAMILLE Z. CHARLES, *Black Immigrants and Black Natives Attending Selective Colleges and Universities in the United States*, 2007 • *The Meeting of Cultures*

AP® SKILLS WORKSHOP ▸ Individual Student Project: *Evidence-Based Argument* *SW16-A*

AP® EXAM PRACTICE *EP16-A*

CHAPTER 17 African Americans in the Twenty-First Century, 2000–Present *676*

Jim Watson/AFP/Getty Images.

Contextualizing African American Stories: **Barack Hussein Obama, America's Forty-Fourth President** *677*

The State of Black America *679*
- The Black "Community" *680*
- Solidarity, Culture, and the Meaning of Blackness *683*
- Diversity in Politics and Religion *685*

Trying Times *688*
- The Carceral State, or "the New Jim Crow" *688*
- 9/11 and the Wars in Afghanistan and Iraq *691*
- Hurricane Katrina *692*

Change Comes to America *694*
- Obama's Forerunners, Campaign, and Victory *695*
- The New Obama Administration *697*
- Racism Confronts Obama in His First Term *700*
- The 2012 Election *702*

Moving Forward *703*
- Obama's Second Term *703*
- African Americans in the Shadow of Ferguson *707*

Backlash, Again: African Americans in the Age of Trump *708*
- Making America Great Again *708*
- Renewed Solidarity and Grassroots Organizing *711*

Conclusion: The Persistence of the Color Line *713*

Chapter 17 Review ▸ Practicing AP® Skills *715*

AP® WORKING WITH SOURCES ▸ #BlackLivesMatter *717*

ALICIA GARZA, *A Herstory of the #BlackLivesMatter Movement*, 2014 • *#SayHerName* • *Citizen–Police Confrontation in Ferguson* • *"We Can't Breathe": 2014, 2020* • *The Police See It Differently* • PHILONISE FLOYD, *Testimony Before the House Judiciary Committee Hearing on "Policing Practices and Law Enforcement Accountability,"* 2020

AP® SKILLS WORKSHOP ▸ **Individual Student Project: *Presentation and Oral Defense*** *SW17-A*

AP® EXAM PRACTICE *EP17-A*

UNIT **4** AP® EXAM PRACTICE *U4EP-A*

PRACTICE AP® ▸ African American Studies Exam *PE-1*

Appendix *A-1*

Documents *A-1*

The Declaration of Independence *A-1*
The Constitution of the United States of America *A-3*
Amendments to the Constitution *A-10*
Selected Legislative Acts *A-14*
Selected Supreme Court Decisions *A-20*
Dred Scott v. Sandford [1857] *A-20*
Plessy v. Ferguson [1896] *A-21*
Brown v. Board of Education of Topeka [1954] *A-22*
Griggs v. Duke Power Co. [1971] *A-22*
Regents of the University of California v. Bakke [1978] *A-23*
Selected Documents *A-24*
Booker T. Washington, *The Atlanta Compromise Speech* [1895] *A-24*
Barack Obama, *A More Perfect Union* [2008] *A-26*

Tables and Charts *A-33*

African American Population of the United States, 1790–2010 *A-33*
Historically Black Colleges and Universities, 1865–Present *A-34*

Glossary/Glosario *G-1*

Notes and Text Credits *N-1*

Index *I-1*

Maps and Figures

Maps

MAP 1.1 Africa's Diverse Geography *5*
MAP 1.2 Ancient Societies of Africa *9*
MAP 1.3 Medieval West Africa and the Trans-Saharan Trade *16*
MAP 2.1 Trade of Enslaved Africans, 1501–1867 *46*
MAP 2.2 The Triangle Trade *48*
MAP 3.1 Distribution of Blacks and Whites, 1680 and 1740 *78*
MAP 4.1 Patriots and Loyalists *139*
MAP 4.2 African Americans across the Developing Nation, 1770 and 1800 *149*
MAP 5.1 The Northwest Ordinance *167*
MAP 5.2 The Louisiana Purchase *174*
MAP 6.1 Agriculture and Industry in the Slave South, 1860 *210*
MAP 6.2 The Missouri Compromise *213*
MAP 6.3 The Domestic Slave Trade, 1808–1865 *216*
MAP 7.1 The Underground Railroad *275*
MAP 7.2 The Kansas-Nebraska Act, 1854 *279*
MAP 8.1 African Americans in Battle *312*
MAP 8.2 Emancipation from Slavery *320*
MAP 9.1 Black Political Participation in the Reconstruction South, 1867–1868 *357*
MAP 9.2 African American Population Distribution, 1860 and 1890 *361*
MAP 10.1 Jim Crow and Disfranchisement in Former Confederate States *385*
MAP 10.2 African American Lynching Victims by State, 1877–1950 *390*
MAP 10.3 School Segregation in the North and West *413*
MAP 11.1 The Great Migration, 1910–1929 *433*
MAP 11.2 Cultural Harlem *454*
MAP 13.1 African American Migration, 1930–1970 *514*
MAP 13.2 The Persistence of Lynching, 1940–1946 *524*
MAP 14.1 The Routes of the Freedom Rides, 1961 *563*
MAP 15.1 The Impact of the Voting Rights Act of 1965 *603*
MAP 16.1 All Black Americans and Foreign-Born Blacks by State, 2017 *665*

By the Numbers

Black and White Populations in the Seventeenth-Century Chesapeake *84*
The Growth of Slavery and Cotton, 1820–1860 *170*
Percent Change in Free Black Population, 1830–1860 *257*
African Americans in the Union Military *308*
Lynchings Every Five Years, 1885–1950 *391*
African Americans in the Vietnam War *615*
Incarceration Rates for Blacks and Whites, 1974–2001 *643*
Black and White Prison Population, 2000–2017 *689*

Introduction: The Study of African American History

It is a joy to offer *Freedom on My Mind* to enhance your knowledge of both African American history and the craft of history. For us, the authors, history has never been just a series of dates and names. It is not just memorizable facts, consumed only to pass a test or complete an assignment. For us, history is adventure; it's a puzzle that must be both unraveled and put together. Being a historian is like being a time-traveling detective. To be able to use our sleuthing skills to unveil the history of African Americans — a history that for too long was dismissed but tells us so much about American democracy — is not just a delight but a serious responsibility.

The History of African American History

Although Black Americans first came to North America in 1619, before the *Mayflower* brought Pilgrims, the history of African American history has a relatively recent past. For most of U.S. history, Black history was ignored, overlooked, exploited, demeaned, discounted, or ridiculed — much as African Americans were. Worse yet, history was often used to justify the mistreatment of African Americans: the history of Africans was used to justify slavery, and the history of slavery was used to justify the subsequent disfranchisement, discrimination, rape, and lynching of African Americans.

American Blacks understood this connection between a history that misrepresented them and their citizenship, and they fought not only to free themselves from bondage but also to create a legacy that future generations could be proud of: a legacy that championed their self-inspired "uplift" and that countered the negative images that prevailed in American society. Take just one example: D. W. Griffith's film *The Birth of a Nation* (1915) used revolutionary cinematography to disseminate a history that represented slaves as happy and race relations as rosy, until the Civil War and Reconstruction unleashed Black criminals and sexual predators on an innocent South. Many used Griffith's film to justify the lynching of Black men and the segregation of the races. Indeed, President Woodrow Wilson, the historian who as president introduced segregation into the government offices of Washington, D.C., premiered the film in the White House and praised its historical accuracy.

The same year that *The Birth of a Nation* premiered, Harvard-trained Black historian Carter G. Woodson founded the Association for the Study of Negro Life and History (ASNLH). Woodson's ASNLH was the culmination of what has become known as the New Negro history movement, begun in the late nineteenth century. The organization's goal was to counter Griffith-type images by resurrecting a positive Black history and recounting all that African Americans had done for themselves and for America. Because professional American historical journals generally did not publish Black history, the ASNLH, with Woodson as editor, issued the *Journal of Negro History* and the *Negro History Bulletin*. During the 1920s, the *Journal of Negro History* and the ASNLH focused much of their attention on proving Griffith wrong. Professionally researched articles and scholarly convention panels demonstrated that Black people were not criminals or sexually dangerous. Black scholars wrote a history that showed how Blacks, despite being mercilessly degraded, had in the one generation after slavery's end become a mostly literate people who voted responsibly and elected representatives who practiced fiscal responsibility and pursued educational and democratic reforms. Because Black history was excluded from public school curricula, the ASNLH also spearheaded the movement that brought about Negro History Week, observed first in African American communities and then in the nation at large. The second week of February was chosen because it marked the birthdays of the Great Emancipator, Abraham Lincoln, and the great Black freedom fighter, Frederick Douglass. Black leaders believed that a celebration of the lives of Lincoln and Douglass would evolve into the study of African Americans in general.

Black scholars did this because they understood the connection between their history and their status in America. The preeminent twentieth-century Black historian W. E. B. Du Bois sternly warned against the erasure and/or distortion of the role played by African Americans in the building of the American nation. "We the darker ones come . . . not altogether empty-handed," he said.[1] African Americans had much to offer this country, much to teach America about humanitarianism and morality, and thus Du Bois pleaded for the study of Black history and its inclusion in the national consciousness. Black history was even more important to African Americans, he instructed. Black people needed to know their history "for positive advance, . . . for negative defense," and to have "implicit trust in our ability and worth." "No people that laughs at itself, and ridicules itself, and wishes to God it was anything but itself ever wrote its name in history," counseled Du Bois at the turn of the twentieth century.[2] For him, Black history, Black freedom, and American democracy were all of a piece.

It should come as no surprise that when the freedom struggle moved onto the national stage in the mid-twentieth century, African American history became a central focus. Activists demanded not just an end to white terrorism, desegregation in all areas of American life, equality in the job market, voting rights, and the freedom to marry regardless of race, but also that nondistorted African American history and studies be included in elementary through high school public school curricula and textbooks, as well as in college courses. They insisted that colleges and universities offer degrees in African American studies and that traditional disciplines offer courses that treated black subjects as legitimate areas of study. In the 1960s, demands were made to extend Negro History Week to a full month, and in 1976, Woodson's organization, by then renamed the Association for the Study of African American Life and History (1972), designated February as Black History Month — a move acknowledged and approved by the federal government.

Debating African American History and Its Sources

Historians rely on documents written in the past. Before we can analyze a period, we must locate and unearth our sources. Primary sources originate during the period under study. Some are official or unofficial documents issued by public and private institutions; items as varied as church records, government census records, newspapers and magazines, probate records, court transcripts, and schoolbooks are exceptionally revelatory of the past. Other records come from individuals. Personal letters and diaries, bank statements, photographs, and even gravestone inscriptions help historians figure out what happened during a particular time period. Once we assemble all of our documents, we write history based on our analysis of them. Our histories become part of a body of secondary sources for the period under study — secondary because they originate from someone who has secondarily written an account that relied on first, or primary, sources.

Researching African American history has always presented a challenge for scholars. During their almost 250 years of enslavement, Africans and African Americans had few belongings they could call their own; thus they left few of the personal records that historians depend on to write history. Added to this obstacle is the fact that during slavery, Black literacy was outlawed. Schools for free Blacks were regularly destroyed, and anyone teaching an enslaved person to read could be arrested, fined, whipped, or jailed for corrupting a labor force that was considered most efficient when it was illiterate. Black Americans, therefore, developed a rich oral tradition. Certainly, as you will see from the sources presented in this book, some Blacks — mostly those who were not enslaved — wrote letters, gave speeches, kept diaries, or wrote narratives of their experiences. However, most Black communication and communion took place through personal interaction and via the spoken word. Before Black history was committed to paper, it was committed to memory and passed down through folklore, art, and secular and religious music. This continued long into the twentieth century as segregation, disfranchisement, and attacks on Black education forced African Americans to depend on their oral tradition.

For historians, who rely heavily on written sources, this presented a problem — as did the fact that many thought it unfair to write Black history using only those sources emanating from the very people and institutions responsible for the African American's second-class citizenship. For example, in his 1935 post–Civil War history, *Black Reconstruction*, Du Bois, a Harvard-trained historian, railed against the professional historians who had written about the period using only the sources that came from the defeated South. It was to be expected, argued Du Bois, that these historians, who were mostly white, male, and southern, would find fault with the freedmen; their sources were those of defeated enslavers and others who had a stake in painting formerly enslaved people as unworthy of freedom. "The chief witness in Reconstruction, the emancipated slave himself, has been almost barred from court," argued Du Bois.[3] In presenting a case for using the written records of Black representatives, which included the few biographies of Black leaders and the unedited debates of the Reconstruction conventions, Du Bois called for true fairness: "If history is going to be scientific, if the record of human action is going to be set down with that accuracy and faithfulness of detail which will allow its use as a measuring rod and guidepost for the future of nations, there must be set some standards of ethics in research and interpretation."[4] In other words, history could not be written from just one point of view or with sources that were highly prejudicial or exclusionary. But who was to say which sources were best, and who was best qualified to write African American history? Could not those sympathetic to Black causes also use history for their own purposes and bend it to their needs? And given that so many African American sources were oral and not preserved in archives or were personal artifacts packed away in family storage, how could the existing sources be accessed to produce written history?

These issues were hotly debated during the mid-twentieth-century freedom struggle, and out of that debate came a new consensus about African American history and history in general. For as African Americans, traditionally the lowest in the

American social strata, demonstrated how important their history was to them and to the nation, other Americans followed suit. Women, workers, and members of America's many ethnic groups expanded the study of their pasts and insisted on inclusion in the narrative of American history. Rather than focus on presidents, or the nation's wars, or the institutions at the top of America's political, economic, and social systems, ordinary American citizens called for a study of America from the "bottom up." Everyone made history, these advocates argued. The daily lives of average Americans were as important for historians as the decisions made by heads of state. It was not just the rich and famous, not just men, not just whites, not just Anglo-Saxon Protestants, and not just heterosexuals who made history. As women, Native Americans, Asian Americans, Hispanic Americans, and gay, lesbian, bisexual, and transgendered citizens demanded equal inclusion in American society, they demanded that their history be included as well. In response, scholars began to change their research methods by including different kinds of sources and asking different kinds of questions; consequently, their histories changed. The midcentury rights movements birthed not just new and expanded citizenship rights, but also a new way of thinking about and doing history. Sometimes history from the "bottom up" looks very different from "top-down" history. Sometimes the differences are reconcilable, but often they are not. Adding sources from rank-and-file Americans made a difference in how the past was written and understood.

The Craft of African American History

Historians of slavery pioneered the "new" African American history in the 1970s. Following the advice of Du Bois, they ceased barring the "chief witness" from their studies and began integrating the experiences of formerly enslaved people into their work and writing some histories from the enslaved person's point of view. This necessitated using different kinds of sources, which, not surprisingly, were oral interviews conducted after slavery or oral testimony given to the Freedmen's Bureau, the government agency established to aid freedpeople in their transition from slavery to freedom. Because Black testimony differed significantly from most white testimony, historians were now tasked with recounting a history that looked at slavery from different vantage points.

Once historians added African American testimony, it changed the way many interpreted seemingly objective sources like census and probate records, court cases, and congressional debates. For example, Harriet Brent Jacobs's account of her enslaver's attempt at rape and her recounting of the sexual exploitation of enslaved women changed the way some historians looked at plantation lists that showed a preponderance of single females with children. This was once assumed to indicate the promiscuity of Black women, but historians now had to consider the sexual profligacy of white men. Plantation records were also combed to trace Black family lineages, a laborious process that revealed, for example, that not all enslaved people took the last names of their enslavers. In addition, although the law did not recognize marriages of enslaved people, these records showed that many enslaved people partnered carefully and with intention — not in a willy-nilly fashion, as had previously been assumed. In the 1970s, historians studied previously excluded Black folktales and Black music and art as a way to discern enslaved people's belief systems and culture. The new sources stimulated different answers to age-old questions and prompted serious reconsideration of previously held historical assumptions. Whereas enslavers had maintained that Blacks were happy under slavery and unfit for freedom, Black-originated sources spoke of ever-present Black resistance to slavery. Whereas most white-originated sources gave Abraham Lincoln and other whites credit for Black emancipation, Black-originated sources showed how African Americans stole themselves from slavery, joined Union armies, and fought for their own freedom and for the Union cause. These new sources showed how a people who were once African became African American, and how and why a people so excluded embraced American democratic principles.

African American sources opened a window not just on slavery and, more broadly, the African American experience, but on the entire American experience. They allowed historians to present a total history: not just one that looked at Black oppression and race relations, but a rich history that included nearly four hundred years of Black cultural production, Black faith and religious communion, Black family history, Black politics, and connections to the African diaspora — that is, the dispersal and movement of peoples of African descent to different parts of the world. In the 1970s, as other groups demanded the inclusion of their own sources in the historical record, their histories grew into fields of study that challenged historians to integrate race, class, gender, and sexuality into American history. Soon, African Americans at the intersection of many of these groups — for example, African American women — also insisted that their particular history be told. Today, many Americans object to what they see as the fractionalization of American history, preferring a more unified history that downplays difference and emphasizes the unity of the American people and the development of a unique American character. Others are comfortable with an American history that is complicated and revealing of Americans' diverse experiences.

Freedom on My Mind: History and Documents

Freedom on My Mind offers a balance between a top-down approach and a bottom-up approach to history. Using both primary and secondary sources, we have written a narrative of African American history that is presented in the context of American history and the evolution of American democracy. Our narrative includes the voices of Blacks and whites, of leaders as well as followers, of men as well as women, and of the well-to-do, the middle classes, and the poor. In creating this narrative, we have used both primary sources that originate in American and African American institutions and primary sources from individuals. We have used secondary sources that present the latest research and analysis of the African American past. We have shown how African Americans were represented by others and how they represented themselves. When enabled by our sources, we have noted the different experiences and perspectives of native-born African Americans, Caribbean and African Blacks, and Blacks in the lesbian, gay, bisexual, and transgender (LGBT) community.

Equal to our narrative in importance are the Document Projects that allow you, the student, to be a time-traveling detective and "do" history. We've offered our analysis of the sources, but we want you to be more than passive recipients of the secondary source that is this book: We want you to participate. We want you to investigate primary sources and create a narrative of your own, as if you, too, were a historian.

As you will discover, sleuthing the past is complicated. Take, for example, the narrative of Olaudah Equiano, a prominent eighteenth-century abolitionist and former enslaved person. As a child, Equiano was stolen from Africa and enslaved, but through a unique set of circumstances, he became a free and outspoken opponent of slavery. Reading his narrative will provide you with insight into what it must have been like to be an eighteenth-century West African and allow you to empathize with those who were involuntarily separated from all that they knew and understood about life. However, you will quickly realize that being a historian requires much more than empathy. Questions will arise, such as "What does Equiano's narrative tell us about his region of Africa, and how did things change over time?" You may also ask questions like "Was Equiano typical?" or "Might Equiano have fabricated or embellished his story to gain support for abolitionism?"

Invariably, one question and answer leads to others. If you pursue your inquiry — and we encourage you to do so — you will find yourself needing additional sources, both primary and secondary. Gradually, a picture of West Africa and the slave trade will emerge — one that you have created from the sources you unearthed. If you decide to compare your study with the secondary works produced by others, you might find differences in approach and perspective. Perhaps you focused on the everyday lives of enslaved eighteenth-century Africans and wrote a bottom-up history, while others focused on the leaders of the abolitionist movement and used a more top-down approach. One thing you will note is that two historians seldom write exactly the same history. This will become apparent when you and your classmates compare your answers to the questions that accompany the sources in *Freedom on My Mind*. Your stations in life, your personal identities, the time period you live in — all of these factors influence the questions you ask and the way you interpret the sources you read.

Freedom on My Mind includes a wide variety of sources to enable you to practice history while learning about African Americans and American democracy. This is what we think makes this text special. Although we have included many events and the names of many people and places, we have tried not to overwhelm you with such information; rather, we have included sources that allow you to reach conclusions on your own and thereby analyze the conclusions we have drawn. This is what excites us about our text, and we invite you to explore and get excited with us.

UNIT 1

Origins of the African Diaspora

1 African Origins
Beginnings to ca. 1600 C.E.

2 From Africa to America
1441–1808

For centuries, African American writers highlighted the importance of ancient Africa in their work. They used examples from ancient Africa to challenge racist stereotypes of African societies as lacking governance or culture, working diligently to reconstruct and represent an authentic history that emphasizes African contributions to the world. They also voiced the varied experiences of the descendants of the African **diaspora**, highlighting aspects of the identities they formed, lives they lived, and art they produced in the centuries since they first arrived in the Americas. These texts, artworks, and artifacts became integral to the initial canon of African American Studies. Establishing the discipline was a long and difficult journey. During the Black Power movement and the Black Campus movement of the late 1960s, and following the increased enrollment of Black college students in predominantly white institutions, African American History and Black Studies scholars' and students' rejection of the flawed Eurocentric depiction of Africa and its descendants as a monolithic place and people devoid of history gained momentum. In 1968, student protests at San Francisco State College paved the way for the first Black Studies department at a four-year college. They demanded to study art, history, and cultures that were not part of traditional courses. Some important examples include ancient civilizations like the Swahili city-states. Their ideal location between the African hinterland and the Indian Ocean made them a trade pipeline that contributed both to their rise and fall, for it eventually captured the attention of the Portuguese in the sixteenth century. Another example is the South African kingdom of Great Zimbabwe, with its architecturally impressive Great Enclosure, a stone structure used for military defense and long-distance trade. These topics were just as important as the study of Egypt and its pyramids.

The AP® African American Studies course is a result of the efforts of the many scholars and activists who advocated for opportunities for students to learn about the history, culture, and contributions of people of African descent in the United States and throughout the African diaspora. It explores Black freedom struggles through an **interdisciplinary** lens, incorporating art, music, literature, science and technology, religion, and politics across eras and continents. It also investigates how people have historically viewed Africa's history and how children of the diaspora remained connected to the continent of Africa. One important example of this relationship between the past and present can be found

In 1968, students at San Francisco State College went on strike against the administration. Led by the Black Student Union and an organization called the Third World Liberation Front, the strike lasted five months and led to the formation of the College of Ethnic Studies, the first Black Studies program in the United States. *Ted Streshinsky Photographic Archive/Getty Images.*

in an iconic sixteenth-century ivory mask representing Queen Idia, Queen mother of Benin, who led armies into battle in the 1500s. Centuries later, in 1977, this mask became the symbol of Black women's leadership adopted by attendees of the Second World Black and African Festival of Arts and Culture.

Each of the four units of *Freedom on My Mind* aims to present a truthful account of the history and the lived encounters of African Americans and Black communities across the diaspora, emphasizing their global influence. Much like the suggested courses for one of the earliest established Black and Puerto Rican Studies program at Hunter College in 1969, **Chapter 1** (African Origins, Beginnings to 1600 C.E.) begins its narrative with a description of Africa in roughly 3.2 million B.C.E. as the cradle of humanity and the ancestral homeland of African Americans. This chapter delves into Africa's unique geography and climate, examining their influence on African settlements, migration patterns, and trade routes. It also chronicles the rise and fall of ancient kingdoms in East and West Africa, as well as the formation of West African medieval empires. This chapter also underscores several developments that are central to AP® African American Studies and especially relevant to **Unit 1:** Origins of the African Diaspora. It challenges the outdated depictions of Africa by emphasizing three key points. First, you'll learn that before the arrival of Europeans and the beginning of the transatlantic slave trade, Africa was home to complex civilizations that played major roles in transcontinental and global trading networks. Second, Africa was a wellspring of rich cultural, intellectual, and linguistic diversity—and is the home of thousands of ethnic groups and languages. Finally, you'll learn how the histories of ancient African societies remain historically and culturally important to their descendants throughout the world.

Chapter 2 (From Africa to America, 1441–1808) explores the beginnings and effects of the

AP® source

This depiction of Queen Njinga (c. 1583–1663) shows her with a military entourage. It is from the Araldi Manuscript, written by Italian missionary Giovanni Antonio Cavazzi da Montecuccolo between 1665 and 1668. *HIP/Art Resource, NY.*

transatlantic slave trade. Early in the history of the trade, West Central Africa was the primary origin of enslaved individuals because the Portuguese gained a foothold in the kingdom of Kongo, then ruled by King Nzinga a Nkuwu. Seeking to strengthen a trade relationship between kingdoms, King Nzinga and his son converted to Christianity. The relationship, however, soon proved to be one of subjugation. The king of Portugal insisted on gaining access to the existing West African slave trade as a condition for providing military assistance to Kongo for protection from neighboring African states and internal rivals. The result was devastating. Although skilled monarchs like Queen Njinga of Angola were able to maintain control over their kingdoms through fierce military resistance, roughly 25 percent of enslaved Africans brought to the future United States would originate from West Central Africa. In this chapter, you'll learn about the causes, the scope, and the chronological events of the transatlantic slave trade, but these events do not come close to telling the full story. You'll also study the impact the slave trade had on African societies. Finally, you'll read about the experiences of African captives along the Middle Passage and their resistance to enslavement.

AP®

UNIT 1 THEMATIC TIMELINE

All of the following developments can be found in the AP® Course Framework.

B.C.E.: 3500 | 1500 | 500 ▼ 1500 | 1600 | 1700 ▼ 1970 | 1980

Migration and the African Diaspora

- **c. 3500 B.C.E.** Bantu expansion begins; central, eastern, and southern Africa adopt metallurgy and farming over next millennia
- **c. 1500–500 B.C.E.** Bantu language speakers undertake a series of migrations throughout Africa
- **c. 500 B.C.E.** Start of trans-Saharan trade connecting West Africa with North Africa and Mediterranean
- **c. 100 C.E.** Aksum rises to power as a naval and trading empire
- **c. 1324 C.E.** Mansa Musa's hajj

Intersections of Identity

- **c. 3000 B.C.E.** Kingdom of Kush develops in Nubia
- **c. 750 B.C.E.** Kushites seize control of Egypt and rule for almost a century
- **c. 830–1230 C.E.** Ghana empire rules western and central Africa
- **c. 1230–1500 C.E.** Mali empire rules western and central Africa
- **c. 1460–1645 C.E.** Songhai empire replaces Mali as the most powerful state in West Africa
- **Late 1400s C.E.** Queen Idia becomes first *iyoba* (queen mother) in the kingdom of Benin (present-day Nigeria)
- **c. 1491 C.E.** King Nzinga a Nkuwu (João I) and his son Nzinga Mbemba (Afonso I) of Kongo voluntarily convert to Christianity
- **1965–1972** Black Campus movement protests at colleges nationwide demand Black Studies courses
- **1968** San Francisco State College strike leads to first Black Studies program in U.S.
- **1976** Negro History Week becomes Black History Month

Creativity, Expression, and the Arts

- **c. 500 B.C.E.** Nok people practice iron technology and create sophisticated fired clay objects
- **c. 1230–1500 C.E.** Learning community flourishes in Mali, drawing astronomers, mathematicians, architects, and jurists to Timbuktu
- **1977** Ivory mask of Queen Idia adopted as symbol for Second World Black Festival of Arts and Culture

Resistance and Resilience

- **1526** Transatlantic slave trade begins
- **1526** Africans enslaved in Santo Domingo lead the earliest known slave revolt in North America
- **1965** Black college students enter predominately white institutions in large numbers for the first time

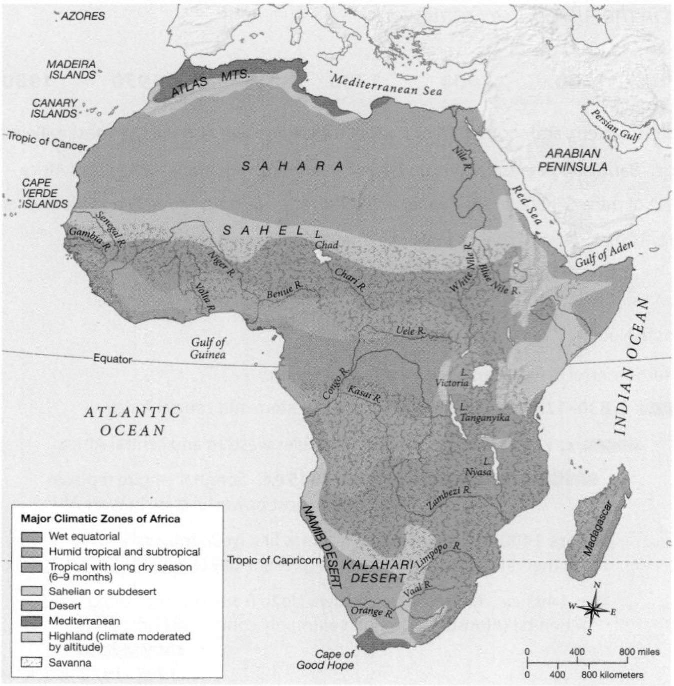

AP® skill Source Analysis (2D)

Describe and draw conclusions from patterns, trends, and limitations in data, making connections to relevant course content.

AP® source Key Context: The second-largest continent, Africa boasts significant geographical diversity. It has five main climate zones: deserts (such as the Sahara), semiarid regions (like the Sahel), savannah grasslands, tropical rain forests, and the Mediterranean zone.

PREDICT

- How do you think the diverse landscape of Africa influenced settlement patterns, trade, and the emergence of culturally distinct ancient and medieval societies? What clues from the map help support your prediction?

SOURCE: *Erich Lessing/Art Resource, NY.*

AP® skill Argumentation (3A)

Formulate a defensible claim.

AP® source Key Context: The *Catalan Atlas* (1375) highlights the wealth and influence of Mansa Musa, the ruler of Mali, a West African medieval empire, from the perspective of a Spanish cartographer.

PREDICT

- How do you think gold and trade molded the political, economic, and religious evolution of the ancient West African empires of Ghana, Mali, and Songhai? What clues from the image help support your prediction?

Source: *From 'History of Indians' (1579) by Diego Duran (1537–1588)/ Biblioteca Nacional, Madrid, Spain/De Agostini Picture Library/Gianni Dagli Orti/Bridgeman Images.*

AP® skill **Source Analysis (2B)**

Describe a source's perspective, purpose, context, and audience.

AP® source **Key Context:** *Black Conquistadors* depicts the first Africans in the Americas, who arrived with Spanish military expeditions. In Mexico, Africans initially came with Hernan Cortes.

PREDICT

- What roles do you believe Africans assumed in the Americas during the sixteenth century, and what impact do you think they had on the colonization of the Americas? What clues from the image help support your prediction?

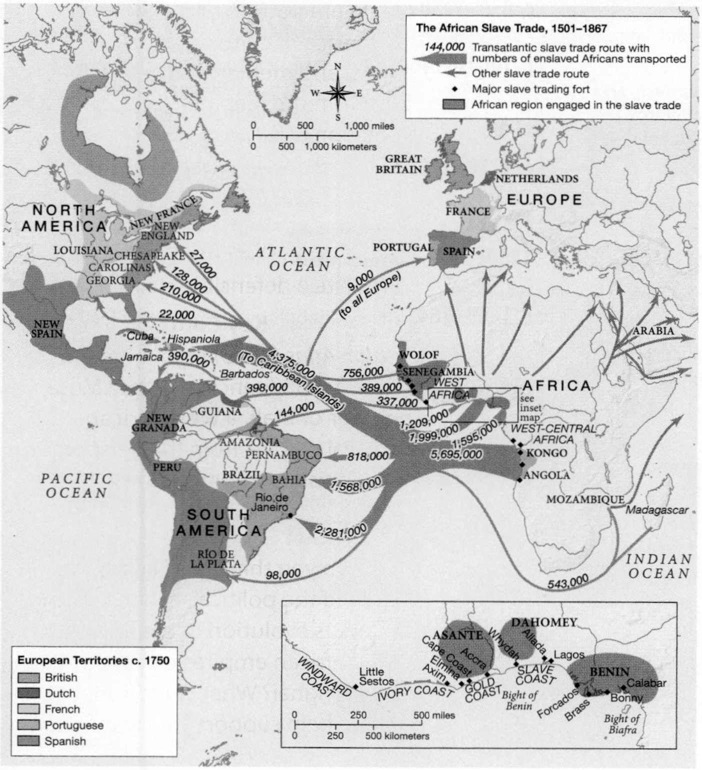

AP® skill **Applying Disciplinary Knowledge (1A)**

Identify and explain course concepts, developments, and processes.

AP® source **Key Context:** *Trade of Enslaved Africans, 1501–1867* illustrates the many routes slave traders used to carry millions of enslaved Africans to the Americas between 1501 and 1867. It also documents the trading routes that took far fewer African captives to Europe and the Middle East during the period.

PREDICT

- How do you think the loss of over 12.5 million Africans impacted African society? What clues from the map help support your prediction?

CHAPTER **1**

African Origins

Beginnings to ca. 1600 C.E.

CHAPTER TIMELINE

Events specific to African history are in purple. General world history events are in black. Events from the AP® Course Framework are marked with an asterisk.

c. 200,000 years ago Anatomically modern humans (*Homo sapiens*) appear in Africa

c. 70,000 years ago *Homo sapiens* begin migrations beyond Africa

c. 20,000 years ago San people emerge as hunter-gatherers in southern Africa

c. 6000–3000 B.C.E. Farming begins in Egypt and, later, West Africa

c. 3500 B.C.E. Bantu expansion begins; central, eastern, and southern parts of Africa adopt metallurgy and farming over the following millennia*

c. 3100 B.C.E. Rule by pharaohs established in Egypt

Egyptian empire endures in various forms until 332 B.C.E.*

c. 3000 B.C.E. Kingdom of Kush develops in Nubia*

c. 2200–2000 B.C.E. Complex societies emerge in China, India, and Central Asia

c. 1500–500 B.C.E. Bantu language speakers undertake a series of migrations throughout Africa*

c. 750 B.C.E. Kushites seize control of Egypt and rule for almost a century*

c. 500 B.C.E. Nok people practice iron technology and create sophisticated fired clay objects*

Beginnings of the trans-Saharan trade connecting West Africa with North Africa and the Mediterranean world*

c. 100 C.E. Aksum rises to power as a naval and trading empire*

479 C.E. Fall of Rome marks the beginning of the medieval period in Europe

610 C.E. Prophet Mohammad introduces Islam

c. 830–1230 C.E. Ghana empire rules western and central Africa*

c. 1000s–1400s C.E. Swahili Coast city-states united by shared language (Swahili, a Bantu lingua franca) and shared religion (Islam)*

c. 1230–1500 C.E. Mali empire rules western and central Africa*

c. 1324 C.E. Mansa Musa's hajj*

1400s C.E. Aztecs rule in Central America; Incas rule in part of South America

c. 1460–1645 C.E. Songhai empire replaces Mali as the most powerful state in West Africa*

Late 1400s C.E. Queen Idia becomes the first iyoba (queen mother) in the kingdom of Benin (present-day Nigeria)*

c. 1491 C.E. King Nzinga a Nkuwu (João I) and his son Nzinga Mbemba (Afonso I) voluntarily convert to Christianity*

"What Is Africa to Me?" The Ancestral Origins of Black Americans

"What is Africa to me?" the Harlem Renaissance writer Countee Cullen asked in a 1925 poem, reflecting on how he should understand the ancestral heritage of African Americans. As a Black American, should he align himself with the "Strong bronzed men and regal black / Women from whose loins I sprang / When the birds of Eden sang?" Or was Africa just a distant point of origin? *"One three centuries removed / From the scenes his fathers loved / Spicy grove and banyan tree, / What is Africa to me?"*[1] Cullen was not alone in asking this question. From the earliest days of the forced migration of African peoples to European colonies in the Americas, Black Americans have maintained a sense of ancestral identity in which the idea of Africa has a place. However, the connections they have drawn have been complicated. Descendants of African peoples who hailed from many different homelands and belonged to many different ethnic groups, African Americans came together as a people in the context of a transatlantic slave trade that lasted for generations. Consequently, many, if not most, modern-day African Americans cannot trace the lineage of their families to the specific African societies in which their ancestors originated. Instead, African Americans tend to embrace an ancestral lineage that encompasses many different locations and epochs in Africa's long and eventful history.

While most modern-day African Americans are descendants of West African and west-central African peoples, Black Americans have long seen their ancestral past inscribed across the African continent writ large rather than confined to this region. For instance, even though she was kidnapped from Senegambia as a child, the eighteenth-century poet Phillis Wheatley did not describe herself as originating there specifically. Instead, she understood her life story to be shaped by "Being Brought from Africa to America."[2] Similarly, when John Russwurm, who cofounded Black America's first newspaper in 1827, looked back on the history of his people, he traced his roots to ancient Egypt and Ethiopia rather than to any of the West African societies where the ancestors of most American Blacks originated.[3]

The affinities African Americans express for ancient Egypt and Ethiopia, as well as the idea of an African homeland, should not surprise us. For just as Europe's historically divided peoples have long come together around a common European identity, **diasporic** Africans have also embraced a transnational homeland and lineage. And while Europeans in the past frequently dismissed Africa as a "Dark Continent" with few claims to distinction, Africans in the Americas have often revered their heritage and rejected European characterizations and stereotypes.

African Americans have nourished cultural and symbolic ties to African civilizations and peoples ever since they first departed the continent. African-born Blacks cherished direct connections to the homelands they left behind, which in turn shaped the African American culture and traditions they passed along to their descendants. Accordingly, any discussion of African American history must begin in Africa. This chapter traces the broad outlines of Africa's history, providing an overview of the rich ancestral heritage of African Americans.

Africa: Humanity's Homeland

What are the most prominent geographic features of the African continent?
How did Africa's varied landscape affect patterns of settlement and trade between diverse cultural regions?

diaspora (p. U1-A)
The dispersion of a people from their homeland. Applied to Africans, this term usually describes the mass movement of Africans and their descendants to the Americas during the slave trade.

interdisciplinary (p. U1-A)
Incorporating multiple academic disciplines, including history, art, music, literature, science and technology, religion, and politics.

Over 11 million square miles in size, Africa is the second-largest continent on earth and the only one to lie in all four hemispheres. Not surprisingly, given its size and central location, modern Africa is home to more countries than any other continent. Combined, these 54 countries are home to 3,000 different ethnic groups, whose members speak more than 2,100 different languages. The peoples of Africa practice a variety of religions, including Christianity, Islam, Judaism, Hinduism, and many traditional African religions. Many of Africa's countries are of relatively recent origin, but the continent's social, political, and ethnic diversity has truly ancient roots. As the homeland of all humankind, Africa has the longest record of human habitation, beginning with the emergence of anatomically modern humans (*Homo sapiens*) around 200,000 years ago. The archaic ancestors of Europeans, Asians, aboriginal Australians, American Indians, and other far-flung populations once lived there, as did the ancestors of other groups that never left the continent, such as Africa's pygmy populations and Khoisan hunter-gatherers.

A Varied Landscape

AP® exam tip

Be sure you're able to explain how the complex societies that emerged in East and West Africa relate to the study of the African American experience.

The many linguistic, ethnic, and cultural differences that divide Africa's populations have been shaped by the continent's long history and varied landscape (Map 1.1). The world's largest desert and the world's most impenetrable rain forest, as well as nearly every other kind of natural environment, can be found in Africa. The prime meridian and the equator run through the continent, which encompasses climates that vary dramatically, ranging from tropical to glacial. For the most part, Africa's terrain is challenging.

Mild in climate only at its northern and southern ends, Africa is a hot continent, where desert and tropical climates predominate and periodic droughts parch many regions. Its topography is less obviously daunting than its climate. Although home to a few mountainous areas, it is composed largely of flatlands that sit on a vast plateau of ancient rocks. However, its soils are as ancient as its rocks and do not easily

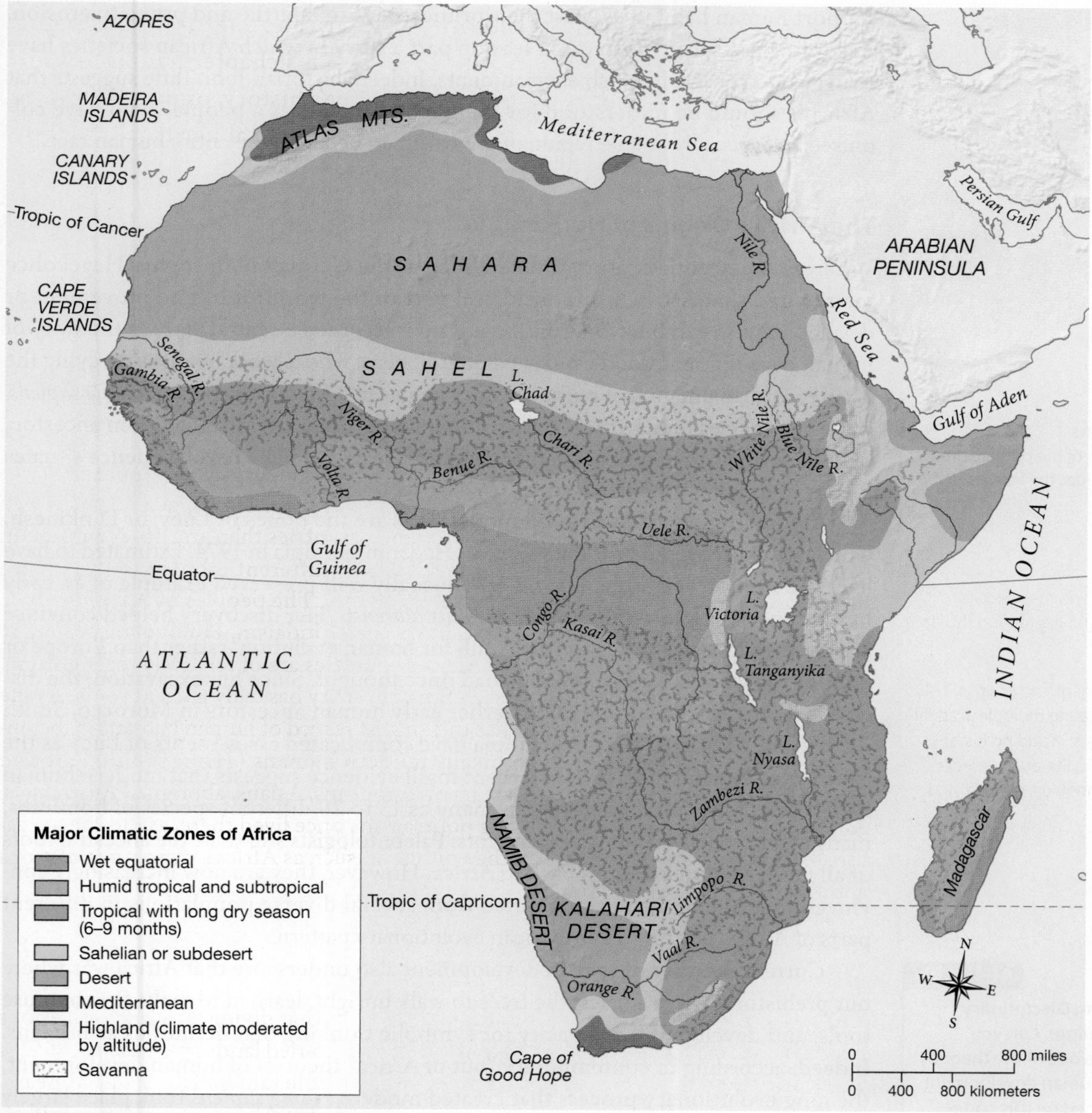

AP® source **MAP 1.1** **Africa's Diverse Geography**

The world's second-largest continent after Asia, Africa is bisected by the equator and subject to a variety of very different climates. This map divides the continent into eight climate regions that range in temperature from desert to tropical rain forest to chilly highlands. **How would this diverse geography be a factor in the continent's cultural diversity?**

ACTIVITY ▸ **Revisit Your Prediction**

In the AP® Unit Warmup (p. U1-E), you made a prediction about this image. **How do you think the diverse landscape of Africa influenced settlement patterns, trade, and the emergence of culturally distinct ancient and medieval societies? What clues from the map help support your prediction? Support or revise your original prediction using evidence from this chapter.**

support human habitation. Past their prime, they are infertile and prone to erosion. Accordingly, African history is at least in part a story in which African societies have struggled to survive in harsh environments. Indeed, historian John Iliffe suggests that Africans should be understood for their achievements as a people "who have colonised an especially hostile region of the world on behalf of the entire human race."[4]

The African Origins of Humankind

Whereas nineteenth-century thinkers such as the German philosopher Hegel once maintained that Africa "is no historical part of the world; it has no movement or development to exhibit,"[5] the continent is now accorded a central place in the story of human development. Modern-day paleontologists, whose work involves studying the fossil record, maintain that human history begins in Africa. Our species, *Homo sapiens*, is the last species in the group known as **hominins**; hominins diverged from ancestors of chimps and other apes some 6 or 7 million years ago. The fossil evidence situates the evolution of hominins in Africa.

hominins
Members of the primate group that includes the species *Homo sapiens*.

Among the oldest-known hominin fossils are the bones of Lucy, or Dinkinesh, which were discovered near the village of Hadar in Ethiopia in 1974. Estimated to have lived 3.2 million years ago, Lucy is an unusually well-preserved example of an early human ancestor known as *Australopithecus afarensis*. Her discovery helped convince scientists that Africa was the crucial hub for human evolution, rather than Europe or Asia, as the world's leading scholars had once thought. Since her excavation, the discovery of the fossilized remains of other early human ancestors in Morocco, South Africa, and additional sites in Ethiopia have complicated assessments of Lucy as the "mother of humankind." Instead, recent fossil evidence suggests that modern human beings may have descended from as many as 15 to 20 different species of hominins, many of whom left no living descendants. Paleontologists still trace the ancestral roots of all modern human beings back to Africa. However, they are now increasingly convinced that human beings originated from several diverse populations in different parts of Africa, positing a Pan-African evolutionary pattern.

Current theories of human development also underscore that Africa was where our prehistoric ancestors left the trees to walk upright, learned to make fires and use tools, and developed the capacity for symbolic thinking that defines us as humans. Indeed, according to contemporary "out of Africa" theories of human development, the long evolutionary process that created modern *Homo sapiens* took place largely in Africa. Anatomically modern humans lived and developed new skills and abilities within Africa for more than 100,000 years before beginning to migrate across the rest of the world starting some 70,000 years ago.

AP® skills

Applying Disciplinary Knowledge: Can you describe one of the theories about human development mentioned on this page?

Peopling a Continent

As this immensely long history suggests, mobility and migration have always been central to Africa's history. The continent pumped out countless waves of emigrants who settled the rest of the world, and it is also home to a cultural geography that has

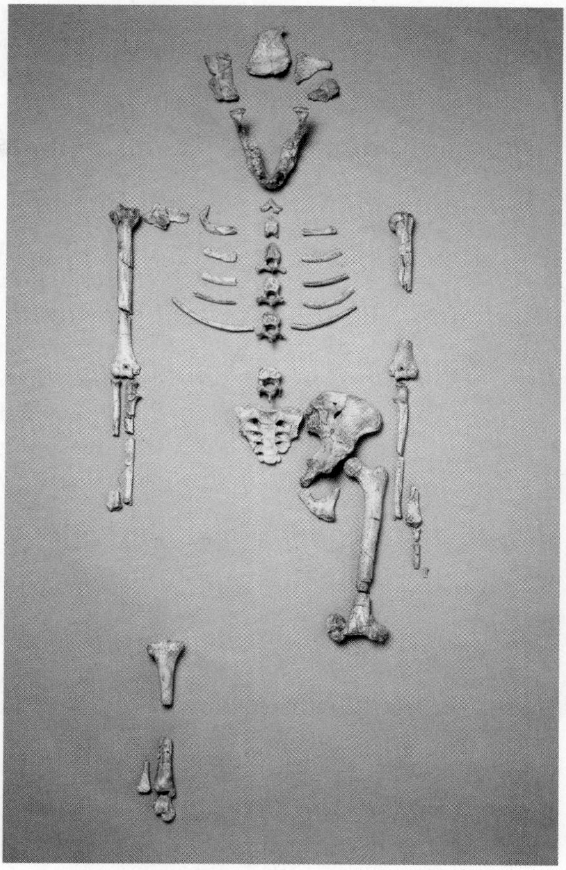

Bones of Lucy, a Hominin Ancestor
The researchers who found the skeletal remains of this early hominin named her after the Beatles song "Lucy in the Sky with Diamonds." A member of the *Australopithecus afarensis* species, Lucy is estimated to have lived around 3.2 million years ago. She was about three feet tall, walked upright, and had flexible thumbs and fingers. Lucy is one of many finds that support the idea that Africa was the home of human evolution. **How can the *Bones of Lucy* be used as evidence to support the claim that human life started in Africa?** *The Natural History Museum, London/Science Source.*

been shaped and reshaped by the migratory movements of Africa's peoples. The continent's earliest inhabitants were **hunter-gatherers** who were kept on the move by their method of subsistence. They followed game, tracked down plant foods as they ripened, and handled the scarcities in their food supply caused by competition or climate fluctuations by expanding their traditional hunting grounds. Among them were the San peoples. Estimated to have lived in southern Africa for well over 20,000 years, the San are thought to have been the first fully human inhabitants of the region; they once populated territories that span modern-day Botswana, Namibia, Angola, Zambia, Zimbabwe, Lesotho, and South Africa. Other early hunter-gatherers include the Ndorobo of the Kenyan highlands, the Aka or Efe pygmies of Africa's equatorial forests, and the Hadza and Sandawe of Tanzania.

hunter-gatherers
People kept on the move by their method of subsistence, which involves following game and tracking down plant foods as they ripen.

Like the hunter-gatherers, the earliest people to raise livestock on the continent were also mobile. Originally from the northern end of Botswana, the Khoikhoi are among the most well-known of these groups. Descendants of the San, they diverged from their hunter-gatherer ancestors when they began to rely on domesticated animals rather than game as their primary source of food. However, raising animals on farms on the savannahs of Africa is difficult, as water is only intermittently available. Instead, peoples such as the Khoikhoi moved their animals from pasture to pasture, in search of areas where water and food were abundant. The Khoikhoi's success in supporting their herds this way would lead them to expand into territory well beyond Botswana and ultimately reunite with their San ancestors. Now recognized as the "first nations" of South Africa, today these groups claim a common identity, identifying as Khoisan peoples.

AP® skills

Applying Disciplinary Knowledge: Why are the Khoikhoi now recognized as among the "first nations" of South Africa?

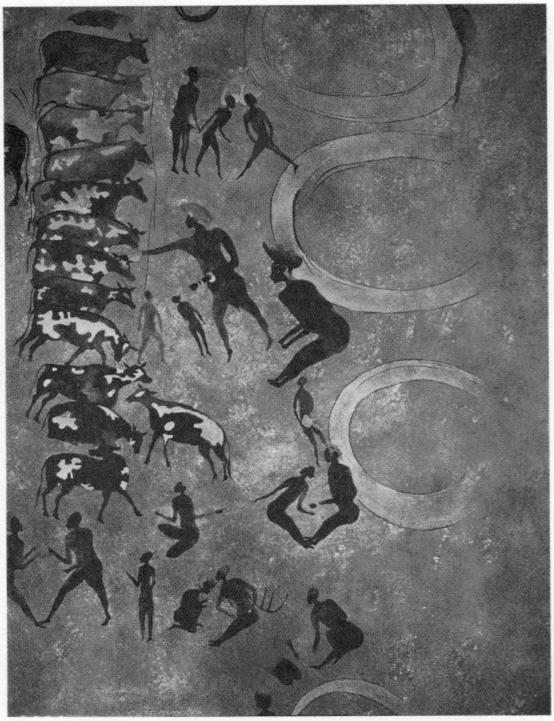

Domesticated Livestock
This image was painted on rock in the Tassili-n-Ajjer region of Algeria in the second millennium B.C.E. The women in this scene tend cattle, while the children play nearby. **What characteristics of early African societies are evident in this image?**
Musee de l'Homme, Paris, France/Erich Lessing/Art Resource, NY.

Even since the development of more sedentary forms of food production, Africa's challenging physical environment has fostered continuing movement among its people. Scientists debate exactly when and where the cultivation of domesticated wild grains and legumes first took hold among Africans. Current archeological evidence suggests that Egyptians began growing such crops as early as 6000 B.C.E. In West Africa, the domestication of native plants such as sorghum, millet, and cowpeas began later, first becoming common sometime around 3000 B.C.E. Both of these developments were likely facilitated by cyclical changes in the climate of North Africa and West Africa, which experienced a wet period following the last ice age. Starting around 8000 B.C.E., the retreat of that era's glaciers and ice sheets left behind humid conditions that fostered population growth across both regions. Summer monsoon rains watered even the Sahara, where ancient herders were able to raise livestock, harvest wild grasses and legumes, and develop West Africa's first domesticated crops. Moreover, this climate change continued to reshape life along the Sahara and its borders even when the monsoons began to stop and dry conditions returned starting sometime in the fourth millennium B.C.E. As northern Africa dried up, people there began to cluster around the Nile River and valleys in concentrated areas of settlements that would form the foundation for the rise of ancient Egypt — an agricultural empire that depended on the waters of the Nile.

Ancient Societies of Africa

What were the features of, and goods produced by, complex societies that emerged in ancient East and West Africa?

What were the causes of Bantu expansion across the African continent?

AP® exam tip

Be sure you can explain why Africa's ancient societies are culturally and historically significant to Black communities.

The ancient era saw the development of complex societies around the world. One of the earliest was ancient Egypt. Located in the northeastern corner of Africa, Egypt was most the prominent complex society in the Mediterranean world between its emergence as an empire around 3100 B.C.E. and its conquest by Alexander the Great in 332 B.C.E. Egypt developed a system of hieroglyphic writing around 3200 B.C.E. and was home to some of the world's first city-states and earliest seats of imperial power.

Africa's ancient history begins with the rise of Egypt; however, Egypt was far from the only notable society in ancient Africa (Map 1.2). The millennia during which Egyptian rulers built an empire on the banks of the Nile also saw the emergence of the kingdoms of Nubia, Kush, and Aksum in East Africa and the development of Iron Age societies in West Africa. Meanwhile, migration continued to create new patterns of settlement across much of the continent. Particularly important in this regard was the millennia-long migration of small groups of Bantu-speaking people from southern West Africa to central, eastern, and southern parts of the continent that took place between approximately 3500 B.C.E. and 1100 C.E. Known as the Bantu expansion, this mass movement reshaped the cultural geography of the continent.

AP® exam tip

You will need to be able to describe the features of, and goods produced by, complex societies that emerged in ancient East and West Africa.

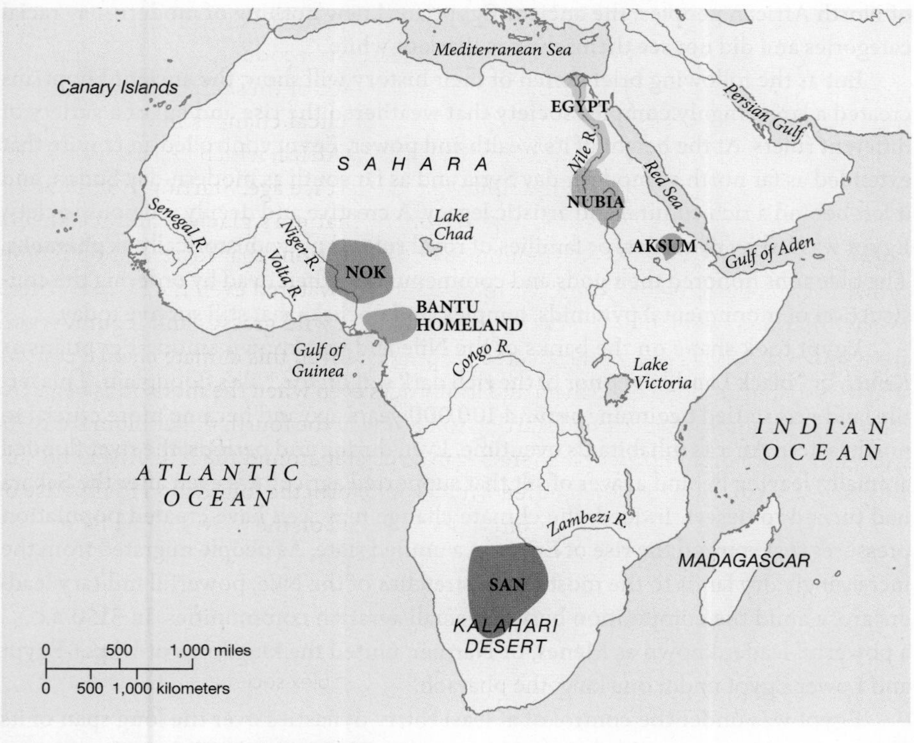

MAP 1.2 Ancient Societies of Africa

During the ancient period, Africa was home to some of the world's first large-scale states, as well as societies that pioneered new ones. This map locates some of the earliest world societies that emerged in Africa during the ancient period. **What geographic features do Egypt, Nubia, and Aksum have in common? How do these commonalities help explain the development of each society?**

Egypt

AP® skills

Applying Disciplinary Knowledge: What contributed to the rise and decline of the Egyptian empire?

The most famous African civilization, Egypt, is also the most controversial, at least with regard to the question of who can lay claim to Egypt's lineage and legacy. Although ancient Greek writers such as Herodotus routinely described the Egyptians as "black-skinned with woolly hair," Euro-American thinkers reclassified the Egyptians as a Caucasian people starting in the nineteenth century. This shift took place when antislavery activists were beginning to point to the accomplishments of the Egyptians to counter claims that people of African descent had never sustained any kind of civilization. White scientists such as Philadelphia's Samuel Morton sought to reclaim white superiority by measuring the skulls of ancient Egyptians and pronouncing them to be Caucasians. While Morton's skull measurements are now considered scientifically meaningless, debates about the race of the ancient Egyptians still persist today — as do arguments over the relative accomplishments of Blacks and whites. However, these debates and arguments would have puzzled ancient Egyptians. A heterogeneous blend of North African peoples, the ancient Egyptians knew nothing of modern-day racial categories and did not see themselves as Black or white.

But as the following brief sketch of their history will show, the ancient Egyptians created a large, highly complex society that weathered the rise and fall of a variety of different rulers. At the height of its wealth and power, Egypt controlled an empire that extended as far north as modern-day Syria and as far south as modern-day Sudan, and it left behind a rich cultural and artistic legacy. A creative and deeply religious society, Egypt was led by **dynasties**, or families of royal rulers known historically as **pharaohs**. The pharaohs honored their gods and commemorated their dead by ordering the construction of monumental pyramids, temples, and obelisks that still survive today.

dynasty
A family of royal rulers.

pharaoh
An Egyptian ruler during the period of empire, recognized as the ultimate source of power.

Egypt took shape on the banks of the Nile and was known among Egyptians as *Kemet*, or "Black Land," in honor of the rich dark soil on the Nile's floodplain. This fertile land was settled beginning around 100,000 years ago and became more crucial to northeastern Africa's inhabitants over time. Even during arid periods, the river flooded annually, leaving behind a layer of silt that supported agriculture even after the Sahara had turned to desert. Indeed, the climate change may well have created population pressures that spurred the rise of Egypt as a unified state. As people migrated from the increasingly dry lands to the most fertile stretches of the Nile, powerful military leaders arose amid the competition between small agrarian communities. In 3150 B.C.E., a powerful leader known as Menes, or Narmer, united the kingdoms of Upper Egypt and Lower Egypt under one king, the pharaoh.

Egypt was under the control of at least thirty dynasties over the long span of its existence and has a complex political history that scholars typically describe in terms of the rise and fall of three distinct kingdoms. The first of these, the Old Kingdom, saw Egypt establish itself as a great power and also marked the reigns of its great pyramid builders, before ending in a period of decentralization and weak leadership. Then came reunification in the Middle Kingdom, a period in which city-states governed by local rulers recognized the pharaoh as the ultimate source of power. However, after a

The Pharaoh and the Goddess
In this mural from an Egyptian tomb, the pharaoh makes an offering to the goddess Hathor-Imentet, whose role is to welcome the deceased. The pharaohs' power came from the belief that they were themselves divinity, members of the sacred universe that controlled Egyptian life. **How can this mural be used to explain the religious beliefs of Egyptians?** *Vestibule, Tomb of Horemheb, Thebes, Egypt/De Agostini Picture Library/S. Vannini/Bridgeman Images.*

period of disunity and decline, the Hyksos of West Asia conquered many of these local rulers, gaining control over much of Lower Egypt. They were eventually driven out of Egypt by Ahmose I (reign c. 1570–1544 B.C.E.), founder of the Eighteenth Dynasty, whose rise to power ushered in the New Kingdom. His ascent marked the beginning of an age of empire in which Egypt expanded deeper into Africa along the Nile and also encroached into Southwest Asia.

Religion was essential to the survival and periodic renewal of Egypt's dynastic rule over its long history. Egypt's pharaohs were both the spiritual and political leaders of their people. They governed by divine authority and were understood to serve as intermediaries between the gods and the people. Egypt's dynastic leaders owned its lands, decreed its laws, and led the armies that protected its borders; they also officiated over religious ceremonies and built temples. Considered high priests, the pharaohs were also held responsible for maintaining peace and order in the kingdom, which they did by aligning themselves with powerful deities. Empowered to rule by the gods, they were obligated to maintain their favor with rituals, prayers, and offerings of food, drink, and goods. They also used Egypt's resources to build temples and monuments in the gods' honor. Closely linked to natural forces and phenomena, Egyptian gods included figures that lent power and authority to its rulers. Among the most notable were Horus, a sky god venerated for vanquishing chaos; Maat, the goddess of truth, justice, harmony, and order; and Osiris, who was both the ruler of the underworld and the god of resurrection and fertility.

Egypt's crops and other agricultural riches were taxed on a yearly basis, giving its leaders the means to develop a highly centralized government and support a strong military. Indeed, all of Egypt's most famous achievements occurred under a government that commanded vast resources. The early development of literacy in ancient Egypt, for example, arose out of the administrative and record-keeping needs created by its empire, and its monuments marked the full power of that empire. Constructed during the Old Kingdom, the pyramid complex in Giza and the famous Sphinx required elaborate planning and a workforce of many thousands of people. Much of the unskilled labor was provided by Egyptian peasants, whose work on the pyramids took place during Egypt's flooding season, when farming was impossible. But the construction of the pyramids also required skilled builders and artisans who worked year-round, architects and engineers who did design work, and administrators who procured supplies and coordinated the building work.

Starting in the first millennium B.C.E., food scarcity, droughts, expensive wars, and civil unrest began to once again fragment Egypt's dynastic rule. As local officials grew more powerful, they challenged the pharaoh's leadership, creating civil conflicts and making Egypt vulnerable to a series of outside invaders. After being conquered by Alexander the Great's Macedonian army in 332 B.C.E., Egypt never fully regained its independence. It was ruled by a new dynasty of Greek rulers after Alexander's death in 323 B.C.E. and became a province of Rome in 30 B.C.E.

Nubia, Kush, and Aksum

As Egypt's prominence declined, the residents of Nubia began to regain independence. Nubia was a region located at the south end of the Nile River, on land now encompassed by southern Egypt and north-central Sudan (see Map 1.2). First settled as early as 8000 B.C.E., Nubia was home to several ancient kingdoms, including Kush, which developed around 3000 B.C.E. The region was more sparsely populated than Egypt.

AP® exam tip

Make sure you can identify the differences between the Nubian and Aksum societies.

Kushites and other Nubians had a complex relationship with their powerful northern neighbor Egypt. Nubia was an agricultural region with rich stores of copper and gold; it was also a gateway to the riches of African societies south of its border. The trade goods that Egyptians could acquire there included treasures from the tropics such as ivory, ebony, and panther skins. In times of peace, Nubians did business with Egypt, but Egyptian rulers such as the New Kingdom's Ramesses II (r. 1279–1213 B.C.E.) raided and plundered Nubia. When they did, they seized both goods and people, enslaving the Nubian soldiers they overpowered. The enslaved Nubians were then used as mercenaries in the pharaoh's armies or as domestic servants in the households of Egyptian noble families. However, Egyptians were also sometimes enslaved in Nubia, which also subjugated its captives of war. Never entirely dominated by its neighbor to the north, Nubia tended to prosper when Egypt was weak. For example, with the collapse of Egypt's New Kingdom at the beginning of the first millennium B.C.E., the Nubian kingdom of Kush not only secured its independence but invaded and conquered Lower Egypt and Upper Egypt. Around 750 B.C.E., the Kushite Piye became pharaoh and established a new line of Kushite dynastic rulers who controlled Egypt for almost a century.

Driven out of Egypt by the Assyrians in 670 B.C.E., the Kushites retreated to Kush, where they retained their independence until about 350, before falling under control of the kingdom of Aksum (also known as Axum). Located south of Kush (on land now occupied by Eritrea and northern Ethiopia), Aksum rose to power as a naval and trading empire starting around 100 C.E. It took shape around Adulis, a port city on the Red Sea that attracted traders from Egypt, Arabia, the eastern Mediterranean, Persia, and India. At the height of its powers between approximately 300 and 600 C.E., Aksum's empire included present-day Somalia, Djibouti, Somaliland, and portions of the Arabian Peninsula. During this period, it also converted to Christianity, under the leadership of King Ezana (r. 320s–c. 360 C.E.), whose conversion inspired him to declare Aksum a Christian state. Wealthy, powerful, and culturally complex, Aksum developed its own currency and written language, known as Geʿez. Still used today as the liturgical, or ceremonial, language of the Ethiopian Orthodox Church, Geʿez is the ancestor of the modern Tigrinya and Tigré languages of Eritrea and Ethiopia.

The Nok and the Bantu

The early history of West Africa is far less well documented than that of East Africa. Although settled for almost as long, it was home to small agricultural societies that left behind little direct evidence of their existence. When and where West Africans first began to make and use iron, for example, was unknown until the 1960s, when archeologists working in northeastern Nigeria uncovered iron artifacts and iron slag — one of the by-products of iron production. This discovery suggested that iron smelting and forging technology may have emerged among the Nok people of Nigeria as early as 500 B.C.E. (see Map 1.2). Also skilled in the creation of fired clay objects, the Nok created remarkable terracotta sculptures, many of which depicted near-life-sized human figures. These highly stylized figures typically have oversized heads that feature large triangular eyes with perforated pupils, flared nostrils, and mouths that protrude outward. Most Nok figures feature elaborate hairstyles and ornate jewelry, possibly depicting important people and ancestors. However, little is known about the function of these pieces or about daily life among the people who produced them, whose recorded history is largely limited to the objects they left behind.

> **AP® skills**
> **Applying Disciplinary Knowledge:** Why are the Nok people credited with the earliest form of iron smelting and forging?

Historians have used evidence drawn from archeological studies, linguistic analyses, and oral traditions to track broad patterns in the movement of West Africa's peoples. Among the most important findings is evidence of extensive geographic dispersion among Bantu-speaking people starting around 3500 B.C.E. Much like population shifts that contributed to the rise of ancient Egypt, the migratory movements

Museum of Fine Arts, Houston, Texas/Museum purchase funded by Brown Foundation Accessions Endowment Fund/Bridgeman Images.

AP® source ***Nok Sculpture***

Found near the Jos Plateau region of modern Nigeria, this ancient terracotta figure displays the oversized head, stylized facial features, elaborate hairstyle, and bold jewelry characteristic of Nok sculpture. This artifact is a fragment of the original; the complete work likely would have depicted the entire body. **How can this image be used to understand the complex societies in Africa?**

of the Bantu may have been shaped by climate change along the Sahara, which forced people who had once flourished within its borders to find new territory. The Bantu, an agricultural people who likely originated in the region now occupied by northern Cameroon and southern Nigeria (see Map 1.2), seem to have been pushed out of their original homeland by population pressures related to the drying up of the Sahara's grasslands. And if not, they clearly had other reasons to seek new territory, as their migration lasted more than two millennia and resulted in the diffusion of Bantu-speaking agriculturalists across much of sub-Saharan Africa.

AP® exam tip

Be sure you can explain the significance of the Bantu expansion.

The Bantu expansion saw Bantu speakers fan out of West Africa in at least two distinct waves. Based on linguistic analyses of the spread of the Bantu language, it seems that the first wave saw migrants head east into the Congo forest region and then south through the Great Lakes region and on to present-day Uganda, Kenya, and Tanzania. The second wave, by contrast, took an entirely different route — or possibly more than one. Second-wave migrants trekked south across central West Africa through modern-day Gabon, the Democratic Republic of the Congo, and Angola, eventually terminating in modern-day South Africa. In addition, some of these migrants may have traveled south along the tributaries of the Congo River.

Regardless of which route they took, the Bantu travelers helped create new communities and patterns of living. This prolonged and slow migration of small groups of people into new territories extended Bantu languages, crops, agricultural know-how, and iron-working technology into central, southern, and southeastern Africa; it also introduced the migrants to the customs and expertise of the foragers, herders, and hunter-gatherers who populated these regions. Over time, these exchanges created new communities whose technological skills and methods of food production were enhanced by the combined expertise of both groups. In addition, some local communities adopted new technologies without having direct contact with Bantu migrants in a process of diffusion; other communities may have developed new technologies on their own. Bantu speakers were a linguistic group rather than a united people, and they lived in loose political formations, or clans, organized by lineage, and were open to making alliances with other African peoples. Although rebuffed by some of the central and southern African peoples they encountered on their migration routes, the Bantu were able to join forces with most. They settled in small communities alongside the indigenous residents of the regions, both hunter-gatherers and herders, and they intermarried and intermixed with many of them. Their language ultimately predominated: today approximately one in three Africans is Bantu speaking. However, the Bantu are a thoroughly mixed and culturally diverse people who live in many different African societies; modern Bantu speak 500 distinct Bantu languages and incorporate 400 different ethnic groups.

AP® exam tip

Be sure you can explain how the Bantu expansion affected the linguistic diversity of West and Central Africa and the genetic heritage of African Americans.

West Africa's Medieval Empires

How did the influence of gold and trade shape the political, economic, and religious development of the ancient West African empires of Ghana, Mali, and Songhai?

The decline of the Nile valley civilizations in Egypt, Kush, and Aksum did not mark the end of Africa's age of empires. In fact, the years between approximately 830 and 1645 saw the rise and fall of a series of empires in West Africa (Map 1.3). This period coincides roughly with Europe's medieval era and is sometimes known as West Africa's medieval era. However, while Europe's medieval era began with the dissolution of the Roman empire and its networks of long-distance exchange, West Africa's medieval period saw the formation of larger states and a growth in long-distance networks. With the rise of its medieval empires, West Africa experienced periods of extraordinary prosperity and cultural ferment that were largely fueled by the expansion of its trade routes across the Sahara.

West Africa's great medieval empires of Ghana, Mali, and Songhai all took shape along the **Sahel**, a stretch of semi-arid land that cuts across the continent, dividing the Sahara desert to its north from the Sudanian savanna (grasslands) to its south. Assigned a name that refers to the "shore" of the desert in Arabic, the Sahel is where the Sahara's great sea of sand and rocks comes to an end, and it marked a crucial point of exchange on the **trans-Saharan trade** routes that began to connect West Africa with North Africa and the Mediterranean world starting around the sixth century B.C.E. There, Berber-speaking merchants could begin to exchange goods with West African merchants. Strategically located, the West African empires that rose to power on the Sahel derived much of their wealth and power from controlling the trade routes across the desert. Moreover, the trade not only enriched the ruling elites of Ghana, Mali, and Songhai, it reshaped West African society by forging new cultural, social, and religious connections with other regions of the world.

Sahel
A stretch of semi-arid land that cuts across the African continent, dividing the Sahara desert to its north from the savannah (grasslands) to its south.

trans-Saharan trade
Trade that connected Berber-speaking merchants of North Africa with West African merchants of the Sahel.

Ghana

Ghana is one of the first West African states of which there is any record. Located outside the bounds of present-day Ghana in an area now occupied by southeastern Mauritania, western Mali, and eastern Senegal, Ghana sustained a powerful kingdom on the Sahel between approximately 830 and 1230 (see Map 1.3).

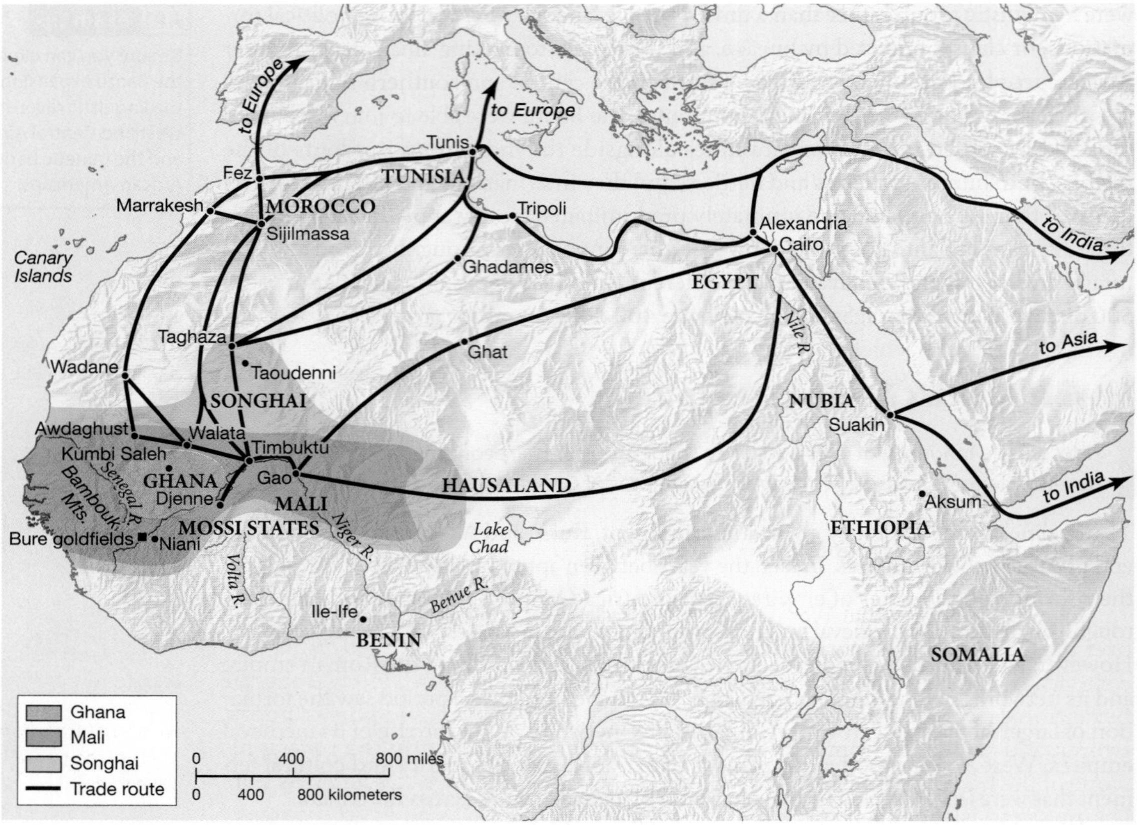

MAP 1.3 Medieval West Africa and the Trans-Saharan Trade

Prior to the era when it became enmeshed in a transatlantic trade with Europe and the Americas, West Africa had a vital place in the trans-Saharan trade. As a result, a number of empires and smaller states and confederacies flourished during this period. **What is one conclusion that can be drawn about the trade network beyond Africa?**

AP® skills

Applying Disciplinary Knowledge: Why is Ghana considered the first West African state of which there is any record?

People have inhabited Ghana since the Paleolithic era (c. 40,000–30,000 B.C.E.). This region's path to empire began with the formation of a loose confederation of clans among the Soninke, a Mande-speaking group that farmed and raised livestock on the grasslands surrounding the Senegal and Niger Rivers. Their communities grew into large villages, which were governed by chieftains as early as 600 B.C.E. and expanded steadily thereafter.

The Soninke were one of the first groups to take advantage of the iron technology that developed in West Africa around 500 B.C.E.; they also made early use of horses and camels, acquiring them from the nomads of the Sahara. Traders as well as farmers, the Soninke first rose to power as intermediaries between the Arab and Berber merchants to their north and the producers of gold to the south. They established Kumbi

Saleh (or Koumbi Saleh), Ghana's capital, right on the edge of the Sahara, and the city quickly became the most dynamic and important southern terminus for the trans-Saharan trade. The Arab geographer Yaqut al-Hamawi described this site of exchange as crucial to the export of African goods. "Merchants meet in Ghana," he wrote, "and from there one enters the arid wastes towards the land of Gold. Were it not for Ghana, this journey would be impossible, because the land of Gold is in a place isolated from the west in the land of the Sudan. From Ghana the merchants take provisions on the way to the land of Gold."[6]

While gold was much in demand in North Africa, salt was almost equally sought after south of the Sahara. Salt was a rarity in the West African grasslands and forests south of the Sahara, which have few naturally occurring deposits of this mineral. But it is abundant in the Sahara, where the droughts that created the region's vast desert left behind vast salt deposits in areas once covered by water. Indeed, in desert salt mining centers such as Taghaza and Taoudenni, salt was so plentiful that slabs of rock salt were used to build homes. Not surprisingly, these areas supplied Berber traders with one of the commodities most crucial to trans-Saharan trade. So precious that it was sometimes exchanged for gold dust, salt fueled the rise of trade for a number of other goods.

AP® skills

Applying Disciplinary Knowledge: What two natural resources were in high demand from the major kingdoms of West Africa? Why?

The commodities that West Africans received in return for their gold expanded over time and came to include silver, tin, lead, perfumes, bracelets, books, stone and coral beads, glass jewelry, and drinking implements from southern Morocco and the Byzantine empire; European and Moroccan cloth and clothing; and horses, books, swords, and chain mail from North Africa. By the fourteenth century, the geographic scope of the trade was immense. Among the new trade goods were cowrie shells from Indian Ocean islands such as the Maldives; these shells began to be used as currency on West African markets.

AP® exam tip

Be prepared to explain the reasons why Africans went to Europe and Europeans went to Africa before the onset of the transatlantic slave trade.

Meanwhile, the goods that Ghana's traders sent north in exchange grew to include not just gold but also copper, ivory, kola nuts, and animal hides. More troublingly, they also sold enslaved people. It is difficult to say exactly when the trans-Saharan slave trade originated, but historians believe it reached its peak between the eighth and sixteenth centuries. A business that took shape around the camel-powered web of trade routes that linked sub-Saharan societies and the Arab world, this trade expanded with the growth of Africa's medieval empire. These societies practiced slavery and enslaved captives of war, and the rise of the trans-Saharan slave trade allowed them to commodify these captives.

All these exchanges enhanced the wealth and power of Ghana's rulers, who taxed their empire's import and exports. But gold — the preferred metal for coins in both Europe and Southwest Asia — remained the region's most crucial export and Ghana's most important source of wealth and power. Derived largely from gold mines located on the upper Senegal River, Ghana's gold supply was controlled by its Soninke kings, who kept the location of their empire's gold mines a closely guarded secret. They claimed a monopoly over the ownership of the gold nuggets they produced by

AP® skills

Applying Disciplinary Knowledge: How did Ghana develop their economy?

permitting only gold dust to be freely traded. This policy both enriched them and elevated the market value of gold by limiting its supply.

A rich and powerful trading empire, medieval Ghana reshaped the West African world around it. Its exchange of goods across the Sahara created a variety of other new trans-Saharan connections, most consequentially the expansion of the Islamic religious faith into West Africa.

AP® skills

Applying Disciplinary Knowledge: How did Islam spread in the kingdom of Ghana?

Originating in early seventh-century Arabia with the prophet Mohammad, Islam spread rapidly across North Africa under the military leadership of Mohammad's successors and reached West Africa primarily by way of the trans-Saharan trade. Most of the North African merchants who participated in the trade were Muslims, as were many of the Berbers who transported its goods. As a result, Muslims became an accepted part of the cultural world of ancient Ghana, especially in key trading sites such as Ghana's capital. Although initially segregated in their own separate neighborhoods, Muslims in cosmopolitan West African cities such as Kumbi Saleh were welcome on both sides of town and even held important positions in its government. Moreover, over time, many of the indigenous residents of Kumbi Saleh and other commercial centers gravitated toward Islam.

Ghana maintained its imperial power for several centuries. At the height of its power, its Soninke rulers commanded a territory that extended from the southern borders of present-day Mauritania to the Bambouk Mountains in present-day Senegal and Mali. They defended their domain with a formidable army, which Arab traveler Al Bakri maintained was capable of putting "200,000 men into the field, more than 40,000 of them archers."[7] However, the wealth and power of Ghana's rulers continued to depend heavily on their monopoly over Africa's gold trade, which did not last forever. Starting in the eleventh and twelfth centuries, new gold fields began to be mined at Bure (modern Guinea) out of the commercial reach of Ghana, and new trade routes were opening up further east. These changes were all the more disastrous because they came at a time when Ghana was beset by a drought that curbed agricultural production and when it was also divided by a string of civil wars. Impoverished and politically unstable, Ghana became the target of attacks by the Sosso ruler Soumaoro, who conquered many of its peoples. Out of this conflict, Mali emerged in 1235 under a new dynamic ruler, Sundiata Keita.

AP® skills

Applying Disciplinary Knowledge: Describe how the rise of the Mali empire coincided with the decline of the kingdom of Ghana.

Mali

griot
Prestigious historians, storytellers, and musicians who maintained and shared a community's history, traditions, and cultural practices.

From the small Malinke kingdom of Kangaba, near the present Mali–Guinea border, came Sundiata, a legendary figure whose name means "lion prince." The story of his exploits was passed down by generations of **griots**, or storytellers, whose stories also may have served as inspiration for Disney's *The Lion King*. Many of the details are impossible to confirm, but the account of his early life in the *Epic of Sundiata* describes him as the twelfth son and sole survivor of Kangaba ruler Nare Maghan.

His father and eleven brothers were all killed off by Soumaoro, a cruel ruler who secured his claim to the kingdom of Kangaba by eliminating not only its king but also all of his sons. He spared only Sundiata, who was unable to walk as a child and therefore seemed unlikely to challenge his leadership. Sundiata overcame his disability by sheer willpower and proved equally resolute about reclaiming his father's kingdom. Exiled after Soumaoro took control of Kangaba, he organized an army by forging alliances with other nearby Malinke peoples and vanquished Soumaoro in the battle of Kirina in 1235. According to the griots, Sundiata prevailed over Soumaoro because he was the more powerful magician of the two. However, modern historians tend to credit Sundiata's victory to his skills as a military leader and strategist, which are evident in his subsequent career.

AP® skills

Applying Disciplinary Knowledge: What is a *griot*? How do *griots* connect to the experiences of Sundiata?

After his initial victory, Sundiata moved quickly to expand his power by founding the empire of Mali (see Map 1.3). After emerging as the leader of the conquered peoples once ruled by the Sossi, Sundiata went on to conquer other states and created an empire even larger and richer than that of ancient Ghana. Centered slighter farther south than Ghana, Mali included all territories once ruled by Ghana as well as the Bure goldfields; the great cities of Timbuktu, Djenne, and Gao on the Niger River; and the salt mines of Taghaza. At its height, it spanned the modern-day countries of Senegal, southern Mauritania, Mali, northern Burkina Faso, western Niger, the Gambia, Guinea-Bissau, Guinea, the Ivory Coast, and northern Ghana. Although he rose to power as Mali's Mansa, or king, Sundiata was not an absolutist monarch. Instead, he set up Mali as a federation of largely autonomous states, led by their own clans and chiefs. Members of a common court all reported to the Mansa and also participated in the Great Gbara Assembly, a deliberative body charged with enforcing the Mansa's edicts and selecting his successor.

A transitional leader, Sundiata is also notable for finding a way to build bridges between the indigenous beliefs of his ancestors and the Islamic faith of Mali's North African trading partners. Although Sundiata himself was probably not Muslim, many of his descendants were, and Sundiata cultivated close ties with Muslim trading partners while also retaining spiritual beliefs and powers traditional to his people. Indeed, some scholars see the *Epic of Sundiata*'s account of his magical victory over Soumaoro as a story about the real powers of a leader who managed to command the loyalties of both his region's Muslim merchant elites and more religiously traditional masses.

AP® skills

Applying Disciplinary Knowledge: How did Sundiata set up political structures in his kingdom?

Sundiata's descendants would continue to straddle this divide. His son Mansa Uli converted to Islam and went on a pilgrimage to Mecca around 1260 or 1270 C.E. However, Uli's conversion did not mark a major shift away from traditional religious beliefs among the empire's peoples. Instead, Islam became the religion of the empire's ruling class, and most of his successors were Muslim and supported the spread of Islam. Most influential in this regard was Mansa Musa I (r. 1312–1337 C.E.), a devout Muslim who became well known throughout Europe and the

AP® skills

Applying Disciplinary Knowledge: How did Islam contribute to the success of the Mali empire?

AP® skills

Applying Disciplinary Knowledge: Careful analysis of the *Catalan Atlas* can be used to describe the significance of Mali's wealth.

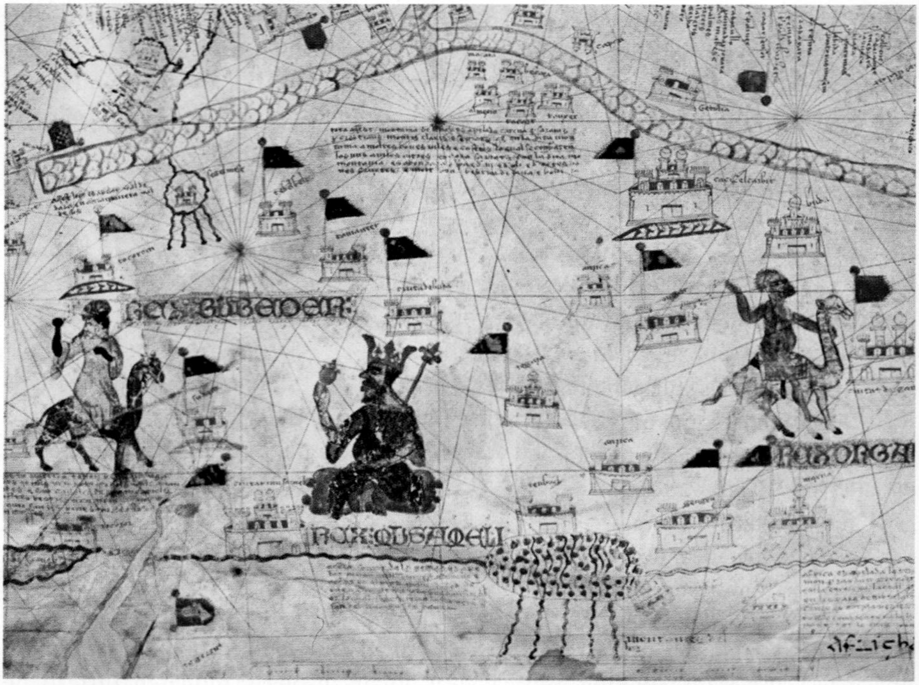

AP® source ***Facsimile of the Catalan Atlas Showing the King of Mali Holding a Gold Nugget, 1375***

Largely devoid of geographic detail, this Spanish nautical map of the known world is adorned with pictures, including sketches of camels, as well as a large and lavish illustration of an African ruler identified as "Muse Melley," "lord of the Negroes of Guinea." This illustration likely refers to Mansa Musa, who ruled the Mali empire between 1312 and 1337, although his placement on the map is closer to North Africa than to West Africa. A devout Muslim, Musa caught the attention of the Islamic and European worlds in 1324, when he made a pilgrimage to Mecca. His caravan included twelve hundred servants and eighty camels carrying two tons of gold, which he distributed to the needy along his route. Not soon forgotten, Musa was depicted in several fourteenth-century maps of the world. ◣ **What does the map convey about the influence of Islam?** *Erich Lessing/Art Resource, NY.*

ACTIVITY ▸ Revisit Your Prediction

In the AP® Unit Warmup (p. U1-E), you made a prediction about this image. ◣ **How do you think gold and trade molded the political, economic, and religious evolution of the ancient West African empires of Ghana, Mali, and Songhai? What clues from the image help support your prediction? Support or revise your original prediction using evidence from this chapter.**

Middle East as a result of his 1324 pilgrimage to Mecca. He made the four-thousand-mile journey with an opulent personal caravan that included twelve hundred servants and eighty camels carrying two tons of gold, which he distributed to the needy along his route. Musa was thereafter pictured in several European maps of the world, which emphasized his wealth by depicting him wearing a large gold crown and holding a gold nugget and scepter. Not surprisingly, stories of Musa's wealth helped inspire Portuguese explorations of Africa's west coast, which started in the first half of the fifteenth century.

Musa's pilgrimage was also influential in his home, where it fostered closer connections between Mali and the Islamic world. Musa returned from Mecca accompanied by Islamic scholars, bureaucrats, and architects, whose expertise had an enduring impact on his administration's political and aesthetic legacies. Among them was the architect Abu Ishaq Ibrahim Al-Sahili from Granada, who built some of the empire's most important mosques and palaces. His creations included the great mosque at Timbuktu, which is still standing.

Meanwhile, some of the other newcomers boosted Islamic education in Mali by helping Mansu create new universities, libraries, and other institutions dedicated to the study of Islam. It was during his reign that Timbuktu first became a center for Islamic scholarship. A trading town populated by Muslim merchants from throughout the Mediterranean world, it was home to three mosques, 150 Islamic schools, and a flourishing book market. "In Timbuktu there are numerous judges, scholars and

AP® exam tip

Be sure you can explain how Mali's wealth and power created opportunities for the empire to expand its reach to other societies within Africa and across the Mediterranean.

AP® exam tip

Be prepared to describe the institutional and community-based models of education present in early West African societies such as Mali.

Sankore Mosque, Timbuktu, Mali

This photograph shows the mosque's pyramid-shaped minaret surrounded by mud-brick walls that enclose a courtyard. The mosque is part of the University of Sankore, which is one of several universities that comprise the larger university complex known as the University of Timbuktu.

In addition to allowing the practice of Islam, what other purpose did the city of Timbuktu serve?

age fotostock/Alamy Stock Photo.

priests, all well paid by the king, who greatly honours learned men," sixteenth-century visitor Leo Africanus wrote, describing the book market. "Many manuscript books coming from Barbary are sold. Such sales are more profitable than any other goods."[8]

However, by the time Africanus, a Berber-Andalusian traveler and author, visited Timbuktu in the early 1500s, Mali had collapsed. Timbuktu remained impressive, but Musa's sons had proved unable to maintain control of either the city or their subjects. In 1468, the Songhai captured Timbuktu and began building a new West African empire.

The Songhai

AP® skills

Applying Disciplinary Knowledge: How did the Songhai come to power in West Africa?

AP® exam tip

Be prepared to explain how the political structure of the Songhai was similar to and different from that of the Ghana kingdom.

AP® skills

Applying Disciplinary Knowledge: Why were there tensions about the social structure in the Songhai kingdom?

A group with roots in the Gao region of the Niger River, the Songhai had once been among Mali's subject peoples but were able to reclaim their independence under the leadership of the Sonni dynasty. Like West Africa's previous rulers, the Songhai dynastic leaders were traders and warriors who derived much of their wealth and power from the trans-Saharan trade and who rose to power by gaining control of its traditional routes. Sonni Ali, the dynasty's first ruler, captured much of the empire of Mali, and one of his successors, Askia al-Hajj Muhammad (r. 1493–1528), expanded its borders north into the Sahara and east into Hausaland (see Map 1.3).

The Songhai rulers created a far more centralized empire than had Ghana's and Mali's rulers. As absolute monarchs, they commanded large armies and developed a highly bureaucratic system of ministers and regional governors to supervise the regions they commanded rather than extending any power or recognition to local rulers. But despite their autocratic powers, Songhai's rulers were never entirely secure. Of the nine kings who ruled the Songhai empire, six were either overthrown in rebellions or killed by their rivals — who were usually close relatives.

Tensions over religion undermined the power of some of Songhai's leaders, who like their predecessors in Mali had to find ways to maintain leadership over the region's Muslim population. Songhai's leaders had to lead the urban elites — without alienating the vast majority of their subjects, who were mostly rural and retained traditional West African religious beliefs and practices. Sonni Ali, who was not a devout Muslim, offended Muslim critics by drinking alcohol and failing to pray in public, and he eventually faced a challenge to his legitimacy from Islamic scholars, who argued that this lack of adherence to Islam made him unfit for his position. This argument did not prevail, but when Ali drowned in the Niger River shortly after his leadership began to be challenged, some of his Muslim critics saw his death as an act of God. His son and successor Sonni Baru faced similar critiques, and he was eventually overthrown by Askia al-Hajj Muhammad, one of the empire's generals.

The ascension of Askia al-Hajj Muhammad, a devout Muslim, was a turning point in West African history in so far as it was one of the first documented examples of an African society in that region demanding a leader who met Muslim standards of piety. But Askia's commitment to Islam did not secure the Songhai's command over their region — or convert most of the empire to Islam. Although he established

Sharia law and further strengthened Muslim education in Songhai by building schools and expanding Timbuktu's University of Sankore throughout his rule and for many decades afterward, most of Songhai's inhabitants remained small farmers with few ties to their country's Muslim elite.

Indigenous religions and local centers of power persisted in Songhai, making the empire vulnerable to civil wars, imperial rivalries, and outside invaders. In the end, Songhai would fall to all three. In 1528, Askia al-Hajj Muhammad was dethroned by his son, who was later dethroned by his brother, and even though the empire's dynastic conflicts waned during the second half of the sixteenth century, a civil war divided the kingdom again in 1591, opening it up to foreign invasion. That year, Morocco, which had recently fallen under control of an expansionist Islamic dynasty, captured and sacked Timbuktu and other Songhai seats of power, causing the once-powerful empire to collapse. Morocco never secured dominion over the vast territories once controlled by the Songhai, and with their retreat, the region split into many small, independent kingdoms.

With the collapse of Songhai, West Africa lost its most powerful and centralized state during a time when the power balance in the region was already in flux. The Portuguese began exploring Africa's coast in the fifteenth century, and by the sixteenth century, they had established trading centers on West Africa's coast that competed with the region's venerable trans-Saharan trade. The caravans that had so long enriched West Africa's medieval empires would shrink, but the long-distance trade in goods, people, and ideas they pioneered would persist — and set the stage for the transatlantic slave trade.

West Africa in the Sixteenth Century

How did syncretic (religious) practices in early West and West Central African societies develop?

What was the function of kinship in early West and Central African societies, and what varied roles did women play?

By the sixteenth century, most of West Africa was populated by many different societies of people who spoke different languages, had diverse cultures, and worshipped different deities. And it was from this diverse world that the first forced migrants to the Americas were uprooted as West Africa became enmeshed in the transatlantic slave trade that began in the early 1500s (the topic of chapter 2).

Religious Beliefs and Practices

Most of the people of sixteenth-century West Africa practiced one of a variety of indigenous religions that recognized many deities and spirits, as well as a more remote, all-powerful creator. Most of these traditional belief systems also attributed life or consciousness to natural objects or phenomena. The Lobi-Dagarti people of southwestern Burkina Faso, for example, worshiped the earth, whose glory they honored by paying

AP® skills

Applying Disciplinary Knowledge: What were the religious practices in West Africa prior to the adoption of Christianity or Islam?

respect to sacred stones, and hill spirits; the gods recognized by the Akan people of Ghana and the Ivory Coast include river deities, and the Igbo's spiritual universe included a god of thunder and lightning known as Amadioha ("owner of the sky"). Adherents of these religions saw the force of God in all things and often invoked the spirits of their ancestors, as well as a spirit world associated with their natural surroundings. But these similar beliefs did not lead West Africans to unite around a single church or religious doctrine.

The region also remained home to a significant population of Muslims, who rejected these indigenous beliefs and embraced a strictly monotheistic idea of God. But with the collapse of the Mali and Songhai empires, their influence diminished — at least for a time. Islam remained the religion of West Africa's commercial elite, but Morocco's Islamic leaders were not powerful enough to maintain religious or political control over the vast empire once controlled by the Songhai. Instead, political power in the region splintered, allowing for the survival and resurgence of many smaller kingdoms in which indigenous African religions and customs flourished.

Kinship Ties and Political Alliances

As Europe's age of exploration dawned, only about one-third of the entire African continent was ruled by large-scale organized states. Most people lived in kingdoms of modest size, city-states, or self-governing villages. Self-governing villages, sometimes known as "stateless societies," typically occupied plots of land no larger than a thousand square miles. Due to the tiny size of self-governing villages and the fact that they generated few written records, the history of such societies is not well understood.

Historians estimate that as many as one-quarter of West Africans lived in such stateless societies.[9] Especially numerous in both central and coastal West Africa, these societies were typically made up of members of related clans and held together by extended family ties rather than claims to common ethnic identity or nationality. Led by chiefs or councils of elders, most were agricultural societies in which property and political leadership usually passed from generation to generation along **matrilineal** or **patrilineal** lines — from mother to daughter or from father to son. Examples of stateless societies include Igboland, a densely populated region along the Niger River in what is today southeastern Nigeria, which was home to many self-governing villages. Although the Igbo people who lived there shared a common language, as well as many of the same customs, traditions, and religious beliefs, they never established a central government or coordinating authority. Ties between villages did exist, but they were social rather than political.

West Africa was also home to a variety of larger states in which **kinship** affiliations led to political affiliations. Larger African polities, such as the kingdoms of the West African interior, were often the product of strategic alliances between closely related royal families. Typical in this regard were the Mossi states, a confederacy of independent kingdoms that took shape in the Upper Volta River region of modern-day Burkina Faso in the middle of the eleventh century (see Map 1.3).

matrilineal succession The practice of passing property and/or leadership from generation to generation from mother to daughter.

patrilineal succession The practice of passing property and/or leadership from generation to generation from father to son.

kinship Political alliances with other African communities that did not include blood ties.

AP® skills

Applying Disciplinary Knowledge: What is an example of kinship from this section of the chapter?

This complex of five kingdoms shared kinship ties and a common military and political system, but the kingdoms were otherwise largely autonomous. They came together around the principle of safety in numbers. Their leaders allied to defend their region from attacks by Mali and Songhai and were successful in retaining independence from other powerful neighboring states until the late nineteenth century, when the Mossi states were conquered by the French. Ruled by an emperor and a council of state made up of the governors of its kingdoms, the Mossi states had no standing army. Instead, local chiefs led cavalry units that could be rapidly mobilized in times of need. The autonomy achieved by the Mossi states had cultural as well as political import. The Mossi kingdoms were among the few sizable polities in West Africa to remain free of Islamic leadership, and they largely retained their traditional religious and ritual practices.

AP® skills

Applying Disciplinary Knowledge: What were the major characteristics of the Mossi kingdoms?

Much like the Mossi kingdoms, the city-states of Hausaland were a closely allied group of neighbors who shared resources while retaining independence. Indigenous to the Sahel and Sahara, the Hausa were farmers and traders whose traditional villages expanded when their lands became the southern terminus in the Sahara trade. Each of the seven city-states in the Hausa confederation specialized in a product or service essential to participation in that trade. The cotton cloth–producing cities of Kano and Rano became known as the "Chiefs of Indigo." Biram was the confederation's original seat of government. Katsina and Daura were known as "Chiefs of the Market" because their geographic location allowed them direct access to the caravans coming across the desert from the north. Gobir, or the "Chief of War," was the city held responsible for protecting the empire from potential invasive neighbors such as Ghana and Songhai. Zaria, which specialized in acquiring enslaved people for the trans-Saharan trade, was known as the "Chief of Slaves."

Hausa leadership was based on ancestry and rooted in an oral tradition that traced the origins of the region's rulers to a common founding family that had seven sons. Less centralized than the Mossi states, the Hausa city-states never conjoined their governments or established an effective army. As a result, they remained vulnerable to domination from outside forces. Several became tributaries of the Songhai empire during the reign of Askia Muhammad (r. 1494–1528 C.E.), and in 1804 all of the Hausa city-states fell under the control of Fulani leader Usman dan Fodio, who established the Sokoto Caliphate.

AP® skills

Applying Disciplinary Knowledge: Explain the difference between the Mossi kingdoms and the city-states of Hausaland.

Benin, Wealth, and Power

Although the Hausa never unified, confederacies among West African peoples could result in the formation of highly centralized states. Sometime before the eleventh century, Edo-speaking people of Yoruba extraction banded together to found the kingdom of Benin, located in what is now southwestern Nigeria (see Map 1.3). According to oral tradition, Benin originated when a group of Edo chiefs asked Prince Oranmiyan of Ile-Ife, a neighboring town ruled by

The oba of Benin, with Attendants This bronze plaque depicts the oba (king), at center, wearing coral beaded regalia and holding the royal scepters. Second to him in scale are two warriors, and other attendants are smaller still, representing their rank. This plaque would have been hung in the royal palace along with others depicting previous obas, providing a visual account of the royal lineage. **What features stand out in this plaque? How does it portray Benin's political and military leadership?** *Peter Horree/Alamy Stock Photo.*

descendants of the divine king of Yorubas, to send them a king. The prince's son, Eweka, became first in a long line of Benin kings, or **obas**.

oba
A royal title in the ancient kingdom of Benin.

Advised by a group of titled and hereditary chiefs, the obas would become more powerful over time. They successfully laid claim to the divine right of kings and expanded Benin's borders by mobilizing a well-equipped army that claimed domination over neighboring Yoruba-, Igbo-, and Edo-speaking populations. Notably, their authority, like that of many less powerful West African leaders, remained rooted in an oral tradition that stressed the common lineage of the kingdom's founders and legitimated its chosen rulers. These ties were also commemorated in the remarkable art created by Benin's metal workers and carvers, who created sculptures designed to glorify the oba and to pay homage to the kingdom's sacred past and collective values. Among these works were magnificent metal plaques hung in the royal palace that depicted the oba flanked by two or more smaller-scale attendants. These figures offer a vivid sense of the hierarchical nature of the oba's royal authority, but the close-knit configuration also suggests that the king's power relies on the support of his people.

As these examples show, West Africa's many states had a variety of sizes and structures, but the region's rulers generally derived power from the network of kinship ties that bound individuals to their communities. The West African proverb "I am because we are, and because we are therefore I am" expresses the collective nature of African social identity.[10]

These values were also built into the region's systems of land ownership, which tended to be collective rather than individual. Land held a spiritual significance among West African peoples, who regarded themselves as custodians of the land of their ancestors rather than as owners of any particular plot. Accordingly, their communities formed around common lands whose use was administrated by their chiefs or elders. People were entitled to cultivate their ancestral homelands and raise livestock on their community's grasslands, but they did not own any of the land they used, and they could not sell it. Instead, land rights revolved around usage, and families controlled only as much land as they could cultivate. As a result of these arrangements, West African societies tended to figure wealth and power not in land but in people. In these kinship-based societies, landownership offered no path to private wealth. Instead, close ties with an abundance of people made ruling families powerful, and these ties could be enhanced by institutions, such as slavery, that gave rulers control over people.

Slavery in West Africa

Slavery has ancient roots in Africa, as it does in most other regions of the world. Practiced by the ancient Egyptians and Nubians, slavery likely emerged in some societies in West Africa as early at 300 B.C.E. Slavery in this region could take many forms and had many different points of origin.

AP® skills

Applying Disciplinary Knowledge: How did enslavement function in West Africa prior to the transatlantic slave trade?

In African societies, as elsewhere around the world, enslavement was often a by-product of war. As outsiders, captives had no status in West Africa's kinship-based societies and could be killed with impunity. But with the rise of settled agriculture, conquered people became a valuable source of labor that many African societies chose to exploit. Female captives were particularly valuable because they could be exploited for both their labor and reproductive potential. But enslaved people, regardless of gender, alike were valuable resources to rulers and ruling families whose power lay in their control over large numbers of people. Moreover, as slavery grew more widespread, even enemies who might once have been regarded as too dangerous to be enslaved gained market value. Captives with allies nearby and powerful warriors who might be difficult to subdue could be sold off to distant lands.

As the slave trade became a source of revenue, some African rulers relied on the sale of enslaved captives to boost their military power by procuring horses, weapons, and other military necessities; other rulers used those who were enslaved as soldiers. Usually conscripted into permanent military service at an early age, such soldiers provided crucial support to the armies in which they served and could rise to positions of high rank. The use of enslaved people to fund or wage war was particularly common in the Islamic world and helped fuel the rise of a trans-Saharan trade in which Arab merchants purchased enslaved people as well as gold; the West African rulers of Ghana, Mali, Songhai, and other states sold their captives of war to fund their armies and maintain and expand their power.

But war was not the only route to enslavement. In many West African societies, those convicted of serious crimes such as adultery, murder, or sorcery were enslaved. People reduced to slavery for these crimes not only lost their freedom but were usually sold away from their families as well — a harsh punishment in these kinship-based societies. Debtors were also enslaved. Some were pawns, debtors who voluntarily submitted to temporary slavery in order to pay off their debts.

Members of most of these groups could move in and out of slavery, although not all of them succeeded in doing so. Pawns, for example, could work off their debts, while female captives of war frequently became members of their enslavers' families via concubinage — a form of sexual slavery that typically ended in freedom if the concubine bore a freeman's child. Two other routes out of slavery were assimilation into an enslaver's kinship network by marriage and **manumission** — a legal process that enslavers could initiate to grant freedom to a favored enslaved person.

manumission
A legal process that enslavers could initiate to grant freedom to an enslaved person.

In West Africa, since enslaved status was rarely inherited, slavery did not create a permanent class of enslaved people or enslavers. Indeed, in years immediately leading to the arrival of Europeans in the 1440s, enslaving others and slave trading were relatively modest sources of wealth in West African societies. West Africans had long sold enslaved people to slave traders, who transported them across the Sahara to North Africa for resale in the Arab world, but this trans-Saharan trade did not expand greatly over time. Likewise, the expansion of slavery within West Africa was limited by the decentralized character of the region's political regimes and its lack of commerce in goods produced by enslaved people. Agriculture was a collective pursuit dedicated to subsistence rather than trade, and it did not require the harsh work regimes that would come to characterize enslaved labor in the Americas.

Enslaved people in African societies were socially marginal and powerless, but there were limits to their subjugation. As elsewhere, enslaved people in West Africa suffered a loss of social status that was nothing less than "social death" in these kinship-based societies.[11] But enslaved people were generally employed in the same agricultural and domestic work that occupied other members of these small communities. Indeed, according to Olaudah Equiano, an eighteenth-century African who experienced slavery both in his homeland and in European colonies, African captives do "no more work than other member of the community including their master. Their food, clothing and lodging were nearly the same as theirs, except that they were not permitted to eat with the free born."[12] They also retained a number of civic rights and privileges. In most African communities, enslaved people were permitted to educate themselves and were generally able to marry and raise children. Slavery also varied across the region, sometimes taking the form of domestic servitude, in which enslaved women predominated. Larger West African polities such as Songhai employed enslaved soldiers and bureaucrats, whose status did not keep them from becoming wealthy and powerful servants of the state.

However different African slavery was from the slavery that developed in the Americas, the fact that it was an entrenched and dynamic institution would have tragic and far-reaching consequences. The European trade with West Africa, which began shortly before Europeans first crossed the Atlantic, would create a new kind of slave trade to supply the workers needed to exploit these new lands.

CONCLUSION

Transatlantic Ties

With the rise of the transatlantic slave trade, millions of Africans entered an enforced migration that led to generations in slavery. Generations of West African captives left their homelands behind and became diasporic Africans, whose ties to the countries of their birth were attenuated by time, distance, and the many hardships they faced in the Americas. Yet Africa and the idea of Africa traveled with them and often served as a source of comfort and strength to enslaved Africans and their American-born descendants. From many different homelands, Africans in the Americas left behind loved ones and the communities in which they were raised, but they also nourished ties to Africa that they passed on to their descendants. (See AP® Working with Sources: Imagining Africa, pp. 31–35.)

CHAPTER 1 REVIEW ▸ PRACTICING AP® SKILLS

AP® ESSENTIAL VOCABULARY AND SOURCES

Essential terms and required sources from the AP® Course are marked with an asterisk.

diaspora* p. U1-A
interdisciplinary* p. U1-A
MAP 1.1 Africa's Diverse Geography (Major Climate Regions of Africa)* p. 5
hominins p. 6
hunter-gatherers p. 7
dynasty p. 10
pharaoh p. 10
Nok Sculpture* (Image of Nok Sculpture, Circa 900 B.C.E.–200 C.E.) p. 14
Sahel* p. 15
trans-Saharan trade* p. 15
griot* p. 18
Facsimile of the Catalan Atlas Showing the King of Mali Holding a Gold Nugget, 1375 (Catalan Atlas* by Abraham Cresques, 1375) p. 20
matrilineal p. 24
patrilineal p. 24
kinship* p. 24
oba p. 26
manumission* p. 28
Phillis Wheatley, *On Being Brought from Africa to America*, 1773 ("On Being Brought from Africa to America" by Phillis Wheatley, 1773)* p. 31

APPLYING DISCIPLINARY KNOWLEDGE: ESSENTIAL QUESTIONS

1. When does African American history begin? To what extent is it necessary to study the history of the African continent to understand the experiences of diasporic African peoples such as African Americans? How far back in time should accounts of African American history begin?
2. Africa is home to many different climate zones and types of terrain, and it has experienced significant climate change over time. How has the continent's environment influenced the history of its peoples?
3. Describe the impact of the trans-Saharan trade on the history of West Africa.
4. Slavery has a long history in Africa. What were the different ways in which it was practiced in African societies?

SUGGESTED REFERENCES

Africa: Humanity's Homeland

Blyden, Nemata Amelia Ibitayo. *African Americans and Africa: A New History*. New Haven: Yale University Press, 2019.

Gilbert, Erik T., and Jonathan T. Reynolds. *Africa in World History*, 3rd ed. Boston: Pearson, 2011.

Harms, Robert. *Africa in Global History with Sources*. New York: W. W. Norton & Company, 2018.

Hoffecker, John. *Modern Humans: Their African Origin and Global Dispersal*. New York: Columbia University Press, 2017.

Iliffe, John. *Africans: The History of a Continent*, 3rd ed. Cambridge: Cambridge University Press, 2017.

Parker, John, and Richard Rathbone. *African History: A Very Short Introduction*. Oxford: Oxford University Press, 2007.

Ancient Societies of Africa

Breunig, Peter. *Nok: African Sculpture in Archaeological Context*, tr. ed. Frankfurt: Africa Magna Verlag, 2014.

Fourshey, Catherine Cymone, Rhonda M. Gonzales, and Christine Saidi. *Bantu Africa: 3500 BCE to Present*. New York: Oxford University Press, 2017.

Higgins, Chester, Jr., and Zahi Hawass. *Ancient Nubia: African Kingdoms on the Nile*, ed. Marjorie M. Fisher et al. Cairo: The American University in Cairo Press, 2012.

Tignor, Robert L. *Egypt: A Short History*. Princeton: Princeton University Press, 2010.

West Africa's Medieval Empires

Conrad, David C. *Empires of Medieval West Africa: Ghana, Mali, and Songhai*. New York: Facts on File, Inc., 2005.

Gomez, Michael. *African Dominion: A New History of Empire in Early and Medieval West Africa*. Princeton: Princeton University Press, 2019.

Wright, John. *The Trans-Saharan Slave Trade*. London: Routledge, 2007.

West Africa in the Sixteenth Century

Green, Toby. *The Rise of the Trans-Atlantic Slave Trade in Western Africa, 1300–1589*. Cambridge: Cambridge University Press, 2014.

Gunsch, Kathryn Wysocki. *The Benin Plaques: A 16th Century Imperial Monument*. London: Routledge, 2017.

Lovejoy, Paul E. *Transformations in Slavery: A History of Slavery in Africa*, 3rd ed. Cambridge: Cambridge University Press, 2011.

Mbiti, John S. *African Religions and Philosophy*. New York: Praeger, 1969.

Salamone, Frank A. *The Hausa of Nigeria*. Lanham, MD: University Press of America, 2009.

Skinner, Elliott P. *The Mossi of Burkina Faso: Chiefs, Politicians and Soldiers*. Prospect Heights, IL: Waveland Press, 1989.

Imagining Africa

Africa has always loomed large in the Black American imagination. As subsequent chapters in this book will show, survivors of the Middle Passage maintained ties to West African societies they left behind by incorporating African folklore, language, music, religious beliefs, and agricultural expertise into the diasporic culture they were forced to create in a new land. Most of their descendants would never see Africa, but they sustained its traditions in the folktales they told, the African vernacular that shaped their speech, the music they created, and the religious rituals they practiced. In addition, the idea of Africa would remain important among African Americans, who have often looked at the continent as a homeland and embraced its culture and history as a source of identity, wisdom, and community.

Accordingly, representations of Africa and its history and culture figure prominently in African American literature, art, and material culture. The following selection of documents and images represents a small sampling of works by African American writers and artists that focus on Africa as a central theme. They include writings by African-born survivors of the Middle Passage; a discussion of Egypt and Ethiopia by a nineteenth-century Black abolitionist; an editorial cartoon from the early twentieth century that invokes the accomplishments of the ancient Egyptians to critique segregation and Jim Crow; a meditation on Africa in a Harlem Renaissance–era poem; and an image of kente cloth that celebrates graduating students' accomplishments in Afrocentric terms. Taken together, they demonstrate the persistent place of Africa in the African American imagination.

key point

The culture and history of Africa are important to many African Americans, both past and present. Many African American writers and artists have explored and celebrated their African ancestry. Representations of Africa permeate African American literature, art, and material culture.

AP® argumentation

DBQ Practice: Explain how representations of Africa contribute to an understanding of the role Africa plays in African American literature, art, and material culture.

DOCUMENT 1
AP® source

Phillis Wheatley | *On Being Brought from Africa to America, 1773*

Born in West Africa in or around 1753, PHILLIS WHEATLEY (d. 1784) was captured and sold into slavery when she was seven or eight years old. Transported to Boston aboard the slave ship *Phillis* in 1761, she was purchased by a local merchant and tailor named John Wheatley, who was looking for a personal servant for his wife, Susannah Wheatley. Once she arrived in her new home, Wheatley was taught to read and write by the Wheatley family, who named her Phillis after the ship that carried her from Africa. The young girl proved a quick study. By age 12, she had mastered not only English but Greek and Latin as well, and by 14, she was writing poetry. Also trained in religion and theology, Wheatley attended church with her enslavers and became a devout Christian. In the following poem, she describes her journey from Africa to America as a journey to salvation.

Breaking it Down Read the background information about Phillis Wheatley first! What is the status of Black Christians as described in Wheatley's poem, and how does she portray her African past? Remember, the intended audience is the group or groups of people the author intends to reach. Ask yourself, who would read and respond to this source? Why?

’Twas mercy brought me from my *Pagan* land,
Taught my benighted soul to understand
That there’s a God, that there’s a *Saviour* too:
Once I redemption neither sought nor knew.
Some view our sable race with scornful eye,
“Their colour is a diabolic die.”
Remember, *Christians, Negros,* black as *Cain,*
May be refin’d, and join th’ angelic train.

SOURCE: Phillis Wheatley, *Poems on Various Subjects, Religious and Moral* (1773; repr. W.H. Lawrence, 1887).

DOCUMENT 2 Belinda | *The Petition of Belinda, 1782*

Born in West Africa, BELINDA SUTTON (b. 1713) was abducted from a village near the Volta River (in modern Ghana) and sold into slavery when she was twelve years old. She ended up in Medford, Massachusetts, where she was enslaved by Isaac Royall, a British loyalist, who fled to Nova Scotia during the Revolutionary War. Abandoned without support by her enslaver after fifty-eight years of enslavement, Belinda petitioned the Commonwealth of Massachusetts in 1783, requesting an “allowance” from the estate of her former enslaver. Likely written by someone other than Belinda, who signed her name with an X, Belinda’s petition is remarkable for recording the wishes and thoughts of an illiterate Africa-born veteran of the Middle Passage. In it, she both makes a claim for a payment, or reparations, for the years she spent in slavery, and discusses her childhood in Africa.

> **Breaking it Down** As you read, make note of each time Belinda describes African society. How does she describe the African society in which she originated? Why does she choose to look back on her childhood in an appeal for financial support?

To the honourable the senate and house of representatives, in general court assembled:

The petition of Belinda, an African,
Humbly shews,

That seventy years have rolled away, since she, on the banks of the Rio de Valta, received her existence. The mountains, covered with spicy forests — the vallies, loaded with the richest fruits, spontaneously produced — joined to that happy temperature of air, which excludes excess, would have yielded her the most complete felicity, had not her mind received early impressions of the cruelty of men, whose faces were like the moon, and whose bows and arrows were like the thunder and the lightning of the clouds. The idea of these, the most dreadful of all enemies, filled her infant slumbers with horror, and her noontide moments with cruel apprehensions! But her affrighted imagination, in its most alarming extension, never represented distresses equal to what she has since really experienced: for before she had twelve years enjoyed the fragrance of her native groves, and ere she realized that Europeans placed their happiness in the yellow dust, which she carelessly marked with her infant footsteps — even when she, in a sacred grove, with each hand in that of a tender parent, was paying her devotion to the great Orisa, who made all things, an armed band of white men, driving many of her countrymen in chains, rushed into the hallowed shades! Could the tears, the sighs, and supplications, bursted from the tortured parental affection, have blunted the keen edge of avarice, she might have been rescued from agony, which many of her country’s children have felt, but which none have ever described. In vain she lifted her supplicating voice to an insulted father, and her guiltless hands to a dishonoured deity! She was ravished from the bosom of her country, from the arms of her friends, while the advanced age of her parents, rendering them unfit for servitude, cruelly separated her from them for ever.

SOURCE: "Petition of an African slave, to the Legislature of Massachusetts," *The American Museum, or Repository of Ancient and Modern Fugitive Pieces, Prose and Poetical* 1, no. 6 (June 1787): 538–40.

DOCUMENT 3 John Russwurm | *On the Egyptians as Africans, 1827*

Born in Jamaica in 1799, JOHN BROWN RUSSWURM (d. 1851) was raised in Quebec and moved to the United States as a young adult. One of the first Blacks to receive a degree from an American college, he graduated from Bowdoin College in 1826 and went on to become an abolitionist, writer, and newspaper publisher. Together with Black New Yorker Samuel Cornish, he founded *Freedom's Journal* (1827–1829), the first African American newspaper in United States. A man with ties to Jamaica, Canada, and the United States, Russwurm also felt strongly drawn to Africa, so much so that he would support the American Colonization Society's effort to create a colony for African Americans there by moving to Liberia in 1829. Published in *Freedom's Journal* in 1827, his essay "The Mutability of Human Affairs" traces the history of African Americans back to Egypt, and it emphasizes that Egypt had close ties to Ethiopia.

Breaking it Down John Russwurm wrote an argument to persuade his audience. As you read, make note of each time he provides evidence or uses reasoning to support his claim of the link of ancient history to modern-day events. How does Russwurm link his discussion of ancient history to modern-day events? Why does he draw ties between Ethiopians and Egyptians?

During a recent visit to the Egyptian Mummy, my thoughts were insensibly carried back to former times, when Egypt was in her splendor, and the only seat of chivalry, science, arts and civilization. As a descendant of Cush [in the Bible, Cush is the son of Ham, Noah's eldest son], I could not but mourn over her present degradation, while reflecting upon the mutability of human affairs, and upon the present condition of a people, who, for more than one thousand years, were the most civilized and enlightened. . . .

Mankind generally allow that all nations are indebted to the Egyptians for the introduction of the arts and sciences; but they are not willing to acknowledge to the present race of Africans; though Herodotus, "the father of history," expressly declares that the "Egyptians had black skins and frizzled hair." All we know of Ethiopia, strengthens us in the belief, that it was early inhabited by a people, whose manners and customs nearly resembled those of the Egyptians. Many of their divinities were the same: they had the same orders of priesthood and religious ceremonies: they made use of the same characters in writing: their dress was alike: and the regal sceptre in both countries was in the form of a plough. Of their philosophy little is known, their wise men, like those of the Indians, were called Gymnosophists: they discharged the sacred functions like Egyptian priests; had their distinct colleges and classes of disciples; taught their dogmas in obscure and mythological language; and were remarkable for their contempt of death. Other writers of a later date than Herodotus, have asserted that the resemblance between the two nations, as it regarded their features, was as striking, as their doctrines were similar. The celebrated Mr. Salt, in his travels in Abyssinia, discovered several monumental remains, the hieroglyphics on which bore a strong resemblance to those engraved on the sarcophagi of Egyptian mummies.

SOURCE: John Russwurm, "Mutability of Human Affairs," *Freedom's Journal*, April 6, 1827.

DOCUMENT 4 George H. Johnson | *The Sphinx Builder Speaks, 1919*

A mail carrier in Richmond, Virginia, GEORGE H. JOHNSON (1888–1970) was also a self-taught artist who created editorial cartoons for his city's leading Black newspaper, the *Richmond Planet*. His cartoons denounced segregation and racial violence and sometimes used African imagery to analyze American race relations.

Breaking it Down Divide the image into four quadrants and list two or more observations from each quadrant. How do these observations connect to the source's message? What message do you think Johnson conveyed to readers by using Egyptian imagery? What does this cartoon tell us about popular understandings of African American history among Black readers during Johnson's era?

The speech bubble reads: "No Power could Lynch, Outrage, and Humiliate 14,000,000 EDUCATED Blacks. Get much learning. Make 'Not a Black Illiterate,' your slogan." *Library of Virginia.*

DOCUMENT 5 Claude McKay | *Outcast, 1922*

A Jamaican-born writer and poet, CLAUDE MCKAY (1889–1948) moved to the United States in 1912 and settled in New York City in 1914. A life-long traveler, he also lived in Europe and North Africa, but retained close enough ties to New York to establish himself as one of the leading luminaries of the Harlem Renaissance. As such, McKay was best known for poems and novels that explored issues of Black identity and attacked American racism. Like Countee Cullen and other Harlem Renaissance contemporaries, he wondered what Africa meant to him, and he explored that subject in the poem titled "Outcast," which looks back on Africa as a lost homeland.

Breaking it Down Reread pages 23–24 for context on the adoption of monotheistic religions in West Africa. This will help you understand Claude McKay's tone and message in this poem. You can also try the "in other words" method to summarize each stanza's main idea as you read. As you read, consider how McKay portrays Africa in his poem. Does he believe that he could ever regain his African identity?

For the dim regions whence my fathers came
My spirit, bondaged by the body, longs.
Words felt, but never heard, my lips would
frame;
My soul would sing forgotten jungle songs.
I would go back to darkness and to peace,
But the great western world holds me in fee,
And I may never hope for full release
While to its alien gods I bend my knee.
Something in me is lost, forever lost,
Some vital thing has gone out of my heart,

And I must walk the way of life a ghost
Among the sons of earth, a thing apart;
For I was born, far from my native clime,
Under the white man's menace, out of time.

SOURCE: From "Three Sonnets," *The Literary Digest*, October 28, 1922.

DOCUMENT 6 *Honoring African American History with a Kente Cloth Stole*

Developed by Asante weavers during the seventeenth century, kente cloth is created from interwoven strips of brightly colored cotton or rayon fabric. First created as an Akan royal and sacred cloth, it was traditionally worn on special occasions by kings and other nobles. However, it was popularized in the United States in the late 1950s by African leaders such as Kwame Nkrumah, the first prime minister of independent Ghana, who wore a kente cloth when he met with President Eisenhower at the White House. During this era of civil rights and African decolonization, Black Americans quickly came to see the cloth as a proud symbol of their African heritage. This symbolism lives on among modern Black college students, who wear the cloth to honor the history and accomplishments of their ancestors and their race. In the following photograph, a professor at Marshall University speaks about this symbolism in the school's annual Donning of the Kente Celebration of Achievement for graduating students.

Breaking it Down What details reveal that this is an important occasion? What does the importance of the occasion suggest about the symbolism of the stole?

Mark Webb, The Herald-Dispatch/Associated Press/AP Images.

PRACTICING AP® SKILLS

1. **AP® Comparison.** Compare and contrast the tone and message of McKay's "Outcast" and Wheatley's "On Being Brought from Africa to America." How do the differences reflect these poets' different audiences? What do the similarities reveal about the importance of African culture and history to the writers?
2. **AP® Causation.** Describe the events that led to the "Petition of Belinda, 1782."
3. **AP® Comparison.** Compare Russworm's and McKay's perspectives on the meaning of Black Americans' ancestral African roots. What is the purpose of each document? How does that purpose connect to each author's perspective?
4. **Connecting to AP® Themes.** Explain how the symbolism of the kente cloth in Document 6 connects to both the theme of Creativity, Expression, and the Arts and the theme of Migration and the African Diaspora.
5. **Class Discussion.** Historians often link the study of history to a search for a "usable past." To what extent do the representations of Africa contained in the documents and images presented here serve this purpose, and why is the past that they present useful?

Visual Texts:
Active Reading

As you move through the AP® African American Studies course, you will be surrounded by **texts**. By "texts," we don't just mean this textbook and other written sources like novels or articles. We also mean speeches, photographs, videos, political cartoons, maps, and cultural artifacts like works of art. Those sources are texts, too, because they can all be "read"; they can be analyzed to better understand the people, events, and movements that led up to and followed their creation.

Regardless of the type of text you're encountering, reading should always be an active process. Active reading is about not only taking in information, but also noticing small details, making connections to prior knowledge, and uncovering deeper meaning.

Active reading isn't something anyone knows how to do automatically. It's a skill you learn and develop over time through practice and the use of targeted strategies. In this workshop, we'll focus on strategies you can use to actively read visual texts, and in the first workshop for Chapter 2 (p. SW2-A), we'll cover complementary strategies for written texts.

As you may have learned in past courses, there are both **primary sources** created during a specific time period from the past and **secondary sources** that provide an account of the past after the fact. Visual primary sources include texts like sculptures, paintings, photographs, and architecture, while visual secondary sources include texts like charts and maps. We'll begin with an active reading strategy best suited to visual primary sources.

Actively Reading Visual Primary Sources

To actively read a visual primary source, it can be helpful to use a strategy called OPTIC:

Overview: How would you describe the visual in one or two sentences to someone who couldn't see it?

Parts: What parts make up the visual? First, describe concrete elements: What people, symbols, or locations do you recognize? Then, consider abstract elements: What stands out to you about the visual's colors, materials, and layout? Try to focus on description rather than interpretation at this stage — stick to the facts.

Title: What is the piece called? Can you tell who created it and when it was made?

Interrelationships: Start putting the pieces together. Look over your Overview, your description of Parts, and the information you gathered about the Title, and then consider how these components connect to course content. Does the visual text remind you of any people, events, or movements you've studied? Explain the connections you see.

Conclusion: Make a claim about the visual text as a whole. Having investigated the components of the visual text and considered connections to broader concepts or developments, what's your main takeaway?

We can practice applying OPTIC to a visual text found on page 20 of this textbook.

Erich Lessing/Art Resource, NY.

Facsimile of the Catalan Atlas Showing the King of Mali Holding a Gold Nugget, 1375

Overview: This visual appears to be part of a map highlighting important people and places and showing how they connect to one another.

Parts: There are three figures on the map. Two smaller figures are riding camels, while the largest figure is sitting on a cushion and wearing a crown. The figure wearing the crown is holding a scepter in one hand and an unknown object in the other hand. There are also small buildings scattered across the map, some of which have flags raised above them.

Title: This map is labeled as a facsimile, so it's a modern reproduction of a map originally drawn in 1375. Based on the title, it seems the crowned figure is meant to be the King of Mali, and the unknown object in his hand is a piece of gold.

Interrelationships: The Catalan Atlas is a medieval map drawn in Spain, so it conveys a European perspective on the rest of the known world. Because the King of Mali is shown holding a gold nugget, it's safe to assume he is Mansa Musa, the king who became famous for his wealth after taking a pilgrimage to Mecca with an elaborate personal caravan. He stands out compared to the other people and places on the map, who are smaller and less colorful.

Conclusion: Mansa Musa's colorful robes, the scepter and gold nugget in his hands, and his large size relative to the other people and places on the map all depict him as a powerful figure with awe-inspiring wealth. Overall, this section of the Catalan Atlas shows European interest in African kingdoms as potential trading partners and sources of gold.

As this example demonstrates, when analyzed deeply, visual primary sources can help you to synthesize previously learned material and emerge with new insights.

recap

Actively Reading Visual Primary Sources

The OPTIC strategy can help you analyze visual primary sources like photographs, political cartoons, maps, works of art, architecture, and other cultural artifacts.

Overview **Parts** **Title** **Interrelationships** **Conclusion**

Activity ▸ Actively Reading Visual Primary Sources

Use the OPTIC strategy to analyze the visual text *The Oba of Benin, with Attendants*, also shown on page 26.

Peter Horree/Alamy Stock Photo.

Actively Reading Visual Secondary Sources

Similarly to how the OPTIC strategy can help you analyze visual primary sources, the Triple I strategy can help you engage with visual secondary sources like charts and maps:

Investigate: Complete a quick visual scan and record at least three details that stand out to you.

Identify: Use contextualizing information (like the title and/or legend) and your course knowledge to identify at least two concepts or developments associated with the visual.

Infer: Based on the details you've investigated and the relevant information you've identified, summarize what you can infer from the visual.

Let's practice applying Triple I to a map also found on page 16 of this textbook.

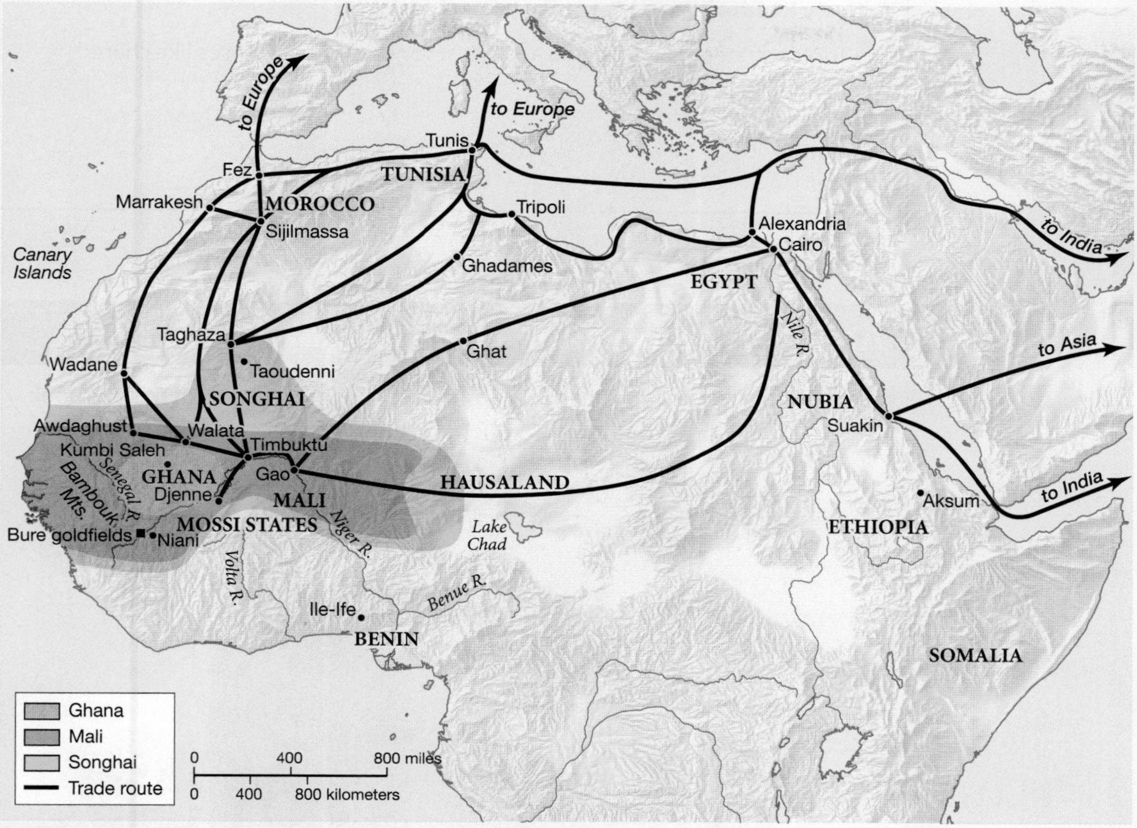

Medieval West Africa and the Trans-Saharan Trade

Investigate

- Three empires are labeled: Ghana, Mali, and Songhai.
- All three empires are in northwest Africa.
- There are lines leading from the empires to Europe, India, and the rest of Asia.

Identify

- Ghani, Mali, and Songhai are known as the Sudanic empires or Sahelian empires because of their location between the Sahara desert and sub-Saharan grasslands.
- All three kingdoms were rich in gold, and their period of prominence roughly overlapped with Europe's medieval era.

Infer

- The strategic location of West Africa's medieval empires and their abundance of gold facilitated trade within and beyond the African continent.

This same approach can be applied to other visual secondary sources like charts and graphs.

recap

Actively Reading Visual Secondary Sources

The Triple I strategy can help you analyze secondary visual sources like charts and maps.

Investigate
Identify
Infer

Activity ▸ Actively Reading Visual Secondary Sources

Use the Triple I strategy to analyze Map 1.1, also shown on page 5 of this textbook.

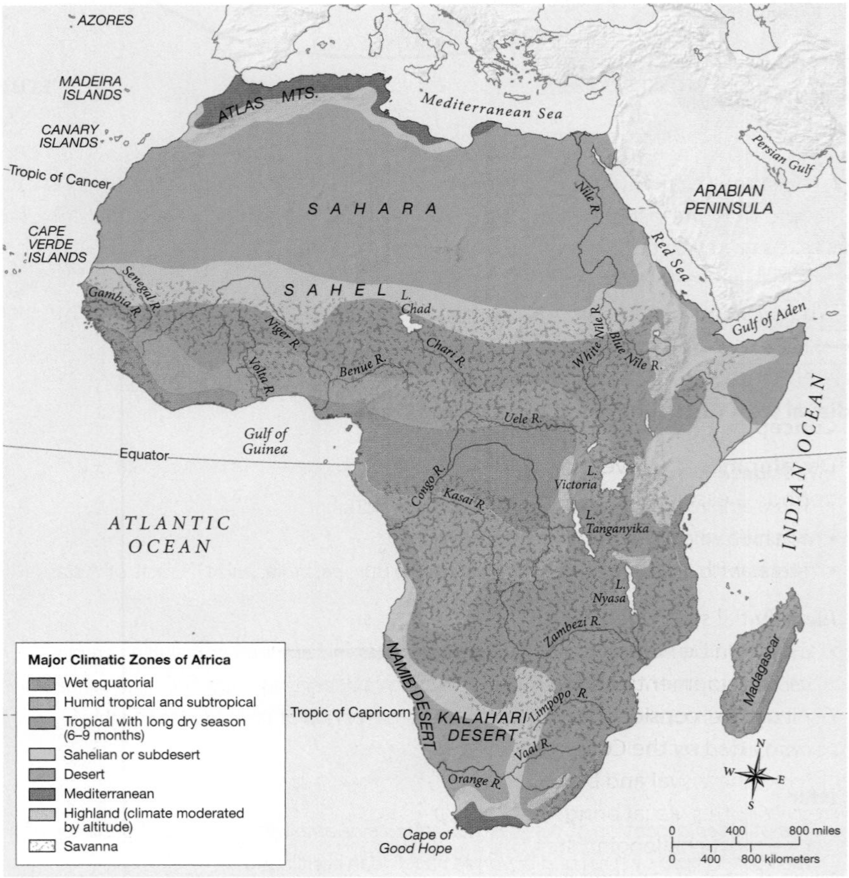

Africa's Diverse Geography

Visual Texts:
Multiple-Choice Questions

The multiple-choice section of the AP® African American Studies Exam is stimulus-based. This means multiple-choice questions will appear in sets of two to three, with each set tied to either a primary or a secondary source. Often, this source will be a visual text — a photograph, map, political cartoon, example of architecture, work of art, or other cultural artifact connected to the field of African American Studies.

As you learned in the previous workshop, the OPTIC and Triple I strategies are designed to help you use course knowledge to deeply analyze visual primary and secondary sources. While practicing those strategies will help you build muscle memory with your analysis skills, you likely won't have time to apply them during the the AP® Exam. During that timed testing environment, you'll need to take a more streamlined approach. That's why this workshop will walk through a few strategies you can use to answer multiple-choice questions with a visual stimulus efficiently and confidently.

Strategy 1: Activate relevant concepts, developments, and processes.

When the stimulus for multiple-choice questions is a visual text, your primary task is to understand how the visual connects to the course content you've studied. Think of the visual text as a key to unlock the concepts, developments, and processes that will be relevant to the questions to follow.

What exactly are concepts, developments, and processes? They are the important figures, events, and trends you learn about in AP® African American Studies. Here's a quick reference guide:

Concept: a person, place, theory, or theme

Development: an event; a political, social, or cultural movement; or a time period — essentially, anything important that happens

Process: two or more related developments — the developments might cause, contrast with, or have commonalities with one another

As an initial step when approaching a visual stimulus for multiple-choice questions, it can be helpful to give the visual a quick initial scan and take note of the concepts, developments, and processes it brings to mind.

For instance, consider the following map, which resembles one of the required sources provided by the College Board. Before even looking at a question set, we can preview the visual and begin to brainstorm some concepts, developments, and processes this visual brings to mind. Brainstorming examples of processes is usually the most challenging step. One useful approach is to explain how two of the developments you identified relate to each other. Does one development cause, contrast with, or have commonalities with another?

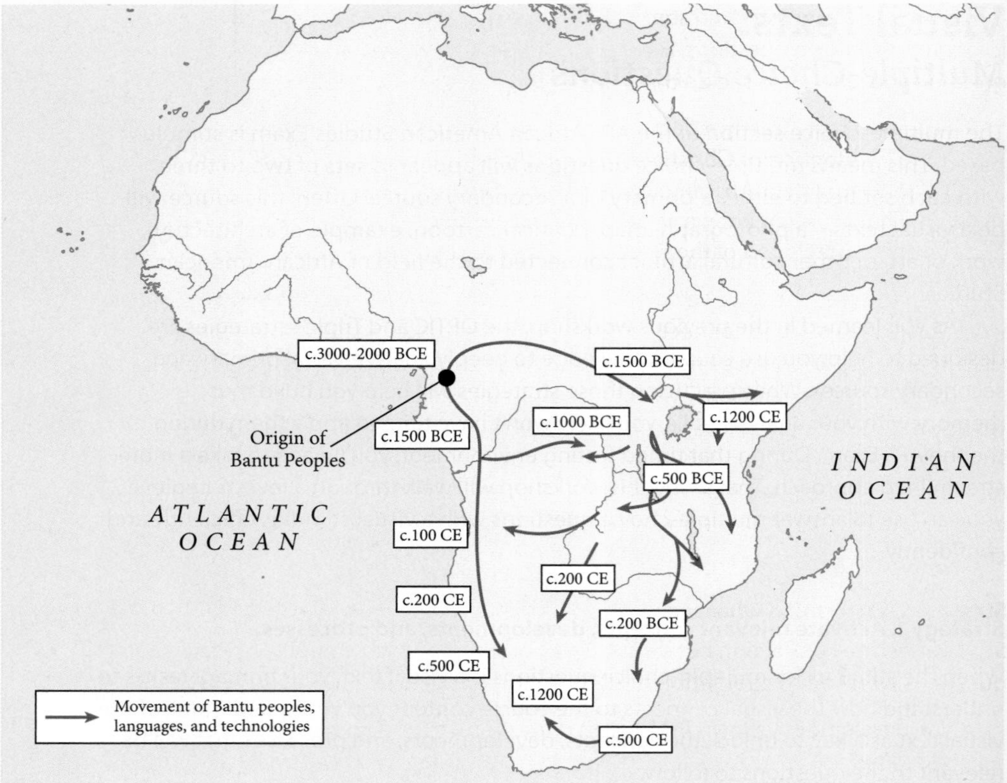

Concepts

- Migration and the African diaspora
- Ancient African societies
- Settlements by bodies of water

Developments

- Time period of 3000 B.C.E.–1200 C.E.
- Bantu migration/expansion
- Cultural exchange between Bantu people and local communities

Processes

- The Bantu migration caused cultural exchange between Bantu people and local communities.

Now that we've activated some knowledge from the course, we're ready to apply it to multiple-choice questions. Here's an example of one kind of multiple-choice question you're likely to see on the AP® African American Studies Exam:

The map most directly reflects which of the following developments?
A. The adoption of Christianity in ancient Africa
B. The growth of African maritime trade
C. The migration known as the Bantu expansion
D. The completion of the first African road systems

Thanks to the prep work we've done, this question is quite easy to answer! Because we were able to identify the connection between the map and the development known as the Bantu expansion, we know the correct answer is C.

As you build up familiarity with stimulus-based multiple-choice questions, you won't need to write out relevant concepts, developments, and processes each time you encounter a visual text. However, the core of the approach still stands: Before reading the question set, look over the visual text to activate your awareness of related course content. This initial step will prime you to recognize relevant, accurate answer choices.

Strategy 2: Determine what the question is really asking using the Four Cs.

Sometimes, the connection between the visual stimulus and its multiple-choice questions won't be so straightforward. For example, consider this sample question:

The development shown in the map most directly contributed to which of the following?
A. Technological and agricultural advancements
B. Changes in weather and climate in the Sahara region
C. The establishment of settlements in Egypt
D. The rejection of Bantu people by most Indigenous residents

None of the answer choices are directly represented in our notes for Strategy 1, so we can't use our prep work as an on-ramp to a correct answer. Instead, we can break down the question to make it more approachable.

While the precise phrasing varies from question to question, many complex questions on the AP® African American Studies Exam are really asking you to approach a concept or development through one of the Four Cs:

Comparison: How are two figures, events, movements, or time periods similar or different?

Causation: What factors *directly* contributed to an event or a movement? What effects did this event or movement *directly* bring about?

Continuity & Change: What changed and what stayed the same between different time periods?

When you're not sure what a question is asking, it can be helpful to try to reframe it in simpler language through reference to one of the Four Cs. In this case, we can rephrase the question as follows:

> *Causation — which answer choice is an effect of the Bantu migration?*

This simpler version of the question will help guide us: the correct answer must reference a development that results from the Bantu migration.

Strategy 3: Eliminate wrong answers.

Even with the rephrased question, there still isn't a clear parallel between the concepts, developments, and process we brainstormed and the answer choices. So, we can then use the process of elimination to cross out choices that are:

False: Are any choices factually incorrect?

Outside the time period: Do any choices pertain to a different time period from the one the question discusses?

Irrelevant: Do any choices fail to answer the question? It's not enough for an answer choice to be true; answers are correct only if they directly address the question asked.

Let's eliminate wrong answers using these principles.

False	D. The rejection of Bantu people by most Indigenous residents *In this textbook, you've learned the Bantu peacefully intermixed with most of the local communities they encountered.*
Outside the time period	C. The establishment of settlements in Egypt *As mentioned earlier in this chapter, the first settlements in Egypt emerged about 100,000 years ago, well before the Bantu migration.*
Irrelevant	B. Changes in weather and climate in the Sahara region *While it's true that changes in climate likely contributed to the Bantu migration, the question is asking for an effect of the Bantu migration, not a cause.*

Having eliminated these answer options, it becomes clear that A is the correct answer.

recap

Answering Multiple-Choice Questions with a Visual Stimulus

The strategies to efficiently and accurately answer multiple-choice question sets build off of one another:

Strategy 1: Activate relevant concepts, developments, and processes.

Concept:
a person, place, theory, or theme

Development:
an event; a political, social, or cultural movement; or a time period — essentially, anything important that happens

Process:
two or more related developments — the developments might cause, contrast with, or have commonalities with one another

Strategy 2: Determine what the question is really asking using the Four Cs.

Comparison:
How are two figures, events, movements, or time periods similar or different?

Causation:
What factors *directly* contributed to an event or a movement? What effects did this event or movement *directly* bring about?

Continuity & Change:
What changed and what stayed the same between different time periods?

Strategy 3: Eliminate wrong answers.

False:
Are any choices factually incorrect?

Outside the time period:
Do any choices pertain to a different time period from the one the question discusses?

Irrelevant:
Do any choices fail to answer the question? It's not enough for an answer choice to be true; answers are correct only if they directly address the question asked.

Activity ▸ Answering Multiple-Choice Questions with a Visual Stimulus

Prepare to answer multiple-choice questions on the following artwork, also shown on page 14 of this textbook.

Museum of Fine Arts, Houston, Texas/Museum purchase funded by Brown Foundation Accessions Endowment Fund/Bridgeman Images.

Nok Sculpture

1. Which of the following best describes historians' understanding of the Nok people?

A. The Nok worked skillfully with iron and clay, but little is known about their daily life.

B. The Nok maintained a matriarchal society centered around female elders.

C. The Nok produced gold jewelry and fine clothing to be traded with other societies.

D. The Nok adhered to strict religious practices and prepared altars honoring their gods.

2. Which of the following best captures the significance of archaeological discoveries like this sculpture?

A. The sculpture is an ancient terracotta figure with exaggerated facial features, an elaborate hairstyle, and bold jewelry.

B. The sculpture was likely discovered in modern-day Nigeria in the late twentieth century.

C. The sculpture shows the Nok had a distinct artistic style and talented craftspeople.

D. The sculpture provides evidence of the earliest-known complex society in ancient Africa.

Before approaching the question set, activate your awareness of relevant course content using a graphic organizer like the one shown below.

Concepts	
Developments	
Processes	

Next, review the questions and rephrase them using the Four Cs.

Question 1	Question 2
☐ Comparison ☐ Causation ☐ Continuity & change	☐ Comparison ☐ Causation ☐ Continuity & change
Rephrasing:	Rephrasing:

Finally, categorize the answer choices to eliminate wrong answers. Make sure to explain your reasoning.

False	
Outside the time period	
Irrelevant	
Correct	

Multiple-Choice Questions

Questions 1–2 refer to the following.

AP® source ***Facsimile of the Catalan Atlas showing the King of Mali Holding a Gold Nugget, 1375***

Erich Lessing/Art Resource, NY.

1. The purpose of this detail from the Catalan Atlas can best be described as

(A) Celebrating the expansion of Islam throughout North Africa and the Middle East

(B) Illustrating a collection of valuable artifacts

(C) Highlighting the architecture of the era

(D) Emphasizing the wealth and power of an African Muslim ruler

2. Which of the following pieces of evidence best supports the depiction of Mansa Musa in the image?

(A) Mansa Musa was depicted in many European maps as a wealthy man wearing a crown and holding a scepter.

(B) Mansa Musa's vast kingdom and accumulated wealth were the main causes of Portuguese incursions into West Africa.

(C) Mansa Musa's pilgrimage to Mecca attracted interest from merchants, prompting plans to trade manufactured goods for gold.

(D) Mansa Musa was a devout Muslim who traveled to the city of Mecca in a well-publicized pilgrimage.

Short-Answer Question

Medieval West Africa and the Trans-Saharan Trade

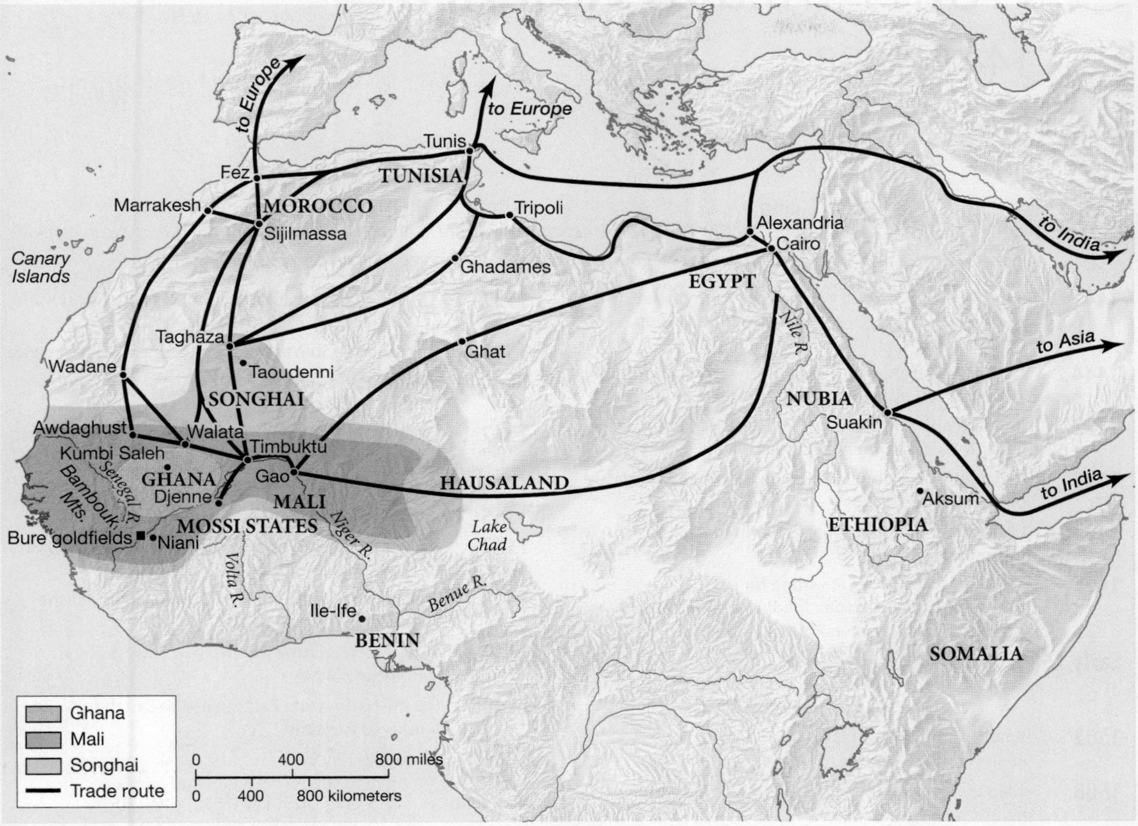

1. Using the map, answer A, B, C, and D.

(A) Describe how the trade routes depicted on this map impacted the Ghana kingdom.

(B) Explain one difference between the trade route for the Songhai empire and the trade route for the Mali kingdom.

(C) Explain how the geographic features of western Africa impacted the trade route of the Mali kingdom.

(D) Explain why the Songhai were the last and largest Sudanic empire.

CHAPTER 2

From Africa to America

1441–1808

CHAPTER TIMELINE

Events specific to African American history are in purple. General U.S. history events are in black. Events from the AP® Course Framework are marked with an asterisk.

1441	Expedition sponsored by Portugal's Prince Henry the Navigator picks up ten enslaved people on African coast
1444	Portuguese expedition returns from Africa with 235 enslaved people; Atlantic slave trade begins
1452	Pope Nicholas V proclaims that Christian kingdoms may enslave Muslim and pagan "enemies of Christ"
1488	Portuguese explorer Bartolomeu Dias rounds Cape of Good Hope
1492	Christopher Columbus makes world's first transatlantic voyage
1494	Treaty of Tordesillas sets stage for early transatlantic slave trade, dividing power in the Atlantic world between Portugal and Spain
Early 1500s	Spain begins to issue contracts to European merchants, permitting them to sell enslaved people in Spanish colonies
1502	Spanish soldier Nicolás de Ovando brings ten enslaved Black people to Hispaniola
1508	Juan Ponce de León employs armed Africans in invasion of Puerto Rico
	Diego Velázquez employs Black auxiliaries in conquest of Cuba
1516	Bartolomé de Las Casas encourages Spanish to replace enslaved American Indians with Africans
1518	First Africans arrive in Mexico with Hernán Cortés
1519	Ferdinand Magellan sets off to sail around world
1519–1521	Hernán Cortés conquers Aztecs
1526	Transatlantic slave trade begins*
1526	Africans enslaved in Santo Domingo (present-day Dominican Republic) and brought to aid Spanish exploration along the South Carolina–Georgia coastline lead earliest known slave revolt in North America, escaping into nearby Indigenous communities*
1528	Juan Garrido issues his petition for freedom*
	Estevanico (also called Esteban), an enslaved African healer from Morocco, forced to work as an explorer and translator in Texas and in territory that became the southwestern U.S.*
1532–1535	Francisco Pizarro conquers Peru, vanquishes Incas
1539	Hernando de Soto explores southeastern North America
1540	Francisco Vásquez de Coronado explores Southwest and Great Plains
1542	Spanish government bans enslavement of American Indian peoples within its territories
1550	First slave ship lands in Brazil
1565	Spanish Florida founded
1587	Sir Walter Raleigh establishes Roanoke, first English settlement in New World
1608	French explorer Samuel de Champlain establishes Quebec
1619	First enslaved Africans arrive in English North American colonies
1640s	Spanish turn from Portuguese to Dutch for enslaved Africans
1656	Elizabeth Key becomes first Black woman in North America to sue for freedom and win*
1724	Louisiana Slave Code (Code Noir, or Black Code) created*
1738	Fort Mose, first sanctioned free Black town in present-day U.S., founded*
1756	Olaudah Equiano kidnapped and sold into slavery
1773	Phillis Wheatley's "On Being Brought from Africa to America" published*
1783	U.S. Constitution refers to slavery but avoids using terms "slave" or "slavery"*
1788	British government restricts number of enslaved people British ships may carry
1789	*The Interesting Narrative of the Life of Olaudah Equiano, or Gustavus Vassa, the African. Written by Himself*, published*
1797	Enslaved women steal weapons in insurrection aboard British ship *Thomas*
1805	Article 14 of the 1805 Haitian Constitution reverses prevailing functions of racial categories in the Atlantic world*
1807	British ban on the slave trade goes into effect
1808	U.S. withdraws from international slave trade, continues domestic slave trade

Enslaved Africans and the Portuguese Prince

On August 8, 1444, in the maritime town of Lagos, Portugal, 235 people disembarked from a Portuguese ship that had taken them from their African homeland. Bound in the first European expedition specifically aimed at enslaving people, these Africans were paraded from the docks to the town gates as a crowd of curious onlookers gathered. Among the onlookers was Prince Henry, the Portuguese monarch who had opened Europe's age of exploration several decades earlier by sponsoring a series of voyages down the West African coast. The enslaved men, women, and children of all complexions and colors were distressed and disoriented as they walked through the streets of Lagos. "Some kept their heads low, and their faces [were] bathed with tears, looking upon one another," noted Henry's court chronicler, while others were "looking up to the heavens and crying out loudly, as if asking for help from the Father of nature." The spectacle ended with an auction that moved even the chronicler, a steadfast admirer of his monarch, to pity. Before their sale, the captives were divided into lots in order to help the merchants split the proceeds of their voyage — and to pay Henry the required 20 percent royal tax. The separation was bound to "increase their suffering still more," the chronicler noted, since it parted "fathers from sons, husbands from wives, brothers from brothers. No respect was shown either to friends or relations, but each fell where his lot took him."[1]

The scene marked the beginning of an African diaspora, or mass dispersion of a people from their homeland, that would carry millions of Africans across the ocean in slavery under European and Euro-American enslavers. Although this first set of captives would land in Portugal, most ended up much farther away. With European settlement of the Americas in the 1500s, a highly profitable transatlantic exchange of goods and enslaved labor began to take shape. Now known as the transatlantic slave trade, this expansive commercial enterprise involved three continents: European merchants exchanged manufactured goods for enslaved people in Africa, shipped the enslaved people to colonies in the Americas to exchange for commodities produced there, and brought those materials to Europe for use in the manufacture of more goods.

This immensely lucrative trade transformed both Africa and the American colonies. Although a long-standing internal slave trade had existed in West Africa prior to the arrival of Europeans, the new triangle trade both exploited and expanded it, ultimately leaving many parts of the region depopulated. Moreover, the transatlantic slave trade forever changed the lives of the millions of Africans it dispersed. Most captives hailed from vibrant West African communities that had had little contact with Europe prior to the rise of the slave trade, and most were enslaved before they ever left Africa. Once early European slave traders began to meet with armed resistance from the peoples who lived on the West African coast, they quickly turned to African traders to supply them with enslaved people.

Although the men, women, and children they purchased were not free in Africa, once they were swept into the transatlantic slave trade, these diasporic Africans would encounter a new kind of slavery. Crowded aboard slave ships for the long and often lethal voyage across the Atlantic, the Africans who ended up in the Americas entered a system of bondage unlike anything that existed in Africa. Whereas slavery in Africa was often temporary and rarely heritable, in the Americas, slavery was lifelong and passed from parent to child. Thus, for those who survived, the transatlantic voyage marked the beginning of a captivity that would pass from one generation to the next.

Dispersed across the Americas, these enslaved people set about rebuilding their lives and creating new communities. As members of many different ethnic and linguistic groups, the slave trade's victims came from a variety of villages and kingdoms. Few, if any, thought of themselves as *Africans* when they first boarded the slave ships. Only in the Americas would they take on a collective identity imposed on them by slavery, forced migration, and the strange new world in which they found themselves.

The Rise of the Transatlantic Slave Trade

Why did Europeans travel to Africa before the onset of the transatlantic slave trade?

How did early forms of enslaved labor by the Portuguese shape slave-based economies in the Americas?

Although Europeans and West Africans lived on neighboring continents separated only by the Arab Islamic societies of North Africa, they were virtual strangers prior to the fifteenth century. Small numbers of people and small quantities of goods had moved between the two continents via overland trade networks for centuries, but prior to the expeditions pioneered by Prince Henry, Europe and West Africa were largely sealed off from each other by massive natural barriers. The Sahara desert made overland travel between the two regions so difficult and dangerous that even after the trans-Saharan trade expanded during the imperial eras of Ghana, Mali, and Songhai, few people made the passage across the desert other than Berber traders and the enslaved Africans they transported north for resale in the Islamic world. Although a lucrative point of connection between West Africa and the Mediterranean world, the trade fostered few direct contacts between Europeans and West Africans. Maritime contact between the two groups was even more limited due to the powerful winds and currents off the Saharan coast, which had long prevented sea travel between Europe and Africa. Separated by desert and sea, West Africa and western Europe were home to two distinct societies that came together abruptly in the fifteenth century — with tragic consequences. Their encounters would foster a transatlantic trade in African peoples that would last several hundred years and depopulate many regions of West Africa.

Europe on the Eve of the Slave Trade

When the Portuguese first began raiding West Africa's sub-Saharan coast, Europe was not yet the conglomeration of powerful empires it would later become. Ruled by a variety of monarchs, city-states, and feuding nobles, European societies were larger, more far-flung, and more economically interconnected than most precolonial West African societies. But they were also divided and socially unstable. European rulers, such as the Portuguese royal family, were still in the process of inventing powerful nation-states that could maintain social order — a development that would be greatly facilitated by the exploitation of Africa and the Americas.

By the fifteenth century, monarchies had risen to replace Europe's feuding nobility, offering their subjects a more secure and politically stable social order. These monarchs forged identities as the protectors of Christendom against Muslim usurpers, waging both the Crusades in the Middle East and eastern Europe and the Reconquista in Iberia (Spain and Portugal). They created royalty-based nation-states in England, France, and Iberia, securing their influence by building powerful bureaucracies and establishing standing armies and navies. But these new state powers were expensive to maintain and difficult to protect, and to sustain their influence, rulers soon needed to explore and exploit new lands.

In Africa, European monarchs such as Prince Henry hoped to find sources of gold and other luxury goods they could use to enrich their treasuries, pay their armies, and increase the commercial power of their nations. Europeans were unfamiliar with the African coast south of Cape Bojador, a headland west of the Sahara marked by treacherous winds that prevented European sailors from traveling farther down the coast. But they hoped that in crossing the unknown lands that lay south of the cape, they would find a route to the riches of Asia that would avoid the powerful Ottoman empire.

Maritime Expeditions and First Contacts

Portugal, one of Europe's earliest nation-states, pioneered the navigation of the West African coast. As the most accomplished shipbuilders in Europe, the Portuguese were the first to develop oceangoing vessels suitable for long exploratory voyages. Called **carracks** and **caravels**, these small sailing ships had two or three masts and were powered by both triangular and square sails. An innovation borrowed from the Arab dhow, the triangular sails that graced Portuguese ships allowed them to brave strong winds and travel faster and farther than any other vessels of their day. In particular, they allowed Portuguese mariners to cut through the dangerous northeasterly winds blowing off Cape Bojador.

carracks/caravels Small sailing ships used by the Portuguese to explore Africa and the Atlantic world. Lightweight, fast, and easy to maneuver, they generally had two or three masts.

Between 1418 and the 1470s, the Portuguese launched a series of exploratory expeditions that remapped the oceans south of Portugal, charting new territories that one explorer described as "oceans where none had ever sailed before."[2] They also discovered several uninhabited islands only a few hundred miles off Africa's west coast, which they began to settle and cultivate. These islands — christened Madeira, the Azores, Arguin, the Cape Verde Islands, and São Tomé and Príncipe — provided the

Portuguese a stepping-off point for expeditions farther down the coast, allowing them to round the Cape of Good Hope in 1488.

The Atlantic slave trade first took shape in conjunction with these expeditions, as Portuguese seamen began to bring back enslaved Africans to sell both in Portugal and in its Atlantic islands. Spain was also active in this early trade and established its own Atlantic colony in the Canary Islands during the fifteenth century. Located off the northwest coast of Africa, the ten islands that make up the Canaries were not as easily settled as the uninhabited islands claimed by Portugal. They were home to an Indigenous people known as the **Guanches**, whose ancestors likely originated among the Berber peoples of North Africa. The Guanches fought off the Spanish from 1402, when the first Spanish expedition arrived, to the 1490s, when the last of the Guanches were finally conquered. Even before that, however, the Spanish began exploiting the fertile soil and temperate weather of the islands by planting sugarcane, wheat, and other crops. The Canaries proved ideal for the production of sugar, which also flourished on the Portuguese islands of Madeira and São Tomé.

Guanches
The aboriginal inhabitants of the Canary Islands.

AP® exam tip

Be prepared to explain why European demand for African laborers increased in the late 1400s.

Sugarcane, a valuable crop previously grown primarily in Cyprus, Sicily, and parts of southern Spain, demanded far more labor than the islands' small Guanche population could provide. First cultivated in the Pacific Rim more than 10,000 years ago, sugar was introduced to Europe in the eleventh century and became an immediate hit. It was in demand among cooks as a spice, sweetener, and preservative and was used by physicians and pharmacists as a remedy for disorders of the blood, stomach, and lungs. As a crop requiring both warm weather and intensive labor, however, sugar was in short supply in Europe. In the Mediterranean, sugarcane was cultivated on large plantations by enslaved workers from Russia and the Balkans — traditional sources of European forced labor. But with the emergence of Portuguese and Spanish colonies in the Atlantic, this plantation system moved offshore and became increasingly dependent on the labor of enslaved Africans. By the 1490s, Madeira was the largest European sugar producer. In the sixteenth century, sugar production boomed in the Azores, the Canaries, Cape Verde, and São Tomé — all of which required imported laborers.

Despite the successful slave raids that took place on some of the earliest Portuguese expeditions to Africa, kidnappings would not remain the means by which the Portuguese secured these laborers. After the early raids, West African rulers quickly organized to defend their coast. By the 1450s, Portuguese slaving expeditions along the Senegambian and Gambian coast were driven offshore by fleets of African canoe men armed with arrows and javelins. Although these African canoes lacked the firepower of the caravels, which were equipped with cannons, they could easily outmaneuver the much larger European vessels, and the canoe men could use their weapons to pick off Europeans who attempted to land. After 1456, the Portuguese crown began negotiating commercial treaties with West African rulers, who agreed to supply the Portuguese with enslaved people in return for European goods. Thus, the slave trade first emerged as a commercial relationship between coastal peoples: African merchants tapped the internal slave trade, which had existed in Africa since ancient times, to supply European traders with thousands of enslaved people each year.

Slave Traders Seizing People in Guinea, Africa, 1789
This engraving of a painting by the artist Richard Westall is titled *A View Taken near Bain on the Coast of Guinea in West Africa. Dedicated to the FEELING HEARTS in All Civilized Nations.* Westall was inspired by the work of Carl Bernhard Wadström, a Swedish industrialist who toured the coast of West Africa in 1787 and 1788 and sketched what he saw there. During his visit, Wadström witnessed firsthand the slave raiding and warfare caused by the slave trade and became an abolitionist as a result of this experience. ■ **What role did coastal African merchants play in the transatlantic slave trade, and what groups were often left vulnerable to slave traders?** *Private Collection/© Michael Graham-Stewart/Bridgeman Images.*

The Enslavement of Indigenous Peoples

If the Portuguese trade in enslaved Africans had served only Europe, the Atlantic slave trade might well have been short-lived. Europe's population boomed in the second half of the fifteenth century, making labor abundant and enslaved imports unnecessary. But the cultivation of Europe's Atlantic colonies created an additional labor market, which was soon complemented by similar markets in the Americas. Indeed, the first Africans arrived in the Americas either with or shortly after Columbus, who may have employed African seamen on some of his voyages. As Spaniards began to populate Hispaniola — the colony Columbus established in 1492 on the island that is now divided between Haiti and the Dominican Republic — enslaved Africans joined them. Nicolás de Ovando, a Spanish soldier who replaced Columbus as governor of Hispaniola in 1502, brought several Iberian-born enslaved Blacks, and he hoped they would both provide labor and help subdue Hispaniola's Indigenous population. His hopes evidently disappointed, Ovando banned the further importation of Blacks shortly thereafter, "on the grounds that they incited native rebellion."[3] But Spain's colonies in the "New World," as Europeans viewed these lands previously unknown to them, would prove far too hungry for labor for any such ban to persist.

African workers were first used in the copper and gold mines of Hispaniola, which resumed importing them in 1505. These workers were needed because Spanish attempts to exploit the labor of the island's native inhabitants, the **Taino Indians**, had met with limited success. During the first few decades of Spanish settlement, the conquistadors were able to extract forced labor from the Tainos under the ***encomienda*** system, which permitted the Spaniards to collect tribute — in the form of labor, gold, or other goods — from the native peoples they controlled. The colonists demanded both labor and gold from the Tainos, whom they put to work mining the island's rivers and streams. But the Tainos did not flourish under Spanish rule.

Taino Indians
One of the Indigenous peoples of the Caribbean.

encomienda
A labor system used by the Spanish in their colonization of the Americas. Under this system, the crown granted colonists control over a specified number of Indigenous Americans from whom they could extract labor.

Some Tainos resisted working for the Spaniards and were slaughtered by them, and many more succumbed to the Old World diseases that the Spanish interlopers carried with them. Not having been exposed to common European illnesses such as influenza, smallpox, chicken pox, mumps, and measles, the Tainos possessed no resistance to these diseases and began to die in droves. By the first decade of the sixteenth century, their population had dropped from 500,000 to 60,000; by 1514, it was down to 28,000; and by 1542, there were only a few hundred Tainos left on the island.

The rapid decline of the native population in Hispaniola was repeated throughout the Americas and set the stage for the development of the transatlantic slave trade. With their settlements triggering large population losses among the hemisphere's Indigenous peoples, European colonists had to look elsewhere for workers. Not surprisingly, they turned to the African slave trade to supply their needs. African slavery was already an established enterprise, offered an almost limitless supply of workers, and had several advantages over American Indian slavery. Most important among them was that African peoples, who lived in the same hemisphere as the Europeans, had some immunity to Old World diseases. Moreover, African laborers were strangers to the New World, which made them more manageable than the region's native populations. Unfamiliar with the local peoples and surrounding terrain, they could not easily escape their confinement.

African slavery was also sanctioned by the Catholic Church, while the enslavement of American Indians was more controversial. The Old World practice of African enslavement had received explicit license in a papal bull (formal proclamation) issued by Pope Nicholas V in 1452. Titled *Dum Diversas*, this proclamation granted the kings of Spain and Portugal permission "to invade, search out, capture, vanquish, and subdue all the Saracens [Muslims] and pagans . . . and other enemies of Christ wheresoever placed," as well as "their kingdoms, duchies, counties, principalities, [and other] possessions . . . and to reduce their persons into perpetual slavery."[4]

Issued before Columbus's voyages, *Dum Diversas* was designed to sanction European attacks on the Islamic societies of North Africa and the Middle East. It did not address the Spanish enslavement of Indigenous peoples of the Americas. Troubled by Spanish mistreatment of these peoples, Dominican missionaries were quick to challenge the legitimacy of American Indian slavery. "Tell me by what right of justice do you hold these Indians in such a cruel and horrible servitude?" Antonio de Montesinos, a Dominican priest stationed on Hispaniola, asked in a sermon delivered in 1511. "Why do you keep them so oppressed and exhausted, without giving them enough to eat or curing them of the sicknesses they incur from the excessive labor you give them, and they die, or rather you kill them, in order to extract and acquire gold every day?"[5] His critique was taken up by other Dominicans, most notably Bartolomé de Las Casas, who pressured both the Spanish crown and the pope to protect the Tainos. Concerned about their rapidly declining populations, Las Casas, starting in 1516, encouraged the Spanish to replace enslaved American Indians with those imported from Africa — a position he later came to regret. He was not then aware, he explained in 1560, of "how unjustly and tyrannically Africans were taken as slaves, in the same fashion as Indians."[6]

How much Las Casas could have done to curb African slavery had he come to this realization earlier remains an open question. But as it was, his campaign put American Indian rather than African slavery under contention. In 1537, Pope Paul III issued another papal bull, declaring that American Indians were rational beings who should be converted rather than enslaved, and in 1542, the Spanish government banned the enslavement of Indigenous peoples within its territories. Although both rulings were largely ignored by colonists and ineffective in curbing the abuses of the encomienda system, they facilitated the expansion of the transatlantic slave trade, which took shape alongside European settlement of the New World and displacement of the region's Indigenous peoples.

The First Africans in the Americas

Roughly 300,000 Africans landed in the Americas before 1620. Most came after 1550, when their numbers began to exceed those of Portuguese and Spanish migrants. By then, the Spanish conquest of the Americas had extended to include the islands of Puerto Rico, Cuba, Guadeloupe, Trinidad, and Jamaica, as well as the mainland regions of Mexico and Peru; the Portuguese had laid claim to Brazil. Enslaved Africans supplied labor for all these colonies. The Africans' presence expanded outward from Hispaniola, which served as the staging ground for further Spanish incursions into the New World. There they worked on sugar plantations after the island's small store of precious metals had been tapped out and accompanied the Spanish on military expeditions. The Spanish explorer Juan Ponce de León employed armed Africans to supplement his forces when he invaded Puerto Rico in 1508, and Diego Velázquez used Black auxiliaries in his 1511–1512 conquest of Cuba. Likewise, the first Africans to arrive in Mexico accompanied Hernán Cortés, who in 1519–1521 conquered the Aztecs with a force that included Juan Garrido, a free Black conquistador who had fought with Ponce de León.

AP® exam tip

Be sure you can explain how Africans helped Europeans lay claim to Indigenous lands.

AP® exam tip

Be prepared to explain how Juan Garrido maintained his freedom by serving in the Spanish military forces, participating in efforts to conquer Indigenous populations.

Garrido lived a long and eventful life that illustrates some of the many roles played by Africans in the conquest and settlement of New Spain. Born around 1480 in West Africa, Garrido was likely sold to Portuguese slave traders as a boy. However, he achieved his freedom sometime after arriving in Portugal, where he lived in Lisbon and converted to Catholicism — taking a Christian name that means "Handsome John." Subsequently a resident of Seville, he was a free man by the time he traveled to the New World in 1503. Once there, he participated in Diego Velázquez's subjugation of Cuba; served on Spanish expeditions to Puerto Rico, Guadeloupe, and Dominica; and became a personal attendant to Hernán Cortés, in whose service he fought in the siege of Tenochtitlan (Mexico City) and crossed the continent on a journey of exploration that ended in Baja California. In between missions, Garrido settled in Tenochtitlan, where he raised a family and planted the first wheat grown in New Spain.

AP® source ***Black Conquistadors***

Some of the first Africans in the Americas arrived with Spanish military expeditions. In Mexico, Africans initially came with Hernán Cortés, whose forces included the free Black conquistador Juan Garrido. In this illustration from a sixteenth-century manuscript, Cortés is depicted meeting the Indigenous peoples of the Tlaxcala region. Garrido is pictured at the far left. **What message does this image convey about the relationship between the Spanish, the ladinos, and the Indigenous peoples of the Tlaxcala region?** *From 'History of Indians' (1579) by Diego Duran (1537–1588)/Biblioteca Nacional, Madrid, Spain/De Agostini Picture Library/Gianni Dagli Orti/Bridgeman Images.*

ACTIVITY ▸ Revisit Your Prediction

In the AP® Unit Warmup (p. U1-F), you made a prediction about this image. **What roles do you believe Africans will assume in the Americas during the sixteenth century, and what impact do you think they will have on the colonization of the Americas? What clues from the image help support your prediction? Support or revise your original prediction using evidence from this chapter.**

Like Juan Garrido, many of the earliest Africans in the New World were ***ladinos***, Latinized Blacks who had lived most if not all of their early lives in Spain or Portugal or in those countries' Atlantic or American colonies. Already acculturated to European ways, ladinos spoke Spanish or Portuguese and had no sympathy for the Indigenous peoples of the Americas. Such attributes made them safe companions for European travelers to the New World and made them useful as domestic servants as well. Many European migrants to New Spain and Brazil brought Black or mulatto (mixed-race) servants with them when they first settled these regions.

ladinos
Latinized Blacks who were born or raised in Spain, Portugal, or these nations' Atlantic or American colonies and who spoke fluent Spanish or Portuguese, worked as intermediaries, and were essential in European colonization of the Americas.

The Spanish colonists began replacing their declining supply of Indigenous laborers with enslaved people imported directly from Africa as early as 1518, and the first enslaved ship arrived in Portuguese Brazil in 1550. Known in New Spain as ***bozales***, these African-born enslaved people quickly accounted for the majority of the New World's enslaved population. They were also the most downtrodden, forced to do the dirtiest, most dangerous, and most demanding work. Employed to extract the silver and gold the Spanish found in Mexico and Peru, they toiled in underground tunnels that sometimes collapsed on top of them and acquired lung disease from the toxic mineral dust. Diving for pearls off the coast of Veracruz, Mexico, Africans drowned in such numbers that their bodies attracted sharks. Some worked on sugar plantations, typically laboring from dawn until dusk planting, harvesting, and refining sugar. In particular, they suffered high mortality rates due to the long hours and hazards involved in boiling the cane at high temperatures to produce sugar. The cultivation of sugarcane, one of the earliest crops grown by enslaved people, was first introduced on Hispaniola and eventually spread throughout the Caribbean. But the largest sixteenth-century sugar producers were Brazil and Mexico, which imported tens of thousands of Africans to plant and process sugar during this period.

AP® skills

Applying Disciplinary Knowledge: What roles did *ladinos* play in the territory that became the United States?

bozales
A term used by the Spanish for recently imported African captives.

The demand for such labor would only increase over time, giving rise to an international slave trade that would last more than three centuries and carry approximately 12.5 million enslaved people to the New World. The African American population of the Americas took shape around these forced migrations.

AP® skills

Applying Disciplinary Knowledge: Identify the diverse roles Africans played during colonization of the Americas in the sixteenth century. How do these roles relate to the slave system that emerged in the Americas?

The Business of Slave Trading

By the beginning of the seventeenth century, the Spanish and Portuguese had begun to lose their monopoly on the exploration and settlement of the New World. Drawn by the riches that their predecessors had extracted from these lands, other European powers such as the Dutch, English, and French began to claim territory in the Americas. They also followed the example set by the Spanish and Portuguese when it came to importing enslaved Africans to help build and sustain their New World settlements.

As a result, the transatlantic slave trade expanded rapidly. Average annual exports of enslaved people from Africa increased from a little over ten thousand enslaved people at the beginning of the seventeenth century to nearly sixty thousand by the eighteenth century.

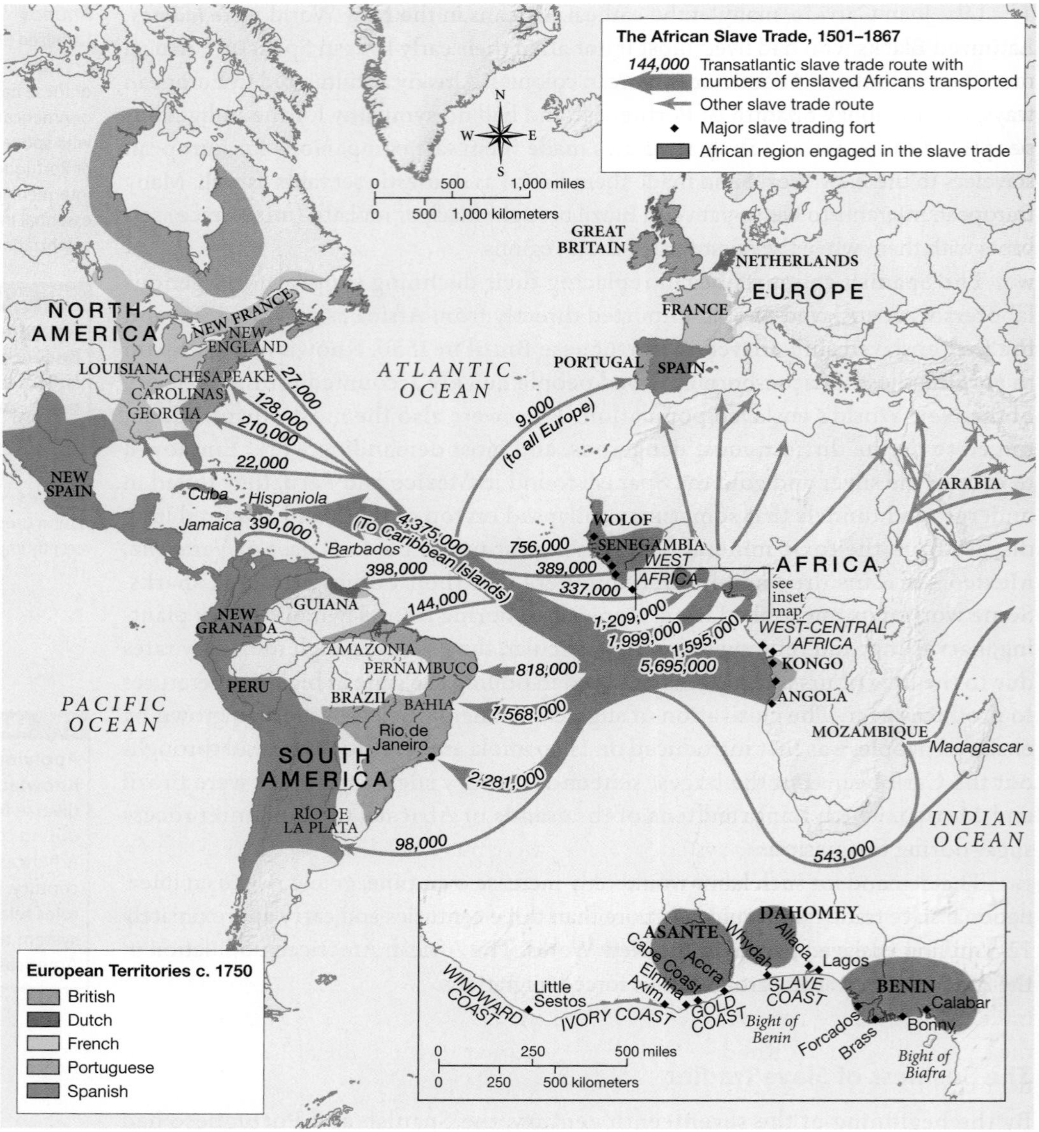

AP® source **MAP 2.1 Trade of Enslaved Africans, 1501–1867**

This map shows the many routes that slave traders used to carry millions of enslaved Africans to the Americas between 1501 and 1867. It also documents the trading routes that took far fewer African captives to Europe and the Middle East during this period. **Why did European traders send enslaved people to the Americas in higher numbers? Which locations in the Americas imported the most enslaved Africans? Which imported the least?**

ACTIVITY ▸ Revisit Your Prediction

In the AP® Unit Warmup (p. U1-F), you made a prediction about this image. **How will the loss of over 12.5 million Africans impact African society? What clues from the map help support your prediction? Support or revise your original prediction using evidence from this chapter.**

The transatlantic trade exploited and expanded on the existing internal slave trade in Africa, pitting African leaders against one another and making the capture and enslavement of prisoners of war more profitable than ever before. Europeans also expanded the trade by traversing larger stretches of the African coast. Whereas early European traders sought their cargo largely along the Senegambian coast, the trade eventually extended south to include Guinea-Bissau, the Gold Coast, Benin, Kongo, and Angola. Some traders even did business with the East African country of Mozambique. The captives brought to these places were drawn from an expansive interior trade that extended into west-central Africa and as far east as Madagascar (Map 2.1).

AP® skills

Applying Disciplinary Knowledge: What were the primary trading zones in Africa from which Africans were forcibly taken? What impact do you think this left on these settlements?

For Europeans, the slave trade remained a coastal exchange that took place largely in their West African trading centers. The earliest such center was **Elmina Castle** on the southern coast of present-day Ghana. Built as a Portuguese trading post in 1482, Elmina — the first of several forts the European powers established on the West African coast — began, by the early seventeenth century, to serve a far more enduring trade in human beings. Like later European trading forts, it had been erected with the agreement or license of local rulers in exchange for access to European commodities and military support. The castles on present-day Ghana's Gold Coast offered European merchants a secure harbor for their vessels and access to African markets trading in goods as well as people. Controlled by the Dutch after 1637, Elmina Castle remained an active slave trading post until the Dutch withdrew from the trade in 1814.

Elmina Castle
A fortress in present-day Ghana, built by the Portuguese as a trading post in 1482 and used as a major slave trading center by the Dutch from 1637 to 1814.

AP® exam tip

Be sure you can describe the scale and geographic scope of the transatlantic slave trade.

The Portuguese controlled the early transatlantic slave trade by virtue of the 1494 Treaty of Tordesillas — an agreement between Spain and Portugal granting the Western Hemisphere to Spain and Africa and Asia to Portugal. The earliest enslaved Africans were shipped to the New World from Lisbon and other European ports, but direct trade between Africa and European colonies in the Americas began in the early 1500s, under Spain's ***asiento*** system. Asientos were trade agreements, and this system authorized European merchants to ship enslaved Africans directly from Africa to New Spain. The Portuguese dominated the asiento system until the 1640s, when Spain and Portugal became enemies. After that, the Spanish transferred their business first to the Dutch and then to the British, who dominated the eighteenth-century transatlantic trade. American colonists eventually participated in the trade as well; over the course of the eighteenth century, Rhode Island traders sponsored at least a thousand transatlantic trips carrying enslaved Africans from their homeland.

asiento
A contract or trade agreement created by the Spanish crown.

European slave ships carried on a **triangle trade** that began with the transport of European copper, beads, guns, ammunition, textiles, and other manufactured goods to the West African coast. After these goods were exchanged for enslaved people, the second leg of the triangle trade — which slave traders called the **Middle Passage** — began. During this most infamous and dangerous phase, slave ships transported enslaved blacks from the West African coast to the slave ports of the New World. The ships then returned to their European ports of origin, laden with profitable crops grown by enslaved people, including sugar, tobacco, rice, and indigo and later cotton (Map 2.2). This trade fueled the economic development of Europe, supplying much of the raw material and capital that propelled European powers

triangle trade
The trade system that propelled the transatlantic slave trade, in which European merchants exchanged manufactured goods for enslaved Africans, whom they shipped to the Americas to exchange for New World commodities, which they then shipped back to European markets.

Middle Passage
Second part of the three-part journey to the Americas in the transatlantic slave trade in which slave ships transported enslaved people from the West African coast to slave ports in the Americas.

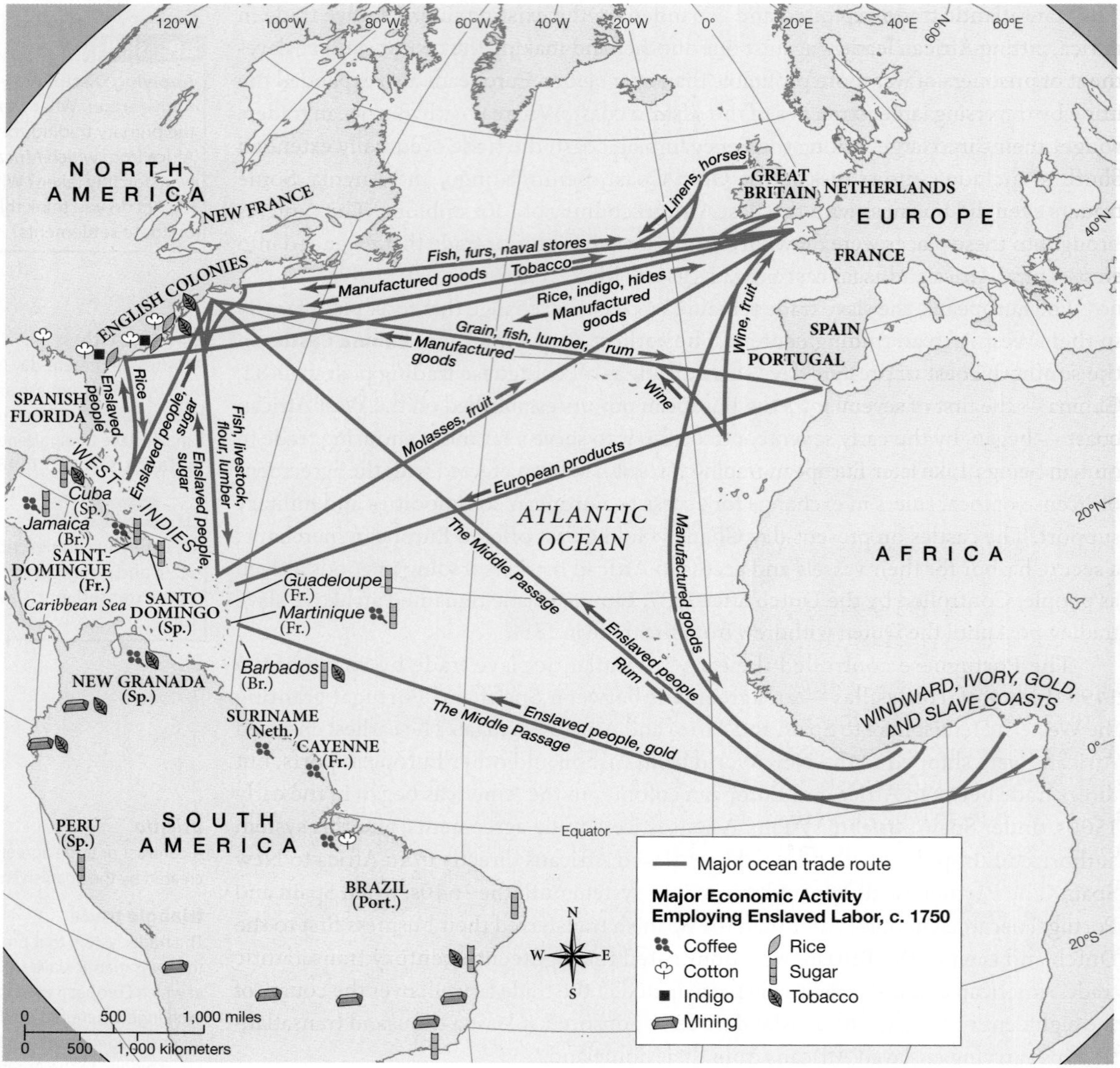

MAP 2.2 The Triangle Trade

The transatlantic slave trade is known as a triangle trade because it took shape around an exchange of goods that involved ports in three different parts of the world. As illustrated in this map, the first leg of the trade took traders from Europe to Africa, where they exchanged manufactured goods such as cloth, copper, beads, guns, and ammunition for enslaved Africans, whom they then sold to buyers in American ports in return for commodities such as sugar, tobacco, and cotton. **What parts of this trade were the English colonies directly involved in? How were they connected to the larger trade?**

into the industrial age. The trade was equally crucial to the economic growth of the Americas, supplying European colonists with much of the labor they needed to make the New World settlements profitable.

For Africans, however, the trade was largely tragic. Although the African rulers, merchants, and middlemen who participated in the trade profited from it, most of the continent's inhabitants did not. By the early nineteenth century, Britain and other imperial powers had begun to withdraw from the slave trade — a process that started with Britain's ban on the trade in 1807 and the U.S. Act to Prohibit the Importation of Slaves, which took effect in 1808. Nevertheless, several hundred years of forced migration had taken a severe toll on Africa and its peoples.

The slave trade fostered warfare and weakened social bonds within Africa by encouraging African villages and states to raid each other. Even African rulers who did not wish to participate in the trade found it difficult to avoid since Europe's slave traders supplied their enemies with guns, which were crucial to resisting the trade's depredations. They had to raid or be raided. The demographic costs of the trade were massive. Generations of young people were lost, and many of them perished as a result of the trade. The transatlantic slave trade also imposed almost unimaginable suffering on the millions of individual Africans who survived their capture and sale.

AP® exam tip

Be sure you can explain how the transatlantic slave trade destabilized West African societies.

The Middle Passage

What conditions did enslaved Africans endure along the three-part journey of the transatlantic slave trade?

For African captives, the journey into transatlantic slavery began long before they saw a European ship. Most of them came from regions outside the West African coast. The African communities that surrounded the European slave trading settlements rarely sold their own people into slavery. The trade was an African enterprise until it reached the coast; only in Angola were Europeans ever really involved in capturing people themselves. Instead, African traders enslaved others by way of an increasingly far-flung network that extended through much of western and west-central Africa.

Separated from their families and cultures, captives endured a long trek to the coast, where they were often imprisoned for months before embarking on the horrifying transatlantic voyage. Underfed and brutally treated throughout their journey, many captives died before ever leaving Africa. Still more perished aboard the slave ships, where they were confined in filthy, overcrowded conditions. But others survived, and some even resisted their circumstances by engaging in revolts and other subversive acts on board ship. Whatever the circumstances, the transatlantic slave trade had tragic consequences and lasting effects for both the Africans who remained at home and those who endured the forced migration abroad. (See AP® Working with Sources: Firsthand Accounts of the Slave Trade, pp. 63–75.)

Capture and Confinement

The transatlantic slave trade was a dirty and dangerous business for everyone involved. It began in the interior of Africa, where African traders purchased enslaved people

AP® skills

Applying Disciplinary Knowledge: What were the conditions like along the march to the coast, and how long could this portion of the journey take? Why do you think knowledge of this segment of the journey is essential to understanding the experience Africans endured along the transatlantic slave trade?

and marched them to the coast. In addition to prisoners of war, the enslaved Africans included individuals who were kidnapped from their homes by African slave raiders. Children were especially vulnerable to such raids, as illustrated in the story of Olaudah Equiano. Born around 1745, Equiano was eleven years old when he and his sister were taken from their family compound by "robbers," who carried them off on a journey that lasted many days.[7] The children of an Igbo village leader in the kingdom of Benin, Equiano and his sister were separated long before they reached the West African coast. Like many other enslaved Africans, Equiano was sold several times by African traders before he ended up in the hands of European traders on the coast.

Equiano and other African captives reached the coast by way of a long overland trek of up to a thousand miles, which often took them through parts of Africa they had never seen. Usually poorly fed and harshly treated during the journey, they marched in **coffles**, or chained groups, bound together to prevent escape. The slave traders secured the coffles using a variety of brutal restraints, including sets of iron collars and chains that strung the enslaved people together, as well as interconnected wooden yokes that served a similar purpose. In addition to wearing these restraints, members of the coffles were often forced to work as porters for the traders, carrying loads of food and other goods. Those who were not up to the rigors of the journey were whipped and dragged along, and captives too weak to continue were left to die by the road.

coffle
A group of animals, prisoners, or slaves enslaved people chained together in a line.

As many as one in ten of the captured Africans died before they reached the coast, where new dangers awaited the survivors. On the final leg of the forced march, many captives saw the ocean for the first time and had to brace themselves for a journey into the unknown. Thirteen-year-old Samuel Ajayi Crowther, who was kidnapped from his Oyo County home (in modern-day Nigeria) nearly a century after Olaudah Equiano entered the trade, had never seen a river before reaching the inland tributary where his captors loaded him on a canoe bound for Lagos, Nigeria, which was then a major slave trading port. He had originally planned to drown himself rather than be sold to the Portuguese, but he was far too frightened of the river to do so. "I had never seen anything like it in my life," he later recalled. "Nothing now terrified me more than the river and the thought of going into another world. . . . During the whole night's voyage on the canoe, not a single thought of leaping into the river had entered my mind, but on the contrary the fear of the river occupied my thoughts."[8]

New terrors confronted the African prisoners when they reached the coast, where they were held in **barracoons**, or temporary barracks. Some barracoons were little more than exposed pens built near the European trading forts, while others were sturdier structures deep inside the forts. Debilitated by the long journey, some captives succumbed to infections they developed after being exposed to European diseases for the first time. Whether confined in pens or in the dank dungeons below one of the coastal castles, the captives who survived were then put on display before African and European traders, who stripped them naked and inspected every inch of their bodies. The Portuguese were especially picky buyers, sometimes spending up to four hours scrutinizing the captives. They would sniff each captive's throat and make each one laugh and sing to ensure that his or her lungs were sound. They also would attempt to

barracoons
Barracks or sheds where some enslaved people were confined before boarding slave ships during the second leg of the three-part journey to the Americas.

Chaine d'esclaves venant de l'intérieure.

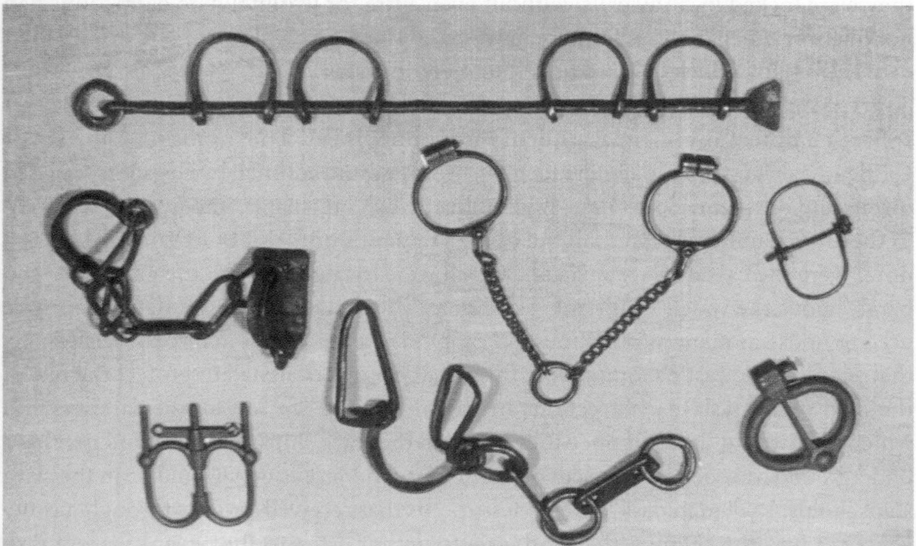

Coffles and Leg Irons

In the top engraving, traders lead enslaved people to the West African coast. The enslaved are nude and bound together at the neck, forming a coffle. Armed, fully clothed traders are positioned at the head and the end of the coffle. The bottom photograph depicts some eighteenth- and nineteenth-century slave fetters and shackles. Made of iron, these brutal restraints provided a variety of ways to secure captives and prevent escapes or rebellions during the long trek to the coast. **How did the tools used to restrain enslaved Africans also attempt to dehumanize them?** *Top: Bibliotheque de L'Arsenal, Paris, France/Archives Charmet/Bridgeman Images; Bottom: Granger/Granger — All rights reserved.*

guess each male captive's age by licking or rubbing his chin to measure the amount of facial hair.

These inspections determined which captives would be marketed to the European and American slave ships that cruised the West African coast. Certain types of enslaved people were unlikely to attract European buyers and were resold on the African market instead. John Barbot, an agent for the French Royal Africa Company, noted that European traders were usually willing to buy only young and relatively healthy enslaved people: They "rejected those above thirty-five years of age, or defective in their limbs, eyes or teeth; or grown grey, or that have the venereal disease, or any other imperfection." According to Barbot, captives who were unlucky enough to meet these requirements were "marked on the breast, with a red-hot iron, imprinting the mark of the French, English, or Dutch companies, that so each nation may distinguish their own, and to prevent their being chang'd by the natives for worse, as they are apt enough to do. In this particular, care is taken that the women, as tenderest, be not burnt too hard."[9]

AP® skills

Applying Disciplinary Knowledge: What were the conditions like for enslaved Africans at the coast, and how long did they remain there before the final leg of the trip? Why do you think knowledge of this segment of the journey is essential to understanding the experience Africans endured along the transatlantic slave trade?

Life in the barracoons was another horror of the long Middle Passage. Fed only enough to keep them alive, the captives were typically confined on the coast for several months as the traders awaited European buyers. Often stripped of their clothes, they lived in quarters that became ever more crowded as the traders accumulated potential cargo. Those in the outdoor pens escaped the elements only at night, when they were locked in filthy cells, without even a fire for warmth. The barracoons had no toilets or other facilities for human waste, so the captives also had to live with their own excrement, which covered the ground of the pens.

The enslaved people confined in the underground dungeons of the slave castles suffered a different but equally horrifying confinement. The imposing Cape Coast Castle — a magnificent triangular fortress, protected and adorned by elegantly designed turrets and other fortifications — housed the British merchants who lived and worked in the airy chambers located on the castle's upper floors. All but invisible (then and now) were the castle's slave quarters, which were located beneath the ground — and barely above the water. This dank "slave hole," divided into three vaulted cellars, was used to house as many as one thousand captives at a time. Carved into the rocky cliffs that supplied the castle's foundation, the slave hole was designed to protect the rest of the garrison from slave insurrections and to prepare the captives for the darkness into which they would descend once they boarded the slave ships. Shackled and confined underground, the victims were cut off from the world just as they would be in the slave ships' holds. Packed in dark, windowless rooms that received air only through narrow vents cut into the ceilings, they had little to do but listen to the ocean's waves crash against the rocks and anticipate the next stage of their journey.

The harsh living conditions in the barracoons and slave castles often killed as many as 5 percent of the captives detained in their confines — a figure often left unmentioned in mortality statistics. In 1684, one official at the Cape Coast Castle matter-of-factly noted, "Sundry of our slaves being lately dead and others falling sick daily makes me get to think that they are to[o] much crowded in their lodging and besides have not the benefit of Air."[10]

If they were healthy enough to do so, some captives tried to escape, but their attempts met with limited success. The barracoons and other enclosures in which they found themselves were usually securely constructed and guarded by armed men. Moreover, by the time they reached the barracoons, most of the slave trade's captives were already far from home and could not rely on local people to shelter them even if they somehow managed to escape confinement. The towns that grew up around European settlements such as Elmina Castle and Cape Coast Castle were populated by Africans who made their living off the slave trade and would likely return freedom seekers to their European enslavers for a small fee. Those who eluded immediate capture risked being reenslaved and even resold by other coastal Africans, who saw them as commodities rather than countrymen.

On the Slave Coast

The slave castles and barracoons offered little hope for successful escape. Once purchased, the enslaved captives held in the barracoons usually parted company with the African middlemen and were paddled out to new prisons aboard the slave ships. Those confined in slave castles such as Elmina, the home of the famous "door of no

The Door of No Return
The Door of No Return is part of a memorial to the Atlantic slave trade on Goree Island, off the coast of Senegal. The claustrophobic corridor opening onto the vast Atlantic invokes a sense of the horror experienced by enslaved people about to be wrenched away from their homelands.
How did conditions such as these in slave castles and barracoons make escape nearly impossible? *Dereje Belachew/Alamy Stock Photo.*

return," exited their dungeons through doors that opened to the sea. Olaudah Equiano was terrified when he boarded the slave ship and saw its captain and crew, whom he thought might have "no country, but . . . this *hollow* place." The white men and their vessel were unlike anything he had seen before, and he was convinced that he "had gotten into a world of bad spirits, and that they were going to kill me."[11]

Although Equiano was only eleven when he was kidnapped, this fear and confusion struck captives of all ages. A Muslim ironworker named Mahommah G. Baquaqua, who was kidnapped from his home as an adult in Benin almost a century later, was equally disoriented. "I had never seen a ship before," he recalled, and "my idea of it was that it was some sort of object of worship of the white man. I imagined that we were all to be slaughtered, and were being led there for that purpose."[12]

With no knowledge of the New World or the brutal profit-based forms of agriculture that drove white men to travel the West African coast in search of enslaved laborers, many African captives suspected the slave traders of being cannibals who had already consumed their own people and were in search of more human flesh. African fears of cannibalism were so widespread that Portuguese slave ship owners instructed their captains to avoid letting the captives see the large metal cauldrons used to cook food, lest the Africans become convinced that they were to be boiled alive. Such fears were an expression of traditional African anxieties about dangerous foreign peoples, which often centered on fears of cannibalism. But they also speak to the social dislocation resulting from the slave trade, which produced suffering so great that some Africans associated the trade with human-eating witches or sorcerers. What else, they thought, could account for the social and physical traumas of the barracoons or the mysterious and demoralizing future that faced the captives once they boarded the slave ships?

The ships' captains and crews had their own reasons to feel uneasy as long as their ships lingered on the West African coast. Although the captains were sometimes under instructions to bring back cargoes of enslaved people from specific areas or specific proportions of men and women, they were anxious to load their ships with a full complement of marketable enslaved people healthy enough to survive the ocean voyage. Unless they could secure a complete cargo of salable enslaved people at the first barracoon they visited — which was often not the case — they had to travel from port to port for several weeks, collecting human cargo along the way.

For the slave ships' largely European seamen, these sojourns along the coast were among the most dangerous phases of the triangle trade. Exposed to tropical fevers, they worried about falling sick, especially since their proximity to the coast created other hazards that required strength and awareness. While anchored in the deep waters off the coast, slave ships were targets for marauding pirates and the naval ships of hostile European powers. Slave ships anchored close to shore were sometimes attacked by African forces that accused them of kidnapping free Africans.

> **AP® exam tip**
>
> Be sure you can describe how enslaved Africans resisted their commodification and enslavement before boarding ships for the Americas while being confined at the coast.

But internal mutiny was the slave traders' paramount concern. As long as the mainland remained in view, their terrified captives had one last hope of escape. During the dangerous days and weeks of travel along the coast, enslaved resistance had to be contained through the use of physical restraints that kept the captives all but immobilized in the holds of the ships. "There is put aboard . . . 30 paire of shackles and boults for such of your negers as are rebellious and we pray you be veary careful to keepe them under . . . that they ryse not against you as they have done in other ships," the Guinea Company advised the slave trader Bartholomew Hayward in 1651.[13]

Iron hand and leg cuffs known as **bilboes**, among the central tools of the trade, were always in short supply. Used primarily on enslaved men, bilboes consisted of two iron shackles locked on a post and usually fastened around the ankles of two men. Joined in this way, the captives were hobbled like competitors in some macabre three-legged race. In the packed hold of a slave ship, the bilboes' heavy iron bars all but immobilized both men, making any attempt to rebel or swim to shore impossible — although they did not prevent some captives from throwing themselves overboard, shackles and all. Similarly, throughout the voyage, the captives required careful supervision, since suicides and other deaths caused by depression were not uncommon.

bilboes
Iron hand and leg cuffs used to shackle enslaved people.

Inside the Slave Ship

Once they had gathered their cargo and caught favorable winds, the slave ship's captain and crew were happy to leave the African coast behind. The journey from Guinea to Caribbean island ports, which were generally the first stop for slave ships bound for North America, lasted fifty to ninety days. Portuguese slave ships could traverse the ocean between Angola and Brazil in thirty to sixty days. Sailing times varied based on weather, ocean currents, and the size of the ship. Advances in shipbuilding and navigation resulted in shorter crossing times.

The worst part of the long Middle Passage began as men, women, and children were packed, nearly naked, into ships designed to accommodate the maximum number of enslaved people in the least amount of space. Slave ships varied in size from 11-ton sloops that could accommodate only thirty enslaved people to 566-ton behemoths that carried up to seven hundred captives.[14] Throughout the slave trade's history, these were the most crowded oceangoing vessels in the Atlantic world.[15] By the time they were fully loaded, most ships were overflowing with naked Africans. There was some debate among ship owners over the virtues of **tight packing**, to maximize profits by packing the ship to capacity, versus "loose packing," in hopes that a slightly smaller cargo would reduce the death rate. However, prior to 1788, when the British government restricted the number of enslaved people British ships could carry, slave traders generally loaded as many enslaved people as they could fit on their ships.

tight packing
Crowding the human cargo carried on slave ships to maximize profits. By contrast, "loose packing" involved carrying fewer enslaved people in better conditions in an effort to keep mortality rates low.

Throughout the slave trade, men outnumbered women by a ratio of roughly 2:1, while children under age fifteen became increasingly common over time, probably as a result of changes in the internal African slave trade. Before 1700, children accounted for roughly 12 percent of slave ships' cargo, but by 1810, the proportion had risen to an average of 46 percent. The women and children on board slave ships did not constitute family groupings. As was the case with Olaudah Equiano and his sister, enslaved family members were often separated long before they boarded the ships, and once aboard, the captives were segregated by gender.

Enslaved men were generally kept in the ship's hold, where they experienced the worst of the crowding. They were shackled together during much of the voyage and were often accommodated one on top of another on crudely constructed bunks, like "rows of books on shelves."[16] The captives stationed on the floor beneath low-lying bunks could barely move and spent much of the voyage pinned to the floorboards, which could, over time, wear the skin on their elbows down to the bone.

The men belowdecks were the biggest worry. Mutinies were not uncommon aboard slave ships, and enslaved men were most likely to mutiny when they were on deck. To protect themselves from their cargo, crews were often twice as large as usual. Armed crew members closely watched the shackled men whenever they were brought on deck, which was normally for only a few hours each day, primarily for meals, exercise, makeshift saltwater baths, and medical inspections. During rough or rainy weather, they stayed below all day.

The Middle Passage
Enslaved Africans belowdecks lived for months in conditions of squalor and indescribable horror. Ill health and impossibly close quarters were a perfect breeding ground for contagious diseases. Mortality rates were high, and death made conditions belowdecks even worse. Although the corpses of the dead were eventually thrown overboard, crew members avoided the ship's hold, so enslaved people who had succumbed to sickness were not always discovered immediately. The living could remain shackled to the dead for hours and sometimes days. **Describe the conditions aboard the slave ships as illustrated here. How did enslavers' attempts at maximizing profits affect the physical and mental welfare of enslaved Africans?** *The Art Archive/Shutterstock.*

Danse de Nègres

Captives aboard slave ships were brought on deck for daily exercise in fair weather. Sometimes still in chains, they were often forced to exert themselves by dancing. In this engraving from a book titled *La France maritime, fondée et dirigée par Amédée Gréhan* . . . (Paris: Postel, 1837–1842), three enslaved Africans are spurred into a reluctant, cowering dance by two sailors holding whips. **What does this illustration convey about the rights enslaved Africans lost during the Middle Passage?** *Photo © CCI/Bridgeman Images.*

During their time on deck, the captives often received exercise through a practice called "dancing the slaves." The crew forced the enslaved people, under close supervision, to jump or dance as best they could in their leg irons, while one of them played a drum or an African banjo or while a sailor played the bagpipes. Exercise was not optional. "If they go about it reluctantly or do not move with agility," one eighteenth-century ship's surgeon observed, "they are flogged; a person standing by them all the time with a cat-o'-nine-tails in his hands for the purpose."[17]

Women and children, by contrast, were usually housed in rooms set apart from the main hold — sometimes together, sometimes separately. Generally indifferent to family ties, the slave traders honored only the relationship between infants and nursing mothers, whom they rarely separated. Regardless of where they slept, women and children — considered less dangerous than men, though they sometimes aided in slave revolts — were usually allowed to move about the ship more freely.

These arrangements also gave the seamen easy access to enslaved women, which the men regarded as one of the perks of the trade. One seaman noted that "on board some ships, the common sailors are allowed to have intercourse with such black women whose consent they can procure."[18] Other witnesses described the sexual violence inherent in such exchanges in more explicit terms. The eighteenth-century British slave trader turned abolitionist John Newton maintained that enslaved women were often "exposed to the wanton rudeness of white savages." "Naked, trembling, terrified and perhaps already exhausted with fatigue and hunger," he wrote, "the poor creatures cannot understand the language they hear, but the looks are sufficient. . . . The prey is provided on the spot and reserved till opportunity offers."[19] Though presented in an antislavery publication, Newton's description does not seem exaggerated. In a more prosaic diary entry written when he was still working in the trade, Newton recorded a sexual assault he witnessed in matter-of-fact terms: "William Cooney seduced a woman slave down into the room and lay with her brutelike in view of the whole quarter deck. . . . If anything happens to her I shall impute to him, for she is big with child. Her number is 83."[20] Likewise, witnesses such as the formerly enslaved Ottobah Cugoano recalled that "it was common for the dirty filthy sailors to take African women and lie upon their bodies."[21]

AP® exam tip

Be sure you can describe how Africans resisted their commodification and enslavement *collectively* during the Middle Passage. What organizational obstacles do you think they faced based upon the diversity that existed among African captives?

Such practices must have infuriated and demoralized the enslaved men confined belowdecks, as Cugoano's bitter comment suggests. But the segregation of the sexes during the Middle Passage limited interaction between African men and women. Far more mobile than men, enslaved women had better access to information on the ship's crew, fortifications, and daily routine, but they had little opportunity to communicate it to the men confined in the ship's hold. On the rare occasions that captive women did find ways to contact their male counterparts, they often played important roles in slave revolts. Women, for example, instigated a 1797 insurrection aboard the British ship *Thomas* by stealing weapons and passing them to the men below, and they engaged in hand-to-hand combat with slave ship crews during several other revolts.

Hardship and Misery on Board

AP® exam tip

Be sure you can describe how Africans resisted their commodification and enslavement *individually* during the Middle Passage. How does this impact your understanding of the conditions and experience Africans endured along the Middle Passage?

Suicides were common both during the Middle Passage and after the captives arrived in the New World. (See AP® Working with Sources: Firsthand Accounts of the Slave Trade, pp. 63–73.) One observer noted that captives were often "so willful and loth to leave their own country that, they have often leap'd out of canoes, boat and ship, into the sea, and kept under water till they were drowned."[22] Many were fueled by the West African religious belief that the dead join the spirits of their ancestors — a formulation that led some slave ship captains to mutilate their charges on the basis of the conviction that "many of the Blacks believe that if they are put to death and not dismembered, they shall return again to their own country, after they are thrown overboard."[23]

Suicidal thoughts among captives were no doubt influenced by depression as much as by any hope for a happier afterlife. During the ocean passage, many captives were either unwilling or unable to eat enough to stay alive, and they resisted their captors' attempts to force-feed them. The slave trader John Barbot, who considered himself "naturally compassionate," noted that he was "necessitated sometimes to cause the teeth of those wretches to be broken, because they would not open their mouths, or be prevailed upon by any entreaties to feed themselves; and thus have forced some sustenance into their throats."[24] Traders also forced enslaved people to exercise, which they mistakenly thought would prevent both melancholy and scurvy (a disease caused by vitamin C deficiency).

The greatest cause of death during the Middle Passage, however, was disease. Estimates of average mortality on slave ships, which rest on scholarly calculations drawn from a slave ship database that is not yet complete, currently range from 15 to 20 percent. Such figures, however, obscure the wide variation in mortality rates seen on different ships. Rates ranged from 4 percent to 55 percent but could be even higher. In 1773, for example, the Dutch slave ship *Nooitgedacht* lost 89 percent of its 157 enslaved people to scurvy.[25]

The single biggest killer was dysentery, a gastrointestinal disorder that routinely swept through the packed holds. An inflammation of the intestines caused by a bacterial infection, dysentery was more evocatively known in the trade as the "bloody flux." Enslaved people boarded ships already malnourished and weakened by the forced march to the West African coast and their time in the barracoons, making them highly susceptible to this infection, which could also be caused or aggravated by the poor food and water on board. Highly contagious, dysentery was one of the great horrors of the voyage, even among those who survived its ravages. The holds of the slave ships had no toilets, bathing areas, or facilities set aside for the sick, so the African captives who came down with the infection had to endure the acute cramping and diarrhea caused by it while shackled to one another in airless confinement. Cooped up in these unsanitary conditions, captives also died from outbreaks of other communicable diseases, including smallpox, measles, and ophthalmia (a blinding eye infection). Any of these diseases could decimate crews and cargoes, which is one reason mortality rates on ships varied so widely.

The holds were so filthy by the time the ships docked that they gave off a stench that could be detected from the shore. The smell must have made life belowdecks even more unendurable — as did the deaths that took place there. Since the crews avoided the pestilence below as much as possible, even death did not always separate the living from the dead. Some enslaved people were forced to spend hours or even days chained to a dead companion. Indeed, death was an overwhelming and ubiquitous presence during the ocean voyage. Confined in close quarters, the captives watched their shipmates die in increasing numbers as the voyage progressed. High mortality rates were so common, even on voyages that escaped any major influx of disease, that contemporaries considered any slave trade voyage on which less than 20 percent of the enslaved died to be a financial success.

The historian Stephanie Smallwood has suggested that the high mortality rates on slave ships produced "an extraordinary social crisis" among the captives because the deaths took place outside any social context that might allow the living to understand and make peace with them. The Akan captives imported to the Americas from the Gold Coast, for example, believed that mortuary rites were essential for a complete death. How could they make sense of the spiritual fate of shipmates, or even kinfolk, who perished and were summarily tossed overboard by the crew? To the Akan, their shipmates' deaths were spiritually incomplete. Surrounded by death and powerless to protect the dead, the Akan and other African captives faced what Smallwood has described as a "dual crisis: the trauma of death, and also of the inability to respond appropriately to death."[26]

The dying did not end with landfall. Even after the ships landed in Barbados, which was often their first stop, the enslaved people who disembarked there and at other New World ports continued to die despite the traders' attempts to revive them with fresh food and water. In the New World, the survivors of the long Middle Passage encountered more new diseases, which killed as many as 30 percent of them after they arrived. Estimates of how many Africans boarded slave ships vary, but current research suggests that upwards of twelve million were dispatched from Africa on more than forty thousand voyages that killed almost two million people.[27] Taking into account the deaths that occurred on the overland trek to the West African coast and in the barracoons — which killed up to 15 percent of the captives — some scholars estimate that only half of the Africans destined for New World slavery survived.

CONCLUSION
The Slave Trade's Diaspora

Between the sixteenth century and the nineteenth century, when the slave trade finally ended, more than twelve million Black captives departed Africa for the New World. Most came from West Africa, where they were captured or purchased by West African slave traders, who sold them to European traders operating along the coast. Although the early trade was dominated by the Spanish and Portuguese, by the 1600s, Dutch, French, English, Danish, Swedish, and other European traders were all visiting Africa's west coast. After 1730, traders based in North America also began to participate in the transatlantic trade. The slave trade did not take shape overnight but instead grew in conjunction with European settlement of the New World. Approximately 3 percent of African captives arrived in the Americas before 1600; about 16 percent came in the seventeenth century, more than 50 percent in the eighteenth century, and about 30 percent in the nineteenth century.

The number of enslaved Africans in the New World began to increase in the seventeenth century as other European powers joined the Spanish and Portuguese in establishing settlements there. Intent on exploiting the hemisphere's rich resources, these newcomers depended on enslaved Africans for much of the labor they needed to sustain their colonies.

The forced migration of Africans to the Americas lasted for generations and created enduring African American communities throughout the hemisphere. Brought to the Americas in chains, slave trade survivors took on new identities in the New World. Whether of Igbo, Akan, Wolof, Mandinka, or other descent, enslaved captives were initially separated by barriers of national affiliation, ethnic group, and language. Once in the Americas, through shared experience, they would forge a collective identity as Africans — and, eventually, as African Americans.

First imported to what is now the United States to clear and cultivate early English and Dutch settlements in Virginia and New York, enslaved Africans were central to the survival and success of these early settlements. They would continue to play vital roles in many other colonies throughout the region in the coming years.

CHAPTER 2 REVIEW ▸ PRACTICING AP® SKILLS

AP® ESSENTIAL VOCABULARY AND SOURCES

**Essential terms and required sources from the AP® Course are marked with an asterisk.*

carracks/caravels p. 39
Guanches p. 40
Taino Indians p. 42
encomienda p. 42
Black Conquistadors* (Image of Juan Garrido on a Spanish Expedition, Sixteenth Century) p. 44
ladinos* p. 45
bozales p. 45
Elmina Castle p. 46
asiento p. 46
triangle trade p. 46
Middle Passage* p. 46
MAP 2.1 Trade of Enslaved Africans, 1501–1867 (Map Showing an Overview of the Slave Trade out of Africa)* p. 47
coffles p. 50
barracoons p. 50
bilboes p. 55
tight packing p. 55
Olaudah Equiano, *The Interesting Narrative of the Life of Olaudah Equiano, or Gustavus Vassa, the African*, 1789 (Excerpt from Chapter 2 of *The Interesting Narrative of the Life of Olaudah Equiano, or Gustavus Vassa, the African. Written by Himself*, 1789)* p. 63

APPLYING DISCIPLINARY KNOWLEDGE: ESSENTIAL QUESTIONS

1. To what factors can we attribute the initial development and eventual expansion of African slavery in Europe's New World colonies? How would you describe this progression?
2. How did traditional West African beliefs — about death, foreigners, and cannibalism, for example — serve to shape enslaved Africans' experience of the Middle Passage?
3. Why did the diasporic Africans brought to the New World not consider themselves members of the same group? How might their shared experience have helped them form a new, collective African American identity?
4. Provide several examples of Africans' resistance to European intrusions in the early slave trade. How did Africans fight back, both individually and collectively, against slave raids, kidnappings, and their own captivity?

SUGGESTED REFERENCES

The Rise of the Transatlantic Slave Trade

Eltis, David. *The Rise of African Slavery in the Americas.* Cambridge: Cambridge University Press, 1999.

Green, Toby. *The Rise of the Trans-Atlantic Slave Trade in Western Africa, 1300–1589.* New York: Cambridge University Press, 2011.

Heywood, Linda M., and John K. Thornton. *Central Africans, Atlantic Creoles, and the Foundation of the Americas, 1585–1660.* New York: Cambridge University Press, 2007.

Lovejoy, Paul E. *Transformations in Slavery: A History of Slavery in Africa.* Cambridge: Cambridge University Press, 2000.

Northrup, David. *Africa's Discovery of Europe, 1450–1850.* New York: Oxford University Press, 2002.

Schwartz, Stuart B. *Tropical Babylons: Sugar and the Making of the Atlantic World, 1450–1680.* Chapel Hill: University of North Carolina Press, 2004.

Thornton, John. *Africa and Africans in the Making of the Atlantic World, 1400–1800.* Cambridge: Cambridge University Press, 1998.

The Middle Passage

Berlin, Ira. *Many Thousands Gone: The First Two Centuries of Slavery in North America.* Cambridge: Belknap Press of Harvard University Press, 2000.

Christopher, Emma. *Slave Ship Sailors and Their Captive Cargoes, 1730–1807.* Cambridge: Cambridge University Press, 2006.

Eltis, David, and David Richardson. *Atlas of the Transatlantic Slave Trade.* New Haven, CT: Yale University Press, 2010.

Inikori, Joseph E., and Stanley L. Engerman, eds. *The Atlantic Slave Trade: Effects on Economies, Societies, and Peoples in Africa, the Americas, and Europe.* Durham: Duke University Press, 1992.

Klein, Herbert S. *The Atlantic Slave Trade.* Cambridge: Cambridge University Press, 1999.

Rediker, Marcus. *The Slave Ship: A Human History.* New York: Viking, 2007.

Restall, Matthew. "Black Conquistadors: Armed Africans in Early Spanish America." *Americas* 57, no. 2 (October 2000).

Smallwood, Stephanie E. *Saltwater Slavery: A Middle Passage from Africa to American Diaspora.* Cambridge: Harvard University Press, 2007.

St Clair, William. *The Door of No Return: The History of Cape Coast Castle and the Atlantic Slave Trade.* New York: BlueBridge, 2007.

Taylor, Eric Robert. *If We Must Die: Shipboard Insurrections in the Era of the Atlantic Slave Trade.* Baton Rouge: LSU Press, 2006.

Firsthand Accounts of the Slave Trade

The slave trade was a grueling and often lethal business that left behind a historical record consisting largely of logs kept by slave ship captains and business records documenting profits and losses. Some firsthand accounts of the Middle Passage do exist. They include accounts of slave trade voyages written by Europeans who worked aboard the slave ships, as well as a handful of narratives that record the experiences of the African captives who made the journey largely belowdecks.

The following documents provide examples of these different sources. Two record the Middle Passage experiences of eighteenth-century Africans who were captured and sold into slavery as children. They include a vivid account of the long journey into slavery endured by Olaudah Equiano, a formerly enslaved man who authored one of the first slave narratives, and a brief account of the capture, enslavement, and terrifying transatlantic voyage of Akeiso, an Igbo girl who was sold into slavery in Jamaica, where she was renamed Florence Hall. Another pair of documents records life aboard the slave ships from the perspective of two men who worked in the slave trade: James Barbot Jr., who served as a ship's officer aboard several slave ships, and Alexander Falconbridge, a surgeon who took part in four slave trade voyages between 1780 and 1787.

The visual sources show just how dangerous these voyages were for all concerned. Included here is an artist's depiction of a slave revolt aboard ship, as well as two pages taken from a slave ship's logbook. Kept by the captain for the ship's owners, the logbook provided a daily record of the important events during each voyage, documenting where the ship traveled, where it picked up cargo, what it carried, and any illnesses or other casualties on board. On the slave ships, death was a routine matter, as can be seen in the pages from the brig *Sally*'s log.

key point

The transatlantic slave journey had three parts, from the march from enslaved Africans' villages to the African coast, to confinement in barracoons, to the voyage to the Americans along the middle passage. The total journey could last nine months. Enslaved people endured immense hardships and abuse throughout the journey while collectively and individually resisting their commodification.

AP® argumentation

DBQ Practice: Explain how enslaved Africans were commodified during the transatlantic slave trade. Use at least two of the documents to support your response.

DOCUMENT 1
AP® source

Olaudah Equiano | *The Interesting Narrative of the Life of Olaudah Equiano, or Gustavus Vassa, the African*, 1789

Born in what is today southeast Nigeria, OLAUDAH EQUIANO (1745–1797) was the youngest son of an Igbo village leader in the kingdom of Benin. Kidnapped into slavery at age eleven, he was resold several times by African enslavers during his six-month journey to the African coast, where he was sold to a slave trader who carried him to the West Indies and into slavery in Virginia. Written after Equiano purchased his own freedom and became active in the British antislavery movement, *The Interesting Narrative of the Life of Olaudah Equiano* has long been considered the

best African account of enslavement, the Middle Passage, and eighteenth-century life in an African village — although one scholar has suggested that Equiano's description of his African past is fictional.[28]

> **Breaking it Down** How does Equiano describe the horrors of the Middle Passage? Why is his perspective important to understand the transatlantic slave trade? What insight does it provide into the way enslaved Africans resisted their commodification? What limitations does Equiano's account present?

One day, when all our people were gone out to their works as usual, and only I and my dear sister were left to mind the house, two men and a woman got over our walls, and in a moment seized us both; and, without giving us time to cry out, or make resistance, they stopped our mouths, tied our hands, and ran off with us into the nearest wood. . . . At the end of six or seven months after I had been kidnapped, I arrived at the sea coast. . . .

The first object which saluted my eyes when I arrived on the coast was the sea, and a slave-ship, which was then riding at anchor, and waiting for its cargo. These filled me with astonishment, which was soon converted into terror. . . . When I was carried on board I was immediately handled, and tossed up, to see if I were sound, by some of the crew; and I was now persuaded that I had got into a world of bad spirits, and that they were going to kill me. Their complexions too differing so much from ours, their long hair, and the language they spoke, which was very different from any I had ever heard, united to confirm me in this belief. Indeed, such were the horrors of my views and fears at the moment, that, if ten thousand worlds had been my own, I would have freely parted with them all to have exchanged my condition with that of the meanest slave in my own country. When I looked round the ship too, and saw a large furnace of copper boiling, and a multitude of black people of every description chained together, every one of their countenances expressing dejection and sorrow, I no longer doubted of my fate, and, quite overpowered with horror and anguish, I fell motionless on the deck and fainted. When I recovered a little, I found some black people about me, who I believed were some of those who brought me on board, and had been receiving their pay; they talked to me in order to cheer me, but all in vain. I asked them if we were not to be eaten by those white men with horrible looks, red faces, and long hair? They told me I was not; and one of the crew brought me a small portion of spirituous liquor in a wine glass; but, being afraid of him, I would not take it out of his hand. One of the blacks therefore took it from him and gave it to me, and I took a little down my palate, which, instead of reviving me, as they thought it would, threw me into the greatest consternation at the strange feeling it produced having never tasted any such liquor before. Soon after this, the blacks who brought me on board went off, and left me abandoned to despair. I now saw myself deprived of all chance of returning to my native country, or even the least glimpse of hope of gaining the shore, which I now considered as friendly: and even wished for my former slavery, in preference to my present situation, which was filled with horrors of every kind, still heightened by my ignorance of what I was to undergo. I was not long suffered to indulge my grief; I was soon put down under the decks, and there I received such a salutation in my nostrils as I had never experienced in my life: so that with the loathsomeness of the stench, and crying together, I became so sick and low that I was not able to eat, nor had I the least desire to taste any thing. I now wished for the last friend, Death, to relieve me; but soon, to my grief, two of the white men offered me eatables; and, on my refusing to eat, one of them held me fast by the hands, and laid me across, I think, the windlass, and tied my feet, while the other flogged me severely. I had never experienced any thing of this kind before; and although not being used to the water, I naturally feared that element the first time I saw it; yet, nevertheless, could I have got over the nettings, I would have jumped over the side; but I could not; and, besides, the crew used to watch us very closely who were not chained down to the decks, lest we should leap into the water; and I have seen some of these poor African prisoners most severely cut for attempting to do so, and hourly whipped for not eating. This indeed was often the case with myself. In a little time after, amongst the poor chained men, I found some of my own nation, which in a small degree gave ease to my mind. I inquired of them what was to be done with us? they gave me to understand we were to be carried to these white people's country to work for them. I then was a little revived, and thought, if it were no worse than working, my situation was not so desperate: but still I feared I should be put to death, the white people looked and acted, as I thought, in so savage a manner; for I had never seen among any people such instances of brutal cruelty; and this not only shewn towards us blacks, but also to some of the whites themselves. One white man in particular I saw, when we were permitted to be on deck, flogged so unmercifully with a large rope near the foremast, that he died in consequence of it; and they tossed him over the side as they would have done a brute. This made me fear these people the more; and I expected nothing less than to be treated in the same manner. I could not help expressing my fears and apprehensions to some of my countrymen: I asked them if these people had no country, but lived in this hollow place the ship? they told me they did not, but came from a distant one. "Then," said I, "how comes it in all our country we never heard of them?" They told me, because they lived so very far off. I then asked, where were their women? had they any like themselves? I was told they had: "And why," said I, "do we not see them?" they answered, because they were left behind. I asked how the vessel could go? they told me they could not tell; but that there were cloth put upon the masts by the help of the ropes I saw, and then the vessel went on; and the white men had some spell or magic they put in the water when they liked in order to stop the vessel. I was exceedingly amazed at this account, and really thought they were spirits. I therefore wished much to be from amongst them, for I expected they would sacrifice me: but my wishes were vain; for we were so quartered that it was impossible for any of us to make our escape. . . . At last, when the ship we were in had got in all her cargo, they made ready with many fearful noises, and we were all put under deck, so that we could not see how they managed the vessel. But this disappointment was the least of my sorrow. The stench of the hold while we were on the coast was so intolerably loathsome, that it was dangerous to remain there for any time, and some of us had been permitted to stay on the deck for the fresh air; but now that the whole ship's cargo were confined together, it became absolutely pestilential. The closeness of the place, and the heat of the climate, added to the number in the ship, which was so crowded that each had scarcely room to turn himself, almost suffocated us. This produced copious perspirations, so that the air soon became unfit for respiration, from a variety of loathsome smells, and brought on a sickness amongst the slaves, of which many died, thus falling victims to the improvident avarice, as I may call it, of their purchasers. This wretched situation was again aggravated by the galling of the chains, now become insupportable; and the filth of the necessary tubs, into which the children often fell, and were almost suffocated. The shrieks of the women, and the groans of the dying, rendered the whole a scene of horror almost inconceiveable. Happily perhaps for myself I was soon reduced so low here that it was thought necessary to keep me almost always on deck; and from my extreme youth I was not put in fetters. In this situation I expected every hour to share the fate of my companions, some of whom were almost daily brought upon deck at the point of death, which I began to hope would soon put an end to my miseries. Often did I think many of the inhabitants of the deep much more happy than myself; I envied them the freedom they enjoyed, and as often wished I could change my condition for theirs. Every circumstance I met with served only to render my state more painful, and heighten my apprehensions and my opinion of the cruelty of the whites. One day they had taken a number of fishes; and when they had killed and satisfied themselves with as many as they thought fit, to our astonishment who were on the deck, rather than give any of them to us to eat, as we expected, they tossed the remaining fish into the sea again, although we begged and prayed for some as well as we could, but in vain; and some of my countrymen, being pressed by hunger, took an opportunity, when they thought no one saw them, of trying to get a little privately; but they were discovered, and the attempt procured them some very severe floggings.

One day, when we had a smooth sea, and moderate wind, two of my wearied countrymen, who were chained together (I was near them at the time), preferring death to such a life of misery, somehow made through the nettings, and jumped into the sea; immediately another quite dejected fellow, who, on account of his illness, was suffered to be out of irons, also followed their example; and I believe many more would very soon have done the same, if they had not been prevented by the ship's crew, who were instantly alarmed. . . . At last, we came in sight of the island of Barbadoes, at which the whites on board gave a great shout, and made many signs of joy to us. We did not know what to think of this; but, as the vessel drew nearer, we plainly saw the harbour, and other ships of different kinds and sizes: and we soon anchored amongst them off Bridge Town. Many merchants and planters now came on board, though it was in the evening. They put us in separate parcels, and examined us attentively. They also made us jump, and pointed to the land, signifying we were to go there. We thought by this we should be eaten by these ugly men, as they appeared to us; and when, soon after we were all put down under the deck again, there was much dread and trembling among us, and nothing but bitter cries to be heard all the night from these apprehensions, insomuch that at last the white people got some old slaves from the land to pacify us. They told us we were not to be eaten, but to work, and were soon to go on land, where we should see many of our country people. This report eased us much; and sure enough, soon after we landed, there came to us Africans of all languages. . . . We were not many days in the merchant's custody before we were sold after their usual manner, which is this: — On a signal given, (as the beat of a drum), the buyers rush at once into the yard where the slaves are confined, and make choice of that parcel they like best. The noise and clamour with which this is attended, and the eagerness visible in the countenances of the buyers, serve not a little to increase the apprehension of the terrified Africans, who may well be supposed to consider them as the ministers of that destruction to which they think themselves devoted. In this manner, without scruple, are relations and friends separated, most of them never to see each other again.

SOURCE: Olaudah Equiano, *The Interesting Narrative of the Life of Olaudah Equiano, or Gustavus Vassa, the African. Written by Himself.* (London: printed for the author, 1789), 32, 45, 46–50, 51–53, 54–55, 56.

DOCUMENT 2 Florence Hall | *Memoirs of the Life of Florence Hall, 1810*

The following is a transcription of a four-page handwritten document found inside a notebook believed to date to 1810. The narrator, FLORENCE HALL, tells the story of her capture, trek to the coast, and experience of the Middle Passage.

Breaking it Down How is Hall's account of the transatlantic journey similar to Equiano's? What perspective is she able to provide that Equiano does not, and why?

Africa is my Country — In the Country of the Eboe [Igbo], on the banks of the great [missing word] river, my people lived. The manner of my life before I was taken, and sold to the white people, I can scarcely remember beyond that I was still unclothed, sometimes employed in attending our people, while engaged in fishing, at other times guarding the fowls and chickens from hawks, or more frequently at play with other children. In one of those evening plays, while at a distance from our houses a party of the enemy came around and drove us, into an enclosed place, and immediately secured us — our hands were tied — while in vain our cries and screams were raised, but raised unheard, if heard, unattended, and by force we were hurried along and rested not until the sun arose, and marked our [illegible word] and distance from our homes. The day we lay concealed, and in the night our journey was performed. Day and night succeeded each other, in hunger, weariness, and grief at the end of the 15th night, our travelling was at an end and the dawn of day shewed us the Great Sea, and the ship, [on? in?] which we were soon embarked, and at once left our Country, and our freedom, and consigned to foreigners and Slavery. The enemies of our Country seized and sold us to the White people, for the love of drink, and from the quarrels of their Chiefs — The white people received, and stripped us of all our beads, and shells, and while the naked children were permitted to walk about the ship, the men and women were chained and kept in darkness below. Our food was sparing, and ever bad. Our punishment was frequent and severe, and death became so frequent an occurrence, that at last it [illegible word] on, without fear on the dying, or grief on those left behind, as we believed that those who died, were restored to their people and Country. A long voyage at length brought the ship to Jamaica. My Eboe name was Akeiso, the loss of which soon put an end to all recollections of my people — another name — a strange language, & a new master, confused my mind, and while ignorance of each, made my labour more troublesome, yet the dread of punishment compelled me to work, [end of existing manuscript]

SOURCE: Florence Hall (Akeiso). *Memoir of the Life of Florence Hall.* The Powel Family Papers. The Historical Society of Pennsylvania. 1808–1820?

DOCUMENT 3 James Barbot Jr. | *General Observations on the Management of Slaves, 1700*

The son and nephew of slave traders, JAMES BARBOT JR. worked aboard slave ships for much of his life and recorded his experiences in several published works. Employed on the Don Carlos as the supercargo (officer) in charge of the purchase and sale of enslaved people, Barbot wrote the following description of how best to manage the captives on board. Despite the precautions described here, an onboard rebellion took place on the ship's first day at sea. At least twenty-eight captives were "lost" — either killed in battle or through suicide by drowning.

Breaking it Down How does Barbot's account of the conditions of the Middle Passage support or counter Equiano's or Hall's? What perspective does he provide as a white male crewman?

As to the management of our slaves aboard, we lodge the two sexes apart, by means of a strong partition at the main mast; the forepart is for men, the other behind the mast for the women. If it be in large ships carrying five or six hundred slaves, the deck in such ships ought to be at least five and a half or six foot high, which is very requisite for driving a continual trade of slaves: for the greater height it has, the more airy and convenient it is for such a considerable number of human creatures; and consequently far the more healthy for them, and fitter to look after them. We build a sort of half-decks along the sides with deals and spars° provided for that purpose in *Europe*, that half-deck extending no farther than the sides of our scuttles, and so the slaves lie in two rows, one above

°Deals and spars are planks and poles.

the other, and as close together as they can be crouded. . . .

. . . The planks, or deals, contract some dampness more or less, either from the deck being so often wash'd to keep it clean and sweet, or from the rain that gets in now and then through the scuttles or other openings, and even from the very sweat of the slaves; which being so crouded in a low place, is perpetual, and occasions many distempers, or at best great inconveniences dangerous to their health. . . .

It has been observ'd before, that some slaves fancy they are carry'd to be eaten, which makes them desperate; and others are so on account of their captivity: so that if care be not taken, they will mutiny and destroy the ship's crew in hopes to get away.

To prevent such misfortunes, we use to visit them daily, narrowly searching every corner between decks, to see whether they have not found means, to gather any pieces of iron, or wood, or knives, about the ship, notwithstanding the great care we take not to leave any tools or nails, or other things in the way: which, however, cannot be always so exactly observ'd, where so many people are in the narrow compass of a ship.

We cause as many of our men as is convenient to lie in the quarter-deck and gun-room, and our principal officers in the great cabbin, where we keep all our small arms in a readiness, with sentinels constantly at the door and avenues to it; being thus ready to disappoint any attempts our slaves might make on a sudden.

These precautions contribute very much to keep them in awe; and if all those who carry slaves duly observ'd them, we should not hear of so many revolts as have happen'd. Where I was concern'd, we always kept our slaves in such order, that we did not perceive the least inclination in any of them to revolt, or mutiny, and lost very few of our number in the voyage.

It is true, we allow'd them much more liberty, and us'd them with more tenderness than most other Europeans would think prudent to do; as, to have them all upon deck every day in good weather; to take their meals twice a-day, at fix'd hours, that is, at ten in the morning, and at five at night; which being ended, we made the men go down again between decks; for the women were almost entirely at their own discretion, to be upon deck as long as they pleas'd, nay even many of the males had the same liberty by turns, successively; few or none being fetter'd or kept in shackles, and that only on account of some disturbances, or injuries, offer'd to their fellow captives, as will unavoidably happen among a numerous croud of such savage people. Besides, we allow'd each of them betwixt their meals a handful of Indian wheat and Mandioca, and now and then short pipes and tobacco to smoak upon deck by turns, and some cocoa-nuts; and to the women a piece of coarse cloth to cover them, and the same to many of the men, which we took care they did wash from time to time, to prevent vermin, which they are very subject to; and because it look'd sweeter and more agreeable. Towards the evening they diverted themselves on the deck, as they thought fit, some conversing together, others dancing, singing, and sporting after their manner, which pleased them highly, and often made us pastime; especially the female sex, who being a-part from the males, on the quarter-deck, and many of them young sprightly maidens, full of jollity and good-humour, afforded us abundance of recreation; as did several little fine boys, which we mostly kept to attend on us about the ship. . . .

Much more might be said relating to the preservation and maintenance of slaves in such voyages, which I leave to the prudence of the officers that govern aboard, if they value their own reputation and their owners advantage; and shall only add these few particulars, that tho' we ought to be circumspect in watching the slaves narrowly, to prevent or disappoint their ill designs for our own conservation, yet must we not be too severe and haughty with them, but on the contrary, caress and humour them in every reasonable thing. Some commanders, of a morose peevish temper are perpetually beating and curbing them, even without the least offence, and will not suffer any upon deck but when unavoidable necessity to ease themselves does require; under pretence it hinders the work of the ship and sailors, and that they are troublesome by their nasty nauseous stench, or their noise; which makes those poor wretches desperate, and besides their falling into distempers thro' melancholy, often is the occasion of their destroying themselves.

Such officers should consider, those unfortunate creatures are men as well as themselves, tho' of a different colour, and pagans; and that they ought to do to others as they would be done by in like circumstances.

SOURCE: James Barbot Jr., "An Abstract of a Voyage to Congo River, or the Zair, and to Cabinde, in the Year 1700," in *A Collection of Voyages and Travels*, ed. Awnsham Churchill and John Churchill (London: J. Walthoe, 1732), 5:546–48.

DOCUMENT 4 Alexander Falconbridge | *An Account of the Slave Trade on the Coast of Africa, 1788*

The British surgeon ALEXANDER FALCONBRIDGE (d. 1792) served as a ship's surgeon on four slave trade voyages between 1780 and 1787 before rejecting the slave trade and becoming an abolitionist. He wrote *An Account of the Slave Trade on the Coast of Africa*, an unflinching account of the brutality of the transatlantic trade, in 1788.

Breaking it Down What insight does his perspective offer into the conditions of the Middle Passage? What is the purpose of this account, and who is the intended audience?

When the ships arrive in the West-Indies, (the chief mart for this inhuman merchandize), the slaves are disposed of, as I have before observed, by different methods. Sometimes the mode of disposal, is that of selling them by what is termed a *scramble*; and a day is soon fixed for that purpose. But previously thereto, the sick, or refuse slaves, of which there are frequently many, are usually conveyed on shore, and sold at a tavern by . . . public auction. These, in general, are purchased . . . upon speculation, at so low a price as five or six dollars a head. I was informed by a mulatto woman, that she purchased a sick slave at Grenada, upon speculation, for the small sum of one dollar, as the poor wretch was apparently dying of the flux. It seldom happens that any, who are carried ashore in the emaciated state to which they are generally reduced by that disorder, long survive their landing. I once saw sixteen conveyed on shore, and sold in the foregoing manner, the whole of whom died before I left the island, which was within a short time after. Sometimes the captains march their slaves through the town at which they intend to dispose of them; and then place them in rows where they are examined and purchased.

The mode of selling them by scramble having fallen under my observation the oftenest, I shal[l] be more particular in describing it. Being some years ago, at one of the islands in the West-Indies, I was witness to a sale by scramble. . . .

On a day appointed, the negroes were landed, and placed altogether in a large yard, belonging to the merchants to whom the ship was consigned. As soon as the hour agreed on arrived, the doors of the yard were suddenly thrown open, and in rushed a considerable number of purchasers, with all the ferocity of brutes. Some instantly seized such of the negroes as they could conveniently lay hold of with their hands. Others, being prepared with several handkerchiefs tied together, encircled with these as many as they were able. While others, by means of a rope, effected the same purpose.

It is scarcely possible to describe the confusion of which this mode of selling is productive. It likewise causes much animosity among the purchasers, who, not unfrequently upon these occasions, fall out and quarrel with each other. The poor astonished negroes were so much terrified by these proceedings, that several of them, through fear, climbed over the walls of the court yard, and ran wild about the town; but were soon hunted down and retaken. . . .

Various are the deceptions made use of in the disposal of sick slaves; and many of these, such as must excite in every humane mind, the liveliest sensations of horror. I have been well informed, that a Liverpool captain boasted of his having cheated some Jews by the following stratagem: A lot of slaves, afflicted with the flux, being about to be landed for sale, he directed the surgeon to stop the anus of each of them with oakum. Thus prepared, they were landed, and taken to the accustomed place of sale; where, being unable to stand but for a very short time, they are usually permitted to sit. The Jews, when they examine them, oblige them to stand up, in order to see if there be any discharge; and when they do not perceive this appearance, they consider it as a symptom of recovery. In the present instance, such an appearance being prevented, the bargain was struck, and they were accordingly sold. But it was not long before a discovery ensued. The excruciating pain which the prevention of a discharge of such an acrimonious nature occasioned, not being to be borne by the poor wretches, the temporary obstruction was removed, and the deluded purchasers were speedily convinced of the imposition.

SOURCE: Alexander Falconbridge, *An Account of the Slave Trade on the Coast of Africa* (London: J. Phillips, 1788), 33–36.

DOCUMENT 5 *The Brig Sally's Log, 1765*

These pages are drawn from an account book kept by ESEK HOPKINS, the captain of a hundred-ton brigantine called *Sally*, which left Providence, Rhode Island, for West Africa on a slaving voyage on September 11, 1764. The *Sally* reached the coast of what is today Guinea-Bissau one month later and spent many months anchored there, acquiring goods and enslaved people. Not until August 20, 1765, more than nine months after reaching Africa, was the *Sally* finally ready to return. All told, Hopkins secured 196 enslaved people, but he sold off 29 of them to other traders before ever leaving Africa. Some 19 captives died before the ship left the coast, and another captive was left for dead on the day the *Sally* set sail, reducing Hopkins's remaining human cargo to about 147 people. An additional 68 Africans perished during *Sally*'s transatlantic voyage; 20 more died shortly after the ship docked in the West Indies in October 1765, and the *Sally* lost 1 last enslaved person between the West Indies and Providence, bringing the death toll among her cargo to 109. Hopkins's log records these deaths and also notes the dates on which they took place.

Breaking it Down How does *The Brig* Sally*'s Log* help to support or counter the claims made by the other authors? What insight does it provide that the other documents do not? What questions does the log answer or raise about the transatlantic slave journey?

1 garle [girl] Slave Dyed [died]
1 boye [boy] Slave Dyed
1 Woman & 1 boye, Dyed
Slaves rose on us was obliged fire on them and destroyed 8 and several more wounded badly I think & ones [ribs?] broke
1 boye & 1 garle Slaves Dyed
1 Woman Slave Dyed
1 Woman & 1 garle Slaves Dyed
1 Woman Slaves Dyed
1 boy Slave Dyed
1 boye Slave Dyed
1 man Slave Dyed
3 boys & 1 garle Dyed
2 Woman and 2 boys Dyed
1 Woman & 1 garle Slave Dyed
1 boye Slave Dyed
1 boye Slave Dyed
1 garle Slave Dyed
1 garle Slave Dyed
1 Woman Slave Dyed
1 Man Slave Dyed of his wounds on the [ribs?] when slaves rose
1 boye Slave Dyed
1 Woman Slave Dyed
2 Women & 1 garle Slaves Dyed
1 man & 1 Woman Slaves Dyed
2 men & 1 garle Slaves Dyed

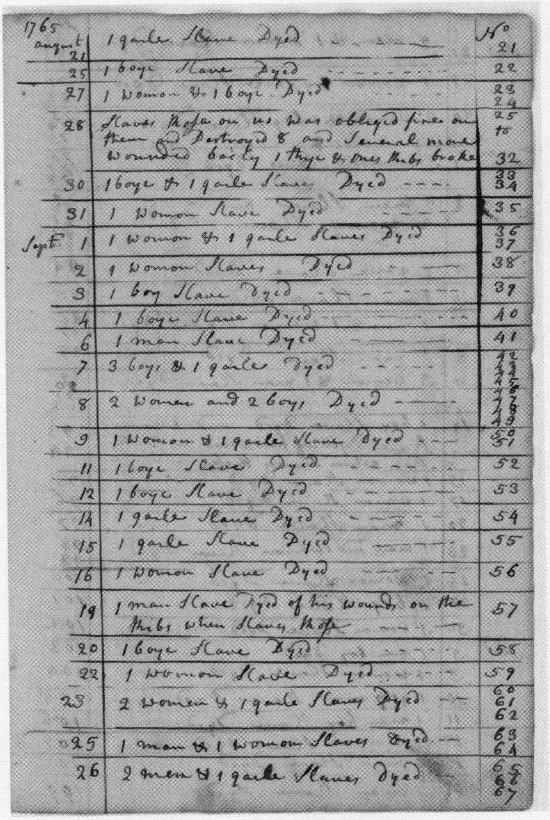

1765		No
august 21	1 garle Slave Dyed	21
25	1 boye Slave Dyed	22
27	1 Woman & 1 boye Dyed	23 24
28	Slaves rose on us was obliged fire on them and Destroyed 8 and Several more wounded badly 1 thye & ones ribs broke	25 to 32
30	1 boye & 1 garle Slaves Dyed	33 34
31	1 Woman Slave Dyed	35
Sept 1	1 woman & 1 garle Slaves Dyed	36 37
2	1 woman Slaves Dyed	38
3	1 boy Slave Dyed	39
4	1 boye Slave Dyed	40
6	1 man Slave Dyed	41
7	3 boys & 1 garle Dyed	42 43 44 45
8	2 women and 2 boys Dyed	46 47 48 49
9	1 woman & 1 garle Slave Dyed	50 51
11	1 boye Slave Dyed	52
12	1 boye Slave Dyed	53
14	1 garle Slave Dyed	54
15	1 garle Slave Dyed	55
16	1 woman Slave Dyed	56
19	1 man Slave Dyed of his wounds on the ribs when Slaves rose	57
20	1 boye Slave Dyed	58
22	1 woman Slave Dyed	59
23	2 women & 1 garle Slaves Dyed	60 61 62
25	1 man & 1 woman Slaves Dyed	63 64
26	2 men & 1 garle Slaves Dyed	65 66 67

Courtesy of the John Carter Brown Library, Brown University.

2 Men & 1 Woman Slaves Dyed

1 Woman & 1 garle Slaves dyed

2 Woman Slaves Dyed

3 Woman Slaves Dyed

3 Men Slaves and 2 Woman Slaves and
2 Woman Slaves Dyed

1 garle Slave Dyed
1 Man Slave Dyed
1 Man & 1 Woman Slave Dyed
1 Man Slave Dyed
3 Woman & 1 Man Slave Dyed

1 boy Slave Dyed and 1 Man
Slave Dyed of his wounds, in the thy [thigh?]
Recd [received] when Slaves Rose
1 Woman Slave Dyed
1 Woman Slave Dyed
1 Man Slave Dyed
1 Man and 1 Woman Slaves Dyed
1 Woman Slave Dyed
1 boy Slave Dyed
1 Woman Slave Dyed
1 Man boy Dyed
1 Woman Slave Dyed
1 young man Slave Dyed
1 Man boy Slave Dyed
1 Woman Slave Dyed
1 Man Slave Dyed
1 Man Slave Dyed

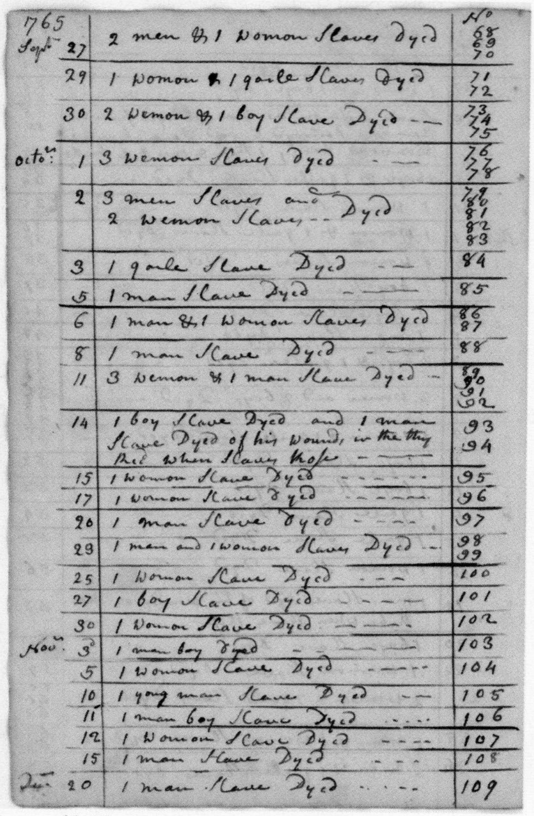

Courtesy of the John Carter Brown Library, Brown University.

PRACTICING AP® SKILLS

1. **AP® Comparison.** Compare Equiano and Hall's details about the transatlantic slave journey and the transatlantic slave trade. To what extent do their accounts support or counter each other?
2. **AP® Causation.** Describe and analyze the various roles Europeans and Africans played in the slave trade. What details from the documents support your analysis?
3. **AP® Causation.** Explain how these documents reveal the effects of the transatlantic slave trade on West African communities.
4. **Connecting to AP® Themes.** Explain how the documents collectively provide insight into both the commodification of enslaved Africans during the transatlantic journey as well as the resilience and resistance of enslaved Africans.
5. **Class Discussion.** What are the benefits and limitations in using firsthand accounts of the transatlantic slave journey to better understand the transatlantic slave trade?

Written Texts:
Active Reading

In the first AP® Skills Workshop for Chapter 1 (p. SW1-A), we practiced applying an active reading process to visual texts to uncover deeper meaning and make connections to course knowledge. Now, we can extend the same skill of active reading to written texts.

Some written texts are **primary sources** created in the moment during a specific time period, while others are **secondary sources** written about the past after the fact. Written primary sources include literary works like poems and excerpts from novels, and nonfiction like journal entries and court cases; while written secondary sources include nonfiction like academic articles and the textbook you're reading right now.

The active reading strategy we'll explore in this workshop can be used for all nonfiction texts, whether they're primary or secondary sources. We'll consider literary texts in later workshops.

Actively Reading Nonfiction

The AP® African American Studies course will introduce you to nonfiction of various eras and genres. Whether you're reading a speech from the 1800s or a magazine article from the modern day, it's helpful to remember that every nonfiction text makes at least one **claim**, an arguable position with which some people might agree and others disagree. When actively reading a nonfiction text, your initial goal will be understanding its claims and determining how they fit together into an overarching **argument**. The following steps will help you achieve that goal:

Step 1: Skim through the source one time. Then, summarize it in a sentence as if you were describing it to a friend who'd never read it before.

Step 2: Read the source more thoroughly. What claims do you spot? In other words, what positions is the writer taking?

Step 3: Skim through the source one more time. What evidence supports each claim?

Step 4: Look over your notes and use them to flesh out your summary. What is the text really arguing?

Written Primary Sources

Let's apply this approach to a primary source relevant to the era of this chapter. Read through the text to follow, which also appears on page 32 of this textbook. Use the four steps above to investigate the source's claims, evidence, and overall argument.

"To the honourable the senate and house of representatives, in general court assembled:

The petition of Belinda, an African,

Humbly shews,

That seventy years have rolled away, since she, on the banks of the Rio de Valta, received her existence. . . . Before she had twelve years enjoyed the fragrance of her native groves, and ere she realized that Europeans placed their happiness in the yellow dust, which she carelessly marked with her infant footsteps — even when she, in a sacred grove, with each hand in that of a tender parent, was paying her devotion to the great Orisa, who made all things, an armed band of white men, driving many of her countrymen in chains, rushed into the hallowed shades! . . . In vain she lifted her supplicating voice to an insulted father, and her guiltless hands to a dishonoured deity! She was ravished from the bosom of her country, from the arms of her friends, while the advanced age of her parents, rendering them unfit for servitude, cruelly separated her from them for ever. . . .

The face of your Petitioner, is now marked with the furrows of time, and her frame feebly bending under the oppression of years, while she, by the Laws of the Land, is denied the enjoyment of one morsel of that immense wealth, apart whereof hath been accumilated by her own industry, and the whole augmented by her servitude.

WHEREFORE, casting herself at the feet of your honours, as to a body of men, formed for the extirpation of vassalage, for the reward of Virtue, and the just return of honest industry – she prays, that such allowance may be made her . . . as will prevent her and her more infirm daughter from misery in the greatest extreme, and scatter comfort over the short and downward path of their Lives – and she will ever Pray."

SOURCE: Belinda Sutton, "The Petition of Belinda," requesting a payment from the Commonwealth of Massachusetts, 1782

We can collect our initial impressions of the source using a graphic organizer:

Summary: A petition written in 1782 describes the tragedies an enslaved woman named Belinda experienced.

Claim	Evidence
Belinda lived a good life before Europeans kidnapped and enslaved her.	"even when she, in a sacred grove, with each hand in that of a tender parent, was paying her devotion to the great Orisa, who made all things, an armed band of white men, driving many of her countrymen in chains, rushed into the hallowed shades!"

(Continued)

Claim	Evidence
Belinda has not received any compensation for her years of servitude.	"she, by the Laws of the Land, is denied the enjoyment of one morsel of that immense wealth, apart whereof hath been accumilated by her own industry, and the whole augmented by her servitude"
Belinda needs payment for her labor.	"she prays, that such allowance may be made her . . . as will prevent her and her more infirm daughter from misery in the greatest extreme"
Revised summary: This petition by an enslaved woman named Belinda argues that she suffered irreparable damage at the hands of Europeans, and that she deserves to be compensated for her suffering and for her labor while enslaved.	

Overall, breaking a primary source into claims and evidence helps us look beyond distractions like complex language and unfamiliar references to see what really matters: the main ideas that drive the source's argument.

Written Secondary Sources

This same process of breaking texts down into claims and evidence can be applied to written secondary sources. Consider the following excerpt:

"The early historical narratives of North America were not uniquely centered on Black women until now; instead, it was about discovery, colonization, and conquest. The history emphasized the "discovery" of land — a geography of multiple meanings depending on who occupied it. . . .

The first Black women who stepped foot on what we now consider American soil were not enslaved. . . . They came with Spanish and Portuguese explorers, and many could be classified as indentured servants, missionaries, interpreters, or simply leaders. . . .

We learn about them through reports authored by explorers such as Vazquez Nunez de Balboa, Hernan Cortes, Francisco Vazquez de Coronado, Lucas Vazquez de Ayllon, Hernando de Soto, and Juan de Onate. Accounts of explorers' journeys sometimes mention women, and those that left silences in the historical record force us to construct Black women's lives through traces, conjectures, and sometimes speculation."

SOURCE: Daina Ramey Berry and Kali Nicole Gross, historians, *A Black Women's History of the United States*, 2020

As with nonfiction primary sources, nonfiction secondary sources can be summarized, broken down into claims and evidence, and re-summarized with greater accuracy.

Summary: The passage notes that Black women in the early Americas were not all enslaved.	
Claim	**Evidence**
History has not adequately considered the history of Black women in the Americas.	"The early historical narratives of North America were not uniquely centered on Black women until now; instead, it was about discovery, colonization, and conquest"
The First Black women to come to the Americas were not enslaved.	"They came with Spanish and Portuguese explorers, and many could be classified as indentured servants, missionaries, interpreters, or simply leaders"
There is evidence backing up the theory that Black women accompanied explorers.	"We learn about them through reports authored by explorers such as Vazquez Nunez de Balboa, Hernan Cortes, Francisco Vazquez de Coronado, Lucas Vazquez de Ayllon, Hernando de Soto, and Juan de Onate."
Historians often have to piece together the story of Black women in the early Americas.	"Accounts of explorers' journeys sometimes mention women, and those that left silences in the historical record force us to construct Black women's lives through traces, conjectures, and sometimes speculation."
Revised summary: This passage argues that despite gaps in the historical archive, there is compelling evidence that the first Black women in the Americas accompanied explorers as indentured servants, missionaries, interpreters, and more, not solely as enslaved people.	

recap

Actively Reading Nonfiction

To understand a nonfiction text, it can be helpful to summarize it, identify its claims and the evidence that supports each claim, and revise your summary to better reflect the text's main idea.

Activity ▸ Actively Reading Nonfiction

Actively read the passage on page SW2-E. Fill in a graphic organizer like the one to follow to guide your work.

Summary:	
Claim	**Evidence**
Revised summary:	

(Continued)

"The course of things in the neighboring islands of the West Indies appears to have given a considerable impulse to the minds of the slaves in different parts of the US. A great disposition to insurgency has manifested itself among them, which, in one instance, in the state of Virginia broke out into actual insurrection. This was easily suppressed: but many of those concerned . . . fell victims to the law. So extensive an execution could not but excite sensibility in the public mind, and beget a regret that the laws had not provided, for such cases, some alternative, combining more mildness with equal efficacy. The legislature of the state . . . have communicated to me through the Governor of the state, their wish that some place could be provided, out of the limits of the U.S. to which slaves guilty of insurgency might be transported; and they have particularly looked to Africa as offering the most desirable receptacle. We might, for this purpose, enter into negotiations with the natives, on some part of the coast, to obtain a settlement, and, by establishing an African company, combine with it commercial operations, which might not only reimburse expenses but procure profit also. . . . The object of this letter therefore is to ask the favor of you to enter into conference with such persons private & public as would be necessary to give us permission to send thither the persons under contemplation."

SOURCE: Thomas Jefferson, letter to Rufus King, Minister to Great Britain, July 13, 1802

Written Texts:
Multiple-Choice Questions

In the second AP® Skills Workshop for Chapter 1 (p. SW1-F), we explored three strategies to tackle multiple-choice questions with a visual stimulus:

Strategy 1: Activate relevant concepts, developments, and processes.

Concept: a person, place, theory, or theme

Development: an event; a political, social, or cultural movement; or a time period — essentially, anything important that happens

Process: two or more related developments — the developments might cause, contrast with, or have commonalities with one another

Strategy 2: Determine what the question is really asking using the Four Cs.

Comparison. How are two figures, events, movements, or time periods similar or different?

Causation. What factors *directly* contributed to an event or a movement? What effects did this event or movement *directly* bring about?

Continuity & Change. What changed and what stayed the same between different time periods?

Strategy 3: Eliminate wrong answers.

False. Are any choices factually incorrect?

Outside the time period. Do any choices pertain to a different time period from the one the question discusses?

Irrelevant. Do any choices fail to answer the question? True answers are correct only if they *directly* address the question asked.

Fortunately, each of these strategies also applies to multiple-choice questions with a written stimulus. To demonstrate this carryover, we can work through a question set tied to an excerpt from Olaudah Equiano's autobiography, which also appears on page 63 of this textbook.

> "The first object which saluted my eyes when I arrived on the coast was the sea, and a slave ship, which was then riding at anchor, and waiting for its cargo. . . . I was immediately handled and tossed up to see if I were sound by some of the crew; and I was now persuaded that I had gotten into a world of bad spirits, and that they were going to kill me. . . . Soon after this the blacks who brought me on board went off, and left me abandoned to despair. I now saw myself deprived of all chance of returning to my native country. . . . I was soon put down under the decks, and there I received such a salutation in my nostrils as I had never experienced in my life: so that, with the loathsomeness of the

(Continued)

> stench, and crying together, I became so sick and low that I was not able to eat, nor had I the least desire to taste anything. I now wished for the last friend, death, to relieve me; but soon, to my grief, two of the white men offered me eatables, and, on my refusing to eat, one of them held me fast by the hands, and laid me across I think the windlass, and tied my feet, while the other flogged me severely. I had never experienced anything of this kind before; and although, not being used to the water . . . could I have got over the nettings, I would have jumped over the side, but I could not; and, besides, the crew used to watch us very closely who were not chained down to the decks, lest we should leap into the water: and I have seen some of these poor African prisoners most severely cut for attempting to do so, and hourly whipped for not eating."
>
> SOURCE: Olaudah Equiano, abolitionist and writer, *The Interesting Narrative of the Life of Olaudah Equiano, or Gustavus Vassa, the African*, 1789

Before approaching the question set associated with this text stimulus, it's important to first activate awareness of related course content. Read through the text to get its main ideas, and then consider what concepts, developments, and processes covered in this chapter might be relevant. Some of the following course knowledge may come to mind:

Concepts/Themes

- Migration and the African diaspora
- The Middle Passage
- Slave narratives

Developments

- The transatlantic slave trade rapidly expanded in the seventeenth and eighteenth centuries.
- Europeans established West African slave trading posts.
- Equiano purchased his freedom and became active in the British abolitionist movement.

Processes

- The rapid expansion of the transatlantic slave trade coincided with the establishment of West African slave trading posts and led to the capture of enslaved people like Equiano.

After previewing the text stimulus, we can turn to the questions and rephrase them using the Four Cs.

1. Which of the following most likely motivated Equiano's abduction?
- A. Children were easier to smuggle after the abolition of the slave trade, compared to adults.
- B. Children were worth more money to enslavers, compared to adults.
- C. He had never seen the coast and could not swim.
- D. His age made him especially vulnerable to village raids.

2. Which of the following best explains how the experience of children during the Middle Passage differed from the experience of other enslaved groups?
- A. Children were permitted to move about the ships more freely.
- B. Children were later able to purchase their freedom.
- C. Enslavers selected the people most likely to survive the journey.
- D. Enslavers kept children and their mothers together during the journey.

Question 1	Question 2
☐ Comparison ☒ Causation ☐ Continuity & change	☒ Comparison ☐ Causation ☐ Continuity & change
Rephrasing: Which of the choices was a likely reason for Equiano's kidnapping?	**Rephrasing:** Which of the choices describes a difference in how enslaved children were treated during the Middle Passage, compared to other groups?

Finally, we can categorize the answer choices to eliminate wrong answers.

Question 1	
False	**B.** Children were worth more money to enslavers, compared to adults. *Enslaved children were not sold for higher prices than enslaved adults.*
Outside the time period	**A.** Children were easier to smuggle after the abolition of the slave trade, compared to adults. *Equiano was abducted well before the abolition of the slave trade in 1808.*
Irrelevant	**C.** He had never seen the coast and could not swim. *Equiano's abduction was unrelated to his lack of familiarity with water.*
Correct	**D.** His age made him especially vulnerable to village raids. *As pointed out in this textbook, children were at greater risk of abduction during raids.*

Question 2	
False	**D.** Enslavers kept children and their mothers together during the journey. *Enslavers often separated families.*
Outside the time period	*None of the answer choices are outside the time period.*
Irrelevant	**B.** Children were later able to purchase their freedom. *The question asks about children's experiences during the Middle Passage, not afterwards.* **C.** Enslavers selected the people most likely to survive the journey. *The question asks about children's experiences during the Middle Passage, not enslavers' motivation to abduct children.*
Correct	**A.** Children were permitted to move about the ships more freely. *As noted in this textbook, enslavers allowed children more freedom on slave ships.*

Keep practicing these strategies each time you encounter multiple-choice question sets. As you become more experienced, you won't need to write out your full thought process each time; applying the strategies will become more automatic. By the time it's exam day, you'll be prepared to tackle the multiple-choice section with confidence!

recap

Answering Multiple-Choice Questions with a Written Stimulus

The same strategies apply for all multiple-choice question sets, whether the stimulus is visual or written.

Strategy 1: Activate relevant concepts, developments, and processes.

Strategy 2: Determine what the question is really asking using the Four Cs.

Strategy 3: Eliminate wrong answers.

Activity ▸ Answering Multiple-Choice Questions with a Written Stimulus

Prepare to answer multiple-choice questions on the following passage.

> "When the ships arrive in the West-Indies, (the chief mart for this inhuman merchandize), the slaves are disposed of, as I have before observed, by different methods. Sometimes the mode of disposal, is that of selling them by what is termed a scramble; and a day is soon fixed for that purpose. But previously thereto, the sick, or refuse slaves, of which there are frequently many, are usually conveyed on shore, and sold at a tavern by . . . public auction. These, in general, are purchased . . . upon speculation, at so low a price as five or six dollars a head. I was informed by a mulatto woman, that she purchased a sick slave at Grenada, upon speculation, for the small sum of one dollar, as the poor wretch was apparently dying of the flux. It seldom happens that any, who are carried ashore in the emaciated state to which they are generally reduced by that disorder, long survive their landing. I once saw sixteen conveyed on shore, and sold in the foregoing manner, the whole of whom died before I left the island, which was within a short time after."
>
> SOURCE: Alexander Falconbridge, abolitionist and former surgeon on slave voyages, *An Account of the Slave Trade on the Coast of Africa*, 1788

Before approaching the question set, activate your awareness of relevant course content using a graphic organizer like the one shown below.

Concepts	
Developments	
Processes	

Next, review the questions and rephrase them using the Four Cs.

1. Which of the following contributed most significantly to the physical state of Africans arriving in the West Indies?
   A. Malnourishment and unsanitary conditions during the Middle Passage
   B. Lack of immunity to common diseases like scurvy and dysentery
   C. Dehumanization and physical abuse during the auction process
   D. Financial motivation for traders to keep enslaved people in good health

2. Which of the following best describes a perspective on the transatlantic slave trade that Equiano and Falconbridge shared?
   A. It contributed to the emergence of Afro-descended communities and religions.
   B. It justified the creation of an African safe haven colony for the formerly enslaved.
   C. It highlighted the importance of building stronger community ties within Africa.
   D. It was an inhumane and traumatic experience that caused irreparable damage.

Question 1	Question 2
☐ Comparison ☐ Causation ☐ Continuity & change	☐ Comparison ☐ Causation ☐ Continuity & change
Rephrasing:	**Rephrasing:**

Finally, categorize the answer choices to eliminate wrong answers. Make sure to explain your reasoning.

False	
Outside the time period	
Irrelevant	
Correct	

Multiple-Choice Questions

Questions 1–2 refer to the following.

The Middle Passage

The Art Archive/Shutterstock.

1. The conditions depicted in the image most directly contributed to which of the following during the transatlantic slave trade?

(A) The transmission of dysentery and high fatalities

(B) The sinking of slave ships and loss of their cargo

(C) The eruption of conflict between members of different African tribes and nations

(D) The escape of enslaved people and their return to Africa

2. Based on the image, which of the following claims can be made regarding nineteenth-century depictions of the Middle Passage?

(A) They clearly portrayed the diversity among African tribes being transported to the Americas.

(B) They rarely included accommodations made by the crew to prevent slave rebellions.

(C) They repeatedly were used by proslavery supporters to challenge accusations that slavery was inhumane.

(D) They infrequently showed the methods enslavers used to maximize profits.

Short-Answer Question

The Triangle Trade

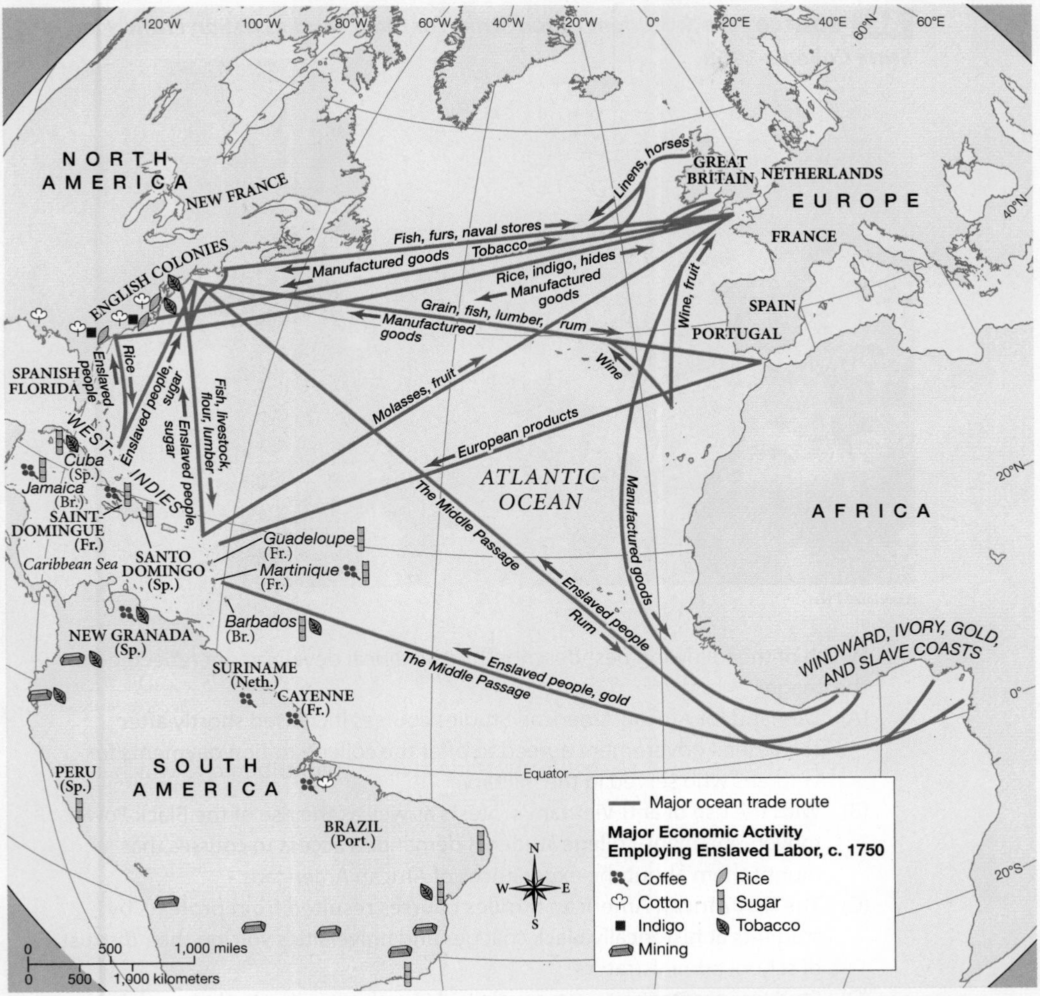

1. Using the map, answer A, B, C, and D.

(A) Describe the pattern of trade depicted in the map.

(B) Describe the role this trading system played in the African diaspora.

(C) Explain one cause of the development of the trading pattern depicted in the map.

(D) Explain the economic effects of the system depicted in the map of Africa, Europe, and the Americas.

Multiple-Choice Questions

Questions 1–2 refer to the following.

AP® source ***Black Student Union Strike for Black Studies at San Francisco State College*, 1968**

Associated Press

1. Which of the following best describes the historical development reflected in the image?

(A) Demand for African American Studies courses increased shortly after the federal government agreed to offer the college tuition payments for veterans who served in the military.

(B) With the rise of anti-Vietnam protests as well as the rise of the Black Power movement, many college students demanded access to courses that taught them about the experiences of African Americans.

(C) The first African American Studies courses resulted from protests by students at historically Black colleges and universities voicing their distrust of school administrators.

(D) Students across the country gathered together to discuss their social and economic future during the peak of the Vietnam War, resulting in calls for greater education about African American history.

2. Which is the best explanation of why the study of African history is relevant to understanding the African American experience?

(A) To challenge the myth that, prior to their experiences in the Americas, Black people did not have a history worth knowing and that their history started with slavery.

(B) To assuage the feelings of many African Americans who felt conflicted about their complicated heritage and history.

(C) To serve the needs of Black college students who felt alienated from mainstream white culture and thus sought a better understanding of their ancestors' experiences.

(D) To give Black students new opportunities and resources that would help them trace their ancestral African roots.

Questions 3–5 refer to the following.

SOURCE 1

Ancient Societies of Africa

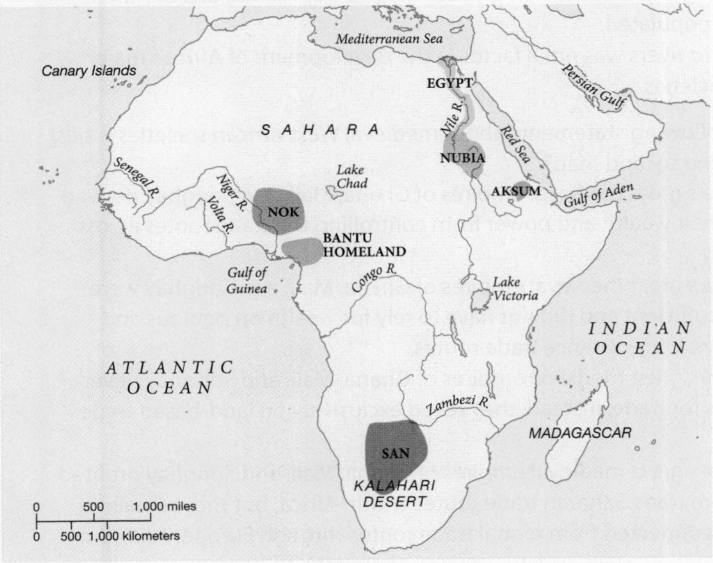

SOURCE 2

Medieval West Africa and the Trans-Saharan Trade

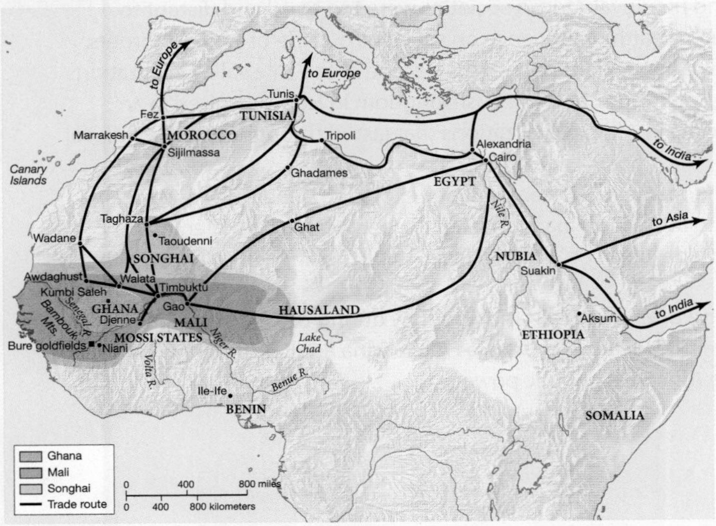

3. Which of the following best describes how Africa's geographic features influenced the ancient societies reflected in the first map?

(A) Africa's size and geographic diversity meant that ancient African civilizations were spread out and rarely traded or interacted.

(B) Access to both the Atlantic and Indian Oceans as well as the Mediterranean and Red Seas gave African societies many opportunities for interaction with other civilizations, facilitating global trade and cultural exchange.

(C) Access to both the Atlantic and Indian Oceans as well as the Mediterranean and Red Seas meant that most African societies evolved along the coastlines, leaving the vast deserts, grasslands, and tropical regions of Africa mostly unpopulated.

(D) Proximity to rivers was not a factor in the development of Africa's major ancient societies.

4. Which of the following statements about medieval West African societies is best supported by the second map?

(A) West Africa's great medieval empires of Ghana, Mali, and Songhay derived much of their wealth and power from controlling the trade routes across the desert.

(B) West Africa's great medieval empires of Ghana, Mali, and Songhay were each self-sufficient and did not have to rely for wealth on perilous and inconsistent long-distance trade routes.

(C) West Africa's great medieval empires of Ghana, Mali, and Songhay never used rivers for trade; instead, they relied exclusively on land-based trade routes.

(D) West Africa's great medieval empires of Ghana, Mali, and Songhay profited greatly from trans-Saharan trade routes within Africa, but they remained largely disconnected from global trade routes through Europe, Asia, and India.

5. Which of the following claims about ancient and medieval African societies is best supported by both maps?

(A) Ancient and medieval African societies were too small and distant to obtain much wealth or influence on societies outside of Africa's borders.

(B) At the end of the ancient period, the decline of the Nile valley civilizations such as Egypt, Aksum, and the Kush kingdom in Nubia resulted in an overall decline in African civilizations that lasted throughout the medieval period.

(C) Ancient and medieval African societies exploited geography and local resources to attain dominance in their respective regions, then they exploited trade, often on a global level, to further increase their wealth and influence.

(D) After the rise of Ghana, Mali, and Songhay during the medieval period, cities in the Nile River valley such as Alexandria and Cairo were no longer relevant to African economic power.

Questions 6–8 refer to the following.

Mankind generally allow that all nations are indebted to the Egyptians for the introduction of the arts and sciences; but they are not willing to acknowledge to the present race of Africans; though Horodotus, "the father of history," expressly declares that the "Egyptians had black skins and frizzled hair." All we know of Ethiopia, strengthens us in the belief, that it was early inhabited by a people, whose manners and customs nearly resembled those of the Egyptians. Many of their divinities were the same: they had the same orders of priesthood and religious ceremonies: they made use of the same characters in writing: their dress was alike: and the regal sceptre in both countries was in the form of a plough.

SOURCE: John Russwurm, *On the Egyptians as Africans*, 1827

6. Which of the following best explains why Russwurm attempts to compare Egyptians to other African groups?
(A) To educate the general public about African civilizations like the Egyptians.
(B) To challenge the evidence that Egyptians were not African.
(C) To highlight the physical features of the average Egyptian.
(D) To provide new evidence of the rich history of Egyptians.

7. Which of the following best explains Russwurm's description of Egyptians as having "black skins and frizzled hair"?
(A) He wanted to clarify what Egyptians looked like.
(B) He wanted to challenge the common belief that Egyptians had fair skin and straight hair.
(C) He wanted to promote the idea that Egyptians were similar to their Arab neighbors.
(D) He wanted to describe the features that Egyptians had prior to implementing their religious practices.

8. Which of the following best describes the historical situation at the time of the excerpt's publication in 1827?
(A) At the time, many European countries had banned some forms of transatlantic trade yet still allowed for the institution of slavery to thrive.
(B) At the time, many enslavers and those who benefited from slavery used scholarly texts to insinuate African inferiority in order to justify their actions.
(C) At the time, although the United States had recently doubled in size, slavery was growing out of fashion, allowing for more perspectives like the excerpt to be published.
(D) At the time, Brazil was still importing kidnapped Africans and forcing them into hard labor; these injustices inspired writers like Russwurm to promote counternarratives of African excellence.

Questions 9–11 refer to the following.

The appalling realities of the Atlantic slave trade, New World slavery, colonial domination, and poverty stigmatized African-descended people. . . . [T]he whole apparatus of learned knowledge decried Africans' lack of civilization, beauty, and wealth. In the nineteenth and early twentieth centuries, well educated people believed Africa to be a dark continent full of ugly people who offered nothing positive to history. Knowledge about black people did not figure in college or high school curricula. . . . Even black Americans' own words were enlisted against Africa. The West African-born Boston poet Phillis Wheatley (ca. 1753–1874) published volumes of poetry, including poems advocating the abolition of slavery. Yet only one of her poems, "On Being Brought from Africa to America" was endlessly quoted — as proof of all black people's preference for America over Africa. The larger body of Wheatley's work, advocating the equal rights of all people, was ignored.

SOURCE: Nell Irvin Painter, *Creating Black Americans: African-American History and Its Meanings, 1619 to the Present*, 2006

9. According to the excerpt, which of the following best describes the conflicting views of Africa held by African Americans?

(A) In schools, African Americans were taught explicitly about the high achievements of African societies, but this conflicted with their experience of racism in the United States.

(B) Most African Americans knew Africa to be a land with rich natural resources and therefore the potential to generate wealth from trade, but these opportunities were being exploited by European and North American colonial powers, with little benefit going to actual Africans or African Americans.

(C) Having grown distrustful of Eurocentric and proslavery histories of Africa that highlighted African inferiority, African Americans turned instead to African American poets like Phyllis Wheatley for historical guidance because they celebrated African excellence.

(D) Many African Americans were told that Africa was uncivilized and that Africans offered little to human history, and this viewpoint conflicted with the many distinct and important cultures and achievements that actually characterizes African history.

10. What claim is the author making about the poetry of Phillis Wheatley?

(A) All of Wheatley's poems offered authentic and personal descriptions of her experiences of living in West Africa.

(B) Wheatley's poem, "On Being Brought from Africa," described Wheatley's journey across the Atlantic Ocean.

(C) Wheatley's poem, "On Being Brought from Africa," was used to celebrate African excellence at a time when few other African American writers were doing so.

(D) Wheatley's poem, "On Being Brought from Africa," was used as evidence that Black Americans were ashamed of their African heritage.

11. Based on the excerpt, why would African Americans seek to learn more about Africa?

(A) Because Africa, African history, and Africans themselves were so often described in racist and disparaging terms, many Black Americans sought out new resources to understand the complex African societies that predated transatlantic slavery.

(B) Because all African Americans knew a great deal about their African heritage before the slave trade, they sought to reinforce it by studying more African history.

(C) The abolitionist movement and the demand for more equality pushed many African Americans to demand that public schools incorporate more African history into the curriculum.

(D) Because African Americans knew so much about Africa and its history already, African Americans' interest in learning more about Africa and its history was only a casual pastime or hobby.

Questions 12–15 refer to the following.

***Detail from the Tomb of Horemheb*, c. 1292 BCE**

About the source: This image depicts the pharaoh making an offering to Goddess Hathor-Imentet, whose role is to welcome the deceased.

Vestibule, Tomb of Horemheb, Thebes, Egypt/De Agostini Picture Library/S. Vannini/Bridgeman Images

12. Based on the image, which of the following best describes the social structure of Egyptian society?

(A) Ancient Egyptian societies were mostly unconcerned with religious ritual; Egyptian pharaohs were much more concerned with maximizing agricultural and economic output.

(B) Social life in Egypt revolved around elaborate gift-making and gift-presenting, which deepened the interpersonal bonds between Egyptian workers and rulers.

(C) The people of Egypt held most of the power in their society, with the pharaoh acting mostly as a powerless figurehead.

(D) The people of Egypt under the leadership of their pharaohs honored their gods and commemorated their dead by ordering the construction of monumental pyramids, temples, and obelisks.

13. What best explains both the cooperation and the conflict between the two ancient African kingdoms of Egypt and Nubia?

(A) Nubia supplied Egypt with gold and luxury items, fostering both a cooperative as well as a competitive relationship between the two kingdoms.

(B) Egyptians and Nubians worshipped different gods, which initially brought them closer economically but ultimately led to religious conflict.

(C) The dynasties that ruled Egypt were subject to political turmoil, so the relationship with their southern neighbor Nubia was always fluctuating between peaceful trade and overt war.

(D) The annual flooding of the Nile led to booms in agricultural production followed by droughts, and this cycle corresponded with peace and conflict between the two Nile River kingdoms.

14. Which of the following best captures a significant difference between the ancient African kingdoms of Egypt and Mali?

(A) While the Egyptian pharaohs were known for their great accumulations of wealth, the rulers of Mali remained economically weak.

(B) The ancient Egyptians converted to Islam long before the people of the kingdom of Mali did.

(C) The people of Mali adopted Islam as their primary religious practice, whereas ancient Egyptians retained their belief in multiple gods.

(D) The pharaohs of Egypt traveled in large caravans to various destinations to honor their gods, whereas the rulers of Mali were known to have rarely left their palaces.

15. Which of the following best describes how geography influenced the formation of the ancient Egyptian kingdom?

(A) The Nile River rarely flooded, allowing Egyptian agriculture to thrive while avoiding the damaging floods that affected other river-dependent kingdoms.

(B) Due to the favorable farmlands along the Nile River, many people migrated to Egypt to seek out new opportunities, and this natural accumulation of immigrants became the power base for the Egyptian ruling class.

(C) The persistent flooding of the Nile River during increasingly arid periods drove people out of the dry surrounding lands, putting population pressure on military leaders like Menes, a.k.a. Narmer, to unite the kingdoms of Upper and Lower Egypt under one ruler, the pharaoh.

(D) Egypt was settled along the poor agricultural lands of the Nile River delta, forcing the early pharaohs to employ elaborate religious rituals and communal building projects like the pyramids to project power in the region.

Short-Answer Questions

1. Using the image, answer A, B, C, and D.

Harmonia Rosales, *Crucifixion* (Oil on Wood Panel, 48″ x 36″), 2020

About the source: Amidst the public display of humiliation and warnings to follow society's rules, as suggested by the figure of Adam on the cross, hope continues to shine. His golden Orí, indicating the spiritual self and destiny, radiates brightly, cutting through the darkness of racism and disempowerment. On the left is the figure of Yemayá, whose Orí also blazes in the night. Dressed in a luxurious golden-patterned blue robe, she looks after Adam, staying present during his crucifixion.

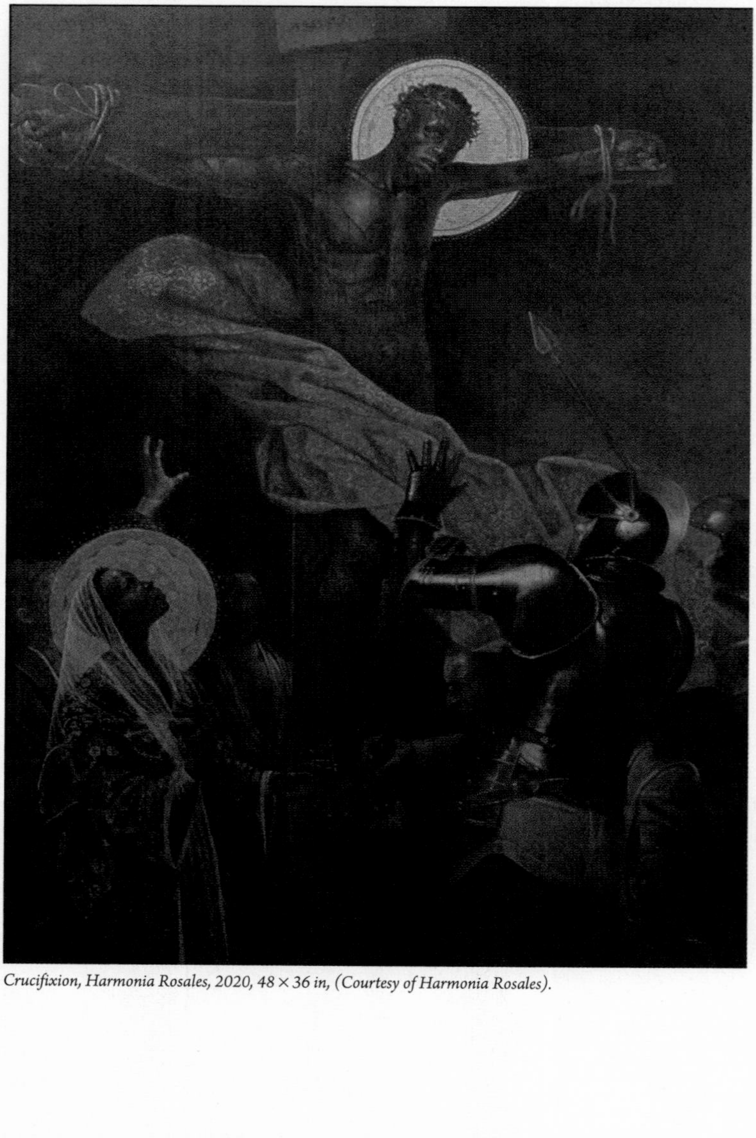

Crucifixion, Harmonia Rosales, 2020, 48 × 36 in, (Courtesy of Harmonia Rosales).

(A) Describe at least one aspect of the image that reflects religious syncretism, i.e., the blending of Africans' local spiritual practices with Christianity.
(B) Describe one short-term impact of the conversion to Christianity by the kingdom of Kongo.
(C) Describe one long-term impact of the blending of African traditions to the practice of Christianity.
(D) Explain how religious beliefs impacted the experiences of captured Africans during the Middle Passage.

2. Using the excerpt, answer A, B, C, and D.

"Black intellectual history has always been the root of Black Studies. This does not exclude important contributions by, and dialogues with, scholars outside of the Black community. But Black Studies is fundamentally a product of Black intellectuals. . . . These academic high achievers earned degrees at the most outstanding institutions of higher education. . . . Many of them spent very productive careers at historically Black colleges and universities, particularly Howard University, Fisk University, and Atlanta University. . . . Black intellectuals and artists kept the community informed about the issues of the day, rethinking historical experience and comparing African Americans to the entire African Diaspora."

SOURCE: Abdul Alkalimat, *The History of Black Studies*, 2021

(A) Describe the argument that Alkalimat makes about the history of Black Studies.
(B) Considering the loss of connection to African history experienced by those who endured the African diaspora, describe the social purpose of studying African history and African American history.
(C) Using one example of ritual, music, art, or religious syncretization, explain how African Americans helped preserve African history and culture during the early African diaspora.
(D) Explain how attempts to preserve African history during the early African diaspora mirrors the work done later by the Black intellectuals that Alkalimat discusses.

3. Answer A, B, C, and D.

(A) Describe the purpose of a griot.
(B) Describe one epic tale that would have been shared by a griot.
(C) Explain how the experiences of West African societies influenced the culture of African Americans.
(D) Explain one other example of a West African tradition that survived the Middle Passage.

Document-Based Question

1. Explain how the development of African American Studies impacted public understanding of history of ancient and medieval African societies.

In your response you should do the following:

- **Respond to the prompt with a defensible thesis or claim that establishes a line of reasoning.**
- **Describe a broader historical or disciplinary context relevant to the topic of the prompt.**
- **Support an argument in response to the prompt using at least three of the sources.**
- **Use at least one additional piece of specific evidence (beyond the evidence found in the sources) relevant to your argument.**
- **For at least two sources, explain how or why the perspective, purpose, context, and/or audience for each source is relevant to your argument.**
- **Reference or cite the sources you use in your argument. You can reference or cite the source letter, title, or author.**

SOURCE A

Black Studies Curriculum, San Francisco State College, Spring 1968

About the source: This source shows cover for the first Black Studies curriculum at San Francisco State College. Two of the course descriptions are also excerpted here.

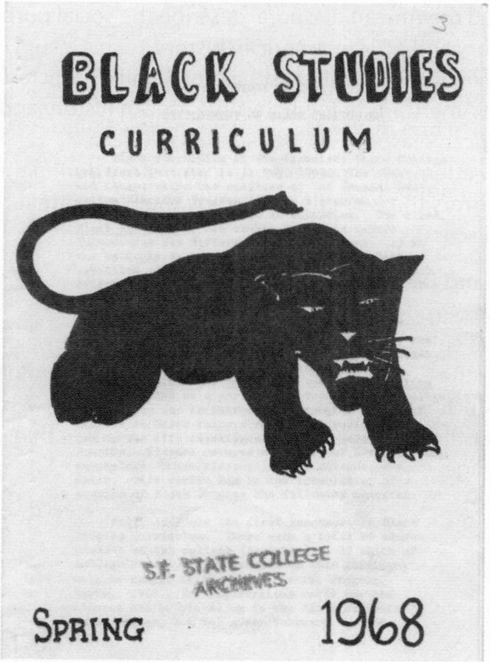

Courtesy of the San Francisco State University Archives.

English

Modern African Thought and Literature **Harold Head**

. . . A study of the recent literature of the black continent is not possible in isolation. It demands the more general context of the whole African cultural revival — African writers and research workers being linked to so many communal preoccupations and characteristics.

The first characteristic common to both these groups, if not to all African thinkers, is their political commitment. However, complementing their politically committed literature, present-day Africans exhibit a committed history, a committed ethnology, and a committed theology.

The student . . . should find the African commitment to Black Power stimulating in its obvious comparative implications. . . .

History

Ancient Black History **Rolland Snellings**

The course in Ancient Black History is extremely important to Black college youth, not only as a positive salve upon the wound of past and present racial oppressions and cultural degradation which has been the lot [of] Black people everywhere, but also as an honest scholarly effort to complete the complex puzzle of human civilization confronting modern man. Modern civilization, contrary to prejudiced views, has resulted from the collective efforts of countless generations of the Races of men, daily pursuing their aim: dreaming, planning, working out their life tasks under indifferent skies. This view of history — which is obvious to the scientific scholar — has been, and in many cases, still is, hotly contested by sterile academics who feel their world-view threatened; by fresh, non-prejudiced approaches. One cannot truly know man until one has known him in all sizes, shapes, and colors upon the isles and continents of earth.

This course will not only outline and sketch the various dynasties, empires, political conflicts, etc. of the Ancient Black World, but also its concrete artistic and scientific achievements and discoveries so that the Black student can realistically "see, feel, or touch" the contributions of the Black peoples, of Africa, to Modern World Culture. . . .

SOURCE B

Medieval West Africa and the Trans-Saharan Trade

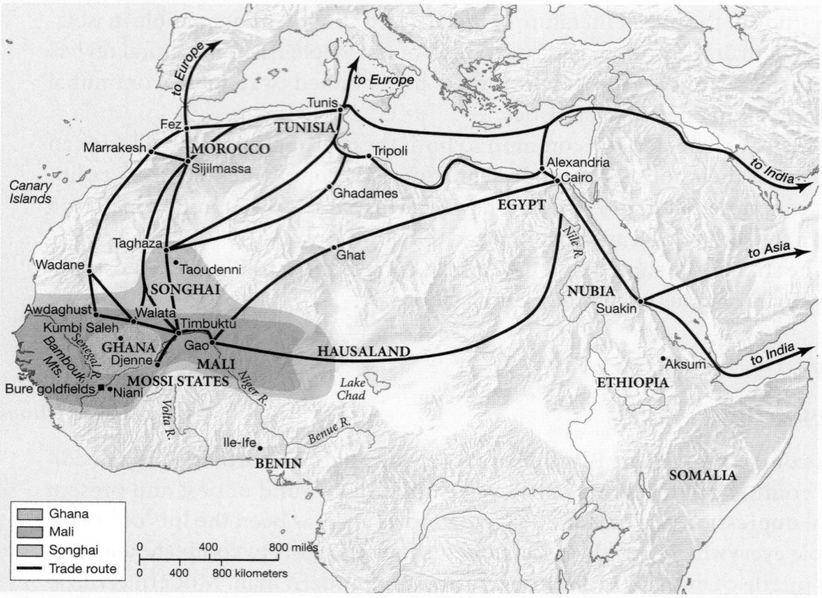

SOURCE C

AP® source Queen Idia Masks, Sixteenth Century and 1977

About the source: The mask on the left was created in the sixteenth century and depicts Queen Idia, the Oba (ruler) of Benin from circa 1504 to 1550. Queen Idia became an iconic symbol of Black women's leadership throughout the African diaspora in 1977, when an ivory mask of her face (shown at right) was adopted as the symbol for FESTAC (Second World Black Festival of Arts and Culture).

Universal History Archive/Getty Images

PIUS UTOMI EKPEI/Getty Images

SOURCE D

AP® source **Carter Godwin Woodson, *The Mis-Education of the Negro*, 1933**

About the source: Born in rural Virginia during Reconstruction, Carter G. Woodson (1875–1950) was a central figure in Black history and an important American scholar. In 1912, he became the first and only person born to enslaved parents to earn a Ph.D. In 1915, he founded the Association for the Study of Negro (now African-American) Life and History, and he devoted the remainder of his life to the study and advancement of Black history.

No thought was given to the history of Africa except so far as it had been a field of exploitation for the Caucasian. You might study the history as it was offered in our system . . . and you would never hear Africa mentioned except in the negative. You would never thereby learn that Africans first domesticated the sheep, goat, and cow, developed the idea of trial by jury, produced the first stringed instruments, and gave the world its greatest boon in the discovery of iron. You would never know that prior to the Mohammedan invasion about 1000 A.D. these natives in the heart of Africa had developed powerful kingdoms which were later organized as the Songhay Empire on the order of that of the Romans and boasting of similar grandeur.

Unlike other people, then, the Negro, according to this point of view, was an exception to the natural plan of things, and he had no such mission as that of an outstanding contribution to culture. The status of the Negro, then, was justly fixed as that of an inferior. Teachers of Negroes in their first schools after Emancipation did not proclaim any such doctrine, but the content of their curricula justified these inferences.

An observer from outside of the situation naturally inquires why the Negroes, many of whom serve their race as teachers, have not changed this program. These teachers, however, are powerless. Negroes have no control over their education and have little voice in their other affairs pertaining thereto. . . . The education of the Negroes, then, the most important thing in the uplift of the Negroes, is almost entirely in the hands of those who have enslaved them and now segregate them.

SOURCE E

Nell Irvin Painter, *Creating Black Americans: African-American History and Its Meanings, 1619 to the Present*, 2006

In the nineteenth century, before many African Americans enjoyed access to higher education or were able to travel, depictions of black people depended heavily upon Eurocentric Western learning. Westerners . . . measured African worth in European terms. . . . Westerners judged Africa as "benighted," or shrouded in darkness. . . . [D]uring the nineteenth-century reign of so-called "scientific" racism, Europeans and Americans of European descent denied black Africa any history worth the name and claimed the ancient civilizations of Egypt and Ethiopia for white people. . . . African Americans constantly disputed the negative and commonplace evaluations of Africa and the Negro race circulating in Western culture. . . .

In the face of racist insult, African Americans shaped their own versions of Africa. The process unfolded across the nineteenth and twentieth centuries, as knowledge of the African past increased and as black Americans discussed the meaning of African history among themselves. They often put several ancient African civilizations together as a single, glorious past they claimed as their own.

UNIT 2

Freedom, Enslavement, and Resistance

3 Slavery in North America
1619–1740

4 African Americans in the Age of Revolution
1741–1783

5 Slavery and Freedom in the New Republic
1775–1820

6 Black Life in the Slave South
1820–1860

7 The Northern Black Freedom Struggle and the Coming of the Civil War
1830–1860

8 Freedom Rising: The Civil War
1861–1865

The transatlantic slave trade lasted for over 350 years, spanning from the early 1500s to the mid-1800s. Within that period, over 12.5 million Africans from Senegambia, Sierra Leone, Liberia, Côte d'Ivoire, Ghana, Benin, Nigeria, Angola, and Mozambique were forcibly transported to the Americas. Approximately 5 percent (around 388,000) of those who survived the arduous journey across the Atlantic were directly transported from Africa to what would later become the United States, while the majority were brought to the Caribbean and Brazil, which would in fact become the last nation to abolish slavery in 1888. Nevertheless, the narrative of all the men, women, and children who endured this difficult three-part voyage, along with the narrative of their descendants, encompasses more than just enslavement. It also includes tales of resistance that began within the dungeons of West African slave citadels like Elmina Castle in Ghana where African captives tried to escape. You can also find it on slave ships like the *Amistad*, where enslaved Africans staged mutinies, forcing enslavers to reconfigure slave ship designs. Enslaved people also resisted covertly, via religious and cultural practices like the congada, a Brazilian religious ceremony combining the celebration of historic African royal figures such as the king of Kongo with the Catholic ritual observation of Our Lady of the Rosary.

Enslaved Africans in the United States also resisted through artistic expression. Potters like David Drake openly defied South Carolinian slave codes that prohibited enslaved people from learning to read and write by inscribing poems about love, life, slavery, and spirituality on jars he created. Free Blacks like Sojourner Truth and Frederick Douglass, the most photographed man of the nineteenth century, used the power of photography to challenge stereotypes about Black people by presenting themselves as deserving of dignity, respect, and equal rights as citizens. With that respect came the right to identify themselves. This sparked the debate over what they would call themselves and be called, and whether to embrace terms such as Colored, African, and African American. While chapters 3 through 8 in *Freedom on My Mind* delve into the key topics typically covered in most U.S. History courses regarding the institution of slavery — such as the economic, political, social, and regional dynamics of the slave system that emerged in seventeenth-century America, the driving forces behind the expansion of slavery in the nineteenth century, and the eventual abolition of slavery with the Thirteenth Amendment in 1865 — the central focus of each chapter seeks to answer a central question posed by Unit 2: How did both free and enslaved Black people resist slavery and strive to secure their own freedom?

AP® source

Potter David Drake created this storage jar in 1857. It is just one example of how he defied slave codes by inscribing poems on his works of pottery.

Storage Jar, 1857 (glazed stoneware)/Drake, Dave (Dave the Potter) (c.1800-70)/MUSEUM OF FINE ARTS, BOSTON/Museum of Fine Arts, Boston, Massachusetts, USA/Bridgeman Images.

In **chapter 3** (Slavery in North America, 1619–1740) you will learn about the first Africans to arrive in Jamestown, Virginia, in 1619 on the Dutch warship *White Lion*. This chapter also explains how slavery expanded throughout the thirteen British colonies, where various factors contributed to the differences that emerged within the institution across the regions of the colonies. It was during this time that many laws were passed to govern enslaved people. In response, many enslaved people resisted these laws and the effects of the institution of slavery in many ways, aiming to secure their own freedom and demonstrating their resilience.

Chapter 4 (African Americans in the Age of Revolution, 1741–1783) explores the appearance of a new African American culture as the population of native-born Black Americans increased among the steady importation of West Africans. One key development is the

In this photograph taken between 1863 and 1865, an unidentified Black Union soldier poses for a picture with his wife and two daughters. *Library of Congress, LC-DIG-ppmsca-36454.*

emergence of culturally diverse **syncretic** (religious) practices, as more Blacks inspired by the Great Awakening began to accept Christianity. This chapter also discusses the dual effects of the Revolutionary War on Black people as they seized the opportunity to fight for their own independence and contribute to the war effort.

Chapter 5 (Slavery and Freedom in the New Republic, 1775–1820) and **chapter 6** (Black Life in the Slave South, 1820–1860) investigate how and why slavery became entrenched and expanded among the southern states while gradually becoming illegal in the northern states after the Revolutionary War. You will learn how Black people continued the fight to make the principles of the American Revolution, such as freedom and equality, a reality for all in a variety of ways. This era saw the publication of Black-run newspapers alongside political efforts undertaken by Black organizations. Black people also continued to resist slavery, establishing the Underground Railroad participating in slave rebellions, and endeavoring to protect their families and forge new kinship networks. Finally, the establishment of Black religious denominations and African-influenced religious practices animated religious life of this era.

Chapter 7 (The Northern Black Freedom Struggle and the Coming of the Civil War, 1830–1860) details the historical events that led to the eventual outbreak of the Civil War but maintains the focus on Black people as the center of abolitionist movement, while **chapter 8** (Freedom Rising: The Civil War, 1861–1865) highlights the experiences and roles Black men and women played in securing their own freedom during the Civil War as soldiers, contrabands, refugees, nurses, teachers, runaways, and civilians. This chapter also describes the legislation that officially changed their position in society.

AP® UNIT 2 THEMATIC TIMELINE

All of the following developments can be found in the AP® Course Framework.

1500 | 1600 | 1700 | 1800 | 1850 | 1900

Migration and the African Diaspora

- **1526** Transatlantic slave trade begins
- **1738** Fort Mose, first sanctioned free Black town in present-day U.S., founded
- **1815** Paul Cuffee takes thirty-eight Black Bostonians to Sierra Leone
- **1820–1860** Forced migration of 1.2 million African Americans from Upper South to Lower South
- **1852** Martin Delany advocates establishing Black nation outside U.S.

Intersections of Identity

- **1816** American Colonization Society (ACS) first meets in Washington, D.C.
- **1832** Maria Stewart's *Why Sit Here and Die* published
- **1861** Harriet A. Jacobs's *Incidents in the Life of a Slave Girl, Written by Herself* published

Creativity, Expression, and the Arts

- **1773** Phillis Wheatley's "On Being Brought from Africa to America" published
- **1827** *Freedom's Journal*, nation's first Black newspaper, founded
- **1841** Frederick Douglass begins career as abolitionist lecturer
- **1843** Sojourner Truth begins career as abolitionist lecturer
- **1858** Enslaved potter David Drake defies South Carolina slave law by signing his name on his pottery

Resistance and Resilience

- **1526** Africans enslaved in Santo Domingo lead earliest known slave revolt in North America
- **1656** Elizabeth Key becomes first Black woman in North America to sue for freedom and win
- **1662** Virginia pronounces slavery to be heritable through mother
- **1687** First freedom seekers arrive in Spanish Florida
- **1724** Louisiana Slave Code (Code Noir, or Black Code) created
- **1739** Stono Rebellion
- **1791–1804** Haitian Revolution
- **1793** Fugitive Slave Act
- **1831** Nat Turner's rebellion
- **1839** *Amistad* revolt
- **1850** Fugitive Slave Act
- **1857** *Dred Scott v. Sandford*
- **1861–1865** Civil War
- **1863** Emancipation Proclamation; U.S. Colored Troops established
- **1865–1877** Reconstruction
- **1865** Thirteenth Amendment abolishes slavery; First celebration of Juneteenth in Texas
- **1888** Brazil becomes last country in the Americas to abolish slavery

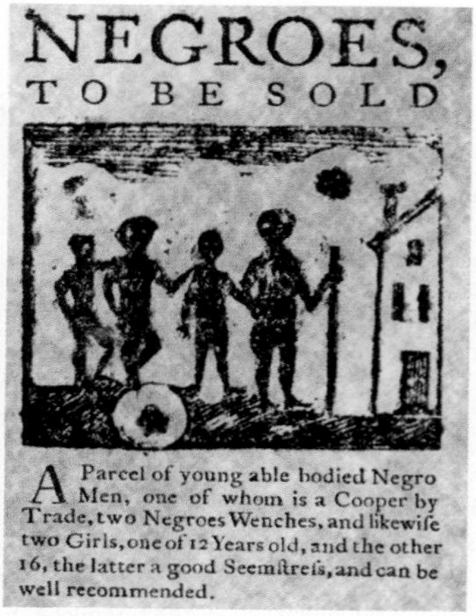

NEGROES,
TO BE SOLD
A Parcel of young able bodied Negro Men, one of whom is a Cooper by Trade, two Negroes Wenches, and likewife two Girls, one of 12 Years old, and the other 16, the latter a good Seemftrefs, and can be well recommended.

AP® skill **Argumentation (3B)**

Support a claim or argument using specific and relevant evidence.

Key Context: This advertisement for a New York slave auction dates to the eighteenth century. In that era, the letter "f" was often used for the letter "s," and many spellings were not standardized. For example, "Seemftrefs" in this ad refers to a seamstress.

PREDICT

- What were some key characteristics of slave auctions? What details from the ad support your response?
- What impact did slave auctions have on enslaved families?

SOURCE: *Granger/Granger — All rights reserved.*

SOURCE: *The Old Plantation, attributed to John Rose, Beaufort County, South Carolina, c. 1785–1790/The Colonial Williamsburg Foundation, Gift of Abby Aldrich Rockefeller.*

AP® skill **Applying Disciplinary Knowledge (1C)**

Identify and explain patterns, connections, or other relationships (causation, changes, continuities, comparison).

Key Context: *The Old Plantation* is a late eighteenth-century painting that depicts a group of enslaved people on a South Carolina plantation.

PREDICT

- How do you think African American forms of self-expression in art, music, and language combined influences from diverse African cultures with local sources? What details in this painting help support your prediction?
- How can self-expression be considered a form of resistance and a demonstration of resilience?

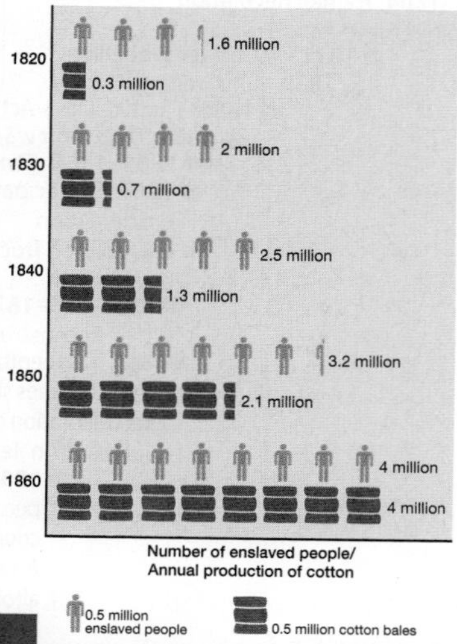

AP® skill **Applying Disciplinary Knowledge (1B)**

Identify and explain the context of a specific event, development, or process.

Key Context: This chart depicts the growth of slavery and cotton production from 1820 to 1860.

PREDICT

- How did the growth of the cotton industry in the United States affect enslaved African American families? What evidence supports your position?
- How did the growth of the cotton industry impact the forced migration patterns of enslaved people? What details in the graph support your prediction?

I Sell the Shadow to Support the Substance.
SOJOURNER TRUTH.

AP® skill **Argumentation (3A)**

Formulate a defensible claim.

Key Context: This photograph shows Sojourner Truth, one of the most famous and influential Black women of the nineteenth century. Her "Ain't I a Woman" speech, delivered in 1851, is one of the most famous abolitionist and women's rights speeches.

PREDICT

- What role and impact do you think women and their narratives about their experience in slavery had on political movements of the nineteenth century?
- How do you think Black women's experiences in the nineteenth century relate to their perspectives on slavery and its effects?

SOURCE: *University of Florida, Smathers Library Special and Area Studies Collections, Rare Books Collections.*

AP® skill **Applying Disciplinary Knowledge (1C)**

Identify and explain patterns, connections, or other relationships (causation, changes, continuities, comparison).

AP® source **Key Context:** This engraving, titled *Gopher John, Seminole Interpreter*, first appeared in an 1848 history of the Second Seminole War.

PREDICT

- How do you think the expansion of slavery in the U.S. South affected relations between Black and Indigenous people and impacted enslaved people's ability to secure their own freedom? What does this image tell you about the relations between Black and Indigenous people in the U.S. South during the expansion of slavery?
- What role do you think maroons played in Seminole resistance to American incursion on their land?

SOURCE: *Library of Congress, Prints and Photographs Division, Washington, D.C., LC- USZC4-6165.*

PRESENTED
to the 4th Regt
U.S.
COLORED TROOPS
BY THE
COLORED LADIES OF BALTIMORE

AP® skill **Applying Disciplinary Knowledge (1B)**

Identify and explain the context of a specific event, development, or process.

AP® skill **Source Analysis (2C)**

Explain the significance of a source's perspective, purpose, context, and audience.

Key Context: This is a remnant of a flag made by the Colored Ladies of Baltimore for the Fourth Regiment, U.S. Colored Troops, during the Civil War.

PREDICT

- What were African American soldiers' motivations for enlisting during the Civil War? What inequities do you think they faced?
- How do you think Black soldiers' service affected Black communities during and after the Civil War?
- What clues does this image reveal about the contributions of enslaved and free African Americans made during the Civil War?

SOURCE: *Regimental flag: Silk mounted on a wooden pole (with the eagle missing). Museum Department, Courtesy of the Maryland Historical Society, image ID 2004.22. Confederate flag: Private Collection/Photo © Don Troiani/Bridgeman Images.*

CHAPTER 3

Slavery in North America

1619–1740

CHAPTER TIMELINE *Events specific to African history are in purple. General U.S. history events are in black. Events from the AP® Course are marked with an asterisk.*

1606	Virginia Company receives royal charter
1607	English found Jamestown colony
1611	Jamestown settlers begin cultivating tobacco
1614	Dutch claim New Netherland
	English settler John Rolfe marries Pocahontas, daughter of Powhatan
1619	First enslaved Africans arrive in English North American colonies
1620	Pilgrims found Plymouth colony
1622	Opechancanough, chief of Powhatan's confederacy, leads Indian uprising against Virginia colonists
1624	Virginia becomes royal colony
1625	Dutch West India Company establishes North American headquarters on island of Manhattan
1626	Dutch begin importing enslaved people to New Netherland
1630	Massachusetts Bay colony founded
1634	Settlers arrive in Maryland
1635–1664	Blacks in New Netherland petition for freedom, win half-freedom
1636	Rhode Island and Connecticut colonies established
1641	Massachusetts becomes first North American colony to legally recognize slavery
1643	Plymouth, Connecticut, and New Haven colonies legally recognize slavery
1644	Opechancanough leads second uprising against English colonists
1656	Quakers arrive in Massachusetts
1656	Elizabeth Key becomes first Black woman in North America to sue for freedom and win*
1660	Royal African Company established; English enter slave trade
1662	Virginia pronounces slavery to be heritable through mother in Laws of Virginia, Act XII, General Assembly*
1663	Carolina becomes royal colony
1664	English seize New Netherland from Dutch, rename it New York
1676	Nathaniel Bacon leads attack on Virginia's government in Bacon's Rebellion
1681	William Penn founds Pennsylvania
1686	Dominion of New England created
1687	First freedom seekers arrive in Spanish Florida*
1688	Germantown Quakers issue first American antislavery petition
1689–1713	England, France, and Spain at war
1690	South Carolina adopts harsh Barbadian slave code
1691	Virginia restricts marriage between Blacks and whites
1692–1693	Salem witch trials
1693	Spain grants liberty to all freedom seekers who convert to Catholicism*
1700	Samuel Sewall issues first New England antislavery tract
1705	Massachusetts outlaws marriage between Blacks and whites
1724	Louisiana Slave Code (Code Noir, or Black Code) created*
1729–1730	Natchez uprising against French; Blacks fight on both sides
1730	Three hundred enslaved people in Virginia organize mass escape
	Approximately four hundred enslaved people in Louisiana conspire to kill French and seize colony
1732	Georgia colony founded
1738	Fort Mose, first sanctioned free Black town in present-day U.S., founded*
1739	Stono rebellion*
1739–1748	British war with Spain in Caribbean, with France in Canada and Europe
1740	South Carolina passes Negro Act

"20. and Odd Negroes": The Story of Virginia's First African Americans

Late in August 1619, the Dutch warship *White Lion* docked in Jamestown, Virginia, with a cargo of "20. and odd negroes."[1] These Africans had begun their transatlantic journey in Luanda, a slave trading port in the Portuguese colony of Angola, where they were loaded onto the slave ship *São João Bautista* with more than three hundred other enslaved people. They survived the harrowing Middle Passage, with illness killing almost a third of the ship's human cargo before they reached the New World. When the ship docked briefly in Jamaica to buy medicine and supplies, Captain Manuel Mendes da Cunha paused to report that he still "had many sick aboard" before hurrying on to the Mexican port of Veracruz, his final destination.[2] But the *Bautista*'s long journey was interrupted when, less than five hundred miles from Veracruz, it was captured by the *Treasurer* and the *White Lion*, two English ships sailing under the Dutch flag. Both ships were heavily armed privateers. Privateers were private warships commissioned by European powers to attack their enemies' ships and seize their cargo. Such piracy could be highly profitable; Spanish ships, for example, often carried gold. But the *Bautista* carried only African captives, so the privateers had to content themselves with seizing as many healthy enslaved people as they could carry. Among them were twenty enslaved people that the *White Lion*'s captain would exchange for provisions when he docked in Jamestown.

The seventeen men and three women who arrived in the Chesapeake in 1619 were the first of many generations of African captives to land in English North America. They likely hailed from one of the African kingdoms along Angola's borders — which included Kongo, Ndongo, and Benguela — before being sold in Angola, a small coastal colony where Portuguese traders exported enslaved people purchased elsewhere.[3] But their exact origins are difficult to reconstruct because the Virginia colonists who noted their arrival did not record the names or histories of the region's first Black settlers. The lives they led in Virginia are also largely undocumented.

Colonial records do reveal that Virginia governor George Yeardley and a prominent merchant named Abraham Pierson purchased all twenty of these early arrivals in exchange for corn and other supplies. Both men owned large plantations, where they put their new Africans to work growing tobacco and other crops. Less clear, however, is whether all twenty of these involuntary migrants remained enslaved for life. They had landed in one of the few New World colonies where slavery had yet to take root, and individual Africans could still move from slavery to freedom with relative ease.

Slavery took several decades to develop in Virginia. The English migrants who settled there initially preferred to hire white servants, who were more familiar to them. But white laborers were not always available and often proved unwilling to work as servants for any great length of time. Enslaved Africans, who could be held in bondage for life, presented no such limitations.

By the end of the seventeenth century, enslaved labor had become crucial to southern colonies such as Virginia and common in European settlements throughout North America.

Enslaved workers were already living in Spanish Florida when the English first arrived. They had come with the Spanish explorer Pedro Menéndez de Avilés, who imported five hundred enslaved Africans to construct the town of St. Augustine in 1565. The Dutch entrepreneurs who settled New Netherland starting in 1625 brought in enslaved workers to clear land and help build their roads and towns, as did the French in Louisiana after 1719. European immigrants to North America were never plentiful enough to meet the colonies' labor needs, and colonists throughout the region imported enslaved Africans to provide additional labor.

With few rights under European law, African workers could be far more brutally exploited than European immigrants and were often used to perform the most grueling tasks. Once the European colonies began to take shape, enslaved Black people continued to provide much of the backbreaking labor needed to make these settlements profitable, especially in the plantation colonies that developed in the South. Meanwhile, their presence shaped the character of the communities in which they lived, creating multicultural societies in which European colonists assigned enslaved Africans a distinct and inferior legal and political status.

The character of North American slavery changed dramatically between 1619 and 1740. As African captives arrived in ever-larger numbers and racial slavery became more entrenched, it became increasingly difficult for the enslaved to secure their freedom or cast off the growing stigma that Blackness and slavery held among the English colonists. Nevertheless, African people throughout the region slowly became African Americans. They developed a distinctive culture forged by the cross-cultural exchanges and biological intermixture that took place among Africans, Europeans, and American Indians; by the legal and social barriers that defined their caste; and by the experience of enslavement.

Slavery and Freedom in Early English North America

What range and variety of specialized roles did enslaved people perform in seventeenth- and early eighteenth-century English North America?

Seventeenth-century English colonists did not arrive in the New World expecting to people their settlements with enslaved Africans. In fact, they hailed from a nation where slavery was no longer practiced. "As for slaves and bondmen we have none," one English historian boasted in the 1570s. "Nay, such is the privilege of our country . . . that if any come hither from other realms, so soon as they set foot on land they become so free . . . all note of servile bondage is utterly removed from them."[4] Although enslaved Africans were not unknown in England, this claim was correct in underscoring that

English common law recognized no form of slavery. Villenage, an English form of serfdom, was extinct by the 1600s and would not be revived in the English colonies.

Instead, the earliest enslavers in the colonies adopted a new system of racial slavery that took several decades to emerge and still longer to give rise to the plantation societies that ultimately became established in the colonial South. For much of the 1600s, Africans who arrived in these colonies entered societies where servitude was far more common than slavery, and enslaved people and servants occupied a similar status. But by the beginning of the eighteenth century, enslaved Black people, who had proved to be more profitable, more plentiful, and far easier to exploit than white servants, predominated in the Chesapeake colonies of Virginia and Maryland. Meanwhile, slavery appeared in New England, where the Puritans and Pilgrims held small numbers of people enslaved, and fueled the growth of a plantation economy in colonial Carolina (Map 3.1).

Settlers, Servants, and the Enslaved in the Chesapeake

England's first successful permanent settlement in North America was founded in 1607 on Jamestown Island, about thirty miles from the mouth of Chesapeake Bay. Financed by the Virginia Company, a joint-stock company chartered by King James I in 1606 to establish an English settlement in the New World, Jamestown was not established with slavery in mind. The company's investors hoped to earn a profit on their shares, and the king hoped to expand England's imperial power.

Indeed, advocates of English colonization, such as the explorer Sir Francis Drake and the writer and armchair traveler Richard Hakluyt, had long maintained that English settlement of the New World could help rescue both Blacks and American Indians from the "Spanish tyranny" described by Bartolomé de Las Casas. Drake, who spent much of his career raiding the Spanish colonies for gold, undermined slavery whenever he could. For instance, he allied with a community of freedom seekers, or **maroons**, in his attack on the Spanish at Panama in 1572, and he liberated the enslaved when he sacked the Spanish town of St. Augustine in 1586.

maroons
Members of freedom-seeking communities; also known as cimarrons, from the Spanish *cimarrón*.

The first English colonists, not unlike Drake, hoped to live off the riches of the New World. Known as "adventurers," they consisted largely of gentlemen and soldiers. However, they would find no precious metals or valuable commodities in Virginia. Instead, they could barely feed themselves. Jamestown was surrounded by a fertile environment full of game and fish, but the colonists were unprepared to fend for themselves in Virginia's alien landscape. Inexperienced in hunting, fishing, or farming, they initially relied on local American Indians to supply them with corn. As a result, they soon wore out their welcome among the Indigenous inhabitants.

AP® skills

Applying Disciplinary Knowledge: How labor intensive was tobacco, and how important was tobacco to the Chesapeake economy?

On the verge of extinction by 1611, the colony was revived by the development of a lucrative **cash crop** that also created a new market for labor. The colonists experimented with planting a type of tobacco imported from South America. The experiment proved so successful that when Captain Samuel Argall arrived to take over Virginia's

cash crops
Readily salable crops grown for commercial sale and export rather than for local use.

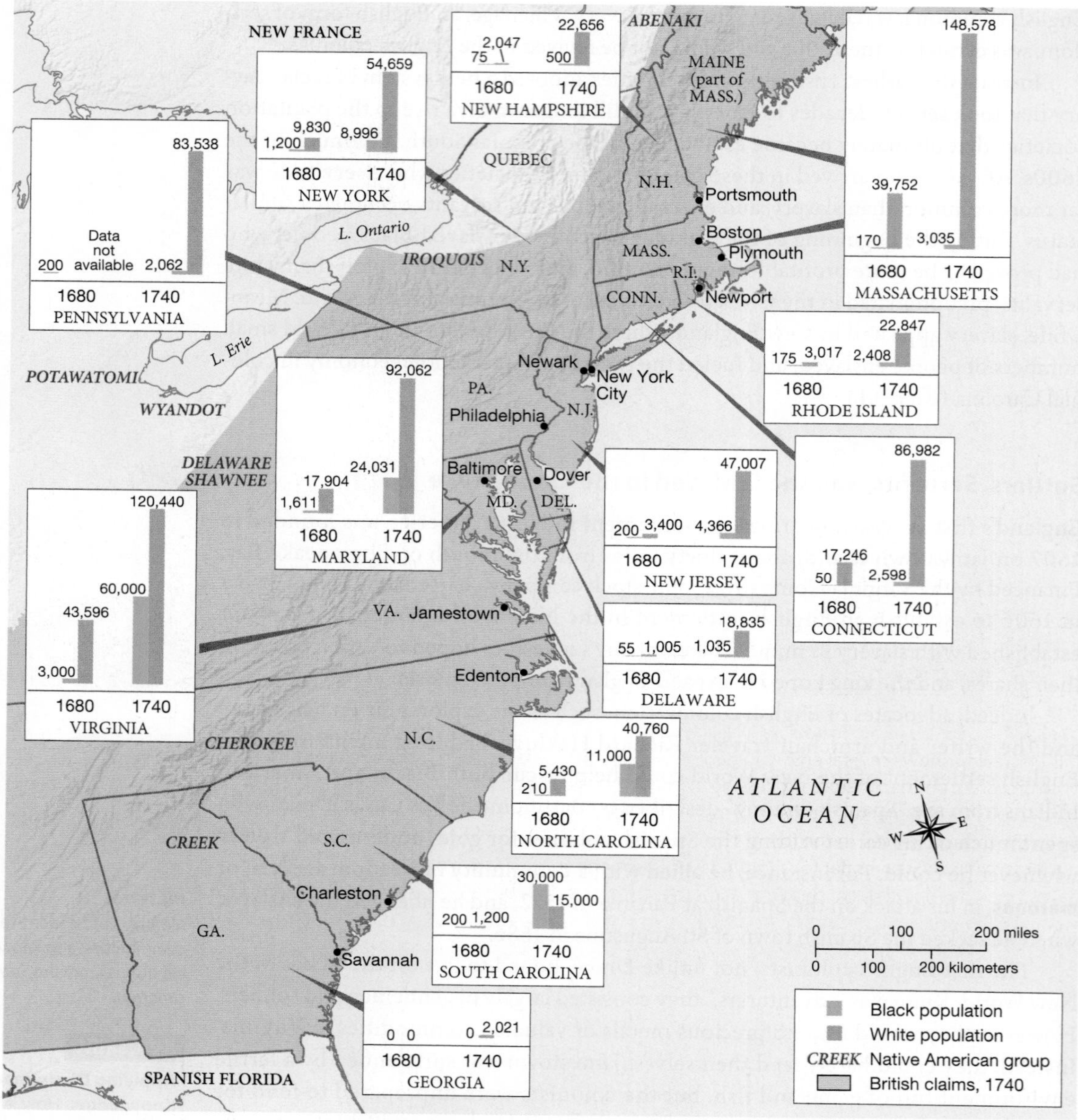

MAP 3.1 Distribution of Blacks and Whites, 1680 and 1740

This map shows the distribution of Blacks and whites in British North America in 1680 and 1740. **In which colonies did the vast majority of Black people live?**

Engraving of a Virginia Tobacco Farm, 1725
This engraving shows several enslaved people working in a tobacco shed. Tobacco leaves, which must be cured, or dried, before processing, hang above them, and the enslaved people prepare these dried leaves for the market. At the far end of the shed, an enslaved woman and child are pulling down the tobacco leaves. In the foreground, another woman strips the leaves off the stems. Behind her, a man rolls the leaves flat for shipping. To his left, another man cuts pieces of rope to tie up the leaves. **What details from this engraving reveal how essential enslaved labor was to the Chesapeake economy? Do you think the omission of the white overseer or supervisor was deliberate on the part of the artist? Explain why or why not.** *Pierre Pomet, A Complete History of Drugs, London, 1725 edition/Image Select/Art Resource, NY.*

governorship in 1617, he found "the market-place, and streets, and all other spare places planted with Tobacco."[5] Tobacco requires constant care throughout its long growing season and must be cleaned, rolled, and dried after it is harvested. But whereas the Spanish had been able to force the Aztecs, Incas, and other Indigenous populations to work for them, the English never managed to subjugate the Eastern Woodlands Indians in Powhatan's confederacy. Other Chesapeake tribes also resisted English rule and enslavement, although the colonists did acquire small numbers of enslaved American Indians from other regions. After 1619, they began to purchase enslaved Africans as well, but even enslaved Africans were in short supply during the colony's early years.

White servitude, rather than Black or American Indian slavery, initially predominated in colonial Virginia and its close neighbor Maryland, which English colonists founded in 1634. Both colonies were established at a time when England had an oversupply of landless rural laborers and urban paupers. Impoverished and unemployed, thousands of English and Scots-Irish servants were willing to travel abroad to cultivate tobacco in the Chesapeake. Most arrived in Virginia as **indentured servants**. As such, they were required to work for four to seven years to pay the cost of their transportation and maintenance.

indentured servants
White laborers who came to the English North American colonies under contract to work for a specified amount of time, usually four to seven years.

The enslaved Africans who ended up in the Chesapeake arrived no more than a few dozen at a time aboard privateers and other small boats. By all evidence, these early arrivals were initially incorporated into a labor force that was at least nominally free. African and European workers labored and lived alongside one another, ran away together, cohabited, and even intermarried. Early colonial documents list both groups as servants, which has long made the legal status of slavery in the early Chesapeake a matter of debate. During this time, enslaved Africans moved from slavery to freedom far more easily than they would in later generations.

Planters were not legally obligated to release Blacks from servitude, however, and by 1640, Virginia courts had at least tacitly recognized this fact. That year, when two white servants and one Black servant were captured in Maryland after running away from a Virginia farmer, they received dramatically different sentences. All three were sentenced to thirty lashes and extended terms of service. But whereas the white servants were assigned only an additional year of servitude, the Black servant — a man named John Punch — was ordered to "serve his said master or his assigns for the time of his natural Life here or elsewhere."[6]

AP® skills
Applying Disciplinary Knowledge: How did the legal status and rights of enslaved Africans begin to change in the Virginia colony in the mid-to-late 1600s?

Subsequent laws suggest that Blacks began to acquire a uniquely inferior status in the colony. A 1643 law decreed that African women — who were often assigned to field work rather than domestic labor — would, unlike English women, be taxed as laborers. A 1662 law made the enslaved status of Black women heritable, decreeing that "all children borne in this country shall be held bond or free only according to the condition of the mother."[7] Both laws ran contrary to the patriarchal assumptions of English common law, which defined women's work as domestic, and therefore not subject to tax, and used paternity rather than maternity to determine inheritance and assign fathers legal jurisdiction over their children. But the system of **chattel slavery** under development in Virginia required a different set of assumptions. Purchased as chattel, or movable personal property, enslaved Africans were legally equivalent to other forms of chattel, such as domestic animals and furniture. They had no rights of any kind and no legal authority over anyone — even their children, who belonged to their enslavers. (See AP® Working with Sources: Making Slaves, pp. 108–117.)

chattel slavery
A system by which enslaved people were considered portable property and denied all rights or legal authority over themselves or their children.

AP® exam tip
Be prepared to explain how American law affected the lives and citizenship rights of enslaved Blacks in the 1600s.

By using the mother's status to determine whether a child would be enslaved or free, Virginia legislators also resolved a number of practical questions. For instance, English law required servant women who became pregnant to work extra time to compensate their enslavers for the loss of their labor and expenses associated with the birth — sanctions that could not be imposed on enslaved women, who were already enslaved for life. Moreover, in making slavery heritable through the mother, the legislators prevented enslaved women from seeking liberty for their children by claiming freemen as the fathers, and they shielded white men from paternity claims. Finally, the new legislation clarified the legal status of enslaved women's children, which had previously been ambiguous. This ambiguity is evident in the case of Elizabeth Key, the illegitimate daughter of an enslaved mother and English father who petitioned for her freedom in 1656. Several courts ruled on her case, handing down different verdicts. She gained her freedom only after she married her English lawyer, who won her case before the colony's general assembly.

By the early 1690s, both Key's victory and her marriage would have been impossible. In addition to passing the 1662 law that made enslaved status heritable through the mother, Virginia lawmakers in 1691 all but outlawed interracial marriage. The new law decreed that any white person who married a "negroe, mulatto, or Indian" would be forever banished from the colony "within three months of such marriage." Ironically, though expressly designed to prevent "that abominable mixture and spurious issue which hereafter may encrease in this dominion," this measure attacked legitimate unions between the races rather than race mixture.[8] Intermarriage became a crime, but white men were neither barred nor discouraged from entering into sexual relationships with enslaved women.

As lawmakers created new laws, they also eliminated legal uncertainties that the colony's first generation of Black residents had used to seek freedom in the courts. As late as the 1660s, for example, Chesapeake courts remained undecided about the compatibility between slavery and Christianity. Black and American Indian converts became Christians with baptism, which gave them legal standing in colonial courts. But Christianity lost any further association with freedom in 1667, when the Virginia legislature passed an act explicitly exempting enslaved people from the freedoms normally extended to Christians. The "blessed sacrament of baptisme," the act noted, "doth not alter the condition of the person as to his bondage or freedome."[9]

As Virginia lawmakers solidified the legal status of slavery, forces outside the colony gave the institution new economic advantages. By midcentury, Virginia's supply of white servants was declining. The colony's reputation for exploiting and abusing servants had made it increasingly unappealing to immigrants, who were also in short supply as a result of the English Civil Wars, which diverted large numbers of Englishmen into military service. Meanwhile, local supplies of enslaved Africans were slowly increasing. The Dutch, who had established settlements on the Middle Atlantic coast starting in the 1620s, took advantage of shipping disruptions caused by the English Civil Wars to secure new commercial markets in the English colonies. They began to supply enslaved laborers to the Chesapeake, where the Black population soared from a few hundred in 1650 to four thousand in 1680. The English themselves entered the slave trade with the 1660 establishment of the Royal African Company, which held a monopoly over English trade with Africa until 1698, transporting between 90,000 and

AP® skills

Applying Disciplinary Knowledge: Can you explain the change that occurred in the number of white indentured servants willing to come to the Chesapeake colonies in the late 1600s? How did it impact the region's dependence upon the labor of enslaved Africans?

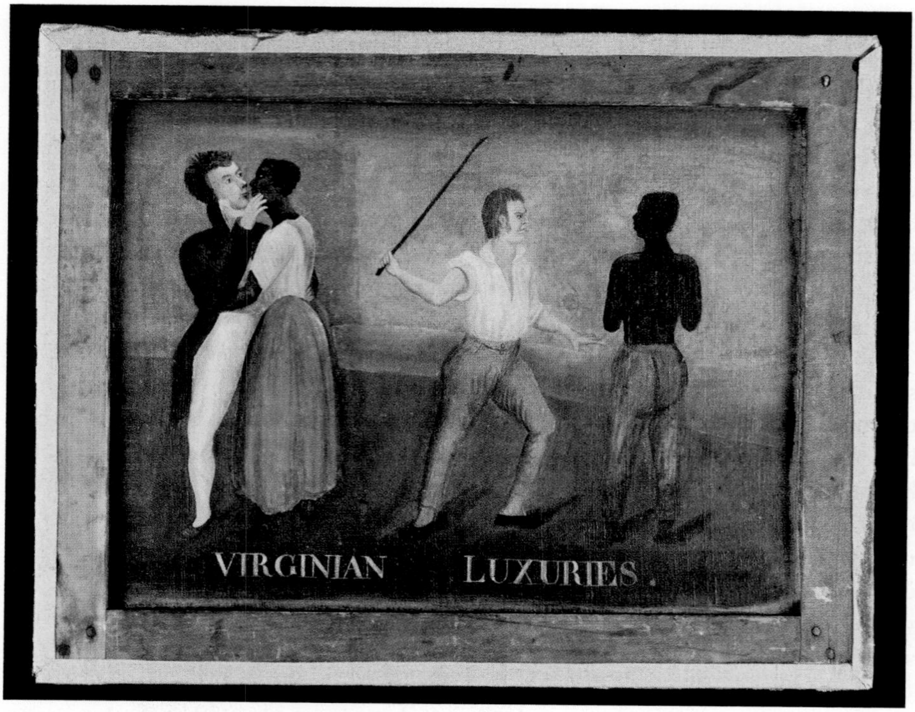

Sex, Power, and Slavery in Virginia
Painted on the back of another painting by an anonymous artist, this piece of art is unusual in its frank depiction of the two kinds of power white enslavers wielded over those they enslaved. On the left is an image of sexual power, which shows a well-dressed enslaver embracing an enslaved woman. On the right is an illustration of physical, brute power, seen as an owner or overseer prepares to whip an enslaved man's bare back. Although Virginia prohibited marriage between whites and Blacks and fined white women who gave birth to mulatto children, it did not discourage sexual relationships between white men and Black women, leaving much room for enslavers to take advantage of enslaved girls and women. **Explain how slave laws left enslaved girls and women open to abuse by their enslavers.** *Virginian Luxuries, c. 1825/The Colonial Williamsburg Foundation, Museum Purchase.*

100,000 enslaved people to English colonies in the New World. The rise of the Royal African Company and of other English entities after 1698 offered English colonists a steady and affordable supply of enslaved labor.

Chattel slavery also offered a variety of noneconomic advantages. Both enslaved people and servants ran away, but enslaved Africans were far easier to recover. Once they escaped beyond neighborhoods where they were known, white English-speaking servants could easily blend in with other European settlers and live as free people. By contrast, Black freedom seekers' color marked them as likely enslaved, making them easy to recapture. One newly arrived African discovered this in 1739 when he was committed to the James City County Jail. According to the *Virginia Gazette*, he was "a new Negro" who could not "speak English; his Name is understood to be Tom."

He was soon picked up by local authorities, who "suppos'd [him] to be a Runaway," and imprisoned to ensure that his "Owner may have him again."[10]

Enslaved Africans offered significant long-term advantages over servant laborers. Their bondage was permanent and hereditary, which meant enslavers could invest in a labor supply that could reproduce itself. Enslaved people also were subject to far stricter social controls than freemen, which made them appealing to white planters intent on maintaining their power. In contrast, by the 1670s, landless white ex-servants had become a disruptive force in the Chesapeake. Largely male, young, and discontented, they competed with more established colonists for land and often drifted from county to county, challenging colonial authorities, encouraging enslaved people to run away, and antagonizing local American Indian populations by encroaching on their land.

The dangers posed by ex-servants and their allies were vividly illustrated in a 1676 upheaval in Virginia known as Bacon's Rebellion. Led by Nathaniel Bacon, a wealthy colonist who commanded the support of an army largely made up of landless freemen, servants, and enslaved people, the rebellion pitted land-hungry colonists against the royal authority of Governor William Berkeley. At issue was the colony's American Indian policy, which was not aggressive enough to suit the many landless men who rallied around Bacon to make war on "Indians in generall," and especially nearby American Indian allies.[11] Charged with treason after an attack on several such groups, Bacon and his makeshift army attacked the colony's royal government, managing to capture Jamestown and set it on fire before English troops arrived to crush the rebellion.

Bacon's Rebellion underscored the dangers of importing thousands of white male servants into a colony that held few opportunities for them. The fact that Bacon had managed to mobilize both poor whites and Black bondmen also left officials worried about the common grievances uniting these two groups. Virginia's colonial government thus moved to forestall further challenges to its authority by sharpening the distinctions between servants and enslaved people. The legislature enacted harsh new laws allowing enslavers to kill anyone enslaved whom they deemed rebellious with impunity. At the same time, it curbed planters' power over white servants and freedmen by limiting the years of service that could be imposed on white servants and lowering the poll taxes that kept poor whites from voting. By empowering whites and subjecting Blacks to ever-stricter systems of control, the colonial legislature took significant steps toward deepening the racial divide and creating an entrenched system of racial slavery.

AP® skills

Applying Disciplinary Knowledge: How do you think the outcome of Bacon's Rebellion further impacted the Chesapeake's dependence on the labor of enslaved Africans?

The Expansion of Slavery in the Chesapeake

"They import so Many Negroes hither," the Virginia planter William Byrd wrote in 1736, "that I fear this Colony will some time or other be confirmed by the name of New Guinea."[12] Byrd's statement reflects an extraordinary demographic shift in the

BY THE NUMBERS Black and White Populations in the Seventeenth-Century Chesapeake

This graph underscores the fact that Blacks remained rare in the Chesapeake prior to the 1660s. While the number of Blacks increased steadily over the decades, this region's Black population nevertheless grew more slowly than its white population throughout most of the seventeenth century. **Describe the difference in the rate of population growth between Black and white colonists. Identify the reasons for the difference.**

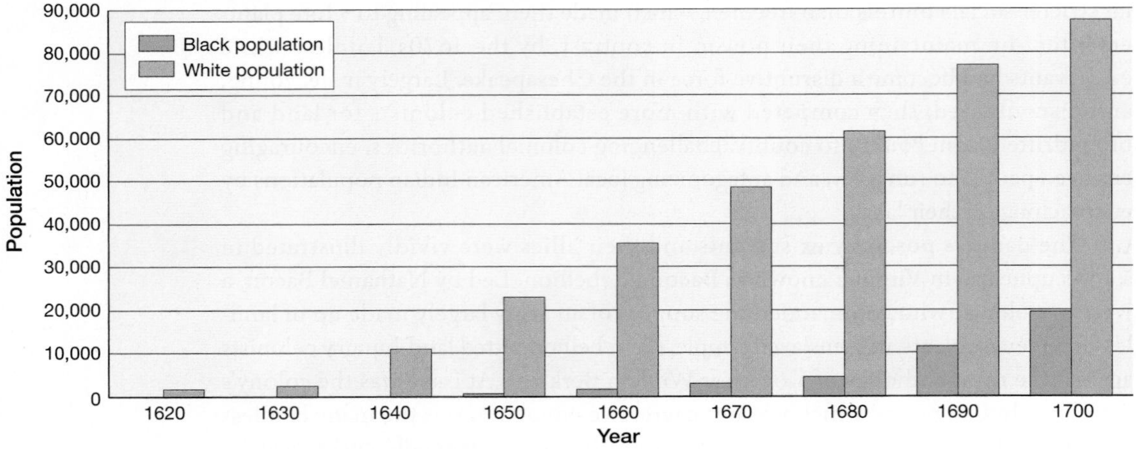

eighteenth-century Chesapeake. In 1680, Blacks constituted approximately 7 percent of Virginia's population, but by 1750, the colony's population was 44 percent Black. Maryland's Black population likewise increased from 9 percent to 30 percent during the same time span. (See By the Numbers: Black and White Populations in the Seventeenth-Century Chesapeake.) Both colonies, although initially populated largely by white servants, had built plantation economies that revolved around Black slavery.

The Africans who flooded the Chesapeake after 1680 had few of the opportunities afforded to early arrivals. Not many would achieve freedom, own property, or establish families. Increasingly drawn from the interior of Africa, the "new Negroes," as they were known, arrived by the boatload and were sold in small lots at numerous riverside wharfs bordering the Chesapeake. The region's farming was dispersed; even large landholders generally owned several small plantations, and few employed more than ten enslaved people on any single holding. The people they enslaved were thus widely dispersed as well, and planters usually assigned new arrivals to unskilled labor on their most remote upcountry holdings. The newcomers, who were not yet conversant in English or trained to do other work, cleared land and cultivated tobacco and other crops under the supervision of white overseers. Still ravaged by the transatlantic journey, one-quarter died within a year of arrival, and few managed to reproduce. In addition, two-thirds of the new arrivals were men, and many planters assigned those they enslaved to sex-segregated quarters where they had little chance to form family ties.

Drawn from different parts of Africa, the newcomers could not always converse with more acculturated enslaved people — or even with each other. The young Olaudah Equiano, who was shipped to Virginia in the 1750s, ended up in complete linguistic isolation. Most of his countrymen had been sold in Barbados, and he and his remaining shipmates landed in a part of Virginia where "we saw few or none of our native Africans, and not one soul who could talk to me."[13] Often the only English words the newcomers knew were the names assigned to them by their enslavers. They received no other instruction in the language.

Linguistically isolated, subjected to a harsh work regime, and forced to abandon even the names that tied them to their homelands, the newcomers struggled but somehow managed to survive. They forged a common language, which one Anglican minister described as "a wild confused medley of negro and corrupt English."[14] These Americanized, or **creole**, forms of communication probably represented a blend of English and several African languages. Newcomers also formed close bonds within their quarters. African-born enslaved people were far less likely to run away than American-born ones, and they rarely ran away alone. Instead, they fled with other Africans, sometimes with the goal of creating their own communities on the frontier.

Groups of African-born enslaved people sometimes conspired to revolt and escape together. When word of planned revolts in 1710 and 1722 reached the colonists, they arrested and executed the conspirators before the rebellions could take place. But one Sunday in the fall of 1730, when most plantation owners were in church, more than three hundred enslaved people organized into military groups and left their plantations for the **Dismal Swamp** — a coastal plain on Virginia's southeastern border. Taking shelter on the frontier, the freedom seekers "did a great deal of Mischief in that Province [of Virginia]," a visitor to the colony reported, before the colonists recruited some Pasquotank Indians to hunt them down.[15]

The defiance of the enslaved affected the colony's free people of color, who were often suspected of fostering slave rebellions. Virginia's small free Black population, mostly descended from the enslaved people who had secured their freedom during the colony's early years, also included **mulatto**, or mixed-race, descendants of unions between enslaved people and whites — some of whom had been born to a white mother and an enslaved father. Regardless of their origins, all lost some of their freedoms as a result of the slave revolts of the early 1700s, which led white colonists to define all Blacks as dangerous. The laws that Virginia passed in the 1720s disarming and disfranchising free Blacks and mulattoes reflected this conviction. With such laws, Virginia transformed a society once overrun by discontented white servants into a racially divided democracy in which only white people could be fully free.

The Creation of the Carolinas

Unlike the Chesapeake settlers, the planters who in 1663 established the colony of Carolina — which would split into the separate colonies of North Carolina and South

AP® exam tip

Be sure you can explain how African American language combined influences from diverse African cultures with local sources. How did this demonstrate the resilience of enslaved Africans?

creole
A language that originated as a combination of other languages; the term *creole* can also refer to people who are racially or culturally mixed.

Dismal Swamp
A coastal plain on Virginia's southeastern border that became a refuge for runaway freedom seekers in 1730.

mulatto
A person with mixed white and African ancestry.

Carolina in 1729 — arrived with plans to use a workforce of enslaved Africans to clear and cultivate their settlement. About half of these settlers hailed from the English colony of Barbados, where slavery was already an established institution. By the mid-seventeenth century, this Caribbean island was dominated by sugar plantations, where wealthy planters used enslaved labor to grow and harvest the demanding crop. The whites emigrating from Barbados to Carolina came in search of new land to plant and brought enslaved people with them. The major challenge for them was finding a suitable staple crop.

AP® skills

Applying Disciplinary Knowledge: Can you describe how African skills and agricultural knowledge helped the Chesapeake colonies prosper?

Rice cultivation, long popular in West Africa, flourished in South Carolina largely as a result of African expertise. The crop was unfamiliar to most English planters, who nonetheless saw its potential and consulted their enslaved workers on the possibility of growing it in Virginia as early as 1648. "The ground and Climate is very proper for it [rice] as our *Negroes* affirme," one colonist reported that year, explaining that "in their Country [it] is most of their food."[16] Experiments in rice cultivation foundered in Virginia but were far more successful in Carolina, which by the 1720s had begun to export nearly ten million pounds of rice a year. Drawing on their own expertise, enslaved Africans grew, harvested, and processed the crop using the equipment and techniques first perfected in West Africa.

task system
A system of enslaved labor in which enslaved workers were assigned daily tasks and permitted to work unsupervised as long as they completed their tasks.

driver
An enslaved person assigned to oversee the work of other enslaved people

Enslaved people on rice plantations worked under a **task system**, which involved minimal white supervision. Unlike enslavers in the Chesapeake, Carolina rice planters did not employ white overseers to direct gangs of enslaved laborers. Instead, low-country enslaved people worked largely under their own direction, completing daily tasks laid out by a Black **driver** — a bondman chosen to oversee the work of other enslaved people. Used only in rice-growing regions, the task system reflected Carolina planters' reliance on their bondpeople's knowledge of African cultivation methods. This reliance is also evident in planters' demand for enslaved workers from rice-growing parts of Africa, such as the Upper Guinea coast, Senegambia, and the Windward Coast. In response, slave traders promoted shipments from these regions, advertising "choice cargo[s] of Windward and Gold Coast Negroes, who have been accustomed to the planting of rice."[17]

AP® skills

Applying Disciplinary Knowledge: How did the task system offer enslaved Africans a degree of independence? How did enslavers try to use the task system to their advantage?

Under the task system, enslaved laborers were required to carry out specific agricultural tasks each day, after which they were free to work on their own behalf. This small measure of independence gave these workers an incentive to complete their daily tasks quickly, but it proved a mixed blessing. From the settlement of Carolina onward, enslaved people there were permitted to farm small allotments of land where they could raise livestock and grow provisions to feed themselves. But with the adoption of rice culture, the practice grew increasingly exploitative. Rather than supplying any rations to their enslaved workers, planters expected them to provision themselves during whatever time they had left after completing their grueling tasks in the rice fields. While whites observed the Sabbath, most enslaved people needed to work on Sundays just to survive.

As in the Chesapeake, Carolina enslavers had little interest in providing those they enslaved with religious instruction. Frustrated missionaries dispatched by the

TO BE SOLD on board the
Ship *Bance-Yland*, on tuesday the 6th
of *May* next, at *Ashley-Ferry*; a choice
cargo of about 250 fine healthy
NEGROES,
just arrived from the
Windward & Rice Coast.
—The utmost care has
already been taken, and
shall be continued, to keep them free from
the least danger of being infected with the
SMALL-POX, no boat having been on
board, and all other communication with
people from *Charles-Town* prevented.
Austin, Laurens, & Appleby.
N. B. Full one Half of the above Negroes have had the
SMALL-POX in their own Country.

Enslaved Africans and Rice Cultivation in Carolina
Carolina planters relied on African slaves' knowledge of and experience with cultivating rice to grow this challenging and lucrative crop. The extent to which the planters valued African expertise is illustrated in advertisements placed by slave traders promoting the fact that the slaves on a particular ship came from rice-cultivating regions of Africa. This advertisement, which appeared in an eighteenth-century newspaper during a smallpox epidemic, also assured potential buyers that careful measures had been taken to keep the slaves free of the disease. **What words, phrases, and marketing strategies does this advertisement use to advance the sale of enslaved people? How does it further contribute to enslavers' attempt to commodify African enslaved people?** *Sarin Images/Granger — All rights reserved.*

Anglican Church routinely proclaimed that the seven-day workweek of the enslaved made conversion "scarcely possible." "The slaves have not time to be instructed by the minister but on the Lord's Day," reported the minister Gideon Johnston in 1713, who noted the additional difficulty of gathering enslaved people together for religious instruction when "the plantations are so many and so remote and distant from one another." He was also not sure that such gatherings would be wise, given that they would provide the enslaved an "opportunity of knowing their own strength and superiority in point of number" and make them "tempted to recover their liberty."[18] Enslavers shared Johnston's worries and often discouraged missionary work among the people they enslaved as a result.

AP® skills

Applying Disciplinary Knowledge: How did enslaved Africans maintain aspects of their culture in the Carolinas?

Enslaved people in Carolina remained isolated and numerous enough to create a distinctly African world of their own. Many lived in self-contained enslaved communities on plantations that housed as many as one hundred enslaved people. Responsible for building their own quarters, they crafted mud-walled homes with palmetto roofs using techniques and materials that were common in sub-Saharan Africa. They cooked their food in handmade earthenware pots, similar to those used in Africa, which they either made themselves or purchased from American Indians. Predominantly African-born until the 1760s, some also bore physical marks of their heritage. These included facial scars known as **country marks**, which members of some African ethnic groups received at puberty to mark their origins, and filed or clipped teeth, which often served a similar purpose. African in their speech as well as their appearance, low-country enslaved people rarely mastered standard English.

country marks
Facial scars indicating particular African origins.

Enslaved Carolinians also retained African religious traditions, although their new environment may have reshaped some of their beliefs. The religious practices of early Black Carolinians are difficult to reconstruct in detail, since most white observers simply dismissed the enslaved as pagans "who knew nothing of the true God."[19] Like other West African peoples, the forced migrants often believed in magic and the existence of conjurers, who could heal the sick and kill their enemies. Such figures served as "Negro doctors" among the enslaved Carolinians, dispensing medicine, charms, and sometimes even poison. Conjurers were powerful figures, respected and feared even by whites, who when they fell ill sometimes accused Black conjurers of having caused their illnesses.

But other beliefs accorded with those of white Christians. One Anglican missionary reported that "our negro-pagans have a notion of God and of a Devil" and interviewed a "negro-pagan woman" who described her God as an omnipotent being who controlled "all things."[20] Such a God was a feature of many West African religions, which usually recognized a multitude of lesser gods and powerful ancestral spirits as well, but enslaved people in the New World may have placed an increasing emphasis on the idea of a single Supreme Being. Far from their villages and sacred places, with few priests to guide them, African-born captives and their descendants did not hold the same religious beliefs as their ancestors. Instead, they developed new, communal belief systems shaped by their experiences of exile, forced migration, and enslavement.

A brutal labor regime also shaped the character of Carolina's enslaved community. In Barbados, where many of the colony's enslavers originated, enslaved people began "work as soon as the day is light, or sometimes two hours before," and did not stop until sunset. Worked literally to death, the enslaved people who labored on the Barbados sugar plantations often died young and rarely left children behind. Subject to grueling labor clearing land and cultivating crops in swamps, African-born enslaved people in Carolina experienced similarly high mortality rates. Throughout much of the eighteenth century, deaths in the colony's enslaved population routinely outnumbered births. But low-country Blacks, like their counterparts in both Barbados and Virginia, did not always submit to their subjugation. Enslaved Carolinians sometimes escaped alone or with others to live in maroon communities on the colony's frontiers. By the early decades of the eighteenth century, however, the expansion of white settlement into North Carolina and Georgia made it increasingly difficult to avoid detection. As in Virginia, Carolina planters paid American Indian slave catchers to capture and return freedom seekers. Planters also instituted measures intended to prevent flight or rebellions. In 1690, South Carolina adopted the Barbadian slave code, which provided that enslaved people who ran away or defied their enslavers more than once could be whipped, slit through the nose, and branded with a hot iron. Three-time offenders could be castrated or hamstrung (have their leg tendons cut). Such punishments were not uncommon, according to one Huguenot missionary, who noted that enslaved people in South Carolina were often crippled or disfigured for "small faults."[21]

Africans in New England

The New England colonies, first settled in the 1620s and 1630s, never became home to a large number of enslaved people or relied on enslaved labor to sustain their economies. The region's cold climate and short growing season prohibited the cultivation of labor-intensive crops such as sugar, tobacco, and rice, resulting in little need for enslaved workers. Instead, most New England agriculture took the form of small family farms dedicated to the production of crops and livestock that could be tended by household members. Prior to 1700, Blacks constituted less than 1 percent of the region's population (or fewer than one thousand people), and they never amounted to more than 3 percent.

These limits to slavery's growth in New England were more a result of geography than of antislavery measures. The Pilgrims and Puritans who established the New England colonies came to the Americas to escape religious persecution in Europe, but their religious ideals did not preclude enslaving others. They looked to the Bible for guidance in establishing exemplary Protestant communities and accepted the slavery of both prisoners of war and foreign peoples as practices sanctioned by the Scriptures.

Accordingly, the Puritans and Pilgrims, who were frequently at odds with their American Indian neighbors, enslaved American Indians whenever they could. Early New England communities, which comprised a collection of coastal settlements, were also drawn into African slavery as a result of their commercial relationships with slaveholding colonies in the Caribbean. New Englanders shipped provisions such as wheat, beef, butter, fish, and cheese to these island colonies and received molasses, sugar, indigo, and other goods grown by enslaved people in return. Occasionally, they purchased Black people as well.

AP® skills

Applying Disciplinary Knowledge: Can you describe the New England colonies' legal position on slavery?

In addition, New England colonists also acquired enslaved Africans in exchange for American Indian prisoners of war, whom they often shipped off to slavery in the Caribbean. These exchanges required New Englanders to address slavery's legality earlier than other English colonists. Massachusetts was the first North American colony to legally recognize chattel slavery, which was sanctioned in the Body of Liberties the colonists compiled in 1641. This document, an enumeration of colonists' rights, permitted them to enslave "Captives taken in just warres" and purchase "such strangers as willingly selle themselves or are sold to us."[22] With the formation of the New England Confederation in 1643, the Plymouth, Connecticut, and New Haven colonies legally recognized slavery as well. New Hampshire, under the legal jurisdiction of Massachusetts until 1679, also began importing small numbers of enslaved people. Only Rhode Island, founded as a haven for religious dissenters in 1636, hesitated. Rhode Island colonists initially rejected permanent bondage, passing a law that limited the servitude of both Blacks and whites to ten years. But the law was never enforced, and Rhode Island went on to import more enslaved people per capita than any other New England colony. Moreover, Rhode Island merchants also entered the slave trade. Starting in 1700, they began sponsoring slaving voyages to Africa, which would ultimately carry more than 100,000 enslaved Africans from their homelands to mainland North America.

By the beginning of the eighteenth century, Boston's enslaved population had grown large enough to trouble some Puritans. "Numerousness of Slaves at this day in the Province, and the Uneasiness of them under their Slavery, hath put many upon thinking whether the Foundation of it be firmly and well laid," wrote the wealthy Boston merchant and judge Samuel Sewall, who had presided over the Salem witch trials in 1692–1693. The only one of three Salem judges to publicly regret his role in the conviction and execution of nineteen accused witches, Sewall issued a formal apology in 1697. But after quieting his conscience on that score, he became increasingly uneasy with himself for having "long neglected doing anything" about slavery.[23] In 1700, he issued the first antislavery tract published in New England, a pamphlet titled *The Selling of Joseph: A Memorial*, which questioned the morality of slavery.

Sewall's pamphlet may have been inspired by the freedom struggles of an enslaved man named Adam, who belonged to John Saffin, a New England merchant and politician. Saffin had pledged to free Adam after he completed a seven-year term of servitude, but Saffin later reneged on his promise, forcing Adam to petition for his freedom and inspiring white Bostonians to circulate a petition on his behalf. Sewall's antislavery tract did not take up Adam's case, however. Instead, it questioned the legitimacy of slavery as an institution, invoking the biblical tale of Joseph, who was sold into slavery by his jealous brothers. Joseph's enslavement was not lawful, natural, or just, wrote Sewall, who suggested that African slavery might be equally illegitimate. New England enslavers had no reason to believe that their bondmen and bondwomen were captured in just wars, Sewall maintained: "Every War is upon one side Unjust." Moreover, given the central role that European slave traders played in "forcing the *Africans* to become

Slaves amongst our selves," slavery as practiced in the Americas was little more than theft, with Africans being abducted from their homes and shipped abroad to enrich those who participated in the trade. Sewall argued that, though Africans might look different from Europeans, as "Sons of Adam" they should have full title to the rights of other men, including an "equal Right unto Liberty, and all other outward Comforts of Life."[24]

Sewall's challenge to the religious morality of slavery fell on deaf ears. Saffin spoke out in his own defense, issuing a pamphlet titled *A Brief and Candid Answer to a Late Printed Sheet, Entitled, The Selling of Joseph* (1701), which insisted that the Bible sanctioned "different Orders and Degrees of Men in the World." Blacks shared few of Joseph's virtues, Saffin maintained; they were "*Cowardly and cruel . . . Libidinous, Deceitful, False and Rude.*"[25] Saffin's invective provides an early example of the racist attacks on the character of Black people that whites frequently invoked to justify slavery. But most of Sewall's contemporaries did not even bother to respond to his argument that slavery was immoral and unchristian: they simply ignored his pamphlet.

The colonists saw slavery as a time-honored institution that had spiritual sanction. Even the colony's Puritan clergy were confident that Massachusetts provided enslaved people "all the liberties and Christian usages which the law of god established in Israell concerning such persons doeth morally require." Though subject to some forms of segregation, enslaved Africans were permitted to legally marry, were entitled to a trial by jury when accused of a crime, and were welcome to join New England churches. The influential Puritan minister Cotton Mather claimed that as long as enslavers were conscientious about providing religious instruction to enslaved people, Christianity "wonderfully Dulcifies, and Mollifies, and Moderates the Circumstances of [slavery]." An enslaver himself, Mather supplied special catechisms that other enslavers could use to guide enslaved Africans toward salvation and told them to promise those they enslaved that "*if they Serve God patiently and cheerfully in the Condition which he orders for them,*" they will be rewarded with "*Eternal Happiness*" in heaven. Mather also took pains to reassure enslavers that the "*Law of Christianity*" did not set the "*Baptised slave at Liberty.*"[26]

Though sanctioned by spiritual authorities such as Mather, the practice of enslaving grew only modestly in New England. Few African captives were imported into the region by New England slave merchants, who typically delivered their shipments to the lucrative slave markets of the Caribbean or the American South rather than to northern slave trading ports. Instead, New England remained a secondary market for enslavement, where traders disposed of a small number of Blacks who were too young, old, or sick to be sold elsewhere. Known in the trade as "refuse slaves," most of them arrived in the region after their shipmates had been sold in the Caribbean.

AP® skills

Applying Disciplinary Knowledge: What was New England's role in the triangular slave trade?

Venture Smith, a native of Guinea who was captured and sold into slavery at age eight, was shipped to Barbados with approximately 260 other African captives, only 200 of whom survived after smallpox broke out on board. All but four of the survivors attracted West Indian buyers; the rest sailed on to Rhode Island. Purchased and employed by the steward of the slave ship that brought him there, Smith was typical of the enslaved people who ended up in New England: He was too young to appeal to planters in the West Indies or in Britain's southern colonies, who sought brawny adult laborers for plantation work. Bought for four gallons of rum and a piece of calico, he was a speculative investment on the part of the ship's steward, who named him Venture and sent him home to his family to work as a domestic servant.

Young enslaved people such as Venture Smith, who were more affordable than adults, were welcome in northern markets. Buyers sometimes expressed a preference for young enslaved people — "the younger the better if not quite children," one buyer specified.[27] These people were often trained to perform domestic service and skilled work. Young Africans were in a better position to learn English, achieve a measure of acculturation, and master domestic tasks and other new skills than were the adult field hands the planters preferred. Young Venture's enslavers put him to work carding wool and pounding dried corn into meal until he grew old enough for farmwork; then he switched to working both in and out of doors.

Venture Smith grew up to be a strong, healthy, and hardworking man who married, fathered three children, and ultimately managed to purchase his own and his family's freedom. But many Blacks in New England did not share his fate. Mortality rates were high and birthrates low among the region's Black population during the eighteenth century. Those who survived had trouble finding partners and establishing families because most were male, and they tended to be employed by different households scattered across the region, which limited their contact with other Blacks. Although some Black men found African or American Indian spouses, marriage between Blacks and whites was outlawed in Massachusetts in 1705 and discouraged virtually everywhere else.

AP® exam tip

Be sure you can explain how the institution of slavery impacted enslaved African families in the New England colonies.

Even enslaved New Englanders who were lucky enough to find partners often lived in different households and may have hesitated to have children because they could not raise a family together. Enslaved children were not prized by northern enslavers, whose households were rarely large enough to accommodate enslaved families. Enslaved women were sometimes sold because of their reproductive potential, as one Connecticut ad for a sixteen-year-old girl indicates. Her enslaver wished to dispose of her "for no other fault but because she is like[ly] to be a good breeder."[28] Meanwhile, enslaved women who did have children could not always count on keeping them. New England newspapers also carried ads placed by enslavers who were anxious to get rid of the offspring of their enslaved women. "A Negro Child a few Days old, to be given away," stated as advertisement that appeared in the June 11, June 25, and July 4, 1730, editions of the *Boston Gazette*, while later the same year an ad in the *Boston Evening-Post* offered "a likely Negroe Child to give away" to "Any Person that has an Inclination to take it."[29] Usually "given away" rather than sold, these children were regarded as unwanted expenses by their enslavers who sometimes even offered a small fee to anyone willing take such a child off their hands.

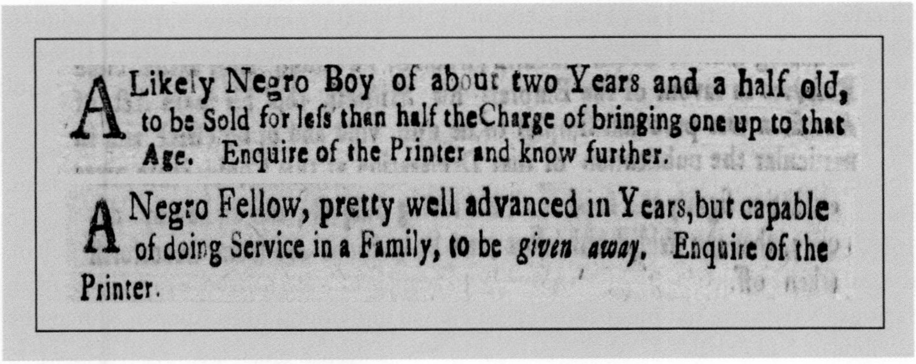

A Likely Negro Boy of about two Years and a half old, to be Sold for less than half theCharge of bringing one up to that Age. Enquire of the Printer and know further.

A Negro Fellow, pretty well advanced in Years,but capable of doing Service in a Family, to be *given away*. Enquire of the Printer.

Ads Posted by Enslavers in New England
In these two ads, from the *Boston Weekly New-Letter* of October 1748, enslavers attempt to rid themselves of an elderly Black man and the child of an enslaved woman. **What do these ads tell us about the value enslavers placed on the very young and elderly and of these enslavers' attitude toward enslaved families? How do they attempt to attract new enslavers for these people?** *The Massachusetts Historical Society.*

Family life was precarious for elderly Black New Englanders as well. While enslaved people in the prime of life had market value, like the very young, enslaved people who were too old to work were often regarded as liabilities by their enslavers. They, too, were sometimes given away or freed to take care of themselves when no longer useful.

Slavery in the Middle Atlantic Colonies

What range and variety of specialized roles did enslaved people perform in the Middle Atlantic colonies?

The settlement of North America's Middle Atlantic coast was pioneered by the Dutch, who began importing enslaved workers to the region in 1626, just a few years after the first white settlers arrived. Known as New Netherland, the region the Dutch settled included large portions of present-day New York, Connecticut, Delaware, and New Jersey, as well as parts of Pennsylvania. This land remained under Dutch rule only until 1664, when England, at war with the Dutch throughout much of the seventeenth century, seized the colony and opened the region to English settlement. Slavery continued and became more repressive under English rule.

Slavery and Half-Freedom in New Netherland

The Dutch colonization of New Netherland was led by the West India Company, a group of Dutch merchants who held a royal monopoly over Dutch trade in the Caribbean and the Americas, as well as dominion over Dutch participation in the African slave trade.

Chartered in 1621, the West India Company established its North American headquarters on the island of Manhattan in 1625. The settlement, known as New Amsterdam, was designed as a fur trading center that also supplied timber for Dutch ships and developed farms to feed Dutch settlers and sell food to the Netherlands. Anxious to reduce their tiny nation's need to import food from other European powers, the company's directors hoped that Dutch farmers would lead the agricultural settlement of New Netherland. But such hopes were dashed when the colony attracted only itinerant fur traders. In 1626, the West India Company began importing Black people to build New Amsterdam, the colony's capital. Owned by the company, the enslaved laborers were drawn from various Dutch slave trading regions and included individuals from Angola, Kongo, the Caribbean, and Brazil.

AP® exam tip

Be prepared to explain how essential African labor was to the establishment of New Netherland.

These laborers were crucial to New Netherland's survival. They cleared land and built New Amsterdam's fort, church, warehouses, sawmills, and farms. Unable to attract European migrants willing to clear, cultivate, and occupy their colony, the company's directors soon resolved that "Negroes would accomplish more work for their masters and at less expense, than farm servants, who must be bribed to go thither by a great deal of money and promises."[30] After 1629, the company's attempts to attract white immigrants included a promise "to supply the colonists with as many Blacks as they conveniently can."[31] The offer encouraged settlers to fan out throughout the lower Hudson Valley, creating settlements in what would later become Manhattan's five boroughs and moving across the river to present-day New Jersey as well. Slavery was even adopted by the Swedish colonists who established settlements along Delaware Bay in 1638. New Netherland's widely dispersed enslaved population grew steadily, rising to approximately 25 percent of the colony's population by midcentury.

That many of the enslaved people in the colony were considered the property of the West India Company rather than of individual enslavers complicated the status of the enslaved under Dutch law and left the terms of their service open to challenge. People enslaved by the company were quick to take advantage of this ambiguity and began petitioning for wages and suing for their freedom as early as the 1630s. Their litigation had mixed results: It won them wages but not freedom, and it further confused the legal status of slavery in the colony. But their efforts did establish that enslaved Blacks had the right to petition colonial authorities and gain access to Dutch courts. Between 1635 and 1664, Black colonists in New Netherland took legal action to gain the rights to earn money, buy land, and petition for freedom.

half-freedom

A status allotted primarily to people enslaved by the Dutch who helped defend New Netherland against American Indian attacks. Half-freedom liberated enslaved adults but not their children.

In the 1640s, such petitions led to a status called **half-freedom**. Primarily allotted to Blacks who had helped defend the colony against American Indian attacks, half-freedom liberated enslaved adults but not their children. These adults maintained obligations to the West India Company and were required to serve as wage laborers for the company when needed, but they were free to work for themselves at all other times, provided they paid a yearly tribute of "one hog, 23 bushels of corn, wampum, or fur pelts worth 20 guilders" to the company.[32]

Nieu Amsterdam, c. 1642–1643
Enslaved workers constructed roads and buildings in early colonial urban settlements such as New Amsterdam, which would later become New York City. Though rarely mentioned in modern-day histories of Manhattan, Black laborers can be seen in this depiction of early New Amsterdam. The central figures in this engraving are a Dutch woman, who appears to be holding a tray of fruits and vegetables, and a Dutch man holding a sheaf of tobacco. But behind them are several busy Black figures, as well as a view of the city's harbor. **How does this image portray the range and variety of labor enslaved people performed in New Amsterdam? What does it reveal about the role of enslaved labor in urban life during this era?** *New York Public Library/Bridgeman Images.*

Half-freedom was exploitative in that it exempted the Dutch West India Company from having to take responsibility for the enslaved adults it freed while allowing the company to retain the labor of their children and require enslaved families to pay corporate tribute. But it ultimately enhanced Black liberty in the Middle Atlantic region because many half-free Blacks successfully petitioned the company for full freedom shortly before the English took over New Netherland in 1664. Anxious to retain their allegiance, the company freed the Blacks' children and removed all other restrictions on their liberty. Some petitioners even received small plots of farmland. The legacy of

AP® skills

Applying Disciplinary Knowledge: What was half-freedom, what opportunities did it offer enslaved Africans, and how did it influence the size of the free Black population in the Middle Atlantic region?

half-freedom enabled one in five New Netherland Blacks to claim freedom when the Dutch surrendered the colony to the English.

Slavery in England's Middle Colonies

In 1664, the English seized New Netherland from the Dutch, laying permanent claim to New York, New Jersey, Delaware, and land that would later be incorporated into Pennsylvania. Since slavery was already well established in Dutch America, this acquisition greatly expanded the geographic and demographic scope of slavery throughout England's northern colonies. New Netherland was home to approximately 300 enslaved people and 75 free Blacks, who altogether constituted around 25 percent of the colony's 1,500 inhabitants. When the English took over, they continued to rely on enslaved Africans to supply much of the region's labor. King Charles II granted control of the colony to his brother James, Duke of York, and renamed the colony New York in James's honor.

Eager to develop New York as a market for enslaved people, James — who held a controlling interest in the Royal African Company — developed policies that favored the purchase of enslaved people from the company, such as the abolition of any property tax on enslaved people and the imposition of tariffs on domestic imports of enslaved people. James also put the colony under the control of English administrators, who made few efforts to attract European workers and permitted the Royal African Company to sell large cargoes of enslaved Africans directly to New Yorkers at fixed prices. When New Yorkers proved to be more interested in buying seasoned and acculturated enslaved people from the West Indies, the company accommodated their preferences by exchanging locally grown provisions for enslaved people from the Caribbean. New York's enslaved population grew steadily as a result of these measures, increasing at a faster pace than the colony's white population between 1698 and 1738.

Slavery in the other Middle Atlantic colonies developed along much the same lines. New Jersey and Delaware had enslaved populations when the English arrived and continued to import enslaved people thereafter. New Jersey, which was initially controlled by English proprietors appointed by Charles II, sought to encourage the settlement and cultivation of farmland by offering sixty acres per enslaved person to any colonist who imported enslaved people. New Jersey maintained a similar policy even after it became a formal colony in 1702. At this time, England's Queen Anne, who saw slavery as crucial to the success of the North American colonies, instructed the royal governors of all the colonies to make sure that the colonists had access to "a constant and sufficient supply of Merchantable Negroes at moderate prices."[33]

New York, New Jersey, Delaware, and Pennsylvania all contained agricultural areas where Dutch and English farmers used a mixture of enslaved and servant workers to grow a variety of crops. Farms throughout the region were small and largely dedicated to the production of wheat, corn, and other provisions, rather than tobacco, rice, or any of the other labor-intensive crops that predominated in the slave South. Even in

NEGROES,
TO BE SOLD
A Parcel of young able bodied Negro Men, one of whom is a Cooper by Trade, two Negroes Wenches, and likewiſe two Girls, one of 12 Years old, and the other 16, the latter a good Seemſtreſs, and can be well recommended.

Northern Slave Markets
Britain's Middle Atlantic colonies became lucrative markets for enslavers in the eighteenth century. Enslaved people proliferated in Northern port cities, where they performed a variety of skilled and unskilled jobs. They also played an important role in developing and cultivating the region's agricultural areas. This advertisement for a New York slave auction, which was published in the *New York Journal* or *General Advertiser*, announces the availability of five slaves, one a cooper by trade and another a seamstress. **Describe the types of skilled jobs enslaved people assumed in the northern colonies near port cities. To what extent were these skilled positions gender based?** *Granger/Granger — All rights reserved.*

ACTIVITY ▸ Revisit Your Prediction

In the AP® Unit Warmup (p. U2-E), you made a prediction about this image. **What were some key characteristics of slave auctions? What details from the ad support your response? What impact did slave auctions have on enslaved families? Support or revise your original prediction using evidence from this chapter.**

Delaware, where tobacco production flourished during the late seventeenth and early eighteenth centuries, large enslavers remained rare. Most of the colony's tobacco was grown by small farmers who enslaved only a few people.

In addition to working in the fields, the enslaved people of the Middle Atlantic cleared land; tended livestock; chopped wood; pressed cider; maintained fences, buildings, and grounds; and served as domestic workers as needed. Like the indentured servants with whom they often worked, they did not have their own quarters but were relegated to the household's back rooms, attics, closets, kitchens, and outbuildings. Enslaved people usually occupied the least appealing spaces, as noted in a 1742 advertisement for a Long Island estate whose farmhouse included "a room of 14 by 16 foot for white servants, over it lodging rooms and a back stairs; behind it a kitchen with a room fit for negroes."[34] Despite the importance of enslaved labor in these agricultural areas, port cities remained the largest enslaving communities in both the Middle Atlantic and New England colonies.

Founded in 1681 with the establishment of the Commonwealth of Pennsylvania, Philadelphia is a case in point. Both the city and the commonwealth were the brainchild of William Penn, an English-born **Quaker**, or member of the egalitarian English Protestant sect also known as the Religious Society of Friends. Penn and other Quakers embraced religious freedom as one of the commonwealth's founding principles. But they were slower to embrace other universal freedoms, and enslaved laborers soon proliferated in the port city of Philadelphia, which was home to a lively trade with England's Caribbean colonies. Among the many Philadelphia Quakers who

AP® skills
Applying Disciplinary Knowledge: How did the labor and living conditions of enslaved Africans in the middle colonies compare with the labor and living conditions of enslaved Africans in the Chesapeake and New England colonies?

AP® skills
Applying Disciplinary Knowledge: How did African skills and agricultural knowledge help the Louisiana colony prosper?

Quaker
A member of the Religious Society of Friends, a pacifist Protestant sect known for its commitment to social justice.

owned and employed enslaved people was Penn himself, who noted that he preferred enslaved Blacks to white indentured servants, "for *then a man has them while they live*."[35]

But slavery became controversial among the Quakers even during Penn's lifetime, which may help explain why Penn, who died in 1718, freed those he enslaved in his will. A group of Germantown Quakers issued the first American antislavery petition in 1688. Its authors were four Dutch-speaking Quakers who had left Europe to escape religious persecution. Dismayed to hear that some of their Quaker neighbors had decided to use enslaved labor, they drafted a petition deploring what they called "the traffik of men-body." "Is there any that would be done or handled at this manner?" they wrote in a document that displayed remarkable empathy for the enslaved. "We should do to all men like as we will be done ourselves; making no difference of what generation, descent, or colour they are. . . . To bring men hither [to America], or to rob and sell them against their will, we stand against. In Europe there are many oppressed for conscience-sake; and here there are those oppressed which are of a black colour."[36]

This early petition did not gain a broad audience or wide support. Instead, slavery continued to flourish in Philadelphia, where many Quaker merchants enslaved people, and imports of enslaved Africans helped sustain Pennsylvania's economic growth during periods when European wars curtailed white immigration.

Frontiers and Forced Labor

What range and variety of specialized roles did enslaved people perform on the colonial frontier?

In the early eighteenth century, slavery began to extend farther west and south into the frontier colonies located on the periphery of European settlement. These colonies, which included French Louisiana and Spanish Florida, were short of labor but too isolated and sparsely settled to maintain a secure enslaved labor force. Between 1717 and 1731, thousands of enslaved people were imported into the Mississippi valley, where the French had claimed a vast stretch of land known as Louisiana. But Louisiana planters were neither numerous enough nor powerful enough to establish a well-regulated plantation society, and they struggled to maintain control of the people they enslaved.

AP® skills

Applying Disciplinary Knowledge: What opportunities awaited freedom seekers from the Carolinas in Spanish Florida?

Colonists in Spanish Florida, founded in 1565, took a less ambitious approach, permitting slavery but never establishing plantations. The colony was instead founded as a military outpost to defend Spain's New World empire, and by the eighteenth century, it had also become a haven for freedom seekers from Carolina. The Spanish permitted these maroons to establish free Black communities; in return, the freedom seekers joined the colony's militia and helped protect its borders.

The British colony of Georgia, founded in 1732, was likewise founded to protect Britain's New World colonies and initially prohibited slavery for that reason. Georgia was meant to serve as a buffer zone between Carolina and Spanish Florida, and its crown-appointed trustees believed that slavery would threaten its military security.

They banned slavery until 1750, when they reversed the ban in response to a sustained campaign among the colonists to legalize slavery.

The early history of slavery in these three frontier settlements illustrates the immense importance of enslaved African laborers in the settlement of the American South, as well as the security risks such workers posed.

Slavery in French Louisiana

France's Louisiana colony, situated on the western frontier of most European settlements in the New World, extended from the Gulf of Mexico to the Canadian border. Claimed by the French explorer Robert de La Salle, who traveled down the Mississippi River in 1682, the colony attracted few European immigrants, but it facilitated a lucrative fur trade with the region's American Indian nations. By 1700, French investors and the French crown were eager to set up plantation settlements. They had established profitable sugar colonies on the West Indian islands of Guadeloupe, Martinique, and Saint Domingue during the seventeenth century and hoped to grow lucrative crops in Louisiana as well.

At this time, however, Louisiana lacked the workforce to sustain commercial agriculture. As of 1706, the colony had fewer than one hundred French and Canadian inhabitants, most of whom were fur traders and soldiers. The Company of the West Indies, which was granted a trade monopoly in the colony by France's King Louis XV in 1719, needed workers to clear land; build fortifications, roads, levees, and irrigation works; and cultivate the plantations that the company hoped to establish. But few French people were willing to immigrate to this frontier outpost. Virtually the only white migrants to the region were a few thousand convicts exiled from France for serious crimes, but even with these new additions, the colony's white population remained well under two thousand throughout the 1720s. Mortality rates among the immigrants were high, and those who survived often fled. Meanwhile, experiments with American Indian labor were disappointing. The American Indian of the region, who maintained an indigenous slave trade of their own, supplied Louisiana with more than two hundred enslaved people during its early years. But the enslaved American Indians provided "very little service," a French official complained in a 1709 letter to the French Ministry of the Colonies, adding that "they are not appropriate for hard labor like the blacks."[37]

With the colony teetering on the brink of collapse, France responded to the colonists' complaints by sending them shiploads of enslaved people directly from Africa. Most of the ships originated in Senegal, where the French controlled the slave trade, and they delivered almost six thousand enslaved people to Louisiana between 1719 and 1731. These forced migrants were crucial to the colony's survival. Approximately two-thirds came from Senegambia, where they had cultivated many of the same crops they would be required to grow in Louisiana. Officials from the Company of the West Indies were aware that rice cultivation was practiced in Africa, and they capitalized on their enslaved workers' familiarity with the crop. They instructed the captains who delivered the colony's first shiploads of enslaved people to deliver several barrels of rice seed as well and to make sure their human cargo included captives who knew how to grow rice. Within a year, rice was growing along large stretches of the Mississippi River.

Enslaved people from Senegambia were also likely crucial to the success of Louisiana's indigo and tobacco plantations. Whereas the French were unfamiliar with the cultivation of these crops, in Senegambia and other regions of West Africa, as one European traveler observed, "tobacco is planted about every man's house."[38] Most Senegambians knew how to plant and grow tobacco seedlings, which they cultivated alongside corn and beans, as was also customary among American Indians. Louisiana's indigo production was even more dependent on African expertise. A powerful blue textile dye most famously used for coloring denim, indigo is the product of a leafy subtropical shrub that originated in India but was grown in Africa during the era of the slave trade. Indigo plants could be cultivated and harvested by unskilled field hands, but transforming indigo into dye required skilled workers. Enslaved people in Louisiana and in other French colonies such as Saint Domingue, Guadeloupe, and Martinique pioneered the New World production of indigo dye in the seventeenth century, using techniques similar to those used in Africa.

Despite the success of the colony's crops grown by enslaved people, the future of Louisiana remained far from secure. Nearly one-third of the Africans imported to the colony died, and the remainder proved hard to control. Louisiana's Black majority outnumbered the colonists by a ratio of 2:1 and never fully accepted French rule. Some ran away and formed fugitive communities in Louisiana's dense woods and tidal wetlands; others sought refuge among their Natchez Indian neighbors, who were hostile to the French. Blacks fought on both sides of the Natchez uprising against the French in 1729–1730, and they plotted their own uprising shortly after the French defeated the Natchez. In 1731, a group of approximately four hundred Bambara captives (members of a Malinke-speaking people whose homeland was on the northern banks of the Senegal River) conspired to kill the French and take over the colony, but their plot was discovered. Even after the leaders of the conspiracy were publicly executed in the center of New Orleans, however, slavery in Louisiana remained a disturbing force. Imports of enslaved people all but ceased after 1731, when the Company of the West Indies resigned its monopoly over the region. The colony's enslaved population eroded further when colonists established a free Black militia to secure the colony from slave uprisings and American Indian attacks.

Code Noir
The slave code used in France's colonies in the Americas.

AP® exam tip

Be prepared to explain how the Code Noir impacted the lives and legal rights of enslaved Africans in the Louisiana colony.

Thus, instead of becoming a lucrative plantation society, French Louisiana remained a chaotic frontier settlement. Consequently, its racial hierarchies remained somewhat fluid. As a French colony, Louisiana had strict slave laws known as the **Code Noir**, or "Black Code," which had been issued in 1685 by Louis XIV for use throughout France's empire. (See AP® Working with Sources: Making Slaves, pp. 108–117.) Under the code, enslaved people who ran away three times were subject to capital punishment, but the French colonists were too few and too poor to kill off their workers — or even capture the enslaved when they ran away. Many freedom seekers ended up living out their lives in Bas du Fleuve, a maroon community located on the outskirts of New Orleans. One of the colony's fastest-growing settlements, Bas du Fleuve housed almost a third of Louisiana's Black population by 1763. Its residents, fugitives from slavery, were subservient to no one and made their living farming and supplying lumber to New Orleans sawmills.

Black Society in Spanish Florida

Like French Louisiana, Spanish Florida never developed large-scale plantation agriculture. The thinly populated military outpost had been established with the help of enslaved African workers supplied by the Spanish crown, but its enslaved population remained small after that. Given its military purpose, Spanish Florida needed soldiers more than it needed field hands. Enslaved people constructed and maintained the region's forts, grew their own food, were assigned tasks as needed, and served in the colony's militia, which also enlisted free Blacks. But both free and enslaved Black people had a high degree of autonomy in Spanish Florida, which made the colony an attractive destination for freedom seekers from Carolina. The first arrived in 1687, just a few decades after Carolina was founded. That year, eight men, two women, and a nursing child made their way to St. Augustine in a stolen canoe, requesting baptism in the "true faith" of the Catholic Church.

These freedom seekers successfully appealed to the church, which claimed religious authority over the lives of all its members, both free and enslaved. The Spanish governor Diego de Quiroga y Losada welcomed them and refused to return them to their English enslavers, maintaining that they were religious refugees and even offering to buy them from the Carolina official who traveled to St. Augustine to reclaim them. When word of these negotiations spread to enslaved people back in Carolina, they began making their way to the Spanish colony in greater numbers. In 1690, Carolina's governor complained to the Spanish that his colony's enslaved people ran off "dayly to your towns."[39] He received little satisfaction. Intent on defending their own colony and more than willing to undermine English colonies in the New World, the Spanish continued to welcome the refugees. In 1693, Spain's King Charles II issued a royal proclamation granting liberty to all freedom seekers who wished to convert to Catholicism. Not surprisingly, this policy infuriated English officials in Carolina, who launched military assaults on St. Augustine in 1702 and 1728. The Spanish colony was able to draw on its growing population of freedom seekers to rebuff these attacks and to retaliate against the English.

Freedom seekers from Carolina also joined and sometimes even led raids on their former enslavers, freeing more enslaved people, who they brought back to St. Augustine. They also fought for their own freedom and autonomy in Florida. Freedom seekers were initially subject to reenslavement by Spanish colonists who

AP® exam tip

Be sure you can explain the historical significance of Fort Mose.

Africans in St. Augustine
This 1673 engraving shows enslaved Black people engaged in a variety of tasks, including escorting the Spanish to their ships. A little over a decade later, the first recorded freedom seekers from Carolina would successfully seek sanctuary in Spanish Florida, where they were welcomed by Spanish officials. Spanish authorities refused to return such fugitives to the English, which made St. Augustine a prime destination for those fleeing slavery. **Explain the significance of Fort Mose and how it provides insight into the different ways in which enslaved Africans resisted the institution of slavery.** *Private Collection/Peter Newark American Pictures/Bridgeman Images.*

ignored the king's promise to free enslaved people seeking religious sanctuary. After petitioning colonial officials for decades, the freedom seekers finally received a grant of unconditional freedom in 1738. That year, they also established their own settlement, the town of Gracia Real de Santa Teresa de Mose, which became known as **Fort Mose**. Located two miles outside St. Augustine, this settlement was the first free Black town within the present-day borders of the United States. Founded by a population of about a hundred freedom seekers, it served the interests of its inhabitants as well as those of the Spanish crown. The town was strategically situated to warn St. Augustine residents of any foreign attack, and it offered the refugees a comfortable home on land where they could support themselves. Surrounded by fertile fields and forests, Fort Mose was bisected by a saltwater river with an abundant supply of fish and shellfish. The freedom seekers' sanctuary would not survive for long, however. Captured and destroyed by the British in 1739 during the War of Jenkins's Ear — a dispute between Britain and Spain over land claims — the fort was resettled only briefly in the 1750s.

Fort Mose
The first free Black town within the present-day borders of the United States, located within what is now Florida and founded by Blacks who had escaped enslavement in the Carolina colony.

Slavery and Servitude in Early Georgia

Just north of Spanish Florida lay a frontier colony designed to act as a buffer and protect its founders' imperial interests. Georgia's colonization was led by a group of British trustees who envisioned a colony populated by lower-class whites. Indentured servants were welcome, but enslaved laborers were not, since they could not be expected to defend the colony against its American Indian and Spanish enemies. If slavery was permitted in Georgia, one of the colony's founders noted in 1732, "there would not be 50 out of 500 remain[ing] in two months time, for they would fly to the Spaniards [in Florida]."[40] Royal officials agreed, instituting a ban on slavery. But few of Georgia's early settlers ended up supporting the ban. No whites could be found to perform the backbreaking work required to clear Georgia's land for production. Even the indentured servants fled to South Carolina and other British colonies rather than serve out their terms in Georgia. Meanwhile, the settlers who stayed lobbied relentlessly to end the ban on enslaved labor. Enslaved Africans were, they maintained, "the only human Creatures proper to improve our Soil," and without them, the colonists were doomed to live in "Primitive Poverty."[41]

AP® skills

Applying Disciplinary Knowledge: What factors contributed to the change in the Georgia colony's legal stance on slavery?

Other than the trustees, the only colonists in favor of maintaining the ban on slavery were the Salzburgers, a group of approximately three hundred German-speaking Protestants who migrated to Georgia in 1734. The Salzburgers hailed from the Catholic principality of Salzburg, Austria, which expelled its Protestant population in 1731. This small, hardworking community of friends and relatives, who came to Georgia with the support of the region's trustees, saw no reason to object to the ban even after their British neighbors told them that it was "impossible and dangerous for White People to plant and manufacture any rice, being a Work only for Negroes."[42] Instead, to prove that the colony could prosper without forced labor, they planted rice and soon mastered its cultivation to the point of producing a surplus.

Their opposition to slavery, however, was more practical than moral. They worried that slavery would weaken their close-knit sect by scattering its members across large plantations. They were also alarmed by reports of Black uprisings in the West Indies, which convinced them that slavery was a dangerous institution. Shortly after the Salzburgers arrived in America, their pastor, Johann Martin Bolzius, heard that enslaved people on St. John in the Virgin Islands had massacred "all the white people that were their masters," and he wondered whether the "great convenience" of enslaved labor was not offset by the dangers that it posed. His worries were compounded a few weeks later when one of the Salzburgers' supporters in South Carolina lent them a dozen enslaved Africans to help them clear land and build roads in their settlement of Ebenezer, Georgia. Bolzius was dismayed by the violent conflicts between the Black workers and the white overseer who was sent to supervise them. He objected when the overseer whipped several of the Blacks and was still more horrified when one enslaved man threatened the overseer with an ax.

"The departure of the Negroes has deprived us of some advantage," Bolzius wrote after the enslaved people returned to South Carolina, "but it has also freed us of much disquietude and worry."[43] Similar anxieties colored the Salzburgers' anti-slavery petitions. They knew "by Experience," they told the Georgia trustees, "that Houses and Gardens will be robbed always by them, and White People are in Danger of Life because of them."[44]

The Stono Rebellion

AP® exam tip

On the AP® Exam, you will need to be able to explain how enslaved Africans resisted the institution of slavery.

In 1739, the Salzburgers' fears were borne out by a slave uprising that began near the Stono River in St. Paul's Parish, South Carolina, and took the lives of about twenty whites and more than forty African Americans. On the morning of Sunday, September 9, approximately twenty enslaved people gathered on the banks of the Stono. They broke into a nearby store that sold guns and ammunition, killed the shopkeepers, and armed themselves with guns, axes, and clubs. They then headed south, killing the whites they encountered and burning their homes to the ground. The rebels spared the life of a local tavern owner who was known to be kind to those he enslaved and overlooked one planter who was hidden by the people he enslaved, but they were otherwise merciless, massacring entire families. Joined by other enslaved people as they marched, the rebels were approximately sixty strong and ten miles from home when they were finally tracked down by a hastily assembled patrol of armed whites late that afternoon. More than forty enslaved people were killed before the **Stono rebellion** was finally suppressed. Most of those who escaped were eventually captured or killed.

Stono rebellion
(1739): A slave rebellion that took place near South Carolina's Stono River in 1739. It was led by enslaved people who hoped to find freedom in Spanish Florida. The rebels killed about twenty whites before they were captured and subdued.

The rebels, who were executed without trial, left little evidence of what had inspired the largest uprising of enslaved people in the British colonies. The rebellion occurred at the end of a long, hot summer marked by a malaria epidemic in Charleston, and amid heightened political tensions between Britain and Spain. Exhausted by the heat, depleted by the epidemic, and apprehensive about a possible war with Spain, the colony's white population was unusually troubled, which may have influenced the timing of the rebellion. The early eighteenth century's traffic in Black Christians from Kongo also could have played a role. The kingdom of Kongo, once ruled by a Catholic king and his son, had collapsed by the 1710s, leaving many Catholic converts in its wake. Enslaved people brought to South Carolina from this region would have been alert to Spanish proclamations offering freedom and sanctuary to Catholics. The rebels also may have seized on colonial troubles as an opportunity to fight their way to refuge in St. Augustine. Few made it that far, but their rebellion was a wake-up call to white colonists across the South. "Evil brought home to us, within our very Doors, awaken'd the Attention of the most Unthinking," a committee of South Carolina legislators noted, summarizing the impact of the rebellion.[45]

However, the colonists' commitment to slavery remained unshaken. Colonial officials were convinced that "the *Negroes* would not have made this Insurrection had they not depended on *St. Augustine* for a Place of Reception afterwards," which allowed them to blame the Spanish. The officials moved quickly to pass a slave code to discourage further uprisings.[46] South Carolina's 1740 Negro Act was designed to keep the colonists' enslaved people in "due subjection and obedience" and underscored that whites were free to kill rebellious Blacks without a trial. It also allowed colonists to keep enslaved people under constant surveillance by empowering all whites to police enslaved people's movements. After 1740, enslaved people could no longer travel beyond the boundaries of their enslavers' plantations without a ticket or pass granting permission. All whites were authorized to investigate and whip enslaved people caught without a pass and could "lawfully" kill any enslaved person who physically resisted interrogation or punishment.[47] Moreover, the colony's governor also enlisted the help of local indigenous tribes to retrieve people who did manage to escape by instituting a system of rewards that encouraged Chickasaw and Catawba Indians to hunt down freedom seekers.[48]

Despite these precautions, the Stono rebellion was not British America's first slave revolt, nor would it be the last. "Freedom wears a cap that Can without a Tongue, Call together those who wish to shake of[f] the fetters of slavery," Lieutenant Governor Alexander Spotswood warned Virginia planters in 1710 after they hanged, quartered, and decapitated two enslaved people who had conspired to revolt. The planters divided the miscreants' corpses over several counties to ensure that their body parts were on display in all of the "most publick places" — reserving the head of one rebel for exhibition in the colony's capital. Their goal was to "inspire such a terror in the other Negroes, as will keep them from forming such designs for the future," but Spotswood was not convinced that violence alone could secure the safety of the colonists. After all, even the "Babel of Languages" spoken among the African rebels had not prevented them from conspiring to revolt. The colonists must suppress all "consultations" among Black people, Spotswood argued, lest they come together around a common love of liberty.[49]

CONCLUSION
Regional Variations of Early American Slavery

In the first half of the eighteenth century, slavery became ever more entrenched in British America. Though unfamiliar to the continent's earliest English settlers, slavery was eventually adopted by colonists from New England to Georgia, who employed enslaved people to perform many different kinds of work. Enslaved labor was most vital to sustaining the settlement and growth of the southern colonies, where landowning enslavers built a plantation economy dedicated to the production of lucrative cash crops. Colonists farther north were less dependent on enslaved labor, but enslaved people were common in the region's port cities and in its most productive agricultural areas.

Africans in early America led lives that were shaped by the regional economies in which they found themselves. Culturally isolated enslaved New Englanders were more likely to learn English and adopt European ways than their counterparts in Georgia and South Carolina, who often lived in African enclaves on remote plantations and retained many of their West African cultural practices and beliefs. Most enslaved people in the southern colonies worked as field hands, while those in New England and the Middle Atlantic were as likely to perform domestic service as farmwork.

Regardless of region, however, enslaved life remained a struggle. Enslaved men predominated in many areas, and not all of them were able to find mates or establish families. New shipments of captive Africans became increasingly common in the southern colonies, bringing in people for whom the traumas of the Middle Passage were still fresh. Moreover, both recent arrivals and native-born enslaved people were increasingly subjected to harsh discipline and careful surveillance. Faced with a growing enslaved population, colonial legislatures across British America enacted strict slave codes that outlawed gatherings of enslaved people, punished slave rebellions, and instituted armed slave patrols. Only in sparsely populated frontier settlements such as French Louisiana and Spanish Florida, where whites relied on people of color to help them defend their borders, did enslaved Blacks retain some degree of freedom.

Even so, throughout the colonies, enslaved Africans proved difficult to control. The strict slave codes introduced in Carolina and other British colonies did little to suppress enslaved resistance. Instead, during the second half of the eighteenth century, freedom would only become more alluring to African Americans. As the social and political turmoil of the Revolutionary era disrupted slavery and the slave trade, it offered large numbers of individual bondmen and bondwomen opportunities to escape their condition. The era's debates over slavery, liberty, and the rights of man would supply enslaved Africans throughout the colonies with an even more dangerous weapon: a revolutionary rhetoric that could be mobilized against all forms of tyranny, including slavery.

CHAPTER 3 REVIEW ▸ PRACTICING AP® SKILLS

AP® ESSENTIAL VOCABULARY AND SOURCES

**Essential terms and required sources from the AP® Course are marked with an asterisk.*

maroons* p. 77
cash crop p. 77
indentured servants p. 80
chattel slavery* p. 80
creole* p. 85
Dismal Swamp* p. 85
mulatto p. 85
task system* p. 86
driver* p. 86
country marks p. 88
half-freedom p. 94
Quaker p. 97
Code Noir* p. 100
Fort Mose* p. 102
Stono rebellion (1739)* p. 104

The Codification of Slavery and Race in Seventeenth-Century Virginia, 1630–1680 **(Laws of Virginia, Act XII, General Assembly, 1662)*** p. 110

The South Carolina Slave Code*, 1740 (Excerpts from the South Carolina Slave Code, 1740) p. 113

The Black Code of Louisiana*, 1724 (Articles 1–10 from the Louisiana Slave Code [Code Noir, or Black Code], 1724) p. 115

partus sequitur ventrem* p. G-17

APPLYING DISCIPLINARY KNOWLEDGE: ESSENTIAL QUESTIONS

1. Describe the regional variations of enslaved labor and systems throughout Britain's North American colonies. What were the causes for variations among the regions?
2. Explain how colonial slave codes impacted the rights, freedoms, and securities of enslaved people and families.
3. What tactics and strategies did enslaved people use in the colonies to secure their freedom? Was freedom more accessible in certain regions? If so, where and why?
4. Explain key effects of the asylum offered by Spanish Florida in the seventeenth and eighteenth centuries.

SUGGESTED REFERENCES

Slavery and Freedom in Early English North America

Berlin, Ira. *Generations of Captivity: A History of African-American Slaves.* Cambridge: Belknap Press of Harvard University Press, 2003.

Breen, T. H., and Stephen Innes. *"Myne Owne Ground": Race and Freedom on Virginia's Eastern Shore, 1640–1676.* New York: Oxford University Press, 1982.

Brown, Kathleen M. *Good Wives, Nasty Wenches, and Anxious Patriarchs: Gender, Race, and Power in Colonial Virginia.* Chapel Hill: University of North Carolina, 1996.

Carney, Judith Ann. *Black Rice: The African Origins of Rice Cultivation in the Americas.* Cambridge: Harvard University Press, 2001.

Gomez, Michael A. *Exchanging Our Country Marks: The Transformation of African Identities in the Colonial and Antebellum South.* Chapel Hill: University of North Carolina Press, 1998.

Knight, Frederick. *Working the Diaspora: The Impact of African Labor on the Anglo-American World, 1650–1850.* New York: New York University Press, 2010.

Morgan, Jennifer L. *Laboring Women: Reproduction and Gender in New World Slavery*. Philadelphia: University of Pennsylvania Press, 2004.

Morgan, Philip D. *Slave Counterpoint: Black Culture in the Eighteenth-Century Chesapeake and Lowcountry.* Chapel Hill: University of North Carolina Press, 1998.

Parent, Anthony S., Jr. *Foul Means: The Formation of a Slave Society in Virginia, 1660–1740.* Chapel Hill: University of North Carolina Press, 2003.

Warren, Wendy. *New England Bound: Slavery and Colonization in Early America* (New York: Liveright, 2017).

______. "'Thrown Upon the World': Valuing Infants in the Eighteenth-Century North American Slave Market," *Slavery and Abolition* 39, no. 4 (2018): 623–841.

Wood, Peter H. *Black Majority: Negroes in Colonial South Carolina from 1670 through the Stono Rebellion.* New York: Norton, 1996.

Slavery in the Middle Atlantic Colonies

Berlin, Ira, and Leslie Harris, eds. *Slavery in New York.* New York: New Press, 2005.

Essah, Patience. *A House Divided: Slavery and Emancipation in Delaware, 1638–1865.* Charlottesville: University of Virginia Press, 1996.

Foote, Thelma Wills. *Black and White Manhattan: The History of Racial Formation in Colonial New York City.* New York: Oxford University Press, 2004.

Harris, Leslie M. *In the Shadow of Slavery: African Americans in New York City, 1626–1863.* Chicago: University of Chicago Press, 2004.

Hodges, Graham Russell. *Root and Branch: African Americans in New York and East Jersey, 1613–1863.* Chapel Hill: University of North Carolina Press, 1999.

______. *Slavery and Freedom in the Rural North: African Americans in Monmouth County, New Jersey, 1665–1865.* Lanham, MD: Rowman & Littlefield Publishers, 1997.

Williams, Oscar. *African Americans and Colonial Legislation in the Middle Colonies.* London: Routledge, 1998.

Williams, William H. *Slavery and Freedom in Delaware, 1639–1865.* Lanham, MD: Rowman & Littlefield Publishers, 1999.

Frontiers and Forced Labor

Deagan, Kathleen A., and Darcie A. MacMahon. *Fort Mose: Colonial America's Black Fortress of Freedom.* Gainesville: University Press of Florida, 1995.

Hall, Gwendolyn Midlo. *Africans in Colonial Louisiana: The Development of Afro-Creole Culture in the Eighteenth Century.* Baton Rouge: LSU Press, 1995.

Hoffer, Peter Charles. *Cry Liberty: The Great Stono River Slave Rebellion of 1739.* New York: Oxford University Press, 2010.

Landers, Jane. *Black Society in Spanish Florida.* Urbana: University of Illinois Press, 1999.

Smith, Mark Michael, ed. *Stono: Documenting and Interpreting a Southern Slave Revolt.* Columbia: University of South Carolina Press, 2005.

Usner, Daniel H., Jr. "From African Captivity to American Slavery: The Introduction of Black Laborers to Colonial Louisiana." *Louisiana History* 20, no. 1 (1979).

Wood, Betty. *Slavery in Colonial Georgia, 1730–1775.* Athens: University of Georgia Press, 2007.

Young, Jeffrey Robert. *Domesticating Slavery: The Master Class in Georgia and South Carolina, 1670–1837.* Chapel Hill: University of North Carolina Press, 1999.

Making Slaves

To transform African captives into chattel slaves, the English colonists developed legal codes that established slavery, regulated who could be enslaved, and assigned free Blacks a distinctive legal status. Virginia, one of the first colonies to codify slavery, led the way by passing laws determining how slavery would pass from parent to child and establishing that enslaved Africans who converted to Christianity would not be entitled to the same freedoms as other Christians. The colony's law books also include several rulings that some historians have read as clear evidence that the English colonists always disapproved of interracial sex. Other scholars have suggested that cases such as the 1630 ruling sanctioning Hugh Davis for "lying with a negro" might have been judgments against extramarital sex or homosexuality. Since the legal proceedings were not recorded, the specific circumstances they addressed remain unknown. How much definitive information can we draw from such legal cases?

Meanwhile, the Massachusetts Bay colony's Puritan rulers also addressed slavery in their laws. Enslaved people were not numerous in early Massachusetts, but the colony's first legal code did authorize the enslavement of "Captives taken in just warres, and such strangers as willingly selle themselves or are sold to us."[50] Enslavers this code further stipulated, should follow biblical precepts on the "Christian usages" of enslaved people.

key point

Although the specific characteristics of the institution of slavery within each of the 13 colonies were shaped by regional factors, all of the 13 colonies established legal codes to regulate the freedoms and rights of enslaved people. Quiet often, these laws also impacted the rights of white colonists in efforts to minimize interracial relations.

In the long run, however, slavery would require far more complicated legal relations and would generate laws regulating every aspect of enslaved people's behavior. These laws governed the behavior of whites as well and typically included sanctions against interracial marriage, measures prohibiting whites from sheltering freedom seekers, and provisions requiring enslavers to supply food and clothing to enslaved people. Though frequently disregarded by both enslavers and the enslaved, the legal codes regulating slavery gave enslavers license to govern those they enslaved and almost unlimited powers of discipline.

The following documents include excerpts from laws developed by English colonists to regulate the slave systems in Virginia, Massachusetts, New Jersey, and South Carolina, as well as an image and excerpt from the legal Code Noir — or Black Code — used to regulate slavery in France's colonies.

AP® argumentation

DBQ Practice: Explain how colonial slave laws restricted the lives of enslaved people. Use at least two of the documents to support your response.

DOCUMENT 1
AP® source

The Codification of Slavery and Race in Seventeenth-Century Virginia, 1630–1680

Determining the legal status of Blacks in early Virginia remains controversial because laws regulating slavery do not appear in the colony's legal statutes until the 1660s — more than forty years after the first enslaved Africans arrived. However, cases prosecuted in Virginia in 1630 and 1640 suggest that Africans may not have received equal justice even before then, while excerpts from laws passed in the 1660s and beyond are clearly discriminatory. The relatively gradual appearance of such laws has led some historians to argue that racial prejudice was crucial to the development of Black slavery.

> **Breaking it Down** What issues or major debates did Virginia slave laws attempt to address in this excerpt? How did Virginia slave laws limit the opportunities for the emancipation of enslaved people? How did these laws also restrict the liberties of white colonists? To what extent were penalties for the same offense influenced by race?

[1630]
September 17th, 1630. Hugh Davis to be soundly whipped, before an assembly of Negroes and others for abusing himself to the dishonor of God and shame of Christians, by defiling his body in lying with a negro; which fault he is to acknowledge next Sabbath day.

[1640]
October 17, 1640. *Whereas Robert Sweat* hath begotten with child a negro woman servant belonging unto Lieutenant *Sheppard, the court hath therefore ordered* that the said negro woman shall be whipt at the whipping post and the said *Sweat* shall tomorrow in the forenoon do public penance for his offence at *James City* church in the time of divine service according to the laws of *England* in that case provided.

[1662]
WHEREAS some doubts have arisen whether children got by any Englishman upon a negro woman should be slave or free, *Be it therefore enacted and declared by this present grand assembly,* that all children borne in this country shall be held bond or free only according to the condition of the mother, *And* that if any christian shall commit fornication with a negro man or woman, he or she so offending shall pay double the fines imposed by the former act.

[1667]
WHEREAS some doubts have risen whether children that are slaves by birth, and by the charity and piety of their owners made pertakers of the blessed sacrament of baptisme, should by vertue of their baptisme be made free; *It is enacted and declared by this grand assembly, and the authority thereof,* that the conferring of baptisme doth not alter the condition of the person as to his bondage or freedome; that diverse masters, freed from this doubt, may more carefully endeavour the propagation of christianity by permitting children, though slaves, or those of greater growth if capable to be admitted to that sacrament.

[1668]
WHEREAS some doubts, have arisen whether negro women set free were still to be accompted [accounted] tithable according to a former act, *It is declared by this grand assembly* that negro women, though permitted to enjoy their freedome yet ought not in all respects to be admitted to a full fruition of the exemptions and impunities of the English, and are still lyable to payment of taxes.

[1669]
WHEREAS the only law in force for the punishment of refractory servants (*a*) resisting their

master, mistris or overseer cannot be inflicted upon negroes, nor the obstinacy of many of them by other then [than] violent meanes suppress, *Be it enacted and declared by this grand assembly*, if any slave resist his master (or other by his masters order correcting him) and by the extremity of the correction should chance to die, that his death shall not be accompted [accounted] felony, but the master (or that other person appointed by the master to punish him) be acquit from molestation, since it cannot be presumed that prepensed malice (which alone makes murther felony) should induce any man to destroy his owne estate.

[June 1670]
WHEREAS it hath beene questioned whither Indians or negroes manumited, or otherwise free, could be capable of purchasing christian servants, *It is enacted* that noe negroe or Indian though baptised and enjoyned their owne freedome shall be capable of any such purchase of christians, but yet not debarred from buying any of their owne nation.

SOURCE: William Waller Hening, ed., *The Statutes at Large; Being a Collection of All the Laws of Virginia* (Richmond, VA: Samuel Pleasants, 1810), 1:146, 552; 2:170, 260, 267, 270, 280–81.

DOCUMENT 2 *The Massachusetts Body of Liberties, 1641*

Adopted in 1641, the Massachusetts Body of Liberties was New England's first legal code. Drafted by the Puritan lawyer Nathan Ward of Ipswich, it drew on both English common law and biblical law to define the rights of the region's European colonists. Enslaved "Forreiners and Strangers," however, were not entitled to freedom under the Body of Liberties.

Breaking it Down What major issue or debate did the laws in this excerpt seek to resolve? What role did religion play? How did the status and rights of enslaved people in Massachusetts compare to non-Black Christian visitors to the colony, and to enslaved people in Virginia?

LIBERTIES OF FORREINERS AND STRANGERS.

89. If any people of other Nations professing the true Christian Religion shall flee to us from the Tiranny or oppression of their persecutors, or from famyne, warres, or the like necessary and compulsorie cause, They shall be entertayned and succoured amongst us, according to that power and prudence, god shall give us.

90. If any ships or other vessels, be it freind or enemy, shall suffer shipwrack upon our Coast, there shall be no violence or wrong offerred to their persons or goods. But their persons shall be harboured, and relieved, and their goods preserved in safety till Authoritie may be certified thereof, and shall take further order therein.

91. There shall never be any bond slaverie, villinage or Captivitie amongst us unles[s] it be lawfull Captives taken in just warres, and such strangers as willingly selle themselves or are sold to us. And these shall have all the liberties and Christian usages which the law of god established in Israell concerning such persons doeth morally require. This exempts none from servitude who shall be Judged thereto by Authoritie.

SOURCE: Charles W. Eliot, ed., *American Historical Documents, 1000–1904*, The Harvard Classics (New York: P. F. Collier & Son, 1910), 43:83–84.

DOCUMENT 3 *An Act for Regulating of Slaves in New Jersey, 1713–1714*

Colonial statutes regulated the status of individual enslaved people and the workings of the slave system as a whole. New Jersey legislators enacted the following law to prohibit the colony's citizens from engaging in any kind of commercial transaction with enslaved people without first securing the permission of the enslaver. It also prohibited citizens from sheltering anyone who might be a fugitive from slavery or from freeing the people they enslaved without pledging "security" funds to the colony should the formerly enslaved ever require public support.

Breaking it Down What issues or major debates are addressed in this excerpt? How did these laws limit the freedoms and rights of enslaved people? How do these laws reflect the New Jersey colony's regional characteristics? Can you identify any shared characteristics or themes with other slave laws?

[§1] *Be it Enacted by the Governour, Council and General Assembly, and by the Authority of the same,* That all and every Person or Persons within this Province, who shall at any time after Publication hereof, buy, sell, barter, trade or traffick with any *Negro, Indian* or *Mullatto Slave,* for any Rum, Wine, Beer, Syder, or other strong Drink, or any other Chattels, Goods, Wares or Commodities whatsoever, unless it be by the consent of his, her or their Master or Mistress, or the person under whose care they are, shall pay for the first Offence *Twenty Shillings,* and for the second and every other Offence, *forty Shillings,* Money according to the Queens Proclamation, the one half to the Informer, the other half to the use of the Poor of that Place where the Fact is committed, to be recovered by Action of Debt before any one of Her Majesties Justices of the Peace.

[§2] *And be it further Enacted by the Authority aforesaid,* That all and every Person or Persons within this Province, who shall find or take up any Negro, Indian or Mullato Slave or Slaves, five Miles from his, her or their Master or Mistresses habitation, who hath not leave in writing from his, her or their Master or Mistress, or are not known to be on their service, he, she or they, so taken up, shall be Whipt by the party that takes them up, or by his order, on the bare back, not exceeding Twenty Lashes; and the Taker up shall have for his reward Five Shillings, Money aforesaid, for every one taken up as aforesaid, with reasonable Charges for carrying him, her or them home, paid him by the Master or Mistress of the Slave or Slaves so taken up; and if above the said five Miles, *six pence per Mile* for every Mile over and above, to be recovered before any one Justice of the Peace, if it exceeds not Forty Shillings, and if more, by Action of Debt in the Court of Common Pleas in the County where the fact shall arise. . . .

[§12] *Be it further Enacted by the Authority aforesaid,* That no Person or Persons whatsoever shall hereafter imploy, harbour, Conceal or entertain other Peoples Slaves at their Houses, Out-Houses or Plantation, without the consent of their Master or Mistress, either signified to them Verbally, or by Certificate in writing under the said Master or Mistresses Hand, excepting in Distress of Weather, or other extraordinary Occasions, upon the forfeiture of *Forty Shillings* for every Time they are so entertained and concealed, to be paid to the Master or Mistress of such Slave or Slaves (so that the Penalty for entertaining such Slave exceeds not the Value of the said Slave) And if any Person or Persons whatsoever shall be found guilty [of] so harbouring, entertaining or concealing of any Slave, or assisting to the conveying them away, if such Slave shall happen to be lost, Dead, or otherways rendered Unserviceable, such Person or Persons so harbouring, entertaining, concealing, assisting or conveying them away, shall be also liable to pay the value of such Slave to the Master or Mistress, to be recovered by Action of Debt in any Court of Record within this Province. . . .

[§14] *And Whereas* it is found by experience, that Free Negroes are an Idle Sloathful People, and prove very often a charge to the Place where they are,

Be it therefore further Enacted by the Authority aforesaid, That any Master or Mistress, manumitting and setting at Liberty any Negro or Mullatto Slave, shall enter into sufficient Security unto Her Majesty, Her Heirs and Successors, with two Sureties, in the Sum of *Two Hundred Pounds,* to pay yearly and every year to such Negro or Mullatto Slave, during their Lives, the Sum of *Twenty Pounds.* And if such Negro or Mullatto Slave shall be made Free by the Will and Testament of any Person deceased, that then the Executors of such Person shall enter into Security, as above, immediately upon proving the said Will and Testament, which if refused to be given, the said Manumission to be void, and of none Effect.

SOURCE: "An Act for Regulating of Slaves," in *The Law of Slavery in New Jersey,* comp. Paul Axel-Lute, rev. October 8, 2009, New Jersey Digital Legal Library, http://njlegallib.rutgers.edu/slavery/acts/A13.html.

DOCUMENT 4 AP® source The South Carolina Slave Code, 1740

Punishment was an important function of slave law. In the aftermath of the Stono rebellion, the South Carolina legislature strengthened its already severe code of slave punishment by passing the following legislation.

Breaking it Down What issue or major debates were the slave laws in this excerpt attempting to address? How did South Carolina slave laws limit the freedoms and rights of enslaved people? Describe the severity of punishment for violation of the laws. Can you identify any shared characteristics or themes with other slave laws? How did these laws also restrict the liberties of white colonists?

AN ACT FOR THE BETTER ORDERING AND GOVERNING [OF] NEGROES AND OTHER SLAVES IN THIS PROVINCE

4. *Whereas* in his majesty's plantations in America, slavery has been introduced and allowed; and the people commonly called negroes, Indians, mulattoes and mestizos, have been deemed absolute slaves, and the subjects of property in the hands of particular persons; the extent of whose power over such slaves, ought to be settled and limited by positive laws, so that the slaves may be kept in due subjection and obedience, and the owners and other persons having the care and government of slaves, may be restrained from exercising too great rigour and cruelty over them; and that the public peace and order of this province may be preserved. . . .

7. *Provided,* that in any action or suit to be brought in pursuance of the direction of this act, the burthen of the proof shall lay upon the plaintiff, and it shall be always presumed, that every negro, Indian, mulatto and mestizo, is a slave, unless the contrary can be made appear. (The Indians in amity with this government excepted) in which case the burthen of the proof shall lie on the defendant. . . .

12. If any slave, who shall be out of the house or plantation where such slave shall live or shall be usually employed, or without some white person in company with such slave, shall refuse to submit to or undergo the examination of any white

SOURCE: Joseph Brevard, *An Alphabetical Digest of the Public Statute Law of South-Carolina* (Charleston, SC: John Hoff, 1816), 2:229–31, 233, 238, 240–41, 243.

person, it shall be lawful for any such white person to pursue, apprehend and moderately correct such slave; and if such slave shall assault and strike such white person, such slave may be lawfully killed. . . .

20. . . . *Be it therefore enacted*, that the several crimes and offences herein after particularly enumerated, are hereby declared to be felony without the benefit of the clergy, *that is to say*, if any slave, free negro, mulatto, Indian or mestizo, shall wilfully and maliciously burn or destroy any stack of rice, corn or other grain, of the product, growth or manufacture of this province; or shall wilfully and maliciously set fire to, burn or destroy any tar kiln, barrels of pitch, tar, turpentine or rosin, or any other [of] the goods or commodities of the growth, produce or manufacture of this province; or shall feloniously steal, take or carry away any slave, being the property of another, with intent to carry such slave out of this province; or shall wilfully and maliciously poison, or administer any poison to any person, freeman, woman, servant or slave; every such slave, free negro, mulatto, Indian, (except as before excepted) and mestizo, shall suffer death as a felon.

21. Any slave who shall be guilty of homicide of any sort, upon any white person, except by misadventure, or in defence of his master or other person under whose care and government such slave shall be, shall upon conviction thereof as aforesaid suffer death.

22. And every slave who shall raise or attempt to raise an insurrection in this province, *or shall endeavour to delude or entice any slave to run away and leave this province; every such slave and slaves, and his and their accomplices, aiders and abettors, shall upon conviction as aforesaid suffer death. . . .*

35. *And whereas* several owners of slaves do suffer their slaves to go and work where they please, upon conditions of paying to their owners certain sums of money agreed upon between the owner and slave; which practice has occasioned such slaves to pilfer and steal, to raise money for their owners, as well as to maintain themselves in drunkenness and evil courses; for prevention of which practices for the future, *Be it enacted*, That no owner, master or mistress of any slave, after the passing of this act, shall permit or suffer any of his, her or their slaves to go and work out of their respective houses or families, without a ticket in writing, under pain of forfeiting the sum of ten pounds, current money, for every such offence. . . .

41. And for that as it is absolutely necessary to the safety of this province, that all due care be taken to restrain the wanderings and meetings of negroes and other slaves, at all times, and more especially on Saturday nights, Sundays and other holidays, and their using and carrying wooden swords, and other mischievous and dangerous weapons, or using or keeping of drums, horns, or other loud instruments, which may call together or give sign or notice to one another of their wicked designs and purposes; and that all masters, overseers and others may be enjoined diligently and carefully to prevent the same:

42. *Be it enacted*, That it shall be lawful for all masters, overseers and other persons whomsoever, to apprehend and take up any negro or other slave that shall be found out of the plantation of his or their master or owner, at any time, especially on Saturday nights, Sundays or other holidays, not being on lawful business, and with a letter from their master or a ticket, or not having a white person with them, and the said negro or other slave or slaves correct by a moderate whipping. . . .

43. *And whereas* cruelty is not only highly unbecoming those who profess themselves Christians, but is odious in the eyes of all men who have any sense of virtue or humanity; therefore to restrain and prevent barbarity being exercised towards slaves, *Be it enacted*, That if any person or persons whosoever, shall wilfully murder his own slave, or the slave of any other person, every such person shall upon conviction thereof, forfeit and pay the sum of seven hundred pounds current money, and shall be rendered, and is hereby declared altogether and for ever incapable of holding, exercising, enjoying or receiving the profits of any office, place or employment civil or military within this province. . . .

45. And if any person shall, on a sudden heat [of] passion, or by undue correction, kill his own slave or the slave of any other person, he shall forfeit the sum of three hundred and fifty pounds current money. And in case any person or persons shall wilfully cut out the tongue, put out the eye, castrate, or cruelly scald, burn, or deprive any slave of any limb or member, or shall inflict any other cruel punishment, other than by whipping or beating with a horse-whip, cow-skin, switch or small stick, or by putting irons on, or confining or imprisoning such slave; every such person shall for every such offence, forfeit the sum of one hundred pounds current money.

46. That in case any person in this province, who shall be owner, or who shall have the care, government or charge of any slave or slaves shall deny, neglect or refuse to allow such slave or slaves under his or her charge, sufficient cloathing, covering or food, it shall and may be lawful for any person or persons, on behalf of such slave or slaves, to make complaint to the next neighbouring justice in the parish where such slave or slaves live or are usually employed; . . . and shall and may set and impose a fine or penalty on any person who shall offend in the premises, in any sum not exceeding twenty pounds current money, for each offence. . . .

52. *And whereas* many owners of slaves, and others who have the care, management and overseeing of slaves, do confine them so closely to hard labour, that they have not sufficient time for natural rest; *Be it therefore enacted,* That if any owner of slaves, or other person who shall have the care, management or overseeing of any slaves, shall work or put any such slave or slaves to labour, more than fifteen hours in twenty-four hours, from the twenty-fifth day of March to the twenty-fifth day of September, or more than fourteen hours in twenty-four hours, from the twenty-fifth day of September to the twenty-fifth day of March; every such person shall forfeit any sum not exceeding twenty pounds, nor under five pounds current money, for every time he, she or they shall offend herein, at the discretion of the justice before whom the complaint shall be made.

53. *And whereas* the having of slaves taught to write, or suffering them to be employed in writing, may be attended with great inconveniencies; *Be it enacted,* That all and every person and persons whatsoever, who shall hereafter teach, or cause any slave or slaves to be taught to write, or shall use or employ any slave as a scribe in any manner of writing whatsoever, hereafter taught to write; every such person and persons shall, for every such offence, forfeit the sum of one hundred pounds current money.

DOCUMENT 5 AP® source *The Black Code of Louisiana, 1724*

The Code Noir, or "Black Code," originated with a decree issued by the French king Louis XIV in 1685. Like the slave codes adopted in the British colonies, the Code Noir regulated the legal status of enslaved and free Blacks, as well as the relationship between enslaved people and enslavers. Enslavers were given almost unlimited physical control over their slaves but were also obliged to make sure the people they enslaved were baptized and permitted to practice the Roman Catholic faith. The Code Noir also regulated marriages between enslaved people. Its regulations regarding enslaved spiritual and family life are excerpted below.

Breaking it Down What issue or major debates were the slave laws in this excerpt attempting to address? What role did religion play in Louisiana slave laws, and how did that compare with the role religion played in Massachusetts slave laws? Can you identify any shared characteristics or themes with other slave laws?

CODE NOIR,

OU

RECUEIL D'EDITS,

DÉCLARATIONS ET ARRETS

CONCERNANT

Les Esclaves Négres de l'Amérique,

AVEC

Un Recueil de Réglemens, concernant la police des Isles Françoises de l'Amérique & les Engagés.

A PARIS,

Chez les LIBRAIRES ASSOCIEZ.

M. DCC. XLIII.

The British Library, London, UK/akg-images.

2. Makes it imperative on masters to impart religious instruction to their slaves.

3. Permits the exercise of the Roman Catholic creed only. Every other mode of worship is prohibited.

4. Negroes placed under the direction or supervision of any other person than a Catholic, are liable to confiscation.

5. Sundays and holidays are to be strictly observed. All negroes found at work on these days are to be confiscated.

6. We forbid our white subjects, of both sexes, to marry with the blacks, under the penalty of being fined and subjected to some other arbitrary punishment. We forbid all curates, priests, or missionaries of our secular or regular clergy, and even our chaplains in our navy to sanction such marriages. We also forbid all our white subjects, and even the manumitted or free-born blacks, to live in a state of concubinage with blacks. Should there be any issue from this kind of intercourse, it is our will that the person so offending, and the master of the slave, should pay each a fine of three hundred livres. Should said issue be the result of the concubinage of the master with his slave, said master shall not only pay the fine, but be deprived of the slave and of the children, who shall be adjudged to the hospital of the locality, and said slaves shall be forever incapable of being set free. But should this illicit intercourse have existed between a free black and his slave, when said free black had no legitimate wife, and should said black marry said slave according to the forms prescribed by the church, said slave shall be thereby set free, and the children shall also become free and legitimate; and in such a case, there shall be no application of the penalties mentioned in the present article.

7. The ceremonies and forms prescribed by the ordinance of Blois, and by the edict of 1639 [French laws], for marriages, shall be observed both with regard to free persons and to slaves. But the consent of the father and mother of the slave is not necessary; that of the master shall be the only one required.

8. We forbid all curates to proceed to effect marriages between slaves without proof of the consent of their masters; and we also forbid all masters to force their slaves into any marriage against their will.

9. Children, issued from the marriage of slaves, shall follow the condition of their parents, and shall belong to the master of the wife and not of the husband, if the husband and wife have different masters.

10. If the husband be a slave, and the wife a free woman, it is our will that their children, of whatever sex they may be, shall share the condition of their mother, and be as free as she, notwithstanding the servitude of their father; and if the father be free and the mother a slave, the children shall all be slaves.

11. Masters shall have their Christian slaves buried in consecrated ground. . . .

43. Husbands and wives shall not be seized and sold separately when belonging to the same master; and their children, when under fourteen years of age, shall not be separated from their parents, and such seizures and sales shall be null and void. The present article shall apply to voluntary sales, and in case such sales should take place in violation of the law, the seller shall be deprived of the slave he has illegally retained, and said slave shall be adjudged to the purchaser without any additional price being required.

Source: Charles Gayarré, *Louisiana: Its Colonial History and Romance*. New York: Harper, 1851.

PRACTICING AP® SKILLS

1. **AP® Causation.** Identify three different factors that shaped and influenced colonial slave laws. Where are each of those factors reflected in these documents?
2. **AP® Continuity and Change.** Explain the extent to which slave regulations varied over time and place. Use evidence from at least two of the documents to support your response.
3. **AP® Causation.** Explain how slave codes developed in response to African Americans' resistance to slavery.
4. **Connecting to AP® Themes.** Explain how American laws impacted the lives and citizenship rights of enslaved Americans between the seventeenth and eighteenth centuries.
5. **Classroom Discussion.** To what extent did slave codes harden the color line in American society? To what degree do you think the perspectives on race reflected in these codes will influence the American legal system after slavery is abolished in 1865?

Sourcing

As you learned in previous workshops, **primary sources** from a certain era include all of the visual and written texts created at that point in the past. So far, you've learned to actively read primary sources using tools like OPTIC for visual texts like architecture and artwork, and summaries of claims and evidence for written texts like letters and speeches. These strategies help you understand a primary source's main components — essentially, what elements convey its meaning?

To succeed on the AP® African American Studies Exam, you'll need to go one step further than simply understanding a primary source's meaning. You'll also need to read between the lines to interpret how a source conveys information about a broader historical and cultural context. This process of analysis is called "sourcing," and it involves using information beyond a visual or written text to flesh out its meaning and then its significance.

Practicing Sourcing

The HIPPO strategy can help you remember the steps to source any primary source document:

Historical Context: When and where was the source created, based on its source line and any other clues? What developments, like movements or events, might have influenced the source's creation?

Intended Audience: Can you figure out the person or people for whom the source was created? How does this affect the source's content and tone?

Purpose: Why was the source created? What message might its creator have been trying to get across, and how can you tell?

Perspective: Can you tell who created the source and what their position in society was like? How might their background, beliefs, and biases have influenced the source's creation?

Outside Information: What course concepts, developments, and processes does the source bring to mind? What does the source *not* tell you, and what other sources might fill in those gaps?

We can practice applying HIPPO to the South Carolina Slave Code, which also appears on page 113 of this textbook.

> "12. If any slave, who shall be out of the house or plantation where such slave shall live or shall be usually employed, or without some white person in company with such slave, shall refuse to submit to or undergo the examination of any white person, it shall be lawful for any such white person to pursue, apprehend and moderately correct such slave; and if such slave shall assault and strike such white person, such slave may be lawfully killed. . . .

22. And every slave who shall raise or attempt to raise an insurrection in this province, *or shall endeavour to delude or entice any slave to run away and leave this province . . . shall upon conviction as aforesaid suffer death* . . . .

41. And for that as it is absolutely necessary to the safety of this province, that all due care be taken to restrain the wanderings and meetings of negroes and other slaves . . . and their using and carrying wooden swords, and other mischievous and dangerous weapons, or using or keeping of drums, horns, or other loud instruments, which may call together or give sign or notice to one another of their wicked designs and purposes. . . .

53. *And whereas* the having of slaves taught to write, or suffering them to be employed in writing, may be attended with great inconveniencies; *Be it enacted,* That all and every person and persons whatsoever, who shall hereafter teach, or cause any slave or slaves to be taught to write, or shall use or employ any slave as a scribe in any manner of writing whatsoever, hereafter taught to write; every such person and persons shall, for every such offence, forfeit the sum of one hundred pounds current money."

SOURCE: The South Carolina Slave Code, 1740

Using course knowledge covered in this chapter, we can complete each step of HIPPO as follows:

Historical Context: In 1739, about fifty enslaved Africans led the Stono Rebellion. Although the rebellion lasted for only a day, its participants marched over ten miles and killed over twenty-five white people. After a white armed patrol captured and killed most of the rebels, South Carolina officials revised the colony's already severe slave code to include even more stringent laws.

Intended Audience: All inhabitants of the South Carolina colony

Purpose: To disempower enslaved people and isolate them from one another, and to strengthen the institution of slavery

Perspective: White male South Carolina officials frightened by the Stono Rebellion and wary of the growing African population as the colony became increasingly dependent on enslaved labor

Outside Information:

- The Code's restrictions on enslaved people's movement were likely intended to discourage escape attempts to St. Augustine in Spanish Florida, where enslaved people could become free by converting to Catholicism.
- The code's prohibitions on drumming and gathering reflect how South Carolina's enslaved population was numerous enough to build self-contained slave communities that maintained aspects of African heritage.

Having collected these clues about when, where, why, for whom, and by whom the source was created, we're set up well for further stages of analysis.

recap

Practicing Sourcing

The HIPPO strategy can help you source any visual or written primary source.

Historical Context
Intended Audience
Purpose
Perspective
Outside Information

Activity ▸ Practicing Sourcing

Use the HIPPO strategy to analyze the following primary source. Fill in a graphic organizer like the one to follow to guide your work.

Historical Context	
Intended Audience	
Purpose	
Perspective	
Outside Information	

"My Lords,

I beg leave to lay before your Lordships an account of our Affairs, first in regard to the Desertion of our Negroes . . . . On the 9th of September last at Night a great Number of Negroes Arose in Rebellion, broke open a Store where they got arms, killed twenty one White Persons, and were marching the next morning in a Daring manner out of the Province, killing all they met and burning several Houses as they passed along the Road. I was returning from Granville County with four Gentlemen and met these Rebels at eleven o'clock in the forenoon and fortunately deserned the approaching danger time enough to avoid it, and to give notice to the Militia who on the Occasion behaved with so much expedition and bravery, as by four a'Clock the same day to come up with them and killed and took so many as put a stop to any further mischief at that time, forty four of them have been killed and Executed; some few yet remain concealed in the Woods expecting the same fate, seem desperate . . . .

It was the Opinion of His Majesty's Council with several other Gentlemen that one of the most effectual means that could be used at present to prevent such desertion of our Negroes is to encourage some Indians by a suitable reward to pursue and if possible to bring back the Deserters, and while the

Indians are thus employed they would be in the way ready to intercept others that might attempt to follow and I have sent for the Chiefs of the Chickasaws living at New Windsor and the Catawbaw Indians for that purpose. . . .

My Lords,
Your Lordships Most Obedient and Most Humble Servant
Wm Bull"

SOURCE: William Bull, South Carolina Lieutenant Governor, letter to British Board of Trade, October 5, 1739

Multiple-Choice Questions

Questions 1–2 refer to the following.

Enslaved Africans and Rice Cultivation in Carolina

TO BE SOLD on board the
Ship *Bance-Yſland*, on tueſday the 6th
of *May* next, at *Aſhley-Ferry*; a choice
cargo of about 250 fine healthy
NEGROES,
juſt arrived from the
Windward & Rice Coaſt.
—The utmoſt care has
already been taken, and
ſhall be continued, to keep them free from
the leaſt danger of being infected with the
SMALL-POX, no boat having been on
board, and all other communication with
people from *Charles-Town* prevented.
Auſtin, Laurens, & Appleby.
N. B. Full one Half of the above Negroes have had the
SMALL-POX in their own Country.

1. Which of the following statements about enslaved laborers in the American colonies does the image best support?

(A) The colonial South Carolina workforce did not rely heavily on enslaved labor.

(B) Most enslaved African laborers were immune to smallpox and other major diseases of the time.

(C) The banning of the transatlantic slave trade during the colonial period diminished the demand for enslaved African laborers.

(D) Many enslaved African laborers possessed agricultural skills that were of high value to planters.

2. Based on the image, an outcome for the enslaved Africans advertised in the image would most likely include working under which of the following conditions?

(A) Individually with less oversight until they finished their task or met their daily quota in task system

(B) Cultivating sugar under brutal circumstances with high casualty rates

(C) Forging metal as blacksmiths for major southern institutions with freedom to live off the plantation

(D) Collectively from sunup to sundown in a gang labor system, under the watch and discipline of an overseer

Short-Answer Question

1. Answer A, B, C, and D.

(A) Describe the different kinds of labor that enslaved people performed in the British colonies.

(B) Describe the variations that emerged in the legal status and political rights of enslaved people who settled in French Louisiana versus the enslaved people who settled in the British colonies.

(C) Explain how the reliance upon enslaved labor economically impacted the British colonies.

(D) Explain how the legal code and customs of Spanish Florida affected enslaved people living in the British colonies.

CHAPTER 4

African Americans in the Age of Revolution

1741–1783

CHAPTER TIMELINE *Events specific to African history are in purple. General U.S. history events are in black. Events from the AP® Course Framework are marked with an asterisk.*

1720 Britain eliminates duties on enslaved people imported directly from Africa

Mid-1730s–1740s Great Awakening begins, then spreads south

1741 Series of fires in New York prompts conspiracy trials of enslaved people

1750 Georgia lifts ban on importing enslaved people

1754–1763 French and Indian War (called Seven Years' War in Europe)

1765 Britain passes Stamp Act

1770 Boston Massacre

Crispus Attucks becomes first casualty of American Revolution

1772 Somerset case inspires challenges to slavery throughout British empire

1773 Boston Tea Party

1773 Phillis Wheatley's "On Being Brought from Africa to America" published*

1774 Britain passes Intolerable Acts

First Continental Congress

1775 British and colonists engage in battles at Lexington and Concord, Massachusetts Second Continental Congress

1775 George Washington appointed commander in chief of Continental army, bans enlistment of Black men

Lord Dunmore offers freedom to enslaved people who will join British forces

Continental army reverses position and declares Blacks eligible for service

1776 Thomas Paine publishes *Common Sense*, arguing for independence

Continental Congress adopts Declaration of Independence

1777–1820s Northern states begin to abolish slavery

1778 British adopt southern strategy

1779 Philipsburg Proclamation promises to free enslaved people serving Britain in any capacity

1781 Colonists adopt Articles of Confederation

British surrender at Yorktown, Virginia

1783 U.S. and Great Britain sign Treaty of Paris

Virginia law directs attorney general to seek manumission for all enslaved soldiers still held in bondage

Massachusetts Supreme Court rules that slavery is incompatible with state constitution

The New York Slave Plot of 1741

During the winter of 1741, British colonists were quick to blame a series of fires that swept lower Manhattan on a massive conspiracy of enslaved people. In the wake of a recent maroon war in Jamaica and slave revolts in Antigua and South Carolina, white New Yorkers were nervous about the two thousand enslaved people who made up one-fifth of the city's population. Enslaved New Yorkers had good reason to be discontented during that unusually cold winter, when food and fuel were scarce. The first fire took place inside Fort George and threatened Lieutenant Governor George Clarke's mansion. Soldiers stationed there rescued Clarke and his family, and citizens gathered with buckets to douse the flames. But onlookers were disturbed to note that although some Blacks pitched in to help, not all of them tried to fight the fire. One enslaved man confided to another that he "wished the governor had been burnt in the middle of it," and a third, a man named Cuffee, danced as the fire spread.[1]

The Fort George fire was only the first in a series of conflagrations. One week later, flames scorched a nearby house, and a week after that, a warehouse burned to the ground. The first week of April saw seven fires, one next to the house of Captain Jacob Sarly. The captain owned an enslaved man named Juan de la Silva, who along with several of his shipmates had been captured and sold into slavery after an attack on a Spanish ship. All of the men swore that they were sailors rather than enslaved people and "free subjects of Spain" as well. They had also publicly threatened to roast John Lush, the privateer who had captured their ship, like "a piece of beef." Moreover, de la Silva had vowed to burn Sarly's house. After the fire at Sarly's neighbor's house broke out, some New Yorkers assumed that de la Silva and his shipmates had started all the fires in a plot to "ruin the city." A cry swept through the city: "Take up the Spanish negroes."[2] But even as de la Silva and his compatriots were rounded up and dragged off to City Hall, another fire broke out in a warehouse on New Street. Cuffee, the enslaved man who had danced while Fort George burned, was seen leaving the building. A huge mob chased him down and carried him to the city jail, shouting, "The Negroes are rising!"[3]

More than one hundred Blacks and several whites were arrested and imprisoned as authorities investigated the alleged conspiracy, coercing confessions from the people they tried and convicted. By the end of the trials, seventeen Blacks and four whites had been hanged, thirteen Blacks had been burned at the stake, and seventy Blacks and seven whites had been banished from the colony. How many of them were guilty of arson — or anything else — remains an open question. The trials took place at a moment when New Yorkers were alert to the dangers of slave rebellion, embroiled in an imperial war with Spain, and suffering the economic effects of a deep recession. One witness reported that Blacks planned "to burn the town, kill the white men, and take their wives and daughters as mistresses." Others maintained that the fires had been set by Blacks and poor whites who had united against the wealthier classes. But once the hysteria of the trials died down, many New Yorkers wondered whether they had been caught in "the merciless Flames of an Imaginary Plot."[4]

Planned or not, the fires provoked fears that illuminated the dangers of slavery, as well as the dangers of interracial freedom struggles in colonial America. Trial testimony reveals a world of discontented enslaved people, servants, and white workers, whose grievances could easily swell into outright rebellion. Most of the accused were people who worked on New York's racially mixed waterfront, where they socialized together, slept together, and shared a common resentment toward more prosperous New Yorkers and the city's social order. But such allegiances did not prevent Blacks from becoming the primary scapegoats. Some of the alleged ringleaders, such as the dancing Cuffee, were criminals whose traffic in stolen goods may have made them easy targets of property owners. Others, such as the hapless "Spanish Negroes," were men who were primarily focused on securing their own freedom.

As the eighteenth century progressed and American colonists battled for independence from Britain, freedom-seeking Blacks would become important foot soldiers in what one historian has described as "the motley crew" of the American Revolution.[5] Discontented Blacks, with no property or privileges to preserve, saw the Revolution as an opportunity to win their own freedom. They fought on both sides of the conflict and participated in all of the Revolution's major battles. White patriots were initially reluctant to enlist Black soldiers, fearing a slave revolt, but after the British began enlisting enslaved people in 1775, most of the colonies followed suit. While securing Black freedom was not among the colonists' Revolutionary goals, they and the British usually freed people who served in their armed forces. African Americans on both sides of the conflict were quick to embrace these opportunities.

The Revolutionary era offered African Americans other routes to freedom as well. The religious revivals of the Great Awakening fostered a spirit of egalitarianism that was appealing to both Blacks and whites. Moreover, as white Americans struggled to free themselves from British domination, many began to question the legitimacy of slavery. Whites manumitted, or freed, more than twenty thousand enslaved people during the final decades of the eighteenth century. Some were inspired to do so by their religious convictions, and others were influenced by the Revolution's democratic ideals.

Thus, the American Revolution fueled the freedom dreams of African Americans, who took advantage of the war's social and political dislocation to join the patriot or British forces, run away, or challenge the terms of their enslavement in court. Their actions helped to erode slavery in America, resulting in a new nation where slavery was permitted in some states but not in others.

African American Life in Eighteenth-Century North America

How did the growth of the cotton industry in the United States displace enslaved African American families?

What were the economic effects of enslaved people's commodification and labor, both within and outside of their communities?

During the 1741 trials, New York chief justice Daniel Horsmanden warned enslavers that they had "enemies of their own household," who should be replaced and "replenished with white people."[6] But New York enslavers proved no more willing to relinquish those they enslaved than had their counterparts in South Carolina, even in the wake of the bloody Stono rebellion. As the supply of white workers shrank, North America's British colonies imported even more captive Africans. Sixty percent of all the African captives imported into the American colonies, most of whom ended up in the South, arrived between the 1720s and the 1780s. In the North, the newcomers joined an existing Black population in which American-born Blacks predominated. English-speaking and comfortable living among whites, many American-born Black northerners had become Christians as well. During these years, African Americans forged a distinct and evolving identity, combining the contributions of the continuous flow of African newcomers with those of the large population of American-born Blacks.

Enslaved and Free Blacks across the Colonies

By the mid-eighteenth century, white laborers were in short supply throughout the colonies, especially after Europe's Seven Years' War of 1756–1763 reduced the flow of European indentured servants and increased the rate of military enlistment in Europe. This shortage led colonists to embrace slavery with greater enthusiasm than ever before. Whereas the total number of enslaved shipped from Africa to North America between 1700 and 1720 was roughly twenty thousand, colonists imported more than fifty thousand captives per decade in the 1740s and 1750s and maintained similar rates, with only a slight drop-off, in the years immediately preceding the Revolution. Most of these newcomers ended up in the southern colonies, but imports of enslaved people in the North increased as well, enlarging and Africanizing the region's small Black population.

In the South, the newcomers populated an expanding plantation frontier. Georgia, which was founded with a ban on importing enslaved people, was home to only 500 enslaved people in 1750. That year, however, its trustees agreed to lift the ban as of January 1, 1751, and after that, the colony quickly became a slave society. Its unfree population soared, reaching 18,000 in 1775. South Carolina also resumed massive imports of enslaved Africans in the 1750s, bringing in 56,000 between 1751 and 1775, even as the colony's enslaved population began to expand by natural increase. Only in the Chesapeake, which was already home to almost 500,000 people of African descent, did enslaved imports slow. As a result of robust rates of natural increase, most Chesapeake planters could expect enslaved families to grow on their own. Planters did continue to bring enslaved Africans to recently settled areas, such as the Virginia Piedmont and western Maryland, but those imports declined over time and amounted to less than 1,000 per year by the 1770s.

By contrast, the enslaved population in the northern colonies was never self-sustaining. Northern employers had to import enslaved people to meet their labor needs. Scattered across the region, Black northerners were rarely able to find partners, so their numbers were not replenished by reproduction. Although the enslaved population in the North remained modest in comparison to that in the South, between 1732 and 1754 captive Africans made up a third of all immigrants (voluntary and involuntary) entering New York City, and Black New Yorkers accounted for almost 20 percent of the city's population. Likewise, one in five Philadelphia laborers and one in ten of all Bostonians were enslaved by midcentury. Massachusetts as a whole saw its Black population increase by 50 percent during each decade between 1700 and 1750.

During the mid-eighteenth century, the use of enslaved labor expanded into new occupational sectors in New England and the middle colonies. Enslaved people had long been common in northern port cities such as New York, Boston, and Philadelphia, where they served as domestic and maritime workers. But urban artisans who had traditionally employed white apprentices now began to train Black enslaved people to work in their shops. Increasing numbers of enslaved Africans were also employed in agriculture, both in southern New England and in the grain-producing regions of the middle colonies — areas that had previously relied on white immigrant workers. Landowning enslavers in regions such as Narragansett County, Rhode Island, became more dependent on enslaved labor, and farmers in Pennsylvania, northern New Jersey, the Hudson Valley, and Long Island began to import large numbers of enslaved Africans for the first time.

As enslaved people became integral to the northern labor force, both American and African American society changed. Since enslaved birthrates remained extremely low in the North, slavery there was sustained by "a continual supply . . . from Africa," as Benjamin Franklin noted.[7] As this observation indicates, by the 1740s, northern merchants had begun to import boatloads of enslaved West Africans. Prior to 1741, 70 percent of the enslaved people shipped to New York originated in the Caribbean, and only 30 percent came directly from Africa. After 1741, the proportions were reversed.[8] Changes in both demand and supply shaped this shift in the composition of imported enslaved people. As the demand for enslaved laborers rose in northern cities, the slave market there could no longer rely on the small-scale trade in "refuse slaves" from the West Indies. In addition, in 1720, the British crown eliminated duties

AP® skills

Applying Disciplinary Knowledge: How did the British colonial policies allow for the expansion of the transport of captured Africans?

on enslaved people imported directly from Africa, making it easier for American merchants to buy shiploads of enslaved Africans.

As slavery expanded in eighteenth-century America, Black freedom contracted. Both the northern and southern colonies had long been home to small numbers of free Blacks, whose populations were increasingly dwarfed by the steady influx of enslaved migrants. By 1775, one observer recalled, "the number of free negroes [in Virginia] was so small that they were seldom to be met with."[9] Free Blacks were even scarcer in South Carolina. Laws discouraging **manumission** and requiring African Americans who did gain freedom to leave the state also limited the free Black population in the South. Free Blacks were somewhat more common in the North, where such restrictions were rare, but as of 1760, they still totaled only 10 percent of the region's small Black population — or a few thousand people.

manumission
A legal process that enslavers could initiate to grant freedom to an enslaved person.

Shaping an African American Culture

The steady importation of thousands of West African captives ensured that African culture shaped the lives of Blacks throughout the colonies, even as the American-born Black population also increased. The cultural impact of these migrants varied by region. It was most striking in areas where American- and Caribbean-born Blacks predominated, such as the Northeast, and weakest in the colonies of the Lower South, where African-born enslaved people had long formed a majority.

AP® exam tip
Be sure you can explain how African Americans combined influences from diverse African cultures with local sources to express themselves through art, music, and language.

African American communities in the North were transformed when shiploads of Africans began docking in northeastern port cities in the 1740s. The newcomers infused African culture into these increasingly acculturated Black communities, made up of English-speaking enslaved people who had long lived and worked among whites and maintained only limited ties to their African roots. But northern Blacks were sufficiently set apart from the white world to enjoy their own evolving culture. Both African and American, they welcomed the new migrants and embraced their African traditions. By midcentury, Blacks across the North began to adopt a self-consciously African identity, which shaped the naming of early Black organizations such as the African Lodge No. 1, a Black Masonic lodge founded in 1776.

During this period, Africans and African Americans in the North united across cultural and linguistic divides in a boisterous annual celebration known as **Negro Election Day**. Largely a New England phenomenon, Negro Election Day combined the Puritan tradition of an election day holiday with African rituals of festive role reversals, in which the powerless temporarily played the role of the powerful. This holiday saw Black New Englanders elect their own kings and governors in elaborate ceremonies that included royal processions, political parades, and inaugural parties. Those ceremonies, which partly spoofed white behavior on official election days, were often regarded with amused disdain by whites, who tended not to grasp the extent to which Negro Election Day parodied its white counterpart. In fact, white

Negro Election Day
An annual New England celebration in which Black communities elected their own kings and governors in elaborate ceremonies that included royal processions, political parades, and inaugural parties.

The Creation of an African American Culture
This late-eighteenth-century painting, *The Old Plantation*, depicts a group of enslaved people on a South Carolina plantation. Their activities strongly suggest the persistence of West African cultural traditions and practices in the Lower South. This painting may depict a wedding, which sometimes featured the tradition of "jumping the broom," or it may depict a dance. Many of the participants' accoutrements — the women's head ties and the players' instruments, for example — are West African in origin. But the other garments shown are typical of American working-class attire during this period, and the slave cabins and other plantation buildings remind us of the setting in which this distinctly African American culture was taking shape. **What does this painting reveal about how the forced labor systems affected the formation of African American musical and linguistic practices?** *The Old Plantation, attributed to John Rose, Beaufort County, South Carolina, c. 1785–1790/The Colonial Williamsburg Foundation, Gift of Abby Aldrich Rockefeller.*

ACTIVITY ▸ Revisit Your Prediction

In the AP® Unit Warmup (p. U2-E), you made a prediction about this image. **How do you think African American forms of self-expression in art, music, and language combined influences from diverse African cultures with local sources? What details in this painting help support your prediction? How can self-expression be considered a form of resistance and a demonstration of resilience? Support or revise your original prediction using evidence from this chapter.**

municipal authorities sanctioned the festivities. On this day, one white observer noted, "all the various languages of Africa, mixed with broken and ludicrous English, filled the air, accompanied with the music of the fiddle, tambourine, the banjo, drum, etc."[10]

But the elections were at least semiserious in their public recognition of local Black leaders' authority. Black governors and kings were often African-born men of royal lineage, and many had the added distinction of serving wealthy and powerful white men, who supplied them with the food, liquor, and elegant clothing required to compete for these offices. Although these were primarily ceremonial positions, some Black governors and kings were authorized to speak on behalf of their communities and were called on to preside over informal trials of enslaved people accused of petty crimes.

Black northerners also came together for African-influenced funeral ceremonies, which struck white observers as alarmingly pagan. Drawing on West African mortuary rites that celebrated the dead with music and song designed to ease their journey into the spirit world, Black funerals confounded white New Englanders. "They did not express so much sorrow at the funeral," a white observer named William Bentley wrote of a Black funeral in Salem, Massachusetts, "as real gratification at appearing so well, a greater sympathy with living happily than the bereaved."[11] Such celebrations made far more sense to the Black people who participated in them. Bentley's comments suggest that, while white northerners found African religious traditions alien, Black northerners did not. Instead, such traditions were a shared point of connection between African newcomers and Blacks who had spent many years in America.

The brisk slave trade in the Chesapeake ensured that Blacks there, like their northern counterparts, did not become wholly estranged from their African cultural heritage. Between 1720 and the 1770s, the planters who settled in the Virginia Piedmont imported approximately fifteen thousand African captives. Most of these settlers came from the tidewater region on Virginia's eastern coast, where decades of tobacco production had exhausted the soil, forcing planters to seek more fertile land farther west. As the settlers fanned out, they carved new plantations out of the wilderness, using the labor of both American Blacks and recent African migrants, who worked and lived together. The African-born enslaved people helped sustain African cultural practices and beliefs among the American-born Blacks throughout the region. In turn, the American Blacks helped the newcomers assimilate. Over time, the two groups blended and intermixed, creating an enslaved culture that was simultaneously African and American.

This blended culture was also evident in linguistic patterns that developed in the Upper South, where Blacks spoke English but also continued to use African idioms and syntax. According to John Smyth, an Englishman who immigrated to Virginia shortly before the Revolution, these cultural hybrids spoke "a mixed dialect between the Guinea and English."[12] Local whites, who in turn adopted some of the Black idioms, called the regional variation of English spoken by Chesapeake Blacks "Virginian," a term that recognized the influence of the blend of African and American culture on the region as a whole.

African cultural beliefs and customs also remained common in the Upper South. Like northern Blacks, even highly acculturated southern Blacks often insisted on

conjure
Traditional African folk magic in which people called conjurers draw on the powers of the spirit world to influence human affairs.

honoring the dead by singing, dancing, and rejoicing at funerals. They also honored traditional African beliefs in the power of **conjure**. Rooted in West African religious traditions and rituals recognizing the existence of magic and the influence of ancestral spirits and other occult powers in daily life, conjure was also influenced by the surroundings in which it took shape in North America, drawing on American Indian knowledge of natural remedies. Conjurers, who could be men or women, were also known as "root doctors" or "Negro doctors" and were often skilled in the use of botanical medicines. Black and white southerners alike consulted them to heal the sick with spells and charms as well as roots and herbs. Conjurers also created love potions and were thought to be able to predict the future. On a more sinister note, many people believed that they poisoned their enemies.

AP® exam tip

Be sure to maintain an understanding of the terms *African diaspora* and *religious syncretism*. What aspects of diasporic experience characterized enslaved peoples' experiences in the Upper South? What religious syncretic practices are described on this page?

Conjure and other African traditions were most entrenched in the Lower South, where acculturation was minimal. Most Blacks in eighteenth-century South Carolina, for example, lived in an increasingly Africanized world. Enslaved birthrates remained low there for much of the century, forcing the colony's planters to import thousands of enslaved West Africans each year to meet the needs of the growing plantation economy. The new arrivals reinforced African cultural practices and spiritual beliefs among low-country enslaved people, even after the number of American-born Blacks in the region slowly began to increase.

Many low-country Blacks never mastered the English language. Isolated on large plantations and put to work under the supervision of Black drivers, they had little contact with English speakers. As a result, even the region's native-born Blacks often spoke a creole language known as **Gullah**, which whites found difficult to understand. Gullah speakers mixed English with West African syntax and words. For instance, using a term from the Efik-Ibibio language spoken by many people in what is today southeastern Nigeria, they referred to white people as "backra" or "buckra," meaning "he who surrounds or governs."[13]

Gullah
A creole language composed of a blend of West African languages and English.

The Great Awakening and Slavery

The enduring influence of African traditions and beliefs and the influx of new arrivals limited the spread of Christianity among African Americans in the eighteenth century. So, too, did the lack of enthusiasm that many enslavers expressed toward conversion of enslaved people. But the period also saw the slow beginnings of Afro-Christianity in both the North and the South, inspired by the **Great Awakening**, a wave of religious revivals that began in New England in the mid-1730s and spread south during the Revolutionary era. This multidenominational movement was led by evangelical ministers from various Protestant sects, attracting Presbyterian, Congregationalist, Baptist, and Methodist participants, as well as members of German, Dutch Reformed, and Moravian churches. These ministers, known as **New Lights**, rejected Protestantism's traditional emphasis on doctrine and ritual in favor of emotional sermons that urged listeners to repent and find spiritual salvation in Christ. New Lights did not seek out

Great Awakening
A multidenominational series of evangelical revivals that took place in North America between the 1730s and the 1780s.

New Lights
Protestant ministers who, during the Great Awakening, challenged traditional religious practices by delivering emotional sermons that urged listeners to repent and find salvation in Christ.

A Moravian Baptism Ceremony
This drawing appears in a German history of the Moravians in Pennsylvania from 1757. A white pastor and two deacons lay their hands on the enslaved man who is being baptized; baptismal water is in the bucket by the windows. Women who have already been baptized surround the ministers. The congregation bearing witness is entirely composed of what the illustrator refers to as "Negro-Germans." **What characteristics of the Great Awakening are visible in this drawing? Why did the Great Awakening appeal to many enslaved people?** *Heritage Images/Getty Images.*

Black converts, but they welcomed Black and American Indian congregants, and their emotional preaching drew spectators of all colors and faiths.

Their message was also appealing. New Light ministers stressed that the liberating effects of faith were open to all. "You that are servants," Benjamin Colman of Boston's Brattle Street Church told his congregants in 1740, "and the meanest of our Household Servants, even our poor Negroes, chuse you the Service of CHRIST; He will make you his Freemen; The SON OF GOD, shall make you free, and you shall be free indeed."[14] At revival meetings, ministers encouraged Blacks and women to relate their conversion experiences and serve as religious examples for other worshippers, opening up new religious roles for both groups. Moreover, Baptist churches allowed Blacks to serve as exhorters, deacons, or even elders (church leaders). While few Black worshippers ever achieved these leadership roles, their growing prominence in church affairs did not go unnoticed. "Women and girls; yea, Negroes, have taken it upon them to do the business of preachers," one hostile observer complained in 1743.[15]

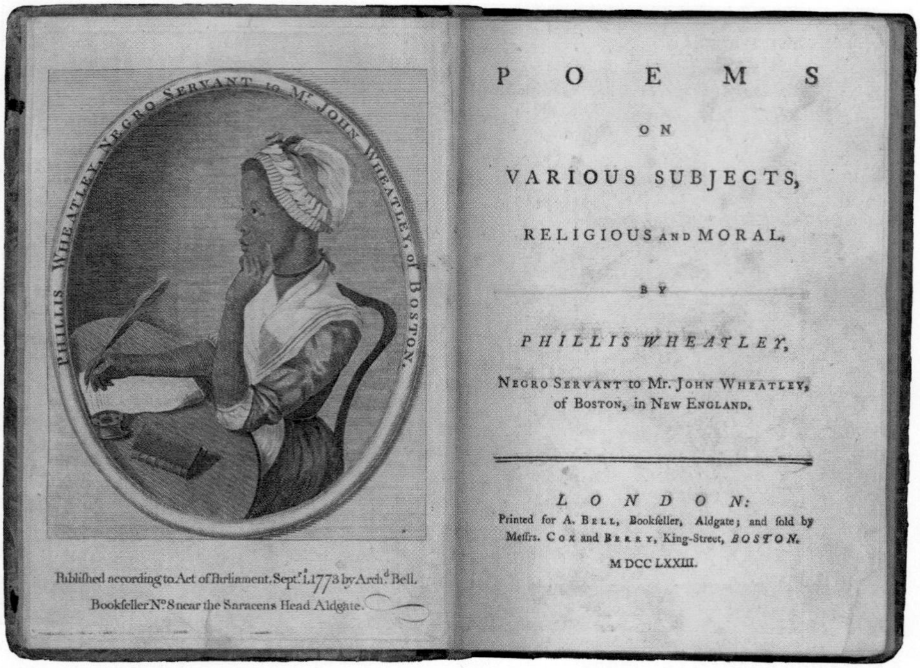

Phillis Wheatley

Poet and antislavery activist Phillis Wheatley published her first book of poems, *Poems on Various Subjects, Religious and Moral*, in 1773 at age twenty. The title page and frontispiece, shown here, feature an engraving of a dignified, intellectual Wheatley engaged in her craft. The frame around her portrait identifies her as "Phillis Wheatley, Negro Servant to Mr. John Wheatley, of Boston." Later that year, John Wheatley would free her. **How does this artist portray Wheatley? How might events in Wheatley's life have affected her perspective on Africa?** *© Massachusetts Historical Society, Boston, MA/Bridgeman Images.*

The egalitarian spirit of the Great Awakening fostered the education, conversion, and eventual manumission of several notable Black northerners, including the famous poet Phillis Wheatley. Wheatley, who was seven or eight years old when she was sold into slavery in the Senegal/Gambia region, was converted and educated by the devout family who purchased her from a slave ship in 1761. Her pious enslaver, Susannah Wheatley, loved the "spellbinding sermon[s]" of evangelical leaders and took their message to heart, encouraging her daughter, Mary, to teach the enslaved girl to read, write, and commit much of the Bible to memory. Phillis Wheatley began writing poetry in her teens, and she published her first book of poems in London when she was twenty years old. *Poems on Various Subjects, Religious and Moral* won her a following among British antislavery activists and also helped her win her own freedom. Later that year, Wheatley's enslaver freed her "at the desire of [his] friends in England."[16]

Likewise, the road to religious awakening began for Nigerian-born James Albert Ukawsaw Gronniosaw when he was purchased by Theodore Frelinghuysen, one of

New Jersey's leading New Light ministers, who sent Gronniosaw to school to learn to read. Initially reluctant to accept Frelinghuysen's notion of a divine father, Gronniosaw told the minister that "my father liv'd at Bournou, and that I wanted very much to see him, and likewise my dear mother, and sister, and I wish'd he would be so good as to send me home to them."[17]

But once he learned to read English, Gronniosaw proved more receptive to Frelinghuysen's instruction. He devoured spiritual classics such as John Bunyan's *The Pilgrim's Progress* and embraced the evangelical wisdom of Richard Baxter's fire-and-brimstone *A Call to the Unconverted*. Meanwhile, Gronniosaw's enslaver seems to have also embraced evangelicalism's liberatory message. Convinced that "the largest portion of the faithful have been poor and of little account," Frelinghuysen freed Gronniosaw in his will, leaving the formerly enslaved man ten pounds to support himself as he continued his spiritual journey.[18]

Wheatley and Gronniosaw were not the only enslaved people to find a religious path to freedom. As the Great Awakening moved south, it inspired thousands of enslavers to take a new interest in enslaved people's religious education and inspired an uptick in manumissions among devout enslavers. But the revival movement posed only a limited challenge to slavery as an institution. Although New Light ministers welcomed Black worshippers, few challenged slavery. In fact, the movement's leading luminaries, the Connecticut Congregationalist Jonathan Edwards and George Whitefield, an itinerant Anglican minister from Gloucester, England, both enslaved people themselves. These evangelical leaders had little trouble reconciling slavery with their religious faith. Edwards, who held several people enslaved for domestic tasks, criticized enslavers who mistreated those they enslaved, but he also maintained that enslaved people flourished under the guidance of a good Christian "master." Whitefield, once he moved from England to preach in Savannah, Georgia, developed similar convictions. Although he openly chided some Georgia enslavers who abused the people they enslaved, calling them "Monsters of Barbarity,"[19] he also remained convinced that slavery was compatible with Christianity as long as enslavers were careful to attend to the spiritual needs of the people they enslaved. He seems to have been terrified by the prospect of a slave revolt, having traveled through South Carolina shortly after the Stono rebellion in 1739. Whitefield encouraged enslaved Blacks to "stay in your calling at all costs . . . [and] give up the thought of seeking freedom from your masters." He also "pray[ed] God, they may never be permitted to get the upper hand."[20]

Whitefield was not alone in worrying that religion might overturn the South's social order. Indeed, in South Carolina, his message of conversion was largely suppressed after it moved two of his most enthusiastic converts to flout the colony's long-standing ban on gatherings of enslaved people. Wealthy siblings Hugh and Jonathan Bryan, who owned plantations in St. Helena's Parish, South Carolina, took to heart Whitefield's critique of enslavers who failed to offer religious instruction to enslaved people. But when the Bryan brothers resolved to organize a Negro school, they were soon investigated for calling together "great numbers of Negroes and other slaves."

AP® skills

Applying Disciplinary Knowledge: Explain the significance of Whitefield's perspective on the effect religion might have on the southern social order.

A committee assembled by the South Carolina Commons House of Assembly in 1742 concluded that, "however commendable" it may be for planters to instruct enslaved people on the "Principles of Religion or Morality, in their own Plantations," anyone who encouraged enslaved people from different plantations to congregate was endangering the "Safety of the Province."[21] Fined and threatened with arrest, the Bryan brothers repented and thereafter confined their religious proselytizing to the people they enslaved.

In the Chesapeake, where white colonists greatly outnumbered people of color, there was less opposition to Black participation in the revivals. Enslaved people in Virginia and Maryland, who were primarily native-born and spoke English, had no trouble understanding the evangelical movement's message and were drawn to its emotional style of worship. Evangelical revival services, which often took place in tent encampments, usually included songs and testimonials as well as prayer. They were more lively and open to innovation than the highly ritualized services offered in the Chesapeake's traditional churches, and they provided Black participants with opportunities to incorporate African music and styles of expression. Although some white ministers deplored the "groans, cries, screams, and agonies" heard from Blacks and other enthusiastic worshippers, most welcomed such congregants. "Ethiopia has . . . stretched forth her hands to God," the Presbyterian revivalist Samuel Davies declared after more than a hundred African Americans attended a revival he held in Hanover County, Virginia, in 1751. Anxious to instruct enslaved people in the Christian faith, Davies distributed Bibles and other religious literature at his revivals. Many of his enslaved congregants, hungry for literacy as well as salvation, spent "every leisure hour" learning to read.[22]

AP® skills

Applying Disciplinary Knowledge: How did the practice of Christianity evolve among Black worshipers? What aspects of the historical situation help contextualize this development?

By the late eighteenth century, Black lay preachers were leading conversions of their own. Many kept their calling largely silent and led congregations that met in secret. Enslaved preachers and their followers were members of a multidenominational Black church that one historian has called the "invisible institution."[23] The product of an era when enslaved people were generally forbidden to hold public gatherings, enslaved congregations often met only under the veil of night. As a result, the activities of enslaved preachers are not well documented.

Even free Black preachers were often forbidden to lead public forms of worship, as the Virginia-born John Marrant found out. A lay preacher, he was eager to share his religious faith with the enslaved people on the Charleston, South Carolina, plantation where he worked as a carpenter, but the plantation's mistress objected. She insisted that Christianity would only result in "negroes ruined," Marrant later recalled. He defied her wishes by leading covert prayer meetings, until her husband launched a surprise raid on one such meeting, bringing in neighbors and employees who helped him flog the congregants until "blood ran from their backs and sides to the floor to make them leave off praying." Thereafter, Marrant's followers prayed only in secret.[24]

Despite white opposition, African Americans' "invisible institution" flourished, offering worshippers a buffer against the white racism they faced on a daily basis.

Whereas the South's white evangelicals hoped that Christianity would school Blacks in obedience and submission, Black converts took other lessons from their newfound faith. Drawn in by the egalitarian spirit of the evangelical movement, they embraced Christianity's message that all people are equal before God, and they saw in the Bible's promises of spiritual deliverance some hope of eventually achieving freedom on earth as well as in heaven. In doing so, they crafted a distinctly Afro-Christian religious faith that helped them survive slavery while praying for freedom.

The African American Revolution

How did colonial laws affect the lives and citizenship rights of enslaved and free African Americans during the late colonial era?

The Revolutionary era was a time of remarkable **ideological** ferment among African Americans. The Great Awakening offered both a new religious faith and educational opportunities to many Black converts, who often found a critique of slavery in the revivalists' message of religious equality. African Americans found the egalitarian principles on which the colonists based their struggles against the British to be equally liberating. The American Revolution took place during the Enlightenment, a time when thinkers throughout the Americas and western Europe questioned traditional institutions, customs, and morals. The discontented colonists framed their complaints in terms of philosophical principles with far-reaching implications.

ideology
A system of ideas and beliefs.

The colonists' rift with Britain took shape over the taxes, import duties, and other obligations the British Parliament imposed on the American colonies. But the colonists went beyond financial disputes to insist that all men had a natural right to self-government. In doing so, they opened up new questions about the legitimacy of slavery. The Revolutionary leader James Otis Jr. maintained that "the colonists are by the law of nature freeborn, as indeed all men are, white or black," and many of Otis's fellow patriots opposed American participation in the African slave trade.[25] But the Revolution's leaders avoided direct attacks on American slavery for fear that internal controversies might derail their attempts to unite the colonies in the common cause. African Americans did not share these fears and approached the Revolution as an antislavery struggle from the outset. They drew on both Revolutionary ideology and the social and political chaos of war to challenge slavery by petitioning for freedom, running away, and fighting for their own liberty on both sides of the conflict.

The Road to Independence

The American colonists' discontent with British rule began in the early 1760s, when the British Parliament levied a new series of taxes on the colonies. The taxes, designed to raise money to pay off British debts incurred during the French and Indian War (1754–1763), when British troops were deployed to protect the colonists' land, were not excessive. But they represented a shift from Britain's previous policy of benign neglect toward the colonies. Colonists had long controlled their own affairs and paid only local taxes. They also had no say in British imperial policy and no political representation in Parliament, which they felt entitled to as British subjects. In particular, they insisted that they should not be subject to "taxation without representation." Taxes imposed on the colonies by Parliament, the rebellious colonists maintained, deprived them of their property without their consent, making them little better than enslaved people.

African Americans were largely unaffected by British taxes because most Blacks were either enslaved or impoverished and, therefore, had little access to the goods that were taxed. But colonists' protests against British tyranny nonetheless held a powerful appeal for African Americans. White patriots cast their opposition to British authority as a struggle for freedom, denouncing the "vile, ignominious slavery" imposed on them by Britain's new policies.[26] Their protests drew on the natural rights philosophy articulated by thinkers such as Britain's own John Locke, who maintained that "men being . . . by nature all free, equal, and independent, no one can be put out of this estate and subjected to the political power of another without his own consent."[27]

AP® skills

Applying Disciplinary Knowledge: Who was blamed for chattel slavery, and why?

Although rarely intended to challenge slavery, white colonists' rhetoric gave enslaved people a powerful new political language with which to address their own condition. When white colonists in Charleston protested passage of the Stamp Act of 1765 — which required colonists to print most documents on a special stamped paper that was issued and taxed by the British government — with chants of "Liberty! Liberty and stamp'd paper," local enslaved people also called for "Liberty, liberty," much to the horror of white observers. A South Carolina politician, recording the incident, dismissed the enslaved people's chant as "a thoughtless imitation" of whites.[28] But enslaved unrest mounted throughout the years leading up to the Revolution, as the conflict inspired African Americans to stage freedom struggles of their own.

In the pre-Revolution years, as American colonists boycotted British goods; protested taxes on stamped documents, sugar, and tea; and scuffled with British soldiers stationed on American soil, enslaved people across the colonies took advantage of the unrest to escape from their enslavers. In Georgia and South Carolina, they fled to swamplands and other unsettled frontier areas to form maroon communities. In the more densely populated North, they often headed for urban areas. According to Boston patriot John Adams, some of the enslaved people already living in northern cities took advantage of the social disorder to free themselves. As the colonies moved toward declaring their independence, he later recalled, enslaved Bostonians pushed for their own freedom by becoming "lazy, idle, proud, vicious and at length wholly useless to their masters, to such a degree that the abolition of slavery became a measure of economy."[29]

Other Black northerners publicly embraced the Revolutionary struggle. In 1772, while still enslaved herself, Phillis Wheatley wrote a poem dedicated to the Earl of Dartmouth, the British king's newly appointed secretary of state for North

America — and a man the colonists hoped might remedy their discontent. In verses linking the patriots' tribulations with those of the enslaved Blacks. Wheatley heralded Dartmouth's appointment as a sign that New England would once more see "Freedom's charms unfold." She went on to explain that having been "young in life" when she was "snatch'd from Afric's fancy'd happy seat," she knew the pain of slavery all too well and could "but pray / Others may never feel tyrannic sway." After her emancipation, Wheatley continued publicly to question how the colonists could reconcile their "cry of liberty" with "the exercise of oppressive power over others."[30] (See AP® Working with Sources: Black Freedom Fighters, pp. 153–61.)

Most of Wheatley's Black contemporaries did not possess her writing skills, but some managed to take such questions to the courts by initiating **freedom suits** that challenged local magistrates and colonial legislatures to recognize their natural rights. "Attended Court; heard the trial of an action of trespass, brought by a mulatto woman, for damages, for restraining her of her liberty," John Adams wrote in his diary in 1766, after witnessing a freedom suit brought by Jenny Slew of Ipswich, Massachusetts. "This is called suing for liberty; the first action that ever I knew of the sort, though I have heard there have been many."[31] As the daughter of a free white woman, Slew claimed her liberty as a birthright, but later enslaved litigants claimed freedom as a natural right, sometimes winning their liberty as a result.

freedom suits
Legal actions by which enslaved people sought to achieve freedom in British and American courts.

Some of the impetus for the freedom suits came from events in Britain rather than America. The **Somerset case**, which freed an enslaved American named James Somerset in 1772, inspired new challenges to slavery throughout the British empire. Somerset was born in Africa and sold into slavery in Virginia, where he lived until his owner, Charles Stewart, brought him to London while traveling on business. Somerset ran away but was caught and imprisoned on a ship bound for Jamaica, where Stewart planned to sell him. The British antislavery activist Granville Sharp, a municipal official, hired lawyers who issued a writ of **habeas corpus** challenging Stewart's right to detain Somerset. Designed to prevent false imprisonment, writs of habeas corpus (Latin for "you should have the body") request the legal review of prisoners detained without trial. The Somerset case ended up in the court of Britain's lord chief justice William Murray, Earl of Mansfield, who was aware that it could challenge the legal status of British slavery. He nonetheless ruled in favor of freeing Somerset, although his ruling was carefully worded to apply only to Somerset's case.

Somerset case (1772)
A British legal case that freed an enslaved American named James Somerset and inspired other enslaved people to sue for their freedom.

habeas corpus
A feature of English common law that protects prisoners from being detained without trial. Translated literally, the Latin phrase means "you should have the body."

The Somerset case did not make slavery illegal in Britain or even address its status anywhere else, but when British antislavery activists celebrated Somerset's release, enslaved people in Britain and the Americas drew on the case to make their own claims to liberty. In January 1773, Massachusetts Blacks collectively petitioned the colony's governor and legislature for the first time. Signed by one author, Felix [Holbrook], but written on behalf of enslaved people throughout Massachusetts, the document appealed to legislators to relieve the "unhappy state and condition" of the enslaved. Invoking the Somerset case as a precedent for their own emancipation, petitioners noted that "men of Great note and Influence . . . have pleaded our cause with arguments which we hope will have their weight with this honorable court."[32] Meanwhile, in Virginia, news of the Somerset case may have prompted an enslaved man named Bacchus to begin a long journey to England in 1774. Bacchus's enslaver, a Virginia lawyer named Gabriel Jones, certainly suspected as much. The runaway slave advertisement that Jones submitted to the *Virginia Gazette* on June 18, 1774, described the appearance of the thirty-year-old freedom seeker and predicted that "he will probably endeavour to pass for a Freeman by the Name of *John Christian*, and attempt to get on Board some Vessel bound for *Great Britain*, from the Knowledge he has of the late Determination of *Somerset*'s Case."[33]

What became of Bacchus is unknown, but the Massachusetts legislature tabled Felix's petition. They received another petition a month later. The new petition listed several authors: Peter Bestes, Sambo Freeman, Felix Holbrook, and Chester Joie. It also bypassed the colony's unpopular governor to speak directly to the patriots in the rebellious house of representatives. "We expect great things from men who have made such a noble stand against the designs of their *fellow-men* to enslave them," they wrote, before requesting the representatives' "assistance in our peaceable and lawful attempts to gain our freedom . . . which, *as men*, we have a natural right to."[34] Framed in the Revolutionary rhetoric of the day, the petitioners' request echoed the expansive natural rights philosophy celebrated by Massachusetts patriots such as James Otis Jr. But Otis never even freed his own enslaved manservant, and Massachusetts legislators proved equally unwilling to link the petitioners' freedom struggles to their own. They ignored the second petition and several subsequent appeals.

Black Patriots

Despite the disappointments, many Black northerners joined the patriot cause. Once the conflict began, fugitives from slavery could often secure their freedom through military service. More than five thousand African Americans are estimated to have fought alongside American forces during the Revolution, and other Blacks sided with the patriots without actually enlisting. Among the best known of these unofficial patriots is Crispus Attucks, a Black seaman who was in all likelihood a fugitive from slavery. Attucks was the American Revolution's first casualty.

The son of an African father and a Natick Indian mother, Attucks was likely born into slavery in Framingham, Massachusetts, sometime in the early 1720s, and fled a farm there in 1750. After his escape, Attucks may have kept a low profile to avoid capture. But as a sailor and dockworker who lived and worked on the Boston waterfront when he was not at sea, Attucks was among the many Bostonians who resented the growing British military presence in New England's premier port city. The British "redcoats" were especially unpopular among men in Attucks's profession because they often supplemented their meager military salaries by working part-time at lower wages than American workers were willing to accept. The soldiers' presence on the docks also discouraged the brisk business in smuggled goods that had long

AP® exam tip

You'll need to know how to explain the purpose of a source. A good first step is summarizing the historical situation at the time. Consider how the story of Crispus Attucks can help you explain the purpose of the advertisement on page 135.

allowed colonial shippers to avoid British taxes. Finally, the British troops threatened the liberty of American sailors and dockworkers, who were often impressed or forced into service in the British navy. These discontented American workers figured prominently in igniting what became known as the Boston Massacre.

The conflict took place on the afternoon of March 5, 1770, beginning in a tavern on Boston's waterfront, where a group of men that one observer described as a "motley rabble of saucy boys, Negroes and mulattoes, Irish teagues [a derogatory term for Catholics] and outlandish jacktars [sailors]" encountered a British soldier who came in to inquire about part-time work.[35] Later that day, outraged by this intrusion onto their turf, more than thirty men from the bar gathered outside the port's customhouse to taunt and heckle the British soldiers stationed outside. The scuffle ended when the redcoats fired on the crowd, killing five men and wounding eleven more. The first to die was Attucks, who was forty-seven years old at the time of his death. More than six feet tall and powerfully built, Attucks was one of the mob's leaders. He may not have been fighting for freedom, but as a member of a close-knit community of workingmen, he was willing to defend his livelihood and died a hero as a result. Attucks and the massacre's other martyrs were honored with a funeral procession that attracted ten thousand mourners, and they were buried together in a common grave.

Attucks was widely celebrated as the "first to defy, the first to die," but his race was rarely noted in Revolutionary-era commemorations of the Boston Massacre.[36] As a man of color who was probably a fugitive from slavery, Attucks embodied contradictions that might divide the former colonists as they fought to establish a slaveholding republic. Accordingly, the famous silversmith and engraver Paul Revere chose not to

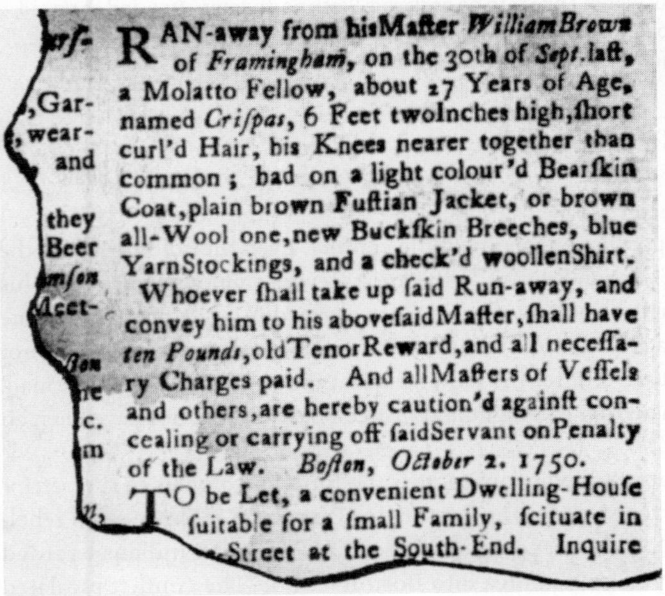
RAN-away from his Maſter *William Brown* of *Framingham*, on the 30th of *Sept.* laſt, a Molatto Fellow, about 27 Years of Age, named *Criſpas*, 6 Feet two Inches high, ſhort curl'd Hair, his Knees nearer together than common; had on a light colour'd Bearſkin Coat, plain brown Fuſtian Jacket, or brown all-Wool one, new Buckſkin Breeches, blue Yarn Stockings, and a check'd woollen Shirt.

Whoever ſhall take up ſaid Run-away, and convey him to his abovesaid Maſter, ſhall have *ten Pounds*, old Tenor Reward, and all neceſſary Charges paid. And all Maſters of Veſſels and others, are hereby caution'd againſt concealing or carrying off ſaid Servant on Penalty of the Law. *Boſton, October* 2. 1750.

TO be Let, a convenient Dwelling-Houſe ſuitable for a ſmall Family, ſcituate in Street at the South-End. Inquire

Wanted Ad for Crispus Attucks

In what is believed to be an ad for Crispus Attucks that ran in the *Boston Gazette* in October 1750, an enslaver described him as "Run-away from his Master." He both offers a reward and warns of punishment to those helping the man escape. Twenty years later, Attucks was a leader in the effort to defy British troops who patrolled Boston harbor. The first to die in the Boston Massacre, he is widely celebrated as the first casualty of the American Revolution. **What does this ad reveal about how Crispus Attucks resisted enslavement?** *Granger/ Granger — All rights reserved.*

African Americans in the Revolution
On July 9, 1776, a group of New York patriots pulled down and destroyed an equestrian statue of Britain's King George III. This French print shows one artist's attempt to depict the event. Although the image has some flaws — rather than being mounted on horseback as he was in the actual statue, for example, the king is shown standing in the print — it is significant in its portrayal of the patriots, most of whom appear to be enslaved. Black northerners, free and enslaved, were a vital force in the patriot struggle. They hoped that in casting off British rule, the colonists would also renounce African slavery. **Compare and contrast the actions depicted in this image to the Contextualizing African American Stories vignette at the beginning of this chapter.** *'La Destruction de la statue royale a Nouvelle Yorck', published in Paris, 1777/Library of Congress, Prints and Photographs Division, Washington, D.C. LC-USZ62-2202.*

include Attucks in his popular engraving of the conflict. Even the color prints of the engraving created by Christian Remick — the artist Revere employed to colorize his broadside — feature British soldiers shooting into a crowd of white patriots. As one nineteenth-century Black abolitionist would later put it, white Americans were not ready to acknowledge that "but for the blow struck at the right time by a black man, the United States, with all that it of right and justice boasts, might not have been an independent republic."[37]

The Boston Massacre rallied people across the thirteen colonies to the patriot cause. In Boston, it set the stage for the Boston Tea Party in 1773. In an open rebellion against the British Tea Act, colonists dressed as American Indians boarded British ships and dumped boxes of tea into Boston harbor. The conflict escalated when Britain passed a series of laws known as the Intolerable Acts. These included the Massachusetts Government Act and the Administration of Justice Act, which curtailed the colonial government's power; the Boston Port Act, which closed Boston's port until its citizens reimbursed British officials for the tea they had destroyed; and the Quartering Act, which stationed British troops in Boston. The British hoped that this punitive legislation would isolate the Massachusetts rebels, but instead it united the American colonists in outrage. In 1774, they organized the First Continental Congress to lobby Britain for the reversal of the Intolerable Acts. The congress threatened to boycott British goods if the acts were not repealed and pledged to support Massachusetts in the event of a British attack, which was not long in coming. On April 19, 1775, the British marched on the towns of Lexington and Concord in a surprise attack designed to subdue the rebellious colony's leaders. Instead, it started a war.

Black northerners were among the patriots who rallied against the British, often joining the struggle in hopes of encouraging the colonists to reject African slavery as well as British tyranny. For instance, a free Black resident of Massachusetts named Lemuel Haynes joined the Granville minutemen and fought in several battles before he fell ill. Horrified when the British invaded Lexington and Concord, the twenty-two-year-old Haynes had recently been freed from indentured servitude and saw the Battle of Lexington as a fight between "tyrants" and the "Liberty [for which] each freeman strives."[38] He also wished to expand the boundaries of that freedom. Although the Declaration of Independence, issued in 1776, maintained that "all men are created equal," it did not free enslaved people (see Appendix: The Declaration of Independence). That omission inspired the studious Haynes, who became a Congregationalist minister, to write his own addendum to the Declaration later that year. Titled "Liberty Further Extended," Haynes's unpublished manuscript called for the abolition of slavery in the American colonies. (See AP® Working with Sources: Black Freedom Fighters, pp. 153–61.)

AP® skills

Applying Disciplinary Knowledge: How did Lemuel Haynes help foster support for the war against the British?

As Haynes's actions illustrate, even before the Second Continental Congress met in May 1775 to organize the war effort, colonial militias mobilized all over New England, enlisting Blacks as well as whites. The Massachusetts Safety Committee, formed in the summer of 1774 to protect citizens from British tyranny, had initially barred enlistment of the enslaved as "inconsistent with the principles [of freedom] that are to be supported."[39] But bans had little practical effect after the British marched on Lexington. As the redcoats approached, Peter Salem, a local enslaved man, was freed to help defend the town. Salem went on to become one of the approximately one hundred patriots of color who served during the Battle of Bunker Hill, where he was widely credited with firing the shot that killed the unpopular British leader Major John Pitcairn.[40] Many of the Revolution's Black soldiers probably entered the patriot forces on similar terms. Militia rosters across New England listed men such as "Joshua Boylston's Prince" and "Isaac Gardner's Adam," whose names suggest that they, too, had only recently been freed from slavery.[41]

Haynes hoped that military service would win Black Americans their "*undeniable right to . . . liberty*," and many enslaved combatants clearly shared his hope.[42]

Enslaved people enlisted in large numbers after northern colonies from Rhode Island to New York passed legislation pledging to free Blacks willing to serve for the duration of the conflict. Shortly before the war, the enslaved Connecticut man Boyrereau Brinch, whose autobiography later recorded his ambivalence about fighting "to liberate freemen, my tyrants," was drafted into the Sixth Connecticut Regiment while still enslaved. He fought for five years before finally receiving his freedom.[43]

For other Black northerners, military service brought immediate freedom. In Rhode Island, where slavery was entrenched, the promise of freedom prompted Blacks to enlist at twice the rate of whites — despite their enslavers' warnings that the British would ship them off to the West Indies if they were captured. Undeterred, enslaved people abandoned their enslavers to enlist until the state began offering enslavers up to 120 pounds for each enslaved person they liberated for military service. In addition to paying for enslaved soldiers, northern states encouraged enslaved enlistments by allowing enslavers to send enslaved substitutes into battle rather than fight themselves.

AP® skills

Applying Disciplinary Knowledge: Why were Black patriots less common in the South? What caused white southerners to question the loyalty of enslaved people?

Black patriots were far less common in the South, where widespread opposition to enslaved soldiers prohibited Black enlistments during the early years of the conflict. As the war began, white southerners understandably questioned enslaved people's loyalty to the cause. As early as 1774, enslaved people in Virginia had conspired to run away in groups when British troops arrived, convincing enslavers that enslaved people would side with the British. "If America & Britain come to a hostile rupture," Virginian James Madison worried, "an Insurrection among the slaves may and will be promoted."[44]

Appointed commander in chief of the newly established Continental army on June 15, 1775, General George Washington shared Madison's sentiments. When he traveled to Cambridge, Massachusetts, to assume command of the patriot forces, he was horrified to find armed Black men among them. He issued general orders barring their enlistment, which he renewed in December. But there is little evidence that Washington's prohibitions, which he later reversed, had a significant effect on Blacks' service. Many New England troops were integrated from the start of the conflict, and after 1776, other colonies used enslaved soldiers to fill enlistment quotas. Only South Carolina and Georgia never mobilized their Black populations. Enslavers who resisted the use of Black soldiers feared slave insurrections and were also afraid of losing their human property. As the Revolution spread south, both outcomes quickly became real possibilities. In 1775, long before the southern colonies had begun to enlist enslaved Blacks, the British organized their first regiment of freedom seekers. They also encouraged freedom seekers to join their armies throughout the conflict. In doing so, they created thousands of Black **loyalists**, as those who remained loyal to the British were called. In this war, African Americans sought freedom on both sides of the conflict (Map 4.1).

loyalists
Colonists who remained loyal to Britain during the American Revolution.

Black Loyalists

Approximately fifteen thousand Black loyalists served with the British. They first entered the war early, at the request of Virginia's royal governor John Murray, the Earl

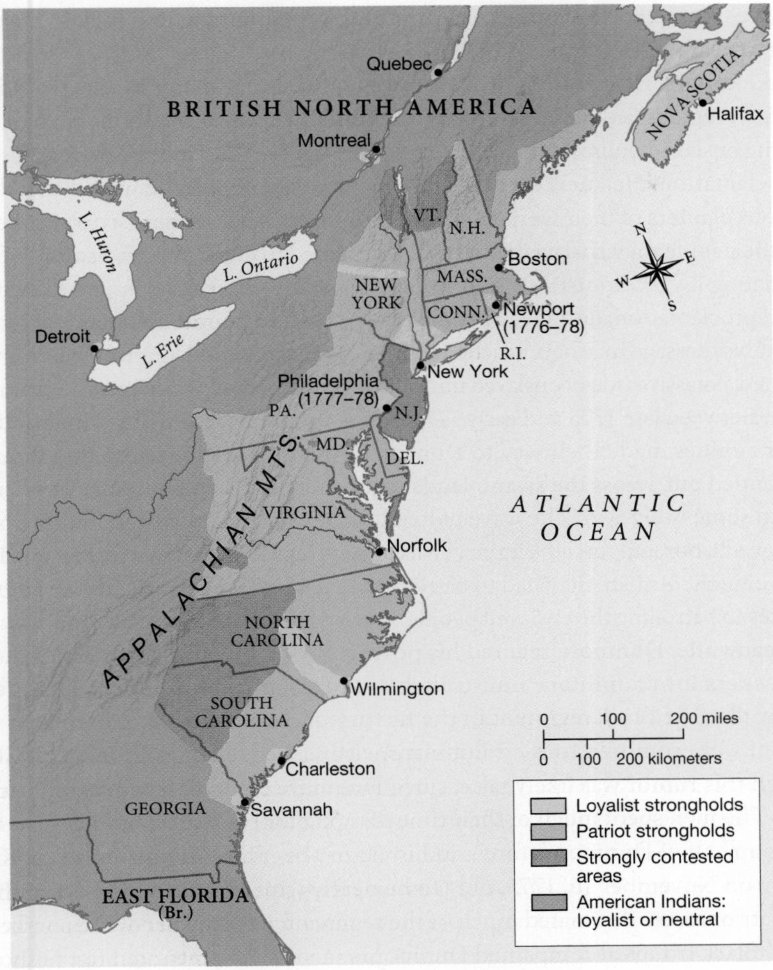

MAP 4.1 Patriots and Loyalists

The American Revolution divided the eastern seaboard's inhabitants into loyalists and patriots, whose sympathies varied from place to place. Patriots were in the majority in most of the colonies; loyalists were widely dispersed, but their strongholds were limited. These political allegiances were hard to track and shifted often, making it difficult to pinpoint the exact numbers of patriots and loyalists at any given point. **Why were so many port cities loyalist strongholds?**

of Dunmore, whom patriot forces had driven out in June 1775. Determined to recapture the colony, Dunmore took refuge on a British ship patrolling the waters outside Yorktown. With only three hundred men at his disposal, he desperately needed reinforcements. On November 7, he reached out to local allies by issuing what became known as **Lord Dunmore's Proclamation**. This published broadside offered freedom

Lord Dunmore's Proclamation (1775) A document issued by Virginia's royal governor John Murray, the Earl of Dunmore, in November 1775, offering freedom to those enslaved by "rebel" colonists if they joined his forces.

to all "indentured Servants, Negroes, or others, (appertaining to Rebels) . . . able and willing to bear Arms" for the British.

Like other British officials, Dunmore realized that many Blacks would serve on whichever side would allow them to fight for their own freedom. He had begun receiving enslaved volunteers as early as April 1775 — many months before he issued his proclamation. He knew that by enlisting enslaved people, he would also deprive rebellious planters of their workers — and send some rebel soldiers scurrying home to guard the people they enslaved. But he still hesitated to enlist enslaved soldiers for fear of alienating loyal colonists. By November, he had no choice and issued the carefully worded proclamation, designed to recruit only enslaved people belonging to rebels.

But his message may have reached a larger audience. Lord Dunmore's Proclamation unleashed a massive tide of enslaved unrest that fundamentally reshaped the character of the war. Between late 1775 and early 1776, some eight hundred enslaved men and many of their families made their way to Dunmore's floating headquarters, and thousands more fanned out across the swamplands in an effort to reach Dunmore or seize their freedom some other way. The wave of freedom seekers disrupted agriculture powered by enslaved labor and forced Virginia enslavers to wage a war on two fronts: in addition to defeating the British, they had to battle armed enslaved rebels and devote additional resources to patrolling the enslaved people who remained on their plantations.

AP® skills

Applying Disciplinary Knowledge: What impact did Lord Dunmore's Proclamation have on the war in 1775 and 1776?

Meanwhile, Dunmore secured his position by organizing the fittest of the freedom seekers into a military unit called Lord Dunmore's Ethiopian Regiment — possibly the first Black regiment in the history of British America. Members of the regiment were rumored to wear uniforms with sashes reading "Liberty for Slaves," although this rumor was likely false, since Dunmore could barely outfit his existing troops. The men spent much of their time foraging for supplies. They also saw battle, making up half of Dunmore's forces in his victory over the Virginia militia at Kemp's Landing on November 16, 1775, only to be nearly wiped out less than a month later, when patriot forces decimated much of the regiment. Replenished with new freedom seekers, Black troops accompanied Dunmore's men as they retreated to the shores of Chesapeake Bay, but smallpox killed off many of the new recruits and their families.

Dunmore failed to hold on to Virginia, and in the summer of 1776, just as the Continental Congress began circulating the Declaration of Independence, he abandoned Virginia to join British forces in New York. But his proclamation had an important and enduring effect on patriot military policy. The prospect of the enslaved people of Virginia fighting for the British convinced General Washington that the outcome of the war now depended on "which side can arm the Negroes faster," and with his support, the congress declared all Blacks eligible for service in the Continental army a week after Dunmore issued his proclamation.[45]

Lord Dunmore's Proclamation also attracted freedom-seeking Black loyalists from as far away as New York and New Jersey. One was a twenty-two-year-old enslaved man named Titus, who ran away from a farmer in Monmouth County, New Jersey, to join the Ethiopian Regiment. He was shipped out when Dunmore retreated to New York

"Bucks of America" flag

Congress declared that Blacks were eligible for service in the Continental army a week after the British army offered freedom to Blacks who would join their ranks. In Massachusetts, an all-Black militia, known as the "Bucks of America," fought as patriots in the Revolutionary War. Years later, in 1789, the Massachusetts governor presented this flag to them during a war commemoration. The flag displays thirteen stars on a blue field, with a buck at the center, leaping under a pine tree, which was a symbol of New England. **Why is this flag historically significant?** *'Bucks of America' flag, c.1787/Massachusetts Historical Society, Boston, MA/Bridgeman Images.*

and soon ended up less than a hundred miles from his home. Undeterred, Titus joined New Jersey's loyalist troops and fought in the Battle of Monmouth County in June 1778, capturing the head of the Monmouth militia. Although he was never officially commissioned as an officer, Titus earned the name "Colonel Tye" for his successful raids. He organized his own commando unit, known as the Black Brigade, with New Jersey Blacks who knew the countryside well. The brigade raided the homes of farmers, making off with their cattle, horses, and enslaved people. Tye and his men turned over their captives to the British and sold to the British the food and supplies they had seized. By the spring of 1780, Tye had New Jersey patriots so terrified that they prevailed on their governor to declare martial law — to little avail. Tye's men continued to terrorize New Jersey until the fall of that year, when Tye died after being wounded in battle.

Lord Dunmore's Proclamation had its most significant impact in the South. Most of the Blacks who served with loyalist forces were southerners, and the proclamation also triggered a mass exodus of freedom seekers, who escaped their plantations by crossing British lines. Historians estimate that 80,000 to 100,000 southern enslaved people fled their enslavers during the Revolution. Not all remained with

AP® skills

Applying Disciplinary Knowledge: What impact did Lord Dunmore's Proclamation have on the Continental army?

the British, however. Some freed themselves and headed to places where they were likely to remain free, such as cities and towns with large free Black populations or frontier areas where slavery had yet to take hold. Moreover, the British did not offer shelter to all the freedom seekers who crossed their lines. British officers were obliged to return any freedom seekers who had escaped from loyalist enslavers, and some British officers sold enslaved people who had escaped from patriot enslavers.

Despite such risks, the chance to find freedom with the British appealed to African Americans throughout the war. Most refugees did not end up in British uniforms because British commanders had little time to train new troops and were often unable to supply their Black volunteers with food and shelter, let alone arms. Instead, they put the refugees to work foraging for food and supplies. Although such duties frequently required the freedom seekers to carry arms and fight any patriots they encountered, they did so without recognition or military pay. Refugees worked behind the lines as well, building fortifications, transporting munitions, cooking for troops, and doing their laundry. British commanders also employed refugees as domestic servants, often supplying their officers with an entire staff of Black domestics.

> **AP® skills**
>
> **Applying Disciplinary Knowledge:** Why was the "certificate of freedom" significant? What challenges did Black refugees still face despite it?

Black refugees were entitled to a "certificate of freedom" for their work but received few other benefits and often had to provide food and shelter for themselves. They also faced other dangers. Food and clean water were often in short supply, and disease remained endemic in the British camps. Thousands escaped slavery only to die of smallpox and what contemporaries called "camp fever," which was likely typhus. Despite these harrowing conditions, many African Americans took their chances with the British, who offered them their only opportunity to achieve freedom.

The service of these freedom seekers was crucial to Britain's war effort and helped reshape British military strategy — and not a moment too soon. In 1778, after three years' worth of military action in the North, the British had yet to win a decisive victory. Worse still for the British, after patriot forces defeated General John Burgoyne's army at Saratoga, New York, in 1777, the French entered the war on the side of the Americans, raising fears that Spain would join their cause as well. France and Spain were Britain's chief imperial rivals, and both countries saw the American rebellion as a chance to challenge Britain's power in America and the Caribbean. With an increasingly international war now under way, Britain's military resources were overextended. Even the mighty British navy could not defend the Caribbean as long as Britain devoted most of its military resources to subduing the die-hard patriots.

Slavery, Soldiers, and the Outcome of the Revolution

How did American law affect the lives and citizenship rights of enslaved and free African Americans during the Revolutionary War?

As the Revolutionary War dragged on, Britain's decision to free enslaved people in exchange for service angered enslavers and weakened loyalist support in the South. When the British abandoned the American colonies in defeat, they also abandoned many Black allies who had fought valiantly in hopes of gaining their freedom. The American Revolution set the northern states on a path to ending slavery — immediately (1777) in some states and more gradually in others, until it was almost entirely eliminated by the 1820s. The free Black population of both the North and the Chesapeake increased significantly throughout this period. Only elsewhere in the South did slavery remain entrenched.

American Victory, British Defeat

Toward the end of 1778, the British Parliament adopted a new battle plan known as the **southern strategy**. Its goal was to crush the rebellion by retaking the South, which was home to far more loyalists than the Northeast and would therefore, the British hoped, be far easier to conquer. The plan depended partly on enlisting help from the region's enslaved people, whose loyalties lay with the British rather than the patriots. Moving the war south also allowed the British to monitor French and Spanish activities in the Caribbean, as well as to blockade southern ports to prevent the delivery of French aid to the patriots.

southern strategy An unsuccessful British military plan, adopted in late 1778, that was designed to defeat the patriots by recapturing the American South.

Britain's southern strategy initially paid off. British troops captured Savannah in 1778 and Charleston in 1779. Black loyalists were crucial to their efforts from the start. In Georgia, a Black sailor named Samson guided the British fleet over shoals at the mouth of the Savannah River. When British troops disembarked, they discovered that the patriots had destroyed a bridge leading to the city and guarded the only remaining road. An elderly enslaved man named Quamino Dolly approached a lieutenant colonel with his plans for an alternative approach and showed troops a route through a nearby swamp, which allowed the British to stage a surprise attack and capture Savannah.

Sir Henry Clinton, who became commander in chief of the British forces later that year, was eager to enlist similar support from enslaved people. In June 1779, as he prepared for an assault on Charleston, he issued the Philipsburg Proclamation. It expanded Lord Dunmore's Proclamation by promising to free all enslaved people willing to serve in any capacity rather than just those who joined the fighting. It also recognized the growing importance of African American patriot combatants by declaring that any Blacks found serving the patriots would be sold for the benefit of the crown.

In the end, however, Britain's southern strategy failed. The vast geographic scope of the southern states ensured that the British would never have enough troops to defend the areas they conquered, while the loyalist support they had hoped for failed to materialize. Instead of finding allies among the former colonists, the British were thwarted by determined opposition from patriot forces. In addition, the embattled new nation had no crucial center of power that British forces could capture and subdue. Even though the British twice seized Philadelphia, the new nation's original capital, they could not derail the Americans.

Moreover, the growing presence of Black soldiers in the Continental army often undermined British attempts to use the people the patriots enslaved against them. In the summer of 1781, for example, a Black patriot spy double-crossed the British by infiltrating their headquarters on behalf of the Marquis de Lafayette, a French volunteer who became a general in George Washington's army. Lafayette was desperate to drive the British general Charles Cornwallis out of Virginia and had been trying for months, without success, to gain advance information about his troop movements. He finally succeeded when he dispatched a formerly enslaved man named James Armistead, who easily infiltrated Cornwallis's camp at Yorktown by posing as a refugee looking for work. Armistead won the trust of Cornwallis, who invited him to spy for the British, at which point Armistead became a double agent. He supplied true information to the Americans and false information to the British, and he remained undiscovered until the day the defeated Cornwallis encountered Armistead in Lafayette's camp and realized that he had been duped.

Still more fatal to Britain's southern strategy was the distinctly mixed success of the British policy of freeing the people enslaved by the rebels. Although the British desperately needed manpower, by enlisting enslaved support, both Dunmore and Clinton eroded their loyalist support in the South and stiffened the resolve of southern patriots. Many southerners were ambivalent about independence when the fighting began, but after Dunmore issued his proclamation, the British never commanded the widespread southern support they envisioned. Clinton's Philipsburg Proclamation only compounded the problem. In the Carolinas and Georgia especially, where most whites were enslavers, loyalists were regarded as traitors to public safety, and patriots were as dedicated to protecting slavery as they were to achieving independence. With support for the war wavering at home, the British abandoned America to the patriots rather than continue the fight. Cornwallis's 1781 surrender at Yorktown was the beginning of the war's end and set the stage for a military retreat that largely devastated Britain's Black allies.

The Fate of Black Loyalists

> **AP® exam tip**
>
> Task verbs identify the action that has to be taken within the prompt. For example, "Describe the fate of Black Loyalists" requires you to write two relevant characteristics of what happened to Black Loyalists after the end of the Revolutionary War. "Explain the fate of Black Loyalists" requires you to contextualize what happened by discussing how or why specific things happened to Black Loyalists after the war ended.

At the siege of Yorktown, a major defeat for Britain, Cornwallis provided no protection for the thousands of African Americans serving in his forces. Under a sustained assault from French and American forces that began in late September 1781, his headquarters were crowded, ravaged by smallpox, and cut off from British supply lines. Desperately short of food by mid-October, Cornwallis first slaughtered his horses to prevent his troops from starving and then issued orders expelling his African American allies to fend for themselves. "It is not to be done," mourned the senior British officer who took the orders and was all too aware that the refugees would be reenslaved. "We drove back to the enemy all of our black friends," another soldier later reflected. "We had used them to good advantage and set them free and now, with fear and trembling they had to face the reward of their cruel masters."[46] The British surrendered a week later, evacuating their troops and leaving their Black allies behind. As the British boarded their boats, American troops patrolled the banks of the York River to ensure that no African Americans escaped.

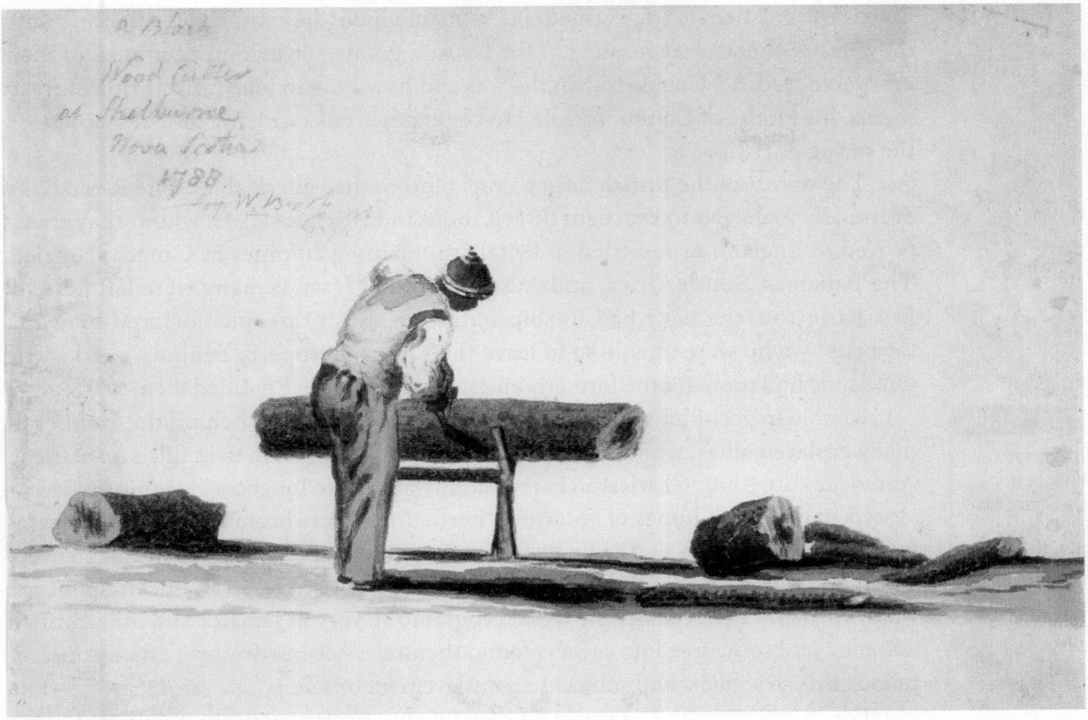

A Black Loyalist in Canada
African Americans served valiantly on both sides of the Revolution, often allying themselves with the side they felt provided the best opportunity for securing their own freedom. The woodcutter at work in this watercolor is a loyalist who sought refuge in Canada after the war. When the British retreated, Black loyalists scrambled to avoid reenslavement. Many resettled in British colonies in Canada, Jamaica, The Bahamas, South Africa, and Australia. **Explain how this image captures the experiences of some of the formerly enslaved population after the end of the Revolutionary War. What details from the painting support your explanation?** *William Booth, A Black Wood Cutter at Shelburne, 1788. Library and Archives Canada/W.H. Coverdale Collection of Canadiana/e008438313.*

Other loyalist troops held their positions as late as 1783. In 1782, Lord Dunmore and other "fight-to-the-end" generals who still hoped to reverse the Yorktown defeat made desperate appeals for ten thousand Black troops. But Britain's military leaders remained unwilling to make full use of their Black allies, even as defeat stared them in the face. Parliament had never intended to abolish American slavery — or to compromise Britain's multimillion-dollar investment in the slave trade and its West Indian sugar colonies. Profits from the slave trade and the export of manufactured goods to Britain's slave colonies were crucial to Britain's prosperity and economic growth during the eighteenth century. British statesman Edmund Burke warned Parliament that freeing enslaved people to fight might unleash a conflict even more ruinous than the American bid for independence. For example, as of 1775, the British West Indies was home to 450,000 enslaved people, who might revolt if given a chance to do so.

Once enslaved people were armed, Burke maintained, they would keep fighting until they "made themselves masters of the houses, goods, wives, and daughters of their murdered lords."[47] Unable to win the war and unwilling to jeopardize British investments, the House of Commons voted to begin peace talks with the former colonists in the spring of 1782.

The retreat of the British dealt a cruel blow to their Black allies. The Royal Navy eventually managed to evacuate fifteen thousand Black loyalists, whom they transported to England or resettled in Britain's remaining colonies in Canada, Jamaica, The Bahamas, South Africa, and Australia. But at least as many were left behind. In Charleston, the navy had to ship out thousands of people enslaved by white loyalists — who were unwilling to leave their human property behind — and at the same time find room for the formerly enslaved whose service entitled them to freedom.

AP® skills

Applying Disciplinary Knowledge: What actions did the British take after the Revolutionary War? What happened to refugees?

Unable to accommodate all the refugees, the British left behind the families of many enslaved allies, who faced reenslavement. As the British fleet filled up, African Americans dove into Charleston harbor and swam out to longboats loading the navy's vessels in desperate hopes of securing a berth. Most were beaten back with cutlasses by the British soldiers on the boats. Some clung to the boats until their fingers were sliced off their hands. Even the Blacks who made it aboard faced an uncertain future. Many formerly enslaved people were resold into slavery in Jamaica and other British colonies, and some freedom seekers found themselves claimed as property by unscrupulous British soldiers and subject to reenslavement or sale.

For most refugees, the prospect of returning to slavery in the South was more fearsome than the uncertainties of relocation. When the British evacuation of New York in 1783 inspired rumors that the enslaved people who fought with the British would be returned to their enslavers, many freedom seekers were terrified. As Boston King, a freedom seeker from South Carolina who fought with the British in New York, later recalled, "Many of the slaves had very cruel masters, so that the thoughts of returning home with them embittered life to us. For some days, we lost our appetite for food, and sleep departed from our eyes."[48] To King's great relief, loyalists in New York offered more generous shelter than their southern counterparts: between three thousand and four thousand Blacks accompanied the British troops when they left. However, Nova Scotia, Canada, where most of the Black evacuees were taken, was no promised land. Located on a chilly stretch of Canada's Atlantic coast, Nova Scotia was overcrowded with loyalist refugees and unwelcoming to people of African descent. The Black loyalists who resettled there were granted small plots of largely barren land to farm and were soon reduced to abject poverty. (See AP® Working with Sources: Black Freedom Fighters, pp. 153–61.)

Meanwhile, other Black loyalists had it worse. Those abandoned in the South continued to defend their territory in the low-country swamps as late as 1786 — three years after the Treaty of Paris, the agreement that formally ended the war and recognized the United States. On Bear Creek, which runs through the Savannah River marshes that once divided South Carolina and Georgia along the coast, freedom seekers built a fortified village one mile long and four hundred feet wide. From there, they raided nearby plantations in both states until May 1789, when the South Carolina governor dispatched a coalition of troops from South Carolina and Georgia, as well as some Catawba Indians, to destroy the settlement. Vanquished after a four-day battle, the Bear Creek settlers, who called themselves "the King of England's Soldiers," were branded a gang of common criminals by the governor.[49]

Closer to Freedom

Despite the crushing losses suffered by Black loyalists, the American Revolution brought African Americans closer to freedom. Most of the five thousand Blacks who served among the American forces ended up free, although some struggled to achieve their freedom. James Armistead, the double agent who spied for Lafayette, was briefly reenslaved after the British left. Despite having supplied invaluable intelligence, he never held an official position in the patriot forces and did not qualify for manumission. He was not freed until 1786, after Lafayette wrote a letter of commendation for him that he used to secure his freedom. Black patriots on the muster rolls were not generally subject to reenslavement, even in the southern states — with the notable exception of Virginia, where some enslavers tried to retain the enslaved substitutes who had fought for them during the war. This caused public outcry and inspired a 1783 legislative decree that declared the actions of such enslavers "contrary to principles of justice and to their own solemn promise" and directed the state's attorney general to seek manumission for any enslaved former soldiers.[50]

> **AP® skills**
>
> **Applying Disciplinary Knowledge:** What happened to James Armistead, and why did his experience cause public outcry?

Black veterans formed only part of the greatly enlarged free Black community that emerged in the decades following the war. Concentrated largely in the North and the Upper South, free Blacks, who had numbered only a few thousand in 1760, reached 60,000 in 1790 and 110,000 in 1800. These remarkable increases reflect a number of developments. Thousands had seized their liberty during the war by running away or pursuing successful freedom suits. In 1780, Mum Bett, an enslaved woman in Sheffield, Massachusetts, filed a suit that helped push her state toward abandoning slavery for good. Having endured years of physical abuse at the hands of her enslaver, she sued for her freedom after hearing public discussions of the Declaration of Independence and the Massachusetts state constitution. "I heard that paper read yesterday that says, all men are born equal, and that every man has a right to freedom. I am not a dumb critter; won't the law give me my freedom?" Bett asked a local lawyer named Theodore Sedgwick, who agreed to represent her in court.[51] Bett's successful suit transformed her into Elizabeth Freeman, a name she took as a symbol of her liberty. Three years later, her lawsuit provided a precedent for the state's final freedom suit — the Quock Walker case of 1783, in which the Massachusetts Supreme Court ruled that slavery was incompatible with the state's new constitution.

After the war, the number of free Blacks in the new nation increased steadily through the abolition of slavery in the northern states. Vermont, which had never

Mum Bett and Freedom Suits
After suffering ongoing physical abuse while enslaved, Mum Bett, depicted here, worked with lawyer Theodore Sedgwick to win her freedom in a 1781 court case. Between 1781 and 1783, her case served as a precedent for a series of cases involving an enslaved man named Quock Walker. Adjudicated by the Massachusetts Supreme Court in 1783, the final Quock Walker case ruled that slavery was incompatible with the state's new constitution.
What factors may have influenced the outcome of Mum Bett's freedom suit? *Portrait of Elizabeth 'Mumbet' Freeman (c.1742–1829) 1811 by Susan Anne Livingston Ridley Sedgwick (fl.1811)/© Massachusetts Historical Society, Boston, MA/ Bridgeman Images.*

had a large enslaved population, banned slavery in 1777. Pennsylvania began planning to end slavery shortly thereafter, although its Act for the Gradual Abolition of Slavery of 1780 was far from generous. It freed only enslaved persons born after 1780, who had to pay for their freedom by serving their enslavers for the first twenty-eight years of their lives. Still, this ground-breaking law advanced the cause of freedom in the new nation and set the stage for gradual abolition in other northern states, which was largely complete by the 1820s.

The free Black population in the South also increased dramatically, largely as a result of manumissions in the Upper South between the 1770s and the early 1800s. The Great Awakening, combined with antislavery sentiments inspired by the American Revolution, prompted enslavers across the region to free large numbers of enslaved people. Quakers throughout the Upper South abandoned slavery during this period, and they encouraged non-Quakers to do so as well. In some states, Quakers also helped make manumissions possible by successfully lobbying for the elimination of statutory restrictions on the emancipation of individual enslaved people by their enslavers. Whereas manumissions had previously required permission of the legislature in Virginia and a financial commitment in Delaware, under the new laws, enslavers could manumit the people they enslaved at will.

The increase in the Upper South's free Black population was also facilitated by the declining profitability of plantation agriculture in the Chesapeake during the second half of the eighteenth century. These years saw declining returns on tobacco, prompting many of the region's planters to abandon this labor-intensive cash crop. They turned instead to wheat and other less demanding crops, which were most profitably grown using seasonal laborers rather than enslaved workers. Manumissions rose, and so too did out-of-state sales of these who remained enslaved. Whereas free Blacks had constituted a tiny percentage of the region's Black population for much of the century, by the 1790s, about 10 percent of Chesapeake Blacks were free. Only in the Lower South did free Blacks remain a rarity (Map 4.2).

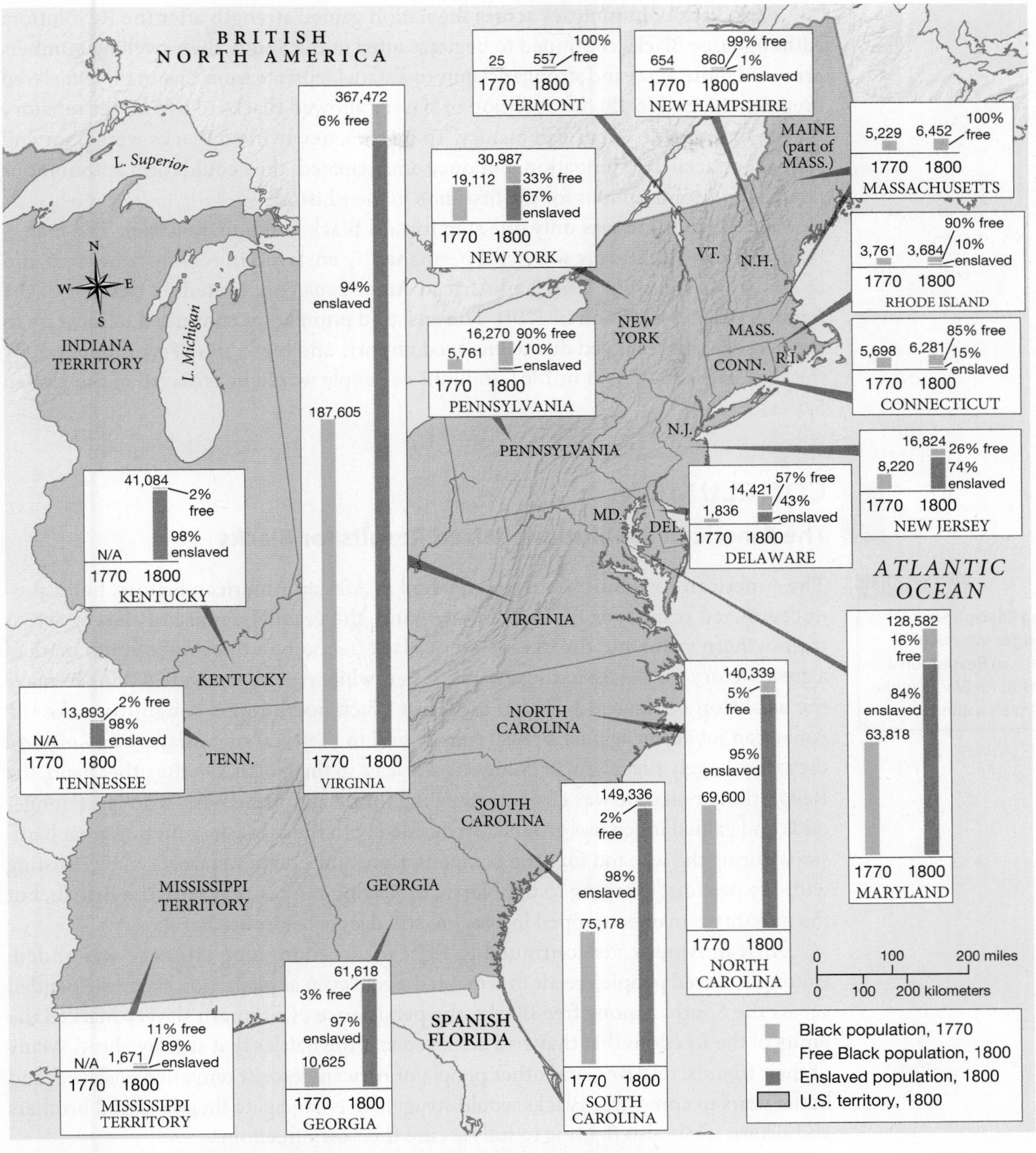

MAP 4.2 African Americans across the Developing Nation, 1770 and 1800

This map illustrates the distribution of the new nation's Black population, which varied across regions. The gold bars show each state's Black population in 1770. The light and dark blue bars show each state's enslaved population and free Black population in 1800. **Which states saw the biggest jumps in the number of enslaved people? Which states had the largest percentages of free Black people? What events contributed to the population change?**

Free Black communities across the nation gained strength after the Revolution. Although free Blacks continued to be persecuted in the South, their swelling numbers provided more allies and stronger claims to a status separate from that of their enslaved brethren. In the North, the abolition of slavery allowed Blacks to live in free territory for the first time in American history. To be sure, newly freed Blacks were poor and subject to racial discrimination, but once emancipated, they could form autonomous families and communities for the first time in their history.

The Revolution was only one step toward Black freedom, however. The majority of African Americans were still permanently enslaved in regions where no end to slavery was in sight. Enslaved African Americans constituted 92 percent of the nation's Black population in 1790. The enslaved population continued to increase in the decades that followed due to enslaved imports and high rates of reproduction. By the start of the Civil War in 1861, millions of people would be enslaved in the United States.

CONCLUSION

The American Revolution's Mixed Results for Blacks

AP® skills

Applying Disciplinary Knowledge: Why was the American Revolution a mixed result for Blacks in the former British colonies?

The American Revolution was a watershed in African American history, but it produced mixed results for Blacks. On one hand, the gradual demise of slavery across the northern states and the expansion of Black freedom in the Upper South marked a great victory for Blacks in these regions. Few white Americans were willing to make the abolition of slavery a central goal, but Black northerners sought to make the American rebellion against British rule an end to the tyranny of slavery as well, and they were largely successful in doing so — at least in the North. On the other hand, the Revolution's outcome was far less rewarding for Black southerners, who faced longer odds and gained much less ground. Most sided with the loyalists, suffering great hardships during the war and for little compensation. Some achieved freedom by enlisting with the patriots, escaping to the North, or leaving the country with the British, but the majority remained trapped in a region still deeply committed to slavery.

African Americans continued to fight for freedom long after the war ended. Among enslaved people, freedom remained a goal even as plantation slavery expanded across the South. Among free Blacks, the persistence of southern slavery marked the limits of the freedom that they had achieved and the battles that still lay ahead. Many of their friends, relatives, and other people of African descent remained enslaved, and in the years to come, free Blacks would struggle to emancipate their enslaved brothers and sisters, while also fighting to fully secure their own freedom.

In their struggles, Blacks throughout America would continue to embrace the egalitarian principles of both the Great Awakening and the patriot cause. In the years to come, enslaved and free Blacks continued to join evangelical churches and embrace an Afro-Christian faith that stressed the equality of all people before God. Free Black communities established their own churches, which became central to the antislavery movement that took shape among northern free Blacks. So, too, did the democratic principles of the American Revolution, as post-Revolutionary African American leaders stressed that their "fathers fought, bled and died for liberty which neither they nor their children have yet received."[52]

CHAPTER 4 REVIEW ▸ PRACTICING AP® SKILLS

AP® ESSENTIAL VOCABULARY AND SOURCES

** Essential terms and required sources from the AP® Course are marked with an asterisk.*

manumission p. 123
Negro Election Day p. 123
conjure p. 126
Gullah* p. 126
Great Awakening p. 126
New Lights p. 126
ideology p. 131
freedom suits* p. 133
Somerset case (1772) p. 133
habeas corpus p. 133
loyalists p. 138
Lord Dunmore's Proclamation (1775) p. 139
southern strategy p. 143

APPLYING DISCIPLINARY KNOWLEDGE: ESSENTIAL QUESTIONS

1. What role did religion — both traditional West African beliefs and practices and Christianity — play in the shaping of an African American culture during the eighteenth century?
2. How did African Americans on both the patriot and loyalist sides use the Revolution to pursue and secure their own freedom? How did they draw on the conflict's ideology to do so? Choose several examples from the chapter to support your argument.
3. Overall, how would you assess African Americans' gains and losses during the Revolutionary era? Consider the outcomes for patriots and loyalists, northerners and southerners, and free and enslaved Blacks. Who benefited the most and the least? What factors were responsible for these results?
4. How did African Americans' participation on both sides of the war change its course? How might the progression or outcome of the conflict have been different had Blacks been barred from service?

SUGGESTED REFERENCES

African American Life in Eighteenth-Century North America

Gomez, Michael A. *Exchanging Our Country Marks: The Transformation of African Identities in the Colonial and Antebellum South.* Chapel Hill: University of North Carolina Press, 1998.

Hodges, Graham Russell. *Root and Branch: African Americans in New York and East Jersey, 1613–1863.* Chapel Hill: University of North Carolina Press, 1999.

Lepore, Jill. *New York Burning: Liberty, Slavery, and Conspiracy in Eighteenth-Century Manhattan.* New York: Knopf, 2005.

Morgan, Philip D. *Slave Counterpoint: Black Culture in the Eighteenth-Century Chesapeake and Lowcountry.* Chapel Hill: University of North Carolina Press, 1998.

Olwell, Robert. *Masters, Slaves, and Subjects: The Culture of Power in the South Carolina Low Country, 1740–1790.* Ithaca: Cornell University Press, 1998.

Piersen, William Dillon. *Black Yankees: The Development of an Afro-American Subculture in Eighteenth-Century New England.* Amherst: University of Massachusetts Press, 1988.

Sidbury, James. *Becoming African in America: Race and Nation in the Early Black Atlantic.* New York: Oxford University Press, 2009.

Sweet, John Wood. *Bodies Politic: Negotiating Race in the American North, 1730–1830.* Philadelphia: University of Pennsylvania Press, 2006.

The African American Revolution

Bradley, Patricia. *Slavery, Propaganda, and the American Revolution.* Jackson: University Press of Mississippi, 1999.

Countryman, Edward. *Enjoy the Same Liberty: Black Americans and the Revolutionary Era.* Lanham, MD: Rowman & Littlefield Publishers, 2012.

Egerton, Douglas R. *Death or Liberty: African Americans and Revolutionary America.* New York: Oxford University Press, 2009.

Gates, Henry Louis, Jr. *The Trials of Phillis Wheatley: America's First Black Poet and Her Encounters with the Founding Fathers.* New York: Basic Civitas Books, 2003.

Holton, Woody. *Black Americans in the Revolutionary Era: A Brief History with Documents.* Boston: Bedford/St. Martin's, 2009.

Kaplan, Sidney, and Emma Nogrady Kaplan. *The Black Presence in the Era of the American Revolution.* Amherst: University of Massachusetts Press, 1989.

Nash, Gary B. *The Forgotten Fifth: African Americans in the Age of Revolution.* Cambridge: Harvard University Press, 2006.

______. *The Unknown American Revolution: The Unruly Birth of Democracy and the Struggle to Create America.* New York: Penguin, 2006.

Saillant, John. *Black Puritan, Black Republican: The Life and Thought of Lemuel Haynes, 1753–1833.* New York: Oxford University Press, 2002.

Slavery, Soldiers, and the Outcome of the Revolution

Frey, Sylvia R. *Water from the Rock: Black Resistance in a Revolutionary Age.* Princeton: Princeton University Press, 1993.

Gilbert, Alan. *Black Patriots and Loyalists: Fighting for Emancipation in the War for Independence.* Chicago: University of Chicago Press, 2012.

Hochschild, Adam. *Bury the Chains: Prophets and Rebels in the Fight to Free an Empire's Slaves.* New York: Mariner Books, 2006.

Jasanoff, Maya. *Liberty's Exiles: American Loyalists in the Revolutionary World.* New York: Knopf, 2011.

Piecuch, Jim. *Three Peoples, One King: Loyalists, Indians, and Slaves in the Revolutionary South, 1775–1782.* Columbia: University of South Carolina Press, 2008.

Pulis, John W., ed. *Moving On: Black Loyalists in the Afro-Atlantic World.* London: Routledge, 1999.

Pybus, Cassandra. *Epic Journeys of Freedom: Runaway Slaves of the American Revolution and Their Global Quest for Liberty.* Boston: Beacon Press, 2007.

Quarles, Benjamin. *The Negro in the American Revolution.* Chapel Hill: University of North Carolina Press, 1996.

Schama, Simon. *Rough Crossings: The Slaves, the British, and the American Revolution.* New York: HarperCollins, 2007.

Taylor, Alan, *The Internal Enemy: Slavery and War in Virginia, 1772–1832.* New York: W. W. Norton & Company, 2013.

Black Freedom Fighters

African Americans fought for their own freedom with the pen and the sword during the American Revolution. Black soldiers joined both the patriot and loyalist forces, and both free and enslaved Blacks were drawn into the natural rights debates engendered by the Revolution. Enslaved people who petitioned for freedom in patriot courts articulated claims to the "Natural and Unaliable [inalienable] Right to that freedom which the Grat Parent of the Unavers hath Bestowed equalley on all menkind," but Black loyalists also fought for freedom.[53] The following documents present Black perspectives from both sides of the conflict. They include writings by the poet Phillis Wheatley and the free Black soldier Lemuel Haynes, both of whom supported the patriots; an excerpt from the memoirs of Boston King, a Black loyalist; and artwork depicting Revolutionary-era African American soldiers.

Born around 1753 and freed in 1773, the poet Phillis Wheatley was still very young when the war was beginning to take shape, but she kept a close eye on the Revolution's ideological conflicts. In 1772, a year before she was emancipated, she wrote a poem addressed to King George's secretary of state for North America, the Earl of Dartmouth, in which she supported the patriot cause while also mourning the freedom that Blacks had not yet won. Two years later, she expressed similar sentiments as a free woman in a letter written to the American Indian leader Samson Occom. Both pieces are included here.

Wheatley's compositions are followed by an essay by Lemuel Haynes, a free Black man who was born in Connecticut and raised in Massachusetts and who served with both the minutemen and the Continental army. Although he fought with the patriots, Haynes was dissatisfied with the new nation's political principles and called for Americans to extend liberty to Blacks as well as whites.

Enslaved in South Carolina when the British invaded Charleston, Boston King had a very different perspective on the Revolution than either Wheatley or Haynes. His only chance of liberty lay in joining the English forces. His memoirs, written nearly twenty years after the Revolution, describes his wartime thoughts and experiences.

Sketched by a French officer who fought with the patriots, the image *Soldiers in Uniform* illustrates the American opponents that King might have confronted, including French soldiers, formerly enslaved men, state militiamen, and frontier fighters, and the painting *The Death of Major Peirson* depicts a Black loyalist fighting among British forces.

key point

The Revolutionary War enabled the British North American colonists to gain political independence. Although many Black colonists also fought in the war on both sides, their motivations and contributions are often excluded from the origin story of America.

AP® argumentation

DBQ Practice: Evaluate the relative importance of the effects of the American Revolution on the lives of Black Americans during the early history of the United States. Use at least two of the documents to support your response.

DOCUMENT 1 Phillis Wheatley | *A Poem to the Earl of Dartmouth, 1772*

Born in Gambia, PHILLIS WHEATLEY (c. 1753–1784) was only seven or eight years old when she was sold into slavery. Her enslavers encouraged her to learn how to read and write and were so impressed by her intelligence that they permitted her to devote her time largely to her education and to developing her gift for poetry. Wheatley wrote and published her first poems as a teenager, attracting attention and controversy as an early Black author who spoke on behalf of a people whom many whites saw as illiterate by nature.

Breaking it Down Pause after reading each stanza and identify how each one reveals causes of the American Revolution. What was Wheatley trying to accomplish with this poem, addressed to Britain's secretary of state for North America? How does she go about it in the poem?

TO THE RIGHT HONORABLE WILLIAM, EARL OF DARTMOUTH

His Majesty's Principal Secretary of State for North America, etc.

Hail, happy day, when smiling like the morn,
Fair *Freedom* rose New England to adorn;
The northern clime beneath her genial ray,
Dartmouth congratulates thy blissful sway;
Elate with hope her race no longer mourns,
Each soul expands, each grateful bosom burns,
While in thine hand with pleasure we behold
The silken reins, and Freedom's charms unfold.
Long lost to realms beneath the northern skies
She shines supreme, while hated faction dies;
Soon as appeared the *Goddess* long desir'd,
Sick at the view, she languish'd and expir'd;
Thus from the splendor of the morning light
The owl in sadness seeks the caves of night.

No more *America*, in mournful strain
Of wrongs, and grievance unredress'd complain,
No longer shall thou dread the iron chain,
Which wanton Tyranny with lawless hand
Had made, and with it meant to enslave the land.
Should you, my lord, while you peruse my song,
Wonder from whence my love of Freedom sprung,
Whence flow these wishes for the common good,
By feeling hearts alone best understood,
I, young in life, by seeming cruel fate
Was snatch'd from Afric's fancy'd happy seat;
What pangs excruciatingly must molest,
What sorrows labour in my parent's breast?
Steel'd was that soul and by no misery mov'd
That from a father seized his babe belov'd;
Such, such my case. And can I then but pray
Others may never feel tyrannic sway?

For favors past, great Sir, our thanks are due,
And thee we ask thy favors to renew,
Since in thy pow'r, as in thy will before,
To sooth the griefs, which thou didst once deplore.
May heav'nly grace the sacred sanction give
To all thy works, and thou forever live
Not only on the wings of fleeting *Fame*,
Though praise immortal crowns the patriot's name,
But to conduct to heav'n's refulgent fane
May fiery coursers sweep th' etherial plain,
And bear thee upwards to the blest abode,
Where, like the prophet, thou shalt find thy God.

SOURCE: Phillis Wheatley, *Poems on Various Subjects, Religious and Moral* (1773; repr., Denver: W. H. Lawrence, 1887), 66–68.

DOCUMENT 2 Phillis Wheatley | *Letter to the Reverend Samson Occom, 1774*

PHILLIS WHEATLEY's letter to the Reverend Samson Occom, a Mohegan Indian and ordained minister with whom she had a correspondence, was in response to a piece that Occom had written in condemnation of Christian ministers who were also enslavers. It was first printed in the Connecticut Gazette on March 11, 1774.

Breaking it Down Some of the terms used in the text are not common to modern conversation. For instance, *avarice* is extreme greed for wealth. As you read, identify words you do not know and use context clues to guess their meaning. After reading, look up these words. How do they add to your understanding of the sort of a future Wheatley foresees for slavery in the letter? What justifications does she offer for her views?

Boston, February 11th, 1774.

Rever'd & Honoured Sir,

I this day received your kind obliging epistle, and am greatly satisfied with your reasons respecting the Negroes, and think highly reasonable what you offer in vindication of their natural rights. Those that invade them cannot be insensible that the divine light is insensibly chasing away the thick darkness which broods over the land of Africa, and the chaos which has reigned so long is converting into beautiful order, and reveals more and more clearly the glorious dispensation of civil and religious liberty, which are so inseparably united, that there is little or no enjoyment of one without the other; otherwise the Israelites had been less solicitous for their freedom from Egyptian slavery. I do not say they would have been contented without it — by no means: for in every human breast God has implanted a principle which we call, love of freedom. It is impatient of oppression, and pants for deliverance; and, by the leave of our modern Egyptians, I will assert that the principle lives in us — God grant deliverance in his own way and time, and get him honour upon all those whose avarice compels them to countenance and help forward the calamities of their fellow creatures. This I desire not for the hurt, but to convince them of the strange absurdities of their conduct whose words and actions are so diametrically opposite. How well the cry of liberty and the reverse disposition for the exercise of oppressive power over others agree, I humbly think it does not require the penetration of a philosopher to determine.

SOURCE: *Connecticut Gazette*, March 11, 1774, 188.

DOCUMENT 3 Lemuel Haynes | *Liberty Further Extended, 1776*

Born in Connecticut, LEMUEL HAYNES (1753–1833) was abandoned by his white mother and African father. He grew up in Massachusetts, where he was bound out as an indentured servant at the age of six months. He joined the Granville minutemen and fought with patriot forces until 1776, when he caught typhus and had to return home. That year, he wrote the following unpublished and recently

discovered manuscript. Probably composed shortly after the publication of the Declaration of Independence, it expands on that document, calling for an antislavery revolution. Haynes was self-educated and became ordained as a Congregationalist minister.

Breaking it Down It may help to read the Declaration of Independence (p. A-1) after reading the headnote but before reading this text. It will help anchor your understanding of Haynes's claims. How does he use the Declaration of Independence to argue his point here?

We hold these truths to be self-Evident, that all men are created Equal, that they are Endowed By their Creator with Ceartain unalienable rights, that among these are Life, Liberty, and the pursuit of happyness.

Congress.

The Preface [of the Declaration of Independence]. As *tyrony* had its Origin from the infernal regions: so it is the Deuty, and honner of Every son of freedom to repel her first motions. But while we are Engaged in the important struggle, it cannot Be tho't impertinent for us to turn one Eye into our own Breast, for a little moment, and See, whether thro' some inadvertency, or a self-contracted Spirit, we Do not find the monster Lurking in our own Bosom; that now while we are inspir'd with so noble a Spirit and Becoming Zeal, we may Be Disposed to tear her from us. If the following would produce such an Effect the auther should rejoice. . . .

Liberty, & freedom, is an innate principle, which is unmoveably placed in the human Species; and to see a man aspire after it, is not Enigmatical, seeing he acts no ways incompatible with his own Nature; consequently, he that would infring upon a mans Liberty may reasonably Expect to meet with oposision, seeing the Defendant cannot Comply to Non-resistance, unless he Counteracts the very Laws of nature.

Liberty is a Jewel which was handed Down to man from the cabinet of heaven, and is Coaeval [originated at the same time] with his Existance. And as it proceed from the Supreme Legislature of the univers, so it is he which hath a sole right to take away; therefore, he that would take away a mans Liberty assumes a prerogative that Belongs to another, and acts out of his own domain.

One man may bost a superorety above another in point of Natural previledg; yet if he can produse no convincive arguments in vindication of this preheminence his hypothesis is to Be Suspected. To affirm, that an Englishman has a right to his Liberty, is a truth which has Been so clearly Evinced, Especially of Late, that to spend time in illustrating this, would be But Superfluous tautology. But I query, whether Liberty is so contracted a principle as to be Confin'd to any nation under Heaven; nay, I think it not hyperbolical to affirm, that Even an affrican, has Equally as good a right to his Liberty in common with Englishmen.

I know that those that are concerned in the Slave-trade, Do pretend to Bring arguments in vindication of their practise; yet if we give them a candid Examination, we shall find them (Even those of the most cogent kind) to be Essencially Deficient. We live in a day wherein *Liberty* & *freedom* is the subject of many millions Concern; and the important Struggle hath alread caused great Effusion of Blood; men seem to manifest the most sanguine resolution not to Let their natural rights go without their Lives go with them; a resolution, one would think Every one that has the Least Love to his country, or futer posterity, would fully confide in, yet while we are so zelous to maintain, and foster our own invaded rights, it cannot be tho't impertinent for us Candidly to reflect on our own conduct, and I doubt not But that we shall find that subsisting in the midst of us, that may with propriety be stiled *Opression*, nay, much greater opression, than that which Englishmen seem so much to spurn at. I mean an oppression which they, themselves, impose upon others. . . .

. . . There is Not the Least precept, or practise, in the Sacred Scriptures, that constitutes a Black man a Slave, any more than a white one.

Shall a mans Couler Be the Decisive Criterion whereby to Judg of his natural right? or Becaus a man is not of the same couler with his Neighbour, shall he Be Deprived of those things that Distuingsheth [Distinguisheth] him from the Beasts of the field?

I would ask, whence is it that an Englishman is so far Distinguished from an Affrican in point of Natural privilege? Did he recieve it in his origenal constitution? or By Some Subsequent grant? Or Does he Bost of some hygher Descent that gives him this pre-heminance? for my part I can find no such revelation. It is a Lamantable consequence of the fall, that mankind, have an insatiable thurst after Superorety one over another: So that however common or prevalent the practise may be, it Does not amount, Even to a Surcomstance, that the practise is ~~Legal~~° warrentable.

° The strikethrough is part of the original document.

SOURCE: Ruth Bogin, " 'Liberty Further Extended': A 1776 Antislavery Manuscript by Lemuel Haynes," *William and Mary Quarterly*, 3rd ser., 40, no. 1 (1983): 94–96. Reprinted by permission of the Omohundro Institute of Early American History and Culture.

DOCUMENT 4 Jean Baptiste Antoine de Verger | *Soldiers in Uniform, 1781*

The following watercolor sketch by French sub-lieutenant JEAN BAPTISTE ANTOINE DE VERGER (1762–1851) documents the diversity of the troops in George Washington's colonial forces at the siege of Yorktown. It depicts (left to right) a Black soldier of the First Rhode Island Regiment, a New England militiaman, a frontier rifleman, and a French officer.

Breaking it Down How does the contextual information provided in the headnote inform your observations of this sketch? Why do you think de Verger chose to sketch this group of soldiers? Based on your reading of the chapter, how common do you think it was for an African American to serve alongside a white soldier?

'Soldiers in Uniform', 1781–1784, by Jean Baptiste Antoine de Verger (1762–1851)/Brown University Library, Providence, Rhode Island/Bridgeman Images.

DOCUMENT 5 Boston King | *Memoirs of a Black Loyalist, 1798*

Born on a plantation near Charleston, South Carolina, BOSTON KING (c. 1760–1802) joined the loyalists rather than returning to the carpenter to whom his enslaver had apprenticed him and who beat him brutally. The following excerpt describes King's experiences with British and American forces in South Carolina.

Breaking it Down Keep Lord Dunmore's Proclamation (p. 139) in mind as you read the text. How might the proclamation have affected Boston King's perspective?

To escape [my master's] cruelty, I determined to go to Charles-Town, and throw myself into the hands of the English. They received me readily, and I began to feel the happiness of liberty, of which I knew nothing before, altho' I was much grieved at first, to be obliged to leave my friends, and reside among strangers. In this situation I was seized with the small-pox, and suffered great hardships; for all the Blacks affected with that disease, were ordered to be carried a mile from the camp, lest the soldiers should be infected, and disabled from marching. This was a grievous circumstance to me and many others. We lay sometimes a whole day without any thing to eat or drink; but Providence sent a man, who belonged to the York volunteers whom I was acquainted with, to my relief. He brought me such things as I stood in need of; and by the blessing of the Lord I began to recover.

By this time, the English left the place; but as I was unable to march with the army, I expected to be taken by the enemy. However when they came, and understood that we were ill of the small-pox, they precipitately left us for fear of the infection. Two days after, the waggons were sent to convey us to the English Army, and we were put into a little cottage, (being 25 in number) about a quarter of a mile from the Hospital.

Being recovered, I marched with the army to Chamblem [Camden, New Jersey]. . . . Upon returning to the camp, to my great astonishment, I found all the English were gone, and had left only a few [loyalist] militia. I felt my mind greatly alarmed, but Captain Lewes, who commanded the militia, said, "You need not be uneasy, for you will see your regiment before 7 o'clock to-night." This satisfied me for the present, and in two hours we set off. As we were on the march, the Captain asked, "How will you like me to be your master?" I answered that I was Captain Grey's servant. "Yes," said he; "but I expect they are all taken prisoners before now; and I have been long enough in the English service, and am determined to leave them." These words roused my indignation, and I spoke some sharp things to him. But he calmly replied, "If you do not behave well, I will put you in irons, and give you a dozen stripes every morning." I now perceived that my case was desperate, and that I had nothing to trust to, but to wait the first opportunity for making my escape. The next morning, I was sent with a little boy over the river to an island to fetch the Captain some horses. When we came to the Island we found about fifty of the English horses, that Captain Lewes had stolen from them at different times while they were at Rockmount [Rocky Mount]. Upon our return to the Captain with the horses we were sent for, he immediately set off by himself. I stayed till about 10 o'clock and then resolved to go to the English army.

SOURCE: "Memoirs of the Life of Boston King, a Black Preacher," *Methodist Magazine*, March 1798, 107–8.

DOCUMENT 6 John Singleton Copley | *The Death of Major Peirson, 1782–1784*

Massachusetts loyalist JOHN SINGLETON COPLEY (1738–1815) included a Black loyalist soldier in his painting The Death of Major Peirson, which portrays the death of fellow loyalist Major Francis Peirson, who was killed at the Battle of Jersey in the Channel Islands. A British island off the coast of Normandy, Jersey was far from the Revolution's main theater of operations, but it became part of the conflict in 1781, when France invaded the island in the hope of limiting the British naval threat to French and American shipping. France failed to gain control of Jersey, which was defended by loyalist forces led by Peirson. In the painting, the death of Peirson, a British army officer who served in the Revolutionary War, is avenged by his servant Pompey, an armed Black loyalist. Whether or not Pompey actually existed is not known, but Copley's painting is perhaps the only Revolutionary-era portrait of a Black loyalist. The Black figure wears the colors of the Royal Ethiopian Regiment organized by Lord Dunmore in Virginia, suggesting that Copley imagined him as one of the African American loyalists evacuated by British forces.

Breaking it Down How does the contextual information provided in the headnote inform your understanding of the painting's message to its audience? How is the Black soldier in this painting portrayed?

Detail. 'The Death of Major Peirson' (1782–1784) by John Singleton Copley (1738–1815)/Universal Images Group/Getty Images.

PRACTICING AP® SKILLS

1. **AP® Causation.** How did Lord Dunmore's Proclamation impact Boston King's experience of the American Revolution? Use evidence from the text to support your response.
2. **AP® Comparison.** Compare Lemual Haynes's perspective on the effects of the American Revolution (p. 155) with that of Boston King (p. 158). How does each document reveal the significance and shortcomings of the Declaration of Independence (p. A-1)?
3. **AP® Comparison.** Compare the sketch by Jean Baptiste Antoine de Verger to John Singleton Copley. To what extent do their portrayals support or counter each other?
4. **Connecting to AP® Themes.** Select two sources and explain how they support the theme of African American Resistance and Resilience during the American Revolution.
5. **Paired Discussion.** Choose two of the sources and explain how each one supports the idea of Black Americans who fought on both sides of the Revolutionary War as "Freedom Fighters."

Short-Answer Questions

In the AP® Skills Workshop on Written Texts: Active Reading (p. SW2-A), you learned to break down **arguments** written by others into **claims** and **evidence**. Now, it's time to write arguments of your own. This skill will be instrumental to success on the AP® African American Studies Exam, where you'll have to develop defensible arguments to effectively answer four short-answer questions (SAQs) — the focus of this workshop — and a document-based question (DBQ) — the focus of the AP® Skills Workshops in Chapters 5–11.

Let's consider the three kinds of short-answer questions you'll encounter on the AP® Exam:

1. **SAQ 1:** involves a required source (and may also involve a closely connected second source)
2. **SAQ 2:** involves a non-required source (and may also involve a closely connected second source)
3. **SAQ 3:** does not involve a source

As we'll model below, you can apply the same basic strategy to confidently and efficiently answer each of these question types.

Strategy 1: Read and break down the question.

Each short-answer question will appear in three to four parts. The parts each count for one point and are graded independently, so you'll want to make sure to provide a short, direct reply to each one. Make sure to read the full question carefully before beginning any brainstorming, because each part will include a specific *task* and may also include hints to a specific *time period* and *topic*. Getting a grasp on these question components will clarify the purpose of your response and ultimately streamline the drafting process.

Time period and topic should be straightforward to spot. If the topic doesn't immediately ring a bell, remember it may just be a different label for a course **concept**, **development**, or **process** you've studied.

To determine each part's task, it can be useful to remember that each part of a short-answer question will likely include one of the following task verbs:

Compare: Provide similarities and differences

Describe: Provide two or more details

Draw a conclusion: Use evidence to determine an accurate takeaway

Evaluate: Provide judgment on significance or accuracy

Explain how: Provide information on a development or process

Explain why: Provide information on the causes of a development or process

Identify: Provide a specific detail without further elaboration

Support *(a claim)*: Provide a specific example and comment on how it backs up the claim

Let's consider a short-answer question similar to those that will appear on the AP® Exam

'Twas mercy brought me from my *Pagan* land,
Taught my benighted soul to understand
That there's a God, that there's a *Saviour* too:
Once I redemption neither sought nor knew.
Some view our sable race with scornful eye,
"Their colour is a diabolic die."
Remember, *Christians, Negros,* black as *Cain,*
May be refin'd, and join th' angelic train.

Source: Phillis Wheatley, "On Being Brought from Africa to America," 1773

"Wheatley's move into [literary circles] hinged on her ability to produce written work acceptable to an audience not invested in her intelligence. . . . She carefully mimicked the forms, including language and stereotypes regarding enslaved Africans, which she inherited. However, she uses these forms to call out the inconsistency of Christian slave ownership."

Source: MaryCatherine Loving, "Uncovering Subversion in Phillis Wheatley's Signature Poem: 'On Being Brought from AFRICA to AMERICA,'" 2016

Using the poem and excerpt, respond to parts A, B, and C.

A. Describe the broader historical context of the poem.
B. Explain why Wheatley's poetry is significant within the field of African American Studies.
C. Explain how enslaved people used one other form of artistic expression beyond poetry during the eighteenth century.

We can break down this short-answer question using a graphic organizer:

Part	Time Period	Topic	Task
A	Late eighteenth century	• Transatlantic slave trade • Theme: Migration and the African Diaspora	Provide 2+ details about the late eighteenth century that are relevant to Wheatley's poem.
B	Late twentieth century – early twenty-first century	• Phillis Wheatley's modern-day significance • Theme: Resistance and Resilience	Provide reasons why Wheatley's poetry is important within African American studies.
C	Eighteenth century	• Art/music/literature • Theme: Creativity, Expression, and the Arts	Provide information on one other form of creativity among enslaved people.

Ultimately, not only does your response to each part need to be *correct* in order to earn the point; it also needs to *directly* answer that part of the question. If a part of your response addresses an irrelevant time period or topic, or if you don't fully complete the task, that part of your response will not earn a point. Therefore, breaking down the full question will set you up well to provide relevant responses that earn full points.

Strategy 2: Source the primary source *(if applicable)*.

If you're working on a short-answer question involving a visual or written primary source, it's safe to assume at least one part of the question will ask you to explain the source's historical **context**, intended **audience**, **purpose**, or **perspective**. Therefore, it will be useful to apply the HIPPO strategy covered in the AP® Skills Workshop for Chapter 3 (p. SW3-A):

Historical Context: When and where was the source created, based on its source line and any other clues? What developments, like movements or events, might have influenced the source's creation?

Intended Audience: Can you figure out the person or people for whom the source was created? How does this affect the source's content and tone?

Purpose: Why was the source created? What message might its creator have been trying to get across, and how can you tell?

Perspective: Can you tell who created the source and what their position in society was like? How might their background, beliefs, and biases have influenced the source's creation?

Outside Information: What course concepts, developments, and processes does the source bring to mind? What does the source *not* tell you, and what other sources might fill in those gaps?

Let's consider how we might source Wheatley's poem:

Historical Context:

At the time of Wheatley's writing in 1773, the transatlantic slave trade was nearly at its peak. The nation was experiencing a religious revival known as the Great Awakening, which popularized the ideal of egalitarianism. Ideals like liberty and equality were also gaining traction; the American Revolution was soon to break out.

Intended Audience: Christians who are enslavers, as well as those who are bystanders

Purpose: To explain Wheatley's connection to Christianity and to her African heritage

Perspective: Phillis Wheatley was an enslaved woman native to Africa and also a devout Christian.

Outside Information:

- Wheatley's enslaver, Susannah Wheatley, was the person who taught her Christianity in addition to other academic subjects.
- Wheatley ultimately gained her freedom following the publishing of her poetry.

Strategy 3: Organize your evidence.

To earn full points on a short-answer question, you'll need to provide **evidence** to back up each part of your response. As a preparatory step, try to identify and categorize relevant information from your course knowledge or, if applicable, from the source(s) included in the prompt.

If you're working with a primary source, you should have already sourced it. Now is the time to pull out the parts of that sourcing that are most significant in the context of the prompt. In this case, part A of the prompt asks you to consider the historical context, so your interpretation of that aspect of sourcing is most significant.

If you're working with a secondary source, ensure you pull in the claims and evidence that are most closely tied to the part of the question you're answering. The passage by Loving complements part B especially well, as it analyzes the significance of Wheatley's poetry from a modern perspective.

Part A: *Describe the broader historical context of the poem.*	Part B: *Explain why Wheatley's poetry is significant within the field of African American Studies.*	Part C: *Explain how enslaved people used one other form of artistic expression beyond poetry during the eighteenth century.*
• Transatlantic slave trade • Great Awakening	• Exposing hypocrisy of Christian enslavers • First Black American woman to have a book published	• Music – banjos and drums rooted in African culture • Celebration of African heritage and building community among enslaved people

This brainstorming step will set you up well to select the strongest examples to use in your completed response.

Strategy 4: Respond to each part of the question.

Now that we've collected some ideas, it's time to assemble them into a complete response that answers each part of the short-answer question. To ensure you fully answer each part, try using the strategy TEA:

Topic sentence: Clearly state an answer that directly responds to the prompt.

Evidence: Back up your answer with relevant details from your course knowledge and/or from the source(s).

Analysis: Provide commentary explaining how your evidence supports your answer.

Pay particular attention to the last step of TEA: Analysis. You will need to lay out exactly how the evidence you've provided logically leads to the claim you've made in your topic sentence.

In this case, a response that aligns with the TEA strategy might look something like this:

A. Wheatley published "On Being Brought from Africa to America" in 1773, when racial prejudice and devout Christianity coexisted at the forefront of American culture. At the time, the transatlantic slave trade was in full swing, and waves of the Great Awakening were revitalizing religious enthusiasm. These developments help explain why Wheatley's poem focuses on racialized stereotypes shaped by the slave trade and on the Christian ideal of salvation.

B. As the first published African American female poet, Wheatley was a ground-breaking figure whose impact continues to resonate. MaryCatherine Loving notes that Wheatley both engaged with and subverted traditional literary structures and Christian themes in her writing, highlighting the contradictions in white Americans' views on race and morality. Ultimately, Wheatley stands out for her ability to use her writing to challenge prevailing stereotypes about enslaved people.

C. In addition to poetry as a form of self-expression, many Africans who had been forcibly brought to America used music to honor and sustain their culture. Often, enslaved people played instruments rooted in their African heritage, such as the banjo or drum. In this way, many enslaved Africans were able to use artistic expression as a way to maintain cultural continuity and strengthen community bonds.

Notice that this response is essentially the TEA strategy three times, in complete sentences. In general, you should aim for about three to four sentences per part.

recap

Responding to Short-Answer Questions

The strategies to efficiently and accurately answer a short-answer question build off of one another:

Strategy 1: Read and annotate the question for its task, topic, and time period. Remember, these are the most common task verbs found on the AP® African American Studies Exam:

Compare	Provide similarities and differences
Describe	Provide two or more details
Draw a conclusion	Use evidence to determine an accurate takeaway
Evaluate	Provide judgment on significance or accuracy
Explain how	Provide information on a development or process
Explain why	Provide information on the causes of a development or process
Identify	Provide a detail without further elaboration
Support (*a claim*)	Provide a specific example and comment on how it backs up the claim

Strategy 2: Source the primary source (if applicable).

Historical Context
Intended Audience
Purpose
Perspective
Outside Information

Strategy 3: Organize your information.

- If you're working with a primary source, ensure you pull in the parts of your sourcing that are most significant in the context of the prompt.
- If you're working with a secondary source, ensure you pull in the claims and evidence that are most closely tied to the part of the question you're answering.

Strategy 4: Respond to each part of the question.

T̲opic sentence
E̲vidence
A̲nalysis

Activity ▸ Responding to Short-Answer Questions

Using the excerpt, respond to parts A, B, and C.

> "We hold these truths to be self-Evident, that all men are created Equal, that they are Endowed By their Creator with Ceartain unalienable rights, that among these are Life, Liberty, and the pursuit of happyness.
>
> *Congress.*
>
> The Preface [of the Declaration of Independence]. As *tyrony* had its Origin from the infernal regions: so it is the Deuty, and honner of Every son of freedom to repel her first motions. But while we are Engaged in the important struggle, it cannot Be tho't impertinent for us to turn one Eye into our own Breast, for a little moment, and See, whether thro' some inadvertency, or a self-contracted Spirit, we Do not find the monster Lurking in our own Bosom. . . .
>
> Even an affrican, has Equally as good a right to his Liberty in common with Englishmen.
>
> I know that those that are concerned in the Slave-trade, Do pretend to Bring arguments in vindication of their practise; yet if we give them a candid Examination, we shall find them (Even those of the most cogent kind) to be Essencially Deficient. We live in a day wherein *Liberty* & *freedom* is the subject of many millions Concern . . . yet while we are so zelous to maintain, and foster our own invaded rights, it cannot be tho't impertinent for us Candidly to reflect on our own conduct."
>
> SOURCE: Lemuel Haynes, a Black veteran of the American Revolution, *Liberty Further Extended: Or Free Thoughts on the Illegality of Slave-Keeping*, unpublished manuscript, 1776

(*Continued*)

A. Describe the broader historical context of Haynes's argument.
B. Describe the ideology that reinforced the institution of slavery in the period between 1754 and 1776.
C. Explain how revolutionary ideals contributed to emancipation claims in the period leading up to the Revolutionary War.

First, break down the prompt using a graphic organizer like the one shown below.

Part	Time Period	Topic	Task
A			
B			
C			

Next, organize your evidence using a graphic organizer like the one shown below.

Part A: Describe the broader historical context of the poem.	**Part B:** Explain why Wheatley's poetry is significant within the field of African American Studies.	**Part C:** Explain how enslaved people used one other form of artistic expression beyond poetry during the eighteenth century.
• •	• •	• •

Finally, draft a complete response to each part of the prompt, making sure that each section of your response provides a topic sentence, evidence, and analysis.

NOTES

Multiple-Choice Questions

Questions 1–3 refer to the following.

> "To escape [my enslaver's] cruelty, I determined to go to Charles-Town, and throw myself into the hands of the English. They received me readily, and I began to feel the happiness of liberty, of which I knew nothing before. . . . In this situation I was seized with the small-pox, and suffered great hardships; for all the Blacks affected with that disease. . . . We lay sometimes a whole day without any thing to eat or drink; but Providence sent a man, who belonged to the York volunteers whom I was acquainted with, to my relief. . . . By this time, the English left the place; but as I was unable to march with the army, I expected to be taken by the enemy. However when they came, and understood that we were ill of the small-pox, they precipitately left us for fear of the infection. Two days after, the waggons were sent to convey us to the English Army, and we were put into a little cottage, (being 25 in number) about a quarter of a mile from the Hospital. Being recovered, I marched with the army to Chamblem [Camden, New Jersey]. . . . Upon returning to the camp, to my great astonishment, I found all the English were gone, and had left only a few [loyalist] militia. I felt my mind greatly alarmed, but Captain Lewes, who commanded the militia, said, "You need not be uneasy, for you will see your regiment before 7 o'clock to-night." This satisfied me for the present, and in two hours we set off. As we were on the march, the Captain asked, "How will you like me to be your master?" I answered that I was Captain Grey's servant. "Yes," said he; "but I expect they are all taken prisoners before now; and I have been long enough in the English service, and am determined to leave them."
>
> These words roused my indignation, and I spoke some sharp things to him. But he calmly replied, "If you do not behave well, I will put you in irons, and give you a dozen stripes every morning." . . .

SOURCE: *"Memoirs of the Life of Boston King, a Black Preacher,"* Methodist Magazine, *March 1798*

1. Which of the following best describes Boston King's experiences with British and American forces in South Carolina?

(A) As a Black soldier in the American colonies, Boston King describes his fear of being captured by loyalists and explains how he used his knowledge of the area to avoid being caught.

(B) Boston King describes his positive interactions with American military leadership while he recovered from smallpox.

(C) As a formerly enslaved man, Boston King describes being a loyalist who had a brief exposure to liberty, then recounts how his recovery from smallpox led him back into forced servitude to American patriots.

(D) Boston King describes becoming ill with smallpox and was forced to leave the British army. Later, he agreed to be a servant to Captain Grey.

2. Which of the following claims is best supported by Boston King's perspective?
- (A) Boston King, like many other enslaved people at the time, sought freedom and believed that joining the British army could help him gain it.
- (B) Smallpox led Boston King to support the American patriots.
- (C) The American colonists were willing to emancipate enslaved Africans in exchange for their military support.
- (D) The British army did little to support Black loyalists.

3. Which of the following events best supports the perspective of Boston King?
- (A) British Parliament's passage of the Intolerable Acts resulting in colonists' outrage
- (B) Lord Dunmore's offer of freedom to enslaved people willing to join British forces
- (C) The signing of the Treaty of Paris in 1783 ending the Revolutionary War
- (D) The Haitian Revolution's attainment of liberty for the enslaved

Short-Answer Question

John Rose, *The Old Plantation*, Beaufort County, South Carolina, c. 1785–1790

The Old Plantation, attributed to John Rose, Beaufort County, South Carolina, c. 1785–1790/The Colonial Williamsburg Foundation, Gift of Abby Aldrich Rockefeller.

1. Using the image, answer A, B, C, and D.
- (A) Using the image as evidence, describe the factors that led to the emergence of African American culture.
- (B) Explain how the transatlantic slave trade impacted interactions among African Americans.
- (C) Explain why the development of African American culture led to the rise of antislavery resistance in the United States.
- (D) Explain why the activity depicted in the image is an example of African diasporic cultural traditions.

CHAPTER 5

Slavery and Freedom in the New Republic

1775–1820

CHAPTER TIMELINE

Events specific to African American history are in purple. General U.S. history events are in black. Events from the AP® Course Framework are marked with an asterisk.

1775 Nation's first antislavery organization founded in Pennsylvania

1776–1787 Ten states ban importation of enslaved people from outside U.S.

1780–1804 Pennsylvania, Connecticut, Rhode Island, New York, and New Jersey enact gradual emancipation laws

1785 Thomas Jefferson writes *Notes on the State of Virginia*, positing Black inferiority

1786–1787 Armed militia of farmers seeks economic reform in Shays's Rebellion

1787 Absalom Jones and Richard Allen found Free African Society

Constitutional Convention meets in Philadelphia

Northwest Ordinance bans slavery north of Ohio River and east of Mississippi River

New York Manumission Society founds New York African Free School

1789 George Washington inaugurated as first U.S. president

First U.S. Congress meets

1790s Southern planters begin cultivating sugar and cotton

Naturalization Act of 1790, first U.S. immigration law, passed

1791 Vermont becomes state

Bill of Rights ratified

1791–1804 Haitian Revolution*

1792–1821 New slave states established: Kentucky, Tennessee, Louisiana, Mississippi, Alabama, and Missouri

1793 Fugitive Slave Act establishes legal mechanisms for capture and return of freedom seekers*

Eli Whitney invents cotton gin

1794 African Methodist Episcopal (AME) Church established*

1798 Alien and Sedition Acts tighten restrictions on aliens in U.S., limit speech criticizing government

1800 Gabriel's rebellion

1803 Louisiana Purchase doubles size of U.S.

1804 Ohio passes black laws

1806 Virginia imposes new restrictions on manumission

1808 International slave trade ends

1812–1815 War of 1812

1815 Paul Cuffe takes thirty-eight Black Bostonians to Sierra Leone*

1816 American Colonization Society (ACS) first meets in Washington, D.C.*

1817 Free Blacks reject colonization at mass meeting in Philadelphia

Please note that this chapter includes primary sources that use the N-word, which we have chosen not to reprint in full here. We wish to accurately reflect both the sources' original intent as well as the racism of the time period, but we also recognize that this word has a long history as a derogatory and deeply hurtful expression when used by white people toward Black people, as it is in the context of these sources. We have replaced the term without hindering understanding of these sources. Be mindful of context, both historical and contemporary, as you read and discuss this chapter.

Benjamin Banneker Questions Thomas Jefferson about Slavery in the New Republic

In 1791, a fifty-nine-year-old Black man named Benjamin Banneker composed a carefully worded letter to Thomas Jefferson, the new nation's first secretary of state. Born free, Banneker owned a small farm just outside Baltimore, where he made his living growing fruit and raising cattle and bees. He was also a self-educated scientist, inventor, and author who had recently published an almanac, which he sent to Jefferson along with his letter. Although he enjoyed "those blessings which proceed from that free and unequalled liberty," Banneker told Jefferson, he was well aware that most of his fellow Black Americans remained enslaved. After winning a war dedicated to protecting their own liberties, white Americans had offered few rights to Blacks. Instead, they dismissed them, Banneker complained, as "a race of beings" more "brutish than human, and scarcely capable of mental endowments." Banneker appealed to Jefferson to help African Americans "eradicate that train of absurd and false ideas and opinions, which so generally prevails with respect to us."[1]

As a Virginia planter who enslaved hundreds of people, Jefferson might seem to have been an unlikely choice of correspondent. But Banneker addressed Jefferson as a revolutionary rather than as a planter, reminding him that he had once had reservations about the injustices of slavery. Indeed, when faced with the "arms and tyranny of the British crown," Banneker wrote, Jefferson had composed the Declaration of Independence, asserting that "all men are created equal, and that they are endowed by their creator with certain inalienable rights, that among these are life, liberty, and the pursuit of happiness."[2]

Jefferson's brief reply to Banneker was courteous but noncommittal. "Nobody wishes more than I do," he wrote, "to see such proofs as you exhibit, that nature has given to our black brethren, talents equal to those of the other colors of men, and that the appearance of a want of them is owing merely to the degraded condition of their existence, both in Africa and America." He even forwarded Banneker's almanac to the French Academy of Sciences as evidence of one Black man's accomplishments.[3] But Jefferson did not address Banneker's critique of his support for slavery. The Virginia planter had never managed to reconcile slavery with the egalitarian ideals that he articulated in the Declaration of Independence, so he had good reason to ignore Banneker's charges against him.

Instead, Jefferson's reply centered on the question of Black racial inferiority, which would become a central issue in the post-Revolutionary debate over slavery, liberty, and equal rights. He told Banneker that while he, too, hoped to see conditions for Blacks improve, he remained unsure that the race could rise very far. In *Notes on the State of Virginia* (1785), Jefferson advanced the "suspicion" that Blacks were "inferior to the whites in the endowments both of body and mind," and he would never admit otherwise.[4] In a private letter written to a friend in 1809, Jefferson even questioned Banneker's intellect, writing, "I have a long letter from Banneker, which shows him to have had a mind of very common stature indeed."[5]

Both Banneker's 1791 letter and Jefferson's response speak to the limits of Black freedom in the new nation. The Revolution marked the beginning of slavery's abolition in the northern states and provided many African Americans throughout the country with the possibility of freedom through military service, manumission, or escape. But slavery still persisted throughout the South. Fueled by the production of cotton and sugar, the region's plantation economy expanded west and south into new territories. As Jefferson's guarded response to Banneker indicates, although he and other enslavers of his era often deplored slavery, they were even more opposed to emancipation and questioned whether Blacks were fit for freedom. For example, Jefferson's friend and fellow Founding Father James Madison, who deemed slavery "the most oppressive dominion ever exercised by man over man," nevertheless considered Blacks "degraded" and abolition impractical.[6]

Not all Americans agreed with Jefferson and Madison. In the aftermath of the Revolution, thousands of white southerners liberated those they had enslaved, and white northerners began eliminating slavery altogether. Massachusetts and Vermont abolished slavery during the Revolution, and New Hampshire had fewer than fifty enslaved people by 1786. The citizens of Pennsylvania, Connecticut, Rhode Island, New York, and New Jersey also enacted gradual emancipation laws between 1780 and 1804. These laws dictated an emancipation process that was far from swift, however. They freed only those born after the laws were passed, and these people were emancipated only after they had served their enslavers for decades.

Manuscript by Benjamin Banneker. Printed and sold by John Fisher, Stationer, Baltimore. Special Collections/Courtesy of the Maryland Historical Society, image ID MS2700

Cover of Benjamin Banneker's Almanac, 1795
This cover of the 1795 edition of Benjamin Banneker's almanac features a woodcut portraying the sixty-four-year-old author. Created by an unknown artist, the portrait depicts Banneker as a dignified figure dressed in simple black-and-white clothing. Although never a Quaker himself, Banneker was closely associated with the antislavery sect, and like many Quakers, he avoided clothing colored with indigo and other dye stuffs, which were often produced by enslaved people. **How does this cover depict Banneker's status and role in American culture?**

Moreover, free Blacks in the North and the South did not have the same liberties as whites. Once the political idealism that ran high during the Revolution died down, many whites proved unwilling to embrace free Blacks as their political or social equals. Whites, as citizens of a republic in which most free Blacks were formerly enslaved and hundreds of thousands of African Americans were still in slavery, tended to associate Blackness with slavery and degradation. To combat these prejudices, free Blacks established separate Black churches, schools, and social organizations and focused their efforts on building their own communities.

Both prejudice and slavery persisted in the Republic, calling into question whether Blacks would ever be granted the liberties enshrined in the Declaration of Independence. This question remained largely unresolved during the new nation's early decades, which saw both Black slavery and Black freedom expand and the Founders adopt a Constitution that neither endorsed nor outlawed slavery. The result left African Americans, both enslaved and free, on the fringes of American democracy.

The Limits of Democracy

How did American law affect the lives and citizenship rights of enslaved and free African Americans in the aftermath of the American Revolution?

How did the growth of the cotton industry in the United States displace enslaved African American families?

The circumscribed nature of Black freedom in the post-Revolutionary era was bitterly disappointing to African Americans, who during and immediately after the Revolution had some reason to hope that slavery might collapse. Between 1776 and 1787, all but three of the new nation's thirteen states banned the importation of enslaved people from outside the United States — although South Carolina suspended the trade for only three years. Among the three states that did not ban the trade, only Georgia, which had suffered massive losses of enslaved people during the war, resumed the trade uninterrupted. North Carolina, which also had no ban, nevertheless discouraged participation in the slave trade by putting prohibitive duties on enslaved imports. New Hampshire had no ban because it did not import enough enslaved people to need one.

Yet the politicians who met to draft the U.S. Constitution in 1787 extended both slavery and the slave trade by agreeing that the United States would not withdraw from the international slave trade prior to 1808 and by creating few checks on the institution within the United States. Slavery quickly rebounded in Georgia and South Carolina and expanded rapidly across the Lower South starting in the 1790s, as planters developed lucrative new cash crops. The expansion of slavery was also facilitated by a vast expanse of new land that the United States acquired when it bought Louisiana from the French in 1803.

The Status of Slavery in the New Nation

In the decade following the Revolution, even the new nation's federal government seemed willing to take action to prohibit the growth of slavery. When the Congress of the Confederation, which served as the country's governing body prior to the ratification of the Constitution in 1790, met in July 1787 to organize the U.S. territories northwest of the Ohio River into prospective states (and auction off some of the land to pay its debts), leaders from across the nation agreed to ban slavery in these territories, which included the present-day states of Illinois, Indiana, Michigan, Ohio, and Wisconsin, as well as part of Minnesota. The congress approved the resulting legislation, known as the **Northwest Ordinance**, when it met to draft the Constitution a month later. But the Northwest Ordinance was not an antislavery triumph. It lent tacit approval to slavery south of the Ohio River, allowing the institution to expand there and specifying that enslaved people who escaped to those territories should be "lawfully reclaimed and conveyed" to their enslavers (Map 5.1).

Northwest Ordinance (1787) An act of the Confederation Congress organizing the region known as the Old Northwest, which included U.S. territories north of the Ohio River and east of the Mississippi River. Slavery was banned in these territories.

Moreover, the Constitutional Convention put no further constraints on slavery. The framers of the Constitution left the status of slavery in the states where it existed under the jurisdiction of the state legislatures. The fifty-five delegates were charged with strengthening the new nation's first system of government rather than addressing the issue of slavery, and they were willing to compromise on divisive issues in order to form a viable federal union. Accordingly, they rejected Pennsylvania delegate Gouverneur Morris's suggestion for a compensated gradual emancipation, which would have required enslavers to free the people they enslaved after a set number of years and used federal funding to reimburse them for the loss of their property. With Georgia's and South Carolina's delegates threatening to leave the Union if the Constitution included such a measure, the delegates crafted a document that made no explicit reference to enslaved people or slavery and included several measures to preserve both.

AP® skills

Applying Disciplinary Knowledge: Why did the authors of the Constitution use the phrase "person[s] held in service or labour"?

The Founders protected the interests of the slave states with a clause forbidding all states to shelter or emancipate freedom seekers — or, as termed in the Constitution, "Person[s] held to Service or Labour." This **fugitive slave clause** was later reinforced by the Fugitive Slave Act of 1793, which established the legal mechanisms by which freedom seekers could be seized and returned. The Constitution also offered enslavers federal aid to subdue slave rebellions in a clause providing federal protection against "domestic violence" within a state's borders.

fugitive slave clause A constitutional clause permitting enslavers of any state to retrieve freedom seekers they had previously enslaved from any other state.

The delegates balanced the opposing interests of slaveholding and nonslaveholding states when it came to the thorny issue of how enslaved people would be counted toward each state's federal representation and tax burden. Would enslaved people be enumerated in the tallies that determined the number of political representatives allotted to each state? Would enslaved people be taxed? Representatives from slave states wanted their enslaved population counted for

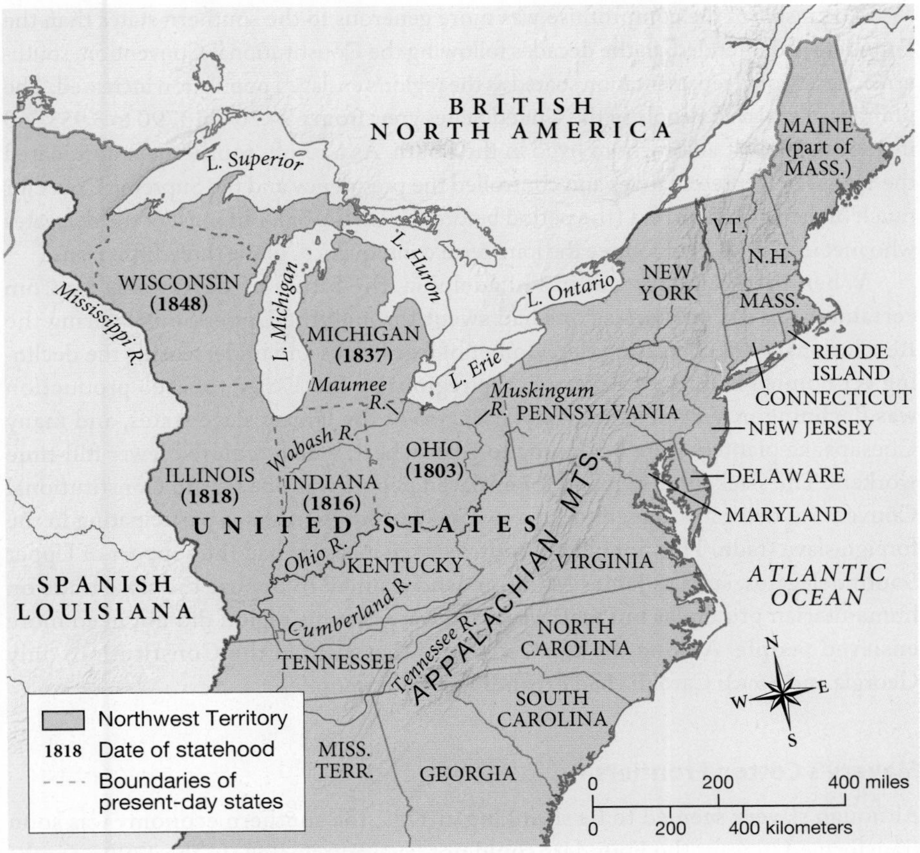

MAP 5.1 The Northwest Ordinance

Passed by the Congress of the Confederation on July 13, 1787, the Northwest Ordinance organized U.S. lands north and west of the Ohio River and east of the Mississippi River into a region known as the Northwest Territory. The Northwest Ordinance also prohibited slavery in this region. **What lands did enslavers gain from the Northwest Ordinance? How did the acquisition of land impact the growth of slavery?**

the purposes of representation but left untaxed; delegates from the other states wanted enslaved people to be taxed but not represented. The **Three-Fifths Compromise** split the difference: Three-fifths of each state's enslaved population would be counted in determining each state's tax burden and representation in the House of Representatives. The compromise was spelled out in the three-fifths clause of the Constitution. (This clause is highlighted in the copy of the Constitution in the Appendix.)

Three-Fifths Compromise
A compromise between the northern and southern states, reached during the Constitutional Convention, establishing that three-fifths of each state's enslaved population would be counted in determining federal taxes and representation in the House of Representatives.

The result of the compromise was more generous to the southern states than the Founders had intended. In the decades following the Constitutional Convention, southern congressional representation soared as the region's enslaved population increased. The number of enslaved people in the United States grew from 694,207 in 1790 to 3,953,760 in 1860 — almost all of whom lived in the South. As a result, southerners dominated the House of Representatives and controlled the presidency and the Supreme Court for much of the antebellum era (the period before the Civil War). But most of the delegates who met in 1787 did not foresee the long-term consequences of the three-fifths clause.

When the Founders met in Philadelphia, the future of slavery was far from certain. A wave of manumissions had swept through the Upper South during the Revolutionary era, increasing the number of free Blacks and underscoring the declining economic viability of slavery in the region. By the 1780s, tobacco production was declining in Virginia and Maryland, two of the largest slave states, and many Chesapeake planters were beginning to grow wheat, which required fewer full-time workers. The slackening demand for enslaved people was one reason Constitutional Convention delegates agreed to set a twenty-year limit on states participating in the foreign slave trade. This potentially controversial measure had the support of Upper South delegates, such as James Madison, who claimed to oppose the slave trade on humanitarian principles but who was also aware that his region did not need more enslaved people. Among the thirteen states that ratified the Constitution, only Georgia and South Carolina had expanding slave economies.

Slavery's Cotton Frontiers

Although slavery seemed to be shrinking in 1787, the southern economy was soon transformed in ways the Founders could not have anticipated. In the 1790s, southern planters developed two new cash crops, sugar and cotton, that secured the future of slavery and turned the South into a growing slave power. As Florida and Louisiana came under U.S. control, American planters expanded into those regions, which became the nation's primary sugar-producing areas. But the expansion of the southern border of the United States was above all fueled by the 1793 invention of Eli Whitney's cotton gin, a machine that facilitated the processing of cotton. Cotton became the most widely cultivated crop grown by enslaved people, flourishing throughout the lower Mississippi valley and beyond and leading to the establishment of new slave states, including Kentucky (1792), Tennessee (1796), Louisiana (1812), Mississippi (1817), Alabama (1819), Missouri (1821), and Arkansas (1836). The early decades of the nineteenth century also saw Americans establish cotton plantations in northern Florida, which became a U.S. territory in 1821.

AP® exam tip

To illustrate the impact of the growth of the cotton industry, you will need to know the causes and effects of the trends and patterns described in this section.

The cultivation of cotton was not new to the Lower South. During the first half of the eighteenth century, Carolina's early proprietors and Georgia's colonial trustees had encouraged the colonists to diversify the emerging plantation economy by growing cotton, hemp, flax, and foodstuffs rather than producing only cash crops such as rice and indigo. But most planters took little interest in cotton, which was then a garden crop rather than an export staple. Enslaved people and small farmers tended small cotton patches, but the fibrous cotton bolls, or seedpods, that they yielded took much of the winter to clean, card, and spin. Only enslaved people and whites too poor to buy ready-made British textiles bothered to produce homespun cotton fabric. Cotton farming had little commercial appeal because salable cotton required far too much work to be cost-effective.

Southern landowners became more interested in producing cotton and other textiles in the years leading up to the Revolution. As the conflict took shape, rebellious colonists began to boycott British goods. Once a badge of poverty, homespun clothing became a symbol of patriotism. It was a necessity during the war, when British imports were no longer available and British warships blockaded the southern colonies, cutting off most of their exports of rice, tobacco, and indigo. Cotton thus became more marketable and useful than ever before, expanding even before Whitney patented his famous gin and soaring thereafter.

The commercial cultivation of cotton first took hold in the Sea Islands of coastal Georgia and South Carolina, where the weather was consistently warm enough to support the cultivation of long-staple, or long-fibered, cotton — an easily cleaned, premium variety. But only a short-staple variety known as "upland cotton," whose fuzzy green seeds had to be carefully combed out, flourished on the mainland. The cotton gin, which used wire spikes, brushes, and a pair of rollers to separate the cotton from its seeds, revolutionized cotton production by transforming mainland cotton into a commercial crop. Whereas cleaning a pound or two of cotton had once taken a full day, the cotton gin allowed a single worker to clean as many as fifty pounds in that time. Upland cotton was also a hardy plant that could be grown throughout much of the South, and as a labor-intensive, profitable crop, it quickly proved to be an ideal crop for enslaved labor.

The South's upland cotton production skyrocketed from 150,000 pounds a year in 1793 to 6.5 million pounds in 1795, and by 1815 the region was producing well over 100 million pounds annually. Because its cultivation depended on enslaved labor, cotton sustained slavery as well, creating an enduring demand for enslaved people throughout the Lower South. The quest for cotton profits drove enslavers farther south and west in search of new land, creating an expanding frontier where forced labor predominated. Between 1790 and 1820, more than 250,000 white migrants from Virginia and Maryland settled in the backcountry regions of South Carolina and Georgia and on the frontiers of Alabama, Mississippi, Louisiana, and Missouri. The wealthiest settlers brought hundreds of enslaved people with them; others used the profits from growing cotton to buy foreign and domestic enslaved people. (See By the Numbers: The Growth of Slavery and Cotton, 1820–1860.)

As the cotton boom began, enslaved people were especially in demand in Georgia and South Carolina, which had both been short of enslaved people even before the boom. Georgia had lost two-thirds of its enslaved population during the Revolutionary War, and South Carolina may have lost up to one-quarter. To recoup

AP® skills

Applying Disciplinary Knowledge: How did the expansion of the United States influence the growth of the cotton industry? To what extent did the Fugitive Slave Act of 1793 also contribute to the economic success of the cotton industry?

BY THE NUMBERS The Growth of Slavery and Cotton, 1820–1860

Enslaved laborers played a crucial role in the production of U.S. cotton crops. As this figure indicates, cotton production expanded tremendously as the enslaved population grew. As slavery fostered the growth of cotton, cotton also promoted the expansion of slavery: The demanding crop required forced labor to clear the land and plant, cultivate, and prepare the cotton for sale. White migrants to the expanding cotton frontiers brought enslaved laborers with them and purchased both foreign and domestic enslaved people to meet their growing needs. **What conclusions can you draw about the growth of slavery and cotton in the United States from 1820 to 1860? How did the participation of enslaved people play a role in the growth?**

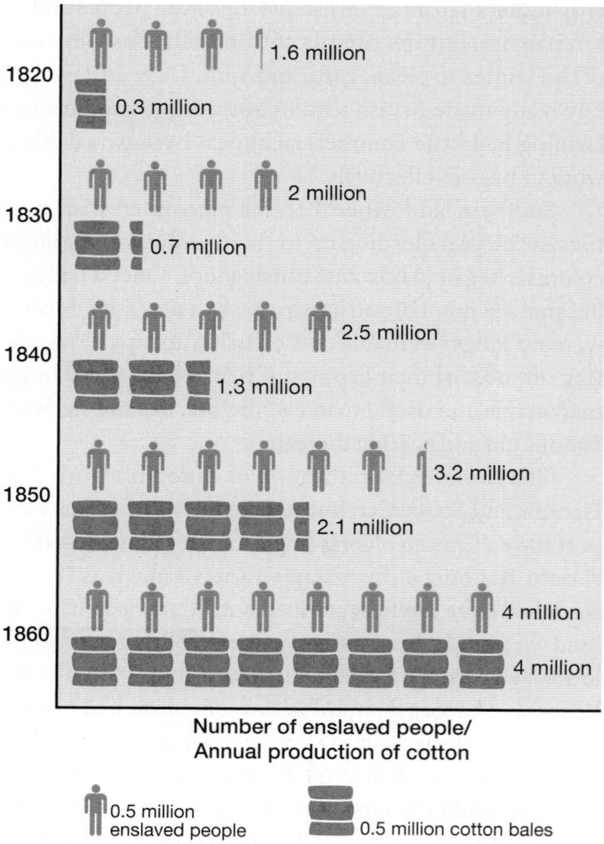

ACTIVITY ▸ Revisit Your Prediction

In the AP® Unit Warmup (p. U2-E), you made a prediction about this image. **How did the growth of the cotton industry in the United States affect enslaved African American families? What evidence supports your position? How did the growth of the cotton industry impact the forced migration patterns of enslaved people? What details in the graph support your prediction? Support or revise your original prediction using evidence from this chapter.**

their losses, planters in these states tracked down wartime fugitives who had escaped to other states and used their militias and American Indian slave catchers to hunt down maroon communities living in the region's backwoods and most inaccessible swamps. Before 1808, when the United States withdrew from the international slave trade, planters in the Lower South imported most of the new enslaved people they purchased from Africa and the Caribbean. But as the international slave trade came to an end, such buyers increasingly sought enslaved people in the Chesapeake and the North, where many enslavers were anxious to unload the people they enslaved while slavery was still legal in their states. Between 1790 and 1820, nearly 170,000 enslaved people were transferred to frontier plantations in an internal migration that continued to increase thereafter.

AP® exam tip

Be sure you can explain how the growth of the cotton industry in the United States displaced enslaved African American families.

The cotton frontier provided planters in the Upper South with a profitable market for people they wanted to sell, as birthrates had grown among the enslaved but planters' labor needs had not. Cotton also enriched the nation as a whole, fueling the

Enslaved People Processing Cotton
This image depicts early-nineteenth-century enslaved people picking, baling, and ginning cotton. Cotton and the invention of the cotton gin transformed the American South and rendered its economy ever more dependent on enslaved labor. As you examine this image, consider what the artist chose to depict and how the artist chose to depict it. **What is included, and what has been left out? What is the general feeling of the image, and where do its accuracies and/or inaccuracies lie?** *North Wind Picture Archives/Alamy Stock Photo.*

growth of northern industry and quickly becoming the country's premier export crop. The impact of cotton on African Americans in the South was equally far-reaching but also far more tragic. As the cotton frontier expanded west, families were scattered in sales that forever separated siblings, husbands and wives, and children and parents. For African Americans consigned to the cotton fields, enslaved labor grew more mind-numbing than ever before.

Unlike other skilled or seasonal work, tending cotton crops demanded unremitting menial labor. Clearing new land was backbreaking, and planting and raising cotton was nearly as arduous. Cotton has a 180- to 200-day growing season, and once the plants matured, enslaved people spent several more months picking the cotton, carefully ginning it, and pressing it into bales. By the time they finished, it was almost time to return to the cotton fields and beat down the stems of the old plants to prepare the new crop. Cotton planters typically planted and harvested corn during breaks in the cotton-growing season, ensuring that enslaved people worked all year round.

This unrelenting regime left little time for enslaved people to cultivate their own food or take care of their families. Thus, while their official workday ended at nightfall, their labors continued long afterward. On returning home, the average enslaved field worker, one observer noted, "does not lose his time. He goes to work at a bit of the land which he has planted with provisions for his own use, while his companion, if he has one, busies herself in preparing [some food] for him, herself, and their children."[7]

Between sundown and sunrise, Black people also had to build new communities within plantations. Newly imported African- and Caribbean-born captives were far from home, and American-born bondpeople from the Upper South or the North had little hope of reconnecting with their kin. Planters who migrated to the new cotton frontiers sometimes brought all the enslaved workers they owned, but they were usually more selective and often ended up separating married couples and breaking up families. Planter migrants needed strong workers who could clear their new land and survive the rigors of the long trip south, often made on foot. As a result, planters favored young adults over their parents and grandparents, and left young children and nursing mothers behind.

Enslaved families in the Upper South also were broken up by sale. One example is the family of Charles Ball, who lived in Calvert County, Maryland, until age four. After his enslaver died in the 1780s, his mother and all of his siblings were sold to separate purchasers, including a Georgia trader who drove Ball's mother away from him with a rawhide whip. Ball survived his childhood and went on to have a family of his own. But in 1805, he, too, was sold to a slave trader without warning and never saw his wife and children again. As he was dragged away from his former enslaver's home, Ball begged to "be allowed to go to see my wife and children" one last time, but the trader told Ball that he "would be able to get another wife."[8] Ball ended up in Georgia, along with numerous other enslaved people who had left behind families in the Chesapeake. He eventually escaped from slavery and settled in Pennsylvania, where he wrote his memoir and remained "fearful, at this day, to let my place of residence be known."[9]

Slavery and Empire

For most of the eighteenth century, the westward expansion of the United States was limited by Spanish, French, and American Indian claims to much of the continent's interior. At the turn of the century, the new nation took advantage of imperial conflicts in Europe and the Caribbean to expand its national boundaries. The most notable of these conflicts was the Haitian Revolution in the French colony of Saint-Domingue, which had far-reaching effects for France's New World empire. This massive slave rebellion scared enslavers across the hemispheres and provided African American populations with an enduring vision of political freedom. It also reshaped the New World's commodity markets and imperial borders in ways that helped expand slavery in the United States.

AP® skills

Applying Disciplinary Knowledge: How was the Haitian Revolution an act of resistance to slavery?

Incendie du Cap.
Révolte générale des Nègres. Massacre des Blancs.
SAINT-DOMINGUE,
OU
HISTOIRE
DE SES RÉVOLUTIONS;
CONTENANT
Le récit effroyable des divisions, des troubles, des ravages, des meurtres, des incendies, des dévastations et des massacres qui eurent lieu dans cette île, depuis 1789 jusqu'à la perte de la colonie.
A PARIS,
Chez TIGER, Imprimeur-Libraire; rue du Petit-Pont St-Jacques, n. 10.
Au Pilier littéraire.

The Haitian Revolution

The Haitian Revolution (1791–1804) in the French colony of Saint-Domingue inspired enslaved people internationally and terrified their enslavers. The frontispiece of this 1815 history of the revolution conveys enslavers' greatest fears, depicting white men, women, and children running helplessly from armed Blacks. Note, in particular, how the women are portrayed. There are many mothers with small children, a wife mourning her collapsed husband, an elderly woman with a cane, and a young woman who appears to be partially naked from the waist up. **How is white womanhood used here to illustrate the dangers of a slave revolt? How is it being used to justify the actions of enslavers?** *Schomburg Center, NYPL/Art Resource, NY.*

The **Haitian Revolution** (1791–1804) took place in the wake of the French Revolution (1789), when France's grasp on its colonies was already weakened by internal turmoil. Enslaved rebels, who numbered 100,000, burned their plantations, executed their enslavers, and shut down sugar production in Haiti, then one of the world's largest sugar producers. Their actions reverberated across the Atlantic world, with sugar in short supply and whites fleeing Haiti. Many of Haiti's sugar planters took refuge in the lower Mississippi valley and began to cultivate sugar there. France never regained control of Haiti. The powerful French general Napoleon Bonaparte, who unseated France's revolutionary leaders at the beginning of the nineteenth century, tried to reenslave Haiti's formerly enslaved people. But even after he captured their leader, Toussaint Louverture, who died in a French jail in 1803, Haiti's Black population resisted reenslavement and declared the country's independence in 1804. The loss of this most lucrative New World colony prompted Napoleon to reevaluate how many colonies France could maintain. He decided to sell off some of its least valuable assets, including Louisiana.

Haitian Revolution (1791–1804)
A rebellion against slavery and colonialism in the French colony of Saint Domingue that led to the establishment of an independent country with Black rule.

Thomas Jefferson, elected president in 1800, profited from France's shrinking imperial ambitions. In 1802, Jefferson dispatched James Monroe to France to offer to buy the port city of New Orleans, which was vital to U.S. trade.

AP® exam tip

Be sure you can explain the global impacts of the Haitian Revolution.

Jefferson authorized Monroe to pay $10 million for the city, along with as much land west of the Mississippi River as the French government could be persuaded to surrender. When Monroe arrived in France, he found Napoleon's foreign minister willing to sell all of Louisiana for the bargain price of $15 million. "They ask for only one town of Louisiana," Napoleon said, "but I consider the whole colony as completely lost."[10] Monroe was quick to agree, for the purchase would give the United States dominion over a vast section of North America's interior, extending from the Gulf of Mexico to the Canadian border and including large swaths of land on the western banks of the Mississippi River.

Louisiana Purchase (1803) The federal government's purchase of Louisiana from France, which doubled the size of the United States and fostered the spread of slavery.

The **Louisiana Purchase** (1803) doubled the size of the United States, adding 828,000 square miles of land, and fostered the spread of slavery in what Jefferson called the "empire for liberty." It included territory that would later become the slave states of Arkansas and Missouri, as well as present-day Oklahoma and portions of Texas (Map 5.2). This new land was well suited to the cultivation of cotton, adding

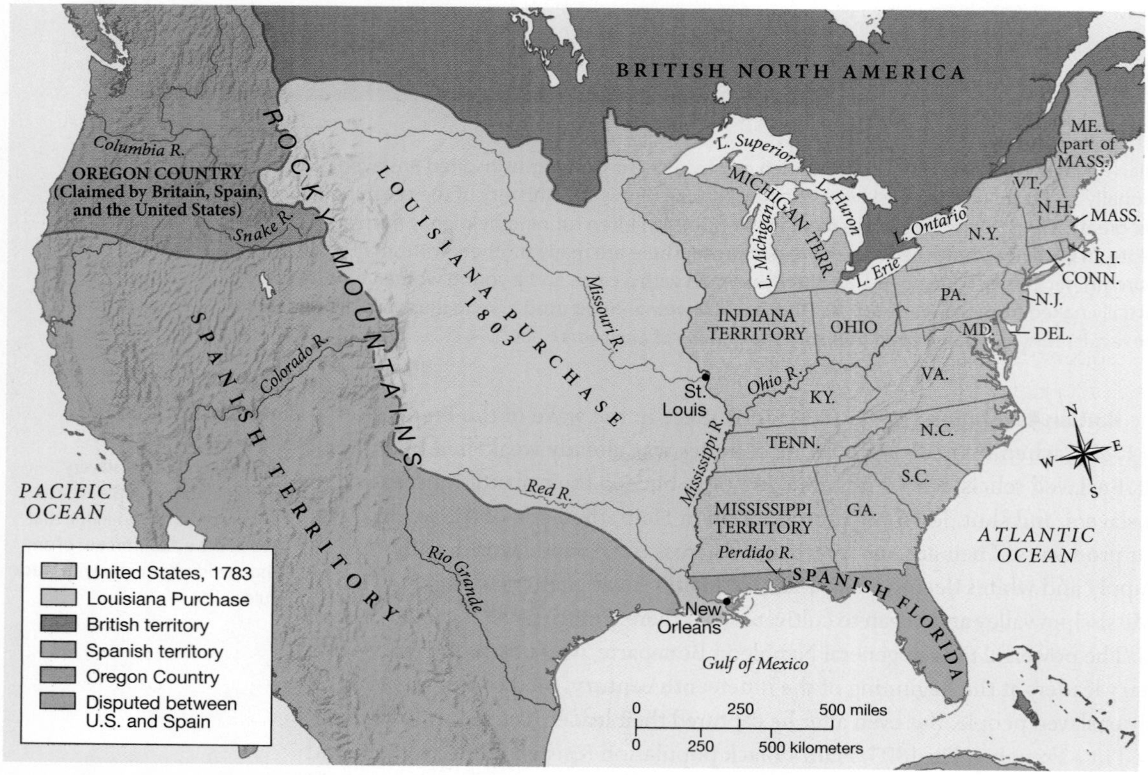

MAP 5.2 The Louisiana Purchase

The 828,000 square miles of land that the United States purchased from France in 1803 extended from the Gulf of Mexico to Canada and included all of present-day Arkansas, Missouri, Iowa, Oklahoma, Kansas, and Nebraska, most of North and South Dakota, and parts of Minnesota, New Mexico, Texas, Colorado, and Louisiana. The acquisition, which doubled the size of the United States, also had a tremendous impact on slavery: it opened new lands for the cultivation of cotton and sugar crops grown by enslaved people and sparked a westward migration of planters, facilitating the growth of the slave trade. **Why is the location of New Orleans a prime area for chattel slavery?**

millions of acres to the South's growing cotton frontier. Southeastern Louisiana also contained terrain suitable for the cultivation of sugar, an even more profitable cash crop. The Louisiana Purchase spurred new waves of westward migration among the planters of the Upper South and offered lucrative new markets for the domestic slave trade, which increased from the thirty thousand enslaved people already living in Louisiana. New Orleans quickly became a principal port for the resale of enslaved Africans. (To evade the congressional ban on importing foreign enslaved people into New Orleans, traders first sold the enslaved people in South Carolina and then resold them in New Orleans.)

Slavery and Freedom outside the Plantation South

How did free Black people in the South organize to support their communities?

What were the inspirations, goals, and struggles of different revolts and abolitionist organizing led by enslaved and free Afro-descendants throughout the Americas?

If cotton gave slavery a new lease on life in the plantation South, the status of slavery elsewhere was more mixed. In southern cities, slavery first expanded and then contracted after the Revolution. The acquisition of New Orleans greatly enlarged the South's enslaved urban population, as did the rapid growth of other urban areas. Thriving markets for cotton and other crops grown by enslaved people fueled the growth of these cities, which shipped the commodities out of their harbors. Urban businessmen employed enslaved workers to haul, load, and unload goods and to build the barrels, crates, and storehouses that contained them, and enslaved people also worked in port cities as tradesmen's assistants and domestics.

But slavery never became as entrenched in urban areas as it did in the countryside, and over time, the use of free Black workers became increasingly common in southern cities. In urban areas, unfree workers were more expensive to maintain than free workers — and potentially more dangerous as well. They often achieved a greater degree of independence than enslaved people on plantations, which made southerners uneasy, especially in the wake of Gabriel's rebellion, an abortive slave plot that took place in Richmond, Virginia, in 1800.

Meanwhile, in the North, slavery was outlawed in every state in the decades following the Revolution. But slavery was slow to die because several states adopted gradual emancipation laws that kept African Americans enslaved well into the early decades of the nineteenth century. Moreover, not all enslavers honored these laws, and some enslaved people were forced to seek their freedom in court.

Urban Slavery and Southern Free Blacks

The enslaved population in most nineteenth-century southern cities either declined or leveled off over time. Most of the enslaved people who passed through the commercial hubs and major slave trading centers such as New Orleans and Charleston were sold to rural enslavers. Southern cities tended to be sites of exchange rather than industry and did not require a large population of enslaved laborers. One major exception was Richmond, which became Virginia's state capital in 1780 and produced a variety of manufactured goods. The success of industrial slavery in Richmond was widespread enough to sustain a growing population of enslaved laborers, but the city was unusual in this regard.

AP® skills

Applying Disciplinary Knowledge: Compare the experiences of laborers in rural and urban areas and explain how these led to increased resistance to slavery in both environments.

Blacks did not disappear from such cities, however. Instead, in cities where enslaved populations declined, the number of free Blacks usually increased. In Baltimore, which saw the earliest and most dramatic shift of this kind, slavery boomed in the decades immediately after the Revolution and declined after 1810. But the city's free Black population soared thereafter.

During the Revolution, Baltimore expanded when Maryland planters abandoned tobacco, which no longer fetched high prices, in favor of wheat and other grains. The city profited enormously from this shift and became a center for milling grain into flour. Baltimore workers also produced the barrels used to store the flour and supplied the labor needed to transport, package, and ship all of Maryland's agricultural exports, as well as to construct roads, warehouses, and other buildings. Between 1790 and 1810, the city's enslaved population expanded rapidly as a result of these developments. "Surplus" enslaved people brought in from the surrounding countryside were cheap and plentiful in a region where tobacco no longer occupied most of the labor force, and they initially supplied much of the labor needed to sustain the city's economic growth. But the rise of cotton, combined with the closing of the international slave trade in 1808, soon made such enslaved people increasingly expensive. Maryland planters with surplus enslaved people began selling them to planters on the cotton frontier rather than to local buyers, and the number of enslaved people in Baltimore shrank.

AP® skills

Applying Disciplinary Knowledge: Why did free Black Americans relocate to Baltimore, Maryland? What types of job opportunities did they seek there?

Meanwhile, free Blacks flocked to Baltimore. The city's growing free Black population, like its economic growth, was a product of forces in the countryside. The declining labor needs of Maryland's planters inspired a wave of manumissions, especially among Baptist and Methodist planters. Many still chose to sell rather than free their surplus enslaved people, however, and the fear of being sold inspired some enslaved people to free themselves — either by working to purchase their freedom or by escaping. Freedom seekers and free Blacks alike migrated to Baltimore, where jobs were plentiful and the large free Black population could provide a community for freemen and shelter freedom seekers. Maryland enslavers often suspected that missing enslaved people were in Baltimore, passing as free Blacks. In 1789, one enslaver ran a newspaper ad seeking the whereabouts of a missing enslaved woman named Charity. His ad maintained that he was all but certain she "is in or near Baltimore-town, passes for a free woman, practices midwifery, and goes by the name of Sarah Dorsey, or Dawson, the Granny."[11]

The economics of slavery in urban areas were never as clear-cut as they were in the rural South. On one hand, the rise of the domestic slave trade after 1808 ensured that urban enslaved people commanded a good price, which encouraged enslavers to retain the people they enslaved as investments. On the other hand, urban enslaved people tended to produce fewer goods than their agricultural counterparts. Whether they worked as domestic laborers or served under tradesmen, enslaved people in cities were rarely subjected to the unremitting labor regime that prevailed in the countryside. Moreover, urban enslaved people could put a strain on their enslavers' finances if they were not fully employed because they were more expensive to clothe, house, and feed in the city than on the plantation.

Thus, a system of **hiring out** was developed to exploit urban enslaved people's labor, allowing some enslavers to make a good living by contracting out the people they enslaved. The practice allowed businessmen who could not afford to buy slaves or needed their labor for only a short time to employ enslaved workers for anywhere from one day to one year. Unlike enslavers, these employers had no obligation to house their workers or supervise them after they left work. Although enslaved workers who were hired out for domestic jobs might live in their employers' homes, many others lived independently. They were allowed to keep a portion of their earnings to cover their room and board and were given the freedom to find their own lodging. This practice, known as **living out**, evolved because many urban employers had no place to house enslaved workers.

hiring out
The practice of enslavers contracting out those they enslaved to work for other employers.

living out
The practice of allowing enslaved people who were hired out in urban areas to keep part of their wages to pay for their rented lodgings.

The hiring-out system gave these workers a degree of freedom that often worried white southerners, who enacted but rarely enforced laws banning the system. Enslaved Blacks who were hired out in southern cities typically made their own work arrangements, remained largely unsupervised, and were often in close contact with free Blacks. This could reduce their value, as one enslaver discovered when he tried to sell an enslaved family he had long hired out. Its members attracted no offers because other enslavers were wary of purchasing enslaved people who had known independence. By contrast, this autonomy benefited enslaved people, who sometimes accumulated enough money to buy their freedom by living cheaply and working extra hours. It could also tempt them to free themselves by either running away or rebelling.

Gabriel's Rebellion

Although city life offered some degree of freedom, it was not enough for an urban bondman known as Prosser's Gabriel, who led a plot to overturn slavery in Richmond in the summer of 1800. The abiding discontent among Richmond's enslaved population led to **Gabriel's rebellion**. At a time when the memory of the American Revolution was very much alive, the more recent Haitian Revolution underscored the possibility that an enslaved people could overthrow their oppressors. Gabriel was among the Black Virginians who embraced this possibility. A blacksmith, he lived outside Richmond with his brothers, Solomon and Martin, on a tobacco plantation belonging to his enslaver, Thomas Prosser. Aware that divisions among the French had helped set the stage for the Haitian Revolution, Gabriel hoped that Virginia's enslaved people could exploit the social and political tensions among whites in their state, which were then running high in anticipation of the election of 1800.

Gabriel's rebellion
An abortive slave revolt plot that took place in Richmond, Virginia, in 1800. It was led by an enslaved man known as Prosser's Gabriel.

AP® skills

Applying Disciplinary Knowledge: Why was Gabriel's plan an act of overt resistance? Why did Gabriel's plot collapse?

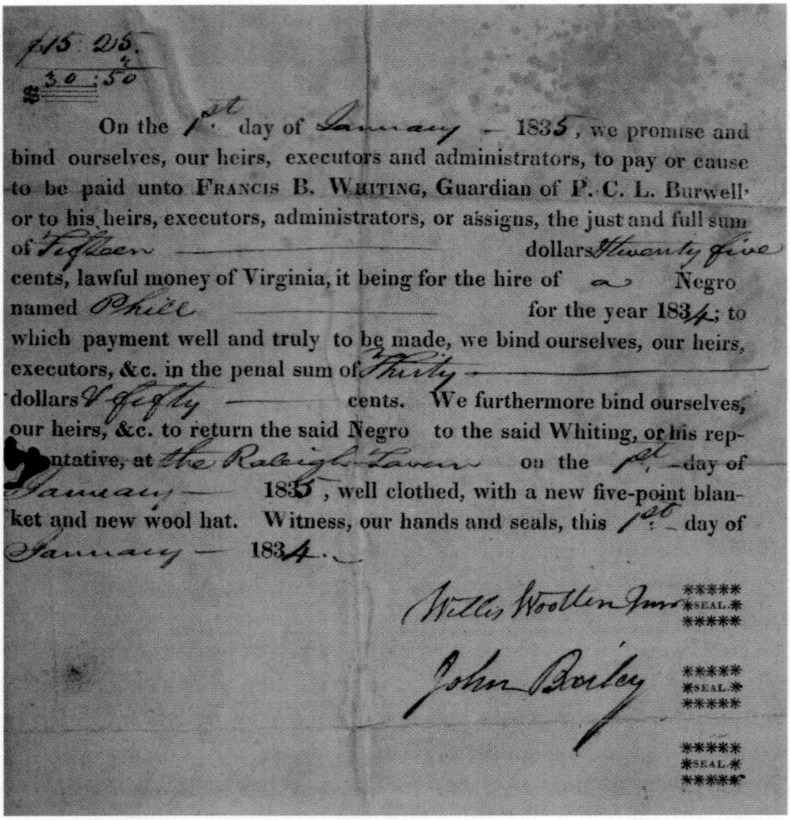

$15.25
$30.50

On the 1st day of January 1835, we promise and bind ourselves, our heirs, executors and administrators, to pay or cause to be paid unto FRANCIS B. WHITING, Guardian of P. C. L. Burwell or to his heirs, executors, administrators, or assigns, the just and full sum of Fifteen dollars & twenty five cents, lawful money of Virginia, it being for the hire of a Negro named Phill for the year 1834; to which payment well and truly to be made, we bind ourselves, our heirs, executors, &c. in the penal sum of Thirty dollars & fifty cents. We furthermore bind ourselves, our heirs, &c. to return the said Negro to the said Whiting, or his rep-[illegible]ntative, at the Raleigh Tavern on the 1st day of January 1835, well clothed, with a new five-point blanket and new wool hat. Witness, our hands and seals, this 1st day of January 1834.

Willis Wootten Junr SEAL.

John Bailey SEAL.

SEAL.

Receipt for the Hire of an Enslaved Person

Dated January 1, 1834, this receipt for the hire of an enslaved person in Virginia is written in a standardized legal form that lists the expenses and obligations involved in renting human property. Slave hiring was a popular practice that allowed enslavers who did not need to use those they enslaved to profit from enslaved labor for others. It also supplied enslaved labor to those who could not afford to enslave others or who needed enslaved labor for only a limited time period. **How does this image exemplify the ways in which enslavers commodified enslaved Black Americans?** *Private Collection/© Michael Graham-Steward/ Bridgeman Images.*

With the aid of his brothers and other enslaved confederates, Gabriel planned to enlist about a thousand enslaved people to attack Richmond's wealthy citizens, while sparing the city's poor whites. He hoped that these discontented Virginians, as well as antislavery whites such as the city's Methodists and Quakers, would join the rebels and help them take control of the state. Most of Gabriel's enslaved recruits worked in or around Richmond and were American-born and highly acculturated. Many were artisans whose labor was not closely supervised. They saw themselves as workingmen united around a cause, much as the colonists had been a quarter century earlier. Gabriel even planned to carry a flag reading "Death or liberty," evoking well-known Revolutionary-era language. Gabriel and his followers took advantage of their freedom of movement to hold secret planning meetings in local taverns and shops and even traveled to the countryside to recruit rural followers at barbecues and revival meetings. They were also able to amass a small cache of weapons, which they hoped to use to seize more weapons in Richmond.

In the end, Gabriel's plot collapsed. As word of the revolt spread to hundreds of enslaved people across the Virginia countryside, two disclosed the plot to their enslaver, who alerted Virginia governor James Monroe. Between this betrayal and a torrential storm that delayed implementation of the plan, the rebellion failed. Six of the ringleaders were captured immediately, and a militia assembled by the governor tracked down the remaining twenty. Among the last to surrender was Gabriel, who eluded the militia for almost three weeks before he was captured and taken back to Richmond in chains. There he was tried and executed along with the twenty-five others. More participants also were indicted, but by mid-October, a state law requiring Virginia to compensate enslavers convicted of capital crimes made the executions prohibitively expensive. The state had paid $8,899.91 to the enslavers of the condemned men, and many more suspects awaited trial. Governor Monroe suspended the executions after Thomas Jefferson suggested that the rebels might instead be sold outside the United States.

Even though Gabriel's rebellion failed, white Virginians lived in fear of an uprising, especially after another slave plot was uncovered in 1802. Some members of the Virginia General Assembly even contemplated abandoning slavery completely, commissioning the governor to confer with President Jefferson about locating a place where "such negroes or mulattoes, as may be emancipated, may be sent or choose to remove as a place of asylum."[12] Instead, most enslavers called for laws that would discourage slave revolts.

Virginia authorities responded by eliminating much of the independence and mobility that urban Blacks enjoyed. In Richmond, Monroe secured the state capital's arsenals and public buildings by instituting a nightly police patrol. The officers were responsible for rounding up any enslaved people caught on the street after nine o'clock. According to the law, these enslaved people would receive "as many stripes" as the officer "might see proper to inflict."[13] In addition, African American laborers were regulated much more carefully than before. Although it was already illegal, enslaved people's hiring out of their own time was outlawed once more, and this time the legislature mandated stiff fines for enslavers and severe whippings for enslaved people who broke the law. The general assembly also cracked down on the "unlawful assemblages" of enslaved people who gathered to relax after work or on Sundays, ordering the state's justices of the peace to break up all such gatherings and to punish enslaved people who participated in them. Even attending church became difficult because enslaved people could no longer go anywhere without written passes from their enslavers, who were often unwilling to supply them.

AP® skills

Applying Disciplinary Knowledge: How did acts of resistance to slavery lead to more codes and laws to restrict both enslaved and free Black Americans? Why were free Black Americans considered a threat to chattel slavery?

Free Blacks found themselves more confined in the aftermath of Gabriel's rebellion as well. Although none were implicated, free Blacks were suspected of helping the rebels promote their plot and steal from their enslavers. Moreover, many white Virginians were convinced that free Blacks' very existence endangered slavery. "If blacks see all their color as slaves," one lawmaker explained, "it will seem to them a disposition of Providence, and they will be content. But if they see others like themselves free, and enjoying the rights they are deprived of, they will repine."[14] So when the state assembly clamped down on the network of Black boatmen who had helped spread word of the planned revolts of 1800 and 1802, it targeted both free and enslaved Blacks. An 1802 law banned any "negro or mulatto" from obtaining a ship pilot's license, and Black pilots whose licenses were issued prior to the law were confined to their boats as they traveled through Virginia. As slave patrols proliferated, free Blacks came under scrutiny in their own neighborhoods. They could no longer survive without papers and had to register with their towns as "Free Negroes & Mulattoes."[15]

In the wake of Gabriel's rebellion, opportunities to pass from slavery to freedom began to decrease across the South. In 1806, Virginia legislators reversed the liberal manumission law the state had adopted during the Revolutionary era, which made manumission a private matter, and replaced it with a new law that made manumission very difficult. The law also required newly emancipated enslaved people to leave the state within twelve months or forfeit their freedom and become subject to reenslavement and sale. Newly freed Blacks and their enslavers could petition the legislature to exempt individuals from the law, but self-purchase and manumission no longer offered enslaved people in Virginia a direct route to lasting freedom. Unless they could secure permission from the legislature to remain in state, newly freed Blacks now had to migrate north and forever separate themselves from their enslaved family members and friends. Not surprisingly, many were unwilling to leave on these terms. By 1815, the state legislature was so overwhelmed by petitions from free Blacks who wanted to remain in Virginia that they authorized the county courts to permit any Black person freed for "extraordinary merit" to stay.[16]

Achieving Emancipation in the North

In addition to expanding the boundaries of America's slave South, the Louisiana Purchase added more land to the free territory of the Old Northwest. The Northwest Ordinance had banned slavery in U.S. territories north of the Ohio River and east of the Mississippi River. In the short term, the ban did not prevent some early settlers from keeping enslaved people in those areas: it did not apply to enslaved people already living there and did not keep some settlers from importing more. But the gradual emancipation of enslaved people in the northern states discouraged such imports, paving the way for the creation of other free states throughout the region.

> **AP® skills**
>
> **Applying Disciplinary Knowledge:** How was liberation from chattel slavery denied in certain parts of the North? How were laws used to both liberate enslaved people while at the same time keep others in bondage?

By 1804, every northern state had either abolished slavery outright or passed a plan to eliminate slavery over time, and the new states that emerged in the Old

Northwest followed suit. But Black freedom was not easily gained or maintained in these states. In Indiana Territory, which included much of the upper Mississippi valley, gradual emancipation meant brutal forms of indentured servitude for up to thirty years before enslaved people became free. To avoid becoming a haven for freedom seekers, Ohio, which became a free state in 1803, policed the border along the Ohio River between the slave South and the free North. In 1804, Ohio passed **black laws** requiring all free Blacks to supply legal proof of their free status and to post a $500 bond to guarantee their good behavior. Indiana, which became a state in 1816, and Illinois, which gained statehood in 1818, entered the Union as free states with similar laws. Though not uniformly enforced, such laws were common in the western states and imposed bond requirements for free Blacks that eventually reached $1,000 — a sum well beyond the reach of most African Americans.

black laws
Laws adopted in some midwestern states requiring all free Black residents to supply legal proof of their free status and post a cash bond of up to $1,000 to guarantee their good behavior.

Federal legislation passed during the early national period also solidified the limits on Black freedom. The nation's first immigration law, the **Naturalization Act of 1790**, instituted residence and racial requirements for potential citizens. Naturalization was available to "free white person[s]" who had been in the United States for at least two years. Free Blacks, by contrast, were not classified as full citizens under the laws of the Republic: They were barred from joining the national militia, carrying federal mail, or holding elected office in the District of Columbia. Moreover, the Constitution did not protect Blacks from racially discriminatory laws imposed by individual states. Emancipation would not bring full freedom for Black northerners, and just achieving emancipation was a struggle for many Blacks.

Naturalization Act of 1790
The nation's first immigration law, which instituted a two-year residency requirement for immigrants who wished to become U.S. citizens and limited naturalization to free white people.

Throughout the North, formerly enslaved people were liberated on terms that were neither swift nor generous. Slavery was outlawed in Massachusetts and Vermont during the Revolution, and it was abolished by means of gradual emancipation laws in the other northern states — with the exception of New Hampshire, which passed no abolition law and instead let its tiny enslaved population dwindle to nothing through manumission and attrition. The first state to adopt a gradual emancipation law was Pennsylvania. Passed in 1780, Pennsylvania's Act for the Gradual Abolition of Slavery provided a model for similar laws in Connecticut and Rhode Island in 1784, New York in 1799, and New Jersey in 1804. These laws applied only to enslaved Blacks born after the legislation was passed — those born before then generally remained enslaved for life — and liberated those it freed in their mid- to late twenties, after they had labored long enough, in effect, to pay for their own freedom. As a result, despite their efforts to speed the application of these laws, thousands of Black northerners remained in bondage through the 1820s.

Many enslavers were reluctant to emancipate their unfree workers even after they had completed the terms of service required. Isabella Baumfree, who later renamed herself Sojourner Truth, was one of many Black northerners who struggled to achieve the freedom promised her by law. Born in upstate New York in 1797, two years too early to qualify for gradual emancipation, Baumfree had little hope of ever obtaining her freedom until 1817, when the New York legislature revised state law, setting July 4, 1827, as the date by which all enslaved people in New York would achieve

AP® skills

Applying Disciplinary Knowledge: How did Sojourner Truth gain her initial freedom from slavery?

freedom, regardless of birth date. This revision did not release enslaved children born before that date from their service obligation, but it reduced the term to twenty-one years. Baumfree, who endured several abusive enslavers and many hardships as an enslaved woman, was understandably eager to be freed, and she no doubt welcomed the law's reduction of the terms of service for her five children. As 1827 approached, she even managed to get her enslaver, John Dumont, to agree to release her a year early if she behaved well and served him faithfully. But July 4, 1827, came and went, and Baumfree remained enslaved. Dumont insisted that Baumfree owed him more time because she had worked less than usual that year due to a "badly diseased hand."[17]

That fall, Baumfree freed herself by sneaking out of Dumont's house early one morning with a baby in one arm and her clothing in the other. She left behind her husband, whom Dumont had picked for her, and the rest of her children, who still owed Dumont many years of labor. But she did not travel far from her family. She took refuge with two antislavery neighbors, Maria and Isaac Van Wagenen, who sheltered Baumfree despite her enslaver's objections. When Dumont tried to drag Baumfree and her baby back to his home, Isaac Van Wagenen told his neighbor that even though he had "never been in the practice of buying and selling slaves; [and] he did not believe in slavery," he would buy out the remainder of Baumfree's time rather than see her return. Dumont accepted his offer of $20 for Baumfree's freedom and $5 for her baby's. Baumfree, who could hardly believe her good fortune, initially assumed that she had changed hands once more. Only after Van Wagenen assured her that "there is but *one* master; and he who is *your* master is *my* master" did she believe that she was free.[18] Baumfree still had to fight to free her other children, who remained with Dumont, and even took him to court to achieve that end.

AP® exam tip

On the AP® Exam, you will likely be required to explain the broad historical context, perspective, and purpose as well as the intended audience of the personal narratives of survivors of slavery.

Gradual emancipation laws gave northern enslavers many years to devise ways to sell the people they enslaved out of state rather than set them free. Unscrupulous enslavers sold thousands of Black northerners illegally in the South. Northern Blacks resisted such sales and sought the assistance of antislavery whites in recovering friends and family members who had been sold illegally. In Pennsylvania, African Americans' struggles to recover friends and family members who had been illegally sold helped inspire the birth of the nation's first antislavery organization. Founded in 1775 by French-born abolitionist Anthony Benezet, the Society for the Relief of Free Negroes Unlawfully Held in Bondage, which was later reorganized as the Pennsylvania Society for Promoting the Abolition of Slavery and for the Relief of Free Negroes Unlawfully Held in Bondage, was a white organization with a predominantly Quaker membership. The American revolutionary Thomas Paine was also a founding member, and Benjamin Franklin joined the organization in the mid-1780s and for a time served as its president. The New York Manumission Society, founded in 1785 by American statesman and Founding Father John Jay, took shape around similar concerns. Its members protested the kidnapping of Blacks, both enslaved and free, in the years immediately following the Revolution and pushed the legislature to prevent New Yorkers from evading gradual emancipation by exporting their enslaved people. But such practices were difficult to police.

Kidnapping of an African American Mother and Child, c. 1840
This engraving from an abolitionist publication dramatizes the kidnapping of a free Black mother and child. Known as "blackbirding," this sinister practice was a threat to the liberties of all northern free Blacks. Blackbirders could earn easy money by abducting free Blacks and selling them to slave traders. Children were particularly popular targets since they could easily be overpowered. **What does this engraving reveal about the experience of free Black Americans in the 1840s?** *The Library Company of Philadelphia.*

Over time, however, the illegal sale and exportation of enslaved northern Blacks ended along with slavery itself. Although some enslavers managed to evade gradual emancipation, northern emancipation statutes also provided many of the region's enslaved people with unprecedented opportunities for negotiation. Enslavers were most willing to offer early emancipation to the very young and very old, who were their least profitable workers, but eventually they had to free all their enslaved people and were sometimes willing to free them early. The region was home to almost 50,000 enslaved people in 1770, but that number declined rapidly thereafter. By 1820, fewer than 20,000 enslaved people, most of whom lived in New York and New Jersey, remained in the North. By 1840, the number of enslaved people in the North had dwindled to just over 1,000.

Free Black Life in the New Republic

How did free Black people in the North organize to support their communities?

How did nineteenth-century emigrationists aim to achieve the goal of Black freedom and self-determination?

As northern Blacks achieved emancipation, free Black communities took shape across the region. Whereas free Blacks in the North never numbered more than a few thousand during the colonial era, by 1810, there were 50,000 of them. That number doubled by 1820 and reached 170,728 in 1840. Most free Blacks lived in port cities, which had had large Black communities even during the colonial era. No longer bound to rural enslavers, the formerly enslaved population congregated in major northern cities such as New York, Philadelphia, and Boston, all of which attracted fugitives from slavery as well. City life offered safety in numbers to freedom seekers and also held significant advantages for free Blacks, including greater opportunities for independence and employment. With their new freedom, African Americans sought to build their own households and sustain larger Black communities that could support churches, schools, and social organizations.

Free Black Organizations

AP® skills

Applying Disciplinary Knowledge: What steps did Black Americans take to adapt to life in the urban North while still developing their own culture?

mutual aid society An organization or voluntary association in which members agreed to assist one another in securing benefits such as insurance.

Black life in the larger northern cities was not without promise for ambitious formerly enslaved people such as Absalom Jones and Richard Allen. Both were born in Delaware, where slavery declined to very low levels after the Revolution but had not been formally abolished. The two men, both Methodist converts enslaved by evangelicals who allowed them to purchase their freedom in the early 1780s, met in Philadelphia and became lifelong friends and allies. They also prospered in business: Jones was a shoemaker, and Allen owned a chimney-sweeping business. They became prominent members of Philadelphia's rapidly growing free Black community and founded the city's first Black **mutual aid society** in 1787. Members of the Free African Society pledged to support one another "in sickness, and for the benefit of their widows and fatherless children."[19]

AP® skills

Applying Disciplinary Knowledge: How did Black organizations contribute to cultural development during the nineteenth century?

The Free African Society was one of several similar free Black organizations established during the late eighteenth and early nineteenth centuries. Others included the African Union Society of Providence, Rhode Island, established in 1780; the Brown Fellowship Society of Charleston, South Carolina, founded in 1790; Boston's African Society, organized in 1796; New York's African Society for Mutual Relief, established in 1808; and the Resolute Beneficial Society of Washington, D.C., founded in 1818. All of these organizations were funded by dues and other fees collected from members, which they used to provide a social safety net for their community. The specific benefits offered varied by organization, but they typically included sickness and disability benefits, burial insurance, and pensions to widows and orphans. Mutual aid societies also helped free Blacks establish other institutions that would be crucial to their community's well-being. Most notable among these were Black churches.

Although many early members of the Black mutual aid societies initially belonged to white churches, they often ended up establishing their own — a move usually inspired by the prejudices they encountered. Richard Allen, Absalom Jones, and other early members of Philadelphia's Free African Society, for example, attended St. George's Methodist Church. Allen, who was a gifted preacher, even led special services for African Americans there. But as Allen's sermons drew more Black worshippers

Bethel AME Church
Black churches such as the Bethel AME Church in Philadelphia provided far more than church services. They met a variety of needs for their communities and congregations, also serving as schools, meetinghouses, clubhouses, lecture halls, and sites for social and political gatherings. Black churches flourished in northern cities during the early nineteenth century, serving both African Americans who were already well established and the recently arrived migrants and newly freed people who came in need of education, work, and community support. **Why is the Bethel AME Church a significant location to the emerging Black culture during the early nineteenth century?** *The Library Company of Philadelphia.*

to St. George's, these congregants became increasingly unwelcome. White leaders began to segregate them, asking them first to sit along the walls and then moving them to seats in the balcony. "You must not kneel here," a church trustee told Absalom Jones when he and several others defied this segregated seating plan, claiming seats on the first floor and kneeling to join the rest of the congregation in prayer one Sunday morning in 1792.[20] Heads still bowed, Jones and his followers refused to move until the prayer was over, at which point the trustee summoned several white men to help him force the Black congregants to the balcony. Disgusted, the Black members of St. George's got up and walked out of the church.

"We never entered it again!" remembered Allen, who had been soliciting funds for the creation of a separate Black church in Philadelphia even before the walkout.[21] The group worshipped in a rented storefront until July 29, 1794, when the African Methodist Episcopal (AME) Church — led by Allen and later renamed the Bethel AME Church — finally opened its doors. Bethel AME joined several other Black Methodist churches to form an independent AME denomination in 1816, at which point the new denomination's congregants elected Allen to serve as the AME's first bishop.

But not all African Americans who had attended St. George's joined Bethel AME. Some abandoned Methodism altogether, registering a permanent protest against the

Absalom Jones, 1810
Painted by Philadelphia artist Raphaelle Peale, this portrait depicts one of Black Philadelphia's most important leaders. Absalom Jones escaped from slavery to become a founding member of the city's Free African Society, as well as the nation's first Black priest of the Episcopal denomination. Peale's depiction of Jones is respectful and underscores Jones's status as a man of God by portraying him in ecclesiastical robes, with Bible in hand. **What features of the painting demonstrate Raphaelle Peale's perspective on Absalom Jones?** *Absalom Jones, 1810, by Raphaelle Peale (1774–1825)/Delaware Art Museum, Wilmington, Delaware/Gift of Absalom Jones School/ Bridgeman Images.*

segregationist policies of white Methodists. Among them was Absalom Jones, who with help from Allen and other members of the Free African Society founded the African Episcopal Church of St. Thomas, the nation's first African American Episcopal church, and became an ordained Episcopal minister in 1804.

AP® skills
Applying Disciplinary Knowledge: How did the Black community reshape Christian worship? What role did Black women play in the development of the Black Christian church community?

Black churches, most of them Methodist or Baptist, proliferated in other cities as well during the early 1800s. Many were funded and built with help from Black mutual aid societies, with which the churches often remained closely affiliated. Boston's first Black Baptist church, the African Meeting House, was founded in 1805 with the help of Boston's African Society and the city's oldest Black fraternal order, the Prince Hall Masonic Lodge. Early Black churches hosted mutual aid society meetings, public lectures, protest meetings, and other gatherings and served the needs of newly freed people who came in search of educational opportunities and economic assistance as well as Sunday services. Virtually all early Black churches also served as schools at various points in their history. Richard Allen founded the nation's first Black Sunday school in his church in 1795, and he opened a night school for adults a few years later. Meanwhile, the African Union Society of Providence built its African Union Meeting House in 1821 to serve as both a school and a Baptist church.

While the leaders of all these early Black churches were men, African American women were crucial to the survival and success of these institutions. Black female worshipers frequently outnumbered their male counterparts in both Black and biracial congregations. Some were drawn to institutions such as the Methodist church because of its support for the education of Black children.

But many were also eager for instruction themselves and attended church classes as well as services. Among them was Jarena Lee, a young Black woman from Cape May, New Jersey, who worked as a domestic servant in Philadelphia. Lee first became interested in religion after hearing a Presbyterian minister speak in 1804. Although she was raised "wholly ignorant of God," Lee was captivated and became anxious to cast off the "weight of my sins, and sinful nature." She sought religious instruction, eventually making her way to Richard Allen's Bethel AME Church, where her "soul was gloriously converted to God." Lee's conversion would propel her toward religious leadership. She became a faithful member of Mother Bethel, and five years after her sanctification, she felt called to preach. A persistent voice told her to "Preach the Gospel; I will put words in your mouth." However, when Lee sought Richard Allen's permission to address his congregation, he discouraged her. Methodism, he told her, "did not call for women preachers."[22] But not long after the founding of the African Methodist Episcopal Church in 1816, Allen relented, granting Lee permission to lead prayers meeting outside the church and address congregations as an exhorter, or lay preacher. As a new denomination composed exclusively of Black Methodist churches such as Allen's Mother Bethel, the AME needed members. Lee began preaching in 1818 and sustained a successful itinerant ministry for decades. Still, despite her efforts, the AME would not ordain its first female minister until 1889.

Free Black Education and Employment

Black northerners emerged from slavery eager to support themselves, and the difficulties they often faced in finding work made them doubly anxious to educate their children. The gradual emancipation acts passed in Pennsylvania, Connecticut, Rhode Island, New York, and New Jersey freed enslaved people only after they had devoted many of their most productive years to working without pay and without any opportunity to educate themselves or acquire property. In an era when most people started working in their teens and did not live much past forty, these formerly enslaved people began their lives as free adults far poorer than even the poor whites beside whom they often worked. Some of the formerly enslaved became destitute and swelled the rolls of northern poorhouses.

Even young and healthy free Blacks had great difficulty finding anything but low-paying menial jobs. Whereas enslaved people had once been used in a variety of occupations, the slow progress of gradual emancipation allowed former enslavers and working-class whites time to craft racially discriminatory statutes and practices designed to keep Blacks at the bottom of the northern labor market. As enslaved people, Black northerners had not competed directly with white workers for paying jobs. Now white workers saw them as a threat. Many whites were unwilling to work alongside Blacks, and many white employers were reluctant to hire formerly enslaved

Juliann Jane Tilman, 1844
Much like Jarena Lee, Juliann Jane Tillman reported that she was called by God's messengers to spread the Gospel. She too preached at the AME Church in Philadelphia, decades after Lee. In this image, Tillman looks directly at the viewer and gestures to prepare for the Second Coming of Christ that has been prophesized in the Book of Revelation. This image was made into a lithograph that could be mass produced. **Why was this image mass produced?** *Sarin Images/Granger — All rights reserved.*

ACTIVITY ▸ Revisit Your Prediction

In the AP® Unit Warmup (p. U2-F), you made a prediction about this image. **What role and impact do you think women and their narratives about their experience in slavery had on political movements of the nineteenth century? How do you think Black women's experiences in the nineteenth century relate to their perspectives on slavery and its effects? Support or revise your original prediction using evidence from this chapter.**

people for anything other than menial labor, so even formerly enslaved people who were highly skilled had difficulty securing well-paying jobs. Instead, free Blacks were welcome only in service trades that were closely associated with slavery. Black women worked as washerwomen, seamstresses, and cooks, and Black men were employed as laborers, mariners, barbers, coachmen, porters, and bootblacks. Northern whites were quick to blame free Blacks' poverty and low occupational status on inherent racial inferiority rather than on social forces, which only compounded the discrimination that free Blacks faced.

AP® skills

Applying Disciplinary Knowledge: Why did Black Americans value education? How did the New York Manumission Society (NYMS) undermine the goals of Black parents?

Still, Black northerners remained hopeful that education would improve the status of their race and help their children succeed in life, and they worked hard to create educational opportunities for their offspring. Most northern municipalities did not have public schools until the 1830s, however, and the ones that existed were not always welcoming to Black children. Boston established a public school system as early as the 1790s, but the African Americans who attended were treated poorly. The Black minister Hosea Easton, who attended school in Boston in the early 1800s, later recalled his teachers' blatant racism. Pupils who misbehaved, Black or white, were banished to the "n***** seat," and those who did not complete their lessons were deemed as "poor or ignorant as a *n******" or as having "no more credit than a *n******." According to Easton, this training had a "disastrous [effect] upon the mind of the community; having been instructed from youth to look upon a black man in no other light than a slave." It also

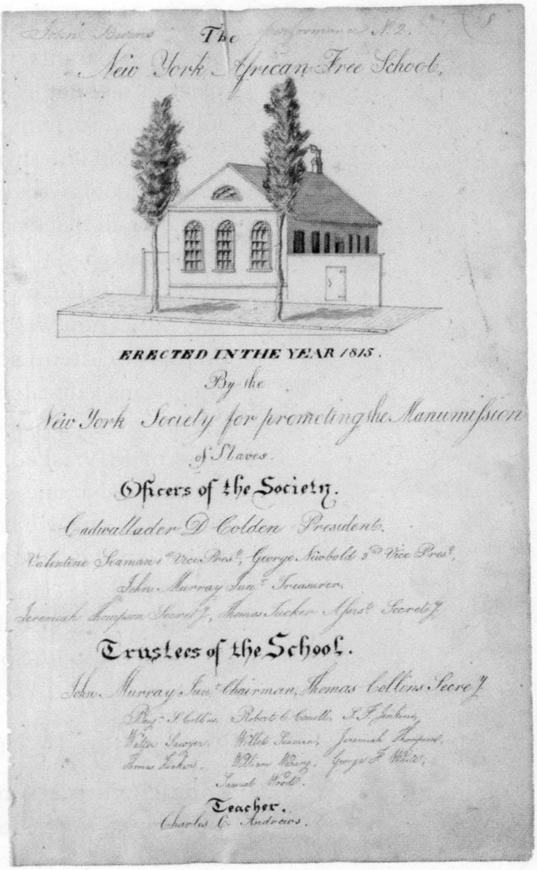

The New York African Free School
The New York African Free School, established in 1787 by the New York Manumission Society, began as a one-room schoolhouse with forty students, most of whose parents were enslaved. In 1835, it was incorporated into the New York City public school system. The African Free School had by then graduated more than fourteen hundred students, many of whom went on to achieve distinction in a variety of professions and to advance the cause of abolitionism. The building depicted here is most likely the replacement for the original schoolhouse, which was destroyed in a fire in 1814. **How did the establishment of the New York African Free School show resistance to inequality?** *Drawing of the Exterior of the New York African Free School with Penmanship. Manuscripts, Penmanship and Drawing Book, AFS, 1822, vol. 4, p. 6, negative #59134/Collection of the New-York Historical Society.*

drove Black parents in Boston to establish their own African School in 1798.[23]

In Philadelphia, African Americans who wished to educate their children faced different obstacles. The city had no public schools prior to 1818, and although the Pennsylvania Society for Promoting the Abolition of Slavery (PAS), a white philanthropic organization, founded a private school for Black children at the beginning of the nineteenth century, many parents could not afford to pay the tuition. The fact that PAS leaders decided not to fund schools taught by Black teachers — withdrawing the support they had once provided to Richard Allen's church — may have alienated Black parents as well, and many continued to send their children to Allen's church to be educated.

In New York, the New York Manumission Society (NYMS) established the New York African Free School in 1787, creating perhaps the most successful early Black school established by white reformers. Its distinguished graduates included Ira Aldridge, who became a renowned Black actor, and James McCune Smith, the first African American to receive a medical degree. But the NYMS's ideas about education were not always in accord with those of Black parents and teachers, and they highlighted the divisions separating early-nineteenth-century Blacks from their white allies.

The NYMS, an exclusively white organization founded by some of New York's wealthiest men, had relatively modest antislavery goals. It supported the education and careful supervision of New York's free Black population in the hope of fostering public support for abolition. The organization's members resolved to "keep a watchful eye over the conduct of such Negroes as have been or may be liberated; and . . . to prevent them from running into immorality or sinking into idleness." In 1788, they even established the Committee for Preventing Irregular Conduct among

Free Negroes. The New York African Free School set similar goals for both its pupils and their parents, to the point where school administrators reserved the right to place former pupils in jobs or apprenticeships rather than let them "waste their time in idleness . . . [or] mingle in bad company" once they left school.[24]

Even in cities with Black schools, securing an education remained challenging. These schools were chronically underfunded and short of books and supplies. In addition, not all Black parents could afford to send their children to school. Many Black youngsters had to work to support their families, and others stayed home because their parents had no money for school clothing or shoes.

Education was a double-edged sword even for those Black northerners lucky enough to attend school. Subject to the same racial prejudices as other African Americans, educated Blacks were shut out of most jobs, both skilled and unskilled. "What are my prospects?" the valedictorian of the New York African Free School's class of 1819 asked rhetorically when he addressed his classmates. "Shall I be a mechanic? No one will employ me; white boys won't work with me. Shall I be a merchant? No one will have me in his office; white clerks won't associate with me."[25] But education would nevertheless be crucial. During the early decades of the nineteenth century, Black schools educated important Black leaders whose speeches and publications helped sustain their community's struggle for abolition and civil rights. (See AP® Working with Sources: Free Black Activism, pp. 197–205.)

Rising White Hostility

Ironically, African Americans faced more rather than less racial hostility as they moved from slavery to freedom at the turn of the nineteenth century. Many whites continued to see Blacks as an economic threat and a social menace. Emancipated Blacks, concentrated in urban areas and often impoverished, formed a highly visible underclass in northern cities, where they performed much of the noisiest, dirtiest work. White New Yorkers complained that the "army of black sweeps" left the city filled with dust, that Black street vendors were the source of New York's most hideous and outlandish crimes, and that the Black tubmen who emptied New York's privies left the houses they passed "filled with stinking stench."[26] Even the activities of more prosperous Blacks made many northern whites nervous. Blacks' establishment of their own institutions, as well as the public events they staged to celebrate emancipation, suggested that Blacks were beginning to succeed in raising their social status. Consequently, whites regarded free Blacks with alarm and subjected them to relentless hostility, mockery, and violence.

AP® skills

Applying Disciplinary Knowledge: Describe the experiences of free Black Americans at the turn of the nineteenth century as they moved from slavery to freedom in the North. What caused the rising hostility they experienced?

Blacks met "daily insults . . . in the streets of Boston," the Revolutionary War veteran Prince Hall complained in 1797. This harassment only escalated on "public days of recreation," when drunken white ruffians celebrated special occasions such as Independence Day by beating Black men and stripping "helpless old women."[27] Such actions finally forced African Americans to move their own Independence Day celebrations from July 4 to July 5. Racial violence increased in the early nineteenth century as white troublemakers and mobs began targeting Black institutions, disrupting services at Black churches, and sometimes even attacking Black congregations. They also began to mock emancipation itself. Racist broadsides made fun of Black gatherings to commemorate the abolition of slavery by calling these events **Bobalition** (a deliberate garbling of *abolition*) celebrations.

Bobalition
A rendition of the word *abolition*, based on what whites heard as a mispronunciation by Blacks. It was used on broadsides and in newspapers to mock free Black celebrations of abolition.

Northern free Blacks and their white allies did not always agree on how best to combat growing prejudice and the persistence of slavery elsewhere in the nation. Members of early white antislavery organizations such as the PAS and NYMS, convinced that prejudice could be addressed only by reforming African Americans, sponsored schools dedicated to young Blacks' moral and religious education and urged African Americans to avoid any behavior that might offend whites. Moreover, these white reformers remained cautious about challenging other Americans' property rights and condemned slavery without calling for enslavers to free the people they enslaved. Instead, they supported the withdrawal of the United States from the international slave trade and gradual emancipation within their home states.

By contrast, as early as the 1790s, Black activists appealed to Congress to end what one petition called slavery's "unconstitutional bondage."[28] Although ignored by Congress, such petitions articulated a vision of American citizenship in which African Americans qualified for the same federal protection offered to all other Americans. African American leaders also parted company with white antislavery reformers in identifying white racism as one of the greatest obstacles facing the antislavery movement. Richard Allen and Absalom Jones addressed this issue in a 1794 protest pamphlet condemning the racist arguments that whites used to justify slavery. "Will you . . . plead our incapacity for freedom, and our contented condition under oppression, as a sufficient cause for keeping us under the grievous yoke?" they asked.[29]

Black Soldiers and Civilians in the War of 1812

As the egalitarian spirit of the Revolutionary era waned at the beginning of the nineteenth century, African American civil rights contracted, and Black leaders had reason to fear that racism would undermine Black freedom even in the North. However, Black soldiers who served in the War of 1812 hoped that their patriotism would help them win full citizenship. Celebrated by many Americans as the "second war of Independence," the War of 1812 (1812–1815) was caused by conflicts between the United States and Britain over trade rights, the U.S. expansion into British and American Indian lands in the Northwest, and Britain's practice of forcibly conscripting American sailors into the British Royal Navy. The war came at a time when the United States had all but eliminated Black soldiers from its army. Not only did Congress restrict militia service to "free, able-bodied white male citizens," but most states' militias had similar restrictions, as did the Marine Corps, which was established in 1798.[30]

But the War of 1812 was largely a naval war, and the new nation's navy was too short of personnel to turn away experienced sailors of any color. Instead, African Americans, who had long been one of the shipping industry's major sources of labor, made up 10 to 20 percent of the crews that defended America's coasts and Great Lakes and often fought with notable valor. Assigned to reclaim Lake Erie from the British, American commodore Oliver Hazard Perry initially expressed little confidence in some 150 reinforcements sent by his superior officer, Commodore Isaac Chauncey, complaining that they were "a motley set, blacks, Soldiers, and boys." He later changed his appraisal of the African American sailors, however, and reported to Chauncey that he was impressed by the "bravery and good conduct of the negroes," who formed a considerable part of his crew. Captain Isaac Hull, commander of the USS *Constitution*, expressed similar sentiments, albeit in language that underscored that Black military service did not always diminish white racial prejudices. "I never had any better fighters than those n*****s," Hull later recalled; "they stripped to the waist and fought like devils."[31]

Free Black civilians also supported the war effort. In Philadelphia, the Committee of Defense, composed of 2,500 Black volunteers, built fortifications designed to secure the city from British naval attack. Moreover, African Americans joined the war as combatants at the Battle of New Orleans, the war's final conflict. In the fall of 1814, with one of the nation's most important seaports under siege, General Andrew Jackson issued a call to arms to free Blacks, appealing for their support as fellow citizens. The more than 500 free Blacks who responded to his call fought in a segregated regiment that formed one-twelfth of the general's forces.

AP® skills

Applying Disciplinary Knowledge: How did Black Americans contribute to the U.S. victory over the British in the War of 1812?

But despite the many contributions of African Americans to the war effort, their civil rights continued to erode. New Jersey Blacks lost the right to vote in 1807, even before the war. Blacks also were disfranchised in Connecticut in 1814 and in Pennsylvania in 1838. Even in states where free Blacks retained the right to vote, they faced voter discrimination. New York, for example, imposed prohibitively high property requirements on Black voters, even after abolishing all such requirements for white voters in 1821.

The Colonization Debate

Given the abiding prejudices that African Americans faced during the post-Revolutionary era, some members of both races began to question Blacks' long-term prospects for success in the United States. Fearing they would never achieve full citizenship, Blacks occasionally contemplated abandoning the United States altogether. Some whites expressed great enthusiasm for their departure, proposing **colonization** schemes designed to send African Americans back to Africa.

colonization
The action of appropriating a place or domain for one's own use. In the context of nineteenth-century emigrationism, colonization refers to the idea that Blacks should be sent back to Africa or moved to another territory outside the United States.

During the late eighteenth century, when many Blacks were still relatively recent arrivals, some were eager to return to the land of their ancestors. In 1787, a group of Massachusetts Blacks petitioned the state legislature to help them migrate to Africa. They asked for help in raising money to "procure lands to settle upon; and to obtain a passage for us and our families."[32] Their petition was never answered, but the idea resurfaced in 1815, when a wealthy Black businessman and ship captain named

Paul Cuffe, or Cuffee, took thirty-eight Black Bostonians to the West African colony of Sierra Leone.

Sierra Leone, founded in 1787 by British reformer Granville Sharp as a refuge for some of London's Black poor, was also home to approximately twelve hundred Black loyalists from Nova Scotia, many of whom had fled slavery in the United States. Although the main intent of the colony was the repatriation of formerly enslaved people to West Africa, it was of interest to Cuffe because his father, Cuffe Slocum, had been born in West Africa. After visiting Sierra Leone in 1811, Cuffe began to consider taking "to Africa some Sober Stedy habited peopel of Colour in order to incourage Soberiety and industry and to interduce culteriantion and Commersce."[33] Cuffe knew a number of African-born people who wished to return to the continent, and in 1812, he began to make arrangements to transport a group of them to the colony.

AP® skills

Applying Disciplinary Knowledge: Why did Paul Cuffe plan to travel to Sierra Leone?

Cuffe's voyage in 1815, however, was not a success. His commercial plans were foiled by British officials who refused to allow him to unload the cargo he had hoped to sell to finance the trip, leaving him $1,700 in debt. He had never planned to lead a mass movement of Blacks back to Africa and vowed not to travel there again without assurances that British officials would be more cooperative in the future. He also cautioned other colonization supporters that Sierra Leone was unlikely to welcome large numbers of American expatriates. Cuffe himself never returned to Sierra Leone; he became sick in the summer of 1817 and died that fall.

Although Cuffe's expedition had the support of Black leaders such as Absalom Jones, it did not foster a colonization movement among American Blacks. Instead, it captured the imagination of white reformers, whose enthusiasm soon had free Black communities across the North worried about a forced migration. Reform-minded whites had long "indulge[d] a hope that . . . free people of color be removed to the coast of Africa with their own consent," the Presbyterian minister Robert Finley wrote Cuffe in 1816, appealing to the ship captain to help him plan a mass migration.[34] With Cuffe's voyage standing as testimony to the practical possibility of colonization, Finley founded a national organization to promote the colonization of free Blacks.

The American Society for Colonizing the Free People of Color of the United States, more popularly known as the American Colonization Society (ACS), first met in Washington, D.C., in 1816. Made up of prominent white clergymen, lawyers, financiers, and politicians — including Speaker of the House Henry Clay — the ACS appealed to both enslavers and those opposed to slavery. Although Finley hoped colonization would eventually bring an end to slavery, the ACS planned to colonize free Blacks only. Its members agreed to avoid the "delicate question" of emancipation, instead assuring southerners that colonization would help secure their enslaved property by ridding the region of free Blacks.[35] Meanwhile, antislavery advocates believed that colonization would facilitate manumissions, allowing planters to free the people they enslaved without enlarging the region's already unpopular free Black population or violating the states' manumission laws. By 1819, the ACS's influential white supporters included President James Monroe, who helped the organization secure a congressional appropriation of $100,000 for its cause. In 1821, the ACS used the money to establish the colony of Liberia on the west coast of Africa and to recruit potential migrants.

AP® skills

Applying Disciplinary Knowledge: Why did the American Society for Colonizing appeal to both enslavers and abolitionists?

Most of the Blacks the ACS shipped to Liberia were formerly enslaved people liberated by the organization in order to allow their emigration. Although the ACS was eager to recruit free Blacks, most were both unwilling to move and deeply suspicious. Less than a month after the first ACS meeting in 1816, three thousand free Blacks gathered in Richard Allen's Philadelphia church to adopt a set of resolutions denouncing colonization as an "unmerited stigma attempted to be cast upon the reputation of the free people of color." Many of those gathered were American-born Blacks with few ties to Africa, and many suspected that colonization was merely a plan to prop up slavery by shipping America's free Blacks out of the United States. They issued a statement saying, "We never will separate ourselves voluntarily from the slave in this country."[36] Although the Black leader James Forten, who presided over the meeting and recorded the resolutions, had previously supported Cuffe's voyage to Sierra Leone on the grounds that Black Americans would "never become a people untell they com[e] out from amongst the white people," Black Philadelphians' mass opposition to the ACS changed his mind.[37] (See AP® Working with Sources: Free Black Activism, pp. 197–205.)

Most African Americans remained suspicious of colonization throughout the antebellum era. But white enthusiasm for the idea did not depend on Black support, and the American Colonization Society continued to attract white members.

CONCLUSION

African American Freedom

Faced with the threat of forced removal, northern free Blacks saw the idea of colonization as an assault on their community. Like Benjamin Banneker several decades earlier, they were convinced that African Americans were entitled to the rights and freedoms that Americans had defended during the Revolution, and they believed that immediate emancipation was the only way to end slavery in the United States.

AP® skills

Applying Disciplinary Knowledge: What did it mean to be free and Black in the United States during the first half of the nineteenth century?

After 1817, northern free Blacks drew on the network of mutual aid societies and churches they had founded as they fought their way out of slavery. The anticolonization campaign that they mounted linked the future of all African Americans, both enslaved and free, to a freedom struggle that would not end until slavery was abolished throughout the United States. Laying new and stronger claims to the United States as "the land of our nativity," northern Blacks drew on their own recent history to insist that slavery could be defeated. "Every year, many of us have restored to us by the gradual, but certain march of the cause of abolition — Parents from whom we have long been separated — Wives and Children whom we had left in servitude — and Brothers, in blood as well as in early sufferings, from whom we had long been parted," Philadelphia's anticolonizationist Blacks maintained.[38]

The new Republic's Black southerners, by contrast, had much less cause for optimism. Although free Black communities expanded in some parts of the South during the nation's early decades, slavery experienced more spectacular gains with the growth of plantation agriculture. Slavery was protected by federal laws mandating the return of freedom seekers and sanctioned in the Constitution, which gave enslavers additional political representation under the three-fifths clause. With the acquisition of Louisiana from France, the United States further guaranteed the institutional strength of slavery by acquiring vast new territories that would soon become home to enslavers looking to settle there. As slavery's cotton frontier expanded into Louisiana, Mississippi, and Alabama during the first half of the nineteenth century, the expansion of plantation agriculture brought wealth and power to the region's enslavers and tremendous anguish to the enslaved. Once the United States ceased importing enslaved people from Africa in 1808, most of the enslaved people who cleared the land and cultivated the crops in these new states were American-born. The majority hailed from the Chesapeake or the northern states and had to leave behind families, friends, and neighbors as they embarked on the forced migration to plantations in the deep South.

CHAPTER 5 REVIEW ▸ PRACTICING AP® SKILLS

AP® ESSENTIAL VOCABULARY AND SOURCES

** Essential terms and required sources from the AP® Course are marked with an asterisk.*

Northwest Ordinance (1787) p. 166
fugitive slave clause p. 166
Three-Fifths Compromise p. 167
Haitian Revolution (1791–1804) p. 173
Louisiana Purchase (1803) p. 174
hiring out p. 177
living out p. 177
Gabriel's rebellion p. 177
black laws p. 181
Naturalization Act of 1790 p. 181
mutual aid society p. 184
Bobalition p. 191
colonization p. 192

APPLYING DISCIPLINARY KNOWLEDGE: ESSENTIAL QUESTIONS

1. Describe the fate of slavery in the post-Revolutionary years and the various factors — political, social, and economic — that contributed to this state of affairs. Would it have been possible to predict in 1783 that things would turn out this way? Why or why not? How might things have been different if political, social, or economic circumstances had been different?
2. Describe the various freedoms allowed, and the restrictions placed on, urban enslaved people, southern free Blacks, northern enslaved people, and newly emancipated northern free Blacks. What limits to their freedom and mobility did each group experience? Which groups were the most and the least restricted, and why?
3. Why did whites grow increasingly hostile toward African Americans as they moved from slavery to freedom? How did the proliferation of free Black organizations help African Americans combat this hostility?
4. How did the colonization effort change from a small, Black-led initiative to a large, white-led movement? What initial appeal did colonization have for its Black supporters? How was this different from the appeal it held for whites, both enslavers and abolitionists?

SUGGESTED REFERENCES

The Limits of Democracy

Adams, Catherine, and Elizabeth H. Pleck. *Love of Freedom: Black Women in Colonial and Revolutionary New England*. New York: Oxford University Press, 2010.

Berlin, Ira. *Generations of Captivity: A History of African-American Slaves*. Cambridge: Belknap Press of Harvard University Press, 2003.

Dain, Bruce. *A Hideous Monster of the Mind: American Race Theory in the Early Republic*. Cambridge: Harvard University Press, 2003.

Fischer, Sibylle. *Modernity Disavowed: Haiti and the Cultures of Slavery in the Age of Revolution*. Durham: Duke University Press, 2004.

Kornblith, Gary J. *Slavery and Sectional Strife in the Early American Republic, 1776–1821*. Lanham, MD: Rowman & Littlefield, 2009.

Mason, Matthew. *Slavery and Politics in the Early American Republic*. Chapel Hill: University of North Carolina Press, 2008.

Morrison, Michael A., and James Brewer Stewart, eds. *Race and the Early Republic: Racial Consciousness and Nation-Building in the Early Republic*. Lanham, MD: Rowman & Littlefield, 2002.

Van Cleve, George William. *A Slaveholders' Union: Slavery, Politics, and the Constitution in the Early American Republic*. Chicago: University of Chicago Press, 2010.

Waldstreicher, David. *Slavery's Constitution: From Revolution to Ratification*. New York: Hill and Wang, 2009.

Slavery and Freedom outside the Plantation South

Berlin, Ira. *Slaves without Masters: The Free Negro in the Antebellum South*. New York: New Press, 2007.

Curry, Leonard P. *The Free Black in Urban America, 1800–1850: The Shadow of the Dream*. Chicago: University of Chicago Press, 1986.

Egerton, Douglas R. *Gabriel's Rebellion: The Virginia Slave Conspiracies of 1800 and 1802*. Chapel Hill: University of North Carolina Press, 1993.

Horton, James Oliver, and Lois E. Horton. *Black Bostonians: Family Life and Community Struggle in the Antebellum North*, rev. ed. New York: Holmes & Meier, 2000.

King, Wilma. *The Essence of Liberty: Free Black Women during the Slave Era*. Columbia: University of Missouri Press, 2006.

Litwack, Leon F. *North of Slavery: The Negro in the Free States, 1790–1860*. Chicago: University of Chicago Press, 1961.

Melish, Joanne Pope. *Disowning Slavery: Gradual Emancipation and "Race" in New England, 1780–1860*. Ithaca: Cornell University Press, 2000.

Painter, Nell Irvin. *Sojourner Truth: A Life, a Symbol*. New York: Norton, 1996.

Rockman, Seth. *Scraping By: Wage Labor, Slavery, and Survival in Early Baltimore*. Baltimore: Johns Hopkins University Press, 2008.

Wade, Richard C. *Slavery in the Cities: The South, 1820–1860*. New York: Oxford University Press, 1967.

Zilversmit, Arthur. *The First Emancipation: The Abolition of Slavery in the North*, 3rd ed. Chicago: University of Chicago Press, 1969.

Free Black Life in the New Republic

Alexander, Leslie M. *African or American? Black Identity and Political Activism in New York City, 1784–1861*. Urbana: University of Illinois Press, 2008.

Collier-Thomas, Bettye. *Jesus, Jobs, and Justice; African American Women and Religion*. New York: Alfred A. Knopf, 2010.

Dunbar, Erica Armstrong. *A Fragile Freedom: African American Women and Emancipation in the Antebellum City*. New Haven: Yale University Press, 2008.

Horton, James Oliver, and Lois E. Horton. *In Hope of Liberty: Culture, Community, and Protest among Northern Free Blacks, 1700–1860*. New York: Oxford University Press, 1997.

Nash, Gary B. *Forging Freedom: The Formation of Philadelphia's Black Community, 1720–1840*. Cambridge: Harvard University Press, 1991.

Newman, Richard S. *Freedom's Prophet: Bishop Richard Allen, the AME Church, and the Black Founding Fathers*. New York: New York University Press, 2008.

______. *The Transformation of American Abolitionism: Fighting Slavery in the Early Republic*. Chapel Hill: University of North Carolina Press, 2002.

Sweet, John Wood. *Bodies Politic: Negotiating Race in the American North, 1730–1830*. Philadelphia: University of Pennsylvania Press, 2006.

White, Shane. *Stories of Freedom in Black New York*. Cambridge: Harvard University Press, 2007.

Winch, Julie. *A Gentleman of Color: The Life of James Forten*. New York: Oxford University Press, 2002.

Free Black Activism

While the American Revolution greatly enlarged the size of the free Black population, the rights that free Blacks obtained were never secure. Free Blacks could not testify on their own behalf in southern courts, which meant that they had no legal means to free themselves if they were abducted by slave traders, and even in northern states such as Pennsylvania, they were required to document their freedom. By the early nineteenth century, many whites had begun to embrace colonization rather than civil rights as a remedy for the discrimination that free Blacks faced, forcing free Blacks to fight for a place in the United States.

The following documents include a 1799 petition to Congress composed by the Philadelphia clergyman Absalom Jones, which protested the fact that the federal government's fugitive slave law made free Blacks vulnerable to illegal enslavement; a selection from an 1813 pamphlet condemning a discriminatory bill under consideration in Pennsylvania; and a list of resolutions opposing colonization from a meeting of free Blacks in 1817. They also include two accounts of individuals acting to secure their freedom in the face of threats of reenslavement, one by a woman who abandoned her enslaver during the Revolutionary War, and another by a woman who had escaped from George Washington's household. They are supplemented by a racist cartoon mocking African American celebrations of the "Bobalition" of slavery. Taken together, these documents show free Blacks' efforts to secure their status by expressing their views on slavery, racial discrimination, and African American civil rights, as well as portraying some of the physical and psychological dangers they faced.

key point

In the years following the American Revolution, free Blacks made strides to obtain equal rights, but these were not secure. These documents show free Blacks' efforts to fortify their status by sharing their views on slavery, racism, and civil rights, as well as the dangers they faced in so doing.

AP® argumentation

DBQ Practice: Explain how Black Americans advocated for equal rights in the years following the American Revolution. Use at least two of the documents to support your response.

DOCUMENT 1 Jane Coggeshall | *Petition for Freedom, 1785*

The following record from the State of Rhode Island describes the petition of JANE COGGESHALL to have her status as a free person affirmed in order to avoid being reenslaved by the heirs of her former enslaver.

Breaking it Down What arguments and appeals did Coggeshall make to secure her freedom? Consider that at the time of the petition, the new republic had emerged as a unique champion of liberty and freedom from tyranny.

Whereas, Jane Coggeshall, of Providence, a negro woman preferred a petition and represented unto this Assembly, that she was a slave to Captain Daniel Coggeshall, of Newport; that in March, A. D. 1777, the enemy being then in possession of Rhode Island, she, together with others, at every risk, effected their escape to Point Judith; that they were carried before the General Assembly, then sitting in South Kingstown, who did thereupon give them their liberty, together with a pass to go to any part of the country to procure a livelihood; that she hath lived at Woodstock and at Providence ever since; that during the whole time she hath maintained herself decently and with reputation, and can appeal to the families wherein she hath lived with respect to her industry, sobriety of manners, and fidelity; that of late she hath been greatly alarmed with a claim of some of the heirs of the said Daniel Coggeshall upon her still as a slave; that as she has enjoyed the inestimable blessing of liberty for near eight years, she feels the most dreadful apprehensions at the idea of again falling into a state of slavery; and thereupon she prayed this Assembly to take her case into consideration, and pass such an act, declaring her free, as was passed for a negro man named Quaco Honeyman, who in like manner made his escape. And the premises being duly considered, —

It is voted and resolved, that the said Jane Coggeshall be, and she is, hereby entirely emancipated and made free.

SOURCE: *Jane Coggeshall's Petition.* Records of the colony of Rhode Island and Providence Plantations, in New England: Printed by order of the General Assembly/Ed. by John Russell Bartlett, Secretary of State of Rhode Island. 1856.

DOCUMENT 2 Absalom Jones and Others | *Petition to Congress on the Fugitive Slave Act, 1799*

The following petition is one of the earliest surviving free Black petitions to the U.S. Congress. Written by ABSALOM JONES (1746–1818) and signed by more than seventy others, it was submitted on December 30, 1799. Its authors contend that the Fugitive Slave Act of 1793, which was passed to enforce the Constitution's fugitive slave clause and allowed slave catchers to detain enslaved and free Blacks, threatened the lives and welfare of African Americans. The petitioners sought protection for free Blacks abducted by slave catchers and challenged the constitutional basis of slavery. Congress ignored their appeal.

Breaking it Down The Constitution upheld the institution of slavery for many reasons, including the desire to appease those who benefited from the inhumane labor system. Yet, many free and enslaved Black Americans used the legal system to seek liberation. How do the petitioners use the Constitution to make their argument?

To the President, Senate, and House of Representatives.

The Petition of the People of Colour, free men, within the City and Suburbs of Philadelphia, humbly sheweth,

That, thankful to God, our Creator, and to the Government under which we live, for the blessings and benefits granted to us in the enjoyment of our natural right to liberty, and the protection of our persons and property, from the oppression and violence which so great a number of like colour and national descent are subject to, we feel ourselves bound, from a sense of these blessings, to continue in our respective allotments, and to lead honest and peaceable lives, rendering due submission unto the laws, and exciting and encouraging each other thereto, agreeable to the uniform advice of our friends, of every denomination; yet while we feel impressed with grateful sensations for the Providential favour we ourselves enjoy, we cannot be insensible of the condition of our afflicted brethren, suffering under various circumstances, in different parts of these states; but deeply sympathizing with them, are incited by a sense of social duty, and humbly conceive ourselves authorized to address and petition you on their behalf, believing them to be objects of your representation in your public councils, in common with ourselves and every other class of citizens within the jurisdiction of the United States, according to the design of the present Constitution, formed by the General Convention, and ratified in the different states, as set forth in the preamble thereto in the following words, viz. "We, the people of the United States, in order to form a more perfect union, establish justice, insure domestic tranquillity, provide for the common defence, and to secure the blessings of liberty to ourselves and posterity, do ordain, &c." We apprehend this solemn compact is violated, by a trade carried on in a clandestine manner, to the coast of Guinea, and another equally wicked, practised openly by citizens of some of the southern states, upon the waters of Maryland and Delaware; men sufficiently callous to qualify them for the brutal purpose, are employed in kidnapping those of our brethren that are free, and purchasing others of such as claim a property in them: thus, those poor helpless victims, like droves of cattle, are seized, fettered, and hurried into places provided for this most horrid traffic, such as dark cellars and garrets, as is notorious at Northwest-fork, Chestertown, Eastown, and divers other places. After a sufficient number is obtained, they are forced on board vessels, crouded under hatches, without the least commiseration, left to deplore the sad separation of the dearest ties in nature, husband from wife, and parents from children; thus packed together, they are transported to Georgia and other places, and there inhumanly exposed to sale. Can any commerce, trade, or transaction, so detestably shock the feeling of man, or degrade the dignity of his nature equal to this? And how increasingly is the evil aggravated, when practised in a land high in profession of the benign doctrines of our Blessed Lord, who taught his followers to do unto others as they would they should do unto them. Your petitioners desire not to enlarge, though volumes might be filled with the sufferings of this grossly abused part of the human species, seven hundred thousand of whom, it is said, are now in unconditional bondage in these states: but conscious of the rectitude of our motives in a concern so nearly affecting us, and so effectually interesting to the welfare of this country, we cannot but address you as guardians of our rights, and patrons of equal and national liberties, hoping you will view the subject in an impartial, unprejudiced light. We do not ask for an immediate emancipation of all, knowing that the degraded state of many, and their want of education, would greatly disqualify for such a change; yet, humbly desire you may exert every means in your power to undo the heavy burdens, and prepare the way for the oppressed to go free, that every yoke may be broken. The law not long since enacted by Congress, called the Fugitive Bill, is in its execution found to be attended with circumstances peculiarly hard and distressing; for many of our afflicted brethren, in order to avoid the barbarities wantonly exercised upon them, or through fear of being carried off by those men-stealers, being forced to seek refuge by flight, they are then, by armed men, under colour of this law, cruelly treated, or brought back in chains to those that have no claim upon them. In the Constitution and the Fugitive Bill, no mention is made of black people, or slaves; therefore, if the Bill of Rights, or the Declaration of Congress are of any validity, we beseech, that as we are men, we may be admitted to partake of the liberties and unalienable rights therein held forth; firmly believing that the extending of justice and equity to all classes, would be a means of drawing down the blessing of Heaven upon this land, for the peace and prosperity of which, and the real happiness of every member of the community, we fervently pray.

Source: Petition of Absalom Jones and others, December 30, 1799, *Records of the U.S. House of Representatives*, Record Group 233 (4~HR6A-F4.2. Jan. 2, 1800), National Archives, Washington, DC.

DOCUMENT 3 James Forten | *Letters from a Man of Colour*, 1813

Published anonymously in 1813, the pamphlet *Letters from a Man of Colour* was written by JAMES FORTEN (1766–1842), a prosperous Black businessman. It contained a series of letters condemning a bill then under consideration before the Pennsylvania Senate that would have required all Blacks who entered Pennsylvania to register with the state. Proposed at a time when anti-Black hostility was on the rise throughout the North, the bill, which did not pass, aimed to make it more difficult for both freedom seekers and free Blacks to settle in Pennsylvania.

> **Breaking it Down** How does Forten use the history of the state as well as the Constitution to create an argument to challenge the bill that would have made it difficult for Blacks to live without the fear of being enslaved? As the following letter makes clear, Forten was outraged by the bill. What was the source of his outrage?

We hold this truth to be self-evident, that GOD created all men equal, and is one of the most prominent features in the Declaration of Independence, and in that glorious fabrick of collected wisdom, our noble Constitution. This idea embraces the Indian and the European, the Savage and the Saint, the Peruvian and the Laplander, the white Man and the African, and whatever measures are adopted subversive of this inestimable privilege, are in direct violation of the letter and the spirit of our Constitution, and become subject to the animadversion of all, particularly those who are deeply interested in the measure.

These thoughts were suggested by the promulgation of a late bill, before the Senate of Pennsylvania, to prevent the emigration of people of colour into this state. It was not passed into a law at this session and must in consequence lay over until the next, before when we sincerely hope, the white men, whom we should look upon as our protectors, will have become convinced of the inhumanity and impolicy of such a measure, and forbear to deprive us of those inestimable treasures, Liberty and Independence. This is almost the only state in the Union wherein the African race have justly boasted of rational liberty and the protection of the laws, and shall it now be said they have been deprived of that liberty, and publickly exposed for sale to the highest bidder? Shall colonial inhumanity that has marked many of us with shameful stripes, become the practice of the people of Pennsylvania, while Mercy stands weeping at the miserable spectacle? People of Pennsylvania, descendants of the immortal Penn, doom us not to the unhappy fate of thousands of our countrymen in the Southern States and the West Indies; despise the traffick in blood, and the blessing of the African will for ever be around you. Many of us are men of property, for the security of which, we have hitherto looked to the laws of our blessed state, but should this become a law, our property is jeopardized, since the same power which can expose to sale an unfortunate fellow creature, can wrest from him those estates, which years of honest industry have accumulated. Where shall the poor African look for protection, should the people of Pennsylvania consent to oppress him? We grant there are a number of worthless men belonging to our colour, but there are laws of sufficient rigour for their punishment, if properly and duly enforced. We wish not to screen the guilty from punishment, but with the guilty do not permit the innocent to suffer. If there are worthless men, there are also men of merit among the African race, who are useful members of Society. The truth of this let their benevolent institutions and the numbers clothed and fed by them witness. Punish the guilty man of colour to the utmost limit of the laws, but sell him not slavery! If he is in danger of becoming a publick charge prevent him! If he is too indolent to labour for his own subsistence, compel him to do so; but sell him not to slavery. By selling him you do not make him better, but commit a wrong, without benefitting the object of it or society at large. Many of our ancestors were brought here more than one hundred years ago; many of our fathers, many of ourselves, have fought and bled for the Independence of our country. Do not then expose us to sale. Let not the spirit of the father behold the son robbed of that Liberty which he died to establish, but let the motto of our legislators, be: "The Law knows no distinction."

SOURCE: [James Forten], *Letters from a Man of Colour, on a Late Bill before the Senate of Pennsylvania* (Pennsylvania: n.p., 1813), 1–3.

DOCUMENT 4 *Sentiments of the People of Color, 1817*

In January 1817, free Blacks gathered at Richard Allen's Bethel AME Church in Philadelphia to voice their opposition to colonization and to articulate their claims to a permanent place in the United States. The meeting adopted the following resolutions.

Breaking it Down Given that most people of African descent were born in the United States and had little to no direct ties to their ancestral African roots due to the transatlantic slave trade, why would the authors of this document oppose colonization?

Whereas our ancestors (not of choice) were the first successful cultivators of the wilds of America, we their descendants feel ourselves entitled to participate in the blessings of her luxuriant soil, which their blood and sweat manured; and that any measure or system of measures, having a tendency to banish us from her bosom, would not only be cruel, but in direct violation of those principles, which have been the boast of this republic.

Resolved, That we view with deep abhorrence the unmerited stigma attempted to be cast upon the reputation of the free people of color, by the promoters of this measure, "that they are a dangerous and useless part of the community," when in the state of disfranchisement in which they live, in the hour of danger they ceased to remember their wrongs, and rallied around the standard of their country.

Resolved, That we never will separate ourselves voluntarily from the slave population in this country; they are our brethren by the ties of consanguinity, of suffering, and of wrong; and we feel that there is more virtue in suffering privations with them, than fancied advantages for a season.

Resolved, That without arts, without science, without a proper knowledge of government, to cast into the savage wilds of Africa the free people of color, seems to us the circuitous route through which they must return to perpetual bondage.

Resolved, That having the strongest confidence in the justice of God, and philanthropy of the free states, we cheerfully submit our destinies to the guidance of Him who suffers not a sparrow to fall, without his special providence.

Resolved, That a committee of eleven persons be appointed to open a correspondence with the honorable Joseph Hopkinson, member of Congress from this city, and likewise to inform him of the sentiments of this meeting, and that the following named persons constitute the committee, and that they have power to call a general meeting, when they in their judgment may deem it proper.

Rev. Absalom Jones, Rev. Richard Allen, James Forten, Robert Douglass, Francis Perkins, Rev. John Gloucester, Robert Gorden, James Johnson, Quamoney Clarkson, John Summersett, Randall Shepherd.

JAMES FORTEN, Chairman.

Russell Parrott, Secretary.

SOURCE: "Sentiments of the People of Color" (1817), reprinted in William Lloyd Garrison, *Thoughts on African Colonization*, Part II (Boston: Garrison and Knapp, 1832), 9–10.

DOCUMENT 5 Ona Judge | *Washington's Runaway Slave*, 1845

In May 1845, the abolitionist newspaper *The Granite Freeman* published a sensational interview with ONA JUDGE (1773–1848), who had been enslaved by George Washington and who had escaped from his household several decades earlier. The interview was reprinted in other abolitionist newspapers, including *The Liberator*. Judge (whose married name was Staines) tells the story of her escape and Washington's efforts to capture her. How does Judge stand firm against such a powerful figure, both in her escape and in her description of Washington's piety?

> **Breaking it Down** The narrative outlines the reasons why Ona Judge self-liberated and refused to allow George Washington to re-enslave her. Before you read this document, review the headnote carefully. How and why was Ona Judge's story recorded? Who is the audience for this document, and what purpose does her story serve for that audience?

There is now living, in the borders of the town of Greenland, N.H., a runaway slave of Gen. Washington, at present supported by the County of Rockingham. Her name at the time of her elopement was ONA MARIA JUDGE. She is not able to give the year of her escape, but says that she came from Philadelphia just after the close of Washington's second term of the Presidency, which must fix it somewhere in the first part of the year 1797.

Being a waiting maid of Mrs. Washington, she was not exposed to any peculiar hardships. If asked why she did not remain in his service, she gives two reasons, first, that she wanted to be free; secondly that she understood that after the decease of her master and mistress, she was to become the property of a grand-daughter of theirs, by name of Custis, and that she was determined never to be her slave.

Being asked how she escaped, she replied substantially as follows, "Whilst they were packing up to go to Virginia, I was packing to go, I didn't know where; for I knew that if I went back to Virginia, I should never get my liberty. I had friends among the colored people of Philadelphia, had my things carried there beforehand, and left Washington's house while they were eating dinner." . . .

She came on board a ship commanded by CAPT. JOHN BOLLES, and bound to Portsmouth, N.H. In relating it, she added, "I never told his name till after he died, a few years since, lest they should punish him for bringing me away." Had she disclosed it, he might have shared the fate of Jonathan Walker in our own day. . . .

Washington made two attempts to recover her. First, he sent a man by the name of Bassett to persuade her to return; but she resisted all the argument he employed for this end. He told her they would set her free when she arrived at Mount Vernon, to which she replied, "I am free now and choose to remain so."

Finding all attempts to seduce her to slavery again in this manner useless, Bassett was sent once more by Washington, with orders to bring her and her infant child by force. The messenger, being acquainted with Gov. Langdon, then of Portsmouth, took up lodgings with him, and disclosed to him the object of his mission. The good old Governor (to his honor be it spoken), must have possessed something of the spirit of modern anti-slavery. He entertained Bassett very handsomely, and in the meantime sent word to Mrs. Staines [Ona Judge], to leave town before twelve o'clock at night, which she did, retired to a place of concealment, and escaped the clutches of the oppressor. Shortly after this, Washington died, and, said she, "they never troubled me any more after he was gone."

The facts here related are known through this region, and may be relied on as substantially correct. Probably they were not for years given to the public, through fear of her recapture; but this reason no longer exists, since she is too old and infirm to be of sufficient value to repay the expense of search.

Though a house servant, she had no education, nor any valuable religious instruction; says she never heard Washington pray, and does not believe that he was accustomed to. "Mrs. Washington used to read prayers, but I don't call that praying." Since her escape she has learned to read, trusts she has been made "wise unto salvation," and is, I think, connected with a church in Portsmouth.

When asked if she is not sorry she left Washington, as she has labored so much harder since, than before, her reply is, "No, I am free, and have, I trust been made a child of God by the means."

SOURCE: "Washington's Runaway Slave." Reported by T.H. Adams. *The Granite Freeman*. May 22, 1845. Reprinted in the *Liberator*, August 22, 1845.

DOCUMENT 6 Edward Williams Clay | *Bobalition*, 1833

In the 1820s, Philadelphia-born artist EDWARD WILLIAMS CLAY (1799–1857) produced a series of cartoons under the title *Life in Philadelphia*, in which he made fun of the city's African American population. The cartoon reproduced here, titled "Grand Celebration ob de Bobalition ob African Slabery," satirizes Black celebrations of the prohibition of the international slave trade. Bobalition cartoons and other documents that were also common in Massachusetts lampooned the manners, speech, and political aspirations of northern free Blacks. In "Grand Celebration," a group of drunken Black men make absurd toasts.

Note: This cartoon includes the N-word, which we have chosen not to reprint in full in the following description of the cartoon's text. We wish to accurately reflect both Clay's original intent as well as the racism of the time period, but we also recognize that this word has a long history as a derogatory and deeply hurtful expression when used by white people toward Black people, as it is in the context of this cartoon. We have replaced the term without hindering understanding of the work as a whole. Be mindful of context, both Clay's and yours, as you read and discuss this cartoon. The text of the cartoon is:

"De day we Celumbrate! Who he no come sooner? Guess de hard fros & de backward Spring put um back. 29 pop gun & 2 grin."

"De Orator ob de day — When I jus hear him begin he discourse, tink he no great ting, but when he come to de end ob um, I tink he like de scorch cat more better dan he look — Moosick — Possum up de Gum tree"

"White man — mighty anxuius to send n***, to de place dey stole him from, now he got no furder use for him."**

"Gubner Eustas — Cleber old sole as eber wore nee buckle in de shoe — 99 cheer an tree quarter."

"De Genuis de Merica — He invent great many curious ting: wonder who fus invent eating & drinking. 30 cheer & ober."

"De Sun — Wonder why he no shine in de night putting n*** to dispense ob de candle."**

"Joe Gales — He ax massa Adams 'if he be in health my brudder' and den he cut he guts out."

"King Edwards — Guess he no great tings no more nor udder people all he cut such a swell."

Breaking it Down Various forms of propaganda were created to humiliate and dehumanize free Black Americans. This source uses exaggerated text and distorted facial characteristics to demonstrate the creator's perspective on Black Americans. As you analyze the source, consider why free Black Americans were considered a threat to the political and social structures in society at this time.

© Hulton Deutsch Collection/Corbis via Getty Images.

PRACTICING AP® SKILLS

1. **AP® Contextualization.** How do these documents reveal the ways that Black Americans sought freedom and fought for civil rights in the early years of the American Republic?
2. **AP® Causation.** How did events such as the American Revolution and the War of 1812 impact the experiences of Black people in North America? Where are those effects evident in these documents?
3. **AP® Continuity and Change.** How did the Fugitive Slave Act of 1793 reflect continued resistance to abolishing chattel slavery in the United States?
4. **Connecting to AP® Themes.** Select three or more documents and explain how they are examples of resistance to chattel slavery and resilience in abolitionist activism.
5. **Class Discussion.** How similar are the injustices discussed in these sources to the experiences of Black Americans today? What points of continuity do you see? What has changed, and how?

Document-Based Questions:
Prompts

In addition to multiple-choice and short-answer questions, the AP® African American Studies Exam will also include a document-based question (DBQ). Document-based questions can seem intimidating, but actually, you've already learned many of the skills you'll need to successfully respond to any DBQ.

For instance, through practice with stimulus-based multiple-choice questions, you've already become familiar with analyzing visual and written texts and determining their connections to relevant course **concepts**, **developments**, and **processes**. You've also learned to articulate your reasoning in your own words through short-answer responses that make clear claims backed up by **evidence** and analysis. The transition from short-answer questions to document-based questions is really just about scale; you'll be working with more sources, so you'll be able to construct a more complex **claim** and incorporate more thorough evidence and analysis.

On the AP® Exam, you'll have roughly 45 minutes to answer the document-based question. Given this time frame, it can be tempting to skip right to the set of sources to begin reading them over. Try to resist this temptation! In actuality, taking a few minutes upfront to break down the prompt will help you use your time much more efficiently, rather than pursuing dead ends. That's why this AP® Skills Workshop will focus on how to strategically approach any DBQ prompt.

Approaching a DBQ Prompt

Most document-based questions will look something like this:

Explain how the reality of enslavement complicated the ideals of the New Republic.

In your response you should do the following:

- **Respond to the prompt with a defensible thesis or claim that establishes a line of reasoning.**
- **Describe a broader historical or disciplinary context relevant to the topic of the prompt.**
- **Support an argument in response to the prompt using at least three of the sources.**
- **Use at least one additional piece of specific evidence (beyond the evidence found in the sources) relevant to your argument.**
- **For at least two sources, explain how or why the perspective, purpose, context, and/or audience for each source is relevant to your argument.**
- **Reference or cite the sources you use in your argument. You can reference or cite the source letter, title, or author.**

Don't worry about the bulleted list of subtasks for now — that language will remain stable regardless of the prompt. Let's focus solely on the text unique to this prompt. We can break it down based on the following components, using a similar process to the one modeled in the AP® Skills Workshop for Chapter 4 (p. SW4-A):

Time Period. Do you see hints indicating a specific time period to focus on? Keep in mind that the prompt may span multiple time periods.

Topic. How would you sum up what the prompt is about in just a few words?

Task. What is the question really asking you to do?

Relevant Course Knowledge. What are the course concepts, developments, and processes that immediately come to mind?

We can structure our brainstorming using a graphic organizer:

Time Period	Topic	Task
Decades immediately following the Revolutionary War (1783–1820)	Revolutionary ideals and slavery	Provide specific details about the contrast between revolutionary ideals (like liberty) and the injustices of slavery.

Relevant Course Concepts, Developments, Processes
• The Northwest Ordinance of 1787 prohibited slavery in some new territories but facilitated the expansion of slavery south of the Ohio River. • The Constitution (Article I, section 9) barred Congress from prohibiting the migration or importation of Africans before 1808. • The Constitution (Article IV, section 2) required that all self-liberated enslaved people be returned to their enslaver. • The Fugitive Slave Act of 1793 established who can seize and return self-liberated enslaved people. • To account for enslaved people when determining each state's proportional representation in the House of Representatives and number of electoral votes, members of the Constitutional Convention proposed and later ratified the Three-Fifths Compromise.

As with short-answer questions, your response to a document-based question doesn't just need to be *correct* in order to earn full points; it also needs to *directly* address the requested task and center on the correct time period and topic. If your response addresses an irrelevant time period or topic, or if you don't fully complete the task, you will not earn full points. Getting a firm grasp on the prompt and collecting relevant course knowledge will help you stay focused and efficient once you begin analyzing the provided sources.

recap

Approaching a DBQ Prompt

To break down a DBQ prompt, you'll want to pull out the following:

Time Period. Do you see hints indicating a specific time period to focus on? Keep in mind that the prompt may span multiple time periods.

Topic. How would you sum up what the prompt is about in just a few words?

Task. What is the question really asking you to do?

Relevant Course Knowledge. What are the course concepts, developments, and processes that immediately come to mind?

Activity ▸ Approaching a DBQ Prompt

Use a graphic organizer like the one shown below to break down the following prompt:

Explain how the principles presented in the Declaration of Independence fueled resistance to enslavement.

Time Period	Topic	Task
Relevant Course Concepts, Developments, Processes		

NOTES

Multiple-Choice Questions

Questions 1–2 refer to the following.

The Northwest Ordinance

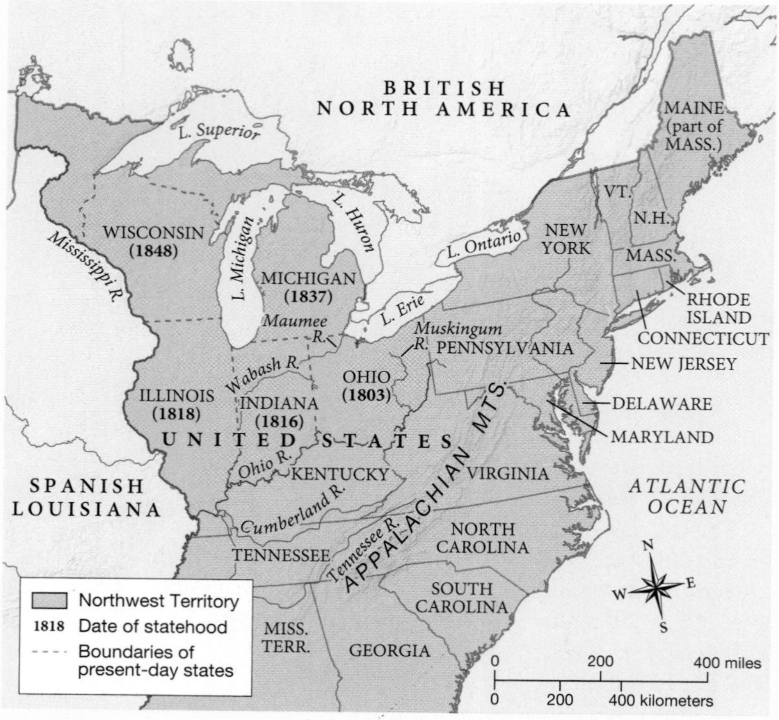

1. Which of the following best describes the purpose of the Northwest Ordinance of 1787?

(A) To organize the U.S. territories northwest of the Ohio River into prospective states while also limiting the expansion of slavery into the Northwest region.

(B) To reallocate land that was occupied by the British and Spanish during the American Revolution.

(C) To determine which land near the Ohio River would be returned to the Spanish monarchy in order to pay off debt from the American Revolution.

(D) To meet the expectations of the fugitive slave clause and thereby increase revenue after the American Revolution.

2. Which of the following statements about the Northwest Ordinance of 1787 does the map best support?

(A) Territories located south of the Ohio River allowed for the gradual emancipation of enslaved people in the United States.

(B) Since the ordinance was intended to address the issue of expansion of slavery, the map identifies only which territories would gain statehood.

(C) The United States gave up the area known as the Northwest Territory to the British in order to appease Americans who had sided with the British.

(D) The adoption of the ordinance would contribute to the Second Middle Passage.

Short-Answer Question

THE 1805 CONSTITUTION OF HAITI
SECOND CONSTITUTION OF HAITI (HAYTI) MAY 20, 1805.
PROMULGATED BY EMPEROR JACQUES I (DESSALINES)

Art. 1. The people inhabiting the island formerly called St. Domingo, hereby agree to form themselves into a free state sovereign and independent of any other power in the universe, under the name of empire of Hayti.

2. Slavery is forever abolished.

3. The Citizens of Hayti are brothers at home; equality in the eyes of the law is incontestably acknowledged, and there cannot exist any titles, advantages, or privileges, other than those necessarily resulting from the consideration and reward of services rendered to liberty and independence.

23. The crown is elective not hereditary.

50. The law admits of no predominant religion.

51. The freedom of worship is tolerated.

5. No person shall be judged without having been legally heard in his defense.

AP® source *The 1805 Constitution of Haiti, printed in the* New York Evening Post, *July 15, 1805*

1. Using the excerpt, answer A, B, C, and D.

(A) Describe the purpose of the 1805 Constitution of Haiti.

(B) Describe one development that influenced the Constitution of Haiti.

(C) Explain the perspective of the founders of Haiti on the role and purpose of its government.

(D) Explain why the 1805 Constitution of Haiti is historically significant.

CHAPTER 6

Black Life in the Slave South

1820–1860

CHAPTER TIMELINE

Events specific to African American history are in purple. General U.S. history events are in black. Events from the AP® Course Framework are marked with an asterisk.

1790–1840s	Second Great Awakening prompts wave of religious revivals
1812	Louisiana admitted as slave state
1814–1858	Seminole wars*
1815–1860	More than five million Europeans immigrate to U.S.
1819	Alabama admitted as slave state
	U.S. and Spain sign Adams–Onís Treaty
1820	Missouri Compromise: Maine admitted as free state (1820), Missouri to be admitted as slave state (1821)
1820–1860	Migration of 1.2 million African Americans from Upper South to Lower South*
1821	Adams–Onís Treaty takes effect; Spain formally cedes Florida to U.S.
1822	Denmark Vesey's planned rebellion discovered; Vesey hanged*
1827	*Freedom's Journal*, nation's first Black newspaper, founded*
1828	Andrew Jackson elected president
1829	*State v. Mann* gives whites who employ or supervise (but do not own) enslaved people authority over those enslaved people's bodies
	David Walker publishes *Walker's Appeal . . . to the Coloured Citizens of the World**
1830	Indian Removal Act
1831	William Lloyd Garrison founds abolitionist newspaper the *Liberator**
	Nat Turner's rebellion*
1835	Eight hundred Black Seminoles help Seminole tribe repel U.S. troops*
	Gag rule prohibits reading of antislavery petitions in Congress
1836	Texas settlers clash with Mexican troops at Alamo and San Jacinto
	Arkansas admitted as slave state
1837	Panic of 1837
1838	Trail of Tears
1841	U.S. Supreme Court frees *Amistad* rebels*
	Solomon Northup kidnapped and sold into slavery*
	Creole insurrection*
1845	Texas annexed, admitted as slave state
	Florida admitted as slave state
1848	Ellen and William Craft escape from slavery
1849	Harriet Tubman and Henry "Box" Brown escape from slavery*
1854	*John v. State* rules that any killing of a white person by an enslaved person is murder

Please note that this chapter includes primary sources by Black writers and speakers that use the N-word, which we have chosen to reprint in this textbook to accurately reflect these speakers' original intent as well as the time period, culture, and racism discussed in each source. We recognize that this word has a long history as a derogatory and deeply hurtful expression when used by white people toward Black people. Black speakers' and writers' choice to use this word relates not only to that history but to a larger cultural tradition in which the N-word can take on different meanings, emphasize shared experience, and be repurposed as a term of endearment within Black communities. This chapter also includes primary sources by white writers and speakers that use the N-word, which we have chosen not to reprint in full here. We have replaced the term without hindering understanding of these sources. Be mindful of context, both historical and contemporary, as you read and discuss this chapter.

William Wells Brown and Growing Up in the Slave South

William Wells Brown was born into slavery on a Kentucky plantation in 1814. His early experiences in bondage were varied and painful. Until he was twelve, he lived in rural Missouri, where his enslaver, Dr. Young, moved his household of forty enslaved people shortly after Brown was born. Young employed Brown's mother and four older siblings on a tobacco and hemp plantation outside St. Louis, where Brown observed the brutal discipline imposed on plantation field hands. As an infant, he often rode on his mother's back while she worked in the fields because she was not allowed to leave the fields to nurse. As a young boy, he was routinely awakened by the sounds of the whippings that Young's overseer gave field hands — including Brown's mother and siblings — who were not at work by 4:30 a.m. He was close enough to the fields to "hear every crack of the whip, and every groan and cry," and he wept at the sounds.[1] More sorrow lay ahead after Young sold Brown's mother and siblings but kept Brown himself because he was the son of Young's cousin and fellow planter George Higgins.

Young hired the boy out to a variety of enslavers, leaving him with a broad understanding of enslaved life and labor in the antebellum South. His first employer, a tavern owner named Major Freeland, was short-tempered, unstable, and prone to lashing out at people he enslaved without warning. To punish those he deemed disobedient, Freeland employed a technique he had learned in his home state of Virginia. Brown recalled that "he would tie them up in the smokehouse, and whip them; after which, he would cause a fire to be made of tobacco stems, and smoke them. This he called '*Virginia play*.'"[2] Brown was so terrified of Freeland that he ran away and hid in the woods, where another local enslaver who kept a pack of bloodhounds for this purpose recaptured him. On his return to Freeland's tavern, Brown, too, was whipped and smoked.

After Freeland's business failed, Brown was promptly hired out again. He ended up working as a steward for a slave trader named Mr. Walker, who employed Brown to tend to the enslaved cargo he shipped from St. Louis to New Orleans. Brown's twelve months in Walker's employ, which he called "the longest year I ever lived," left him with a renewed determination to escape. On the journey south, Brown worried that he would be sold himself once the boat reached New Orleans, and he loathed his duties, which included preventing people enslaved by Walker from escaping whenever the boat stopped. One woman who had been sold away from her husband and children committed suicide by flinging herself into the Mississippi River. Brown was also in charge of doling out rations during the journey and preparing the enslaved people for market once the boat docked. After shaving the old men and blackening their whiskers to make them look younger, Brown had to have them all "dressed and driven out into the yard," where "some were set to dancing, some to jumping, some to singing, and some to playing cards" to make them appear cheerful and happy.[3] Brown eventually escaped from Walker, but he was forever haunted by what he had witnessed and became an abolitionist who fought to end slavery.

Brown was a captive spectator to the rapid expansion of a system built around the brutal forced migration and sale of enslaved Blacks. With the closing of the international slave trade in 1808, enslaved Americans became a predominantly U.S.-born population. They maintained a robust rate of reproduction, growing in number from a little over 1.5 million in 1820 to almost 4 million in 1860. And they continued to be bought and sold in an expanding domestic slave trade that supplied Black workers to the new slave states and territories taking shape in the South.

Enslaved labor predominated throughout the South, which maintained a largely agricultural economy even as industrialization moved many northern workers from fields to factories. As a result, the North and South became increasingly distinct and divided by the 1820s, especially with regard to the expansion of slavery. But strong economic ties also connected the regions. The South was crucial to American industrialization: Enslaved African Americans cultivated and harvested many of the raw materials used in northern factories. Likewise, the South depended on the North for textiles and manufactured goods — and provided the North with a lucrative market for those goods.

Enslaved African Americans rarely profited from their labor. In addition to working for their enslavers from sunup to sundown, they had to sustain themselves and their families. They also nurtured their communities and forged a distinctive culture within the confines of an oppressive system of bondage. Successful escapes were rare, and slave uprisings still more so. Enslaved people fought back by means of truancy, malingering, theft, and outright defiance under the watchful eyes of their enslavers and overseers. They also followed the sectional debates that divided the slave and free states. Those debates encouraged them to pray for freedom and hope that northern opposition would help topple the slave system. But until that day came, they would have to settle for survival.

The Expansion and Consolidation of Slavery

How did the expansion of slavery in the U.S. South affected relations between Black and Indigenous people?

How did the growth of the cotton industry in the United States displace enslaved African American families?

By 1820, slavery was all but dead in the North and banned throughout the Old Northwest. But it never came close to dying out completely, as many of the Founding Fathers had once predicted it would. Instead, the rise of cotton cultivation in the 1790s fostered the steady expansion of southern plantation agriculture. Moreover, during the first half of the nineteenth century, the Louisiana Purchase, Spain's cession of Spanish Florida, and the annexation of Texas opened new territory to American settlement and expanded the region within which slavery could be practiced. The expansion of the southern states took place at the expense of the American Indian inhabitants of the Southeast, whom white settlers pushed off their land. As white settlers moved into this territory, southern slavery became more entrenched.

The domestic slave trade expanded as the Upper South sold its surplus bondpeople in the Lower South, displacing hundreds of thousands of African Americans and tearing apart Black families and communities. The South's most lucrative crops required a large supply of enslaved workers, which strengthened white southerners' commitment to slavery in an era when many northerners were increasingly committed to free labor. These regional differences became a source of major sectional conflict during the late 1810s, when Missouri's petition for statehood threatened to upset the balance between states with and without slavery, and they remained divisive throughout the antebellum era.

AP® exam tip

Be prepared to explain how the expansion of the cotton industry impacted the social, political, and economic structures in the United States.

Slavery, Cotton, and American Industrialization

By the 1820s, stark regional differences were emerging between the North and South. Although these years saw the start of a transportation revolution that would link both regions to a shared national market, the new railroads, turnpikes, and shipping routes connected two increasingly distinct societies. With gradual emancipation all but complete, the North was committed to free labor; the South's investment in slavery only increased over time. Both regions expanded steadily, adding new people and new territory. Whereas population growth in the South relied primarily on natural increase, however, growth in the North also resulted from immigration. Between 1815 and 1860, more than five million Europeans immigrated to the United States, but fewer than one-eighth of them settled in southern slave states.

Slavery itself discouraged immigration to the South because there were few jobs for white immigrants. A majority of white southerners were not enslavers. They were largely small farmers with no employees. The region's major employers and wealthiest men were planters who favored enslaved over white workers. In addition to the labor they provided, enslaved people were a profitable investment: their prices rose steadily throughout the antebellum era, as did the return that enslavers could expect when enslaved people reproduced. Enslaved people also could be forced to do any type of work, including the grueling year-round labor needed to produce the South's lucrative cash crops.

AP® skills

Applying Disciplinary Knowledge: How did slavery impact immigration in the South?

The production of tobacco, rice, sugar, hemp, and above all cotton sustained the South's economy. By 1850, 55 percent of the South's enslaved population worked on cotton plantations, where they grew 75 percent of the world's supply of cotton (Map 6.1). Their labor enriched both the South and the nation as a whole: that year, cotton constituted more than 50 percent of all U.S. exports. Sugar, produced primarily

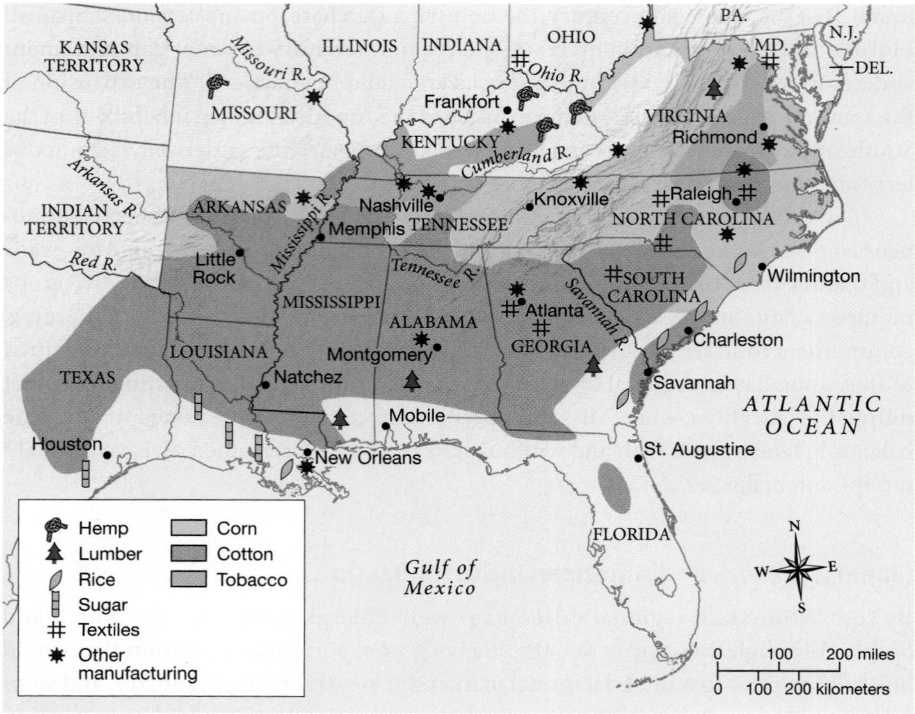

MAP 6.1 Agriculture and Industry in the Slave South, 1860

The economy of the antebellum South was dominated by cotton production, but southern planters also cultivated corn and tobacco in the Upper South, sugar in parts of Louisiana and Texas, and rice along the coasts of North and South Carolina, Georgia, and Louisiana. In addition, southern workers also produced hemp, lumber, textiles, and small quantities of other kinds of manufactured goods. **Where was manufacturing the sparsest, and why might that be?**

in Louisiana, was another highly profitable crop. Used throughout the United States, Louisiana sugar was also exported, making up as much as one-quarter of the world's sugar production during years when the crop flourished.

Southern businessmen used enslaved labor in the region's small industrial sector as well. Enslaved workers produced chewing tobacco in Richmond and Petersburg, Virginia; salt in western Virginia; and iron in a variety of ironworks located along Virginia's and Maryland's waterways. They also staffed lumber camps in forests and swamps across the South.

The North, by contrast, was home to a much larger nonagricultural sector. The first half of the nineteenth century saw northern farmers adopt new machinery that allowed them to increase production while reducing the number of workers they employed. Moreover, they took advantage of the reduced transportation costs and increased shipping speeds resulting from the transportation revolution to expand their markets. Food no longer had to be grown locally. Instead, large commercial farms in the Midwest began to monopolize the North's agricultural sector, and other parts of the region industrialized. Major manufacturing centers emerged in Boston, New York, and Philadelphia, and factory towns sprang up across the Northeast. Wages were high enough in these industrial areas to attract European immigrants, providing the northern states with a rapidly expanding free white labor force.

The different regional economies that emerged in the North and South were by no means autonomous. Southerners produced few manufactured goods and relied on the North — and, to a lesser extent, Europe — to supply them with furniture, tools, clothing, shoes, and other products. Likewise, northern industrialists imported raw materials such as cotton and indigo from the South. They used these materials to produce textiles, including fabrics manufactured specifically for the southern market, such as "negro cloth," a coarse cotton fabric used for enslaved people's clothing. Northern manufacturers also imported other crucial raw materials from the South. The most important was lumber, which factories used to make furniture, paper, buttons, bobbins, and many other household items and supplies that were then shipped to the South as finished products.

Despite such ties, the North and South had different economic and political interests. As the regions' economies diverged, northerners favored government measures designed to support American industrial production, such as protective tariffs on manufactured goods. Southerners, who produced few manufactured goods and imported many from abroad, opposed tariffs. Underlying such divergent interests were even deeper divisions over slavery.

The Missouri Compromise Crisis

With Alabama already scheduled for admission to the Union as a slave state in 1819, the nation was made up of eleven free states and eleven slave states. The admission of Missouri threatened to upset the balance. Missouri Territory had no restrictions on slavery, and some of its most fertile farmland had been settled by enslavers such as William Wells Brown's enslaver. By 1818, when Missouri applied for statehood, the territory was home to more than two thousand enslaved people. Nevertheless, northern congressmen were reluctant to admit Missouri as a slave state. The admission of another slave state would increase the South's power in Congress at a time when northern politicians had already begun to regret the Constitution's Three-Fifths Compromise.

> **AP® skills**
>
> **Applying Disciplinary Knowledge:** Why did the admission of Missouri threaten to upset the balance of free and slave states?

Although more than 60 percent of white Americans lived in the North, by 1818, northern representatives held only a slim majority of congressional seats. The additional political representation allotted to the South as a result of the

Three-Fifths Compromise gave southerners many more seats in the House of Representatives than they would have had if the number of representatives had been based on just the free population. Moreover, since each state had two Senate seats, Missouri's admission as a slave state would result in more southern than northern senators.

Many northern legislators also had misgivings about the westward expansion of slavery. One of them was New York representative James Tallmadge, who proposed a radical amendment to Missouri's statehood bill: banning slavery in Missouri and requiring that all enslaved people already in the region be freed by age twenty-five. Tallmadge's amendment set off a storm of sectional controversy that the elderly Thomas Jefferson likened to a "fire bell in the night" because it raised alarming new questions about whether the United States would remain united.[4]

AP® skills

Applying Disciplinary Knowledge: Why did the admission of Missouri to the United States cause significant debate among legislators?

The "Missouri question" inspired the nation's first extended debate over the expansion of slavery, which engaged both Black and white Americans. Anxious to see whether Congress would take action against slavery, free Blacks living in Washington, D.C., crowded the galleries of the House and Senate, while white southerners threatened to secede from the Union, and northern politicians embraced federal action against slavery for the first time.

Tallmadge's amendment was narrowly approved in the House of Representatives, but it stalled in the Senate. The question went unresolved until 1820, when a group led by Kentucky senator Henry Clay embraced a compromise in which Missouri would be admitted as a slave state alongside the new free state of Maine, which had split off from Massachusetts to form an independent territory in 1819. The **Missouri Compromise**, as it became known, retained the balance of power between the regions, but it also included a major concession to antislavery northerners: Congress agreed that slavery throughout the rest of the Louisiana Purchase would be prohibited north of latitude 36°30′, which runs along Missouri's southern border (Map 6.2). Slavery would not travel north, as many northern whites feared. But the Missouri Compromise was deeply disappointing to African Americans in both regions. It stopped the southward progression of gradual emancipation at Missouri's southern border and shored up slavery in the South.

Missouri Compromise (1820)
An agreement balancing the admission of Missouri as a slave state with the admission of Maine as a free state and prohibiting slavery north of latitude 36°30′ in any state except Missouri.

Slavery Expands into Indian Territory

The relentless expansion of the slave South also had a devastating effect on the region's American Indian peoples. White settlers and federal officials used a combination of treaties, warfare, and forced migration to drive the Cherokee, Creek, Choctaw, Chickasaw, and Seminole tribes from their homelands. Known among whites as the Five Civilized Tribes, because they had adopted European institutions in an attempt to live peacefully alongside their white neighbors, these tribes occupied large amounts of land that became increasingly appealing to settlers as the South's

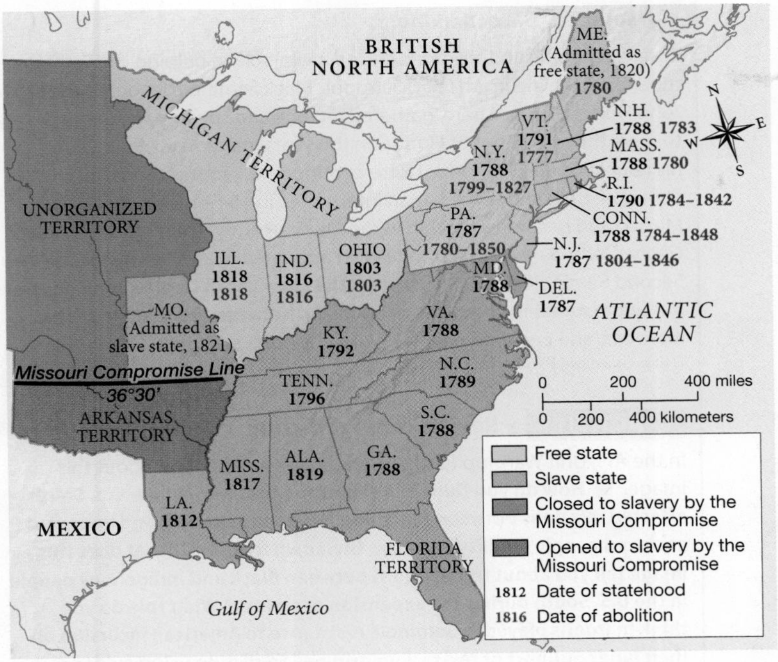

MAP 6.2 The Missouri Compromise

Passed in 1820, the Missouri Compromise prohibited slavery north of latitude 36°30′, except within the boundaries of the state of Missouri. As this map shows, the passage of the Missouri Compromise solidified the sectional divide between the slaveholding states of the South and the free states of the North, which had all passed abolition laws well before 1820. The year in which these laws were passed is also indicated, along with the year in which slavery actually ended in states that used gradual emancipation laws to abolish slavery. **How might the compromise impact the liberation of enslaved people in the southern region of the country?**

plantation economy expanded. The conflicts that white encroachment created culminated in the federal government's passage of the **Indian Removal Act** in 1830, which forced Indians living east of the Mississippi River to relocate to Indian Territory (present-day Oklahoma).

Indian Removal Act (1830) An act signed into law by President Andrew Jackson that forced American Indians living east of the Mississippi River to relocate to Indian Territory (present-day Oklahoma).

This act came on the heels of several decades of conflict, most of which involved disputes over the Indians' traditional homelands, which were coveted by white settlers. But the Seminole tribe, which lived in northern Florida, also clashed with state and federal authorities on the issue of slavery. Although the Seminole people practiced slavery, their system of bondage differed dramatically from that of the other four tribes, whose slavery practices resembled those of southern whites. Among the Seminole, enslaved people were adopted as kin: they could not be sold to whites, and

AP® source ***Black Seminoles***

Enslaved people and maroons played a vital role in helping the Seminole tribe resist the incursions of U.S. troops. Black Seminole leaders such as John Horse, pictured here, gathered recruits and spearheaded efforts to drive the troops out of Florida. In the years immediately following his relocation to Oklahoma, Horse continued to work on behalf of the Seminole tribe and served as an interpreter. In 1849, he emigrated to Mexico and became a captain in the Mexican army. This engraving, titled *Gopher John, Seminole Interpreter*, first appeared in an 1848 history of the Second Seminole War. **How does the story about Gopher John deepen our understanding about the relationship between Indigenous people, maroons, and enslaved people?** *University of Florida, Smathers Library Special and Area Studies Collections, Rare Books Collections.*

ACTIVITY ▸ Revisit Your Prediction

In the AP® Unit Warmup (p. U2-F), you made a prediction about this image. **How do you think the expansion of slavery in the U.S. South affected relations between Black and Indigenous people and impacted enslaved people's ability to secure their own freedom? What does this image tell you about the relations between Black and Indigenous people in the U.S. South during the expansion of slavery? What role do you think maroons played in Seminole resistance to American incursion on their land? Support or revise your original prediction using evidence from this chapter.**

they rarely passed their enslaved status on to their children. The tribe also allied with fugitives from slavery and sheltered entire communities of freedom seekers. Known today as Black Seminoles, the members of these maroon communities remained free by paying their Seminole hosts an annual tribute in livestock or crops, and they helped the Seminole tribe defend their land from white squatters.

AP® skills

Applying Disciplinary Knowledge: How did the Seminoles' use of enslaved labor differ from that of most white Americans? Why is this distinction significant?

By the late 1820s, however, all five tribes were having trouble holding on to their land. As white settlers proliferated, they drove the Indians out by squatting on their territory, stealing their livestock, and burning their towns. The Indians complained to both state and federal officials, who resolved the conflict by dispossessing the Indians. The Indian Removal Act of 1830 was designed by Andrew Jackson, who had been elected president in 1828, and called for the Five Civilized Tribes to sign treaties giving up their homelands in the Southeast in return for payments and new land in the West. The army forcibly displaced Indians who refused to relocate. Among them were most of the Cherokee tribe, who remained on their land until 1838, when federal troops marched them west on a brutal journey known as the Trail of Tears. As the tribes moved west, they took the people they enslaved with them.

AP® skills

Applying Disciplinary Knowledge: Describe the historical situation of the Trail of Tears.

The Seminole nation was the only tribe to resist with force. Enslaved and maroon allies helped the Seminole repel the U.S. troops who arrived to drive them out of Florida in 1835. The Seminole tribe numbered only four thousand, but the tribe had eight hundred Black Seminole allies who fiercely opposed relocation. Some of the Black Seminoles were freedom seekers who knew they would be returned to their enslavers if the tribe agreed to move. Others feared that relocation would lead to the reenslavement of all Black Seminoles. Black Seminole leaders such as John Horse, fighting alongside Seminole leaders such as Osceola, enlisted several hundred rebellious enslaved people on plantations to join the Seminole cause. When Osceola's forces were defeated in the spring of 1838, Horse was forced west along with most of his Seminole allies. Several hundred Seminoles remained behind in the Florida swamps, however, and they waged another war to resist displacement between 1855 and 1858.

AP® exam tip

Be sure you are able to describe the role some African American freedom seekers played in Seminole resistance to relocation during the Second Seminole War.

The Domestic Slave Trade

Most enslaved African Americans were owned by white southerners. Louisiana and Alabama joined the Union in 1812 and 1819, respectively, further expanding the South's cotton belt. Cotton planters migrated into the territories of Arkansas and Missouri and also established settlements in Spanish Florida, which Spain ceded to the United States in the 1819 Adams–Onís Treaty. (The agreement took effect two years later, in 1821.) Settler enslavers also began arriving in Texas as early as the 1820s, when the region still belonged to Mexico, which had abolished slavery. They supported Texas's war for independence in the 1830s and the U.S. annexation of Texas in 1845, which brought Texas into the Union as a slave state. As the last of the four new slave states to enter the Union between 1820 and 1860, Texas followed Missouri (1821), Arkansas (1836), and Florida (1845).

Slavery was most important in the Lower South. Between 1820 and 1860, 1.2 million African Americans moved from the Upper South to the Lower South in a mass migration that relocated almost half of the region's enslaved population. Approximately one-third of these involuntary migrants belonged to Upper South enslavers who took the people they enslaved with them as they migrated west and south to establish new plantations in South Carolina, Georgia, Alabama, Mississippi, Louisiana, Florida, Arkansas, and Texas. The remaining two-thirds were bought, transported, and resold in the Lower South by slave traders (Map 6.3).

Most enslaved people made the grueling journey on foot, in coffles that could contain anywhere from thirty to three hundred men, women, and children. The men were usually chained together in handcuffed pairs, while the women and children trailed behind them or were carried in wagons. Traders on horseback, with whips and guns, accompanied the coffles. After walking twenty to twenty-five miles during the day, enslaved people often slept outdoors, sometimes under tents or just huddled together on the ground. As the South's transportation network improved,

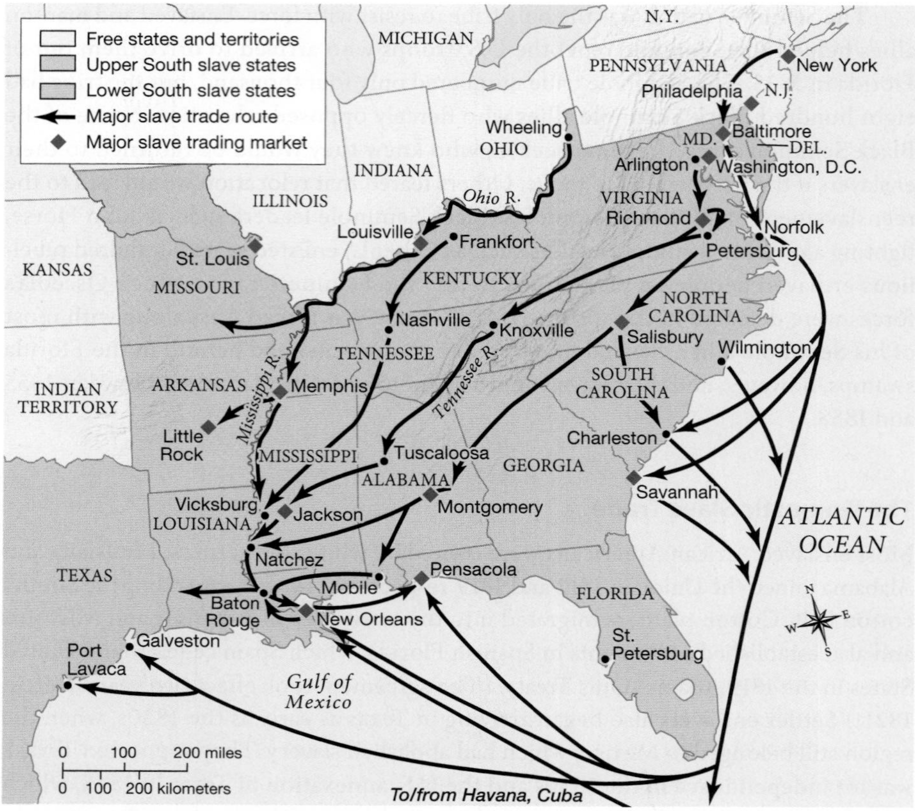

MAP 6.3 The Domestic Slave Trade, 1808–1865

With the termination of the international slave trade in 1808, an extensive domestic slave trade developed to transfer enslaved people from the North and Upper South, where free labor was increasingly predominant, to the Lower South's ever-expanding plantation frontier. This map illustrates the various routes by which the forced migrants traveled south: some were carried in railroad cars, and others were loaded onto riverboats and oceangoing vessels and shipped to slave ports such as New Orleans. Many more made the long journey on foot, marching south under the supervision of armed slave traders.

How and why did enslavers create a new system to continue the domestic slave trade?

DATA SOURCE: *The Atlas of African-American History and Politics: From the Slave Trade to Modern Times, by Arwin Smallwood and Jeffrey Elliot.* Copyright © 1998 The McGraw-Hill Companies, Inc.

some traders began to ship enslaved people south on steamships that chugged down the Mississippi or on oceangoing ships that docked in New Orleans. By the 1850s, transporting enslaved people by rail was also common. Lyman Abbott, a northerner who visited the region in 1856, found that "every train going south has . . . slaves on board, twenty or more, and a 'n***** car,' which is very generally also the smoking-car, and sometimes the baggage-car."[5]

Regardless of how the enslaved people traveled, the journey represented a new Middle Passage for them. Enslaved people dreaded being "sold down the river" to the Lower South, knowing, above all, that such sales usually meant permanent separation from their families and friends. The majority of people who entered the trade were under thirty; most left their parents behind, although very young children were usually sold with their mothers. The trade also split up many young enslaved couples, disrupting one in five enslaved marriages in the Upper South, and divided siblings, extended families, and friends. These losses were all the more devastating because they came without warning: enslavers usually sold enslaved people in secret to avoid giving them a chance to object. Charity Bowery's female enslaver, for example, made sure that Bowery was out running errands when she sold Bowery's twelve-year-old son. "She didn't want to be troubled with our cries," Bowery later remembered.[6] Enslavers routinely used the ever-present threat of sale to control the people they enslaved and suppress dissent. According to one enslaved man, his enslaver would threaten "that if we didn't suit him, he would put us in his pocket quick — meaning he would sell us."[7]

Once in the Lower South, enslaved people faced new traumas. On arrival, they were marketed at auction houses and slave trading centers across the region. Prospective buyers appraised them as if they were farm animals, inspecting their bodies for signs of illness or other physical weakness and for scars from frequent whippings, which might indicate a rebellious nature. Virtually all buyers were men, since even widowed white women often bought enslaved people through male intermediaries rather than entering into the trade themselves. Prospective buyers subjected enslaved people to a level of scrutiny considered too indelicate for white women to witness. Men examined enslaved people's teeth to determine their age and pushed back their clothes to look at their muscles. They also "felt all over the women folks," one formerly enslaved recalled, to try to determine whether they were fertile.[8] Not surprisingly, enslaved people found the whole procedure deeply degrading. But some also tried to shape its outcome. Henry Bibb, whose Kentucky enslaver punished him for being a chronic runaway by selling his entire family to a slave trader, was so intent on keeping his family together that he told a prospective buyer he had run away only once.

AP® exam tip

Be sure you can describe the context in which the "Second Middle Passage" took place. What were its primary causes? What effect did this forced migration have on enslaved families?

Black Challenges to Slavery

What were the inspirations, goals, and struggles of different revolts and abolitionist organizing led by enslaved and free Afro-descendants throughout the Americas during the nineteenth century?

As slavery expanded, Black discontent heightened. In 1820, the disappointing outcome of the Missouri crisis helped inspire a free Black man named Denmark Vesey to denounce slavery and exhort enslaved South Carolinians to rebel. Divine inspiration moved an enslaved preacher named Nat Turner to lead a bloody attack on slavery in Southampton, Virginia, in 1831. Neither of these men's actions succeeded in overturning slavery, but both had an enduring impact. Within the region, Vesey and Turner's actions

SALE OF ESTATES, PICTURES AND SLAVES IN THE ROTUNDA, NEW ORLEANS.

Auctioning People
Enslaved people experienced tremendous degradation in the process of their auction and sale. Potential buyers, almost all of whom were white men, inspected them bodily and subjected them to questioning. Enslaved couples and parents of enslaved children were burdened with the additional fear of having their families torn asunder. In this engraving of an auction house in New Orleans, a family is on the auction block. The auctioneers and buyers treat them merely as goods to be sold, on par with the sale of paintings, deeds, and various agricultural commodities shown in the picture. **Explain the potential long-term impact of slave auctions on enslaved families. Use details from the engraving to support your explanation.** *The Historic New Orleans Collection/Bridgeman Images.*

inspired new repressive measures to forestall any future rebellions. Outside the South, their actions fueled Black abolitionist critiques of slavery. In particular, David Walker, a free Black man who fled the South after Vesey's planned revolt was suppressed, insisted that the enslaved rebels were heroes and called for others to follow in their footsteps.

Denmark Vesey's Plot

Originally named Telemarque, Denmark Vesey hailed from St. Thomas in the Danish West Indies. As a teenager, he relocated to Charleston, South Carolina, with his enslaver in 1793. Fluent in both French and English, the young enslaved man had taught himself to read and write by the time he reached Charleston, where his enslaver employed him as a clerk and domestic servant. As an enslaved man who was highly skilled and valuable, Vesey might have remained in bondage all his life but for

Remembering Denmark Vesey
African American artist Ed Dwight was commissioned to create this life-size bronze sculpture of Vesey for Hampton Park in Charleston, South Carolina. Speaking at the unveiling ceremony in 2014, the Rev. Joe Darby of the AME Church said, "Some people see Denmark Vesey as a dangerous terrorist. Most see him as a freedom fighter. My hope is that this monument will add to the full story of our southern heritage."
How does this monument portray Vesey? Based on the evidence in the chapter, how do you view his role in American history? *Quotation source: Adam Parker, "Denmark Vesey Monument Unveiled before Hundreds,"* The Post and Courier *(February 14, 2014). Photo credit: Tony Cenicola/The New York Times/Redux Pictures.*

an extraordinary stroke of good luck in 1799. That year, he purchased a lottery ticket — likely with money earned from taking on extra work during his free hours — and won the princely sum of $1,500. He used $600 of it to purchase his own freedom and the remainder to move out of his enslaver's house and establish a carpentry business.

Vesey continued to socialize and identify with enslaved people, and he became increasingly eager to see all of his enslaved friends set free. In 1819, when congressional debates over the status of Missouri appeared in the Charleston newspapers, Vesey was delighted to see slavery under attack. His plot took at least some inspiration from these debates, the news of which reached Black communities across the country. As one Charleston enslaver complained, "By the Missouri question, our slaves thought, there was a charter of liberties granted them by Congress."[9]

By 1820, with the help of several enslaved friends, Vesey had begun planning a rebellion. They spent more than a year recruiting other men. Armed with stolen guns and knives, they planned to raid Charleston's Meeting Street Arsenal and a nearby shop to gather additional weapons for their supporters, whom they expected to number in the thousands. Vesey was a lay preacher in Charleston's African Methodist Episcopal (AME) church, and he reviewed the details of the plot at religious classes held in his home, in which he likened the planned rebellion to the delivery of the children of Israel from Egyptian slavery.

The conspirators dreamed of freeing themselves and sailing off to Haiti, but more than a month before the scheduled rebellion, two enslaved people in Charleston divulged the plan to their enslavers. Local authorities swiftly suppressed the uprising. Over the next month, officials arrested 131 enslaved and free Blacks, 72 of whom were tried, convicted, and sentenced to death. More died in custody, and 27 were ultimately released. Vesey was hanged on July 2, 1822, with five other men in a public spectacle that drew thousands of Black and white Charlestonians. The event was followed by several other mass hangings the same month.

The rebels were deliberately denied funerals or proper burials. Aware that Africans and African Americans cherished funeral rites as a way to free the spirit of the deceased, Charleston authorities had the rebels cut down and dismembered after they were hanged. As the death toll mounted, however, it became clear that the costly executions could not proceed indefinitely. The loss of enslaved property and labor imposed a severe economic burden on both the enslavers and the state. By late July, Carolinians were ready to see the hangings come to an end. As a lawyer told one of Charleston's magistrates, "You must take care and save negroes enough for the Rice crop."[10] The remaining thirty-seven rebels were transported to slave societies outside the United States at their enslavers' expense.

Neither death nor deportation could erase the memory of Vesey's plot, however, and like Richmond whites in the aftermath of Gabriel's rebellion in 1800, white South Carolinians moved quickly to limit the mobility and autonomy of the state's enslaved population. State officials banned enslaved people from hiring themselves out, and they forbade free Blacks to hire enslaved people. The City of Charleston took the additional precaution of hiring a permanent force of 150 guardsmen to patrol the city around the clock. Any enslaved person caught on the street after 9 p.m. without a written pass could be arrested and whipped or, worse, assigned to walk on a prison treadmill installed at the Charleston jail in 1823. The treadmill consisted of a wheel with steps, which was propelled by a group of manacled enslaved people, who climbed the rotating steps under the supervision of a driver brandishing a cat-o'-nine-tails. The mill was used to grind corn sold to offset the jail's daily expenses, but even when there was no grain to grind, prisoners could be assigned to hard labor on the treadmill.

AP® skills

Applying Disciplinary Knowledge: Why were free Black Americans considered a threat to chattel slavery?

Bitterly aware that Vesey and most of his key collaborators could read and write, South Carolina officials reinforced existing laws against teaching enslaved people to read, and the state legislature adopted new legislation forbidding free Black education. In the fall of 1822, municipal authorities also razed the AME church where Vesey had preached, although they could find no evidence that church leaders had participated in the plot. As one nineteenth-century commentator later noted, the church was threatening because it "tended to spread the dangerous infection of the alphabet."[11]

AP® exam tip

Be sure you can explain how acts of resistance led to increased codes and laws used to restrict both enslaved and free Black Americans.

Free Blacks were also subject to new legislation and surveillance designed to make them feel unwelcome in the state. One law required all free Black males over age fifteen to find white guardians willing to post bonds for their good behavior, and another barred free Blacks who left the state from returning. The state also put new restrictions on the free Black sailors who worked on ships that docked in South Carolina. Passed in 1822, The South Carolina Negro Seamen Act required Black sailors to be incarcerated while in South Carolina. The ship captains who employed free Black sailors were responsible for jail costs, and if they did not pay them, or if they left any of their sailors behind, these Black men could be sold into slavery.

David Walker's Exile

Even as Charleston whites moved to ensure that no new Vesey would threaten their safety, Vesey's memory lived on. Among the free Blacks who fled Charleston in the wake of the plot was David Walker, who moved north and made a name for himself as the most militant Black abolitionist of his era. The rising hostility toward free Blacks in Charleston had convinced him that "if I remain in this bloody land . . . I will not live long."[12] By 1825, the forty-year-old Walker had resettled in Boston, where he ran a used clothing store near the harbor, outfitting the sailors and other mariners who passed through the city. In Boston, Walker found a lively Black community, married, and joined the African Lodge of the Honorable Society of Free and Accepted Masons. Members included local leaders such as the Reverend Thomas Paul, the minister of Boston's First African Baptist Church.

But moving to Massachusetts did not allow Walker to escape white oppression. He found most African American northerners "ignorant and poor" and unable "to obtain the comforts of life, but by cleaning their [white people's] boots and shoes, old clothes, [and] waiting on them." He also found African Americans hard-pressed to secure their position in the face of the American Colonization Society's plans.[13]

The American Colonization Society (ACS), though opposed by Blacks, had become steadily more popular among whites. At their most polite, ACS members continued to champion colonization as a step toward the eradication of slavery. But after founding the West African colony of Liberia in 1821, they began to focus their attention on free Blacks. While many Blacks were not opposed to emigration in theory, they questioned the motives of the ACS and believed that the organization's propaganda hurt Black prospects for freedom in America. ACS members rejected the views of an earlier generation of antislavery whites who embraced Black education as the road to self-improvement. Instead, colonizationists such as ACS secretary Elias Caldwell contended that improving the condition of African Americans would only give them more "relish for those privileges which they can never attain."[14]

AP® exam tip

Be sure you can explain the purpose of the American Colonization Society. How did Black people respond to it? How does this response reflect popular debates about Black self-identification during the nineteenth century?

David Walker was appalled by the ACS, viewing colonization as a doctrine designed to perpetuate slavery by banishing free Blacks. Walker advocated abolition instead of emigration and denounced colonization as a proslavery plot. Convinced that all Blacks should fight for freedom within the United States, he sheltered fugitives from slavery in his home and became a contributor to the nation's first Black newspaper, *Freedom's Journal* (founded in 1827), which opposed both colonization and slavery. Like the *Journal*'s editors, Walker was convinced that African Americans could not defeat slavery and racism without pleading their own cause. This conviction inspired him to publish an abolitionist manifesto of his own in 1829, titled *Walker's Appeal . . . to the Coloured Citizens of the World*. A fiery protest against slavery and colonization, *Walker's Appeal* lambasted white people for enslaving and oppressing people of color, and it also critiqued Blacks for acquiescing to white domination. "Are we MEN!! — I ask you, O my brethren! Are we MEN?" asked Walker, addressing his fellow Blacks.

AP® skills

Applying Disciplinary Knowledge: Describe David Walker's perspective on the American Colonization Society.

AP® skills

Applying Disciplinary Knowledge: How did David Walker's *Appeal* shift the focus from colonization to emancipation?

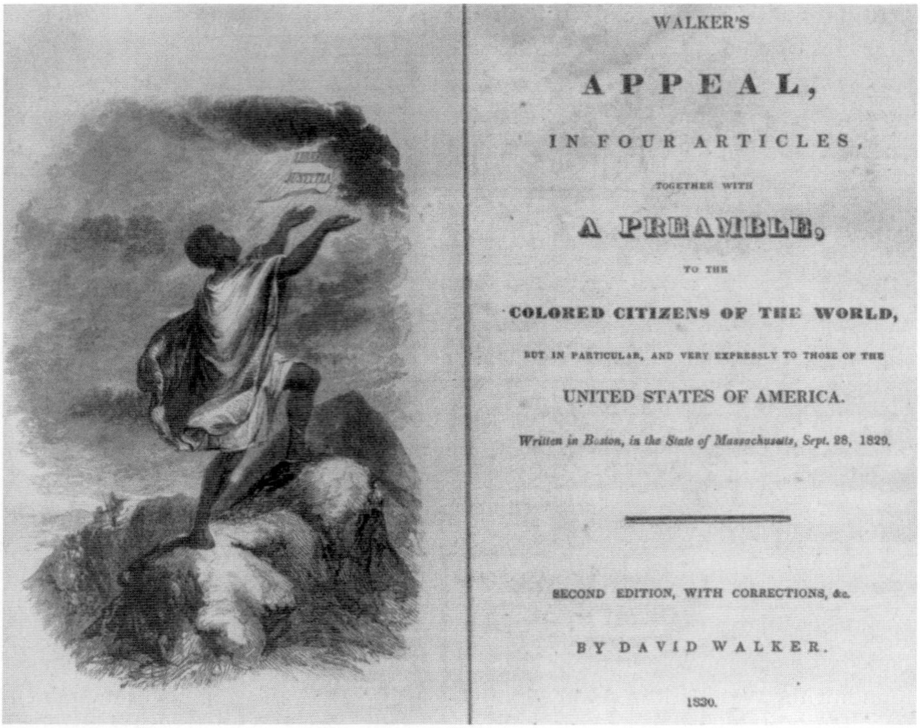

Frontispiece and Title Page of Walker's Appeal, 1830
Printed from an engraving by an unknown artist, the frontispiece for the second edition of *Walker's Appeal* shows an enslaved man standing on top of a mountain, his hands raised toward a piece of paper that floats directly above him. Inscribed on the paper are the Latin words *libertas justitia* —"liberty and justice." **Why did the artist depict the man with his hands raised? What message does this pose convey to its audience?** *Library of Congress, Prints and Photographs Division, Washington, D.C., LC-USZ62-63775.*

"How we could be so *submissive* to a gang of men, . . . I never could conceive." But he reserved his harshest critique for American enslavers whom he described as "tyrants and devils."[15]

Walker's controversial pamphlet was influential on several counts. It galvanized a new generation of radical Blacks who would lobby for abolition and civil rights for many years to come. Among whites, it helped shift the focus of the antislavery movement from colonization to emancipation. Walker's call for enslaved people to commit violence was widely condemned by white abolitionists, most of whom were political moderates who supported the ACS, but these reformers proved more open to his critique of colonization. The influential white abolitionist William Lloyd Garrison, who still held moderate views when he first encountered Walker's pamphlet, criticized "the spirit and tendency of this *Appeal*" but also acknowledged that it contained many "valuable truths."[16] Shortly after its publication, Garrison renounced colonization and dedicated himself to the immediate abolition of slavery.

In the South, Walker's *Appeal* strengthened the determination of whites to suppress Black dissent. By 1830, the pamphlet had reached Virginia, North Carolina, Georgia, Louisiana, and Alabama, where whites discovered copies in the hands of Black seamen and enslaved people. Terrified by its message, they offered a $3,000 bounty for Walker's death and a $10,000 reward for anyone willing to kidnap Walker and deliver him alive. His pamphlet was the subject of special meetings of several southern state legislatures, and it inspired new laws restricting the rights of enslaved and free Blacks in Georgia and North Carolina.

In the midst of this controversy, Walker was found dead in the doorway of his home in June 1830, just after the publication of the third edition of his *Appeal*. He probably succumbed to tuberculosis, which was rampant in nineteenth-century Boston. But given the size of the reward that Walker's enemies offered to see him dead, many free Blacks were convinced that he was the victim of foul play. Either way, Walker's death did not end his influence. His pamphlet had shown that slavery had enemies throughout the nation.

Nat Turner's Rebellion, the *Amistad* Case, and the *Creole* Insurrection

Walker's message received additional support just a few years later, when an enslaved lay preacher named Nat Turner led one of the bloodiest slave rebellions in American history. Born in 1800, Turner was a lifelong resident of Southampton County, Virginia, and grew up during a time when many Blacks and whites in the Upper South were embracing evangelical Christianity. The first few decades of the nineteenth century saw the **Second Great Awakening**, similar to the Great Awakening of the eighteenth century. Once again, a wave of Baptist and Methodist revivals swept through the nation. But Black and white congregants often understood the message of religious equality quite differently, especially in the South.

Second Great Awakening A Christian revival movement that took place during the first half of the nineteenth century.

Raised in a Methodist household, Turner was a pious young man who spent much of his spare time praying and fasting. He experienced powerful religious visions, which eventually convinced him that "the great day of judgment" was at hand. Turner bided his time for years, waiting for "signs in the heavens that it would make known to me when I should commence the great work." On the evening of August 21, 1831, he struck, accompanied by a small band of fellow enslaved people who shared his vision of "slay[ing] my enemies with their own weapons."[17]

Armed with axes and hatchets, Turner and his men began by murdering Turner's enslaver, Joseph Travis, and his family and stealing their small cache of guns. They then moved from plantation to plantation freeing enslaved people; killing white men, women, and children; and gathering more weapons and recruits. Turner's force grew to more than fifty enslaved and free Blacks who managed to kill sixty whites before a Virginia militia tracked them down two days later. The rebels scattered but were pursued by a growing force of armed whites, who went on a killing spree that lasted more than two weeks and resulted in the deaths of more than a hundred Blacks — all of whom died without trial. An additional forty-eight suspects were captured, tried, and executed by the state, including Turner himself, who had managed to evade capture for three months until a white farmer discovered him in hiding.

Turner's rebellion terrified whites across the South. Turner was soon rumored to have an army of 1,200 co-conspirators located as far away as North Carolina. In Virginia, as one plantation mistress put it, fears of revolt were "agonizing." Virginia legislators were even willing to consider the abolition of slavery rather than continue to contemplate "the horrors of servile war which will not end until . . . the slaves or the whites are totally exterminated."[18] They debated a gradual emancipation plan but quickly decided that emancipation was not the solution.

AP® skills

Applying Disciplinary Knowledge: How did Nat Turner's actions impact gradual emancipation?

Convinced that Turner's uprising was caused by the abolitionist agitation of men such as David Walker, Virginia's leaders instead revised the state's legal code to bar enslaved and free Blacks from preaching or even attending religious meetings without white supervision. Virginia legislators also targeted free Blacks with a colonization bill, which allocated new funding to remove them, and a police bill that denied free Blacks trial by jury and subjected any free Black person convicted of a crime to sale and relocation.

gag rule
A series of congressional resolutions passed by the House of Representatives between 1836 and 1840 that tabled, without discussion, petitions regarding slavery; the gag rule was instituted to silence dissent over slavery. It was repealed in 1844.

Lawmakers also took precautions that were unprecedented in scope. In 1835, southern legislators silenced congressional debates over slavery for almost a decade by passing a **gag rule** prohibiting the reading of antislavery petitions in Congress. Former president John Quincy Adams, now a representative from Massachusetts, tirelessly opposed this rule, believing that it imposed unconstitutional limitations on petitioners' freedom of speech. He also saw congressional support for the rule as evidence that the nation was falling under the control of a dangerous "slavocracy" led by wealthy southern enslavers. Known as "Old Man Eloquent" for his rhetorical skills, Adams called for rescinding the gag rule every year until 1844, when he finally prevailed.

AP® skills

Applying Disciplinary Knowledge: What was the outcome of the *Amistad* case? How did it affect the public attitude toward abolition?

Still, no gag rule or law could fully suppress Black dissent. In the years following Nat Turner's rebellion, two slave insurrections at sea intensified whites' fears and called the security of the slave system into question. In 1839, a group of Africans who had just been kidnapped and enslaved seized control of the Spanish slave ship *Amistad* in international waters near Cuba. The U.S. navy captured the ship and made the rebels prisoners of the U.S. government, at which point Spain demanded their return. But the rebels' enslavement violated treaties prohibiting the international slave trade, and their status had to be determined in court. The ***Amistad* case** became a widely publicized abolitionist cause and ultimately reached the U.S. Supreme Court, which freed the rebels in 1841.

***Amistad* case**
An 1839 slave insurrection aboard the *Amistad*, a Spanish ship, in international waters near Cuba. The case became a widely publicized abolitionist cause and ultimately reached the U.S. Supreme Court, which freed the rebels in 1841.

A similar revolt in 1841 had a comparable outcome. Led by Madison Washington, enslaved people aboard the *Creole,* an American ship engaged in the internal slave trade, seized the vessel, sailed to British waters, and declared themselves free. The British accepted the enslaved people's emancipation declaration, enabling them to go free in the Bahamas. Speaking for the U.S. government, Secretary of State Daniel Webster honored the rebels' claims to freedom in the ***Creole* insurrection** but insisted unsuccessfully that the British government compensate the enslavers for their lost property.

***Creole* insurrection**
An 1841 slave insurrection aboard the *Creole*, a ship carrying 135 enslaved people from Hampton Roads, Virginia, to New Orleans, Louisiana.

Although both incidents took place at sea, the *Amistad* and *Creole* revolts reinforced the insecurity that southern enslavers felt. Like the actions of Denmark Vesey, David Walker, and Nat Turner, these enslaved people's endeavors suggested that Black dissent could never be fully subdued. Moreover, the fact that the *Amistad* rebels went on to win their freedom in U.S. courts underscored the limited support slavery enjoyed outside the South.

Everyday Resistance to Slavery

What were the daily forms of resistance demonstrated by enslaved and free African Americans?

Both external and internal opposition to slavery unnerved white southerners, whose control over their enslaved population was precarious and hard-won. Although they used repressive slave codes, vigilant slave patrols, brutal punishments, and the threat of sale to keep their bondmen and bondwomen subdued, they could never eradicate Black resistance to slavery. Instead, individual resistance was nearly an everyday occurrence. Organized rebellions became rare in the wake of Nat Turner's revolt, but enslaved discontent remained ubiquitous. Enslaved African Americans protested their condition in many ways, such as by stealing plantation property, feigning illness, refusing to work, defying their enslavers, and running away.

Disobedience and Defiance

Theft was perhaps the most common form of disobedience, although few enslaved people regarded it as a crime. "Po' nigger had to steal back dar in slav'y eben to git 'nuf t'eat. . . . Ef it hadn't been fo' dem [whites], nigger wouldn't know nothin' 'bout stealin'," explained one formerly enslaved person from Virginia. Rosa Barnwell, a formerly enslaved woman in South Carolina, reported that her enslavers expected enslaved people to survive on a weekly allowance of approximately eight quarts of corn and four quarts of sweet potatoes. Given no meat, they sometimes took "a hog on their own account." Louisa Gause, who was also enslaved in South Carolina, concluded, "If [an enslaved person] did [steal], he never take nothin, but what been belong to him."[19]

Enslaved people also feigned illness to avoid unpleasant work assignments. Planters often complained of enslaved people who were "lazy . . . and affected to be sick," and some even employed doctors to determine whether the people they enslaved were "really ill or merely 'playing possum.' "[20] Such determinations were not always possible, however, and some enslaved people managed to evade work by refusing to eat for days and pretending to be too weak to stand up.

AP® skills
Applying Disciplinary Knowledge: Describe some examples of covert resistance to slavery on this page.

AP® source ***Harriet Tubman***

Harriet Tubman, born Araminta "Minty" Ross, endured a brutal childhood and young adulthood in slavery. Following her final, permanent escape in 1849, she helped many more enslaved people — including members of her own family — escape to freedom and spoke out against the horrors of slavery. During the Civil War, she served the Union as a cook, nurse, teacher, scout, and spy. **What is the significance of visual depictions of African American leaders in photography and art — as with Harriet Tubman's portrait — during this time?** *Library of Congress, Prints and Photographs Division, Washington, D.C., LC-USZ62-7816.*

Some enslaved people defied their enslavers by running away and hiding to avoid punishment or other harsh measures. Mostly temporary, such escapes were often propelled by despair and fear rather than being carefully planned. Araminta "Minty" Ross, who later renamed herself Harriet Tubman, fled her female enslaver in terror at age seven after stealing a lump of sugar. Miss Susan, the brutal enslaver for whom Tubman worked as a nursemaid, was a merciless taskmaster who beat Tubman every day, lashing out at the girl every time the baby she tended cried. Caught in the act of stealing, Tubman was afraid to face whatever punishment this far graver transgression might bring. When she saw her enslaver grab her rawhide whip, she ran as far as she could and then took shelter in a pigpen, where she hid for five days, braving the muck of the pen and competing with the pigs for scraps to eat. She stayed there until hunger and her increasing fear of the adult pigs drove her to return home and face the wrath of her enslaver. Not until 1849, two decades later, did she finally manage to escape permanently.

truant
An enslaved person who ran away for a limited period of time to visit loved ones; attend religious meetings or other social events; or escape punishment, abusive treatment, or undesirable work assignments.

In escaping from slavery only temporarily, the seven-year-old Tubman became what enslavers deemed a **truant** — an enslaved person who absconded for a matter of days, weeks, or sometimes months. Although truants were generally adults, many were like Tubman in that they fled to avoid punishment. Others sought to escape especially onerous work assignments or abusive treatment, and they would sometimes agree to return after negotiating better conditions with their enslavers. Truants often hid in local swamps or woods — a form of resistance also known as **lying out**. In many cases, these people received support from other enslaved people who brought them food and supplies and who sometimes even hid the truants in their homes. But truants also included more short-term escapees, who left to visit loved ones or attend religious meetings, dances, or other social events.

AP® skills

Applying Disciplinary Knowledge: Describe the different reasons enslaved people turned to truancy or lying out to resist their enslavers.

lying out
A form of resistance in which enslaved people hid near their home plantations, often to escape undesirable work assignments or abusive treatment by their enslavers.

Some enslaved people countered harsh treatment with outright resistance. The famous freedom seeker Frederick Douglass almost lost his life at age sixteen when he physically resisted a whipping from a particularly brutal enslaver. Born on a Maryland plantation, Douglass spent much of his youth in Baltimore, working as a house servant. But when he became an unruly teenager, Douglass's enslaver sent him out of the city to work for a poor white farmer named Mr. Covey, who was known for his ability to subdue even the most recalcitrant enslaved people. Covey subjected Douglass to a brutal work regime and terrible weekly beatings that left Douglass feeling utterly "broken in body, soul, and spirit." One day, however, he found himself fighting back against his tormentor. "From whence came the spirit I don't know," Douglass later recalled. The two men exchanged blows until both were exhausted, and thereafter Douglass recovered his "long-crushed spirit." He took no more beatings from Covey and "let it be known . . . that the white man who expected to succeed in whipping, must also succeed in killing me."[21]

Douglass was lucky to survive this resolution, given that enslaved people who physically resisted risked death. They had no right to self-defense under southern law, which gave white people uncontrolled authority over enslaved people's bodies. Even whites who merely supervised the people enslaved by others had this authority, as the North Carolina Supreme Court justice Thomas Ruffin ruled in the influential 1829 case *State v. Mann*. Ruffin overturned the enslaver Elizabeth Jones's attempt to impose criminal sanctions on John Mann, to whom she had hired out Lydia, a woman she enslaved. When Lydia disobeyed Mann, he whipped her, and when she tried to escape, he shot and wounded her. Mann's acquittal shored up the power of southern whites who employed or even supervised enslaved people. Subsequent rulings across the South reinforced these principles. Georgia's Supreme Court ruled in *John v. State* (1854) that any enslaved person accused of killing a white person had to be charged with murder, even if he or she had acted in self-defense (an act that would normally carry a manslaughter charge).[22]

Escaping Slavery

Successful permanent escapes were rare. Whites patrolled plantation districts on a nightly basis, severely punishing enslaved people who left their quarters. "Run Nigger, run, Patty Roller will catch you . . . I'll shoot you with my flintlock gun," enslaved African Americans would sing, sometimes in an effort to warn others that patrollers were nearby.[23] Some of slavery's successful freedom seekers, such as Frederick Douglass, William Wells Brown, and Harriet Tubman, went on to provide eloquent testimony about the brutality of slavery and become some of the nation's most influential antislavery activists. Although most freedom seekers were caught before they made it out of the South, even unsuccessful escape attempts had an impact on the slave system because they cost enslavers time and money and reminded southern whites that African Americans were held in bondage against their will.

AP® exam tip

Be sure you can explain the significance of Harriet Tubman's contributions to abolitionism and African Americans' pursuit of freedom.

One difficulty of permanent escape was that although freedom seekers could hide in nearby woods or swamps with relative ease, they could not travel on roads without a pass. A few exceptionally enterprising freedom seekers learned to read and write so that they could forge their own passes, but even procuring paper and ink could be challenging. Solomon Northup, a free Black man from New York, learned this first-hand when he was kidnapped and sold into slavery in 1841. Northup was drugged and ended up in a slave pen after traveling to Washington, D.C., with two white men who had offered him a job as a musician. The men sold him to a slave trader, who believed, despite Northup's protests to the contrary, that he was a fugitive from slavery from Georgia. Neither the trader nor any of Northup's subsequent enslavers had any incentive to believe that he was free, and he was eventually sold as far south as Louisiana, where he toiled on cotton plantations for many years.

AP® skills

Applying Disciplinary Knowledge: What happened to Soloman Northup? How does his experience relate to the changes in the domestic slave trade during the nineteenth century?

Literate and legally free, Northup had white friends in New York who could vouch for his identity, but plantation life made it almost impossible for him to write or mail a letter. He explained his difficulty in his autobiography, *Twelve Years a Slave*: "In the first place, I was deprived of pen, ink, and paper. In the second place, a slave cannot leave his plantation without a pass, nor will a post-master mail a letter for one without written instructions from his owner. I was in slavery nine years, and always watchful and on the alert, before I met with the good fortune of obtaining a sheet of paper." Even after that, Northup had to figure out how to make ink to write his letter and find a white man he trusted to mail it.[24]

Geographic distance created another obstacle. Enslaved Blacks who lived in Texas sometimes managed to escape to Mexico, but freedom seekers from other regions generally made their way north. Those who attempted to leave the Lower South faced a trek of hundreds of miles and had to navigate their way through vast expanses of strange territory without getting lost. Uneducated and for the most part illiterate, freedom seekers had no maps and had to hide during the day and travel at night, guided only by the **North Star**.

North Star
A star, also known as Polaris, that always points north and was used by freedom seekers to navigate their way to freedom.

Skilled freedom seekers had slightly better opportunities to escape. They could blend in with free Blacks more easily in southern cities than could scantily dressed field hands, which gave them opportunities to travel north by boat or train. Although steamboats were often inspected for fugitives from slavery, and Blacks on trains had to carry passes or papers documenting their free status, successful freedom seekers, such as the enslaved couple Ellen and William Craft, found ingenious ways to evade detection. The Crafts, who left a plantation in Macon, Georgia, in 1848, escaped by passing off the light-skinned Ellen as a sickly young enslaver traveling north to seek medical attention. Her husband played the role of the young invalid's faithful attendant. With Ellen swathed in bandages and pretending to be too ill to speak, the couple rode by train to Savannah, where they boarded a steamship bound for Philadelphia. A year later, the enslaved tobacco factory worker Henry "Box" Brown made an equally daring escape from Richmond. With help from a sympathetic white shopkeeper, Brown had himself shipped to Philadelphia in a large wooden crate, which traveled by steamboat, rail, ferry, and delivery wagon before finally arriving at its destination twenty-seven hours later. Such escapes were well publicized, leaving white southerners ever more vigilant.

Deposited January 10. 1850.
THE RESURRECTION OF HENRY BOX BROWN AT PHILADELPHIA.
Who escaped from Richmond Va. in a Box 3 feet long 2½ ft. deep and 2 ft wide.

Henry "Box" Brown
Henry "Box" Brown, a man enslaved in Virginia, made a daring escape by having himself shipped to Philadelphia in a crate. His example serves as one of the more creative and surprising examples of enslaved people's determination to be free. After winning his freedom, Brown published an autobiography and became a popular abolitionist speaker and entertainer. Some abolitionists, however, including Frederick Douglass, disapproved of Brown's disclosure of his escape method, feeling that it prevented other enslaved people from escaping by similar means. ◣ **Why is Brown featured in the box in this depiction? What does this image, and Douglass's reaction to it, reveal about the audience for Brown's story?** *Library of Congress, Prints and Photographs Division, Washington, D.C., LC-USZCN4-225.*

Enslaved people who lived in or traveled through border states and territories had the best chance to escape because of their proximity to free soil. Enslaved people in Kentucky could cross the Ohio River to seek freedom to the north, while those in Missouri could try their luck in Iowa or Illinois. These enslaved people were also much closer to the **Underground Railroad**, a network of Black and white antislavery activists who routinely sheltered freedom seekers. But to contact the Underground Railroad, enslaved people first had to elude patrollers, slave catchers, and the hunting dogs white southerners used to track them down.

AP® exam tip
Be sure you can describe the role and scale of the Underground Railroad.

Underground Railroad
A network of antislavery activists who helped freedom seekers escape to the North and Canada.

Family ties kept many enslaved people from attempting escape. Most successful freedom seekers were young men from the Upper South and border states who, in addition to being strong enough to withstand the trek, were either childless or already separated from their families due to sale or migration. They also had a better chance of traveling undetected because planters typically employed young enslaved men to run errands. Women, by contrast, were far less likely to be given jobs that took them away from their enslavers' property. Childbearing and motherhood limited their options even further. Enslaved women bore an average of seven children, beginning in their late teens, and spent much of their twenties and thirties either pregnant or nursing. They maintained close ties with their children through to adulthood and frequently cared for grandchildren when they became too old to work in the fields. Few women were willing to escape without their offspring, and few freedom seekers made it far when accompanied by children. Female freedom seekers who traveled with children could not "walk so far or so fast as scores of *men* that are constantly leaving," one Underground Railroad volunteer observed, while another estimated that such women were three times more likely to be caught than men who traveled alone.[25]

AP® skills

Applying Disciplinary Knowledge: What unique challenges did Black women face when attempting to self-liberate?

Survival, Community, and Culture

What role did religious services and churches play in daily forms of resistance to slavery?

How did enslaved African Americans adapt African musical elements from their ancestors and influence the development of American musical genres?

Since permanent escape was not a viable option for most unfree African Americans, they increasingly turned to Christianity to help them bear slavery's hardships. They also counted on fellow enslaved people. Most nineteenth-century enslaved people lived and worked on holdings large enough to sustain small enslaved communities. As of 1850, 73.4 percent of all enslaved people were held in bondage by planters who enslaved ten or more people, and 51.6 percent were enslaved by planters who held more than twenty people in bondage. Work took up much of their time and fostered bonds among enslaved laborers, who often worked in gender-segregated work gangs. Meanwhile, even though African American families were often scattered by sale, kinship remained central to enslaved people's cultural and social life, and family ties were extensive and resilient. Enslaved people sustained loving relationships with relatives and created new connections with nonrelatives to endure life under slavery and seek refuge from complete domination by their enslavers.

Religion

By the early 1800s, many enslaved communities had embraced evangelical Christianity, but young enslaved people received much of their religious education in the slave quarters rather than in church. Drawn to the emotional forms of worship common in

Baptist and Methodist revivals and churches, African Americans continued to favor these denominations over Presbyterian and Episcopal churches, where Sunday services tended to be more restrained. They rarely relied solely on white religious leaders for guidance, however. In rural areas, many Blacks lacked access to religious services, and even in areas where churches were more plentiful, enslavers did not always permit enslaved people to attend church. (See AP® Working with Sources: Testimony of Enslaved People, pp. 242–249.)

Even Blacks who worshipped alongside whites or received religious instruction from their enslavers tended to distrust white Christianity. Relegated to segregated pews or sometimes required to listen to the minister's sermon from outside the church, African Americans had few opportunities to worship on equal terms. In the "white folks' church," one formerly enslaved person remembered, the enslaved "couldn't do nuthin' — jes sit dere. Dey could sing, an' take de sacrement; but didn't have no voice — jes like animals!"[26] The character of the religious instruction that enslaved people received made matters worse. White ministers often stressed obedience and humility, with popular teachings centering on scriptural passages such as "Servants be obedient to their masters" and "Let as many servants as are under the yoke count their own masters worthy of all honor." Enslaved people understood the obvious self-interest animating such teachings. As the formerly enslaved Wes Brady recalled, "You ought to have heard that 'Hellish' preaching. . . . 'Obey your Master and Mistress, don't steal chickens, don't steal eggs and meat,' and nary word 'bout having a soul to save."[27]

AP® skills

Applying Disciplinary Knowledge: Why did Black people tend to distrust white Christianity during this time period?

Rather than accept the instruction of white ministers, enslaved Blacks across the South often belonged to what historians have termed the **invisible church**. Enslaved Christianity stressed the equality of all men under God, drawing on the Bible as inspiration for spirituals that expressed enslaved people's own humanity, capacity for freedom, and hope of justice for an oppressed people. Enslaved people also embraced scriptural stories that held out the promise of liberation under a just God. Their favorite was the Old Testament's book of Exodus, which tells of how Moses freed the children of Israel from slavery in Egypt. This story was celebrated in slave spirituals such as "Go Down, Moses," which drew a direct parallel between the enslavement of African Americans and the enslavement of the Israelites. "Go down, Moses," its chorus commanded, "Away down to Egypt's land, / And tell King Pharaoh / To let my people go."

invisible church
A term used to describe groups of enslaved African Americans who met in secret for Christian worship.

Enslaved people gathered in their homes to hold their own religious ceremonies or assembled in secret "hush harbors" in the woods. Often led by community elders, these ceremonies might incorporate African spiritual practices such as juju and voodoo. Most common was the **ring shout**, often known simply as the "shout." In this form of worship, congregants formed a circle and moved counterclockwise while shuffling their feet, clapping, singing, calling out, or praying aloud. Practiced in both the West Indies and North America, the ring shout combined West African–based music and dance traditions with the passionate Protestantism of the Second Great Awakening to create a powerful new ritual that offered emotional and physical release. The formerly enslaved Mose Hursey, who witnessed these ceremonies as a child in Red River, Texas, recalled,

ring shout
A religious ritual developed by enslaved people in the West Indies and North America that involved forming a circle and shuffling counter-clockwise while singing and praying.

A Plantation Burial
Enslaved people gather at sunset in a secluded forest for a funeral on the plantation of Mississippi governor Tilghman Tucker. A Black preacher, at center, delivers an emotional address to the mourners; before him is the casket, and in the foreground is the dug grave. In the distance on the right, a white couple — presumably the governor and his wife — is hidden among the trees. **How does this painting portray the significance of religious practices for enslaved people?** *GL Archive/Alamy Stock Photo.*

"I heard them [enslaved people] get up with a powerful force of spirit, clappin' they hands and walking around the place. They'd shout, 'I got the glory. I got the old time religion in my heart.'"[28] The expressive, rhythmic music produced during the shouts lives on today in musical genres such as the blues and gospel.

Gender, Age, and Work

In communities forbidden any form of formal education, family structures allowed enslaved people to pass on wisdom, knowledge, and skills from one generation to the next. Enslaved elders usually played a vital role in schooling their communities. Few could teach their young people to read or write because literacy was discouraged or banned for enslaved people in the southern states. But elderly enslaved people passed on other valuable lessons to youngsters, such as how to handle their enslavers, negotiate with overseers and other white authorities, and resolve disputes within their quarters. Generally respected for their extensive life experience, many served as the spiritual leaders of their communities as well.

Older enslaved people taught younger ones the agricultural techniques used to cultivate the planters' crops and the gardens that sustained enslaved families. They also helped young people master other survival skills. Adult men taught young boys how to fish, hunt, and forage for food, and women taught girls how to cook, sew, clean, take care of children, and help deliver babies. These tasks were not strictly divided by gender. Frederick Douglass recalled that his grandmother was not only a skilled nurse but also "a capital hand at making nets for catching shad and herring" and equally good at using her nets to catch these fish.[29] Children of both sexes performed housework and took care of other children. But once they were old enough for adult labor, typically at puberty, girls and boys often worked separately and learned different tasks.

Although enslaved people both worked in the fields on plantations regardless of their gender, tasks were commonly divided by gender. Field hands were usually split into sex-segregated work gangs and assigned different work regimes. Women were classified as three-quarters of a hand (rather than as a full hand), and on plantations with sufficient male workers, women were spared some of the most physically taxing labor. During planting season, women hoed the fields, and men plowed. When enslaved workers erected fences, the men split the rails, and the women assembled the fences.

When additional labor was needed, however, enslaved women might be assigned to any task. On Louisiana sugar plantations, for example, female work gangs toiled alongside male gangs. They worked sixty to seventy hours per week, under conditions that compromised their capacity to conceive, deliver, and nurture healthy children. Whereas enslaved populations grew swiftly throughout the rest of the South, in southeastern Louisiana, the natural growth rate among enslaved people declined by 13 percent per decade. During the grinding season, when enslaved people of both sexes worked almost around the clock cutting cane for the sugar mills, and during planting, which involved hand-planting thousands of seed cane stems, women had trouble conceiving and carrying babies to term. In addition, the cane workers' spare diet of salt pork, molasses, and corn bread did not supply women with enough calories or vitamins to have healthy babies or, in some cases, even sustain their fertility. Stillbirths and miscarriages were common, and many infants died. One woman named Rachel, who worked on Joseph Kleinpeter's Variety Plantation in Louisiana, gave birth to nine children between 1836 and 1849, and only four of them survived. Such losses were psychologically devastating for enslaved women, whose numerous pregnancies and miscarriages often took place under conditions that could be lethal to their own health. "My ma died 'bout three hours after I was born," noted the formerly enslaved Edward De Bieuw. She was hoeing cane when she went into labor, he explained, and "she told the driver she was sick; he told her to just hoe-right-on. Soon, I was born, and my ma die[d] a few minutes after dey brung her to the house."[30]

AP® skills

Applying Disciplinary Knowledge: Describe the tasks "work gangs" were forced to do.

Wealthy Louisiana sugar planters could afford to purchase new enslaved people when theirs did not reproduce, but planters elsewhere generally had a vested interest in encouraging enslaved reproduction. Some enslavers reduced the daily work required of pregnant and nursing women, reclassifying them as one-half hands rather than three-quarter hands and assigning them to lighter tasks. Some enslavers also increased their food allotment. Such measures helped maintain a robust rate of reproduction throughout much of the antebellum South.

Many enslavers and overseers were convinced that Black women were naturally immune to the rigors of pregnancy, which often kept white women confined to their beds for months. One Mississippi planter told a northern visitor that the exercise that Black women received performing field work spared them "the difficulty, danger, and pain which attended women of the better classes in giving birth to their offspring." Such beliefs often made enslavers quick to suspect enslaved people who were pregnant or nursing of faking or "playing the lady" when they complained of pain or fatigue.[31] Some even whipped pregnant enslaved women, and such whippings were common enough that enslavers developed a special method for administering them. According to one formerly enslaved person, enslaved pregnant women were made to "lie face down in a specially dug depression in the ground," which protected the fetus while the mother was abused.[32]

AP® skills

Applying Disciplinary Knowledge: Why did enslavers have a vested interest in encouraging enslaved people to reproduce? To what extent was this interest reflected in enslavers' treatment of pregnant enslaved women?

Sent back to work shortly after giving birth, enslaved women then had to juggle infant care and the grueling labor regime. Some field workers, such as William Wells Brown's mother, were allowed no time to nurse and thus were forced to carry their infants with them in the fields. Even when pregnant or nurturing newborns, enslaved women faced many hours of domestic work upon returning home, where they had to feed their families, take care of their children, and tend to domestic tasks such as sewing and housecleaning. Enslaved men often supplemented their families' meager diets by catching game and fish, raising vegetables, and keeping domestic animals such as pigs and chickens. But women performed much of the domestic labor in the slave quarters.

Enslaved women shouldered their burdens by taking care of one another and developing a sense of independence that made them more similar to their husbands than were most antebellum wives. Whereas freemen of that era had considerable power over their wives' behavior and possessions, enslaved men had virtually no authority over enslaved women. Black men were not breadwinners and often performed the same kind of work as their wives. Gender norms in the quarters, therefore, tended to recognize Black men and women as equal partners with similar abilities.

Marriage and Family

Southern courts never recognized enslaved marriages because, according to slave codes, enslaved people were " 'not ranked among sentient beings, but among things,' and things are not married."[33] In practice, however, enslaved African Americans courted, loved, and formed lasting unions. Enslaved couples came together and remained together largely at the discretion of their enslavers, many of whom had little interest in their happiness. Enslavers were anxious for enslaved women to reproduce and for enslaved men to be tied down by family loyalties; they generally encouraged their slaves to marry informally and often conducted the ceremonies themselves.

"The marsters married the slaves without any papers," a formerly enslaved man named John Bectom remembered. "All they did was to say . . . 'Frank, I pronounce you and Jane man and wife.' "[34] Some enslavers hosted big weddings for enslaved people, even hiring preachers to lead the ceremonies. Such weddings were popular among the enslaved, who regarded them as occasions for celebration. Many years after slavery ended, the formerly enslaved man Richard Moring still had good memories of the weddings held on his enslaver's North Carolina plantation. "When dere wus a weddin' dar wus fun fer all," he recalled. "Dey wus all dressed up in new clothes, an' marster's dinin' room wus decorated wid flowers fer de 'casion. . . . De preacher married 'em up good an' tight jist lak he done de white folks."[35] But wedding ceremonies were not always officiated by enslavers, and some took place within the slave quarters.[36]

However they were celebrated, enslaved unions lacked the sanctity, and sometimes even the consensual character, of marriages among whites. Sexual partners could be imposed on enslaved people in appallingly brutal ways. Louisa Everett's marriage began when her enslaver came into her cabin with an enslaved man named Sam and forced Sam to undress. According to Louisa, her enslaver then asked her, " 'Do you think you can stand this big nigger?' He had that old bull whip flung acrost his

A Wedding of Enslaved People
This early photograph was taken at a wedding of enslaved people at Hurricane Plantation, a five-thousand-acre estate on the Mississippi River that enslaved more than three hundred people. Hurricane's enslaver prided himself on being enlightened, as he supported community gatherings. **How does this image showcase the experiences of enslaved people?** *J. Mack Moore Collection/Old Court Jouse Museum, Vicksburg, MS.*

shoulder, and Lawd, that man could hit so hard! So I jes said 'yassur, I guess so,' and tried to hide my face so I couldn't see Sam's nakedness, but he made me look at him anyhow. Well he told us what we must git busy and do in his presence, and we had to do it. After that we were considered man and wife. Me and Sam was a healthy pair and had fine, big babies, so I never had another man forced on me, thank God. Sam was kind to me and I learnt to love him."[37] Of course, not all enslaved women could say the same. When Rose Williams was sixteen, she was told to share a cabin occupied by an enslaved man named Rufus, whose sexual advances she did not welcome. When she complained to her enslaver, he threatened to beat her if she did not have sex with Rufus. He had paid "big money" for her, he said, "cause I wants you to raise me childrens."[38]

All enslaved women, single or married, were vulnerable to sexual abuse, and enslaved men could offer them little protection from white men's sexual advances. "WHY does the slave ever love?" wrote the freedom seeker Harriet Jacobs when she learned that, in order to keep her as his mistress, her enslaver had rebuffed the free Black carpenter who wished to marry her and buy her freedom.[39] Such abuses were so common that one critic of slavery charged that "one of the reasons why wicked men in the South uphold slavery is the facility which it affords for a licentious life."[40] These violations also complicated the family ties between enslaved couples and their children. Enslaved men ended up raising children who were not their own, and fatherless children were all too common. Henry Bibb never knew his father, Kentucky state senator James Bibb, but he grew up knowing that he and his seven brothers were all children of enslavers, none of whom prevented any of them from being bought and sold.

AP® skills

Applying Disciplinary Knowledge: How does Harriet Jacobs's recounting of her experience on this page illustrate the unique vulnerabilities and injustices faced by enslaved women?

Not all enslaved families were the products of an owner's coercion, however. The prevalence of marriages between enslaved people on different plantations, known as **abroad marriages**, suggests that many enslavers allowed enslaved people to choose their own partners. Though never particularly popular with enslavers, such marriages may have accounted for as many as a third of all enslaved marriages in mid-nineteenth-century South Carolina.[41] Abroad marriages required a strong commitment because enslaved men had to secure their enslavers' permission to visit their wives and then brave the slave patrols en route. "My pa would have to git a pass to come see my mammy. He sometimes come without a pass," recalled the formerly enslaved Millie Barbie.[42] But these marriages had the advantage of sheltering spouses from witnessing their loved ones' harsh treatment. Newly married Henry Bibb was initially happy to be purchased by Mr. Gatewood, who owned his wife, Malinda, but he soon found himself "much dissatisfied," because "to live where I must be eye witness to her insults, scourgings and abuses, such as are common to be inflicted upon slaves, was more than I could bear."[43]

abroad marriages Marriages between enslaved people who belonged to different enslavers and lived on different plantations.

Parenthood posed similar dilemmas for the enslaved, whose children could be disciplined or brutalized by their enslavers. The abuse of Bibb's daughter

Mary Frances made his family life under slavery still more unbearable. Once the child grew old enough to be weaned, her parents were no longer permitted to look after her during the day. Instead, they had to work in the fields, leaving their little girl in the home of a cruel and impatient plantation mistress who would often "slap with her hand the face of little Frances, for crying after her mother,

An Enslaved Family in a Georgia Cotton Field, c. 1860
Taken shortly before the Civil War, this photograph shows a family of enslaved people picking cotton on a plantation outside Savannah. Cotton picking typically required the labor of the entire family, including young children. **What is the historical significance of this photograph? What does it reveal about the gang or task system of labor?** *Private Collection/Peter Newark American Pictures/Bridgeman Images.*

until her little face was left black and blue." As much as he loved his daughter, Bibb also regretted fatherhood, stating that he "could never look upon the dear child without being filled with sorrow and fearful apprehensions . . . because she was a slave, regarded as property."[44]

Although enslaved adults had little control over the actions of their enslavers, they did their best to shield their children from abuse. Some subjected their family's children to physical punishment at home, in the hopes of mitigating any punishment administered by an enslaver, as Eliza Adams found out when she sought out her grandmother after a conflict with her enslaver. Believing that her grandmother might protect her from punishment, Adams was surprised to receive a whipping from her instead. Enslaved adults also tried to protect children by teaching them to stay out of trouble. Children learned to obey their enslavers at an early age and received careful instruction on the intricacies of their region's racial etiquette, like stepping aside for white people and not doing anything that might irritate or alarm them. Aware that children are naturally curious, enslaved parents taught their offspring never to be caught staring at whites or, worse still, eavesdropping on their conversations. But enslaved children, who were barely noticed by whites, could also amass valuable information, and their elders instructed them in the fine art of "listenin widout no ears en seein widout no eyes," as the formerly enslaved Julia Woodberry put it.[45]

fictive kin
People regarded as family even though they were not related by blood or marriage.

Enslaved children also received protection and advice from enslaved people who did not have the opportunity to raise their own children. Although African American family members were frequently scattered by sale, family units remained important even when their members were not united by blood. African Americans who lost their kinfolk to sale or migration often created new family connections by embracing nonrelatives as **fictive kin**. Orphaned children were taken in by nonrelatives, as young Laura Clark learned when she and her mother were sold to different enslavers. Although bereft at the loss of her daughter, Laura's mother acted quickly to secure a substitute parent. According to Laura, her mother asked a woman who had been sold to the same enslaver to "take kier of my baby Chile . . . and if fen I never sees her no mo' raise her for God."[46] Young migrant teenagers likewise claimed older enslaved people as foster parents and grandparents. When such migrants had children of their own, they named them after both the family members they had left behind and their adopted relatives. These new family ties eased, but did not erase, the pain felt by enslaved people separated from their families by sale.

CONCLUSION
Surviving Slavery

Whether a matter of blood or otherwise, families helped African Americans survive and endure slavery. These powerful social ties united an enslaved people who had originated in many different West African societies and survived the Middle

Passage, only to form new communities that also fell prey to slavery and sale. As one prominent scholar has put it, throughout "generations of captivity," African Americans endured by building communities strong enough to overcome these adversities.[47] Enslaved communities nurtured their children, cherished their elders, passed down African traditions, and provided members with a supportive environment.

No amount of community, however, could spare enslaved Blacks from slavery's worst sorrows. Enslaved families lived in constant fear of separation by sale. Most enslaved people faced terrible hardships on a daily basis, working long hours under grueling conditions. They were subjected to brutal corporal punishment meted out not only by their enslavers but also by other whites, such as overseers and employers. Enslaved parents could not protect their children from such punishment or other forms of mistreatment, and enslaved spouses could not defend each other in the face of whippings and sexual abuse.

Enslaved people often resisted such abuses, but their resistance was usually covert. Enslaved rebels who offered direct physical opposition to their oppressors rarely survived their confrontations. Truancy as well as more serious escape attempts were common, as were stealing and avoiding work. Supervised by their enslavers and overseers during the day and watched by armed patrollers at night, most enslaved people had few opportunities to plan any form of organized resistance, and those who attempted it were often caught in the act. Still, African American resistance to slavery could never be completely suppressed. Successful slave insurrections or advanced plots, when they did occur, further illuminated the impossibility of completely silencing Black dissent.

Antebellum enslaved communities sustained their hopes for freedom by embracing an egalitarian form of Christianity that assured them that all people were equal under God. In addition to providing spiritual comfort and emotional release, enslaved people's religion nourished freedom dreams by emphasizing biblical texts such as the book of Exodus. As sectional struggles increasingly pitted the free North against the slave South, enslaved African Americans began to cherish more secular hopes for freedom as well. Joined by a growing cadre of Black abolitionists in the North, they kept a close, hopeful watch on the widening rift between white northerners and southerners, and they stood ready to cast off their chains should freedom ever come.

CHAPTER 6 REVIEW ▸ PRACTICING AP® SKILLS

AP® ESSENTIAL VOCABULARY AND SOURCES

**Essential terms and required sources from the AP® Course are marked with an asterisk.*

Missouri Compromise (1820) p. 212
Indian Removal Act (1830) p. 213
Black Seminoles **(*Gopher John*, a Black Seminole leader and interpreter, 1863)*** p. 214
Second Great Awakening p. 223
gag rule p. 224
Amistad **case*** p. 224
Creole **insurrection*** p. 225
truant p. 226
lying out p. 226
Harriet Tubman **(Photographs of Harriet Tubman Throughout Her Life: Matte Collodion Print of Harriet Tubman, 1871–1876)*** p. 226
North Star p. 228
Underground Railroad* p. 229
invisible church p. 231
ring shout* p. 231
abroad marriages p. 236
fictive kin p. 238

APPLYING DISCIPLINARY KNOWLEDGE: ESSENTIAL QUESTIONS

1. Discuss the deepening political, economic, social, and slavery-related divisions between the North and South in the years 1820 to 1860. How was each region becoming more distinctive, and how were the two regions becoming more opposed to each other? In what ways did the two regions remain linked despite the growing divide between them?
2. How did the actions of Denmark Vesey, Nat Turner, David Walker, and the enslaved people aboard the *Amistad* and the *Creole* resonate throughout the country? Compare the effects of their actions in the North and in the South and discuss the implications for enslaved and free Blacks. What do these effects and implications tell you about the state of the nation during this period?
3. Discuss the various types of enslaved resistance. How did individual enslaved people's circumstances — their age, gender, location, or skill level, for example — make it more or less difficult to defy their enslavers or escape permanently?
4. How did gender affect enslaved people's experiences? In what ways were enslaved women's hardships different from enslaved men's? In what ways were enslaved women and men arguably more equal than white women and men of this period?

SUGGESTED REFERENCES

The Expansion and Consolidation of Slavery

Baptist, Edward E. *The Half Has Never Been Told: Slavery and the Making of American Capitalism.* New York: Basic Books, 2014.

Berry, Daina Ramey. *The Price for Their Pound of Flesh: The Value of the Enslaved, from Womb to Grave, in the Building of a Nation.* Boston: Beacon Press, 2017.

Campbell, Randolph B. *An Empire for Slavery: The Peculiar Institution in Texas, 1821–1865.* Baton Rouge: LSU Press, 1991.

Deyle, Steven. *Carry Me Back: The Domestic Slave Trade in American Life.* New York: Oxford University Press, 2006.

Follett, Richard. *The Sugar Masters: Planters and Slaves in Louisiana's Cane World, 1820–1860.* Baton Rouge: LSU Press, 2007.

Johnson, Walter. *Soul by Soul: Life Inside the Antebellum Slave Market.* Cambridge: Harvard University Press, 1999.

Morrison, Michael A. *Slavery and the American West: The Eclipse of Manifest Destiny.* Chapel Hill: University of North Carolina Press, 1997.

Rothman, Adam. *Slave Country: American Expansion and the Origins of the Deep South.* Cambridge: Harvard University Press, 2005.

Black Challenges to Slavery

Aptheker, Herbert. *American Negro Slave Revolts*, 5th ed. New York: International Publishers, 1983.

Dillon, Merton L. *Slavery Attacked: Southern States and Their Allies, 1619–1865.* Baton Rouge: LSU Press, 1991.

Egerton, Douglas R. *He Shall Go Out Free: The Lives of Denmark Vesey.* Lanham, MD: Rowman & Littlefield, 2004.

Greenberg, Kenneth S., ed. *Nat Turner: A Slave Rebellion in History and Memory.* New York: Oxford University Press, 2003.

Hinks, Peter P. *To Awaken My Afflicted Brethren: David Walker and the Problem of Antebellum Slave Resistance.* University Park: Pennsylvania State University Press, 1997.

Jones, Howard. *Mutiny on the* Amistad*: The Saga of a Slave Revolt and Its Impact on American Abolition, Law, and Diplomacy.* New York: Oxford University Press, 1997.

Kly, Y. N., ed. *The Invisible War: The African American Anti-Slavery Resistance from the Stono Rebellion through the Seminole Wars.* Atlanta: Clarity Press, 2006.

Rucker, Walter C. *The River Flows On: Black Resistance, Culture, and Identity Formation in Early America.* Baton Rouge: LSU Press, 2006.

Everyday Resistance to Slavery

Berry, Daina Ramey. *"Swing the Sickle for the Harvest Is Ripe": Gender and Slavery in Antebellum Georgia.* Urbana: University of Illinois Press, 2007.

Camp, Stephanie M. H. *Closer to Freedom: Enslaved Women and Everyday Resistance in the Plantation South.* Chapel Hill: University of North Carolina Press, 2004.

Franklin, John Hope, and Loren Schweninger. *Runaway Slaves: Rebels on the Plantation.* New York: Oxford University Press, 1999.

Glymph, Thavolia. *Out of the House of Bondage: The Transformation of the Plantation Household.* Cambridge: Cambridge University Press, 2008.

Jones, Norrece T., Jr. *Born a Child of Freedom, Yet a Slave: Mechanisms of Control and Strategies of Resistance in Antebellum South Carolina.* Hanover: University Press of New England/Wesleyan University Press, 1990.

McLaurin, Melton A. *Celia, a Slave.* New York: Avon, 1999.

Rivers, Larry Eugene. *Rebels and Runaways: Slave Resistance in Nineteenth-Century Florida.* Urbana: University of Illinois Press, 2012.

Schermerhorn, Calvin. *Money over Mastery, Family over Freedom: Slavery in the Antebellum Upper South.* Baltimore: Johns Hopkins University Press, 2011.

Webber, Thomas L. *Deep Like the Rivers: Education in the Slave Quarter Community, 1831–1865.* New York: Norton, 1978.

Survival, Community, and Culture

Blassingame, John W. *The Slave Community: Plantation Life in the Antebellum South*, rev. ed. New York: Oxford University Press, 1979.

Fett, Sharla M. *Working Cures: Healing, Health, and Power on Southern Slave Plantations.* Chapel Hill: University of North Carolina Press, 2002.

Hunter, Tera W. *Bound in Wedlock: Slave and Free Black Marriage in the Nineteenth Century.* Cambridge: Harvard University Press, 2017.

Irons, Charles F. *The Origins of Proslavery Christianity: White and Black Evangelicals in Colonial and Antebellum Virginia.* Chapel Hill: University of North Carolina Press, 2008.

Kaye, Anthony E. *Joining Places: Slave Neighborhoods in the Old South.* Chapel Hill: University of North Carolina Press, 2009.

Levine, Lawrence W. *Black Culture and Black Consciousness: Afro-American Folk Thought from Slavery to Freedom.* New York: Oxford University Press, 1978.

Raboteau, Albert J. *Slave Religion: The "Invisible Institution" in the Antebellum South.* New York: Oxford University Press, 1978.

Schwartz, Marie Jenkins. *Born in Bondage: Growing Up Enslaved in the Antebellum South.* Cambridge: Harvard University Press, 2001.

West, Emily. *Chains of Love: Slave Couples in Antebellum South Carolina.* Urbana: University of Illinois Press, 2004.

White, Deborah Gray. *Ar'n't I a Woman? Female Slaves in the Plantation South*, rev. ed. New York: Norton, 1999.

Testimony of Enslaved People

Enslaved African Americans had few opportunities to express their views on slavery. Rarely permitted to learn to read or write, they were usually unable to record their stories even after slavery was abolished. Some formerly enslaved people, such as William Wells Brown and Frederick Douglass, published autobiographies known as fugitive slave narratives. Often written with the help of white editors, these book-length works constitute some of the richest testimony we have about the enslaved experience. Such narratives must, however, be read with caution, with an eye toward the influence white editors might have had on the Black authors.

Similar interpretive issues relate to shorter documents that shed light on the enslaved experience. "Slave Punishment" provides a visual representation of the brutal treatment described in slave narratives such as Brown's. Lewis Clarke's questions and answers about slavery follow. A freedom seeker from Kentucky, Clarke describes slavery from his personal experience. The next document excerpted here is from the memoir of Bethany, who was enslaved in Virginia from birth until her purchase as an adult by a northerner; her story was recorded by "M.W.G.," who notes in the preface to the memoir that the "language and personal characteristics of Bethany cannot be transcribed," but the narrative is an "unvarnished tale."[48] The last document is an excerpt from an interview with the formerly enslaved Mary Reynolds, one of more than 2,300 formerly enslaved people interviewed between 1936 and 1938 under the Federal Writers' Project. Part of the federally funded Works Progress Administration (WPA), this Great Depression–era initiative employed mostly white writers and journalists, whom the elderly formerly enslaved people often regarded with suspicion. Even so, the interviews provide a crucial record of more than two thousand individuals' perspectives on slavery.

key point

These narratives all convey the experiences of formerly enslaved people. However, many reached audiences via white editors or interviewers. Keep in mind what influence or effect white editors or interviewers may have had on the accounts and perspectives shared. Even so, these documents provide a crucial record of the firsthand experience of enslavement.

AP® argumentation

DBQ Practice: Explain how the testimonies of enslaved Africans and African Americans impacted the narrative of chattel slavery in America. Use at least two of the documents to support your response.

DOCUMENT 1 *Slave Punishment*

Enslaved people of all ages, male and female, endured a wide range of horrific abuses. Difficult as these were to bear individually, they were made all the worse when enslaved people had to witness the cruel treatment of their loved ones. This early-nineteenth-century engraving depicts a group of enslaved people of all ages enduring different kinds of physical abuse, suffering alone as well as witnessing others' pain. At the far right, a young man tries to shield two children from the whip, attempting to halt their tormentor with a gesture.

Content note: This document includes a graphic depiction of violence.

Breaking it Down As you read, consider what factors may have shaped the perspective of the artist. What details reveal the artist's perspective?

Snark/Art Resource, NY.

DOCUMENT 2 Lewis Clarke | *Questions and Answers about Slavery, 1845*

Born into slavery in Kentucky, LEWIS GARRARD CLARKE (1815–1897) escaped to Canada in 1841 and eventually resettled in Ohio. He became an antislavery lecturer, sharing the story of his life under slavery with audiences across the Northeast. Clarke also published his autobiography, and in one of the book's appendices, he supplemented his life story with a series of answers to the questions that audiences most frequently asked him about slavery.

Breaking it Down What does this document reveal about the impact of the system of slavery on the family structure of the enslaved? What is significant about the audience for this source, and what does that tell you about its purpose?

The following questions are often asked me, when I meet the people in public, and I have thought it would be well to put down the answers here.

How many holidays in a year do the slaves in Kentucky have? — They usually have six days at Christmas, and two or three others in the course of the year. Public opinion generally seems to require this much of slaveholders; a few give more, some less; some *none*, not a day nor an hour.

How do slaves spend the Sabbath? — Every way the master pleases. There are certain kinds of work which are respectable for Sabbath day. Slaves are often sent out to salt the cattle, collect and count the pigs and sheep, mend fences, drive the stock from one pasture to another. Breaking young horses and mules, to send them to market, yoking young oxen, and training them, is proper Sabbath work; piling and burning brush, on the back part of the lot, grubbing brier patches that are out of the way, and where they will not be seen. Sometimes corn must be shelled in the corn-crib; hemp is baled in the hemp-house. The still-house must be attended on the Sabbath. In these, and various other such like employments, the more avaricious slaveholders keep their slaves busy a good part of every Sabbath. It is a great day for visiting and eating, and the house servants often have more to do on that than on any other day. . . .

What proportion of slaves attend church on the Sabbath? — In the country, not *more* than *one in ten on an average.*

How many slaves have you ever known that could read? — I never saw more than three or four that could properly read at all. I never saw but one that could write.

What do slaves know about the Bible? — They generally believe there is somewhere a real Bible, that came from God; but they frequently say the Bible now used is master's Bible; most that they hear from it being, "Servants, obey your masters."

Are families often separated? How many such cases have you personally known? — *I never knew a whole family to live together till all were grown up, in my life.* There is almost always, in every family, some one or more keen and bright, or else sullen and stubborn slave, whose influence they are afraid of on the rest of the family, and such a one must take a walking ticket to the south.

There are other causes of separation. The death of a large owner is the occasion usually of many families being broken up. Bankruptcy is another cause of separation, and the hard-heartedness of a majority of slaveholders another and a more fruitful cause than either or all the rest. *Generally* there is but little more scruple about separating families than there is with a man who keeps sheep in selling off the lambs in the fall.

SOURCE: Lewis Garrard Clarke, *Narratives of the Sufferings of Lewis and Milton Clarke, Sons of a Soldier of the Revolution, during a Captivity of More Than Twenty Years among the Slaveholders of Kentucky, One of the So Called Christian States of North America* (Boston: Bela Marsh, 1846), 103–5.

DOCUMENT 3 Bethany Veney | *Narrative of Bethany Veney, a Slave Woman, 1889*

BETHANY VENEY (1815–1916) was born into slavery in Virginia in 1815. She was eventually purchased by a northern businessman, who sent her to his home in Rhode Island; she lived the rest of her life as a freed person in New England. Veney's memoir, written more than twenty years after the end of the Civil War, offers a rare first-person narrative by an enslaved woman. When this excerpt begins, she is living in the household of David Kibbler, brother-in-law of her enslaver Lucy Fletcher. Bethany's husband had recently been sold south.

Breaking it Down As you read this document, consider the perspective of Veney compared to that of Clarke (p. 233). What aspects of these documents point to areas of similarity in their experiences? Is there anywhere each author's perspective on their experiences differ?

Several months passed, and I became a mother.

My dear white lady, in your pleasant home made joyous by the tender love of husband and children all your own, you can never understand the slave mother's emotions as she clasps her newborn child, and knows that a master's word can at any moment take it from her embrace; and when, as was mine, that child is a girl, and from her own experience she sees its almost certain doom is to minister to the unbridled lust of the slave-owner, and feels that the law holds over her no protecting arm, it is not strange that, rude and uncultured as I was, I felt all this, and would have been glad if we could have died together there and then.

Master Kibbler was still hard and cruel, and I was in constant trouble. Miss Lucy was kind as ever, and it grieved her to see me unhappy. At last, she told me that perhaps, if I should have some other home and some other master, I should not be so wretched, and, if I chose, I might look about and see what I could do. I soon heard that John Prince, at Luray, was wanting to buy a woman. Miss Lucy told me, if it was agreeable to me, I might go to him and work for a fortnight, and if at the end of that time he wanted me, and I chose to stay, she would arrange terms with him; but, if I did not want to stay, not to believe anything that any one might tell me, but come back at once to her.

At the end of two weeks, Master John said he was going over to have a talk with Miss Lucy; and did I think, if he should conclude to buy me, that I should steal from him? I answered that, if I worked for him, I ought to expect him to give me enough to eat, and then I should have no need to steal. "You wouldn't want me to go over yonder, into the garden of another man, and steal his chickens, when I am working for you, would you, Master John? I expect, of course, you will give me enough to eat and to wear, and then I shall have no reason to steal from anybody." He seemed satisfied and pleased, and bargained with Miss Lucy, both for me and my little girl. Both master and Mrs. Prince were kind and pleasant to me, and my little Charlotte played with the little Princes, and had a good time. I worked very hard, but I was strong and well, and willing to work; and for several years there was little to interrupt this state of things.

At last, I can't say how long, I was told that John O'Neile, the jailer, had bought me; and he soon took me to his home, which was in one part of the jail. He, however, was not the real purchaser. This was David McCoy. . . . and he had bought me with the idea of taking me to Richmond, thinking he could make a speculation on me. I was well known in all the parts around as a faithful, hard-working woman, when well treated, but ugly and wilful, if abused beyond a certain point. McCoy had bought me away from my child; and now, he thought, he could sell me, if carried to Richmond, at a good advantage. I did not think so; and I determined, if possible, to disappoint him. . . .

I had never in my life felt so sad and so completely forsaken. I thought my heart was really breaking. Mr. O'Neile called me; and, as I passed out of the door, I heard Jackoline, the jailer's daughter, singing in a loud, clear voice, -

> *"When through the deep waters I call thee to go,*
> *The rivers of woe shall not thee overflow;*
> *For I will be with thee, and cause thee to stand,*
> *Upheld by my righteous, omnipotent hand."*

I can never forget the impression these *words* and the *music* and the tones of Jackoline's voice made upon me. It seemed to me as if they all came directly out of heaven. It was my Saviour speaking directly to me. Was not *I* passing the deep waters? What rivers of woe could be sorer than these through which I was passing? Would not this righteous, omnipotent hand uphold me and help me? Yes, here was His word for it. I would trust it; and I was comforted.

We mounted the stage, and were off for Charlotteville, where we stopped over night, and took the cars next morning for Richmond.

Arrived in Richmond, we were again shut up in jail, all around which was a very high fence, so high that no communication with the outside world was possible. I say we, for there was a young slave girl

[Eliza] whom McCoy had taken with me to the Richmond market. The next day, as the hour for the auction drew near, Jailer O'Neile came to us, with a man, whom he told to take us along to the dressmaker and to charge her to "fix us up fine." This dressmaker was a most disagreeable woman, whose business it was to array such poor creatures as we in the gaudiest and most striking attire conceivable, that, when placed upon the auction stand, we should attract the attention of all present, if not in one way, why, in another. She put a white muslin apron on me, and a large cape, with great pink bows on each shoulder, and a similar rig also on Eliza. Thus equipped, we were led through a crowd of rude men and boys to the place of sale, which was a large open space on a prominent square, under cover.

I had been told by an old negro woman certain tricks that I could resort to, when placed upon the stand, that would be likely to hinder my sale; and when the doctor, who was employed to examine the slaves on such occasions, told me to let him see my tongue, he found it coated and feverish, and, turning from me with a shiver of disgust, said he was obliged to admit that at that moment I was in a very bilious condition. One after another of the crowd felt of my limbs, asked me all manner of questions, to which I replied in the ugliest manner I dared; and when the auctioneer raised his hammer, and cried, "How much do I hear for this woman?" the bids were so low I was ordered down from the stand, and . . . taken back [to her master's home].

SOURCE: Bethany Veney, *The Narrative of Bethany Veney: A Slave Woman.* (Boston: Press of Geo. H. Ellis), 1889.

DOCUMENT 4 Mary Reynolds | *The Days of Slavery, 1937*

The daughter of a free Black father and an enslaved mother, MARY REYNOLDS grew up on the Kilpatrick family plantation in Black River, Louisiana. Although her father was willing to buy Reynolds's mother and children, their enslaver refused to sell them, so the family remained enslaved until the Union army took control of Louisiana during the Civil War. Reynolds told her story in the mid-1930s to a writer working for the Federal Writers' Project of the Works Progress Administration. Interviewed in the Dallas County (Texas) Convalescent Home, she claimed to be over one hundred years old, and although she appeared feeble and frail, Reynolds was still lively and alert and able to describe her early life in striking detail.

Note: This testimony includes the N-word, which we have chosen to reprint in this textbook to accurately reflect Reynolds's original intent as well as the time period, culture, and racism discussed in the testimony. We recognize that this word has a long history as a derogatory and deeply hurtful expression when used by white people toward Black people. Reynolds's choice to use this word relates not only to that history but to a larger cultural tradition in which the N-word can take on different meanings, emphasize shared experience, and be repurposed as a term of endearment within Black communities. While the use of that word in Reynolds's context might not be hurtful, the use of it in our current context very often is. Be mindful of context, both Reynolds's and yours, as you read and discuss this testimony.

Breaking it Down Primary sources provide a direct connection to the past and offer a unique window into individuals' lived experiences. As you read, note the similarities and differences between Reynolds's testimony and that of Veney (p. 234) and Clarke (p. 233). How do the details in each document speak to the different purposes they serve?

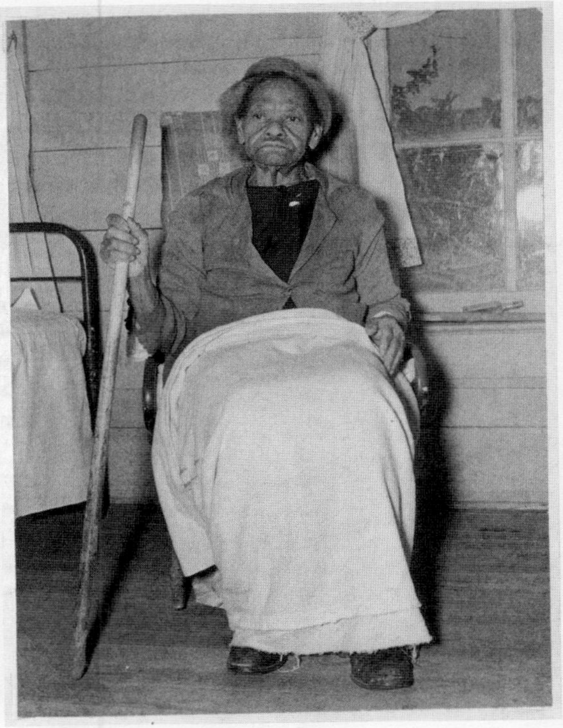

Mary Reynolds, Age 105, at the Dallas County Convalescent Home, Texas, c. 1937
Mary Reynolds was one of more than 2,300 formerly enslaved people interviewed by the Federal Writers' Project, a New Deal agency sponsored by the federal government's Works Progress Administration during the 1930s. Despite her advanced age, her memories of slavery were vivid. *Library of Congress, Manuscript Division, WPA Slave Narrative Project (Texas Narratives, vol. 16, page 3), Federal Writers' Project, U.S. Works Progress Administration (USWPA).*

Massa Kilpatrick wasn't no piddlin' man. He was a man of plenty. He had a big house with no more style to it than a crib, but it could room plenty people. He was a medicine doctor and they was rooms in the second story for sick folks what come to lay in. It would take two days to go all over the land he owned. He had cattle and stock and sheep and more'n a hundred slaves and more besides. He bought the bes' of niggers near every time the spec'lators come that way. He'd make a swap of the old ones and give money for young ones what could work.

He raised corn and cotton and cane and 'taters and goobers,° 'sides the peas and other feedin' for the niggers. I 'member I helt a hoe handle mighty onsteady when they put a old woman to larn me and some other chillun to scrape the fields. That old woman would be in a frantic. She'd show me and then turn 'bout to show some other li'l nigger, and I'd have the young corn cut clean as the grass. She say, "For the love of Gawd, you better larn it right, or Solomon will beat the breath out you body." Old man Solomon was the nigger driver.

Slavery was the worst days was ever seed in the world. They was things past tellin', but I got the scars on my old body to show to this day. I seed worse than what happened to me. I seed them put the men and women in the stock with they hands screwed down through holes in the board and they feets tied together and they naked behinds to the world. Solomon the overseer beat them with a big whip and massa look on. The niggers better not stop in the fields when they hear them yellin'. They cut the flesh most to the bones and some they was when they taken them out of stock and put them on the beds, they never got up again. . . .

The times I hated most was pickin' cotton when the frost was on the bolls. My hands git sore and crack open and bleed. We'd have a li'l fire in the fields and iffen the ones with tender hands couldn't stand it no longer, we'd run and warm our hands a li'l bit. When I could steal a 'tater, I used to slip it in the ashes and when I'd run to the fire I'd take it out and eat it on the sly.

° 'Taters and goobers are potatoes and peanuts. The word *goober* probably comes from *n-guba*, a Kongolese or Kimbundu term for "peanut."

In the cabins it was nice and warm. They was built of pine boardin' and they was one long rom [room] of them up the hill back of the big house. Near one side of the cabins was a fireplace. They'd bring in two, three big logs and put on the fire and they'd last near a week. The beds was made out of puncheons [wooden posts] fitted in holes bored in the wall, and planks laid 'cross them poles. We had tickin' mattresses filled with corn shucks. Sometimes the men build chairs at night. We didn't know much 'bout havin' nothin', though. . . .

Once in a while they'd give us a li'l piece of Sat'day evenin' to wash out clothes. . . . When they'd git through with the clothes . . . the niggers which sold they goobers and 'taters brung fiddles and guitars and come out and play. The others clap they hands and stomp they feet. . . .

We was scart of Solomon and his whip, though, and he didn't like frolickin'. He didn't like for us niggers to pray, either. We never heared of no church, but us have prayin' in the cabins. We'd set on the floor and pray with our heads down low and sing low, but if Solomon heared he'd come and beat on the wall with the stock of his whip. He'd say, "I'll come in there and tear the hide off you backs." But some [of] the old niggers tell us we got to pray to Gawd that he don't think different of the blacks and the whites. I know that Solomon is burnin' in hell today, and it pleasures me to know it.

SOURCE: "Ex-slave Stories (Texas): Mary Reynolds," in *Born in Slavery: Slave Narratives from the Federal Writers' Project, 1936–1938*, American Memory, Library of Congress, 238–40.

PRACTICING AP® SKILLS

1. **AP® Contextualization.** Choose two of the documents and explain how developments and processes from this chapter can be used to contextualize each. What aspects of context, if any, are shared between the documents you chose?
2. **AP® Causation.** What factors influenced the perspective of slavery by enslavers during the antebellum era? Use evidence from at least one of the documents to support your response.
3. **AP® Continuity and Change.** The document describing Clarke's experience dates to the antebellum era, whereas Veney and Reynolds remember slavery years after emancipation. What do these documents suggest about how enslaved and free African Americans' perspectives on the institution of slavery changed over time? Why might this have been the case?
4. **Connecting to AP® Themes.** Although most enslaved testimony, including Veney's memoir and Reynolds's interview, was not written by themselves, their survival story still offers insight into the experiences of enslaved people during the era of chattel slavery. What do these documents reveal about how enslaved people viewed the conditions of enslavement and their enslavers — and to what extent can these accounts be considered a direct transcription of their lived experiences? In your response, explain why these testimonies of formerly enslaved Africans are significant historical documents.
5. **Class Discussion.** Some view personal testimony like the WPA recordings and memoirs as a means to bring about justice. Others see these as helpful in healing from the trauma of the past. Still others might argue that the primary purpose of such testimony is to educate for the future to prevent similar atrocities from ever occurring again. What do you think is the primary purpose of the testimony and firsthand experience detailed in these documents? How effective are they in achieving that purpose?

Document-Based Questions:
Skillful Skimming

In the AP® Skills Workshop for Chapter 5 (p. SW5-A), we practiced breaking down a DBQ prompt to accurately identify the time period, topic, task, and course knowledge that will be relevant to your response. Now, it's time to consider how to approach the sources themselves.

If we had all the time in the world, we'd recommend a close reading of each of the sources using the techniques in the Visual Texts: Active Reading (p. SW1-A) and Written Texts: Active Reading (p. SW2-A) workshops. The AP® Exam will be a timed writing environment, though, so we'll have to condense our initial source review to catch important points as efficiently as possible. We can think of this streamlined process as skillful skimming — we're reading the sources quickly, but we're aiming to read them well.

Preparing for Skillful Skimming

To illustrate efficient source review, we can work with this sample DBQ prompt:

Explain how Black Americans resisted chattel slavery in the period from 1820 to 1860.

In your response you should do the following:

- **Respond to the prompt with a defensible thesis or claim that establishes a line of reasoning.**
- **Describe a broader historical or disciplinary context relevant to the topic of the prompt.**
- **Support an argument in response to the prompt using at least three of the sources.**
- **Use at least one additional piece of specific evidence (beyond the evidence found in the sources) relevant to your argument.**
- **For at least two sources, explain how or why the perspective, purpose, context, and/or audience for each source is relevant to your argument.**
- **Reference or cite the sources you use in your argument. You can reference or cite the source letter, title, or author.**

As we noted in the previous workshop, there's no need to worry about the bulleted subtasks for now. Let's focus on breaking down the unique portion of the prompt as a preliminary step.

Time Period	Topic	Task
1820–1860	Resistance to slavery	Provide specific details about overt and covert resistance to chattel slavery.

Relevant Course Concepts, Developments, Processes

- The *Amistad* case and the *Creole* insurrection secured freedom for enslaved Africans who had staged revolts.
- Truants, or people who fled enslavement, often hid close to their owner's property in a form of resistance called "lying out."
- Abolitionists formed a network now known as the Underground Railroad to help enslaved people resettle in free territories.
- Enslaved people often strengthened kinship and community through religious worship.

This pre-work should prime the most important course knowledge to keep in mind as we approach the sources for this document-based question:

Source A: Am I Not a Woman and a Sister?, 1832

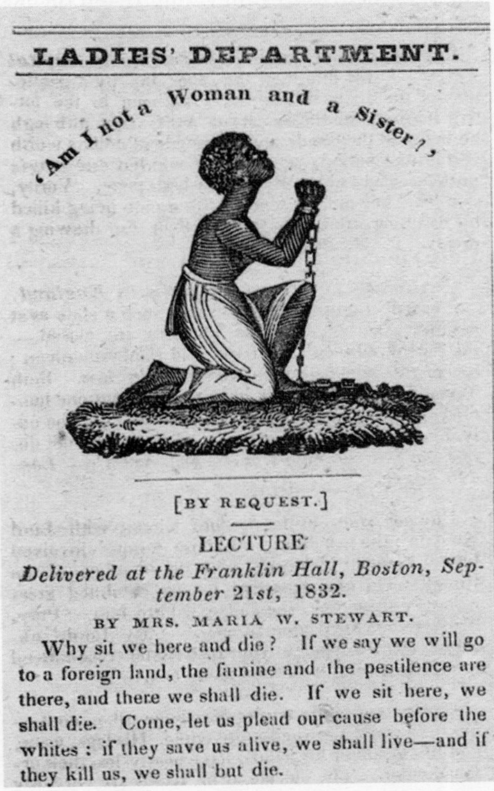
LADIES' DEPARTMENT.

'Am I not a Woman and a Sister?'

[BY REQUEST.]

LECTURE

Delivered at the Franklin Hall, Boston, September 21st, 1832.

BY MRS. MARIA W. STEWART.

Why sit we here and die? If we say we will go to a foreign land, the famine and the pestilence are there, and there we shall die. If we sit here, we shall die. Come, let us plead our cause before the whites: if they save us alive, we shall live—and if they kill us, we shall but die.

"Am I not a Woman and a Sister?", A lecture delivered by Maria Stewart on September 21, 1832, as reprinted in The Liberator*, vol. 2, no. 46, November 17, 1832.*

SOURCE: "Am I Not a Woman and a Sister?", illustration for a lecture delivered by Maria Stewart on September 21, 1832, as reprinted in *The Liberator*

Source B: What, to the Slave, Is the Fourth of July?, 1852

"At a time like this, scorching irony, not convincing argument, is needed. O! had I the ability, and could I reach the nation's ear, I would, to-day, pour out a fiery stream of biting ridicule, blasting reproach, withering sarcasm, and stern rebuke. For it is not light that is needed, but fire; it is not the gentle shower, but thunder. We need the storm, the whirlwind, and the earthquake. The feeling of the nation must be quickened; the conscience of the nation must be roused; the propriety of the nation must be startled; the hypocrisy of the nation must be exposed; and its crimes against God and man must be proclaimed and denounced.

What, to the American slave, is your 4th of July? I answer: a day that reveals to him, more than all other days in the year, the gross injustice and cruelty to which he is the constant victim. To him, your celebration is a sham; your boasted liberty, an unholy license; your national greatness, swelling vanity; your sounds of rejoicing are empty and heartless; your denunciations of tyrants, brass fronted impudence; your shouts of liberty and equality, hollow mockery; your prayers and hymns, your sermons and thanksgivings, with all your religious parade, and solemnity, are, to him, mere bombast, fraud, deception, impiety, and hypocrisy — a thin veil to cover up crimes which would disgrace a nation of savages. There is not a nation on the earth guilty of practices, more shocking and bloody, than are the people of these United States, at this very hour."

SOURCE: Frederick Douglass, "What, to the Slave, Is the Fourth of July?," keynote address for Independence Day celebration, Rochester, New York, July 5, 1852

Source C: The Condition, Elevation, Emigration, and Destiny of the Colored People of the United States, 1852

"That there have been people in all ages under certain circumstances, that may be benefited by emigration, will be admitted; and that there are circumstances under which emigration is absolutely necessary to their political elevation, cannot be disputed. . . .

This may be acknowledged; but to advocate the emigration of the colored people of the United States from their native homes, is a new feature in our history, and at first view, may be considered objectionable, as pernicious to our interests. This objection is at once removed, when reflecting on our condition as incontrovertibly shown in a foregoing part of this work. And we shall proceed at once to give the advantages to be derived from emigration, to us as a people, in preference to any other policy that we may adopt."

SOURCE: Martin R. Delany, *The Condition, Elevation, Emigration, and Destiny of the Colored People of the United States*, 1852

Source D: Go Down, Moses, c. 1853

When Israel was in Egypt's land
Let my people go
Oppressed so hard they could not stand
Let my people go

Go down, Moses
Way down in Egypt land
Tell old Pharaoh,
"Let my people go"

"Thus spoke the Lord," bold Moses said
Let my people go
"If not I'll smite your first born dead"
Let my people go

"No more in bondage shall they toil"
Let my people go
"Let them come out with Egypt's spoil"
Let my people go

SOURCE: "Go Down, Moses," African American spiritual, c. 1853

Source E: Percent Change in Free Black Population, 1830–1860

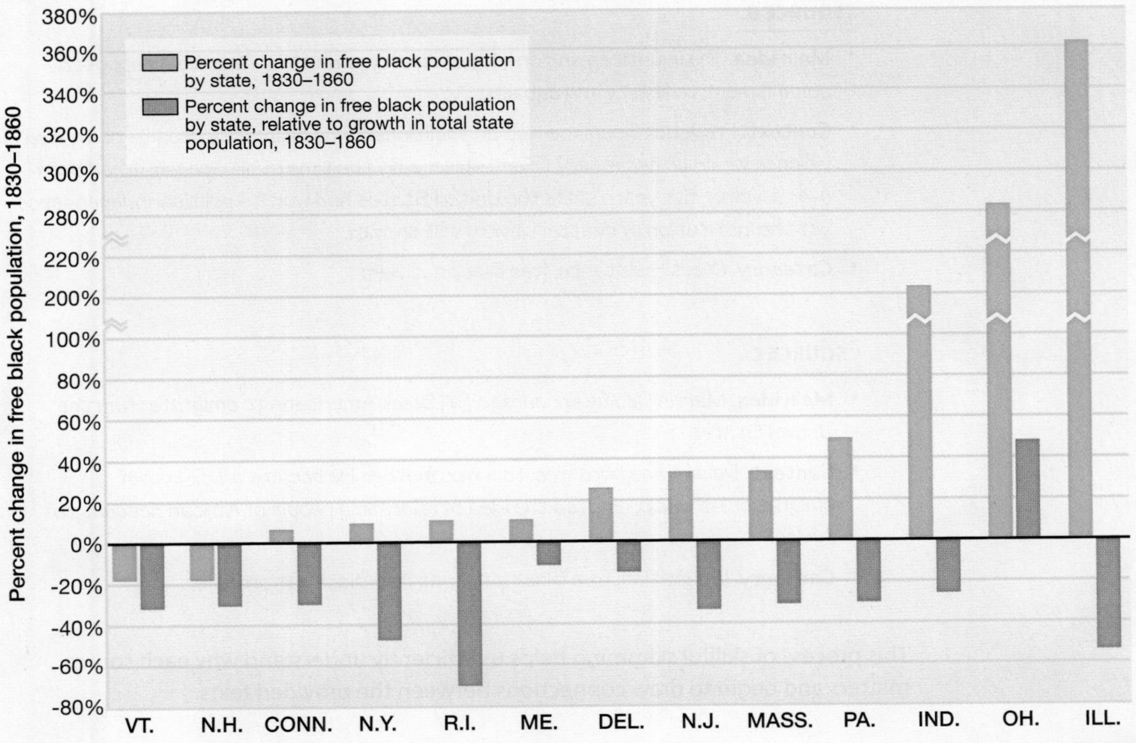

Taking only a minute or so per source, we can skim each of the sources and use scratch paper to take quick notes on the following:

Main idea. How would you summarize the source in one sentence?

Context. What course knowledge seems directly connected to this particular source? What's the most relevant outside knowledge about its topic, its time period, or its creator?

Category. How would you generalize the point of the source in just a few words? Does this category align or contrast with other sources for the same DBQ?

Here's how that might play out for the first three sources:

SOURCE A

- **Main idea.** Black people have as much intellectual potential as white people and should take action to end enslavement and servitude.
- **Context.** Born free in Hartford, Connecticut, Stewart was one of the first American women to lecture in public on political issues and the first Black woman to publish a political manifesto.
- **Category.** Abolitionist events; free Black activism; feminism

SOURCE B

- **Main idea.** The injustices and cruelty of slavery undermine America's supposed commitment to liberty and equality.
- **Context.** Frederick Douglass was an abolitionist who ultimately became convinced violence would be necessary to end slavery. By the time of his speech, it had been over seventy-five years since the United States had won its political independence, yet the institution of chattel slavery still thrived.
- **Category.** Overt resistance; free Black activism

SOURCE C

- **Main idea.** Martin Delany encouraged all Black Americans to emigrate from the United States.
- **Context.** Delany was born free, to a free mother. He became a well-known emigrationist who promoted the idea of relocating people of African descent to Africa.
- **Category.** Emigration; free Black activism; free Black nationalism

This process of skillful skimming helps us efficiently understand why each source matters and begin to draw connections between the provided texts.

recap

Skillful Skimming

Prepare to respond to a document-based question by taking notes on the following in each source:

Main idea. How would you summarize the source in one sentence?

Context. What course knowledge seems directly connected to this particular source? What's the most relevant outside knowledge about its topic, its time period, or its creator?

Category. How would you generalize the point of the source in just a few words? Does this category align or contrast with other sources for the same DBQ?

Activity ▸ Skillful Skimming

Use a graphic organizer like the one shown below to practice skillful skimming on Sources D and E.

	Source D	Source E
Main idea		
Context		
Category		

Multiple-Choice Questions

Questions 1–2 refer to the following.

"Are we MEN!! — I ask you, O my brethren! are we MEN? Did our Creator make us to be slaves to dust and ashes like ourselves? Are they not dying worms as well as we? Have they not to make their appearance before the tribunal of Heaven, to answer for the deeds done in the body, as well as we? Have we any other Master but Jesus Christ alone? Is he not their Master as well as ours? — What right then, have we to obey and call any other Master, but Himself? How we could be so submissive to a gang of men, whom we cannot tell whether they are as good as ourselves or not, I never could conceive. However, this is shut up with the Lord, and we cannot precisely tell — but I declare, we judge men by their works.

The whites have always been an unjust, jealous, unmerciful, avaricious and blood-thirsty set of beings, always seeking after power and authority. — We view them all over the confederacy of Greece, where they were first known to be anything, (in consequence of education) we see them there, cutting each other's throats — trying to subject each other to wretchedness and misery — to effect which, they used all kinds of deceitful, unfair, and unmerciful means."

AP® source David Walker, *Appeal to the Colored Citizens of the World,* 1829

1. Which statement best reflects David Walker's perspective in this excerpt?

(A) David Walker challenged the obedience of enslaved men to white enslavers.

(B) David Walker called Black Americans to be seen as human beings and given immediate emancipation.

(C) David Walker criticized the actions of Americans and considered them to be "tyrants."

(D) David Walker shared a reflection about his experience as an enslaved man in the United States.

2. What factors may have contributed to David Walker's views?

(A) The revision of the Fugitive Slave Act as well as the increased number of restrictions of northern enslaved people

(B) Walker's experience living under the restrictions placed on "free" Black people of the North despite not being enslaved himself

(C) The increased number of overt acts of antislavery resistance and the harsh responses by the U.S. government

(D) The brutality of the Second Middle Passage as well as the publication of *Uncle Tom's Cabin*

Short-Answer Question

1. Answer A, B, C, and D.

(A) Advocates of radical resistance used a variety of methods — from publishing detailed accounts of the horrors of slavery to pushing for outright revolt or violence — to encourage Black Americans to achieve their freedom by any means necessary. Describe one historically significant example of this radical resistance.

(B) Describe the significance of the North Star to enslaved people seeking freedom.

(C) Explain how the practice of Christianity influenced the antislavery resistance movement in the United States.

(D) Explain the connection between the concept of kinship and resistance to slavery.

CHAPTER 7

The Northern Black Freedom Struggle and the Coming of the Civil War

1830–1860

CHAPTER TIMELINE

Events specific to African American history are in purple. General U.S. history events are in black. Events from the AP® Course Framework are marked with an asterisk.

1829	Riots in Cincinnati drive out half the Black population
1830	First National Negro Convention
1831	Maria Stewart begins writing and speaking on Black moral reform*
	Mary Prince's *The History of Mary Prince, a West Indian Slave* published*
1833	American Anti-Slavery Society established
	Philadelphia Female Anti-Slavery Society established
	Slavery ends in the British West Indian colonies
	Great Britain enacts compensated emancipation of all enslaved people in its empire
1836	American Moral Reform Society established
1837	White mob burns abolitionist print shop in Alton, Illinois, and murders editor
1838	White mob destroys Philadelphia's Pennsylvania Hall
1840	Liberty Party founded
1841	Frederick Douglass begins career as abolitionist lecturer
	Madison Washington leads a slave mutiny aboard the slave ship *Creole**
1842	*Prigg v. Pennsylvania* finds personal liberty laws unconstitutional
1843	Henry Highland Garnet calls on enslaved people to revolt*
	Sojourner Truth begins career as abolitionist lecturer*
1845	Frederick Douglass's first autobiography published
1846	American Missionary Association established
1846–1848	Mexican-American War
1847	Douglass begins publishing the *North Star*
1848	Douglass attends women's rights convention in Seneca Falls, New York
1849	*Roberts v. City* of Boston upholds segregated schools in Massachusetts
1850	Compromise of 1850
	Fugitive Slave Act*
1851	Christiana Resistance
	Mary Ann Shadd emigrates to Canada
1852	Harriet Beecher Stowe's *Uncle Tom's Cabin* published
	Martin Delany advocates establishing Black nation outside U.S.*
1854	Elizabeth Jennings sues New York streetcar company to end segregated seating
	Kansas-Nebraska Act
	Republican Party founded
	Anthony Burns captured and returned to slavery
1855	Massachusetts becomes first state to prohibit segregation by race in public schools
	Douglass's expanded autobiography *My Bondage and My Freedom* published*
1856	Violence erupts in Kansas between proslavery and antislavery settlers
	Harriet Tubman's reflection in *The Refugee* by Benjamin Drew published*
1857	Black community of Seneca Village razed to make way for Central Park in New York City
	Dred Scott v. Sandford decision denies African American citizenship*
	Frederick Douglass gives West India Emancipation speech*
1859	Delany begins search for site of African American emigrant settlement in Africa*
	John Brown's raid on Harpers Ferry, Virginia
1860	Abraham Lincoln elected president
	South Carolina secedes from Union

Please note that this chapter includes a place name that includes the N-word, which we have chosen not to reprint in full here. We wish to accurately reflect the racism of the time period, but we also recognize that this word has a long history as a derogatory and deeply hurtful expression when used by white people toward Black people, as it is in the context of this place name. We have replaced the term without hindering understanding of the content. Be mindful of context, both historical and contemporary, as you read and discuss this chapter.

Mary Ann Shadd and the Black Liberation Struggle before the Civil War

In January 1849, twenty-five-year-old Mary Ann Shadd weighed in on the enduring debate among free Blacks in the North about how best to advance their cause. A veteran schoolteacher who had benefited from her private education and her family's political activism, Shadd spoke in a self-confident and independent voice. She was also impatient. "We have been holding conventions for years — have been assembling together and whining over our difficulties and afflictions, passing resolutions on resolutions . . . but it does really seem that we have made but little progress, considering our resolves." Her solution was clear and pointed: "We should do more, and talk less."[1]

Shadd was both a doer and a talker. Despairing of African American prospects in the United States, she left her teaching job in New York City in 1851 and moved to Canada. In Windsor, Ontario, where African Americans had already formed a small community, she took another teaching job and soon also became cofounder and editor of the *Provincial Freeman*, a weekly Black newspaper whose masthead announced its devotion "to anti-slavery, temperance, and general literature." Attending the 1855 National Negro Convention in Philadelphia as one of only two female delegates, she gave a speech that electrified the audience. An observer described it as "one of the most convincing and telling speeches in favor of Canadian emigration I ever heard."[2]

Teacher, journalist, abolitionist, proponent of emigration to Canada, and women's rights activist, Mary Ann Shadd (later Cary) represents many of the different liberation paths that African Americans pursued after 1830. In the 1830s and 1840s, free Blacks in northern cities focused on building their own communities and on promoting moral reform, education, and Black unity to beat back anti-Black prejudice and discrimination. Increasingly, leading men and women formed organizations to accomplish the paired goals of securing equal rights in the North and ending slavery in the South. They met in local, regional, and national conventions to debate their goals and strategies, and they established and wrote for Black newspapers that linked communities and ideas throughout the North. The formerly enslaved among them described the horrors of slavery to persuade whites to join their efforts. Some Black activists mounted legal challenges to the discrimination they endured even in states that had abolished slavery. Some participated in petition campaigns and, though generally barred from voting, joined new political parties that aimed to prohibit the spread of slavery to new territories in the West.

Black activists pushed abolition onto the national and international agenda, joining forces with the unprecedented and gathering Western campaign to abolish slavery rooted in Great Britain, France, and the United States. In the 1840s and 1850s, the issue of slavery in the territories increasingly threatened to tear apart the nation. Activists deliberately disobeyed a strict new fugitive slave law, continuing to shepherd fugitives from slavery to freedom by way of the Underground Railroad. Increasingly, that meant fleeing to Canada, as in the 1850s a growing number of free Blacks came to believe there was no place for them in the United States. Others chose to stay and to confront injustice directly, a few through violent resistance and even insurrection. By 1860, Black activism had helped force a catastrophic national showdown over slavery. As the states of the slave South and the free North grew increasingly discontented, each side convinced that the other was conspiring to take over the federal government, the sectional struggle descended into disunion and civil war.

The Boundaries of Freedom

How did free Black people in the North and South organize to support their communities?

Describe the techniques used by Black women activists to advocate for social justice and reform.

In the three decades before the Civil War, free Blacks in the North sought to make viable lives for themselves and their children while their communities fought against increasing white hostility. Prejudice, law, and custom increasingly limited Black opportunities for participation in the political, economic, and social life of the American Republic. As a consequence, Black communities turned inward, focusing on building attitudes and institutions that would make them self-reliant. Yet, their very success often provoked an angry, even violent, response among whites. More and more, free Blacks in the North saw their struggle for self-improvement and full citizenship as inseparable from the struggle of enslaved Blacks to end their bondage.

Racial Discrimination in the Era of the Common Man

AP® skills

Applying Disciplinary Knowledge: How prevalent was the existence of slavery in the North by the 1830s?

By 1830, slavery existed almost exclusively in the South. Starting in the 1780s, northern states had abolished slavery, primarily through gradual emancipation laws that freed enslaved people after they reached a certain age. In 1830, New Jersey was the only northern state with a significant number of enslaved people: 2,254. By 1850, that number was 236, and slavery in the North was fast becoming a distant memory.

Yet, the end of slavery brought an increase, not a decrease, in anti-Black prejudice, discrimination, and violence. After visiting the United States in 1831, the French writer Alexis de Tocqueville noted that "the prejudice of race appears to be stronger in the states that have abolished slavery than in those where it still exists; and nowhere is it so intolerant as in those states where servitude has never been known."[3] There are several explanations for this intensification of racial hostility. Tocqueville was ignorant of the fact that slavery had existed previously throughout the North. Indeed, the legacy of Black enslavement and its associated racism shaped northern Black life. Whites created structures of discrimination and repression to enforce Black submission. Increasingly, they viewed Blacks as racially inferior, and studies in the emerging social sciences investigating human origins reinforced their views. In the 1820s and 1830s, Dr. Samuel G. Morton of Philadelphia collected human skulls from all over the world and classified them according to race. Measuring skull cavities, he proposed in *Crania Americana* (1839) that Europeans had the most brain capacity, Africans the least. His studies in craniology claimed to prove racial hierarchies popularized in studies such as *Types of Mankind, or Ethnological Researches* (1854) by Josiah Clark Nott and George Robins Gliddon, with a contribution by Louis Agassiz. Agassiz, a Swiss zoologist and geologist who taught at Harvard, lectured widely on the separate origins of the races and their distinctive characteristics.

Throughout the nineteenth century, leading scholars in Europe and America investigated and debated racial origins and character. For American enslavers, these early studies in the field that would become anthropology helped justify the enslavement of African Americans. For white northerners, these ideas fed notions of white supremacy and suggested reasons to view free Blacks as a problem population. Many favored schemes to remove the problem by colonizing African Americans outside the United States, but the American Colonization Society's efforts to sponsor the emigration of free Blacks to Liberia were largely unsuccessful. Most free Blacks opposed the idea of colonization, as they believed that the United States was their home. A group of Rochester Blacks asserted, "We do not consider Africa to be our home, any more than the present whites do England, Scotland, or Ireland."[4]

Unable to pressure or force free Blacks to leave the country, whites circumscribed African Americans' freedom and undermined their impact through segregation and exclusion. Black laws discouraged or forbade Blacks from entering or settling in Ohio, Indiana, and Illinois — free states bordering on slave states — as well as in Wisconsin and the slave state of Missouri. By law and by custom, whites severely restricted Blacks' access to jobs, public institutions and accommodations, and white neighborhoods. Black passengers on stagecoaches, steamboats, trains, streetcars, and omnibuses were required to sit in separate sections or relegated to separate cars.

The legal system, too, discriminated against Blacks. Law enforcement officers routinely left Black life, liberty, and property unprotected, and Blacks had little redress in the courts. A white Cincinnati lawyer admitted to Tocqueville that the lack of legal protection for local Blacks often led to "the most revolting injustices."[5] Blacks were also imprisoned at far higher rates than whites for all kinds of offenses — real and imagined, minor and major — in part because of racist views that held them

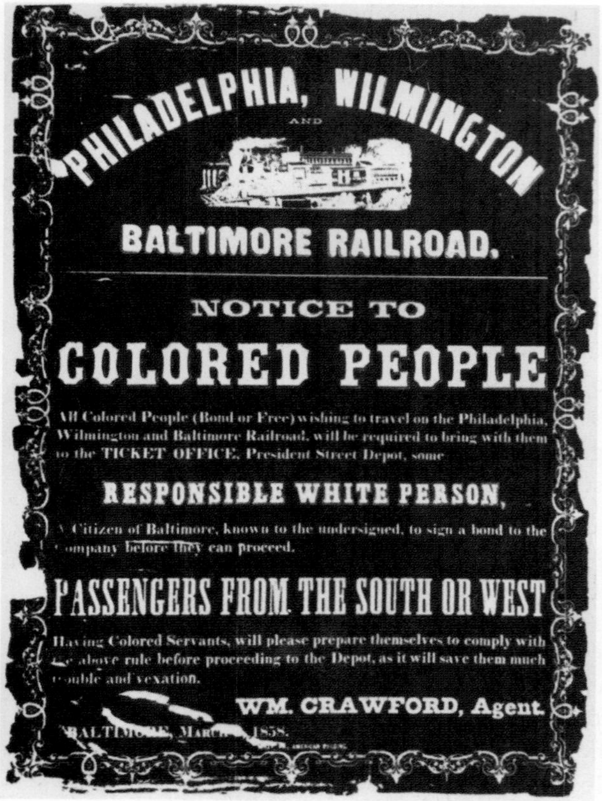

"Notice to Colored People"
During the 1850s, free Blacks in the South and in parts of the North bordering on the South experienced growing restrictions on their movements between cities, as did the enslaved. These restrictions reflected heightened anti-Black racism and racial tensions that stemmed from white anxieties about how best to control Blacks in a period of intensifying regional conflict over slavery, as well as from white concern about the place of Blacks in a country increasingly seen by whites as a white nation. The 1850 Fugitive Slave Act epitomized the national commitment to constraining the mobility of enslaved people and solidifying slavery. This 1858 poster declares that every Black traveling on the Philadelphia, Wilmington and Baltimore Railroad must have a bond posted by a white Baltimorean. White passengers traveling with enslaved Blacks are notified to have papers ready for their "servants" as well. Philadelphia and Wilmington were key stops along the Underground Railroad, which spirited freedom seekers to freedom. The poster is a graphic illustration of the increasing surveillance and repression of enslaved and free Blacks in the Upper South and free Blacks in the North on the eve of the Civil War. **How does this 1858 poster demonstrate the increased level of restrictions Blacks people faced following passage of the Compromise of 1850?** *Spencer Collection, New York Public Library/Bridgeman Images.*

prone to criminality. In a most alarming pattern that would only expand over time, Blacks tended to be overrepresented in crime statistics, including arrests, convictions, and imprisonment rates. As a result, Black women and men have historically been incarcerated at rates that exceed their percentage of the population at local, state, and national levels, owing principally to anti-Black racism. Relatedly, because Blacks could not serve on juries or function as witnesses or lawyers, Blacks accused of crimes were more likely to be convicted and sentenced than whites similarly accused. Not until the late 1850s were Blacks permitted to serve on juries, and then only in Massachusetts.

AP® skills

Applying Disciplinary Knowledge: How were Black people living in the North legally discriminated against?

For whites, this was the era of the common man. Universal white male suffrage became the norm after 1830, while Black men lost the right to vote. In 1837, Pennsylvania disfranchised Black men, and every state that entered the Union after 1819, except Maine, prohibited Black suffrage. In 1860, Black men could vote only in Maine, New Hampshire, Vermont, Massachusetts, and Rhode Island. Blacks constituted just 6 percent of the population in these five states.

Black political exclusion solidified white male supremacy. Fearing that voting by allegedly ignorant and untrustworthy Black men would pollute the political system, white men and state laws effectively removed Black interests from political representation. Whites degraded the status of Blacks and then punished them for it. Excluding Blacks from political life also had the effect of marginalizing them in the nation's economic life. Thrown into competition with American-born working-class whites and new white immigrants looking to establish themselves, free Blacks were often the targets of hostility that flared into violence. Racially motivated riots were almost commonplace in northern cities, as white mobs attacked Black neighborhoods with much loss of property and even loss of life.

AP® skills

Applying Disciplinary Knowledge: Can you identify any differences in the political opportunities made available to white and Black men in the 1830s?

A series of riots in Cincinnati offers an example. Directly across the Ohio River from the slave state of Kentucky, Cincinnati was where southern Blacks who had been emancipated or had purchased their freedom often relocated. It was also a common destination for freedom seekers and, in time, a key stop along the Underground Railroad. The city's Black population grew so rapidly as to alarm its white population, and in late June 1829, local officials announced that they would rigorously apply Ohio's black laws. As the city's Blacks began to investigate the possibility of resettling in Canada, white mobs attacked them. Over the summer, half the Black population was driven from the city. Some two hundred eventually settled in Upper Canada, where they named their new community Wilberforce, after the British abolitionist William Wilberforce, who led the effort to end slavery in Britain's colonies. His goal was accomplished in 1833, when Parliament passed a compensated emancipation law that applied to the entire British empire.

But the violence was not over in Cincinnati. In 1836, white mobs destroyed the shop that printed an abolitionist newspaper and moved on to destroy houses and churches belonging to African Americans. In 1841, fights between unemployed Black and white dockworkers escalated into a battle in which Blacks mobilized to protect their neighborhood. After police and militia disarmed these Blacks, the whites returned, leading to additional loss of life and greater devastation of property.

Boston, New York, and Providence, Rhode Island, also experienced anti-Black riots, but no city had more than Philadelphia, which, not coincidentally, had the largest Black population. Riots rocked the city in 1820, 1829, 1834, 1835, 1838, 1842, and 1849. During the 1834 riot, both prosperous and poor Blacks were attacked; many died, and hundreds fled the city. Roving white mobs vandalized the African Presbyterian Church and devastated a Black Methodist church, while also attacking white supporters of Black rights. In 1838, a mob assaulted Black and white abolitionists meeting in Philadelphia's Pennsylvania Hall, which had just been dedicated to the cause of abolitionism, and burned the building to the ground. The year before, proslavery activists in Alton, Illinois, hurled the printing presses of a white antislavery newspaper into the Mississippi River, burned the print shop, and murdered the editor, Elijah P. Lovejoy. These race riots, which targeted white abolitionists as well as Blacks, formed part of a larger pattern of racial and ethnic hostility that was also evident in politics.

AP® exam tip

You should be able to explain the causes for northern race riots in the early to mid-1800s, and describe how Black people responded.

During the 1840s and 1850s, anti-immigrant, anti-Catholic Know-Nothings, so-called for the secret nature of their party organization, won local and state offices in New England, New York, and Pennsylvania. The era of the common man was also an era of intense white nationalism, which defined the United States as Anglo-Saxon and Protestant, a land in which Black people, free and enslaved, had no place.

The Growth of Free Black Communities in the North

AP® exam tip

Be sure you can describe the economic vulnerabilities and obstacles Black people faced in the North.

Racial hostility, economic discrimination, political and social exclusion, and violence had severe consequences for Black communities in the North in the decades after 1830. These forces constrained the efforts of northern free Blacks to make a living and improve themselves and undermined their communities. The jobs available to Black people were primarily unskilled and paid the lowest wages. Often the work was seasonal, with periods of unemployment. Between 1820 and 1860, the percentages and relative numbers of Black men in skilled and semiskilled jobs actually declined, as these jobs increasingly went to native-born whites and the growing numbers of white immigrants. Between 1830 and 1860, the U.S. population increased from 13 million to 32 million, almost 5 million of whom were immigrants. Most newcomers settled in the cities of the North, where their numbers increased competition for scarce jobs. Serious economic downturns in each decade between 1830 and 1860 further eroded the already-declining economic status of northern Blacks.

Black women formed a little more than half the population in urban Black communities. The shorter life expectancy of Black males — owing to disease as well as both overwork and poverty from lack of work — and the consistently high demand for Black women as domestic servants help explain their greater numbers. There were more widows than widowers in the Black communities in Philadelphia, Boston, and Cincinnati, and the number of female-headed households grew. These households were generally poorer than dual-headed households.

AP® skills

Applying Disciplinary Knowledge: How was Black northerners' health impacted by their economic conditions?

Blacks had shorter life expectancies and higher death rates than whites due to accidents, disease, and a lack of adequate health care. They had higher infant mortality rates and fewer children. After 1840, urban Black families in the North were smaller in size than rural Black families in the North and southern Black families. In the short term, smaller families had a positive impact, as they meant fewer demands on limited family budgets. In the longer term, smaller families had a more negative impact, for there were fewer young people to contribute to the family income.

Overall, however, the number of free Blacks in the North continued to grow through natural increase, the migration of free Blacks from the South, and the arrival of fugitives from slavery. By 1860, half the nation's free Black population (226,152) lived in cities in the North. In 1860, Boston had 2,261 Blacks, New York 12,472, and Philadelphia 22,185. As a proportion of the population, however, these Black communities were shrinking, for the white population was rising more rapidly due to the influx of European immigrants, especially from Ireland, which suffered from widespread

BY THE NUMBERS **Percent Change in Free Black Population, 1830–1860**

As this figure illustrates, the free Black population rose significantly in the vast majority of northern states during the period from 1830 to 1860. Despite these increases, however, free Black representation in the general population decreased during this same period, owing largely to the influx of white European immigrants to the United States. While the northern enslaved population became statistically insignificant during these years, it is important to remember that most Blacks remained enslaved — and that most free Blacks still lived in the South.

To what extent do you believe free Black people were able to wield more or less economic and political power in the North by 1860? Use details from the map to support your answers.

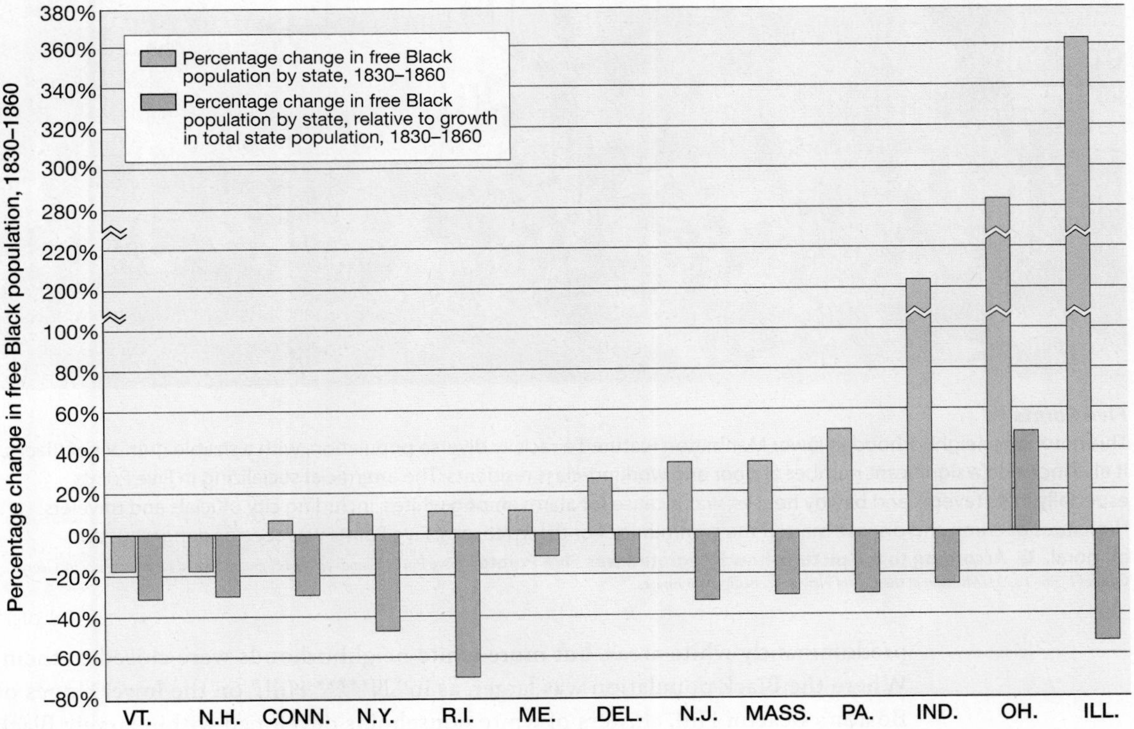

famine in the 1840s. Increasingly, the newer western cities, such as Pittsburgh and St. Louis, also had large Black populations. Cincinnati, for example, counted 3,737 Blacks in 1860.[6] (See By the Numbers: Percentage Change in Free Black Population, 1830–1860.)

In northern cities, Black neighborhoods evolved close to, but mostly separate from, white neighborhoods. Cities were still small and densely settled, and Blacks, as one observer noted, found themselves "crammed into lofts, garrets and cellars, in blind alleys and narrow courts." Some neighborhoods were racially diverse, with Blacks living among poor and working-class whites, especially recent immigrants. The inhabitants of New York City's Five Points district in lower Manhattan consisted "of all colors, white, yellow, brown and ebony black."[7] Some affluent Blacks lived in

Five Points
This notorious neighborhood in lower Manhattan featured a racially diverse population, with a sizable number of Blacks. It also included a significant number of poor and working-class residents. The interracial socializing in Five Points, especially in its taverns and bawdy houses, was a cause for alarm among whites, including city officials and travelers. High rates of crime and disease marred the community. For these reasons, Five Points was seen as dangerous and immoral. **According to the picture, how integrated was Five Points?** Five Points, *hand- colored engraving based on an original by George Catlin (1796–1872)/Museum of the City of New York/Bridgeman Images.*

predominantly white areas, but more white neighborhoods were closed to them. Where the Black population was larger, as in "N***** Hill," on the lower slopes of Boston's Beacon Hill, clusters of white households developed within largely Black areas. Black neighborhoods almost everywhere were crowded and lacked clean streets and public services such as police and fire protection. Poor sanitation was one reason life expectancies were shorter for Blacks than for whites.

Although the economic and physical security of Black communities generally declined from 1830 to 1860, some individuals and families succeeded in pulling themselves out of poverty, primarily by establishing small businesses that grew into larger enterprises. The Forten family of Philadelphia is one example. At the end of the eighteenth century, James Forten, a second-generation free Black man, purchased a sail loft from the man with whom he had apprenticed. By the 1830s, his sail-making business was highly respected and prosperous, with twenty to thirty employees.[8] Forten was a wealthy man who was able to give his daughters and granddaughters a good education. Most became teachers, and all were active abolitionists and strong advocates of free Black **uplift**: the idea, especially popular among the elite, that Black self-help, leadership, and autonomy were necessary to elevate the race as a whole. Like Forten, other free Blacks who prospered usually came from families that had been free for more than one generation.

uplift
The idea that racial progress demands autonomous Black efforts; especially seen as the responsibility of the more fortunate of the race to help lift up the less fortunate.

Ironically, the very success of Black entrepreneurs attracted the animosity of whites, and successful communities were often victims of violence. Seneca Village, in upper Manhattan, was a thriving Black community in the 1830s and 1840s, with churches, schools, businesses, cemeteries, and various community institutions. Wealthy Blacks invested in it because of its promise; poorer Blacks lived there because of its affordability and welcoming atmosphere. Community gardens, with "cabbage, and melon-patches, with hills of corn and cucumbers, and beds of beets, [and] parsnips,"[9] sustained those who lived there. Known as a haven for freedom seekers, Seneca Village was also a center of abolitionism and growing agitation for Black rights. In 1857, city officials razed it to make way for Central Park.

AP® exam tip
On the AP® Exam, you will need to be able to identify the main goal of racial uplift.

Black Self-Help in an Era of Moral Reform

The day-to-day struggles of northern Blacks to overcome oppression created an internal focus on self-improvement and community building. Excluded from the political, economic, and social worlds of whites, Blacks looked to one another for emotional, psychological, and spiritual support as well as for material and institutional resources. Their profound and ubiquitous sense of racial unity built crucially on a bedrock need and desire for affirmation as a people. Out of this pervasive struggle for affirmation as a people came the necessary and growing commitment to self-help — the belief that they themselves must take responsibility for their destinies, regardless of external forces. As the influential Black journalist, doctor, and writer Martin R. Delany observed in 1852, "Our elevation must be the result of self-efforts, and work of our own hands. No other human power can accomplish it. If we but determine it shall be so, it will be so."[10]

Mutual aid societies, independent Black churches, and Black schools knit Black communities together. A range of benevolent institutions for women and men, including male lodges and fraternal orders, as well as their women's auxiliaries, helped individuals look out for one another. Female benevolent societies aimed especially to assist the many widows in Black communities. By 1840, there were more than sixty such societies in Philadelphia alone. Black orphanages took care of children whose parents had died or could not support them. In New York City, the Colored Orphan Asylum, set up by white Quaker women in 1836, quickly became an important Black community institution that provided education, apprenticeships, and job opportunities. In 1846, James McCune Smith was appointed its medical director. Denied admission to American colleges, he had received his medical training in Scotland but had returned to the United States to serve African Americans. His commitment was typical of the way privileged Black people helped support their communities.

AP® skills
Applying Disciplinary Knowledge: How did Black mutual aid and benevolent societies support racial uplift?

Colored Orphan Asylum
Founded in 1836 by three Quaker women — Anna and Hanna Shotwell and Mary Murray — the Colored Orphan Asylum (COA) cared for and educated New York City's African American orphans, who were excluded from white orphan asylums. The facility included up to 400 African American orphans, who after reaching the age of twelve, were mostly indentured out to work for rural families. On July 13, during the 1863 Draft Riots, a racist white mob burned down the COA. Fortunately, it was rebuilt. **How does the history of the Colored Orphan Asylum and the eventual fate of the children who resided there reflect the unique obstacles Black people faced in New York?** *Collection of the New-York Historical Society/ Bridgeman Images.*

Independent Black churches sustained their communities with a range of services. Philadelphia's Mother Bethel AME Church was among the most active. Like other Black churches, Mother Bethel sponsored schools in the belief that education would both improve the lives of future generations and decrease white hostility. "If we ever expect to see the influence of prejudice decrease, and ourselves respected," maintained one spokesman in 1832, "it must be by the blessings of an enlightened education."[11] Attending schools with white children was rarely an option, as white families, associating integrated schools with abolition and racial mixing, vigorously opposed them. Sunday schools, which enhanced religious education with basic training in reading, writing, and arithmetic, helped advance Black literacy and numeracy.

Northern Black communities pushed for separate Black public schools and created private schools, often with the assistance of supportive whites, especially Quakers and abolitionists. Yet even white assistance brought little assurance of success. In 1832, when Prudence Crandall, a young Quaker teacher in Canterbury, Connecticut, admitted an African American girl to her female academy, white parents withdrew their students. Crandall responded by closing her school and then reopening it for Black girls only. Local opposition escalated, and Connecticut passed a law that made the school illegal. Crandall was arrested, and her school was vandalized and eventually burned. Under pressure from abolitionists, Connecticut repealed the law, but Miss Crandall's School for Young Ladies and Little Misses of Color never reopened.

Though appreciative of the commitment of white teachers, Blacks increasingly sought to establish their own schools, with Black teachers who could more closely identify with their students. By the 1830s, the New York African Free School had more than 1,400 students. Yet most Black schools were poorly equipped, lacking books and unable to pay teachers the salaries white teachers received. An assessment in 1848 concluded that the state of Black education "has been shamefully limited."[12] Slowly, however, the spread of the common school movement — the effort to create public schools open to all — and court challenges to discrimination in education opened some public schools to African Americans. In Cincinnati, for example, Blacks created a community-based Black high school in the face of extreme white opposition. The city later built a Black public high school.

AP® exam tip

Be sure you can describe the obstacles Black people faced when trying to obtain an education for their children and explain how they worked to overcome these obstacles.

To meet the expanding need for teachers, northern Black secondary education focused on teacher training. The Institute for Colored Youth in Philadelphia trained teachers, as did Charles Avery's Allegheny Institute, established near Pittsburgh in 1849. Avery's school emphasized vocational training, but in the 1850s, two new Black colleges focused on the arts and sciences. In Chester County, Pennsylvania, the Ashmun Institute opened in 1854 to provide higher education "for male youth of African descent"; it was renamed Lincoln University after the Civil War. In Ohio in 1856, the Methodist Church founded Wilberforce University, named for the British abolitionist. Also in Ohio, Oberlin College, founded by abolitionists and a major stop along the Underground Railroad, was committed to progressive causes and had been open to both African Americans and women for twenty years by the mid-1850s.

Teaching attracted many of the most talented Black women of the era precisely because it was one of the few professions open to women. Sarah Mapps Douglass, for example, born into a comfortable Black Philadelphia family and educated by private tutors, founded a high school for girls that included training in science, atypical of education for girls in the period. In 1853, Douglass began running the girls' department of the Institute for Colored Youth. After taking classes at the Female Medical College of Pennsylvania and Penn Medical University in the late 1850s, she began a series of medical education classes for women in her home.

Douglass was committed to Black uplift, and her uplift activities are representative of educated Black women. Such women were generally deeply religious and were deeply engaged in the reform spirit of the antebellum era, seeking to remake and perfect society by promoting virtuous living. Using women's role as guardian of the family, home, and culture more broadly, these women argued for temperance to end the abuses of alcoholism. They also called for an end to prostitution and for more humane treatment of prisoners and the mentally ill. For Black women, social reform had the particular aim of improving Black communities and elevating the status of Blacks.

AP® exam tip

You should be prepared to explain how Black women activists contributed to racial uplift and furthered the cause for women's rights.

Among the first to articulate this message of uplift was Maria W. Stewart, who, in Boston in the early 1830s, was the first American woman, white or Black, to speak before a mixed audience of men and women — at the time a brave and highly controversial act. She had been influenced by David Walker, who encouraged her brief but electrifying public speaking career. Intensely religious, Stewart rejected Walker's call for violence, emphasizing the moral reform of the Black community instead. Beginning in 1831, in speeches, essays, and editorials, she stressed the importance of education, especially that of girls, and Black elevation generally. "How long shall the fair daughters of Africa be compelled to bury their minds and talents beneath a load of iron pots and kettles?" she asked. She also urged African American women to understand their duty as mothers to "create in the minds of your little girls and boys a thirst for knowledge." She implored men to "flee from the gambling board and the dance-hall; for we are poor, and have no money to throw away. . . . Let our money, instead . . . be appropriated for schools and seminaries of learning for our children and youth."[13]

Stewart firmly believed that Black moral and intellectual improvement would decrease white prejudice,[14] and other Black leaders made similar arguments. Writing in the *Colored American*, the Pittsburgh AME minister and educator Lewis Woodson expressed the commonly held belief that deportment and dress reflect inner character: "Every one must agree that the moral effect of mean dress is, to degrade us in our own eyes and in the eyes of all who behold us." Articulating a particular concern among Black women and men, Woodson maintained that "colored females should be extremely attentive to cleanliness and neatness of dress" because "of the prejudices which exist against them in the community in which they live; and they should consider how imprudent it is, by neglecting their personal appearance, to heighten and aggravate that prejudice."[15]

But Black leaders recognized that it was not only Black people who needed improvement. In 1836, James Forten and others founded the Christian-inspired American Moral Reform Society. The society was dedicated to the equality of all, including Blacks, whites, and women, and promoted various initiatives — such as public education, peace activism, and temperance — to elevate all Americans, regardless of race. They proposed to advance African Americans' struggle as a way of "improving the condition of mankind,"[16] an expression of a globalist **human rights** sensibility that increasingly shaped Black thought and action. Thus they sought an end to slavery and urged members to boycott goods produced using enslaved labor. The society's program was indicative not only of antebellum reform generally but also of the difficult situation of a free people striving to work with white allies to achieve respect and dignity in a nation that sanctioned Black enslavement.

human rights
Rights that apply universally to all people, regardless of nation, history, and culture.

Forging a Black Freedom Struggle

How did gender affect the genre and themes of slave narratives in the nineteenth century?

What were the features of radical resistance strategies promoted by Black activists to demand change during the nineteenth century?

The far-reaching commitment of northern Black communities to collective affirmation, self-improvement, and moral reform was inextricably linked to the abolition of slavery. Free Blacks recognized that they could not elevate their own people unless all Black people were free. This core belief necessitated Black activism, as Blacks and their leaders more and more worked together both within and outside their communities. Only a concerted and widespread effort could bring about fundamental change in the nation's racial conscience, laws, and practices. Through speeches, meetings, annual conventions, and newspapers, Black leaders formed networks that connected their communities and sharpened their message of moral reform to address the nation's moral conscience as a means to advance their people's cause. Casting slavery as an evil institution, they wrote and lectured on the ways it debased individual lives and corrupted the nation as a whole. They argued for the importance of equal rights not only for Blacks but often also for women, and they challenged Blacks' status in the larger society. The arrival of fugitives from slavery brought new and powerful voices to strengthen their ranks. Black activists participated in and supported the white abolitionist organizations founded in this era, but they also operated independently. Although largely disfranchised, they engaged in political actions to advance the uplift of free Blacks as well as the cause of abolitionism.

Building a National Black Community: The Black Convention Movement and the Black Press

In September 1830, Bishop Richard Allen called Black clergy and other leaders to gather at Philadelphia's Mother Bethel AME Church to consider the issues that were of primary concern to their communities, including abolitionism. Some forty responded, from nine states, including the slave states of Delaware, Maryland, and Virginia. The First National Negro Convention was the first in a series of gatherings that constituted the **Black convention movement**. In national meetings called annually through 1835 and occasionally thereafter, and especially in a far more prolific series of state and local conventions, Black leaders built networks and helped forge a Black national consciousness. They discussed and debated the state of their communities and what they could do to improve them. They framed resolutions and undertook projects that sought to elevate the status of free Blacks and to promote abolitionism. Many were ministers, and their proposals reflected Christian values and the importance of an upright moral character.

Black convention movement
A series of national, regional, and local conventions, starting in 1830, where Black leaders addressed the concerns of free and enslaved Blacks.

The 1830 convention set an agenda for future meetings. In light of the recent Cincinnati riots, migration to Canada was under discussion, as was Black education, especially Black vocational schools. At the early conventions, attendees expressed support for programs that enhanced Blacks' job prospects and looked for ways to move Blacks from menial to vocational jobs, although a proposal for a manual labor school for Black boys never materialized. They went on record as promoting cooperative economic enterprises, such as Black businesses and mutual savings banks. They also promoted the moral virtue of farm life. In fact, churchgoing and righteous living — including temperance, sexual morality, and thrift — would, they argued, ensure the social and moral reform of individual lives that would benefit the community as a whole.

AP® exam tip
Be sure you can explain how Black organizations helped Black people organize and fight for equal rights.

In the 1840s, conventions met in other cities, including Cleveland, New York City, and Rochester and Troy in upstate New York. Discussions were increasingly political and militant. A new generation of leaders was emerging, men and women who had formerly been enslaved and whose frank descriptions of enslaved life riveted audiences and won converts to abolition among reform-minded white people. Speaking at the 1843 convention in Buffalo, New York, were two former enslaved men from Maryland. Henry Highland Garnet, minister of the Liberty Street Presbyterian Church in Troy, called openly for a slave rebellion, while Frederick Douglass, a lecturer on the abolitionist circuit, advocated a more tempered response, believing it would be better to appeal to the conscience of the nation and to end slavery peaceably. (See AP® Working with Sources: Forging an African American Nation — Enslaved and Free, North and South, pp. 286–93.)

These Black conventions, especially the national ones, helped foster a sense of African Americans as a distinct people. Although debates were often spirited and proposals ranged from conservative to radical, they strengthened Black identity through a unity of purpose. These conventions amounted to a significant and alternative Black political movement with a core agenda that united free Black uplift and abolition. Meeting in Cleveland in 1848, one convention stressed this powerful sense of African American peoplehood: "We are as a people, chained together. We are one people — one in general complexion, one in a common degradation, one in popular estimation. As one rises, all must rise, and as one falls all must fall."[17]

The Black press was another vital element in the growing network of Black leaders and institutions with a unified purpose. Similarly, the Black press functioned as a critical element in the creation of a sense of Blacks as a distinctive people, as a nation within a nation. In 1827, Samuel Cornish and John Russwurm began publishing *Freedom's Journal*, the nation's first African American newspaper. It was, the first issue announced, "devoted to the dissemination of useful knowledge among our brethren, and to their moral and religious improvement." The *Journal* continued, "We wish to plead our own cause. Too long have others spoken for us."[18] The paper lasted only two years, and in 1829 Cornish began publishing *The Rights of All*, primarily to argue against colonization. This paper, too, was short-lived, its brief run indicative of how difficult it was to sustain any newspaper at this time, but especially a Black one. Agents were required to distribute copies and enlist subscribers. Owing to the small base of Black subscribers, Black papers survived long term only with the help of wealthy patrons and the support of white subscribers.

AP® exam tip

Be prepared to explain why the Black press was an essential tool within Black communities.

Nevertheless, between 1830 and 1860, more than forty Black newspapers provided a weekly or monthly perspective on current events and a forum for discussing the fight for abolition as well as issues relevant to free Black uplift, such as suffrage, jobs, housing, schools, and fair treatment on public transportation. Because copies were passed from one person to another and often discussed within group contexts, such as taverns and meetings, the papers had a widespread influence. Stories in one were reprinted in others, building a sense of Black unity and contributing to the emergence of a powerful national Black press tradition.

Frederick Douglass
This engraving of a smartly dressed young Douglass vividly captures his self-confidence and middle-class bearing. Douglass's emergence as the preeminent Black leader and Black abolitionist of his era owed significantly to his intelligence, hard work, and ambition. His rise to prominence also owed to his uncanny ability to articulate not only his people's cause, but also how that cause shaped America's past, present, and future. As a social reformer dedicated to a wide range of issues, including woman suffrage, Douglass helped bring people together across barriers of race, gender, and class. Analyze Douglass's clothes, countenance, and posture. ■ **What impression do you think he is trying to leave for anyone who will view his portrait, and why?** *British Library, London, UK/Bridgeman Images.*

The most influential newspaper was published by Frederick Douglass. In 1847, he launched the *North Star* as an explicitly abolitionist paper aiming to "attack slavery in all its forms and aspects; advocate universal emancipation; exalt the standard of public morality; promote the moral and intellectual improvement of the colored people; and hasten the day of freedom to the three millions of our enslaved fellow countrymen."[19] The *North Star* attracted white readers as well as Black. In 1851, it merged with the *Liberty Party Paper* to become *Frederick Douglass' Paper,* which continued in publication until 1863. Its longevity both derived from and contributed to Douglass's stature as the preeminent Black leader of his day. The paper also published contributions from well-known correspondents, such as James McCune Smith, who in 1855 argued vigorously for race pride. "We must learn to love, respect and glory in our Negro nature," he asserted.[20]

Growing Black Activism in Literature, Politics, and the Justice System

In addition to the influential role Frederick Douglass played in the newspaper business, he was a powerful lecturer who captivated audiences by recounting the realities of his life as an enslaved man. He had escaped slavery in 1838 and settled in New Bedford, Massachusetts, where he worked as a day laborer. In 1841, while attending an antislavery meeting in Nantucket, he agreed to say a few words. The audience was riveted, and the meeting's organizers urged him to begin lecturing regularly for the abolitionist cause. One of these organizers was the prominent white abolitionist William Lloyd Garrison, who soon encouraged Douglass to make lecturing a career and to publish the story of his life.

In 1845, Douglass published *Narrative of the Life of Frederick Douglass, an American Slave.* It sold more than 30,000 copies in its first five years in print, and in 1855, he published an expanded version, *My Bondage and My Freedom.* Douglass's books reached a wide range of readers and exemplify the genre of slave narratives that emerged as this era's most original and significant form of African American literary expression. Addressed largely to white audiences, these narratives charted individual yet representative journeys from enslavement in the South to free Black person. By revealing the details of what it meant to be enslaved, they affirmed the humanity of enslaved African Americans. Notable narratives of slavery and escape were written by William Wells Brown, Henry "Box" Brown, and Henry Bibb. Equally noteworthy was Harriet Jacobs's *Incidents in the Life of a Slave Girl* (published in 1861), which treated explicitly the sexual exploitation of enslaved women by white enslavers.[21]

AP® exam tip

You will need to be able to explain the impact of Black women's enslavement narratives on the political movements of this era.

AP® exam tip

Be sure you can explain the significance of slave narratives to abolitionist activism.

This outpouring of African American literature was in a real sense a renaissance. Jarena Lee, a member of Mother Bethel, wrote a spiritual autobiography (originally published in 1836; expanded and updated in 1849) that recorded her struggles in the male-dominated world of preaching. Frances Ellen Watkins (later Harper) published *Poems on Miscellaneous Subjects* (1854), a collection that included "The Slave Mother," which examined the unique pain enslaved mothers endured. Frederick Douglass and Martin Delany published novels with plots centered on slave insurrections, and William Wells Brown's novel *Clotel* (1853) helped establish the character type of the "tragic mulatta," a white-looking Black woman whose mixed-race identity typically led to tragedy. Both Clotel, allegedly Thomas Jefferson's daughter, and her mother, Currer, Jefferson's alleged mistress, were tragic mulattas. In *Our Nig, or Sketches from the Life of a Free Black* (1859), Harriet E. Wilson explored prejudice in the North through a coming-of-age narrative remarkably like her own life story. James W. C. Pennington wrote both a slave narrative and a study of the history of Black people in the United States, and William Cooper Nell recorded the contributions of Black soldiers to the nation's wars. Hosea Easton published his challenge to racism in *A Treatise on the Intellectual Character, and Civil and Political Condition of the Colored People of the U. States* (1837).

AP® skills

Applying Disciplinary Knowledge: Can you describe the characteristics of slave narratives of the 1830s and explain what made them unique from previous narratives?

These works exhibited significantly less of the deference to white leadership that had marked the writings of the first post-Revolutionary generation. Pioneering this increasing Black militancy, David Walker's *Appeal* (1829) had called on enslaved people to revolt, and Robert Alexander Young's pamphlet *The Ethiopian Manifesto* (1829) had warned enslavers of a terrible punishment from God unless they freed the people they enslaved and sought God's forgiveness. The new generation of Black leaders carried forward this militant approach. They sought to reform not only the Black community but also the nation. Their strategy of **moral suasion** aimed to convince the white majority that slavery and the oppression of free Blacks were immoral, offensive to God, and contrary to the nation's ideals. In turn, they said, given the workings of the moral universe, God's wrath would destroy the nation if it did not repent, abolish slavery, and treat Blacks equally.

moral suasion
A primary strategy in the abolitionist movement that relied on vigorous appeals to the nation's moral and Christian conscience.

Frederick Douglass was certainly the most well-known African American speaker on the abolitionist lecture circuit, but Sojourner Truth may have been the most compelling. Born enslaved and named Isabella Baumfree, she had achieved freedom and secured custody of her son, who had been sold illegally, through a lawsuit. In 1843, she transformed herself by taking a new name and occupation. As a lecturer-spiritualist-preacher, she was both outspoken and plainspoken, powerful and fearless. In 1847, before a packed audience in Boston's Faneuil Hall, she challenged even Douglass, who had despaired of God's ability to bring about a peaceful end to slavery. Truth stood up and asked, "Frederick, is God dead?" The audience enthusiastically shouted support for her position.[22]

For Truth, as for many of her religiously motivated reform colleagues, the abolition of slavery was both part of God's divine plan and necessary for America to realize its democratic ideals. But as a woman, Truth also argued powerfully and effectively for

I Sell the Shadow to Support the Substance.
SOJOURNER TRUTH.

Sojourner Truth
One of the most famous and influential Black women of the nineteenth century, Sojourner Truth (born Isabella Baumfree) both embodied and spoke powerfully to the intersection of the struggles of Blacks, women, and the dispossessed. Truth's wide-ranging influence and popularity owed heavily to her piercing intelligence, Christian spirituality, striking speaking ability, and commanding sense of self. Notwithstanding her illiteracy, Truth's voice resonated with insight and the power of personal witness. This image was printed on a small card. The caption underneath it, "I Sell the Shadow to Support the Substance," illustrates her willingness to help support herself however she could. Photographs were a powerful tool to defy stereotypes. During slavery, Black women's femininity was often called into question or denied. **What elements in the picture can you find that speak to Truth's femininity or status as a woman?** *Library of Congress, Prints and Photographs Division, Washington, D.C., LC- USZC4-6165.*

women's rights. In an 1851 speech in Akron, Ohio, she made a powerful case for women's equality: "I have plowed and reaped and husked and chopped and mowed. . . . I can carry as much as any man, and can eat as much too, if I can get it."[23] Truth did not present herself as a respectable middle-class reformer who argued for abolition and equality in the abstract. Her words grew out of her own experience as an enslaved person, a wage earner, and a mother. Her directness won both followers and detractors. In an 1858 speech in a small Indiana town, when hecklers questioned whether so forceful a speaker could actually be a woman, Truth bared her breast.[24]

The experience and approach of Sarah Parker Remond was entirely different. She was born into an affluent free Black family in Salem, Massachusetts, but when she was barred from attending a girls' academy there, her family moved to Newport, Rhode Island, where she received an education. She chose a career as an antislavery lecturer, speaking locally, then nationally, and eventually traveling to England to help push forward a global campaign against slavery. Remond and other female abolitionist speakers braved strong opposition not just to Blacks speaking in public but also to women speaking in public. Their perseverance is testimony to their commitment to the abolitionist crusade and offers insight into their support for women's rights.

Elizabeth Jennings, a teacher in New York City's Black schools who had also lectured on behalf of Black women, took her activism to a new level when, in 1854, she was forcibly removed from a streetcar on her way to church. The Third Avenue Railroad, she was told, had separate cars for Black customers. With the support of her congregation, she sued the railroad company, claiming that as public conveyances, streetcars could not refuse to serve passengers on the basis of race. The jury ruled in her favor and awarded her damages. Jennings's unquestioned respectability, especially as an exemplary Black woman, played a key role in the judge's ruling: "*Colored persons, if sober, well-behaved, and free from disease,* had the same rights as others: and could neither be excluded *by any rules of the Company, nor by force of violence,* and in case of such expulsion or exclusion, the Company was liable." The Third Avenue Railroad apparently stopped segregating its cars, and the case, reported in *Frederick Douglass' Paper*, received considerable attention.[25]

AP® skills

Applying Disciplinary Knowledge: How did Black northerners use the courts to aid in their fight for equal rights?

Jennings's case, and a few others in the 1840s and early 1850s, seemed to signal that respectable free Blacks could use the courts to end discrimination. Benjamin Roberts initiated one of the most important legal cases. In 1848, Roberts sued the city of Boston on behalf of his daughter Sarah, who was forced to attend a mediocre all-Black school when there was a better all-white school closer to the family's home. Robert Morris, one of the nation's first Black lawyers, and the white lawyer Charles Sumner, later a U.S. senator, argued the *Roberts* case. In *Roberts v. City of Boston* (1849), the Massachusetts Supreme Court upheld Boston's public school statute requiring racially segregated schools. But the argument presented by Sumner, that "a school, exclusively devoted to one class, must differ essentially, in its spirit and character, from that public school . . . where all classes meet together in equality,"[26] did not go unheeded. Boston Blacks organized the Equal School Rights Committee to continue the fight for integrated public schools locally and statewide, and in 1855 Massachusetts became the first state to prohibit segregation of public schools on the basis of race.

Abolitionism: Moral Suasion, Political Action, Race, and Gender

Black abolitionists were innumerable and varied and often operated independently of any organization. From many different perspectives — female and male, formerly enslaved and freeborn — they urged their own communities and Americans in general to reform themselves and to better society by ensuring equal rights and ending slavery. Some cooperated with sympathetic white people who also organized against slavery. Some broke away from white organizations. Regardless, the agendas of Black activists helped shape the growing **abolitionist movement**, which increasingly commanded the attention of white citizens, politicians, and the national government. Abolitionists in the United States also linked themselves to a transatlantic movement, notably in Great Britain and France, to abolish slavery.

abolitionist movement A loose coalition of organizations with Black and white members that worked in various ways to end slavery immediately.

In the 1830s, the momentum of abolitionism shifted away from groups advocating gradual emancipation, the compensation of enslavers for freeing the people they enslaved, and the colonization of Blacks outside the United States. The new abolitionist movement sought to end slavery immediately rather than gradually, and without compensation, through moral suasion and **political action** — working within the political system. Despite their exclusion from political life, Black activists supported the latter approach as well as the former. Indeed, Blacks continued to mount vigorous and widespread opposition to slavery, working within their own organizations as well as within more influential and better-funded (and mostly white) abolitionist groups.

political action A primary strategy in the abolitionist movement that relied on working through political channels to force changes in the law and political practices.

William Lloyd Garrison led the moral suasion wing of the abolitionist movement, and the wealthy brothers Arthur and Lewis Tappan led the political action wing. Together the three men founded the American Anti-Slavery Society in 1833. Among the sixty-three delegates from eleven states at the society's first meeting in Philadelphia were three African Americans: Robert Purvis, James McCrummell, and James G. Barbadoes. The delegates framed two goals: "the entire abolition of slavery in the United States" and the elevation of "the character and condition of the people of color."[27]

AP® skills

Applying Disciplinary Knowledge: How did abolitionist demands change by the 1830s?

Garrison's moral suasion approach had been shaped by the arguments of Black abolitionists, and in 1831, with their support, he began publishing the *Liberator*, the most famous antislavery newspaper of the era. James Forten signed up subscribers in Philadelphia and sent Garrison's Boston office an advance payment on their subscriptions. Writing as "A Colored Philadelphian," he was also a frequent contributor to the paper's early issues.[28] Garrison worked well with Black activists and counted them among his friends. He published Maria Stewart's speeches in the *Liberator* and promoted the speaking career of Frederick Douglass, writing a preface to Douglass's slave narrative.

In the pages of the *Liberator*, Garrison condemned slavery as immoral and contrary to Christian principles, and he called for immediate, uncompensated emancipation.

He stated his opposition to colonization, and he promoted many of the era's reforms, including women's rights, prison reform, and temperance. Garrison believed that slavery could be ended and society perfected through a change in the human heart, not through political action. In fact, he perceived the Constitution as a proslavery document and the federal government as fouled by its proslavery connections.

The Tappan brothers, by contrast, saw the Constitution as an antislavery document. Consequently, they fought to end slavery through political action, including electing antislavery candidates and creating antislavery political parties. They believed it best to work within the political system to build a climate favorable to abolition. Political abolitionists gained growing influence as increasing numbers of northern politicians took a stand against slavery. Their strong support for the antislavery wing of the national Whig Party enhanced their impact, and they were actively involved in two antislavery parties: the Liberty Party, founded in 1840, and the Free-Soil Party, which absorbed the Liberty Party upon its founding in 1848.

AP® skills

Applying Disciplinary Knowledge: How did the abolitionist movement provide to Black Americans, regardless of gender, opportunities for civic engagement denied to them by the American political system?

Although Black men and all women were excluded from the nation's political life, they were active in abolitionist organizations. Women worked through women's auxiliaries of the American Anti-Slavery Society, which set up numerous regional affiliates, and also formed separate organizations. In 1833, the white Quaker abolitionist Lucretia Mott founded the Philadelphia Female Anti-Slavery Society; among its members were the Black activist Grace Douglass and her daughter Sarah Mapps Douglass, as well as women from the Forten family. There was also a Female Anti-Slavery Society in Boston. Women in these organizations signed petitions, distributed literature, sponsored bazaars to raise money, and vigilantly supported the cause of freedom seekers from the South. Many participated in the free produce movement, which encouraged boycotting of goods produced by enslaved labor. Female abolitionists often felt a special empathy for enslaved families torn apart by slave sales, and their concern for the plight of enslaved women, especially enslaved mothers, informed their antislavery arguments.

Women's participation in the abolitionist movement contributed significantly to the emergence of the women's rights movement. As women organized petition campaigns and formulated antislavery arguments, they gained confidence in their ability to work in the public arena and felt more keenly the limitations male abolitionist organizers placed on their participation. Women were usually prohibited from speaking in public and routinely denied leadership positions.

The issue of women's role in the abolitionist movement became so contentious that in 1840, when Garrison appointed a woman to the executive committee of the American Anti-Slavery Society, the organization split in two. The Tappans and a group of Black ministers, including Henry Highland Garnet, founded the rival American and Foreign Anti-Slavery Society (AFAS), which was committed to political abolitionism and to male leadership at the top levels. At an international meeting of abolitionist organizations in London in June 1840, the AFAS joined with like-minded British abolitionists to prohibit women from participating in policymaking.

Lucretia Mott, representing the Philadelphia Female Anti-Slavery Society, had to observe the proceedings from a railed-off space reserved for women.

Eight years later, in Seneca Falls, New York, Mott and Elizabeth Cady Stanton organized the nation's first women's rights convention. Frederick Douglass was in attendance, and some Black male activists, including the formerly enslaved Jermain W. Loguen, lent their support to women's rights, notably woman suffrage.

AP® skills

Applying Disciplinary Knowledge: Can you identify the connection between the abolitionist movement and the woman suffrage movement?

By this time, the abolitionist movement was further divided by a split between Garrison and Douglass, who came to agree with Garnet that political action was the most effective means of mobilizing public opposition to slavery. Douglass's decision in 1847 to publish his own newspaper, the *North Star*, also indicated his increasing independence from his mentor. Even the most zealous white abolitionists, including Garrison, did not always treat Black activists as equals. Many seemed more committed to freeing enslaved people than to securing equal rights for free Blacks.

Though fraught with divisions, the abolitionist movement won converts to its cause, especially among white evangelical northerners. For many, Christian principles seemed synonymous with concern for enslaved people. In the 1830s and

Fugitive Slave Law Convention

This group portrait taken at the Fugitive Slave Law Convention in Cazenovia, New York, in August 1850 captures the diversity of the participants. At center are Frederick Douglass and pioneering women's rights activist and abolitionist Angelina Grimké.

How does this photograph demonstrate the degree in which women were active participants in the abolitionist movement? *The Art Archive at Shutterstock.*

1840s, the Baptist, Methodist, and Presbyterian Churches forbade their members to enslave people, and the issue caused proslavery southern churches to withdraw from these denominations and organize separately. In 1846, several white abolitionist missionary societies merged with the Black Union Missionary Society to form the **American Missionary Association (AMA)**. With widespread support from Black leaders and members, including Samuel Cornish, Henry Highland Garnet, Jermain Loguen, James Pennington, and Mary Ann Shadd, the AMA promoted not only abolition but Christian-based education for African Americans as well. The abolitionist movement also succeeded in pushing slavery onto the national political agenda. In 1846, when war with Mexico began, the contest over whether enslaved people should be allowed in the West intensified, giving the slavery issue an urgent and decidedly political cast.

American Missionary Association
A Protestant missionary organization resulting from the merger of Black and white missionary societies in 1846 to promote abolition and Black education.

Slavery and the Coming of the Civil War

How did Black people aim to achieve the goal of Black freedom and self-determination through emigration in the nineteenth century?

What to do about the existence of slavery in a democratic nation that professed freedom and equality was a question that would not go away. Delegates at the Constitutional Convention in 1787 had devised a series of compromises that protected slavery even as some states took steps to end it. As the nation expanded, another compromise in 1820 protected slavery in territories south of Missouri's southern border while prohibiting it to the north. A few decades later, the Compromise of 1850 sought to hold together the increasingly disaffected North and South. But as a consequence, the Missouri Compromise was undone, first by popular sovereignty, a new plan for letting the people themselves decide whether the territory in which they lived would be slave or free, and then by a U.S. Supreme Court ruling that Congress did not have and had never had the authority to prohibit slavery in the territories. Northerners feared that a vast southern enslaver, or "Slave Power," conspiracy had triumphed, taking away their rights and allowing the detested slave system to undercut their free labor system. With the election of Abraham Lincoln as president in 1860, southerners feared that the incoming Republican administration would implement a vast northern conspiracy to end the slave system. Politics and compromise could no longer hold the Union together. African Americans had more than a political stake in the tumultuous events of the 1850s, as their rights and protections increasingly eroded. Some responded with resistance, even violence. Some saw emigration as the only solution. And some hoped that war, if it came, would end slavery and advance Black equality.

AP® skills
Applying Disciplinary Knowledge: Why did many abolitionists fear there was a growing "Slave Power" conspiracy in the United States by 1860?

Westward Expansion and Slavery in the Territories

Between 1830 and 1860, hundreds of thousands of Americans moved west, including enslaved Blacks and American Indians who were forcibly relocated (see chapter 6).

While the Missouri Compromise had, for the Louisiana Territory, settled the issue of which regions would permit slavery and which would not, American incursions into Mexican territory raised the issue anew. By 1830, the more than 20,000 Americans who had settled in Mexican Texas had reintroduced slavery — and 2,000 enslaved people — into an area where Mexico had formally abolished it. In 1836, these proslavery Americans seceded from Mexico, declared themselves the Lone Star Republic, and sought annexation to the United States. They were at first refused, but in 1845, Texas was admitted to the Union as a slave state. Northerners' opposition to a move they perceived as growing evidence of a "Slave Power" conspiracy invigorated the Liberty Party, which in 1844 received nearly nine times the number of votes it had in 1840 — 62,000 of the more than 2.5 million votes cast.

By this time, many Americans enthusiastically supported the notion that it was the "manifest destiny" of the nation to rule the continent from the Atlantic to the Pacific. The Oregon Treaty of 1846 between the United States and Great Britain settled a boundary dispute in the Oregon Country, clearing the way for official territorial recognition by the United States. Still, congressional factions wrangled over whether to forbid slavery in the territory, as the Oregon provisional government had already done in 1844, before finally voting to establish the Oregon Territory as a free territory in 1848.

Northern and southern politicians closely watched the number of potential slave and free states, lest one section dominate the other in Congress. Even before the Oregon negotiation with Great Britain was settled, however, the United States was at war with Mexico, following a failed attempt to purchase the Mexican provinces of Upper California and New Mexico. The prospect that these areas would become U.S. possessions ignited the issue of slavery in the territories once again. In the House of Representatives, Pennsylvania Democrat David Wilmot introduced a proviso that "neither slavery nor involuntary servitude shall ever exist in any part" of any territory gained from the Mexican-American War. Wilmot was against slavery, but he was not pro-Black. He aimed to keep slavery out of the territories so that free white labor would have a chance to thrive there and to prevent Blacks from coming into the area. The **Wilmot Proviso** failed to pass the Senate, but the angry debate it sparked intensified tensions between the North and South.

In 1848, the Treaty of Guadalupe Hidalgo sealed the U.S. victory over Mexico. In the treaty, Mexico ceded what became the territories of California, New Mexico, and Utah, as well as all of Texas north of the Rio Grande. Meanwhile, the discovery of gold in California drew so many prospectors to that territory (including more than 4,000 free Blacks) that in 1850 it applied for admission to the Union as a free state. If admitted, California would tip the balance in the Senate to the free states.

The vote on California statehood was one of the issues finally settled by the **Compromise of 1850**, which consisted of a series of separate bills. Neither side got all it wanted. Antislavery northerners succeeded in abolishing the slave trade in the District of Columbia, while southerners prevented the abolition of slavery there. California entered the Union as a free state, but the decision of whether slavery would be allowed

Wilmot Proviso (1846)
A controversial congressional proposal that sought to prohibit slavery in the new territories gained as a result of the Mexican-American War. Although it did not pass the Senate, it sparked angry debate between the North and South.

Compromise of 1850
A compromise aimed at reducing sectional tensions by admitting California as a free state; permitting the question of slavery to be settled by popular sovereignty in New Mexico and Utah Territories; abolishing the slave trade in the District of Columbia; resolving the Texas debt issue; and enacting a new fugitive slave law.

popular sovereignty
An approach to resolving the question of whether to allow slavery in new states by letting residents of the territories decide.

Fugitive Slave Act (1850)
Part of the Compromise of 1850, this law strengthened federal authority over freedom seekers.

personal liberty laws
A series of state laws in the North aimed at preventing the return of freedom seekers to the South.

in the territories of New Mexico and Utah was left to the people living in those areas, a policy known as **popular sovereignty**. The federal government assumed the debt contracted by the Lone Star Republic, and, as a concession to the South, a new fugitive slave law was enacted.

The **Fugitive Slave Act** of 1850 made it easier for freedom seekers to be captured and returned to their enslavers by strengthening federal authority over the capture and return of freedom seekers. Many northerners had long objected to the actions of slave catchers, and some northern states had passed **personal liberty laws** forbidding the kidnapping and forced return of freedom seekers. These laws were ruled unconstitutional in *Prigg v. Pennsylvania* (1842), but in that decision the U.S. Supreme Court also affirmed that the return of freedom seekers was a federal matter, in which state officials could not be required to assist. Northern states had then passed new personal liberty laws that forbade state officials to assist in fugitive cases and prohibited the use of state courts and jails for alleged fugitives from slavery. Under the Fugitive Slave Act of 1850, federal marshals were required to pursue alleged fugitives from slavery, and federal commissioners were appointed to oversee such cases. The fees these officials received — $10 for a freedom seeker returned to the claimant, $5 for a freedom seeker set free — reflected the law's bias.

But it was the authorizing of federal marshals to call on citizen bystanders to aid in the capture of alleged fugitives from slavery that especially angered northerners. Citizens who refused or who in any way aided an alleged fugitive from slavery could be fined $1,000 and sent to prison for six months. Many in the North who had not given much thought to slavery now felt that the federal government had far exceeded its powers. They perceived the federal effort to protect enslaved property as an attack on their own personal liberty, forcing them to act against their conscience. Wisconsin challenged the constitutionality of the law, and a Massachusetts statute sought to nullify it.

AP® skills

Applying Disciplinary Knowledge: How did the compromises made over the expansion of slavery impact the rights of free Black people?

For Black Americans, however, the implications of the law were far more menacing. Those who had escaped slavery, even years before, were no longer safe in the North. They were subject to arrest, denied jury trials, and forbidden to testify on their own behalf. A statement by an enslaver making a claim, together with an identification of the alleged fugitive from slavery, was all that was needed to return a person to slavery. A growing number of former fugitives from slavery left the United States for Canada, Mexico, Europe, and elsewhere. Given the provisions of the law, free Blacks were also at risk, as there was little to prevent unscrupulous slave hunters from seizing and enslaving them. An unknowable number of free Blacks as well as freedom seekers suffered enslavement or reenslavement at the hands of slave hunters. During the 1850s, 296 of 330 freedom seekers formally arrested, or 90 percent, suffered reenslavement.[29]

The Fugitive Slave Law Crisis and Civil Disobedience

Northern Black communities, where many fugitives from slavery lived, responded to the Fugitive Slave Act of 1850 with protest meetings, resolutions, and petitions. Blacks and their white allies demanded repeal of the act and mounted vigorous resistance against it. Jermain Loguen, born enslaved in Tennessee, proclaimed, "I will not live a slave, and if force is employed to reenslave me, I shall make preparations to meet the crisis as becomes a man."[30]

As a young man, Loguen had escaped to freedom on the Underground Railroad (Map 7.1). In the North, **vigilance committees**, an aboveground arm of the Underground Railroad, assisted arriving freedom seekers by providing temporary shelter, food, clothing, and sometimes legal assistance and jobs. The Black printer David Ruggles led the New York Vigilance Committee, which was widely admired for its militancy and effectiveness. Abolitionist Quakers joined the effort, but in the 1830s and 1840s, vigilance committees consisted primarily of Blacks. After the Fugitive Slave Act was passed in 1850, however, northern white support for the Underground Railroad

vigilance committees
Groups led by free Blacks and their allies in the North to assist freedom seekers.

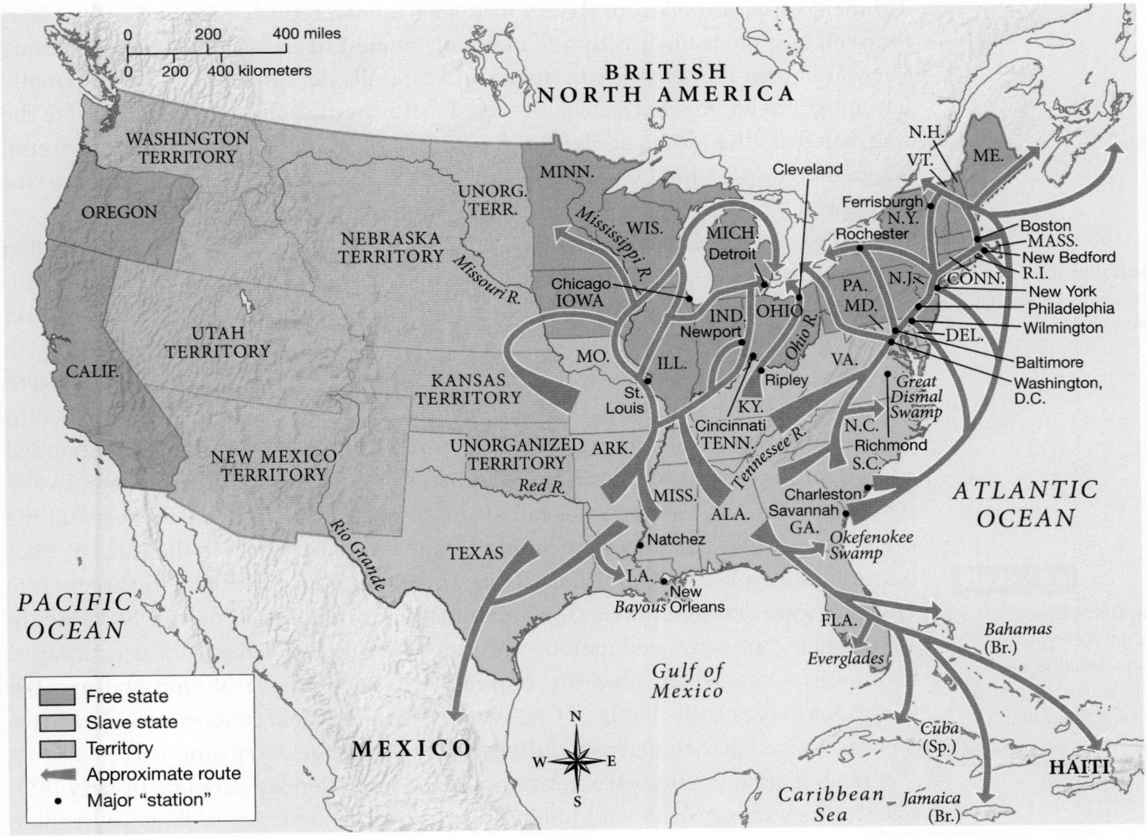

MAP 7.1 The Underground Railroad

The Underground Railroad consisted of an intricate secret network of people, routes, and safe places that allowed thousands of enslaved people to escape bondage. Freedom fighters such as Harriet Tubman placed themselves — and their own freedom — at great risk to help others reach the North. **Where did the Underground Railroad extend beyond the borders of the United States?**

grew, and vigilance committees became increasingly interracial. They expanded the networks of cellars, attics, church basements, and other safe spaces where freedom seekers could take refuge before being shepherded to freedom, often in Canada. Although their operations were of necessity covert because they were illegal, the vigilance committee and Underground Railroad networks helped an untold number of freedom seekers. For example, the Boston Vigilance Committee acknowledged helping sixty-nine freedom seekers to escape in 1851 alone.

The best-known "agent" on the Underground Railroad was William Still. As head of the Philadelphia Vigilance Committee, he kept records on the freedom seekers he assisted and later published their stories in *The Underground Rail Road* (1872). (See AP® Working with Sources: Forging an African American Nation — Enslaved and Free, North and South, pp. 286–93.) The most famous "conductor" was Harriet Tubman, who escaped from slavery in 1849. Tubman returned to the South at least fourteen times to lead, directly and indirectly, some 130 enslaved people to freedom. She was known for her strict discipline and carefully developed plans and reputedly never lost a freedom seeker. Deeply revered in northern abolitionist circles, where she was hailed as "the Moses of Her People," Tubman was intensely hated in the South, where there was a $40,000 bounty (the equivalent of more than $1 million today) for her capture.[31]

civil disobedience
The refusal to obey a law that one believes is unjust.

Those who aided freedom seekers or refused to help in their capture engaged in **civil disobedience** — refusal to obey a law that one considers unjust — a form of militant protest with a long history among African Americans. Their resolve was soon tested. On September 11, 1851, William Parker, a fugitive from slavery who lived with his wife, Eliza, also a fugitive from slavery, near Christiana, Pennsylvania, refused to allow a U.S. marshal and a party of Maryland enslavers led by Edward Gorsuch to search the Parker home for recent fugitives from Gorsuch's plantation. Eliza sounded a large dinner horn, summoning more than seventy-five local supporters. In the fight that followed, Gorsuch was killed and his son wounded. The Parkers and the other freedom seekers they were hiding escaped to Canada, but in the wake of what became known as the Christiana Resistance, thirty-five Blacks and three white Quakers were arrested for treason and conspiracy under the Fugitive Slave Act of 1850. Their cause attracted nationwide attention. Support came from as far away as Columbus, Ohio, where a meeting of free Blacks adopted a resolution praising "the victorious heroes at the battle of Christiana."[32] Pennsylvania congressman Thaddeus Stevens assisted in their defense, and eventually the charges were dropped.

AP® skills

Applying Disciplinary Knowledge: Can you identify and describe ways abolitionist activists engaged in civil disobedience in the 1850s?

Boston became a hotbed of resistance to the hated fugitive slave law. In early 1851, slave hunters seized Shadrach Minkins (also known as Frederick Wilkins), a freedom seeker working at a coffeehouse, and dragged him to a federal courthouse. Almost instantly, the Boston Vigilance Committee mobilized, and a crowd surrounded the courthouse while a group of Black men liberated Minkins and sent him on to freedom in Canada. In late May 1854, a similar effort to save Anthony Burns, another local African American who had been seized and jailed as a fugitive from slavery, failed.

Anthony Burns

This moving poster centers on an amiable portrait of the young freedom seeker Anthony Burns, surrounded by scenes that feature his tragic reenslavement in Boston in 1854. **What details does the poster use to convey the full impact of the Fugitive Slave Act on the lives of Black people?** *Library of Congress, Prints and Photographs Division, Washington, D.C., LC-USZ62-90750.*

President Franklin Pierce sent federal troops to Boston, and as they escorted Burns to the wharf for his return to slavery, some 50,000 protesters lined the streets and draped Boston's buildings in black. Although Burns was returned to slavery, Boston abolitionists eventually raised enough money to purchase his freedom.

This crisis intensified the conflict between the North and South over slavery. Southerners perceived the confrontations as part of a well-orchestrated northern campaign to defy the law and destroy slavery and the southern way of life that depended on it. For northerners, the confrontations forced an awareness of the reality of slavery and its impact on their lives. So did publication of the best-selling novel ***Uncle Tom's Cabin*** in 1852. Its white evangelical author, Harriet Beecher Stowe, crafted a sentimental yet graphic depiction of slavery's devastating effects on families, building empathy with slavery's victims in order to increase support for abolition.

Uncle Tom's Cabin (1852)
A best-selling novel by Harriet Beecher Stowe that portrayed the horrors of slavery, boosted the abolitionist cause, and angered the proslavery South.

Confrontations in "Bleeding Kansas" and the Courts

In 1854, Illinois senator Stephen A. Douglas, who had engineered passage of the Compromise of 1850, reopened the issue of slavery in the territories by promoting popular sovereignty for Kansas and Nebraska. By the terms of the **Kansas-Nebraska Act** (1854), the people who settled those territories would vote to determine whether, as states, they would be slave or free (Map 7.2). The result was a series of violent confrontations between proslavery and antislavery settlers. In May 1856, when proslavery forces from Missouri attacked the antislavery town of Lawrence, Kansas, John Brown, the self-appointed "captain" of antislavery forces, took revenge by murdering five proslavery settlers at Pottawatomie Creek. The furor over "Bleeding Kansas" also brought violence to the floor of the Senate when South Carolina representative Preston S. Brooks beat Massachusetts senator Charles Sumner into unconsciousness at his desk. Brooks claimed to be upholding the honor of his kinsman, South Carolina senator Andrew P. Butler, whom Sumner had singled out for insult in his earlier speech "The Crime against Kansas."

Kansas-Nebraska Act (1854)
A law that allowed the residents of Kansas and Nebraska Territories to decide whether slavery should be allowed.

AP® skills

Applying Disciplinary Knowledge: To what extent had violence become an increasingly popular strategy for settling the debate over slavery?

The national political system and the methods of civil debate, negotiation, and compromise proved increasingly ineffective in managing the slavery question. The issue eventually split the Whig Party, and it disintegrated. After 1856, the Democratic Party, ever more wedded to proslavery interests, was the only national political party left. Meanwhile, a number of sectional parties related to the slavery issue had merged. The abolitionist Liberty Party, formed in 1840, had called for an end to slavery in the District of Columbia and to the domestic slave trade. In 1848, it became part of the Free-Soil Party, founded that year. With the motto "Free Soil, Free Speech, Free Labor, Free Men," this party announced its opposition to the extension of slavery into the territories. To discourage the spread of plantation agriculture, the party also supported a homestead law that would distribute federal land in small plots to settlers (preferably whites) who would actually farm it, rather than to speculators. Although the party's motivations were often racist and many members were not abolitionists, it did attract influential abolitionist politicians and supporters of civil rights for free Blacks, such as

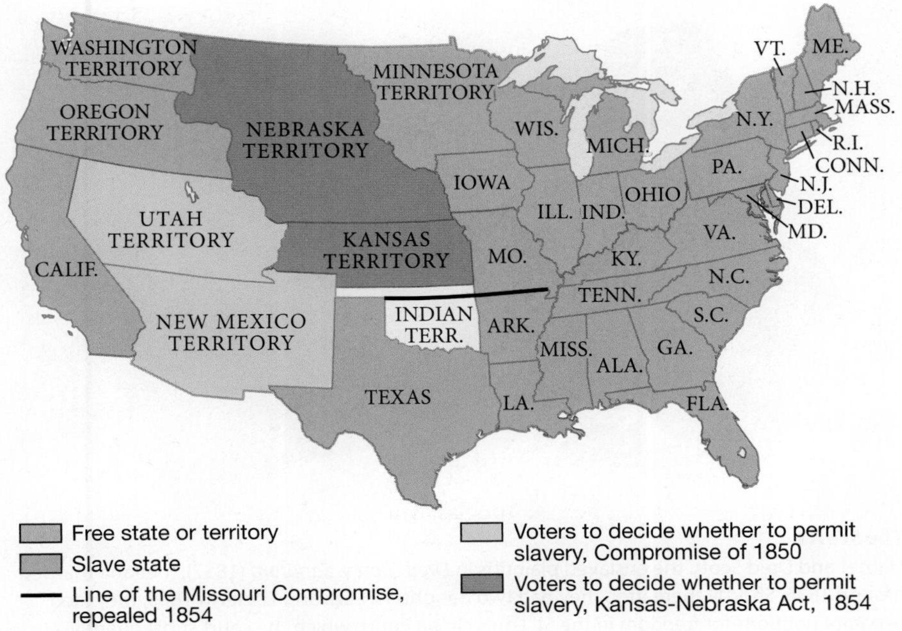

MAP 7.2 The Kansas-Nebraska Act, 1854

This map shows the free and slave states following the passage of the Kansas-Nebraska Act, as well as the areas where both this act and the Compromise of 1850 allowed popular sovereignty to rule the day. As the map indicates, the Kansas-Nebraska Act promoted the increasingly stark sectional divide between the slave South and the free North. **Why would this redrawn map spark a bloody fight over Kansas?**

Charles Sumner. Free-Soilers, Black and white, helped Massachusetts Blacks in their successful battles against discrimination in schools and transportation and in overturning state laws prohibiting interracial marriage.

In 1854, Free-Soilers joined with northern opponents of the Kansas-Nebraska Act and others opposed to the spread of slavery to form the Republican Party. Like the Liberty and Free-Soil Parties, the Republican Party was solely a northern party, with no southern support. Its 1856 presidential election slogan, "Free Soil, Free Labor, Free Speech, Free Men, Frémont" (for Republican presidential candidate John Frémont), highlighted Republicans' opposition to the extension of slavery into the territories, but the party made no commitment to end slavery. Nevertheless, Frederick Douglass and a growing number of Blacks joined the party, believing it could energize the abolitionist crusade. Through the Republican Party, the northern Black political struggle connected with the national political system. White southerners, observing Black support for the Republicans, feared that the party was conspiring to destroy slavery.

Meanwhile, a case making its way through the courts addressed the issue of slavery in the territories head-on. In 1846, enslaved people named Dred and Harriet

AP® skills

Applying Disciplinary Knowledge: What impact did the *Dred Scott* case have on the debate over slavery?

The Scotts
Harriet and Dred Scott, the enslaved plaintiffs in *Dred Scott v. Sandford* (1857), met and married around 1836. Shortly thereafter, they had two daughters, Eliza and Lizzie. In 1846, they filed separate petitions for freedom in the St. Louis circuit court, which the court subsequently combined, with Dred as the plaintiff. In fact, the U.S. Supreme Court's ruling in the case applied to all the Scotts, including the girls. In its 1857 decision, the Court determined that the Scotts and other African Americans were not citizens of the United States and did not share the same rights that whites enjoyed. Although they were freed almost immediately after the Court announced its decision, Dred died of tuberculosis a year later. Harriet died in 1876. **How did the Scotts attempt to use the courts to secure their freedom? What widespread implications did their case have for other African Americans?** *Library of Congress, Prints and Photographs Division, Washington, D.C., LC-USZ62-79305.*

Dred Scott v. Sandford (1857)
A controversial U.S. Supreme Court decision ruling that Scott, an enslaved man, was not entitled to sue in the Missouri courts and was not free even though he had been taken into a free territory; that no person of African descent could be a citizen; that enslaved people were property; and that Congress had no authority to regulate slavery in the territories.

Scott sued for their freedom because they had lived with their enslaver in Wisconsin Territory, where slavery was forbidden, before he moved them back to the slave state of Missouri. After a series of technical issues and split decisions in the Missouri courts, the U.S. Supreme Court took the case and in 1857 rendered its decision. In ***Dred Scott v. Sandford***, the Court ruled against Scott, and by extension his wife, Harriet. First, said the Court, Scott was not entitled to sue in the courts of Missouri because he was not a citizen. No person of African descent could be a citizen of the United States. Further, from the time of the nation's founding, "negroes of the African race" had been "regarded as beings of an inferior order, and altogether unfit to associate with the white race, either in social or political relations; and so far inferior, that they had no rights which the white man was bound to respect."[33] Enslaved people were legally protected property, and under the Constitution, Congress had no authority to deny the right of property. Thus it could not forbid slavery anywhere. All laws that forbade slavery in the territories were unconstitutional, including the Missouri Compromise of 1820. (See Appendix: *Dred Scott v. Sandford* for the text of this ruling.)

Emigration and John Brown's Raid on Harpers Ferry

The effect of the *Dred Scott* decision was instantaneous and inflammatory. Not only abolitionists but also many northerners generally saw the decision as more evidence of a massive "Slave Power" conspiracy, now authorized by the courts, to extend slavery into new territories. For many northerners, there appeared to be nothing to prevent southern enslaved labor from undermining northern free labor. Like the Fugitive Slave Act of 1850, the *Dred Scott* decision turned an increasing number of northerners, even whites opposed to abolition and Black civil rights, against the Supreme Court's position on slavery, which they saw as eroding their personal liberties.

For Black people, the decision was devastating. Their citizenship denied and their status declared inferior, they began to question more seriously their ties to the nation in which they lived. Robert Purvis declared that he owed no allegiance to a nation in which Black men possessed no rights that whites must respect. Frederick Douglass blasted the decision as "judicial wolfishness." Speaking to African Americans from Canada, Mary Ann Shadd Cary exclaimed, "Your national ship is rotten and sinking, why not leave it?"[34]

The *Dred Scott* decision clearly diminished Blacks' prospects for a viable life and meaningful future in the United States. They also had more reason than ever before to fear for their personal safety. Many decided to leave the country, with most going to Canada. By 1860, several thousand former African Americans lived in communities there. Proponents of emigration to Canada included H. Ford Douglas, a prominent Black leader from Ohio, and Mary Ann Shadd Cary, who had emigrated shortly after Congress passed the Fugitive Slave Act of 1850. Also residing in Canada in the late 1850s was the family of Martin R. Delany.

AP® exam tip

Be prepared to explain how the *Dred Scott* case influenced Black people's existing opinions on emigration to other countries.

Thoroughly disillusioned with the United States, Delany became the era's most prominent champion of emigration. He spoke for a loose-knit yet committed group that promoted emigration to Canada, Central and South America, the West Indies, and West Africa. In a series of national emigration conventions, the first and most important of which occurred in Cleveland in 1854, Delany tapped into an emigrationist sentiment that grew stronger and more vocal by the end of the 1850s. In speeches and especially in his influential book *The Condition, Elevation, Emigration, and Destiny of the Colored People of the United States* (1852), he explained how Black self-definition, self-regard, and self-reliance demanded Black self-determination, proposing the establishment of a Black nation outside the United States. In this regard, he can be considered a father of **Black nationalism**: the belief that African Americans were a nation within a nation that required self-determination.

Black nationalism
A diffuse ideology founded on the idea that Black people constituted a nation within a nation. It fostered Black pride and encouraged Black people to control the economy of their communities.

Toward the end of the decade, Delany focused on the prospects for Black emigration to West Africa, where he hoped to establish an unnamed though "thriving and prosperous Republic." Africa was "the native home of the African race," he argued, "and there he can enjoy the dignity of manhood, the rights of citizenship, and all the advantages of civilization and freedom."[35] In 1859 and 1860, joined by Robert Campbell, a Jamaican chemist, Delany explored the Niger River valley in search of a site for a Black American emigrant settlement. Like most other such efforts, the enormous financial, political, and logistical difficulties of this plan led to its failure, and Delany returned to the United States.

AP® skills

Applying Disciplinary Knowledge: What were the arguments in favor of emigrating to Liberia?

Interest in emigration remained widespread, however. In the 1850s, the white-dominated American Colonization Society sponsored the migration of several thousand Blacks to Liberia, while the Black press featured a vigorous debate on Liberia's benefits and drawbacks. Proponents stressed Black self-rule; opponents stressed Liberia's high mortality rate and inefficient government. Henry Highland Garnet came out in favor of emigration and worked on a plan — ultimately unsuccessful — to establish an emigrant Black American colony in West Africa funded by whites. The Episcopal priest and missionary James Theodore Holly promoted emigration to Haiti, and in 1861, he led a group of 101 people to an ill-fated and short-lived settlement there. But most northern Blacks remained in the United States. Despite the intensification of racial hostility and legal exclusion, they dared to hope that, as William Still expressed it, "great evils must be consummated that good might come."[36]

Some were not content to wait. In 1859, upon learning that John Brown secretly planned to incite a slave insurrection, five Black men joined his effort. Brown's plan was to seize arms and ammunition at the federal arsenal at Harpers Ferry, Virginia, thereby inspiring local enslaved people to join in an uprising that would trigger a series of slave revolts throughout the South and destroy the institution. On the night of October 16, Brown and his band of twenty-one men slipped into Harpers Ferry from a nearby farm, where they had been hiding out and planning. The poorly conceived plan unraveled as quickly as it unfolded. In the federal troops' hastily organized counterattack, ten of Brown's comrades were killed, including two of his sons. Five others escaped; seven, including Brown, were captured.

John Brown's raid (1859) An unsuccessful attempt by the white abolitionist John Brown to seize the federal arsenal at Harpers Ferry, Virginia, and incite a slave insurrection.

News of **John Brown's raid** on Harpers Ferry inflamed the conspiratorial views that the slave South and free North increasingly had of each other. Proslavery forces saw Brown as a madman. They perceived the botched though frightful insurrection as evidence of a "Black Republican Conspiracy" bent on destroying slavery and the southern way of life. Yet abolitionists, particularly Black abolitionists — even those opposed to violence as a means of emancipation — viewed Brown and his comrades as martyrs. Frances Ellen Watkins called Brown "the hero of the nineteenth century." Frederick Douglass praised him as "a human soul illuminated with divine qualities." A group of Providence Blacks applauded him as an "unflinching champion of liberty."[37]

Yet at the time, most Americans supported the restoration of order, swift and harsh justice for the guilty, and renewed efforts to moderate the slavery crisis. Thus Brown's speedy trial and treason conviction were, for them, a relief. On December 2, he went calmly to his hanging death, but not before he handed a note to a jail guard, offering this prediction:

> *Charlestown, Va. 2nd, December, 1859.*
> *I John Brown am now quite certain that the crimes of this guilty, land: will never be purged away; but with Blood. I had as I now think: vainly flattered myself that without verry [sic] much bloodshed; it might be done.*[38]

The next year, when Republican Abraham Lincoln won the presidency, the slavery question seemed less likely than ever before to be resolved. Lincoln's appeal was clearly sectional: all his electoral votes came from the free states of the North and West. Most of the electorate voted against him. In a four-way race, with northern and southern wings of the Democratic Party running separate candidates and a hastily organized Constitutional Union Party offering yet another choice, Lincoln won just 39 percent of the popular vote. Although he repeatedly stated that neither he as president nor the Republican Party would disturb slavery where it already existed, the slave states of the South made plans to withdraw from the Union.

CONCLUSION

Whose Country Is It?

Who belongs in the United States of America? When the contest over slavery reached a crisis with the election of Abraham Lincoln, the slave states believed they no longer belonged. But northern free Blacks had persistently debated that question throughout the preceding three decades. Most felt they were Americans precisely because they had been born in the United States, functioned as solid citizens, and served bravely in the nation's wars, even though that service had typically been scorned and rejected. Free Blacks argued that the *Dred Scott* decision notwithstanding, their birth and residency on U.S. soil, in combination with their unquestioned patriotism and firm commitment to the best of American ideals, made them U.S. citizens. Consequently, they vigorously resisted white supremacist efforts to deny their equality, especially their claim to U.S. citizenship. They fiercely maintained their allegiance to a nation that circumscribed and excluded them, demanding that America live up to its democratic and egalitarian promise.

At the beginning of the 1830s, northern Black communities turned inward. In the face of racial prejudice that cast them as inferiors, they cultivated self-regard and self-reliance. They cared for one another through mutual aid societies; they built independent churches and supported Black schools. Black leaders promoted moral reform, arguing that Christian ideals and virtuous living would strengthen their communities and win the approval of whites.

Blacks also turned outward, dedicating themselves to elevation within the larger society and to the abolition of slavery. Only by freeing the enslaved, they concluded, could they truly free and elevate themselves. At conventions, they debated strategies. Through newspapers, they built networks. They formed organizations. They boycotted goods produced by enslaved labor. The arrival of freedom seekers magnified the voices of Black abolitionists and emboldened them. They asserted that white attitudes and practices toward Blacks urgently needed to be reformed. They lectured and wrote books. They petitioned the government and sued for equal treatment in schools and on public conveyances. Still, they continued to be hemmed in by laws and practices that denied them representation in the nation's political life and pushed them to the margins of its economic and social life. Segregation and Black exclusion from white circles was the social norm. Studies in the emerging and pseudoscientific social sciences defined racial hierarchies that placed Blacks at the bottom. Most whites avoided Blacks, fearing contamination.

In the 1850s, Black prospects for a future in the United States narrowed further. A new law meant that freedom seekers could not be secure in the free states, and a U.S. Supreme Court ruling asserted that African Americans could not be, and never had been, citizens of the land of their birth. Many concluded that they no longer belonged in such a nation, and some emigrated — to Canada, Africa, Haiti, and elsewhere.

Yet Black claims to equality and freedom had pushed the slavery issue onto the national agenda, and the very crisis that undermined their allegiance to the nation also split the nation apart. Following the election of a president whose support was entirely in the North, the states of the South began to withdraw. The coming civil war would prove that African Americans, as free people, indeed belonged in the United States. In fact, that war would redefine the very nature of the nation. Frederick Douglass understood this. In 1849, he wrote, "We deem it a settled point that the destiny of the colored man is bound up with that of the white people of this country. . . . *We are here*, and here we are likely to be. . . . This is *our* country; and the question for the philosophers and statesmen of the land ought to be, What principles should dictate the policy of the action toward us?"[39] That question would not, however, be settled by the war. It would continue to be asked, again and again.

CHAPTER 7 REVIEW ▸ PRACTICING AP® SKILLS

AP® ESSENTIAL VOCABULARY AND SOURCES

**Essential terms and required sources from the AP® Course are marked with an asterisk.*

uplift* p. 259
human rights p. 262
Black convention movement* p. 263
moral suasion p. 266
abolitionist movement* p. 269
political action p. 269
American Missionary Association (AMA) p. 272
Wilmot Proviso (1846) p. 273
Compromise of 1850 p. 273
popular sovereignty p. 274
Fugitive Slave Act (1850)* p. 274
personal liberty laws p. 274
vigilance committees p. 275
civil disobedience* p. 276
Uncle Tom's Cabin (1852) p. 278
Kansas-Nebraska Act (1854) p. 278
Dred Scott v. Sandford (1857)* p. 280
Black nationalism* p. 281
John Brown's raid (1859) p. 282
Henry Highland Garnet, *An Address to the Slaves of the United States of America*, 1843 ("An Address to the Slaves of the United States" by Henry Highland Garnet, 1843)*
Frederick Douglass, *What to the Slave Is the Fourth of July?* 1852 ("What to the Slave Is the Fourth of July": Descendants Read Frederick Douglass's Speech, 2020)* p. 290

APPLYING DISCIPLINARY KNOWLEDGE: ESSENTIAL QUESTIONS

1. In what ways did the end of slavery in the North bring about an increase in anti-Black prejudice? What strategies did free Black northerners develop to combat discrimination and fortify their communities?

2. How did free Black northerners begin to link their plight to that of enslaved southerners?
3. What techniques did free Blacks employ, and what organizations and institutions did they found, to advance the developing Black freedom movement?
4. Describe the various legal and political battles surrounding slavery during the years 1850 to 1860. How did Black northerners respond? What impact did these events have on the Black freedom struggle?
5. How did the events of 1830 to 1860 fuel the mounting tensions between the North and South?

SUGGESTED REFERENCES

The Boundaries of Freedom

Alexander, Leslie M. *African or American? Black Identity and Political Activism in New York City, 1784–1861*. Urbana: University of Illinois Press, 2008.

Curry, Leonard P. *The Free Black in Urban America, 1800–1850: The Shadow of the Dream*. Chicago: University of Chicago Press, 1986.

Harris, Leslie M. *In the Shadow of Slavery: African Americans in New York City, 1626–1863*. Chicago: University of Chicago Press, 2003.

Hodges, Graham Russell. *Root and Branch: African Americans in New York and East Jersey, 1613–1863*. Chapel Hill: University of North Carolina Press, 1999.

Horton, James O., and Lois E. Horton. *Black Bostonians: Family Life and Community Struggle in the Antebellum North*. New York: Holmes & Meier, 1979.

———. *In Hope of Liberty: Culture, Community, and Protest among Northern Free Blacks, 1700–1860*. New York: Oxford University Press, 1997.

Litwack, Leon. *North of Slavery: The Negro in the Free States, 1790–1860*. Chicago: University of Chicago Press, 1961.

Melish, Joanne Pope. *Disowning Slavery: Gradual Emancipation and "Race" in New England, 1780–1860*. Ithaca: Cornell University Press, 1998.

Forging a Black Freedom Struggle

Bell, Howard H. *A Survey of the Negro Convention Movement, 1830–1861*. New York: Arno Press, 1969.

Blackett, Richard. *Building an Antislavery Wall: Black Americans in the Atlantic Abolitionist Movement, 1830–1860*. Ithaca: Cornell University Press, 1989.

Hall, Stephen G. *A Faithful Account of the Race: African American Historical Writing in Nineteenth-Century America*. Chapel Hill: University of North Carolina Press, 2009.

Jones, Martha S. *Birthright Citizens: A History of Race and Rights in Antebellum America*. New York: Cambridge University Press, 2018.

McCarthy, Timothy Patrick, and John Stauffer, eds. *Prophets of Protest: Reconsidering the History of American Abolitionism*. New York: New Press, 2006.

Painter, Nell Irvin. *Sojourner Truth: A Life, a Symbol*. New York: Norton, 1996.

Pease, Jane H., and William H. Pease. *They Who Would Be Free: Blacks' Search for Freedom, 1830–1861*. New York: Atheneum, 1974.

Pryor, Elizabeth Stordeur, *Colored Travelers: Mobility and the Fight for Citizenship before the Civil War*. Chapel Hill: University of North Carolina Press, 2016.

Quarles, Benjamin. *Black Abolitionists*. New York: Oxford University Press, 1969.

Rael, Patrick. *Black Identity and Black Protest in the Antebellum North*. Chapel Hill: University of North Carolina Press, 2002.

Rhodes, Jane. *Mary Ann Shadd Cary: The Black Press and Protest in the Nineteenth Century*. Bloomington: Indiana University Press, 1998.

Winch, Julie. *Philadelphia's Black Elite: Activism, Accommodation, and the Struggle for Autonomy, 1787–1848*. Philadelphia: Temple University Press, 1988.

Yee, Shirley. *Black Women Abolitionists: A Study in Activism, 1828–1860*. Knoxville: University of Tennessee Press, 1992.

Slavery and the Coming of the Civil War

Bordewich, Fergus. *Bound for Canaan: The Underground Railroad and the War for the Soul of America*. New York: Amistad, 2005.

Fehrenbacher, Don. *The Dred Scott Case: Its Significance in American Law and Politics*. New York: Oxford University Press, 1978.

Finkelman, Paul. Dred Scott v. Sandford: *A Brief History with Documents*. Boston: Bedford/St. Martin's, 1997.

Foner, Eric. *Free Soil, Free Labor, Free Men: The Ideology of the Republican Party before the Civil War*. New York: Oxford University Press, 1995.

Holt, Michael F. *The Fate of Their Country: Politicians, Slavery Extension, and the Coming of the Civil War*. New York: Hill and Wang, 2004.

McPherson, James M. *Battle Cry of Freedom: The Civil War Era*. New York: Oxford University Press, 1988.

Miller, Floyd J. *The Search for a Black Nationality: Black Emigration and Colonization, 1787–1863*. Urbana: University of Illinois Press, 1975.

Slaughter, Thomas P. *Bloody Dawn: The Christiana Riot and Racial Violence in the Antebellum North*. New York: Oxford University Press, 1991.

Still, William. *The Underground Rail Road*. 1872. Reprint, Chicago: Johnson, 1970.

Taylor, Quintard. *In Search of the Racial Frontier: African Americans in the American West, 1528–1990*. New York: Norton, 1998.

Forging an African American Nation—Enslaved and Free, North and South

In antebellum America, African Americans—North and South, enslaved and free—built over time and place the powerful bonds that united them as a people, a community, and a "nation within a nation." These bonds were neither natural nor God given; rather, African Americans' shared origins and their shared experiences in America helped solidify their ties to each other. These deep-seated connections intensified over time as subsequent generations of African-descended peoples, enslaved and free, increasingly identified with one another, enabling them to forge fundamental social, cultural, political, and economic networks—such as churches, schools, and mutual benefit societies—that unified them as a singular people. Primary to this evolving sense of African American identity were the core beliefs, commitments, and actions of African Americans themselves. Secondary but still crucial factors that often influenced this evolving racial identification were Black enslavement and anti-Black repression.

The following documents testify to African Americans' deepening sense of unity as a people, regardless of their location or status, in the middle decades of the nineteenth century. The written documents are from northern Blacks, who were relatively more at liberty than their southern brothers and sisters, whether free or enslaved, to express themselves and to mount an open liberation struggle. The excerpt from a speech by Sarah Mapps Douglass, an elite northern free Black woman, describes the evolution of her identification with enslaved southern Blacks. The African American liberation struggle required both this identification and various liberation strategies and tactics. The speech by Henry Highland Garnet, a formerly enslaved person who as a child escaped to Pennsylvania with his family, underscores the profound tie between enslaved and free African Americans. It also issues a revolutionary and highly controversial call for armed slave insurrection to emancipate the enslaved. Like Garnet, Frederick Douglass also escaped enslavement as a young man, though he later purchased his freedom with the help of English abolitionists. Douglass's speech is a scorching condemnation of the rank hypocrisy of Black enslavement in an America wedded to freedom, equality, and democracy.

Similarly, the visual documents highlight important aspects of the developing antebellum African American liberation struggle, which in large part grew out of Blacks' evolving identification as an African American people. "Escaping Slavery via the Underground Railroad" illustrates the centrality of active grassroots resistance to enslavement. The depiction of "Jim Crow" vividly represents the racist stereotypes that African Americans continually fought on the cultural battlefront of their freedom struggle.

key point

Although descended from many different ancestral tribes with unique cultural beliefs and practices who were often at war with each other, by the 1830s, both enslaved and free African Americans began to see themselves as a unified people and forged important networks to fight the institution of slavery.

AP® argumentation

DBQ Practice: Explain how the African American freedom struggle evolved during the early to mid-nineteenth century. Use at least two of the documents to support your response.

DOCUMENT 1 Sarah Mapps Douglass | *To Make the Slaves' Cause Our Own*, 1832

The majority of Black women in the antebellum North were poor, working class, and illiterate; thus, firsthand written accounts of their attitudes and experiences are rare. It is possible, however, to learn something of the attitudes and experiences of Black women in this era from the few who were well educated and whose family backgrounds and opportunities afforded them elite status. SARAH MAPPS DOUGLASS (1806–1882) was a founding member of the Female Literary Society of Philadelphia and the Philadelphia Female Anti-Slavery Society. A well-regarded lecturer and political essayist, she also established a high school for Black girls and taught at the Institute for Colored Youth. Her life and activism reflected her deep commitment to Quakerism. In the speech excerpted here, which she gave at one of the first meetings of the Female Literary Society, she describes the awakening of her compassion for enslaved Blacks.

> **Breaking it Down** To what extent do Sarah Mapps Douglass's racial, class, and gender identities influence her identification with the enslaved?

My friends — my sisters: How important is the occasion for which we have assembled ourselves together this evening, to hold a feast, to feed our never-dying minds, to excite each other to deeds of mercy, words of peace; to stir up in the bosom of each, gratitude to God for his increasing goodness, and feeling of deep sympathy for our brethren and sisters, who are in this land of christian light and liberty held in bondage the most cruel and degrading — to make their cause our own!

An English writer has said, "We must feel deeply before we can act rightly; from that absorbing, heart-rendering [*sic*] compassion for ourselves springs a deeper sympathy for others, and from a sense of our weakness and our own upbraidings arises a disposition to be indulgent, to forbear, to forgive." This is my experience. One short year ago, how different were my feelings on the subject of slavery! It is true, the wail of the captive sometimes came to my ear in the midst of my happiness, and caused my heart to bleed for his wrongs; but, alas! the impression was as evanescent as the early cloud and morning dew. I had formed a little world of my own, and cared not to move beyond its precincts. But how was the scene changed when I beheld the oppressor° lurking on the border of my own peaceful home! I saw his iron hand stretched forth to seize me as his prey, and the cause of the slave became my own. I started up, and with one mighty effort threw from me the lethargy which had covered me as a mantle for years; and determined, by the help of the Almighty, to use every exertion in my power to elevate the character of my wronged and neglected race. One year ago, I detested the slaveholder; now I can pity and pray for him. Has not this been your experience, my sisters? Have you not felt as I have felt upon this thrilling subject? My heart assures me some of you have.

° Douglass may be referring to a slave hunter or to discussions in the Pennsylvania legislature regarding the return of fugitives from slavery.

SOURCE: C. Peter Ripley, ed., *The Black Abolitionist Papers* (Chapel Hill: University of North Carolina Press, 1991), 3: 122–23.

DOCUMENT 2
AP® source

Henry Highland Garnet | *An Address to the Slaves of the United States of America, 1843*

At the time he delivered this speech, HENRY HIGHLAND GARNET (1815–1882) had been involved in abolitionist activities for more than ten years. He had studied theology at the Oneida Institute in Whitesboro, New York, where he sharpened his intellectual and rhetorical skills. As a pastor, he mastered public speaking. In 1843, he was one of seventy delegates from twelve states who attended the National Negro Convention in Buffalo, New York. There he gave a controversial speech that called on the enslaved to revolt. Notice a crucial rhetorical technique: he addressed his speech to the enslaved, although of course no enslaved people were present.

Breaking it Down How does Highland's rhetoric demonstrate the new direction the abolitionist movement was taking in the 1830s and 1840s?

Brethren and fellow citizens: Your brethren of the North, East and West have been accustomed to meet together in national conventions, to sympathize with each other, and to weep over your unhappy condition. In these meetings we have addressed all classes of the free, but we have never, until this time, sent a word of consolation and advice to you. We have been contented in sitting still and mourning over your sorrows, earnestly hoping that before this day your sacred liberties would have been restored. But we have hoped in vain. Years have rolled on, and tens of thousands have been borne on streams of blood and tears to the shores of eternity. While you have been oppressed, we have also been partakers with you; nor can we be free while you are enslaved. We, therefore, write to you as being bound with you.

Many of you are bound to us, not only by the ties of a common humanity, but we are connected by the more tender relations of parents, wives, husbands and sisters and friends. As such we most affectionately address you. . . .

Two hundred and twenty-seven years ago the first of our injured race were brought to the shores of America. They came not with glad spirits to select their homes in the New World. They came not with their own consent, to find an unmolested enjoyment of the blessings of this fruitful soil. The first dealings they had with men calling themselves Christians exhibited to them the worst features of corrupt and sordid hearts, and convinced them that no cruelty is too great, no villainy and no robbery too abhorrent for even enlightened men to perform, when influenced by avarice and lust. Neither did they come flying upon the wings of Liberty to a land of freedom. But they came with broken hearts from their beloved native land and were doomed to unrequited toil and deep degradation. Nor did the evil of their bondage end at their emancipation by death. Succeeding generations inherited their chains, and millions have come from eternity into time, and have returned again to the world of spirits, cursed and ruined by American Slavery.

The propagators of the system, or their immediate successors, very soon discovered its growing evil and its tremendous wickedness, and secret promises were made to destroy it. The gross inconsistency of a people holding slaves, who had themselves "ferried o'er the wave" for freedom's sake, was too apparent to be entirely overlooked. The voice of Freedom cried, "Emancipate your slaves." . . . But all was [in] vain. Slavery had stretched its dark wings of death over the land, the Church stood silently by, the priests prophesied falsely, and the people loved to have it so. Its throne is established, and now it reigns triumphantly.

Nearly three millions of your fellow citizens are prohibited by law and public opinion (which in this country is stronger than law) from reading the Book of Life. Your intellect has been destroyed as much as possible, and every ray of light they have attempted to shut out from your minds. The oppressors themselves

SOURCE: Philip S. Foner and Robert James Branham, eds., *Lift Every Voice: African American Oratory, 1787–1900* (Tuscaloosa: University of Alabama Press, 1998), 198–202, 204–5.

have become involved in the ruin. They have become weak, sensual and rapacious; they have cursed you; they have cursed themselves; they have cursed the earth which they have trod. . . .

Brethren, it is as wrong for your lordly oppressors to keep you in slavery as it was for the man thief to steal our ancestors from the coast of Africa. You should therefore now use the same manner of resistance as would have been just in our ancestors when the bloody footprints of the first remorseless soul thief was placed upon the shores of our fatherland. The humblest peasant is as free in the sight of God as the proudest monarch that ever swayed a scepter. Liberty is a spirit sent out from God and, like its great Author, is no respecter of persons.

Brethren, the time has come when you must act for yourselves. It is an old and true saying that, "if hereditary bondsmen would be free, they must themselves strike the blow."° You can plead your own cause and do the work of emancipation better than any others. The nations of the Old World are moving in the great cause of universal freedom, and some of them at least will, ere long, do you justice. The combined powers of Europe have placed their broad seal of disapprobation upon the African slave trade. But in the slaveholding parts of the United States the trade is as brisk as ever. They buy and sell you as though you were brute beasts. The North has done much; her opinion of slavery in the abstract is known. But in regard to the South, we adopt the opinion of the *New York Evangelist* — "We have advanced so far, that the cause apparently waits for a more effectual door to be thrown open than has been yet." We are about to point you to that more effectual door. Look around you and behold the bosoms of your loving wives heaving with untold agonies! Hear the cries of your poor children! Remember the stripes your fathers bore. Think of the torture and disgrace of your noble mothers. Think of your wretched sisters, loving virtue and purity, as they are driven into concubinage and are exposed to the unbridled lusts of incarnate devils. Think of the undying glory that hangs around the ancient name of Africa — and forget not that you are native-born American citizens, and as such you are justly entitled to all the rights that are granted to the freest. Think how many tears you have poured out upon the soil which you have cultivated with unrequited toil and enriched with your blood; and then go to your lordly enslavers and tell them plainly that you *are determined to be free.* Appeal to their sense of justice and tell them that they have no more right to oppress you than you have to enslave them. Entreat them to remove the grievous burdens which they have imposed upon you, and to remunerate you for your labor. Promise them renewed diligence in the cultivation of the soil, if they will render to you an equivalent for your services. Point them to the increase of happiness and prosperity in the British West Indies since the Act of Emancipation.° Tell them, in language which they cannot misunderstand, of the exceeding sinfulness of slavery and of a future judgment and of the righteous retributions of an indignant God. Inform them that all you desire is freedom, and that nothing else will suffice. Do this, and forever after cease to toil for the heartless tyrants, who give you no other reward but stripes and abuse. If they then commence the work of death, they, and not you, will be responsible for the consequences. You had far better all die — *die immediately* — than live slaves and entail your wretchedness upon your posterity. If you would be free in this generation, here is your only hope. However much you and all of us may desire it, there is not much hope of redemption without the shedding of blood. If you must bleed, let it all come at once — rather *die freemen than live to be slaves.* . . .

Brethren, arise, arise! Strike for your lives and liberties. Now is the day and the hour. Let every slave throughout the land do this, and the days of slavery are numbered. You cannot be more oppressed than you have been; you cannot suffer greater cruelties than you have already. *Rather die freemen than live to be slaves.* Remember that you are three *millions!* . . .

Let your motto be Resistance! *Resistance!* RESISTANCE! No oppressed people have ever secured their liberty without resistance.

° Paraphrased from Lord Byron, *Childe Harold's Pilgrimage* (1818).

° Slavery had been abolished in the British West Indies by an act of Parliament in 1833.

DOCUMENT 3
AP® source

Frederick Douglass | *What to the Slave Is the Fourth of July?*, 1852

In 1843, when FREDERICK DOUGLASS (1818–1895) opposed Henry Highland Garnet's call for an armed slave revolt to overthrow slavery, he was relatively new to abolitionist organizing; he had been on the lecture circuit for only two years and a freeman for five. Less than a decade later, he was as seasoned a speaker as Garnet and was better known and more influential. On July 5, 1852, Douglass delivered one of his most famous speeches, to the Ladies' Anti-Slavery Society of Rochester, New York, which had invited him to address an Independence Day celebration in Corinthian Hall. Some five hundred to six hundred people each paid 12½ cents to hear the renowned abolitionist. Like many other community celebrations at the time, this event began with a prayer and a reading of the Declaration of Independence. Douglass made the most of the occasion to drive home his message. The audience, the local press reported, reacted with much applause.

Breaking it Down How is Douglass able to offer a perspective unique from that of Henry Highland Garnet (p. 288) and Sarah Mapps Douglass (p. 287)?

Fellow-Citizens — Pardon me, and allow me to ask, why am I called upon to speak here to-day? What have I, or those I represent, to do with your national independence? Are the great principles of political freedom and of natural justice, embodied in that Declaration of Independence, extended to us? and am I, therefore, called upon to bring our humble offering to the national altar, and to confess the benefits, and express devout gratitude for the blessings, resulting from your independence to us?

Would to God, both for your sakes and ours, that an affirmative answer could be truthfully returned to these questions! . . .

But, such is not the state of the case. I say it with a sad sense of the disparity between us. I am not included within the pale of this glorious anniversary! Your high independence only reveals the immeasurable distance between us. The blessings in which you this day rejoice, are not enjoyed in common. The rich inheritance of justice, liberty, prosperity, and independence, bequeathed by your fathers, is shared by you, not by me. The sunlight that brought life and healing to you, has brought stripes and death to me. This Fourth of July is *yours*, not *mine*. *You* may rejoice, *I* must mourn. To drag a man in fetters into the grand illuminated temple of liberty, and call upon him to join you in joyous anthems, were inhuman mockery and sacrilegious irony. Do you mean, citizens, to mock me, by asking me to speak to-day? . . .

Fellow-citizens, above your national, tumultuous joy, I hear the mournful wail of millions, whose chains, heavy and grievous yesterday, are to-day rendered more intolerable by the jubilant shouts that reach them. If I do forget, if I do not faithfully remember those bleeding children of sorrow this day, "may my right hand forget her cunning, and may my tongue cleave to the roof of my mouth!" To forget them, to pass lightly over their wrongs, and to chime in with the popular theme, would be treason most scandalous and shocking, and would make me a reproach before God and the world. My subject, then, fellow-citizens, is American Slavery. I shall see this day and its popular characteristics from the slave's point of view. Standing here, identified with the American bondman, making his wrongs mine, I do not hesitate to declare, with all my soul, that the character and conduct of this nation never looked blacker to me than on this Fourth of July. Whether we turn to the declarations of the past, or to the professions of the present, the conduct of the nation seems equally hideous and revolting. America is false to the past, false to the present, and solemnly binds herself to be false to the future. Standing with God and the crushed and bleeding slave on this occasion, I will, in the name of humanity which is outraged, in the name of liberty which is fettered, in the name of the constitution and the bible, which are disregarded and trampled upon, dare to call in question and to denounce, with all the emphasis I can command, everything that serves to perpetuate slavery — the great sin and shame of America! "I will not equivocate; I will not excuse"; I will use the severest language I can command; and yet not one word shall escape me that any man, whose judgment is not blinded by prejudice, or who is not at heart a slaveholder, shall not confess to be right and just.

But I fancy I hear some of my audience say, it is just in this circumstance that you and your brother abolitionists fail to make a favorable impression on the public mind. Would you argue more, and denounce less, would you persuade more and rebuke less, your cause would be much more likely to succeed. But, I submit, where all is plain there is nothing to be argued. . . .

For the present, it is enough to affirm the equal manhood of the Negro race. Is it not astonishing that, while we are plowing, planting, and reaping, using all kinds of mechanical tools, erecting houses, constructing bridges, building ships, working in metals of brass, iron, copper, silver, and gold; that, while we are reading, writing, and cyphering, acting as clerks, merchants, and secretaries, having among us lawyers, doctors, ministers, poets, authors, editors, orators, and teachers; that, while we are engaged in all manner of enterprises common to other men — digging gold in California, capturing the whale in the Pacific, feeding sheep and cattle on the hillside, living, moving, acting, thinking, planning, living in families as husbands, wives, and children, and, above all, confessing and worshiping the Christian's God, and looking hopefully for life and immortality beyond the grave — we are called upon to prove that we are men!

Would you have me argue that man is entitled to liberty? that he is the rightful owner of his own body? You have already declared it. Must I argue the wrongfulness of slavery? Is that a question for republicans? . . . There is not a man beneath the canopy of heaven that does not know that slavery is wrong *for him.*

What! am I to argue that it is wrong to make men brutes, to rob them of their liberty, to work them without wages, to keep them ignorant of their relations to their fellow-men, to beat them with sticks, to flay their flesh with the lash, to load their limbs with irons, to hunt them with dogs, to sell them at auction, to sunder their families, to knock out their teeth, to burn their flesh, to starve them into obedience and submission to their masters? Must I argue that a system, thus marked with blood and stained with pollution, is wrong? No; I will not. I have better employment for my time and strength than such arguments would imply.

What, then, remains to be argued? Is it that slavery is not divine; that God did not establish it; that our doctors of divinity are mistaken? There is blasphemy in the thought. That which is inhuman cannot be divine. Who can reason on such a proposition! They that can, may! I cannot. The time for such argument is past.

At a time like this, scorching irony, not convincing argument, is needed. Oh! had I the ability, and could I reach the nation's ear, I would to-day pour out a fiery stream of biting ridicule, blasting reproach, withering sarcasm, and stern rebuke. For it is not light that is needed, but fire; it is not the gentle shower, but thunder. We need the storm, the whirlwind, and the earthquake. The feeling of the nation must be quickened; the conscience of the nation must be roused; the propriety of the nation must be startled; the hypocrisy of the nation must be exposed; and its crimes against God and man must be proclaimed and denounced.

What to the American slave is your Fourth of July? I answer, a day that reveals to him, more than all other days in the year, the gross injustice and cruelty to which he is the constant victim. To him, your celebration is a sham; your boasted liberty, an unholy license; your national greatness, swelling vanity; your sounds of rejoicing are empty and heartless; your denunciations of tyrants, brass-fronted impudence; your shouts of liberty and equality, hollow mockery; your prayers and hymns, your sermons and thanksgivings, with all your religious parade and solemnity, are to him mere bombast, fraud, deception, impiety, and hypocrisy — a thin veil to cover up crimes which would disgrace a nation of savages. There is not a nation on the earth guilty of practices more shocking and bloody, than are the people of these United States, at this very hour.

Source: Frederick Douglass, *What to the Slave Is the Fourth of July? Frederick Douglass, Oration, Delivered in Corinthian Hall, Rochester, July 5, 1852* (Rochester, NY: Lee, Mann, 1852), 14–15.

DOCUMENT 4 *Escaping Slavery via the Underground Railroad*

The Underground Railroad was a network of individuals and groups throughout the South and North who secretly assisted freedom seekers in making their way to freedom. In this engraving, taken from William Still's *The Underground Rail Road* (1872), a group of exhausted freedom seekers, including a mother and an infant, arrive at League Island, Philadelphia, from Norfolk, Virginia. Carriages stand by as volunteers help them up the hill to safety. The engraving is a compelling illustration of enslaved resistance: the lengths to which the enslaved themselves went in their quest for freedom. It also shows their committed and courageous allies in the struggle against slavery. Indeed, the Underground Railroad has come to symbolize the extraordinary difficulties of the fight for both human rights and Black freedom.

Breaking it Down How does the image show the lengths to which the enslaved went in their quest to free themselves? What does it suggest about the level of commitment and courage of their allies in the struggle against slavery?

Newberry Library, Chicago, Illinois/Bridgeman Images.

DOCUMENT 5 Jim Crow

White blackface minstrelsy, which caricatured and denigrated Blacks, grew out of 1820s urban street entertainments in which young Black and white men performed for coins and food in public places such as wharves, markets, street corners, and parks. T. D. (Thomas Dartmouth) "Daddy" Rice, the white traveling actor most closely associated with early minstrelsy, developed blackface routines that featured singing, dancing, and humor. His most famous Black character was an enslaved person dressed in rags named Jim

Crow, who, Rice claimed, was inspired by the dance of a disabled Black man. The Jim Crow character made Rice famous, and in time "Jim Crow" became a common racial epithet. By the late nineteenth century, the term was used to refer to the whole range of laws and customs related to racial segregation.

Breaking it Down How does the depiction of Black people in minstrel shows dehumanize and reinforce stereotypes of Black people? To what extent do you think this dehumanization influenced white acceptance of racist laws and policies?

Collection of the New-York Historical Society/Bridgeman Images.

PRACTICING AP® SKILLS

1. **AP® Contextualization.** Describe the role Black organizations and conventions played in the fight against slavery from the 1830s to the 1860s. How do these documents illustrate that role?
2. **AP® Comparison.** Compare and contrast the techniques all three activists in this source collection used to advocate for an end to slavery.
3. **AP® Contextualization.** Explain how the historical events of the 1830s–1860s influenced the outlook and message of Black abolitionists like Mapps Douglass, Garnet, and Douglass.
4. **Exploring AP® Themes.** How do the documents demonstrate the range of methods Black abolitionists developed to assert agency in the fight against slavery?
5. **Class Discussion.** Discuss how the diverse backgrounds of each speaker in this source collection reflect the diversity of the Black abolitionist movement.

Document-Based Questions:
Thesis Statements

So far, our exploration of document-based questions has focused on pre-writing steps: how to break down prompts (p. SW5-A) and how to skillfully skim sources (p. SW6-A). We're now prepared to approach the drafting process itself, beginning with the thesis statement.

A **thesis statement** is the core of any strong essay, including a successful response to a document-based question. Your essay's thesis statement will be the central claim that allows the reader to understand your view or position on the topic at hand. It's your opportunity to directly assert the opinion that you will later support with specific pieces of **evidence**. As we'll demonstrate in this workshop, the strongest thesis statements are those that preview a logical train of thought that will structure the remainder of the **argument**.

Examining the AP® Rubric

Thankfully, there's clear guidance on what, exactly, a thesis must do in order to earn full points on the AP® African American Studies Exam. According to that rubric, you'll earn a point if your essay:

- Responds to the prompt with a defensible thesis or claim that establishes a line of reasoning. *To earn this point, the thesis must make a claim that responds to the prompt rather than restate or rephrase the prompt. The thesis must consist of one or more sentences located in one place, either in the introduction or the conclusion.*

You'll earn an additional point if your essay:

- Uses reasoning (e.g., causation, comparison, change or continuity across time or geography) to set up an argument that addresses the prompt. *To earn this point, the response must demonstrate the use of reasoning to frame or structure an argument, even if the reasoning is uneven or the evidence lacks specificity.*

Taken together, these guidelines let us know a successful thesis will:

1. **Make a claim that incorporates one of the 4 Cs**
   a. Comparison
   b. Causation
   c. Continuity & Change
2. **Establish a line of reasoning**

We can break down each of these requirements and then put them together to craft a complete thesis statement.

Reviewing Skillful Skimming

This workshop will build directly off of your work in the AP® Skills Workshop for Chapter 6 (p. SW6-A), so we will practice with the same prompt:

Explain how Black Americans resisted chattel slavery in the period from 1820 to 1860.

As always, our first step will be breaking down the prompt to bring the proper time period, topic, task, and course knowledge to front of mind.

Time Period	Topic	Task
1820–1860	Resistance to slavery	Provide specific details about overt and covert resistance to chattel slavery.
Relevant Course Concepts, Developments, Processes		
• The *Amistad* case and the *Creole* insurrection secured freedom for enslaved Africans who had staged revolts. • Truants, or people who fled enslavement, often hid close to their owner's property in a form of resistance known as "lying out." • Abolitionists formed a network now known as the Underground Railroad to help enslaved people resettle in free territories. • Enslaved people often strengthened kinship and community through religious worship.		

Next, we can approach the sources themselves. In the previous workshop, we practiced skillful skimming to efficiently identify key information about each source. If you have access to your notes from that workshop, look them over to refresh your memory. If not, give the sources a skim using these principles:

Main idea. How would you summarize the source in one sentence?

Context. What course knowledge seems directly connected to this particular source? What's the most relevant outside knowledge about its topic, its time period, or its creator?

Category. How would you generalize the point of the source in just a few words? Does this category align or contrast with other sources for the same DBQ?

Source A: Am I Not a Woman and a Sister?, 1832

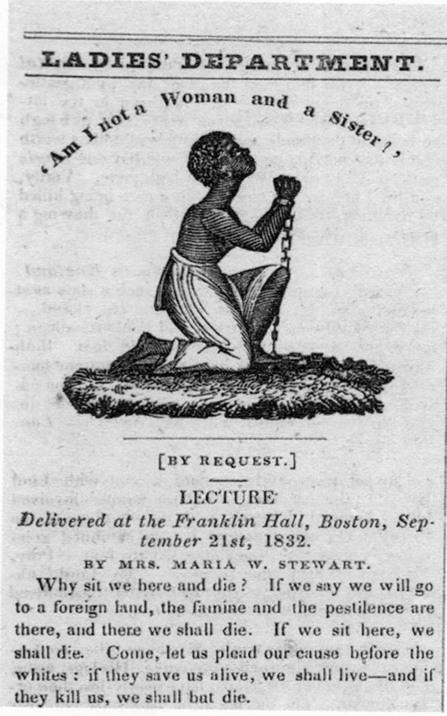
LADIES' DEPARTMENT.

"Am I not a Woman and a Sister?"

[BY REQUEST.]

LECTURE

Delivered at the Franklin Hall, Boston, September 21st, 1832.

BY MRS. MARIA W. STEWART.

Why sit we here and die? If we say we will go to a foreign land, the famine and the pestilence are there, and there we shall die. If we sit here, we shall die. Come, let us plead our cause before the whites: if they save us alive, we shall live—and if they kill us, we shall but die.

"Am I not a Woman and a Sister?", A lecture delivered by Maria Stewart on September 21, 1832, as reprinted in The Liberator, *vol. 2, no. 46, November 17, 1832.*

SOURCE: "Am I Not a Woman and a Sister?," illustration for a lecture delivered by Maria Stewart on September 21, 1832, as reprinted in *The Liberator*

Source B: What, to the Slave, Is the Fourth of July?, 1852

"At a time like this, scorching irony, not convincing argument, is needed. O! had I the ability, and could I reach the nation's ear, I would, to-day, pour out a fiery stream of biting ridicule, blasting reproach, withering sarcasm, and stern rebuke. For it is not light that is needed, but fire; it is not the gentle shower, but thunder. We need the storm, the whirlwind, and the earthquake. The feeling of the nation must be quickened; the conscience of the nation must be roused; the propriety of the nation must be startled; the hypocrisy of the nation must be exposed; and its crimes against God and man must be proclaimed and denounced.

What, to the American slave, is your 4th of July? I answer: a day that reveals to him, more than all other days in the year, the gross injustice and cruelty to which he is the constant victim. To him, your celebration is a sham; your boasted liberty, an unholy license; your national greatness, swelling vanity; your sounds of rejoicing are empty and heartless; your denunciations of tyrants, brass fronted impudence; your shouts of liberty and equality, hollow mockery; your prayers and hymns, your sermons and thanksgivings, with all your religious parade, and solemnity, are, to him, mere bombast, fraud, deception, impiety, and hypocrisy

— a thin veil to cover up crimes which would disgrace a nation of savages. There is not a nation on the earth guilty of practices, more shocking and bloody, than are the people of these United States, at this very hour."

SOURCE: Frederick Douglass, "What, to the Slave, Is the Fourth of July?," keynote address for Independence Day celebration, Rochester, New York, July 5, 1852

Source C: The Condition, Elevation, Emigration, and Destiny of the Colored People of the United States, 1852

"That there have been people in all ages under certain circumstances, that may be benefited by emigration, will be admitted; and that there are circumstances under which emigration is absolutely necessary to their political elevation, cannot be disputed. . . .

This may be acknowledged; but to advocate the emigration of the colored people of the United States from their native homes, is a new feature in our history, and at first view, may be considered objectionable, as pernicious to our interests. This objection is at once removed, when reflecting on our condition as incontrovertibly shown in a foregoing part of this work. And we shall proceed at once to give the advantages to be derived from emigration, to us as a people, in preference to any other policy that we may adopt."

SOURCE: Martin R. Delany, *The Condition, Elevation, Emigration, and Destiny of the Colored People of the United States*, 1852

Source D: Go Down, Moses, c. 1853

When Israel was in Egypt's land
Let my people go
Oppressed so hard they could not stand
Let my people go

Go down, Moses
Way down in Egypt land
Tell old Pharaoh,
"Let my people go"

"Thus spoke the Lord," bold Moses said
Let my people go
"If not I'll smite your first born dead"
Let my people go
"No more in bondage shall they toil"
Let my people go
"Let them come out with Egypt's spoil"
Let my people go

SOURCE: "Go Down, Moses," African American spiritual, c. 1853

Source E: Percent Change in Free Black Population, 1830–1860

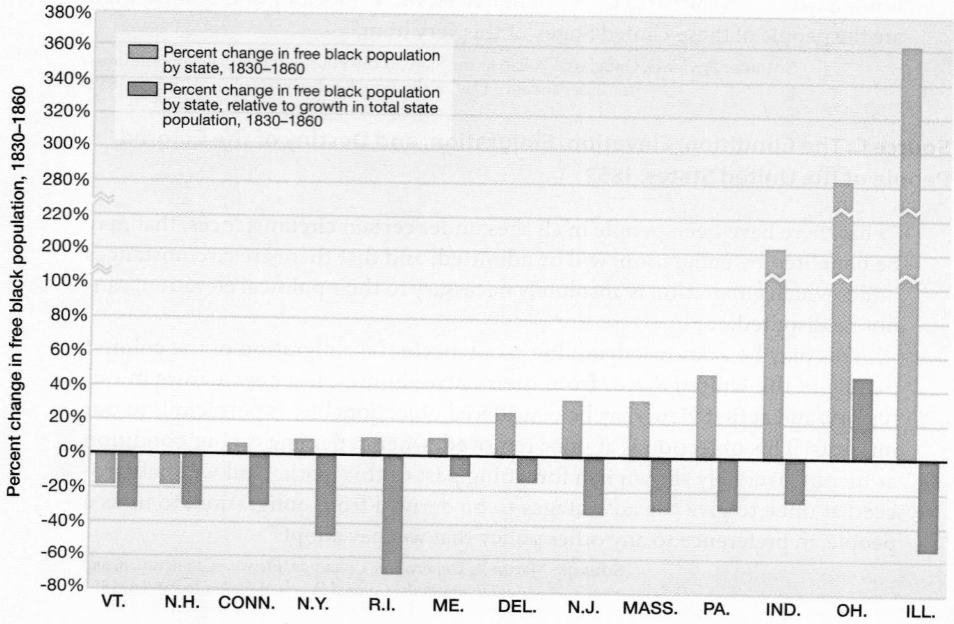

Having reviewed the sources, you should now have a better sense of how they connect to one another and to the topic of the document-based question: resistance to slavery. It's now time to shape our initial observations into a **claim**.

Making a Claim

As you learned in the AP® Skills Workshop for Chapter 2 (p. SW2-A), a claim is an assertion that requires a defense — it has to state a position that some people might disagree with. You make claims in your day-to-day life whenever you take a position instead of just stating a fact. For instance:

> **Statement of Fact.** Some high school students take Advanced Placement courses.
>
> **Claim.** More high school students should take Advanced Placement courses.

The first statement isn't a claim — it just makes an assertion that can be easily verified as true. It's not possible to argue for or against the idea that some students take AP® courses, because it's a neutral fact.

The second statement, on the other hand, takes a position that's arguable. Some people might agree that more students should take Advanced Placement courses, while others might disagree. Because the second statement would need to be backed up by evidence to become convincing, it's an example of a claim.

An effective thesis statement will always be a claim, not a statement of fact. That's why it's not enough to restate the prompt topic — you need to clearly assert your own arguable opinion to earn full points on the AP® Exam.

Finding an arguable claim becomes easier if you use one of the Four Cs, the reasoning processes you've been practicing throughout this course.

Comparison. How are two figures, events, movements, or time periods similar or different?

Causation. What factors directly contributed to an event or a movement? What effects did this event or movement directly bring about?

Continuity & Change. What changed and what stayed the same between different time periods?

To see what we mean, consider how we can convert a statement of fact into a claim by applying each of the reasoning processes:

Statement of Fact. Many Black people resisted slavery and the slave trade in the period from 1820 to 1860.

Comparison. Overt rebellion was the most impactful form of resistance, compared to other actions like abolitionist events or emigration.

Causation. Religious principles drove resistance efforts by strengthening community ties.

Continuity & Change. The rise of Black nationalists like Martin R. Delany reflected a change from white-led emigration efforts like the American Colonization Society.

In this way, applying one of the Four Cs can help you move from discussing facts to making an arguable claim.

When crafting a claim in response to a document-based question, you'll need to decide which reasoning process aligns best with the prompt. Some prompts point clearly to one process over another — for instance, a prompt asking you to explain why a movement came to be would align better with causation than with comparison — but often, there isn't one right approach. Usually, you'll be able to simply go with your gut and select the process that jumps out to you as a promising framework. In this case, the prompt task asks us to explain the ways in which Black Americans resisted slavery within one specific time period, so continuity and change is off the table (as that process addresses multiple time periods). Instead, we could use comparison to point out the degree of similarity between resistance methods, or causation to explore the factors that brought about resistance.

Establishing a Line of Reasoning

As mentioned previously, a claim becomes compelling only if it's backed up by evidence. Of course, it's not enough to throw evidence at a wall and hope it sticks. Instead, you'll need to create a chain of logic that guides your reader through your main points in an organized fashion. That's the function of a **line of reasoning**, the connections you draw between a claim and the evidence presented to support it.

When placed at the beginning of an essay, a thesis statement is the perfect opportunity to preview the line of reasoning that will structure the remainder of your response. Take a look at the following thesis statement template to see what we mean:

X *because* A, B, *and* C.

Based solely on a thesis statement in this format, you can predict the basic shape of the essay to follow. X is the writer's main claim, while A, B, and C hint at the categories of evidence the writer will use to support their claim. As long as the essay remains faithful to this outline, it will have a clear line of reasoning that keeps the essay organized and cohesive.

In the previous section, we used three different reasoning processes to craft arguable claims. Here, let's use the claim based on the reasoning process of causation:

Religious principles drove resistance efforts by strengthening community ties.

We can flesh out this claim using the thesis statement template and some of the information we collected while skillfully skimming:

Religion drove resistance efforts among Black Americans in the period from 1820 to 1860, because it inspired abolitionists like Maria Stewart, provided motivation during journeys on the Underground Railroad, and promoted unity among Black Americans.

Because this thesis statement lays out an arguable claim and establishes a clear line of reasoning, it sets the stage well for a convincing, organized DBQ response.

recap

Crafting a Thesis Statement

A thesis statement is a type of claim. A claim is an arguable position that requires a defense. To move from a statement of fact to an arguable claim, it can be helpful to apply one of the reasoning processes outlined in the Four Cs:

Comparison. How are two figures, events, movements, or time periods similar or different?

Causation. What factors *directly* contributed to an event or a movement? What effects did this event or movement *directly* bring about?

Continuity & Change. What changed and what stayed the same between different time periods?

To establish a line of reasoning in your thesis statement, try using the following format:

X because **A**, **B**, and **C**.

Activity ▸ Crafting a Thesis Statement

Write a thesis statement in response to the prompt on page SW7-B. You may wish to use the template ***X** because **A**, **B**, and **C**.*

NOTES

Multiple-Choice Questions

Questions 1–2 refer to the following.

The Underground Railroad

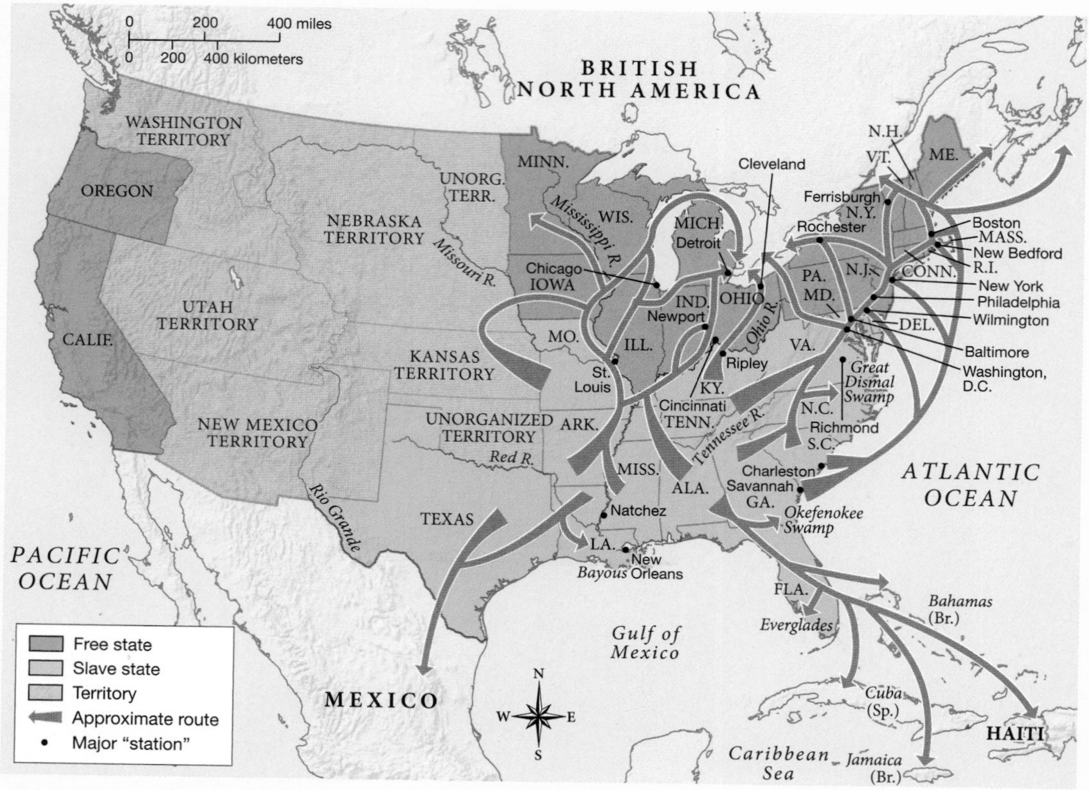

1. Which of the following best describes a consequence of the activities depicted on the map?
   (A) Congress enacted the Fugitive Slave Acts of 1793 and 1850.
   (B) Napoleon sold the colony of Louisiana to the United States.
   (C) The United States declared war against Mexico.
   (D) The American Colonization Society campaigned for free Black emigration to Liberia.

2. The patterns depicted on the map reflect which of the following historically significant developments in the struggle for Black freedom?
   (A) The Civil War battles that led to the signing of the Emancipation Proclamation
   (B) The slave rebellions that took place during the 1830s
   (C) The location of maroons that existed well after the start of the Civil War
   (D) The covert network of abolitionists who provided resources to help enslaved people resettle in free territories

Short-Answer Question

Sojourner Truth, *"I Sell the Shadow to Support the Substance."*

I Sell the Shadow to Support the Substance.
SOJOURNER TRUTH.

Library of Congress, Prints and Photographs Division, Washington, D.C., LC- USZC4-6165.

1. Using the image, answer A, B, C, and D.

(A) Describe the impact that Sojourner Truth had on both the fight against slavery and the fight for women's rights.

(B) Explain why visual depictions of African American leaders in photography and art were significant during the era of slavery.

(C) Explain why Black women's activism in the nineteenth century was historically and culturally significant.

(D) Explain how Black women in the nineteenth century advocated for social justice and reform.

CHAPTER 8

Freedom Rising: The Civil War

1861–1865

CHAPTER TIMELINE

Events specific to African American history are in purple. General U.S. history events are in black. Events from the AP® Course Framework are marked with an asterisk.

1861	Confederate States of America established
	Confederates fire on Fort Sumter; Civil War begins
	Lincoln calls for military volunteers to put down rebellion
	Freedom seekers designated contraband of war
	Confederates defeat Union troops at Bull Run
	First Confiscation Act
	Mary S. Peake begins teaching contrabands in Hampton, Virginia
	Union troops control Sea Islands, begin Port Royal Experiment
1862	Congress ends slavery in District of Columbia and U.S. territories
	Robert Smalls pilots *Planter* to Union navy and secures his own freedom
	Second Confiscation Act
	Elizabeth Keckley founds Contraband Relief Association
	Black army unit organized in Sea Islands
	Union army defeats Confederates at Antietam
	Preliminary Emancipation Proclamation
	Black army units organized in Louisiana
	Charlotte Forten arrives in Sea Islands to teach contrabands
1863	Emancipation Proclamation*
	Petition drive in California ends restriction on Blacks testifying against whites in court
	Union institutes military draft
	U.S. Colored Troops established
1863	Black army units fight at Port Hudson, Louisiana
	Harriet Tubman serves as Union scout*
	Union victory at Gettysburg ends Confederate offensive in North
	Draft riots in New York City*
	Black army unit leads assault on Fort Wagner, South Carolina
	Lincoln's Gettysburg Address
	Lincoln announces "10 percent plan"
1864	Confederate troops murder Black prisoners of war at Fort Pillow, Tennessee
	Congress equalizes pay of Black and white soldiers
	Congress passes Wade–Davis Bill in opposition to Lincoln's Reconstruction plan
	National Equal Rights League founded
	Lincoln reelected on National Union ticket, with former Democrat Andrew Johnson as vice president
1865	General William T. Sherman issues Special Field Order 15
	Black lawyer John S. Rock accepted to argue cases before U.S. Supreme Court
	Petition drive leads to repeal of Illinois law requiring Black settlers to pay a fine
	Congress establishes Freedmen's Bureau*
	Confederate Congress authorizes arming of enslaved people
	Confederate general Robert E. Lee surrenders to Union general Ulysses S. Grant Lincoln assassinated
	Thirteenth Amendment abolishes slavery*

Please note that this chapter includes primary sources that use the N-word, which we have chosen not to reprint in full here. We wish to accurately reflect both the sources' original intent as well as the racism of the time period, but we also recognize that this word has a long history as a derogatory and deeply hurtful expression when used by white people toward Black people, as it is in the context of these sources. We have replaced the term without hindering understanding of these sources. Be mindful of context, both historical and contemporary, as you read and discuss this chapter.

Robert Smalls and the African American Freedom Struggle during the Civil War

Around three o'clock in the morning on May 13, 1862, the *Planter*, a Confederate steamer loaded with supplies for nearby Confederate outposts, made its way up Charleston harbor with the enslaved pilot Robert Smalls at the helm. Confederate lookouts, accustomed to seeing Black pilots, took little note of the fact that there were no white men on deck.

Once outside the harbor, Smalls revved up the steamer's engine and sped in the direction of the Union blockade. Hoisting a white flag of surrender, he hoped the Union navy would permit the *Planter* to enter Union lines as a fugitive vessel and, more important, that his family members and friends on board would be protected as fugitives from slavery. After several tense moments, the Union sailors turned their guns and cannons away, received the surrender of the *Planter*, and welcomed the freedom seekers as free people.

Smalls had devised a cunning plan to secure freedom for himself and his family. Smalls and those around him had heard that Union forces were using freedom seekers to help fight the Confederacy. Once behind Union lines, he provided the Union navy with important information about Confederate units in Charleston harbor. Before long, he was piloting the *Planter* for the Union navy, transporting people and supplies within the Union zone. Not long afterward, Congress gave Smalls and his band of freedom fighters a financial reward for surrendering the *Planter* to Union forces.

The story of Smalls's daring escape captured the attention of African Americans and the northern white press. In October 1862, a meeting of Blacks at New York City's Shiloh Presbyterian Church, pastored by the Reverend Henry Highland Garnet, welcomed him "with deafening cheers." A resolution adopted by the meeting claimed that Smalls's bold action demonstrated "a faithful devotedness to the cause of the American union."[1] For Black and their allies, the exploit became one of the most celebrated events of the Civil War. It is also just one instance in what turned out to be a massive defection of enslaved people from the Confederacy to Union lines. The ever-growing number of enslaved men, women, and children who seized their freedom by joining the Union cause ultimately contributed to the collapse of the Confederacy.

The Civil War began as a southern war for Confederate independence and a northern war to defeat the Confederate rebellion and restore the Union. At the outset, neither side thought that the war would last very long or eventually lead to the destruction of slavery. The Confederacy was founded to protect slavery. The Union was willing to accept slavery where it already existed, opposing only the extension of slavery into the territories.

The transformation of the Union cause from a war to restore the Union to a war with the additional aim of abolishing slavery owed much to the actions of the enslaved people themselves. Their escape from slavery and their presence behind Union lines, together with the advocacy of northern free Blacks and their white abolitionist allies, put pressure on the Lincoln administration and the U.S. Congress for policy changes and new laws that would address the issue of slavery directly and end it. The Union victory also owed much to the Black men — both free and recently freed — who served in the Union army and navy, as well as to the many Black men and women who worked alongside the troops and, as civilians, supported the Union cause. Their dedication and service, they believed, would earn them the rights of U.S. citizens. But as free Blacks in the North and South had known for decades, freedom did not mean fair treatment and equality, and it was apparent at the war's end that the Black freedom struggle was far from over.

The Coming of War and the Seizing of Freedom, 1861–1862

What were enslaved and free African American men and women's contributions during the United States Civil War?

In hindsight, the Civil War seems to have been inevitable, but following the election of Abraham Lincoln as president in November 1860, the war came in a series of small steps, the consequences of which were not fully apparent at the time. As the states of the Confederacy withdrew from the Union to protect slavery, northern free Blacks and their allies increasingly expressed the hope that if war came, it would be a war to end slavery everywhere. That was not the Union's initial war aim, but when enslaved people began pressing the issue by fleeing to Union lines, Union commanders were forced to respond, and in time they moved to protect the refugees' freedom. Slowly, Lincoln and Congress, too, were forced to respond by putting in place policies and practices that pointed toward a general emancipation.

War Aims and Battlefield Realities

With the election of Lincoln, sectional tensions over slavery reached a crisis. Believing they owed no loyalty to a Union that could elect a president without any southern support, the slave states made plans to withdraw from the Union. On November 10, 1860, South Carolina called a secession convention, and on December 20, it declared that "the union now subsisting between South Carolina and other States, under the name of the 'United States of America' is hereby dissolved." Four days later, the convention passed a declaration listing the causes justifying secession: the North's interference with slavery; repeated northern condemnations of slavery as sinful; northern support for abolitionism; northerners' aiding and abetting the escape of southern freedom seekers; northern promotion of slave insurrections through "emissaries, books, and pictures"; and the election of Lincoln, a leader "whose opinions and purposes are hostile to slavery."[2]

South Carolina's secession ordinance declared the state independent, but already a movement was underway for the formation of a confederacy of slave states. By February 1, 1861, Mississippi, Florida, Alabama, Georgia, Louisiana, and Texas also had seceded, and on February 4, delegates from these states met in Montgomery, Alabama, to create the **Confederate States of America**. They wrote a constitution that read much like the U.S. Constitution, with the key difference being that it explicitly protected the right to hold enslaved people as property within its domain. Setting up a provisional government, the Confederacy elected Mississippi senator Jefferson Davis as president.

Confederate States of America
The eleven southern states that seceded from the United States in 1860 and 1861, precipitating the Civil War.

Even as the Confederacy formed, there were two attempts to avert disunion. In Congress, Kentucky senator John J. Crittenden proposed to reinstate the 1820 Missouri Compromise and thus guarantee the protection of slavery in territories south of the southern border of Missouri. After a U.S. Senate committee failed to reach agreement on the proposal, the Virginia legislature called a peace convention. But the delegates in attendance, representing both free and slave states, also failed to find a compromise that would hold the Union together.

While some still hoped for peace, the Confederate States of America prepared for war. They began organizing an army and a navy, and state militias seized federal forts, arsenals, and post offices. Most military posts in the South came under Confederate command. In Charleston, Union major Robert Anderson withdrew from Fort Moultrie to the more easily protected Fort Sumter, on an island in the harbor, and waited for provisions.

On March 4, 1861, Lincoln delivered his inaugural address to a fractured Union. Speaking directly to "the Southern States," he reaffirmed, "I have no purpose, directly or indirectly, to interfere with the institution of slavery in the States where it exists. I believe I have no lawful right to do so, and I have no inclination to do so." At the same time, Lincoln asserted that the Union was a binding and "perpetual" compact. Furthermore, he explained, "no State, upon its own mere motion, can lawfully get out of the Union." He concluded, "Acts of violence, within any State or States, against the authority of the United States, are insurrectionary or revolutionary." Precisely because it was unlawful and thus intolerable, Lincoln believed that secession must be overturned. It was his position that the Union had to be respected and maintained.[3]

In his first cabinet meeting, Lincoln raised the issue of provisioning Fort Sumter, and the matter was discussed often in the following weeks. Eventually, the president determined that the fort should be resupplied, and he informed the governor of South Carolina of this intention. In turn, South Carolina demanded the fort's surrender. When Major Anderson refused, Confederate shore batteries opened fire early on the morning of April 12. The next day, Anderson surrendered. The Civil War had begun.

Anticipating that Anderson was ready to evacuate the fort, Confederate officials did not think their actions would lead to hostilities. After all, back in January, fire from Charleston's shore batteries had forced the withdrawal of a provision ship without further incident. But they miscalculated. On April 15, Lincoln called for 75,000 militia to put down the insurrection and "to repossess the forts, places, and property which have been seized from the Union."[4]

Virginia refused to answer the call. Its first secession convention had rejected leaving the Union, but now a second convention voted for it. By May 20, Arkansas, Tennessee, and North Carolina had also joined the Confederacy, making a total of eleven Confederate states. The slave states Delaware, Maryland, Kentucky, and Missouri, known as the border states, remained in the Union, but not without strife. Federal troops occupied Baltimore; guerrilla fighting ravaged Missouri; and a provisional Confederate government was formed in Kentucky, although the state officially declared its neutrality. Even as Virginia's state capital, Richmond, was selected as the new Confederate capital, the state's western counties seceded from Virginia and organized a Unionist government.

Patriotic fervor pervaded both North and South. Each side felt that its cause was just and believed that it would soon prevail. Lincoln's call for volunteers had anticipated a three-month commitment. With their superior economic, material, military, and human resources (close to two to one), northerners believed that the Confederate rebellion would be quickly put down. With fierce determination and confidence in their formidable military abilities, southerners believed that they would succeed in establishing the Confederate States of America as an independent nation. They would be defending their homeland, while the Union would be forced to take the war into the Confederate states.

Three months into the war, Union forces marched thirty miles into Virginia. On July 21, 1861, along a creek called Bull Run, the Confederates turned them back. Union officials had miscalculated. It was clear that the Confederacy would not back down in the face of Union advantages on and off the battlefield. It was also clear that the war would not be over soon.

Union Policy on Black Soldiers and Black Freedom

AP® exam tip

Explain how Black Americans, regardless of gender, contributed to the Union war effort upon the outbreak of the Civil War.

Free Black men responded enthusiastically to Lincoln's call for volunteers. In Pittsburgh, the Hannibal Guards, a local Black militia, pledged support for the Union cause: "As we consider ourselves American citizens . . . although deprived of all our political rights, we yet wish the government of the United States to be sustained against the tyranny of slavery, and are willing to assist in any honorable way . . . to sustain the present administration."[5] In Albany, Ohio, free Blacks organized the Attucks Guards, naming their regiment after Crispus Attucks, the freedom seeker who was the first person to die in the American Revolution. Albany's Black women gave the volunteer company a handsome homemade flag. And at Boston's Twelfth Baptist Church, those assembled unanimously resolved that "we are ready to stand by and defend the Government with 'our lives, our fortunes, and our sacred honor.' " They resolved further that "the colored women could go as nurses, seamstresses, and warriors if need be."[6]

Regimental flag: Silk mounted on a wooden pole (with the eagle missing). Museum Department, Courtesy of the Maryland Historical Society, image ID 2004.22. Confederate flag: Private Collection/Photo © Don Troiani/Bridgeman Images.

Regimental and Confederate Flags

At left, the remnant of a handsome flag made by the Colored Ladies of Baltimore for the Fourth Regiment U.S. Colored Troops showcases Black patriotism. This regimental flag vividly illustrates the strong Black civilian support for the Union war effort. Even more impressively, it illustrates African Americans' deep pride in and zealous support for Black Union troops during and after the war. This support was particularly strong among women with male relatives and friends serving in the military. Juxtaposed with this emblem of Black Union patriotism is the flag of the Confederacy, which symbolizes both slavery and the Confederate cause. The Confederate flag simultaneously represents two vexing dilemmas that continue to make it intensely controversial, down to the present day: It represents the inherent tension between slavery and freedom, as well as the inherent tension between Confederate patriotism and the treason of Confederate rebellion against the Union. **Compare and contrast the purpose and message of each flag.**

ACTIVITY ▸ Revisit Your Prediction

In the AP® Unit Warmup (p. U2-F), you made a prediction about this image. **What were African American soldiers' motivations for enlisting during the U.S. Civil War? What inequities do you think they faced? How do you think Black soldiers' service affected Black communities during and after the U.S. Civil War? What contributions do you think enslaved and free African Americans made during the U.S. Civil War? Support or revise your original prediction using evidence from this chapter.**

But in all cases, military service by Black men was rejected. For many whites, Black men serving in the Union forces evoked thoughts of slave insurrections and violated notions of white male superiority. When Black men in Cincinnati met to organize a home guard to protect the city, white opposition was fierce. Instead of gratitude, these volunteers received "insults . . . for this simple offer." In Cincinnati, as throughout the North, Blacks encountered a persistent refrain: "We want you d——d n*****s to keep out of this; this is a white man's war."[7] In September 1862, President Lincoln observed that if the Union accepted Black troops, he feared "that in a few weeks the arms would be in the hands of the rebels."[8] Despite the service of Black men in the American Revolution and the War of 1812, the U.S. army had generally excluded Black soldiers, and they were barred from state militias as well.[9]

Nevertheless, from the outset, northern Blacks and abolitionists engaged in vigorous debate about the purposes, possible consequences, and larger meanings of the war. Many worked hard to make emancipation a central war goal. Shortly after the surrender of Fort Sumter, the *Anglo-African Magazine* prophesied that "out of this strife will come freedom, though the methods are not yet clearly apparent." "Justice to the slave," the magazine argued, was "the sure and permanent basis of 'a more perfect Union.' "[10] Frederick Douglass expressed a similarly hopeful vision in May 1861: "Any attempt now to separate the freedom of the slave from the victory of the Government . . . any attempt to secure peace to the whites while leaving the blacks in chains . . . will be labor lost. The American people and the Government at Washington may refuse to recognize it for a time; but the 'inexorable logic of events' will force it upon them in the end; that the war now being waged in this land is a war for and against slavery."[11] (See AP® Working with Sources: Wartime and Emancipation, pp. 325–35.)

Nevertheless, Lincoln continued to frame the conflict as a rebellion that must be put down so the Union could be preserved. As president and commander in chief, he refused to acknowledge slavery as the cause of the war or abolition as its goal. He knew he could not afford to alienate the border states, where slavery still existed. Securing the loyalty of Maryland — to the north of Washington, D.C. — was an especially important goal. Without it, the nation's capital would be surrounded by hostile territory. And Maryland's loyalty was uncertain. In Baltimore, federal troops had been shot at as they had marched through the city. As riots and civil disorder continued, Lincoln suspended habeas corpus on April 27, 1861. Those suspected of disloyal acts could be taken into custody without the right to have a judge rule on the lawfulness of their imprisonment. In other words, they could be held in jail indefinitely without the authorities showing cause.

To help further secure the border states' loyalty, Lincoln developed a plan for gradual, compensated emancipation of enslaved people that allowed the states, not the federal government, to take the initiative. He especially hoped that Delaware, with fewer than 2,000 enslaved people, would view such a plan favorably. But none of the border states adopted emancipation plans. Congress, however, passed legislation to end slavery in the District of Columbia, and on April 16, 1862, Lincoln signed the act into law. It gave enslavers who could prove their loyalty to the Union up to $300 for each person freed, and it gave each freedperson who chose emigration to

Haiti, Liberia, or any country outside the United States up to $100. Nearly 3,000 enslaved people were freed by this act, and several hundred chose to accept payment to relocate to Haiti. In June, Congress ended slavery in U.S. territories — those areas west of the Mississippi River not yet organized as states. For the Union, this crucial action settled once and for all an extremely divisive issue that had caused zealous discord between the South and North before the war and that persisted as a fundamental disagreement between the Confederacy and the Union. For the Confederacy, it suggested that the Union's ultimate goal was to end southern slavery.

The District of Columbia Emancipation Act showed Lincoln's two-pronged approach to the problem of slavery — compensation and colonization — but it did not prove to be the model that Lincoln had hoped for. In the spring and summer of 1862, the war was not going well for the Union. Despite a massive effort, Union attempts to advance on Richmond failed, and by fall the Confederate Army of Northern Virginia was on the offensive. Calls for a general emancipation proliferated, but in a famous exchange with the journalist Horace Greeley of the *New York Tribune*, who urged Lincoln to commit himself to end slavery, Lincoln replied: "My paramount object in this struggle is to save the Union, and is not either to save or to destroy slavery. . . . What I do about slavery, and the colored race, I do because I believe it helps to save the Union. . . . I have here stated my purpose according to my view of official duty; and I intend no modification of my oft-expressed personal wish that all men every where could be free."[12]

AP® skills

Applying Disciplinary Knowledge: Can you describe the purpose of the District of Columbia Emancipation Act and explain how it combined both old and new solutions to the problem of slavery?

Freedom Seekers and Freedpeople

Pressure to address emancipation directly mounted because some enslaved people had already freed themselves. Taking advantage of the unsettled conditions of wartime, enslaved people fled to Union lines and Union-controlled territory, where their presence forced military commanders to determine their status. The first to seize freedom in this way were Frank Baker, James Townsend, and Shepard Mallory, who, just after the hostilities began, had been sent by their enslaver to build Confederate fortifications in Hampton, Virginia. In the middle of the night on May 23, 1861, they commandeered a skiff and crossed the waters of Hampton Roads to Fortress Monroe, which was still in Union hands. There they received protection from the commander, General Benjamin F. Butler, who refused to return them to their enslavers. Instead, using the South's definition of enslaved people as property, Butler designated them **contraband** of war, or confiscated Confederate property. These three men were the first of thousands of freedom seekers — men, women, and children — who would swell the population at Fortress Monroe. By July 1861, there were 900 refugees there, and by August 1862, there were 3,000. By the end of the war, in April 1865, some 10,000 formerly enslaved people lived in camps at Hampton, the village across from the fortress, which had been burned to the ground by retreating Confederates in August 1861.

contraband
A freedom seeker pursuing protection behind Union lines. This designation recognized enslaved people's status as human property and paved the way for their emancipation.

AP® exam tip

Describe how the designation of freedom seekers as contraband(s) influenced federal and military policy regarding enslaved people during the Civil War.

In military terms, *contraband* designated nonhuman property and goods. Butler's use of the term for freedom seekers was unconventional, but it shaped subsequent Union policy. It also implied subordinate status, as the formerly enslaved people were not yet fully emancipated. Butler put them to work as diggers and dockworkers, as servants and laundresses and cooks. They received army rations and eventually wages — $8 a month for males, $4 for females. These refugees deprived the Confederacy of a vital labor source that increasingly contributed to the Union cause.

First Confiscation Act (1861) A congressional act authorizing the confiscation of Confederate property, including enslaved people employed in the rebellion, who were then considered free.

Butler was not the only Union officer to be perplexed by the question of what to do with freedom seekers who fled to Union lines. In early August 1861, Congress sought to clarify the situation through the **First Confiscation Act**, which authorized the confiscation of enslaved people as Confederate property. This act voided enslavers' claims to enslaved people who — like the three who sought refuge at Fortress Monroe — had been working directly for the Confederate military. Later that same month, John C. Frémont, the major general in charge of the Department of the West and an outspoken abolitionist, cited civil disorder in Missouri as his rationale for declaring martial law and freeing the people enslaved by all disloyal enslavers. Lincoln, concerned about securing the loyalty of the border states, voided the order.

Nevertheless, African Americans, by running from slavery to freedom, were already shaping three related developments: the decisions of individual commanders about what to do with the refugees, Union military policy as a whole, and growing acceptance in the North of formerly enslaved people as laborers for the Union military. In March 1862, Congress passed an additional article of war that prohibited Union navy and army officers from returning freedom seekers to slavery. Even before that, however, Union officers in recaptured coastal South Carolina were developing their own innovative policies. Port Royal and the Sea Islands had been taken by Union troops in November 1861, as the Union naval blockade of the South proved increasingly successful. Fleeing plantation owners abandoned their land and some 10,000 enslaved people, who remembered November 7 as "the day of the big gun-shoot."[13]

Port Royal Experiment An attempt by government officials and civilian volunteers to assist Sea Island enslaved people, who had been abandoned by their enslavers, in their transition to freedom.

In what came to be known as the **Port Royal Experiment**, these formerly enslaved people were designated contrabands and began working the abandoned cotton plantations under the supervision of Union military officials. They organized their own time and labor, received wages, and sold surplus crops. A few were able to purchase plots of abandoned land when U.S. Treasury officials auctioned it off, but most of the land went to northern businessmen, who hired the contrabands to farm it. The formerly enslaved people's success in this endeavor could have been a model for the transition from slavery to freedom.

Assisting the contrabands were a group of idealistic missionaries and teachers sent by northern religious and charitable organizations such as the American Missionary Association. Most of the teachers were white women who saw themselves as civilizing and Christianizing a primitive and inferior people. Sea Island Blacks may have resented

STAMPEDE AMONG THE NEGROES IN VIRGINIA—THEIR ARRIVAL AT FORTRESS MONROE.

Enslaved Contrabands

Enslaved Blacks contributed to their emancipation by running away and seeking refuge at Union strongholds such as Fortress Monroe in Virginia, shown here. Union military policies and practices helped shape the freedom journey for tens of thousands of enslaved refugees. By redefining freedom seekers' status as "contraband of war," thus making them subject to seizure by the Union, military officials helped lay the groundwork for employing refugees as non-enslaved workers, further spurring the transition from slavery to freedom. **What inferences can you make regarding the degree to which enslaved people took advantage of the war to obtain their own freedom?** *Library of Congress, Prints and Photographs Division, Washington, D.C., LC- USZ62-31165.*

the women's condescension and racial prejudice, but they were eager to be educated. At makeshift schools in churches and on outdoor benches, they learned to read and write, to understand the Bible and Christian principles, and to master the responsibilities of freedom. One who traveled to the Sea Islands to teach formerly enslaved people was Charlotte Forten, the granddaughter of the successful African American businessman James Forten. An abolitionist, writer, poet, and teacher, she subsequently published a revealing narrative of her experiences that showed her empathy and sympathy

AP® skills

Applying Disciplinary Knowledge: Why might the formerly enslaved Sea Island Blacks have been eager for education despite the treatment they received from white missionaries and teachers?

for the Sea Island freedpeople as well as the class and cultural distance between herself and them.

Even as the Port Royal contrabands were building independent lives, their status was uncertain. On May 19, 1862, the Union commander General David Hunter issued a proclamation freeing all the enslaved people in Florida, Georgia, and South Carolina, but Lincoln again voided the order. Hunter set about organizing the freedmen into a regiment until the War Department forced him to abandon this plan. Finally, on July 17, 1862, Congress clarified the status of freedom seekers. The **Second Confiscation Act** declared freedom for all enslaved people employed in the rebellion and for freedom seekers able to make it to Union-controlled territory. It thereby freed all enslaved people who had been deserted by Confederate enslavers, as well as all those who took refuge behind Union lines or were captured, if their enslavers were waging war against the Union. Slavery in the border states, however, was protected. The act also empowered the federal government to seize and sell all other Confederate property. Finally, it gave the president the power to authorize the use of "persons of African descent" in any way he deemed necessary to put down the rebellion and "to make provision for the transportation, colonization, and settlement, in some tropical country beyond the limits of the United States, of such persons of the African race, made free by the provisions of this act, as may be willing to emigrate."[14]

Second Confiscation Act (1862)
A congressional act declaring freedom for all enslaved people employed in the rebellion and for freedom seekers able to make it to Union-controlled territory.

Union forces in the West were more successful than those in the East, and by mid-1862, they had captured New Orleans and were moving up the Mississippi River. In Louisiana, as elsewhere, enslaved people fled to Union lines. Thousands of refugees arrived from the low-lying rice plantations near New Orleans, the cotton plantations around Baton Rouge, and the sugar plantations along the river and west of New Orleans. General Butler, now the military governor of New Orleans, initially followed a two-pronged policy: he welcomed the people enslaved by anyone disloyal to the Union, but he returned the freedom seekers enslaved by pro-Union planters — some of whom had only recently sworn loyalty to the Union and were looking to Butler to protect their property. In the confusion of wartime conditions, however, it became increasingly difficult, if not impractical, to distinguish between the freedom seekers enslaved by loyal and disloyal enslavers. Butler's solution was to arrange for freedom seekers to provide wage labor for allegedly loyal plantation owners who sought the help, thus avoiding the question of the freedom seekers' status, which was neither enslaved nor free.

A growing body of freedom seekers took over and worked abandoned land and carved out hidden freedom seeker settlements in the bayous. The widening exodus of enslaved people alarmed southern whites, who increasingly feared slave insurrections. As Union forces gained firmer control of the region, however, they instituted systems of labor that, like the Port Royal Experiment, allowed the formerly enslaved people to work the surrounding plantations as independent laborers under the supervision of Union officials.[15]

Turning Points, 1862–1863

What were African American soldiers' motivations for enlisting during the Civil War, and what inequities did they face?

In more than a year of fighting, neither side had achieved its aims. Union forces had secured some coastal areas of the Confederacy, but advances on the capital of Richmond had been checked. Freedom seekers were creating turmoil for Union military officers and forcing the issue of freedom on a cautious Lincoln. But events began to take a decisive turn in the summer of 1862. Within the next twelve months, a military order by the president would decree formal emancipation for enslaved people under Confederate control and authorize Black men to serve in the Union army. Following this change of policy, the use of Black units would contribute to the Union's success, as significant military victories in the summer of 1863 marked a turning point in the war.

The Emancipation Proclamation

Abraham Lincoln fully understood the military and political advantages that freeing fugitives from slavery and employing them as military labor and support personnel gave the Union cause. He was also aware that recasting the war as a fight against slavery could have diplomatic benefits. In Great Britain especially, where antislavery sentiment was strong, a war aim of ending slavery would enhance the political and moral weight of the Union's cause. It would also seriously undercut the Confederacy's push for diplomatic recognition in Europe.

Through the middle of 1862, Lincoln publicly continued his cautious, pragmatic approach to the question of slavery and the status of freedom seekers. Yet, he was privately making plans to take a bolder step. On July 22, he surprised his cabinet by announcing his intention to free all the people enslaved by those in rebellion against the Union. This act would be a military proclamation issued under his authority as commander in chief. At the suggestion of one of his cabinet members, however, Lincoln agreed to withhold the announcement until after a Union victory on the battlefield, so as not to appear desperate or beholden in any way to the freedom seekers or to abolitionist pressure.

The Union victory on September 17, 1862, at Antietam Creek, near Sharpsburg, Maryland, gave Lincoln the occasion he needed. Union forces repelled a Confederate offensive, and General Robert E. Lee's army retreated back into Virginia. The victory proved significant, not only for reversing Union military fortunes but also for dissuading Britain from recognizing the Confederacy. Five days later, on September 22, 1862, Lincoln issued the **preliminary Emancipation Proclamation**.

preliminary Emancipation Proclamation (1862)
A presidential proclamation giving the Confederacy one hundred days to cease the rebellion. If it did not, all its entire enslaved population would be freed.

This proclamation gave the Confederates one hundred days — until January 1, 1863 — to cease their rebellion. If they did not, all the people they enslaved would be freed on that date. The proclamation drew its authority from the additional article of war approved in March 1862 and the Second Confiscation Act. The proclamation maintained Lincoln's two-pronged approach to the problem of slavery: compensation and colonization. It recommended that Congress offer loyal slave states monetary assistance to enable them to adopt gradual or immediate emancipation plans. It also offered continued support for the colonization of freedpeople outside the United States.

Emancipation Proclamation (1863) A presidential proclamation, issued by Abraham Lincoln, freeing all enslaved people under Confederate control and authorizing the use of Black troops in the Civil War.

The Confederacy scorned the preliminary Emancipation Proclamation, and no person or state ceased its rebellion. On January 1, 1863, Lincoln signed the final **Emancipation Proclamation**. (See AP® Working with Sources: Wartime and Emancipation, pp. 325–35.) This proclamation referenced the preliminary one, with its determination to free the enslaved people in states or parts of states still in rebellion against the United States as of January 1, and listed the regions in which the slaves "shall be then, thenceforward, and forever free." Consistent with Lincoln's cautious and pragmatic approach to the war and his strenuous efforts to maintain the loyalty of those within the Union who still enslaved people, the Emancipation Proclamation had clear and functional limits. It did not free the enslaved in places that the Union had actual control over: the border states, pro-Union areas within the Confederacy, and former Confederate areas under Union control.

AP® skills

Applying Disciplinary Knowledge: Can you identify the limitations of the Emancipation Proclamation?

Furthermore, the proclamation said nothing about compensation or colonization, only that military and naval authorities would recognize and maintain the freedom of "said persons," who were urged "to abstain from all violence" and to "labor faithfully for reasonable wages." Finally, it declared that "such persons of suitable condition" were to be "received into the armed service." Lincoln ended the proclamation with an invocation: "Upon this act, sincerely believed to be an act of justice, warranted by the Constitution, upon military necessity, I invoke the considerate judgment of mankind, and the gracious favor of Almighty God." The war to save the Union thus officially also became a war to free enslaved people. It was clear that now, when the Union was restored, it would be a nation of free people, a nation in which slavery would not exist.

In the North, Blacks and their allies ardently embraced the Emancipation Proclamation. At the grand celebration on January 1, 1863, at the Israel Bethel AME Church in Washington, D.C., Pastor Henry McNeal Turner witnessed a community overcome with joy: "Men squealed, women fainted, dogs barked, white and colored people shook hands, songs were sung. . . . Great processions of colored and white men marched to and fro and passed in front of the White House and congratulated President Lincoln on his proclamation. . . . It was indeed a time of times, and a half time, nothing like it will ever be seen again in this life."[16]

For Blacks in captured Confederate territory now under Union control, the Emancipation Proclamation celebrations also were widespread, joyous, and hopeful. In Hampton, Virginia, members of the large free Black community that had grown up around Fortress Monroe gathered for a reading of the proclamation. They met under a large tree — now known as the Emancipation Oak and still standing on the campus of Hampton University — where a school for formerly enslaved people had been conducted since 1861 by Mary S. Peake. In the South Carolina Sea Islands, the high point of the long celebration was unplanned. Colonel Thomas Wentworth Higginson, an abolitionist from Massachusetts and commander of the First Regiment of South Carolina Volunteers, received a Union flag for his unit, which was composed of formerly enslaved people. As he received the flag, the freedpeople burst into a spontaneous rendition of "My Country, 'Tis of Thee." "It was a touching and beautiful incident, and sent a thrill through all our hearts," recalled Charlotte Forten.[17]

Enslaved people under Confederate control who got word of the Emancipation Proclamation kept their responses secret so as not to enrage Confederates and provoke retaliation. Many enslavers worked hard to prevent word of the proclamation from reaching the people they enslaved, some even relocating their operations to more isolated or more secure Confederate areas, where plantation life continued as usual. Felix Haywood, formerly enslaved in Texas, recalled, "The War didn't change nothin'." In fact, he said, "sometimes you didn't knowed it was goin' on. It was the endin' of it that made the difference."[18]

Nevertheless, news of emancipation continued to spread as Union forces advanced. While the proclamation did not immediately free any enslaved people still under Confederate control, it transformed the conflict by making emancipation a central war aim, linking emancipation with Union victory. Outside the United States, emancipation was applauded in Britain and France, and it ended Confederate hopes for European diplomatic recognition.

The U.S. Colored Troops

At the beginning of the war, Black men and Black militia units had been officially excluded from service in the Union army, but some Union commanders in the field had seen the merit of turning contrabands into soldiers. In August 1862, General Hunter finally received permission to recruit freedmen in the Sea Islands, and one hundred signed up to become the First South Carolina Volunteers (later the Thirty-Third U.S. Colored Troops). In September, General Butler organized the First Louisiana Native Guard, composed mostly of formerly enslaved men, into a federal unit. Neither regiment saw action until after the Emancipation Proclamation officially declared that Blacks would be received into the Union army, and the War Department, on May 22, 1863, created a bureau to oversee the new **U.S. Colored Troops**.

U.S. Colored Troops
The official designation for the division of Black units that joined the U.S. army beginning in 1863.

In the North, recruitment of free Blacks was slow at first. While some Black men had already organized militia units, believing that wartime service would help promote emancipation and substantiate their claims to full citizenship, others were less confident. The *Liberator* reported that a well-attended recruitment meeting on April 27, 1863, in New York City's Shiloh Presbyterian Church had produced only one recruit, despite stirring speeches by Henry Highland Garnet and Frederick Douglass. One audience member explained that the problem "was not cowardice . . . but a proper respect for their own manhood. If the Government wanted their services, let it guarantee to them all the rights of citizens and soldiers, and, instead of one man, he would insure them 5,000 men in twenty days."[19] That summer, Douglass stepped up his efforts to promote Black military service, emphasizing its links with citizenship.

AP® exam tip
You will need to be able to describe the motivations behind Black enlistment in the war effort. How do they compare to the motivations of white soldiers to enlist?

"Once let the black man get upon his person the brass letters U.S.," he announced, "let him get an eagle on his button, and a musket on his shoulder, and bullets in his pocket, and there is no power on earth or under the earth which can deny that he has earned the right of citizenship in the United States."[20]

Ultimately, 179,000 Black men enlisted in the U.S. Colored Troops, almost 10 percent of all who served in the Union army. A few, such as Martin R. Delany, were commissioned officers; 7,122 were noncommissioned officers. Another 29,500 Black men served in the Union navy. Among them was Robert Smalls, who by the end of 1863 was captain of a Union vessel. In one estimate, Blacks participated in almost 250 battles. They suffered more than 37,000 casualties. Seventeen Black soldiers and four Black sailors received the Congressional Medal of Honor. (See By the Numbers: African Americans in the Union Military.)

BY THE NUMBERS African Americans in the Union Military

African Americans had a distinguished record of military service and played a significant role in Union victory. Of those who served in the Union army, 33,000 were free Blacks from Union states; 42,000 were formerly enslaved and freemen from border states; 99,000 were formerly enslaved from Confederate states; and the rest were most likely southern free Blacks. Another 29,500 Black men served in the Union navy. Black troops accounted for 10 percent of the Union army and nearly 25 percent of the navy. **To what extent was the fight to win the war and end slavery a combined effort from both the free and enslaved Black communities?**

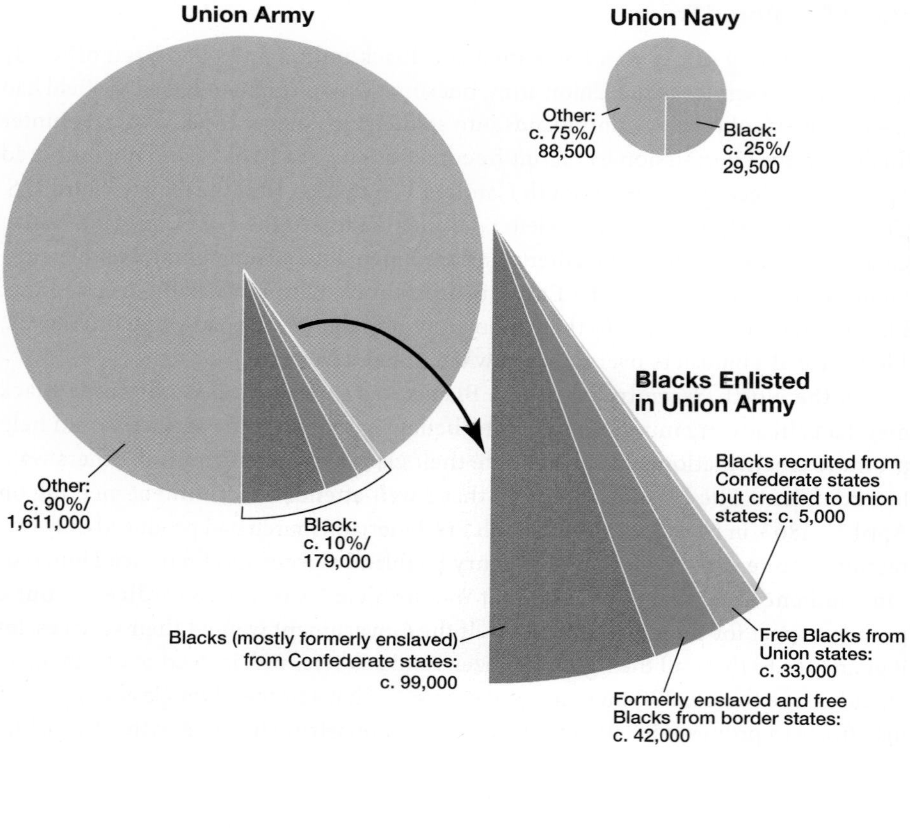

African American Soldiers Storm Fort Wagner

The all-Black Fifty-Fourth Massachusetts Volunteer Infantry Regiment (U.S. Colored Troops) led the famed yet ill-fated July 18, 1863, storming of Fort Wagner, which was vital to the fortifications of Charleston, South Carolina. Most of the volunteers, including Frederick Douglass's sons Lewis and Charles Douglass, were from Massachusetts. Colonel Robert Gould Shaw, Harvard-educated son of a prominent abolitionist family, led the troops, died in the battle along with 272 of the troops and was buried along with them. The bravery, heroism, and patriotism of the troops and their fallen leader were much praised throughout the North at the time. In addition, that glowing view of them has characterized their subsequent historical and cultural representation. **What messages does this image convey about the Fifty-Fourth Massachusetts Volunteer Infantry and Colonel Robert Gould Shaw, their commander? What messages are conveyed here more generally about Black soldiers, Black men, and Black people?** *Private Collection/Peter Newark American Pictures/Bridgeman Images.*

This distinguished record of Black military wartime service evolved within the limits imposed by racial prejudice. The military hierarchy reinforced the racial hierarchy of American society. Black units were invariably led by white officers; the idea of Black officers leading troops, especially white troops, was totally unacceptable. The white officers who led Black troops varied in motivation, quality, and effectiveness, but most barely tolerated their Black subordinates. One exception was Robert Gould Shaw, colonel of the Fifty-Fourth Massachusetts Volunteer Infantry Regiment, a unit raised by abolitionists. The first such Black unit to be organized, it included two of Frederick Douglass's sons.

Black soldiers fighting for the Union endured many inequities. White officers, many of whom questioned the fitness and bravery of Black soldiers, assigned them to the most difficult noncombat duties, such as building fortifications and manning supply lines. These officers too often mismanaged their troops, resulting in inept battlefield maneuvers and excessive casualty rates. Lack of good training and equipment also contributed to the high number of Black fatalities.

Black troops were also at greater risk than white troops because of Confederate policy, which regarded Black Union soldiers as instigators of slave insurrections. As such, they were subject to enslavement or execution upon capture. At Fort Pillow, Tennessee, the killing of scores of Black prisoners of war by their Confederate captors on April 12, 1864, sparked much controversy. The Confederates denied the incident, but the northern press called it a massacre and used it as propaganda to promote the war effort. The threat of capture and possible enslavement, torture, or murder at the hands of Confederates made Black enlistment in the Union army itself an act of courage.

AP® exam tip

You should be able to identify the inequities Black soldiers encountered in the army. What does their continued service in the face of discrimination reveal about their dedication to the United States and the ideals of freedom?

Finally, pay inequities caused considerable resentment. Black soldiers received $10 a month, with $3 deducted for food and clothing, regardless of rank. By contrast, white privates received $13 and free food and clothing, and their pay increased with promotions. So strong was the resentment among the soldiers of the Fifty-Fourth Massachusetts Regiment that they refused to accept any pay at all until the pay for whites and Blacks was equalized. In the Third South Carolina Infantry, the issue of pay inequity sparked a mutiny in which the leader, Sergeant William Walker, a former refugee from slavery, was executed. On June 15, 1864, Congress passed legislation that equalized the pay of Black and white soldiers and offered back pay to all those who had been underpaid or had refused pay in protest. Following this remedy, the recruitment of Black soldiers increased significantly.

African Americans in the Major Battles of 1863

The U.S. Colored Troops helped the Union meet its mounting manpower needs, and when given the opportunity to fight, they fought heroically. The first Black units in combat were the former Louisiana Native Guards, fighting for the Union as the African Brigade and soon designated the First Louisiana. Augmented by contrabands, the unit was assigned to the Mississippi River campaign that aimed to split the Confederacy in two. On May 27, these Black soldiers participated in the assault on Port Hudson, Louisiana, where they proved they were as courageous as any white soldiers. "The undaunted heroism, and the great endurance of the negro, as exhibited that day," the formerly enslaved man William Wells Brown later wrote, "created a new chapter in American history for the colored man."[21] On June 7, armed only with old muskets, they defended the Union outpost at

Milliken's Bend, Louisiana, leading Charles Dana, assistant secretary of war, to observe, "The bravery of the blacks in the battle at Milliken's Bend completely revolutionized the sentiment of the army with regard to the employment of negro troops. I heard prominent officers who . . . had sneered at the idea of the negroes fighting express themselves after that as heartily in favor of it."[22] Nevertheless, the battle at Milliken's Bend also revealed the risks Black troops faced, as several who were captured by Confederates were sold into slavery, and a few were rumored to have been murdered.[23] On July 4, Vicksburg, Mississippi, the last major Confederate stronghold on the Mississippi River, surrendered to General Ulysses S. Grant, and a few days later Lincoln announced that the Mississippi River, now entirely in Union hands, "again goes unvexed to the sea."[24]

Lincoln had much to rejoice about on that Fourth of July. Just days earlier, Union armies had turned back another Confederate invasion. General Lee's march into Maryland and Pennsylvania was stopped at Gettysburg, where a three-day battle, on July 1–3, resulted in a decisive Union victory. No soldiers of the U.S. Colored Troops participated in the battle, and the services of Black units organized in Philadelphia and Harrisburg by Octavius Catto and Thomas Morris Chester, respectively, were rejected. Nevertheless, large numbers of contrabands and free Blacks aided the Army of the Potomac. Fearing capture and enslavement, hundreds of Pennsylvania free Blacks fled in advance of Lee's march north, but a few were seized and sold.

The most notable battle that July for the U.S. Colored Troops took place in South Carolina. On July 18, the Fifty-Fourth Massachusetts led a second assault on Fort Wagner in Charleston harbor. Despite heavy losses, including the death of their commander, Colonel Shaw, the men of the Fifty-Fourth showed uncommon valor, charging the Confederate batteries in waves. Lewis Douglass, one of Frederick Douglass's sons, wrote to his wife, "I wish we had a hundred thousand colored troops," because then "we would put an end to this war."[25] The bravery of the Fifty-Fourth excited the northern imagination. The unit's performance, said the *New York Tribune*, "made Fort Wagner such a name to the colored race as Bunker Hill has been for ninety years to the white Yankees"[26] (Map 8.1).

In November, Lincoln traveled to Gettysburg to dedicate a national cemetery honoring the fallen soldiers buried there. His short speech, delivered on November 19, 1863, is one of the best-known and most cherished speeches in American history. By announcing "a new birth of freedom" for an American nation "conceived in Liberty, and dedicated to the proposition that all men are created equal,"[27] it fixed forever the noblest goal of the war. Originally aimed to suppress a rebellion and preserve the Union, the war was now being fought to preserve democracy and abolish slavery.

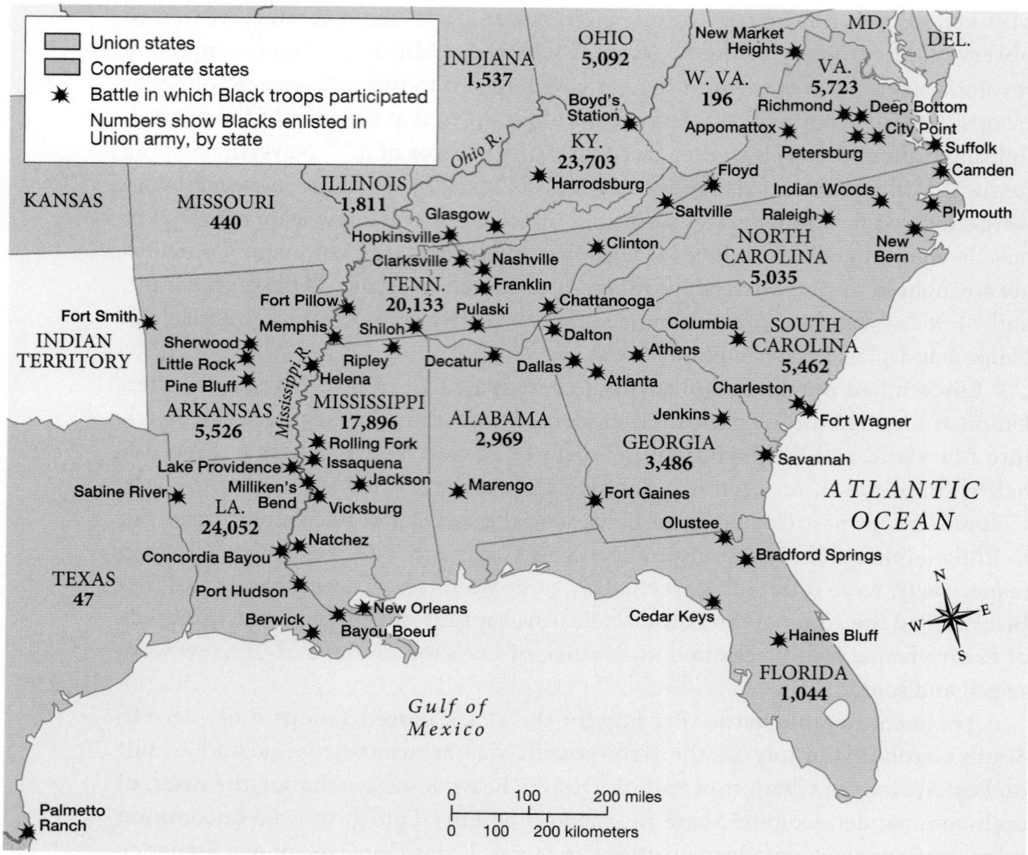

MAP 8.1 African Americans in Battle

Black troops played a pivotal role in the Union war effort, enlisting in the army and navy in significant numbers and participating in close to forty major battles. Their valiant efforts inspired Black civilians to intensify their support for the Union cause. The impressive wartime service of Black troops also sustained their claims and those of their people for full freedom and full U.S. citizenship. **From which states did most Black soldiers come? Why do you think so many of the Civil War battles that Black troops fought in happened along and near the Mississippi River?** DATA SOURCE: *The Atlas of African-American History and Politics: From the Slave Trade to Modern Times, by Arwin Smallwood and Jeffrey Elliot. Copyright © 1998 The McGraw-Hill Companies, Inc.*

Home Fronts and War's End, 1863–1865

How did Black soldiers' service affect Black communities during and after the Civil War? What events officially ended legal enslavement in the United States?

Lincoln's words in the Gettysburg Address reassured many African Americans, but not all were convinced that this change in rhetoric would dramatically change the quality of their lives. Northern Democrats objected to making emancipation a war goal, and in some areas of the North, support for the war faltered. As civilians and resources were increasingly mobilized for the war effort, war-weariness set in, and opposition to Lincoln's conduct of the war grew. Congress tried to block his plans for reintegrating former Confederate areas and people into the Union. At the same time, deaths, desertions, and declining numbers of white volunteers forced the imposition of a military draft, despite the addition of new Black troops. In New York City, resistance to the draft turned violent, and roving mobs of white men targeted Black neighborhoods and institutions. It was clear that any restoration of the Union would need to address civil rights and equality in the North as well as the end of slavery in the South. Black leaders renewed their efforts, recognizing that the freedom struggle would not end with emancipation. In 1865, Union victory and the passage of a constitutional amendment forbidding slavery ensured freedom for all enslaved people. But for northern and southern Blacks, both free and newly freed, the fight for citizenship and equality continued.

Riots and Restoration of the Union

Shortly after the Union's decisive victories at Gettysburg and Vicksburg, and just before the assault on Fort Wagner, Union troops were hastily transferred to New York City to put down a riot. A military draft instituted on March 3, 1863, had proved so unpopular in various parts of the North that it triggered violence. The draft was unpopular not only because many did not want to fight a war to end Black slavery but also because they saw the draft as inequitable. The prosperous could pay $300 to purchase an exemption or hire a substitute, while the poor and working-class had no choice but to serve. On July 13, when newspapers published the names of the first draftees, chosen by lottery, a mob of white men attacked the Manhattan draft office.

AP® exam tip

Be sure you can explain how and why Black communities suffered from anti-Black violence during the war.

The **New York City draft riots** spread quickly, and for four days, roving white mobs, including large numbers of criminals and Irish working-class men, turned to ransacking Black neighborhoods. They burned the Colored Orphan Asylum to the ground. Thousands of Blacks were left homeless and destitute. Dozens were lynched; some were murdered in their homes. By July 15, as more federal troops arrived in the city, some directly from Gettysburg, the violence subsided.

New York City draft riots (1863) Anti-Black riots sparked by white working-class opposition to the Union's military draft.

The causes of the riots were deep-seated. Emancipation may have become a war aim, but for many whites, it was not welcome. Many white soldiers resented being asked to fight and die to free enslaved people. Many white working-class people feared that emancipation would mean a flood of Black laborers coming north to take their jobs and undercut their wages and status.

The racist language of northern white Democratic politicians and the Democratic press inflamed these fears and tensions. Lincoln was denounced as a tyrant and the Emancipation Proclamation as unconstitutional. Democratic legislatures in Indiana, Illinois, and New Jersey raised formal objections to the war and passed peace resolutions. The language of the Illinois resolution revealed northern fears. After questioning the president's authority to proclaim emancipation, it argued that "the sudden, unconditional and violent liberation of 3,000,000 negro slaves" would have consequences that "cannot be contemplated without the most dismal foreboding of horror and dismay."[28]

The disturbances in New York City were not the only anti-Black riots in the North during the war years. In 1862 and 1863, anti-Black riots also rocked Brooklyn, New York — then a separate city — and Detroit. But the New York City riots were the worst, and Black outrage was intense and widespread. "A gloom of infamy and shame will hang over New York for centuries," prophesied the AME Church's *Christian Recorder*.[29] After blasting local and state authorities for their failure to protect Black people and Black property, James W. C. Pennington called on Blacks not to back down but to redouble their efforts for full citizenship rights.[30] Events in New York City and elsewhere made it clear that emancipation would not mean racial equality.

These events also made it clear that the war's end would not mean harmony or even peace. Nevertheless, on December 8, 1863, Lincoln formally began to lay the groundwork for reuniting the Confederate and Union states in a stable postwar nation by issuing his **Proclamation of Amnesty and Reconstruction**. By this time, Louisiana, large stretches along the Mississippi River, and areas of Tennessee and Arkansas were in Union hands. To allow the former Confederate states to form pro-Union governments and reenter the Union, Lincoln officially pardoned all except high-ranking Confederate civil and military officials and decreed that their property should be restored to them "except as to slaves." The proclamation directed that when voters equal to 10 percent of the votes cast in the 1860 election swore an oath of loyalty to the Union, they would be permitted to reestablish a state government. It also expressed the hope that the new state governments would recognize the needs of formerly enslaved people as "a laboring, landless, and homeless class" and would provide for their education.[31] This plan guided the reorganization of defeated Confederate areas until Lincoln's death sixteen months later.

Proclamation of Amnesty and Reconstruction (1863) Lincoln's proposal for the reorganization and readmission into the Union of the defeated Confederate states.

Black Civilians at Work for the War

The Union's 1863 military draft made it clear that the initial enthusiasm for the war was over. Even earlier, in April 1862, the Confederate army had sought to solve its manpower shortage through conscription. The war had gone on much longer than anyone had expected, and shortages in military manpower meant that civilians, too, had to be mobilized for the war effort. Resources were strained on both sides but especially in the South. From the beginning, Black labor — free and enslaved — had been vital to the Confederate war effort. Blacks grew most of the food for Confederate troops. They loaded and carted goods and supplies. Through coercion and impressment, as well as slave hiring and assignment, they worked for the military by building roads, entrenchments, and fortifications. Blacks served as personal servants, cooks, foragers, and spies for Confederate soldiers and officers. But as increasing numbers of enslaved people fled to the Union lines and Union troops controlled increasing

AP® skills

Applying Disciplinary Knowledge: How did Black freedom seekers weaken the Confederacy?

African Americans Laboring for the Union
Here African American men are building a stockade in Alexandria, Virginia, to defend the Union railroad depot there and thus strengthen the defense of nearby Washington, D.C., against Confederate attack. Building such fortifications was essential to the Union war effort. In the Confederacy as well as the Union, African American civilians, both women and men, were an indispensable element of the labor force that performed such vital work as feeding and serving troops and building encampments and roads. **How did Black civilians contribute to the war effort? How essential was their labor to the war effort?** *Historical/Getty Images.*

amounts of Confederate territory, the Confederacy weakened. By mid-1864, roughly 400,000 enslaved people, or almost 10 percent of the enslaved population, were no longer under Confederate control, and many were laboring for the Union.

To stop enslaved people from fleeing and solidify the slave system, southern whites strengthened slave patrols, clamped down on enslaved and free Black mobility, and moved the people they enslaved away from nearby war zones and Union-controlled areas. At the same time, to quell enslaved unrest and defections, particularly in places near Union-held areas, enslavers often yielded to enslaved people's demands. These included continuing, or even expanding, previous understandings that allowed enslaved people to farm their own plots and market their own crops. Some enslavers and enslaved people made arrangements such as dividing or sharing harvests, trading wages for labor, and renting land and houses.

As most freedom seekers, at least early on, were males and wartime conditions further cut into the availability of the labor of enslaved men, the work of enslaved women became increasingly important. Many shouldered additional field work in addition to the domestic work they traditionally performed. More than ever before, they were responsible for sustaining their households. Like all enslaved people who remained under Confederate control, they weighed their options and waited for their chances. Especially toward the end of the war, increasing numbers of enslaved women, with their children, also began to seek freedom behind Union lines. Elizabeth Botume, a northern teacher sent to the Sea Islands by the New England Freedmen's Aid Society, remembered seeing a refugee mother "striding along with her hominy pot, in which was a live chicken, poised on her head. One child was on her back, with its arms tightly clasped around her neck, and its feet about her waist, and under each arm was a smaller child."[32] Women tried to hold together families in refugee camps.

AP® skills

Applying Disciplinary Knowledge: What contributions did Black women make to the Union war effort?

As an increasing number of enslaved people fled the Confederacy, their contributions to the Union war effort grew. Not only Black soldiers and sailors, but also another 200,000 Black women and men ultimately traveled with the Union armies over the course of the war and labored in nonmilitary capacities. Both men and women served as servants and spies; men served primarily as road builders, carpenters, wagon drivers, livestock tenders, and foragers; women served primarily as cooks, laundresses, teachers, and nurses. Many individuals often filled many roles at once, working in various capacities depending on what was needed. For example, Harriet Tubman was a scout, spy, teacher, and nurse during the war, even as she continued to assist enslaved people escaping to freedom. The formerly enslaved Susie King Taylor started a school in the Sea Islands and served as a teacher, nurse, and laundress for the all-Black Thirty-Third U.S. Colored Troops. In the Confederate White House in Richmond, Mary Elizabeth Bowser worked undercover as a house servant and spied for the Union. Before she escaped toward the end of the war, she tried — unsuccessfully — to burn down the Confederate White House. In the Lincoln White House in Washington, Elizabeth Keckley served as the First Lady's dressmaker and confidante.

In 1862, Keckley used her connections to establish a charitable organization for assisting the contrabands who crowded into the Union capital. This Contraband Relief Association was supported by many prominent abolitionists, including Henry Highland Garnet, Frederick Douglass, and Sojourner Truth, who also raised food and money for Black regiments. A report of the association explained, "Our work has been to provide shelter, food, clothing, medicines and nourishments for them, we have also buried their dead, and in fact, done all we could . . . to alleviate their sufferings, and help them on towards a higher plane of civilization."[33] Black women were prominent in the work of northern freedpeople's aid societies as well, such as the Contraband Committee of the Mother Bethel AME Church in Philadelphia and the Freedmen's Friend Society in Brooklyn. From the battlefields and war-torn plantations of the South to the military hospitals and contraband camps in the region, it was often the unpaid work of Black women that alleviated suffering and provided humanitarian aid.

Elizabeth Keckley
Best known as First Lady Mary Todd Lincoln's seamstress and confidante from 1861 to 1868, Elizabeth Keckley was born into slavery but achieved economic success and respectability as a dressmaker for elite white women, a group of whom loaned her the money to buy her freedom. Keckley was an abolitionist, the founder and leader of the Washington, D.C.–based Contraband Relief Association, a member of Washington's Black elite, and a noted memoirist. Her *Behind the Scenes: or, Thirty Years a Slave, and Four Years in the White House* (1868) is an illuminating look at her fascinating life, notably her rise from slavery to freedom and her intimate interactions with the Lincoln family. **How might Elizabeth Keckley's interactions with the white elite have supported the cause of abolition?** *Picture History/ Newscom.*

Union Victory, Emancipation from Slavery, and the Renewed Struggle for Equality

Despite the Union's battlefield successes in 1864, Lincoln's reelection was by no means assured. Congressional opposition to the leniency of his "10 percent plan" for the reintegration of former Confederates and Confederate regions into the Union had culminated in the passage on July 2, 1864, of the **Wade–Davis Bill**, which challenged the president's authority. This bill required that before a state government could be reestablished, a majority of the state's white male citizens had to take an ironclad oath that they had never supported the Confederacy. After Lincoln refused to sign the bill, its sponsors published a manifesto that signaled a looming constitutional crisis between the executive and legislative branches over what came to be called Reconstruction.

Wade–Davis Bill (1864)
A congressional proposal for the reorganization and readmission into the Union of the defeated Confederate states. Lincoln refused to sign the bill.

During the summer of 1864, opposition to the war and to Lincoln's conduct of it grew. Large numbers of Democrats pushed to end the war immediately. Within Lincoln's own Republican Party, John C. Frémont, who had been relieved of his command in Missouri, strenuously criticized the president for his overly cautious prosecution of the war. Frémont ran against Lincoln as a Radical Republican, splitting the party until withdrawing from the race in favor of Lincoln in September 1864. To gain Democratic and border state support, Lincoln chose as his vice presidential running mate the former Democratic senator and military governor of Tennessee, Andrew Johnson. In opposition to the Radical Republicans, Lincoln's faction of the Republican Party renamed itself the National Union Party. The Democratic candidate was former Union general George B. McClellan. Lincoln and Johnson won by only 400,000 votes out of 4 million cast. General William Tecumseh Sherman's victories as he marched through Georgia contributed to Lincoln's slim margin of victory.

At Lincoln's second inauguration, on March 4, 1865, the proud Black regiments that marched in front of him underscored how much had changed in four years of war. In his address, Lincoln acknowledged that slavery had been the cause of the war, which he cast as God's punishment for the national sin of slavery. Yet, he ended with a vision of reconciliation: "With malice toward none, with charity for all, with firmness in the right as God gives us to see the right, let us strive on to finish the work we are in, to bind up the nation's wounds, . . . to do all which may achieve and cherish a just and lasting peace among ourselves and with all nations."[34]

Special Field Order 15 (1865)
A military order by Union general William T. Sherman that granted freedpeople the right to land that had been abandoned by Confederate plantation owners.

While Lincoln's approach to former Confederates was conciliatory, allowing for pardons and the return of property, it was already being countermanded by his generals in the field. On January 16, 1865, General Sherman issued **Special Field Order 15**, which granted confiscated and abandoned Confederate land to formerly enslaved people. Each head of household could receive up to forty acres of land along the Florida, Georgia, and South Carolina coast, and later a few freedpeople received army mules for working the land. These arrangements granted the freedpeople possessory titles to the land until Congress ruled on the validity of the titles. These arrangements also aimed to facilitate the transition of the freedpeople to independent livelihoods by providing them with farms and a stable economic basis to sustain their freedom.

Freedmen's Bureau (1865–1872)
A federal agency created during Reconstruction to aid freedpeople in their transition to freedom.

The same concerns moved Congress, in March 1865, to establish the **Freedmen's Bureau**, a new government agency charged with enabling formerly enslaved people's transition to freedom, assisting them with food, clothing, and shelter. Ultimately, the bureau also supervised and enforced labor contracts, settled disputes, helped establish schools, and set up courts to protect formerly enslaved people's civil rights.[35]

AP® skills

Applying Disciplinary Knowledge: What early steps did the federal government take to help the formerly enslaved transition to freedom?

Meanwhile, the Confederacy tried to avoid the defeat that now seemed inevitable by considering a plan to emancipate and arm enslaved people. Debate over the plan recognized the tremendous military advantage the Union had gained by arming freedom seekers. President Davis initially resisted the idea, but General Robert E. Lee endorsed it. On March 13, the Confederate Congress passed the measure, and Davis signed it, but by then the war was nearly over. On April 9, Lee surrendered to Grant at Appomattox Court House, Virginia, and other Confederate commanders soon followed suit. Before the Confederates' final capitulation, however, President Lincoln was shot on April 14 by Confederate sympathizer John Wilkes Booth and died the next morning. For a nation ravaged by four years of war, peace and reconciliation without a strong national leader would be even more difficult than it would have been with Lincoln at the helm.

COLORED TROOPS, UNDER GENERAL WILD, LIBERATING SLAVES IN NORTH CAROLINA.

Colored Troops under General Wild, Liberating Enslaved People in North Carolina, 1864
Amid the tumult of the Civil War, the enslaved experienced emancipation in various ways. An especially moving moment transpired whenever Black troops, functioning as a Black liberation army, helped free their enslaved brethren. This illustration shows a Black soldier shaking the hand of a newly freed person. The image projects happiness, thanksgiving, and racial solidarity. **How did the formerly enslaved commemorate emancipation?** *Granger/Granger — All rights reserved.*

With the Confederate surrender, enslaved people in the Confederate states were ostensibly freed, but many remained in bondage until Union soldiers reached them to enforce the terms of the Emancipation Proclamation. In Texas, enslaved people did not receive the news of freedom until June 19, 1865, now commemorated as the African American holiday **Juneteenth**. The responses of the formerly enslaved ran the gamut, from joyous celebrations to fear of the unknown. Texan Richard Carruthers recalled, "That the day I shouted," and fellow Texan Felix Haywood remembered that "everybody went wild." Many formerly enslaved people interpreted the moment of emancipation as evidence of God's deliverance. A Virginia woman claimed, "De Lord can make Heaven out of Hell any time, I do believe."[36] But mixed emotions, uncertainty, confusion, and anxiety were common. One freedperson in Mississippi said, "Dey all had dif-fe'nt ways o' thinkin' 'bout it. Mos'ly though dey jus' lak me, dey didn't know zackly what it meant." A freedperson in South Carolina remembered that "some were sorry, some hurt, but a few were silent and glad."[37] Some preferred the comfort of the familiar, even the patterns of mutual dependency between whites and Blacks that slavery bred.

Juneteenth
The June 19 holiday that celebrates the effective end of slavery in the United States.

AP® exam tip
Be sure you can explain why Juneteenth is historically and culturally significant.

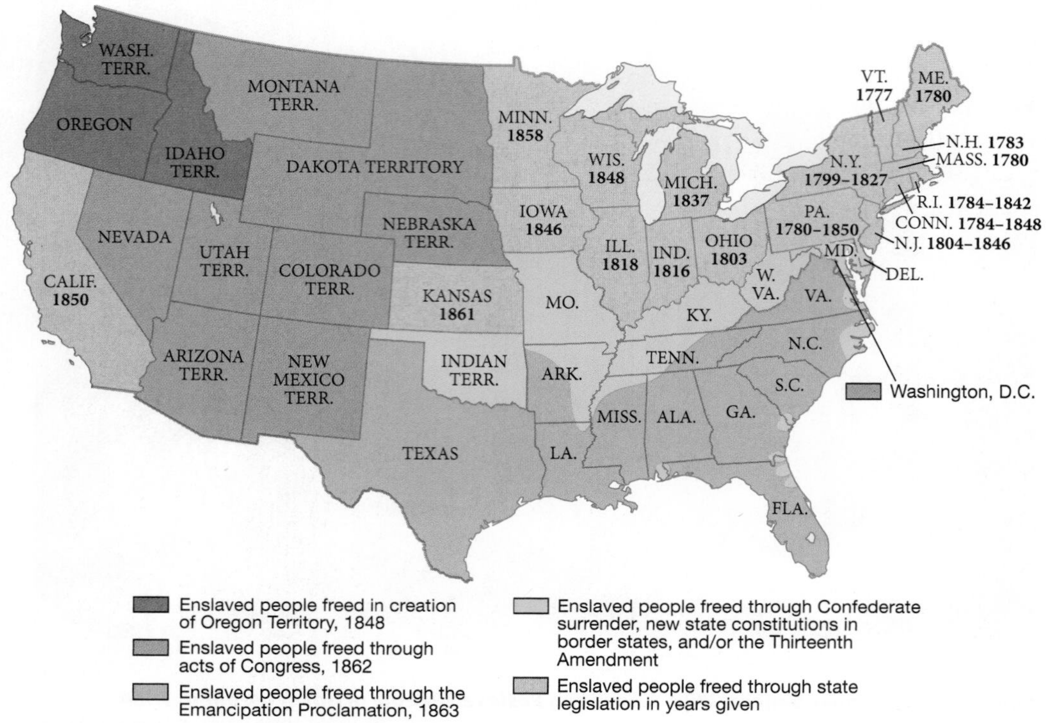

MAP 8.2 Emancipation from Slavery

The role of the federal and state governments in the abolition of slavery was neither simple nor straightforward. This map illustrates key steps in the complex process of national and state-mandated emancipation as it unfolded between 1848 and 1865. In those states with gradual emancipation laws, the date spans show the year in which the initial emancipation statutes were passed followed by the year in which slavery actually ended. **In various regions — North, South, and West — in what ways did government-mandated emancipation happen?**

Thirteenth Amendment (1865) The constitutional amendment that formally abolished slavery.

"I was a-farin' pretty well in de kitchen," Texan Aleck Trimble said. "I didn't tink I eber see better times dan what dem was, and I ain't." But most freedpeople agreed with the Texas woman who concluded that "in slavery I owns nothin' and never owns nothin'. In freedom I's own de home and raise de family. All dat cause worriment and in slavery I have no worriment, but I takes de freedom."[38]

Between September 1864 and February 1865, new state constitutions in Louisiana, Maryland, Missouri, and Tennessee abolished slavery. In February 1865, Congress approved the **Thirteenth Amendment**, which abolished slavery everywhere in the Union, and sent it to the states for ratification. When the amendment was ratified on December 18, 1865, enslaved people in Kentucky and Delaware were finally free (Map 8.2). The amendment was the culmination of a war initially undertaken to preserve the Union before being transformed into a war to end slavery.

But freedom did not mean equality. Free African Americans living in the North had struggled for civil rights for generations, and their efforts had continued during the war. In Philadelphia, for example, Octavius Catto launched a campaign to desegregate the streetcars, which finally succeeded in 1867. Black activism took place at the state and national levels as well. In California, Blacks organized a petition campaign against a state law that prohibited them from testifying against whites in court. Similar laws existed in Oregon, Indiana, Illinois, and Iowa. This overtly discriminatory prohibition allowed unscrupulous whites to take advantage of Blacks in shady court dealings. The California petition drive succeeded in 1863, when the state legislature voided the law.

AP® exam tip

Be prepared to describe the primary effects of the Thirteenth Amendment, which officially ended legal enslavement in the United States.

In Illinois, Blacks challenged an 1853 law that required African Americans settling in the state to pay a heavy fine. If they failed to do so, they were subject to arrest and forced labor for the highest bidder in order to pay the fine. Until 1863, the law was seldom enforced. That year, however, eight Blacks were arrested under it, and seven were incarcerated and then further victimized as forced laborers. In response, the Repeal Association led by John Jones, the wealthiest Black man in Chicago, mounted a vigorous campaign to have the law overturned. The campaign collected more than 11,000 signatures, and in February 1865, the Illinois legislature repealed the law.

At the national level, the National Convention of Colored Men, held in Syracuse, New York, in October 1864, revived the Black convention movement. Frederick Douglass served as president of the Syracuse convention, but other Black leaders, such as John S. Rock and John Mercer Langston, also made their presence felt. The 145 delegates, from both northern and southern states, endorsed emancipation, legal equality without regard to race, and Black male suffrage. They also created the **National Equal Rights League** to advocate for these goals. Like the free Black organizations of the antebellum era, the league emphasized moral reform and self-help, aiming "to encourage sound morality, education, temperance, frugality, industry, and promote everything that pertains to a well-ordered and dignified life."[39] To increase the league's influence, Black leaders quickly formed state and local auxiliaries that attracted many members. The war correspondent Thomas Morris Chester, for example, was able to join the society in Harrisburg, Pennsylvania, directly upon his return from the front.

National Equal Rights League
An organization established by Black leaders in 1864 to promote emancipation, legal equality, and Black male suffrage.

The U.S. government also took steps to reverse some inequities. The State Department began issuing passports to Blacks, ignoring the nullification of black citizenship asserted in the *Dred Scott* decision (1857). In 1865, Massachusetts senator Charles Sumner, a staunch ally of Black citizenship rights, led the successful effort to end the forty-year prohibition against Blacks carrying the U.S. mail. Sumner also paved the way for John S. Rock to become the first Black man accepted to argue cases before the U.S. Supreme Court in early 1865.

Though important, these piecemeal triumphs did not dramatically alter anti-Black prejudice and discrimination in the North. They did, however, solidify Black commitment to the long freedom struggle that would define the next generations of African Americans, both north and south.

CONCLUSION

Emancipation and Equality

On New Year's Eve 1862, Frederick Douglass gathered with more than 3,000 people at the Tremont Temple in Boston, and later at the Twelfth Baptist Church, to celebrate the Emancipation Proclamation. Speaking at Tremont, he called the gathering a "worthy celebration of the first step on the part of the nation in its departure from the thraldom of the ages."[40] As evidenced by this lukewarm statement, many abolitionists were disappointed in the proclamation, for several reasons. It had been too long in coming; it pertained only to enslaved people in regions under Confederate control and so freed almost no one; and it seemed more a military necessity than an affirmation of moral right, the intent being to harm enslavers more than to help enslaved people. Yet, others rejoiced that it made emancipation a war aim and held out hope for the future.[41]

At the beginning of the war, Lincoln avoided addressing slavery directly. He had to move cautiously to retain the loyalty of the border states, where slavery still existed. Although he pressured them to end slavery, none did so. Congress, however, acted to end slavery in all U.S. territories and in the District of Columbia, where Lincoln's preference for the compensation of enslavers and the colonization of enslaved people was written into the legislation.

Yet even as Lincoln moved cautiously, enslaved people were themselves forcing the issue of emancipation. By taking advantage of wartime conditions to flee to Union lines in ever-increasing numbers, they compelled Union commanders to make decisions regarding their status. Weeks after the war began, General Benjamin Butler declared that the enslaved people who had fled to Fortress Monroe for protection were "contraband of war" and refused to return them to their enslavers. Other commanders made similar decisions. In the Sea Islands of coastal South Carolina and Georgia, Union commanders oversaw what came to be called the Port Royal Experiment, a system whereby contrabands worked the plantations abandoned by their former enslavers. Teachers and missionaries from the North helped the formerly enslaved make the transition to independent livelihoods. General David Hunter organized Black fighting units that were eventually recognized by the War Department, and General Butler did the same in Louisiana.

The Emancipation Proclamation authorized the military recruitment of Black men, and eventually Black units constituted one-tenth of the U.S. army. Although they gained distinction for their battlefield successes, many Black soldiers were assigned to work duties rather than to combat, and only when they protested did they receive the same pay as white troops. Nearly 40,000 African American men died for the Union; disease or infection killed 30,000, or three-fourths of those who died. This ultimate sacrifice, the brave wartime service of Black troops, and strong Black civilian support proved crucial to the Union victory and strengthened African American claims for full citizenship.

The Confederate defeat and the Thirteenth Amendment to the Constitution ended slavery forever. But as Frederick Douglass pointed out, emancipation was just the first step; it did not mean equality. African Americans intensified their efforts to achieve civil rights and citizenship. The fractured nation had to be reconstructed, and African Americans were determined that it would incorporate them as equals.

CHAPTER 8 REVIEW ▸ PRACTICING AP® SKILLS

AP® ESSENTIAL VOCABULARY AND SOURCES

**Essential terms and required sources from the AP® Course are marked with an asterisk.*

Confederate States of America p. 297
contraband p. 301
First Confiscation Act (1861) p. 302
Port Royal Experiment p. 302
Second Confiscation Act (1862) p. 304
preliminary Emancipation Proclamation (1862) p. 305
Emancipation Proclamation (1863)* p. 306
U.S. Colored Troops* p. 307
New York City draft riots (1863)* p. 313
Proclamation of Amnesty and Reconstruction (1863)* p. 314
Wade–Davis Bill (1864) p. 317
Special Field Order 15 (1865) p. 318
Freedmen's Bureau (1865–1872)* p. 318
Juneteenth* p. 319
Thirteenth Amendment (ratified 1865)* p. 320
National Equal Rights League p. 321

APPLYING DISCIPLINARY KNOWLEDGE: ESSENTIAL QUESTIONS

1. Describe the attitudes and approaches of President Abraham Lincoln, Congress, and the Union military toward slavery and freedom seekers in the early years of the war. How were their evolving policies and practices shaped by Blacks' actions?
2. How did the war's aims shift from the defeat of the rebellion and the preservation of the Union to include emancipation? How might things have been different had the Confederate states responded differently to the preliminary Emancipation Proclamation?
3. How did the enlistment of Black soldiers both challenge and reinforce existing racial hierarchies?
4. How did the Emancipation Proclamation promote Black equality? In what ways did it fall short?
5. Describe the various contributions of African Americans to the Union war effort — both in the military and on the home front. How did their efforts further the war's aims and their own hopes of achieving freedom and citizenship rights?

SUGGESTED REFERENCES

The Coming of War and the Seizing of Freedom, 1861–1862

Berlin, Ira, Barbara J. Fields, Thavolia Glymph, Joseph P. Reidy, and Leslie S. Rowland, eds. *Freedom: A Documentary History of Emancipation, 1861–1867.* 1st ser., vol. 1, *The Destruction of Slavery*. New York: Cambridge University Press, 1985.

Gerteis, Louis. *From Contraband to Freedman: Federal Policy toward Southern Blacks, 1861–1865.* Greenwood, CT: Greenwood Press, 1973.

Litwack, Leon F. *Been in the Storm So Long: The Aftermath of Slavery*. New York: Knopf, 1979.

McPherson, James M. *The Negro's Civil War: How American Blacks Felt and Acted during the War for the Union.* 1965. Reprint, New York: Vintage, 2003.

Mohr, Clarence L. *On the Threshold of Freedom: Masters and Slaves in Civil War Georgia.* Baton Rouge: LSU Press, 2001.

Nieman, Donald G. *The Day of the Jubilee: The Civil War Experience of Black Southerners*. New York: Garland, 1994.

Quarles, Benjamin. *The Negro in the Civil War*. Boston: Little, Brown, 1953.

Robinson, Armstead. *Bitter Fruits of Bondage: The Demise of Slavery and the Collapse of the Confederacy, 1861–1865*. Charlottesville: University of Virginia Press, 2005.

Rose, Willie Lee. *Rehearsal for Reconstruction: The Port Royal Experiment*. Indianapolis: Bobbs-Merrill, 1964.

Ward, Andrew. *The Slaves' War: The Civil War in the Words of Former Slaves*. Boston: Houghton Mifflin, 2008.

Turning Points, 1862–1863

Berlin, Ira, Joseph P. Reidy, and Leslie S. Rowland, eds. *Freedom: A Documentary History of Emancipation, 1861–1867.* 2nd ser., *The Black Military Experience.* New York: Cambridge University Press, 1982.

Bernstein, Iver. *The New York City Draft Riots: Their Significance for American Society and Politics in the Age of the Civil War*. New York: Oxford University Press, 1990.

Cornish, Dudley Taylor. *The Sable Arm: Negro Troops in the Union Army, 1861–1865*. New York: Longmans, Green, 1956.

Franklin, John Hope. *The Emancipation Proclamation.* Garden City, NY: Doubleday, 1963.

Glatthaar, Joseph T. *Forged in Battle: The Civil War Alliance of Black Soldiers and White Officers*. Baton Rouge: LSU Press, 1990.

Redkey, Edwin S., ed. *A Grand Army of Black Men: Letters from African American Soldiers in the Union Army, 1861–1865*. New York: Cambridge University Press, 1992.

Smith, John David, ed. *Black Soldiers in Blue: African American Troops in the Civil War Era*. Chapel Hill: University of North Carolina Press, 2002.

Trudeau, Noah Andre. *Like Men of War: Black Troops in the Civil War, 1862–1865*. Boston: Little, Brown, 1998.

Home Fronts and War's End, 1863–1865

Bercaw, Nancy. *Gendered Freedoms: Race, Rights, and the Politics of Household in the Delta, 1861–1875.* Gainesville: University Press of Florida, 2003.

Berlin, Ira, and Leslie S. Rowland, eds. *Families and Freedom: A Documentary History of African-American Kinship in the Civil War Era*. New York: New Press, 1997.

Forbes, Ella. *African American Women during the Civil War*. New York: Garland, 1998.

Frankel, Noralee. *Freedom's Women: Black Women and Families in Civil War Era Mississippi*. Bloomington: Indiana University Press, 1999.

Jordan, Ervin L., Jr. *Black Confederates and Afro-Yankees in Civil War Virginia*. Charlottesville: University of Virginia Press, 1995.

Levine, Bruce. *Confederate Emancipation: Southern Plans to Free and Arm Slaves during the Civil War*. New York: Oxford University Press, 2006.

Schwalm, Leslie A. *A Hard Fight for We: Women's Transition from Slavery to Freedom in South Carolina*. Urbana: University of Illinois Press, 1997.

Williams, Heather Andrea. *Self-Taught: African American Education in Slavery and Freedom*. Chapel Hill: University of North Carolina Press, 2005.

Wartime and Emancipation

Wars often bring about huge and unintended social changes, and for African Americans, the outbreak of the Civil War in 1861 was fraught with both opportunities and dilemmas. The central role of slavery in the crises that led to hostilities gave hope to many that the war would end that institution. Yet, the uncertainty surrounding the status of enslaved people who sought freedom by running to Union lines, and the Union's official policy through 1862 of refusing military service by African Americans presented free Blacks with dilemmas about how best to respond to, or even take charge of, events that had the potential to be revolutionary.

The speeches excerpted here were two responses heard in Philadelphia, a city with a large and vigorous free Black community. Alfred M. Green acknowledges that Black men have not been recognized as citizens, yet he urges them to support the Union cause and to respond to President Lincoln's call for volunteers. When Green spoke in April 1861, it was not yet clear that Black units would not be accepted in the Union army. Later in 1861, as Black volunteers were rejected in what was described by many, white and Black, as "a white man's war," Green continued to urge Black men to fight for the right to serve. Some Black men agreed with him, but others questioned the wisdom of seeking to serve in a military that did not want them and considered them more fit for labor than for combat. Isaiah C. Wears addresses the status of free Black men in the American Republic more directly by challenging Lincoln's insinuations about Black people as the cause of the war as well as the president's fondness for colonization schemes.

While some Blacks debated the opportunities and dilemmas of the war, Black women often responded to its uncertainties and demands by assuming new and expanded roles. In the South, as growing numbers of Black men, particularly enslaved people and contrabands, joined the military and the war effort, Black women, particularly enslaved people and contrabands, were called on to do more to keep households and plantations running and to keep their families together. Some used new responsibilities to gain greater control over their lives. Enslaved women who fled to Union lines took on new roles, too, working in a variety of ways to aid the Union cause. Similarly, free Black women in the North strongly supported the war effort on the home front. Susie King Taylor, an enslaved woman and then a contraband, served a Black military unit in the Sea Islands as a teacher and a nurse. Like many Black women during the Civil War, Taylor took on a new, expanded, and empowering set of wartime roles even as she continued to perform the traditional woman's role of serving the needs of others.

Precisely because it ushers in the Union-directed process of emancipation from slavery, the Emancipation Proclamation issued by President Lincoln is significant and revealing. What freedom actually meant was much more complicated, emerging only as it was lived in the months and years after the actual moment of emancipation. The formal Emancipation Proclamation and the images here offer insights into both the moment and the meaning of emancipation. An especially significant moment

key point

During the Civil War, Black people continued to be viewed as noncitizens of the United States and were even blamed for the war. Yet, from the onset of the war, Black Americans showed their support as soldiers and as volunteer civilians.

of freedom in Black memory — though it actually affected only a small number of enslaved people — was New Year's Day 1863, when the Emancipation Proclamation went into effect. In *Watch Meeting — Dec. 31st — Waiting for the Hour* (also called *The Hour of Emancipation*), the New England painter William Tolman Carlton (1816–1888) envisions how enslaved people or contrabands might have looked as they waited for midnight, when the new year would begin and enslaved people (at least in theory) would be freed. Two photographs showing Private Hubbard Pryor before and after enlisting in the U.S. Colored Troops suggest that enlistment helped free him. *Freedmen's Memorial* is one of the most famous artistic representations of Abraham Lincoln as the "Great Emancipator."

AP® argumentation

DBQ Practice: Explain how Black Americans from all backgrounds contributed to the Civil War effort. Use at least two of the documents to support your response.

DOCUMENT 1 Alfred M. Green | *Let Us . . . Take Up the Sword, 1861*

ALFRED M. GREEN, a Philadelphia schoolteacher, gave this speech to an assembly of Black men in Philadelphia on April 20, 1861, just a few days after Lincoln's call for 75,000 volunteers to put down the insurrection. Green urges an enthusiastic response, pointing to the patriotism of Black men who fought in previous wars, despite "past grievances."

Breaking it Down How does this source illustrate Black people's perception of their role in the war effort and their desire to fight for their country and freedom? How does Green's speech support the claim that Black people saw themselves as citizens, even when their country did not?

The time has arrived in the history of the great Republic when we may again give evidence to the world of the bravery and patriotism of a race, in whose hearts burns the love of country, of freedom, and of civil and religious toleration. It is these grand principles that enable men, however proscribed, when possessed of true patriotism, to say: "My country, right or wrong, I love thee still!"

It is true, the brave deeds of our fathers, sworn and subscribed to by the immortal Washington of the Revolution of 1776, and of Jackson and others in the War of 1812, have failed to bring us into recognition as citizens, enjoying those rights so dearly bought by those noble and patriotic sires.

It is true, that our injuries in many respects are great; fugitive-slave laws, Dred Scott decisions, indictments for treason, and long and dreary months of imprisonment. . . .

Our duty, brethren, is not to cavil over past grievances. Let us not be derelict to duty in the time of need. While we remember the past, and regret that our present position in the country is not such as to create within us that burning zeal and enthusiasm for the field of battle, which inspires other men in the full enjoyment of every civil and religious emolument, yet let us endeavor to hope for the future, and improve the present auspicious moment for creating anew our claims upon the justice and honor of the Republic; and, above all, let not the honor and glory achieved by our fathers be blasted or sullied by a want of true heroism among their sons. Let us, then, take up the sword, trusting in God, who will defend the right, remembering that these are other days than those of yore — that the world to-day is on the side of freedom and universal political equality.

That the war-cry of the howling leaders of Secession and treason is, let us drive back the advance guard of civil and religious freedom; let us have more slave territory; let us build stronger the tyrant system of slavery in the great American Republic. Remember, too, that your very presence among the troops of the North would inspire your oppressed brethren of the South with zeal for the overthrow of the tyrant system, and confidence in the armies of the living God — the God of truth, justice, and equality to all men.

SOURCE: *Philadelphia Press*, April 22, 1861, in *Letters and Discussions on the Formation of Colored Regiments*, by Alfred M. Green (1862; repr., Philadelphia: Rhistoric Publications, 1969), 3–4.

DOCUMENT 2 Isaiah C. Wears | *The Evil Injustice of Colonization,* 1862

Lincoln's own racism and his keen awareness of the pervasiveness of white racism prevented him from envisioning a multiracial society. These realities shaped his views on emancipation. Until the Emancipation Proclamation of January 1863, his emancipation plans always involved promoting colonization. Meeting with Black leaders on August 14, 1862, Lincoln stated, "But for your race among us there could not be war, although many men engaged on either side do not care for you one way or the other. Nevertheless, I repeat, without the institution of Slavery and the colored race as a basis, the war could not have an existence. It is better for us both, therefore, to be separated."[42] The next day, at a meeting of the Statistical Association of the Colored People of Philadelphia, the group's president, ISAIAH C. WEARS (1822–1900), challenged Lincoln's ideas.

Breaking it Down What reasons does Wears give for arguing that Lincoln is in error? What are Wears's main counterarguments regarding the cause of the war and against colonization?

To be asked, after so many years of oppression and wrong have been inflicted in a land and by a people who have been so largely enriched by the black man's toil, to pull up stakes in a civilized and Christian nation and to go to an uncivilized and barbarous nation, simply to gratify an unnatural wicked prejudice emanating from slavery, is unreasonable and anti-Christian in the extreme.

How unaccountably strange it seems, that wise men familiar with the history of this country, with the history of slavery, with the rebellion and its merciless outrages, yet are apparently totally ignorant of the true cause of the war — or, if not ignorant, afraid or ashamed to charge the guilt where it belongs. . . .

Says the President: The colored race are the cause of the war. So were the children of Israel the cause of the troubles of Egypt. So was Christ the cause of great commotions in Judea, in this same sense; and those identified with Him were considered of the baser sort, and really unfit for citizenship.

But surely the President did not mean to say that our race was the cause of the war, but the occasion thereof.

If black men are here in the way of white men, they did not come here of their own accord. Their presence is traceable to the white man's lust for power, love of oppression and disregard of the plain teachings of the Lord Jesus Christ, whose rule enjoins upon all men to "do unto others as they would be done by." . . .

But it is not the Negro that is the cause of the war; it is the unwillingness on the part of the American people to do the race simple justice.

It is not social equality to be made the equal of the white man, to have kind masters to provide for him, or to find for him congenial homes in Africa or Central America that he needs, but he desires not to be robbed of his labor — to be deprived of his God-given rights.

The effect of this scheme of colonization, we fear, will be to arouse prejudice and to increase enmity against us, without bringing with it the remedy proposed or designed.

Repentance is more needed on the part of our oppressors than anything else. . . .

. . . And it seems reasonable to infer that the nation shall not again have peace and prosperity until prejudice, selfishness and slavery are sorely punished in the nation.

SOURCE: Philip S. Foner and Robert James Branham, eds., *Lift Every Voice: African American Oratory, 1787–1900* (Tuscaloosa: University of Alabama Press, 1998), 375–77.

DOCUMENT 3 Susie King Taylor | *Reminiscences of My Life in Camp, 1902*

SUSIE KING TAYLOR (1848–1912) was an enslaved woman in Georgia who sought freedom in 1862 with her cousins and uncles to a contraband camp in the Sea Islands. Mature, well spoken, and literate, she organized a school for contrabands. After she married Edward King, a Black non-commissioned officer in the Thirty-Third U.S. Colored Troops, she was attached to the unit as a laundress. She also taught and nursed the soldiers. The following excerpt is from Taylor's memoir, published in 1902, which is the only published account of its kind.

Breaking it Down What did Taylor do for the soldiers, and why? What aspects of Taylor's narrative illustrate a valuable perspective unique from those of Green and Wears?

When we arrived in Beaufort, Captain Trowbridge and the men he had enlisted went to camp at Old Fort, which they named "Camp Saxton." I was enrolled as laundress.

The first suits worn by the boys were red coats and pants, which they disliked very much, for, they said, "The rebels see us, miles away."

The first colored troops did not receive any pay for eighteen months, and the men had to depend wholly on what they received from the commissary, established by General Saxton. A great many of these men had large families, and as they had no money to give them, their wives were obliged to support themselves and children by washing for the officers of the gunboats and the soldiers, and making cakes and pies which they sold to the boys in camp. Finally, in 1863, the government decided to give them half pay, but the men would not accept this. They wanted "full pay" or nothing. They preferred rather to give their services to the state, which they did until 1864, when the government granted them full pay, with all the back pay due. . . .

On the first of January, 1863, we held services for the purpose of listening to the reading of President Lincoln's proclamation by Dr. W. H. Brisbane, and the presentation of two beautiful stands of colors, one from a lady in Connecticut, and the other from Rev. Mr. Cheever. The presentation speech was made by Chaplain French. It was a glorious day for us all, and we enjoyed every minute of it, and as a fitting close and the crowning event of this occasion we had a grand barbecue. A number of oxen were roasted whole, and we had a fine feast. Although not served as tastily or correctly as it would have been at home, yet it was enjoyed with keen appetites and relish. The soldiers had a good time. They sang or shouted "Hurrah!" all through the camp, and seemed overflowing with fun and frolic until taps were sounded, when many, no doubt, dreamt of this memorable day. . . .

I taught a great many of the comrades in Company E to read and write, when they were off duty. Nearly all were anxious to learn. My husband taught some also when it was convenient for him. I was very happy to know my efforts were successful in camp, and also felt grateful for the appreciation of my services. I gave my services willingly for four years and three months without receiving a dollar. I was glad, however, to be allowed to go with the regiment, to care for the sick and afflicted comrades. . . .

I learned to handle a musket very well while in the regiment, and could shoot straight and often hit the target. I assisted in cleaning the guns and used to fire them off, to see if the cartridges were dry, before cleaning and reloading, each day. I thought this great fun. I was also able to take a gun all apart, and put it together again. . . .

Fort Wagner being only a mile from our camp, I went there two or three times a week, and would go up on the ramparts to watch the gunners send their shells into Charleston (which they did every fifteen minutes), and had a full view of the city from that point. Outside of the fort were many skulls lying about; I have often moved them one side out of the path. The comrades and I would have quite a debate as to which side the men fought on. Some thought they were the skulls of our boys; others thought they were the enemy's; but as there was no definite way to know, it was never decided which could lay claim to them. They were a gruesome sight, those fleshless heads and grinning jaws, but by this time I had become accustomed to worse things and did not feel as I might have earlier in my camp life.

It seems strange how our aversion to seeing suffering is overcome in war, — how we are able to see the most sickening sights, such as men with their limbs blown off and mangled by the deadly shells, without a shudder; and instead of turning away, how we hurry to assist in alleviating their pain, bind up their wounds, and press the cool water to their parched lips, with feelings only of sympathy and pity. . . .

Finally orders were received for the boys to prepare to take Fort Gregg. . . . I helped as many as I could to pack haversacks and cartridge boxes. . . .

About four o'clock, July 2, the charge was made. The firing could be plainly heard in camp. I hastened down to the landing and remained there until eight o'clock that morning. When the wounded arrived, or rather began to arrive, the first one brought in was Samuel Anderson of our company. He was badly wounded. Then others of our boys, some with their legs off, arm gone, foot off, and wounds of all kinds imaginable. They had to wade through creeks and marshes, as they were discovered by the enemy and shelled very badly. A number of the men were lost, some got fastened in the mud and had to cut off the legs of their pants, to free themselves. . . .

My work now began. I gave my assistance to try to alleviate their sufferings. I asked the doctor at the hospital what I could get for them to eat. They wanted soup, but that I could not get; but I had a few cans of condensed milk and some turtle eggs, so I thought I would try to make some custard. I had doubts as to my success, for cooking with turtle eggs was something new to me, but the adage has it, "Nothing ventured, nothing done," so I made a venture and the result was a very delicious custard. This I carried to the men, who enjoyed it very much. My services were given at all times for the comfort of these men. I was on hand to assist whenever needed. I was enrolled as company laundress, but I did very little of it, because I was always busy doing other things through camp, and was employed all the time doing something for the officers and comrades.

SOURCE: Susie King Taylor, *Reminiscences of My Life in Camp: An African American Woman's Civil War Memoir*, ed. Catherine Clinton (Athens: University of Georgia Press, 2006), 15–16, 18, 21, 26, 31–32, 34–35.

DOCUMENT 4 *The Emancipation Proclamation, 1863*

The Emancipation Proclamation, issued on January 1, 1863, freed all the enslaved held by the Confederacy. The January 1 date was established in the *preliminary* Emancipation Proclamation, issued on September 22, 1862. That preliminary proclamation had given the Confederacy and its member states 100 days to cease their unlawful rebellion, renounce secession, and return to the Union or else the enslaved within their borders would be freed.

Breaking it Down How did President Abraham Lincoln justify issuing the preliminary Emancipation Proclamation and the actual Emancipation Proclamation? To what extent are some of the claims made by Wears and Green reflected in this document? How do you explain Lincoln's particular admonitions and concessions to the freedpeople within the Emancipation Proclamation, and how is this document an initial step toward acknowledging Black people as citizens?

By the President of the United States of America: a Proclamation.

Whereas, on the twenty-second day of September, in the year of our Lord one thousand eight hundred and sixty-two, a proclamation was issued by the President of the United States, containing, among other things, the following, to wit:

"That on the first day of January, in the year of our Lord one thousand eight hundred and sixty-three, all persons held as slaves within any State or designated part of a State, the people whereof shall then be in rebellion against the United States, shall be then, thenceforward, and forever free; and the Executive Government of the United States, including the military and naval authority thereof, will recognize and maintain the freedom of such persons, and will do no act or acts to repress such persons, or any of them, in any efforts they may make for their actual freedom.

"That the Executive will, on the first day of January aforesaid, by proclamation, designate the States and parts of States, if any, in which the people thereof, respectively, shall then be in rebellion against the United States; and the fact that any State, or the people thereof, shall on that day be, in good faith, represented in the Congress of the United States by members chosen thereto at elections wherein a majority of the qualified voters of such State shall have participated, shall, in the absence of strong countervailing testimony, be deemed conclusive evidence that such State, and the people thereof, are not then in rebellion against the United States."

Now, therefore I, Abraham Lincoln, President of the United States, by virtue of the power in me vested as Commander-in-Chief, of the Army and Navy of the United States in time of actual armed rebellion against the authority and government of the United States, and as a fit and necessary war measure for suppressing said rebellion, do, on this first day of January, in the year of our Lord one thousand eight hundred and sixty-three, and in accordance with my purpose so to do publicly proclaimed for the full period of one hundred days, from the day first above mentioned, order and designate as the States and parts of States wherein the people thereof respectively, are this day in rebellion against the United States, the following, to wit:

Arkansas, Texas, Louisiana, (except the Parishes of St. Bernard, Plaquemines, Jefferson, St. John, St. Charles, St. James Ascension, Assumption, Terrebonne, Lafourche, St. Mary, St. Martin, and Orleans, including the City of New Orleans) Mississippi, Alabama, Florida, Georgia, South Carolina, North Carolina, and Virginia, (except the forty-eight counties designated as West Virginia, and also the counties of Berkley, Accomac, Northampton, Elizabeth City, York, Princess Ann, and Norfolk, including the cities of Norfolk and Portsmouth[)], and which excepted parts, are for the present, left precisely as if this proclamation were not issued.

And by virtue of the power, and for the purpose aforesaid, I do order and declare that all persons held as slaves within said designated States, and parts of States, are, and henceforward shall be free; and that the Executive government of the United States, including the military and naval authorities thereof, will recognize and maintain the freedom of said persons.

And I hereby enjoin upon the people so declared to be free to abstain from all violence, unless in necessary self-defense; and I recommend to them that, in all cases when allowed, they labor faithfully for reasonable wages.

And I further declare and make known, that such persons of suitable condition, will be received into the armed service of the United States to garrison forts, positions, stations, and other places, and to man vessels of all sorts in said service.

And upon this act, sincerely believed to be an act of justice, warranted by the Constitution, upon military necessity, I invoke the considerate judgment of mankind, and the gracious favor of Almighty God.

In witness whereof, I have hereunto set my hand and caused the seal of the United States to be affixed.

Done at the City of Washington, this first day of January, in the year of our Lord one thousand eight hundred and sixty three, and of the Independence of the United States of America the eighty-seventh.

By the President: ABRAHAM LINCOLN
WILLIAM H. SEWARD, Secretary of State.

DOCUMENT 5 William Tolman Carlton | *Watch Meeting—Dec. 31st—Waiting for the Hour*, 1863

In *Watch Meeting — Dec. 31st — Waiting for the Hour* (also called *The Hour of Emancipation*), the white painter WILLIAM TOLMAN CARLTON (1816–1888) depicts a watch night congregation of enslaved people or contrabands located in a barn or an outbuilding. About a dozen figures are gathered around a huge pocket watch illuminated by a flaring torch; the watch says five minutes to twelve. Notice the postures of those who have gathered. What are they doing? What emotions do their expressions convey? One white woman is present. Who is she, and why did the painter place her in the scene? The painting is full of symbols. What book is the central figure looking at? What document is nailed to the wall? How do you interpret the figure of the torch holder with the coffle iron around his neck? After locating the cross in the upper-left rafters, find a flag and a banjo. What do these objects symbolize?

Breaking it Down What claim does the artist make regarding the meaning of emancipation, both to the individuals in this painting and to Black Americans everywhere? Although we can use this painting to understand the moment and meaning of emancipation as a New England abolitionist envisioned it,[43] how might the actual moment of emancipation have differed from its representation here?

The Hour of Emancipation, *1863, by William Tolman Carlton (1816–1888)/Private Collection/Photo © Christie's Images/Bridgeman Images.*

DOCUMENT 6 *Private Hubbard Pryor, before and after Enlisting in the U.S. Colored Troops, 1864*

The following side-by-side photographs show PRIVATE HUBBARD PRYOR (c. 1842–1890) literally transformed by his enlistment in the U.S. Colored Troops. Compare the two images, especially taking note of Pryor's dress, facial expression, and posture in each photo. Keep in mind that it was not yet a convention to smile for the camera.

Breaking it Down These images were consciously staged. What point do you think the photographer was trying to make with the clothing, objects, countenance, and positioning of Private Pryor? Use what you have learned in this chapter to evaluate the picture on the left. What do you see, think, wonder, and predict about his experience as a soldier in the war? What effect might both of these photos have had on those who viewed them?

Courtesy of the National Archives, Records of the Adjutant General's Office, c. 1775–c. 1928, ARC identifiers #849127 and #849136.

DOCUMENT 7 *Freedmen's Memorial, 1876*

Titled *Emancipation* but also known as *Freedmen's Memorial*, this sculpture stands in Lincoln Park on Capitol Hill in Washington, D.C. Created by THOMAS BALL (1819–1911), a white American artist best known for his monumental sculptures of American heroes, *Freedmen's Memorial* was erected with contributions from African Americans, beginning with $5 entrusted to a former enslaver by a formerly enslaved person to build a monument to the martyred president.[44] Significantly, it portrays Lincoln as "the Great Emancipator," holding out his hand over a kneeling, nearly naked freedman. Is Lincoln offering the freedman a blessing? Is he urging him to rise? A twenty-first-century critic has said, "It looks as if the 16th president is about to pet the man." What do you think? The monument has long been controversial. Frederick Douglass, who spoke at the dedication, was reported by one observer to have said that it "showed the Negro on his knees, when a more manly attitude would have been more indicative of freedom."[45]

Breaking it Down What impression does the artist give regarding both Lincoln and the enslaved man's role in emancipation? What clues in the monument support your perception? To what extent does the monument align with what you learned regarding Black people's role in their own emancipation during the war? Explain your answer.

The George F. Landegger Collection of District of Columbia Photographs in Carol M. Highsmith's America, Library of Congress, Prints and Photographs Division, Washington, D.C., LC-DIG-highsm-10341.

PRACTICING AP® SKILLS

1. **AP® Comparison.** How do Wears's claims about colonization counter or support the arguments of influential Black supporters of emigration in the 1860s?
2. **AP® Causation.** Explain the impact the passage of the Emancipation Proclamation had on the outcome of the Civil War. Where is that impact evident in these documents?
3. **AP® Comparison.** Compare how each document supports the claim that Black people saw themselves as citizens even when their country did not.
4. **Connecting to AP® Themes.** Describe African American women's contributions during the U.S. Civil War and explain their significance to the war's outcome. Use the source by Susie King Taylor to support your response.
5. **Class Discussion.** In 1861 and 1862, what choices did the Civil War offer free Black men in the North? Why did Green and Wears argue the positions they did? As a class, discuss how you think the positions of Green and Wears might have changed.

Document-Based Questions:
Introductions

As you learned in the AP® Skills Workshop for Chapter 7 (p. SW7-A), an effective **thesis statement** previews the **argument** you'll make in your response to a document-based question. By making a **claim** that incorporates one of the Four Cs, and by establishing a **line of reasoning** through the *X because A, B, and C* template, you'll be well on your way to an organized and compelling response.

While a thesis statement is essential to a strong response to a document-based question, it shouldn't open your essay on its own. Instead, you'll want to first provide any context your reader needs to fully appreciate your thesis statement and the reasoning that will follow. That's the purpose of an introduction.

In this workshop, we'll focus on how to build a framework of introductory information to situate readers within a historical **context**.

Examining the AP® Rubric

The rubric that will be used to assess DBQ responses states you'll earn a point if your essay:

- Describes a broader historical or disciplinary context relevant to the topic of the prompt. *To earn this point, the response must describe broader events, developments, processes, or disciplinary connections that are relevant to the topic of the prompt. The point is not earned for a passing phrase or reference.*

The introduction of your essay will be the perfect place for the historical context necessary to earn this point. Don't worry about the rubric's mention of "disciplinary context" for now; in the AP® Skills Workshop for Chapter 11 (p. SW11-A), we'll go over how to convey your essay's significance within the field of African American Studies.

Reviewing Prewriting Skills

Let's use a sample document-based question connected to this chapter's time period to review the steps that lead up to an essay introduction:

Explain how Black people's contributions to the Civil War dismantled the institution of slavery.

In the first AP® Skills Workshop on DBQs (p. SW5-A), we went over how to break down a prompt and activate course knowledge so relevant **concepts**, **developments**, and **processes** come to mind. Following those steps for the prompt above will lead to a graphic organizer that looks something like the one to follow.

Time Period	Topic	Task
American Civil War (1861–1865)	Black people's participation in the Civil War and eventual emancipation	Explain the relationship between Black Americans' participation in the Civil War and their eventual emancipation.

Relevant Course Concepts, Developments, Processes
• African American men were initially excluded from serving in the Union army or navy but were eventually allowed to join when labor shortages arose. • Some Black people believed participation in the military would promote emancipation and strengthen their claims to full citizenship. • While the Lincoln administration and the U.S. Congress initially prioritized the preservation of the Union, the actions of Black soldiers and abolitionists placed more attention on the goal of ending slavery. • In 1863, the Emancipation Proclamation decisively linked a Union victory with emancipation and also declared formerly enslaved people would be welcomed into military service. • Black men participated as soldiers, built fortifications, and manned supply lines, while Black women worked as nurses, spies, cooks, and laundresses.

Typically, your next step would be to skillfully skim the sources provided (using the technique outlined in the AP® Skills Workshop for Chapter 6, p. SW6-A), and then draft a thesis statement (following the principles from the AP® Skills Workshop for Chapter 7, p. SW7-A). To save time, we'll provide a thesis statement upfront:

> Black people's many wartime contributions brought about the abolition of slavery because their participation in battle, as medical support, and at camp was critical to the Union's ability to win the war.

With a broken-down prompt and a thesis statement in hand, we're now ready to craft an essay introduction.

Introducing a DBQ

Like we mentioned at the very beginning of this workshop, the introduction is where you'll provide the context your audience needs to follow your essay's argument. This chapter covered a great deal of historical information that could connect to the prompt about Black Americans' impact on the Civil War, but of course, we can't fit all of it into one brief paragraph. And, though our work to break down the prompt articulated a topic, specified a time period, and collected some relevant course knowledge, it didn't create a cohesive narrative.

To narrow our focus to only the historical information that *directly* contextualizes our argument, we can ask ourselves this key question: What historical information does my audience need to grasp in order to understand my thesis statement?

In this case, our thesis statement is about Black people's contributions to the Civil War both on and off the battlefield. So, we can focus on articulating the historical circumstances that set the stage for those contributions.

What happened, in a general sense?	• Both free and enslaved Black people supported the Union cause.
What happened, more specifically?	• African American men were initially excluded from the Union army. • The Emancipation Proclamation made abolition a clear Union goal and approved the recruitment of Black soldiers.
How does this context connect to the thesis statement?	• The Union couldn't have won without combat and non-combat support from African American people.

Adopting this approach makes it easier to progress from a general historical context to the specific information that sets the stage for our thesis statement. We can convert our brainstorming into full sentences that form a complete and cohesive introduction:

> Thousands of free and enslaved African Americans supported the Union's cause during the Civil War of 1861 to 1865. While Black people had contributed to the war effort even while formally excluded from armed service, the Emancipation Proclamation of 1863 welcomed formerly enslaved people into the military. Ultimately, African Americans were instrumental in securing a Union victory and, thus, their liberation. Black people's many wartime contributions brought about the abolition of slavery because their participation in battle, as medical support, and at camp was critical to the Union's ability to win the war.

More than just a passing reference, the historical context offered in an introduction like this one acclimates readers to the argument that will be made in the essay to follow.

recap

Introducing a DBQ

When drafting an introduction for a document-based question, it can be helpful to ask yourself the following questions:

- **What happened, in a general sense?**
- **What happened, more specifically?**
- **How does this context connect to the thesis statement?**

Activity ▸ Introducing a DBQ

Draft your own introduction incorporating the sample thesis statement provided on page SW8-B.

NOTES

Multiple-Choice Questions

Questions 1–2 refer to the following.

> The people are informed that in accordance with a Proclamation from the Executive of the United States, all slaves are free. This involves an absolute equality of personal rights and rights of property, between former masters and slaves, and the connection heretofore existing between them, becomes that between employer and hired labor. The freed are advised to remain at their present homes, and work for wages. They are informed that they will not be allowed to collect at military posts; and that they will not be supported in idleness either there or elsewhere.

AP® source General Order No. 3, *The Galveston Tri-Weekly News*, June 20, 1865

1. The excerpt best illustrates which of the following major developments in the Black freedom struggle?

(A) The signing of the Emancipation Proclamation liberating all enslaved people in Confederate states
(B) The establishment of the Freedmen's Bureau
(C) The end of slavery in the last state of rebellion
(D) The ratification of the Fourteenth Amendment

2. The excerpt contains the first description in an American legal document of which of the following historically significant civil rights principles?

(A) The legal emancipation of all enslaved people
(B) The legal equality of Black and white people
(C) The entitlement of Black people to wages in exchange for labor
(D) The establishment of federal jurisdiction over all former Confederate states

Short-Answer Question

"When the war is over, the country is saved, peace is established, and the black man's rights are secured, as they will be, history with an impartial hand will dispose of that and sundry other questions. . . . Words are now useful only as they stimulate to blows. . . . Liberty won by white men would lose half its luster. "Who would be free themselves must strike the blow." "Better even die free, than to live slaves." This is the sentiment of every brave colored man amongst us. . . . By every consideration which binds you to your enslaved fellow-countrymen, and the peace and welfare of your country; by every aspiration which you cherish for the freedom and equality of yourselves and your children; by all the ties of blood and identity which make us one with the brave black men now fighting our battles in Louisiana and in South Carolina, I urge you to fly to arms, and smite with death the power that would bury the government and your liberty in the same hopeless grave."

SOURCE: Frederick Douglass, *Men of Color, to Arms*, 1863

1. Using the excerpt, answer A, B, C, and D.

(A) Describe the broader historical context that compelled Douglass to make the speech in the excerpt.

(B) Using a specific example, explain how Black soldiers impacted the war.

(C) Explain how Black women responded to Douglass's call to support the war.

(D) Using a specific example, explain to what extent Douglass's claims about the benefits of participating in the war were realized immediately after the war.

Multiple-Choice Questions

Questions 1–3 refer to the following.

***Africans in St. Augustine,* 1673**

Private Collection/Peter Newark American Pictures/Bridgeman Images

1. Which of the following best describes the significance of St. Augustine as a historical place in African American history?

(A) It was the final destination for the enslaved Africans who participated in the Stono Rebellion, fighting their way to freedom from South Carolina.

(B) It was home to the first sanctioned free Black town in what is now the United States.

(C) It was the first city in what would become the United States to abolish slavery.

(D) It was home to a strict slave legal code which became the model for British colonies.

2. An enslaved African from the British colonies fleeing slavery and seeking to arrive in St. Augustine was most likely motivated by which of the following?

(A) Indigenous groups in Spanish Florida protected runaways and gave them refuge.

(B) St. Augustine was a major stop along the Underground Railroad.

(C) Spanish Florida offered emancipation to enslaved people fleeing the British colonies.

(D) St. Augustine-based Spanish missionaries helped enslaved African people return to Africa.

3. The response of enslaved Africans in British colonies to the policies of Spanish Florida resulted in which of the following?

(A) The introduction of South Carolina's restrictive 1740 slave code

(B) The recognition of Fort Mose as a legitimate town by the British colonies

(C) The emancipation of enslaved people in South Carolina

(D) A negotiation between the British and Spanish over the sale of Florida

Questions 4–6 refer to the following.

Steal away, steal away, steal away to Jesus! Steal away, steal away home, I ain't got long to stay here.

1 My Lord, He calls me, He calls me by the thunder; The trumpet sounds within my soul; I ain't got long to stay here. [Refrain]

2 Green trees are bending, Poor sinners stand a trembling; The trumpet sounds within my soul; I ain't got long to stay here. [Refrain]

3 My Lord, He calls me, He calls me by the lightning; The trumpet sounds within my soul; I ain't got long to stay here.

AP® source *Steal Away to Jesus* (song), Wallis Willis, c. 1862

4. Which of the following statements about spirituals does *Steal Away* best support?

(A) They articulated enslaved people's hopes, often focusing on obtaining freedom.

(B) They demonstrated enslaved people's acceptance of Christianity as it was practiced by white Americans.

(C) They contained hidden messages demonstrating that enslaved people rejected American Christianity.

(D) They revealed the deep loss of cultural heritage suffered by enslaved African people.

5. Which of the following best describes the cultural purpose of spirituals like *Steal Away*?

(A) Spirituals were a form of resistance against the dehumanizing conditions and injustice of enslavement.

(B) Spirituals were performed to gain the favor and acceptance of the white clergy.

(C) Spirituals were performed to gain monetary support from white patrons.

(D) Spirituals were intended to fill the same role as African griots.

6. The emergence of spirituals resulted from which of the following historical trends of the 1800s?

(A) The conversion of enslaved communities to Presbyterian and Episcopal churches

(B) The closing of the transatlantic slave trade as Congress banned the importation of enslaved Africans in 1808

(C) The beginning of the Second Middle Passage in the early to mid-nineteenth century

(D) The rise of syncretism, combining African Americans' African cultural practices with their American identity

Questions 7–9 refer to the following.

> "The slaves' narrative gave Northern whites a comprehensive picture of life in slavery, countering easy stereotypes with brutal reality. Along with depictions of mistreatment were portraits of stable slave families presided over by resourceful men and women who acquired skills, created institutions, and satisfied material needs on their own. In recent decades, historians have confirmed the accuracy of these narratives, using them and other data to reconstruct African American culture in slavery. By stressing the slaves' humanity, their cultural vitality, and their accomplishments, slave narratives contested prevailing racial myths far more comprehensively than any other kind of abolitionist literature."
>
> SOURCE: James Brewer Stewart, historian, *Holy Warriors: The Abolitionists and American Slavery*, 1996

7. The excerpt best describes which of the following historical developments of the 1800s?

(A) A surge in the publication of African American literature by formerly enslaved Black men and women

(B) A movement away from the idea of violence as being an accepted form of resistance by Black abolitionists

(C) A greater push for Black abolitionist writers to collaborate with white abolitionists to publish their experiences in the form of narratives

(D) A breakdown in the cohesiveness of the Black abolitionist movement

8. Which of the following most directly contributed to the historical situation described in the excerpt?

(A) The efforts of Black women using publications to call attention to their distinct experiences during slavery

(B) The decriminalization of reading and writing for enslaved people in most states

(C) The increased deference of Black abolitionists to white abolitionists

(D) The emerging strategy of Black abolitionists to convince white Americans that slavery was unconstitutional rather than immoral

9. Which of the following could be best used as evidence to support Stewart's central claim in the excerpt?

(A) Bartolomé de Las Casas's *A Short Account of the Destruction of the Indies* gave enough insight into the devastating effects of slavery to help end the transatlantic slave trade.

(B) Harriet Beecher Stowe's *Uncle Tom's Cabin* bolstered support for abolition by portraying enslaved people sympathetically, although it was later criticized for stereotypical and racist portrayals.

(C) William Lloyd Garrison's *The Liberator* was a popular publication that advocated for the abolition of slavery and featured the work of Black abolitionists like James Forten and Maria Stewart alongside Garrison's own antislavery arguments.

(D) Solomon Northup's *Twelve Years a Slave* sold over 30,000 copies in three years after its publication and continues to be used by historians for its eyewitness account of life under enslavement.

Questions 10–12 refer to the following.

SOURCE 1

African Americans in the Union Military

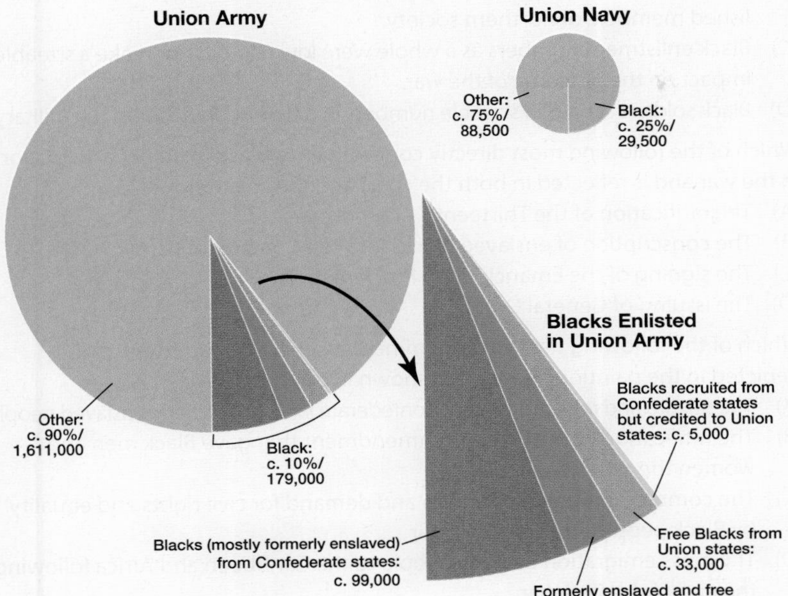

SOURCE 2

Currier & Ives, *The Gallant Charge of the Fifty Fourth Massachusetts Regiment*, 1863

Private Collection/Peter Newark American Pictures/Bridgeman Images

10. Which of the following statements about Black participation in the Civil War does the chart best support?

(A) The majority of able-bodied Black men rejected military service due to pervasive racism in the Union army.

(B) The bulk of Black men who fought in the war were already free and established members of northern society.

(C) Black enlistment numbers as a whole were low and did not make a sizeable impact on the outcome of the war.

(D) Black soldiers served in sizeable numbers in different branches of the military.

11. Which of the following most directly contributed to Black military participation in the war and is reflected in both the chart and the illustration?

(A) The ratification of the Thirteenth Amendment

(B) The conscription of enslaved Blacks into the Confederate army

(C) The signing of the Emancipation Proclamation

(D) The issuing of General Order 3

12. Which of the following describes an immediate effect of both the event depicted in the painting and a trend shown in the chart?

(A) The seizure and redistribution of Confederate lands to formerly enslaved people

(B) The ratification of the Fifteenth Amendment that gave Black men and women the right to vote

(C) The commemoration of freedom and demand for civil rights and equality by Black people after the Civil War

(D) The mass emigration of Black people to the Caribbean and Africa following the end of the Civil War

Questions 13–15 refer to the following.

SOURCE 1

AP® source ***Gopher John, Seminole Interpreter*, engraving, 1848**

Library of Congress, Prints and Photographs Division, Washington, D.C., LC-USZC4-6165.

SOURCE 2

AP® source ***Arkansas Petition for Freedmen's Rights, 1869***

"To the Honorable Senators and Representatives in the Congress of the United States Respecting the State of Arkansas, Gentlemen, We the undersigned Petitioners, Members of the General Assembly of the State of Arkansas, do most respectfully [state] that information has been received that there are Three Thousand Persons of African descent living and residing in the Choctaw and Chickasaw Nations who were formally held in servitude and who are desirous of [emancipation] from said Nations and enjoying all the rights and privileges of citizens. Therefore, we request that you use your influence for the purpose of [enabling] by the Congress of the United States to allow the Choctaws and Chickasaw Nations to agree or [enact] Article III of a treaty entered into by and between the government of the United States and the said Choctaw and Chickasaw Nations dated April 26, 1866, that all persons of African descent in said Nations receive and hold forty (40) acres of land and be entitled to all the rights and privileges of any other class of citizens of said nations, including the right of suffrage . . ."

13. Which of the following statements do both sources best support?

(A) Indigenous groups were ardent supporters of the abolitionist movement and fought to protect freedom seekers in all three Seminole Wars.

(B) Black people found refuge within some Indigenous communities and were enslaved by others.

(C) Black people were employed by the U.S. military to remove Indigenous peoples from their land before the Civil War.

(D) Racial slavery was never codified within Indigenous communities.

14. Which of the following historical situations provides context for Source 2?

(A) The Choctaw were the only tribe to resist federal displacement under the Indian Removal Act.

(B) The Chickasaw had adopted European institutions in an attempt to live peacefully alongside their white neighbors.

(C) The five large Indigenous nations (Creek, Cherokee, Choctaw, Chickasaw, and Seminole) adopted slave codes, created slave patrols, and assisted in recapturing enslaved Black people who fled for freedom.

(D) The Thirteenth Amendment did not apply to Black people enslaved by Indigenous nations or give them equal rights.

15. Which of the following explains the historical significance of Black Seminoles like Gopher John as a historical figure in African American Studies?

(A) Black Seminoles helped provide safe passage to displaced Indigenous people during the Trail of Tears.

(B) Black Seminoles were never welcomed as kin despite their contributions to the Seminole community.

(C) Black Seminoles played a vital role in helping the Seminole tribes resist the incursions of U.S. troops.

(D) Enslaved Black Seminoles were the Seminoles' main source of income.

Short-Answer Questions

1. Using the map, answer A, B, C, and D.

AP® source *Trade of Enslaved Africans, 1501–1867*

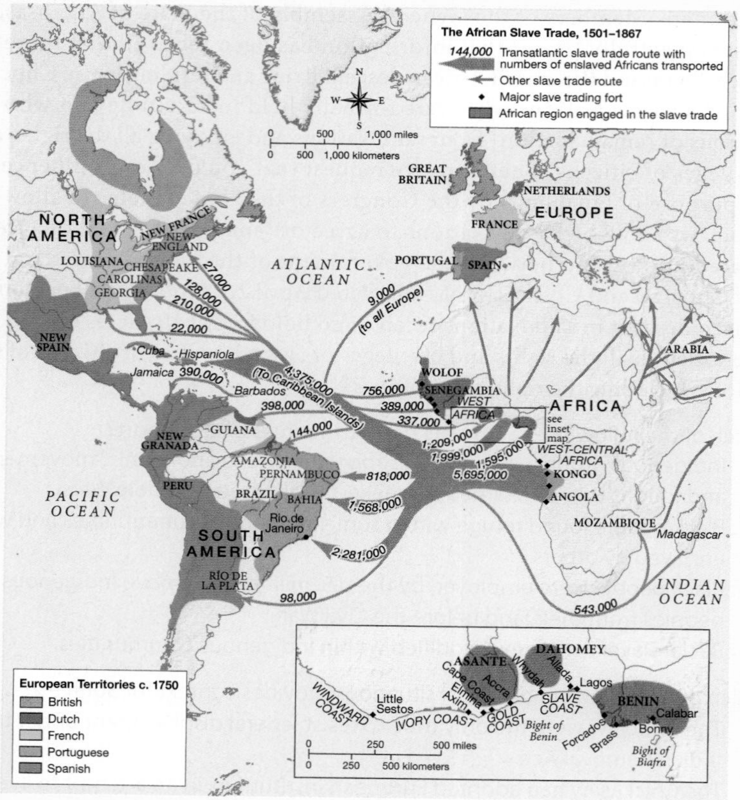

(A) Describe one political or cultural impact that the pattern depicted in the map had on West African communities.

(B) Describe one way in which the distribution of distinct African ethnic groups shaped the cultural or economic development of African American communities in the United States.

(C) Explain why the pattern in the numbers of enslaved Africans brought into Brazil and the United States shifted during the nineteenth century.

(D) Explain how the character of the institution of slavery that developed in the United States compared with the practice of slavery at one other location on the map.

2. Using the excerpt, answer A, B, C, and D.

"Brethren, it is as wrong for your lordly oppressors to keep you in slavery as it was for the man thief to steal our ancestors from the coast of Africa. You should therefore now use the same manner of resistance as would have been just in our ancestors when the bloody footprints of the first remorseless soul thief was placed upon the shores of our fatherland. . . . Think how many tears you have poured out upon the soil which you have cultivated with unrequited toil and enriched with your blood; and then go to your lordly enslavers and tell them plainly that you are determined to be free. . . . Point them to the increase of happiness and prosperity in the British West Indies since the Act of Emancipation. . . . If you would be free in this generation, here is your only hope. However much you and all of us may desire it, there is not much hope of redemption without the shedding of blood. If you must bleed, let it all come at once — rather die freemen than live to be slaves. . . . Brethren, arise, arise! Strike for your lives and liberties. Now is the day and the hour. Let every slave throughout the land do this, and the days of slavery are numbered. You cannot be more oppressed than you have been; you cannot suffer greater cruelties than you have already. Rather die freemen than live to be slaves. Remember that you are three millions! . . . Let your motto be Resistance! Resistance! RESISTANCE! No oppressed people have ever secured their liberty without resistance."

AP® source Henry Highland Garnet, *An Address to the Slaves of the United States of America*, 1843

(A) Describe the broader context of Garnett's speech.

(B) Describe the types of nineteenth-century resistance strategies promoted by Black activists to demand change.

(C) Explain how Garnett's strategy of resistance in 1843 compares to the strategy of resistance adopted by abolitionists in the decades after the Revolutionary War.

(D) Explain how the contributions of one contemporary Black abolitionist who shared Garnett's strategy regarding the struggle for freedom in the 1840s contributed to the effort.

3. Answer A, B, C, and D.

(A) Describe the motivations for Black Americans enlisting in the Civil War.

(B) Describe the inequities Black soldiers faced during the Civil War.

(C) Explain how Black soldiers' service affected Black communities during and after the Civil War.

(D) Explain how free and enslaved Black women contributed to the war effort.

Document-Based Question

1. **Explain how ancestral African cultural elements influenced the artistic expressions of enslaved Africans.**

   In your response you should do the following:
   - **Respond to the prompt with a defensible thesis or claim that establishes a line of reasoning.**
   - **Describe a broader historical or disciplinary context relevant to the topic of the prompt.**
   - **Support an argument in response to the prompt using at least three of the sources.**
   - **Use at least one additional piece of specific evidence (beyond the evidence found in the sources) relevant to your argument.**
   - **For at least two sources, explain how or why the perspective, purpose, context, and/or audience for each source is relevant to your argument.**
   - **Reference or cite the sources you use in your argument. You can reference or cite the source letter, title, or author.**

SOURCE A

William Sidney Mount, *The Banjo Player*, 1856

Art Collection 2/Alamy Stock Photo

SOURCE B

McIntosh County Shouters, *Gullah-Geechee Ring Shout*, Georgia, 2010

American Folklife Center, sponsoring body Library of Congress

SOURCE C

***Follow the Drinking Gourd*, song, first published 1928**

When the sun come back
And the first quail calls.
Follow the drinking gourd.
For the old man is awaitin'
For to carry you to freedom.
Follow the drinking gourd.
Follow the drinking gourd.
Follow the drinking gourd.
For the old man is awaitin'
For to carry you to freedom.
Follow the drinking gourd.
The river bank makes
A very good road
The dead trees will show you the way.
Left foot peg foot
Traveling on.
Follow the drinking gourd.
(Chorus)
The river ends
Between two hills.
Follow the drinking gourd.
There's another river

On the other side
Follow the drinking gourd.
(Chorus)
When the great big river
Meets another river
Follow the drinking gourd
For the old man is awaitin'
For to carry you to freedom.
Follow the drinking gourd.

SOURCE D

Handmade Sweetgrass Baskets at the Charleston City Market in Charleston, South Carolina, 2023

Castle Light Images/Alamy Stock Photo

SOURCE E

Yvonne P. Chireau, *Black Magic: Religion and the African American Conjuring Tradition*, 2006

Among enslaved blacks, older cosmologies gradually merged with concepts that were extracted from newly formed Afro-Christian ideas such as a radical monotheism, dualistic notions of good and evil, and concepts of spiritual intervention. Elements of the older African worldview also intersected with a network of Anglo-American supernatural traditions. The simultaneous emergence of African-based supernaturalism . . . and black Americans' embrace of Christianity resulted in the reinforcement of magic and religion as convergent phenomena. . . .

Religious leaders in slave communities were entrusted with . . . maintaining spiritual traditions. These leaders included both Christian ministers and Conjurers. Occasionally, these offices were shared by a single person. William Webb was one such individual. Enslaved in Kentucky in the early 1800s, Webb recalled how he had prepared special bags of roots for other blacks to carry in order "to keep peace" between masters and slaves on location plantations. The roots, he explained, were to be used in conjunction with prayer. When asked by other bondmen about the bags, he explained, "I told them those roots were able to make them faithful when they were calling on the Supreme Being, and to keep [their] mind at work all the time." . . .

Slave Conjurers offered consolation to other bondspersons who were at risk. . . . The black abolitionist and writer Henry Clay Bruce . . . described a community of slaves that hired the services of a Conjurer to prevent their deportation and removal to a plantation in the Deep South. The Conjurer's powers, they believed, obstructed the slaveowners' attempts to separate them, for at the last minute the scheduled relocation was aborted. The assurance that these individuals supplied . . . was often indispensable. Such defenses against the psychological and physical assaults of slavery were essential for many African Americans, who endured a system in which their humanity was devalued and their collective efforts at self-determination were constantly hindered.

UNIT **3**

The Practice of Freedom

9 Reconstruction: The Making and Unmaking of a Revolution
1865–1877

10 Black Life and Culture during the Nadir
1877–1915

11 The New Negro Comes of Age
1915–1930

Unit 3 covers nearly one hundred years and highlights resilience and reconnection with Black American identities. Following the end of the Civil War in 1865, African Americans, both born free and formerly enslaved, were able to claim social, economic, and political freedom — particularly during the period of Reconstruction from 1865 to 1873. One of the recurring themes in this unit revolves around the question of how African Americans were going to exercise their newfound freedom and economic opportunities. Self-determination took on a deeper meaning as African Americans were able to build on their ancestral roots while thriving in areas of business and education. Intellectual and political differences informed many different approaches to building society, resisting oppression, and ways of being.

In this unit, you will also learn about the steps African Americans took to protect their rights while dealing with the threat of opposition and violence. After the failure of Reconstruction came a period of violence and backlash during the late nineteenth and early twentieth centuries. Many Black Americans left the South, moving to the North for greater opportunities in what became known as the Great Migration. Relocating to new parts of the country during the Great Migration also inspired a new generation of African Americans who challenged the legal status quo while highlighting the talents within the community. Life during this "nadir" of domestic terrorism, disfranchisement, and the loss of family gave rise to movements such as Black nationalism, Black Women's Clubs, and the Harlem Renaissance, a movement of the 1920s and 30s that produced inspirational writing, art, and music exploring Black experiences through Black lenses.

The initial gains made by Black Americans immediately after emancipation are outlined in **chapter 9** (**Reconstruction: The Making and Unmaking of a Revolution, 1865–1877**) with a detailed analysis of the implications of the Thirteenth Amendment, which abolished slavery in the United States. Although African Americans were able to form new connections, establish communities, and work for pay during this time, the work offered generally did not lead to prosperity. Often depicted in white published newsprint as lazy and violent, Black Americans had to partner with allies to gather support for their enfranchisement. These relationships with prominent individuals such as William Lloyd Garrison offer

This photograph, taken circa 1902, shows young Black men and women in a history classroom at the Tuskegee Institute, founded on July 4, 1881. Under the leadership of its first president, Booker T. Washington, the school expanded rapidly from a single room in 1881 to a nearly 2,300-acre campus at the turn of the twentieth century. The school, now known as Tuskegee University, is still one of the top historically Black colleges and universities in the nation. *Library of Congress, Prints & Photographs Division, Reproduction number LC-USZ62-64712 (b&w film copy neg.).*

some insight into the inequality within a nation known for its belief in life, liberty, and the freedom to pursue happiness. This activism eventually led to the passage of the Civil Rights Acts of 1866 and 1871, but the end of Reconstruction stunted many efforts toward further progress. Most importantly, this chapter illustrates what it was to live with the concept, but not the full practice, of freedom — and how racist violence and a lack of support from the federal government limited many of the rights that should have been protected.

Chapter 10 (Black Life and Culture during the Nadir, 1877–1915) expands on the African American experience, walking through the steps that the federal and state governments took to uphold and protect racist practices post-Reconstruction. This chapter also details the rise of lynching throughout most of the country at this time. Despite the daily violence and injustice Black Americans experienced under Jim Crow, they continued to work for true freedom and equality. This chapter highlights advocates such as Ida B. Wells and W. E. B. Du Bois in particular. The exposés penned by Wells describe in detail the injustices white Americans inflicted upon Black Americans during the late nineteenth century. Du Bois, a historian and sociologist, became one of the most powerful intellectual voices of the era. The experiences of Black cowboys, entertainers, and entrepreneurs are also captured in this chapter. Finally, you'll learn about "uplift," a concept that captures many different strategies for social advancement during this era, including industrial education, liberal arts education, civil rights activism, women's suffrage, and more. Perhaps nowhere else is the concept of "uplift" so beautifully encapsulated as in James Weldon Johnson's poem, "Lift Every Voice and Sing," and the flourishing of institutions for higher learning for Black Americans. These efforts often served as beacons of light for Black Americans during times of dread and disfranchisement.

Chapter 11 (The New Negro Comes of Age, 1915–1930) offers an analysis of the prosperity of some Black Americans and the flowering of cultural movements even at the height of lynching in the United States. The exodus from southern states to the North and Midwest during the Great Migration allowed for new economic opportunities. The rebirth and renewal of Black art and culture during the Harlem Renaissance of the 1920s and 30s gave rise to new genres of music, art, and literature. Many Black Americans embraced the Black nationalism of Marcus Garvey — who would go on to inspire later generations of activists, including Malcolm X (more on him in Unit 4). This era also saw the rise of educated African Americans and influx of immigrants from the West Indies, broadening and enriching the concept of Black American identity. As in the Jim Crow South, acts of violence and oppressive federal policies continued to be challenged.

AP® source

James van der Zee (1886–1983) was a photographer who chronicled the lives of Black Americans, especially New Yorkers, throughout the twentieth century. He is best known for his portraits depicting Black people and their lives through the lens of rebirth that permeated the Harlem Renaissance in the 1920s and 30s. He would frequently hand-tint and draw on his portraits to add detail, as in this photograph. Titled "Do Tell," this hand-tinted gelatin silver print was taken in 1930. *© James Van Der Zee Archive, The Metropolitan Museum of Art with respect to James Van Der Zee (American, Lenox, Massachusetts 1886–1983 Washington, D.C.), Do Tell. 1930. Hand tinted gelatin silver print, Image: 24.4 × 19.3 cm (9 5/8 × 7 5/8 in.); Paper: 25.2 × 20.1 cm (9 15/16 × 7 15/16 in.). Art Institute of Chicago, The Mary and Leigh Block Endowment Fund (2002.99) © James Van Der Zee Archive, The Metropolitan Museum of Art.*

Above all, this unit tells the story of how — in the face of many challenges — Black Americans forged their own paths to new freedoms, building vibrant communities and powerful movements, both artistic and political.

UNIT 3 THEMATIC TIMELINE

All of the following developments can be found in the AP® Course Framework.

1850 | 1875 | 1900 | 1925 | 1950

Migration and the African Diaspora

- **1890s–1930s** Over 100,000 Afro-Caribbean immigrants arrive in the U.S.
- **1910s–70s** Thousands of Black people move from the American South to the North during the Great Migration
- **1910** National Urban League founded
- **1921** Marcus Garvey's Universal Negro Improvement Association hits 4 million members worldwide

Intersections of Identity

- **1881** Tuskegee Institute founded
- **1895** Booker T. Washington delivers Atlanta Compromise speech
- **1896** National Association of Colored Women founded
- **1903** W. E. B. Du Bois's *The Souls of Black Folk* published
- **1909** National Association for the Advancement of Colored People founded
- **1925** Alain Locke's *The New Negro* published
- **1933** Carter G. Woodson's *The Mis-Education of the Negro* published

Creativity, Expression, and the Arts

- **1872** Fisk Jubilee Singers perform at White House
- **1900** James Weldon Johnson and John Rosamond Johnson create "Lift Every Voice and Sing"
- **1920s–30s** Black literary, artistic, and intellectual life of Harlem Renaissance creates cultural revolution
- **1940–41** Jacob Lawrence paints *Migration Series*

Resistance and Resilience

- **1865** Thirteenth Amendment abolishes slavery
- **1866** Civil Rights Act defines U.S. citizenship and overturns black codes
- **1868** Fourteenth Amendment defines and guarantees equal citizenship
- **1870** Fifteenth Amendment guarantees Black male suffrage
- **1875** Civil Rights Act requires equal treatment of whites and Blacks
- **1877** Compromise of 1877 ends Reconstruction
- **1883** U.S. Supreme Court overturns Civil Rights Act of 1875
- **1892** Ida B. Wells launches antilynching campaign
- **1896** *Plessy v. Ferguson* establishes separate but equal doctrine
- **1919** Red Summer race riots begin in Chicago, spread nationwide
- **1921** Tulsa race massacre

Source: *From 'The Illustrated London News,' November 18, 1876/Private Collection/Bridgeman Images.*

AP® skill Source Analysis (2C)

Explain the significance of a source's perspective, purpose, context, and audience.

Key Context: This engraving from 1876 shows Black worshippers in church. After Reconstruction, the number of Black churches increased significantly.

PREDICT

- What role do you think churches played in Black cultural life in the decades following the Civil War?
- What opportunities might churches have presented to African Americans during this era?
- What details from the image help support your prediction?

Source: *Chicago History Museum/Archive Photos/Getty Images.*

AP® skill Source Analysis (2C)

Explain the significance of a source's perspective, purpose, context, and audience.

Key Context: The Great Migration transformed African Americans from primarily rural dwellers to primarily urban dwellers. Black southerners forged new connections to their northern environment, such as engaging with nature for leisure rather than livelihood/labor.

PREDICT

- How do you think the Great Migration affected Black communities and American culture?
- What details from the photo help support your prediction?

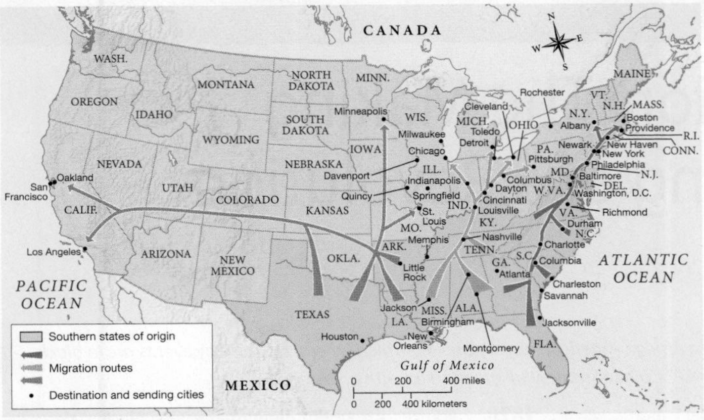

Data from Smallwood and Elliot, The Atlas of African-American History and Politics: From the Slave Trade to Modern Times *(1998).*

AP® skill Applying Disciplinary Knowledge (1C)

Identify and explain patterns, connections, or other relationships (causation, changes, continuities, comparison).

Key Context: This map shows the major railroad routes used by Black migrants to travel from the South to the cities of the North and, to a lesser extent, the West during the Great Migration.

PREDICT

- What does this map suggest about the causes and effects of the Great Migration?

SOURCE: *Photo by Jim Mooney/NY Daily News Archive via Getty Images.*

AP® skill Applying Disciplinary Knowledge (1A)

Identify and explain course concepts, developments, and processes.

AP® skill Argumentation (3A)

Formulate a defensible claim.

Key Context: In response to ongoing exclusion from broader American society, many African Americans created businesses catering to the needs of Black citizens. This photo shows Madam C. J. Walker, the first woman millionaire in the United States.

PREDICT

- What details from the image stand out most? Explain how you think the photo provides a visual narrative of the economic stability and well-being of their communities in the early twentieth century.

CHAPTER 9

Reconstruction: The Making and Unmaking of a Revolution

1865–1877

CHAPTER TIMELINE

Events specific to African American history are in purple. General U.S. history events are in black. Events from the AP® Course Framework are marked with an asterisk.

1865
- General William T. Sherman issues Special Field Order 15*
- Freedmen's Bureau founded*
- Freedman's Savings and Trust Company founded*
- Southern states pass black codes*
- Ku Klux Klan founded*
- Thirteenth Amendment abolishes slavery*

1866
- Civil Rights Act defines U.S. citizenship and overturns black codes
- Congress reauthorizes Freedmen's Bureau with expanded powers
- Southern Homestead Act
- Two Black cavalry regiments and two Black infantry regiments established
- American Equal Rights Association founded

1867–1868
- Reconstruction Acts

1868
- President Andrew Johnson impeached; Senate fails to convict him
- Fourteenth Amendment defines and guarantees equal citizenship*
- Radical Republican Thaddeus Stevens dies

1869
- National Woman Suffrage Association founded
- American Woman Suffrage Association founded
- Knights of Labor founded
- Isaac Myers helps found Colored National Labor Union

1870
- Fifteenth Amendment guarantees Black male suffrage*
- Force Act gives federal troops authority to put down racial disorder
- Hiram Revels becomes first African American U.S. senator*

1872
- Fisk Jubilee Singers perform at White House*
- Freedmen's Bureau disbanded

1873
- Colfax Massacre
- *Slaughterhouse Cases*; U.S. Supreme Court limits Fourteenth Amendment

1874
- Freedman's Savings and Trust Company fails
- Radical Republican Charles Sumner dies
- Robert Smalls elected to U.S. House of Representatives

1875
- Civil Rights Act requires equal treatment of whites and Blacks in public accommodations and on public conveyances

1876
- Hamburg Massacre
- Presidential election disputed

1877
- Disputed election resolved; deal results in federal troops being withdrawn from South
- Henry O. Flipper becomes first Black West Point graduate

Jourdon and Mandy Anderson Find Security in Freedom after Slavery

In the summer after the Civil War ended, freedman Jourdon Anderson of Dayton, Ohio, thought hard about the postwar prospects for himself, his wife Mandy, and their three children. Colonel P. H. Anderson, their "Old Master" in Big Spring, Tennessee, "promising to do better for me than anybody else can," and asked Jourdon and his family to return to the "old home" to work for him. Free since 1864, Jourdon and Mandy had made a nice life for themselves and their family in Dayton. "I get $25 a month, with victuals and clothing; have a comfortable home for Mandy . . . and the children," Jourdon explained in his formal response to Colonel Anderson's invitation. Recalling that Anderson had more than once tried to shoot him, Jourdon demanded "some proof that you are sincerely disposed to treat us justly and kindly" as a condition of return. The terms Jourdon and Mandy laid out were clear and precise:

> We have concluded to test your sincerity by asking you to send us our wages for the time we served you. This will make us forget and forgive old scores, and rely on your justice and friendship in the future. I served you faithfully for thirty-two years and Mandy twenty years. At $25 a month for me, and $2 a week for Mandy, our earnings would amount to $11,680. Add to this the interest for the time our wages has been kept back and deduct what you paid for our clothing and three doctor's visits to me, and pulling a tooth for Mandy, and the balance will show what we are in justice entitled to. Please send the money by Adams Express, in care of V. Winters, esq., Dayton, Ohio. If you fail to pay us for faithful labors in the past we can have little faith in your promises in the future. We trust the good Maker has opened your eyes to the wrongs which you and your fathers have done to me and my fathers, in making us toil for you for generations without recompense.

Besides making sure that their economic situation would be solid, Jourdon and Mandy wanted to know that their domestic and social lives as free people would be protected and dignified. The old patterns of white dominance and Black subordination were unacceptable. Jourdon observed that when "the folks here" talk to Mandy, they "call her Mrs. Anderson." Jourdon and Mandy demanded that their daughters Milly and Jane, "now grown up and both good-looking girls," be safe from rape and sexual exploitation at the hands of white men. "I would rather stay here and starve and die if it comes to that than have my girls brought to shame by the violence and wickedness of their young masters." Mandy and Jourdon were also very proud of their son Grundy, whose teacher had told them that Grundy "has a head for a preacher." They made certain their children attended Sunday school and church, as well as grammar school. Committed to a good education for their children, they asked Colonel Anderson "if there has been any schools opened for the colored children in your neighborhood." Jourdon explained, "The great desire of my life now is to give my children an education, and have them form virtuous habits."[1]

Jourdon Anderson's extraordinary response to his former enslaver's request that he and his family come back to work on the old homestead pointedly reveals the concerns of African Americans as they built new lives for themselves in freedom. Family ties, church and community, dignified labor with fair compensation, and education for their children were top priorities. But these were neither safe nor protected in the immediate aftermath of the Civil War, as many white landowners sought to ensure that formerly enslaved people continued working the land and remained bound by white rule. The tension between Black assertiveness and white racism made interracial conflict inevitable. Freedom brought a revolution in Black economic, social, and political life, but it did not bring equality. As President Andrew Johnson and the Radical Republicans in Congress battled over executive and legislative power, the fate of the freedpeople hung in the balance. When Congress proved more powerful, laws and constitutional amendments sought to ensure African American civil and voting rights. For about a decade from 1867 to 1877, African Americans in the South, even more than in the North, actively and responsibly participated in public life. Intense, often violent, southern white opposition, coupled with a dwindling national concern for freedpeople as the country turned to economic development, undermined the revolutionary period of interracial democracy and the political gains Black people had made during Reconstruction. Some left the South for other regions of the country, but wherever they tried to put down roots — in the U.S. military, in new all-Black towns in Kansas and Oklahoma, and in northern and midwestern cities where they sought jobs in factories — they struggled to achieve equal rights and independent lives.

A Social Revolution

How did the Thirteenth Amendment impact African Americans by defining standards of citizenship?

How did new labor practices impede the ability of African Americans to advance economically after the abolition of slavery?

Thirteenth Amendment (ratified 1865) The constitutional amendment that formally abolished slavery.

For the four million African Americans who had been enslaved, freedom brought new goals and responsibilities. While the **Thirteenth Amendment** (ratified December 1865) formally abolished slavery, the enslaved themselves had spearheaded their own emancipation by running to freedom behind Union lines, supporting the Union war effort, and undermining the Confederate war effort. Foremost for many after emancipation was reuniting with family members from whom they had been separated.

Economic independence wrought immediate changes in family structure and shifting gender roles, as well as hope for the future. Extended families and community structures such as new schools and independent Black churches provided services and support in the new environment of freedom. Labor arrangements had to be renegotiated, even though for most freedpeople, the nature of their work — field work and domestic service — remained largely the same. In freedom, Black people had the right to learn to read and write, and they eagerly pursued education. For those who had been enslaved, the first years of freedom involved a transition — from enslaved households to independent households and from enslaved labor to free labor — that constituted a social revolution.

Freedom and Family

Freedpeople's struggles to create independent and functional families gave meaning to their freedom. Under slavery, enslavers had exercised significant control over enslaved families. With freedom, Black people gained control over their families, even as they tried to remake them. Often the first step was to reunite those who had been separated before the war. One government official observed that "the work of emancipation was incomplete until the families which had been dispersed by slavery were reunited."[2] The war itself also had separated families. As individuals fled to Union lines and traveled with Union armies or enlisted in the U.S. Colored Troops, they lost touch with parents, spouses, children, and relatives who were themselves sometimes scattered. A Missouri official reported that after Black men had enlisted in the military, their wives and children had been "driven from their masters['] homes," and court records indicate that women separated from children sought help to get them back.[3] In short, wartime conditions had made it increasingly hard to hold Black families together.

After the war, thousands of freedpeople traveled great distances at significant material and emotional costs, seeking lost and displaced family members. One middle-aged North Carolina freedman who had been sold away from his wife and children traveled almost six hundred miles on foot to try to find them.[4] People inquired for missing relatives at former plantation homes, contraband camps, churches, and government agencies. Others wrote letters, and those who were not literate asked for help from teachers, preachers, missionaries, and government officials. Many took out ads in Black newspapers.

AP® exam tip

Be prepared to explain how, after abolition and the end of the Civil War, African Americans strengthened family bonds that had been disrupted by enslavement.

Most searches were unsuccessful, owing to time and distance, death, and difficulties that were simply insurmountable, given the lack of records. Family members who did find one another expressed relief and joy. Reunited after having been sold apart twenty years earlier, husband and wife Ben and Betty Dodson embraced, and Ben shouted, "Glory! glory! hallelujah." In some cases, people did not recognize one another after such a long absence. One formerly enslaved woman, sold away as a child, could identify the woman standing before her as her mother only by a distinctive facial scar.[5]

Sometimes new family ties had replaced old ones. Many forcibly separated partners and spouses over time had come to believe they would never see each other again, and they formed new attachments. For them, reunions were heartrending. Some chose their former spouse; others, the new one. One woman gave each of her two husbands a two-week test run before settling on one. Many men stayed with and supported one wife while continuing to support the other.[6] Others remained torn between two loves. One freedman wrote to his first wife, "I thinks of you and my children every day of my life. . . . I do love you the same. My love to you have never failed. . . . I have got another wife, and I am very sorry. . . . You feels and seems to me as much like my dear loving wife, as you ever did."[7]

The tensions following from troubled reunions often proved overwhelming. Many spouses who accused their partners of infidelity or desertion now sought relief through the courts. The number of wives seeking support for their children and themselves from negligent fathers and husbands increased, as did the number of divorce cases and custody battles over children. Battles between birth parents and the adults who had raised their children were confusing and painful for all involved. During slavery, some white women enslavers had taken young enslaved people from their mothers to be raised in the big house as part of the domestic staff. After emancipation, these children were reclaimed. As one freed mother told her former female enslaver, "You took her away from me an' didn' pay no mind to my cryin', so now I'se takin' her back home. We's free now, Mis' Polly, we ain't gwine be slaves no more to nobody."[8]

Legalizing enslaved marriages was a critical step in confirming freedpeople's new identities. Some viewed marriage as a moral and a Christian responsibility; some saw it as a means for legitimating children and becoming eligible for Union veterans' pensions. Preachers, missionaries, and public officials supported marriage as a way to anchor Black families and enhance their moral foundation. The rites themselves varied widely, from traditional "jumping the broom" ceremonies, common under slavery, to church weddings. One freedwoman recalled that while she and her husband had had a broomstick ceremony while enslaved, once freed they "had a real sho' nuff weddin' wid a preacher. Dat cost a dollar."[9] Mass weddings featuring as many as seventy couples were common. In 1866, seventeen North Carolina counties registered 9,000 marriages of freedpeople; four Virginia counties registered 3,000. Yet some couples remained together without formalizing their marriages, being accepted in their local communities as husband and wife.

AP® exam tip

Make sure you can explain how African American family structures changed following emancipation.

Many formerly enslaved people took new names to recognize family ties and to symbolize their independence and their desire for a new life characterized by dignity and respect. In slavery, "we hardly knowed our names," one freedperson recalled. "We was cussed for so many bitches and sons of bitches and bloody bitches, and blood of bitches. We never heard our names scarcely at all."[10] Enslavers had often assigned first names, such as Pompey and Caesar, and refused to recognize the surnames used within enslaved communities. Now, as independent people, freedpeople legally claimed first and last names of their own choosing.

In form, freed families were flexible and adaptive. Although the most common organization was the nuclear family — two parents and their children — families often included extended kin and nonrelated members. Ties of affection and economic need made extended families important. Pooling resources and working collectively sustained these families. Even when dispersed in different households, families tended to live in communities among relatives. Close-knit communities defined women's and men's social and cultural worlds, nurturing a cooperative spirit and a communal folk culture.

Most newly freed families had to meet their household needs with very limited resources, and poverty rendered them fragile. Every person had to work. Immediately after emancipation, large numbers of freedwomen withdrew from field labor and domestic service to manage their own households, but most were soon forced to work outside the home for wages. Although traditional notions of women's and men's roles prevailed — woman as caretaker and homemaker; man as breadwinner and protector — Black men by themselves rarely earned enough to support their families. One consequence was that Black women who were contributing to the family income also participated more fully in family decision making. In addition, Black women felt freer to leave dysfunctional relationships and to divorce or simply live apart from their husbands. But female-headed households were almost always poorer than dual-headed households. Moreover, as legal protectors and guarantors of their wives and children, freedmen exercised the rights of contract and child custody. Men typically made and signed labor contracts on behalf of their wives, and they held the upper hand in child custody disputes.

Church and Community

The explosive growth of independent Black churches in the South during this period reflects freedpeople's desire for dignity, autonomy, and self-expression as well as independent and affirmative religious lives. With emancipation, they rejected white Christianity and exited white churches by the thousands to form congregations of their own. As Matthew Gilbert, a Tennessee Baptist minister, noted, "The emancipation of the colored people made the colored churches and ministry a necessity, both by virtue of the prejudice existing against us and of our essential manhood before the laws of the land."[11] Often with the assistance of missionaries from churches in the North, the major Black denominations — Baptist, African Methodist Episcopal (AME), and African Methodist Episcopal Zion (AME Zion) — became established in the South. By 1880, nationwide there were more than 500,000 people in the Baptist Church, 400,000 in the AME Church, and 250,000 in the AME Zion Church. By 1890, more than half of those belonging to independent Black churches were Baptists.[12]

Next to the family, the Black church provided the most important institutional support in the transition from slavery to freedom. Joining a church was an act of physical and spiritual emancipation, and Black churches united Black communities. They also empowered Blacks because they operated outside white control. In addition, Black churches anchored collective Black identification — a sense of peoplehood, of nationhood. Men dominated church leadership, but women constituted most of the

The Black Church

This 1876 sketch is an evocative presentation of a Black church scene in which serious and well-dressed women, men, and children appear to be engaged in serious reflection on a biblical passage. While the preacher and his assistant are clearly leading the Bible study, the multiple settings within the scene enable us to focus on the congregants. The individuals and groupings — indeed, the collective image — convey authentic Black Christian propriety. **How did the church offer leadership opportunities for Black people denied to them in society?** *From 'The Illustrated London News,' November 18, 1876/Private Collection/Bridgeman Images.*

ACTIVITY ▸ Revisit Your Prediction

In the AP® Unit Warmup (p. U3-E), you made a prediction about this image. **What role do you think churches played in Black cultural life in the decades following the Civil War? What opportunities might churches have presented to African Americans during this era? What details from the image help support your prediction? Support or revise your original prediction using evidence from this chapter.**

members and regular attendees and did most of what was called church work. Women gave and raised money, taught Sunday school, ran women's auxiliaries, welcomed visitors, and led social welfare programs for the needy, sick, and elderly. They were also prominent in domestic and foreign missionary activities. One grateful minister consistently offered "great praise" to the church sisters for all their hard work.[13]

Women derived their authority in churches from their roles as Christian wives, mothers, "sisters," and homemakers. As "church mothers," they exercised informal yet significant influence in church affairs, including matters of governance typically reserved for male members, such as the selection of preachers and the allocation of church funds. Although women were not allowed to become preachers, many preached nevertheless, under titles such as "evangelist."

AP® exam tip

You'll need to be able to describe ways that Black women progressed and supported the advancement of newly freed African Americans.

Black women were also leaders in and practitioners of African-derived forms of popular, or folk, religion — such as conjure and voodoo, or hoodoo — which had evolved during slavery and continued after emancipation. Focusing on magic and the supernatural, they involved healing and harming beliefs and practices. One celebrated voodoo "priestess" was Marie Laveau of New Orleans. Not surprisingly, Black church leaders railed against folk religion as an ignorant and idolatrous relic of slavery. Still, these beliefs and practices were common, especially among rural people, but even in towns and cities and among Christians.

In Black urban neighborhoods, church networks and resources helped fuel institutional growth, including hospitals, clinics, asylums for orphans and the mentally ill, mutual aid societies, lodges, and unions. Churches led Black community efforts to deal with the epidemics of cholera, smallpox, and yellow fever that swept through the South after the war, especially as Blacks who had never traveled much before became more exposed to lethal diseases. With help from the Medical Division of the Freedmen's Bureau, former wartime army hospitals were converted into hospitals to serve African Americans. In Washington, D.C., Freedmen's Hospital was established during the war. In New Orleans and Richmond, Virginia, the existing Black hospitals expanded. By the late 1860s, segregated asylums and hospitals served Black communities in a number of southern cities.

In addition, Black churches, northern white churches, and the American Missionary Association (AMA) founded Black grade schools and high schools during this period. They also established colleges and teacher training institutes, known as normal schools. These **historically Black colleges and universities** reflected their founders' goals, giving great emphasis to religious instruction, Christian morality, and hard work, as well as academic and vocational training. (See Appendix: Historically Black Colleges and Universities, 1865–Present.)

historically Black colleges and universities
Separate institutions of higher learning for African Americans. Most of them were founded in the post-emancipation era.

AP® exam tip

Be prepared to explain how the creation of historically Black colleges and universities (HBCUs) impacted African Americans' lives.

Through their networks and resources, Black churches generated a range of economic organizations. Each church operated as an economic enterprise, undertaking fundraising, buying and maintaining buildings and real estate, promoting businesses, and supporting social programs for the needy. Mutual aid societies rooted in churches evolved into Black insurance companies and banks in the late nineteenth and early twentieth centuries. Church social circles provided ready consumer bases for Black

AP® exam tip

On the AP® Exam, you'll need to be able to explain how the African American church promoted the economic well-being and the political empowerment of their communities during this era.

products and services. Some churches sold Christian products, such as Bibles and religious pamphlets and lithographs. Black ministers served on the boards of Black companies. Churches sponsored business expositions featuring products such as furniture, medicines, and handicrafts to showcase African Americans' economic progress since emancipation.

The church was also the hub of Black political life. At all levels — from within the church to local, state, and national politics — the church functioned as the key forum for political debate and action. It was vital to Black political education and activism, including participation in Black community politics and the white-dominated political mainstream. Among Black ministers' many roles, that of political leader proved central. Preacher-politicians saw themselves both as faithful servants to their congregations and as representatives of their people to white politicians. They believed that their Christian-based leadership would improve the morality of both the political system and secular society. In the 1870s, the Reverend James Poindexter of the Second Baptist Church in Columbus, Ohio, explained that "all the help the preachers and all other good and worthy citizens can give by taking hold of politics is needed in order to keep the government out of bad hands and secure the ends for which governments are formed."[14]

Land and Labor

Special Field Order 15 (1865)
A military order by Union general William T. Sherman that granted freedpeople the right to land that had been abandoned by Confederate plantation owners.

Freedmen's Bureau (1865–1872)
A federal agency created during Reconstruction to aid freedpeople in their transition to freedom.

Landownership was fundamental to freedpeople's aspirations for economic independence. Rebuilding families as independent households required land. Speaking for his people, particularly freedpeople, in the summer of 1864, the AME missionary and minister Richard Cain explained, "We must possess the soil, be the owner of lands and become independent."[15] This message was repeated in January 1865, when several hundred Blacks in the Sea Islands told General William T. Sherman, "We want to be placed on land until we are able to buy it, and make it our own."[16] As part of his **Special Field Order 15**, Sherman settled more than 40,000 freedpeople in coastal areas that had been abandoned by Confederate plantation owners. Unfortunately, what was known as Sherman's Reserve did not last. The Reconstruction plans of President Abraham Lincoln and his successor, Andrew Johnson, directed that former Confederates who swore allegiance to the United States would regain their land, and unclaimed land was auctioned to the highest bidder. Many freedpeople were already working this land under federal supervision; others had simply squatted on abandoned land and worked it to sustain themselves. They were all evicted.

Although the **Freedmen's Bureau** (1865–1872), the vital federal institution created to assist the freedpeople in their transition to freedom, was able to help some enter into contracts to rent the land they were already farming, the bureau was not able to help them purchase land. Few freedpeople or free Blacks possessed the clout, capital, or credit to buy land, and as a result, they lost out to returning ex-Confederate plantation owners and northern and southern investors. The Southern Homestead

Act, passed by Congress in 1866, made public land available to freedmen, but it had little impact and was repealed a decade later. In the end, most land in the former Confederacy was returned to white control, often to the original owners. The rest went to northern white investors, former army officers, and Freedmen's Bureau officials.

This "landless emancipation" devastated freedpeople. "Damm such freedom as that," one angry freedman exclaimed, expressing the frustration of many.[17] Freedpeople believed that they had earned the right to own the land they and their ancestors had worked while enslaved. They argued that freedom without provision for self-sufficiency was a shocking violation of the federal government's economic and moral responsibility. A group of Mississippi Blacks called it "a breach of faith on the part of the government."[18] Some simply refused to leave the property they now considered their own. The freedpeople on the Taylor farm in Norfolk County, Virginia, mounted an armed resistance when their former enslavers returned to reclaim their prewar property, but to no avail. Forced evictions of freedpeople from land and farms they assumed now belonged to them were common.

Lacking the means to own land, most freedpeople were forced into tenancy. They rented and worked land that belonged to white landowners under terms that favored the owners. Black male heads of household entered into contracts with landowners that spelled out the wage or paid labor, as opposed to slave or unfree labor relationship. For their part, freedpeople sought fair compensation for their labor, work organized along family lines, and an end to physical punishment and gang-style labor with overseers. They also wanted guaranteed leisure time and the right to hunt, fish, gather wild food plants, raise farm animals, and cultivate designated plots for their own use. For white landowners, the aim of these contracts was to ensure a steady supply of farm labor so that their landholdings, planted in cash crops, would make a profit. That meant limiting wages, forbidding worker mobility, and suppressing competition. Labor contracts were difficult to break, and because most freedmen could neither read nor write, many relied on Freedmen's Bureau officials to look out for their best interests. The labor contract battles between freedpeople and landowners were at times bitter and divisive, but in the end, the landowners were far more powerful, and labor contracts generally favored their interests.

Despite their landholdings, whites operated within cash-strapped southern economies after the war. Instead of paying farmworkers in cash, most negotiated **sharecropping** arrangements under which farmers worked the land for a "share" of the crop, typically one-third or one-half. Often the landowner supplied the cabin or house in which the family lived, as well as seed, work animals, and tools. If a "cropper" had his own mule and plow, he might warrant a larger share of the crop. This share he would "sell" to the plantation owner or a local merchant — often the same person — following the harvest. But instead of cash changing hands, the sharecropper would get credit to use for buying food and clothing — or whatever his family might need — from the merchant. At the end of the year, when accounts were settled on "countin' day," the sharecropper usually got no more than a bill showing how much he still owed the landowner or merchant.

sharecropping
An agricultural system that emerged during Reconstruction in which a landowner contracts with a farmer to work a parcel of land in return for a share of the crop.

All too often, landowners and merchants cheated workers, forcing them into a pattern of cyclical debt. Even many Black farmers who owned their own land were forced into debt. For example, in a system known as **crop lien**, they had to borrow against anticipated harvests for seed and supplies. Most Black households were thus reduced to a form of coerced labor, a kind of partial slavery, tied to the land they farmed as the only means they had to work off their debt, which every year grew larger instead of smaller. Debtors were also subject to imprisonment, and prisoners were subject to another form of coerced labor, as states contracted out their labor to landowners or businesses in need of a labor force. This **convict lease** system generated income for southern states, but it forced prisoners to work under conditions similar to enslavement that blatantly disregarded their human rights.

crop lien
An agricultural system in which a farmer borrows against his anticipated crop for the seed and supplies he needs and settles his debt after the crop is harvested.

convict lease
A penal system in which convict labor is hired out to landowners or businesses to generate income for the state.

black codes
Laws regulating the labor and behavior of freedpeople passed by southern states in the immediate aftermath of emancipation. These laws were overturned by the Civil Rights Act of 1866.

Immediately after the war, the main goal for white southerners was to reassert control over Blacks. State legislatures passed **black codes** that enforced the labor contracts that once again bound freedpeople, who had few other options, to the land. The codes mandated strict obedience to white employers and set work hours, usually sunup to sundown. Although the codes allowed freedpeople to legalize their marriages, own property, make contracts, and access the courts, their aim was to perpetuate a heavily exploited labor force in conditions of freedom: a kind of neo-slavery. Vagrancy provisions were especially oppressive. Individuals without labor contracts who were unable to prove that they were employed risked fines, imprisonment, and forced labor, as did those who left a job before a contract ended or who were unruly or simply lost. In Mississippi, freedpeople were prohibited from renting urban property, helping to ensure that they would stay on plantations and work in agriculture. In Florida, breaking a labor contract often resulted in physical punishment, such as a whipping, or being hired out for a year to a planter. As one southern white pointedly observed in November 1865, the purpose behind black codes and vagrancy laws was to "teach the negro that if he goes to work, keeps his place, and behaves himself, he will be protected by *our* white laws."[19]

Black codes also permitted the courts to order apprenticeships that removed children from Black families and bound them to white employers, often without their parents' or guardians' consent. In *Adeline Brown v. State* (1865), the Maryland Court of Appeals upheld the state's black apprentice law. Two years later, however, the case *In re Turner* (1867) overturned the law as unconstitutional because its educational provisions for Black youths were different from those for white youths.

The Hope of Education

AP® exam tip

You'll need to be able to describe the founding of historically Black colleges and universities (HBCUs) in the late nineteenth and early twentieth centuries.

To operate as free and independent people, the formerly enslaved — more than 90 percent of whom were illiterate at the moment of emancipation — recognized that they had to learn to read and write, and they did so eagerly. Some began their schooling in the Union military or in contraband camps, where they were sometimes taught by formerly enslaved people, such as Susie King Taylor, or by northern Black women,

Frances Ellen Watkins Harper
Freeborn Frances Ellen Watkins Harper was an influential abolitionist and women's rights advocate, a poet and novelist, and an orator. Her well-received *Poems on Miscellaneous Subjects* (1854) treated gender equality as well as abolitionism. *Minnie's Sacrifice* (1869), a serial novel; *Sketches of Southern Life* (1872), a book of poetry; and her most famous work, the novel *Iola Leroy, or Shadows Uplifted* (1892), all address Reconstruction. Harper's life and work reflect a profound belief in and active commitment to both gender and racial equality. In particular, her activism on behalf of both women's rights and Black rights led her to become a founding vice president of the National Association of Colored Women in 1896. **What developments during Reconstruction might have influenced her focus on gender equality in particular?** *Granger/Granger — All rights reserved.*

such as Charlotte Forten, who went to the Sea Islands to teach. After the war, many makeshift classrooms grew into permanent institutions. On St. Helena Island, so many teachers were from Pennsylvania that the school was named the Penn School, and it expanded to accommodate 1,700 students on a campus that served Black children into the 1940s. In Hampton, Virginia, where thousands of contrabands set up their own community soon after the Civil War began, the teacher was a free Black woman named Mary S. Peake. Under the sponsorship of the AMA, she began her school under a tree later known as the Emancipation Oak. After she died of tuberculosis, General Benjamin Butler stepped in to build the Butler School for Negro Children, again with the assistance of the AMA. Frances Ellen Watkins Harper, who before the war had lectured on behalf of abolition and Black education, captured the excitement and sense of independence that came with achieving literacy. In Harper's 1872 poem "Learning to Read," the narrator, an elderly freeperson, is overjoyed by the prospect of literacy: "So I got a pair of glasses,/And straight to work I went,/And never stopped till I could read/The hymns and Testament./Then I got a little cabin—/A place to call my own—/And I felt as independent/As the queen upon her throne."[20]

Northern teachers, missionaries, and philanthropists helped found hundreds of schools for Black children and adults. Some of these schools were set up in churches and homes. In other cases, freedpeople pooled their resources to buy land, build schoolhouses, and hire teachers. The Freedmen's Bureau assisted by renting facilities, providing books, and transporting teachers, and the AMA helped fund schools and hire teachers, white and Black. The Pennsylvania Branch of the American Freedmen's Union Commission sent out 1,400 teachers to serve 150,000 students. In addition to these privately sponsored organizations, Reconstruction state governments, often led by Black officials, began to establish public school systems — new for the South — that gave Black children access to education, largely in segregated schools that operated only during the winter months, when children were not needed for planting and harvesting. By 1880 Black illiteracy had declined to 70 percent, and by 1910 it was down to 30 percent.[21]

In all these schools, the standard New England curriculum prevailed. The three Rs — reading, writing, and arithmetic — were emphasized. In the best schools, instruction in history, geography, spelling, grammar, and music might also be available. Colleges offered a classical liberal curriculum that included math, science, Latin, and Greek. Given the pressing need for teachers, they usually emphasized teacher training, instructing young people in teaching methods and theory as well as diction, geometry, algebra, and map reading.

By 1868, more than half the teachers in Black schools in the South were Black, and most were women. For them, teaching was a calling, not just a job. "I am myself a colored woman," noted Sarah G. Stanley, "bound to that ignorant, degraded, long enslaved race, by the ties of love and consanguinity; they are socially, and politically, 'my people.'"[22] The increasing preponderance of Black teachers reflected a growing race consciousness and commitment to self-reliance. Despite the fact that white teachers may have had better training and more experience, Black communities preferred Black teachers. The Reverend Richard Cain observed that white "teachers and preachers have feelings, but not as we feel for our kindred."[23] In 1869, a group of Blacks in Petersburg, Virginia, petitioned the school board to replace white teachers with Black ones, asserting, "We do not want our children to be trained to think or feel that they are inferior."[24] Black female teachers became important community leaders and inspirational role models. Like Black schools, they helped build racial solidarity and community identity.

AP® exam tip

Be able to compare and contrast the curricular paths favored by different historically Black colleges and universities.

Although the historically Black colleges and universities emphasized teacher training, early on they took two different curricular paths that reflected the different expectations freedpeople had for themselves in light of their opportunities. Schools such as Fisk University in Nashville, Tennessee, founded in 1866, embraced the classical liberal arts model, whereas schools such as Hampton Institute in Hampton, Virginia, founded in 1868, adopted the vocational-industrial model. When Booker T. Washington helped found Tuskegee Institute in 1881, he modeled it on Hampton, where he had been a student and teacher. In 1871, Alcorn Agricultural and Mechanical College (Alcorn A&M) opened as Alcorn University in Claiborne County, Mississippi. Alcorn was both the nation's first state-supported college for Blacks and the first federal land-grant Black college.

Fisk offered a well-rounded academic program to prepare the best and the brightest of the race for citizenship, leadership, and a wide range of careers. The school boldly aimed for "the highest standards, not of Negro education, but of American education at its best."[25] Within six years, however, Fisk faced a serious financial crisis that threatened its survival. In an effort to raise money, George L. White, school treasurer and music professor, organized a choral ensemble to go on a fundraising tour. Modeling their performances on European presentation styles, but singing slave songs and spirituals little known to white audiences, the Fisk Jubilee Singers were soon famous. In 1872, they performed for President Ulysses S. Grant at the White House, and the next year, while on a European tour, they sang for Britain's Queen Victoria. The money they raised saved the school from bankruptcy and enabled Fisk to build its first

AP® source ***The Fisk Jubilee Singers***

This 1880 photograph illustrates the middle-class refinement of the Fisk Jubilee Singers. This sense of middle-class respectability also revealed the singers' commitment to racial uplift: the presentation of positive images of Blacks as a way to enhance their freedom struggle. As formerly enslaved people and the children of formerly enslaved people, the Jubilee Singers pioneered an African American music tradition that relied on polished versions of enslaved spirituals. Their noble presentation of this Black religious folk music provided a critical counterpoint and challenge to negative stereotypes of Blacks resulting from the minstrel tradition. Over time, the Jubilee Singers' performances for audiences around the world enhanced Black and white respect for Blacks and their culture. **Explain how the Fisk Jubilee Singers reflected the central principles of racial uplift.** *Granger/Granger — All rights reserved.*

permanent building, Jubilee Hall, today a National Historic Landmark. Their performances built worldwide respect and admiration for African American music and culture and inspired other Black colleges to create similar groups.

Hampton Institute had a different mission: "to train selected Negro youth who should go out and teach and lead their people first by example, by getting land and homes; . . . to teach respect for labor, . . . and in this way to build up an industrial system for the sake not only of self-support and intelligent labor, but also for the sake of character."[26] Samuel Chapman Armstrong, Hampton's white founder and Booker T. Washington's mentor, believed that training young people in skilled trades, rather than teaching a classical liberal arts curriculum, would best enable poverty-stricken freedpeople to pull themselves up by their bootstraps. As skilled laborers and highly trained domestic servants, they would earn adequate wages, build self-respect, and win the admiration of whites. Students at Hampton paid their way by working on campus, which helped them learn the occupational skills that would qualify them for jobs after graduation. Many learned to teach trade skills such as carpentry and sewing, and they practice-taught at the successor to the Butler School for Negro Children. The Hampton model of vocational training was akin to that of training schools for poor white children and immigrants at the time, but some Black leaders feared that it would perpetuate Black subordination. The *Louisianian*, a Black newspaper, complained that Armstrong "seems to think that we should only know enough to make good servants."[27] The debate over vocational training versus liberal arts intensified toward the end of the century, and at its center was Washington, the preeminent Black leader of his day.

A Short-Lived Political Revolution

How did the Fourteenth and Fifteenth Amendments impact African Americans by defining standards of citizenship?

How were Reconstruction-era reforms dismantled during the late nineteenth century?

Even as Black people built independent lives, they sought a place in American public life, and for a short period known as **Black Reconstruction**, black men were able to vote in the South and to participate in politics. Radical Republicans in Congress had taken charge of Reconstruction and forced the former Confederate states to hold democratically elected constitutional conventions, which wrote new state constitutions that protected Black suffrage. The consequences were revolutionary. Nowhere else in the world had an emancipated people been integrated into the political system so quickly. Black men elected or appointed to state and local offices proved able and moderate and demonstrated their interest in compromise and progressive reforms such as public schools. But Black Reconstruction was short-lived. Outraged southern whites mobilized a violent and racist counterrevolution that restored white political dominance

Black Reconstruction
The revolutionary political period from 1867 to 1877 when, for the first time ever, Black men actively participated in the mainstream politics of the reconstructed southern states and, in turn, transformed the nation's political life.

by 1877. Congress and the Republican Party abandoned Black interests, and the U.S. Supreme Court reversed gains made by Reconstruction laws and amendments. In its retreat from Black Reconstruction, the national government reflected the expanding white opposition to the evolving Black freedom struggle.

The Political Contest over Reconstruction

Andrew Johnson, who became president after Abraham Lincoln was assassinated, continued Lincoln's lenient policies toward former Confederates. Like Lincoln, Johnson insisted that the war was an insurrection, that the southern states were never out of the Union, and that the organization of a new civil authority in these states was an executive, not a legislative, function. His rapid restoration of civil government in the former Confederate states, amnesty for former Confederates, and lack of interest in protecting the civil rights of freedpeople angered the Radical Republicans in Congress. This faction, led by Representative Thaddeus Stevens and Senator Charles Sumner, had pressed for more aggressive military campaigns during the war and a quicker end to slavery. Challenging Lincoln, it had run John C. Frémont against him for the presidency in 1864 and passed the Wade–Davis Bill aiming to reverse Lincoln's proposed leniency toward Confederates. In December 1865, when Johnson declared that the Union had been restored and it looked as though representatives and senators from former Confederate states would be reseated in Congress, the Radical Republicans balked. Concerned for the civil rights of the freedpeople, they quickly appointed a joint committee to examine issues of suffrage and representation for the former Confederate states. The struggle between the president and Congress escalated in early 1866 when Congress passed two bills over Johnson's veto: the reauthorization of the Freedmen's Bureau and the Civil Rights Act.

> **AP® skills**
>
> **Applying Disciplinary Knowledge:** What caused tension to emerge between Andrew Johnson and the Radical Republicans in Congress?

Established in March 1865, the Freedmen's Bureau aimed to help freedpeople in their economic, social, and political transition to freedom. To prevent them from becoming wards of the state and the bureau from becoming a permanent guardian, it remained a temporary agency that Congress had to renew annually. In reauthorizing the Freedmen's Bureau in February 1866, Congress expanded its powers by establishing military commissions to hear cases of civil rights abuses — of which there were many. The bureau heard shocking reports of whites violently beating and abusing Blacks (even murdering them), cheating them out of their wages, shortchanging them on purchased goods, and stealing their crop shares. In September 1865, for example, the head of the Freedmen's Bureau in Mississippi reported, "Men, who are honorable in their dealings with their white neighbors, will cheat a negro without feeling a single twinge of their honor; to kill a negro they do not deem murder; to debauch a negro woman they do not think fornication; to take property away from a negro they do not deem robbery. . . . They still have the ingrained feeling that the Black people at large belong to the whites at large."[28] When Johnson vetoed the reauthorization bill, stating that the military commissions were unconstitutional,

> **AP® exam tip**
>
> Be sure you can describe the purpose of the Freedmen's Bureau.

Congress passed the bill over his veto. The bureau experienced severe cutbacks in 1869, however, and its reach and effectiveness seriously declined before it was finally ended in 1872.

Civil Rights Act of 1866
An act defining U.S. citizenship and protecting the civil rights of freedpeople.

To further protect the civil rights of freedpeople, Congress passed the **Civil Rights Act of 1866**, again over Johnson's veto. This act defined U.S. citizenship for the first time and affirmed that all citizens were equally protected by the laws. It overturned black codes and ensured that Blacks could make contracts and initiate lawsuits, but it did not protect Black voting rights. In February 1866, Frederick Douglass and a delegation of other Black leaders met with Johnson to try to convince him of the importance of Black suffrage, but without success.

Fourteenth Amendment (ratified 1868)
The constitutional amendment that defined U.S. citizenship to include Blacks and guaranteed citizens due process and equal protection of the law.

Tensions between the stubborn and increasingly isolated Johnson and an energetic Congress escalated over the **Fourteenth Amendment**, which Congress quickly proposed and sent to the states for ratification in 1866. Ratified in 1868, this amendment affirmed the Civil Rights Act's definition of citizenship and guarantee of "equal protection of the laws" to all citizens. Declaring that "all persons born or naturalized in the United States" are "citizens of the United States and of the State wherein they reside," it reversed the *Dred Scott* decision of 1857, which had ruled that Blacks could not be citizens. To protect citizens against civil rights violations by the states, the amendment also declared that "no State shall make or enforce any law which shall abridge the privileges and immunities of citizens of the United States; nor shall any State deprive any person of life, liberty, or property without due process of law; nor deny to any person within its jurisdiction the equal protection of the laws." This clause would ultimately shape the Black freedom struggle, but not before states found ways to craft racially discriminatory laws and practices in the areas in which states were sovereign, such as public education.

Reconstruction Act of 1867 (first)
An act dividing the South into military districts and requiring the former Confederate states to write new constitutions at conventions with delegates elected by universal male suffrage.

AP® skills

Applying Disciplinary Knowledge: What were the contents of the Reconstruction Act of 1867? How did it benefit African Americans?

Outmaneuvered, Johnson took his case to the people, embarking on an unprecedented presidential speaking tour, which proved disastrous. In the midterm elections of 1866, the Radical Republicans captured two-thirds of both houses of Congress, and the next year they moved quickly to take charge of Reconstruction by passing several Reconstruction Acts. The first **Reconstruction Act of 1867**, passed on March 2, 1867, dissolved state governments in the former Confederacy (except for Tennessee) and divided the old Confederacy into five military districts subject to martial law, each with a military governor. To reenter the Union, a state was required to call a constitutional convention, which would be elected by universal male suffrage (including Black male suffrage); to write a new state constitution that guaranteed Black suffrage; and to ratify the Fourteenth Amendment. The other three Reconstruction Acts passed in 1867 and early 1868 empowered the military commander of each district to ensure that the process of reconstruction in each state went forward despite strong ex-Confederate opposition.

On March 2, 1867, Congress also passed — and later passed again, over Johnson's veto — the Tenure of Office Act, which prohibited the president from removing any

Freedmen's Bureau Cartoon

This vicious Democratic Party broadside from 1866 slanders the Freedmen's Bureau as well as freedpeople. Central to the party's widespread effort to get rid of the Freedmen's Bureau specifically and of Reconstruction in its entirety was a racist, vitriolic, and highly calculated public campaign against both. This broadside is a chilling representation of the discredited view that Reconstruction was a tragic mistake because it did too much too soon for the inferior and uncivilized freedpeople, who were incapable of shouldering the responsibilities of freedom. **Describe the purpose of the Freedmen's Bureau and the growing tensions surrounding Reconstruction. How are they reflected in this cartoon?**

Library of Congress, Rare Book and Special Collections Division, Washington, D.C./LC-USZ-62-57340.

cabinet member from office without the Senate's approval. The act was designed to protect Secretary of War Edwin M. Stanton, a Radical Republican who was openly critical of the president. When Johnson dismissed Stanton in February 1868, the House of Representatives impeached Johnson for this violation of the act and other charges. The Senate failed to convict him, but thereafter the president was politically sidelined, and Congress assumed primary responsibility for Reconstruction.

AP® skills

Applying Disciplinary Knowledge: Can you explain the degree of Black political involvement during Reconstruction?

Black Reconstruction

By early March 1867, the military Reconstruction of the South was already under way. Many former Confederates were ineligible to vote in elections for delegates to state constitutional conventions, and up to 30 percent of whites refused to participate in elections in which Black men could vote. Thus in some states, Black voters were in the majority. Of the slightly more than 1,000 delegates elected to write new state constitutions, 268 were Black. In South Carolina and Louisiana, Blacks formed the majority of delegates. Black delegates advocated the interests of freedpeople specifically and of the people of their states and the nation generally. They also argued for curtailing the interests of caste and property. In South Carolina, for example, delegate Robert Smalls proposed that the state sponsor a public school system that was open to all.

The state constitutional conventions initiated a new phase of Reconstruction. (See AP® Working with Sources: The Vote, pp. 370–79.) Decades later, the Black scholar and activist W. E. B. Du Bois called it "Black Reconstruction" in a book by that title. His subtitle, "An Essay toward a History of the Part Which Black Folk Played in the Attempt to Reconstruct Democracy in America," suggests a transformative yet short-lived revolutionary moment during which African Americans participated in southern political life. The constitutions these conventions drafted provided for a range of "firsts" for the South: universal male suffrage, public schools, progressive taxes, improved court and judicial systems, commissions to promote industrial development, state aid for railroad development, and social welfare institutions such as hospitals and asylums for orphans and the mentally ill. In many ways, these were among the most progressive state constitutions and state governments the nation ever had, and they are why Du Bois called Reconstruction a "splendid failure"[29] — splendid for what could have been.

AP® skills

Applying Disciplinary Knowledge: Describe Du Bois's claims about Black Reconstruction. What's one example from this chapter that could prove these claims?

Du Bois also argued that Black Reconstruction was splendid because it did not fail due to alleged Black incompetence and inferiority, as many whites expected. Instead, Black Reconstruction clearly demonstrated African American competence and equality. From the first, white southerners who did not participate in the conventions denigrated the Black delegates as incompetent and the white delegates as "carpetbaggers" and "scalawags." Carpetbaggers were northern whites who were stereotyped as having come to the South with their belongings in travel bags made from carpet. Their aim was allegedly to make money off plantation, railroad, and industrial interests as well as the freedpeople themselves. Scalawags were southern whites who had turned on their fellow white southerners and tied their fortunes to the Republican Party. Such charges were overstated. While Black Reconstruction politicians ranged from liberal to conservative, they were more centrist than radical, more committed to reintegrating former Confederates into the new state governments than punishing them for having waged war against the United States, and more than competent.

During Black Reconstruction, some 2,000 Blacks served as officeholders at the various levels of government in the South.[30] Although a little over half for whom

The First Colored Senator and Representatives, 1872
This dignified group portrait represents the first Black men to serve in Congress as statesmen as well as pioneering Black political leaders. In the back row, from left to right, are Robert C. De Large (South Carolina) and Jefferson F. Long (Georgia). In the front row are Hiram R. Revels (Mississippi), Benjamin S. Turner (Alabama), Josiah T. Walls (Florida), Joseph H. Rainey (South Carolina), and Robert Brown Elliott (South Carolina). Except for Revels, who served in the Senate (1870–1871), all of these men served in the House of Representatives during the Forty-First (1869–1871) and/or Forty-Second Congress (1871–1873). **Describe the political opportunities that were available to African Americans during Reconstruction.** *Library of Congress, Prints and Photographs Division, Washington, D.C., LC-DIG-ppmsca-17564.*

information is available had been enslaved, they were now literate, and they were committed. Among them were artisans, laborers, businessmen, carpenters, barbers, ministers, teachers, editors, publishers, storekeepers, and merchants. They served as sheriffs, police officers, justices of the peace, registrars, city council members, county commissioners, members of boards of education, tax collectors, land office clerks, and postmasters. Wherever they served, they sought to balance the interests of Black and white southerners. In a political era marked by graft and corruption, Black politicians proved to be more ethical than their white counterparts.

> **AP® exam tip**
> Be prepared to explain how the Fifteenth Amendment impacted African Americans' participation in American politics.

A few Black Republicans achieved high state office. In Louisiana, Mississippi, and South Carolina, Blacks served as lieutenant governor. Some were superintendents of education, a post with considerable power. More than six hundred state legislators were Black, including Robert Smalls, who served in the South Carolina House of Representatives and Senate (Map 9.1). In 1874, Smalls was elected to the U.S. House of Representatives. Thirteen other black men served in the U.S. House during this era, and two served in the Senate. Like their colleagues in local and state positions in the South, these black senators and congressmen were moderate politicians who tried hard to balance the often irreconcilable concerns of freedpeople and southern whites. Hiram R. Revels (1870–1871) and Blanche K. Bruce (1875–1881) were both senators from Mississippi. A minister in the AME Church, Revels was known for his oratorical ability and his amnesty program for disfranchised former Confederates, which would have allowed them to vote and hold office with limited penalties. Bruce, a skilled Mississippi delta politician and planter, proved to be a far more vigorous champion of Black civil rights and an unyielding opponent of white resistance to Black political participation.

The widespread political involvement of Blacks, many of whom were freed people who had never before had any political rights, was unprecedented in the United States and unique among nineteenth-century post-emancipation societies, including Jamaica, Cuba, and Brazil. In the United States, Blacks' service in office, as well as the wide range of political activities of thousands of other Black people, amounted to a political revolution. Black politics then and since has included innumerable local, grassroots, and community-based activities outside the realm of formal politics, activities aimed at enhancing Black influence and control. Still, for the Black community, political participation and the vote during Reconstruction represented key expressions of citizenship and national belonging. (See AP® Working with Sources: The Vote, pp. 370–79.) When Black men voted, they cast a family vote — a choice that reflected the collective aspirations of their wives, children, relatives, and extended kin, as well as those of their neighbors and communities.

Union League
An organization founded in 1862 to promote the Republican Party. During Reconstruction, the league recruited freedpeople into the party and advanced their political education.

Freedpeople allied themselves with the Republican Party, the party of emancipation and Abraham Lincoln. They were actively recruited by the **Union League**, which had been created in the North in 1862 to build support for the Republican Party and sent representatives to the South after the war. Along with the Freedmen's Bureau, southern branches of the Union League mobilized Black support for the Republican Party and helped Blacks understand their political rights and responsibilities as citizens.

Fifteenth Amendment
(ratified 1870)
The constitutional amendment that enfranchised Black men.

African Americans viewed the right to vote as the most important of all civil rights and the one on which all other civil rights depended. The vote made economic, social, and political liberties possible and helped protect Blacks. To ensure this right, the overwhelmingly Republican U.S. Congress proposed the **Fifteenth Amendment** in 1869, and it was ratified the next year. It declared, "The right of citizens of the United States to vote shall not be denied or abridged by the United States or by any State on account of race, color, or previous condition of servitude."

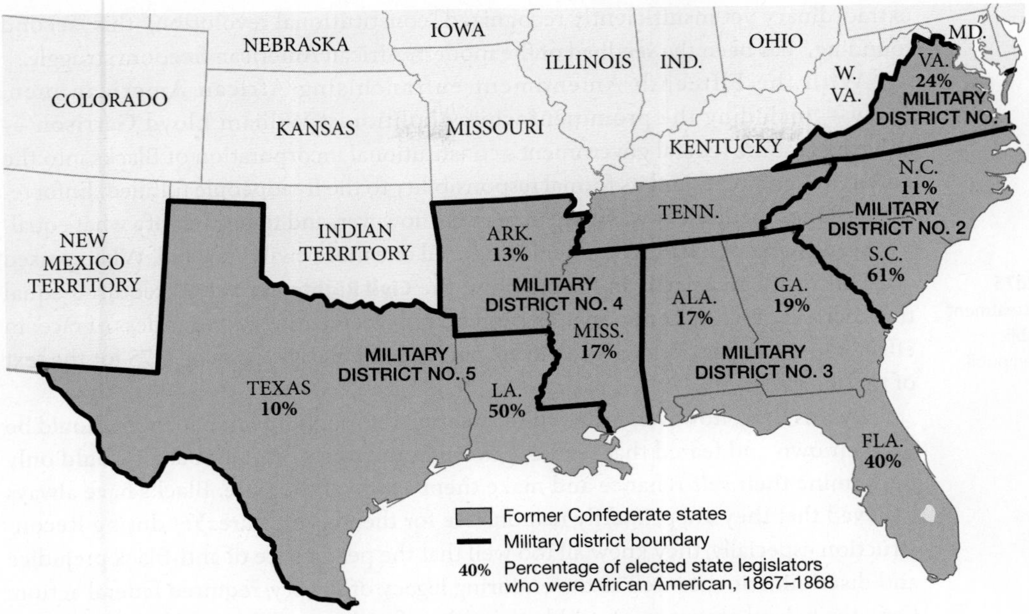

MAP 9.1 Black Political Participation in the Reconstruction South, 1867–1868

During the overlapping years of Congressional Reconstruction and Black Reconstruction, the states of the former Confederacy were reorganized into five military districts under the first Reconstruction Act of 1867. Within these districts, for the first time ever, thousands of newly enfranchised Blacks participated in politics, voted, and held elected offices at all levels of the government. As this map illustrates, the percentages of African Americans elected to the first state legislatures as a result of the four Reconstruction Acts were significant: Half of Louisiana's elected state legislators were Black, and in South Carolina, Black legislators comprised a 61 percent majority. ■ **What made Black political participation at this particular moment "revolutionary"?** *Data from Smallwood and Elliot,* The Atlas of African-American History and Politics: From the Slave Trade to Modern Times *(1998).*

The Thirteenth, Fourteenth, and Fifteenth Amendments — the Reconstruction Amendments — constituted what might be called, according to contemporary historian Eric Foner, a "second founding" of the United States: a revitalization of the late eighteenth-century creation of the nation, the "first founding." Reconstruction as well as these constitutional amendments signified a powerful though tragically flawed historical moment dedicated to both advancing the ongoing African American freedom struggle and helping the United States realize its better self. The deeply inspiring egalitarian and democratic idealism of this "second founding" has influenced world history as well as U.S. history, from that time to today. The Republican, journalist, and politician Carl Schurz, who fought for the Union in the Civil War, labeled Reconstruction a "constitutional revolution" that gave new and enduring meaning to the rights of American citizens, particularly African Americans, freed and free.[31] Indeed, that

> **AP® skills**
>
> **Applying Disciplinary Knowledge:** Describe the evidence Eric Foner uses to support his claim that Reconstruction was "a second founding." To what extent do you agree or disagree with his claim?

extraordinary yet insufficiently recognized "constitutional revolution," this "second founding," has been the seedbed of the modern African American freedom struggle.

With the Fifteenth Amendment enfranchising African American men, many — including the prominent white abolitionist William Lloyd Garrison — believed that the federal government's constitutional incorporation of Blacks into the Union was complete and its formal responsibility to the freedpeople fulfilled. Enforcement of the amendment was a separate issue, however, and to help clarify what equality meant, Senator Charles Sumner introduced one more civil rights bill. When passed after his death and partly in his memory, the **Civil Rights Act of 1875** required equal treatment in public accommodations and on public conveyances regardless of race: in effect a "public rights" guarantee. (See Appendix: Civil Rights Act of 1875 for the text of this federal law.)

Civil Rights Act of 1875
An act requiring equal treatment regardless of race in public accommodations and on public conveyances.

By this time, however, most white Americans thought the freedpeople should be on their own and feared that further government efforts on their behalf would only undermine their self-reliance and make them wards of the state. Blacks have always believed that they are primarily responsible for their own future. Yet during Reconstruction especially, they knew all too well that the persistence of anti-Black prejudice and discrimination, as well as the enduring legacy of slavery, required federal action. Only the federal government could ensure their freedom and their rights in the face of widespread and hostile white opposition.

The Defeat of Reconstruction

While northern whites thought that the Fifteenth Amendment completed Reconstruction, southern whites found Black political involvement intolerable; they were shocked and outraged that their world had been turned upside down. For them, Black political participation represented a "base conspiracy against human nature."[32] Even as many white southerners withdrew from the system, they immediately initiated a counterrevolution that would restore white rule and sought what they called "redemption" through the all-white Democratic Party.

AP® skills

Applying Disciplinary Knowledge: How did "home rule" and "states' rights" policies decrease Black political power?

White opposition movements proceeded differently in each state, but by the late 1860s, they had begun to succeed. As soon as they gained sufficient leverage, southern whites ousted Blacks from political office in an effort to bring back what they called "home rule" under the reinvigorated ideology of states' rights. Home rule and states' rights served as euphemisms for white domination of land, Black labor, and state and local government. Under the guise of restoring fiscal conservatism — trimming taxes and cutting state government functions and budgets — southern Democrats scaled back and ended programs that assisted freedpeople, including, for instance, ending South Carolina's land reform commission.

An essential element of white "redemption" was the intimidation of Blacks through terror, violence, and even murder. White supremacist and vigilante organizations formed throughout the South. While the Ku Klux Klan (KKK), organized in

Tennessee in 1865, was the most notable group, others were the '76 Association, the Knights of the White Camelia, the White Brotherhood, and the Pale Faces. Members of the KKK, called night riders because they conducted their raids at night, wore white robes and hoods to hide their identities. People from all sectors of southern white society joined these groups.

The targets of white attacks were often successful and economically independent Black landowners, storeowners, and small entrepreneurs. Black schools, churches, homes, lodges, business buildings, livestock, barns, and fences were destroyed. Blacks were beaten, raped, murdered, and lynched. So widespread were these vicious attacks in the late 1860s and early 1870s that Congress held hearings to investigate the causes of this widespread lawlessness. "The object of it is to kill out the leading men of the republican party . . . men who have taken a prominent stand," testified Emanuel Fortune, a delegate to Florida's constitutional convention and member of the state house of representatives who had been forced from his home and county by the KKK. In other testimony, Congress learned that Jack Dupree of Monroe County, Mississippi, the strong-willed president of a local Republican club, had been lynched by the KKK in front of his wife and newborn twins.[33]

Force Acts (1870, 1871) Two laws providing federal protection of Blacks' civil rights in the face of white terroristic activities.

To restore order, Congress passed two **Force Acts**, in 1870 and 1871, to protect the civil rights of Blacks as defined in the Fourteenth and Fifteenth Amendments. Federal troops rather than state militias were authorized to put down the widespread lawlessness, and those who conspired to deprive Black people of their civil rights were to be tried in federal rather than state or local courts.

Nevertheless, the violence continued. In Colfax, Louisiana, a disputed election in 1873 prompted whites to use cannon and rifle fire to disband a group of armed freedmen, commanded by Black militia and veterans, who were attempting to maintain Republican control of the town. On Easter Sunday, in the bloodiest racial massacre of the era, more than 280 Blacks were killed, including 50 who had surrendered. The Colfax Massacre demonstrated the limits of armed Black self-defense and the lengths to which whites would go to secure white dominance. A similar white attack occurred in 1876 in Hamburg, South Carolina, where skirmishes between Black militia, armed by the state, and whites, acting on their own authority, escalated into a shoot-out. Six Black men died at the hands of the white mob. The Hamburg Massacre routed local Black political authority and strengthened white resolve to "redeem" South Carolina.

In the end, the Republican Party, the federal government, and northern whites all accepted the return of white ex-Confederates to political and economic power. With the death of Thaddeus Stevens in 1868 and Charles Sumner in 1874, Blacks lost their most effective spokesmen in Congress. Growing numbers of Republicans had wearied of the party's crusade on behalf of Blacks and were happy to turn what they called the "Negro problem" over to southern whites, who were presumed to know best how to handle it. Republicans were confident that the Fifteenth Amendment had secured their Black voting base in the South. As the party gathered strength in the Midwest and West, recruiting Black Republicans — and securing a southern base for the

Republican Party — became less important to the party. Instead, it turned its attention to economic issues, such as support for railroads and industry. Especially after the panic of 1873 set off a deep four-year depression, Black Republicans in the South, and Black civil rights in general, became expendable.

One indication of the federal government's abandonment of the freedpeople was its failure to back the Freedman's Savings and Trust Company, which collapsed during the depression. Chartered by Congress in 1865 to promote thrift and savings among freedpeople, it had many small savings accounts averaging less than $50 each. Its last president was Frederick Douglass, who deposited $10,000 of his own money to bolster the institution. When the bank failed in 1874, thousands of African Americans lost all they had. Eventually, half of the account holders received reimbursements of about 60 percent of their deposits. The other half received nothing.

By 1877, southern whites had retaken political control of all the southern states. That same year, in a political deal that resolved the disputed 1876 presidential election between the Democrat Samuel Tilden and the Republican Rutherford B. Hayes, Black Reconstruction officially ended. In return for a Hayes victory, Republicans agreed to remove federal troops from the South. In April 1877, when the troops withdrew, southern Blacks were left without federal protection.

The U.S. Supreme Court further undermined Black civil rights. In the 1873 ***Slaughterhouse Cases***, the Court, distinguishing between national citizenship and state citizenship, ruled that the Fourteenth Amendment guaranteed only a narrow class of national citizenship rights and did not encompass the array of civil rights pertaining to state citizenship. A decade later, in the ***Civil Rights Cases*** (1883), the Court overturned the Civil Rights Act of 1875, declaring that Congress did not have the authority to protect against the discriminatory conduct of individuals and private groups. As a result, private companies and businesses, such as hotels, restaurants, and theaters, could refuse to serve Black people, and they did. The Court thus legitimized the power of states and private individuals and institutions to discriminate against Black citizens and practically canceled the power of the federal government to intervene. AME bishop Henry McNeal Turner expressed pervasive Black feelings of both outrage and despair. The decision, he proclaimed, "absolves the Negro's allegiance to the general government, makes the American flag to him a rag of contempt instead of a symbol of liberty."[34]

Slaughterhouse Cases (1873)
A U.S. Supreme Court ruling limiting the authority of the Fourteenth Amendment. The ruling expanded the scope of state-level citizenship at the expense of U.S. citizenship.

Civil Rights Cases (1883)
A U.S. Supreme Court ruling that overturned the Civil Rights Act of 1875.

AP® exam tip

You'll need to be able to explain how the Supreme Court helped to dismantle Reconstruction-era reforms during the late nineteenth century.

Opportunities and Limits outside the South

What factors caused newly freed African Americans to go West during and after the Civil War?

During the Civil War, roughly 100,000 Blacks left the South permanently, relocating in the North, Midwest, and West, especially in areas bordering on the former Confederacy (Map 9.2).[35] During Reconstruction, the migration continued, as many African

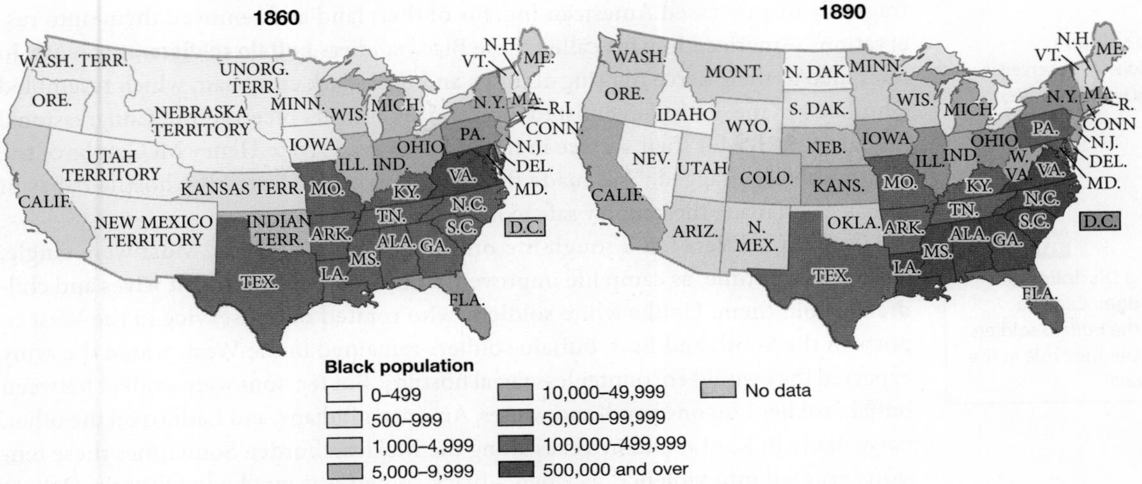

MAP 9.2 African American Population Distribution, 1860 and 1890

In the years following the Civil War, the Black population grew significantly and began to spread across the nation. Nevertheless, the vast majority of Blacks remained wedded to the South. The states that witnessed the largest and most striking growth in their Black populations from 1860 onward, and those with the largest total numbers of blacks in 1890, were those of the former Confederacy — the so-called Black belt states of the antebellum and postbellum South — and the states bordering them. **Outside the states of the former Confederacy, which states and territories had the largest African American population increases in this period?**

Americans believed they had to leave the South to improve their lives. Wherever they went, however, they encountered well-established patterns of anti-Black prejudice and discrimination. Often new patterns developed as well. White military officials, workers, factory owners, and union leaders limited Black opportunities for dignified work and fair wages, further circumscribing Black lives. By the end of the 1870s, national indifference to the plight of Blacks meant that wherever they lived, they knew that they themselves, not the states or the federal government, had to advance their own cause and protect their rights and liberties.

Autonomy in the West

For African Americans, as for all other Americans, the West beckoned as a land of opportunity. Some who envisioned a better future for themselves in the West were young men who joined the army. The U.S. Colored Troops were disbanded after the war, but new Black units (again with white officers) were authorized. Between 1866 and 1917, 25,000 Black men — some former Civil War soldiers and others with no prior military experience — served in the Ninth and Tenth Cavalry Regiments and the Twenty-Fourth and Twenty-Fifth Infantry Regiments (established in 1866), all assigned to military posts in the West. There they fought in the Indian wars that

buffalo soldiers
Black soldiers who served in U.S. army units in the West.

tragically dispossessed American Indians of their land and removed them onto reservations. American Indians called these Black soldiers **buffalo soldiers**, apparently in reference to their fierce fighting abilities and their dark curly hair, which resembled a buffalo's mane. Thirteen enlisted men and six officers received the Congressional Medal of Honor for their service in the Indian wars. Private Henry McCombs of the Tenth Calvary bragged, "We made the West," having "defeated the hostile tribes of Indians; and made the country safe to live in."[36]

AP® skills

Applying Disciplinary Knowledge: Can you identify the buffalo soldiers and explain their role in the Indian wars?

Buffalo soldiers led a rough life on remote military posts. Most were single, although over time, as camp life improved, some married or brought wives and children to join them. Unlike white soldiers, who rotated out of service in the West to posts in the South and East, buffalo soldiers remained in the West, where the army expected they would encounter less racial hostility. But tensions were evident between buffalo soldiers, on one hand, and whites, American Indians, and Latinos on the other, particularly in Kansas and in Texas along the Mexican border. Sometimes these tensions erupted into violence, as when a Black soldier was lynched in Sturgis, Dakota Territory, in 1885. In response, twenty men from the Twenty-Fifth Infantry shot up two saloons, killing one white civilian.

A few Black men became officers, but not without enduring discrimination both within the ranks and from white officers. Henry O. Flipper is one example. Appointed to West Point by a Reconstruction Republican from Georgia, Flipper became the first Black man to graduate from the military academy in 1877. As a second lieutenant in the Tenth Cavalry Regiment, he was often assigned to manual labor instead of command positions. Nevertheless, he served with distinction in the Apache War of 1880. Two years later, however, he was dismissed from the army on a controversial charge of embezzlement. For the rest of his life, he fought to be exonerated and reinstated.

AP® skills

Applying Disciplinary Knowledge: Can you explain why many African Americans moved West? What opportunities did the West offer African Americans that they could not find in the South?

Other African Americans went west as families. An especially notable migration took place from Tennessee and Kentucky to Kansas, where African Americans hoped to claim cheap public land available under the Homestead Act of 1862. In 1876, the Hartwell family of Pulaski, Tennessee (which had been the birthplace of the KKK in 1866), migrated to Kansas because Tennessee was "no place for colored people."[37] In Kansas, Black migrants built all-Black towns that promised freedom from white persecution and an opportunity for self-government. Nicodemus, incorporated in 1877, was the most famous of these towns. "Nicodemus is the most harmonious place on earth," proclaimed one of the town's newspapers in 1887. "Everybody works for the interest of the town and all pull together."[38] It grew out of a development proposal by W. J. Niles, a Black businessman, and a white land developer named W. R. Hill. The first Black settlers came from Lexington, Kentucky, and by 1880, the thriving town, which serviced a growing county, had almost 260 Black and almost 60 white residents, a bank, general stores, hotels, a pharmacy, a millinery, a livery, and a barbershop.[39] One resident was Edward P. McCabe, a talented and ambitious New Yorker and an active Republican who, upon moving to Nicodemus, became a farmer, an attorney, and a land agent. During the years he served as state auditor (1883–1887), he was the highest-ranking Black officeholder in the country.

Benjamin "Pap" Singleton, who detested sharecropping and promoted Black landownership as the most viable basis for Black self-improvement, became the most important proponent of the Black migration to Kansas. Operating out of Edgefield, Tennessee, his Edgefield Real Estate and Homestead Association spread word of available land and a hospitable environment for Blacks in Kansas. Black newspapers, mass meetings, circulars, and letters home from migrants also inspired "emigration fever." Singleton became known as "the Moses of the Colored Exodus." In the spring and summer of 1879, more than 6,000 blacks from Texas, Louisiana, and Mississippi — called **Exodusters** — migrated to Kansas, where they were able to settle on land that became theirs. John Solomon Lewis of Louisiana described the feeling: "When I landed on the soil, I looked on the ground and I says this is free ground. Then I looked on the heavens, and I says them is free and beautiful heavens. Then I looked within my heart, and I says to myself I wonder why I never was free before?"[40]

Exodusters
The name given to the more than 6,000 Blacks from Texas, Louisiana, and Mississippi who migrated to Kansas and were able to settle on land that became theirs.

Landownership made the difference, and the Exodusters established four all-Black farming communities that grew into towns with businesses, churches, and schools. Most Exodusters decided for themselves to take a chance on the West, although grassroots leaders such as Singleton and Henry Adams from Shreveport, Louisiana, helped inspire them. Adams's activities in politics and Black labor organizing were indicative of a growing grassroots Black nationalism. Involved in a variety of regional networks along the Mississippi River, Adams promoted migration to Kansas and also supported the Colonization Council, which sought federal funds for Black migration to Liberia.

Between 1865 and 1920, more than sixty all-Black towns were created in the West, some fifty of them in Oklahoma, where new settlements of southern freedmen joined with people formerly enslaved by American Indians were established in what had been designated Indian Territory. Tullahassee, for example, which began as a Creek settlement in 1850, had become mostly African American by 1881, as the Creeks moved elsewhere. In the late 1880s, when American Indian land in Oklahoma was opened up for settlement, all-Black towns boomed. They offered a freedom unknown elsewhere. But the five- to ten-acre plots on which most Black migrants settled were too small for independent farms, and many ended up working for nearby ranches and larger farms owned by whites.[41] Eventually, most of the Black boomtowns died out.

The Right to Work for Fair Wages

Like Jourdon Anderson, some other freedpeople left the South as soon as they were free, moving north and west in expectation of fair wages for their labor and a good education for their children. Many gravitated to cities, where the hope of better jobs soon faltered. Black newcomers ran into the prejudice and discrimination in hiring and wages that had long hobbled Black workers there. Managers were reluctant to hire them, and white workers, who saw them as competition, were hostile, especially since Blacks were often hired as strikebreakers. White labor unions characteristically excluded Blacks.

Black Homesteaders

Nicodemus, Kansas, founded in 1877, is among the oldest and most famous of the Black towns founded in the late nineteenth century. In these settlements, Black migrants, such as the people shown here, left behind the racial restrictions and horrors of the South for the promise of a new start: a viable homestead in the West. While some whites lived in Nicodemus, the town's population was mostly Black. Nicodemus peaked in the early 1880s before beginning to decline late in the decade. A few hundred people still live there today. This late-nineteenth-century photo of two well-dressed Black couples in Nicodemus reflects a striking sense of frontier commitment and rough-hewn refinement. These couples vividly illustrate the sense of hope and possibility projected by the boosters of Nicodemus at its height. **How were many of the promises of Reconstruction made available to African Americans that moved out West?** *Library of Congress, Prints and Photographs Division, Washington, D.C., HABS KANS, 33-Nico, 1-6, 069503p/.*

AP® skills

Applying Disciplinary Knowledge: Identify the conditions and situations that encouraged African Americans to unionize.

Some individuals were able to set out on their own. In 1865, when white caulkers in the Baltimore shipyards went on strike to force the firing of more than a hundred Black caulkers and longshoremen, Isaac Myers, a highly skilled Black caulker, joined with other Black labor activists and a small group of supportive whites to create the Black-owned and cooperatively run Chesapeake Marine Railway and Dry Dock Company. It was a strong center of Black union activism, and in 1869, Myers helped found the Colored National Labor Union to advance the cause of Black workers. Myers was also a proponent of interracial labor solidarity. Yet his efforts were short-lived. By the mid-1870s, the Colored National Labor Union had dissolved due to internal dissension and the economic depression that followed the panic of 1873. By the mid-1880s, the company Myers had founded also had collapsed.

The idea of interracial labor solidarity was taken up by the Knights of Labor, a broad-based union founded in 1869 that welcomed both skilled and unskilled workers and eventually African Americans and women. With the rise of industry in the North during and after the war, the Knights believed that only a united and inclusive labor movement could stand up to the growing power of industrialists, who, said the Knights, built profits through "wage slavery." The organization's motto was "An injury to one is the concern of all." At its height in 1886, the Knights had more than 700,000 members. Despite the fact that its assemblies in the South were segregated by race, the Knights' commitment to interracial unionism drew African American support. Black workers fully embraced the Knights' major goals: the eight-hour workday, the abolition of child and convict labor, equal pay for equal work, and worker-owned and worker-managed cooperatives. By 1886, two-thirds of Richmond, Virginia's 5,000 tobacco workers — many of them Black — belonged to the organization. But the Knights of Labor's quick decline followed its quick rise to prominence. Failed strikes and disputes between skilled and unskilled workers weakened it internally, and the 1886 Haymarket bombing — a deadly confrontation between striking workers and police in Chicago — damaged its reputation. As southern whites increasingly withdrew from the Knights, it became a largely Black organization that fell victim to racial terrorism. In Richmond, as elsewhere, the demise of the Knights doomed prospects for interracial unionism for decades.

The Struggle for Equal Rights

In the North and West, the fight for dignified work and equal labor rights took place in concert with a growing civil rights struggle that was part of a larger Black freedom struggle that had begun before the war. The National Equal Rights League continued to promote full legal and political equality, land acquisition as a basis for economic independence, education, frugality, and moral rectitude. Local, state, and national conventions kept the tradition of vigorous agitation alive, while petition campaigns and lobbying kept the pressure on local and state governments and the Republican Party to pass legislation and amendments guaranteeing Black civil rights and suffrage.

On the local level, Black campaigns against segregated seating in public conveyances continued, many of them having been initiated by women. In Philadelphia, Frances Ellen Watkins Harper and Harriet Tubman were among those who protested their forcible ejections from streetcars. The long campaign led by Octavius Catto, a teacher at the Institute for Colored Youth, and William Still, the best-known "agent" on the Underground Railroad finally succeeded in getting a desegregation law passed in 1867. Three days later, when a conductor told school principal Caroline Le Count that she could not board a streetcar, she lodged a complaint, and the conductor was fined. Thereafter, Philadelphia's streetcar companies abided by the new law, reversing decades of custom.[42] A similar protest in which Sojourner Truth played a role had ended streetcar segregation in Washington, D.C., in 1865.

AP® skills

Applying Disciplinary Knowledge: Explain how southern legal policies attempted to keep African Americans segregated from public life and institutions, and their impact on African American communities.

Segregated schools were the norm in the North, and as in the South, many Blacks preferred all-Black schools with Black teachers who took to heart the interests of Black students. Catto argued for this position. He also pointed out that white teachers assigned to Black schools were likely to be those not qualified for positions in white schools and, thus, "inferior."[43] In other communities, Black fathers initiated suits so that their children could attend white schools. Cases in Iowa in 1875 and 1876 brought court rulings in the plaintiffs' favor, but local whites blocked their enforcement. In Indiana, despite an 1869 law permitting localities to provide schools for Black children, communities with few Black residents did not do so, and Black children all too often went without an education. The same situation pertained in Illinois and California.[44]

During Black Reconstruction, educational opportunities for Black children may have been more plentiful in the South than in the North, and opportunities for Black voting were better in the South, too. In 1865, Black men in the North could vote without restriction only in Maine, New Hampshire, Vermont, Massachusetts, and Rhode Island. Together these states accounted for just 7 percent of the northern Black population. Some northern states actually took action to deny Black men the vote — Minnesota, Kansas, and Ohio in 1867, and Michigan and New York in 1868. Most northern whites viewed the vote as a white male prerogative. Even where Blacks could vote, they were often intimidated and subjected to violence. In 1871, Octavius Catto was murdered on his way to the polls.

Thus, in 1869 and 1870, ratification of the Fifteenth Amendment proved to be as contentious in the North and West as it was in the South. The former slave states Delaware, Kentucky, Maryland, and Tennessee rejected the amendment, but so did California and New Jersey; New York rescinded its ratification; and Ohio waffled, first rejecting and then ratifying the amendment. Reasons for the opposition varied. Californians, for example, wanted to ensure that the amendment did not enfranchise Chinese residents. The debate in states that eventually ratified the amendment varied. Massachusetts and Connecticut had literacy requirements that they hoped would remain unaffected. Rhode Island wanted to retain its requirement that foreign-born citizens had to own property worth at least $134 to be eligible to vote. These restrictions narrowed the electorate in the North and West by making it difficult for poor and illiterate whites, as well as Blacks, to vote. After the end of Reconstruction, some of the same and similar techniques would be used by southern states to disfranchise Blacks.

The Fifteenth Amendment proved most contentious among many northern women for what it did *not* do: it did not extend the vote to women. Many woman suffrage supporters, especially white women, felt betrayed that Black men would get the vote before women. Abolitionists and feminists had long been allied in the struggle for equal rights, and women had actively worked for abolition, emancipation, and the Thirteenth Amendment. In 1866, to present a united front in support of universal suffrage, women's rights leaders Lucy Stone, Susan B. Anthony, and Elizabeth Cady Stanton joined with Frederick Douglass to found the American Equal Rights Association. But it soon became apparent that members of this organization did not all share the same priorities. (See AP® Working with Sources: The Vote, pp. 370–79.) Douglass and Stone believed that the organization should work to secure the Black male vote first and then seek woman suffrage. Stanton and Anthony detested the idea that the rights of women would take a backseat to those of Black men. Stanton even resorted to using the racist epithet "Sambo" in reference to Black men.[45] Black feminists such as Sojourner Truth and Frances Ellen Watkins Harper took Stanton to task for ignoring the reality of Black women's lives. "You white women speak here of rights," Harper protested. "I speak of wrongs."[46]

Dissension over the Fifteenth Amendment divided old allies, destroyed friendships, and split the American Equal Rights Association (AERA) — and ultimately the women's movement itself. In 1869, in the wake of the AERA's fracturing, Anthony and Stanton organized the National Woman Suffrage Association, which focused on securing voting rights for women at the national level. That same year, Stone organized the rival American Woman Suffrage Association, which included among its members Harper, Truth, and Douglass and developed a state-by-state approach to woman suffrage. The bitter fight over the Fifteenth Amendment revealed deeper divisions in American politics and society over the rights and status of African Americans that would undercut their opportunities for decades to come.

CONCLUSION

Revolutions and Reversals

The end of slavery in the United States was revolutionary. For formerly enslaved people, now free, lives and livelihoods had to be remade. Foremost on the minds of many was reuniting with family members separated by slave sales and war. New Black communities were built and old ones were renewed, centering on independent Black churches, schools, and enterprises. Freedpeople knew that to live independently, they had to be literate, and they placed great faith in education. They learned eagerly, and within a decade, dozens of Black colleges were giving students a formal and expanded education, including the opportunity to acquire job skills, such as teacher training. Freedpeople remade themselves, their families, and their communities, but their hopes for economic independence faded as the reality of emancipation, which had made them free but had not provided them with land, set in. Impoverished and pressed into labor patterns that resembled slavery, most became tenant farmers or sharecroppers, dependent on white landowners, and many became trapped in a cycle of debt.

When the Radical Republicans in Congress took control of Reconstruction in 1867, their efforts to guarantee civil rights for freedpeople effected a political revolution in the South that had the potential for an economic and social revolution, too. With Black votes and officeholding, southern states wrote new constitutions that created state aid for economic development, progressive tax and judicial systems, much-needed social welfare institutions, and the region's first public school systems. But this so-called Black Reconstruction proved short-lived. Southern white opposition was unrelenting and often violent. By 1877, whites had regained control of state and local governments in the South. As the Republican Party, now weary of the campaign for Black rights, increasingly turned its attention to economic development, southern Blacks in particular were left with shockingly little protection and dwindling numbers of effective white advocates of equal rights for Blacks. "When you turned us loose," Frederick Douglass chastised the Republican National Convention in 1876, "you gave us no acres: you turned us loose to the sky, to the storm, to the whirlwind, and, worst of all, you turned us loose to the wrath of our infuriated masters."[47]

Some southern Blacks went west to build new communities or to serve in army units that fought the Indian wars. Others sought work in the expanding factories of the North. But wherever they went, they encountered prejudice and discrimination. Although campaigns for desegregating transportation and schools resulted in the passage of civil rights laws, those laws often went unenforced. U.S. Supreme Court rulings limited the impact of well-intentioned laws and constitutional amendments passed during Black Reconstruction. In 1883, a revived National Equal Rights League, meeting in Louisville, Kentucky, conceded "that many of the laws intended to secure us our rights as citizens are nothing more than dead letters."[48]

Abandoned by the government as they sought to carve out meaningful lives within an increasingly white supremacist nation, African Americans understood more clearly now than ever before what they had always known in their hearts: they were responsible for their own uplift. Thus, freedom's first generations turned inward, practiced self-reliance, and focused even more intently on self-elevation and the building of strong communities that would sustain them going forward.

CHAPTER 9 REVIEW ▸ PRACTICING AP® SKILLS

AP® ESSENTIAL VOCABULARY AND SOURCES

** Essential terms and required sources from the AP® Course are marked with an asterisk.*

Thirteenth Amendment (ratified 1865)* p. 338
historically Black colleges and universities* p. 343
Special Field Order 15* p. 344
Freedmen's Bureau* p. 344
sharecropping* p. 345
crop lien* p. 346
convict lease* p. 346
black codes* p. 346
The Fisk Jubilee Singers*(Jubilee Singers of Fisk University, 1875) p. 349
Black Reconstruction p. 350
Civil Rights Act of 1866 p. 352
Fourteenth Amendment (ratified 1868)* p. 352
Reconstruction Act of 1867 (first) p. 352
Union League p. 356
Fifteenth Amendment (ratified 1870)* p. 356
Civil Rights Act of 1875 p. 358
Force Acts (1870, 1871) p. 359
Slaughterhouse Cases (1873) p. 360
Civil Rights Cases (1883) p. 360
buffalo soldiers p. 362
Exodusters p. 363

APPLYING DISCIPLINARY KNOWLEDGE: ESSENTIAL QUESTIONS

1. What practices, institutions, and organizations did freedpeople develop to facilitate their transition to freedom? How successful were the freedpeople, and what challenges did they face?
2. What factors resulted in the defeat of Reconstruction? Was it inevitable, or might things have turned out differently had any of these circumstances been different? Explain.
3. What kinds of opportunities did freedpeople seek in the North and West? How did they attempt to realize their dreams? What obstacles did they have to overcome?
4. Should we judge Reconstruction on its initial promise or its ultimate failure? What is your assessment of this period?

SUGGESTED REFERENCES

A Social Revolution

Anderson, James D. *The Education of Blacks in the South, 1860–1935*. Chapel Hill: University of North Carolina Press, 1988.

Berlin, Ira, and Leslie S. Rowland, eds. *Families and Freedom: A Documentary History of African-American Kinship in the Civil War Era*. New York: New Press, 1997.

Fairclough, Adam. *A Class of Their Own: Black Teachers in the Segregated South*. Cambridge: Belknap Press of Harvard University Press, 2007.

Hunter, Tera. *To 'Joy My Freedom: Southern Black Women's Lives and Labors after the Civil War*. Cambridge: Harvard University Press, 1997.

Litwack, Leon F. *Been in the Storm So Long: The Aftermath of Slavery*. New York: Knopf, 1979.

Montgomery, William E. *Under Their Own Vine and Fig Tree: The African-American Church in the South, 1865–1900*. Baton Rouge: LSU Press, 1993.

Rachleff, Peter J. *Black Labor in the South: Richmond, Virginia, 1865–1890*. Philadelphia: Temple University Press, 1984.

Saville, Julie. *The Work of Reconstruction: From Slave to Wage Laborer in South Carolina, 1860–1870*. New York: Cambridge University Press, 1994.

Schwalm, Leslie A. *A Hard Fight for We: Women's Transition from Slavery to Freedom in South Carolina*. Urbana: University of Illinois Press, 1997.

Williams, Heather Andrea. *Self-Taught: African American Education in Slavery and Freedom*. Chapel Hill: University of North Carolina Press, 2005.

A Short-Lived Political Revolution

Benedict, Michael Les. *A Compromise of Principle: Congressional Republicans and Reconstruction, 1863–1869*. New York: Norton, 1974.

Du Bois, W. E. B. *Black Reconstruction in America: An Essay toward a History of the Part Which Black Folk Played in the Attempt to Reconstruct Democracy in America, 1860–1880*. 1935. Reprint, New York: Atheneum, 1970.

Dudden, Faye E. *Fighting Chance: The Fight Over Woman Suffrage and Black Suffrage in Reconstruction America*. New York: Oxford University Press, 2011.

Foner, Eric. *Freedom's Lawmakers: A Directory of Black Officeholders during Reconstruction*. Rev. ed. Baton Rouge: LSU Press, 1993.

———. *Reconstruction: America's Unfinished Revolution, 1863–1877*. New York: Harper & Row, 1988.

——— *The Second Founding: How the Civil War and Reconstruction Remade the Constitution*. New York: Norton, 2019.

Gillette, William. *Retreat from Reconstruction, 1869–1879*. Baton Rouge: LSU Press, 1979.

Hahn, Steven. *A Nation under Our Feet: Black Political Struggles in the Rural South from Slavery to the Great Migration*. Cambridge: Belknap Press of Harvard University Press, 2003.

Rabinowitz, Howard N., ed. *Southern Black Leaders of the Reconstruction Era*. Urbana: University of Illinois Press, 1982.

Opportunities and Limits outside the South

Athearn, Robert G. *In Search of Canaan: Black Migration to Kansas, 1879–80*. Lawrence: Regents Press of Kansas, 1978.

Davis, Hugh. *"We Will Be Satisfied with Nothing Less": The African American Struggle for Equal Rights in the North during Reconstruction*. Ithaca: Cornell University Press, 2011.

Painter, Nell Irvin. *Exodusters: Black Migration to Kansas after Reconstruction*. New York: Knopf, 1977.

Richardson, Heather Cox. *The Death of Reconstruction: Race, Labor, and Politics in the Post–Civil War North, 1865–1901*. Cambridge: Harvard University Press, 2001.

Schwalm, Leslie A. *Emancipation's Diaspora: Race and Reconstruction in the Upper Midwest*. Chapel Hill: University of North Carolina Press, 2009.

Taylor, Quintard. *In Search of the Racial Frontier: African Americans in the American West, 1528–1990*. New York: Norton, 1998.

The Vote

After the Thirteenth Amendment ended slavery in 1865, the Fourteenth Amendment, proposed in June 1866, sought to secure Black civil rights by defining citizenship and guaranteeing the equal protection of the laws. In establishing the means by which representation in Congress would be apportioned, this amendment used the word *male* for the first time in the Constitution. Supporters of woman suffrage were dismayed, for they had hoped for universal suffrage — the right of every adult to vote without regard to race or sex. In August 1866, a group of women had joined with Frederick Douglass to found the American Equal Rights Association (AERA) in an effort to create a united front for advancing the causes of Black and women's rights. When it became evident that the Fifteenth Amendment, proposed in February 1869, would secure Black male suffrage but not woman suffrage, the AERA split.

key point

The Fifteenth Amendment was ratified during Reconstruction and protected African American men's right to vote. African American men took advantage of their new political opportunities by not only casting their vote in local, state, and federal elections but also running for office. Black women, on the other hand, continued fighting for the right to vote by organizing, petitioning, and lecturing.

Some AERA members, led by Douglass, believed that Black male suffrage was the most immediate need. Others, including Susan B. Anthony and Elizabeth Cady Stanton, gave priority to woman suffrage. But what did Black women think? Did they ally themselves with Black men or white women? In the following documents, Black women voice their opinions on suffrage, an issue that went to the core of their identities; and, we read how the recognition of Black manhood figured into popular arguments for the Black male vote.

Contemporary visual representations of Black Reconstruction, notably those depicting Black male voters and politicians, reveal the historical moment and the political, racial, and cultural as well as the aesthetic aims of the artists. In the late 1860s, the Radical Republicans were still in their ascendancy, but by 1874, their heyday was over. Within the party and throughout the nation, support for freedpeople and their cause had diminished.

AP® argumentation

DBQ Practice: Explain how some African Americans and African American-led organizations advocated for universal suffrage during the Reconstruction era. Use at least three of the documents to support your response.

DOCUMENT 1 Sojourner Truth | *Equal Voting Rights, 1867*

SOJOURNER TRUTH (1797–1883) was nearly seventy years old when she spoke at the second meeting of the American Equal Rights Association in New York City in May 1867. She had begun life enslaved in New York and become one of the most famous African Americans of the nineteenth century. An abolitionist and a supporter of women's rights, Truth electrified audiences with her insight and candor.

Breaking it Down How does Truth support her argument that women both need and deserve the right to vote? How does she acknowledge her membership in multiple oppressed groups? What rhetorical strategies does she use to appeal to and gain the support of her audience?

I feel that if I have to answer for the deeds done in my body just as much as a man, I have a right to have just as much as a man. There is a great stir about colored men getting their rights, but not a word about the colored women; and if colored men get their rights, and not colored women theirs, you see the colored men will be masters over the women, and it will be just as bad as it was before. So I am for keeping the thing going while things are stirring; because if we wait till it is still, it will take a great while to get it going again. White women are a great deal smarter, and know more than colored women, while colored women do not know scarcely anything. They go out washing, which is about as high as a colored woman gets, and their men go about idle, strutting up and down; and when the women come home, they ask for their money and take it all, and then scold because there is no food. I want you to consider on that, chil'n. I call you chil'n; you are somebody's chil'n, and I am old enough to be mother of all that is here. I want women to have their rights. In the courts women have no right, no voice; nobody speaks for them. I wish woman to have her voice there among the pettifoggers.° If it is not a fit place for women, it is unfit for men to be there.

I am above eighty years old;° it is about time for me to be going. I have been forty years a slave and forty years free, and would be here forty years more to have equal rights for all. I suppose I am kept here because something remains for me to do; I suppose I am yet to help to break the chain. I have done a great deal of work; as much as a man, but did not get so much pay. I used to work in the field and bind grain, keeping up with the cradler;° but men doing no more, got twice as much pay; so with the German women. They work in the field and do as much work, but do not get the pay. We do as much, we eat as much, we want as much. I suppose I am about the only colored woman that goes about to speak for the rights of the colored women. I want to keep the thing stirring, now that the ice is cracked. What we want is a little money. You men know that you get as much again as women when you write, or for what you do. When we get our rights we shall not have to come to you for money, for then we shall have money enough in our own pockets; and may be you will ask us for money. But help us now until we get it. It is a good consolation to know that when we have got this battle once fought we shall not be coming to you any more. You have been having our rights so long, that you think, like a slave-holder, that you own us. I know that it is hard for one who has held the reins for so long to give up; it cuts like a knife. It will feel all the better when it closes up again. I have been in Washington about three years, seeing about these colored people. Now colored men have [will soon attain] the right to vote. There ought to be equal rights now more than ever, since colored people have got their freedom.

°Tricksters.

°She was actually about seventy.

°A machine for binding and bunching grain.

SOURCE: Philip S. Foner and Robert James Branham, eds., *Lift Every Voice: African American Oratory, 1787–1900* (Tuscaloosa: University of Alabama Press, 1998), 464–65.

DOCUMENT 2 Proceedings of the American Equal Rights Association | *A Debate: Negro Male Suffrage vs. Woman Suffrage, 1869*

The May 12, 1869, meeting of the AMERICAN EQUAL RIGHTS ASSOCIATION was its last. By this time, tensions between those who prioritized Black male suffrage and those who prioritized woman suffrage had torn the association apart. In this excerpt from the meeting's proceedings, we hear from Frederick Douglass and Frances Ellen Watkins Harper, two of the most important African American leaders

of the day and key advocates for abolition, African American rights, and women's rights. Susan B. Anthony, Lucy Stone, Pauline W. Davis, Julia Ward Howe, and Elizabeth Cady Stanton were key white advocates for both abolition and women's rights and, to differing extents, supporters of African American rights.

> **Breaking it Down** To what extent are the arguments in this document influenced by racism and sexism? How does this source support or counter Truth's claims in her speech for equal voting rights?

MR. DOUGLASS: I come here more as a listener than to speak and I have listened with a great deal of pleasure. . . . There is no name greater than that of Elizabeth Cady Stanton in the matter of woman's rights and equal rights, but my sentiments are tinged a little against [her remarks in] *The Revolution* [a magazine]. There was in the address to which I allude the employment of certain names, such as "Sambo," and the gardener, and the bootblack, and the daughters of Jefferson and Washington and other daughters. (Laughter.) I must say that I asked what difference there is between the daughters of Jefferson and Washington and other daughters. (Laughter.) I must say that I do not see how any one can pretend that there is the same urgency in giving the ballot to woman as to the negro. With us, the matter is a question of life and death, at least, in fifteen States of the Union. When women, because they are women, are hunted down through the cities of New York and New Orleans; when they are dragged from their houses and hung upon lamp-posts; when their children are torn from their arms, and their brains dashed out upon the pavement; when they are objects of insult and outrage at every turn; when they are in danger of having their homes burnt down over their heads; when their children are not allowed to enter schools; then they will have an urgency to obtain the ballot equal to our own. (Great applause.)

A VOICE: — Is that not all true about black women?

MR. DOUGLASS: — Yes, yes, yes; it is true of the black woman, but not because she is a woman, but because she is black. (Applause.) Julia Ward Howe at the conclusion of her great speech delivered at the convention in Boston last year said: "I am willing that the negro shall get the ballot before me." (Applause.) Woman! why, she has 10,000 modes of grappling with her difficulties. I believe that all the virtue of the world can take care of all the evil. I believe that all the intelligence can take care of all the ignorance. (Applause.) I am in favor of woman's suffrage in order that we shall have all the virtue and vice confronted. Let me tell you that when there were few houses in which the black man could have put his head, this wooly head of mine found a refuge in the house of Mrs. Elizabeth Cady Stanton, and if I had been blacker than sixteen midnights, without a single star, it would have been the same. (Applause.)

MISS [Susan B.] ANTHONY: — The old anti-slavery school says women must stand back and wait until the negroes shall be recognized. But we say, if you will not give the whole loaf of suffrage to the entire people, give it to the most intelligent first. (Applause.) If intelligence, justice, and morality are to have precedence in the Government, let the question of woman be brought up first and that of the negro last. (Applause.) While I was canvassing the State with petitions and had them filled with names for our cause to the Legislature, a man dared to say to me that the freedom of women was all a theory and not a practical thing. (Applause.) When Mr. Douglass mentioned the black man first and the woman last, if he had noticed he would have seen that it was the men that clapped and not the women. There is not the woman born who desires to eat the bread of dependence, no matter whether it be from the hand of father, husband, or brother; for any one who does so eat her bread places herself in the power of the person from whom she takes it. (Applause.) Mr. Douglass talks about the wrongs of the negro; but with all the outrages that he to-day suffers, he would not exchange his sex and take the place of Elizabeth Cady Stanton. (Laughter and applause.)

MR. DOUGLASS: I want to know if granting you the right of suffrage will change the nature of our sexes? (Great laughter.)

MISS ANTHONY: It will change the pecuniary position of woman; it will place her where she can earn her own bread. (Loud applause.) She will not then be driven to such employments only as man chooses for her. . . .

MRS. LUCY STONE: — Mrs. Stanton will, of course, advocate the precedence for her sex, and Mr. Douglass will strive for the first position for his, and both are perhaps right. If it be true that the government derives its authority from the consent of the governed, we are safe in trusting that principle to the uttermost. If one has a right to say that you can not read and therefore can not vote, then it may be said that you are a woman and therefore can not vote. We are lost if we turn away from the middle principle and argue for one class. . . . The gentleman who addressed you claimed that the negroes had the first right to the suffrage, and drew a picture which only his great word-power can do. He again in Massachusetts, when it had cast a majority in favor of Grant and negro suffrage, stood upon the platform and said that woman had better wait for the negro; that is, that both could not be carried, and that the negro had better be the one. But I freely forgave him because he felt as he spoke. But woman suffrage is more imperative than his own; and I want to remind the audience that when he says what the Ku-Kluxes did all over the South, the Ku-Kluxes here in the North in the shape of men, take away the children from the mother, and separate them as completely as if done on the block of the auctioneer. . . . Woman has an ocean of wrongs too deep for any plummet, and the negro, too, has an ocean of wrongs that can not be fathomed. There are two great oceans; in the one is the black man, and in the other is the woman. But I thank God for that XV. Amendment, and hope it will be adopted in every State. I will be thankful in my soul if any body can get out of the terrible pit. But I believe that the safety of the government would be more promoted by the admission of woman as an element of restoration and harmony than the negro. I believe that the influence of woman will save the country before every other power. (Applause.) I see the signs of times pointing to this consummation, and I believe that in some parts of the country women will vote for the President of the United States in 1872. . . .

MRS. PAULINE W. DAVIS said she would not be altogether satisfied to have the XVth Amendment passed without the XVIth, for woman would have a race of tyrants raised above her in the South, and the black women of that country would also receive worse treatment than if the Amendment was not passed. Take any class that have been slaves, and you will find that they are the worst when free, and become the hardest masters. The colored women of the South say they do not want to get married to the negro, as their husbands can take their children away from them, and also appropriate their earnings. The black women are more intelligent than the men, because they have learned something from their mistresses. She then related incidents showing how black men whip and abuse their wives in the South. One of her sister's servants whipped his wife every Sunday regularly. (Laughter.) She thought that sort of men should not have the making of the laws for the government of the women throughout the land. (Applause.)

MR. DOUGLASS said that all disinterested spectators would concede that this Equal Rights meeting had been pre-eminently a Woman's Rights meeting. (Applause.) They had just heard an argument with which he could not agree — that the suffrage to the black men should be postponed to that of the women. . . . "I do not believe the story that the slaves who are enfranchised become the worst of tyrants. (A voice, 'Neither do I.' Applause.) I know how this theory came about. When a slave was made a driver, he made himself more officious than the white driver, so that his master might not suspect that he was favoring those under him. But we do not intend to have any master over us. (Applause.)"

THE PRESIDENT (MRS. STANTON) argued that not another man should be enfranchised until enough women are admitted to the polls to outweigh those already there. (Applause.) She did not believe in allowing ignorant negroes and foreigners to make laws for her to obey. (Applause.)

MRS. [Frances Ellen Watkins] HARPER (colored) said that when it was a question of race, she let the lesser question of sex go. But the white women all go for sex, letting race occupy a minor position. She liked the idea of work-women, but she would like to know if it was broad enough to take colored women.

MISS ANTHONY and several others: Yes, yes.

MRS. HARPER said that when she was at Boston there were sixty women who left work because one colored woman went to gain a livelihood in their midst. (Applause.) If the nation could only handle one question, she would not have the black woman put a single straw in the way, if only the men of the race could obtain what they wanted. (Great applause.)

SOURCE: Philip S. Foner, ed., *Frederick Douglass on Women's Rights* (New York: Da Capo Press, 1992), 86–89.

DOCUMENT 3 Mary Ann Shadd Cary | *Woman's Right to Vote, Early 1870s*

MARY ANN SHADD CARY (1823–1893) was an educator, a journalist, and a reformer who was deeply committed to both Black and women's rights. In the 1850s, she was also a proponent of emigration to Canada. Following the split of the AERA, she sided with Elizabeth Cady Stanton and Susan B. Anthony in founding the National Woman Suffrage Association. At the time she gave this speech, Cary was teaching in Washington, D.C. The speech captures the substance of remarks she made before the Judiciary Committee of the House of Representatives in support of a petition on behalf of enfranchising women in Washington, D.C. In 1883, Cary received a law degree from Howard University.

Breaking it Down How does Cary's argument acknowledge her membership in multiple oppressed groups? How does she attempt to appeal and gain the support of her audience?

By the provisions of the 14th & 15th amendments to the Constitution of the United States, — a logical sequence of which is the representation by colored men of time-honored commonwealths in both houses of Congress, — millions of colored *women*, to-day, share with colored men the responsibilities of freedom from chattel slavery. From the introduction of freedom° African slavery to its extinction, a period of more than two hundred years, *they* shared *equally* with fathers, brothers, denied the right to vote. This fact of their investiture with the privileges of free women of the same time and by the same amendments which disentralled their kinsmen and conferred upon the latter the right of franchise, without so endowing themselves is one of the anomalies of a measure of legislation otherwise grand in conception and consequences beyond comparison. The colored women of this country though heretofore silent, in great measure upon this question of the right to vote by the women of the [copy missing], so long and ardently the cry of the noblest of the land, have neither been indifferent to their own just claims under the amendments, in common with colored men, nor to the demand for political recognition so justly made every where within its borders throughout the land.

The strength and glory of a free nation, is *not so much* in the size and equipments of its armies, as in the *loyal hearts* and willing hands of its *men* and *women*; And this fact has been illustrated in an eminent degree by well-known events in the history of the United States. To the white women of the nation conjointly with the men, it is indebted for arduous and dangerous personal service, and

° The strikethroughs throughout are part of the original document.

generous expenditure of time, wealth and counsel, so indispensable to success in its hour of danger. The colored *women* though humble in sphere, and unendowed with worldly goods, yet, led as by inspiration, — not only fed, and sheltered, and guided in *safety* the prisoner soldiers of the Union when escaping from the enemy, or the soldier who was compelled to risk life *itself* in the struggle to break the back-bone of rebellion, but gave their *sons* and brothers to the armies of the nation and their prayers to high Heaven for the success of the Right.

The surges of fratricidal war have passed we hope never to return; the premonitions of the future, are peace and good will; these blessings, so greatly to be desired, can only be made permanent, in responsible governments, — based as you affirm upon the consent of the governed, — by giving to both sexes practically the equal powers conferred in the provisions of the Constitution as amended. In the District of Columbia the women in common with the women of the states and territories, feel keenly the discrimination against them in the retention of the word *male* in the organic act for the same, and as by reason of its retention, all the evils incident to partial legislation are endured by them, they sincerely, hope that the word *male* may be stricken out by Congress on your recommendation without delay. Taxed, and governed in other respects, without their consent, they respectfully demand, that the principles of the *founders* of the government may *not* be disregarded in their case: but, as there are *laws* by which they are tried, with penalties attached thereto, that they may be invested with the right to vote as do men, that thus as in all Republics *indeed*, they may in future, be governed by their own consent.

SOURCE: Philip S. Foner and Robert James Branham, eds., *Lift Every Voice: African American Oratory, 1787–1900* (Tuscaloosa: University of Alabama Press, 1998), 516–17.

DOCUMENT 4 A. R. Waud | *The First Vote, 1867*

This image by A. R. WAUD (1828–1891), which appeared in *Harper's Weekly*, evokes the revolutionary importance of African Americans' first opportunity to vote. The range of facial expressions, dress, status, and life experiences represented in the line of Black male voters suggests the various meanings and expectations attached to the event. The Black voters are humanized and individualized — a poor laborer, a well-dressed city man, a soldier. This all-male image captures the reality of the vote as a privilege of manhood. The flag overhead, as well as the serious expression of the white man overseeing the voting, reflects the profound political transformation represented by this very special moment.

Breaking it Down This image portrays Black men, of varying walks of life and ages, voting for the first time. What message(s) does this type of portrayal send?

Library of Congress, Prints and Photographs Division, Washington, D.C., LC-DIG-ppmsca-31598.

DOCUMENT 5 A. Clark | *Address of the Colored State Convention to the People of Iowa on Behalf of Their Enfranchisement, 1868*

Throughout the nineteenth century, African Americans met in local, state, regional, and national conventions to discuss their ongoing freedom struggle and develop a united front in terms of liberation and uplift goals, strategies, and tactics. These conventions modeled self-definition and self-reliance. These critical meetings also both helped unite African Americans as a people and present to their white compatriots, notably their allies and friends, a clear and focused understanding of how they could best help advance the concerns of African Americans. This 1868 Iowa convention address makes an argument on behalf of Black male enfranchisement. It was prepared and delivered to the convention by A. CLARK, chairman of the Committee on Address.

Breaking it Down What arguments does Clark use to support his claim that Black men both deserve and need the right to vote? How does gender factor into those arguments? How does this source support or counter Truth's, Harper's, and Shadd's claims?

To the People of Iowa: . . . We ask no privilege; we simply ask you to recognize our claim to manhood by giving to us that right without which we have no power to defend ourselves from unjust legislation, and no voice in the government we have endeavored to preserve. Being men, we claim to be of that number comprehended in the Declaration of Independence, and who are entitled not only to life, but to equal rights in the pursuit and securing of happiness and in the choice of those who are to rule over us. Deprived of this, we are forced to pay taxes without representation; to submit, without appeal, to laws however offensive, without a single voice in framing them; to bear arms without the right to say whether against friend or foe — against loyalty or disloyalty. Without suffrage, we are forced into strict subjection to a government whose councils are to us foreign, and are called by our own countrymen to witness a violence upon the primary principles of a republican government as gross and outrageous as that which justly stirred patriot Americans to throw overboard the tea from English bottoms in a Boston harbor and to wage war for Independence. Let a consistent support be given to this principle of government, founded only "on the consent of the governed" — to this keystone in the arch of American liberty — and our full rights as freemen are secured. Our demands are not excessive; we ask not for social equality with the white man, as is often claimed by the shallow demagogue; for a law higher than human must forever govern social relations. We ask only that privilege which is now given to every white, native-born or adopted, male citizen of our State — the privilege of the ballot-box. We ask that the word "white" be stricken from the Constitution of our State; that the organic law of our State shall give to suffrage irrevocable guarantees that shall know of no distinction at the polls on account of color. . . . We demand this as native born citizens of the United States, and who have never known other allegiance than to its authority and the laws of our State, and as those who have been true and loyal to our government from its foundation to the present time, and who have never deserted its interest whilst even in the midst of treason and under subjection to its most violent enemies. We ask, in the honored name of 200,000 colored troops, five hundred of whom were from our own Iowa, who, with the first opportunity, enlisted under the flag of our country and the banner of our State, and bared their breasts to the remorseless storm of treason, and by hundreds went down to death in the conflict, whilst the franchised rebels and their cowardly friends, the now bitter enemies of our right to suffrage, remained in quiet at home, safe, and fattened on the fruits of our sacrifice, toil and blood. We make these demands as one of right and necessity, if not expediency, and are unwilling to believe that a powerful, ruling people, strengthened by new victories with the aid of our hands, could be less magnanimous in purpose and in action, less consistent with the true theory of a sound democracy, than to concede to us our claims. We believe that with expediency even our demands are not at war, but that with right does public policy strike hands and unite our votes, as it did our muskets, to the maintenance of authority over the disorganizing elements which attend a returning peace. We have too much faith in the permanency of this government to believe that the extension of the elective franchise to a few loyal colored men could unsettle its foundation or violate a single declaration of its rights. . . . In this can the colored men of Iowa take courage, and say to our white friends, we are Americans by birth and we assure you that we are Americans in feeling; and in spite of all the wrongs which we have long and silently endured in this our native country, we would yet exclaim, with a full heart, "O, America! with all thy faults, we love thee still."

SOURCE: Proceedings of the Iowa State Colored Convention, held in the City of Des Moines, February 12th and 13th, 1868 (Muscatine, IA, 1868).

DOCUMENT 6 Thomas Nast | *Colored Rule in a Reconstructed(?) State, 1874*

Colored Rule in a Reconstructed(?) State by THOMAS NAST (1840–1902) appeared on the cover of the March 14, 1874, issue of *Harper's Weekly*. This drawing argues that Black Reconstruction was a tragic mistake owing to Black inferiority and incapacity. The caption reads "The members call each other thieves, liars, rascals, and cowards." Columbia, the goddess at the podium under the banner that says "Let us have peace," is reprimanding the legislators: "You are Aping the lowest Whites. If you disgrace your Race in this way you had better take Back Seats."

Breaking it Down Look at the portrayal of Justice in the top right corner of the image and the message, "Let Us Have Peace." Who would it serve to have Black political participation and representation seen as a disruption of peace?

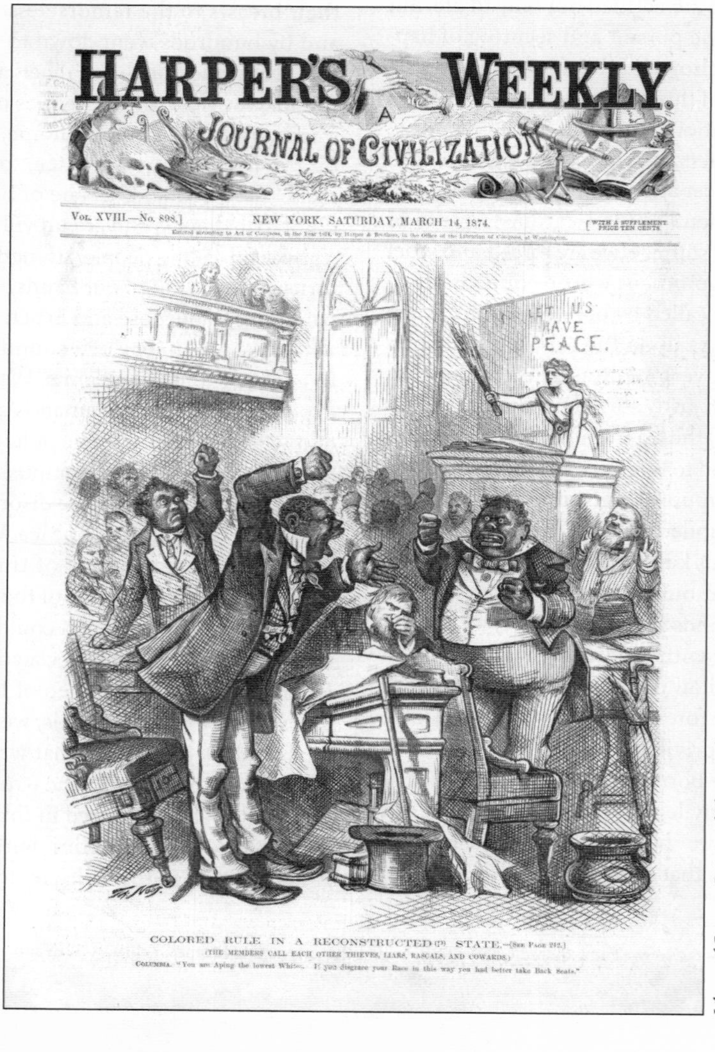

HARPER'S WEEKLY.
A JOURNAL OF CIVILIZATION.

Vol. XVIII.—No. 898.] NEW YORK, SATURDAY, MARCH 14, 1874. [WITH A SUPPLEMENT PRICE TEN CENTS.

Entered according to Act of Congress, in the Year 1874, by Harper & Brothers, in the Office of the Librarian of Congress, at Washington.

COLORED RULE IN A RECONSTRUCTED(?) STATE.—(See Page 242.)
(THE MEMBERS CALL EACH OTHER THIEVES, LIARS, RASCALS, AND COWARDS.)
COLUMBIA. "You are Aping the lowest Whites. If you disgrace your Race in this way you had better take Back Seats."

Library of Congress, Prints and Photographs Division, Washington, D.C., LC-USZ62-102256.

PRACTICING AP® SKILLS

1. **AP® Contextualization.** Describe the major goals of racial uplift during Reconstruction and how they influenced the fight for Black suffrage. What aspects of uplift do you see reflected in these documents?
2. **AP® Causation.** Explain how these documents illustrate some of the political impacts of the ratification of the Fifteenth Amendment during Reconstruction.
3. **AP® Comparison.** Compare African American women and white women's arguments for woman suffrage. Use evidence from at least two of the documents to support your response.
4. **Connecting to AP® Themes.** Explain how the intersections of identity influenced the fight for the right to vote within the African American community during the nineteenth century.
5. **Think-Pair-Share.** Choose a claim Du Bois makes about Black Reconstruction. Support or counter that claim with evidence from at least one of the other texts in this collection.

Document-Based Questions:
Evidence

Like you've learned in previous workshops, a **thesis statement** is essential to a well-constructed response to a document-based question. In order to be effective, however, a thesis must be supported by **evidence**. In fact, the strength of any **argument** is based upon both the *amount* and *quality* of the evidence the writer uses to support their **claim**. This is especially true when responding to a DBQ, since this section of the AP® Exam is meant to assess your ability to interpret multiple sources and synthesize their most relevant details into an argument. We specify that the details must be *relevant* to avoid overwhelming your reader with a lengthy list of random facts. In this workshop, we'll focus on building the skills you'll need to curate the evidence that's best tailored to your thesis and thus most likely to strengthen your argument.

Examining the AP® Rubric

The rubric that will be used to assess DBQ responses makes clear you'll need to incorporate both evidence from the sources *and* evidence beyond the sources. Specifically, it states you'll earn full points only if your essay fulfills both of the criteria below:

- **Two points:** Supports an argument in response to the prompt using at least three sources. *To earn two points, the response must accurately describe—rather than just quote—the content from at least three sources. In addition, the response must use the content of three sources to support an argument in response to the prompt.*
- **One point:** Uses at least one additional piece of specific evidence (beyond the evidence found in the sources) relevant to an argument in response to the prompt. *To earn this point, the response must describe the evidence using more than a phrase or reference. This additional piece of evidence must be relevant to an argument in response to the prompt.*

In other words, the evidence in your essay must be:

1. **Sufficient.** You need at least three pieces of evidence from the provided sources, and at least one piece of evidence beyond the sources.
2. **Descriptive.** You need to paraphrase, not directly quote, at least three of the provided sources.
3. **Relevant.** All evidence must directly support the argument outlined in your thesis statement.

Evidence that meets these criteria will make your thesis, and therefore your essay, more convincing.

Reviewing Prewriting Skills

We can use the following sample prompt to practice gathering evidence:

Evaluate the extent to which the Reconstruction Amendments enabled Black people to socially, politically, and economically advance by 1877.

As you've seen in the AP® Skills Workshop for Chapter 5 (p. SW5-A), you'll want to first break down the prompt into its time period, topic, and task, and then jot down the course knowledge that first comes to mind:

Time Period	Topic	Task
Reconstruction (1865–1877)	Impact of the Reconstruction Amendments	Determine how much the Reconstruction Amendments helped Black people politically, economically, and socially by 1877.

Relevant Course Concepts, Developments, Processes

- The Thirteenth Amendment (1865) abolished slavery, the Fourteenth Amendment (1868) established birthright citizenship and guaranteed equal legal protection to all people, and the Fifteenth Amendment (1870) granted Black men the right to vote.
- Thousands of African American people served in public office during Reconstruction, stretching from local positions to the U.S. Senate.
- Many states enacted Black Codes to counteract Reconstruction's benefits to African Americans. These restrictive laws controlled Black people's movement, labor, and lifestyles.
- Economic advancement was very difficult for formerly enslaved people, as many labor contracts provided very little pay and sharecropping arrangements forced them to return a significant portion of their crops to landowners.
- Under the system of convict leasing, African American men who had been imprisoned on minor charges were forced to work without pay, essentially recreating enslaved labor.
- Southern governments suppressed Black voting through measures like poll taxes, grandfather clauses, and literacy tests.

Next, you'll approach the sources for skillful skimming (p. SW6-A) to identify the most important information:

Main idea. How would you summarize the source in one sentence?

Context. What course knowledge seems directly connected to this particular source? What's the most relevant outside knowledge about its topic, its time period, or its creator?

Category. How would you generalize the point of the source in just a few words? Does this category align or contrast with other sources for the same DBQ?

On exam day, you'll want to take about 30 seconds with each source, so your skillful skimming notes are unlikely to be in full sentences. For now, though, take a bit longer with each source; it's useful to get practice articulating your thoughts in full sentences.

Source A: "Black Codes" of Mississippi, 1865

"An Act to Confer Civil Rights on Freedmen, and for Other Purposes

Section 3. All freedmen, free negroes or mullatoes who do now and have herebefore lived and cohabited together as husband and wife shall be taken and held in law as legally married, and the issue shall be taken and held as legitimate for all purposes; and it shall not be lawful for any freedman, free negro or mulatto to intermarry with any white person; nor for any person to intermarry with any freedman, free negro or mulatto; and any person who shall so intermarry shall be deemed guilty of felony, and on conviction thereof shall be confined in the State penitentiary for life; and those shall be deemed freedmen, free negroes and mulattoes who are of pure negro blood, and those descended from a negro to the third generation, inclusive, though one ancestor in each generation may have been a white person. . . .

An Act to Amend the Vagrant Laws of the State

Section 2. Be it further enacted, That all freedmen, free Negroes, and mulattoes in this state over the age of eighteen years found . . . with no lawful employment or business, or found unlawfully assembling themselves together . . . and all white persons so assembling with freedmen, free Negroes, or mulattoes, or usually associating with freedmen, free Negroes, or mulattoes on terms of equality, or living in adultery or fornication with a freedwoman, free Negro, or mulatto, shall be deemed vagrants; and, on conviction thereof, shall be fined in the sum of not exceeding, in the case of a freedman, free Negro, or mulatto, fifty dollars, and a white man, two hundred dollars, and imprisoned at the discretion of the court, the free Negro not exceeding ten days, and the white man not exceeding six months."

SOURCE: Selections from Mississippi state laws, October–December 1865

Source B: Glimpses at the Freedmen's Bureau, 1866

VTR/Alamy Stock Photo

SOURCE: Frank Leslie's Illustrated Newspaper, *Glimpses at the Freedmen's Bureau — issuing rations to the old and sick — from a sketch by our special artist, Jas. E. Taylor*, September 22, 1866

Source C: Black Political Participation in the Reconstruction South, 1867–1868

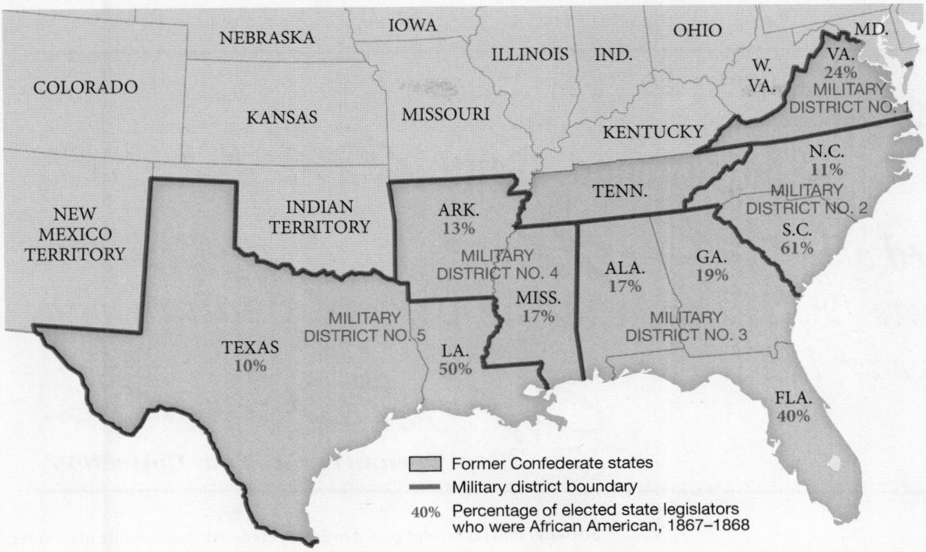

SOURCE: Data from *The Atlas of African-American History and Politics: From the Slave Trade to Modern Times*, 1998

Source D: Statement of Cane Cook, 1870

"I worked for Robert Hodges, last year, who lives about two and-a-half miles from Andersonville, Georgia. I had my own stock, and rented land from him, agreeing to give him one-third of the corn, and one-fourth of the cotton for rent. We divided the corn by the wagon load, and had no trouble about that. . . . He told me he would buy my cotton and pay me the market price, which was twenty-one cents that day, and I told him he might have it. I got some meat and corn and other things from him during the year, and he paid me $50 in cash Christmas. I went to him last Friday a week ago for a settlement. When he read over his account he had a gallon of syrup charged to me, and I told him I had not had any syrup of him. . . . He got up very angry, and took a large hickory stick and came towards me. . . . As I turned to go down the steps — there are four steps — he struck me a powerful blow on the back of my head, and I fell from the porch to the ground. I was not entirely senseless, but I was stiff and could not move hand or foot. . . . My hands, arms, back, and legs are almost useless. I have not been able to lift a bit of food to my mouth. I have to be fed like a baby. I have not gone before any of the courts; I have no money to pay a lawyer, and I know it would do no good. Mr. Hodges has not paid me for my cotton, and says he will not settle with me, but will settle with any man I will send him. While I lay before his door he told me that if I died he would pay my wife $50. I hope there will be some law sometime for us poor oppressed people. If we could only get land and have homes we could get along; but they won't sell us any land."

SOURCE: Cane Cook, African American sharecropper, interview with Reverend H. W. Pierson, 1870

Source E: Poll Tax Receipt, 1871

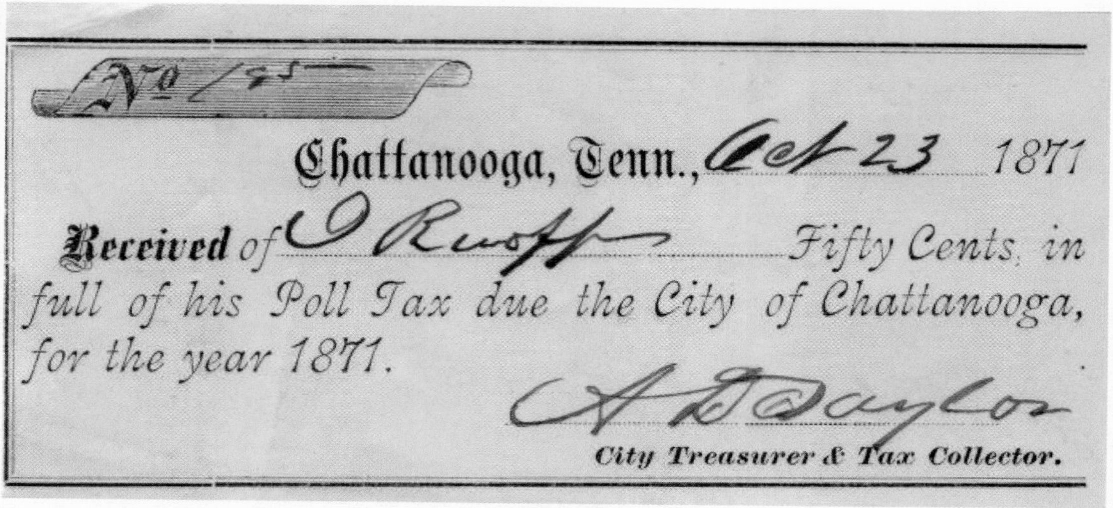

No

Chattanooga, Tenn., Oct 23 1871

Received of J Ruoff Fifty Cents in full of his Poll Tax due the City of Chattanooga, for the year 1871.

A J Taylor

City Treasurer & Tax Collector.

Tennessee State Library & Archives

SOURCE: Poll tax receipt issued to James Frederick Ruoff, white male voter, Chattanooga, Tennessee, October 23, 1871

A skillful skim of the provided sources might look like this:

SOURCE A

Main idea. Despite the Fourteenth Amendment, the Black Codes of Mississippi limited who Black people could marry and penalized them for supposed offenses like being unemployed or congregating.

Context. Many states enacted Black Codes to counteract Reconstruction's benefits to African Americans. These restrictive laws controlled Black people's movement, labor, and lifestyles.

Category. Social; political

SOURCE B

Main idea. The Freedmen's Bureau provided essential services like food and medical care to formerly enslaved people.

Context. In 1865, Congress established the Freedmen's Bureau to assist newly free Black Americans. The Bureau distributed food, established schools and hospitals, settled labor disputes, and even helped people locate their lost relatives.

Category. Economic; social

SOURCE C

Main idea. Black men not only voted but were also elected to a significant portion of state and local offices in former Confederate states.

Context. The Fifteenth Amendment gave Black people the ability to vote and run for office. It's estimated that over 2,000 Black people held political office during Reconstruction.

Category. Political

SOURCE D

Main idea. Sharecroppers were often forced to work for hostile, exploitative landowners under unfair business practices.

Context. The Thirteenth Amendment abolished slavery but did not provide Black people with a means of obtaining and maintaining economic independence, and the Fourteenth Amendment supposedly guaranteed Black people equal protection under the law but did not protect them from white supremacist actions on the local level.

Category. Economic; social

SOURCE E

Main idea. All voters had to pay the city of Chattanooga, Tennessee in order to vote in its elections.

Context. Although the Fifteenth Amendment gave Black men the right to vote, by the 1870s, many former Confederate states had written voter suppression measures like poll taxes, grandfather clauses, and literacy tests into their laws.

Category. Political

On the AP® Exam, you'll next need to collect your thoughts into a thesis statement as outlined in the AP® Skills Workshop for Chapter 7 (p. SW7-A). Here, we'll save time by providing a sample thesis statement:

> The impact of the Reconstruction Amendments was weakened because Black people were left vulnerable to economic exploitation, discriminatory laws that restricted their daily lives, and voter suppression.

Now, we can focus on curating evidence that best supports this thesis statement.

Writing Topic Sentences

To ensure our collection of evidence is as efficient and organized as possible, we'll start by establishing the **topic sentences** that will define each paragraph's focus. Because we have a coherent thesis statement presented in the *X because A, B, and C* format, we can readily break the statement into topic sentences:

Thesis statement	The impact of the Reconstruction amendments was weakened because Black people were left vulnerable to economic exploitation, discriminatory laws that restricted their daily lives, and voter suppression.
Paragraph 1	Despite the Thirteenth Amendment abolishing slavery, Black Americans still faced exploitation that prevented economic independence.
Paragraph 2	Black Americans endured substantial restrictions on their daily activities even after the Fourteenth Amendment established citizens' equality under the law.
Paragraph 3	The Fifteenth Amendment gave Black men the ability to participate in the electoral process; however, they were subjected to voter suppression tactics that counteracted federal protections.

These topic sentences establish the framework that will house each piece of evidence.

Gathering Evidence

Now that we have our topic sentences, let's determine what evidence best aligns with each paragraph. We're not aiming to cram every source into every paragraph (though sources can be used in multiple paragraphs). We're aiming to locate the facts and details that make each topic sentence as convincing as possible. Here, we'll model one paragraph using a graphic organizer:

Topic Sentence: Despite the Thirteenth Amendment abolishing slavery, Black Americans still faced exploitation that prevented economic independence.		
Evidence	**Explanation of How Evidence Supports Your Topic Sentence**	**Source of Evidence**
The Freedmen's Bureau provided essential services like food and medical care to formerly enslaved people.	In the early years of Reconstruction, initiatives like the Freedmen's Bureau improved the economic condition of formerly enslaved people through direct aid as well as education and social support.	Source B
Cane Cook was a sharecropper farming land he did not own. He describes how a white landowner violated the terms of their sharecropping arrangement and how the landowner then violently attacked him, leaving him permanently disabled.	The Thirteenth Amendment abolished slavery but did not provide Black people with a means of obtaining and maintaining economic independence. For instance, while the Union military had aimed to redistribute confiscated and abandoned Confederate land to formerly enslaved people through Special Field Order 15, President Johnson reversed this plan, leaving African Americans in much less advantageous sharecropping arrangements. In this way, Black Americans continued to live under white landowners' economic control.	Source D

It may seem odd to record the source of each piece of evidence in the last column rather than the first, but in fact, that placement reminds us to pull in evidence in an arrangement that best supports each topic sentence, rather than mimicking the sources' order of appearance.

Notice, as well, how outside evidence naturally arises in the second column explaining how each piece of evidence supports the topic sentence. As you'll recall, a DBQ response can receive full points only if it incorporates at least one substantial piece of evidence beyond the sources. You'll want to make sure at least one body paragraph — preferably two — meaningfully engages with outside evidence directly connected to its topic sentence.

recap

Gathering Evidence

Successful responses to document-based questions will include evidence that is:

1. **Sufficient.** You need at least three pieces of evidence from the provided sources, and at least one piece of evidence beyond the sources.
2. **Descriptive.** You need to paraphrase, not directly quote, at least three of the provided sources.
3. **Relevant.** All evidence must directly support the argument outlined in your thesis statement.

Remember, you may address sources in a different order from the one in which they were presented.

Activity ▸ Gathering Evidence

Use a graphic organizer like the one shown below to collect evidence. You may choose to complete this activity using the sample topic sentence provided for either Paragraph 2 or Paragraph 3.

Topic Sentence:		
Evidence	Explanation of How Evidence Supports Your Topic Sentence	Source of Evidence

Multiple-Choice Questions

Questions 1–2 refer to the following.

AP® source ***The Fisk Jubilee Singers,* 1880**

1. The historical situation reflected in this image most directly resulted from which of the following during Reconstruction?
   (A) Redistribution of Confederate lands, assets, and wealth to the formerly enslaved
   (B) Increased emigration to Liberia and Latin America
   (C) Expanded access to education made possible by the emergence of historically Black colleges and universities
   (D) Distribution of generational wealth due to the ratification of the Fourteenth Amendment

2. This image was most likely intended to highlight which of the following during the late nineteenth century?
   (A) Black middle-class sophistication
   (B) The benefits of a vocational education
   (C) The highest standards of "Negro education"
   (D) The influence of classical music on Black culture

Short-Answer Question

1. **Answer A, B, C, and D.**

   (A) Describe the broader context that led to the ratification of the Reconstruction Amendments.

   (B) Explain how one of the Reconstruction Amendments fulfilled the postwar hopes of African Americans who supported Black enlistment in the Union army.

   (C) Explain how one of the Reconstruction Amendments was undermined by state or local laws during Reconstruction.

   (D) Using one specific example, explain how the Thirteenth Amendment impacted Black political participation in politics.

CHAPTER **10**

Black Life and Culture during the Nadir

1877–1915

CHAPTER TIMELINE

Events specific to African American history are in purple. General U.S. history events are in black. Events from the AP® Course Framework are marked with an asterisk.

1879	More than 6,000 Exodusters leave the South for Kansas
1881	Tuskegee Institute founded*
1883	U.S. Supreme Court overturns Civil Rights Act of 1875
1886	Colored Farmers' Alliance founded
1890	*Louisville, New Orleans and Texas Railway v. Mississippi* rules segregation on common carriers lawful
	Land-Grant College Act
	Mississippi's new state constitution provides model for Black disfranchisement
1892	Ida B. Wells launches antilynching campaign*
1893	Blacks boycott Chicago World's Fair
1895	Wells's *A Red Record* published*
	Booker T. Washington delivers *Atlanta Compromise* speech*
1896	Paul Laurence Dunbar's *Lyrics of Lowly Life* published
	Plessy v. Ferguson establishes separate but equal doctrine*
	National Association of Colored Women founded*
	Populist Party dissolves
1897	American Negro Academy founded
1898	*Williams v. Mississippi* upholds voting requirements used to disfranchise Blacks
	U.S. annexes Hawaii
	Wilmington Insurrection
	U.S. annexes Puerto Rico, Guam, and the Philippines
1900	Brothers James Weldon Johnson and John Rosamond Johnson create "Lift Every Voice and Sing"*
	W. E. B. Du Bois addresses Pan-African Congress
	National Negro Business League founded
1901	Booker T. Washington's *Up from Slavery* published
	Charles Chesnutt's *The Marrow of Tradition* published
1903	Maggie L. Walker establishes St. Luke Penny Savings Bank
	Du Bois's *The Souls of Black Folk* published*
1904	Mary McLeod Bethune founds Daytona Normal and Industrial Institute for Negro Girls
1905	Niagara movement founded
1906	Following unproven accusation, 167 Black soldiers discharged without honor in Brownsville, Texas
1909	National Negro Committee founded; renamed National Association for the Advancement of Colored People in 1910*
1910	African American boxer Jack Johnson's defense of world heavyweight title seen as victory for race
	National Urban League founded
	The Crisis, NAACP's journal, begins publication*
1911	*Bailey v. Alabama* overturns Alabama law holding laborers criminally liable for taking money in advance for work not performed
1914	W. C. Handy's "St. Louis Blues"
	United States v. Reynolds outlaws an aspect of debt peonage
1915	NAACP protests *The Birth of a Nation*
	NAACP scores legal victory for voting rights in *Guinn v. United States.*

Please note that this chapter includes a primary source quotation by a Black speaker that uses the N-word, which we have chosen to reprint in this textbook to accurately reflect this speaker's original intent as well as the time period, culture, and racism discussed in the quotation. We recognize that this word has a long history as a derogatory and deeply hurtful expression when used by white people toward Black people. Black speakers' and writers' choice to use this word relates not only to that history but to a larger cultural tradition in which the N-word can take on different meanings, emphasize shared experience, and be repurposed as a term of endearment within Black communities. While the use of that word in such contexts might not be hurtful, the use of it in our current context very often is. Be mindful of context, both historical and contemporary, as you read and discuss this chapter.

Ida B. Wells: Creating Hope and Community amid Extreme Repression

Seated in the ladies' car on the train from Tennessee to Mississippi in 1883, the twenty-one-year-old African American schoolteacher Ida B. Wells settled in for her trip home. When the conductor demanded that she move to the smoking car, she refused. She had paid for a first-class ticket and did not want to sit in the dirty, smelly smoker, where rowdy white men often insulted Black women. When the conductor tried to pry her from her seat, she fought back, biting his hand. Then, as she later described it, "I braced my feet against the seat in front and was holding to the back,"[1] so that the conductor had to call for assistance. It took three white men, including the conductor, to wrench the diminutive Wells, who was less than five feet tall, from her seat. The white ladies in the car applauded the conductor and his crew.

Outraged, Wells filed suit against the Chesapeake, Ohio and Southwestern Railroad, charging the company with discrimination and assault. Despite the violent attack — "the sleeves of my linen duster had been torn out and I had been pretty roughly handled" — she later recalled, "I had not been hurt physically."[2] Before the suit was settled, Wells filed another for a similar incident. But after an initial victory in a lower court in the first case, the Tennessee Supreme Court ruled against her in both cases in 1887, claiming that the smoker and the ladies' car were comparable and that Wells had sued only to harass the railroad.

Wells wrote about her violent expulsion from the ladies' car for Memphis's Black Baptist newspaper *Living Way*. Other Black newspapers reprinted her story, and she began to write regularly for the Black press. In 1889, she bought a one-third interest in the Memphis *Free Speech and Headlight* and turned it into a regional voice for African American concerns. As editor, she protested conditions in the city's Black schools and clauses in Mississippi's new constitution that would effectively prevent Black men from voting.[3] When she denounced white Memphians for the lynching of three friends in 1892, a mob destroyed her newspaper's offices. Wells left Memphis forever, but she had found her life's purpose. As an investigative journalist, she researched and analyzed lynching, and through publications, lectures, and connections with Black leaders and organizations, she helped launch a national and international antilynching crusade that made her one of the most powerful Black activists of her era.

Supporting Wells's efforts were Black leaders from earlier generations, such as Frederick Douglass, and Black leaders from freedom's first generation — those born after emancipation. Among her contemporaries in this first generation were Black teachers, newspaper editors, preachers, and entrepreneurs who contributed to a growing Black middle class that helped reshape the South. They were role models for what could be achieved and also advocates for improving the lives of all African Americans. Their actions helped prepare the way for the founding of powerful organizations that would lead the Black freedom struggle well into the twentieth century.

The trajectory of Wells's life illustrates what Blacks did for themselves and also what they endured when Reconstruction ended and a harsh new reality took shape. At the turn of the century, white supremacists devised new laws that required segregation in schools and public places, demeaning Blacks and circumscribing their participation in the economic, social, and political life of the South. Throughout this especially trying period, terror and violence — particularly lynching (as Wells's campaign publicized) — as well as segregation were used to enforce white supremacy. Nevertheless, despite the many constraints, Black people created rich lives for themselves and viable, self-sufficient communities. They founded businesses that served Black neighborhoods. They built schools dedicated to vocational training, teacher training, and academic curricula. They formed organizations that promoted self-help and racial advancement through Black solidarity. They found new means of self-expression through theater, dance, music, and literature. Performers, musicians, and writers explored the nature of the Black experience and discovered deep sources of inspiration and hope.

Freedom's first generation fought hard to create viable lives and careers in the hostile context of white supremacy that emerged in this low point, or nadir, at the end of the nineteenth century. The persistence and ingenuity of these individuals fostered a powerful culture of struggle and affirmation that in the first decades of the twentieth century renewed collective protest against inequality.

Racism and Black Challenges

How were many Reconstruction-era reforms dismantled during the late nineteenth century?

How did the introduction of Jim Crow laws impact African Americans economically after Reconstruction?

Negotiations between Republicans and Democrats over the contested presidential election of 1876 produced a compromise that restored white rule in the South and ended federal protections for the rights of African Americans. What followed was continued intimidation, violence, and murder aimed at keeping Blacks submissive to whites. New laws required segregation of the races in public places, and new voting requirements disfranchised Black men. Violations, or any behavior that could be interpreted as nonsubmissive, could mean death at the hands of a white mob. Such laws and practices were embedded in a political and social culture built on views of racial hierarchy that were promoted as scientific and used to justify white dominance over peoples of color.

Racial Segregation

Black people had long protested discrimination by streetcar companies that required them to ride in separate cars or in the backs of cars. Stories of forced removal from public conveyances were told in many autobiographies, including those by Frederick Douglass and Harriet Jacobs, and protests were equally numerous. Before the Civil War, Elizabeth Jennings's suit against a New York City streetcar company had desegregated transportation in that city, and more recent campaigns had ended streetcar discrimination in Washington, D.C., in 1865 and in Philadelphia in 1867. But in the South, a different scenario was unfolding.

Custom had long excluded Blacks from public places where whites were likely to be. During Black Reconstruction, however, the new state constitutions that Black men helped write affirmed equal rights, and state laws required equal treatment of whites and Blacks. Louisiana's 1869 civil rights act, for example, specifically forbade segregation on public transportation carriers. Thus in 1872, when Josephine DeCuir was refused a ladies' stateroom on a Mississippi steamboat, she sued. The state court awarded her damages, but in 1878, in *Hall v. DeCuir*, the U.S. Supreme Court overturned the Louisiana statute, reasoning that Louisiana could not prohibit racial segregation on common carriers because matters relating to interstate commerce came under federal jurisdiction. States, according to this logic, could legally segregate intrastate but not interstate passengers. In the Civil Rights Cases (1883), the U.S. Supreme Court overturned the Civil Rights Act of 1875, stating that Congress had no authority to bar discrimination by private individuals and businesses. In *Louisville, New Orleans and Texas Railway v. Mississippi* (1890), the Court ruled that it was actually lawful for states to require racial segregation on common carriers. In the late nineteenth century, this expanding system of spatial and physical racial separation in public transportation and elsewhere came to be called **Jim Crow**, after a popular minstrel show character that ridiculed Black people.

Many streetcar and railroad companies actually opposed Jim Crow because of the extra expense involved in maintaining separate cars, the fear of losing Black customers, and the difficulty of enforcement. But white-dominated southern state legislatures moved to make segregation mandatory. In 1890, Louisiana passed a law stating that "all railway companies carrying passengers in their coaches in this State, shall provide equal but separate accommodations for the white and colored races."[4] Opposition to this Separate Car Act was particularly intense among the light-complexioned African American elite of New Orleans, who in 1891 formed a committee to challenge it. They planned a highly orchestrated act of civil disobedience: a Black citizen would violate

AP® exam tip

As you read this section, consider how the structures of chattel slavery were legally reformed yet systemically remained the same during Reconstruction.

AP® skills

Applying Disciplinary Knowledge: How did the U.S. Supreme Court legalize racial segregation at the state level?

Jim Crow
A system of laws and customs that enforced segregation, the spatial and physical separation of the races.

AP® skills

Applying Disciplinary Knowledge: Why is the term "Jim Crow" used to describe the laws and customs that enforced segregation?

the law, be arrested, and initiate a case they intended to take all the way to the U.S. Supreme Court.

On June 7, 1892, Homer Plessy, a local shoemaker who was seven-eighths white, purchased a first-class ticket and took a seat for a short trip to Covington, just north of New Orleans. When the conductor demanded that he go to the "colored car," Plessy refused and was arrested for violating the Separate Car Act. In court, Plessy maintained that this law violated the Fourteenth Amendment, and after appeals, the Supreme Court agreed to hear the case.

Plessy v. Ferguson (1896)
A U.S. Supreme Court decision upholding the constitutionality of state laws mandating racial segregation in public facilities.

separate but equal
The legal doctrine established in *Plessy v. Ferguson* (1896) stating that as long as they were deemed equal to those of whites, separate (Jim Crow) facilities and accommodations for Blacks did not violate the Fourteenth Amendment's equal protection clause.

In ***Plessy v. Ferguson*** (1896), the Court declared Louisiana's Separate Car Act constitutional and established the **separate but equal** legal doctrine that would protect segregation for more than half a century. (The text of *Plessy v. Ferguson* is in the Appendix.) The justices reasoned that the racially separate but allegedly equal railroad cars did not violate the Fourteenth Amendment's guarantee of equal protection of the laws. Furthermore, they maintained that the Separate Car Act specifically, and Jim Crow segregation generally, respected custom and did not stigmatize African Americans as inferior. They pointed to "the establishment of separate schools for white and colored children" as "a valid exercise of the legislative power" and claimed that state legislatures were "at liberty to act with reference to the established usages, customs, and tradition of the people, and with a view to the promotion of their comfort, and the preservation of the public peace and good order."[5]

AP® skills

Applying Disciplinary Knowledge: How did Black Americans react to the segregation laws?

The *Plessy* decision not only legalized long-standing custom and state-sanctioned discrimination against Black people but also prompted the passage of new and more comprehensive Jim Crow laws. By 1910, all southern states mandated segregated railroad cars, streetcars, and waiting rooms (Map 10.1). Despite the theory of "separate but equal," actual accommodations for Black people were strikingly unequal, and Blacks protested in mass meetings, sermons, editorials, petitions, and lobbying efforts. Between 1900 and 1906, they organized an impressive series of streetcar boycotts in more than twenty-five southern cities. But wherever Blacks protested and boycotted — and despite concessions to Blacks in some places — white elites marshaled their resources to pass more restrictive laws, or they resorted to intimidation and violence to enforce Black submission.

Throughout the South, stores, restaurants, and hotels displayed signs designating "Colored Only" or "Whites Only" sections. Separate entrances, waiting rooms, water fountains, toilets, service counters, and ticket windows became standard. Theater balconies were reserved for "Colored Only." Public parks and recreational facilities might have a special Negro day, but generally Blacks were excluded from them — and from public libraries as well. In courtrooms and city hall buildings, signs directed traffic so as to minimize interracial contact. Work sites were segregated; hospitals, clinics, asylums, and prisons were racially exclusive. In city neighborhoods where Black populations were concentrated, Blacks established their own parks, hospitals, and clinics.

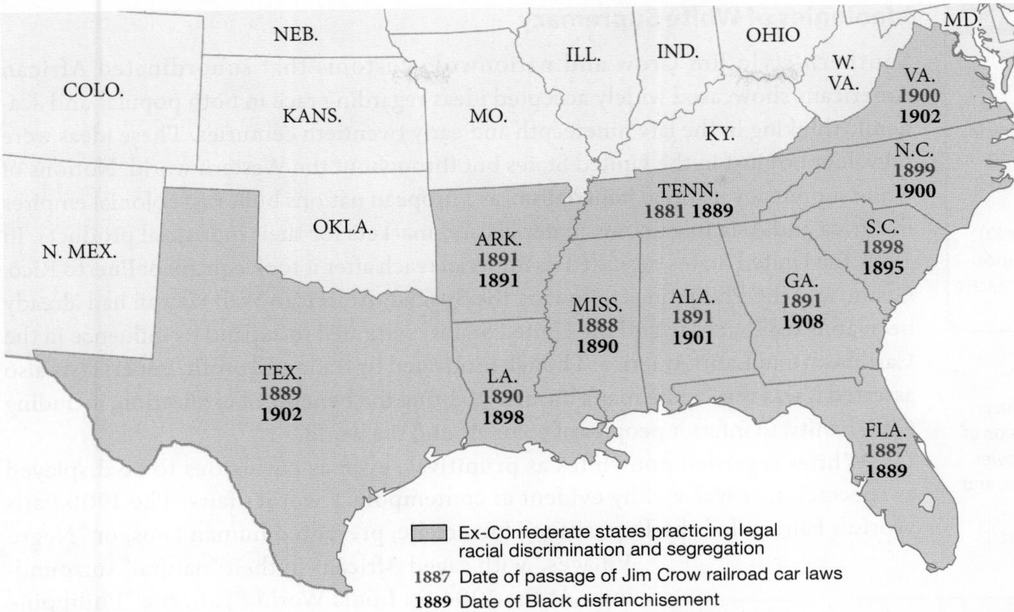

MAP 10.1 Jim Crow and Disfranchisement in Former Confederate States

As shown in this map, each state of the former Confederacy passed laws segregating railroad cars, a critical marker in the evolution of Jim Crow. Each of these states also disfranchised its Black citizens, depriving them of the vote through a variety of strategies. Setting these developments against one another illustrates the links between Jim Crow and disfranchisement. The *Plessy v. Ferguson* decision in 1896 paved the way for the creation and enforcement of new and ever more restrictive Jim Crow laws, further circumscribing Black life in the South. ■ **How many years between railroad car segregation and disfranchisement are most commonly seen here? Why would states use disfranchisement laws as a strategy?**

Essential to Jim Crow was a system of racial etiquette that reinforced patterns of Black subordination. Whenever Blacks came into contact with whites, Blacks were expected to defer. In towns, they had to surrender the sidewalk to whites, and Black men were expected to remove their hats and bow their heads. When spoken to by whites, Blacks diverted their gaze so as not to look at whites directly. Blacks had to refer to whites as “Mr.,” “Miss,” or “Mrs.,” proper titles of deference, while whites addressed Blacks with belittling terms such as “auntie,” “uncle,” “boy,” and “girl.” Family members taught Black children racial etiquette, often using “trickster tales” that traced back to West African and enslaved culture, to show how to survive by one’s wits. The children might laugh when clever Brer Rabbit outsmarted an authority figure, but they also understood the story’s message about the limits of outward resistance and protest in a Jim Crow world.

AP® exam tip

On the AP® Exam, you will need to be able to describe how African Americans were endangered by acts of racial violence such as lynching and retaliation from former Confederates, political terrorist groups like the Ku Klux Klan, and others who embraced white supremacist doctrine.

imperialism
The late-nineteenth-century European and U.S. extension of political and economic power over nations in Africa, Asia, and the Americas.

Ideologies of White Supremacy

Southern-style Jim Crow and nationwide customs that subordinated African Americans showcased widely accepted ideas regarding race in both popular and academic thinking in the late nineteenth and early twentieth centuries. These ideas were prevalent not just in the United States but throughout the Western world. Notions of white supremacy justified **imperialism**, as European nations built vast colonial empires in Africa and Asia to gain raw materials and markets for their industrial products. In 1898, the United States extended its imperial reach after it took control of Puerto Rico, Guam, and the Philippines following the Spanish-American War. Hawaii had already been annexed that year, and the United States continued to expand its influence in the Caribbean and Latin America. Though motivated by trade and profit, imperialists also asserted it was the "white man's burden" to bring the benefits of civilization, including Christianity, to inferior peoples of color around the world.

Whites regarded nonwhites as primitives, even as curiosities to be displayed as spectacles, as was vividly evident at contemporary world's fairs. The 1900 Paris World's Fair, called the Exposition Universelle, presented human zoos, or "Negro Villages," with caged Africans in their "natural" surroundings. At the 1904 St. Louis World's Fair, the "Philippine Reservation" re-created the habitat and lifestyle of the Igorot people to highlight the alleged benefits U.S. governance would bring. Also on display at this fair were the defeated Apache warrior Geronimo, now a prisoner of war, and other conquered Apaches in a tepee village, and Ota Benga, a diminutive Congolese Mbuti, who would later be exhibited in the monkey house at New York City's Bronx Zoo. Protests from Black clergy closed the exhibit at the zoo. "Our race, we think, is depressed enough," wrote James H. Gordon, chairman of the Colored Baptist Ministers' Conference, in the *New York Times*, "without exhibiting one of us with the apes. We think we are worthy of being considered human beings, with souls."[6]

The zoo's backers and board of directors included distinguished anthropologists and zoologists who promoted

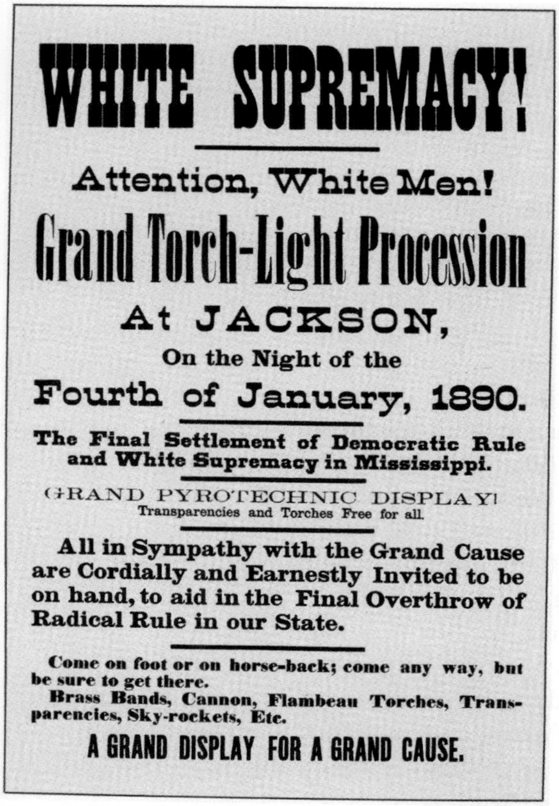
WHITE SUPREMACY!
Attention, White Men!
Grand Torch-Light Procession
At JACKSON,
On the Night of the
Fourth of January, 1890.
The Final Settlement of Democratic Rule and White Supremacy in Mississippi.
GRAND PYROTECHNIC DISPLAY!
Transparencies and Torches Free for all.
All in Sympathy with the Grand Cause are Cordially and Earnestly Invited to be on hand, to aid in the Final Overthrow of Radical Rule in our State.
Come on foot or on horse-back; come any way, but be sure to get there.
Brass Bands, Cannon, Flambeau Torches, Transparencies, Sky-rockets, Etc.
A GRAND DISPLAY FOR A GRAND CAUSE.

White Supremacy
This potent ad graphically illustrates the role of racist intimidation and terrorization in the 1890 campaign to disfranchise Blacks in Mississippi and throughout the South. This kind of campaign was a pillar of the highly orchestrated, formal restoration of white rule in the post-Reconstruction South and the institutionalization of Jim Crow domination. **What was the purpose of this poster?** *Granger/Granger — All rights reserved.*

theories of race and human evolution that drew on craniology studies and Charles Darwin's ideas about natural selection. The view that categorized human populations hierarchically by race and contended that races evolved unequally is today known as **scientific racism** and is recognized as a reflection of white supremacist thinking. In the late nineteenth and early twentieth centuries, the academic establishment supported this pseudoscience. Anthropologists studying so-called primitives concluded that Anglo-Saxons (those most often doing the classifying) were the most advanced humans, while Negroes were at the bottom of the evolutionary scale. Sociologists, psychologists, and pathologists attributed inherent mental and moral characteristics to each race. Again, Anglo-Saxons were mentally and physically superior, while Negroes were believed to have limited intelligence, a tendency toward criminality, and a vulnerability to disease.

scientific racism
Pseudoscientific yet powerful notions of white superiority endorsed by most of the academic and scientific establishment until well into the twentieth century.

AP® skills

Applying Disciplinary Knowledge: What justification was used to limit the political and social rights of Black Americans?

Pseudoscientific theories of racial evolution reinforced notions of white supremacy. Through natural selection, or "the survival of the fittest," Caucasians had risen to the top, according to the scientific establishment. As the most advanced and civilized race, their economic and political dominance of the world was both inevitable and justified. This view, known as **Social Darwinism**, also supported the economic and social order, in which Blacks were deemed fit only for field work, hard labor, and domestic service. Welfare or assistance to Black people, or to the poor generally, was in this view misguided, because those who resided at the bottom of the social hierarchy were fulfilling their natural destiny and thus deserved no better. Wealth and power would naturally go to the fittest, and neither government nor society should interfere.

Social Darwinism
The idea that the evolutionary notion of the survival of the fittest applies to society and the economy, used to justify white domination of both.

But according to this view, government could and should keep the races from mixing, lest the strength of the white race be diluted by inferior races. Jim Crow laws were, of course, one way to do this. To further ensure against racial mixing, a majority of states, not only southern ones, passed anti-miscegenation laws prohibiting interracial sex and marriage. In addition, these states sought to police what was called "racial integrity" by determining who was white and who was Black. Older categorizations had defined race by fractions: a "quadroon" was one-quarter Black (had one Black grandparent); an "octoroon," such as Homer Plessy, was one-eighth Black. Now states adopted the one-drop rule: one drop of Black blood made a person Black. To prevent "black blood" from polluting the white race, state registrars of vital statistics kept track of lineage, and birth records were required to state whether a newborn was white or Black. Marriages were also regulated. South Carolina's 1895 law forbade anyone with one Black great-grandparent to marry a white person. Because state laws differed, moving from one state to another could delegitimize a marriage and the couple's children.

AP® skills

Applying Disciplinary Knowledge: How did race as a social construct evolve during the Jim Crow era?

This line of reasoning braced racist public policies and practices, such as those justifying segregated schools throughout the country, and helped shape white attitudes and practices toward other peoples of color living in the United States. The widespread and virulent idea of white supremacy led to the Chinese Exclusion Act of 1882, which barred immigration from China.

Disfranchisement and Political Activism

In politics, new voting regulations and practices that disfranchised Black men demonstrated the deep-seated commitment to white supremacy. Many of these new policies also disfranchised large numbers of poor white men, seen by white elites as ignorant and unsuited to political participation. Elite white men viewed politics as their special racial and class preserve. In the South, the Democratic Party dominated, and it sought to prevent Black male voters from becoming a voting bloc that might be exploited by one white faction against another. State legislatures also drew district lines to minimize Black voting strength. The myth of the corrupt Black voter — a persistent charge that had been used to undermine Black political participation during Reconstruction — justified disfranchisement. So did **progressivism** — a reform movement that sought to cleanse politics of corruption and bring efficiency to American political life. In the North, progressives tried to break the power of big-city political bosses. In the South, white progressives targeted Black politicians and voters. The ideology of the New South, which promoted the region as forward looking, industrializing, urbanizing, and modernizing, meshed with the ideologies of progressivism and white supremacy.

AP® skills

Applying Disciplinary Knowledge: How did elite white men gain political power during this era?

progressivism
A wide-ranging reform movement that sought to eliminate corruption, bring efficiency to American political and economic life, and improve society.

Wherever violence, intimidation, and coercion did not prevent Black men from exercising the franchise, southern white chicanery — including moving polling places, stuffing ballot boxes, buying and manipulating Black voters, and destroying Black ballots — undermined the black vote. South Carolina's notorious 1882 "eight box law" demanded that voters put separate ballots for each particular issue or candidate in a specially marked box. Many voters, Black and white, had their entire ballots disqualified for failing to follow the rules. Black and many poor white voters were excluded from the Democratic Party when it incorporated itself as a private club that permitted only members to vote in primary elections. In what soon came to be known as a **white primary** — a primary election that effectively excluded Blacks — southern Democrats selected the white candidates who would run on their slate in the general election. Then, because the Democratic Party completely dominated southern politics, whoever won its primary inevitably won the election, too.

white primary
A state primary election in the Democratic Party–controlled South in which the party functioned as a private club that determined its own membership and was thus able to exclude Blacks. This practice was outlawed by *Smith v. Allwright* in 1944.

Other strategies for disfranchising Black voters were written into law. Poll taxes — payments required to vote — were so high as to discourage voting, especially by the poor, and abuses such as shifting payment locations and times further burdened Black voters. Literacy tests required reading and writing sections of the state constitution, and "understanding clauses" demanded that potential voters explain the meaning of often technical constitutional clauses. The fact that white registrars decided who passed these tests and who did not meant that potential Black voters were almost always disqualified. Grandfather clauses limited the right to vote to males who could vote before 1867 and to their sons and grandsons, thus effectively eliminating Black men.

AP® exam tip

Be sure you can describe the measures through which Black voting was suppressed after Reconstruction, including poll taxes, literacy tests, and grandfather clauses.

In 1890, Mississippi's new constitution included a poll tax, a literacy test, and an understanding clause; the U.S. Supreme Court upheld this disfranchisement model in *Williams v. Mississippi* (1898). A decade later, similar voting laws were in place throughout the South, and their effect was dramatic. Before Louisiana's disfranchisement statutes were passed in 1897 and 1898, the state had more than 130,000 Black voters; after the laws were in place, only a little more than 1,300 Black voters remained. Before disfranchisement, Black voters constituted a majority in twenty-six Louisiana parishes; after disfranchisement, they formed a majority in none. Black protest against these discriminatory measures proved unsuccessful.

AP® skills

Applying Disciplinary Knowledge: How did limiting economic opportunity contribute to disfranchisement?

This effective removal of southern Black men from politics came just as agrarian protest movements in the South and Midwest appeared poised to bring Black and white farmers together in a challenge to powerful railroad, financial, and corporate interests. All farmers had been affected by declining crop and commodity prices, especially those for cotton, and by escalating indebtedness. To outmaneuver corporate monopolies through cooperative purchasing and marketing arrangements, farmers established Farmers' Alliances, and some dreamed of a farm-labor coalition that would be inclusive in its call for unified action. But internal divisions were apparent. The Southern Farmers' Alliance (SFA) did not admit Blacks, for example, and in 1886, the **Colored Farmers' Alliance (CFA)** was organized in response. By 1891, the CFA had more than one million members, most of them landless farmers or day laborers, who had a different perspective from that of the white farmers who owned land and hired laborers.

Colored Farmers' Alliance (CFA)
A late-nineteenth-century organization comprised of African American farmers and farm workers, which fought for farmers' rights.

Yet racial divisions persisted when both alliances supported the Populist Party, which grew rapidly in the early 1890s by advocating federal price supports for crops as well as a fairer banking system, currency reform, and railroad regulation. In the 1896 presidential election, the Populists nominated the Democratic candidate, William Jennings Bryan, and when he lost to Republican William McKinley, the Populist Party dissolved.

AP® skills

Applying Disciplinary Knowledge: Why was the Farmers' Alliance formed?

In North Carolina, however, Black and white Populists had united with Republicans to send the Black lawyer George Henry White to the U.S. House of Representatives and win some local and state contests. But the specter of Black and white cooperation threatened southern white elites, and by 1898, the Democrats had beaten back collaborative interracial politics everywhere in the state except Wilmington. A small city that was more than two-thirds Black, Wilmington had a vibrant Black community and a growing Black professional class. In 1898, a white insurrection there took back white rule after Alexander Manly, editor of the *Daily Record* and a Hampton Institute graduate, outraged whites with an editorial arguing that interracial relationships between poor white women and poor Black men were often consensual. In what became known as the **Wilmington Insurrection**, whites killed scores of Blacks and destroyed Black property, including the premises of the *Daily Record*. Enough Blacks were driven out of the city to end their demographic majority. The white insurrectionists overthrew the local government and replaced it with their handpicked leaders.

Wilmington Insurrection (1898)
A race riot in Wilmington, North Carolina, that restored white political power in the city and signaled the end of biracial politics in the city and state.

AP® skills

Applying Disciplinary Knowledge: What caused the Wilmington Insurrection?

Lynching and the Campaign against It

lynching
The public murder, by a lawless mob, of an individual alleged to have committed a crime or a breach of social custom.

The Wilmington Insurrection showed how far whites were willing to go to subordinate Blacks, especially to suppress their rights. When legal means did not suffice, they used intimidation and violence — even murder. Perhaps the most horrific form of violence was **lynching**, the public murder, often a hanging, of an individual by a mob acting outside the law. (See AP® Working with Sources: Agency and Constraint, pp. 419–27.) "Lynching," stated the white investigative journalist Ray Stannard Baker in an article in *McClure's Magazine* in January 1905, "is not a Southern Crime, nor a Western crime, nor a Northern crime: it is an American crime."[7] But a disproportionate number of lynchings took place in the South, and a disproportionate number of the victims were Black (Map 10.2). In 1908, Baker published lynching statistics and concluded that

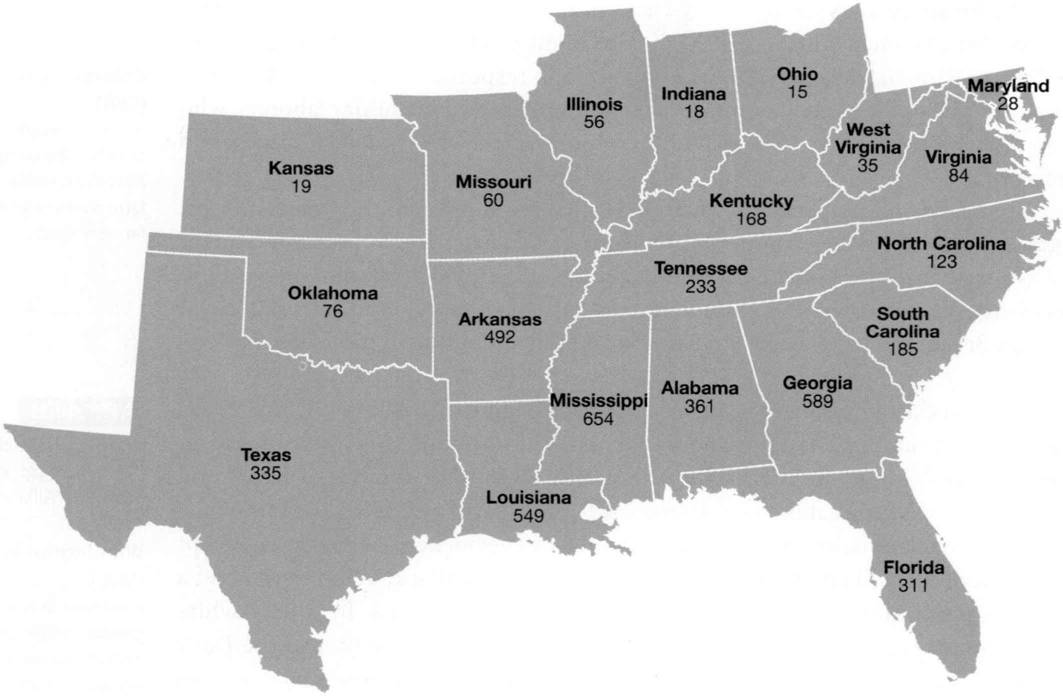

MAP 10.2 African American Lynching Victims by State, 1877–1950

Bryan Stevenson and his colleagues at the Equal Justice Initiative (EJI) have shed new light on the extent of racial terror lynching between 1877 and 1950. This map shows their findings on the states with the highest numbers, but lynching also occurred in other states on a smaller scale. The EJI's National Memorial for Peace and Justice, which opened in 2018, is dedicated to racial terror lynching victims and the larger history of racial inequality and injustice. **How can this map be used to support the claims Ray Stannard Baker made about lynching in 1905 (p. 376) and 1908 (p. 377)?**

BY THE NUMBERS Lynchings Every Five Years, 1885–1950

This graph shows the intensity of lynching in the late nineteenth and early twentieth centuries, with a second spike in the years following World War I (to be discussed in the next chapter). Victims were killed without trial for alleged criminal behavior and were also murdered for perceived insults to white people and other violations of the racial hierarchy. **Use the graph to describe the experiences of Black Americans in the South.** *Data from The Equal Justice Initiative.*

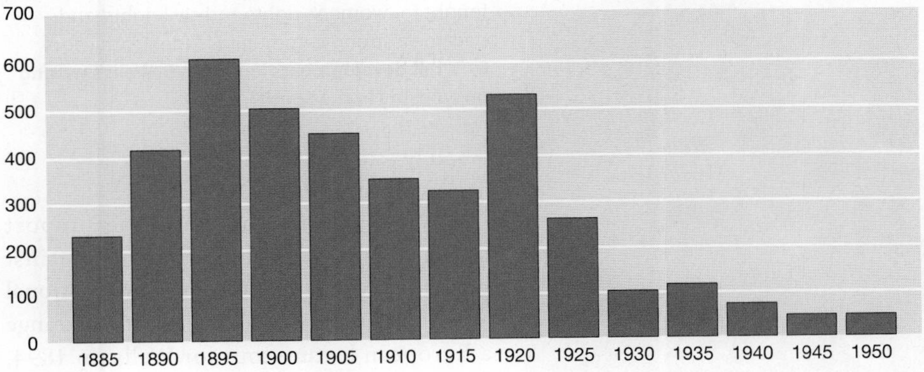

"Mississippi, Alabama, Louisiana and Georgia — the black belt states — are thus seen to have the worst records."[8] For southern whites, the lynching of Blacks was a violent form of social control that had far less to do with punishing Black crimes than with terrorizing Blacks into subordination. (See By the Numbers: Lynchings Every Five Years, 1885–1950.)

AP® skills

Applying Disciplinary Knowledge: What purpose did lynching serve for southern whites?

For Ida B. Wells, lynching assumed a profoundly personal meaning after three of her friends — Thomas Moss, Calvin McDowell, and William Stewart — were lynched. The episode began in a Black community on the outskirts of Memphis, where the Black People's Grocery Company competed with a white grocery store. Feuds and street fights escalated into armed attacks, and when whites were injured, dozens of Blacks were jailed. On March 9, 1892, a white mob broke into the jail; dragged Moss, McDowell, and Stewart from their cells; took them to a field outside the city; and shot them. Afterward, they gouged out McDowell's eyes.[9]

In the Memphis *Free Speech and Headlight*, the newspaper she co-owned, Wells lashed out against the lynching and criticized Memphis officials for not identifying the lynchers. She also revealed findings from research into the alleged causes of lynchings: although victims were most often thought to have raped a white woman, these charges were usually false. Wells's articles enraged the white Memphis establishment, but they came to the attention of the Black editor T. Thomas Fortune, who reprinted them in his newspaper, the *New York Age*. Fortune soon hired Wells to write for his paper and helped her publish her research in a pamphlet titled *Southern Horrors: Lynch Law in All Its Phases* (1892).

Ida B. Wells

In an era perhaps best known for a Booker T. Washington–style accommodationism, Ida B. Wells was among those contemporary African American leaders who offered a militant alternative. This fiery journalist, leader, and activist helped spearhead the campaign against lynching, fought for women's rights and civil rights, and became a strong community leader in Chicago. **What developments led to Ida B. Wells's writing on lynching in the South?** *Private Collection/Prismatic Pictures/Bridgeman Images.*

With Fortune's help and the support of Black women, Wells's campaign against lynching received national and international attention. Frederick Douglass helped arrange a European lecture tour for Wells. In 1894, she helped found the British Anti-Lynching Committee. Douglass also collaborated with Wells on a pamphlet explaining the Black boycott of the 1893 Chicago World's Fair, where white officials rebuffed efforts to include an exhibit on Black progress since emancipation but embraced an ethnographic African village featuring Dahomeyans.[10] In 1895, Wells published *A Red Record*, a more formal study of lynching statistics and the alleged causes of lynchings. Her approach was like that of white progressive reformers who sought to end corruption and lawlessness by exposing the facts. In this, she was disappointed, but her efforts, like those of her Black contemporaries — especially W. E. B. Du Bois and *Boston Guardian* editor William Monroe Trotter — kept the Black protest tradition alive.

AP® skills

Applying Disciplinary Knowledge: Explain what motivated Wells to write *Southern Horrors*.

AP® skills

Applying Disciplinary Knowledge: What was the effect of Wells's campaign against lynching? Describe two conclusions she drew from her investigation of lynching in *A Red Record*?

Wells's analysis of lynching refuted the reasons defenders used to rationalize the practice: to crush Black rebellion, to remove corrupt Black voters and officials, and, most important, to protect white women from Black male rapists. In each case, as Wells showed, the alleged defense was false. Most especially, she argued that the rape of a white woman by a Black man was rare. In fact, it was Black women's virtue that needed to be protected, notably from white men. Her analysis also demonstrated that, contrary to common belief, lynchings often targeted successful Blacks, not misfits and criminals, and occurred not in out-of-the-way settings with weak police and court systems, but in places where such systems were strong. In short, the police and courts that did almost nothing to protect Blacks were often complicit in these murders.

Freedom's First Generation

What were the causes of heightened racial violence in the early twentieth century, and how did African Americans respond to white supremacist attacks?

How did groundbreaking texts — and the dialogue these texts generated — portray Black humanity and the effects of racism on African Americans?

The network of Black activists Wells drew on to support her antilynching campaign was much like the network of Black activists who, before and during the Civil War, mobilized to end slavery and work for equal rights. As in the old antebellum crusade, many activists emerging from freedom's first generation were women. With an emphasis on racial solidarity, they committed themselves to racial advancement. Often part of an emerging southern Black middle class, they worked with business leaders, newspaper editors, and preachers to strengthen Black families and build independent communities. Members of freedom's first generation saw themselves as standing on the shoulders of those who had gone before and committed themselves to making life better for future generations as well as their own generation. At the turn of the twentieth century, a flowering of Black cultural expressions, some new, testified to the creativity unleashed by freedom.

Black Women and Men in the Era of Jim Crow

Wells's candid analysis of the causes of lynching specifically, and her uncompromising activism generally, drew both admirers and critics. One critic was a prominent white Missouri journalist who, in a private letter to one of Wells's British supporters, slandered the morality of Black women, characterizing them as prostitutes. Passed along to Josephine St. Pierre Ruffin, editor of the *Woman's Era*, the nation's first Black women's newspaper, the letter caused an uproar. Ruffin circulated it among her elite Black women friends throughout the North. The result was a call for a national meeting. "There was a time when our mothers and sisters could not protect themselves from such beasts," wrote one who attended the meeting in Boston in 1895, "but a new era has begun and we propose to defend ourselves."[11] Led by Margaret Murray Washington, the wife of Booker T. Washington, the attendees established the National Federation of Afro-American Women, which the next year merged with the National League of Colored Women to form the **National Association of Colored Women (NACW)**. One delegate to the NACW's inaugural meeting in July 1896, in Washington, D.C., was Harriet Tubman, the seventy-five-year-old heroine of the Underground Railroad. The poet Frances Ellen Watkins Harper, then in her early seventies, was also a founding member. The organization's leaders were, however, members of a new generation of women who were determined not only to defend the honor of Black women, but also to advance the cause of their race.

Mary Church Terrell, an Oberlin graduate and a teacher of Latin at Washington's highly regarded M Street High School, was elected NACW president. Like many of her generation, she was the child of formerly enslaved people, but her parents were

National Association of Colored Women (NACW)
A federation of Black women's clubs founded in 1896 to promote the interrelated uplift of Black women and Black people.

AP® skills

Applying Disciplinary Knowledge: Why did the National Association of Colored Women form?

AP® exam tip

Be sure you can describe the ways that Black women promoted the advancement of African Americans. What examples in this chapter can you use to support this description?

freed by the time she was born and were successful in business. Thus, she grew up in an elite Memphis family that stressed education and achievement. With confidence gained through education and organizing skills honed in church work, she and other prominent women assumed new leadership roles in the era of Jim Crow discrimination and disfranchisement that undercut Black male leadership. They dedicated themselves to **uplift** — the notion that Blacks themselves must take primary responsibility for Black progress.

uplift
The idea that racial progress demands autonomous Black efforts; especially seen as the responsibility of the more fortunate of the race to help lift up the less fortunate.

The NACW epitomized the increasing emphasis placed by blacks of the era on the "politics of respectability": the notion that striving for and achieving respectability promoted the cause of their race.[12] The NACW and other club organizations dedicated themselves to programs of self-help and, in the words of Fannie Barrier Williams, to the "social reconstruction" of "the great masses of the colored women in this country." These less fortunate "sisters" of Black club women needed training and time "to complete the work of emancipation," explained Williams, a leader of the Black women's club movement who also did social welfare work in Chicago. She recalled the motivations behind the movement: "Better homes, better schools, better protection for girls of scant home training, better sanitary conditions, better opportunities for competent young women to gain employment, and the need of being better known to the American people appealed to the conscience of progressive colored women from many communities."[13]

AP® skills

Applying Disciplinary Knowledge: What was the mission of the NACW?

A key impetus for the formation of the NACW was the agitation surrounding Wells's research on lynching, but the abolishment of lynching was only one of the organization's objectives. Taking as its motto "Lifting as We Climb," the NACW developed a broad range of programs for advancing Black education through fundraising, scholarships, and grants and for offering community-based assistance to Black women in areas such as jobs, child care, temperance, health, and hygiene. The federation also supported woman suffrage and fought discriminatory Jim Crow laws and practices, including the convict lease system that forced Black people to work on plantations and factories. At its height, around 1920, it had 100,000 members.

Although Wells was a founding member of the NACW, she was not an active member. Her lawsuits and outspokenness, especially her frank statements about women's virtue, made her a little too radical for many of the elite club women of the era, who preferred not to address matters of sexuality so openly. These women worried that behavior perceived to be unladylike might undermine their cause.[14] But the NACW was fully committed to service and self-respect through the kind of leadership advocated — and modeled — by Anna Julia Cooper, another Oberlin graduate teaching Latin at M Street High School, who had been a speaker at both the Boston and the Washington organizational meetings.

The lives of elite Black women — a new class in southern society — were distinct from the lives of those they sought to elevate. Overwhelmingly, Black women in the South had little time or energy for clubs. Those who lived in towns and cities worked outside the home for wages, which were usually about $2 a week. Most often they worked in white women's homes — as cooks, maids, nannies, and nurses. They might have several jobs, sewing for others or taking in laundry on the side. As many as one-fourth of them were widows, and almost 30 percent were heads of households. Black women typically outlived Black men, and in southern cities the ratio of Black men to Black women was 87:100. The years between 1880 and 1900 saw the fertility rates of urban Black women decline. Discrimination and violence against Black men, who seldom made enough money on their own to support families, undermined urban Black family life. In towns and cities, Black men performed low-paying, unskilled, dirty, and physically demanding jobs such as hauling, loading, and unloading goods, and cleaning streets, yards, gardens, buildings, and factories. Hard labor compromised their health and shortened their lives. Thus, Black women typically had to help sustain their families financially.

AP® exam tip

Be prepared to explain why Black women entered the workforce at this time. You should also be able to describe the goals of Black women's labor organizing.

In Atlanta, there were enough Black washerwomen to constitute a labor network with potential for collective action, and in early July 1881, twenty washerwomen met in a church to form the Washing Society and demand higher wages. They called for a strike on July 19, and with the support of Black churches, mutual aid societies, and fraternal organizations, three thousand workers joined in. Despite arrests and threats of tax increases and license fees, the washerwomen did not budge. In the end, they got their raise, and their collective action inspired cooks, maids, and nurses to make similar demands.

AP® skills

Applying Disciplinary Knowledge: How did Black women take collective action in Atlanta in 1881? How did the labor conditions of urban Black women compare to those of rural Black women at this time?

Black women in rural areas lacked such opportunities for collective action. The wives and daughters of sharecroppers and tenant farmers worked around the clock. In the early morning, they prepared a typical breakfast of salt pork, molasses, and corn bread, which they would sometimes have to deliver to the fields, where family members were already at work. At noon, the same meal was carried to the fields. During planting season, women might join their husbands and children in the fields. Throughout the day and evening, women sewed, mended, washed, and cleaned; older women cared for children, and mothers nursed babies. They tended small plots, where they grew vegetables and fruits, or raised chickens and hogs to feed their families or supplement their income. According to the wife of one Mississippi farmer, many women did double duty — "a man's share in the field, and a woman's part at home."[15] As Rosina Hoard of North Carolina explained, "I had my house work and de cookin' to do and to look after de chillun, but I'd go out and still pick my two hunnert pounds ob cotton a day."[16]

For southern Black men toiling in the fields, work was also nonstop. They were responsible for the cash crop — cotton, tobacco, rice, or sugar, depending on the region — and they supplemented their families' diets by hunting and fishing. No matter how hard they worked, however, they rarely got ahead. "Dem sharecroppuhs is jes like slaves," observed Archie Booker, a formerly enslaved man from Virginia. "Dey don' know slavery is ovuh."[17] Another Black man summed it up this way: "White man

Rural Women Washing
Doing the laundry was an extremely labor-intensive task for rural Black women. Although this photograph, from around 1900, shows others helping out, Black women all too often had to combine several jobs at once, such as looking after children and doing the laundry for their own family and for white families. This image also conveys a tension between the dignity of such work and its harshness. **How can this image be used to support an explanation of the intersectionality of Black women around the turn of the twentieth century?**

sit down whole year; Nigger work day and night and make crop; Nigger hardly gits bread and meat; white man sittin' down gits all. It's wrong."[18]

Increasingly, Blacks in the rural South were ensnared in a system of cyclical indebtedness to the landowners whose fields they worked as sharecroppers and to the storeowners from whom they bought supplies. All too often the landowner and the storeowner were the same person. Added to the array of laws and customs that worked against their economic independence was a condition known as **debt peonage**, an entanglement from which they almost never escaped. In this system, those who owed fines and faced prison sentences for infractions of labor contracts or vagrancy laws sold their labor to a third party in exchange for payment of their debts. (See AP® Working with Sources: Agency and Constraint, pp. 419–27.) Ending debt peonage was another cause advocated by racial uplift organizations like the NACW.

debt peonage
A system of forced labor requiring servitude in exchange for payment of one's debts. This system trapped thousands of Black agricultural workers in the South in conditions not unlike those of slavery.

Black Communities in the Cities of the New South

When twenty-one-year-old Ida B. Wells moved to Memphis in 1883, she chose city life over life in Holly Springs, Mississippi, the small town where she had been raised. She was not alone. Between 1880 and 1910, an increasing number of southern Black women, men, and families moved to the cities of the New South, where white progressives were promoting growth and industry. Black women and men helped meet the labor and service needs of urban growth, but they had much to gain as well. For them, cities such as Richmond, Nashville, Atlanta, and Washington, D.C., offered better lives, especially better opportunities for education and employment, as well as the rich array of social, cultural, and intellectual activities that concentrations of Black residents made possible. Between 1880 and 1890, Nashville's Black population grew from 16,337 to more than 29,400, and Atlanta's grew from 16,330 to roughly 28,100.

These burgeoning Black urban communities were what W. E. B. Du Bois described as a "group economy" — "a closed economic circle, largely independent of surrounding whites." He reflected, "There used to be Negro business men in Northern cities and a few even in Southern cities, but they catered to white trade; the Negro business man to-day caters to colored trade. . . . In every city in the United States which has considerable Negro population, the colored group is serving itself in religion, medical care, legal advice and often educating its children. In growing degree also it is serving itself in insurance, houses, books, amusements."[19]

Richmond offers one example. The Black population of the former Confederate capital grew from 27,800 to 46,700 between 1880 and 1910. The city had begun to industrialize before the Civil War, and after the war, Black workers in the construction trades helped rebuild the city as a rail and industrial center. Blacks also worked in the city's long-standing tobacco industry. African Americans lived primarily in Jackson Ward, a neighborhood a mile northwest of the state capitol. Residents liked to think of it as "the Black Wall Street of America." A 1907 publication called *Souvenir Views: Negro Enterprises and Residences* listed four large insurance companies, four banks, four drugstores, five weekly newspapers, fourteen physicians, four dentists, two real estate agents, eight lawyers, ten large barbershops, four butchers, two ice dealers, five paperhangers, three confectionery stores and ice cream manufacturers, two "electric power" shoe repairers, one machinist, more than fifty dressmakers, five transfer companies (short-distance transportation companies), ninety public school teachers, six paint contractors, five building contractors, two brick contractors, two photographers, three "first-class tailors," one grocery, two fish and game stores, one liquor store, one wood and coal yard, one jeweler, one tinner, two upholsterers, two steam laundries, two first-class hotels, two hospitals, one cigar factory, one shoe store, one clothing and gents' "furnishing" store, one dry goods and millinery store, five funeral directors and embalmers, two colleges, one business college, seventeen printers, one automobile company, and four "first-class clubs."[20] This was indeed a lively and self-sufficient city within a city.

AP® skills

Applying Disciplinary Knowledge: Describe how life changed for Black Americans in Richmond, Virginia, during the late nineteenth and early twentieth centuries. Why are these changes significant?

Of the five Black newspapers, the best known was the Richmond *Planet*, a weekly founded in 1883 and edited by John Mitchell Jr. Like so many others in freedom's first generation, Mitchell was born in slavery — in 1863 outside Richmond. In the city, he became a teacher and then an editor, and in the pages of the *Planet*, he addressed the issues of the day, including investigating lynchings and fighting against Black disfranchisement in Virginia. In 1898, he voiced opposition to the Spanish-American War, warning that U.S. control of the Philippines would subject Filipinos to the same kind of racial repression that dominated the South.

AP® skills

Applying Disciplinary Knowledge: Why is the St. Luke Penny Savings Bank historically significant?

Of the four banks, one was the Mechanics Savings Bank, founded by Mitchell in 1902. Another was the St. Luke Penny Savings Bank (later the Consolidated Bank and Trust Company), chartered by Maggie L. Walker in 1903. The nation's first Black woman bank president, Walker was born to formerly enslaved parents in 1867. Like so many other Black women of her generation, she was a teacher — a graduate of the Richmond Colored Normal School. But she also took classes in sales and accounting, and with her keen business sense, she revitalized the Richmond branch of the Independent Order of St. Luke, which had been founded in 1867 as a women's sickness and death benefit association. Led by Walker, this branch was a springboard for an array of enterprises, including a women's insurance company, a department store, a newspaper called the *St. Luke Herald*, a youth educational loan program, and a delinquent girls' school. A vice president of the NACW, Walker was committed to racial uplift and progressive reform. Her good friend Mary McLeod Bethune often visited her in Richmond. Bethune, who had founded the Daytona Normal and Industrial Institute for Negro Girls in Florida in 1904, was also an NACW officer.

Another bank was the True Reformers Bank, founded in 1888 by the Reverend William Washington Browne, an enslaved man from Georgia who escaped to serve in the Union army. A temperance advocate, Browne first established a temperance society in Richmond that offered members life insurance. Expanding to a bank, the True Reformers provided loans and banking services, and its three-story building, built in 1891, had meeting rooms and a concert hall for lectures and entertainment. In 1893, the True Reformers started a newspaper. When Browne died in 1897, the Reverend William Lee Taylor became president of the bank and affiliated enterprises, which included a real estate agency and a retirement home. Unfortunately, owing largely to mismanagement and scandal, the bank closed in 1910.

There were thirty-one churches in Jackson Ward in 1907, twenty-three of them Baptist. The Sixth Mount Zion Baptist Church had been founded in 1867 by the enslaved preacher John Jasper, who later became famous for his "De Sun Do Move" sermon, which he delivered more than 250 times, once before the Virginia General Assembly. Like so many other Black churches, Sixth Mount Zion provided community services to the elderly and destitute. The needs of the poor were also looked after by the Richmond Neighborhood Association and the Richmond Welfare League, founded in 1913 and 1914, respectively. They later joined with other organizations to affiliate with the National Urban League, which had been founded in New York in 1910.

The Freedmen's Bureau established the Richmond Colored Normal School (later Armstrong High School) in 1865; the school became part of the Richmond school system in 1876. In 1865, the American Baptist Home Mission Society founded Virginia Union (later Virginia Union University) in Richmond with a grant from the Freedmen's Bureau. Created in 1882 in nearby Chesterfield County, the Virginia Normal and Collegiate (later Industrial) Institute became Virginia State College for Negroes in 1930 and Virginia State University in 1979. It was funded by the State of Virginia until designated a land-grant college under the Land-Grant College Act of 1890, which required states to open land-grant colleges to all races or establish separate Black colleges emphasizing agriculture and the "mechanic arts." Nearby, too, was the Virginia Industrial School for Colored Girls, set up in 1915 by Janie Porter Barrett.

Emancipation Day Parade
Excitement and joviality characterized Emancipation Day parades in Richmond, Virginia, and in Black communities throughout the United States. These parades, which drew participants and onlookers from miles around, featured marching bands, dignitaries, and local groups. Related activities included formal speeches, cultural performances, picnics, and parties. **What details from this photo suggest the sense of racial solidarity and pride fostered by celebrations like this one?** *Library of Congress, Prints and Photographs Division, LC-D401-18421.*

As president of the Virginia State Federation of Colored Women's Clubs, Barrett had raised funds for this home for delinquent girls, which taught self-direction and basic job skills.

On April 8, 1905, the Richmond *Planet* reported on that year's Emancipation Day celebration in Richmond: "The colored people of this city celebrated the fortieth year of their emancipation on last Monday with a large parade. Excursionists from other cities swelled the crowd and five bands of music mustered into service." Speeches at the Broad Street Baseball Park followed the parade, and in the evening, a banquet and a performance by a "colored" opera company delighted attendees. "The affair was a success," the *Planet* reported, "and the best of good-feeling prevailed."[21]

Good feelings did not always prevail in Richmond, however. Just one year earlier, after the Virginia Passenger and Power Company announced that it would segregate seating on its electric streetcars, the Black community had organized a streetcar boycott. John Mitchell Jr. in the *Planet* and Maggie Walker in the *St. Luke Herald* urged readers to join the boycott. For more than a year, the Black population of Richmond stayed off the city's streetcars, but the streetcar company did not cave in. Instead, the Virginia General Assembly, which in 1904 allowed but did not require streetcar segregation, made the practice mandatory in 1906.

Nevertheless, for the Black people of Richmond, the power of cooperative action had been demonstrated. Black workers in the city's tobacco industry had long joined together in trade unions that recognized the common interests of workers and sought to elevate the dignity of work. But possibilities for interracial unionism had died with the demise of the Knights of Labor in the late 1880s, and Black locals were not affiliated with the National Tobacco Workers' Union of America, an affiliate of the American Federation of Labor, which excluded Blacks. Like so much else in the Jim Crow era, the shared interests of the working class did not cross the color line.

AP® skills

Applying Disciplinary Knowledge: Why did the Black community rally behind Jack Johnson?

In July 1910, Black Richmond united with all of Black America in celebrating the victory of world heavyweight boxing champion Jack Johnson over his white opponent, Jim Jeffries, in Reno, Nevada, in what was billed as the "fight of the century." "Jack Johnson Travels in Style," boasted the Richmond *Planet* on July 16: "Was Offered over $300,000 to Fake the Fight — Wouldn't Give Up the Desire of a Life-time."[22] Johnson's defense of his title against Jeffries had been hyped by both the white and Black press as a contest for racial supremacy. In 1908, with his commanding victory over the reigning champion, the Australian boxer Tommy Burns, Johnson had delivered a resounding blow against the notion of white supremacy. Simultaneously, he became the first Black man to hold the title of world heavyweight boxing champion — an achievement symbolic of global masculine supremacy. Indeed, whenever the hard-hitting and flamboyant Johnson, who was champion from 1908 to 1915, defeated a white opponent, Black Americans proclaimed a victory for their race. In the *Planet*, Lucille Watkins described her feelings in a poem: "Jack Johnson, we have waited long for you / To grow our prayers in this single blow."[23] White response to the Johnson–Jeffries match was swift. Immediately after the fight, a wave of anti-Black violence swept over the country, leaving thirteen Blacks dead and hundreds injured.

Black Richmond exemplified the thriving economic, social, religious, and cultural life that African Americans created in the cities of the New South despite the constraints of Jim Crow. W. E. B. Du Bois found the same spirit animating Durham, North Carolina, and in a 1912 essay titled "The Upbuilding of Black Durham," he praised Black Durham's progress since emancipation. Attributing the city's success to the "vision, knowledge, thrift, and efficiency" of its leaders, he singled out "a minister with college training, a physician with professional training, and a barber who saved his money," along with "a bright hustling young graduate of the public schools."[24] Throughout the cities of the South, the new Black middle class — including business people, entrepreneurs, editors, preachers, and teachers — dedicated themselves to moral reform, literary and cultural affairs, civic improvements, economic development, and mutual welfare. Black civic leaders built networks within their communities and with other communities. They worked with whites to secure concessions, such as jobs and government support for Black schools and services for Black neighborhoods, but they knew that the most productive strategies for sustaining Black community life remained self-help and self-sufficiency.

New Cultural Expressions

In 1914, Jackson Ward's new Hippodrome Theater provided an elegant setting for Black entertainment. Among the illustrious performers who graced its stage was Richmond native Bill Robinson, known to the world as Bojangles. Born in the city in 1878 and soon orphaned, he ran away as a child to Washington, D.C., where minstrel shows fascinated him. He quickly learned the routines, and, incorporating juba and other dances into a rhythmic tap-dancing style, he became famous on the vaudeville circuit and later in films. His development of a unique stage character rooted in tap dance was only one of the new creative expressions that emerged as freedom's first generation established a rich social and cultural life.

> **AP® skills**
>
> **Applying Disciplinary Knowledge:** How did the uplift ideology play a role in Black entertainment during this era?

In San Francisco, street performers George Walker and Bert Williams combined their talents to become Black musical theater's best-known song-and-dance team. Mixing songs, jokes, pantomime, and dance, they took their show to New York, where, in white theaters with balcony seating for Blacks, funnyman Williams performed in blackface opposite straight man Walker. Their musical *The Gold Bug* (1896) popularized the cakewalk, an enslaved parody of white balls and social pretensions in which elegantly attired Black women and men, arm in arm, leaned way back and grandly strutted across the stage. Soon the cakewalk was a nationwide staple of dance and entertainment, and cakewalk contests were all the rage. Other Williams and Walker shows included *In Dahomey* (1903) and *Abyssinia* (1906), both composed by Will Marion Cook. Cook also composed *Clorindy, or The Origin of the Cakewalk* (1898) and *Jes Lak White Folks* (1899). Another composer for the Black musical stage was Bob Cole, known for *A Trip to Coontown* (1898) and for collaborations with the brothers James Weldon Johnson and John Rosamond Johnson, including *The Shoo-Fly Regiment* (1907).

Despite the racist constraints of American culture and the white-controlled theater world, Black artists of the musical stage fought hard to endow with depth and dignity the limited range of characters available to them. As Walker observed in 1909, "We want our folks, the Negroes, to like us. Over and above the money and the prestige is a love for the race. We feel that in a degree we represent the race and every hair's breadth of achievement we make is to its credit."[25] Many Black musical artists were college educated and classically trained and committed to the ideology of uplift. The Johnson brothers expressed this ideology in "Lift Every Voice and Sing," created in 1900 when John Rosamond Johnson set his brother James Weldon Johnson's poem to music: "Sing a song full of the faith that the dark past has taught us, / Sing a song full of the hope that the present has brought us; / Facing the rising sun / Of our new day begun, / Let us march on till victory is won."[26] The song was soon performed in Black churches and schools and at events around the nation, and in 1919, the NAACP adopted it as the Negro national anthem. (For the full lyrics of this song, see chapter 11, AP® Working with Sources: The Harlem/New Negro Renaissance, pp. 460–69.)

AP® exam tip

On the AP® Exam, you'll need to be able to explain how African American literature, poetry, and music encouraged African Americans to take pride in their heritage and cultural achievements.

In Memphis, cornet player and minstrel troupe leader William Christopher "W. C." Handy took a special interest in the mixed ballads (a combination of African American folk music and Anglo-American ballad often centered on a heroic figure like John Henry), field hollers, work songs, moans, and chants he heard in the cotton fields. The music that Handy heard and popularized was the blues, a rich and expressive musical genre dating back to the late nineteenth century and created largely by ordinary Black folk that explores the ups and downs of everyday life. "Southern Negroes sang about everything," Handy later wrote. "Trains, steamboats, steam whistles, sledge hammers, fast women, mean bosses, stubborn mules — all become subjects for their songs. . . . From these materials, they set the mood for what we now call blues."[27] The self-styled "Father of the Blues," Handy reworked this extraordinary vein of Black folk music into his own compositions, such as "St. Louis Blues" (1914), which made him and the blues famous.

Notable for a twelve-bar, three-line structure in which the second line repeats the first and the third line responds to the first two lines, blues songs were performed solo yet engaged the audience in a traditional call-and-response pattern. Ma Rainey, "the Mother of the Blues," was the biggest star on the tent-show circuit, which appealed largely to working-class and poor Blacks. With an earthy, riveting voice, she mesmerized audiences with songs such as "Moonshine Blues." The extraordinary impact of the blues on American music can be heard today in genres as diverse as country, rhythm and blues, rock 'n' roll, gospel, jazz, and soul.

AP® skills

Applying Disciplinary Knowledge: How did Ma Rainey leave a lasting impression on the music industry?

Jazz primarily took shape in turn-of-the-century New Orleans, where a distinctive musical culture showcased African roots: rhythmic complexity, improvisation,

***Bert Williams and George Walker in* In Dahomey**
Bert Williams was a pantomime and comic extraordinaire and a vaudeville superstar. Williams's blackface character, which drew upon the entertainment tradition of Blacks doing blackface minstrelsy, both epitomized and slyly undermined the clownish character he played. Between 1893 and 1909, Williams (second from right) performed in a series of pioneering and popular musical theater shows with partner George Walker (second from left), whose Black dandy character contrasted perfectly with Williams's oafish character. Williams's successful solo career, which included films as well as stints with the Ziegfeld Follies on Broadway, solidified his widespread fame. **How did Black entertainers reshape views of African Americans at the turn of the twentieth century?** *Photofest.*

call and response, and the separation of melody and beat, or swing. African American musicians such as cornetist and bandleader Charles "Buddy" Bolden used European brass horns to combine European harmonies with African polyrhythms in dance band music and drum ensembles. Bolden gave New Orleans jazz a strong blues grounding. Jazz pianist, composer, and arranger Jelly Roll Morton helped popularize jazz, especially in the 1920s. He was also a pioneer player of ragtime, a syncopated piano music made famous by Scott Joplin, the "King of Ragtime," who was born near Texarkana, Texas, and that was commonly associated with Sedalia and St. Louis, Missouri. Joplin's "Maple Leaf Rag" (1899) was one of the most influential and popular ragtime tunes.

Issues of racial identification and race struggle characterized the work of important Black writers of the period. Paul Laurence Dunbar contributed his writing talent to a number of musical stage shows, notably *Clorindy* and *In Dahomey*. But he made a name for himself, and a career, as a poet and writer of fiction. His poems in Black dialect catered to white tastes and stereotypes of happy enslaved people, and they garnered a national following. But Black readers were more likely to favor the currents of protest found in his antilynching poem "The Haunted Oak" and in the poem for

The Banjo Lesson, *1893*
Henry Ossawa Tanner's representation of an attentive male elder (perhaps a doting grandfather) lovingly teaching a young boy how to play the banjo offered a radical alternative to the common racist stereotypes of Black musicians, notably banjo players, as comic, even buffoonish, characters. This popular painting also debunked the myth of innate Black musicality by showing that Black musical talent required training and practice. Despite this warm and deeply humane portrayal of Black sociocultural life, some critics have lamented that most of Tanner's work was nonracial. **What message does this painting convey? Use at least one piece of evidence from the image to support your answer.** The Banjo Lesson, *by Henry Osawa Tanner, 1893, oil on canvas, 49 in. × 35½ in./ Hampton University Museum Collection, Hampton University, Hampton, Virginia.*

which he is best remembered today, "We Wear the Mask" (from his 1896 book *Lyrics of Lowly Life*), which deftly explores the realities behind the public faces put on by Blacks in their efforts to endure and rise above the racist constraints of the era.

Charles Chesnutt likewise attracted support from the white literary establishment, even though his works forthrightly portrayed the lives of southern Blacks. His book *The Marrow of Tradition* (1901) sparked controversy. The setting of the novel was the 1898 Wilmington Insurrection, which some of his relatives had survived. Among the themes it explored were mixed-race identity and racial justice. Like Chesnutt's final novel, *The Colonel's Dream* (1905), *The Marrow of Tradition* generated limited sales, dashing his hopes for a full-time literary career. Chesnutt shifted gears, focusing instead on his legal stenography business in Cleveland, his family, and less ambitious writing projects.

Painter Henry Ossawa Tanner, perhaps best known for *The Banjo Lesson* (1893), discovered as an art student that the racism of the American art establishment made it impossible to sustain a career in his native land. He settled instead in Paris, where he had a successful career that included painting biblical subjects.

Migration, Accommodation, and Protest

How did African American writers and activists respond to racism and anti-Black violence during the nadir?

What strategies for racial uplift (or social advancement) were proposed by African American writers, educators, and leaders at the turn of the twentieth century?

Despite Jim Crow, many Black southerners built satisfying personal lives and successful communities by emphasizing self-reliance and separatism. Some chose to leave the South, moving west to the freer environments of Oklahoma's Black towns and joining the Black army units stationed at western forts. Others went to West Africa, where they hoped to build new lives in an all-Black environment. Concurrently, two Black leaders articulated competing uplift strategies. Booker T. Washington advocated that Blacks accommodate to life in the segregated South while gaining the industrial and vocational training that could bring economic independence. This approach, he argued, would ultimately yield interracial as well as intraracial progress. W. E. B. Du Bois promoted economic self-sufficiency as well as agitation for civil and political rights. Together, these strategies would eventually advance the causes of civil and political equality as well as the cause of economic justice. Du Bois also asserted that the most talented of his race, notably future Black leaders, must avail themselves of the best academic training to achieve at the highest levels, uplift the race, and challenge white supremacy.

AP® exam tip

Be sure you're able to describe how some African American leaders such as Booker T. Washington advocated for industrial education and training as a means of economic advancement and independence.

AP® exam tip

Be prepared to compare and contrast the different strategies for Black advancement that Booker T. Washington and W. E. B. Du Bois debated.

Migration Hopes and Disappointments

In 1892, immediately following the lynching of her friends in Memphis, Ida B. Wells wrote in the *Free Speech and Headlight*, "There is . . . only one thing left that we can do; save our money and leave a town which will neither protect our lives and property, nor give us a fair trial in the courts."[28] Many heeded such advice, and soon Wells, too, left Memphis, one of some 250,000 southern Blacks who left the South between the end of the Civil War and 1910.

Although migration to Kansas subsided after the initial Exoduster movement, it never stopped, and eventually 25,000 Blacks left Arkansas, Alabama, Mississippi, Louisiana, and Texas for Kansas. Black migration to Oklahoma, however, accelerated, and between 1890 and 1910, more than 100,000 Blacks settled there, largely in all-Black towns. The most famous of these towns was Boley, which had more than 1,000 residents in 1907 and some 2,000 Black farm families in its vicinity. Like Black communities elsewhere, Boley featured a range of institutions, including a school, churches, restaurants, fraternal orders, and women's clubs.

The late-nineteenth-century West featured an array of Black women working in various capacities, such as farming, business, journalism, and education. Some of these women defied gender norms, working as gold hunters and mail and freight haulers. Biddy Bridget Mason was a formerly enslaved woman who eventually amassed

AP® skills

Applying Disciplinary Knowledge: What roles did Black women have in the West in the late nineteenth century?

a fortune in Los Angeles real estate, became well known for her charitable and philanthropic work, and helped found the First AME Church in Los Angeles, the oldest African American church in the city. Mary Ellen Pleasant, also formerly enslaved, became an abolitionist and, and upon moving to San Francisco in 1852, a pioneering entrepreneur and civil rights activist. Unfortunately, financial controversy and decline marred her final years.

AP® Skills

Applying Disciplinary Knowledge: Why is Stagecoach Mary a significant figure in American history?

The larger-than-life Mary Fields, better known as "Stagecoach Mary," or "Black Mary," led a very colorful life, including delivering mail in central west Montana from 1895 to 1903. She was the second woman to deliver mail in the West and the first African American woman to deliver the U.S. mail. Wearing men's clothes, carrying both a revolver and a rifle, and radiating a no-nonsense attitude, the swearing, cigar-smoking, hard-drinking, and quick-shooting Fields was a highly dependable mail carrier who beat back would-be mail thieves and braved innumerable and at times unbelievable challenges — including, by one account, a pack of wolves — to do her job. A kind-hearted and generous soul, she became a legendary and beloved local figure in Cascade, Montana.

Black men in the West worked as cowboys as well as farmers. The 1890 U.S. census reported 1,600 western cowboys of color; indeed, roughly one in four cowboys was African American. Working together with white and nonwhite cowboys, they mostly herded cattle on grueling drives to Kansas and other markets across the West. Not surprisingly, however, racist discrimination undercut the interracial camaraderie of the rough-and-tumble world of nineteenth-century American cowboys.

Like white cowboys, Black cowboys loom large in the popular imagination. The African American cowboy Nat Love became particularly well known through his sensational autobiography, in which he battled the dangers of American Indians, storms, and stampedes on cattle drives in the West. Bill Pickett achieved fame in Wild West shows and on the rodeo circuit as the first steer wrestler, pioneering a dangerous event in which a rider chases a steer, dismounts, and pulls the steer to the ground by its horns. Perhaps the most famous of African American frontiersmen was Bass Reeves, the first African American deputy U.S. marshal in Arkansas and the Oklahoma Territory, who bought more than three thousand criminals (including his own son) to justice. Though illiterate, Reeves had a unique set of skills for tracking fugitives: he spoke several indigenous languages, knew the area well, was a master of disguise and intrigue, and was an expert marksman. Standing over six feet tall, the impeccably dressed lawman cut a dashing figure atop his white stallion. Some suggest that Reeves's larger-than-life exploits were the basis of the popular radio and early TV character "The Lone Ranger."

For Blacks in the U.S. army, discrimination was ever present. When the four Black units serving in western forts moved to Florida in preparation for deployment to Cuba in the Spanish-American War, these buffalo soldiers encountered Jim Crow. After racial violence flared in Lakeland and Tampa, Florida, Chaplain George Prioleau of the Ninth Cavalry wrote a letter to the editor of the *Cleveland Gazette*, a prominent Black newspaper: "Why sir, the Negro of this country is a freeman and yet a slave. Talk about fighting and freeing poor Cuba and of Spain's brutality: . . . Is America any better

Black Cowboys
Black men could find employment in the West as cowboys, and they often signed on for cattle drives that involved herding a couple thousand animals across the range for weeks at a time. Cowboys were expert riders, ropers, and outdoorsmen who needed to respond quickly to the dangers they faced along the trail. **What types of jobs did Black men have in the West? What developments help explain the appeal of such jobs?** *Universal History Archive/Getty Images.*

than Spain?"[29] The irony of ostensibly fighting to free Cubans and Filipinos from Spanish oppression was not lost on the soldiers, and Lewis Douglass, son of Frederick Douglass, warned that "injustice to dark races" prevailed wherever the United States took control.[30]

In 1906, an incident in Brownsville, Texas, where the Twenty-Fifth Infantry Regiment was stationed, captured national attention. When an exchange of gunfire left a white man dead and a police officer injured, townspeople immediately blamed the Black soldiers at Fort Brown. Despite a lack of evidence and the absence of a trial or even formal charges, President Theodore Roosevelt discharged all 167 soldiers without honor. Widespread Black protest, including that of the NACW and the Black press, as well as a private message from Booker T. Washington, could not convince Roosevelt to change his mind.

AP® skills

Applying Disciplinary Knowledge: How did the experiences of enlisted men in the South differ from those who lived in the West?

International Migrations

Some southern Blacks left the United States altogether, settling in Liberia, the West African colony founded by the American Colonization Society (ACS) in 1821 for the resettlement of free African Americans. In the late nineteenth century, the

Back-to-Africa movement revived, and roughly 3,800 Blacks, or about 238 annually, emigrated to Liberia, mostly under the auspices of the ACS, which still acted as a trustee. African Methodist Episcopal bishop Henry McNeal Turner, one of the era's most prominent Black supporters of Black emigration, became an honorary vice president of the ACS in 1876. Believing that Blacks would never receive fair treatment in the United States, he also advocated the civilizing and Christianizing mission of African American resettlement and the pride of race a Black nation in Africa could bring. But the two groups of emigrants his International Migration Society sponsored in 1895 and 1896 did not fare well. In Liberia, the new settlers suffered from a lack of jobs, high rates of illness and death, and cultural and political clashes with indigenous Liberians. Dissent among them also reduced their enthusiasm, and many returned to the United States.

Alexander Crummell, a school companion of Henry Highland Garnet, had fought to be ordained in the Episcopal Church, and under the church's auspices, he had gone to Liberia as a missionary. During two decades in Liberia, he and his associate Edward Blyden, who had been born in the West Indies, advanced ideas of Black unity and nationalism. But their efforts were unsuccessful, and in 1871, political strife prompted Crummell to return to the United States. In addition to leading an Episcopal congregation in Washington, D.C., he wrote and spoke extensively, building an impressive scholarly reputation. In 1897, he founded the American Negro Academy, dedicated to advancing Black scholarship and Black intellectual life.

AP® exam tip

Remember, on the AP® Exam you'll need to explain how or why an event occurred. Take the prompt "Explain why international migration appealed to some Black Americans at the turn of the twentieth century." To answer it, you need to analyze the motivation to migrate at that time. That analysis must include a description of the historical situation *and* an explanation of how that situation connects to the reason for migration.

West Indian Blacks like Blyden also sought relief from oppression by immigrating to the cities of the North, where they contributed significantly to the development of communities such as Harlem. In 1900, there were roughly five thousand foreign-born blacks in New York City, and by 1910 almost twelve thousand were living there. Most were from the British Caribbean, notably Jamaica and Barbados, where there was limited economic opportunity. Caribbean immigrant Harold Ellis observed, "You were never able to come out of the class in which you were born down there," while in the United States, "there was prejudice . . . but it was better than having no hope."[31]

The Age of Booker T. Washington

The preeminent African American spokesman between 1895 and 1915 was Booker T. Washington, head of Tuskegee Institute in Alabama, which he helped found. Emphasizing economic nationalism, race pride, racial solidarity, and interracial goodwill, Washington formulated an uplift program that reflected the spirit of the times. He was the era's most powerful race leader because of his ability to voice Black people's concerns and to work with influential whites by preaching racial conciliation.

From his enslaved beginnings, Washington's rise to greatness is a classic American success story, carefully recounted in his iconic 1901 autobiography, *Up from Slavery*. Born in 1856 to an enslaved cook and an unknown white father in Franklin County, Virginia, he was eager to succeed, and his mother supported his desire for an education. The family moved to West Virginia after the Civil War, and there nine-year-old Booker got up early to work in the salt mines so that later in the day he could attend a few hours of school. At age sixteen, he walked five hundred miles to enroll at Hampton Institute, where he took a job as a janitor to pay his room and board. He worked hard to impress those in authority, especially whites, with his moral character, work ethic, ambition, and intelligence.

At Hampton, Washington came under the influence of Samuel Chapman Armstrong, the school's president and a leading promoter of industrial and agricultural education for Blacks. In 1881, after Washington had graduated and returned to Hampton as a teacher, Armstrong arranged for his protégé to head what was being organized as Tuskegee Institute for Negroes in rural southeastern Alabama. Washington first held classes in an AME Zion church. His students, learning bricklaying, literally built the school on the site of an abandoned plantation. Washington's fund-raising and public relations efforts helped achieve not only solvency but also fame for the school. By 1915, when he died, Tuskegee was enrolling fifteen hundred students a year and had a campus of thirty-five hundred acres and some one hundred buildings.

Washington worked hard to secure state funding and the support of northern white philanthropists, who were attracted by the Hampton–Tuskegee model of vocational education for Black youths because it promoted individual and collective advancement within the confines of Jim Crow. Both Andrew Carnegie and John D. Rockefeller, men who had made their fortunes from steel and oil, respectively, contributed to Tuskegee. Julius Rosenwald, part owner of Sears, Roebuck, piloted a program with Washington that ultimately led to the creation of five thousand rural schools for Black children in the South.

With Tuskegee as a base of operations, Washington emerged as an increasingly influential Black educator and spokesman. In 1900, he founded the National Negro Business League, a network of Black business and professional men that encouraged the development of Black-owned and Black-operated enterprises. Washington cultivated loyalists within Black business, church, education, and press circles. His stature allowed him to exercise great power, which he used to sustain his friends and supporters and ruthlessly cut off those who crossed him. His network became known as the Tuskegee Machine and the era he dominated as the Age of Booker T. Washington.

AP® skills

Applying Disciplinary Knowledge: What was the purpose of the National Negro Business League?

In 1895, Washington delivered a speech at the Cotton States and International Exposition in Atlanta that gave classic expression to themes he had refined for more than a decade. Speaking to a largely white audience, he argued that economic uplift, especially through business development and industrial education, was the best course for Black advancement. Portraying Black southerners as loyal and patient, he encouraged them to begin "at the bottom of life" and not "permit our grievances to overshadow our opportunities." "Cast down your bucket where you are," he urged his listeners; Black people should seek to better their condition within the South, and white employers should hire African Americans rather than foreign laborers. Finally, he called Black agitation for social equality "the extremest folly." He concluded, "In all things that are purely social we can be as separate as the fingers, yet one as the hand in all things essential to mutual progress."[32]

Atlanta Compromise speech (1895)
Booker T. Washington's classic statement of racial conciliation and accommodationism.

accommodationism
A strategy, popularized by Booker T. Washington, for achieving Black progress through vocational/industrial training and an acceptance of the racial status quo, including segregation.

AP® skills
Applying Disciplinary Knowledge: Why did Booker T. Washington advocate to work within the existing system?

Washington's **Atlanta Compromise speech** proved masterful precisely because its multiple messages allowed different audiences to hear what they wanted to hear. Most important for Black people were the elements of hope and possibility for a brighter future. The emphasis on self-help, solidarity, economic uplift, and making the most of life within the confines of segregation hit widely popular notes. Most important for whites was **accommodationism**, or working within the racial status quo, including segregation — an approach that Washington publicly urged. (See Appendix: The Atlanta Compromise Speech for the text of this speech.)

Frederick Douglass had died earlier that year, and whites now looked to Washington as the heir apparent: the lead voice of African Americans. Philanthropists relied on his advice regarding which Black institutions and causes to support, and Presidents Theodore Roosevelt and William Howard Taft consulted him before dispensing political patronage positions available to Blacks. But Roosevelt incurred much criticism in 1901 when he invited Washington to dine at the White House, a breach of custom that offended many whites, especially in the South. Nevertheless, Washington continued his public efforts to promote interracial harmony by squaring Black uplift with white goodwill. Privately, he spent large sums of money to defeat Jim Crow legislation and mount legal challenges by secretly retaining lawyers and working through intermediaries. At the time, these efforts were unknown to all but a few highly trusted contemporaries.

The Emergence of W. E. B. Du Bois

Numerous aspects of Washington's leadership — notably his accommodationism, his educational philosophy, and his dictatorial methods — drew increasing Black criticism, especially from northern-based leaders such as William Monroe Trotter. The brilliant and radical, Harvard-educated Trotter edited the *Boston Guardian*, one of the most uncompromising Black newspapers of its day. Trotter viewed accommodationism as a betrayal of Black people and made it a mission of his paper to challenge Washington. When, in 1903, Washington tried to deliver a speech at a Black church in Boston, opponents led by Trotter heckled him. Washington was further incensed when a fight broke out, and he took Trotter to court over what came to be called the Boston Riot. Trotter was fined $500 and sent to jail for a month for his role in the affair.

Soon, W. E. B. Du Bois also became a vocal critic of Washington's accommodationism, but the two Black leaders were not polar opposites. Du Bois's racial uplift ideology in many ways mirrored that of Washington and mainstream Black thought. In light of Du Bois's own emphasis on racial solidarity, economic advancement, and hard work, he initially found much to admire in Washington's program. Also like Washington, Du Bois at times stressed Blacks' responsibilities and duties more than their grievances and rights. Initially, he even praised Washington's Atlanta Compromise speech as a hopeful and viable program for racial progress.

Booker T. Washington and W. E. B. Du Bois
Washington (left) and Du Bois (right), brilliant and ambitious men who were zealously dedicated to their people's elevation, were the preeminent African American leaders of their day. These photographs capture their common seriousness of purpose, unwavering commitment, and laser-like intensity. Despite their differences in philosophy — particularly Washington's accommodationism versus Du Bois's militancy — and the rift that developed between them, they agreed on the ultimate goal for African Americans: full freedom and equality. **What roles did Du Bois and Washington have in shaping the Black American experience?** *Left: Library of Congress, Prints and Photographs Division, Washington, D.C., LC-ppmsca-23961; Right: Library of Congress, Prints and Photographs Division, Washington, D.C., LC-USZ62-16767.*

Yet the two men's lives had been very different. Du Bois had been born in 1868 to a family that had been free for generations. Reared largely by his mother in a small Black community within essentially white Great Barrington, Massachusetts, he was a precocious child and brilliant student. He was also enormously ambitious and disciplined. His stellar academic credentials included an undergraduate degree from Fisk in 1889 and undergraduate and graduate degrees from Harvard, including a Ph.D. in 1895. Trained as a historian, he also did pioneering work in the emerging field of sociology. In the early 1900s, Du Bois taught at Atlanta University, where he conducted a series of pathbreaking studies of Black life.

Du Bois was always far more outspoken than Washington about Black rights and the need for the vote. Their differences grew as Jim Crow laws and Black disfranchisement intensified. Du Bois also placed far more emphasis on the need for liberal arts and advanced scientific and technical education for Blacks. His vision reflected an elitist, top-down leadership style. Advocating the most advanced college curricula for the academically talented, Du Bois thus hoped to prepare what he called the "talented tenth" for the rigors of race leadership.

The bitter break between Du Bois and Washington owed directly to Washington's use of his Tuskegee Machine and the lengths to which he would go to punish opponents, especially Trotter. In *The Souls of Black Folk* (1903), Du Bois spelled out his objections to accommodationism: "Mr. Washington distinctly asks that black people give up, at least for the present, three things, — First, political power, Second, insistence on civil rights, Third, higher education of Negro youth, — and concentrate all their energies on industrial education, and accumulation of wealth, and the conciliation of the South." Yet this approach, Du Bois pointed out, produced only disfranchisement, "civil inferiority," and a "withdrawal of aid from institutions for the higher training of the Negro." Moreover, Washington's approach "has tended to make the whites, North and South, shift the burden of the Negro problem to the Negro's shoulders . . . when in fact the burden belongs to the nation, and the hands of none of us are clean if we bend not our energies to righting these great wrongs."[33] The program Du Bois announced in *The Souls of Black Folk* guided his actions for the rest of his life.

AP® skills

Applying Disciplinary Knowledge: Explain Du Bois's main argument against accommodationism in *The Souls of Black Folk*.

Du Bois's race leadership linked national and international developments. He helped assemble an exhibit for the 1900 Paris World's Fair that summarized African American achievements since emancipation. That summer, he also led the African American delegation, which included Anna Julia Cooper, to the first **Pan-African Congress** in London. The Trinidadian lawyer Henry Sylvester Williams, who called the meeting, promoted the concept of **Pan-Africanism** — the notion, held by those both within and outside the African continent, of a shared global sense of African identity as well as an abiding concern for the welfare of Africans everywhere. Delegates from Great Britain, the United States, the West Indies, and Africa condemned the partition of Africa into European colonies. African American leaders such as Alexander Crummell and Edward Blyden, as well as Martin R. Delany and Henry M. Turner, had not protested the European colonization of Africa because they saw in it a civilizing influence. But Du Bois was among those who clearly perceived its liabilities. In his address to the congress, he warned, "The problem of the twentieth century is the problem of the color line, the question as to how far differences of race, which show themselves chiefly in the color of the skin and the texture of the hair, are going to be made, hereafter, the basis of denying to over half the world the right of sharing to their utmost ability the opportunities and privileges of modern civilization."[34]

Pan-African Congress (1900)
An international meeting in London to address the welfare of Africans around the world and to argue for an end to European colonization of Africa.

Pan-Africanism
A global political movement committed to African self-determination and the end of European domination of the African continent.

Niagara movement (1905)
A militant protest organization committed to revitalizing a national Black civil rights agenda in opposition to Booker T. Washington's accommodationist program.

In 1905, Du Bois helped launch the **Niagara movement**, a militant protest organization of Black intellectuals and professionals that, in opposition to Washington's program, tried to revitalize a national Black civil rights agenda. Local actions by National Equal Rights League auxiliaries, particularly challenges to unequal educational opportunities for Blacks (Map 10.3), had continued in northern states into the 1880s. T. Thomas Fortune had led two previous efforts to resurrect a national civil rights movement, but both foundered. The National Afro-American League lasted from 1889 to 1893 and the National Afro-American Council from 1898 to 1908. Fortune left the latter organization in 1904.

AP® skills

Applying Disciplinary Knowledge: Describe the Niagara movement. What was Du Bois's role in it? What were the movement's goals, and how did it seek to achieve them?

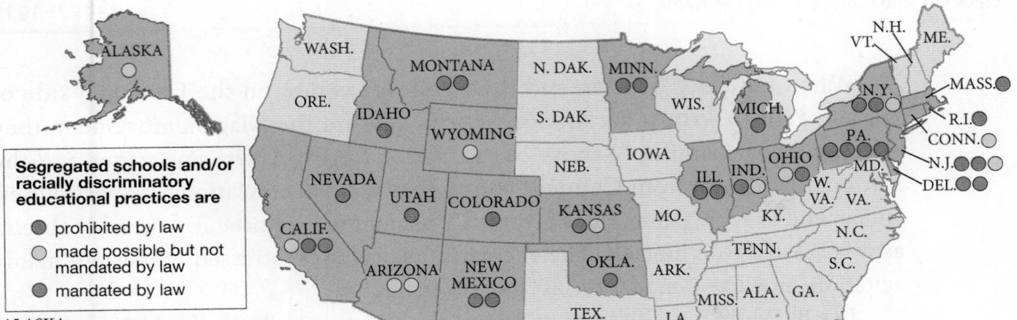

ALASKA
1905: Statute provides for the education of white children and "children of mixed blood who lead a civilized life." Unclear whether full-blooded Black children would be able to attend.

ARIZONA
1909: Statute (passed over governor's veto) gives school district trustees the authority to segregate Black and white schoolchildren in districts with more than 8 Black pupils.
1927: Statute mandates that in areas with 25 or more Black high-school students, an election will determine whether to segregate these students.

CALIFORNIA
1870: Statute mandates that if 10 white children's parents provide a written request, African and American Indian children will be required to attend a separate school.
1880: Statute bans school segregation, mandating that children of any race or nationality can attend public schools.
1902: Statute repeals 1880 law, prohibiting Black, Chinese, and Japanese children from attending schools designated for whites.

COLORADO
1876: State constitution prohibits classification of students in public schools by race.

CONNECTICUT
1933: Statute permits the establishment of separate schools for Black students if the authorities believe that such separation is necessary or proper.

DELAWARE
1877: Statute levies a separate tax on Blacks to fund Black schools.
1915: State code requires that schools be segregated by race.

IDAHO
1889: State constitution prohibits school segregation.

ILLINOIS
1874: Statute prohibits boards of education from excluding children from public school on account of color, establishing a fine of between $5 and $100 for those who exclude children and a fine of up to $25 for those who threaten to exclude them.
1896: Statute prohibits school officers from excluding children from public schools on account of color, establishing a fine of between $5 and $100 for offenders.

INDIANA
1869: Statute mandates the establishment of separate schools for Black children. If there are not enough Black students for this purpose, trustees are directed to find other means of educating Black children.
1877: Statute decrees that Black children shall be admitted to white schools if separate schools cannot be provided for them, or if they advance to a higher grade than is offered by Black schools.

KANSAS
1868: Statute mandates the establishment of separate schools for Black or mixed-race students in cities with more than 150,000 people.
1905: Statute allows Kansas City to organize and maintain separate Black and white schools, including high schools, but orders that "no discrimination on account of color shall be made in high schools, except as provided herein."

MASSACHUSETTS
1894: Statute prohibits students' exclusion from public school on account of race, color, or religion.

MICHIGAN
1871: Statute prohibits separate schools or departments based on race or color.

MINNESOTA
1877: Statute prohibits segregated schools, establishing a $50 penalty per offense and mandating that the offending school district would lose funds.
1905: Statute prohibits school districts from classifying students according to race or color, including by the establishment of separate schools; mandates that the offending school district would lose funds.

MONTANA
1871: Statute establishes separate schools for Black children.
1895: Statute declares all public schools open to all children (without express reference to separate schools or Black children).

NEVADA
1865: Statute prohibits Black, Asian, and American Indian students from attending public schools, empowering any district's Board of Trustees to establish separate schools for these students.

NEW JERSEY
1881: Statute decrees that no child between the ages of 5 and 18 may be excluded from public school on account of religion, nationality, or color.
1903: Statute decrees that no child between the ages of 5 and 18 may be excluded from public school on account of religion, nationality, or color, stipulating punishment with a misdemeanor charge, fine between $50 and $250, and/or imprisonment in a county jail, workhouse, or penitentiary.
1929: Statute authorizes segregated schools.

NEW MEXICO
1907: Statute mandates separate rooms for the teaching of Black children, noting that when "said rooms are so provided, such pupils may not be admitted to the school rooms occupied and used by pupils of Caucasian or other descent."
1911: State constitution establishes free public schools open to all school-aged children, regardless of race.

NEW YORK
1900: Statute repeals an 1864 law establishing segregated schools, making it unlawful to refuse admission to any public school in New York on account of race or color.
1910: Statute prohibits the exclusion of students from public schools on account of race or color.
1930: Statute endows school district trustees with the authority to establish separate schools.

OHIO
1878: Statute allows school districts to organize separate schools if "in their judgment it may be for the advantage of the district to do so."
1887: Statute prohibits school segregation.

OKLAHOMA
1904: Statute orders a fine for instructors teaching in unsegregated schools: "Any instructor who shall teach in any school, college or institution where members of the white and colored race are received and enrolled as pupils for instruction shall be deemed guilty of a misdemeanor, and upon conviction thereof, shall be fined in any sum not less than $10 nor more than $50 for each offense."

PENNSYLVANIA
1869: Statute prohibits Black children from attending Pittsburgh schools.
1872: Statute repeals 1869 Pittsburgh school segregation order.
1881: Statute prohibits any teacher or school administrator from discriminating against students based on race or color.
1911: Statute bans school segregation.

RHODE ISLAND
1882: Statute prohibits students' exclusion from school on account of race or color.

UTAH
1895: State constitution prohibits school segregation.

WYOMING
1887: Statute establishes that separate schools may be provided for Black children in school districts with 15 or more Black children.

MAP 10.3 School Segregation in the North and West

School segregation laws and practices varied from state to state, within states, and across time. In some states and localities, segregated schools were required by law (de jure segregation); in others, they were the result of custom (de facto segregation). The absence of school segregation laws in a few states — often those with few Blacks or influential Black and tolerant white populations — actually fostered limited integration. This map offers a sampling of laws from the northern, midwestern, and western states that mandated, allowed, and prohibited segregated schools. As shown here, these laws at times changed, typically owing to shifting public opinion within these states. **Which states shifted from laws that prohibited segregation to laws that made segregation possible? How did the evolution of segregation impact migration patterns?**

When Du Bois, Trotter, and their colleagues met on the Canadian side of Niagara Falls to write a declaration of principles for the Niagara movement, they expressed goals similar to those of the National Afro-American League and the National Afro-American Council: voting rights, equal educational opportunities, and an end to segregation. But Fortune, a Washington supporter, was notably absent, as was Washington himself. The energetic "Niagaraites" stressed "persistent manly agitation," not accommodation, as "the way to liberty."[35]

Ida B. Wells initially maintained connections with both the National Afro-American Council and the Niagara movement. Early on she headed the council's antilynching bureau and served as convention secretary for three years. In June 1895, she married Ferdinand L. Barnett, founder of the *Conservator*, Chicago's first Black newspaper, becoming Ida B. Wells-Barnett. She and her husband were strong supporters of the Niagara movement. But undermined by money woes, infighting, and Washington's powerful opposition, the movement achieved few tangible results.

In September 1906, Du Bois witnessed firsthand a vicious race riot in Atlanta. Five days of lawlessness devastated Black areas of the city and left ten Blacks and one white dead. Two years later, a race riot in Springfield, Illinois, the hometown of Abraham Lincoln, grabbed the nation's attention. A white woman's false rape accusation against a Black man led rampaging whites to lynch two innocent Black men and wreak havoc on the Black community.

The Springfield race riot made it clear that racial tensions were not just a southern problem but a national problem. In the wake of this riot, a distinguished roster of Black and white progressives issued a call for an interracial organization to end racial discrimination and inequality. Those signing the call and attending the 1909 meeting to establish the National Negro Committee included Du Bois, Wells-Barnett, Mary Church Terrell, and Josephine St. Pierre Ruffin, as well as prominent white reformers such as journalists Mary White Ovington, Oswald Garrison Villard (grandson of William Lloyd Garrison), and Ray Stannard Baker, as well as social workers Jane Addams and Lillian Wald. At its 1910 meeting, the organization became the **National Association for the Advancement of Colored People (NAACP)**.

National Association for the Advancement of Colored People (NAACP) Founded in 1909, the leading advocacy group for Black civil rights up to the present.

With a home office in New York City and branch offices in Baltimore, Boston, Detroit, Kansas City, St. Louis, and Washington, D.C., the NAACP quickly became the nation's leading African American civil rights organization, with notable early successes despite the very limited funds. Filing a brief in *Guinn v. United States* (1915), it helped overturn Oklahoma's grandfather clause, which had contributed to Black disfranchisement. Protesting *The Birth of a Nation*, the 1915 film that glorified the role of the Ku Klux Klan in the overthrow of Black Reconstruction, the NAACP shut down showings in some cities and forced offensive scenes to be edited out. From its beginnings, the NAACP was vital to national efforts to end lynching. As director of publicity and research, Du Bois founded and edited the organization's journal, *The Crisis*, in which he published lynching reports and statistics together with wide-ranging news coverage and opinion pieces on issues important to African Americans.

AP® skills

Applying Disciplinary Knowledge: What were some of the early accomplishments of the NAACP?

The Birth of a Nation, *1915*
D.W. Griffith's silent film *The Birth of a Nation* utilized new filmmaking techniques such as the close-up, the panoramic long shot, fades, and the flashback, which earned Griffin the title "Father of American Cinema." With a run time of three hours and a cast of more than ten thousand people, the spectacular film was a popular sensation and box-office hit. It was also white supremacist propaganda that depicted Reconstruction as a time of suffering for whites at the hands of immoral and ignorant Blacks and their Republican allies. An adaptation of Thomas Dixon's racist novel *The Clansman*, the film fostered white sympathies for the Ku Klux Klan and contributed to the Klan's resurgence and spread. In this scene, the villain Gus (played by a white actor in blackface) is captured by honorable Klansmen who will deliver justice by lynching. While whites largely embraced Griffin's film, Blacks rejected it precisely because of its racism and historical misrepresentations. **This film had a featured screening at the White House during Woodrow Wilson's presidency. What lasting effects did the message of this film, compounded by its endorsement by the American political establishment, have on the perception of Black Americans?** *Courtesy Everett Collection/Shutterstock.*

Under his direction, the journal's circulation grew from 1,000 for the first issue in November 1910 to 100,000 nine years later. When Washington died in 1915, Du Bois had already emerged as the nation's preeminent Black spokesperson for a comprehensive civil rights agenda and a well-supported program of organized protest.

Growing concern among Blacks and their white allies about increasingly serious issues confronting urban Blacks, notably the escalating numbers of rural southern Black migrants to northern cities like New York, led to the establishment in 1910 of the National League on Urban Conditions among Negroes. This new organization folded together three different organizations doing related work: the Committee for the Improvement of Industrial Conditions Among Negroes in New York (founded in 1906), the National League for the Protection of Colored Women (founded in 1906), and the Committee on Urban Conditions among Negroes (founded in 1910). This new organization dedicated itself to assisting Black urban migrants with their social welfare needs: especially employment, housing, education, and healthcare. The Black economist Dr. George Edmund Haynes and white philanthropist Ruth Standish Baldwin helped found the National League on Urban Conditions among Negroes. From 1910 to 1917, Dr. Haynes served as its first executive secretary. In 1920, the organization shortened its name to the **National Urban League (NUL)**. Along with the NAACP, the NUL quickly emerged as a vital organization advancing the concerns of urban Blacks and, more broadly, the Black freedom struggle.

National Urban League (NUL)
An organization founded in the early twentieth century dedicated to assisting Black migrants from the South and to advancing the concerns of urban Blacks.

CONCLUSION
Racial Uplift in the Nadir

"If you want to lift yourself up, lift up someone else." This saying, attributed to Booker T. Washington, exemplifies how Black Americans kept hope alive between 1877 and 1915, sometimes described as the lowest moment, or nadir, in African American history. After Reconstruction, Blacks lost ground in crucial areas. Without land, they struggled for economic independence. Southern states imposed segregation laws and legalized Jim Crow practices that relegated Blacks to second-rate public facilities and branded them as racial inferiors. Disfranchisement, peonage, and lynching structured powerful systems of racial oppression, which kept African Americans at the bottom of every hierarchy in American politics, law, and society.

But many Blacks and the institutions they built avoided these traps, subverted these realities, and surmounted these obstacles. Turning inward, freedom's first generation intensified their emphasis on racial solidarity, self-help, and economic nationalism. They strengthened their communities, seeing the building of robust African American communities as the best way to endure and even thrive in the increasingly restrictive world of Jim Crow. A powerful network of Black institutions — churches, schools, businesses, mutual aid societies, and newspapers — blossomed. A new culture of freedom unleashed new forms of creativity in music, literature, and the arts. Ultimately, Black leaders joined with white progressives to form a new civil rights organization that mobilized against racial injustice. Freedom's first generation thus helped open the way for the New Negro of the twentieth century to forge new and even more productive paths of resistance and achievement. Indeed, in a very real sense, freedom's first generation were New Negroes.

CHAPTER 10 REVIEW ▸ PRACTICING AP® SKILLS

AP® ESSENTIAL VOCABULARY AND SOURCES

** Essential terms and required sources from the AP® Course are marked with an asterisk.*

Jim Crow p. 383
Plessy v. Ferguson (1896)* p. 384
separate but equal* p. 384
imperialism p. 386
scientific racism p. 387
Social Darwinism p. 387
progressivism p. 388
white primary p. 388
Colored Farmers' Alliance (CFA) p. 389
Wilmington Insurrection (1898) p. 389
lynching* p. 390
National Association of Colored Women (NACW) p. 393
uplift* p. 394
debt peonage p. 396
Atlanta Compromise speech (1895)* p. 410
accommodationism* p. 410
Pan-African Congress (1900) p. 412
Pan-Africanism* p. 412
Niagara movement (1905) p. 412
National Association for the Advancement of Colored People (NAACP)* p. 414
National Urban League (NUL)* p. 416
W. E. B. Du Bois, *Along the Color Line*, 1910 (Excerpts from The Souls of Black Folk by W.E.B. Du Bois, 1903 [Selections from "The Forethought," "Of Our Spiritual Strivings," "Of Alexander Crummell," and "The Afterthought"])* p. 425

APPLYING DISCIPLINARY KNOWLEDGE: ESSENTIAL QUESTIONS

1. What connections can be drawn among disfranchisement, the growth of Jim Crow laws and practices, the concept of scientific racism, and American and European imperialism abroad? What underlying philosophies informed these developments?
2. How did Jim Crow laws and lynchings function as a means of social control in the South?
3. In what ways did communities of African Americans focus on racial solidarity and advancement during these years? How did this focus manifest itself socially, culturally, and economically? Consider Jackson Ward, the main Black neighborhood in Richmond, Virginia, as an example. To what would you attribute the post-Reconstruction development of this "city within a city"?
4. Consider the various strains of Black thought surrounding accommodationism and protest. Which individuals and organizations supported which philosophies? In what ways were these different ideas connected to and divergent from one another?

SUGGESTED REFERENCES

Racism and Black Challenges

Allen, James. *Without Sanctuary: Lynching Photography in America*. Santa Fe, NM: Twin Palms, 2000.

Baker, Ray Stannard. *Following the Color Line: American Negro Citizenship in the Progressive Era*. 1908. Repr., New York: Harper & Row, 1964.

Bay, Mia. *To Tell the Truth Freely: The Life of Ida B. Wells*. New York: Hill and Wang, 2009.

Brundage, W. Fitzhugh. *Lynching in the New South: Georgia and Virginia, 1880–1930*. Urbana: University of Illinois Press, 1993.

Cash, Wilbur J. *The Mind of the South*. 1941. Reprint, New York: Vintage, 1991.

Equal Justice Initiative. *Lynching in America: Confronting the Legacy of Racial Terror*, 3rd ed. Montgomery: Equal Justice Initiative, 2017.

Fredrickson, George M. *Racism: A Short History*. Princeton: Princeton University Press, 2002.

Gilmore, Glenda Elizabeth. *Gender and Jim Crow: Women and the Politics of White Supremacy in North Carolina, 1896–1920*. Chapel Hill: University of North Carolina Press, 1996.

Gould, Stephen Jay. *The Mismeasure of Man*. New York: Norton, 1996.

Gross, Kali N. *Colored Amazons: Crime, Violence, and Black Women in the City of Brotherly Love, 1880–1910*. Durham: Duke University Press, 2006.

Hale, Grace Elizabeth. *Making Whiteness: The Culture of Segregation in the South, 1890–1940*. New York: Pantheon, 1998.

Haley, Sarah. *No Mercy Here: Gender, Punishment, and the Making of Jim Crow Modernity*. Chapel Hill: University of North Carolina Press, 2016.

LeFlouria, Talitha L. *Chained in Silence: Black Women and Convict Labor in the New South*. Chapel Hill: University of North Carolina Press, 2015.

Freedom's First Generation

Anderson, James D. *The Education of Blacks in the South, 1860–1935*. Chapel Hill: University of North Carolina Press, 1988.

Brown, Elsa Barkley. "Womanist Consciousness: Maggie Lena Walker and the Independent Order of Saint Luke," *Signs: Journal of Women in Culture and Society* 14, no. 3 (Spring 1989): 610–33.

Brundage, W. Fitzhugh, ed. *Beyond Blackface: African Americans and the Creation of American Popular Culture, 1890–1930*. Chapel Hill: University of North Carolina Press, 2011.

Daniel, Pete. *The Shadow of Slavery: Peonage in the South, 1901–1969*. Urbana: University of Illinois Press, 1972.

Higginbotham, Evelyn Brooks. *Righteous Discontent: The Women's Movement in the Black Baptist Church, 1880–1920*. Cambridge: Harvard University Press, 1993.

Hunter, Tera. *To 'Joy My Freedom: Southern Black Women's Lives and Labors after the Civil War.* Cambridge: Harvard University Press, 1997.

Litwack, Leon. *Trouble in Mind: Black Southerners in the Age of Jim Crow*. New York: Knopf, 1998.

Montgomery, William E. *Under Their Own Vine and Fig Tree: The African-American Church in the South, 1865–1900.* Baton Rouge: LSU Press, 1993.

Shaw, Stephanie J. *What a Woman Ought to Be and to Do: Black Professional Women Workers during the Jim Crow Era.* Chicago: University of Chicago Press, 1996.

Sotiropoulos, Karen. *Staging Race: Black Performers in Turn of the Century America.* Cambridge: Harvard University Press, 2006.

Migration, Accommodation, and Protest

Berlin, Ira. *The Making of African America: The Four Great Migrations*. New York: Viking, 2010.

Gaines, Kevin K. *Uplifting the Race: Black Leadership, Politics, and Culture in the Twentieth Century.* Chapel Hill: University of North Carolina Press, 1996.

Hahn, Steven. *A Nation under Our Feet: Black Political Struggles in the Rural South from Slavery to the Great Migration*. Cambridge: Belknap Press of Harvard University Press, 2003.

Harlan, Louis R. *Booker T. Washington: The Making of a Black Leader, 1856–1901*. New York: Oxford University Press, 1972.

Katz, William Loren. *The Black West: A Documentary and Pictorial History of the African American Role in the Westward Expansion of the United States*. Golden, CO: Fulcrum Publishing, 2019.

Lewis, David Levering. *W. E. B. Du Bois: Biography of a Race*, vol. 1, *1868–1919*. New York: Henry Holt, 1993.

Meier, August. *Negro Thought in America, 1880–1915: Racial Ideologies in the Age of Booker T. Washington*. Ann Arbor: University of Michigan Press, 1963.

Norrell, Robert J. *Up from History: The Life of Booker T. Washington*. Cambridge: Belknap Press of Harvard University Press, 2009.

Painter, Nell Irvin. *Exodusters: Black Migration to Kansas after Reconstruction*. New York: Knopf, 1977.

Taylor, Quintard. *In Search of the Racial Frontier: African Americans in the American West, 1528–1990*. New York: Norton, 1998.

Agency and Constraint

According to one historical axiom, humans throughout history have lived their lives within the limits imposed by the specific contexts they experience. They can and do exercise agency, or purposeful action, in the struggle against the bounds of the worlds within which they operate. Even though the tension between agency and constraint shapes historical experience, ultimately constraints limit agency. African American history in particular, especially the realities of African American freedom after emancipation, vividly illustrates this dynamic tension. While African Americans, notably freedpeople, made remarkable progress at the turn of the twentieth century, it was also one of the worst periods in African American freedom, in which white supremacy tragically impeded Black progress and devastated incalculable numbers of Black lives.

Still, for African Americans specifically and for oppressed peoples generally, it is essential to emphasize the complexity of their historical agency — in particular, what they themselves have done historically and what they continue to do individually and collectively to advance their liberation and alleviate racist oppression. In other words, to understand what has happened and continues to happen to African Americans is not enough: we also must understand what African Americans have done and continue to do for themselves, paying special attention to the small and large ways as well as the complex and simple ways they have fought for freedom and resisted white supremacy.

Lynching functioned as a key mechanism in the violent repression of African Americans in the decades after Reconstruction. Vigilante justice, in which people took the law into their own hands and murdered individuals accused of crimes, had been practiced by mobs in America since colonial times, and during Reconstruction, the Ku Klux Klan and similar groups lynched Blacks as part of their terrorist campaigns. Those who perpetrated lynchings said that the victims were criminals who got what they deserved. Especially if the charge was a Black man's assault on a white woman, lynching was said to be necessary to spare the woman from the ordeal of giving courtroom testimony. In the late nineteenth century, lynching reached epidemic proportions, averaging two or three recorded episodes per week. They were often public spectacles, drawing crowds of onlookers as well as participants. The setting was sometimes a desolate, secluded place, but it was just as likely to be a public square, in front of the local courthouse, with the sheriff and officers of the law among the crowd. Victims were often tortured while alive, and after death their bodies were mutilated. Bystanders took souvenirs and photographs of the event. Such photographs, affixed to postcards, were often sent to friends and relatives until Congress forbade the mailing of such materials in 1908.

The NAACP made a nationwide campaign against lynching a priority. In 1919, it published an analysis of the dire situation titled *Thirty Years of Lynching in the United States*. With each new report of a lynching, NAACP staff hung a banner reading "A man was lynched yesterday" out the window of its New York City headquarters. In 1901, George Henry White — the last Black southerner of the generation born enslaved to serve in Congress — introduced a bill that would have made lynching a federal crime. It failed to pass. In 1918, with NAACP backing, Congressman Leonidas Dyer of St. Louis introduced a bill with the same intent. Neither the Dyer Anti-Lynching Bill, reintroduced numerous times, nor any other antilynching bill ever passed Congress.

Like lynching, peonage helped structure the white supremacist regime of the era. Peonage was a notoriously vicious element in the South's repressive labor regime that impoverished Black agricultural workers while enriching white planters and merchants. Defined as a "condition of compulsory service, based on the indebtedness of the peon to the master,"[36] it resulted when an agricultural worker signed a contract for her or his labor but either failed to fulfill one or more requirements of the contract or, as was all too often the case, was alleged to have failed. Especially if the individual had received an advance on the promise of his or her labor, state laws made the worker liable to arrest, fine, and imprisonment for charges of contract fraud. Vagrancy and other ill-defined allegations also fed the chicanery that characterized this unjust system.

The worker might avoid imprisonment and have her or his fine paid by a third party through a private labor agreement in which the worker agreed to work until the debt was paid off. The problem was that the debt persisted. Often through technicalities and trickery, the person who held the debt manipulated a set of practices ensuring control over the labor of the debtor for as long as possible. It is no wonder that to debt peons, their life and work felt like slavery. In fact, some historians have called it neoslavery.[37] In addition to prison farms, which tended to operate outside public view, a common form of highly visible convict labor that evoked slavery and ensnared many Blacks was chain gangs, in which prisoners shackled together by ankle chains did hard public labor, like clearing land and building roads under strict armed surveillance. Work gangs did similar kinds of labor under comparable surveillance but without the ankle chains.

In *Clyatt v. United States* (1905), the first case challenging debt peonage, the U.S. Supreme Court ruled that the Peonage Abolition Act (1867) was constitutional. More important, in *Bailey v. Alabama* (1911), a case that received secret support from Booker T. Washington, the Court overturned an Alabama law that held a laborer criminally liable for taking money in advance for work not performed. This law, said the Court, was in violation of both the Thirteenth Amendment, which outlawed slavery, and the Fourteenth Amendment, which ensured equal protection of the laws. Finally, in *United States v. Reynolds* (1914), the Court outlawed the criminal surety laws that had perpetuated the peonage system by allowing employers to pay for the release of debtors in exchange for control over the debtors' labor.

key point

Racial terror was used as a tool to enforce the white supremacist regime of the South in the decades after Reconstruction. Lynching served to violently repress African Americans in the decades after Reconstruction. Debt peonage was an oppressive labor system that helped structure the society of the era. During this time, African Americans exercised their agency to challenge these injustices.

As you examine the written and visual documents that follow, consider the environment in which lynching and peonage were practiced. What did participants and observers think of these events and systems? What role if any did gender play in limiting African Americans' agency?

Content note: This set of documents includes a photograph of the lynching of Charles Mitchell, a Black man who was murdered by a white mob in 1897.

AP® argumentation

DBQ Practice: Explain how lynching, debt peonage, chain gangs, and the campaigns to abolish them complicate the meaning of freedom in the decades following Reconstruction. Use at least three of the documents to support your response.

DOCUMENT 1 *The Lynching of Charles Mitchell, 1897*

In June 1897, CHARLES MITCHELL, a twenty-three-year-old Black hotel porter, was accused of robbery by a prominent white woman in Urbana, Ohio; next, she accused him of rape. While he was in jail, a white mob gathered. The sheriff called up the militia, which fired into the crowd, killing several men and wounding others. The militia then withdrew, evidently expecting the Ohio National Guard to arrive, but the mayor had advised the guard to stay away. At that point, the mob broke into the jail, and the sheriff handed over the keys to Mitchell's cell. A noose was placed around Mitchell's neck, and he was hanged from a tree limb in the courthouse yard, as shown here. Later his corpse was displayed in a coffin under the lynching tree. Amid threats of burning the body, it was removed, but not before relic hunters had "nearly cut the coat off the dead man. Every button was gone, and even his shoes and stockings were taken off and carried away." The *New York Times* reported that the "wounding of the jail assailants arouses more local indignation than the murder of the Negro."[38]

Breaking it Down Rather than focusing on the body of Charles Mitchell, take a closer look at the people included in the photo. Notice their clothing, age, facial expressions, and other noteworthy features of the photo. What do these details communicate about the function of lynching in the decades following Reconstruction?

Fogg Art Museum, Harvard Art Museums/On deposit from the Carpenter Center for the Visual Arts/Bridgeman Images.

DOCUMENT 2 The Executive Committee of the State Convention of Colored Citizens of Kentucky | *Call for a Convention* 1885

Throughout the late nineteenth and early twentieth centuries, African Americans continued not only to protest loudly the galling injustices they endured but also to demand forcefully that local, state, and federal governments rectify these horrible wrongs. One of the ways they "spoke truth to power" and demanded redress of their grievances was through the demands and petitions that emerged from their innumerable local, state, regional, and national conventions. Below is an excerpt from the 1885 "call" for a convention of "colored men" of Kentucky to meet and articulate their people's concerns and demands.

Breaking it Down As you note the acts of racism and injustice referenced in this document, focus on the intended audience and the goals of this call for a convention. Pay close attention to both the tone and the substance of the call. How would you characterize both? How do they help achieve the committee's purpose?

When a free people, living in a body-politic, feel that the laws are unjustly administered to them; that discriminations are openly make; that various subterfuges and legal technicalities are constantly used to deprive them of the enjoyment of those rights and immunities belonging to the humblest citizen; when the courts become no refuge for the outraged, and when a sentiment is not found sufficient to do them justice; ***it becomes their bounden duty to protest against such a state of affairs. To do less than vigorously and earnestly enter our protest, is to cringe like hounds before masters, and to show that we are not fit for freedom.*** We are robbed by some of the railroad companion who take our first-class fares and then we are driven into smoking cars, and, if we demur, are cursed and roughly handled. Our women have been beaten by brutal brakemen, and, in many cases, left to ride on platforms at the risk of life and limb.

We are tried in courts controlled entirely by white men, and no colored man sits on a Kentucky jury. This seems no mere accident, but a determined effort to exclude us from fair trials and put us at the mercy of our enemies, from the judge down to the vilest suborned witness.

When charged with grave offenses, the jail is mobbed, and the accused taken out and hanged, and out of the hundreds of such cases since the war, not a single high-handed murderer has been ever brought before a court to answer. Colored men have been deliberately murdered, and few if any murderers have been punished by the law; indecent haste to free the criminal in such cases has made the trial a farce too ridiculous to be called more than a puppet show.

The penitentiary is full of our race who are sent there by wicked and malicious persecutions, and unjust sentences dealt out by judges who deem a colored criminal fit only for the severest and longest sentences for trivial offenses.

In all departments of the State we are systematically deprived of recognition except in menial positions. In our metropolitan city, and even cities of lesser note, we are not considered in the appointments in fire companies, police force, notary publics, etc. In fact, we are the ruled class and have no share in the government.

While grateful for much done in the line of school advantages, yet no system in this enlightened day is complete without normal schools. These the colored people have not, while every other ex-slave State has made provisions for normal training. . . .

SOURCE: *Proceedings of the Colored State Convention assembled in St. Paul's A.M.E. Church*, Lexington, Kentucky, November 26, 1885.

DOCUMENT 3 A Georgia Negro Peon | *The New Slavery in the South*, 1904

This narrative first appeared in February 1904 in the New York magazine the *Independent*. It was told to a representative of the magazine, who then prepared it for publication. The narrative begins with a sharecropper and a storekeeper settling their account, which, not surprisingly, comes out in the storekeeper's favor.

Breaking it Down Remember, the term "peon" refers to an unpaid farm worker who was considered to be unskilled. As you read, look for ways that peonage operated as a system, paying particular attention to how gender factored into the effects of peonage on Black people.

I am a negro and was born some time during the war in Elbert County, Ga., and I reckon by this time I must be a little over forty years old. . . .

. . . The storekeeper took us one by one and read to us statements of our accounts. According to the books there was no man of us who owed the Senator less than $100; some of us were put down for as much as $200. I owed $165, according to the bookkeeper. These debts were not accumulated during one year, but ran back for three and four years, so we were told — in spite of the fact that we understood that we had had a full settlement at the end of each year. But no one of us would have dared to dispute a white man's word — oh, no; not in those days. Besides, we fellows didn't care anything about the amounts — we were after getting away; and we had been told that we might go, if we signed the acknowledgements. We would have signed anything, just to get away. So we stepped up, we did, and made our marks. That same night we were rounded up by a constable and ten or twelve white men, who aided him, and we were locked up, every one of us, in one of the Senator's stockades. The next morning it was explained to us by the two guards appointed to watch us that, in the papers we had signed the day before, we had not only made acknowledgement of our indebtedness, but that we had also agreed to work for the Senator until the debts were paid by hard labor. And from that day forward we were treated just like convicts. Really we had made ourselves lifetime slaves, or peons, as the laws called us. But call it slavery, peonage, or what not, the truth is we lived in a hell on earth what time we spent in the Senator's peon camp.

I lived in that camp, as a peon, for nearly three years. My wife fared better than I did, as did the wives of some of the other Negroes, because the white men about the camp used these unfortunate creatures as their mistresses. When I was first put in the stockade my wife was still kept for a while in the "Big House," but my little boy, who was only nine years old, was given away to a Negro family across the river in South Carolina, and I never saw or heard of him after that. When I left the camp my wife had had two children by some one of the white bosses, and she was living in a fairly good shape in a little house off to herself. But the poor Negro women who were not in the class with my wife fared about as bad as the helpless Negro men. Most of the time the women who were peons or convicts were compelled to wear men's clothes. Sometimes, when I have seen them dressed like men, and plowing or hoeing or hauling logs or working at the blacksmith's trade, just the same as men, my heart would bleed and my blood would boil, but I was powerless to raise a hand. It would have meant death on the spot to have said a word. Of the first six women brought to the camp, two of them gave birth to children after they had been there more than twelve months — and the babies had white men for their fathers!

The stockades in which we slept, were, I believe, the filthiest places in the world. They were cesspools of nastiness. During the thirteen [*sic*] years that I was there I am willing to swear that a mattress was never moved after it had been brought there, except to turn it over once or twice a month. No sheets were used, only dark-colored blankets. Most of the men slept every night in the clothing that they had worked in all day. Some of the worst characters were made to sleep in chairs. The doors were locked and barred, each night, and tallow-candles were the only lights allowed. Really the stockades were but little more than cow sheds, horse stables or hog pens. Strange to say, not a great number of these people died while I was there, though a great many came away maimed and bruised and, in some cases, disabled for life. As far as I can remember only about ten died during the last ten years that I was there, two of these being killed outright by the guards for trivial offenses.

It was a hard school that peon camp was, but I learned more there in a few short months by contact with those poor fellows from the outside world than ever I had known before. Most of what I learned was evil, and I now know that I should have been better off without the knowledge, but much of what I learned was helpful to me. Barring two or three severe and brutal whippings which I received, I got along very well, all things considered; but the system is damnable. A favorite way of whipping a man was to strap him down to a log, flat on his back, and spank him fifty or sixty times on his bare feet with a shingle or a huge piece of plank. When the men [*sic*] would get up with sore and blistered feet and an aching body, if he could not then keep up with the other men at work he would be strapped to the log again, this time face downward, and would be lashed with a buggy trace on his bare back. When a woman had to be whipped it was usually done in private, though they would be compelled to fall down across a barrel or something of the kind and receive the licks on their backsides.

The working day on a peon farm begins with sunrise and ends when the sun goes down; or, in other words, the average peon works from ten to twelve hours each day, with one hour (from 12 o'clock to 1 o'clock) for dinner. Hot or cold, sun or rain, this is the rule. As to their meals, the laborers are divided up into squads or companies, just the same as soldiers in a great military camp would be. . . . Each peon is provided with a great big tin cup, a flat tin pan and two big tin spoons. No knives or forks are ever seen, except those used by the cooks. At meal time the peons pass in single file before the cooks, and hold out their pans and cups to receive their allowances. Cow peas (red or white, which when boiled turn black), fat bacon and old-fashioned Georgia cornbread, baked in pones from one to two and three inches thick, made up the chief articles of food. Black coffee, black molasses and brown sugar are also used abundantly. . . .

Today, I am told, there are six or seven of these private camps in Georgia — that is to say, camps where most of the convicts are leased from the State of Georgia. But there are hundreds and hundreds of farms all over the State where Negroes, and in some cases poor white folks, are held in bondage on the ground that they are working out debts, or where the contract which they have made holds them in a kind of perpetual bondage, because, under those contracts, they may not quit one employer and hire out to another except by and with the knowledge and consent of the former employer.

One of the usual ways to secure laborers for a large peonage camp is for the proprietor to send out an agent to the little courts in the towns and villages, and where a man charged with some petty offense has no friends or money the agent will urge him to plead guilty, with the understanding that the agent will pay his fine, and in that way save him from the disgrace of being sent to jail or the chain-gang! For this high favor the man must sign beforehand a paper signifying his willingness to go to the farm and work out the amount of the fine imposed. When he reaches the farm he has to be fed and clothed, to be sure, and these things are charged up to his account. By the time he has worked out his first debt another is hanging over his head, and so on and so on, by a sort of endless chain, for an indefinite period, as in every case the indebtedness is arbitrarily arranged by the employer. In many cases it is very evident that the court officials are in collusion with the proprietors or agents, and that they divide the "graft" among themselves. . . .

But I didn't tell you how I got out. I didn't get out — they put me out. When I had served as a peon for nearly three years — and you remember that they claimed I owed them only $165 — when I had served for nearly three years one of the bosses came to me and said that my time was up. He happened to be the one who was said to be living with my wife. He gave me a new suit of overalls, which cost about seventy-five cents, took me in a buggy and carried me across the Broad River into South Carolina, set me down and told me to "git." I didn't have a cent of money, and I wasn't feeling well, but somehow I managed to get a move on me. I begged my way to Columbia. In two or three days I ran across a man looking for laborers to carry to Birmingham, and I joined his gang. I have been here in the Birmingham district since they released me, and I reckon I'll die either in a coal mine or an iron furnace. It don't make much difference which. Either is better than a Georgia peon camp. And a Georgia peon camp is hell itself!

SOURCE: Herbert Aptheker, ed., *A Documentary History of the Negro People in the United States*, vol. 2, *From the Reconstruction Era to 1910*, 5th ed. (New York: Citadel Press, 1970), 832, 835–38.

DOCUMENT 4 | W. E. B. Du Bois | *Along the Color Line*, 1910

AP® source

W. E. B. DU BOIS (1868–1963), a founder of the NAACP and editor of its journal, *The Crisis*, wrote this editorial on *Bailey v. Alabama* in the journal's second issue, in December 1910. At the time, the case was making its way through the courts. Notice the position of the U.S. Department of Justice in relation to Alabama's contract labor law. The Supreme Court ruling, issued in 1911, declared Alabama's peonage law unconstitutional.

Breaking it Down Before you read the text, consider reviewing the Fifth, Eighth, and Thirteenth Amendments to the Constitution.

Several Southern laws, which have reduced Negro farm hands to virtual peonage, are to be tested before the United States Supreme Court. The case is the appeal of an Alabama Negro convicted of violating the contract law, upheld by the State Supreme Court, under which he was sentenced to a fine equivalent to 126 days' hard labor for the county. The Federal Department of Justice believes that the law imposes compulsory service in satisfaction of debt, reducing the Negroes to actual slavery.

The law provides that in contracts of service entered into by a laborer, where money was advanced, and the contract broken without just cause, and the money not refunded, the laborer is guilty, and may be sentenced to hard labor until the fine is worked out. The Federal Department contends that the purpose and effect of the law is not to stop fraudulent practices so much as to impose compulsory service upon the Negroes who constitute the bulk of the farm labor of the State. The point that will be attacked most vigorously is the Alabama rule of evidence in such cases, which, in practice, assumes the Negro accused was guilty of intent to defraud, "contrary to the axiomatic and elementary principle of presumption of innocence in a criminal procedure."

The reports of the abuses existing under this contract system in the South have aroused widespread indignation as they have appeared from time to time when some exceptionally flagrant case was forced into publicity. Now that the Department of Justice has become interested, and the issue is to be placed before the supreme tribunal, a definite pronouncement may be expected.

SOURCE: Herbert Aptheker, ed., *A Documentary History of the Negro People in the United States*, vol. 3, *1910–1932* (New York: Citadel Press, 1977), 31–32.

DOCUMENT 5 Letter to the Editor | *From the South, 1911*

In August 1911, W. E. B. DU BOIS published this letter sent to him as editor of *The Crisis*. It provides details about the peonage system and life in the Jim Crow South.

Breaking it Down As you read, notice what the writer has to say about *The Crisis* itself. How might Jim Crow laws have shaped the author's view of peonage and its consequences for the author personally?

Kind Sir:

I am not an educated man. I will give you the peonage system as it is practised here in the name of the law.

If a colored man is arrested here and hasn't any money, whether he is guilty or not, he has to pay just the same. A man of color is never tried in this country. It is simply a farce. Everything is fixed before he enters the courtroom. I will try to give you an illustration of how it is done:

I am brought in a prisoner, go through the farce of being tried. The whole of my fine may amount to fifty dollars. A kindly appearing man will come up and pay my fine and take me to his farm to allow me to work it out. At the end of a month I find that I owe him more than I did when I went there. The debt is increased year in and year out. You would ask, "How is that?" It is simply that he is charging you more for your board, lodging and washing than they allow you for your work, and you can't help yourself either, nor can anyone else help you, because you are still a prisoner and never get your fine worked out. If you do as they say and be a good Negro, you are allowed to marry, provided you can get someone to have you, and of course the debt still increases. This is in the United States, where it is supposed that every man has equal rights before the law, and we are held in bondage by this same outfit.

Of course we can't prove anything. Our word is nothing. If we state things as they are, the powers that be make a different statement, and that sets ours aside at Washington and, I suppose, in Heaven, too.

Now, I have tried to tell you how we are made servants here according to law. I will tell you in my next letter how the lawmakers keep the colored children out of schools, how that pressure is brought to bear on their parents in such a manner they cannot help themselves. The cheapest way we can borrow money here is at the rate of twenty-five cents on the dollar per year.

Your paper is the best I have read of the kind. I never dreamed there was such a paper in the world. I will subscribe soon. I think there are a great many here that will take your paper. I haven't had the chance to show your paper to any yet, but will as soon as I can. You know we have to be careful with such literature as this in this country.

What I have told you is strictly confidential. If you publish it, don't put my name to it. I would be dead in a short time after the news reached here.

One word more about the peonage. The court and the man you work for are always partners. One makes the fine and the other one works you and holds you, and if you leave you are tracked up with bloodhounds and brought back.

SOURCE: Herbert Aptheker, ed., *A Documentary History of the Negro People in the United States*, vol. 3, *1910–1932* (New York: Citadel Press, 1977), 31–32.

DOCUMENT 6 Chain Gang

Convict labor in the South assumed two major forms: prison farms and chain gangs. Both were elements of a racist "criminal injustice system" in which Black people were unfairly and disproportionately tried, convicted, and imprisoned. Southern states instituted the use of chain gangs in the late nineteenth century, and chain gangs were a grim feature of southern urban and rural life until the 1950s, when these states formally abolished the practice. This photograph

of members of a southern Black chain gang reveals both their humanity and their dehumanization. The image invites the viewer's attention and concern because the subjects are looking directly yet nonthreateningly at the camera. Their youth is signaled by their lack of facial hair; and the chains, striped uniforms, and work axes clearly convey their criminalization.

Breaking it Down What specific details from this image can be used to explain the climate of the time?

Library of Congress, Prints and Photographs Division, Washington, D.C., LC-D401-16155.

PRACTICING AP® SKILLS

1. **AP® Contextualization.** Describe peonage. What was its role in the society of the post-Reconstruction South? How significant was that role? Use evidence from at least one of the documents to support your response.
2. **AP® Comparison.** How did the conditions of peonage and the chain gang compare with the conditions of slavery? In your response, consider whose interests peonage and chain gangs served. Use at least two of the documents to support your comparison.
3. **AP® Continuity and Change.** To what extent did the labor system in the southern United States change after Reconstruction? Use evidence from at least two of the documents to support your response.
4. **Connecting to AP® Themes.** Explain how Black people organized and worked to end peonage and lynching in the United States after the end of Reconstruction. How do these tactics illustrate resistance and resilience?
5. **Class Discussion.** What continuities and/or discontinuities do you see between today's mass incarceration crisis afflicting Black and brown people in particular and earlier alarming patterns illustrating disproportionate and unjust incarceration rates for Blacks?

Document-Based Questions
Commentary

Over the course of the past few workshops, we've covered most of the skills you'll need to write a full response to a document-based question. We've gone over how to break down a prompt, skillfully skim sources, craft a **thesis statement**, build a full introduction, and organize evidence into body paragraphs. We're almost ready to begin writing a full response! First, though, we need to review the importance of providing quality **commentary** in each body paragraph.

When trying to construct body paragraphs, students often fall into the trap of just listing all their **evidence** for one paragraph and then the next. It's a common misconception that body paragraphs fulfill the AP® rubric as long as they reference the required number of sources. In actuality, the main purpose of the DBQ is to evaluate your ability to formulate a *claim* that synthesizes multiple sources and defend it with a detailed *analysis* of those sources. Commentary is what makes the difference between scattered evidence and a cohesive **argument** in support of a **claim**, and you'll need commentary if you hope to earn full points on the AP® Exam.

Examining the AP® Rubric

In the AP® Skills Workshop for Chapter 9 (p. SW9-A), we used the AP® rubric to determine that the evidence used in response to a document-based question must be:

1. **Sufficient.** You need at least three pieces of evidence from the provided sources, and at least one piece of evidence beyond the sources.
2. **Descriptive.** You need to paraphrase, not directly quote, at least three of the provided sources.
3. **Relevant.** All evidence must directly support the argument outlined in your thesis statement.

Having clarified the kind of evidence you'll need to include, we can now consider the rubric's complementary standard for commentary on that evidence:

- **One point:** For at least two sources, explains how or why the perspective, purpose, context, and/or audience of each source is relevant to an argument.
  To earn this point, the response must explain how or why (rather than simply identify) the perspective, purpose, context, or audience of each source (for at least two sources) is relevant to an argument about the prompt.

The mention of **context**, **audience**, **purpose**, and **perspective** likely brings to mind the sourcing strategy HIPPO from the AP® Skills Workshop for Chapter 3 (p. SW3-A):

Historical Context. When and where was the source created, based on its source line and any other clues? What developments, like movements or events, might have influenced the source's creation?

Intended Audience. Can you figure out the person or people for whom the source was created? How does this affect the source's content and tone?

Purpose. Why was the source created? What message might its creator have been trying to get across, and how can you tell?

Perspective. Can you tell who created the source and what their position in society was like? How might their background, beliefs, and biases have influenced the source's creation?

Outside Information. What course concepts, developments, and processes does the source bring to mind? What does the source *not* tell you, and what other sources might fill in those gaps?

It's key to note, however, that it's not enough to simply *identify* source information using the technique with which you're already familiar. Instead, for two sources, your commentary will need to explain *how* or *why* the source information supports the argument outlined in your thesis.

Reviewing Prewriting Skills

We can use the following sample prompt to practice building commentary:

Explain how African American entrepreneurs, businesses, and organizations promoted the economic stability and well-being of Black communities in the late nineteenth and early twentieth centuries.

As you've seen in the AP® Skills Workshop for Chapter 5 (p. SW5-A), you'll want to first break down the prompt into its task, time period, and topic, and then jot down the course knowledge that first comes to mind:

Time Period	Topic	Task
The nadir (1877–1915)	Impact of Black entrepreneurs, businesses, and organizations	Explain the relationship between Black entrepreneurs, businesses, and organizations and the welfare of the Black community.

Relevant Course Concepts, Developments, Processes

- After Reconstruction, Black people struggled for economic independence and faced exploitative work arrangements like sharecropping and debt peonage.
- Because white hostility excluded many African Americans from full participation in American economic and social life, Black people created their own businesses tailored to the needs of their communities.
- Especially in Southern cities like Richmond and Atlanta, it became common for the Black community to function as a self-sufficient "city within a city."
- Madam C. J. Walker, the first female American millionaire, is one notable example of the many African American inventors and entrepreneurs who hired Black workers and financially supported Black institutions.
- Several Black business organizations formed networks to advance Black-owned and Black-operated enterprises.

Next, you'll approach the sources for skillful skimming (p. SW6-A). On exam day, you'll want to take about 30 seconds to a minute with each source, so your skillful skimming notes are unlikely to be in full sentences. For now, though, take a bit longer with each source; it's useful to get practice articulating your thoughts in full sentences. As usual, try to identify the most important information:

Main idea. How would you summarize the source in one sentence?

Context. What course knowledge seems directly connected to this particular source? What's the most relevant outside knowledge about its topic, its time period, or its creator?

Category. How would you generalize the point of the source in just a few words? Does this category align or contrast with other sources for the same DBQ?

Source A: Proceedings of the National Negro Business League, 1900

"As I have travelled through the country from time to time I have been constantly surprised to note the number of colored men and women, often in small towns and remote districts, who are engaged in various lines of business. Sometimes in many cases the business is very humble, but nevertheless it was sufficiently advanced to indicate the opportunities of the race in this direction. My observation in this regard led me to believe that the time had come for the bringing together of the leading and most successful colored men and women throughout the country who are engaged in business. After consultation with men and women in various parts of the country it was determined to call a meeting in the city of Boston to organize the National Business League. This meeting was held during the 23d and 24th of August, and it was generally believed that it was one of the most successful and helpful meetings that has ever been held among our people. The meeting was called with two objects in view: first, to bring the men and women engaged in business together, in order that they might get acquainted with each other and get information and inspiration from each other; secondly, to form plans for an annual meeting and the organization of local business leagues that should extend throughout the country. Both of these objects, I think, have been admirably accomplished. I think there has never been a time in the history of the race when all feel so much encouraged in relation to their business opportunities as now. The promoters of this organization appreciate very keenly that the race cannot depend upon mere material growth alone for its ultimate success, but they do feel that material prosperity will greatly hasten their recognition in other directions."

SOURCE: Booker T. Washington, president and founder of the National Negro Business League, introduction to "Proceedings of the National Negro Business League," 1900

Source B: The Economic Revolution in the South, 1907

"[T]he rule of agricultural labor in the black belt of the South is not a system of free labor; it is simply a form of peonage. The black peon is held down by perpetual debt or petty criminal judgments; his rent rises with the price of cotton, his chances to buy land are either non-existent or confined to infertile regions. . . .

After freedom came, the Negro made four distinct efforts to reach economic safety. The first effort was by means of the select house-servant class; the second, by means of competitive industry; the third, by land-owning; and the fourth, by what I shall call the group economy. . . .

It [the group economy] consists of a coöperative arrangement of industry and service in a group which tends to make the group a closed economic circle, largely independent of surrounding whites. . . . There used to be Negro business men in Northern cities and a few even in Southern cities, but they catered to white trade; the Negro business man to-day caters to colored trade. So far has this gone to-day that in every city in the United States which has considerable Negro population, the colored group is serving itself in religion, medical care, legal advice and often educating its children. In growing degree also it is serving itself in insurance, houses, books, amusements."

SOURCE: W. E. B. Du Bois, "The Economic Revolution in the South," a chapter from *The Negro in the South*, 1907

Source C: Negro Banks of Virginia, 1910

"Total Resources $886,310.53 — Twelve Institutions in the State — All in Flourishing Condition.
Norfolk, Va., Jan. 25. — Virginia leads the country in colored banking institutions, both in number and resources, divided as follows:

Richmond with Four institutions, to-wit: The Savings Bank of the True Reformers, the Mechanics Savings Bank, St. Luke's Savings Bank and the Nickel Savings Bank.

Newport News has two, namely: The Crown Savings Bank and the Songs and Daughters of Peace Penny, Nickel and Dime Savings Bank.

Norfolk has two—the Brown Savings and Banking Company and the Gideon Savings Bank.

Hampton has one—the G.U.O Fisherman's Savings Bank.

Courtland has the Sussex-Surrey Savings Bank.

Staunton has the Dime Savings Bank and Trust Association.

Waynesboro has the Southern One Cent Savings Bank. . . .

All of these banks do a regular banking business, accepting deposits subject to check. They pay interest on savings accounts, discount commercial paper, make loans on real estate, the majority of them have New York correspondents, maintain splendid connections with the large white local banks, enjoy good credit and are all, without exception, in a flourishing condition."

SOURCE: *The New York Age* newspaper, "Negro Banks of Virginia," 1910

Source D: Fire Insurance Map of Greenwood District, 1915

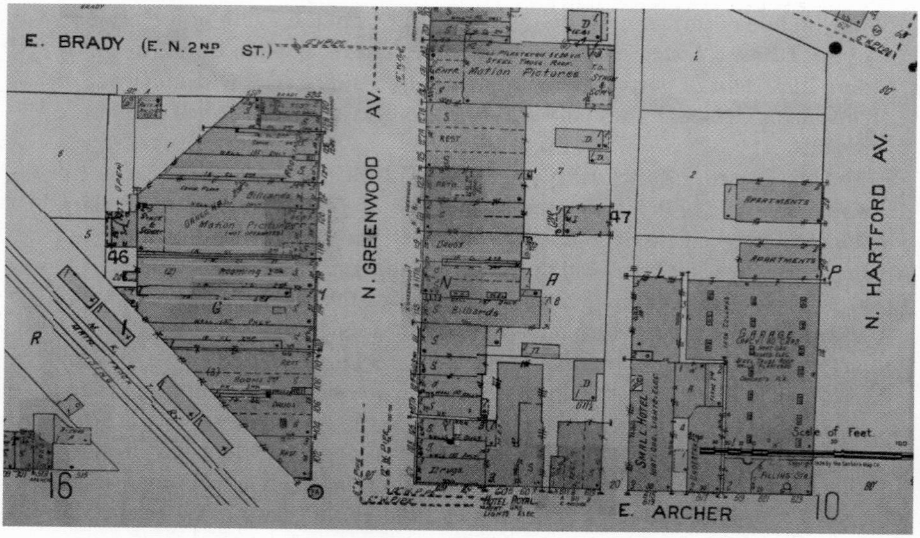

(1939) Sanborn Fire Insurance Map from Tulsa, Tulsa County, Oklahoma. Sanborn Map Company, to 1939 Vol. 1, ; Republished 1939. [Map] Retrieved from the Library of Congress, https://www.loc.gov/item/sanborn07276_010/

SOURCE: Fire insurance map showing businesses like drugstores, hotels, and movie theaters in the Greenwood District of Tulsa, Oklahoma, 1915

Source E: First National Convention of The Madam Walker Beauty Culturists League, 1917

Madam Walker Family Archives/A'Lelia Bundles

Sales agents for The Madam C. J. Walker Manufacturing Company gather at Philadelphia's Union Baptist Church to learn about marketing strategy and business management.

A skillful skim of the sources might look like this:

SOURCE A

Main idea. The National Negro Business League brought together Black entrepreneurs to encourage the economic development of Black businesses.

Context. Booker T. Washington founded the National Negro Business League in 1900, in alignment with his belief that economic independence would protect against the harm of racial discrimination.

Category. Community support

SOURCE B

Main idea. Without equal opportunities to participate in the broader economy, Black people launched businesses specifically catering to their communities.

Context. While W. E. B. Du Bois and Booker T. Washington differed in their opinions on the best path toward Black advancement, they both believed in racial solidarity and economic advancement.

Category. Goods and services, employment

SOURCE C

Main idea. Black people pooled their resources together and created their own banks and financial institutions.

Context. Citizens Savings Bank and Trust Company was a Black-owned bank in the United States and was founded in 1904.

Category. Community support

SOURCE D

Main idea. At the time the map was drawn in 1915, Tulsa's Greenwood District was a thriving center of commerce.

Context. The Greenwood neighborhood in Tulsa, Oklahoma, was home to a prosperous, self-sufficient thriving Black business community nicknamed "Black Wall Street."

Category. Goods and services

SOURCE E

Main idea. Some Black-owned businesses became major employers for the Black community.

Context. Madam C. J. Walker, the first female American millionaire, is one notable example of the many African American inventors and entrepreneurs who hired Black workers and financially supported Black institutions.

Category. Employment

On the AP® Exam, you'll next need to collect your thoughts into a thesis statement as outlined in the AP® Skills Workshop for Chapter 7 (p. SW7-A). Here, we'll save time by providing a sample thesis statement:

> Many Black communities were able to thrive despite the racist policies of the nadir because Black entrepreneurs and businesses provided goods and services, community support, and employment to the Black community.

We can then articulate three **topic sentences** that spring naturally from this thesis statement:

Thesis statement	Many Black communities were able to thrive despite the racist policies of the nadir because Black entrepreneurs and businesses provided essential goods and services, community support, and employment to the Black community.
Paragraph 1	Facing discrimination in the wider economy, African Americans launched businesses to provide their communities with in-demand products and resources.
Paragraph 2	In addition, Black people formed supportive networks that encouraged further economic growth.
Paragraph 3	Furthermore, Black entrepreneurs and businesses provided employment opportunities that helped Black workers build skills and make financial gains.

After that, we can gather the evidence that best supports this thesis statement, tackling one paragraph at a time. An evidence chart for our paragraph on goods and services might look like this:

Topic Sentence: Facing discrimination in the wider economy, African Americans launched businesses to provide their communities with in-demand products and resources.		
Evidence	**Explanation of How Evidence Supports Your Topic Sentence**	**Source of Evidence**
Until Black Americans began starting their own businesses, they often had to secure goods and services through sharecropping and debt peonage.	Black-owned businesses kept money within Black communities instead of forcing African Americans to funnel money back to white landowners through exploitative arrangements. Also, Black-owned businesses filled a gap in the economy, since Jim Crow laws often limited where African Americans could shop.	Source B
The Greenwood neighborhood in Tulsa, Oklahoma, was home to a wide variety of successful establishments like drugstores, hotels, and movie theaters.	Black business districts like Greenwood's "Black Wall Street" became incredibly prosperous during the nadir. In fact, some became affluent enough to reach self-sufficiency.	Source D

Having completed these prewriting steps, we can focus on building out the commentary that will transform this collection of evidence into a cohesive paragraph.

Developing Commentary

We mentioned earlier in this workshop that commentary is your chance to explain exactly how each piece of evidence supports your argument's claim. On the AP® Exam, you'll do this by providing more detail on the perspective, purpose, context, or audience of at least two sources, and by laying out how those details support your topic sentences and thus your thesis.

Again, we'll remind you to resist the common tendency to write out a laundry list of evidence! Commentary is your chance to make your personal perspective clear, so try your best to put evidence into your own words as succinctly as possible so you can devote more time to analyzing sourcing and explaining how the evidence ultimately supports your unique claim.

To drive home the importance of quality commentary, let's consider a sample paragraph that relies too heavily on restating evidence from the provided sources:

> Facing discrimination in the wider economy, African Americans launched businesses to provide their communities with supplies and support. W. E. B. Du Bois notes that before Black Americans began starting their own businesses, they often had to secure goods and services through sharecropping and debt peonage. African Americans gained a great deal of economic independence by building their own business districts. The Greenwood neighborhood in Tulsa, Oklahoma, was home to a wide variety of successful establishments like drugstores, hotels, and movie theaters (Source D).

Aside from the opening sentence, this paragraph simply lists evidence with little elaboration or explanation linking each detail to the writer's claim. Compare that paragraph to the one that follows:

> Facing discrimination in the wider economy, African Americans launched businesses to provide their communities with supplies and support. W. E. B. Du Bois notes that before Black Americans began starting their own businesses, they often had to secure goods and services through sharecropping and debt peonage. Writing from the perspective of a civil rights activist committed to Black advancement, Du Bois explains how economic independence would empower Black people to escape harmful financial arrangements. Indeed, African Americans gained a great deal of economic independence by building their own business districts in cities across the South. For instance, the Greenwood neighborhood in Tulsa, Oklahoma, was home to a wide variety of establishments like drugstores, hotels, and movie theaters (Source D). In fact, at the time the fire insurance map was drawn, Greenwood had become affluent enough to build a reputation as "Black Wall Street." During an era when Jim Crow laws excluded African Americans from participating in the broader economy, Black-owned businesses played a key role in connecting African Americans with the goods and services they needed to live better lives.

This paragraph is successful because it not only includes specific evidence from the sources, but also explains how the evidence connects to the paragraph's overarching topic sentence (and, therefore, to the essay's thesis statement). In other words, there's ample commentary; notice the analysis of how Du Bois's perspective likely influenced his writing, and how the historical context of Greenwood's reputation as "Black Wall Street" explains the map's significance. The paragraph also closes in a way that links back to the topic sentence, reminding readers how the evidence that's been presented fits into a broader argument.

Incorporating Transitions

You may have also noticed that the successful sample body paragraph uses phrases to smooth out the **transitions** between different subtopics. Because your response to a DBQ will be lengthier than SAQ responses, and because you're dealing with multiple sources, you'll need transition words or phrases to create cohesive and coherent paragraphs. You may wish to incorporate transitions like those to follow:

Causation	Combination	Chronology	Contrast	Example
accordingly	additionally	after	after all	as an
as a result	again	afterwards	although	illustration
and so	also	always	and yet	for example
because	as a result	during	at the same time	for instance
consequently	besides	earlier	but	specifically
for that	even more	following	despite	that is
reason	finally	immediately	however	to demonstrate
hence	first, firstly further	in the	in contrast	to illustrate
on account of	furthermore	meantime later	nevertheless	
since	in addition	never	nonetheless	
therefore	in fact	next	notwithstanding	
thus	indeed	now	on the contrary	
	in similar fashion	once	on the other	
	in the first place	simultaneously	hand	
	in the same way	so far	otherwise	
	in the second	sometimes	though	
	place last, lastly	soon	yet	
	likewise	subsequently		
	moreover	then		
	next	until		
	second, secondly	when		
		whenever		
		while		

You can readily apply these phrases to your own writing. For instance, you can use one of the "example" phrases to introduce your first piece of evidence. Before you move onto to another piece of evidence that will further support the same topic sentence, you can then use one of the phrases under "combination."

Documenting Sources

You'll also want to make sure you properly cite your sources to ensure your reader notices the moments you bring in source evidence. You can do this by naming the source's creator, providing the source's title, or simply sharing the source's letter:

- W. E. B. Du Bois noted that before Black Americans began starting their own businesses, they often had to secure goods and services through sharecropping and debt peonage.
- For instance, the Greenwood neighborhood in Tulsa, Oklahoma, was home to a wide variety of successful establishments like drugstores, hotels, and movie theaters (Source D).

recap

Developing Commentary

To develop commentary, provide more detail on the perspective, purpose, context, or audience of at least two sources, and then lay out how those details support your topic sentences and thus your thesis. Remember to use transitions to move smoothly between topics, and remember to cite each source's creator, title, or letter.

Activity ▸ Developing Commentary

First, use a graphic organizer like the one shown below to collect evidence. You may choose to complete this activity using the sample topic sentence provided for either Paragraph 2 or Paragraph 3.

Topic Sentence:		
Evidence	Explanation of How Evidence Supports Your Topic Sentence	Source of Evidence

Then, use your graphic organizer to draft a complete body paragraph that includes commentary on at least two sources, incorporates transitions, and provides appropriate citations.

Multiple-Choice Questions

Questions 1–3 refer to the following.

"The law provides that in contracts of service entered by a laborer, where money was advanced, and the contract broken without just cause, and the money not refunded, the laborer is guilty, and may be sentenced to hard labor until the fine is worked out. The Federal Department contends that the purpose and effect of the law is not to stop fraudulent practices so much as to impose compulsory service upon the Negroes who constitute the bulk of the farm labor of the State."

AP® source W. E. B. Du Bois, *Along the Color Line*, 1910

1. Which of the following Supreme Court cases led most directly to the issue described in the excerpt?

(A) *Dred Scott v. Sandford*, 1857, which denied rights of citizenship to both enslaved and free Black Americans

(B) The *Slaughterhouse Cases*, 1873, which ruled that the Fourteenth Amendment protects only the legal rights associated with federal U.S. citizenship, not those that pertain to state citizenship

(C) *Plessy v. Ferguson*, 1896, which effectively legalized separate and unequal resources, facilities, and rights

(D) *Brown v. Board of Education*, 1954, which outlawed the so-called "separate but equal" rationale for racial segregation

2. Which of the following best describes the viewpoint of W. E. B. Du Bois in the excerpt above?

(A) Du Bois is explaining how the federal government offered remedy to those who dealt with labor abuse as long as they were born in the United States.

(B) Du Bois is describing the terms of labor contracts for sharecroppers in the early twentieth century.

(C) Du Bois is arguing against the use of labor contracts with the federal government as well as state municipalities.

(D) Du Bois is criticizing the inequitable terms of labor contracts for sharecroppers and the lack of support from the federal government.

3. Which of the following statements best reflects the legal issue at stake in the excerpt?

(A) The excerpt highlights the work-related abuses that many Black Americans in the South had to endure due to the decision made in the *Slaughterhouse Cases*.

(B) The excerpt details how the perception that Black Americans were not full citizens led to their being denied restitution from courts during labor disputes.

(C) The excerpt suggests that although there were many instances in which Black Americans were denied equal protection under the law, they were nonetheless able to use the courts to seek justice.

(D) The excerpt argues that the Fourteenth Amendment ensures equal protection of the law for all citizens of the United States, and that its protections cannot be denied for race, creed, or religious practices.

Short-Answer Question

Black Cowboys

Universal History Archive/Getty Images.

1. Using the image, answer A, B, C, and D.

(A) Describe the historical context of the image.

(B) Explain one conclusion that can be drawn about life for African Americans post-Reconstruction based on the image.

(C) Explain how this photograph might challenge stereotypes held by some people about Black Americans, the West, or the cowboy profession.

(D) Explain the influence of Black cowboys on early twentieth-century pop culture.

CHAPTER **11**

The New Negro Comes of Age

1915–1930

CHAPTER TIMELINE *Events specific to African American history are in purple. General U.S. history events are in black. Events from the AP® Course Framework are marked with an asterisk.*

1915	Carter G. Woodson establishes Association for the Study of Negro Life and History*
1916	Woodson begins publishing *Journal of Negro History*
1917	U.S. enters World War I
	Race riot erupts in East St. Louis, Illinois
	Silent march along New York's Fifth Avenue
	Buchanan v. Warley overturns city ordinances mandating where Blacks can live
1918	World War I ends
1919	Red Summer race riots
1920	Nineteenth Amendment guarantees women's suffrage
	James Weldon Johnson becomes first Black executive secretary of NAACP
1921	*Shuffle Along*, first all-Black music and dance revue, opens on Broadway
	Marcus Garvey's Universal Negro Improvement Association hits four million members worldwide*
1922	*The Negro in Chicago* is published, showcasing the sociological insights of the Chicago School
1923	Charles S. Johnson founds *Opportunity*, National Urban League's journal
1924	The Immigration Act of 1924 severely curtails immigration from the West Indies
1925	Alain Locke's *The New Negro* published*
1926	Woodson establishes Negro History Week (expanded to Black History Month in 1976)*
1927	Duke Ellington and his band become regulars at Harlem's Cotton Club
	Jane Edna Hunter opens her largest Phyllis Wheatley Home in Cleveland
1928	Oscar De Priest elected to U.S. House of Representatives
1929	Stock market crashes; Great Depression begins
1930	Reflecting the demographic shift of the Great Migration, all three cities with the largest Black populations are now in the North

Please note that this chapter includes a map of cultural Harlem that includes the N-word, which we have chosen to reprint in this textbook to accurately reflect Black artists' original intent as well as the time period and culture of the era. We recognize that this word has a long history as a derogatory and deeply hurtful expression when used by white people toward Black people. Black people's choice to use this word relates not only to that history but to a larger cultural tradition in which the N-word can take on different meanings, emphasize shared experience, and be repurposed as a term of endearment within Black communities. While the use of that word in such contexts might not be hurtful, the use of it in our current context very often is. Be mindful of context, both historical and contemporary, as you read and discuss this chapter.

Zora Neale Hurston and the Advancement of the Black Freedom Struggle

In 1925, Zora Neale Hurston stood on the street corners of Harlem, conducting social science research. A student at Barnard College, she was taking skull measurements, and she needed to convince African Americans to allow her to place her calipers around their heads. Audacious and persuasive, Hurston succeeded in her data collection. She turned these data over to Franz Boas, a leading anthropologist at Columbia University, who used them to demonstrate that craniology was a false science. Skull measurements, which had been used for a century to argue that Blacks had smaller cranial capacities than other races and thus were intellectually inferior, actually demonstrated nothing more than the biases of the analyst. Boas challenged the entire anthropology establishment with his theories of cultural relativism, overturning the notion that societies could be ranked along an evolutionary scale. He also argued that individual capabilities were determined more by environment than by race. Hurston studied with Boas after she graduated from Barnard, but by that time, she had already embarked on a writing career. Everything she wrote, however, was informed by anthropology and by the core belief in equality that she admired in the social science approach of her mentor.

Hurston burst onto the African American literary scene in Harlem with short stories and plays that revealed a dazzling new talent. Her fiction drew on her memories of growing up in the all-Black town of Eatonville, Florida, where her father was the mayor and her mother encouraged her inquisitiveness. Young Hurston absorbed her surroundings and delighted in the storytelling she heard on neighbors' front porches. For her, African American culture was vibrant, healthy, and the equal of other cultures. Rejecting the dominant white view of African Americans as inferior and the African American experience as tragic, Hurston presented that experience as she knew and understood it: as a life-affirming twist on the resilience and complexity of the human condition.

Hurston's move from Florida to New York City paralleled the migration of more than a million African Americans from the rural and urban South to the metropolises of the North between 1915 and 1940. This migration changed their lives, giving many of them new jobs in industry and new visibility and power as they changed the racial composition of northern cities. Hurston's self-confidence exemplifies the increasingly affirmative spirit of African Americans. In 1917, after the United States entered World War I, Black men served in all-Black regiments overseas. When they returned, many were aggressive, even militant, and determined to achieve the equality so long denied them and their people. This growing defiance increasingly characterized both the national Black mood and Black mass organizations, which advanced the self-help and protest traditions. Black studies in the social sciences broadened understanding of African American lives, the nature of prejudice, and the causes of racial conflict. New expressions in literature, such as Hurston's, explored Black heritage and identity. The Great Migration, the Universal Negro Improvement Association (UNIA), and the New Negro Renaissance, often called the Harlem Renaissance, were the most significant manifestations of the early-twentieth-century New Negro.

The Great Migration

What were the causes of the Great Migration, and what impact did it have on Black communities and American culture?

What were the effects of Afro-Caribbean migration to the United States in the early twentieth century?

Since the beginning of the Civil War, Black people in the South had been on the move. During the war, they fled to Union lines and freedom; after the war, they went in search of families and new lives. During and after Reconstruction, some moved to the New South's growing cities; others moved to new towns, especially all-Black ones, in Kansas and Oklahoma; and a small but steady number went north, seeking better jobs and educational opportunities. Indeed, in the last decade of the nineteenth century, 200,000 Blacks relocated to the North from the South. Starting in the 1910s, the number moving north grew exponentially, dramatically changing the demographic makeup of the nation. These northern migrants also transformed African American identity and national race relations. Initially, they sought jobs in industry, which were increasingly available after the start of World War I in 1914. Moving into "Negro districts" in the North's large cities, they helped create vibrant and self-sufficient communities.

Origins and Patterns of Migration

"The peoples is leaving here by the thousands," wrote a Black man from Atlanta to the *Chicago Defender* on May 2, 1917, as he asked about jobs in Chicago.[1] From Biloxi, Mississippi, a "willen workin woman" explained to the newspaper on April 27, 1917, that she yearned to escape "this land of sufring."[2] From Charleston, South Carolina, on February 10, 1917, came the report that "the times in the south is very hard and one can scarcely live."[3] One resident of Vicksburg, Mississippi, explained on May 7, 1917, "We are working here at starvation wages and some of us are virtually without employment willing to accept any kind of work such as cooking, laundering, or as domestics."[4] A hopeful man from Houston, Texas, declared on April 20, 1917, "I dont Care where [I go] so long as I Go where a man is a man."[5]

The Great Migration
This 1918 photograph captures a well-dressed family that made the journey from the South to the North during World War I. Their dress reflects the importance of both the act of migration and the act of visually recording the moment. The fact that so many African Americans migrated as individuals or in non-kin-based groups only heightens the importance of these kinds of family migration photographs. **Use this image to describe the Black family structure in the United States in the 1900s.** *Chicago History Museum/Archive Photos/Getty Images.*

ACTIVITY ▸ Revisit Your Prediction

In the AP® Unit Warmup (p. U3-E), you made a prediction about this image. **How do you think the Great Migration will impact the Black communities and American culture? What details from the photo help support your prediction? Support or revise your original prediction using evidence from this chapter.**

Great Migration
The migration of 1.5 million African Americans from the South to the metropolises of the North in the years from 1915 to 1940.

The huge numbers of Black people who decided to leave the Jim Crow South constituted one of the largest grassroots migrations in U.S. history. Today that shift in population is called the **Great Migration**. Two million Blacks, according to one estimate, migrated out of the South between 1915 and 1930, most of them headed to the North. While many migrants came from southern cities, many also came from plantations and farms, so this was also a rural-to-urban migration, from sharecropping and tenant farming to urban wage work. Increasing rural-to-urban migration within the South in addition to increasing Black migration from the South to the North led to the southern rural Black population being halved by 1930.

AP® exam tip

Be sure you can describe how racial discrimination and violence, coupled with lack of economic opportunities in the South, spurred the beginnings of the Great Migration.

Asked why they left, migrants described both "push" and "pull" factors. Some, like the woman from Biloxi, were desperate to get away from the South, with its poverty and peonage, its repression and lynchings, its stagnant wages, and the daily violence and indignities of Jim Crow. Also pushing Blacks out of the South were a series of natural disasters. The boll weevil, a cotton-eating beetle that spread from Mexico to Texas in the 1890s and then throughout the South, devastated the cotton crop. Floods in the Mississippi valley during the winter of 1916 and in North Carolina the following summer caused extensive damage. The region was in an economic depression, due in part to the decline of the overseas cotton market following the outbreak of war in Europe. At the same time, the war was creating job opportunities in the North. War industries were expanding just as the immigrant labor pool was shrinking dramatically. In 1914, more than a million Europeans came to the United States, but in 1915, after the outbreak of war, fewer than 200,000 arrived. Northern industries, in desperate need of labor, dispatched agents to recruit Black workers in the South. For Black southerners, the pull of better jobs proved decisive, as men who had been earning 75 cents a day could earn up to $5 a day in the meatpacking, iron, steel, and auto industries.

chain migration
A migration pattern in which initial migrants prepare the way for family members and friends to follow, creating migrant clusters from specific locales in their new settings.

Men often migrated first, setting up a household base for others to follow. A **chain migration** pattern emerged, in which family members, friends, and neighbors joined the first migrants, who reported their satisfaction with their new lives in the North. Through letters home, southern Blacks learned of jobs with higher salaries, good schools for children, and opportunities for political involvement as well as social and cultural activities. Earlier migrants returning to the South for a visit made a big impression with their city clothes, new cars, and cash. Black sleeping car porters and maids were important information sources, as they traveled throughout the country and could make comparisons. They often brought with them and distributed copies of the *Chicago Defender*, a Black newspaper that vigorously promoted migration.

AP® exam tip

On the AP® Exam, you'll need to be able to explain how a new railway system and the Black press made the Great Migration possible.

In Robert Horton's barbershop in Hattiesburg, Mississippi, migration was the topic of conversation as copies of the *Defender* were passed around. When Horton decided to move to Chicago, he did so as part of a migration club that he helped create, drawing on family, church, and barbershop connections. Soon, forty Black migrants from Hattiesburg were encouraging friends and family members to join them and helping newcomers find places to stay.[6] Their experience was common, as clubs, neighborhood groups, and whole churches pooled resources to travel north together. Railroads offered special group rates, and migrations followed the rail lines. Blacks from Florida, Georgia, and the Carolinas traveled East Coast railroads to Philadelphia, Newark, New York, Buffalo, and other cities. Those from Alabama, Louisiana, Mississippi, Arkansas, and Tennessee took trains to cities such as St. Louis, Chicago, Detroit, Cleveland, and Pittsburgh (Map 11.1). As wave upon wave of newcomers arrived, they transformed the cities of the North.

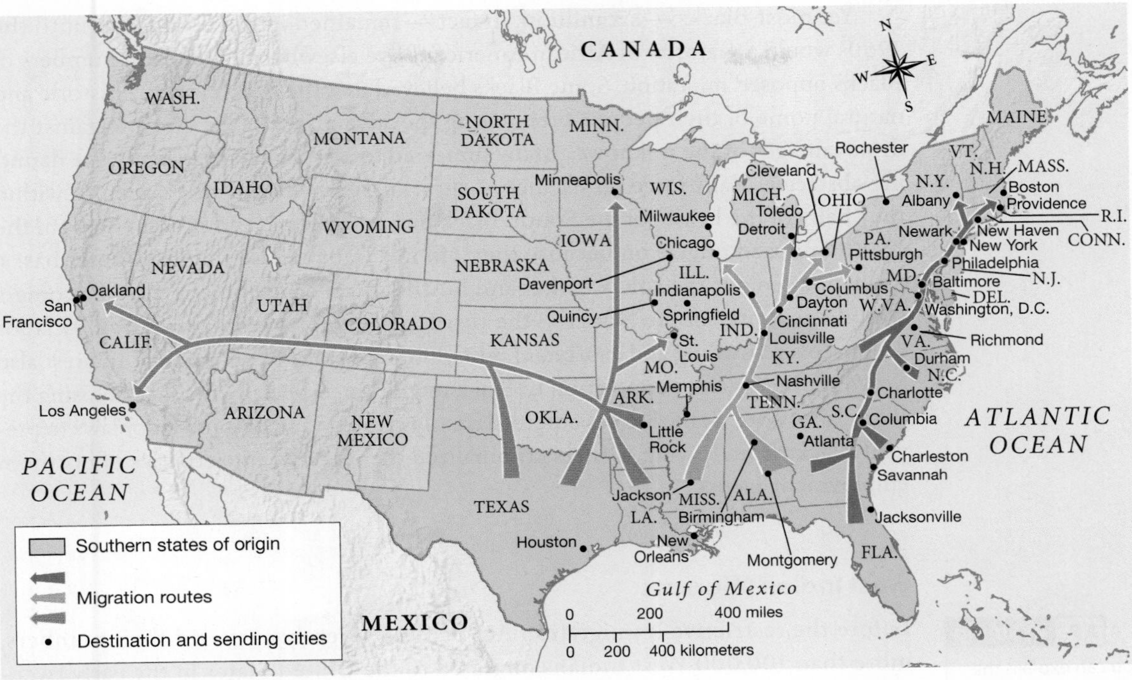

MAP 11.1 The Great Migration, 1910–1929

This map shows the major railroad routes used by Black migrants to travel from the South to the cities of the North and, to a lesser extent, the West. It also shows the increasing national spread of the African American population. (See also Map 13.1.) **Compare this map to Map 10.2 (African American Lynching Victims by State, 1877–1950). Describe the similarities and differences.** *Data from Smallwood and Elliot,* The Atlas of African-American History and Politics: From the Slave Trade to Modern Times *(1998).*

ACTIVITY ▸ Revisit Your Prediction

In the AP® Unit Warmup (p. U3-F), you made a prediction about this image. **What does this map suggest about the causes and effects of the Great Migration? Support or revise your original prediction using evidence from this chapter.**

In 1910, reflecting the fact that the bulk of pre–World War I Black migrants had moved to southern cities, the three U.S. cities with the largest Black populations were all in the South: Washington, D.C. (94,000), New Orleans (89,000), and Baltimore (85,000). The Great Migration dramatically shifted the Black migrant flow not only to cities but northward, transforming the North and the United States as well. In 1930, the three U.S. cities with the largest Black populations were all in the North: Chicago (234,000), New York (225,000), and Philadelphia (220,000). The Black population of Harlem alone had gone from 50,000 in 1915 to 200,000 in 1930. Even more dramatically, the Black population of Detroit mushroomed from 6,000 in 1910 to 120,000 in 1930.

AP® skills

Applying Disciplinary Knowledge: Describe the impacts of chain migration.

Yet most Blacks — six million, in fact — remained in the South; not until the 1960s would a majority of African Americans live elsewhere. Significant numbers of Blacks opposed migration. Some Blacks believed that the South was the historic and natural home of their people, often citing the advantages of the known against the disadvantages of the unknown. Many preferred to stay and fight, despite the daunting obstacles. Many forged resistance — survival, self-help, and affirmation — within the "belly of the beast" of the South. Black business people and professionals in the South opposed migration because they did not want to lose their customer bases. They pointed out the cold weather and hostile social environment that newcomers would encounter in the North — the threat of unemployment, exclusion by labor unions, overcrowding and exorbitant rents, and race riots. Economic self-interest also drove southern white opposition to Black migration, especially the fear of losing the Black labor pool. Some locales enforced hastily created vagrancy and labor laws to prevent Blacks from leaving. Others criminalized the recruitment activities of northern employment agents.

West Indian Migrants

AP® exam tip

Be sure you can explain the reasons for the increase in Black Caribbean migration to the United States during the first half of the twentieth century. You should also be prepared to describe the effects of Afro-Caribbean migration to the United States in the early twentieth century and the migration's effect on African American communities.

Before the restrictive Immigration Act of 1924 severely curtailed their numbers, more than 100,000 West Indians migrated to the United States in the early twentieth century. Indeed, most foreign-born Blacks in the United States at that time hailed from the West Indies. Coming from places like Jamaica, Barbados, Cuba, and Puerto Rico and going to places like Florida and New York, these Afro-Caribbean migrants enhanced the internal ethnic differences within the African American population in the United States. In addition, bringing the imperial, colonial, and distinctive island dimensions of their backgrounds with them, these West Indian migrants, mostly from the Afro-British Caribbean, enriched the international and political as well as cultural dimensions of the African American world in the United States. While most were from English-speaking islands, a significant number were from non-English-speaking islands, notably Spanish-speaking and French-speaking ones. West Indian migrants also contributed to the religious pluralism within the African American world in the United States, as many were Anglican, Episcopalian, and Catholic.

Many West Indian migrants, like innumerable migrants elsewhere, sent remittances to families back home to help out. Many, perhaps most, of these migrants were working class; some were skilled; many had labored on the Panama Canal construction project (1904–1914). Some were middle-class professionals. A striking number, however, were temporary sojourners, as fully a third returned to their original nation. Still, by 1930, roughly 40,000 West Indians called New York City, especially Harlem and Brooklyn, their home. Collectively, like migrants to the United States generally, they were drawn to the American dream of opportunities and better lives.

Black Community Aid Societies

Southern Blacks wrote to the *Chicago Defender* about their hopes for migration not just because the newspaper promoted life in the North, but also because it was familiar. Two-thirds of the *Defender*'s circulation — 230,000 by 1915 — was outside the paper's Chicago base. Passed from one person to another, read aloud in beauty parlors, barbershops, and churches, the *Defender* enjoyed an actual circulation that was several times the official figure. "The Mouthpiece of 14 Million People," proclaimed its masthead. Robert Abbott, who founded the paper in 1905 as a one-man operation, gave it a national presence by taking a militant stance on many race issues of the day. The paper not only promoted migration but also listed jobs and train schedules. "Ride for a day and a night to freedom," proclaimed Abbott. "You tip your hat to no white man. . . . You are a man and are expected to carry yourself as such."[7] Between 1916 and 1920, some 50,000 southern Blacks headed for Chicago.

For them and other migrants, the Black exodus took on biblical proportions. They saw themselves as leaving the land of persecution for the promised land, where they hoped to create new lives. Indeed, they had to rebuild households, develop new work routines, settle their children in school, make new friends, become part of new neighborhoods, establish new church homes, and join new social clubs and organizations. The benevolent societies and established Black churches in the North offered help. In Chicago, the Phyllis Wheatley Home gave young women a safe place to live while they looked for work. The home was opened in 1908 by the Phyllis Wheatley Club, which Elizabeth Lindsay Davis, a teacher and member of the National Association of Colored Women, had founded in 1896. It was one branch of a network of **Black settlement houses** modeled on Jane Addams's Hull House, also in Chicago, which helped immigrant women from Europe adjust to life in America. The Chicago branch of the National Urban League, established in 1916, offered similar services for newly arrived southern Blacks. Its social workers helped with jobs and housing, and at its "stranger meetings," Urban League members instructed newcomers in the dress and conduct appropriate for city life.

Black settlement houses Urban institutions created by progressive women reformers to house migrant women and help them adjust to urban life.

AP® skills

Applying Disciplinary Knowledge: How did the Black settlement houses in Chicago help newly migrated southerners adjust to city living?

Black-led aid organizations like those in Chicago rallied across the North to address the pressing needs of Black migrants. The Urban League assisted with issues like jobs and housing (including landlord–tenant conflicts), medical care, police protection, and recreation. The Urban League, which had origins in connecting local community centers, initiated Big Brothers and Big Sisters clubs to help Black urban youth. Under the auspices of the Urban League and powerful local Black women, institutions like Harlem's White Rose Mission, Philadelphia's Armstrong Association, Chicago's Negro Fellowship League, and the Atlanta Neighborhood Union helped innumerable Black girls and women.

AP® exam tip

Be sure you can describe how the Urban League assisted African Americans migrating from the rural South during the Great Migration.

Phyllis Wheatley Women's Clubs and Homes also had a national reach. Some of them offered classes in domestic skills, some offered nurseries, and some provided residences for Black working women. One such residence was founded by Jane Edna Hunter, a trained nurse from South Carolina who relocated to Cleveland in 1905.

Despite her solid background, in Cleveland she endured severe workplace discrimination and extreme difficulty finding satisfactory housing. These experiences pushed her to start a Phyllis Wheatley Home there in 1911 to help struggling Black women, especially domestic workers and private day nurses. In 1913, she opened a twenty-three-room residence; in 1917, she opened a seventy-two-room building. By 1927, Hunter had led the building of an eleven-story residence for Black women, which also had a dining hall, a nursery school, a beauty training school, and a playground. Hunter's critics claimed that far too many of these girls and women were funneled into dead-end jobs for wealthy whites, some of whom helped finance her work through the Phyllis Wheatley Association. Nevertheless, the association and the Phyllis Wheatley Home assisted many Black girls and women in Cleveland.

Changes in Church Membership and Worship

Long-established Chicago churches also smoothed the transition from the rural South to the urban North. Quinn Chapel African Methodist Episcopal Church, the city's oldest Black church, attracted new members with outreach efforts. More astonishing was the growth of Olivet Baptist Church, whose members met new arrivals at the railroad station and helped them get settled in new homes. In addition to an employment bureau and home locator service, Olivet provided women's groups to aid homemakers and single women, boys' and girls' clubs, a day nursery and kindergarten for working mothers, a workingmen's home, and a food pantry with a dining room. Not surprisingly, the church's membership doubled in just four years, from 4,200 in 1916 to 8,500 in 1919.

AP® exam tip

Be sure you can explain how African Americans continued to transform Christian worship in the United States and created their own institutions during this era, when the number of Black churches increased significantly.

This swift increase did not come without controversy, however, as established church members objected to the emotionalism of southern Black Christians, and southerners felt out of place in sedate worship services. One newcomer confessed that she "couldn't understand the pastor and the words he used" at Olivet, and she "couldn't sing their way."[8] The differences were not just a matter of worship style. There was a class divide between middle-class Chicago natives, many of whom were descendants of free Blacks, and the poorer newcomers from the South. But as newcomers began to outnumber natives in Chicago's established churches, they infused worship with a "folk" religiosity and a southern preaching style. Their spirituals and rhythmic hymn singing merged with blues and secular music to create a new genre called gospel music.

Many Chicago natives viewed with suspicion the storefront churches that southern Pentecostals established and the religious groups that had emerged from the breakaway holiness movement within the Methodist Church. Seeking a personal and life-changing experience of grace, rural Blacks in states along the Mississippi River had been drawn to the holiness movement in the late nineteenth century. One of them, William Seymour, preached that the gift of the Holy Spirit was manifested by speaking in tongues. His Azusa Street Revival, which began in Los Angeles in 1906, is credited with launching the spread of **Pentecostalism**, but by then the Pentecostal Church

Pentecostalism
A religious movement that emphasizes a personal and life-changing experience of grace and promotes the belief that the presence of the Holy Spirit is manifested by speaking in tongues.

of God in Christ was already strong in Tennessee and Mississippi. Migrants from this region brought their religion with them, founding twenty storefront churches in Chicago by 1919 and launching a five-year building project for Roberts Temple Church of God in Christ in 1922.

Segregation, Self-Sufficiency, and Political Power

While escaping the legal segregation and oppression of the Jim Crow South, the newcomers recognized a different kind of segregation at work in the North. In the workplace, southerners often felt too vulnerable to join unions, especially as white workers and trade unions affiliated with the American Federation of Labor did not welcome them. The Stockyards Labor Council tried to organize Chicago's butchering and meatpacking workers in an interracial union, but only Chicago natives joined, not southern newcomers. In 1921, these newcomers, eager for work, took jobs in the stockyards vacated by striking workers, thus helping packinghouses to break the strike and exacerbating tensions in Chicago's Black neighborhoods.

The most serious tensions between Blacks and whites, however, were over housing. Because patterns of residential segregation circumscribed northern Black neighborhoods, their populations soon exceeded what the existing housing stock could handle. Between 1910 and 1920, as Chicago's South Side population tripled, the neighborhood deteriorated. Like the overcrowded Negro districts in other cities in the North, the South Side of Chicago suffered from inferior sewage control, lighting, and police protection. Because housing was scarce, rents were higher than in nearby white neighborhoods, and groceries were more expensive. But when Blacks attempted to move beyond what was called "the Black belt," white homeowners' associations resisted with both legal obstacles and violence. Fifty-eight "race bombings" of Black residences took place in Chicago between July 1, 1917, and March 1, 1921.[9]

In the North, racial segregation was enforced by long-standing custom (de facto) rather than by law (de jure), as in the South. Yet, as in southern cities, Black communities in the North were largely distinct and separate from the white neighborhoods that surrounded and excluded them. And also like their southern counterparts, northern Negro districts were lively and self-sufficient, with businesses, churches, and social clubs and organizations owned or operated by Blacks for Blacks. In Chicago, for example, Black doctors and civic activists established Provident Hospital, where Black physicians could practice and Black nurses could train. Because white funeral homes would not handle Black bodies, Black funeral directors catered to an exclusively Black clientele. They arranged the emotion-rich "homegoing" ceremonies that southerners wanted or helped them plan for the deceased to be buried in the South. Self-contained enterprises such as Chicago's Metropolitan Funeral Home Association encompassed Black funeral homes, casket makers, chemical suppliers, and insurance agents. Chicagoans led the National Negro Funeral Directors Association. Funeral directors were respected community leaders, often members of the National

AP® skills

Applying Disciplinary Knowledge: What is a homegoing ceremony? Why would it be called this rather than being called a funeral?

Madam C. J. Walker
At the wheel of a Model T in 1916, Walker exudes the confidence of the most successful Black business woman of her time. Born in poverty to sharecroppers who had been enslaved in Louisiana in 1910, Walker settled in Indianapolis, where she created a hugely successful hair care business empire catering to Black women. At its height, her hair care business employed 40,000 African Americans. **How does this photo epitomize Black entrepreneurship and financial success?** *Photo by Jim Mooney/NY Daily News Archive via Getty Images.*

ACTIVITY ▸ Revisit Your Prediction

In the AP® Unit Warmup (p. U3-F), you made a prediction about this image. **What details from the image stand out most? Explain how you think the photo provides a visual narrative of the economic stability and well-being of African American communities in the early twentieth century. Support or revise your original prediction using evidence from this chapter.**

Negro Business League and supporters of local NAACP and National Urban League chapters. They frequently opened their funeral parlors for community meetings and family gatherings.

As in the South, segregated funeral homes, beauty parlors, and barbershops were safe places where Blacks could talk freely. Unlike in the South, however, Blacks voted and organized politically in the North. Because Black voting was not legally obstructed, concentrations of northern Black neighborhoods created voting blocs that were able to put Black politicians in office. In 1915, Blacks on Chicago's South Side elected Oscar De Priest, a Republican, as alderman for the Second Ward. After the

Nineteenth Amendment to the U.S. Constitution guaranteed woman suffrage in 1920, the votes of Black women significantly enhanced northern Black political influence. In 1918, the Black vote helped send Republican Adelbert Roberts to the Illinois state house. In 1926, he became the first Black member elected to the Illinois state senate. In 1928, South Side Chicago Blacks sent Oscar De Priest to the U.S. House of Representatives, making him the first African American to serve in Congress since North Carolina's George Henry White completed his final term in 1901.

Black women in Chicago had been politically active long before they could vote. The city was the home of Fannie Barrier Williams, who in 1924 was the first Black woman on Chicago's Library Board. Chicagoan Ida B. Wells, a legendary advocate of woman suffrage, personified the cause of Black woman suffragists, who unapologetically argued on behalf of suffrage for all women. In particular, these women battled the anti-Black racism that suffused the white-dominated suffrage movement of the late nineteenth and early twentieth century.

AP® exam tip

Be prepared to describe how Black women leaders, including churchwomen, created clubs and denominational organizations that countered race and gender stereotypes by exemplifying the dignity, capacity, beauty, and strength of Black women.

Owing to the rapidly expanding Black population, Black women's spaces like beauty parlors proliferated and, like male barbershops, created vital spaces for frank discussions. With their hair-straightening processes and products, these Black beauty salons offered Black women, especially southern newcomers, new styles to signal their urban identity. Black women's evolving beauty culture gave them a sense of dignity and self-worth. It also provided opportunities for jobs and activism. Maggie Wilson, a Chicago sales agent for Madam C. J. Walker's hair products, explained that these jobs "made it possible for thousands of women to give up the washtub, the cook kitchen, the scrub work and that drudgery that was the only way for them to make a living."[10] Meanwhile, Madam C. J. Walker created a nationwide enterprise. Her Hair Culturists Union of America took stands on current issues, and her Walker Clubs for sales agents did community work. She also established schools that taught Black beauty methods and donated much of her considerable fortune to Black institutions.

AP® exam tip

Be sure you can describe how African American inventors and entrepreneurs like Robert S. Abbott, Marjorie Joyner, Ann Lowe, Charles Clinton Spaulding, Madam C. J. Walker, Maggie Lena Walker, and more developed products that highlighted the beauty of Black people, fostered Black economic advancement, and supported community initiatives through philanthropy.

War Abroad, Violence at Home

What were the causes of heightened racial violence during the Red Summer?

How did African Americans respond to white supremacist attacks during the Red Summer?

In April 1917, the United States entered the "Great War" — the conflict between the Allies (chiefly France and Great Britain) and the Central powers (chiefly Germany and Austria-Hungary) that would later become known as World War I. The African American response to the United States joining the Allies was mixed. Most Blacks rallied patriotically to the cause and supported President Woodrow Wilson's effort to "make the world safe for democracy" by enlisting in the armed forces, buying war bonds, and contributing to the American Red Cross. In *The Crisis*, W. E. B. Du Bois urged Blacks to "forget our special grievances and close our ranks shoulder to shoulder with our own white fellow citizens and the allied nations that are fighting for democracy."[11] However, an influential group on the Black radical left objected. Chandler Owen and A. Philip Randolph, editors of the *Messenger*, a socialist magazine, criticized the war as nothing but an effort to advance capitalist interests. In a public letter to President Wilson, they argued, "Lynching, Jim Crow, segregation, discrimination in the armed forces and out, disfranchisement of millions of black souls in the South — all these things make your cry of making the world safe for democracy a sham, a mockery, a rape on decency and a travesty on common justice."[12]

African Americans in the Great War

Although Blacks were 10 percent of the U.S. population, they made up more than 13 percent of the draftees. More than 2.3 million Black men registered for the draft; 380,000 actually served. Only 42,000 Black men, however — about 3 percent of U.S. combat forces — saw actual combat. Most Black servicemen worked in support units that loaded and unloaded supplies, dug trenches, and buried the dead. Army units continued to be segregated, the navy and the coast guard allowed Blacks to serve only in menial positions, and the marines and nursing units excluded Blacks altogether.

The four long-standing Black regiments were not given overseas combat assignments, but under pressure from the NAACP and militant newspapers such as the *Chicago Defender*, the army established two Black combat divisions and began training Black officers at a segregated camp in Des Moines, Iowa. One thousand African Americans received commissions, but few actually commanded troops. Those who were commissioned served only in the lower ranks and led only Black troops. White soldiers refused to salute them, and they were excluded from officers' clubs. Provisions and training for Black troops were also unequal. Many had to train with picks and shovels instead of guns, and their camps lacked bathroom facilities and even blankets in winter. Black soldiers traveled to and from the European war front in the bottom holds of poorly ventilated, segregated ships. U.S. army camps in Europe also were segregated. Black troops faced hostility from their own white officers as well as from white soldiers.

Hell Fighters
The 369th Infantry Regiment, formed from the Fifteenth New York National Guard in Harlem, one of the most highly decorated fighting units of World War I.

Nevertheless, when sent into combat, Black units performed ably. The most famous unit was the 369th Infantry Regiment, known as the **Hell Fighters**, from Harlem's Fifteenth New York National Guard. The Hell Fighters served a record 191 days at the front, fighting alongside the French, who outfitted, armed, and fed them. France awarded the entire unit the Croix de Guerre, the French command's highest military honor. Two other Black regiments also received the Croix de Guerre. No Black soldier in World War I received a medal from the United States until Corporal Freddie Stowers of Company C of the 371st Regiment received the Congressional Medal of Honor posthumously in 1991. Stowers died while courageously rallying his comrades in a September 1918 battle. The 368th of the 92nd Division became

An Ideal Vision of Service

This World War I recruiting poster depicts a farewell scene as a soldier is about to join an African American infantry unit. Captioned "Colored Man Is No Slacker," the image was designed to inspire a sense of civic pride and patriotism. **Who is the intended audience for this image? What is the purpose of addressing this audience?** *Gilder Lehrman Collection, New York/Bridgeman Images.*

embroiled in controversy when it failed in its mission during another battle in late 1918. The white press and white officials laid the blame squarely on Black soldiers, while the Black press and Black officials pointed to fatigue, lack of preparation, and inept white leadership as key reasons for the regiment's failure.

The people of France appreciated both the valor of Black soldiers and their distinctive African American culture. Black soldiers introduced the French to jazz and ragtime. Directing the 369th's regimental band was James Reese Europe, a New York bandleader who played the music of Black composers. While touring in France, the band delighted French audiences with "St. Louis Blues" and other W. C. Handy hits. When the regiment returned to the United States, though, it was not permitted to march in New York City's victory parade. Instead, on February 17, 1919, the 369th held a separate parade on Fifth Avenue, its band led by James Reese Europe and drum major Bill "Bojangles" Robinson. The soldiers marched north to Harlem, where cheering crowds eagerly welcomed them home.

Race Riots and Red Summer

During the war years, the Great Migration hit record numbers, as job opportunities expanded for Black workers in northern industries. The number of African Americans in East St. Louis, an industrial city of 60,000 across the Mississippi River from St. Louis, Missouri, grew from 6,000 in 1910 to 10,000 in 1917. White resentment of Black migrants was stoked by employers who used Black workers to gain the upper hand in labor negotiations. Trouble exploded in February 1917, when the Aluminum Ore Company hired 470 Black workers to replace striking white workers who belonged to the American Federation of Labor local, which excluded Blacks. On May 28, thousands of outraged white workers mercilessly attacked Blacks in the downtown area. After several weeks of relative calm, on July 2 a car of white males shot into a group of Blacks in a Black neighborhood. When two white plainclothes

Silent March, July 28, 1917

An overwhelmingly Black crowd, estimated at 20,000 people, observed the stunning protest march of some 10,000 Blacks, all dressed in white, as they silently moved down New York City's Fifth Avenue on a Saturday afternoon in 1917. Organized and led by the NAACP, the marchers were protesting the shocking spectacle of anti-Black violence in America, particularly the horror of the recent East St. Louis race riot. One young marcher's sign read "Color, blood and suffering have made us one." **Describe the impact of the Silent March of 1917. How does this image contribute to your understanding of it as an example of resistance to white supremacist attacks on Black communities?** *Library of Congress, Prints and Photographs Division, Washington, D.C., LC-DIG-ds-00894.*

policemen passed by in a car, the crowd mistook them for the original attackers and fired on the policemen, killing them. Roving white mobs responded savagely. When authorities finally restored order, 125 Black men, women, and children had been tortured and killed; innumerable Black homes had been destroyed; hundreds had been left homeless; and property damage had amounted to $400,000.

silent march (1917)
A mass march orchestrated by the NAACP down New York City's Fifth Avenue on July 28, 1917, to protest the horrific East St. Louis, Illinois, race riot of July 2.

On July 28, 1917, the NAACP and New York religious leaders organized a **silent march** to protest the East St. Louis riot. It was the first African American mass protest of its kind. To muffled drums, roughly 10,000 Blacks — young and old, women and men, boys and girls, all dressed in white — walked quietly down Fifth Avenue in a funeral-like procession. Typical protest banners read "Mr. President, why not make America safe for democracy?" and "We have fought in six wars, our reward was East St. Louis."[13]

Black troop encampments also raised tensions among white residents. A month after the East St. Louis riot, a riot erupted in Houston, Texas, where the Black Twenty-Fourth Infantry Regiment was stationed. Thirteen Black soldiers were tried for mutiny, convicted, and hanged. The number of lynchings in the country rose as well, from thirty-six in 1917 to sixty in 1918 and seventy-six in 1919. (See chapter 10, By the Numbers: Lynchings Every Five Years, 1885–1950, p. 377.) At least ten veterans in uniform were killed. In Birmingham, Alabama, Sergeant Major Joe Green was shot to death by a white streetcar conductor who became enraged when Green asked for his change. Private Wilbur Little, who wore his army uniform because he owned no other clothes, was murdered in Blakely, Georgia, by whites who demanded that he wear civilian clothes.

The Great War ended in November 1918. Returning veterans, who expected that their sacrifices would be rewarded with respect, were increasingly impatient with discrimination and white hostility. W. E. B. Du Bois, who had earlier counseled cooperation, now demanded action. Tensions rose during the postwar economic readjustment period as competition for scarce housing and jobs grew, and a political atmosphere of fear spread in the wake of the Communist revolution in Russia. In the summer of 1919, racial violence reached the point of national crisis as riots erupted in cities such as Charleston, South Carolina; Omaha, Nebraska; Knoxville, Tennessee; Washington, D.C.; Longview, Texas; and Elaine, Arkansas — roughly twenty-five places in all. James Weldon Johnson, field secretary for the NAACP, referred to it as the **Red Summer**.

AP® exam tip

On the AP® Exam, you'll need to be able to explain how a global flu pandemic, competition for jobs, and racial discrimination against Black First World War veterans all contributed to a rise in hate crimes across the country in 1919.

Red Summer (1919)
The summer of 1919, in the aftermath of World War I, during which a series of more than two dozen race riots, many in northern cities, took place.

The worst rioting took place in Chicago, where five days of street fights, shootings, beatings, and fires took the lives of twenty-three Blacks and fifteen whites. The trouble began on July 27, when a Black teenager floating on a railroad tie in Lake Michigan unwittingly drifted into the whites-only area. In the North, there were often no signs designating "Whites Only" or "Colored Only," but the boundaries were understood. Whites threw stones at the teenager, who drowned. When a white policeman refused to arrest the perpetrators, a fight broke out and then escalated and spread. City police could not stop the violence; only heavy rain and the Illinois National Guard finally restored order. More than five hundred people, most of them Black, suffered serious injuries. At least a thousand Black homes were destroyed.

Walter White, assistant executive secretary of the NAACP, was assigned to report on the riot for *The Crisis* and offered eight reasons for the violence: race prejudice, economic competition, political corruption, police inefficiency, newspaper lies about Black crime, unpunished crimes against Blacks, housing competition, and postwar racial anxieties. He concluded by observing that living in the neighborhood where the fighting took place were more than 9,000 men who had registered for the draft and 1,850 who had been in training camps. "These men," he stated, "with their new outlook on life, injected the same spirit of independence into their companions," surprising whites by fighting back.[14] In Harlem, the young Jamaican-born writer Claude McKay expressed the same thought in a poem. Titling his militant sonnet "If We Must Die," he called for defiance:

AP® skills

Applying Disciplinary Knowledge: What conclusions did Walter White draw from the riot in Chicago?

Like men we'll face the murderous, cowardly pack,
Pressed to the wall, dying, but fighting back![15]

The Rebirth of the KKK

This mounting and widespread wartime and postwar Black assertiveness greatly alarmed the resurgent KKK. Revived at Stone Mountain, Georgia, in 1915, the new Ku Klux Klan (KKK) was only loosely connected with the earlier KKK. Inspired in part by the anti-Reconstruction and white supremacist movie *Birth of a Nation* (1915), the new KKK saw itself as a secret army and fraternal order preparing for the impending race war. Epitomizing the white supremacist backlash against growing Black assertiveness, the revitalized KKK stood proudly for the notion of the United States as a white country: the tradition of racist white nationalism. Pledging to represent the interests of pure white Americans — "100 percent Americans" — the KKK was especially committed to protecting white womanhood.

The modern KKK's expansive commitment to whiteness meant that it was not only anti-Black but also anti-immigrant and antiforeign. The KKK's very narrow view of whiteness led it to oppose accepting "darker" European immigrants from southern and eastern Europe, particularly those they viewed as "swarthy" Jewish people. Fueling this virulent and violent antisemitism was an intense hatred of Jewish people's religious practices (representing Jewish people as "Christ-killing" heathens) as well as racist ideas of white superiority. The KKK's fundamental religious intolerance also fed its intense anti-Catholicism; thus, Klan violence and murders targeted Catholic and Jewish people as well as Black people.

Consistent with its retrogressive whiteness and religious intolerance, the KKK was not only antiforeign and antiradical (which often went together in their worldview) but also anti-urban and antimodern, opposing evolution and supporting prohibition. Cities were especially problematic precisely because they contained so much of what the KKK opposed. The KKK's opposition to alcohol and evolution revealed a religious fundamentalism in which both were seen as undermining the moral fiber of their white Christian nation. Similarly, the KKK strenuously promoted white patriarchal values and practices as vital to "100 percent Americanism."

The 1920s KKK was highly popular and influential nationwide. In 1925, the KKK marched forty thousand strong in Washington, D.C. By that same year, it had three million members all over the country, including the North, West, and Midwest. The organization included white men from all classes and occupations, and it functioned as a lucrative money-making operation. In addition, it encompassed the extremely popular and influential Women's Order, the Junior Order for boys, and the Tri K Klub for girls. Not surprisingly, the KKK exercised significant political influence nationwide. Racked by internal squabbles and scandal, however, the group declined in the late 1920s.

The KKK and their ilk did not deter a bright and determined Ossian Sweet, though. As a five-year-old boy, he had witnessed the lynching of a Black male teenager in his hometown of Bartow, Florida. Years later, as a medical student at Howard University, he was confined to his room during the Washington, D.C., Race Riot of 1919, where five Blacks and ten whites died. In 1921, he moved to Detroit, Michigan, where he opened a successful medical practice, which served the poor, underserved Blacks of the Black Bottom area. The following year he married Gladys Mitchell, who was from a solid Black middle-class Detroit family. In 1924, while studying abroad in Paris and Vienna, the Sweets had a daughter, Margarite, whom they called "Iva."

Seeking a better neighborhood, in 1925 the Sweets decided to buy a home in the all-white Garland Avenue community, despite the fact that several other local Black families had tried unsuccessfully to buy homes in and move into white neighborhoods in Detroit. Hostile whites, including the local KKK, had violently prevented them from doing so. The Sweets remained undaunted. Shortly after moving in, a rock-throwing white mob attacked the Sweets and their friends in their home. When the Sweets fired back in self-defense, one white was killed and another wounded. In the trial that followed, the NAACP hired Clarence Darrow, the most famous defense attorney of the time, who eventually got them acquitted, earning the NAACP much praise and positive publicity for their efforts. Indeed, the legal victory is represented as a civil rights milestone.

AP® skills

Applying Disciplinary Knowledge: How did Dr. Ossian Sweet's actions counter those of white aggressors?

The lengths to which incensed whites would go to police the boundaries of whiteness all too often led to horrific acts of anti-Black terrorism. The Tulsa Race Massacre of 1921 and the Rosewood (Florida) Massacre of 1923 graphically illustrate the extraordinary depth and utter depravity of white supremacist violence, notably in the 1920s. The trigger for both massacres was a false yet incendiary accusation that a white woman had been raped by a Black man. In the Tulsa Race Massacre, the all-Black Greenwood section of Tulsa, whose thriving business district had been dubbed "Black Wall Street," was devastated by white mobs, despite the efforts of local Blacks to protect themselves and their community. Perhaps as many as 300 Blacks and whites lost their lives, and 8,000 Blacks were left homeless. In the Rosewood Massacre, the all-Black town of roughly 350 was destroyed, perhaps as many as 27 Blacks lost their lives, and the remaining Blacks fled for their safety, never to return.

The New Negro Arrives

How did the New Negro movement and the Harlem Renaissance emphasize self-definition, racial pride, and cultural innovation?

What was the impact of Marcus Garvey and the Universal Negro Improvement Association (UNIA) on political thought throughout the African diaspora?

The increasingly assertive spirit of African Americans was expressed in many ways, including in a continuing migration out of the South. An estimated 500,000 moved to the North during the war years; another 700,000 migrated in the 1920s. In northern metropolises, Blacks constituted an increasingly large segment of the population, and they were vocal in demanding their rights. National mass organizations with a wide range of programs, some in service to the welfare of the newcomers and some expanding a research base that propelled Black scholars to the forefront of their fields, strengthened individual and collective efforts. In Black communities such as

New York's Harlem, fresh forms of expression in literature, the visual arts, dance, and music affirmed Black identity and culture and gained recognition for Black creativity in American culture. The activism of Black scholars, writers, and performers had a ripple effect, helping position African Americans as a force to be reckoned with and inspiring them to take pride in their heritage, their accomplishments, and their Black identity.

Institutional Bases for Social Science and Historical Studies

New Negro
A term used increasingly after World War I to describe a growing assertiveness animating African Americans, especially those associated with Marcus Garvey's Universal Negro Improvement Association and the Harlem Renaissance.

AP® exam tip

Be prepared to describe how the New Negro movement encouraged African Americans to define their own identity and to advocate for themselves politically in the midst of the nadir's atrocities.

The term **New Negro** had been around at least since the late nineteenth century. Booker T. Washington had used it in the title of a collection of essays he edited with Fannie Barrier Williams, *A New Negro for a New Century* (1900). But after the beginning of the Great Migration and the end of the Great War, the label was increasingly appropriated by Blacks, mostly those based in northern cities, who rejected Washington's accommodationism. In the *Messenger*, Owen and Randolph defined the New Negro: In politics, he "cannot be lulled into a false sense of security with political spoils and patronage" but demands political equality and universal suffrage; in economics, he "demands the full product of his toil," the ability "to buy in the market, commodities at the lowest possible price," and the right to join labor unions; and in society, "he stands for absolute and unequivocal '*social equality*.' "[16] Not all Black spokespersons were militant, but throughout northern cities especially, a renewed self-confidence gave rise to new and energetic challenges to discrimination.

During the Chicago riot of 1919, the city's Urban League opened its headquarters as an emergency center, and after the fighting subsided, its executive secretary, T. Arnold Hill, was instrumental in establishing the Chicago Commission on Race Relations to investigate the causes of interracial violence. Researching and writing much of the commission's report was Charles S. Johnson, who, as a graduate student in sociology at the University of Chicago, had witnessed the riot firsthand. Under Johnson's supervision, *The Negro in Chicago: A Study of Race Relations and a Race Riot* (1922) became a classic of sociological analysis. This massive 672-page social science study of the conditions of Black life in Chicago and of relations between Blacks and whites built on a wide range of sources, including interviews, charts, photographs, and maps. This work showcased what came to be known as the Chicago School: a famous and influential sociological approach to understanding cities, or urban sociology, developed at the University of Chicago. The Chicago School emphasized environmental and structural factors over genetics to explain urban phenomena, such as how blacks adapted to northern urban life. Another intent of the Chicago School was to inform in order to generate understanding and bring about reform. Like Du Bois, who had written a pioneering study titled *The Philadelphia Negro* in 1899, the Chicago School practitioner Charles Johnson believed that facts would dispel prejudice and advance the race.

AP® skills

Applying Disciplinary Knowledge: Why was the Chicago School important to the cause of Black activism?

In 1921, Johnson was appointed director of research for the National Urban League. Moving to the organization's New York headquarters, he founded the journal

Opportunity in 1923, naming it for the league's slogan, "Not Alms but Opportunity." As editor of the journal, he published both social science research and contributions by Black writers and poets. Hill, promoted to director of industrial relations, developed vocational training and programs for improving race relations in the workplace. Leading the Urban League in the 1920s, its golden era, was executive secretary Eugene K. Jones, another social scientist who, like Johnson and Hill, was a graduate of Virginia Union University in Richmond. The Urban League organized boycotts of businesses that refused to hire Blacks and pressured city schools to provide training for workers. With affiliates in more than thirty cities, including some in the South, the Urban League's efforts to eliminate barriers to employment, ensure fair treatment for workers, and improve housing and sanitation had a lasting effect on individual lives, Black communities, and race relations. Like the NAACP, also headquartered in New York City, the Urban League was reformist and progressive, but unlike the NAACP, it did not seek to become a mass-membership organization.

The NAACP increased its membership significantly during these years, under the leadership of James Weldon Johnson, who in 1920 became its first Black executive secretary. Johnson initiated a nationwide campaign to sign up new members at $1 a year. As a result, the organization became overwhelmingly Black, while remaining committed to interracial cooperation. Throughout the 1920s, the NAACP claimed 100,000 members in more than 300 chapters nationwide. Johnson was particularly successful in the dangerous work of establishing chapters in the deep South, although these were subject to anti-Black violence, and some had to close or go underground.

The NAACP looked to the courts to end housing discrimination and to Congress to end lynching. In 1917, in *Buchanan v. Warley*, it convinced the U.S. Supreme Court to overturn city ordinances mandating where Blacks could live, and in 1926, it successfully defended the Black physician Ossian Sweet against murder charges stemming from the attack on his home in Detroit. The NAACP was less successful in Congress. The Dyer Anti-Lynching Bill, which the NAACP backed and which would have made lynching a federal crime, was introduced year after year but never passed, owing primarily to the opposition of southern white members of Congress.

Both the Urban League and the NAACP drew together broad constituencies of Blacks and sympathetic whites who wanted to end racial violence and discrimination. With Johnson and Du Bois directing research and publications for their respective organizations, sociological studies of Black life became a growing part of a reformist program that had racial equality and integration as its goals. Chicago School–trained Black sociologists built a strong base of scholarship on urban and social problems. Most notable was E. Franklin Frazier, whose Ph.D. dissertation was published as *The Negro Family in Chicago* in 1932. Culminating years of sociological research on Chicago was *Black Metropolis: A Study of Negro Life in a Northern City* (1945) by St. Clair Drake and Horace R. Cayton, considered a masterpiece. The academic establishment had largely ignored Du Bois's early work, but these studies coming out of Chicago commanded acclaim, and both Johnson and Frazier later became officers in the American

Sociological Association. In 1928, Charles Johnson left the Urban League to chair Fisk University's social sciences department, where he trained a new generation of sociologists and turned his attention to the lives and conditions of rural Blacks in the South. He published two important works, *Shadow of the Plantation* (1934) and *Growing Up in the Black Belt* (1941).

AP® skills

Applying Disciplinary Knowledge: What does the term "New Negro" mean, and how did James Weldon Johnson personify it?

James Weldon Johnson was both a renaissance man in the broadest possible sense of the term and a major figure in the Harlem Renaissance. In many ways, he personified the New Negro. In 1930, he left his official position at the NAACP and joined Charles Johnson at Fisk, accepting a professorship in creative writing and literature. Johnson, a distinguished writer, authored the highly acclaimed novel *Autobiography of an Ex-Colored Man* (1912) and the poem "Lift Every Voice and Sing" (1900), which became the Negro national anthem. John Rosamond Johnson, his brother, with whom he collaborated on many songs — notably for Broadway musicals — wrote the music. (See AP® Working with Sources: The Harlem/New Negro Renaissance, pp. 460–69.) While executive secretary of the NAACP, James Weldon Johnson had published collections of Negro spirituals, his own poems, and perhaps his most famous work, *God's Trombones: Seven Negro Sermons in Verse* (1927). He also wrote *Black Manhattan* (1930), which hailed Harlem as "the Negro metropolis." He observed, "The Negro's situation in Harlem is without precedent in all his history in New York; never before has he been so securely anchored, never before has he owned the land, never before has he had so well established a community life."[17]

Like James Weldon Johnson, Du Bois was both a renaissance man in the broadest possible sense and a central figure in the Harlem Renaissance. Du Bois indeed personified the complexity of the New Negro. He promoted the renaissance early on, and he also helped advance it by publishing many of the new writers in *The Crisis*. However, unlike Johnson, who demonstrated a greater appreciation for African American folk culture, Du Bois was an elitist, who preferred what he and like-minded African Americans termed "respectable" art, such as spirituals, as opposed to jazz and blues, which they saw as disreputable. In addition, he argued for art as propaganda — art aimed primarily at advancing African American liberation — rather than advocating for artistic freedom. This attitude ultimately alienated him from many of the young artists of the Harlem Renaissance, who demanded greater choice. In the 1930s, Du Bois focused increasingly on his scholarship. He left the NAACP in 1934 to return to Atlanta University, where he produced his landmark work *Black Reconstruction* (1935) and a history of African peoples titled *Black Folk, Then and Now* (1939).

More than any other individual, Carter G. Woodson promoted the serious study of African American history and culture. An educator who received a Ph.D. in history from Harvard in 1912, Woodson taught at M Street High School (renamed for Paul Laurence Dunbar in 1916) and Howard University in Washington, D.C. In 1915, he established the Association for the Study of Negro Life and History, the foremost organization promoting African American history among the lay public as well as within Black institutions. In 1916, he founded the *Journal of Negro History*, the major

Carter G. Woodson
Carter G. Woodson became known as "the Father of Negro History" for his pioneering and immeasurable contributions to the study and recognition of African American history. These contributions include founding the *Journal of Negro History* in 1915 and, in 1926, creating Negro History Week, which was expanded to Black History Month in 1976. **Why were the actions taken by Carter G. Woodson essential to the New Negro movement?** *Granger/Granger — All rights reserved.*

scholarly journal in its field. His *Negro History Bulletin*, which began publication in 1937, made Black history accessible to educators, students, and general readers. Woodson wrote many scholarly books and articles on Black history, including studies of education, the church, migration, the family, and the professions. His textbook *The Negro in Our History* (1922) was widely used for many years.

To further promote the study of Black history, in 1926 Woodson created Negro History Week, a week in February (the week of Frederick Douglass's and Abraham Lincoln's birthdays) during which African American contributions could be highlighted in schools and organizations. In 1976, the annual celebration was extended to all of February as **Black History Month** and is now widely observed. Woodson donated his large collection of Black history materials to the Library of Congress. For his many accomplishments, he received the NAACP's prestigious Spingarn Medal in 1926 and is remembered as "the Father of Negro History."

Black History Month
A celebration of African American history and culture that began in 1926 as Negro History Week, established by Carter G. Woodson. It became Black History Month in 1976.

Another major archive of Black history was the lifework of Arthur Schomburg, a historian, bibliophile, and activist who collected five thousand books, documents, and other materials. "The American Negro must remake his past in order to make his future," Schomburg argued. "History must restore what slavery took away."[18] Schomburg's collection became the basis for a research center at the Harlem branch of the New York Public Library. Today, the Schomburg Center for Research in Black Culture is one of the foremost research centers for Black history in the world.

The Universal Negro Improvement Association

Universal Negro Improvement Association (UNIA)
The global organization founded by Marcus Garvey in Jamaica in 1914 that promoted race pride, racial unity, Black separatism, and African redemption.

Of all the new organizations and fresh approaches to Black elevation, Marcus Garvey's **Universal Negro Improvement Association (UNIA)** was the largest and most militant. Founded in Kingston, Jamaica, in 1914, it surged after 1916, when Garvey relocated its headquarters to Harlem. By 1919, the UNIA claimed two million members in thirty chapters in the United States and the West Indies. By 1921, the number had grown to four million members worldwide.

AP® exam tip

Make sure you're able to describe the mission and methods of the Universal Negro Improvement Association.

The UNIA's astonishing growth owed not only to Garvey's vision and oratorical skills but also to the brutal racism of the wartime and postwar era. Garvey emphasized race pride and racial unity at a time when these messages resonated deeply with Blacks. He reinvigorated Black nationalism, and even Black separatism, and ignited a grassroots movement, with UNIA chapters forming in rural and urban areas in every part of the country. Some local units focused on practical matters, such as voter registration, health clinics, and adult night schools. Unique to the UNIA, however, was the message of African redemption, the restoration of African independence and greatness, and Pan-Africanism — the essential oneness of all African peoples, wherever they lived. Garveyism helped African Americans to recognize both the American and African components of their identity, to see themselves in an international context, and to feel that they were part of a global Black movement. Unlike the uplift and reformist organizations established in the late nineteenth and early twentieth centuries (such as the NAACP), which were integrationist in ideology, the UNIA was separatist. It emphasized Black self-determination — independent Black nation building — rather than fighting for civil and political rights in the United States.

Born in St. Ann's Bay, Jamaica, in 1887, Garvey was a printer, journalist, and labor organizer in the Caribbean and Central and South America, where he witnessed the crushing oppression of peasants on plantations. He spent a formative period in London, where African nationalists and anticolonial activists such as Duse Muhammed Ali, editor of the *African Times and Orient Review*, strongly influenced him. Garvey was also influenced by Booker T. Washington's autobiography, *Up from Slavery* (1901), and upon his return to Jamaica in 1912, he tried to set up an industrial training school on the Tuskegee model. He initially came to the United States to seek Washington's advice, but Washington died in 1915 before the two could meet. Garvey refocused his vision on prospects for the UNIA in the United States. Excited by what he saw and heard as he traveled among Black communities throughout the country, he returned to his Harlem base to build the organization.

AP® exam tip

Be sure you can explain how Garvey inspired African Americans to embrace their shared African heritage. In particular, be prepared to describe his advocacy for the ideals of industrial, political, and educational advancement and self-determination through separatist Black institutions.

Garvey effectively wielded the rituals and symbols of prestige and power. He captivated followers with inspirational rhetoric, sharp dress, and proud self-presentation. The UNIA had a complex leadership hierarchy, grand titles and military orders, uniforms, and strong women's auxiliaries. It held huge mass meetings and parades and provided many opportunities for organizing and mobilizing. Its militant weekly newspaper, the *Negro World*, began in 1918 with a circulation of around 3,000. Within a year, it had 50,000 readers, and in its heyday in the early 1920s, it claimed more than 200,000 readers. Amy Jacques Garvey, Marcus Garvey's second wife, edited the popular women's page, which spoke to the particular concerns of Black women through the prism of Garveyism.

Garveyites
In their full regalia, these Garveyites, individually and collectively, radiate race pride, confidence, self-reliance, and unity. In particular, the men in their military-style uniforms evoke a sense of proud Black manhood. Garvey and his followers imparted a comforting sense of belonging to a powerful and important organization and being part of a defining historical moment for African people everywhere. **What is Black self-determination? Is the scene in this photograph an example? Explain.** *Granger/Granger — All rights reserved.*

Everywhere Garvey went, he electrified audiences as he roared maxims such as "Up, you mighty race! You can accomplish what you will!"[19] and thundered the UNIA's motto: "One God! One Aim! One Destiny!" Along the crowded Harlem parade route to the 1920 UNIA convention at Madison Square Garden, parading Garveyites carried a striking range of banners, including those proclaiming "We Want a Black Civilization" and "Africa Must Be Free." The lead banner of the Woman's Auxiliary read "God Give Us Real Men!"[20] At the convention, Garvey was crowned the "Provisional President of the African Republic." The convention adopted the Declaration of the Rights of the Negro Peoples of the World, which asserted the right of Africans everywhere to self-definition and self-determination. In his speech, Garvey proclaimed, "We shall raise the banner of democracy in Africa, or 400,000,000 of us will report to God the reason why."[21] Under the UNIA's red, black, and green flag, the themes of race pride, racial unity, and African regeneration were proclaimed.

AP® skills
Applying Disciplinary Knowledge: What do the messages of the UNIA banners have in common?

For many, Garveyism functioned like a religion. Garvey relied heavily on support from Black ministers, who provided an organizational and recruitment network.

In 1924, the African Orthodox Church, an independent Black denomination with a Black nationalist message, became the UNIA's official church.

At the heart of Garvey's efforts, however, was economic nationalism. Compellingly representing a dominant Black position, he argued that a separate Black economy and independent Black enterprises were central to racial advancement. The UNIA established hotels, restaurants, and stores under the Negro Factories Corporation, whose goal was Black business development. One subsidiary manufactured dolls in various shades of brown, from dark to mulatto. For Garveyites, economic enterprise was a matter of race pride.

The Black Star Line steamship company, created with much fanfare in 1919, was the movement's centerpiece, intended to unite African peoples in the Old and New Worlds spiritually, socially, politically, and economically. By undermining Western colonial rule, it would, claimed Garvey, redeem Africa. This grand promotion of commercial and travel links across the Atlantic excited not only Garveyites but also many Blacks outside the movement, who were attracted by Garvey's Pan-African–related "Africa for Africans" idea — the notion that Africans themselves must rule their own nations and continent. Thus inspired, they bought stock in the company at $5 a share. The Black Star Line was to be a key instrument of Black self-determination and Black separatism.

As a self-identified full-blooded Black who opposed racial mixing, Garvey roundly condemned integration. His call for racial purity was not unlike that of the resurgent Ku Klux Klan, and he stirred great controversy when he met with Klan leaders. Du Bois called Garvey "the most dangerous enemy of the Negro race in America and in the world," denouncing him as "either a lunatic or a traitor,"[22] while Garvey distrusted and harshly criticized light-skinned leaders such as Du Bois. Du Bois was not the only Black leader alarmed by Garvey. Many criticized the Back to Africa fever as hysterical and cultlike, and they feared that Garvey was exploiting the hopes and fears of the Black masses. By early 1922, the Black Star Line had sold more than 150,000 shares of stock, but the three ships it purchased and outfitted proved unseaworthy. To many, the project seemed like an ill-conceived scheme to defraud poor Black stockholders. The U.S. Justice Department was also suspicious of Garvey, a foreign national who seemed to be advocating disloyalty on the part of Black Americans at a time when all foreign radicals — as well as American Communists, socialists, and left-wing progressives — were viewed as dangerous.

The immediate pretext for the UNIA's swift fall was evidence of financial impropriety in the Black Star Line. Although Garvey himself was innocent of the charges, in 1923, he was convicted of mail fraud for selling bogus stock in the venture through the mail. In 1925, he began serving a five-year prison sentence, and two years later, he was deported as an "undesirable alien." The UNIA soon faded, but Garveyism as an ideology persisted. The UNIA was the most important mass Black movement before the modern Civil Rights movement.

The Harlem Renaissance

So much of the New Negro spirit, so many of the organizations that represented the New Negro, and so many New Negro leaders and celebrities were centered in Harlem that it was, declared Alain Locke, a "race capital."[23] Two of the preeminent Black newspapers of the era — the *Amsterdam News* and the *New York Age* — were located in Harlem. Many of the Black elite lived on Striver's Row and in Sugar Hill (Map 11.2). Locke, a Rhodes Scholar with a Ph.D. in philosophy from Harvard, taught literature and philosophy at Howard University in Washington, D.C., but he encouraged one of his most talented students, Zora Neale Hurston, to move to New York to study anthropology at Columbia and to write. Locke became both spokesman and promoter for a constellation of writers whose remarkable outpouring of poetry and fiction, often allied with the visual arts, dance, and music, defined a new Black cultural movement. Best known as the **Harlem Renaissance**, this New Negro arts movement encompassed the ferment of Black life in the metropolis and flourished in other places as well, such as Chicago and Washington, D.C. (See AP® Working with Sources: The Harlem/New Negro Renaissance, pp. 460–69.)

Harlem Renaissance
The New Negro arts movement, a flourishing of African American art and culture rooted in Harlem in the 1920s.

Like Woodson and Schomburg, the writers and artists of the Harlem Renaissance sought to present authentic versions of the African American experience. Like the UNIA, they affirmed the value of Blackness and the African heritage. But unlike the UNIA, they were typically integrationist, not separatist, often relying on white patrons and appealing to white audiences. Collectively, they refashioned the Black image. Du Bois, as editor of *The Crisis*, and Johnson, as editor of *Opportunity*, provided a publication base for their writings and enthusiastically promoted their efforts.

AP® skills

Applying Disciplinary Knowledge: How does the Harlem Renaissance relate to the New Negro movement?

AP® exam tip

On the AP® Exam, you'll need to be able to explain how Harlem Renaissance writers — especially poets — expressed their relationships to Africa in their poetry.

In 1925, Locke edited a special issue of the *Survey Graphic*, a social science and cultural journal. In the issue, titled "Harlem: Mecca of the New Negro," he reflected on Harlem's significance. It was not the center of Black education, industry, or finance, "yet here . . . are the forces that make a group known and felt in the world. The reformers, the fighting advocates, the inner spokesmen, the poets, artists and social prophets are here,"[24] he asserted, and the journal issue proved his point. Included were studies in history and sociology by James Weldon Johnson, Arthur Schomburg, and Charles S. Johnson; essays on jazz and art; a reflection on color lines by Walter White; and poems by Claude McKay, Countee Cullen, Jean Toomer, and Langston Hughes. McKay, a socialist, wrote poems of disillusionment; Cullen's textured sonnets were rich with literary allusions. Like so many other Harlem Renaissance writers, these authors expressed Black themes and explored issues in Black identity. Toomer is best known for *Cane* (1923), a haunting prose poem that examines the effects of the past and the present — of slavery, spiritual and material impoverishment, stunted rural and urban environments — on African American identities. Toomer's interest in the rhythms of Black speech reflected a current running throughout Harlem Renaissance work, notably in the poems of Hughes and Sterling Brown.

Locke's next effort was even more spectacular. For the book *The New Negro* (1925), he wrote what might be regarded as the manifesto of the New Negro arts movement

MAP 11.2 Cultural Harlem

This map provides a geographic and neighborhood layout and tour of Harlem. It pinpoints some of the important sites where the vibrant social, cultural, intellectual, religious, and political life of the Harlem Renaissance played out. Also shown are the residences of some of the era's central figures who served as spokespeople for the New Negro through their careers and activism. **What does this map suggest about the range of institutions sustaining the Harlem community?** DATA SOURCE: Jeffrey Brown Ferguson, *The Harlem Renaissance: A Brief History with Documents* (Boston: Bedford/St. Martin's, 2008), 9.

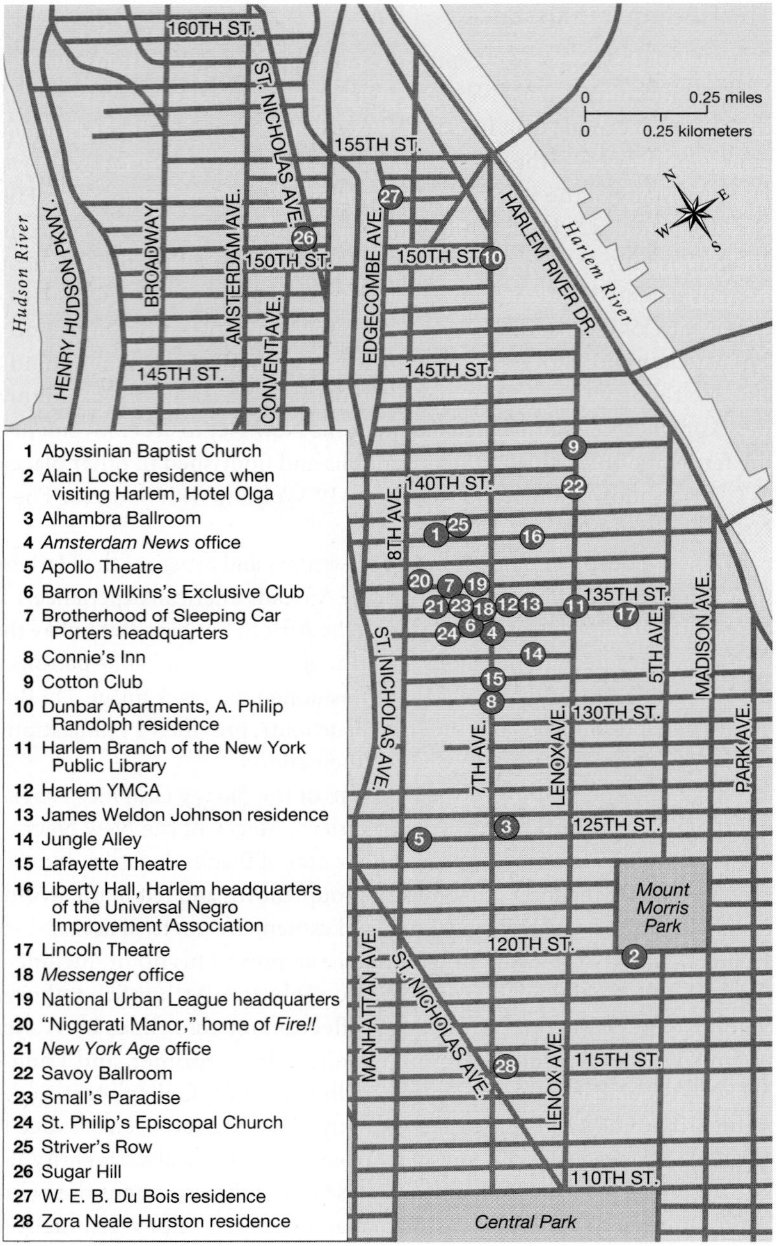

and collected an even wider array of writers and poets, including Gwendolyn Bennett and Zora Neale Hurston. Essays addressed Negro spirituals, dance, and folk literature, including Brer Rabbit tales. Supplying drawings and decorative designs was the young artist Aaron Douglas, who had moved from Kansas City to Harlem after the *Survey Graphic*'s Harlem issue convinced him that Harlem was the place to be. Douglas's distinctive style, drawing on Egyptian and West African sources as well as cubism and Art Deco, captured the attention of Du Bois and Johnson, who asked Douglas to illustrate their journals and draw covers for books by Black authors. Douglas's race-conscious visual art explored themes in African American history and culture, especially folk culture, and connections between African Americans and Africa. Considered the father of modern African American visual art, he is also remembered as a muralist and is known especially for his murals at the Harlem branch of the New York Public Library and at Fisk University, where he founded the art department.

AP® skills

Applying Disciplinary Knowledge: How did Aaron Douglas contribute to the Harlem Renaissance?

The short-lived *Fire!!* (1926), a magazine subtitled *Devoted to Younger Negro Artists*, was indicative of the excitement and creativity of the Harlem Renaissance. Hurston and Hughes, along with Wallace Thurman, the editor of *Fire!!*, led these younger artists, who chafed at artistic visions that aimed to attract white audiences and serve a political purpose. Du Bois had insisted that "all Art is propaganda," by which he meant that art should deal with subjects that would advance the Black freedom struggle.[25] Locke offered a middle position: while rejecting art as propaganda, he called for race-conscious art of the highest order. The writers for *Fire!!* called instead for a more complete freedom of artistic expression. Their art would embrace the lower classes and the gritty realities confronting Blacks, not just genteel, middle-class concerns. Rejecting art that would "pour racial individuality into the mold of American standardization," Hughes spoke for his colleagues: "We younger Negro artists who create now intend to express our individual dark-skinned selves without fear or shame. If white people are pleased we are glad. If they are not, it doesn't matter. We know we are beautiful. And ugly too."[26]

Innovative literature and art were only part of what was happening during the Harlem Renaissance. On Broadway and in Harlem, dance revues with tap dancers such as Bojangles were wildly popular, especially after the success of *Shuffle Along* (1921), the first Broadway musical created, produced, and performed by Blacks. The Chicago-based comedy team Flournoy Miller and Aubrey Lyles wrote the script, and the musical team Noble Sissle and Eubie Blake created hit tunes such as "I'm Just Wild about Harry." *Shuffle Along*'s famous chorus line helped launch the entertainment careers of Florence Mills and Josephine Baker. Mills combined innocence with an edgy sensuality to become the biggest Black musical theater star of the era. Baker achieved her greatest stardom in Paris, where she thrilled audiences with outrageous costumes and exuberant performances of popular dances such as the Charleston and the Black Bottom. In the late 1920s, the Alhambra Ballroom and the Savoy Ballroom became the most popular dance halls in Harlem.

AP® skills

Applying Disciplinary Knowledge: What was the first Broadway musical produced, created, and performed by Black people? Why is this work an example of resilience?

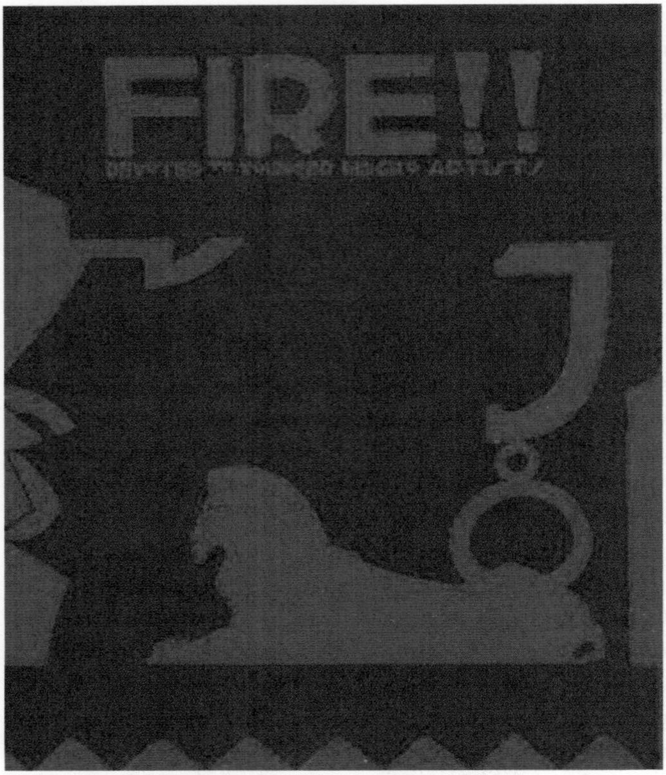

***Aaron Douglas's Cover for* Fire!!**
Aaron Douglas — painter, graphic artist, and muralist — was the preeminent artist of the Harlem Renaissance. He created this cover for *Fire!! Devoted to Younger Negro Artists* in 1926, two years after arriving in Harlem from the Midwest as a young artist himself. The design vividly captures the various influences that shaped his modern African American aesthetic, including Egyptian art, Art Deco, cubism, and modern design. **To what extent does Douglas's perspective in this image challenge that of W. E. B. Du Bois? Use details from this cover image to support your response.** *The Picture Art Collection/Alamy Stock Photo. © 2024 Heirs of Aaron Douglas/Licensed by VAGA at Artists Rights Society (ARS), NY.*

Blues singers long popular on the Black tent circuit now drew huge crowds to the cabarets and nightclubs of Harlem, where whites and Blacks had a good time and illegal booze flowed. Jungle Alley, an area along 133rd Street between Lenox and 7th Avenues, was dotted with nightclubs and cabarets. North of Jungle Alley, many of the best-known Black entertainers of the era, such as Bessie Smith and Duke Ellington, performed at the Cotton Club, the most famous Harlem venue. Like Connie's Inn and Barron Wilkins's Exclusive Club, the Cotton Club catered to all-white audiences.

Harlem Blacks especially enjoyed Small's Paradise and lesser-known clubs like Tillie's Chicken Shack, which featured down-home entertainment, including raucous blues. The Lafayette Theatre and the Lincoln Theatre were highly popular Black entertainment venues, and after 1934, the Apollo Theatre became the most important performance venue for Black entertainers in the United States.

The music of the Harlem Renaissance, particularly jazz and blues, constituted the most original and innovative artistic development of the 1920s. Especially noteworthy was the powerful work of blues singers such as Ma Rainey, "the Mother of the Blues," and Bessie Smith, "the Empress of the Blues." The work of these and other classic blues divas dealt profoundly with life's ups and downs and featured women's points of view, notably those of working-class and struggling women.

The New Orleans–born cornetist and trumpeter Louis "Satchmo" Armstrong pioneered several innovative and fresh developments in jazz. As shown in his classic tune "West End Blues" (1928), Armstrong's stunning technical virtuosity, improvisational skill, and vocal and compositional originality enabled him to help create the instrumental jazz solo and the vocal jazz solo. He also introduced scat singing, in which the singer mimics a musical instrument in a striking call-and-response pattern.

AP® exam tip

Be prepared to describe African Americans' contributions to American music in the first half of the twentieth century. In particular, make sure you can connect the evolution of blues from acoustic music with roots in slavery in the American South to the new, electric version that evolved as African Americans moved north during the Great Migration. Finally, be prepared to explain how blues music conveys its themes of despair and hope, love, and loss.

Duke Ellington and his jazz band were key innovators of orchestral, big band, or what is sometimes called swing, jazz. They shot to fame at the Cotton Club, where they were regulars after 1927. Over a long career, Ellington was recognized as a preeminent American composer. Swank whites-only cabarets like the Cotton Club (there was also one in Chicago), which featured jazz bands, blues singers, and Black dancers, contributed to the mainstream acceptance of jazz and the blues, as did radio performances and recordings on "race labels" that allowed millions who would never see these Black musical stars in person to hear and appreciate their fresh and thrilling music.

The glitter of the Harlem Renaissance crashed along with the stock market and the onset of the Great Depression, although its artists and writers continued to produce important work. In later years, certain limits of the movement came into clearer focus: its social distance from the working-class Black communities it sought to energize and its overreliance on European artistic standards and white patrons. Most important, however, the empowering change in Black identity and expression that it fostered became permanent. The Harlem Renaissance promoted a more accurate and affirmative understanding of African American history and culture, and it also demonstrated the beauty and power of race-conscious art and enriched American culture immeasurably.

CONCLUSION

The New Negro Comes of Age

By 1915, African Americans were becoming both more visible and more powerful. Waves of migrants from the South swelled the metropolises of the North, changing their demographics and the nature of urban life. Black Americans who had served loyally in World War I returned ready to make America pay attention to the New Negro and live up to the promise of democracy. Regrettably, white backlash against blacks, exemplified by the period's anti-Black riots and massacres as well as the renascent Ku Klux Klan, was widespread and deep.

As Black organizations became mass organizations, Black protest, lobbying, and litigation broadened and strengthened. Some groups welcomed white support and cooperation; others rejected it. These organizations and the publications they sponsored provided an institutional base for research into the conditions of Black life that generated a new, nationwide awareness of the New Negro and a new understanding of prejudice and racial conflict. With concentrations of Black voters in Negro districts and Black workers in certain industries, the Black presence could no longer be ignored.

Two of this era's developments stand out: the rise and fall of Marcus Garvey's Universal Negro Improvement Association, and the spectacular flourishing of the writers, visual artists, and musicians of what came to be called the Harlem, or New Negro, Renaissance. Even as African American artists debated the character of the New Negro and the nature of African American identity, the struggles, failures, and achievements of these artists represented a proud and compelling chapter in the increasingly powerful cultural wing of the African American freedom struggle. In addition, innumerable white Americans increasingly reacted with admiration and respect for this bold Black cultural assertiveness, despite white supremacy's dominance.

CHAPTER 11 REVIEW ▸ PRACTICING AP® SKILLS

AP® ESSENTIAL VOCABULARY AND SOURCES

** Essential terms and required sources from the AP® Course are marked with an asterisk.*

Great Migration* p. 431

chain migration p. 432

Black settlement houses p. 435

Pentecostalism p. 436

Hell Fighters p. 440

silent march (1917) p. 442

Red Summer (1919)* p. 443

New Negro* p. 446

Black History Month* p. 449

Universal Negro Improvement Association (UNIA)* p. 449

Harlem Renaissance* p. 453

Alain Locke, Foreword to *The New Negro*, 1925 (Excerpt from *The New Negro: An Interpretation by Alain Locke*, 1925)* p. 461

James Weldon Johnson and John Rosamond Johnson, *Lift Every Voice and Sing*, 1900 ("Lift Every Voice and Sing" by James Weldon Johnson and J. Rosamond Johnson, 1900)* p. 463

James Van Der Zee, *Couple in Raccoon Coats*, 1932 (from James Van Der Zee's Portfolio of Eighteen Photographs, 1905-38; "Harlem Couple," 1932)* p. 467

APPLYING DISCIPLINARY KNOWLEDGE: ESSENTIAL QUESTIONS

1. Describe the tensions — between Blacks and whites and between newer and more established northern Blacks — brought about by the Great Migration. What challenges did the newcomers face, and how did they and northern Blacks generally address these challenges?
2. How did World War I bring about social change both for African Americans who fought in the war and for those who remained on the home front?
3. How do you characterize the state of race relations in this period?
4. Consider the various intellectual, political, social, and cultural developments that accompanied the rise of the New Negro. What did the efforts of the Black social scientists, scholars, artists, writers, and activists who pioneered this movement have in common? What were their goals?

SUGGESTED REFERENCES

The Great Migration

Arnesen, Eric. *Black Protest and the Great Migration: A Brief History with Documents*. Boston: Bedford/St. Martin's, 2003.

Baldwin, Davarian L. *Chicago's New Negroes: Modernity, the Great Migration, and Black Urban Life*. Chapel Hill: University of North Carolina Press, 2007.

Gottlieb, Peter. *Making Their Own Way: Southern Blacks' Migration to Pittsburgh, 1916–30*. Urbana: University of Illinois Press, 1987.

Gregory, James N. *The Southern Diaspora: How the Great Migrations of Black and White Southerners Transformed America*. Chapel Hill: University of North Carolina Press, 2005.

Grossman, James R. *Land of Hope: Chicago, Black Southerners, and the Great Migration*. Chicago: University of Chicago Press, 1989.

Hunter, Jane Edna. *A Nickel and a Prayer*. Edited by Rhondda Robinson Thomas. Morgantown: West Virginia University Press, 2011.

Phillips, Kimberley L. *AlabamaNorth: African-American Migrants, Community, and Working-Class Activism in Cleveland, 1915–45*. Urbana: University of Illinois Press, 1999.

Thomas, Richard W. *Life for Us Is What We Make It: Building Black Community in Detroit, 1915–1945*. Bloomington: Indiana University Press, 1992.

Trotter, Joe William, Jr. *Black Milwaukee: The Making of an Industrial Proletariat, 1915–45*. Urbana: University of Illinois Press, 1985.

Wilkerson, Isabel. *The Warmth of Other Suns: The Epic Story of America's Great Migration*. New York: Random House, 2010.

War Abroad, Violence at Home

Boyle, Kevin. *Arc of Justice: A Saga of Race, Civil Rights, and Murder in the Jazz Age*. New York: Holt, 2004.

D'Orso, Mike. *Like Judgment Day: The Ruin and Redemption of a Town Called Rosewood*. New York: Putnam, 1996.

Ellsworth, Scott. *Death in a Promised Land: The Tulsa Race Riot of 1921*. Baton Rouge: LSU Press, 1992.

MacLean, Nancy. *Behind the Mask of Chivalry: The Making of the Second Ku Klux Klan*. New York: Oxford University Press, 1995.

Schneider, Mark Robert. *"We Return Fighting": The Civil Rights Movement in the Jazz Age*. Boston: Northeastern University Press, 2002.

Williams, Chad L. *Torchbearers of Democracy: African American Soldiers in the World War I Era*. Chapel Hill: University of North Carolina Press, 2010.

The New Negro Arrives

Goggin, Jacqueline. *Carter G. Woodson: A Life in Black History*. Baton Rouge: LSU Press, 1993.

Harold, Claudrena. *The Rise and Fall of the Garvey Movement in the Urban South, 1918–1942*. New York: Routledge, 2007.

Harris, William H. *Keeping the Faith: A. Philip Randolph, Milton P. Webster, and the Brotherhood of Sleeping Car Porters, 1925–37*. Urbana: University of Illinois Press, 1977.

Haygood, Will, et al., *I Too Sing America: The Harlem Renaissance at 100*. New York: Rizzoli/Electra, 2018.

Hill, Robert A., ed. *The Marcus Garvey and Universal Negro Improvement Association Papers*. 10 vols. Berkeley: University of California Press, 1983–2006.

Huggins, Nathan Irvin. *Harlem Renaissance*. New York: Oxford University Press, 1971.

Hutchinson, George T. *The Harlem Renaissance in Black and White*. Cambridge: Belknap Press of Harvard University Press, 1995.

Lewis, David Levering. *When Harlem Was in Vogue*. New York: Vintage, 1982.

Rolinson, Mary G. *Grassroots Garveyism: The Universal Negro Improvement Association in the Rural South, 1920–1927*. Chapel Hill: University of North Carolina Press, 2007.

Stein, Judith. *The World of Marcus Garvey: Race and Class in Modern Society*. Baton Rouge: LSU Press, 1991.

Wall, Cheryl A. *Women of the Harlem Renaissance*. Bloomington: Indiana University Press, 1995.

The Harlem/New Negro Renaissance

The Harlem/New Negro Renaissance (1917–1936) was an extraordinary and audacious time in the twentieth-century African American freedom struggle, reaching its high point in the heady days of the mid-1920s to late 1920s. The renaissance emerged out of the powerful and very influential cultural domain of that continuing freedom struggle. Previously, recently emancipated African Americans had struggled strenuously to give meaning to their freedom, battling a resurgent white supremacy that endeavored to reenslave them through terrorism, Jim Crow, and disfranchisement. In the context of the late nineteenth century and the first decade and a half of the twentieth, then, African Americans of necessity had prioritized the economic, political, and social dimensions of their freedom struggle. Heralding the revitalized race pride, racial self-confidence, militancy, and assertiveness engendered by the hope of the Great Migration and the democratic possibilities of World War I, the Harlem/New Negro Renaissance represented a new and exciting front of that freedom struggle: cultural struggle. From this point forward, the freedom struggle would necessarily be cultural as well as economic, political, and social, precisely because these aspects of the freedom struggle were, paradoxically, at once separable and inextricably interwoven.

The Harlem Renaissance was indeed a New Negro Renaissance. It was a Harlem-centered yet national — even global — phenomenon. African Americans in the United States, like Africans and African peoples throughout the African diaspora, were concurrently and at times interactively engaged in nation-building projects. These significant projects were also fundamentally committed to interrelated race building as well as cultural nationalist projects. At their core, these projects centered on self-definition, self-determination, and self-realization. For African Americans in the United States, this interrelated series of projects meant deeply examining and exuberantly projecting their Africanness as well as their Americanness.

To its critics, the Harlem/New Negro Renaissance was a top-down, elitist series of efforts to jumpstart an African American cultural renaissance too beholden to traditional top-down, Euro-American (white) visions and forms; in their view, it also suffered from an excess of white support. These critics questioned the notion that African Americans producing first-rate literature and art according to Euro-American standards, as well as comparable standards advanced by African American elitists like W. E. B. Du Bois and Alain Locke, would have the power to uplift the race.

As editors of *The Crisis* and *Opportunity* respectively, Du Bois and Charles S. Johnson published the writers, supported their careers, and helped make the New Negro Renaissance. This movement also included a vital assortment of white patrons and supporters like Carl Van Vechten and Charlotte Osgood Mason. These well-connected "friends of the Negro" also encompassed wider networks of influential white editors, publishers, and publicists. They assisted Black writers: editing their work, helping them to get published, spreading positive publicity, and directly financing Black writers. As many then and since have noted, including some of the artists themselves, the times were heady yet troubling. The often crucial white support too often came with controlling and patronizing strings attached, too often undercutting Black independence and originality.

Regardless, the quantity and quality of literature and art produced during this exhilarating, if at times overhyped, moment was monumental, far surpassing collectively the cultural work produced in the preceding post-emancipation years. Historian David Levering Lewis counted "twenty-six novels, ten volumes of poetry, five Broadway plays, countless essays and short stories, three performed ballets and concerti, and a considerable output of canvas and sculpture."[27]

Ultimately, the extraordinary music and the comparably compelling literary work drawing upon African American folk and popular cultures constituted the most original and powerful New Negro Renaissance art. The timeless blues and jazz of the era unfortunately went unheralded by most Black observers, like Du Bois and Locke, whose middle-class, uplift, and Euro-American-influenced aesthetic sensibilities blinded them to the very real and highly original art all around them. They were looking, seeing, and hearing in the wrong places. The most stunningly original and enduring art bubbled up from their own heritage.

key point

The Harlem/New Negro Renaissance (1917–1936) played an important role in the African American freedom struggle, positioning art and culture as interwoven with economic, political, and social aspects of that struggle. Revitalized race pride, racial self-confidence, militancy, and assertiveness characterized this movement. As you interact with the sources, consider the historical situation of the Harlem Renaissance and why the term "renaissance" was used to label the time period.

AP® argumentation

DBQ Practice: Explain how the New Negro movement and Harlem Renaissance encouraged African Americans to define their own identity and to advocate for themselves politically in the midst of the nadir's atrocities. Use at least three of the documents to support your response.

DOCUMENT 1 Alain Locke | *Foreword to* The New Negro, 1925

AP® source

ALAIN LOCKE (1885–1954), a key architect of the Harlem Renaissance, edited the anthology *The New Negro, An Interpretation* as a showcase to introduce the renaissance and a broad cross-section of its artists to the world. Locke's foreword to the volume has several related goals. First, it seeks to define the "New Negro" and the "New Negro Renaissance" as both persuasive evidence and powerful symbols of Negro cultural and social progress since emancipation. Second, in the foreword Locke places the concept of the "New Negro" in its historical context, emphasizing the dominant contemporary and racialist belief that each race had a distinctive "folk spirit" that had to be thoroughly developed for that group to realize its promise and make its full contribution to world history and human civilization. Toward this end, through their cultural work, African American artists in particular had a special role to play by highlighting and exploring the "folk expression" of their people and, in turn, advancing their people's "self-determination." Third, Locke argues why, how, and with what consequences this "New Negro Renaissance" made up an essential cultural wing of the Black Freedom struggle and, thus, necessarily contributed to that struggle.

Breaking it Down As you read, list the goal(s) described in the headnote. How well does Locke achieve these goals? Consider how Marcus Garvey's views influenced Alain Locke's views as well. What evidence can you find for that influence in this text?

This volume aims to document the New Negro culturally and socially, — to register the transformations of the inner and outer life of the Negro in America that have so significantly taken place in the last few years. There is ample evidence of a New Negro in the latest phases of social change and progress, but still more in the internal world of the Negro mind and spirit. Here in the very heart of the folk-spirit are the essential forces, and folk interpretation is truly vital and representative only in terms of these. Of all the voluminous literature on the Negro, so much is mere external view and commentary that we may warrantably say that nine-tenths of it is about the Negro rather than of him, so that it is the Negro problem rather than the Negro that is known and mooted in the general mind. We turn therefore in the other direction to the elements of truest social portraiture, and discover in the artistic self-expression of the Negro to-day a new figure on the national canvas and a new force in the foreground of affairs. Whoever wishes to see the Negro in his essential traits, must seek the enlightenment of that self-portraiture which the present developments of Negro culture are offering. In these pages, without ignoring either the fact that there are important interactions between the national and the race life, or that the attitude of America toward the Negro is as important a factor as the attitude of the Negro toward America, we have nevertheless concentrated upon self-expression and the forces and motives of self-determination. So far as he is culturally articulate, we shall let the Negro speak for himself.

Yet the New Negro must be seen in the perspective of a New World, and especially of a New America. Europe seething in a dozen centers with emergent nationalities, Palestine full of a renascent Judaism — these are no more alive with the progressive forces of our era than the quickened centers of the lives of black folk. America seeking a new spiritual expansion and artistic maturity, trying to found an American literature, a national art, and a national music implies a Negro-American culture seeking the same satisfactions and objectives. Separate as it may be in color and substance, the culture of the Negro is of a pattern integral with the times and with its cultural setting. The achievements of the present generation have eventually made this apparent. Liberal minds to-day cannot be asked to peer with sympathetic curiosity into the darkened Ghetto of a segregated race life. That was yesterday. Nor must they expect to find a mind and soul bizarre and alien as the mind of a savage, or even as naive and refreshing as the mind of the peasant or the child. That too was yesterday, and the day before. Now that there is cultural adolescence and then approach to maturity, — there has come a development that makes these phases of Negro life only an interesting and significant segment of the general American scene.

Until recently, except talent here and there, the main stream of this development has run in the special channels of "race literature" and "race journalism." Particularly as a literary movement, it has gradually gathered momentum in the effort and output of such progressive race periodicals as *The Crisis* under the editorship of Dr. Du Bois and more lately, through the quickening encouragement of Charles Johnson, in the brilliant pages of *Opportunity, a Journal of Negro Life*. But more and more the creative talents of the race have been taken up into the general journalistic, literary and artistic agencies, as the wide range of the acknowledgments of the material here collected will in itself be sufficient to demonstrate. Recently in a project of *The Survey Graphic*, whose Harlem Number of March, 1925, has been taken by kind permission as the nucleus of this book, the whole movement was presented as it is epitomized in the progressive Negro community of the American metropolis. Enlarging this stage we are now presenting the New Negro in a national and even international scope. Although there are few centers that can be pointed out approximating Harlem's significance, the full significance of that even is a racial awakening on a national and perhaps even a world scale.

That is why our comparison is taken with those nascent movements of folk-expression and self-determination which are playing a creative part in the world today. The galvanizing shocks and reactions of the last few years are making by subtle processes of internal reorganization a race out of its own disunited and apathetic elements. A race experience penetrated in this way invariably flowers. As in India, in China, in Egypt, Ireland, Russia, Bohemia, Palestine and Mexico, we are witnessing the resurgence of a people: it has aptly been said, — "For all who read the signs aright, such a dramatic flowering of a new race-spirit is taking place close at home-among American Negroes."

Negro life is not only establishing new contacts and founding new centers, it is finding a new soul. There is a fresh spiritual and cultural focusing. We have, as the heralding sign, an unusual outburst of creative expression. There is a renewed race-spirit that consciously and proudly sets itself apart. Justifiably then, we speak of the offerings of this book embodying these ripening forces as culled from the first fruits of the Negro Renaissance.

SOURCE: Alain Locke, *The New Negro, An Interpretation* (New York: Albert and Charles Boni, 1925), ix.

DOCUMENT 2 AP® source James Weldon Johnson and John Rosamond Johnson | *Lift Every Voice and Sing, 1900*

Also known as the Negro national anthem, "Lift Every Voice and Sing" was written by JAMES WELDON JOHNSON (1871–1938) and set to music by his brother, JOHN ROSAMOND JOHNSON (1873–1954). Beginning in the 1920s, led by the NAACP and Black women's groups, Black organizations and institutions across the country, especially schools and churches, popularized the anthem, which is still sung today. James Weldon Johnson noted a feeling of special joy at hearing his song sung by Black children. Indeed, the song is a stirring symbol and affirmation of the race pride that helped define the New Negro Renaissance.

Breaking it Down Before you read, refresh your memory about the "uplift" ideology. As you read each stanza of the song, identify how it connects to the ideology.

Lift ev'ry voice and sing
Till earth and heaven ring,
Ring with the harmonies of Liberty;
Let our rejoicing rise
High as the list'ning skies,
Let it resound loud as the rolling seas;
Sing a song full of the faith that the dark past has taught us,
Sing a song full of the hope that the present has brought us;
Facing the rising sun
Of our new day begun,
Let us march on till victory is won.

Stony the road we trod,
Bitter the chast'ning rod
Felt in the days when hope had died;
Yet, with a steady beat,
Have not our weary feet
Come to the place for which our fathers sighed,
We have come over a way that with tears has been watered,
We have come, treading our path thro' the blood of the slaughtered,
Out from the gloomy past,
Till now we stand at last
Where the white gleam of our bright star is cast.

God of our weary years,
God of our silent tears,
Thou who hast brought us thus far on the way;
Thou who hast by Thy might,
Led us into the light,
Keep us forever in the path, we pray,
Lest our feet stray from the places, our God, where we met Thee,
Lest, our hearts drunk with the wine of the world, we forget Thee,
Shadowed beneath Thy hand,
May we forever stand,
True to our God, true to our Native Land.

SOURCE: Tuskegee Institute Department of Records and Research, Monroe N. Work, ed., *Negro Year Book: An Annual Encyclopedia of the Negro, 1918–1919* (Tuskegee, AL: Negro Year Book, 1919).

DOCUMENT 3 Ma Rainey | *Prove It on Me Blues, 1928*

MA RAINEY (1886?–1939; born Gertrude Pridgett), "Mother of the Blues," personified the classic African American blues women tradition rooted in the early twentieth century, which blossomed in the 1920s. Noted for her awesome vocal power and energy, she was first recorded in 1923. She both recorded and performed many popular tunes, including "Bad Luck Blues" (1923), "Countin' the Blues" (1925), and "Sissy Blues" (1926). Ma Rainey was also a very popular performer and good businesswoman. The gender and sexual politics of songs like her "Prove It on Me" speak to how blues artists like Ma Rainey in particular and the blues in general revealingly grappled with different identifications and practices in everyday life.

Breaking it Down Number each section of the song and comment on one literary technique Rainey uses to convey her message. How do these contribute to rendering lesbian experience visible to the audience?

Went out last night, had a great big fight
Everything seemed to go on wrong
I looked up, to my surprise
The gal I was with was gone

Where she went, I don't know
I mean to follow everywhere she goes;
Folks say I'm crooked. I didn't know where
she took it
I want the whole world to know

They say I do it, ain't nobody caught me
Sure got to prove it on me;
Went out last night with a crowd of my
friends
They must've been women, 'cause I don't like
no men

It's true I wear a collar and a tie
Makes the wind blow all the while
Don't you say I do it, ain't nobody caught me
You sure got to prove it on me

Say I do it, ain't nobody caught me
Sure got to prove it on me
I went out last night with a crowd of my
friends
It must've been women, 'cause I don't like no
men

Wear my clothes just like a fan
Talk to the gals just like any old man
Cause they say I do it, ain't nobody
caught me
Sure got to prove it on me

SOURCE: Ma Rainey, *Prove It on Me Blues* (lyrics), 1928.

DOCUMENT 4 Langston Hughes | *I, Too, 1926*

Popularly known as the "Poet Laureate of the Negro Race," literary artist and social activist LANGSTON HUGHES (1902–1967) was the most well-known Black writer of his time. He first achieved fame as a major figure in the Harlem Renaissance. In time, Hughes achieved lasting fame as a major figure on the global scene, as well as on the American literary scene. Known as a poet of the people, his work vividly and perceptively explores Black life and culture from the perspective of everyday folk — from the bottom up rather than the top down. As the poem "I, Too" shows, Hughes's work brilliantly illuminates America as well as Black America. In turn, universal and global dimensions of the American and specifically the Black American experiences are insightfully represented.

Breaking it Down What details in this poem reveal the speaker's perspective on his own identity? How might the message of this poem be read as political given the context in which it was written? Does this poem help you understand Hughes's extraordinary popularity as a poet? Why or why not?

I, too, sing America.

I am the darker brother.
They send me to eat in the kitchen
When company comes,
But I laugh,
And eat well,
And grow strong.

Tomorrow,
I'll be at the table
When company comes.
Nobody'll dare
Say to me,
"Eat in the kitchen,"
Then.

Besides,
They'll see how beautiful I am
And be ashamed —

I, too, am America.

SOURCE: Langston Hughes, "I, Too" from The Weary Blues, 1926 (New York: Alfred A. Knopf).

DOCUMENT 5 Gwendolyn Bennett | *To a Dark Girl*, 1927

GWENDOLYN BENNETT (1902–1981) achieved fame as a poet and editor during the Harlem Renaissance. During the Renaissance, she also led Harlem Circles, where young Black artists like Langston Hughes presented their work. With a degree from Pratt Institute, Bennett also had careers as a practicing artist and art teacher. A number of Bennett's poems showcase her race pride, especially her pride in her people's African past. The poem "To a Dark Girl" illustrates another defining feature of her poetry.

Breaking it Down Keep in mind that a simple definition of colorism is the belief that a person is inferior due to their darker complexion. How does this poem address colorism? What literary techniques does Bennett use to counter negative stereotypes? How effective is this poem as a vehicle for the fundamental commitment to Black women's affirmation and uplift?

I love you for your brownness,
And the rounded darkness of your breast;
I love you for the breaking sadness in
your voice
And shadows where your wayward
eyelids rest.

Something of old forgotten queens
Lurks in the lithe abandon of your walk,
And something of the shackled slave
Sobs in the rhythm of your talk.

Oh, little brown girl, born for sorrow's mate,
Keep all you have of queenliness,
Forgetting that you once were slave,
And let your full lips laugh at Fate!

SOURCE: William Stanley Braitwaite, ed., *Anthology of Magazine Verse for 1927, and Yearbook of American Poetry*, 1927 (Boston: B. J. Brimmer Company), 32.

DOCUMENT 6 Augusta Savage | *Gamin*, c. 1930

AUGUSTA SAVAGE (1892–1962) was the most accomplished and prominent sculptor of the Harlem Renaissance, earning a degree from the Cooper Union School of Art and early gaining attention through her sculptures of famous figures like Marcus Garvey and W. E. B. Du Bois. In the 1930s, she became an important arts educator in Harlem. *Gamin*, apparently based on her nephew, helped solidify her artistic reputation, winning her a scholarship that led to several years of art study in Europe. Her sculptures have been lauded for their portrayal of Black facial features.

Breaking it Down Read the headnote carefully before examining the sculpture. What details in this sculpture could be used to support the claim that it emphasizes racial pride?

Smithsonian American Art Museum, Washington, D.C./Art Resource, NY.

DOCUMENT 7

AP® source

James Van Der Zee | *Couple in Raccoon Coats*, 1932

JAMES VAN DER ZEE (1886–1983) was the most famous and successful photographer in Harlem during the 1920s and 1930s. He was also a principal figure of the Harlem Renaissance — indeed, the most popular and accomplished photographer of the renaissance. His subjects also included a 1924 series of photographs documenting the activities and members of Marcus Garvey's Universal Negro Improvement Association. He is particularly well known for photographs of famous Blacks — like Garvey and the entertainer Florence Mills — as well as middle-class Blacks like those captured in this photograph.

Breaking it Down James Van Der Zee's photographs often upended and defied negative stereotypes of Black Americans. What details from this photograph illustrate the qualities of the "new negro"? How does the image highlight the liberated spirit, beauty, and dignity of Black people?

James Van Der Zee Archive, The Metropolitan Museum of Art; Gift of Donna Van Der Zee, 2021. Photo source Bridgeman Images.

DOCUMENT 8 Archibald Motley | *Tongues (Holy Rollers), 1929*

ARCHIBALD MOTLEY (1891–1981) was a highly trained and accomplished visual artist, best known for his paintings of Black urban life, notably in Chicago in the 1920s and 1930s. These works are a critical visual component of the Chicago Renaissance, the New Negro Renaissance as it evolved in this vital center of African American life and culture. (The Chicago Renaissance is discussed in greater depth in the next chapter.) Motley's visual work is praised for its modern and sensitive portrayals of the diversity of African Americans as a people as well as its positive representations of African American life and culture. This painting vividly captures the latter feature in its affirmative representation of the ecstatic dimensions of African American spiritualism.

Breaking it Down Read the headnote that precedes this painting first. Then, list all of the actions you see in the painting. How do these actions relate to the musical innovations of the era? What details contribute to a uniquely Black aesthetic?

Tongues (Holy Rollers), *1929, by Archibald J. Motley Jr., (1891-1981)/Private Collection/(c) Valerie Gerrard Browne / Chicago History Museum/Bridgeman Images.*

PRACTICING AP® SKILLS

1. **AP® Causation.** What concepts, developments, or processes in this chapter contribute to the notion that the painting *Tongues* is an example of rebirth of Black pride in African roots?
2. **AP® Comparison.** How does the sculpture by Augusta Savage compare to the pottery by David Drake (p. 466)? Consider the context, audience, and purpose of each work of art in your response.
3. **AP® Continuity and Change.** Given its widespread popularity, how did the Negro national anthem "Lift Every Voice and Sing" function for African Americans, from the era of the Harlem Renaissance to today?
4. **Connecting to AP® Themes.** Issues of African American self-definition and identity were fundamental to the New Negro/Harlem Renaissance. What light do these documents shed on the multiple and cross-cutting national, racial, class, gender, and sexual identifications of African Americans at the time?
5. **Class Presentation.** Select two sources from this section that aim to reshape views of dark-skinned people. Research and select a book, song, or other form of media (from any era) that promotes positive views of people with darker complexions. Prepare and deliver a short presentation that explains the similarities and differences in how all three sources celebrate darker skin and/or refute the faulty logic of colorism.

Document-Based Questions:
Conclusions

Congratulations! You've reached the final component of a successful DBQ response: the conclusion. Although you may feel as if you have nothing left to discuss by the time you get to the end of your essay, the conclusion is actually the ideal place to emphasize the importance of your **argument** in the broader context of AP® African American Studies.

Examining the AP® Rubric

The rubric that will be used to assess DBQ responses states you'll earn a point if your essay:

- Describes a broader historical or disciplinary context relevant to the topic of the prompt. *To earn this point, the response must describe broader events, developments, processes, or disciplinary connections that are relevant to the topic of the prompt. The point is not earned for a passing phrase or reference.*

It's a common misconception that a conclusion is just "window dressing" and doesn't meaningfully add to an essay's argument. As this excerpt from the rubric demonstrates, that's simply untrue, especially within AP® African American Studies. Within this interdisciplinary course, it's especially important to weave together historical information and disciplinary connections (like references to politics, literature, or media) to contextualize the topic at hand.

You should have already worked toward earning this point by providing historical **context** in your essay's introduction. Now, you can ensure full credit by emphasizing disciplinary connections in your essay's conclusion.

Reviewing Prewriting Skills

In almost every AP® Skills Workshop on document-based questions, we've practiced how to break down a prompt and activate course knowledge so relevant **concepts**, **developments**, and **processes** come to mind. This prep work will come in handy for a conclusion, too, so let's practice it using a sample DBQ prompt:

Evaluate the extent to which the New Negro movement influenced both the artistic and political attitudes of Black people in America from 1915 to 1930.

Breaking down that prompt might result in a graphic organizer along these lines:

Time Period	Topic	Task
1915–1930	The New Negro movement	Explain how much the New Negro movement influenced both the artistic and political attitudes of Black Americans from 1915 to 1930.

Relevant Course Concepts, Developments, Processes
• The New Negro movement arose as a philosophy encouraging African Americans to counter discrimination with pride in their identities and advocacy. • Northern cities blossomed from 1915 to 1930 due to the Great Migration, in which African Americans left the Jim Crow South en masse. • Black artists active during The New Negro movement created a distinct aesthetic reflecting cultural pride. • Artistic innovations associated with the New Negro movement include blues and jazz music, tap dancing, literature exploring Black identity, and African-inspired art. The New Negro arts movement is also known as the Harlem Renaissance.

On the AP® Exam, you'd then skillfully skim the sources, draft a **thesis statement**, articulate **topic sentences**, collect **evidence** to support each topic sentence, and then weave that evidence together through **commentary**. Here, we'll provide a sample thesis statement:

> The New Negro movement significantly influenced both the artistic and political attitudes of African Americans because it encouraged pride in Black identity, sparked new ideas and artistic achievements, and united African Americans around shared struggles.

Concluding a DBQ

To write a strong conclusion, you'll have to go a step beyond *what* your essay has argued to focus on the *so what*, meaning the reasons why your argument matters in the broader context of African American Studies.

Most successful conclusions start off with a restatement of the thesis statement that brings the argument full circle. There isn't a formula dictating how to draft the rest of a concluding paragraph, but the following questions can kickstart your thinking:

- How does your analysis counter prevailing stereotypes or misconceptions about Black history and culture?
- How did developments connected to the essay topic give rise to later events and movements?
- How does the essay topic connect to current events affecting Black Americans?
- What lesson can be drawn from your analysis?

An effective conclusion on our sample essay topic might end up looking like this:

> By instilling pride in African American culture, encouraging innovative forms of expression, and energizing Black Americans to resist discrimination, the New Negro movement significantly impacted Black artistic and political identities in the period from 1915 to 1930. This cultural revolution laid the groundwork for future developments, from the Black Power movement that began in the 1960s to the Black Lives Matter movement that has shaped recent political discourse. Thus, though it has been roughly a century since thinkers like Alain Locke and Jessie Fauset first expressed their groundbreaking philosophies, the New Negro movement continues to shape Black American thought and action.

recap

Concluding a DBQ

When drafting a conclusion for a document-based question, it can be helpful to ask yourself the following questions:

- **How does your analysis counter prevailing stereotypes or misconceptions about Black history and culture?**
- **How did developments connected to the essay topic give rise to later events and movements?**
- **How does the essay topic connect to current events affecting Black Americans?**
- **What lesson can be drawn from your analysis?**

Activity ▸ Concluding a DBQ

Draft your own conclusion responding to the prompt provided on page SW11-A.

NOTES

Multiple-Choice Questions

Questions 1–2 refer to the following.

***Madam C. J. Walker,* 1916**

Photo by Jim Mooney/NY Daily News Archive via Getty Images

1. Which of the following statements best describes the relationship between the above image and the legacy of Madam C. J. Walker?

(A) The photo reflects Madam C. J. Walker's ability to purchase an automobile and drive her friends around town as one of the many wealthy Black women of her era.

(B) The photo captures both Madam C. J. Walker's confident stare and her command of the Model T, reflecting the wealth and power she was able to accumulate due to the success of her Black beauty brand. The photo captures Walker's mentorship of other women and her habit of giving them opportunities to thrive in business.

(C) The photo illustrates how Madam C. J. Walker's mentorship of other Black women entrepreneurs helped cement her legacy.

(D) The photo highlights the glamor of capitalism in America as well as the challenges faced by Black women who sought business opportunities.

2. How did Madam C. J. Walker promote economic opportunities for Black women?

(A) Walker employed Black women in her businesses and often invited them to spend time with her socially, offering them the chance to network.

(B) Walker paid Black women a living wage to travel, promote, and sell her beauty products, giving many of them a chance to escape the drudgery of domestic labor.

(C) Walker was a philanthropist who donated much of her considerable fortune to various Black institutions, which in turn provided more opportunities for Black women.

(D) Walker held entrepreneurial events for Black women to encourage them to start their own companies so they could advance economically.

Short-Answer Question

"Some Garveyites sustained an official relationship with the [Universal Negro Improvement Association]; others confronting harsh political realities, could not. . . . Garveyism provided a powerful organizing principle, a political approach that combined caution and ambition, that proposed both a practical and an inspiring means to confront a postwar world. . . . The characterization of Garveyism as an ideology has never really fit. . . . Garveyism was radical in some moments and reactionary in others, strident in some places and cautious in others."

SOURCE: Adam Ewing, *The Age of Garvey: How a Jamaican Activist Created a Mass Movement and Changed Global Black Politics*, 2016

"The first [Universal Negro Improvement Association (UNIA)] and African Communities League circular emanating from Jamaica in 1914 listed two of its ten objectives as follows: 'To assist in civilizing the backwards tribes of Africa, and to promote a conscientious Christian worship among the native tribes of Africa.' The UNIA constitution, written after the organization's incorporation in New York, included these same objectives. . . . Garvey's adoption of this goal has prompted debates among those who have tried to refute the leader's eligibility to be considered a Black nationalist. . . . Garvey believed modern and Western civilization had much to offer Africans. . . . Garvey consistently argued that the African race had already proved . . . its ability to succeed, innovate, and even dominate other races."

SOURCE: Mary G. Rolinson, *Grassroots Garveyism: The Universal Negro Improvement Association in the Rural South, 1920–1927*, 2012

1. Using the excerpts, answer A, B, C, and D.

(A) Describe one major difference between Ewing's and Rolinson's interpretations of Marcus Garvey and "Garveyism" as a political stance.

(B) Describe the broader historical context of Marcus Garvey and "Garveyism" that is being addressed by both Ewing and Rolinson.

(C) Explain how one historical event, development, or circumstance in the period between 1915 and 1930 that is not explicitly mentioned in the excerpts could be used to support Ewing's argument.

(D) Explain how one historical event, development, or circumstance in the period between 1915 and 1930 that is not explicitly mentioned in the excerpts could be used to support Rolinson's perspective.

Multiple-Choice Questions

Questions 1–3 refer to the following.

SOURCE 1

***The First Colored Senator and Representatives*, 1872**

Library of Congress, Prints and Photographs Division, Washington, D.C., LC-DIG-ppmsca-17564

SOURCE 2

Black Political Participation in the Reconstruction South, 1867–1868

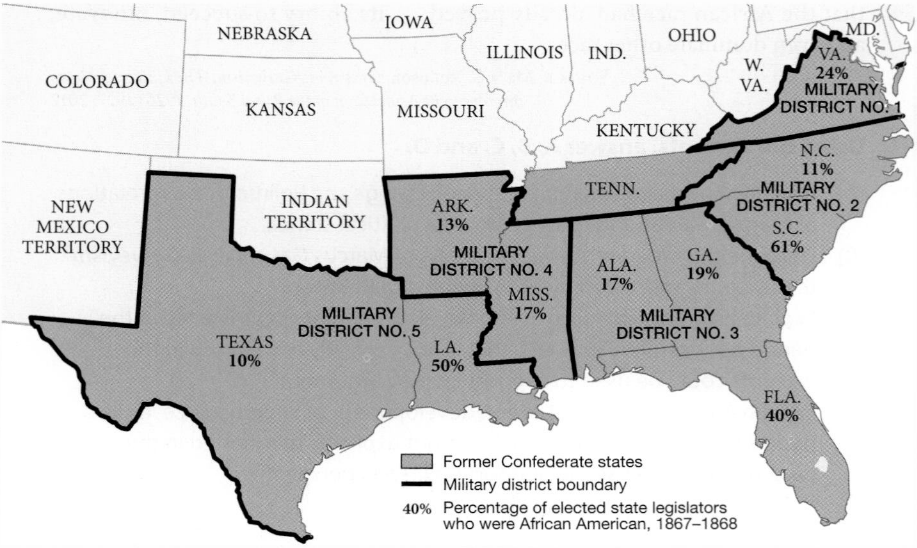

1. Which of the following most directly contributed to the historical development depicted in both the image and map?
(A) The implementation of Special Field Order No. 15
(B) The establishment of the Freedmen's Bureau
(C) The declaration of General Order No. 3
(D) The ratification of the Fifteenth Amendment

2. Which of the following statements about Black political participation during Reconstruction does the map best support?
(A) Black politicians mainly represented districts and states in the North.
(B) Radical Republicans in office provided enough support to gain Black men's votes but not enough to enable them to run for office.
(C) Union military presence was essential to Black political participation in the South.
(D) Black political representation in the federal government eclipsed Black representation on the local and state level during Reconstruction.

3. The Compromise of 1877 had which of the following impacts on Black political participation during Reconstruction?
(A) Voting and political representation declined as Black people were less able to vote and run for office without military protection.
(B) Membership in the Democratic Party increased as Black voters became disillusioned with the Republican Party and switched parties.
(C) Political influence increased as a new wave of Republicans reaffirmed their support for Black suffrage.
(D) Interest in voting declined as Black voters did not feel supported by the Radical Republicans.

Questions 4–6 refer to the following.

Know all Men by these Presents, that John B. Kinard of Sumter County, State of Georgia, held and firmly bound to the United States of America by these presents, in the contract; That he is to furnish the persons whose names are subjoined, (freed laborers,) quarters, fuel, healthy and substantial rations, & is to furnish a sufficiency of land for said laborers to cultivate horses or mules feed for the same & all expenses except [word unclear] to pay said laborers one third of what is made on said plantation as hands or parts of hands in proportions to the number of hands that work on said plantation. The said laborers agree on their part to pay said Kinard for all rations that he furnishes them at their market prices out of their said crop & also to bear their proportionable share of the expenses of the Bagging & Ropes & to receive that portion of the crop as above stated for their share as wages. The said persons are to labor faithfully on his plantation, six days during the week, in the manner customary on a plantation; said persons to forfeit, in whole or in part, their wages, or their interest in the crop, in case they violate this contract. All differences to be referred to an officer or agent of the Bureau of Refugees, Freedmen and Abandoned Lands, for Adjustment.

Cesar Carter 1/3 of the crop that he makes & for his son
for Son Willy Carter. 1/2 hand in proportion as to 1/3 of the crop
John B. Kinard Employer

This contract is to commence with ~~this date~~ this year and close with the year.
Given in duplicate at Americus
this 5th day of October 1867.
Witness W.L. Kinard
J.A.J. Chambles

Contract,
Between ....
J.B. Kinard
and Cesar Carter
Willy Carter
freedmen

Office Agent Bureau R.F. & A.L.
For Sumter County,
October 8th 1867
Approved
J.M. Robinson
Agent.

SOURCE: William A. Gladstone *Sharecropper's contract, to share one-third crop*, 5 Oct. 1867

4. Which of the following most directly contributed to the historical situation presented by the document?
(A) The Freedmen's Bureau guaranteed the labor rights and protection for freedpeople.
(B) The damage done to southern plantations during the Civil War left a shortage of available land.
(C) Congressional Reconstruction plans did not include land redistribution to newly freed African Americans.
(D) Newly freed African Americans emerged from Reconstruction without the skills required to be economically independent.

5. Which of the following best describes an outcome of the historical situation depicted in the document?
(A) The Supreme Court determined such contracts and labor arrangements unconstitutional at the end of Reconstruction.
(B) Landowners that broke the contract forfeited their land and became trapped in the convict lease system.
(C) Black workers were able to save money and advance economically into the middle class.
(D) Landowners and merchants cheated workers, forcing them into a pattern of cyclical debt.

6. Which of the following best explains the significance of sharecropping in the African American experience after the Civil War?

(A) It prevented the reunion of Black families after the Civil War.

(B) It enabled Black people to pool their resources to establish institutions like the Citizens Savings Bank and Trust Company.

(C) It helped the South heal from the racial tensions that lingered after the Civil War.

(D) It was used to systematically keep Black people in an economic situation similar to slavery.

Questions 7–9 refer to the following.

SOURCE 1

Black and white soldiers in Chicago, 1919

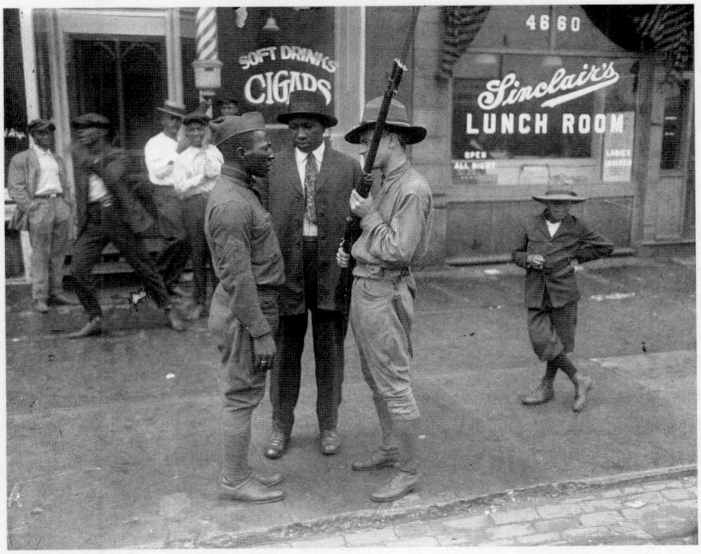

Chicago Tribune/Getty Images

SOURCE 2

Cameron McWhirter, *Red Summer: The Summer of 1919 and the Awakening of Black America*, 2011

"The first months after the war's abrupt end, blacks hoped they had won a new place in American society. It was a 'plastic moment,' as historian Richard Slotkin put it, when racial boundaries seemed to undulate and the social order expanded, possibly to allow a new pace for blacks. . . . But soon race relations frayed and goodwill from the war dissipated. Many whites resorted to threats and violence to reassert their old dominance. Most politicians did not see the rising potential for riots or lynching. Some openly endorsed such anti black violence when it came. Others said there was little they could do to stop it. Most delayed and bungled when faced with crises. Blacks who had seen themselves on the cusp of true equality, became confused and angry. . . ."

7. Which of the following best explains the cause of the historical situation depicted and discussed in both sources?

(A) Competition for jobs and racial discrimination against Black World War I veterans contributed to a rise in hate crimes across the country.

(B) Frustration over distribution of GI Bill benefits along racial lines led to racial violence.

(C) Failure of the federal and local governments to bestow medals of honor on Black World War I veterans led to urban riots.

(D) Discontent over the prevalence of subpar housing in Black northern cities after World War I led to racial tensions.

8. Which of the following earlier developments had an effect most similar to that of the race riots described in the excerpt?

(A) The tensions that emerged during the forced migration of millions of Africans during the Second Middle Passage

(B) The racial violence that occurred during Reconstruction following the end of the Civil War

(C) The protest that ensued after the Supreme Court's ruling in *Plessy v. Ferguson*

(D) The racial attacks on the Black community that ensued after the Emancipation Proclamation was passed

9. Which of the following explains how Black people responded to the historical developments depicted in both sources?

(A) Black people migrated to Latin America in massive numbers not seen before in American history.

(B) Black people resisted white supremacist attacks on their communities through various tactics including armed self-defense.

(C) Black people lobbied and successfully got an antilynching bill passed through Congress.

(D) Black newspaper moguls sold their newspapers and donated their profits to legal funds to help Black veterans unfairly prosecuted during race riots.

Questions 10–12 refer to the following.

"Colored women have a double burden to carry — the burden of race as well as that of sex. White women all over the civilized world showed how great a handicap they thought sex was by the desperate efforts they made to secure suffrage. The extreme and violent methods to which the English wo[m]en especially resorted are fresh in our minds. But those white women had only one handicap to overcome. What would they not have done, if they had been obliged to surmount TWO, as we colored women have to do?

There is no doubt that some of the disadvantages under which colored women labor may be removed by their votes. By casting their ballots properly, by putting good men into office and keeping bad men out colored women can do much to remove some of the disabilities under which we live in those sections where their votes are counted. And even in those sections of the country where the fifteenth amendment is not violated, there are many conditions confronting colored people which should and can be removed."

SOURCE: Mary Church Terrell, *An Appeal to Colored Women to Vote and Do Their Duty in Politics*, 1921

10. Which of the following historical evidence best supports Terrell's claim?

(A) Black women entered the workforce to support their families in high numbers following the Civil War.

(B) The Nineteenth Amendment gave women the right to vote but did not address the racist obstacles that prevented Black women from voting in certain states at the state and local levels.

(C) The vagrancy laws that emerged during Reconstruction applied to Black women only.

(D) Black women were not granted citizenship by the Fourteenth Amendment.

11. Which of the following best describes the purpose of Terrell's speech?

(A) To advocate for the adoption of strategies used by British woman suffrage activists to gain attention for Black woman suffrage.

(B) To sow further division between white and Black woman suffrage and show the hypocrisy of the woman suffrage movement.

(C) To bring attention to the need for the right to vote to address the gendered and racial obstacles Black women faced.

(D) To highlight the strength and talents of Black women during and after the end of slavery.

12. Which of the following best describes how Black women responded to the historical situation depicted in the passage?

(A) Black women organized and created women's clubs for and run by Black women to fight for suffrage.

(B) Black women focused all efforts on removing the state and local laws preventing Black men from voting so that those men could represent the positions of Black women at the ballot box.

(C) Black women rejected the politics of respectability and challenged gender discrimination within the Black church.

(D) Black women refused to join the feminist movement until white women activists championed Black woman suffrage.

Questions 13–15 refer to the following.

Cultural Harlem, 1920s

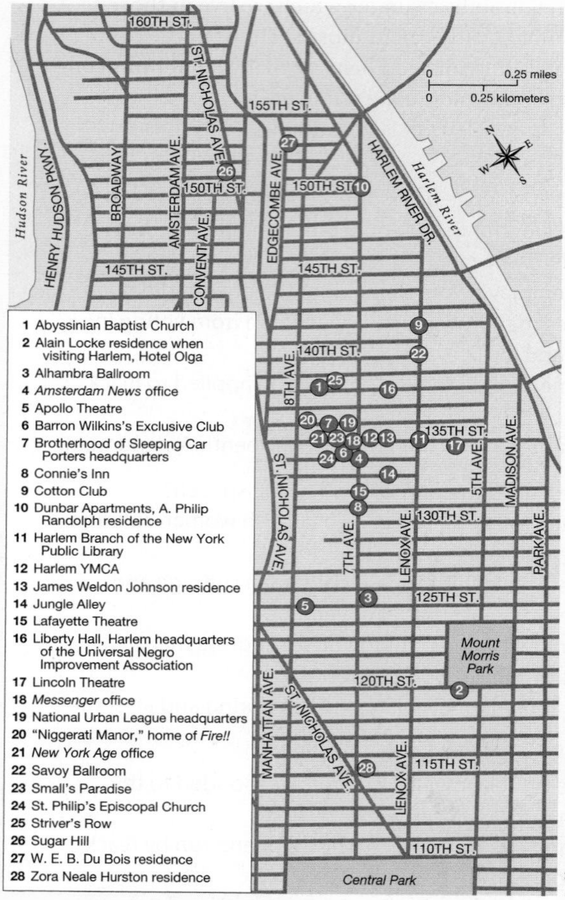

Jeffrey Brown Ferguson, *The Harlem Renaissance: A Brief History with Documents* (Boston: Bedford/St. Martin's, 2008), 9.

13. Which of the following best describes the historical significance of the map and its highlighted locations?

(A) The map is evidence of Black artists' desire to place themselves in locations that would help them create art that would be representative of their race.

(B) The map reflects Black Harlem artists' desire to generate environments where they could create art that would gain validation from the leading white artists of the time.

(C) The map reflects Harlem's status as the only city in the United States with conditions ripe for Black cultural and artistic exploration.

(D) The map reflects the geographic location and conditions of a period of Black cultural renaissance in the United States.

14. Which of the following broader historical contexts best explains the cultural landmarks depicted in the map?

(A) The New Negro movement emerged after World War I and encompassed cultural movements that produced artistic innovations.

(B) The automobile became widely accessible and led to increased geographic mobility for Black artists.

(C) The conclusion of World War I encouraged many artists who had served in the military to describe their experiences.

(D) A cross-cultural artistic revival swept across the United States.

15. The historical development reflected in the map most directly resulted from which of the following?

(A) The establishment of new historically Black colleges in Harlem, making it a prominent center of Black education.

(B) The emergence of Harlem as a major population center resulting from new patterns of Black migration.

(C) The decline in Black employment and businesses due to a slowing postwar economy.

(D) The reduction in racial violence across the North following the conclusion of World War I.

Short-Answer Questions

1. Using the image, answer A, B, C, and D.

AP® source ***Harlem Couple*, James Van Der Zee, 1932**

Couple in Raccoon Coats, 1932, by James Van Der Zee (PHOTOGRAPH) Copyright Donna Mussenden Van Der Zee/Photo Source: Bridgeman Images.

(A) Describe how the image reflects one historical development in African American history during the early to mid-twentieth century.
(B) Using a specific example, describe how early to mid-twentieth-century social activists used photography to enact social change.
(C) Describe one significant feature of Harlem in the early to-mid-twentieth century that is depicted in the image.
(D) Explain how the image challenges one misconception about Black people that some might have held during the twentieth century.

2. Using the excerpt, answer A, B, C, and D.

"If through me, an humble representative, seven millions of my people in the South might be permitted to send a message to Harvard. . . . 'Tell them that by the way of the shop, the field, the skilled hand, habits of thrift and economy, by way of industrial school and college, we are coming. We are crawling up, working up, yea, bursting up. Often through oppression, unjust discrimination and prejudice, but through them all we are coming up, and with proper habits, intelligence and property, there is no power on earth that can permanently stay our progress. . . .' During the next half century and more, my race must continue passing through the severe American crucible. We are to be tested in our patience, our forbearance, our perseverance, our power to endure wrong, to withstand temptations, to economize, to acquire and use skill; our ability to compete. . . . I beg of you to remember that wherever our life touches yours, we help or hinder. . . . There is no escape — man drags man down, or man lifts man up. Thus helped, we of both races in the South, soon shall throw off the shackles of racial and sectional prejudice and rise, as Harvard University has risen and as we all should rise, above the clouds of ignorance, narrowness and selfishness, into that atmosphere, that pure sunshine, where it will be our highest ambition to serve man, our brother, regardless of race or previous condition. . . ."

SOURCE: Booker T. Washington, Address delivered at the alumni dinner of Harvard University after receiving the honorary degree of Master of Arts, 1896

(A) Describe the broader historical context that compelled Washington to make the speech from which this excerpt is taken.
(B) Describe one way that Washington believed Black people could achieve racial uplift.
(C) Using a specific example of one Black leader other than Washington who was devoted to racial uplift, explain how their strategy was similar to or different from Washington's.
(D) Using a specific example, explain the degree to which one of Washington's hopes was fulfilled by the 1930s.

3. Answer A, B, C, and D.

(A) Describe West African educational traditions and the transfer of knowledge prior to the transatlantic slave trade.
(B) Describe how Black educational traditions evolved from 1865 until the 1920s.
(C) Using one example, explain how political and social movements impacted Black educational traditions and curriculum during the 1920s.
(D) Explain the social, economic, or political impact that increased access to higher education had on the Black community in the early twentieth century.

Document-Based Question

1. Explain how Black migration patterns and trends shaped the character of Black communities in the United States during the early twentieth century.

In your response you should do the following:

- **Respond to the prompt with a defensible thesis or claim that establishes a line of reasoning.**
- **Describe a broader historical or disciplinary context relevant to the topic of the prompt.**
- **Support an argument in response to the prompt using at least three of the sources.**
- **Use at least one additional piece of specific evidence (beyond the evidence found in the sources) relevant to your argument.**
- **For at least two sources, explain how or why the perspective, purpose, context, and/or audience for each source is relevant to your argument.**
- **Reference or cite the sources you use in your argument. You can reference or cite the source letter, title, or author.**

SOURCE A

Isabel Wilkerson, *The Warmth of Other Suns: The Epic Story of America's Great Migration*, 2011

From the early years of the twentieth century to well past its middle age, nearly every black family in the American South . . . had a decision to make. There were sharecroppers losing at settlement. Typists wanting to work in an office. Yard boys scared that a single gesture near the planter's wife could leave them hanging from an oak tree. They were all stuck in a caste system as hard and unyielding as the red Georgia clay. . . .

It was during the First World War that a silent pilgrimage took its first steps within the borders of this country. . . . It would not end until the 1970s and would set into motion changes in the North and South that no one . . . could have imagined at the start of it or dreamed would take nearly a lifetime to play out. . . .

Its imprint is everywhere in urban life. The configuration of the cities as we know them, the social geography or black and white neighborhoods, the spread of the housing projects as well as the rise of a well-scrubbed black middle class, along with the alternative waves of white flight and suburbanization — all of these grew, directly or indirectly, from the response of everyone touched by the Great Migration.

So, too, rose the language and music of urban America that sprang from the blues that came with the migrants and dominates our airwaves to this day. So, too, came the people who might not have existed, or become who they did, had there been no Great Migration. People as diverse as James Baldwin and Michelle Obama, Miles Davis and Toni Morrison, Spike Lee and Denzel Washington, and anonymous teachers, store clerks, steelworkers, and physicians. . . . They were all children whose life chances were altered because a parent or grandparent had made the hard decision to leave.

SOURCE B

Ship Manifest of Passengers Traveling from Jamaica to Philadelphia, 1909

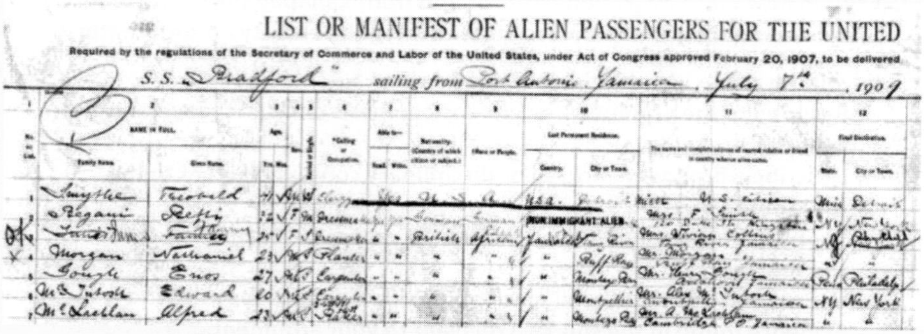
LIST OR MANIFEST OF ALIEN PASSENGERS FOR THE UNITED

Required by the regulations of the Secretary of Commerce and Labor of the United States, under Act of Congress approved February 20, 1907, to be delivered

S. S. "Bradford" sailing from Port Antonio, Jamaica, July 7th, 1909

SOURCE C

Langston Hughes, "The South" (poem), *The Weary Blues*, 1926

The lazy, laughing South
With blood on its mouth.
The sunny-faced South,
    Beast-strong,
    Idiot-brained.
The child-minded South
Scratching in the dead fire's ashes
For a Negro's bones.
    Cotton and the moon,
    Warmth, earth, warmth,
    The sky, the sun, the stars,
    The magnolia-scented South.
Beautiful, like a woman,
Seductive as a dark-eyed whore,
    Passionate, cruel,
    Honey-lipped, syphilitic —
    That is the South.
And I, who am black, would love her
But she spits in my face.
And I, who am black,
Would give her many rare gifts
But she turns her back upon me.
    So now I seek the North —
    The cold-faced North,
    For she, they say,
    Is a kinder mistress,
And in her house my children
May escape the spell of the South.

SOURCE D

AP® source Trade of Enslaved Africans, 1501–1867

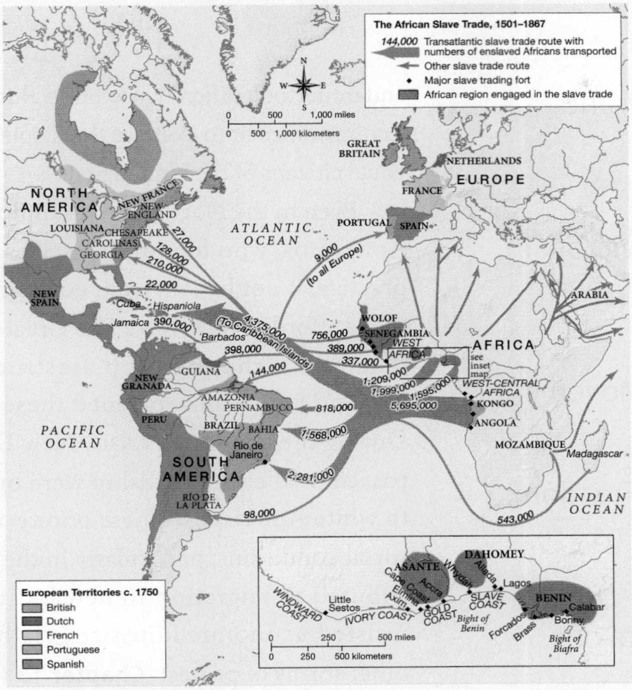

SOURCE E

AP® source Marcus Garvey at His Desk (photograph), August 5, 1924

Library of Congress, Prints & Photographs Division, Reproduction number LC-USZ61-1854 (b&w film copy neg.)

UNIT 4

Movements and Debates

12 Catastrophe, Recovery, and Renewal
1930–1942

13 Fighting for a Double Victory in the World War II Era
1938–1950

14 The Early Civil Rights Movement
1945–1963

15 Multiple Meanings of Freedom: The Movement Broadens
1961–1976

16 Racial Progress in an Era of Backlash and Change
1965–2000

17 African Americans in the Twenty-First Century
2000–Present

Unit 4 covers nearly a century of ground, from the 1930s to the present day. Several chapters in this unit will illustrate African Americans' quest for civil rights and how they found achievement in their goals for the right to vote. In the 1950s through the 1970s especially, various activist groups formed to address the many social, political, and economic injustices that Black Americans had endured since the end of Reconstruction and the height of Jim Crow. These organizations held diverse viewpoints and undertook different methods. But, they shared a common goal: to exercise their rights as true and equal citizens of the United States.

Even in the North, life was difficult for Black Americans, who found themselves excluded in practice, if not by law, from economic opportunities afforded to whites. The Great Depression, detailed in **chapter 12** (Catastrophe, Recovery, and Renewal), worsened these conditions. During the economic crisis, New Deal policies passed to alleviate hardship were only available to white Americans. These poor economic and social conditions, particularly in the South, contributed to migration to new locations. Many resisted economic injustices via boycott and other forms of protest. **Chapter 13** (Fighting for a Double Victory in the World War II Era, 1938–1950) explores the pivotal role African Americans played in World War II. Even amidst a fight to end fascism, many African Americans were still subject to unfair, oppressive treatment in a segregated military. Some in the armed forces sought to achieve change through nonviolent protest, such as the Port Chicago protest and the hunger strike at Camp Rousseau in Port Hueneme, California. The U.S. military finally desegregated in 1948, nearly three years after the end of World War II.

Chapter 14 (The Early Civil Rights Movement, 1945–1963) describes the postwar struggle for freedom, as different political groups came together to protest. Some African Americans joined the Communist Party during this era to participate in the Black freedom struggle. This political affiliation quickly became dangerous during the McCarthy era of the late 1940s and early 1950s. Even loose association with someone accused of Communist Party membership could have negative consequences.

In February 1968, an estimated 1,300 Black sanitation workers went on strike to protest the inhumane working conditions at the Memphis Sanitation Department. The striking men wore signs that said, "I AM A MAN," asserting their right to be treated equitably and with respect. Dr. Martin Luther King traveled to Memphis to show support for the strike. There, he delivered his last speech, "I've Been to the Mountaintop." He was assassinated the next day. *Bettmann/Getty Images.*

In this chapter, you'll also learn about the strategies used by different groups such as the Black Power movement, SNCC, and the Cambridge Nonviolent Action Committee (CNAC). You will have opportunities to compare and contrast their methods, goals, and results. The Black freedom struggle gained steam and some important victories during this time. Judicial gains such as *Brown v. Board of Education* in 1954 required states with segregation laws to desegregate "with all deliberate speed." Federal legislation such as the Civil Rights Act of 1964 and the Voting Rights Act of 1965 were important wins that secured rights for Black Americans throughout the nation.

The increase in nonviolent protest movements came with an increase of violent responses and obstacles, as you'll learn in **chapter 15** (Multiple Meanings of Freedom: The Movement Broadens, 1961–1976). The Mississippi Summer Freedom Project of 1964 is just one example of the relationship between the success of nonviolent protest tactics and racist backlash. Northern volunteers traveled to Mississippi to register Black voters, teach literacy and civics at newly established Freedom Schools, and spread the word about the newly formed Mississippi Freedom Democratic Party. Within days of the first group of volunteers' arrival, three went missing. They were later found murdered. Ultimately, their deaths brought more supporters to the cause of civil rights — but at great cost.

This chapter also examines the resurgence in artistic expression that focused on racial pride and new conceptions of identity, as well as the formation of institutions dedicated to promote political, economic, and social opportunity. Within their communities, African Americans debated about what it meant to be Black in America and how to make progress.

Chapter 16 (Racial Progress in an Era of Backlash and Change, 1965–2000) explores the rise of Black nationalism and its connection to the Black Panther Party as well as the Anti–Vietnam War movement. The economic crisis experienced by

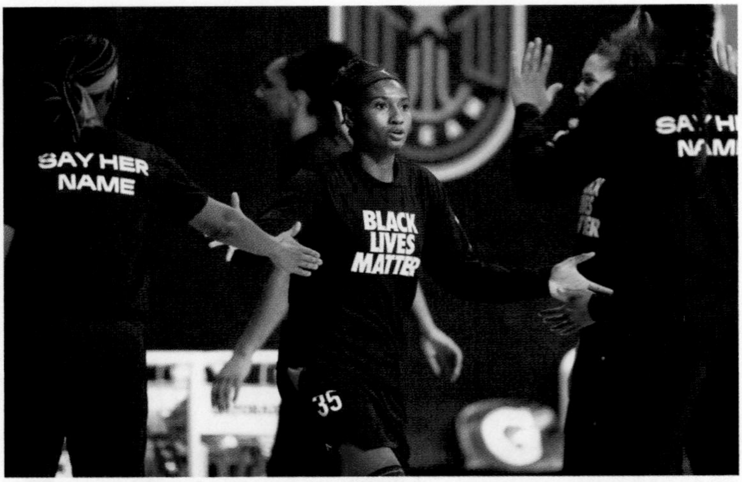

In 2020, the WNBA dedicated their season to the "long history of inequality, implicit bias and racism that disproportionately impacts communities of color." Players including Angel McCoughtry, pictured here, followed in the footsteps of others before them to bring awareness to social and political issues by wearing jerseys with "Black Lives Matter" on the front and "Say Her Name" on the back. An outgrowth of the Black Lives Matter movement, the Say Her Name campaign aims to raise public awareness specifically for the Black women who are victims of police brutality and anti-Black violence. *Ned Dishman/Getty Images.*

many African Americans in rural and urban areas became a priority for many activist groups. These groups — especially the Black Panthers — received intense scrutiny from the Federal Bureau of Investigation. This chapter also details the progress made in the Black freedom struggle during the latter half of the twentieth century. Black Americans made important strides toward social and economic equality, and in turn helped fuel political momentum for other marginalized groups.

Black art and thought continued to flourish in the late twentieth century. Sociologist Patricia Hill Collins, building on the work of others before her, advanced a theory of "interlocking systems of oppression," which treats social categories such as race, gender, class, sexuality, and ability as interconnected and directly related categories of experience that all contribute to individuals' interaction with social systems in all areas of life, ultimately leading to unequal outcomes. The work of writers and scholars such as Alice Walker, Kimberlé Crenshaw, Gwendolyn Brooks, and Audre Lorde built on this foundation in their work, revealing how different aspects of Black people's identities and lived experiences affect how others perceive them and the opportunities they are afforded.

By the twenty-first century, integration in the workplace and higher education had been achieved, but not to the fullest possible extent. The color line remained alive and well. **Chapter 17** (African Americans in the Twenty-First Century) illustrates that America has not moved into a post-racial era, as evidenced by the aftermath of Hurricane Katrina in 2005, the continued mass incarceration of African Americans, increasing police brutality, a persistent wealth gap, and more. Yet this century also saw the first Black president and the first Black woman vice president. In 2020, the Black Lives Matter and Say Her Name movements gained momentum and support from a multiracial coalition in their campaign against police brutality. This renewed solidarity and strength in grassroots protest movements sparked reforms in the police and criminal justice systems. While there is still much ground yet to cover, these recent developments are cause to hope for the future.

AP® UNIT 4 THEMATIC TIMELINE

All of the following developments can be found in the AP® Course Framework.

1925 | 1950 | 1975 | 2000 | 2025

Migration and the African Diaspora

- **1940s** More than 1.5 million African Americans migrate out of South
- **Mid-1970s** Rap music emerges on New York City streets

Intersections of Identity

- **1930** The Nation of Islam (NOI) founded in Detroit
- **1966** Huey Newton and Bobby Seale found Black Panther Party for Self-Defense (BPPSD) in Oakland

Creativity, Expression, and the Arts

- **1936** Track star Jesse Owens wins four gold medals at Berlin Olympics
- **1947** Jackie Robinson becomes first Black major league baseball player
- **1952** Josephine Baker delivers speech criticizing segregation in St. Louis, Missouri
- **1964** Malcolm X gives "The Ballot or the Bullet" speech

Resistance and Resilience

- **1934** Federal Housing Administration founded; its mortgage policies promote redlining and restrictive covenants
- **1941** A. Philip Randolph organizes March on Washington to demand desegregation of armed services Tuskegee Airmen's unit formed
- **1942** *Pittsburgh Courier* launches Double V campaign Congress of Racial Equality (CORE) founded
- **1948** Truman issues Executive Order 9981, ending segregation in armed services
- **1954** *Brown v. Board of Education* overturns segregation in public schools
- **1955** Fourteen-year-old Emmett Till murdered in Mississippi
- **1957** Southern Christian Leadership Conference (SCLC) founded
- **1960** Student Nonviolent Coordinating Committee (SNCC) founded
- **1961** Congress of Racial Equality (CORE) organizes Freedom Rides
- **1963** March on Washington for Jobs and Freedom
- **1964** Mississippi Freedom Democratic Party (MFDP) founded Civil Rights Act
- **1965** Voting Rights Act
- **1968** Fair Housing Act Shirley Chisholm elected to Congress
- **1971** Congressional Black Caucus founded
- **2008** Barack Obama elected first African American president
- **2012** Obama reelected president
- **2020** Kamala Harris becomes first African American vice president

SOURCE: *National Archives and Records Administration, Still Pictures Record Section, NARA-531334/111-SC-238651.*

AP® skill **Applying Disciplinary Knowledge (1C)**

Identify and explain patterns, connections, or other relationships (causation, changes, continuities, comparison).

Key Context: The U.S. armed forces remained segregated at the outset of World War II. Despite this, over two million African Americans served in every branch of the U.S. military. African Americans faced unequal treatment in a segregated military.

PREDICT

- What does this photograph suggest about African Americans' participation in the war effort?

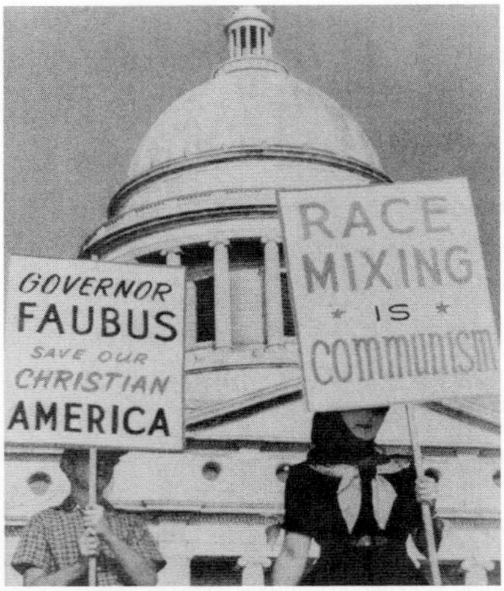

SOURCE: *Everett Collection/AGE Fotostock.*

AP® skill **Applying Disciplinary Knowledge (1B)**

Identify and explain the context of a specific event, development, or process.

Key Context: Through the mid-twentieth century, African Americans in the North and South continued to face racial discrimination, violence, and segregation in education, housing, transportation, and voting. The Civil Rights movement sought to eradicate segregation and ensure federal protection of rights guaranteed by the Reconstruction Amendments and the Civil Rights Act of 1875 (which outlawed racial discrimination in public places).

PREDICT

- What do you think Americans' perspective on issues such as segregation were in the mid-twentieth century? What clues from the image support your response?

SOURCE: © *George Ballis/Take Stock/The Image Works.*

AP® skill **Source Analysis (2C)**

Explain the significance of a source's perspective, purpose, context, and audience.

Key Context: Throughout U.S. history, Black women played central roles in the struggle for freedom and racial and gender equality. In this photo, Fannie Lou Hamer (center) speaks at a protest. She is surrounded by other notable civil rights activists.

PREDICT

- What does this photo suggest about how the roles Black women played in the Civil Rights movement?
- What connections do you see to earlier Black women's activism?

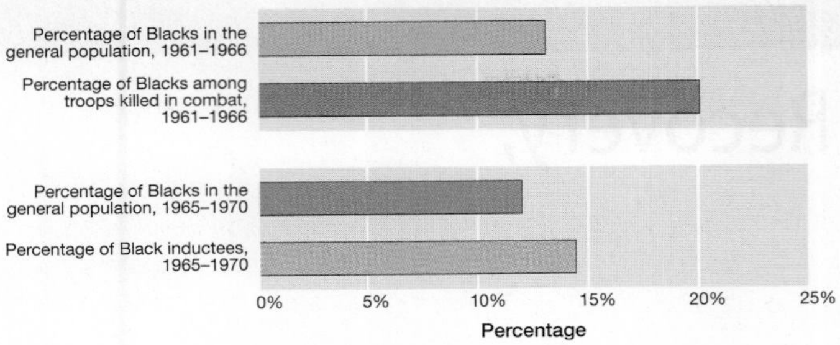

AP® skill **Source Analysis (2D)**

Describe and draw conclusions from patterns, trends, and limitations in data, making connections to relevant course content.

Key Context: Despite fighting and sacrificing their lives for their country, many Black soldiers were subjected to discrimination within the military ranks. Additionally, upon returning home, Black veterans often encountered racism, lack of support, and inadequate access to benefits and resources.

PREDICT

▸ What conclusions can you draw from this graph about the conditions under which African Americans served during the Vietnam War?

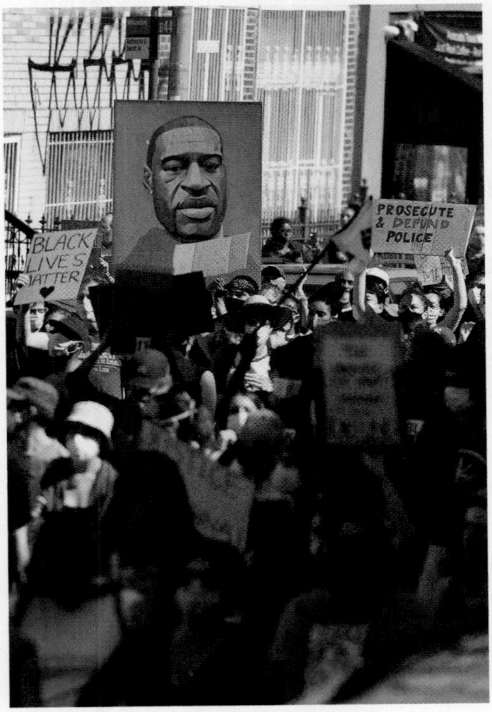

SOURCE: *ANGELA WEISS/Getty Images.*

AP® skill **Applying Disciplinary Knowledge (1C)**

Identify and explain patterns, connections, or other relationships (causation, changes, continuities, comparison).

Key Context: This photograph was taken in 2020 during nationwide protests against the police killing of George Floyd. Protesters in this photo are carrying signs, including a large poster of Floyd.

PREDICT

▸ How do you think this image connects with the Civil Rights movement of the twentieth century? What details from the image support your prediction?

CHAPTER **12**

Catastrophe, Recovery, and Renewal

1930–1942

CHAPTER TIMELINE

Events specific to African American history are in purple. General U.S. history events are in black. Events from the AP® Course Framework are marked with an asterisk.

1929	Stock market crashes; Great Depression begins
1930	Négritude Movement begins*
1931	The Scottsboro Boys arrested
1932	Tuskegee Syphilis Study begins
	Angelo Herndon imprisoned for leading a biracial demonstration of unemployed workers, in violation of Georgia's anti-insurrection statute
1933	Franklin D. Roosevelt becomes president and initiates New Deal
	Paul Robeson stars in film version of *The Emperor Jones*
	Katherine Dunham founds Negro Dance Group*
1934	NAACP begins legal initiative to overturn segregation
	Arthur Mitchell becomes the first African American to be elected to the U.S. Congress as a Democrat
	Federal Housing Administration founded; its mortgage policies promote redlining and restrictive covenants*
1935	American Federation of Labor recognizes Brotherhood of Sleeping Car Porters and Maids
	National Labor Relations Act, also called Wagner Act, passed; Social Security Act passed; both acts exclude farm and domestic workers from coverage
	Fascist Italy invades and annexes Ethiopia
1936	National Negro Congress founded
	Mary McLeod Bethune appointed head of Division of Negro Affairs of National Youth Administration (becomes official division director in 1939)
1936	Track star Jesse Owens wins four gold medals at Berlin Olympics*
	Black voters switch to Democratic Party; 75 percent vote for FDR
1937	Bethune organizes the Federal Council on Negro Affairs, informally known as the Black Cabinet
	The Southern Negro Youth Congress forms to promote youth employment, education, health, and citizenship
	Joe Louis becomes world heavyweight champion
	Japan invades China, igniting World War II in Pacific
	Zora Neale Hurston's *Their Eyes Were Watching God* published
1938	*Missouri ex rel. Gaines v. Canada* requires Missouri to admit qualified Black candidates to state law school
1938	Loïs Mailou Jones paints *Les Fétiches**
1939	Marian Anderson performs at Lincoln Memorial
	Billie Holiday adds "Strange Fruit" to her performances
	The film *Gone with the Wind* premieres, idealizing plantation culture and slavery
	Germany invades Poland, igniting World War II in Europe
1940	NAACP Legal Defense and Education Fund created, with Thurgood Marshall at the helm
	Richard Wright's *Native Son* published
1940–1941	Jacob Lawrence paints *The Migration of the Negro**
1943	Afro-Cuban artist Wifredo Lam paints *The Jungle**

Please note that this chapter includes primary sources by Black writers and speakers that use the N-word, which we have chosen to reprint in this textbook to accurately reflect these speakers' original intent as well as the time period, culture, and racism discussed in each source. We recognize that this word has a long history as a derogatory and deeply hurtful expression when used by white people toward Black people. Black speakers' and writers' choice to use this word relates not only to that history but to a larger cultural tradition in which the N-word can take on different meanings, emphasize shared experience, and be repurposed as a term of endearment within Black communities. This chapter also includes primary sources by white writers and speakers that use the N-word, which we have chosen not to reprint in full here. We have replaced the term without hindering understanding of these sources. Be mindful of context, both historical and contemporary, as you read and discuss this chapter.

Contextualizing African American Stories

The Campaign to Free "the Scottsboro Boys"

Haywood Patterson, Eugene Williams, and brothers LeRoy (Roy) Wright and Andy Wright were poor teenaged friends. On March 25, 1931, they hopped aboard a Southern Railroad freight train headed to Memphis from Chattanooga, looking for work. The teens were among the roughly two million hobos during the Great Depression (most of whom were older men), who stowed away on freight trains without paying; they eluded authorities and sought work wherever they could find it. Skyrocketing youth joblessness — roughly three million Americans between the ages of sixteen and twenty-five were jobless by early 1933 — motivated these young men to leave their homes and take their chances on the rails.

Olen Montgomery, Clarence Norris, Ozie Powell, Willie Robertson, and Charlie Weems were teenagers on the same train as the friends Haywood, Eugene, Roy, and Andy, but Olen, Clarence, Ozie, Willie, and Charlie knew neither one another nor the friends. Haywood was involved in a fight with a group of white teenagers along the way. When the train reached Paint Rock, Alabama, all nine of the Black youths were arrested for assault, even though most of them did not know any of the others.

The assault charge was just the beginning. All nine were also charged with raping Victoria Price and Ruby Bates, two teenaged whites on the freight train. The extreme racist hysteria surrounding the rape accusation, which proved false, sealed the fate of "the Scottsboro Boys," as they soon came to be known (because they were held for trial in Scottsboro, Alabama). Despite compelling evidence that should have freed them, the nine suffered years in jail before eventually being freed. Their lives were never the same. All suffered subsequent hardship and tragedy. Indeed, the fate of the Scottsboro Boys epitomizes a criminal "injustice" system that ensnared innumerable Blacks, especially Black men falsely accused of raping white women.

The International Labor Defense (ILD), the legal wing of the Communist Party, and lead attorney Samuel Leibowitz mounted an intense and complicated defense effort. As a result, many Blacks looked with growing favor on the party and its vigorous antiracism, even though few Blacks actually became Communists. In late 1935, the ILD joined forces with the NAACP and the American Civil Liberties Union (ACLU) to create a joint defense effort: the Scottsboro Defense Committee. The remarkable campaign to free the Scottsboro Boys became an international as well as a national cause and helped save the youths' lives. This critically important campaign also signaled the increasing necessity of a vigorous and vigilant African American freedom struggle, especially in the context of the Great Depression, when hard times for the nation were especially hard for African Americans.

The Great Depression of the 1930s devastated African American lives and communities, but it also led to new and intensified forms of economic, social, and political struggle.

Black self-help necessarily mushroomed at all levels. As Black urban masses created Black voting blocs and Black protest grew, the federal government began responding to African Americans' concerns. For the first time since Reconstruction, Black could look to the federal government for support. Within the government, Black political appointees lobbied for fairness. As African American writers, artists, musicians, and sports heroes got respectful attention from mass audiences, their cultural achievements helped advance the spirit animating the Black freedom struggle.

The Great Depression and the New Deal

What were the enduring forms of segregation and discrimination in daily life that African Americans faced in the first half of the twentieth century?

What were the long-term effects of housing discrimination on African Americans in the first half of the twentieth century?

When the stock market crashed in 1929, the national economic crisis was part of an escalating global depression. For African Americans, whether they were sharecropping in the South or working for wages in the North, the downturn hit with blunt force. Interventions by the federal government offered some immediate relief and long-term hope, but African Americans also understood that they had to take action on their own. As Black organizing became increasingly political, intent on dismantling segregation in unions and the workplace, in schools, and even in stores, white politicians found it increasingly difficult to ignore the growing Black vote and Black economic power. The president began consulting Black leaders more frequently, and Blacks were increasingly placed in federal agencies to help oversee Black interests.

Economic Crisis and Joblessness

The stock market crash of October 1929 precipitated but did not cause the Great Depression. The Depression resulted from a variety of factors: unchecked financial speculation, a severe contraction of cash and credit, declining demand, weakness in the agricultural sector, corporate debt, widespread greed, and gross economic inequality. As businesses and banks failed and factories closed, national income plummeted from $81 billion in 1929 to $40 billion in 1932. By October 1930, four million Americans were unemployed. Within a year, the number increased to seven million, and then to eleven million. By 1932, one-quarter of Americans were out of work. Foreclosures skyrocketed, and millions were rendered homeless.

At one point, twenty million Americans were officially on relief. Dwindling local, state, and federal revenues undercut government assistance. Private relief efforts helped, but they proved woefully insufficient as well. At the height of the Depression, roughly three-fourths of Black families were forced onto public relief. Jobless Blacks were evicted from homes and apartments, and the numbers of drifting hoboes, homeless, and beggars skyrocketed. Poverty, hunger, starvation — indeed, death — stalked the land. It is unsurprising, therefore, that in 1935 bluesman Carl Martin wailed: "Everyone's crying: 'Let's have a New Deal,'/'Cause I've got to make a living./Even if I have to rob and steal."

In the rural South, overproduction of cotton and the loss of overseas markets had kept the price of cotton low all through the 1920s; then it collapsed, plummeting from 18 cents per pound in 1929 to 6 cents in 1933. At the same time, the gradual mechanization of southern agriculture put thousands of Black tenant farmers and sharecroppers out of work. The Great Mississippi Flood of 1927 also displaced African Americans, who headed for cities such as Memphis, New Orleans, and Jackson, Mississippi; but there were no jobs.

Even the most onerous and least desirable jobs in southern cities, typically called "Negro jobs," such as garbage collection and domestic service, were now being taken over by whites. It Atlanta, a white vigilante group calling themselves the "Black Shirts" rallied around the cry "No Jobs for N*****s until Every White Man Has a Job!" Intimidation, violence, and even murder underwrote these sordid campaigns to dislodge Black workers and replace them with white workers.

AP® skills

Applying Disciplinary Knowledge: Can you explain why African American southerners were hit particularly hard during the Depression?

While many Americans had prospered in the 1920s, most Black Americans had not, and the Depression made their lives much more difficult. By 1931, two years after the Depression's official beginning, Black unemployment in the South stood at 33 percent; a year later, it was 50 percent. Black unemployment always outpaced the national average, as Blacks were the last hired and the first fired; unions, which continued to discriminate, offered little protection. In 1932, the Black unemployment rate in Harlem was 50 percent; in Philadelphia it was 56 percent. At one point, Detroit's massive Black unemployment rate reached 60 percent, as auto plants shed workers.

Clearly the picture for northern as well as southern Blacks was bleak. Anna Arnold Hedgeman, Harlem social worker, observed, "Many families had been reduced to living below street level. It was estimated that more than ten thousand Negroes lived in cellars and basements which had been converted into makeshift flats. Packed in damp, ratridden dungeons, they existed in squalor not too different from that of Arkansas sharecroppers."[1]

AP® exam tip

Compare how southern and northern African Americans were impacted by the Great Depression.

In 1934, 43 percent of northern Blacks on relief were domestics. A year later, Black activists Ella Baker and Marvel Cooke wrote a scathing exposé of "The Bronx Slave Market": an extremely abusive labor system in the Bronx, New York that exploited Black women domestics. Desperate Black women domestics lined the

Thirteen-Year-Old Sharecropper
This 1937 photograph of a thirteen-year-old sharecropper near Americus, Georgia, was taken as part of the efforts of the New Deal's Farm Security Administration to publicize and ameliorate the plight of suffering Great Depression–era farmworkers. The boy's youth intensifies the emotional power of the photograph. **To what extent had economic opportunities improved for African American agricultural laborers in the South since Reconstruction?** *Dorothea Lange photograph for the U.S. Farm Security Administration, 1937. Library of Congress, Prints and Photographs Division, Washington, D.C., LCUSF34-017915-C.*

streets to be picked up by white women. These domestics performed a backbreaking array of jobs for shockingly low pay. All too often, an untold number never got paid in this cruel and unregulated labor network. Hardship hit Black businesses, the Black middle and upper classes, and Black community institutions as well. Precisely because their primarily Black clientele suffered massive economic losses, Black professionals, including dentists and doctors, lost clients and revenue. During the 1920s, the estimated number of Black businesses had almost doubled, from 40,000 to 70,000. During the Depression, many of these businesses went under. Black business sales revenue plummeted from $99 million in 1929 to $48 million in 1934. In 1929, there were 134 Black banks; by 1934, only 12 existed. The decline continued; by the outset of World War II, there were only 6.

One sector of Black businesses not only survived but thrived, however. Black insurance companies like Atlanta Life Insurance Company and North Carolina Mutual Life (headquartered in Durham, North Carolina) prospered during the Depression largely because the early Social Security system excluded most Blacks, and thus many, although impoverished and suffering, out of sheer necessity paid their insurance premiums as best they could. Also, these businesses tended to have a wider range of investments and in particular reduced their investments in the hemorrhaging Black mortgage market during the Depression.

The tragic reality that Blacks suffered disproportionately from poor medical care worsened. Many of the 250 pre-Depression era Black clinics, nursing schools, and hospitals went out of business, drastically curtailing already inadequate Black health care options. Suffering was particularly acute among the elderly and the infirm. Disease, malnutrition, complications from severe stress, and premature death rates grew. These problems were especially acute in the rural South, where doctors, nurses, and medical care were relatively rare. Infant death rates grew, life expectancy for women and men shrank, and other indices of Black health declined.

Medical researchers took advantage of the lack of health care options for rural Blacks in the **Tuskegee Syphilis Study**. (See chapter 13, AP® Working with Sources: African Americans and the Tuskegee Experiments, pp. 520–29.) For almost forty years beginning in 1932, the U.S. Public Health Service, with the willing participation of Tuskegee Institute and the Tuskegee Veterans Hospital, both Black institutions, conducted a medical experiment to study the long-term consequences of untreated syphilis. More than 600 Black men were denied medical treatment and relief as part of the notorious study, even though penicillin to treat the disease became widely available in the 1940s. The men thought they were receiving free medical care and did not know the nature of the study. A deeply disturbing and gross example of the racist practice of using Black bodies for medical experimentation, the Tuskegee Syphilis Study highlighted the powerlessness of its poor, Black male subjects. Most suffered and died without ever knowing the full truth, which came to light only after a 1972 news exposé.

Tuskegee Syphilis Study A federally funded study in collaboration with Tuskegee Institute of the long-term consequences of untreated syphilis, now infamous for the horrific and unethical treatment of its subjects, mostly local, poor, and illiterate Black male sharecroppers.

Inequality in the New Deal

Republican president Herbert Hoover's failure to stem the economic disaster swept the Democrat Franklin D. Roosevelt into office in the election of 1932. Hoover had taken a hands-off approach to the economy, believing it would self-correct and rebound. But the crisis of the Depression proved so severe that extraordinary government intervention was necessary. Roosevelt responded by instituting a series of novel federal programs that he called the New Deal.

A massive and unprecedented expansion of federal power, Roosevelt's First New Deal aimed to provide relief and revive the ailing economy. Emphasizing jobs over direct handouts, programs such as the Federal Emergency Relief Administration (FERA; 1933) and the Civilian Conservation Corps (CCC; 1933) helped many families make it through the worst of times. The Securities and Exchange Commission (SEC; 1934) regulated the stock market. Between 1935 and 1938, Roosevelt advanced the more aggressive Second New Deal, financed to a far greater extent by deficit spending. This plan aimed to alleviate poverty, expand jobs programs while curtailing direct relief programs, and create a social safety net.

In 1935, the U.S. Supreme Court ruled unconstitutional the National Recovery Administration (NRA; 1933), which had sought to stabilize industry by setting prices, wages, and working hours. Bolstered by his landslide reelection the next year, Roosevelt unsuccessfully challenged the Court by seeking to "pack" it with additional justices sympathetic to his goals. Congress balked, and the president lost some support. The Court, however, reversed course in 1937 and declared constitutional both the Social Security Act (1935), which provided old-age pensions and disability benefits, and the National Labor Relations Act (1935), known as the Wagner Act, which recognized the right of labor unions to organize, bargain collectively, and strike. That same year, Roosevelt cut back on deficit spending and contracted the New Deal, contributing to a second stock market crash and a serious recession. It took the economic expansion resulting from World War II for the economy to recover fully. Nevertheless, both the First and Second New Deals greatly expanded federal control over American society and the economy.

AP® exam tip

Be sure you are able to describe the enduring forms of segregation and discrimination in daily life that African Americans faced during the Great Depression.

The New Deal did not help all Americans equally, however. The racial discrimination that permeated America permeated New Deal programs as well. Some called the New Deal a "raw deal" for African Americans. Many Blacks quipped that the NRA, which allowed job-shifting from Blacks to whites rather than pay blacks hard-won wage increases, stood for "Negro Removal Agency" or "Negroes Robbed Again." Where New Deal programs were administered locally, especially in the South, Blacks did not benefit at the same rate as whites. The Agricultural Adjustment Administration poured millions of dollars into helping farmers, but almost none of the money benefited Black sharecroppers or tenant farmers or the dwindling number of independent Black farmers. The Social Security Act excluded participation by those working in agriculture, domestic service, or day labor, the types of jobs held by most Black people. Agricultural and domestic workers were also excluded from the Wagner Act and from the Fair Labor Standards Act, which established maximum working hours and minimum wages.

The Federal Housing Administration (FHA) and Home Owners Loan Corporation (HOLC) forbade mortgage loans in integrated areas, promoting the racist policy of redlining. This extremely discriminatory and widespread practice sustained the bank practice of approving mortgage loans only to Blacks who lived in all-Black neighborhoods. The FHA and HOLC likewise endorsed restrictive covenants, which promoted the practice of allowing whites to refuse to sell homes to Blacks in white neighborhoods. Historically, redlining and restrictive covenants have seriously undermined Black economic advancement by preventing Blacks from building up equity in their homes and benefiting from gains in the real estate market that have allowed white homeowners to develop wealth.

Black Voters in the Democratic Party

The National Urban League and the NAACP tried to insert nondiscrimination clauses into New Deal legislation, but lawmakers balked. However, these organizations kept the pressure on the federal government to pay attention to Black concerns, as did a lobbying effort led by the Black lawyer John P. Davis and the Black economist Robert C. Weaver, both Harvard graduates. Black organizations were able to gain some political leverage with the Roosevelt administration, which claimed to be the champion of the poor and the dispossessed. President Roosevelt communicated this message through his fireside chats, radio broadcasts to the nation in which he explained the New Deal in language everyone could understand. African Americans' greatest advocate in the White House, however, was First Lady Eleanor Roosevelt. She spoke out on behalf of Black concerns, built connections with Black leaders and groups, and lobbied her husband, New Dealers, and other influential officials on behalf of African Americans.

Eleanor Roosevelt's efforts pushed the Roosevelt administration to open the door to African Americans in government jobs. The number of Blacks entering the civil service grew from 50,000 in 1933 to more than 150,000 by 1941, and for the first time African Americans received political appointments to government agencies. Particularly visible was Mary McLeod Bethune, whose 1936 appointment to head the Division of Negro Affairs of the National Youth Administration evolved into her appointment to official division director in 1939. In this capacity, she launched opportunities for vocational training and jobs in both the private sector and government for thousands of unemployed Black youths between the ages of sixteen and twenty-four.

AP® skills

Applying Disciplinary Knowledge: Who was Mary McLeod Bethune, and what was her role in the Roosevelt administration?

Mary McLeod Bethune

Civil and women's rights leader Bethune sits in her office at Bethune-Cookman College in this 1943 photo by the African American photographer Gordon Parks. A portrait of FDR is prominently displayed on her wall, surrounded by portraits of African American intellectuals and activists. At the time this photo was taken, Bethune was director of Negro Affairs of the National Youth Organization in Roosevelt's cabinet and vice president of the NAACP. She would become the only woman of color at the founding conference of the United Nations, appointed by Roosevelt's successor, Harry Truman. **To what extent was Mary McLeod Bethune's activism a continuation of the political and community activism of African American women of the past?**

Library of Congress, Prints and Photographs Division, Washington, D.C./LC-USW3-014843-C.

Bethune, an active member of the NAACP, had served as president of the National Association of Colored Women in the 1920s, and in 1935, she had established the National Council of Negro Women, an alliance of Black women's organizations.

AP® exam tip

Be prepared to describe the ways Black women leaders furthered the goals of the major civil rights organizations and grassroots efforts.

Black Cabinet
The informal name of the Federal Council on Negro Affairs, a group of Black New Deal political advisers organized by Mary McLeod Bethune in 1937.

The Black journalist Roi Ottley called Bethune "the First Lady of the Struggle." She used her influence to get the federal government to sponsor conferences highlighting Black problems and devising federal solutions. Perhaps most important, in 1937, Bethune organized the Federal Council on Negro Affairs, informally known as the **Black Cabinet**, a group of influential Black policy advisers who met at her home to discuss civil rights and help shape the New Deal's response to Black concerns. Among them were Robert C. Weaver, Eugene K. Jones from the Commerce Department, William H. Hastie from the Interior Department, A. Philip Randolph, T. Arnold Hill, and Walter White, who, like Bethune, was a personal friend of Eleanor Roosevelt.

For the first time since Reconstruction, Black people received support from the federal government, and they were drawn to the Democratic Party, for Republicans had taken Black voters for granted. In 1932, Robert L. Vann, the editor of the *Pittsburgh Courier*, an influential Black newspaper, called on Black voters to exercise their political muscle: "My friends, go turn Lincoln's picture to the wall. That debt has been paid in full."[2] In 1936, 75 percent of African Americans voted for Roosevelt, and since that time, they have been an important constituency within the Democratic Party. Indicative of the trend, Republican Oscar De Priest lost his seat in the U.S. House of Representatives in 1934 to Democrat Arthur Mitchell, a Black politician who had switched parties.

Throughout the latter half of the 1930s, Mitchell was the only African American in Congress, but in northern metropolises, Blacks increasingly constituted a voting bloc that commanded the attention of white politicians. In previous decades, Black concerns had been almost completely ignored. Now Roosevelt had to balance federal efforts on behalf of Black Americans against the prospect of losing the support of racist white Democrats from the South. As African Americans gained political power, their activism took an increasingly political turn. As was so often the case in the African American experience, this activism was particularly evident in Black churches.

Coming Together to Battle Hardship

What were the primary strategies civil rights organizations used to fight discrimination?

How did grassroots organizing beyond the South advance the goals of the Civil Rights movement?

During the Depression years, Blacks turned to values and practices that reflected their long history of resilience and resourcefulness. They came together to help one another informally, in families and neighborhoods, but they also joined churches and unions that organized on behalf of those hit hard by the dismal economy. Meanwhile, the Communist Party's successful defense of Blacks in several high-profile southern court cases brought heightened attention to racial injustice and the party's antiracist work. Black organizations such as the National Negro Congress, the Southern Negro Youth Congress, and a reenergized NAACP laid the groundwork for the Civil Rights movement.

Surviving through Church and Community

African Americans relied on their core values — their deep commitment to family, kin, friends, neighbors, communities, and religion — to survive the Great Depression. Helping others, even taking in and housing down-and-out family members, was common. Collective child care and elder care arrangements proliferated. The bartering and sharing of essentials — food, clothing, housing, temporary work — expanded, as did the recycling of used clothes, shoes, and other material goods. To save money on groceries, people turned to fishing, hunting, gardening, and canning fruits and vegetables. Potlucks brought families and friends together over shared meals.

The underground economies in Black communities also flourished. Theft, bootlegging, selling illegal alcohol and drugs, gambling, and prostitution thrived. People altered electrical wires and gas pipes in apartment buildings to get power and heat free of charge. Especially popular in cities were "the numbers," illegal gambling operations where people placed small bets with "numbers runners" in hopes of cashing in. These gambling rackets amassed massive profits. In time, many of the largest and most profitable numbers operations were taken over by white mobsters.

In the legitimate and respectable world, Black churches dramatically expanded their aid for the rapidly growing numbers of those in need. Harlem's Abyssinian Baptist Church, led by the Reverend Adam Clayton Powell Sr., fed two thousand people daily in its soup kitchen and handed out clothing and fuel. For many, politics and assistance went hand-in-hand. Powell Sr. had helped organize the silent march of 1917, and his son, Adam Clayton Powell Jr., who succeeded him in the pulpit in 1937, was an outspoken advocate for civil rights, organizing a "Don't Buy Where You Can't Work" campaign to pressure New York stores to hire Black employees. In 1941, Powell Jr. was elected to the city council, and in 1944, he was elected as a Democrat to the U.S. House of Representatives. The Powells' activism was an early sign of the increasing political as well as socioeconomic activism of Black religious leaders.

> **AP® skills**
>
> **Applying Disciplinary Knowledge:** Explain how the African American church worked to alleviate the negative impacts of the Great Depression on African Americans. Were their strategies and methods similar to or different from past efforts to aid their communities?

Equally notable was the rise of independent religious movements that aimed to provide political direction along with spiritual nourishment and material relief. Both Charles Emmanuel Grace, known as "Sweet Daddy Grace" or just "Daddy Grace," and George Baker, known as "Father Divine," projected a sense of their own divinity and preached righteous living and positive thinking. Both had huge interracial followings, and their movements, with subsidiary businesses and investments, amassed great wealth, increasing their influence. Daddy Grace's United House of Prayer for All People drew on the flamboyant personality of its leader, with his crown, shoulder-length hair, purple robes, and extra-long red, white, and blue fingernails. Daddy Grace was a highly dramatic preacher and faith healer who fed the hungry in church cafeterias and housed the homeless in his apartment buildings.

Father Divine's Peace Mission movement was even more extensive. At its height, it had more than 160 mission centers in the United States, Canada, and Europe, where meals were lavish affairs, not just soup and bread. Run mostly by women who were secretaries, the movement preached against smoking and drinking and advocated sexual abstinence. Father Divine's progressive political agenda included support for minimum-wage legislation, curbs on corporate profits, a federal antilynching law, and the abolition of capital punishment. His emphasis on political education contributed to the era's growing Black awareness and political action.

Black Collective Action and Interracial Unionism

Outside the church, Black activism found expression in rent strikes, boycotts, and consumer cooperatives, often organized by women. The Housewives' League in both northern and southern cities coordinated **"Don't Buy Where You Can't Work" boycotts**. These were often related to "Double Duty Dollar" campaigns, which advocated patronizing Black businesses because their profits would get reinvested in Black neighborhoods. In Harlem, the Domestic Workers' Union formed to demand fair pay and hours and to try to end the street corner "slave markets," where unemployed Black women gathered each morning, hoping that white women might drive by and hire them for the day or at least a few hours.

"Don't Buy Where You Can't Work" boycotts 1930s grassroots campaigns that fought for the hiring of Blacks in white-owned stores in Black communities.

Brotherhood of Sleeping Car Porters and Maids The union formed in 1925 to represent the rights of low-paid Black railroad workers.

AP® skills

Applying Disciplinary Knowledge: Can you identify A. Philip Randolph and explain the main goals and objectives of the Brotherhood of Sleeping Car Porters and Maids? To what extent were they similar to the goals of African American labor organizations after Reconstruction?

Building on the Wagner Act, despite its failure to bar racial discrimination in unions, A. Philip Randolph sought to leverage the power of Black wageworkers. He had long advocated interracial unionism, and he had joined the Socialist Party as a young man because of its views on labor. His first efforts to organize Black workers — elevator operators and stevedores — were undermined by the American Federation of Labor (AFL). In 1925, he was elected president of the newly formed **Brotherhood of Sleeping Car Porters and Maids**, commonly referred to as the Brotherhood of Sleeping Car Porters. Jobs as railroad porters and maids were highly coveted, though they involved long hours and low pay. Randolph used the union as an organizational base for promoting both the rights of Blacks and the rights of labor. In 1935, the AFL recognized the union, which won its first contract in 1937.

Interracial unionism gained a significant foothold in the 1930s, despite the persistent anti-Black racism within the labor movement. Crucial to this advance was the Committee for Industrial Organization, which was created in 1935 as part of the AFL and became the independent **Congress of Industrial Organizations (CIO)** in 1938. The CIO promoted mass industrial unionism: the organization of all industrial workers, whether unskilled, semiskilled, or skilled, and without regard to race or ethnicity. Despite the CIO's inclusive aims, however, Black union members and

Congress of Industrial Organizations (CIO) An association of unions based on industry rather than skill. African Americans joined CIO unions in record numbers during World War II.

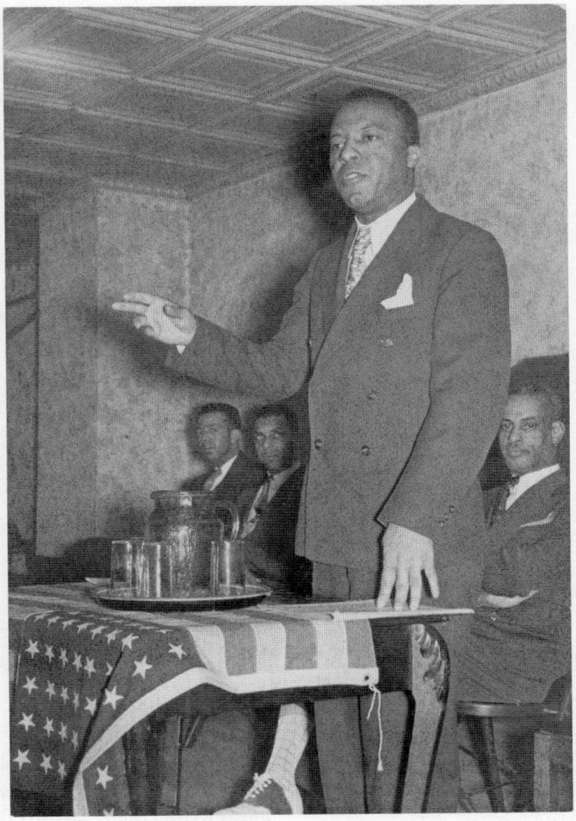

A. Philip Randolph
A. Philip Randolph addresses members of the Brotherhood of Sleeping Car Porters and Maids, the union he led with Milton P. Webster. Among his other leadership positions, Randolph was a member of the Black Cabinet and president of the National Negro Congress. **How did Black people organize and fight for labor rights during this era? How were they able to use their collective power to demand better working conditions?** *Rex Hardy Jr./Getty Images.*

their white allies, notably socialists and Communists, battled the reality of racial discrimination even within CIO unions.

The Communist Party's Appeal

The Socialist Party that Randolph joined in 1916 advocated fairness for workers and social equality, but it did not have a large Black following, in part because of racism within its ranks. After the 1917 revolution in Russia and the establishment of the Soviet Union, the Communist Party broadcast a similar message of social justice and gained some Black followers, notably among Harlem activists and intellectuals. Although Blacks largely rejected the Communist Party's revolutionary ideology, its critique of capitalism aided their understanding of the Depression, and its commitment to equality had significant appeal. (See AP® Working with Sources: Communist Radicalism and Everyday Realities, pp. 495–501.)

The Communist Party's successful defense in the **Scottsboro Boys case** (described in the chapter introduction) enhanced its reputation with innumerable Blacks. More than any other largely white political organization, the Communist Party acted to end racial oppression, modeling white antiracist activism and helping to lead the struggle against white supremacy. As a result, although it had relatively few Black members, it had many Black sympathizers and admirers among its "fellow travelers," and many Blacks participated in party-led activities on behalf of the Scottsboro Boys.

As part of the Communist Party's long-term struggle to save the lives of the Scottsboro Boys, their lawyers brought two especially influential cases to the U.S. Supreme Court. In *Powell v. Alabama* (1932), the Court ruled that defendants in capital trials have a right to counsel, and in *Norris v. Alabama* (1935), it ruled that potential jurors may not be excluded from juries on the basis of race. In another court case, lawyers for the party successfully defended one of its organizers, Angelo Herndon, who in 1932 had been ordered to prison in Georgia for leading a biracial demonstration of unemployed workers. In 1937, the U.S. Supreme Court overturned

AP® skills

Applying Disciplinary Knowledge: Explain why the Communist Party became attractive to many African Americans during the Great Depression.

Scottsboro Boys case (1931) A highly publicized series of trials of Black youths in Scottsboro, Alabama, who were falsely accused of rape and successfully defended by lawyers paid for by the Communist Party.

The Scottsboro Boys
This photograph of the nine Scottsboro Boys was taken while they were being held in the Jefferson County Jail in Birmingham, Alabama, on false charges that they had raped two young white women, Victoria Price and Ruby Bates, on a freight train in March 1931. An international effort to free them, led by the Communist Party's International Labor Defense, eventually helped secure their release. Standing, left to right, are Clarence Norris, age 19; Ozie Powell, 18; Haywood Patterson, 19; Roy Wright, 15; Charlie Weems, 20; and Eugene Williams, 16. Sitting, left to right, are Andrew Wright, 19; Olen Montgomery, 17; and Willie Roberson, 19. **What do you think was the photographers' purpose behind this photograph? Who do you think was the intended audience? How does the image reflect larger trends in the Jim Crow era of violence, racism, and the use of prison to strip away their rights?** *CSU Archives/Everett Collection.*

Herndon's conviction, declaring Georgia's nineteenth-century anti-insurrection statute unconstitutional.

The Communist Party also led efforts to organize the Alabama Sharecroppers Union (ASU; 1931–1936), intended as a biracial union but eventually led by Blacks, who joined because of its commitment to raising agricultural prices and wages and ending discrimination in New Deal agricultural programs. The ASU was part of a larger wave of tenant farming and sharecropper organizing in the South often led by Communists. The ASU demanded that sharecroppers be paid in cash rather than shares or in-kind wages; it lobbied to give sharecroppers direct food advances and the right to market surplus crops. School-aged children of sharecroppers, they argued, should receive nine months of public schooling per term. The ASU also joined the call for the immediate release of the Scottsboro Boys.

The Communist Party, notably its Black members and sympathizers, or fellow travelers, helped advance the fundamental understanding that economic empowerment was essential to the ongoing Black freedom struggle. Black academics such as economist Abram Harris and political scientist Ralph Bunche explored the interlocking nexus between class and race struggle — and especially interracial unionism — as a way to mutually advance these interrelated agendas. Unlike Communists, however, who sought to destroy capitalism, those like Bunche and Harris, representative of a large and growing Black critique of capitalism, sought to reform capitalism structurally and radically.

Organizing for Civil Rights

In 1935, John P. Davis and other Black leaders called for a nationwide Black united front of civil rights organizations that would bring together groups and individuals ranging from left-progressive to centrist-liberal. The need for such a front had been reinforced by a riot in Harlem that year that had targeted white-owned property. This riot signaled a heightened level of anger and frustration in Black communities; previously, racial violence had been instigated mostly by white mobs attacking Black victims. More than eight hundred delegates representing almost five hundred organizations — with the notable exception of the NAACP — met in Chicago in 1936 to found the **National Negro Congress** (NNC; 1936–1947). Participants included intellectuals such as Alain Locke and Ralph Bunche of Howard University, civil rights activists (including dissident NAACP members), Black religious leaders, white and Black labor organizers, and Communists.

National Negro Congress An umbrella organization of Black organizations whose first national meeting in 1936 expressed a commitment to radical politics and militant labor organization and activism.

The NNC functioned as the vanguard of collective Black liberal-left efforts to alleviate New Deal racism. Working interracially wherever possible, the NNC also joined the fight against what many saw as the growing threat of domestic as well as international fascism. Elected as its president, A. Philip Randolph committed the NNC to interracial labor organizing and militant mass action when necessary and viable. Though hamstrung by a lack of money, the NNC went on the offensive. With more than seventy local chapters at its apex, the NNC fought for jobs, fair housing, and fair dispensation of relief. Through a network of local councils, the NNC proved particularly effective at promoting interracial unionism, especially the concerns of Black industrial workers in a number of cities.

AP® skills

Applying Disciplinary Knowledge: How are the goals and strategies of the NNC similar to or different from those of other civil rights organizations you have studied?

Ultimately, however, the big tent politics of the NNC proved unwieldy, and serious internal wrangling undermined the group's effectiveness. For instance, as Communists and labor activists gained influence and the NCC became more militant and secular, certain Black religious groups withdrew their support. Ultimately, the radicals alienated those who believed that Black business owners were undermined by the organization's focus on workers' interests. Randolph resigned in 1940, charging that Communists had infiltrated and overrun the organization.

AP® exam tip

Be sure you can describe the essential methods and strategies of the major civil rights organizations.

Southern Negro Youth Congress
A radical southern-based youth organization that promoted the interrelated concerns of Black youth and their people framed around four core commitments: jobs, education, health, and citizenship.

The **Southern Negro Youth Congress** (SNYC; 1937–1949) was a radical, independent southern-based youth organization that grew out of and aligned itself with the NNC. The SNYC promoted the interrelated concerns of Black youth specifically and Black people generally, framed around four core commitments: jobs, education, health, and citizenship. The SNYC's wide-ranging agenda included union organizing; legal aid; antilynching and antirape activism; voting rights activism, notably voter registration and the campaign to abolish the poll tax; lobbying in Washington, D.C.; and cultural activism throughout the rural Black South. Among the SNYC's most important leaders were Edward E. Strong, Esther and James Jackson, and Lewis and Dorothy Burnham. Anti-Communist hysteria led to the SNYC's demise and contributed to the demise of the NNC as well. In many ways, the SNYC foreshadowed the radical youth politics of the Student Nonviolent Coordinating Committee of the 1960s. Similarly, the NNC foreshadowed the economic, class-based dimensions of the radicalism of the civil rights/Black Power insurgency, especially from the late 1960s through the mid- to late 1970s.

Meanwhile, the NAACP, which denounced the Communist Party and was increasingly critical of racism within the labor movement, was itself criticized for overlooking the needs of Black workers. W. E. B. Du Bois had resigned from *The Crisis* in 1934, and the NAACP was increasingly considered middle class and middle-of-the-road. Its membership had declined as more activist Black organizations arose, but beginning in 1934, a new initiative to overturn segregation, led by special legal counsel Charles Hamilton Houston, reenergized the group. Houston, as dean of Howard University Law School, had pioneered the field of civil rights law and trained a cadre of Black lawyers, among them future U.S. Supreme Court Justice Thurgood Marshall. In 1940, Houston helped create a legal division within the NAACP called the Legal Defense and Educational Fund, headed by Marshall.

Houston's plan was to demonstrate that the separate but equal doctrine established in 1896 by *Plessy v. Ferguson* denied Blacks their Fourteenth Amendment rights to due process and equal protection under the law. He started with a series of suits demanding that all separate Black schools be made equal to white schools and that Black teacher salaries be made the same as white teacher salaries. The purpose of this short-term strategy of equalization was twofold: to show states and localities that they could not afford dual educational systems and to lay the groundwork for a direct challenge to the constitutionality of segregation. NAACP lawyers targeted the common southern state practice of paying the out-of-state tuition for Blacks who agreed to attend graduate and professional schools in other states. In *Pearson v. Murray* (1936), the Maryland Court of Appeals ruled that the University of Maryland's refusal to admit Donald Murray, an Amherst College graduate, to its law school violated Murray's citizenship rights. In another important NAACP legal victory, *Missouri ex rel. Gaines v. Canada* (1938), the U.S. Supreme Court ruled that Lloyd Gaines, a Missouri resident, had to be admitted to Missouri's all-white law school because the state failed to provide an equal legal education for Blacks. These were the first steps in a campaign that would culminate with the overturning of *Plessy* in *Brown v. Board of Education of Topeka* (1954), argued before the Supreme Court by Thurgood Marshall.

Black Culture in Hard Times

Why did proponents of Négritude and **Negrismo** critique colonialism?

How did artists, performers, poets, athletes, and musicians of African descent advocate for racial equality?

Negrismo
Movement that emerged in the Spanish-speaking Caribbean that celebrated African contributions to Latin American art, music, and literature.

One New Deal program with direct benefits for individual African Americans was the Works Progress Administration (WPA), established in 1935 to pump federal money into public works projects that hired people who needed jobs. The WPA not only built roads, bridges, and parks but sponsored programs, such as the Federal Writers' Project, that employed writers, artists, musicians, and actors. The WPA brightened the grim decade of the Great Depression. For some, it was a lifeline. Zora Neale Hurston, for example, was hired by the WPA to collect folklore from Florida's back roads and turpentine camps, where highly exploited Black workers extracting turpentine from pine trees lived and labored, often reduced to peonage. The study to which she contributed, "The Florida Negro," ultimately included slave narratives. Today transcripts of WPA interviews with more than two thousand formerly enslaved people, all of whom were then at least in their seventies, are a rich documentary resource. The work that Hurston did for the WPA paralleled her research interests, and in the 1930s, she published two collections of African American folklore, *Mules and Men* (1935) and *Tell My Horse* (1938). Her most acclaimed work of fiction, *Their Eyes Were Watching God* (1937), is also grounded in African American folk culture, centering on the maturation of Janie, its protagonist, who finds within herself the means to triumph over poverty, sexism, and racism.

AP® skills

Applying Disciplinary Knowledge: Can you identify the WPA and explain how Zora Neale Hurston used it as a tool to help in the preservation and study of African American history and culture?

The cultural struggle so central to both the ongoing African American freedom struggle and the evolving New Negro consciousness continued during the New Deal era. Even as the exuberance of the Harlem Renaissance gave way to the hard, cold realities of the Depression, powerful and important African American cultural work persisted. The literature, music, visual art, and dance of the Chicago Renaissance of the 1930s vividly captured the realism that shaped this period of cultural struggle. Internationally and domestically, cultural and political movements of African-descended peoples contributed significantly to the Black freedom struggles. Similarly, the growing global as well as national recognition of African American artists, performers, and athletes helped advance the African American freedom struggle.

The Chicago Renaissance

AP® skills

Applying Disciplinary Knowledge: Compare and contrast the Chicago and Harlem Renaissances. What characteristics did each movement share? What aspects of each movement were unique?

Richard Wright, a young Black author who also worked for the WPA, criticized Hurston's fiction for its lack of social protest. In "Blueprint for Negro Writing" (1937), he rejected the "humble novels, poems, and plays" of the Harlem Renaissance writers, whom he characterized as pandering to the interests of white audiences. Wright announced a new agenda: "Today the question is: Shall Negro writing be for the Negro masses, molding the lives and consciousness of those masses toward new goals, or shall it continue begging the question of the Negroes' humanity?"[3] Wright was a strong and angry new voice for naturalism and art with a political purpose. He joined the Communist Party in Chicago before moving to New York, where he influenced another young Black writer working for the WPA, Ralph Ellison.

Wright's early fiction reflected a Marxist conception of art, showing how economic forces shaped African American destiny. His 1938 collection of short stories, *Uncle Tom's Children*, probed the racial conflict and violence of the Jim Crow South, and his novel *Native Son* (1940) explored the same forces at work in the Chicago ghetto while plumbing racial, class, gender, and emotional-psychological depths. The first Book-of-the-Month Club selection of a novel by a Black author, *Native Son* was a huge commercial success. Many viewed that success as evidence that there was now a growing audience for serious works by Black writers. Within a few years, Wright publicly repudiated the Communist Party; by 1946, he had turned his back on the United States as well, moving to Paris, where he lived for the rest of his life.

Chicago Renaissance
A rich and wide-ranging Black arts movement of the 1930s and 1940s reflecting the cultural worlds of Black Chicago.

Wright was the most famous artist to emerge within what has come to be known as the **Chicago Renaissance** of the 1930s and 1940s. Like the Harlem Renaissance, the Chicago Renaissance featured an extraordinary and exciting range of Black art. More so than the Harlem Renaissance, though, the Chicago Renaissance featured the experiences of poor, working-class African Americans, notably the experiences of Black factory workers in America's industrial heartland. Writer Arna Bontemps, poet Margaret Walker, and Wright were part of Black creative networks in Chicago that yielded important literary works, including Bontemps's *Black Thunder*, a powerful novel about Gabriel's 1800 slave conspiracy in Richmond, Virginia; Walker's classic and very popular paean to her people's s freedom struggle *For My People* (1942); and the renowned works of Wright. For a time, the WPA sustained a number of Black Chicago artists, including Wright and Walker.

In the 1930s, painters Eldzier Cortor and Archibald Motley also did work for the WPA in Chicago. The works of Motley, best known for his vivid representations of Black Chicago's unique style and exuberance, and those of painter and printmaker Cortor, best known for his representations of the Black female form, epitomized the vitality of the visual arts during Chicago's Renaissance. (See chapter 11, AP® Working with Sources: The Harlem/New Negro Renaissance, p. 460, for an example of Motley's art.)

Extraordinary music — notably jazz, gospel, and blues — pulsated throughout Renaissance Chicago. Louis Armstrong and Lil Hardin exemplified the originality and vitality of the Black South Side Chicago jazz and blues scene. Marrying a wide range of instruments with enthusiastic Black religious musical traditions, Thomas Dorsey pioneered and extensively promoted **gospel music**, whose early epicenter was Chicago. Gospel soon became a staple in Black religious music nationally. He wrote his beloved and widely performed gospel classic "Take My Hand, Precious Lord" (1932) in the throes of grief over the tragic deaths of his wife, Nettie, and their unborn child in a car accident. Earlier, before turning principally to gospel, Dorsey had been a well-known blues pianist, working with the likes of Ma Rainey. He had also worked as "Georgia Tom" with Tampa Red. Their hit recording of the ragtime hit "It's Tight Like That" sold seven million copies.

gospel music
A popular and influential musical genre that achieved prominence in the 1930s and continues to evolve. Gospel marries Black sacred music with popular Black musical forms.

AP® exam tip

Be sure you can explain how faith and music inspired African Americans to combat continued discrimination during this era.

Working in Chicago during the 1930s, Katherine Dunham helped pioneer African American modern dance and soon emerged as a pivotal figure in twentieth-century modern dance broadly. Dunham excelled not only as a performer, dancer, and choreographer but also as an anthropologist, a writer, a global arts ambassador, and a social activist. Many of her dances, such as the famous "L'Ag'Ya" (first performed in 1938) — which combines ballet and elements drawn from a Martinique fighting dance — built upon wide-ranging ethnographic field observations throughout the Caribbean. In that impressive body of scholarship, Dunham's descriptions and analyses emphasized ritual dance, notably its African-derived expressions. Although she finished her undergraduate degree at the University of Chicago, she never completed her advanced degree, despite the extensive fieldwork she had conducted. Instead, by the late 1930s, she prioritized her artistic career.

Dunham's formal dance training featured ballet and included various other dance genres, such as Spanish and Javanese. In 1933, Dunham founded the Negro Dance Group, one of several dance schools she created and ran during her life. At one point, the WPA helped support the Negro Dance Group. Dunham performed widely throughout Chicago, including working with the ballet company of the Chicago Opera. In 1938, she worked for the Federal Theatre Project as dance director of the Chicago Negro Theatre. Her subsequent achievements

AP® source ***Katherine Dunham on Broadway***

Katherine Dunham, center, performs in the all-Black musical *Cabin in the Sky*, which she co-choreographed with George Balanchine. Dunham integrated her research on dance traditions brought by enslaved Africans to the Caribbean into her work as a choreographer and performer. **Explain how Dunham's work helped advance the cultural renaissance and place African American dance in a global context.** *George Karger/ Getty Images.*

are legendary, including important concert, Broadway, and film work, as well as global company tours to more than thirty countries.

African American Art within a Global Context

AP® exam tip

Explain how artists, performers, poets, and musicians of African descent advocated for racial equality and brought international attention to the Black Freedom movement.

Négritude
A cultural movement launched in the 1930s that called for a common identity among Africans dispersed throughout the world, supported decolonization and the liberation of African and African-descended peoples, and generally favored Marxism.

Pan-Africanism
A global political movement committed to African self-determination and the end of European domination of the African continent.

AP® skills

Applying Disciplinary Knowledge: Explain how the political and cultural goals of Pan-Africanism and Négritude overlapped.

Dunham's career illustrates the extent to which this period of cultural renaissance witnessed related global, Pan-African, and international dimensions. **Négritude**, a cultural movement that evolved out of the African and African diasporic French-speaking colonial world, found a home in the cosmopolitan and global world of Paris, the center of the French empire. Négritude was led by Léopold Sédar Senghor of Senegal, Aimé Césaire of Martinique, and Léon Damas of Guiana. The movement called for a common Black identity among Africans dispersed throughout the world, opposed French colonialism, and generally favored Marxism.

Similarly, **Pan-Africanism**, a global political movement organized at the turn of the century by the Trinidadian lawyer-activist Henry Sylvester Williams, found a comparable home in London, the center of the British empire. The Pan-African movement attracted the likes of W. E. B. Du Bois and Ethiopia's legendary ruler Haile Selassie. Increasingly popular in the English-speaking world and committed to African self-determination and the end of European domination of the African continent, Pan-Africanism overlapped politically with the cultural politics of Négritude.

Both Négritude and Pan-Africanism promoted the right of African peoples everywhere to self-determination and, in turn, promoted the self-definition and affirmation of African peoples on the continent and throughout the African diaspora. The cross-pollination of these various African diasporic cultural movements found fertile expression in the works of American artists such as Langston Hughes. Similarly, the American-based Harlem/New Negro Renaissance and the Chicago Renaissance were deeply political. The cultural politics of all these movements embraced self-definition, self-determination, freedom from colonial and imperial rule, and the rediscovery and embrace of Mother Africa.

A growing number of African American visual artists of the period, reflecting an internationalist as well as Euro-American aesthetic bent, studied in Paris. There they found support and encouragement, but their primary subjects and themes often remained African American. Palmer Hayden, for example, returned from study in Paris and worked on WPA art projects depicting scenes of African American life. His *Midsummer Night in Harlem* (1938) invoked a folk style that conveyed the festive atmosphere of neighbors escaping the heat of airless tenements.

The sculptor Augusta Savage brought African American themes to the world stage when she was asked to create a sculpture for the 1939 New York World's Fair. Savage presented *Lift Every Voice and Sing*, inspired by the Negro national anthem, to honor African American musical contributions to the arts. Nearly fifty years earlier, at the 1893 Chicago World's Fair, a display by African Americans had been rejected. That an African American was now commissioned to exhibit her work is indicative of the status that was accorded Black creativity in the 1930s. (See chapter 11, AP® Working with Sources: The Harlem/New Negro Renaissance, p. 460, for an example of Savage's art.) White recognition of Black achievement in the arts and in sports did not translate to civil equality, however.

Cultural Activism and the Arts

White Americans enjoyed Black music, and in the clubs of Harlem, they were moved when jazz vocalist extraordinaire Billie Holiday sang "Strange Fruit," her haunting signature song protesting lynching. Tragically, during the 1930s, more than one hundred Blacks were officially lynched, prompting the civil rights activist Abel Meeropol to compose the song. By 1939, when Holiday began closing her performances with her intensely dramatic and emotionally draining rendition of "Strange Fruit," she was already a highly respected and famous jazz artist. Holiday's insistence on spotlighting the horrors of lynching set her at odds with white racists, however, and she found a powerful enemy in Harry Anslinger, head of the Federal Bureau of Narcotics. After refusing Anslinger's demand to stop performing the song, Holiday was subjected to steady surveillance and harassment from his agency until her death in 1959.

Concurrently, the "First Lady of Song" Ella Fitzgerald, who like Holiday rapidly emerged in the amazing musical world of 1930s Harlem, also became one of the most revered and influential vocalists of the twentieth century. Fitzgerald was "The Singer's Singer," and her vocal qualities and ability to deliver a set of lyrics remain peerless. She came to fame in the 1930s as the singer for drummer Chick Webb's band, and she took over the band's leadership for a number of years after Webb died in 1939. "A-Tisket, A-Tasket," a tune that Fitzgerald co-wrote, based on a nursery rhyme, was one of the decade's biggest hits and helped solidify her fame.

Paul Robeson, a concert singer with a magnificent bass voice, sold out performances worldwide. Robeson, a global superstar, excelled at singing spirituals, folk songs from around the world, and European concert music. Robeson was also a popular actor, but his acting talents, especially in film and musical theater, were all too often fenced in by stereotypes. Still, he met with wide acclaim in performing the role of Othello and the title role in the film version of Eugene O'Neill's *The Emperor Jones* (1933). His rendition of "Ol' Man River" in the movie *Show Boat* (1936) made him famous. Robeson felt constrained by American expectations that he should play only "Negro roles," and he was drawn to the relative absence of race and class prejudice that he personally experienced in the Soviet Union. An ardent internationalist and anticolonialist, Robeson, increasingly a global citizen, contributed to freedom struggles and left-wing causes around the world. Like Holiday's "Strange Fruit" performances, Robeson's left-progressive cultural work epitomized the egalitarian and democratic dimensions of Popular Front cultural politics. Indeed, Robeson was one of the most famous artists of the era, and his wide-ranging, global, and interrelated political and cultural work earmarked him as a key exponent of those radical and activist cultural politics.

Fighting Racial Stereotypes in Popular Culture

AP® skills

Applying Disciplinary Knowledge: Explain how mainstream movies and radio were a form of escape for Black people during the 1930s but also furthered negative stereotypes about African American culture.

Movies and radio were popular pastimes in the 1930s, offering an escape from the decade's hard times. But while they popularized Black culture — notably Black, music, song, and dance — movies and radio also perpetuated demeaning stereotypes. *The Amos 'n' Andy Show*, the most popular radio show of the 1930s, featured the antics of two buffoonish Black men and reflected the enduring influence of minstrelsy and its inherent racism on American culture. Jokes trafficked in the characters' schemes to get ahead, their fractured English, and disturbing gendered, classed, and racialized Black stereotypes. These included the sexist and misogynist characterization of Black women as represented by Sapphire, the overbearing wife of Kingfish, the show's third central character. Created and performed by Charles Correll and Freeman Gosden, two white actors, the show stoked controversy from the outset, especially widespread Black opposition. While many Blacks found the show funny, many others did not. Black protest against the show persisted and helped kill an early 1950s television version featuring a talented Black cast.

The most popular Black actor of the 1930s was Stepin Fetchit (Lincoln Perry), known as "the Laziest Man in the World." Playing the slow-talking, dim-witted, shiftless sidekick to white costars, Stepin Fetchit was the first Black actor to become a millionaire. While Perry himself was quite smart and literate, Stepin Fetchit was exactly the opposite. Although some have seen Stepin Fetchit as a prankster, most have viewed him as a racist and demeaning caricature.

Not surprisingly, the Black characters in the most popular film of the decade and one of the most popular films of all time, *Gone with the Wind* (1939), were "happy slaves" who were loyal to their white folks. In this nostalgic and racist world, these stereotyped roles jibed with the proslavery, prosouthern, pro-white, and Neo-Confederate sympathies of Margaret Mitchell's novel, on which the film was based. "Pork," the house servant played by Oscar Polk, was trifling and dim-witted. "Big Sam," the field foreman played by Everett Brown, was kind-hearted and contented. "Prissy," the house servant played by Thelma "Butterfly" McQueen, was funny yet irresponsible. Most striking of all, "Mammy," the house servant played by Hattie McDaniel, was stern yet intensely loyal. For that portrayal, McDaniel became the first Black person to win an Academy Award (for Best Supporting Actress). Black protest against the movie's idealized view of plantation culture and its demeaning Black characters has consistently hounded the movie from its opening until today.

AP® exam tip

Be sure you can describe the contributions of Black athletes to sports in the twentieth century and beyond.

Even baseball, the most American of pastimes, fell victim to racism. Banned from the major leagues in 1887, Black baseball players got a chance to play ball after Andrew "Rube" Foster founded the Negro National League in 1920. It had an eight-team circuit: the Cuban Stars and seven city-based teams from St. Louis, Kansas City, Indianapolis, Dayton, Detroit, and Chicago (which had two teams). Games were played after folks got off work, with Sunday doubleheaders drawing crowds of up to ten thousand. The Depression and Foster's death in 1930 sent the league into a tailspin, but it was revived in 1934, and by 1937, a second league, the Negro American

Jesse Owens at the Berlin Olympics
Jesse Owens stands on the first-place platform in the 1936 Summer Olympics, which were hosted by Nazi Germany. Lutz Long of Germany gives the Nazi salute behind him; in front is third-place winner Naoto Tajima of Japan. Owens won four gold medals in track and set three world records. His victory was seen as a rebuke to Hitler's theory of Aryan superiority. Once back home, however, he was still subjected to Jim Crow–era racism.
What does this image reveal about the context in which Black athletes made important contributions to sports during this era?
Associated Press/AP Images.

League, had been founded. The giants of the Negro baseball leagues, such as pitcher Satchel Paige and catcher Josh Gibson, were wildly popular.

While all Americans cheered for track-and-field star Jesse Owens when he won four gold medals at the Berlin Olympics in 1936, his fellow African Americans cheered especially loudly. His outstanding performances included tying the world record in the 100-meter sprint and setting world records in the long jump, 200-meter sprint, and 400-meter relay. For Black Americans, Owens's success was a strong refutation of the myth of Aryan supremacy so crucial to Nazism and the totalitarian regime of Adolf Hitler, who had intended that the Berlin games would showcase his racial theories.

Boxing was deeply political. When Joe Louis, "the Brown Bomber," knocked out the Italian heavyweight boxer Primo Carnera in 1935, his victory was seen as a blow to fascist Italy. For Black Americans, it had a special meaning after Italy invaded Ethiopia, an independent African nation that had resisted colonial rule. The invasion was widely denounced in the Black press, and Black Americans supported the Ethiopians with financial contributions, medical supplies, and a hospital for the wounded. The event strengthened African American internationalism, and clearly it signaled the dangers of totalitarian aggression.

Each major achievement by an African American seemed to be not only an individual success but also a step forward in the Black freedom struggle. When Joe Louis defeated Jim Braddock in June 1937 with an eighth-round knockout for the world heavyweight boxing title, Blacks, glued to their radios, erupted in joy. The next year, when Louis defeated Max Schmeling to avenge an earlier loss to the German boxer, the victory was another repudiation of white supremacy. "The Brown Bomber" was embraced as a national hero, but among Blacks, pride in his achievement felt personal. "He belongs to us," noted the popular Black entertainer Lena Horne.[4]

AP® skills

Applying Disciplinary Knowledge: Why was each major achievement by an African American a win for the community as well?

On a cold and windy Easter Sunday in 1939, 75,000 Americans, Black and white, gathered at the Lincoln Memorial to hear the great African American contralto

Marian Anderson at the Lincoln Memorial
This striking image of the crowd assembled to hear the great African American contralto Marian Anderson sing on Easter Sunday, April 9, 1939, captures a transformative moment in African American protest history. As an opera and concert star, Anderson had marvelously represented her country around the world. That fact made the refusal of the Daughters of the American Revolution to permit her to perform at Constitution Hall all the more galling. This mass protest was among the first to use the sacred national space of the Lincoln Memorial to make a powerful statement on behalf of racial equality. **How did African American artists use their art to bring attention to social injustice?** *Courtesy Everett Collection.*

Marian Anderson sing. The concert had been arranged with the help of First Lady Eleanor Roosevelt after the Daughters of the American Revolution, of which Roosevelt was a member, had refused to allow Anderson to perform in its Constitution Hall. Roosevelt resigned from the organization, and as a member of the NAACP, she worked with Walter White to enlist the support of the U.S. secretary of the interior for an outdoor concert in a meaningful public venue. The Lincoln Memorial concert was a strong national protest against discrimination, a vivid demonstration of the increasing influence of the African American freedom struggle, and a resounding success. Standing in front of microphones that broadcast the concert to millions, Anderson opened with the patriotic anthem "America," which begins with the words "My country, 'tis of thee."

CONCLUSION

Freedom Struggle, Mass Movements, and Mass Culture

Ironically, precisely because of their struggle not only to survive but also to rise above the Great Depression, African Americans became both more visible and more powerful. Marian Anderson closed her epic Lincoln Memorial concert with the Negro spiritual "Nobody Knows the Trouble I've Seen." All who heard Anderson knew of the "troubles" that she and other African Americans had long confronted. Earlier, as the nation plunged into the Great Depression, individual and collective Black struggle and broad-based Black activism deepened. Escalating African American demands pushed the federal government to respond more and more to Black concerns, in many ways for the first time since Reconstruction. Black leaders within and outside the federal government increasingly looked out for the national and collective welfare of their race.

The Depression and the New Deal forced African Americans to confront the fundamental reality that their freedom struggle has remained complex and multifaceted: racial, economic, political, social, and cultural. The catastrophe of the New Deal and the wide-ranging yet all too often racially discriminatory New Deal efforts to alleviate that crisis forced African Americans to grapple even more intensely with the complexities of their multifaceted freedom struggle. On one hand, the era forced them to intensify their wide-ranging and deep-seated efforts to come to grips with the interwoven racial and economic, or class, dimensions of that struggle. On the other, this historical moment forced them to intensify their efforts at self-definition, self-help, and self-determination — at realizing full equality.

Despite the hard times of the 1930s, Black culture not only flourished within the confines of racial expectations but also increasingly broke through those confines. Indeed, the cultural front in the larger Black freedom struggle intensified dramatically in this period. Toward the end of the decade, as totalitarian regimes in Germany, Italy, and Japan embarked on conquests that would soon bring on the Second World War, Black Americans were positioned to demand democracy at home as never before.

CHAPTER 12 REVIEW ▸ PRACTICING AP® SKILLS

AP® ESSENTIAL VOCABULARY AND SOURCES

**Essential terms and required sources from the AP® Course are marked with an asterisk.*

Tuskegee Syphilis Study p. 475
Black Cabinet p. 478
"Don't Buy Where You Can't Work" boycotts p. 480
Brotherhood of Sleeping Car Porters and Maids p. 480
Congress of Industrial Organizations (CIO) p. 480
Scottsboro Boys case p. 481
National Negro Congress p. 483
Southern Negro Youth Congress p. 484
Negrismo* p. 485
Chicago Renaissance p. 486
gospel music* p. 487
Katherine Dunham on Broadway* (Katherine Dunham, Cabin in the Sky, 1940) p. 487
Négritude* p. 488
Pan-Africanism* p. 488

APPLYING DISCIPLINARY KNOWLEDGE: ESSENTIAL QUESTIONS

1. How would you characterize and assess the impact of the Great Depression and the New Deal on African Americans?
2. How did ordinary Blacks respond to the extraordinary challenges of the era?
3. How did Black politicians, activists, wageworkers, authors, and artists seek to address the specific problems that the Depression and the New Deal posed for African Americans? What were the results of their efforts?
4. What impact did African American culture have on American culture in this period?
5. In what ways do you see aspects of the ongoing African American freedom struggle evolving into what some have called "the long Civil Rights movement"?

SUGGESTED REFERENCES

The Great Depression and the New Deal

Kirby, John B. *Black Americans in the Roosevelt Era: Liberalism and Race*. Knoxville: University of Tennessee Press, 1980.

Sitkoff, Harvard. *A New Deal for Blacks: The Emergence of Civil Rights as a National Issue*. Vol. 1., *The Depression Decade*. New York: Oxford University Press, 1978.

Sullivan, Patricia. *Days of Hope: Race and Democracy in the New Deal Era*. Chapel Hill: University of North Carolina Press, 1996.

Walker, Juliet E. K. *The History of Black Business in America: Capitalism, Race, Entrepreneurship*. Woodbridge, CT: Twayne Publishers, 1998.

Wolters, Raymond. *Negroes and the Great Depression: The Problem of Economic Recovery*. Westport, CT: Greenwood, 1970.

Coming Together to Battle Hardship

Bates, Beth Tompkins. *Pullman Porters and the Rise of Protest Politics in Black America, 1925–1945*. Chapel Hill: University of North Carolina Press, 2001.

Gellman, Erik S. *Death Blow to Jim Crow: The National Negro Congress and the Rise of Militant Civil Rights*. Chapel Hill: University of North Carolina Press, 2012.

Goodman, James. *Stories of Scottsboro*. New York: Pantheon, 1994.

Harris, William H. *Keeping the Faith: A. Philip Randolph, Milton P. Webster, and the Brotherhood of Sleeping Car Porters, 1925–37*. Urbana: University of Illinois Press, 1977.

Kelley, Robin D. G. *Hammer and Hoe: Alabama Communists during the Great Depression*. Chapel Hill: University of North Carolina Press, 1990.

Naison, Mark. *Communists in Harlem during the Depression*. Urbana: University of Illinois Press, 1983.

Black Culture in Hard Times

Adi, Hakim. *Pan-Africanism: A History*. London: Bloomsbury, 2018.

Ashe, Arthur. *A Hard Road to Glory: A History of the African-American Athlete, 1919–1945*. New York: Warner, 1988.

Chin, Elizabeth, ed. *Katherine Dunham: Recovering an Anthropological Legacy, Choreographing Ethnographic Futures*. Santa Fe: School for Advanced Research Press, 2014.

Cripps, Thomas. *Slow Fade to Black: The Negro in American Film, 1900–1942*. New York: Oxford University Press, 1977.

Hine, Darlene Clark, and John McCluskey Jr., eds. *The Black Chicago Renaissance* Urbana: University of Illinois Press, 2012.

Rabaka, Reiland. *The Negritude Movement: W. E. B. Du Bois, Leon Damas, Aime Cesaire, Leopold Senghor, Frantz Fanon and the Evolution of an Insurgent Idea*. Lanham, MD: Lexington Books, 2016.

Sammons, Jeffrey T. *Beyond the Ring: The Role of Boxing in American Society*. Urbana: University of Illinois Press, 1988.

Sklaroff, Lauren Rebecca. *Black Culture and the New Deal: The Quest for Civil Rights in the Roosevelt Era*. Chapel Hill: University of North Carolina Press, 2009.

Communist Radicalism and Everyday Realities

Founded in 1919, the Communist Party of the United States (CPUSA) pursued an aggressive program for organizing the country's laboring masses while maintaining vital connections to international communism. Despite Red scare repression, when all labor radicalism was equated with communism and socialism, the CPUSA soon committed itself to large and inclusive labor unions. Between 1928 and 1935, the party developed a plan for recruiting African Americans, especially those in the South, whom it viewed as minorities with the right of self-determination and the potential for constituting an all-Black forty-ninth state. Between 1935 and 1939, the party shifted dramatically to a Popular Front platform that sought to unite progressive elements, including the Black freedom struggle, the labor movement, and left-wing organizations under the slogan "Communism is twentieth-century Americanism." After initially throwing its support behind the Soviet Union and opposing the entry of the United States into World War II, the party shifted its position in 1941 to all-out support for the U.S. war effort.

Black support for the CPUSA grew during the Great Depression primarily because of the party's anti-imperialist, anticolonialist, and, most important, antiracist work. The party's strong support for interracial unions, keen opposition to Jim Crow, and striking encouragement of Black culture were crucial to building its small yet committed base of Black members. Communist theories of anticapitalist social and economic organization appealed to many Blacks, including those such as Richard Wright who were party members at one time or another, as well as innumerable supporters and "fellow travelers"—those sympathetic to the party's views and practices who never joined the party.

But it was the party's call for worker solidarity and social equality that appealed to Black sharecroppers and workers, as Angelo Herndon's experience attests. In addition, the party's successful defense of Herndon and the Scottsboro Boys through its legal arm, the International Labor Defense, indicated not only a compelling commitment to racial equality but also an inspiring willingness to defend Blacks charged with criminal offenses at a time when other groups shied away from such involvement.

key point

Support for the Communist Party of the United States (CPUSA) grew as economic conditions of African Americans worsened during the Depression. CPUSA principles such as anti-imperialism, antiracism, worker solidarity, and social equality, along with its defense of the Scottsboro Boys, increasingly appealed at a time when racial violence and discrimination increased in the United States. Support for the party, however, waned by the 1950s during the second Red scare and the Civil Rights movement.

The racial egalitarian or antiracist politics of the CPUSA reflected a broader and increasingly powerful current among the era's progressives. The ongoing crisis of the Great Depression brought together the cultural and political struggles of marginalized groups such as African Americans, who used artistic expressions to promote racial and economic justice. The three photographs included here are representative of the large body of progressive cultural work that emerged during this period. These photographs are part of a collection of sixty thousand photographs taken for the Resettlement Administration (RA) and the Farm Security Administration (FSA) between 1935 and 1942, almost exclusively in rural and small-town America, by a stellar array of white documentary photographers, including Walker Evans, Dorothea Lange, Ben Shahn, and Marion Post Wolcott. The soon-to-be-famous Black photographer and filmmaker Gordon Parks began taking photographs for the FSA in 1942. Two key aims of these photographs in particular and of the massive photo-documentary project in general were to expose problems that the FSA needed to address and to showcase the agency's efforts to address those problems.

Communism's appeal for African Americans did not last. Herndon and Wright repudiated the party in the 1940s, and in the face of a second Red scare in the 1950s and 1960s, many other Blacks took care to distance themselves from the CPUSA, which its enemies saw as fomenting revolution in the United States, sometimes in conspiracy with the evolving modern Civil Rights movement. The following documents, however, reveal much about the party's appeal for a growing number of Blacks at a time when rampant economic inequality, racial injustice, and the Great Depression emboldened Black criticism of capitalism, leading some to reject it altogether in favor of communism.

AP® argumentation

DBQ Practice: Explain how Communism's appeal to African Americans developed and waned during the first half of the twentieth century. Use at least three of the documents to support your response.

DOCUMENT 1 W. E. B. Du Bois | *Negro Editors on Communism: A Symposium of the American Negro Press, 1932*

In 1932, amid the worsening Great Depression, W. E. B. DU BOIS (1868–1963) asked African American newspaper editors to comment on communism for *The Crisis*. Two responses follow. None of the editors who contributed their thoughts were members of the Communist Party, but they clearly understood the appeal of its efforts to bridge the racial divide.

Breaking it Down Describe each author's perception of communism and the Communist Party. What claims do they make regarding communism vs. American democracy and how African Americans are treated under both systems?

Carl Murphy

Baltimore Afro-American

The Communists appear to be the only party going our way. They are as radical as the N.A.A.C.P. were twenty years ago.

Since the abolitionists passed off the scene, no white group of national prominence has openly advocated the economic, political and social equality of black folks.

Mr. Clarence Darrow° speaking in Washington recently declared that we should not care what political candidates think of prohibition, the League of Nations, the tariff or any other general issue. What we should demand, Mr. Darrow said, is candidates who are right on all questions affecting the colored people. I agree with him.

Communism would appeal to Mr. Darrow if he were in my place.

°Clarence Darrow (1857–1938), the most prominent lawyer of his day, was known for defending the underdog. He successfully argued the case of Ossian Sweet for the NAACP but is best remembered for defending John T. Scopes in a 1925 trial in Tennessee involving the teaching of evolution in schools.

Communists in Maryland saved Orphan Jones° from a legal lynching. They secured a change of venue from the mob-ridden Easton [Eastern] Shore. They fought the exclusion of colored men from the jury, and on that ground financed an appeal of the case to Maryland's highest court. They compelled estimable Judge Duncan of Towson, Maryland, to testify that he had never considered colored people in picking jurors in his court for twenty-six years.

The Communists are going our way, for which Allah be praised.

°Euel Lee (1873–1933), known as "Orphan Jones," was accused of murdering a white family in Taylorsville, Maryland, in October 1931. Bernard Ades, a member of a Communist group that was active in racial justice issues, took on Lee's defense and arranged a change of venue for the trial, to Towson, outside Baltimore, where it was heard in the court of Judge Frank I. Duncan. Lee was convicted and, following several unsuccessful appeals, was hanged in October 1933.

W. P. Dabney

Cincinnati Union

It is as hard for people who are prosperous to visualize the great growth of Communism among American Citizens, as it is for them to realize the suffering that drives folk into its folds.

The Negro has, for many reasons, been considered immune to participation in such movement. His good humor and adaptability to vicissitudes of fortune are proverbial. His vast faith in the beatitudes of Eternity that gave birth to this song, "You may have all the world but give me Jesus." Last but not least, the class or caste of white Communists. From the earliest days of slavery, the Negro was taught by his owners to hate the "Po white man," for they knew the value of keeping the enemy divided.

That hatred, almost venomous in its intensity, was so sincerely reciprocated, that though sixty-six years have fled since [Confederate general Robert E.] Lee bowed his head in defeat, caste in the South has lost neither spite nor opportunity for its indulgence. But, "the age of miracles" has not passed! "The unexpected has happened!" Thousands of Colored Citizens have joined the Communists, and far more thousands leniently look in that direction. Poor Negroes now gather in parks and halls. They have lost their humor and their God. "If One exists," they say, "He is the friend of the rich, a patron of preachers, those fatted parasites who should be exterminated."

They argue that they have all to gain, nothing to lose. That better to die fighting like men than starve or fall victims to lynchers, as have thousands of their innocent brethren. *"Equal rights,"* the goal for which they strive. *They are sick,* of the U.S. Constitution with its impotent laws, political parties reeking with hypocrisy, philanthropists whose gold-fed institutions emasculate our intelligentsia and blind the pathetically small number of white friends to "Color" Segregation, that most cruel of all castes.

The Communists came, not bringing charity but brotherhood, not bringing words but deeds! What matters motive? When a man is drowning does he demand reasons for the helping hand? "'Tis an ill wind that blows nobody good." The world is beginning to see the tragedy that rocks and shocks "The Souls of Black Folk." Driven to desperation, they are thinking! Why should they be barred, segregated, deprived of opportunity because of circumstances beyond their control? Is it any wonder that thousands are yielding to Communism's appeal?

There will be no Black Communists in America when fair play rules, merit is recognized, race prejudice ostracised. Will Pharaoh Heed?

SOURCE: W. E. B. Du Bois, "Negro Editors on Communism: A Symposium of the American Negro Press." Bedford St. Martin's wishes to thank the Crisis Publishing Co., Inc., the publisher of the magazine of the National Association of the Advancement of Colored People, for the use of this material first published in the April and May 1932 issue of *Crisis* magazine.

DOCUMENT 2 Angelo Herndon | *You Cannot Kill the Working Class*, 1934

ANGELO HERNDON (1913–1997), the son of an Ohio miner, began working in the mines at age thirteen. By age seventeen, he was in Birmingham, Alabama, working for the Tennessee Coal, Iron and Railroad Company. In this passage from his autobiographical pamphlet, which he wrote in 1934 with the assistance of the International Labor Defense (ILD), the Communist Party's legal defense arm, he describes his introduction to the Communist Party and his reasons for joining. He wrote the pamphlet, titled *You Cannot Kill the Working Class*, while in jail for allegedly inciting an insurrection, a conviction the ILD succeeded in getting the U.S. Supreme Court to overturn in 1937. The pamphlet depicts the hope the party offered to workers who felt they had nowhere to turn during the Great Depression.

Note: This pamphlet includes the N-word, which we have chosen to reprint in this textbook to accurately reflect Herndon's original intent as well as the time period, culture, and racism discussed in the pamphlet. We recognize that this word has a long history as a derogatory and deeply hurtful expression when used by white people toward Black people, as it is in the context of this pamphlet. Be mindful of context, both Herndon's and yours, as you read and discuss this document.

Breaking it Down Describe the author's perception of communism and the Communist Party. What claims does he make regarding communism, Jim Crow, and the degree of opportunities African Americans have under both. How organized was the Communist Party, according to the author?

One day in June, 1930, walking home from work, I came across some handbills put out by the Unemployment Council in Birmingham. They said: "Would you rather fight — or starve?" They called on the workers to come to a mass meeting at 3 o'clock.

Somehow I never thought of missing that meeting. I said to myself over and over: "It's war! It's war! And I might as well get into it right now!" I got to the meeting while a white fellow was speaking. I didn't get everything he said, but this much hit me and stuck with me: that the workers could only get things by fighting for them, and that the Negro and white workers had to stick together to get results. The speaker described the conditions of the Negroes in Birmingham, and I kept saying to myself: "That's it." Then a Negro spoke from the same platform, and somehow I knew that this was what I'd been looking for all my life.

At the end of the meeting I went up and gave my name. From that day to this, every minute of my life has been tied up with the workers' movement.

I joined the Unemployment Council, and some weeks later the Communist Party. I read all the literature of the movement that I could get my hands on, and began to see my way more clearly.

I had some mighty funny ideas at first, but I guess that was only natural. For instance, I thought that we ought to start by getting all the big Negro leaders like De Priest and Du Bois and Walter White into the Communist Party, and then we would have all the support we needed. I didn't know then that De Priest and the rest of the leaders of that type are on the side of the bosses, and fight as hard as they can against the workers. They don't believe in fighting against the system that produces Jim-Crowism. They stand up for that system, and try to preserve it, and so they are really on the side of Jim-Crowism and inequality. I got rid of all these ideas after I heard Oscar Adams and others like him speak in Birmingham. . . .

I look back over what I've written about those days since I picked up the leaflet of the Unemployment Council, and wonder if I've really said what I mean. I don't know if I can get across to you the feeling that came over me whenever I went to a meeting of the Council, or of the Communist Party, and heard their speakers and read their leaflets. All my life I'd been sweated and stepped on and Jim-Crowed. I lay on my belly in the mines for a few dollars a week, and saw my pay stolen and slashed, and my buddies killed. I lived in the worst section of town, and rode behind the "Colored" signs on streetcars, as though there was something disgusting about me. I heard myself called "nigger" and "darky," and I had to say "Yes, sir" to every white man, whether he had my respect or not.

I had always detested it, but I had never known that anything could be done about it. And here, all of a sudden, I had found organizations in which Negroes and whites sat together, and worked together, and knew no difference of race or color. Here were organizations that weren't scared to come out for equality for the Negro people, and for the rights of the workers. The Jim-Crow system, the wage-slave system, weren't everlasting after all! It was like all of a sudden turning a corner on a dirty, old street and finding yourself facing a broad, shining highway. . . .

In June, 1930, I was elected a delegate to the National Unemployment Convention in Chicago. . . .

In Chicago, I got my first broad view of the revolutionary workers' movement. I met workers from almost every state in the union, and I heard about the work of the same kind of organizations in other countries, and it first dawned on me how strong and powerful the working-class was. There wasn't only me and a few others in Birmingham. There were hundreds, thousands, millions of us!

SOURCE: August Meier, Elliott Rudwick, and Francis L. Broderick, eds., *Black Protest Thought in the Twentieth Century*, 2nd ed. (Indianapolis: Bobbs-Merrill, 1971), 138–41.

DOCUMENT 3 Russell Lee | *Negro Drinking at "Colored" Water Cooler in Streetcar Terminal, Oklahoma City, Oklahoma, 1939*

The well-dressed young Black man in this photograph by RUSSELL LEE (1903–1986) must have been thirsty. He drinks from a disposable cup at a primitive water cooler designated "colored" that is neither inviting nor particularly clean. The state of the floor and walls reinforces the overall impression of filth. Interestingly, to his left are bathrooms for "white" and "colored" women, and on the other side are bathrooms for "white" and "colored" men. The photograph, however, does not show what we assume are racially separate bathrooms around each corner.

Breaking it Down What social and economic issues are represented in this photograph and the ones that follow, taken by FSA photographers? How might these photographs be used to support an antidiscrimination campaign?

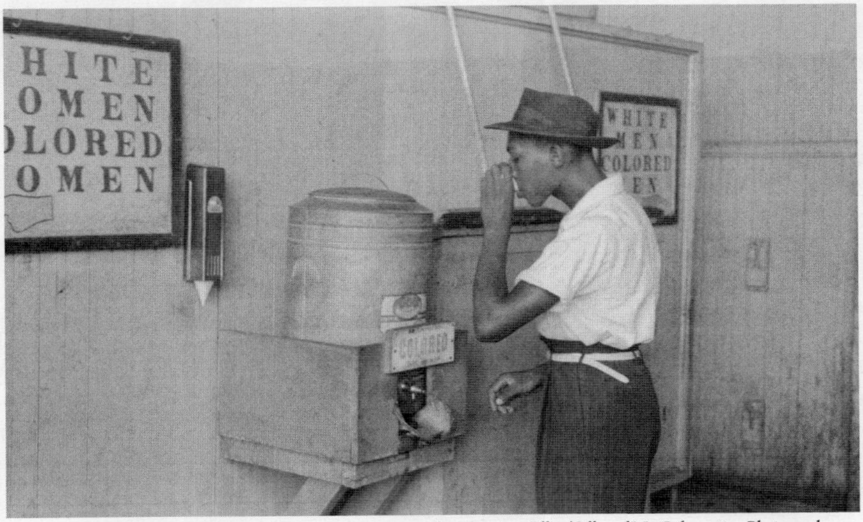

1939 photo by Russell Lee/Library of Congress, Farm Security Administration Office/Office of War Information Photograph Collection, LC-DIG-fas-8a26761.

DOCUMENT 4 Margaret Bourke-White | *The Louisville Flood, 1937*

In the midst of the Great Depression, the residents of Louisville, Kentucky, were hit with a natural disaster when relentless rains swelled the Ohio River to nearly thirty feet above flood stage. An estimated 175,000 people were forced to leave their homes, which were destroyed or damaged by the flooding. Photojournalist MARGARET BOURKE-WHITE (1904–1971) captured this image of Louisville residents lining up to receive food and clothing from a Red Cross relief station.

Breaking it Down What are some of the ironies in this image?

Margaret Bourke-White/Time Life Pictures/Getty Images.

DOCUMENT 5 Marion Post Wolcott | *Negroes Jitterbugging in a Juke Joint on Saturday Afternoon, Clarksdale, Mississippi Delta, 1939*

The well-dressed young Black people having a good time in this photograph by MARION POST WOLCOTT (1910–1990) are a prime example of the social solidarity among youth, the working class, and other ordinary folks. For many, work was too often a site of oppression, sorrow, and pain, and they welcomed the opportunity to let loose and enjoy each other's company. The photo centers on a woman dancing the jitterbug and highlights the human need for pleasure and community.

Breaking it Down Looking carefully at the crowd of observers, what evidence do you see of white surveillance of Black lives under Jim Crow?

1939 photo by Marion Post Wolcott/Library of Congress, Farm Security Administration Office/Office of War Information Photograph Collection, LC-DIG-fsa-8c10917.

PRACTICING AP® SKILLS

1. **AP® Contextualization.** Describe the economic and social conditions of African Americans during the 1930s and explain how they influenced African American support of the Communist Party. Use at least one of the documents in this section as evidence to support your response.
2. **AP® Comparison.** Compare and contrast the different arguments in these documents on African American membership in the Communist Party of the United States.
3. **AP® Continuity and Change.** Using at least two pieces of evidence from the documents, explain why African American support for the Communist Party changed by the 1950s.
4. **Connecting to AP® Themes.** Explain how African American support for the Communist Party of the United States was a display of resistance. To what extent were motives for resistance in earlier eras similar to motives for support of the Communist party in this era?
5. **Class Debate.** Debate the advantages and disadvantages of African American support of the Communist Party of the United States from 1930 to 1950.

Multiple-Choice Questions with Paired Stimuli

As you'll recall from the previous AP® Skills Workshops on multiple-choice questions (pp. SW1-F, SW2-F), all multiple-choice questions on the AP® Exam will be stimulus based. Sometimes, a question set will pertain to a standalone text excerpt or visual. Other times, a question set will connect to a *pair* of sources — either two sources of the same type (e.g., two visuals) or of different types (e.g., one text excerpt and one visual). These questions with paired stimuli are the focus of this workshop.

You've already learned that there are three primary strategies to tackle multiple-choice questions on the AP® Exam:

Strategy 1: Activate relevant concepts, developments, and processes.

Concept: a person, place, theory, or theme

Development: an event; a political, social, or cultural movement; or a time period — essentially, anything important that happens

Process: two or more related developments — the developments might cause, contrast with, or have commonalities with one another

Strategy 2: Determine what the question is really asking using the Four Cs.

Comparison. How are two figures, events, movements, or time periods similar or different?

Causation. What factors *directly* contributed to an event or a movement? What effects did this event or movement *directly* bring about?

Continuity & Change. What changed and what stayed the same between different time periods?

Strategy 3: Eliminate wrong answers.

False. Are any choices factually incorrect?

Outside the time period. Do any choices pertain to a different time period from the one the question discusses?

Irrelevant. Do any choices fail to answer the question? True answers are correct only if they *directly* address the question asked.

Conveniently, all of these strategies are applicable to multiple-choice questions with paired stimuli. In this workshop, we'll review how to activate course knowledge, break down multiple-choice questions, and sift through distractors to find the correct answer choice. Throughout, we'll tailor these strategies to questions with multiple sources.

Let's build our familiarity with paired stimuli using the following question set:

Questions 1–2 refer to the following.

SOURCE 1

Margaret Bourke-White, *The Louisville Flood*, photograph of emergency relief line after flooding in Louisville, Kentucky, 1937

Margaret Bourke-White/Time Life Pictures/Getty Images

SOURCE 2

"The NIRA established the National Recovery Administration (NRA) to stabilize business by setting minimum wages and maximum hours for dozens of industries, issues of obvious concern to black as well as white workers. . . .

The NRA was particularly notorious for its refusal to consider the needs of black workers as it determined and implemented farming and industry regulations. Although NRA codes required equal pay for black and white workers at the same jobs, local administrators routinely ignored those provisions, with no repercussions from above. . . .

Because the NRA generally accepted local wage and hiring practices, African American workers who kept their jobs continued to face the same discrimination they had before the New Deal. . . .

Indeed, because virtually all New Deal programs were administered locally, well-intended rules by agency heads in Washington, D.C., were often ignored on the ground. In the South even government employment services were

(*continued*)

segregated. Black applicants were offered vocational training or employment in only the most menial and poorly paid occupations. . . .

President Roosevelt, who promised equality and opportunity for what he termed 'the forgotten man,' and who was aware of the barriers facing black people, was nevertheless largely unwilling to challenge segregation and discrimination head on. In the 'solid South,' long-serving Democratic elected officials supported white supremacy as well as the New Deal, and their seniority in Congress meant they controlled important committees. Roosevelt feared that taking on segregation would alienate them, which would in turn undermine his carefully constructed political coalition and jeopardize his legislative priorities. He was not willing to take that risk. As a result, Roosevelt did little in the first years of his presidency to enforce or even encourage civil rights provisions."

Source: Cheryl Lynn Greenberg, historian, *To Ask for an Equal Chance: African Americans in the Great Depression*, 2009

1. Which of the following statements is best supported by both sources?
(A) Government relief programs primarily served Black Americans.
(B) Government relief programs were more powerful in the U.S. than abroad.
(C) Government relief programs received support from Democratic politicians.
(D) Government relief programs fell short of securing economic stability.

2. Which of the following best describes the impact of New Deal programs?
(A) New Deal programs provided limited benefits to Black Americans.
(B) New Deal programs were meant to alleviate poverty.
(C) New Deal programs were popular with most Americans.
(D) New Deal programs significantly reduced racial inequality.

First, we can activate our course knowledge by considering what concepts, developments, and processes covered in this chapter might be relevant:

Concepts/Themes	• Resistance and Resilience • Economic inequality
Developments	• The Great Depression • Rise of government relief — Roosevelt's New Deal • Discrimination in New Deal programs
Processes	• The New Deal was meant to address the economic struggles of the Great Depression, but discrimination limited its benefits to Black Americans.

Gathering those details sets us up well to rewrite each question in simpler terms. As you've learned, often, but not always, multiple-choice questions can be rephrased using the Four Cs:

Comparison — How are two figures, events, movements, or time periods similar or different?

Causation — What factors *directly* contributed to an event or a movement? What effects did this event or movement *directly* bring about?

Continuity & Change — What changed and what stayed the same between different time periods?

Here, we can rephrase the questions as follows:

Question 1	Question 2
X Comparison ☐ Causation ☐ Continuity & Change	☐ Comparison X Causation ☐ Continuity & Change
Rephrasing: What conclusion can be drawn from both sources?	**Rephrasing:** Which option is an effect of the New Deal?

So far, we've practiced strategies that should already be familiar to you. Because this particular multiple-choice question set connects to multiple sources, we recommend taking the additional step of comparing the two sources through a Venn diagram:

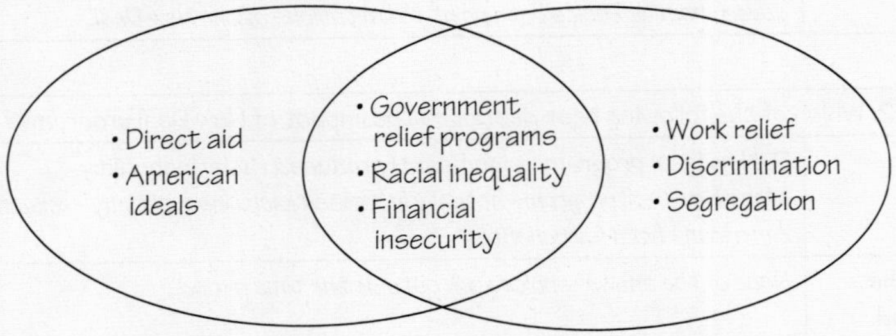

Taking this additional step helps us critically examine why these two sources are paired together for a question set. Often, at least one of the questions pertaining to paired stimuli will invite you to compare or contrast the sources, so it's helpful to begin considering how the sources interact with one another.

Having considered the extent of overlap between the sources, we can return to the answer choices and cross out choices that are:

False	Are any choices factually incorrect?
Outside the time period	Do any choices pertain to a different time period from the one the question discusses?
Irrelevant	Do any choices fail to answer the question? It's not enough for an answer choice to be true; answers are correct only if they directly address the question asked.

That process of elimination can be visualized through charts:

Question 1: Which of the following statements is best supported by both sources?	
False	**A.** Government relief programs primarily served Black Americans. *Government relief programs did not primarily serve Black Americans.*
Outside the time period	*None of the answer choices are outside the time period.*
Irrelevant	**B.** Government relief programs were more powerful in the United States than abroad. *Neither source shares information about foreign relief programs.* **C.** Government relief programs received support from Democratic politicians. *There is no information in Source 1 about who supported relief programs.*
Correct	**D.** Government relief programs fell short of securing economic stability. *The long line of people needing aid and the description of discrimination by government agencies both point to limitations of the New Deal.*

Question 2: Which of the following best describes the impact of New Deal programs?	
False	**D.** New Deal programs significantly reduced racial inequality. *Many New Deal programs actually increased racial inequality by excluding Black Americans from full benefits.*
Outside the time period	*None of the answer choices are outside the time period.*
Irrelevant	**B.** New Deal programs were meant to alleviate poverty. *The question is asking about the impact, not the cause, of the New Deal.* **C.** New Deal programs were popular with most Americans. *The question is asking about the impact, not the popularity, of the New Deal.*
Correct	**A.** New Deal programs provided limited benefits to Black Americans. *Even though the New Deal provided some benefits, Black Americans couldn't take full advantage of its programs.*

Following these steps can help guide you to correct answers for multiple-choice question sets with paired stimuli.

recap

Answering Multiple-Choice Questions with Paired Stimuli

The same strategies apply for all multiple-choice question sets, even when there are paired stimuli.

Strategy 1: Activate relevant concepts, developments, and processes.
Strategy 2: Determine what the question is really asking using the Four Cs.
Strategy 3: Eliminate wrong answers.

When working with paired stimuli, you'll also want to complete a Venn diagram investigating the extent of the overlap between the sources.

Activity ▸ Answering Multiple-Choice Questions with Paired Stimuli

Questions 1–2 refer to the following.

SOURCE 1

***Les Fétiches* [*The Carved Masks*] by Loïs Mailou Jones, 1938**

Smithsonian American Art Museum, Washington, DC/Art Resource, NY

(*continued*)

SOURCE 2

"[T]here is the possibility that the sensitive artistic mind of the American Negro, stimulated by a cultural pride and interest, will receive from African art a profound and galvanizing influence. The legacy is there at least, with prospects of a rich yield. In the first place, there is in the mere knowledge of the skill and unique mastery of the arts of the ancestors the valuable and stimulating realization that the Negro is not a cultural foundling without his own inheritance. Our timid and apologetic imitativeness and overburdening sense of cultural indebtedness have, let us hope, their natural end in such knowledge and realization. . . .

But what the Negro artist of to-day has most to gain from the arts of the forefathers is perhaps not cultural inspiration or technical innovations, but the lesson of a classic background, the lesson of discipline, of style, of technical control pushed to the limits of technical mastery. A more highly stylized art does not exist than the African."

SOURCE: Alain Locke, "The Legacy of the Ancestral Arts" from *The New Negro: An Interpretation*, 1925

Before approaching the question set, activate your awareness of relevant course content using a graphic organizer like the one shown below.

Concepts	
Developments	
Processes	

Next, review the questions and rephrase them using the Four Cs.

1. Which of the following best describes the significance of *Les Fétiches* in African American Studies?

(A) The painting urges viewers to embrace traditional African religious practices.
(B) The painting conveys pride in African ancestral heritage and culture.
(C) The painting celebrates Jones's firsthand experiences as an African-born painter.
(D) The painting commemorates Jones's achievement of displaying artwork in Paris.

2. Jones and Locke provide evidence for which of the following statements about African American art of the early twentieth century?

(A) African American art of the early twentieth century had clear African influences.
(B) African American art of the early twentieth century was more emotional than technical.
(C) African American art of the early twentieth century inspired twenty-first-century pop culture.
(D) African American art of the early twentieth century used controversial techniques.

Question 1:	Question 2:
☐ Comparison ☐ Causation ☐ Continuity & Change	☐ Comparison ☐ Causation ☐ Continuity & Change
Rephrasing:	**Rephrasing:**

Then, compare the two sources using a Venn diagram:

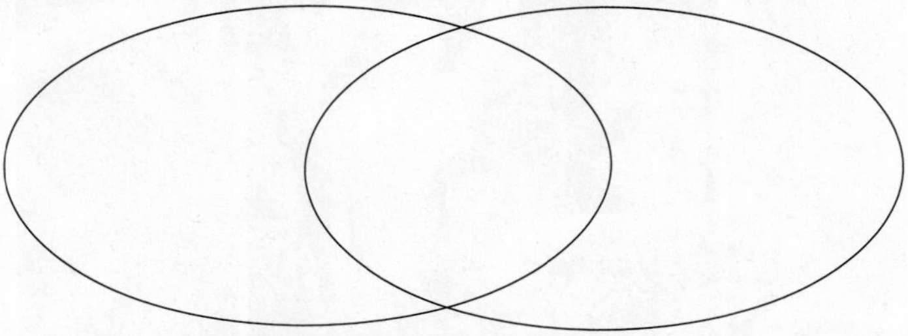

Finally, categorize the answer choices to eliminate wrong answers. Make sure to explain your reasoning.

False	
Outside the time period	
Irrelevant	
Correct	

Multiple-Choice Questions

Questions 1–2 refer to the following.

AP® source ***Katherine Dunham on Broadway*, 1943**

1. Which of the following developments in Black artistic expression during the early 1930s is most directly reflected in the image?
   (A) Waning African American artistic expression in the midst of an economic crisis
   (B) The emergence of a global, Pan-African cultural renaissance
   (C) The beginning of the Black Arts and Black Power movements
   (D) Decreased acceptance among white audiences of performances promoting stereotypes about Black Americans

2. Which of the following creative works best aligns with the perspectives of the artists depicted in the image?

(A) *The Amos 'n' Andy Show*

(B) The television performances of Stepin Fetchit

(C) *Gone with the Wind* by Margaret Mitchell

(D) *Lift Every Voice and Sing* by Augusta Savage

Short-Answer Question

1. Answer A, B, C, and D.

(A) Describe the influence of the New Negro movement on the development of another movement that emerged in the 1930s outside of the United States.

(B) Using a specific example from one movement of the 1930s, explain how Black artists interpreted Black people's connection to Africa and the diaspora.

(C) Using a specific example from the 1800s, explain how Black cultural expression was influenced by the African diaspora.

(D) Using a specific example, explain the extent of the similarity in the artistic goals and methods of Black artists of the 1930s and griots of West Africa.

CHAPTER **13**

Fighting for a Double Victory in the World War II Era

1938–1950

CHAPTER TIMELINE *Events specific to African American history are in purple. General U.S. history events are in black. Events from the AP® Course Framework are marked with an asterisk.*

1938 Charles Houston writes *New York Times* editorial protesting discrimination in armed forces

1939 Germany invades Poland

1940s More than 1.5 million African Americans migrate out of South*

1940 Frederick O'Neal and Abram Hill found American Negro Theatre in Harlem

Walter White, A. Philip Randolph, and T. Arnold Hill demand elimination of segregation and discrimination in armed services

First peacetime draft instituted

1940–1941 Thirteen lynchings reported in South

1941 President Franklin D. Roosevelt delivers Four Freedoms speech

Randolph oversees March on Washington Movement; FDR responds to activism with

Executive Order 8802, creating the Fair Employment Practices Commission

Body of Private Felix Hall found hanging from tree at Fort Benning, Georgia

Roosevelt and Winston Churchill sign Atlantic Charter

Tuskegee Airmen's unit formed*

Japanese bomb Pearl Harbor; United States declares war on Japan and Germany

1942 *Pittsburgh Courier* launches Double V campaign*

Roosevelt authorizes relocation and internment of 110,000 Japanese and Japanese Americans

Twenty thousand white workers walk off job at Packard Motor Car Company to protest promotion of three Black workers

Three hundred fifty white workers shut down Dodge plant in Detroit to protest promotion of twenty-three Black workers

Congress of Racial Equality (CORE) founded*

1942 James G. Thompson writes "Should I Sacrifice to Live 'Half-American'?" in *Pittsburgh Courier**

1943 Black membership in CIO unions grows to 400,000

William Hastie resigns as adviser to War Secretary

By year's end, 242 racial battles have taken place in 47 cities

1944 Black regiments of Second Cavalry Division assigned to noncombat jobs in North Africa

Smith v. Allwright declares all-white Texas Democratic primary illegal

Servicemen's Readjustment Act, known as GI Bill, passed

United States navy admits Black women to WAVES

1945 Black WACs strike at Fort Devens to protest discriminatory work assignments

Roosevelt dies; Truman becomes president

Germany surrenders

United States drops atomic bombs on Hiroshima and Nagasaki; Japan surrenders

1946 Race riot in Columbia, Tennessee

Morgan v. Virginia declares segregation in interstate bus travel illegal

1947 Jackie Robinson becomes first Black major league baseball player*

Eight Blacks and eight whites from CORE test *Morgan v. Virginia* by initiating first Freedom Rides*

President's Committee on Civil Rights issues report, *To Secure These Rights*

1948 Truman issues Executive Order 9981, requiring equal opportunity in the armed services

1950 Althea Gibson becomes first African American to compete in the United States National Tennis Championship

National Basketball Association drafts its first Black player, Charles "Chuck" Cooper

James Tillman and Evelyn Bates Mobilize for War

In 1941, twenty-one-year-old James Tillman of Pittsburgh signed up for what he thought would be a noncombat truck-driving job in the U.S. army. He ended up in the Ninety-Second Infantry Division, the only Black unit to see ground combat in Europe in World War II. After joining the army, Tillman, like many other northern Black men, was sent south for training. From Maryland, he traveled to the Louisiana swamps to prepare for action in the South Pacific. Then he found himself at Fort Huachuca, Arizona, training for desert fighting in Africa. A year and a half later, Tillman was still training, this time in northern Arizona for combat in the mountains of Italy. Most army units trained for three to six months, but not the "buffalo soldiers" of the Ninety-Second Infantry. Although their nickname came from the nineteenth-century Black troops who fought courageously in the Indian wars and the Spanish-American War, U.S. officials doubted their courage and abilities and were reluctant to send them into combat.

Tillman knew that Black politicians were fighting for the Ninety-Second Infantry to see combat, however. As he put it, they wanted Black soldiers to "get recognition," so that the prestige of fighting on the frontline would not go only to white men.[1] Tillman and his division finally saw combat in Italy, where Tillman manned the heavy guns that pushed the Germans back from Rome to Florence to Milan. Although many Black men died in the battles that eventually forced the German surrender, neither Tillman nor the Ninety-Second Infantry got the recognition they deserved.

When Tillman landed in Norfolk, Virginia, after the war, his unit was unceremoniously left on the docks for hours, with no way to get to camp. While other returning troops were cheered and paraded, Tillman's unit was subjected to the strange looks of whites, who treated them as if they were convicts, and to the anxious gazes of Blacks, who wondered if they would be lynched. As a sergeant, Tillman wouldn't let his men walk through town with their heads down; he had them march proudly, with their shoulders back and their heads held high.

Afraid that local whites would instigate a violent confrontation, the army sent the soldiers home without fanfare the following day. Tillman returned to Pittsburgh, where he could not find a job. Still, he thought his unit had accomplished much. He explained, "We were fighting . . . for our people . . . we had to prove that Blacks would fight. . . . If we failed, the whole Black race would fail. We were fighting for the flag and for our rights. We knew that this would be the beginning of breaking down segregation."[2]

While Tillman fought in Italy, Evelyn Bates waged her own battle at home. A native of Memphis, Tennessee, Bates took advantage of the wartime industrial expansion and got a job at the Firestone Tire and Rubber Company in her hometown. In the absence of men, Firestone, like most other factories, had to rely on women for both domestic and war production. Bates was one of the few Black women to land one of these jobs, but like Tillman, she had to fight entrenched ideas about Blacks in general and Black women in particular.

Unlike white women, Black women were thought to be suited for the same heavy labor as men. Bates initially found herself working in a field full of wasps and snakes, sorting and cutting tires. Many of her friends quit because the work was so hard, and Bates almost joined them when she had to stand outside in the cold and sweep nearly frozen water. "In that factory, the attitude was bad," she recalled. When she complained, she was reassigned to a job lifting slabs of rubber weighing up to 125 pounds onto trays that rolled along a nonstop conveyor belt. As Bates recollected, "They had mens doing it before they hired black womens. Didn't any women do it but black womens."[3]

But Bates persevered, despite the eight-hour-a-day, seven-day-a-week grind, because her weekly salary of $25 was much higher than the pittance she had made doing domestic work. At war's end, Firestone fired most of the Black women it had hired in order to rehire the white men who had gone off to war. Although Bates felt fortunate to get a job sweeping the floor of the room where she had once hauled rubber, she resented the fact that white women workers were not summarily dismissed as well. Firestone had begun hiring white women five years before Black women, and in typical "last hired, first fired" fashion, the company laid off the Black women first. Some, like Bates, were kept on as maids because, as Bates said, "white women didn't want to sweep, she didn't want to clean up no restroom, so that was a Black woman's job."[4]

Still, the war had pried open factory doors for African Americans. Bates joined the union and, with seniority, was able to apply for jobs typically reserved for white women. Although she took much abuse from white supervisors, she endured; over time, she attained better-paying, less demanding, and more rewarding positions.

The war spurred changes in the lives of Tillman, Bates, and millions of other African Americans who enlisted in the armed forces or sought work in the expanded war industries. World War II, Black leaders maintained, would not be like World War I. Black people would not just "close ranks" with white Americans and forget their special grievances. Instead, they would fight, announced the *Pittsburgh Courier* in February 1942, for a "Double Victory" against fascism abroad and racism at home. As the experiences of Tillman and Bates made clear, achieving the "Double V" would not be easy for African Americans. But their wartime challenges prepared them for the postwar Civil Rights movement, which would prove to be the most important social and economic justice movement the United States had ever experienced.

Please note that this chapter includes primary sources by Black writers and speakers that use the N-word, which we have chosen to reprint in this textbook to accurately reflect these speakers' original intent as well as the time period, culture, and racism discussed in each source. We recognize that this word has a long history as a derogatory and deeply hurtful expression when used by white people toward Black people. Black speakers' and writers' choice to use this word relates not only to that history but to a larger cultural tradition in which the N-word can take on different meanings, emphasize shared experience, and be repurposed as a term of endearment within Black communities. This chapter also includes primary sources by white writers and speakers that use the N-word, which we have chosen not to reprint in full here. We have replaced the term without hindering understanding of these sources. Be mindful of context, both historical and contemporary, as you read and discuss this chapter.

The Crisis of World War II

How did African American soldiers participate in the Second World War?

How did the Double V Campaign emerge during the Second World War?

World War I — the Great War, as it was termed — did not end all wars, as so many had hoped. Just twenty years later, German armies, under the command of Adolf Hitler, again tore across Europe, conquering nations and subduing people. As it had in World War I, the United States entered the conflict belatedly, this time after an attack by Germany's ally Japan. At home, the war spotlighted issues of democracy and racial prejudice that could not be ignored. America thus faced a dual crisis: it had to help its allies stop German and Japanese aggression abroad, and it needed to make its own ideology of democracy and equality a reality at home.

AP® skills

Applying Disciplinary Knowledge: What was the dual crisis America faced during World War II?

America Enters the War and States Its Goals

December 7, 1941 — the day the Japanese bombed the U.S. naval base at Pearl Harbor, Hawaii — marked the entry of the United States into World War II. But it did not mark the beginning of that war or America's involvement in it. Europe had been fully embroiled in war since Hitler invaded Poland in September 1939. By the time the United States declared war on Japan, the **Axis powers** — Japan, Germany, and Italy — had formed a military alliance. Hitler had annexed Austria and overrun most of Europe and was attempting to defeat Britain and the Soviet Union, the two nations that along with the United States would become the **Allies**. In Asia, Japan had invaded China and Indochina. Hitler's aggression had emboldened the Japanese, who wanted to expel Europeans from Asia and become the dominant power in the region. From Japan's perspective, only the United States stood in its way. Yet, Japan depended on American raw materials, and when the United States placed an embargo on oil and steel, the Japanese attacked.

Axis powers
The nations that fought against the United States and the other Allies in World War II. The principal Axis powers were Germany, Italy, and Japan.

Allies
The nations that fought against the Axis powers in World War II. Among the Allies were the United States, Canada, France, Great Britain, Mexico, and the Soviet Union.

President Franklin D. Roosevelt and the U.S. Congress had not stood idly by as the world had devolved into chaos. Although they knew that most Americans wanted to stay out of the war and that only a direct attack on the country would convince Americans that the United States should join the conflict, they did everything they could to support Britain in its fight to save western Europe and to prepare the nation for war. In September 1940, the first peacetime draft was instituted, compelling all men

Four Freedoms
The four essential human rights that, in January 1941, President Franklin Roosevelt proclaimed people everywhere ought to have: freedom of speech and religion, and freedom from want and fear.

Atlantic Charter (1941)
A document signed by President Franklin Roosevelt and British prime minister Winston Churchill in August 1941. Among other things, it declared that all people had the right to economic advancement, to social security, and to choose their own form of government.

Nazism
A racist totalitarian ideology proclaiming certain non-Jewish Germans to be a superior race destined to rule the world.

between the ages of twenty-one and thirty-five to register with local draft boards and mobilizing an army of 900,000. Congress appropriated money for American industries to produce arms and prepare military forces, and it gave Roosevelt the power to lease arms and lend ships to Britain and the Soviet Union.

American leaders also began the very careful process of explaining to the public what was at stake. The principles that America upheld were outlined in Roosevelt's **Four Freedoms** speech, delivered in January 1941, and in the **Atlantic Charter**, a document signed in August of that year by Roosevelt and British prime minister Winston Churchill. In his January speech, Roosevelt argued that people everywhere ought to have freedom of speech, freedom of religion, and freedom from want and fear. The Atlantic Charter reiterated these freedoms and also stated that people had the right to economic advancement, to social security, and to choose the form of government they would live under. It also denounced **Nazism**, the racist totalitarian ideology expounded by the German chancellor, Adolf Hitler. Nazism proclaimed Germans to be a superior people destined to lead the world. The only thing standing in their way, Nazis said, was the Jewish people. Roosevelt's signature on the Atlantic Charter made American opposition to racism and totalitarianism official goals of the war.

African Americans Respond to the War

African Americans had been fighting racism and fascist-like southern governments since the days of slavery. As a people who had been brutalized, enslaved, raped, lynched, robbed of their property, and segregated in the workplace and society, African Americans could identify with Jewish Europeans. For centuries, European nations had terrorized and discriminated against Jewish people. Hitler had now gone further and stripped them of their citizenship rights, corralled them into ghettos and concentration camps, and murdered them outright — all in the name of racial supremacy. African Americans heard in Roosevelt's goals a call to end racism and fascism not only abroad, but in America as well.

AP® skills

Applying Disciplinary Knowledge: What discrimination did African Americans endure in the armed services at the beginning of the war?

Early on, Black leaders protested discrimination in the armed forces. In 1938, Charles Hamilton Houston — a former army officer in World War I and now special legal counsel to the NAACP — wrote a letter to the editor of the *New York Times* warning that if the army's general staff "thinks that Negroes in the next war are going to be content with peeling potatoes and washing dishes," they had badly misread the minds of African Americans.[5] African Americans had only recently started voting for the Democratic Party, and Black leaders sought to use the Black vote to pressure the administration for concessions. In September 1940, Walter White, NAACP executive secretary; A. Philip Randolph, head of the Brotherhood of Sleeping Car Porters; and T. Arnold Hill, adviser on Negro affairs for the National Youth Administration, met with Secretary of the Navy Frank Knox and Assistant Secretary of War Robert P. Patterson to push their demands for the elimination of segregation and discrimination in the armed services.

For the most part, President Roosevelt's response was disappointing. His press secretary noted that he refused "to intermingle the colored and white enlisted personnel in the same regimental organizations." According to Roosevelt, separate units "had proven satisfactory over a long period of years, and to make changes now would produce a situation destructive to morale and detrimental to the preparation for national defense."[6] In addition to this disappointing news, Black leaders were frustrated by the directive that Black units would have no Black officers other than medics and chaplains. Colonel Benjamin O. Davis Sr., the senior Black officer in the nation's armed forces, was promoted to brigadier general, and Judge William H. Hastie, the dean of Howard University Law School, was appointed civilian aide on Negro affairs to Secretary of War Henry L. Stimson. But the administration held fast to the idea that Black men could not lead and would serve best under the direction of white men, especially southern white men.

African Americans did not accept these decisions without protest. "We asked Mr. Roosevelt to change the rules of the game and he countered by giving us some new uniforms," complained the *Baltimore Afro-American*. The American Red Cross's separation of Black and white blood prompted Charles Drew, the African American physician who developed the process of storing and shipping blood plasma to be used in blood banks, to resign from that organization. The navy's announcement in 1940 that it would accept Blacks only as mess attendants, cooks, and stewards inspired protest and an angry NAACP editorial, asking how Blacks were supposed to feel about "what our white fellow citizens declare to be the 'vast difference' between American Democracy and Hitlerism." When the Army Air Corps refused the application of a Howard University student named Yancey Williams, the NAACP initiated a lawsuit on his behalf.[7]

AP® skills

Applying Disciplinary Knowledge: Explain how African Americans fought back against the discrimination they faced in the armed services. To what extent did their methods of resistance differ from past methods of resistance?

Mass protests replaced unorganized actions when Black leaders, guided by Randolph, created the **March on Washington Movement**. In January 1941, Randolph called for a gathering of 50,000 to 100,000 Black Americans in the nation's capital on July 1 to demand equal opportunity for Blacks in defense industries and an end to "their humiliation in the armed services."[8] The president, fearing international embarrassment, lobbied hard to get Randolph to call off the increasingly popular march, but Randolph held firmly to his demands. Just five days before the scheduled march, Roosevelt issued **Executive Order 8802**, which banned racial discrimination in defense industries and created the Fair Employment Practices Commission (FEPC) to ensure compliance.

March on Washington Movement (1941)
A. Philip Randolph's call for 50,000 to 100,000 Black Americans to gather in Washington, D.C., on July 1, 1941, to demand equal opportunity for Blacks in defense industries and the armed services.

Executive Order 8802 (1941)
President Franklin Roosevelt's response to the March on Washington Movement. It banned racial discrimination in defense industries and created the Fair Employment Practices Commission (FEPC).

Randolph did call off the march, but the contradictions inherent in America's international and national postures remained. It seemed hypocritical to fight racism abroad with a segregated army and terribly unfair to ask African Americans to fight for democracy and citizenship rights overseas when they were accorded only second-class citizenship at home. African Americans debated these issues and tried to resolve them so that neither they nor the nation would be cheated.

Behind the debates were bitter memories of the way Black Americans had been treated during and after World War I. Some Blacks were so angry that they supported

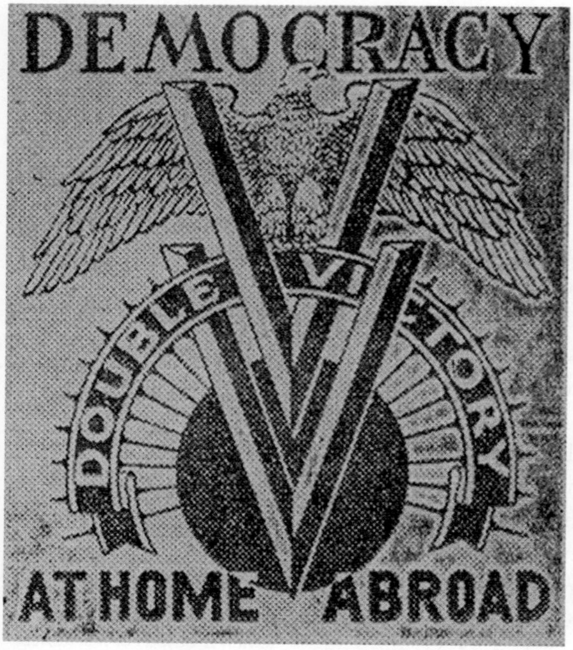

AP® source ***African Americans' Double Victory***

On February 7, 1942, the *Pittsburgh Courier* published a letter to the editor from James G. Thompson. In it, he proclaimed, "Let we colored Americans adopt the double VV for a double victory." The first V was "for victory over our enemies from without," while the second V stood "for victory over our enemies from within." After this letter was published, the Double V symbol became popular among African Americans. **Based on the clues from the image and information you have learned from the chapter, describe the main objective of the Double V Campaign.** *Pittsburgh Courier Archives.*

and admired the Japanese, if only because Japan was a nonwhite nation challenging white supremacy, and Japanese Americans also confronted discrimination. Some believed that a Japanese victory "would be the first step in the darker races coming back into their own."[9] Even Black Americans who opposed Japan could not bring themselves to support the United States uncritically. Some African Americans argued that it was American racism that had made the country vulnerable to the Japanese. According to the Black activist and writer George Schuyler, "Race prejudice and only race prejudice caused our complacence toward Japan."[10]

These sentiments made many African American leaders nervous. Once the United States declared war on Japan in 1941, African American dissent could easily be interpreted as disloyalty, and protest could be seen as sedition. The Japanese had launched an intensive propaganda campaign to gain Black Americans' support, and the Federal Bureau of Investigation and the U.S. army's Military Intelligence Division were keeping a close watch on African American leaders and newspapers for evidence of treason. If the U.S. government thought that Black people posed a threat of internal subversion, they might curtail Black civil liberties. The detainment of many German Americans and Italian Americans, as well as the internment of Japanese Americans beginning in 1942, served as vivid examples of what could happen to those deemed security risks.[11]

Double V campaign Nickname for the "Double Victory" campaign, a World War II strategy committing African Americans to fight for liberty both at home and abroad.

The **Double V campaign** provided a masterful way to fight racism without endangering civil liberties. Even before its official declaration by the *Pittsburgh Courier* in February 1942, Black leaders insisted that African Americans could simultaneously be patriotic and fight for Black rights. A. Philip Randolph wrote an article two weeks after the bombing of Pearl Harbor, reminding African Americans that the principles of democracy were at stake both at home and abroad. The fight to defeat the Axis powers involved "the obligation, responsibility, and task for the Negro people to fight with all their might for their constitutional, democratic rights and freedoms here in America." The Jamaican American historian and journalist J. A. Rogers acknowledged that World War I had left Blacks with lukewarm loyalty, but he urged them to "enter the fight with all the zest, thrill and patriotism of every other American group, at the same time preparing ourselves mentally and otherwise, to demand, and if necessary to seize, our rights as citizens during the conflict, and especially after it."[12]

AP® exam tip

Be sure you can explain how the Double V Campaign emerged during the Second World War.

Racial Violence and Discrimination in the Military

Fighting on two fronts would not be easy, not least because the U.S. military would not let Blacks fight. Despite Black leaders' best efforts, for most of the war, segregation persisted in the armed forces. Few Blacks were appointed to selective service boards, and Blacks did not receive a proportionate share of deferments. Throughout the draft's early years, Blacks were largely passed over until white soldiers began to complain that they should not be the only ones forced to sacrifice. During the last years of the war, the number of Black inductees steadily increased, but 50 to 75 percent of them were assigned to noncombat and unskilled work. Only three Black divisions, among them James Tillman's Ninety-Second Infantry, saw combat. Even highly trained Black pilots were discriminated against. The Army Air Corps initially would not let **Tuskegee Airmen** — named for Tuskegee Institute and trained as separate units apart from white pilots — fly combat missions and only belatedly allowed them to engage in air-to-air combat, for which they were trained. Although the fighter and bomber units earned distinguished service citations, and individual airmen were decorated with the highest medals, it was not until the beginning of 1944 that the Army Air Corps deployed them in a meaningful way. (See AP® Working with Sources: African Americans and the Tuskegee Experiments, pp. 534–43.)

Tuskegee Airmen
Black pilots trained by the Army Air Corps at Tuskegee Institute during World War II. The pilots earned distinction despite efforts to disband and malign them.

Black officers were similarly mistreated. The army integrated its twenty officer training camps, and by the end of the war in August 1945, almost eight thousand Black officers had been commissioned. Still, as of March 1945, their number represented only 1 percent of Black servicemen — compared to 11 percent of white servicemen receiving commissions. Army policy did not allow a Black officer to outrank a white officer in his unit, which severely limited Black officers' opportunities. They could not use the white officers' clubs to which they paid dues. Even enemy prisoners of war were treated better than Black soldiers and officers. In one instance, Black officers stationed in Italy were required to sit in the back of an army theater, where the seats in front were reserved for white officers and Italian prisoners.[13]

This humiliating treatment was something that Black soldiers grappled with. Captain Luther Smith was taken prisoner of war by the Germans and later remembered being confronted by a German officer who said, "You are Black American. You volunteered to fight for a country that lynches your people." Smith recalled that he was "floored" by this comment, saying that his first thought was, "You are absolutely correct. . . . Yes, I had volunteered to fight for a country that lynched my people." But Smith retorted with the kind of optimism expressed by James Tillman: "I am Black American. It is my home. I will fight for it because I have no other home, and by fighting for it I can make America better."[14]

Black Women in the Military
Sixty-five hundred Black women volunteered for the Women's Army Corps (WAC). Although they faced humiliating discrimination, they wore the uniform and served their country with pride. Here, the first African American WACs officer, Captain Charity Adams, leads her company at the Fort Des Moines Training Center in Iowa. **What contributions to the military did Black women make during World War II, and what obstacles did they face?** *National Archives and Records Administration, Still Pictures Record Section, NARA-531334/111-SC-238651.*

ACTIVITY ▸ **Revisit Your Prediction**

In the AP® Unit Warmup (p. U4-E), you made a prediction about this image. **What does this photograph suggest about African Americans' participation in the war effort? Support or revise your original prediction using evidence from this chapter.**

For men like Smith, conditions got worse before they got better. Not until early 1944 did the navy change its employment policy and consider individual performance rather than race in recruitment, assignments, and promotions. By the end of the war, of the nearly 168,000 Black men employed in the navy, 90 percent were still messmen, and only a handful had been assigned crew positions. The U.S. Marine Corps accepted no Blacks until August 1942, when it set up a separate training facility for them in North Carolina.

Black women fared no better in the military. Sixty-five hundred Black women volunteered for the Women's Army Corps (WAC), but most found themselves doing service work that required none of the skills for which they had been trained. At Fort Breckinridge, Kentucky, white WACs did clerical and technical work, while Blacks swept warehouse floors, served food, or endured the heat and humidity of the laundry. Of the 50,000 women who served as nurses in the wartime army, only about 500 were Black. At first, army policy was to have Black nurses care only for Black soldiers. But since few Blacks saw combat and the need for nurses escalated precipitously as the war wore on, the army revised this policy in 1944.

AP® skills

Applying Disciplinary Knowledge: Describe the types of discrimination African American women endured in the armed services during the war. How did their gender and race impact their experience during the war?

As for the navy, the Roosevelt administration banned Black women from its volunteer female unit, Women Accepted for Volunteer Emergency Service (WAVES), until Republican presidential candidate Thomas Dewey made the ban a campaign issue in 1944. Still, the administration's policies were so distasteful to Black women that few volunteered, and at war's end, the navy had just two Black female officers and seventy-two Black enlisted women. Of the almost eleven thousand navy nurses, only four were Black.[15]

Black women who volunteered for the United Service Organizations (USO) met with similar discrimination. When the USO was founded in 1941 to provide wholesome recreation for soldiers in their off-duty hours, no thought was given to the needs of Black soldiers or to the community of women who wanted to boost their morale. African American women often had to create separate USOs because Blacks were prohibited from entering white facilities.

In addition to the official policies limiting their opportunities, black soldiers were subjected to an endless array of insults and indignities. At Fort Bragg, North Carolina, Black troops could not board white buses; they had to wait for the infrequent buses marked "Colored Troops." White civilian bus drivers would often not transport them, and train agents would not sell them tickets. Black soldiers on leave sometimes had to wait for days to reach their destinations, and while waiting, they could not eat at the station restaurants or use facilities that even German prisoners of war could use.[16] When Black soldiers left base, local whites often shouted racial slurs and epithets at them. In conflicts involving white civilians, Black troops were usually presumed to be at fault and in many cases were jailed, court-martialed, or dishonorably discharged.[17]

The racism Black soldiers experienced extended beyond verbal abuse and segregation. Although racial violence was by no means restricted to the South, southern towns and police officers were the most belligerent toward Black soldiers. Countless acts of violence occurred. In March 1941, the body of Private Felix Hall of Montgomery, Alabama, was found hanging from a tree at Fort Benning, Georgia. The War Department would not rule out suicide, even though Hall's hands and feet were bound.[18] In 1942, a white bus driver killed a Black soldier in Mobile, Alabama; a white policeman clubbed and shot a Black soldier in Beaumont, Texas; and a Black army nurse in Montgomery was brutally beaten and jailed for defying the Jim Crow seating arrangements on a bus. In 1943, a white policeman in Little Rock, Arkansas, killed a Black sergeant, and the white sheriff of Centreville, Mississippi, shot a Black soldier

AP® skills

Applying Disciplinary Knowledge: What racial violence did African American soldiers endure while deployed in southern towns?

at point-blank range. The sheriff was heard to ask a white military policeman after the shooting, "Any more n*****s you want killed?"[19] According to the Black writer and activist James Baldwin, northern Black families experienced "a peculiar kind of relief when they knew that their boys were being shipped out of the south, to do battle overseas. It was, perhaps, like feeling that the most dangerous part of a dangerous journey had been passed and that now, even if death should come, it would come with honor and without the complicity of their countrymen."[20]

AP® skills

Applying Disciplinary Knowledge: How did the War Department handle the racial violence against Black soldiers in the armed services? How effective was that response?

When provoked by racism, Black soldiers either bolted the army or fought back. In Alexandria, Louisiana, the attempted arrest of a drunken Black soldier led to a race riot that resulted in the shooting of twenty-eight Blacks and the arrest of nearly three thousand. In Fort Devens, Massachusetts, fifty-four Black WACs staged a strike in protest of their consistent assignment to maid-type work, work that white WACs were usually exempted from. In Prescott, Arizona, forty-three Black soldiers went absent without leave (AWOL) to escape being terrorized by whites, and at Camp Rousseau, in Port Hueneme, California, Blacks staged a hunger strike to protest the discrimination they faced. To counter Black resistance, the governor of Mississippi asked the War Department to move Black regiments out of his state and requested that the army remove the firing pins from Black soldiers' rifles. Even the War Department was forced to admit it had a problem. In 1942, at the end of a particularly violent summer, it issued a memorandum instructing white officers to treat Blacks with care and diplomacy.[21]

The War Department's ineffectiveness in addressing racial violence and discrimination was just one factor in William Hastie's decision to resign his post as adviser on Negro affairs to Secretary of War Henry Stimson in January 1943. Hastie was disgusted with the overall treatment of Blacks in the military, including the refusal of the Army Air Corps to deploy the Ninety-Ninth Pursuit Squadron, the first all-Black flying unit trained at Tuskegee Army Air Field, and the employment of other Black aviators as trash collectors and groundskeepers.[22] (See AP® Working with Sources: African Americans and the Tuskegee Experiments, pp. 534–43.) He condemned Stimson's well-publicized comments on Black inferiority and the War Department's adoption of what he called "the traditional mores of the South." At his resignation press conference, he said, "It is difficult to see how a Negro in this position, with all his superiors maintaining or inaugurating racial segregation, can accomplish anything of value."[23]

A year later, it came as no surprise when, after two years of combat training, Black regiments of the Second Cavalry Division — who had been shipped to North Africa because of an urgent need for combat troops — were instead assigned to jobs unloading ships, repairing roads, and driving trucks. One Black soldier reasoned that Black soldiers were denied the right to fight so that "after the war is over demands couldn't be so great." Whites would be able to say, "Didn't his white brother (?) die on the front line, while he was comparatively safe in the rear echelon?"[24] Indeed, when the military's segregation policy was under review after the war, South Carolina senator Burnet R. Maybank invoked that argument. "The wars of this country have been won by white soldiers," he said. "Negro soldiers have rendered their greatest service as cooks, drivers, maintenance men, mechanics and such positions for which they are well qualified."[25]

Black soldiers, however, saw their service to their country as the beginning of the end of segregation. One discharged army corporal said, "I spent four years in the army to free a bunch of Dutchmen and Frenchmen, and I'm hanged if I'm going to let the Alabama version of the Germans kick me around when I get home. No sirree-bob! I went into the Army a nigger; I'm comin' out a man."[26]

Despite all that they endured, more than 2.5 million African Americans served in the military during World War II. From the beginning, they knew theirs was a double fight: their fight for freedom would be for both their nation and their race. They faced not only the weapons of the Germans, Italians, and Japanese, but also the belligerence of their own compatriots. Still they fought, confident that American racism would sooner or later give way.

African Americans on the Home Front

How were African Americans involved in the home front effort during the Second World War?

World War II brought the decade-long Great Depression to a halt. As factories retooled in preparation for war, millions of unemployed Americans returned to work, and many who had been fortunate enough to be employed during the Depression found new work that was more fulfilling, more interesting, and better paying. For African Americans who had been bound to agricultural labor and service work, the war opened up new employment opportunities. Generally shut out of jobs in the South, they migrated to the North, Midwest, and West Coast for work. Like Evelyn Bates, they met resistance at every turn. For those who worked in the war industries making munitions; building aircraft, boats, and armored vehicles; sewing uniforms; and meeting the various needs of a nation at war, the Double Victory meant not only producing the goods that allowed America to triumph overseas, but also fighting for economic rights at home.[27]

New Jobs and Wartime Migration

During the 1940s, more than 1.5 million African Americans migrated out of the South. Another million moved from rural to urban areas within the South, transforming a predominantly rural people into an urban population almost overnight (Map 13.1). Those who moved did so because of limited work opportunities. Blacks throughout the South were relegated to low-wage agricultural and forestry work. Ultimately, whether it was in the shipyards of Mobile, Alabama, the aircraft plants of Oakland, California, or the automobile factories of Detroit, Blacks had to fight for the chance to work — especially at high-paying skilled jobs.[28]

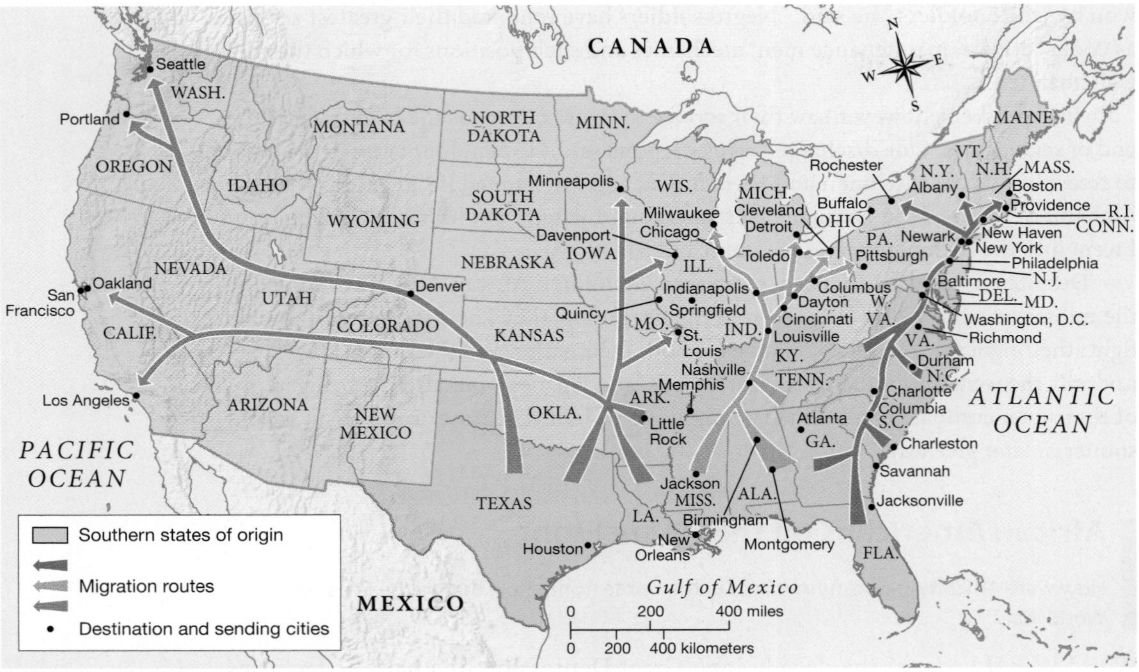

MAP 13.1 African American Migration, 1930–1970

During World War II, African Americans continued their mass migration from the South to the North, Midwest, and West Coast. Some stayed in the South but moved from rural to urban areas. This trend continued in the decades following the war, transplanting more than five million Blacks over the course of thirty years and turning African Americans into a predominantly urban population. The wartime migration prompted an increase in racial tensions in the North and West, areas usually perceived to be racially tolerant. **What changes in migration routes are apparent since the first wave of the Great Migration (see Map 11.1)?**

AP® exam tip

Be prepared to describe the enduring forms of segregation and discrimination in daily life that African Americans faced during the war.

With few exceptions, southern governors and white laborers worked together to maintain a segregated labor force that kept Blacks as a continual source of cheap labor. Despite the country's war needs, most whites resisted federal encroachment that threatened to topple this labor hierarchy. Nothing demonstrated this fact better than the antimigration and "work or jail" laws passed by several states. Texas legislator Rogers Kelly, for example, drafted a state law prohibiting recruiting agents from talking to Black laborers about moving north to Michigan for work. In 1942, to ensure the sugarcane harvest, New Orleans ordered police to arrest vagrants. These included Blacks looking for meaningful employment outside agricultural work, who were compelled to either work in the fields or go to jail. Similarly, in 1943, sheriffs in Macon, Georgia, rounded up Black women and men and forced them to do farm and domestic work. If they objected, they were arrested as vagrants and jailed. A *Louisiana Weekly* editorial titled "Slavery 1942" described these laws as an attempt to "maintain control of the vast Southern reservoir of cheap labor." Southerners, the editorial charged, "don't want to lose their Black labor."[29]

But the South did lose much of its cheap Black labor. In 1940, 77 percent of the total U.S. Black population lived in the South, with more than 49 percent in rural areas; two out of five Blacks worked as farmers, sharecroppers, or farm laborers. By 1950, only 68 percent of the total Black population remained in the South, a percentage that continued to drop through 1970. In what some have called a jobs movement, at least a million Black workers entered the industrial labor force during World War II, swelling their numbers from a meager 3 percent of defense workers in 1942 to 8.3 percent in 1944. Twenty-five percent of these laborers worked in foundries, and 12 percent worked in shipbuilding and steel mills. In 1943, 55,000 of the 450,000 members of the Detroit United Auto Workers were Black.[30]

Some of those who left the South had been trained by New Deal and war agencies. In 1942, for example, the War Manpower Commission (the federal agency that balanced labor needs across industries) began placing graduates from Xavier University of Louisiana's welding program in shipyards outside Louisiana. Before the war, local Black activist Paul Dixon demanded that Blacks be given a chance at nonagricultural work, but his pleas fell on deaf ears. Shortly after the war began, however, the U.S. Employment Service used Dixon's referrals to supply skilled workers to plants outside the South. Southerners' worst fears were realized when war needs forced government agencies to team with Black activist organizations to fill skilled jobs throughout the nation. From the Florida War Training Center in Jacksonville, Black workers were placed in shipyards and airports in places such as Chester, Pennsylvania, and Bridgeport, Connecticut. By May 1944, the Houston Works Progress Administration had trained close to eight hundred Black shipyard workers. Only a few found work in the South; the rest migrated to the West Coast.[31]

AP® skills

Applying Disciplinary Knowledge: Describe how African American civilians were impacted by the war. How does this impact compare to that of World War I?

The main route out of the South led due north to Chicago, Detroit, and other midwestern cities, but World War II also opened new routes west, giving the region its first significant Black population outside Los Angeles. Western migrants hailed mostly from Texas, Louisiana, and Arkansas, but East Coast southerners also found their way west. As the sociologist Charles S. Johnson explained, "To the romantic appeal of the west, has been added the real and actual opportunity for gainful employment, setting in motion a war-time migration of huge proportions."[32] In fact, during the 1940s, the West Coast's Black population grew by 443,000 (33 percent). Most migrants settled in five major metropolitan areas: Seattle-Tacoma and Portland-Vancouver in the Pacific Northwest, and the San Francisco Bay area, the Los Angeles–Long Beach area, and San Diego in California. Initially, representatives of the shipbuilding and aircraft industries recruited these workers, but African Americans soon made their way west on their own. The region's mild climate, greater freedom, and high wages promised a future that could not be realized in the South.[33]

Both skilled and unskilled workers left the South for better lives elsewhere. In what was quickly becoming a civil rights issue, Black Americans protested "work or jail" orders and exercised their right to move. They tapped into what became known as the "underground railroad," a network of Black activists, union representatives, and

Black Women in War Industries
The war gave African American women the opportunity to trade domestic work for higher-paying, more interesting jobs. Among the growing West Coast Black population was Ann Bland, pictured here, who worked as a burner (a worker who cut metal with a torch) on the second U.S. navy ship named for an African American, the SS *George Washington Carver*. She was among the six thousand African Americans employed at the Kaiser Shipyards in Richmond, California. **What does this photograph reveal about how the war impacted employment opportunities for Black women?** *Schomburg Center, NYPL/Art Resource, NY.*

northern and western recruiting agents who helped place black farmworkers in industries. For example, with the help of the United Cannery, Agricultural, Packing, and Allied Workers of America, Campbell's soup plants in New Jersey arranged contracts for, and paid the transportation of, farmworkers from Florida, Arkansas, and Tennessee.[34]

Women were among the first to leave the South. Of the 1 million or so Blacks who entered defense employment during the war years, 60 percent were women. For them, factory work meant an escape from domestic work in white homes, where the pay was low and the threat of sexual assault ever present. Factory worker Lyn Childs asked, "Do you think that if you did domestic work all of your life, where you'd clean somebody's toilets and did all the cooking for some lazy characters who were sitting on top, and you finally got a chance where you can get a dignified job, you wouldn't fly through the door?"[35] Fanny Christina Hill felt the same way. The 60 cents an hour she made during her training at North American Aviation was more than she had ever made doing domestic work. As her salary increased, she gained economic security and bought a home, something she said she would never have been able to do had the war not transformed her circumstances. Quoting her sister, she reflected, "Hitler was the one that got us out of the white folks' kitchen."[36]

zoot suit riots
World War II riots in Los Angeles that pitted white sailors and civilians against African American as well as Hispanic and Latino men. So called because of the Blacks' and Latinos' broad felt hats, pegged trousers, and gold chains, which were popularly referred to as zoot suits.

Race Riots during the War Years

During the war, as a result of the new competition for jobs and tensions over migration, riots erupted in cities large and small. Several cities were racked by violence that pitted white sailors and civilians against African Americans and Latinos. In Los Angeles, the conflict was called the **zoot suit riots**, after the "zoot suits" — broad felt hats, pegged trousers, and gold chains — worn by Black and Latino men there.

San Diego, Long Beach, Chicago, Detroit, and Philadelphia also saw conflict. In 1943, a particularly volatile year, there were 242 racial battles in 47 cities.[37]

One of the worst riots started on June 16 in Beaumont, Texas, when between two thousand and three thousand white workers, mostly from the Pennsylvania Shipyards there, beat and robbed Black pedestrians, overturned cars, and burned Black homes. While the immediate cause was a rumor that a Black man had raped a white woman, the underlying cause was tensions sparked by the migration of more than thirty thousand whites and Blacks who competed for the limited available housing and recreational space in Beaumont.[38]

AP® skills

Applying Disciplinary Knowledge: Identify the common causes for the race riots that occurred during World War II.

Detroit presented a similar situation. White workers held massive strikes to prevent the promotion of Black workers and resisted allowing Black housing in white neighborhoods. They excluded Black residents from two new federal housing projects, one of which was named for the Black abolitionist and feminist Sojourner Truth. Tempers flared in the summer of 1943 when a fight broke out between a white man and a Black man on the Belle Isle Bridge. Fighting spread as rumors circulated among Blacks that whites had killed a Black woman and her baby and among whites that a Black man had raped and killed a white woman. It took 6,000 federal troops to restore peace after three days of rioting that led to 34 deaths, 675 injuries, 1,900 arrests, and $2 million in property damage. Although white storeowners suffered property damage, of the 34 people who died, 25 were African American. Most of those who were injured and/or arrested also were Black. Not long afterward, a riot erupted in Harlem after police shot a Black soldier. The result was 6 deaths, 500 injuries, hundreds of arrests, and property damage totaling $5 million.

Thus, as the war created opportunities for African Americans, it also spawned racial conflict. The nation needed workers to build weapons, tanks, boats, and airplanes. It needed to feed and clothe its more than 16 million troops. African Americans took advantage of these opportunities, picking up and leaving the South despite the best efforts of legislators, governors, and the police to stop them. Although African Americans welcomed the chance to serve their country on the home front, not all Americans were welcoming toward them.

Organizing for Economic Opportunity

AP® skills

Applying Disciplinary Knowledge: How were African Americans able to push for more rights and economic opportunities during World War II?

Getting a job was one thing. Being treated fairly, paid equitably, and given room to advance was another. African Americans had to organize in order to gain the economic rights that white Americans often took for granted. As Fanny Christina Hill discovered, getting a job was just the beginning of an uphill struggle. Although Hill worked in California, her experiences were similar to those of Evelyn Bates, who stayed in the South. Hill trained with white workers, but once she arrived on the factory floor, she, like Bates, was relegated to physically grueling assignments and denied the opportunity to perform skilled labor based on misconceptions about Black women's abilities. As she recalled, "All the Negroes went to Department 17 because there was nothing but shooting and bucking rivets. You stood on one side of the panel and your partner stood on this side, and he would shoot the rivets with a gun and you'd buck them with the bar."[39] She found that "white girls . . . went to better departments where the work was not as strenuous." Hill remembered that in some departments at North American Aviation, "they didn't even allow a black person to walk through there let alone work in there."[40]

AP® skills

Applying Disciplinary Knowledge: How did the conditions that contributed to the increase in race riots during World War II compare with the conditions that led to the race riots during the Red Summer after World War I?

Across America, conflict and violence erupted as white workers sought to maintain their privileged work status. Herbert Ward recalled that at the Lockheed-Vega aircraft factory in Burbank, California, white men made racial slurs in the restrooms "to scare you if possible, or to embarrass you to such an extent that you wouldn't want to stay." He said that fights were not uncommon.[41] In Mobile, Alabama, federal troops had to quell the rioting of 20,000 white men who took to the streets in 1943 to protest the promotion of Black welders at the Alabama Dry Dock and Shipbuilding Company.[42] When one Black man, John Gutter — a graduate of Xavier University of Louisiana's welding program — was promoted at the Todd-Johnson Dry Docks in New Orleans, more than three thousand white workers walked off the job.

In the industrial powerhouse of Detroit, tensions between Black and white workers were palpable. In September 1941, 250 whites staged a sit-down strike at the Packard Motor Car Company to protest the promotion of two Blacks from polishing work to assembly work. In May 1942, twenty thousand white workers at Packard walked off the job and stopped production for almost a week to protest the promotion of three Blacks. Shortly after that, 350 white workers shut down the Dodge plant after twenty-three African Americans were promoted from unskilled to skilled jobs. When two Blacks were promoted from janitorial work to machine operation at the Hudson Naval Ordnance Plant, white workers staged a work stoppage, and the Black workers were demoted. An Office of War Information investigation found that white workers resented the economic gains being made by Blacks and felt that "the Negro must be kept in his place."[43]

But African Americans had other ideas. During the 1941 March on Washington negotiations with President Roosevelt, A. Philip Randolph was explicit in his requests that Blacks be considered for jobs in defense industries. "Our people," he said, "are being turned away at factory gates because they are colored."[44] Although Roosevelt's Executive Order 8802 established the FEPC to investigate complaints of discrimination and address grievances, Roosevelt crippled the agency from the start by providing no enforcement apparatus, a very limited budget, and some leaders who were less than sympathetic to African American complaints. A 1943 editorial titled "Open Letter to the President" in the NAACP's journal, *The Crisis,* noted what African Americans knew all too well: "Executive Order 8802 is being defied and sabotaged by management and labor alike."[45]

The ineffectiveness of the FEPC was a setback for African American workers but not a fatal blow. Throughout the war, Blacks turned to unions, especially the new unions of the Congress of Industrial Organizations (CIO; founded in 1935 as the Committee for Industrial Organization), for support. Because CIO unions were organized by industry, they tended to be more inclusive than the American Federation of Labor unions that organized workers on the basis of skill. The National Maritime Union; International Longshore and Warehouse Union; United Cannery, Agricultural, Packing, and Allied Workers of America; and United Packinghouse Workers of America were generally helpful in finding work for Blacks, moving them between cities, and fighting for better positions for them. Often union representatives worked in coordination with regional FEPC offices, African American organizations, and government agencies to advance economic equality.

Nevertheless, regional customs, politics, and the ideological leanings of union leadership determined how helpful a union would or could be. Depending on the region, for example, the United Automobile Workers (UAW) could be a help or a hindrance to Black workers. On one hand, despite the white "hate strikes" at the Packard Motor Car Company in 1942, union officials continued to support Black upgrades. The predominantly African American UAW Local 600 in Detroit allied with the Detroit NAACP and put civil rights at the top of its agenda.[46] On the other hand, Blacks at North American Aviation in Dallas were reluctant to take their grievances to the union. According to the union representative, "Here in Texas there shall be no social equality. . . . No one is going to tell us that we will have to accept our Negroes as equals."[47] This feeling prevailed in most UAW locals in the South and Southwest.

Blacks confronted similar union policies on the West Coast, where a huge obstacle to fair employment was the International Brotherhood of Boilermakers (IBB), the umbrella union that organized shipyard workers. Before 1937, the IBB had excluded Black workers from its unions. When it changed this policy, it created all-Black "auxiliary" unions denying Blacks full insurance rights, employment opportunities, seniority protection, and equal participation in labor guarantees and privileges. In 1943, African Americans protested these Jim Crow unions. In response, the IBB forced shipyard employers to fire Black workers. Hundreds were fired in California and Oregon, including Joseph James, president of the San Francisco chapter of the NAACP. With the support of the CIO and the NAACP, James initiated a lawsuit against the Marinship shipyards in Sausalito, California. In 1944, the California Supreme Court ruled in his favor and ordered the IBB to dismantle its auxiliary structure.[48]

Throughout the country, Black organizations such as the NAACP and the National Urban League worked unceasingly — not just for civil rights but also for economic justice. NAACP branches organized protests against discrimination in defense plants nationwide. In the South, the Urban League pushed for African American training, teaming up wherever possible with the War Manpower Commission, local FEPC offices, and the U.S. Employment Service to place skilled and unskilled Black workers in industrial jobs. Progress was always relative. In some places, especially in the South, negotiations ended with Black workers accepting equal pay but segregated employment. In other places, negotiated settlements resulted in integrated unions fighting for across-the-board improvements for Black and white workers alike.

AP® skills

Applying Disciplinary Knowledge: Identify the methods and strategies African Americans used to obtain more rights and economic opportunities during the war. To what extent were their methods a continuation of or a break from past methods?

To further their efforts, African Americans increasingly joined unions and other types of organizations in the 1940s. Those who could took the Urban League's advice to "get into somebody's union and stay there."[49] By 1943, some 400,000 Black workers had joined CIO unions and, as members, gained access to collective bargaining, seniority rights, grievance systems to appeal violations of their rights, and national representation. Many of them also joined the NAACP. From 355 branches and a membership of about 55,000 in 1940, the NAACP grew to 1,073 branches and more than 450,000 members in 1946.[50] As its membership increased, its infrastructure grew more sophisticated. With new local branches linked to statewide networks, the NAACP could mount political campaigns and stage local protests. In 1942, a new organization, the Congress of Racial Equality (CORE), was founded for the purpose of mounting civil disobedience or direct-action campaigns to end segregation. CORE staged the first sit-down strikes to end segregation in northern restaurants and other public and private places.

The Black press emerged as one of the most important institutions in the Black urban community. Newspapers increased their circulation by 40 percent, becoming the main channel for expressing Black protest and building community. Called **soldiers without swords** for their role on the frontlines of the Double V campaign, Black journalists facilitated the flow of information relevant to African Americans. For example, the *Pittsburgh Courier* provided a detailed analysis of Nazism and racism by comparing Germany and Georgia. Foreign correspondents for the *Pittsburgh Courier, Baltimore Afro-American, Chicago Defender,* and *Norfolk (Virginia) Journal and Guide* covered the deployment and treatment of Black troops. The National Newspaper Publishers Association and the Associated Negro Press reported on issues ranging from Blacks in the military to employment at home. As African Americans in one part of the country learned about and were inspired by those in another part, solidarity grew.[51] Being Black extended beyond one's racial identity; Black people thought of themselves as a nation within a nation. During the war years, Blacks became what the poet LeRoi Jones (later Amiri Baraka) would refer to as "a country."

soldiers without swords The name given to African American journalists because of their relentless reporting of the injustices Blacks suffered during World War II.

The Struggle for Citizenship Rights

To what extent did African American veterans have access to the benefits of the GI Bill? What were the enduring forms of segregation and discrimination in daily life that African Americans faced in the first half of the twentieth century?

The more African Americans thought of themselves as a nation within a nation, the more they considered themselves worthy of the consideration and respect invoked by the Atlantic Charter that the Allies signed in January 1942. This document pledged the Allies to "respect the right of all peoples to choose the form of government under which they will live." It stated that Allied nations had to work for "improved labour standards, economic advancement, and social security," as well as to see "sovereign rights and self-government restored to those who have been forcibly deprived of them." These principles sparked revolutions in Africa and Asia, as colonial subjects asserted their right to be independent of colonial rulers.

As a people who had consistently been "forcibly deprived" of their constitutional rights, African Americans also used the war as an opportunity to assert their right to self-determination and liberty. This meant not only the right to fight for their country and to work without discrimination, but also fundamental citizenship rights such as rights to vote, hold office, and serve on juries. In addition, it meant the right to participate in the social and cultural life of America as free and equal human beings.

Fighting and Dying for the Right to Vote

Unlike the millions of African Americans who gained the right to vote when they moved north or west, those who stayed in the South remained under the political and economic domination of southern whites, who used legal tactics such as the white primary, literacy tests, poll taxes, grandfather clauses, and outright terror to keep Blacks disfranchised. But southern Blacks understood the importance of electoral politics and knew that fighting for the right to vote meant challenging a regional culture built on Black dependence and subordination. The international crisis provided the philosophical and ideological foundation for an all-out fight for the franchise. Begun during World War II, it was a fight that would continue long after that conflict ended.

Southern whites and Blacks thought differently about the Black vote. One southern white cotton gin owner told a *New York Times* reporter, "The n*****s would take over the county if they could vote in full numbers. They'd stick together and vote blacks into every office in the county. Why you'd have a n***** judge, n***** sheriff, a n***** tax assessor — think what the black SOB's would do to you."[52] Mississippi senator Theodore Bilbo openly invited white registrars to illegally prevent Blacks from voting: "You know and I know what's the best way to keep the n***** from voting. You do it the night before the election. I don't have to tell you any more than that. Red-blooded men know what I mean."[53] African Americans believed that the vote would allow them to oust the anti-union and anti-Black officials who dominated southern politics and would help them secure economic rights. "Politics IS food, clothes, and housing," preached some Black activists.[54]

AP® skills

Applying Disciplinary Knowledge: Why was the right to vote a powerful tool for securing essential rights during World War II?

Just as nations such as Britain and France were slow to realize that the days when they could subjugate the people of India, Africa, and Southeast Asia were coming to a close, southern whites were slow to understand African Americans' determination to gain the vote. Blacks were better organized than before the war and had gained many white allies, including some CIO union leaders and Washington insiders, such as the president's influential wife, Eleanor Roosevelt. The First Lady supported efforts to eliminate voting barriers and rid the nation of the poll tax, which unfairly kept Blacks and poor whites from voting. Many others agreed, such as Florida senator Claude Pepper, who thought it was time for the "wave of democracy" to touch

America's shores. Likewise, Senate Majority Leader Alben Barkley of Kentucky said that he could think of "no more opportune time to try to spread democracy in our country than at a time when we are trying to spread it in other countries and throughout the world."[55]

AP® skills

Applying Disciplinary Knowledge: What was the outcome of the *Smith v. Allwright* case (1944)? How did it impact African Americans' ability to push for voting rights immediately after the war?

Spreading democracy in the United States turned out to be a long, drawn-out fight, especially in the South. But with unions, white liberals, and a newly invigorated NAACP on their side, African Americans made a lot of headway during the war, especially after *Smith v. Allwright* (1944), in which the U.S. Supreme Court declared the all-white Texas Democratic primary illegal. That case, said the Black activist Luther Porter Jackson, "was the beginning of a complete revolution in our thinking on the right of suffrage."[56] Two weeks after the ruling, thirty-six Black delegates representing every southern state met to establish the National Progressive Voters League, which aimed to help southern Blacks register and vote and to coordinate the efforts of Black voters throughout the United States. Just in time for the 1944 election, the ruling reinvigorated the CIO's Political Action Committee, which helped Blacks pay their poll taxes and sent Black and white fieldworkers into Black areas to get out the vote. Activists in South Carolina organized the Progressive Democratic Party and sent a slate of delegates to the 1944 Democratic National Convention. By the end of 1944, the Progressive Democratic Party had 45,000 members.

Progressive Democratic Party leaders knew that their delegates would not be seated at the convention, but they wanted to bring attention to increasingly unacceptable contradictions in American society. One was the fact that Blacks were fighting for democracy abroad yet could not participate fully in democracy at home. Another was that the Democratic Party, political home of liberal Americans and President Roosevelt, also comprised the most rabid segregationists in the nation. From the Black perspective, this unholy alliance, which had persisted since the end of Reconstruction, had to go. But southern whites were of the same mind as South Carolina senator Burnet Maybank, who said, "As a Southern Democrat, I do not propose to be run out of my Party by . . . the Negroes . . . it will be my purpose to see that our Party stands where it always has — [for] states rights and white supremacy."[57]

In small towns and on city streets, Blacks and their white allies met resistance from a revived Ku Klux Klan and other white terrorist organizations. In 1940–1941, there were thirteen reported lynchings in the South. Some were political in nature. For instance, Elbert Williams, the founder of the Brownsville, Tennessee, chapter of the NAACP, was murdered shortly after he launched a voter registration campaign in 1940.

Soldiers especially were targeted. Having acquired a level of self-esteem that made accepting second-class citizenship intolerable, they were among the first to register to vote when they returned home from the war. Segregationists feared their assertiveness, and the Ku Klux Klan thought they were "getting out of their place." In 1946, shortly after he returned from the war to Wrightsville, Georgia, veteran Isaac Newton was shot dead when he went to register to vote. In February 1946, a race

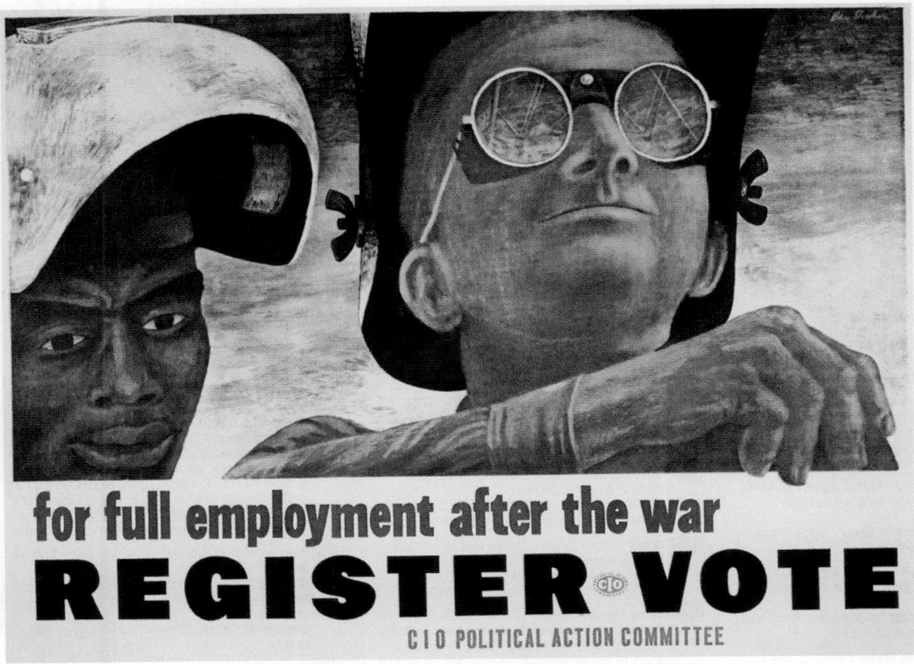

for full employment after the war
REGISTER VOTE
CIO
CIO POLITICAL ACTION COMMITTEE

Voter Registration Poster
Most African Americans did not separate civil rights from economic justice. They believed that the right to vote and the right to earn a fair wage were rights they were entitled to as U.S. citizens. Not all CIO unions worked with Blacks to achieve equality on both fronts, but many did. This 1944 CIO Political Action Committee poster is an example of CIO efforts to help Blacks achieve full economic and political rights. **To what degree was the fight for political rights and the fight for economic rights one and the same for African Americans during World War II?**
Granger/Granger — All rights reserved.

riot in Columbia, Tennessee, pitted Black veterans and their community against the police and the National Guard. When the dust settled, two Black men were dead, four white policemen were wounded, and more than one hundred Blacks had been arrested. The two months following the 1946 southern primary elections saw nine lynchings. Veteran Macio Snipes, the only Black person from his district to vote in the Georgia primary, was shot the next day while sitting on his porch. A week later, a white mob killed two Black veterans and their wives in Monroe, Georgia (Map 13.2).

Segregationists killed African Americans who sought the vote, but they could not kill African Americans' determination to vote. Many more would die before Congress finally passed voting rights legislation. However, as law-abiding, taxpaying citizens of the United States, Black people understood the folly of fighting and dying abroad so that others could enjoy rights that they could not enjoy at home.

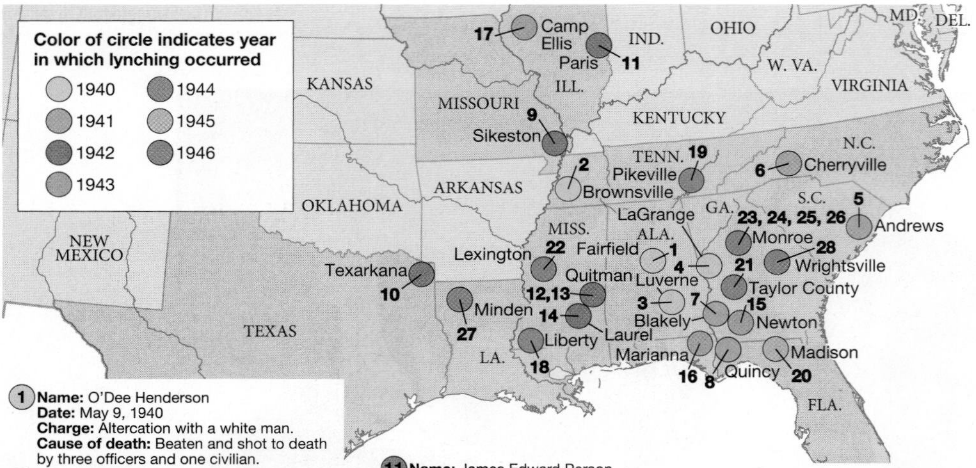

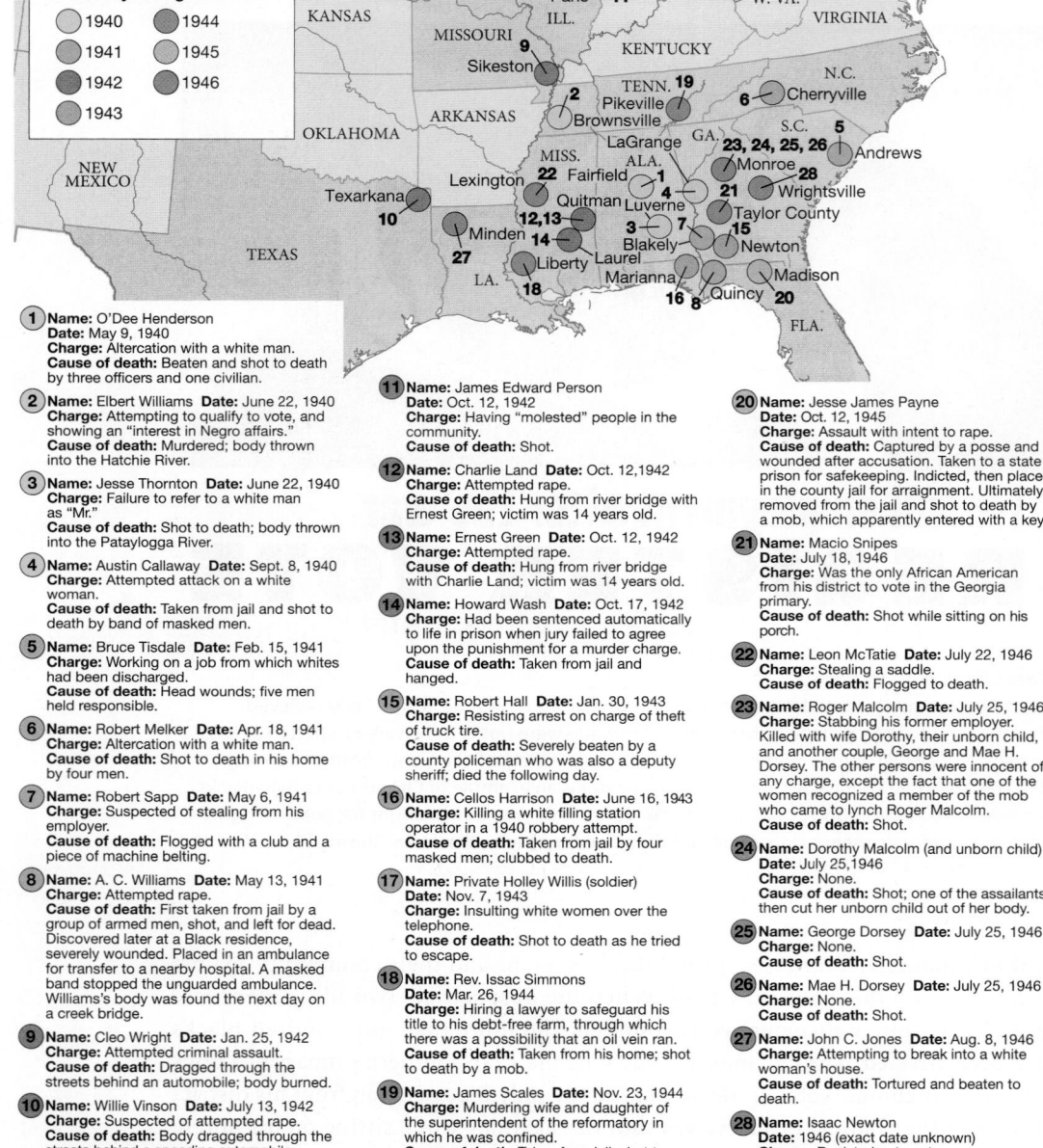

1 **Name:** O'Dee Henderson
Date: May 9, 1940
Charge: Altercation with a white man.
Cause of death: Beaten and shot to death by three officers and one civilian.

2 **Name:** Elbert Williams **Date:** June 22, 1940
Charge: Attempting to qualify to vote, and showing an "interest in Negro affairs."
Cause of death: Murdered; body thrown into the Hatchie River.

3 **Name:** Jesse Thornton **Date:** June 22, 1940
Charge: Failure to refer to a white man as "Mr."
Cause of death: Shot to death; body thrown into the Pataylogga River.

4 **Name:** Austin Callaway **Date:** Sept. 8, 1940
Charge: Attempted attack on a white woman.
Cause of death: Taken from jail and shot to death by band of masked men.

5 **Name:** Bruce Tisdale **Date:** Feb. 15, 1941
Charge: Working on a job from which whites had been discharged.
Cause of death: Head wounds; five men held responsible.

6 **Name:** Robert Melker **Date:** Apr. 18, 1941
Charge: Altercation with a white man.
Cause of death: Shot to death in his home by four men.

7 **Name:** Robert Sapp **Date:** May 6, 1941
Charge: Suspected of stealing from his employer.
Cause of death: Flogged with a club and a piece of machine belting.

8 **Name:** A. C. Williams **Date:** May 13, 1941
Charge: Attempted rape.
Cause of death: First taken from jail by a group of armed men, shot, and left for dead. Discovered later at a Black residence, severely wounded. Placed in an ambulance for transfer to a nearby hospital. A masked band stopped the unguarded ambulance. Williams's body was found the next day on a creek bridge.

9 **Name:** Cleo Wright **Date:** Jan. 25, 1942
Charge: Attempted criminal assault.
Cause of death: Dragged through the streets behind an automobile; body burned.

10 **Name:** Willie Vinson **Date:** July 13, 1942
Charge: Suspected of attempted rape.
Cause of death: Body dragged through the streets behind a speeding automobile; hanged from a cotton gin winch.

11 **Name:** James Edward Person
Date: Oct. 12, 1942
Charge: Having "molested" people in the community.
Cause of death: Shot.

12 **Name:** Charlie Land **Date:** Oct. 12,1942
Charge: Attempted rape.
Cause of death: Hung from river bridge with Ernest Green; victim was 14 years old.

13 **Name:** Ernest Green **Date:** Oct. 12, 1942
Charge: Attempted rape.
Cause of death: Hung from river bridge with Charlie Land; victim was 14 years old.

14 **Name:** Howard Wash **Date:** Oct. 17, 1942
Charge: Had been sentenced automatically to life in prison when jury failed to agree upon the punishment for a murder charge.
Cause of death: Taken from jail and hanged.

15 **Name:** Robert Hall **Date:** Jan. 30, 1943
Charge: Resisting arrest on charge of theft of truck tire.
Cause of death: Severely beaten by a county policeman who was also a deputy sheriff; died the following day.

16 **Name:** Cellos Harrison **Date:** June 16, 1943
Charge: Killing a white filling station operator in a 1940 robbery attempt.
Cause of death: Taken from jail by four masked men; clubbed to death.

17 **Name:** Private Holley Willis (soldier)
Date: Nov. 7, 1943
Charge: Insulting white women over the telephone.
Cause of death: Shot to death as he tried to escape.

18 **Name:** Rev. Issac Simmons
Date: Mar. 26, 1944
Charge: Hiring a lawyer to safeguard his title to his debt-free farm, through which there was a possibility that an oil vein ran.
Cause of death: Taken from his home; shot to death by a mob.

19 **Name:** James Scales **Date:** Nov. 23, 1944
Charge: Murdering wife and daughter of the superintendent of the reformatory in which he was confined.
Cause of death: Taken from jail; shot to death by a mob.

20 **Name:** Jesse James Payne
Date: Oct. 12, 1945
Charge: Assault with intent to rape.
Cause of death: Captured by a posse and wounded after accusation. Taken to a state prison for safekeeping. Indicted, then placed in the county jail for arraignment. Ultimately, removed from the jail and shot to death by a mob, which apparently entered with a key.

21 **Name:** Macio Snipes
Date: July 18, 1946
Charge: Was the only African American from his district to vote in the Georgia primary.
Cause of death: Shot while sitting on his porch.

22 **Name:** Leon McTatie **Date:** July 22, 1946
Charge: Stealing a saddle.
Cause of death: Flogged to death.

23 **Name:** Roger Malcolm **Date:** July 25, 1946
Charge: Stabbing his former employer. Killed with wife Dorothy, their unborn child, and another couple, George and Mae H. Dorsey. The other persons were innocent of any charge, except the fact that one of the women recognized a member of the mob who came to lynch Roger Malcolm.
Cause of death: Shot.

24 **Name:** Dorothy Malcolm (and unborn child)
Date: July 25,1946
Charge: None.
Cause of death: Shot; one of the assailants then cut her unborn child out of her body.

25 **Name:** George Dorsey **Date:** July 25, 1946
Charge: None.
Cause of death: Shot.

26 **Name:** Mae H. Dorsey **Date:** July 25, 1946
Charge: None.
Cause of death: Shot.

27 **Name:** John C. Jones **Date:** Aug. 8, 1946
Charge: Attempting to break into a white woman's house.
Cause of death: Tortured and beaten to death.

28 **Name:** Isaac Newton
Date: 1946 (exact date unknown)
Charge: Registering to vote.
Cause of death: Shot.

MAP 13.2 The Persistence of Lynching, 1940–1946

Lynching persisted in the South throughout the war years. Often its victims were African Americans who had fought for their country or asserted other citizenship rights, such as voting. Statistics on lynching are not exact, in part because experts disagree on its definition and in part because many lynchings went unreported or suspected murders were not investigated. In 1947, the President's Committee on Civil Rights proposed a host of ameliorative measures to Congress, including an antilynching law that was not enacted. **What do the charges associated with these lynchings reveal about race relations and the American judicial system? To what extent had that changed since Reconstruction?** DATA SOURCE: "Lynching — Crime," *Negro Year Book: A Review of Events Affecting Negro Life, 1944–1946*, by Jessie P. Guzman and W. Hardin Hughes, National Humanities Center Resource Toolbox, The Making of African American Identity: Volume 3, 1917–1968 (http://nationalhumanitiescenter.org/pds/maai3/segregation/text2/lynchingcrime.pdf).

New Beginnings in Political Life

World War II marked a turning point for African Americans. Those who had migrated and found meaningful and satisfying work, as well as those who had visited foreign countries where they were not demeaned, were unwilling to return to their prewar oppression. A defense worker named Margaret Wright captured the hope of the era when she noted that after the war, "a lot of blacks that were share cropping, doing menial work and stuff, got into the army and saw how other things were and how things could be. They decided they did not want to go back to what they were doing before. They did not want to walk behind a plow, they wouldn't get on the back of the bus anymore."[58] Despite the conflict, violence, and bloodshed, the period was also marked by an exuberance and optimism expressed in Black political, social, and cultural life.

AP® skills

Applying Disciplinary Knowledge: How did participation in the war effort encourage and energize African Americans? What predictions can you make regarding the link between returning African American soldiers and the Civil Rights movement that would take shape in the 1950s and 1960s?

Following the Allied victory in 1945, Blacks rejected second-class citizenship more than they had during the war. The "new consciousness" that Wright noticed was nourished by the courageous examples set by individual African Americans. This was especially evident in the South, where usually acquiescent Blacks turned out in increasing numbers to register and vote despite white terrorism. The number of Blacks who voted tripled to 600,000 between the 1940 election and the 1946 Democratic primaries. When Mississippi's segregationist senator Theodore Bilbo's 1946 campaign was investigated, two hundred Blacks from across the state appeared for the hearings, and sixty-eight Black men and women testified to the tactics the senator had used to keep Blacks from voting.

African Americans also grew more assertive in society. When Irene Morgan refused to give up her seat to a white passenger during a bus ride from Gloucester County, Virginia, to Baltimore, she was arrested, found guilty, and fined. Defiantly, she took her case to NAACP attorneys Thurgood Marshall and William Hastie, who argued it before the U.S. Supreme Court. In ***Morgan v. Virginia*** (1946), the Court declared segregation in interstate bus travel illegal. Blacks could no longer be made to sit in the back of the bus behind whites when crossing state lines. In 1947, eight Blacks and eight whites from CORE tested the case in the first of many nonviolent direct-action campaigns to end segregation. In what they called the Journey of Reconciliation, they rode Greyhound and Trailways buses from Washington, D.C., through Virginia, North Carolina, and Kentucky, with the Blacks sitting in front of the whites. Several of them were arrested, and more than once they were dragged from the bus by angry whites. Although their protest did not end interstate segregation, it did become a model for the Freedom Rides of the 1960s.[59]

Morgan v. Virginia (1946)
A U.S. Supreme Court ruling that declared illegal the practice of making Blacks sit in the back of the bus behind whites in interstate bus travel.

AP® skills

Applying Disciplinary Knowledge: What was the historical significance of *Morgan v. Virginia* (1946)?

African Americans also fought to end segregation in national professional organizations. Mabel Staupers, the executive secretary of the National Association of Colored Graduate Nurses, led a successful letter-writing campaign to end discrimination in the army and navy nursing corps. When both branches accepted Black nurses on an equal basis with whites in January 1945, Staupers continued her crusade for full integration of Black nurses into the profession at large. Her lobbying efforts paid off in 1948, when the American Nurses Association eliminated the color bar and allowed Black nurses to become members.[60]

Social and Cultural Changes

AP® skills

Applying Disciplinary Knowledge: How did athletes use their platforms to help fight Jim Crow?

Perhaps nothing symbolized the hope of the era more than the desegregation of baseball, America's favorite pastime. Until 1945, talented African Americans could play professionally only on Negro league ball clubs. Although future Hall of Famers such as Josh Gibson and Satchel Paige were revered for their skills in Black America, where regional leagues were a major source of entertainment, Black ballplayers wanted a chance to compete with white players and earn similar salaries. In 1945, the Brooklyn Dodgers signed Jackie Robinson, who had played for the Kansas City Monarchs in the Negro American League. After proving himself able to withstand malicious heckling from segregationists, Jim Crow accommodations during spring training, and the ever-present threats on his life, Robinson took the field on opening day in 1947 to the cheers of Black and white Americans who hoped that this was the first step in the desegregation of all sports. Robinson was soon followed by other Black baseball players, most notably Willie Mays of the New York Giants, Ernie Banks of the Chicago Cubs, and Hank Aaron of the Milwaukee Braves.

Other sports desegregated. In tennis, Althea Gibson in 1950 became the first African American to compete in the invitation-only U.S. National Tennis Championship. In 1951, she became the first Black tennis player to play at Wimbledon, the sport's premier tournament. In 1950, the National Basketball Association drafted its first Black player, Charles "Chuck" Cooper. Barriers in football fell, too. By 1946, six teams in what would become the All-America Football Conference had signed eight Black players, but it took the National Football League until 1949 to draft a Black player and until the mid-1960s to regularly play signed players. Black boxers had long dominated prizefighting. Joe Louis thrilled Black and white crowds alike, especially in 1938, when his defeat of the German heavyweight boxer Max Schmeling made him the pride not only of Black Americans but of the nation as a whole.

Cities nurtured Black culture and made Black talent visible. In 1940, the writer Frederick O'Neal and the actor Abram Hill founded the American Negro Theatre (ANT) in Harlem as a way to expand the limited opportunities available to Black entertainers and the entertainment available to Black audiences. In Hollywood films, for example, Black actors were restricted to stereotypical roles. Most were not allowed to play anything but handkerchief-headed mammies or sluggish, pop-eyed, superstitious buffoons. Black actors who rejected these parts found little or no work. The light-skinned Lena Horne was the exception that proved the rule, landing small roles in the 1943 films *Cabin in the Sky* and *Stormy Weather.* She was mostly allowed only to sing — even then with the understanding that her scenes would be cut when the films were shown in states that forbade the presence of nonstereotypical Black actors

Breaking the Race Barrier in Sports
In 1947, Jackie Robinson left the Negro American League's Kansas City Monarchs and became a starter for the Brooklyn Dodgers, the first major league baseball team to sign an African American. Though his hire angered some of his teammates, here three of them pose with him to document what proved to be the beginning of the integration of all major league sports. **How does this image reveal the ways the fight for racial equality extended into sports in the 1940s and 1950s?** *Bettmann/Getty Images.*

on the screen. Though advised to pass for white or Latino in order to get more roles, Horne never did so, and focused instead on her singing career.

Besides producing plays written by Black authors and featuring Black actors, the ANT offered classes in acting, voice, speech, and many aspects of theater production. From 1940 to 1949, more than 50,000 people attended ANT productions in which Black actors played the parts of fully developed, complicated human beings. The most successful production by far was the 1944 play *Anna Lucasta*, written by the white playwright Philip Yordan about a Polish American family. The ANT revised the play and made it suitable for a Black cast. It was an immediate success, moving to Broadway after five weeks and subsequently touring to Chicago and London. *Anna Lucasta* offered an opportunity to showcase the array of untapped talent in Black America.

AP® skills

Applying Disciplinary Knowledge: How did African Americans use the arts as a medium to fight against injustice after World War II?

At the center of Black migrant culture was Black music. Full of the expectations characteristic of the war era, this music reflected an African America that was on the move both physically and emotionally. The lyrics to the jazz tune "Take the 'A' Train" told people that if they rode the New York subway uptown, they would get to "Sugar Hill in Harlem." A metaphor for a people who became mostly urban during the 1940s, the song suggested that a sweeter life awaited them if they would just "Hurry, get on now." Bebop, a new form of jazz, also reflected a people on the road to independence and in the process of breaking the mold sculpted by white America. In contrast to the big band music it grew out of, bebop featured small groups and improvisational soloists. The sound was irregular and frenetic. More suitable for listening than for dancing, it was featured in the many small nightclubs that dotted the urban landscape. Trumpeter Dizzy Gillespie and saxophonist Charlie Parker pioneered bebop, which also featured trumpeter Miles Davis, pianist Thelonious Monk, and many others.

Blacks, therefore, did not give up their fight for victory at the end of World War II. They continued to press for the domestic "V" in the Double V campaign launched at the beginning of the war. From voting to bebop, everything signaled a new beginning. Once the Allies had defeated the Axis powers, African Americans were determined to defeat injustice at home.

Desegregating the Military and the GI Bill

The efforts of Black people to resist Jim Crow conditions in the military began to pay off toward the end of the war. For example, in March 1945, the men of the decorated 34th Seabee Battalion, a Black unit that had lost men while constructing airship hangers and other war infrastructure overseas, staged a hunger strike in protest of segregated living and eating conditions and the demeaned status of its petty officers. The navy responded by replacing the southern white commanding officer and 20 percent of the original officers with personnel screened for nonprejudicial racial attitudes. Shortly thereafter, as America closed in on Japan, several Seabee battalions were successfully integrated.

Similarly, African American sailors forced the issue of fairness at Port Chicago, where forty-five survivors of a munitions explosion that killed more than two hundred Black sailors were tried and convicted for refusing to resume loading ammunition. Their appeal, taken up by Thurgood Marshall and the NAACP, exposed some basic inequities, such as the assignment of Blacks to dangerous work for which they had not been trained. In the aftermath of the Port Chicago disaster, both Black *and* white units were assigned to Port Chicago and other ammunition dumps. Blacks were thereafter admitted to the Naval Academy, and separate facilities and quotas for Blacks who qualified for advanced training were eliminated.

The Fort Devens strike of fifty-four African American WACs also bore fruit. Although most who struck returned to work when commanded to do so, four women

Innovating in the Performing Arts

Despite the continued setbacks in achieving racial equality, shows like "Jivin' in Be-Bop" signaled the optimism in urban African America. New York City had been a mecca for artists of the Harlem Renaissance, and it continued to attract cultural icons like Dizzy Gillespie in the postwar period. **Who was the audience for this poster? What message does it convey? How does it reveal the role the arts played in the fight for racial equality?** *LMPC/Getty Images.*

refused. They were court-martialed and convicted for disobeying orders. As happened with the Port Chicago sailors, African Americans applied pressure. This time much of it came from African American women who marshaled emotional and financial support from their members in the NAACP, the National Council of Negro Women, and the National Association of Colored Women. Although WAC officials refused to back away from the charges of insubordination, they dropped the appeal, released the four women (three with honorable discharges and one with a general discharge), and when they subsequently assigned WACs to a Chicago hospital, officials took care to establish proper living conditions and work opportunities that included a variety of medical technician jobs.[61]

Executive Order 9981 (1948)
Issued by President Harry Truman, this order called for "equality of treatment and opportunity for all persons in the armed services without regard to race, color, religion, or national origin."

AP® skills

Applying Disciplinary Knowledge: What was the historical significance of Executive Order 9981? What role did African American activists both during and after the war play in its creation?

GI Bill (1944)
The popular name of the Servicemen's Readjustment Act, which provided returning soldiers with educational benefits, low-interest home loans, and unemployment benefits. African Americans were disproportionately denied these benefits.

AP® exam tip

Be sure you can describe African Americans' access to the benefits of the GI Bill.

President Harry S. Truman was not unmindful of the pressure African Americans were exerting or how important their vote would be in the 1948 election. In 1946, he established the President's Committee on Civil Rights, which included two African Americans. In October 1947, the committee issued a report, *To Secure These Rights*, which endorsed, among other things, a permanent FEPC, an antilynching law, and an end to segregation and discrimination in the military. In 1948, Truman issued **Executive Order 9981**. "It is hereby declared," the order read, "that there shall be equality of treatment and opportunity for all persons in the armed services without regard to race, color, religion, or national origin."[62] It would take several years for Truman's order to be fully implemented, and although discrimination in the armed services would not disappear, neither would African American resistance to it.

Even as the military opened doors, other avenues of opportunity remained closed. The most significant and far-reaching example of continuing discrimination was the way the Servicemen's Readjustment Act, commonly known as the **GI Bill**, was applied to African Americans. Passed by Congress in 1944, the GI Bill was designed to help returning veterans reenter American society as productive citizens. It allowed them to complete a college education at the government's expense, take out low-interest home loans, and collect unemployment compensation. The GI Bill transformed the nature of higher education in the United States. Before the war, few working-class or even middle-class Americans attended college. As millions of returning veterans entered college classrooms, higher education ceased to be the preserve of the rich. The GI Bill also transformed the housing market, making home ownership more commonplace. As white veterans bought homes with government loans, they facilitated America's suburbanization and the rise of the white middle class.[63]

Black Americans experienced no such boon. The bill itself did not discriminate, but its administration both stifled Black advancement and widened the economic gap between Black and white Americans. Black soldiers, for example, received a disproportionate share of dishonorable and Section VIII, or "blue," discharges. (A blue discharge was neither honorable nor dishonorable but was widely presumed to be less than honorable.) Usually issued without provocation, these blue discharges not only disqualified Black veterans from receiving GI Bill benefits but also stigmatized them in the job market and in society at large. A 1946 congressional investigation found that the blue discharge "procedure lends itself to dismissals based on prejudice and antagonism," but this finding did not undo the damage done by such discriminatory policies.[64]

The GI Bill's insidious administration by the Veterans Administration (VA) placed even Black veterans with honorable discharges at a severe disadvantage.

The VA granted low-interest home loans to Black veterans only if they purchased homes in black neighborhoods, and such homes were few in number. It forced Black veterans to take service jobs by refusing to pay unemployment benefits to those who declined unskilled jobs while looking for something less dead-end. Furthermore, because most white colleges in the North and South held fast to segregation and accepted few African Americans, Blacks were effectively shut out of the educational benefits of the GI Bill. Out of the 9,000 students enrolled at the University of Pennsylvania in 1946, only 46 were Black. Segregation policies forced Blacks to seek admission primarily to historically black colleges and universities, which quickly became overcrowded. Limited facilities forced Black colleges to turn away an estimated 20,000 veterans. Meanwhile, the VA consistently refused to pay the tuition of the few Blacks who were accepted by white colleges.[65]

In the end, African American soldiers were catastrophically shortchanged by the administration of the GI Bill. By contrast, whites who received VA home loans and/or college tuition payments obtained a boost to their earnings and status that they and their offspring benefited from. With the equity they built up in their homes, they were able to put the next generation through college, start businesses, and otherwise invest for the future.[66]

Although Black Americans achieved a victory with the postwar desegregation of the armed forces, they nevertheless suffered gravely in the postwar era from the VA's poor treatment of them. Examples of **systemic or institutionalized racism**, the government's military policies demonstrated that its discrimination could be as destructive as that practiced by individuals. In many ways, the VA's policies were more disabling than the acts of violence perpetrated by individual racists, because its financial effects would be felt for generations.

systemic racism (also known as **institutionalized racism**)
Discrimination practiced by corporations and governments.

CONCLUSION

A Partial Victory

In May 1945, Germany surrendered to the Allies. Three months later, in August, after the United States dropped atomic bombs on Hiroshima and Nagasaki, Japan surrendered as well. Although African Americans had played a crucial role in winning the war, they could declare only a partial victory. In 1942, they had vowed to fight for victory both abroad and at home, and although the government and war industries had limited their contributions, they had given all that the nation would allow them to. At war's end, despite a few hard-won advances, they had yet to win the fight against injustice in America.

Throughout the war, despite the violence they encountered, African Americans had persisted in their fight for domestic victory. Millions had left the South, and in the next two decades, millions more would leave the region. Like immigrants from abroad, they sought out new places in the North and Midwest, and for the first time, they became a significant presence on the West Coast. Though discriminated against in the workforce, Black Americans expanded their work experience and were often successful in their attempt to join unions. Even so, they met resistance at every turn. White workers went on strike when Blacks entered the workplace, when they were promoted out of unskilled jobs, or when they joined unions. Hate crimes, violent reprisals, and even riots followed when Blacks moved into decent neighborhoods or when they wore the uniform of their country, which they had fought for the same as other Americans.

Despite the challenges and setbacks, World War II opened doors, and Blacks were determined not to let those doors close again. They wanted first-class citizenship. They wanted to vote, to serve on juries, and to be elected to public office. They wanted jobs for which they were qualified. They wanted to compete in sports against white athletes, and they wanted to be portrayed in movies as real human beings. World War II had given African Americans a peek at what life could be like, and it had raised their expectations of equal opportunity. The challenge for them would be to make those expectations a reality.

CHAPTER 13 REVIEW ▸ PRACTICING AP® SKILLS

AP® ESSENTIAL VOCABULARY AND SOURCES

**Essential terms and required sources from the AP® Course are marked with an asterisk.*

Axis powers p. 505
Allies p. 505
Four Freedoms p. 506
Atlantic Charter (1941) p. 506
Nazism p. 506
March on Washington Movement (1941)* p. 507
Executive Order 8802 (1941) p. 507
African Americans' Double Victory* (Poster on the Double V Campaign, *Pittsburgh Courier*) p. 508
Double V campaign* p. 508
Tuskegee Airmen* p. 509
zoot suit riots p. 516
soldiers without swords p. 520
Morgan v. Virginia (1946) p. 525
Executive Order 9981 (1948) p. 530
GI Bill (1944)* p. 530
systemic or institutionalized racism p. 531

APPLYING DISCIPLINARY KNOWLEDGE: ESSENTIAL QUESTIONS

1. Describe the strategy behind the Double V campaign. How did it enable African Americans to protest their circumstances without risking accusations of disloyalty?
2. How did wartime conditions, both in the service and on the home front, shed light on the injustices and restrictions African Americans faced? How did Black individuals and organizations address these challenges?
3. What factors during the war promoted Black solidarity? How did this bring about the sense of Blacks becoming a nation within a nation?
4. How did African Americans use the war to advance themselves politically, socially, and culturally? What were the results of their efforts?
5. How did Black migration affect the national Democratic Party? Most white southerners were Democrats. How did they react to the new concerns of their political party?

SUGGESTED REFERENCES

The Crisis of World War II

Bolzenius, Sandra M. *Glory in Their Spirit: How Four Black Women Took on the Army During World War II*. Urbana: University of Illinois Press, 2018.

Dixon, Chris. *African Americans and the Pacific War, 1941–1945: Race, Nationality, and the Fight for Freedom*. United Kingdom: Cambridge University Press, 2018.

Edgerton, Robert B. *Hidden Heroism: Black Soldiers in America's Wars*. Boulder, CO: Westview Press, 2001.

Foner, Jack D. *Blacks and the Military in American History*. New York: Praeger, 1974.

Gallicchio, Marc. *The African American Encounter with Japan and China: Black Internationalism in Asia, 1895–1945*. Chapel Hill: University of North Carolina Press, 2000.

Honey, Michael Keith. *Black Workers Remember: An Oral History of Segregation, Unionism, and the Freedom Struggle*. Berkeley: University of California Press, 1999.

Latty, Yvonne. *We Were There: Voices of African American Veterans, from World War II to the War in Iraq*. New York: Amistad, 2004.

Miller, Richard E. *The Messman Chronicles: African Americans in the U.S. Navy, 1932–1943*. Annapolis, MD: Naval Institute Press, 2004.

Nalty, Bernard C. *Strength for the Fight: A History of Black Americans in the Military*. New York: Free Press, 1986.

Sitkoff, Harvard. "Racial Militancy and Interracial Violence in the Second World War." *Journal of American History* 58, no. 3 (1971): 661–81.

Sullivan, Patricia. *Days of Hope: Race and Democracy in the New Deal Era*. Chapel Hill: University of North Carolina Press, 1996.

African Americans on the Home Front

The Black Press: Soldiers without Swords. DVD. South Burlington, VT: California Newsreel, 1998.

Chamberlain, Charles D. *Victory at Home: Manpower and Race in the American South during World War II*. Athens: University of Georgia Press, 2003.

Dalfiume, Richard M. "The 'Forgotten Years' of the Negro Revolution." *Journal of American History* 55, no. 1 (1968): 90–106.

Gregory, James N. *The Southern Diaspora: How the Great Migrations of Black and White Southerners Transformed America*. Chapel Hill: University of North Carolina Press, 2005.

Harding, Vincent, Robin D. G. Kelley, and Earl Lewis. *We Changed the World: African Americans, 1945–1970*. New York: Oxford University Press, 1997.

Johnson, Marilynn. "Gender, Race, and Rumors." *Gender and History* 10, no. 2 (1998): 252–77.

MacLean, Nancy. *Freedom Is Not Enough: The Opening of the American Workplace*. Cambridge: Harvard University Press, 2006.

Murch, Donna Jean. *Living for the City: Migration, Education, and the Rise of the Black Panther Party in Oakland, California*. Chapel Hill: University of North Carolina Press, 2010.

Savage, Barbara Dianne. *Broadcasting Freedom: Radio, War, and the Politics of Race, 1938–1948*. Chapel Hill: University of North Carolina Press, 1999.

Takaki, Ronald. *Double Victory: A Multicultural History of America in World War II*. Boston: Little, Brown, 2000.

Taylor, Quintard. "African American Men in the American West, 1528–1990." *Annals of the American Academy of Political and Social Science* 569 (May 2000): 102–19.

The Struggle for Citizenship Rights

Bolzenius, Sandra. *Glory in Their Spirit: How Four Black Women Took on the Army During World War II*. Urbana: University of Illinois Press, 2018.

Bullock, Henry Allen. *A History of Negro Education in the South: From 1619 to the Present*. Cambridge: Harvard University Press, 1967.

Herbold, Hilary. *"Never a Level Playing Field: Blacks and the GI Bill."* Journal of Blacks in Higher Education 6 (Winter 1994–1995): 104–8.

Hine, Darlene Clark. *Black Women in White: Racial Conflict and Cooperation in the Nursing Profession, 1890–1950*. Bloomington: Indiana University Press, 1989.

Katznelson, Ira. *When Affirmative Action Was White: An Untold History of Racial Inequality in Twentieth-Century America*. New York: Norton, 2005.

Korstad, Robert, and Nelson Lichtenstein. "Opportunities Found and Lost: Labor, Radicals, and the Early Civil Rights Movement." *Journal of American History* 75, no. 3 (1988): 786–811.

McGuire, Phillip, ed. *Taps for a Jim Crow Army: Letters from Black Soldiers in World War II*. Lexington: University Press of Kentucky, 1993.

Sacks, Karen Brodkin. "How Did Jews Become White Folks?" In *Race*, edited by Steven Gregory and Roger Sanjek (pp. 78–102). New Brunswick: Rutgers University Press, 1994.

Turner, Sarah, and John Bound. "Closing the Gap or Widening the Divide: The Effects of the G.I. Bill and World War II on the Educational Outcomes of Black Americans." Working Paper 9044, National Bureau of Economic Research, Cambridge, MA, 2002.

Washburn, Patrick S. *A Question of Sedition: The Federal Government's Investigation of the Black Press during World War II*. New York: Oxford University Press, 1986.

African Americans and the Tuskegee Experiments

Tuskegee Institute was founded in 1881 as a school for Blacks in Macon County, Alabama. During the Great Depression and World War II, it was chosen as the site of two disparate experiments. One, the infamous Tuskegee Syphilis Study, showed how expendable Black lives were perceived to be. The other, the launching of the famed Tuskegee Airmen, demonstrated how much Blacks could achieve if given the opportunity.

The syphilis experiment began in 1932. The American medical community had long been convinced that syphilis, a contagious disease transmitted through sexual intercourse and from mother to fetus, affected whites and Blacks differently. It was thought that whites, by dint of their more highly developed brains, suffered more neurological symptoms in the later stages of the disease, while Blacks, ruled more by their bodies, suffered more cardiovascular complications. The Study of Untreated Syphilis in the Male Negro, sponsored by the Public Health Service (PHS), presented researchers with a chance to test their theories.

The subjects were desperately poor, uneducated male sharecroppers scattered throughout rural Macon County. Although women showed up for medical care, the PHS chose men because women required internal gynecological exams, which were more costly than the visual examinations used to confirm men's symptoms. Because most had never visited a doctor or received any kind of medical care, they welcomed the free treatment for minor ailments, the meals during treatment, and the free burial arrangements in the event of their death. The true nature of the study was never explained; in fact, health officials told the farmers they were being treated for "bad blood," and they used Black doctors, local pastors and teachers, and community leaders as recruiters. Since Alabama law prevented white nurses from caring for Black patients, a Black public health nurse named Eunice Rivers was recruited to serve as a liaison between the men and the doctors conducting the study.

Though health officials never intended to treat the participants for syphilis, the study took a turn in 1933 when a decision was made to follow the men until death because only an autopsy could determine the true effect of syphilis. In practice, this meant that when penicillin emerged as a cure for the disease in the early 1940s, instead of treating all of the syphilitic participants (and their sexual partners and their children) and closing the study or splitting off a control group for testing with penicillin, PHS scientists withheld the cure and continued to give the Tuskegee men arsenic and mercury, medications that they knew were ineffective and that had side effects similar to the lethal effects associated with today's chemotherapy treatments. The spinal taps the men received were especially painful and debilitating. Though they thought they were patients of the PHS, they actually became specimens whose bodies upon death could be autopsied to determine the ravages of the disease. The men were even prevented from fighting in World War II because the military would have tested them and administered the cure where necessary. In the late 1960s, Peter Buxtun, a PHS venereal disease investigator in San Francisco, raised questions about the morality of the study. The story broke on July 26, 1972, and quickly became front-page news. The study was terminated shortly thereafter. Congressional hearings followed, and in 1974, the NAACP filed a class action suit on behalf of the study victims.

Even as the syphilis study was being conducted in Macon County, decisions were being made in Washington that would bring another, more fortunate group of African American men to the area. In 1939, in response to civil rights leaders' protests against the exclusion of Blacks from military pilot training programs, Congress passed an appropriations bill designating funds for training African American pilots. Opposed to this idea, the War Department diverted the money into funding civilian flight schools willing to train Blacks. One such school was inaugurated at Tuskegee Institute. Two years later, in 1941, when Congress passed legislation forcing the Army Air Corps to form an all-Black unit, the Tuskegee Airmen, as they would come to be called, were ready. Admissions requirements for the all-Black units were high, requiring flight experience or a college degree — criteria intended to exclude most applicants. Instead, the Army Air Corps was flooded with qualified applicants. The men accepted constituted an elite, highly educated group. They completed both their basic training and their flight training at the newly christened Tuskegee Army Air Field.

Despite continuing segregation and discrimination, the Tuskegee Airmen went on to win 3 Distinguished Unit Citations by war's end and various individual awards, including at least 1 Silver Star, an estimated 150 Distinguished Flying Crosses, 14 Bronze Stars, and 8 Purple Hearts. When President Harry Truman finally ended segregation in the military in 1948, the veteran Tuskegee Airmen found themselves in high demand throughout the newly formed U.S. air force. Benjamin O. Davis Jr., the African American commander of the Ninety-Ninth and 332nd Fighter Groups, helped draft the air force plan for implementing integration and later became the first African American air force general. (He was the son of Brigadier General Benjamin O. Davis Sr.; see p. 492). The air force was the first armed service to fully integrate in the postwar period.

key point

During the Double V campaign, African Americans defied stereotypes as they fought for racial justice and equality in the midst of World War II. At the same time, African Americans continued to suffer from racist medical practices that had devastating effects.

AP® argumentation

DBQ Practice: Evaluate the extent to which the federal government's treatment of African Americans in the 1940s represents a continuation of earlier racial policies. Use at least three of the documents to support your response.

DOCUMENT 1 *Interview with a Tuskegee Syphilis Study Participant, 1972*

In these notes, an interviewer records a study participant's experiences after the close of the study. As the interviewer notes, participants were told they were being treated for "bad blood," a local term used to describe several illnesses. The men were offered free medical exams, meals, and burial insurance. To allay any fears, the study employed many Macon County, Alabama, residents, including the Black public health nurse Eunice Rivers, mentioned in this interview. Her public health background persuaded her that partial health care for this impoverished community was better than none at all.

Breaking it Down How did the federal government provide the illusion that Tuskegee Syphilis Study participants were receiving treatment? Why was the federal government's treatment of the participants unethical and inhumane? How does this document characterize the discrimination African Americans endured in the 1940s?

Subject was asked what the study meant to the people involved, how it started, etc.

SUBJECT: Started with a blood test. Clinic met at Shiloh Church. They gave us shots. Nurse (Rivers) came out and took us in (to John Andrews Hospital). One time I had a spinal puncture — had to stay in bed for 10 days afterward. Had headaches from that. Several others did too (and stayed in bed awhile). I wore a rubber belt for a long time afterward. Had ointment to run in under the belt.

Doctors came every year or so. After 25 years they gave everyone in the study $25.00 and a certificate. They told him he was in pretty good health.

At the beginning, he thought he had "bad blood." They said that was syphilis. (He) just thought it was an "incurable disease." He was booked for Birmingham for "606" shots° but "nurse stopped it." Some other doctor took blood that time and he was signed up to go to Birmingham. Nurse Rivers said he wasn't due to take the shots . . . he went to get on the bus to Birmingham and they turned him down. This was some time between 1942–1947.

He did not know he was sick before 1932. They gave them a bunch of shots — about once a month. Then they did a spinal. Nurse would notify them about the blood tests and bring them down.

He had not talked to any of the other participants lately.

He had the shots in his arm. In 1961, he had a growth removed from his bladder. (He is 66.) Health insurance paid for it. He paid his bill and his insurance paid back all but $20.

QUESTION: *Could all the people in the group afford hospitalization? What would others have done?*

SUBJECT: I don't know. I asked the (government) doctors about it (the growth) and they sent me to my family doctor. The government people didn't know I had insurance.

He didn't know of any others in the study who had been in the hospital although one man had become blind after awhile. He hadn't thought much about whether his disease had been cured. The doctor was seeing him every year, and he was feeling pretty good. He was not told what the disease might do to him. He stayed in the program because they asked him to. Nurse came and got him. He thought they all had the same disease. The blind man had been blind nearly 20 years — had worn glasses awhile, then had become blind.

QUESTION: *Did anyone do anything about the blind man's eyes?*

SUBJECT: I think he told nurse. They talked one time about sending him somewhere. Wasn't treated that he knew of. He (the blind man) never went anywhere and he (subject) didn't know the details. The blind man is about 75 now.

°Arsphenamine, or compound 606, a drug containing arsenic that was used to treat syphilis prior to the use of penicillin.

SOURCE: U.S. Department of Health, Education, and Welfare, "Interview Notes, 11/01/1972," Tuskegee Syphilis Study Administrative Records, Records of the Centers for Disease Control and Prevention, 1921–2006, NARA's Southeast Region (Atlanta), Morrow, GA.

DOCUMENT 2 *Tuskegee Study Participants*

The Tuskegee Syphilis Study began in the early years of the Depression, a period marked by the poverty of most Americans and the desperate poverty of African Americans. In Macon County, Alabama, as in most of the South, Black sharecroppers were pushed off the land as the government paid landowners not to plant cotton and other crops. Tenants who still worked the land received low wages, and

those who still sharecropped got little cash for their crops. Many were caught in a cycle of debt that amounted to peonage. Their houses mostly resembled shacks and lacked running water or indoor toilets. Medical care was almost nonexistent, and many whites believed that Black people did not need medical care. In fact, the attitude of Dr. John Heller, the director of venereal diseases at the Public Health Service from 1943 to 1948, toward the study participants was that they were "subjects, not patients; clinical material, not sick people."[67]

Breaking it Down Examine this picture of the study participants. Why would Heller describe them so? What demeanor do the men project? Based on this photo and your background knowledge, how would you describe the demographic makeup of the Tuskegee participants? How do you think their social and economic positions in society influenced both their willingness to participate in the study and the way they were treated by the medical community and government?

National Archives at Atlanta, Tuskegee Syphilis Study Administrative Records, 1929–1972, ARC Identifier 956097, Agency-Assigned Identifier 18868.

DOCUMENT 3 *Letter from U.S. Public Health Service to Surgeon General*

The Tuskegee Study was sanctioned by the highest offices in the nation's public health structure. The study was begun during the Depression, a time when money for such experiments was scare. However, both the Alabama State Board of Health and the U.S. Public Health Service thought the Tuskegee project worthy of the limited expenditures. In the letter below, the Director of the Bureau of Preventable Diseases indicates a willingness to treat the minor ailments of the projects' subjects but not the syphilis itself.

Breaking it Down What does this letter reveal about the nature of the study? How does this document reveal the type of institutional or systemic discrimination African Americans endured in the 1940s? What role did the federal government play? How does this document validate or contradict the account from the "Interview with a Tuskegee Syphilis Study Participant, 1972"?

U. S. PUBLIC HEALTH SERVICE
COOPERATING WITH
Alabama State Board of Health
STATE CAPITOL

J. N. BAKER, M. D.
STATE HEALTH OFFICER

D. G. GILL, M. D.
ACTING ASSISTANT SURGEON
U. S. PUBLIC HEALTH SERVICE

Montgomery

August 15, 1933.

File
cw.

U. S. Public Health Service
AUG 1 ... 1933
Division of Venereal Diseases

Surgeon General H.S.Cumming,
U.S.Public Health Service,
Washington, D.C.

Dear Dr. Cumming:

Beg to acknowledge receipt of the report sent Dr. Baker relating to the study of untreated syphilis conducted by Passed Assistant Surgeon R.A.Vonderlehr.

The high percentage of these people showing a positive serological test for syphilis again emphasizes the problem of control of this disease amongst the negro. The amount of treatment administered during this study was highly commendable, particularly since treatment was not the prime objective.

Respectfully,

DGG/H

D. G. Gill

D.G.Gill, M.D., Director,
Bureau of Preventable Diseases.
A.A.S., U.S.Public Health Service.

National Archives and Records Administration, NAID 564684.

DOCUMENT 4 Alexander Jefferson | *Interview with a Tuskegee Airman, 2006*

LIEUTENANT COLONEL ALEXANDER JEFFERSON (b. 1921), a Tuskegee Airman who served in the 332nd Fighter Group of the U.S. Army Air Corps during World War II, gave an interview in 2006 describing his experiences. In it, he described his training, the experience of being shot down and taken prisoner of war by the Germans, his observations of Europe, and his return home. During the war, the white commander of Jefferson's unit, General William W. Momyer, claimed that the 332nd "failed to display the aggressiveness and desire for combat that are necessary for a first-class fighting organization."

Note: This interview includes the N-word, which we have chosen to reprint in this textbook to accurately reflect Jefferson's original intent as well as the time period, culture, and racism discussed in the interview. We recognize that this word has a long history as a derogatory and deeply hurtful expression when used by white people toward Black people, as it is in the context of this interview. Be mindful of context, both Jefferson's and yours, as you read and discuss this source.

Breaking it Down What challenges did Tuskegee Airmen face and overcome during their service? How did their performance challenge racial stereotypes? How did their experiences in the war and when they came home support the main arguments of the Double V Campaign? How do Jefferson's recollections compare with General Momyer's account of the Tuskegee Airmen's capabilities?

This is June 1944. The Americans have just liberated Rome. Our job is to escort these bombers. It's B17s and B24s, [they're] going to Germany. They're 21,000/22,000 feet up to the target.

[And by that time, more than likely, we would have to turn them loose and come] back and another group would take over and bring them back home.

I was trying to explain to someone, if you look up at 12 o'clock to the horizon [to see contrails, to look behind you at six o'clock to the horizon to see] contrails of bombers going to Germany. And fighters all over the sky. Bombers in front of you, bombers behind you. It was unbelievable.

Sometimes we'd take the B17s to the target. You look up ahead, there's a big black cloud over the target.

The black cloud would extend from 15,000 feet to 25,000 feet, round like a hockey puck — flak [anti-aircraft fire]. And the bombers would fly straight into that black cloud and sometimes we got caught in that flak.

Where it was so close so they would actually hit the plane and actually knock the plane out of control. It sounds like somebody would take pebbles and throw it on a tin roof.

If you're that close and those things hit your plane, blowing holes, knocking holes in your wings and in your fuselage, you were too darn close.

Many times, we'd see the bombers go into the flak, [and out] the bottom of the cloud would come a bomber, half on fire, wing blown off. You'd hear the radio: bail out, damn it. Bail out. Bail out.

And out of this plane would come one cloud, one chute — you'd see a guy come out. And another guy came out. And all of a sudden, boosh(ph), explode.

First time was realization — I saw eight men die. I got sick. I'm sitting up there at 24,000 feet. And I got sick inside that oxygen mask. I puked and vomited. First time I ever got sick in an airplane.

[August the 12th, 1944: they simply said, some big towers and some buildings, you go over] and use your 50-calibers and shoot it up and destroy it. That's what we did.

The guys went in, down on the deck, 400 miles an hour. The first 12 guys got through okay. The side of the cliff was lighted up with anti-aircraft fire. We got down within a thousand yards, 1,500 yards, 800 yards, 600 yards. I got hits on the target and I went across the top of the target at treetop height.

Something says, boom — I looked up and there's a hole on top of the canopy. And I pulled up off of the deck and fire came out of the floor, because the shell had come up through the floor in front of the stick.

Out of the nine months of training, we never had one minute on training on how to get out [of] an airplane. I remember the tail going by and I pulled the D-ring on a parachute. Ordinarily, they'd say count one, two, three, pull it. No, I pulled that son of a gun, bang, right then. When the parachute popped, I'm in the trees and quite naturally the guys who shot me down were sitting over there about 200 or 300 yards away.

The German interrogator came down and said 332nd Fighter Group, Negroes, red tails. I looked at his book and said what the heck. He opened it up and thumbed through it, had all the pictures of all the classes that had graduated before me. They had all my marks at Clark University. They had my high school marks at Chadsey High School in Detroit. They knew how much taxes my dad paid on his house in Detroit. They knew more about me than I knew about myself.

When I got to Stalag Luft III, which is 80 miles east of Berlin, I was treated as a POW with all the rights and privileges of an American officer. No segregation, no discrimination. I was only there four months or five months when the Russians started coming west and the Germans put us out on the road and we walked 80 kilometers, temperature — 20 below zero.

Further west we wound up at Stalag 7A. I was there for about four months until April where Patton's Third Army liberated the camp I was in.

The next day after that, somebody said, hey Jeff, there's a place down there with a lot of dead people. I said what are you talking about? He said man, they've gotten people down there stacked up like cordwood. So we got a jeep and we went down to see this place, Dachau.

The ovens were still warm. The odor of human flesh is something I'll never forget. A table, 20 or 30-feet long covered with amalgam and gold teeth where they cut off the hair for seat cushions.

Man's inhumanity to man.

Coming down the gangplank by boat from London — a boat across from Le Havre to London. When you walked — [Unintelligible] down the gangplank in New York City, a big sign in front of you says: whites to the right, colored to the left. And a white soldier down at the bottom indicated whites to the right and niggers to the left. Coming back home — racist segregation.

Malcolm [X], Martin Luther King, Rosa Parks — I am part of the Civil Rights Movement. America — United States: best country in the world. You don't like it? Leave it. The only obligation, make it better. It ain't perfect but it's home.

DOCUMENT 5 *Tuskegee Airmen*

The military established the flight training program at Tuskegee expecting it to fail. The top brass held the belief, expressed in a 1925 report by the U.S. Army War College, that African Americans were cowards, that they lacked initiative and would not accept responsibility, and that leadership qualities and intelligence were beyond them.[68] The Tuskegee Airmen, both pilots and ground support units, worked hard to show the higher-ups just how wrong they were. Black airmen came to Tuskegee from all parts of the country but especially from New York City, Washington, Los Angeles, Chicago, Philadelphia, and Detroit. Most had at least some college education, and many had college degrees. They trained the same way white pilots trained and took the same courses and tests in operations, meteorology, intelligence, engineering, medicine, and other officer fields. Enlisted members were trained to be aircraft and engine mechanics, armament specialists, radio repairmen, parachute riggers, control tower operators, policemen, or administrative clerks — all the skills needed so that they could fully function as an Army Air Corps flying squadron or ground support unit.[69] Look at this picture and think about the Army War College report and about the other documents in this Document Project.

Breaking it Down Describe the composure and the positioning of the men in the picture. How does this picture demonstrate the way Tuskegee Airmen represented their race? How did they challenge twentieth-century stereotypes of Black men and their abilities?

Afro Newspaper/Gado/Archive Photos/Getty Images.

DOCUMENT 6 William H. Hastie and George E. Stratemeyer | *Resignation Memo and Response, 1943*

When WILLIAM H. HASTIE (1904–1976) resigned his post as civilian aide to Secretary of War HENRY L. STIMSON (1867–1950), he explained his reasons in a detailed memo dated January 5, 1943. Among those reasons were "segregation within Army theatres, the blood plasma issue and the unvarying pattern of separate Negro units." He was especially disturbed by the Army Air Corps' policies at Tuskegee. Major General GEORGE E. STRATEMEYER (1890–1969), U.S. army chief of the air staff, responded to Hastie's memo on January 12, 1943. Following are excerpts from their correspondence.

Breaking it Down How does this document reveal the types of discrimination African Americans endured in the armed services? Were any of these types of discrimination similar to those suffered during previous wars? What role did the federal government play? How did their experience in the war and when they came home support the main arguments of the Double V Campaign?

William H. Hastie: As you know, I have believed for some time that my presence in the War Department is no longer essential to the maintenance of the several substantial gains made during the past two years in the handling of racial issues and particular problems of Negro military and civilian personnel. At the same time I have believed that there remain areas in which changes of racial policy should be made but will not be made in response to advocacy within the Department but only as a result of strong and manifest public opinion. . . .

Compelling new considerations have now arisen. In one very important branch of the Army, the Air Forces, where the handling of racial issues has been reactionary and unsatisfactory from the outset, further retrogression is now so apparent and recent occurrences are so objectionable and inexcusable that I have no alternative but to resign in protest and to give public expression to my views. This ultimate decision has been forced upon me by . . . the humiliating and morale shattering mistreatment which, with at least the tacit approval of the Air Command, continues to be imposed upon Negro military personnel at the Tuskegee Air Base. . . .

. . . The Negro program began with the organization of several so-called Aviation Squadrons (Separate). Of these units . . . it is sufficient to say, that they were organized to serve no specific military need . . . and that . . . their characteristic assignment has been the performance of such odd jobs of common labor as may arise from time to time at air fields. . . .

. . . Two Negro officers were sent by the Ground Forces to the Air Forces school for Aerial Observers. They successfully completed their course. But such information as I have been able to get reveals no plans for their utilization and no intention of training additional Negro officers in Aerial Observation. . . .

. . . To date no application of a Negro for appointment as an army service pilot has been accepted. . . .

. . . The racial impositions upon Negro personnel at Tuskegee have become so severe and demoralizing that, in my judgment, they jeopardize the entire future of the Negro in combat aviation.

George E. Stratemeyer: I have caused an analysis to be made of the statements contained in the memorandum to the Secretary of War . . . from Judge William H. Hastie. . . .

. . . Judge Hastie's statement that Aviation Squadrons (Separate) would never have existed except for the necessity of making some provision for Negro enlisted men in the Air Forces is bluntly true. Judge Hastie, however, fails to analyze or recognize the necessity for the creation of these units. . . . Fifty-four per cent of white selectees scored 100 or better on the Army General Classification Test; 8.5% of the Negroes attained that score. Forty-eight per cent of white selectees scored 100 or better on the Mechanical Aptitude Test; 7.1% of the Negroes attained that score. Experience has shown that the soldier who fails to meet the standard of 100 or better on both these tests has difficulty in absorbing instruction at technical schools. . . . The white soldier in the lower intelligence brackets, while not assigned to Aviation Squadrons (Separate), finds himself detailed to "the performance of odd jobs of common labor as may arise from time to time at air fields." These facts clearly indicate that Judge Hastie's position with reference to Aviation Squadrons (Separate) is not well taken.

. . . The school at Tuskegee was established after most careful study and conferences with officials of Tuskegee Institute. These same officials urged the establishment of the Army Air Forces School at that location to include a Negro Contract Primary Flying School. . . . Although certain white contractors objected . . . , the program has been carried through with excellent results. . . .

. . . The two Negro officers who received training as Aerial Observers were returned to the Ground Forces for duty in consonance with current policy as were white officers similarly detailed for this training. The War Department policy with reference to the assignment of Negro officers to white units precludes the training of Negro Observers for duty with the Air Forces inasmuch as there are no Negro Observation Units. . . .

. . . The statement of Judge Hastie that racial impositions upon Negro personnel at Tuskegee are so severe and demoralizing as to jeopardize the future of the Negro in combat aviation does not appear to be borne out by fact. The report of the Inspector General . . . and the statement by the Commanding General . . . that the 99th Fighter Squadron is in a superior state of training, indicates that the mission of the Army Air Forces installation at Tuskegee is being successfully accomplished.

SOURCE: Morris J. MacGregor and Bernard C. Nalty, eds., *Blacks in the United States Armed Forces: Basic Documents*, vol. 5, *Black Soldiers in World War II* (Wilmington, DE: Scholarly Resources, 1977), 178–81, 183–85.

PRACTICING AP® SKILLS

1. **AP® Contextualization.** Describe the opportunities and racial discrimination African Americans faced during World War II. What evidence from these documents support your description?
2. **AP® Causation.** Explain why African Americans launched the Double V Campaign. How do these documents illustrate the necessity of that campaign?
3. **AP® Comparison.** Compare the manner in which African American soldiers were treated in World Wars I and II. Did they face similar or different obstacles?
4. **Connecting to AP® Themes.** To what extent did the Double V campaign fall under the tradition of African American resistance?
5. **Think/Pair/Share.** Discuss to what extent democracy increased at home while the United States fought fascism abroad. How do the documents that address the Tuskegee Study factor into your position? What about the documents covering the experiences of Tuskegee Airmen?

Responding to Short-Answer Questions without Stimuli

Back in Chapter 4, the AP® Skills Workshop (p. SW4-A) introduced you to four strategies to help craft accurate and thorough responses to short-answer questions (SAQs) on the AP® Exam. As you might recall, SAQs might involve a required source (or sources), a non-required source (or sources), or no source at all. In this workshop, we'll be focusing solely on the final category of short-answer question, in which you'll approach a prompt with no associated stimulus.

While we won't need to use our sourcing skills, the other SAQ strategies you've already practiced will carry over. Let's review those strategies and then practice applying them to a sample short-answer question with no stimulus.

Strategy 1: Read and break down the question.

As you know, each short-answer question will appear in three to four parts that are graded independently. Each part will include a specific *task* and may also include hints to a specific *time period* and *topic*.

The time period and topic should be straightforward to spot. If the topic doesn't immediately ring a bell, remember it may just be a different label for a course **concept**, **development**, or **process** you've studied.

To determine each part's task, it can be useful to remember that each part of a short-answer question will likely include one of the following task verbs:

Compare	Provide similarities and differences
Describe	Provide two or more details
Draw a conclusion	Use evidence to determine an accurate takeaway
Evaluate	Provide judgment on significance or accuracy
Explain how	Provide information on a development or process with an example
Explain why	Provide information on the causes of a development or process with an example
Identify	Provide specific detail without further elaboration
Support (*a claim*)	Provide a specific example and comment on how it backs up the claim

As with all short-answer questions, it's important to identify each part's time period, topic, and task before beginning to craft your response. Students often make the mistake of reading a prompt too quickly and then providing a response that may be well constructed and thoroughly explained but doesn't directly address the question. This error is especially dangerous when answering a short-answer question with no stimulus; without a source providing hints to an appropriate topic and time period, it's easy to lose focus.

Let's practice responding to a short-answer question with no stimulus. We can use the following sample question:

Respond to parts A, B, C, and D.

(A) Describe one specific example of Black Americans' contributions to World War II.

(B) Describe one enduring form of discrimination Black people experienced in the five years following the end of World War II.

(C) Using a specific example, explain how Black people individually or collectively resisted discrimination in the five years following the end of World War II.

(D) Evaluate the extent to which Black Americans' efforts to resist discrimination changed from the 1940s to the 1950s.

We can break down this short-answer question using a graphic organizer:

Part	Time Period	Topic	Task
A	World War II (1941–1945)	Black Americans participating in the war effort	Give details about one way Black Americans participated in the war effort.
B	Postwar years (1945–1950)	Discrimination against Black Americans	Give details about a form of discrimination that persisted throughout the 1940s.
C	Postwar years (1945–1950)	Resistance to discrimination	Provide information on one way that Black people pushed back against postwar discrimination, either individually or in groups.
D	1940s–1950s	Changes in resistance strategies	Judge how significantly Black people's resistance efforts changed from the 1940s to the 1950s.

As we reinforced in Chapter 4's workshop, not only does your response to each part need to be *correct* in order to earn the point; it also needs to *directly* answer that part of the question. If a part of your response addresses an irrelevant time period or topic, or if you don't fully complete the task, that part of your response will not earn a point. Therefore, breaking down the full question will set you up well to provide relevant responses that earn full points.

Strategy 3: Organize your evidence.
Because our sample prompt has no associated stimulus, we're skipping right over Strategy 2, which focuses on sourcing. Instead, we'll jump straight into the process of identifying and categorizing relevant information from your course knowledge.

Part A: Describe one specific example of Black Americans' contributions to World War II.	Part B: Describe one enduring form of discrimination Black people experienced in the five years following the end of World War II.	Part C: Using a specific example, explain how Black people individually or collectively resisted discrimination in the five years following the end of World War II.	Part D: Evaluate the extent to which Black Americans' efforts to resist discrimination changed from the 1940s to the 1950s.
• Over two million Black men and women served in the U.S. military during World War II • The Tuskegee Airmen, also known as the "Red Tails," were the first Black pilots	• Local Jim Crow discrimination blocked many Black veterans from receiving the full benefits of the GI Bill • White Americans sometimes violently attacked Black veterans • Discriminatory housing practices (such as redlining) blocked African Americans from accessing public transportation, healthy food, clean water, and health care and excluded them from home ownership	• James J. Thompson initiated the "Double Victory" campaign against fascism abroad and segregation at home • Black people joined organizations such as the NAACP, Urban League, and the Brotherhood of Sleeping Car Porters	• World War II was a turning point and caused more Black Americans than ever to reject second-class citizenship. • The number of Black voters significantly increased after the end of World War II • Group advocacy led to the desegregation of the U.S. military as well as sports like baseball

This brainstorming step will set you up well to select the strongest examples to use in your completed response.

Strategy 4: Respond to each part of the question.
As we've practiced before, we can use the strategy TEA to assemble a complete response:

Topic sentence	Clearly state an answer that directly responds to the prompt.
Evidence	Cite relevant details from your course knowledge and/or from the source(s).
Analysis	Provide commentary explaining how your evidence backs up your answer.

As always, an effective short-answer response will begin with an arguable claim and not a statement of fact. Remember, the short-answer question evaluates your ability to participate in a historical debate, not just repeat facts. Further, make sure to pay particular attention to the last step of TEA: Analysis. You will need to lay out exactly how the evidence you've provided logically leads to the claim you've made in your topic sentence.

In this case, a response to part A that aligns with the TEA strategy might look something like this:

> Black Americans directly contributed to the United States' success in World War II through service in the armed forces. For instance, the all-Black unit known as the Tuskegee Airmen earned military distinctions for their exceptional efforts in Europe and North Africa. Despite segregation within the military and discriminatory treatment of Black veterans, African Americans persisted in supporting the war effort and ultimately contributed to an Allied victory.

In general, you should aim for about three to four sentences per part, totaling about nine to twelve sentences for the complete response.

recap

Responding to Short-Answer Questions without Stimuli

The strategies to efficiently and accurately answer a short-answer question with no stimulus mimic those used for other kinds of short-answer questions:

Strategy 1: Read and annotate the question for its task, topic, and time period. Remember, these are the most common task verbs found on the AP® African American Studies Exam:

Compare	Provide similarities and differences
Describe	Provide two or more details
Draw a conclusion	Use evidence to determine an accurate takeaway
Evaluate	Provide judgment on significance or accuracy
Explain how	Provide information on a development or process
Explain why	Provide information on the causes of a development or process
Identify	Provide information without further elaboration
Support *(a claim)*	Provide a specific example and comment on how it backs up the claim

Skip Strategy 2, as there will be no stimulus to source.

(continued)

Strategy 3: Organize your information.

Strategy 4: Respond to each part of the question.

Topic sentence

Evidence

Analysis

Activity ▸ Responding to Short-Answer Questions without Stimuli

Draft a complete response to parts B, C, and D of the sample prompt, making sure that each section of your response provides a topic sentence, evidence, and analysis.

NOTES

Multiple-Choice Questions

Questions 1–2 refer to the following.

AP® source *African Americans' Double Victory,* 1942

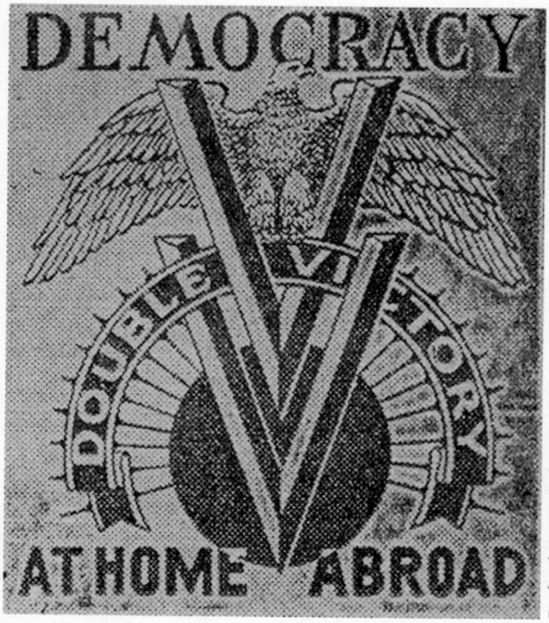

Pittsburgh Courier Archives.

1. The image best reflects which of the following developments of the 1940s?

(A) Labor unions' determination to fight communism and labor discrimination

(B) Veterans' dedication to fight fascism and racial oppression

(C) Women's rights activists' resolve to condemn racism and gender discrimination

(D) Immigrant organizations' determination to end immigration laws that discriminated against Afro-Caribbeans

2. Which of the following historical developments most directly resulted from the Double V campaign?

(A) The increased awareness among Black Americans that fighting for the United States during World War II entitled them to demand civil rights reform at home

(B) The passage of the GI Bill of 1944, which rewarded returning American veterans, including 1.2 million Black veterans, by providing funds for college tuition, low-cost home mortgages, and low-interest business startup loans

(C) The success of the Tuskegee Airmen, the first Black American pilots in the U.S. military, in combating fascism through their service in Europe and North Africa during World War II

(D) The immediate end of Jim Crow segregation throughout schools, businesses, and public services in the southern states

Short-Answer Question

***African American Migration,* 1930–1970**

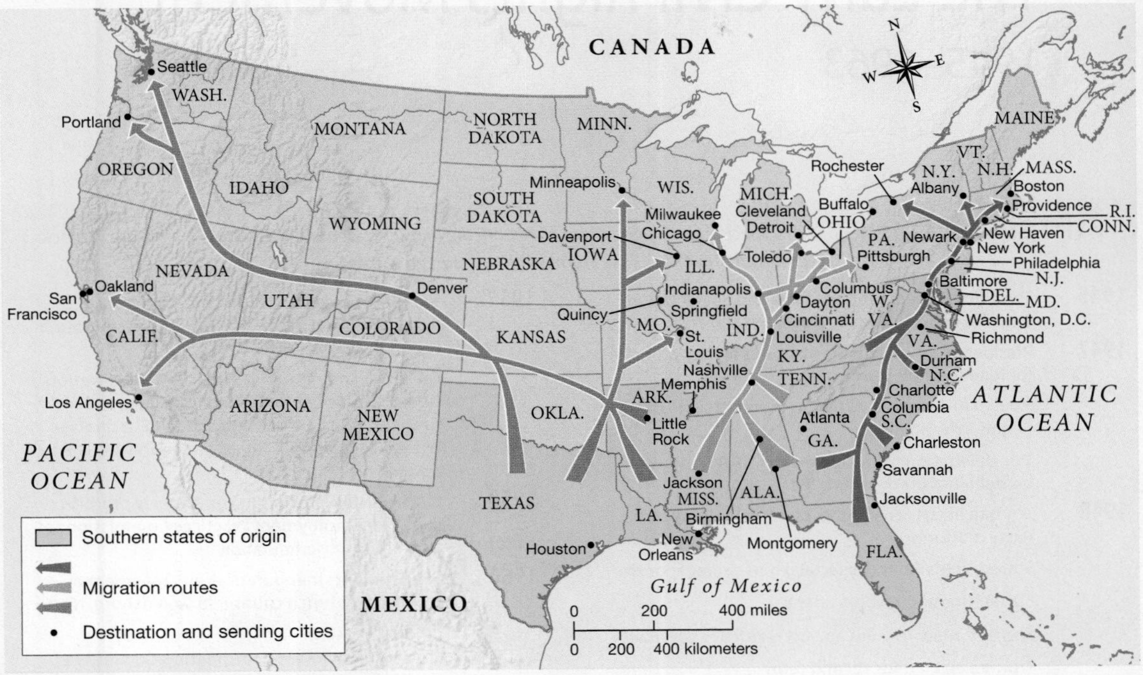

1. Using the map, answer A, B, C, and D.

(A) Describe the historical situation depicted on the map.

(B) Describe one difference between the pattern and period of migration depicted on the map and one other migration that took place in the history of the African diaspora or involving African-descended peoples in the nineteenth century.

(C) Explain one cause of the historical situation depicted on the map.

(D) Explain one economic, social, or political effect that occurred as a result of the historical situation depicted by the map.

CHAPTER **14**

The Early Civil Rights Movement

1945–1963

CHAPTER TIMELINE

Events specific to African American history are in purple. General U.S. history events are in black. Events from the AP® Course Framework are marked with an asterisk.

1945 Tensions between United States and Soviet Union begin to escalate in early stages of Cold War

1947 President Harry S. Truman institutes loyalty program for federal employees

House Un-American Activities Committee (HUAC) begins investigations

U.S. delegation to the UN rejects NAACP petition on behalf of Black civil rights

1948 Truman inserts civil rights plank into Democratic Party platform

States' Rights Party (Dixiecrats) runs segregationist Strom Thurmond for president

Shelley v. Kraemer rules against restrictive covenants

Truman elected for second term

1949 North Atlantic Treaty Organization (NATO) founded

Soviet Union detonates atomic bomb

1950–1953 Korean War

1950 NAACP passes loyalty resolution

McCarran Internal Security Act establishes loyalty review boards in executive branch

1951 NAACP files class action suit, *Brown v. Board of Education of Topeka*, challenging educational segregation*

1952 Dwight D. Eisenhower elected president

1954 *Brown v. Board of Education of Topeka* declares separate public educational facilities unconstitutional*

1955 Fourteen-year-old Emmett Till murdered in Mississippi*

Montgomery bus boycott begins when Rosa Parks refuses to relinquish her seat to a white passenger*

1956 *Browder v. Gayle* declares segregated buses illegal; Montgomery bus boycott ends

1957 Southern Christian Leadership Conference (SCLC) founded in Atlanta; Martin Luther King Jr. becomes first president*

Governor Orval Faubus orders Arkansas National Guard to block entrance of nine Black students to Little Rock Central High School; Eisenhower federalizes National Guard and mobilizes U.S. army to protect students*

1958 Black elected officials in Los Angeles produce state Fair Employment Practices Commission to address job discrimination

1960 Four students inaugurate sit-in movement at Woolworth's lunch counter in Greensboro, North Carolina*

Student Nonviolent Coordinating Committee (SNCC) founded*

John F. Kennedy elected president

Seventeen newly formed African nations join the United Nations

1961 Congress of Racial Equality (CORE) organizes Freedom Rides*

1962 Kennedy sends troops to Oxford, Mississippi, to quell riots after James Meredith wins right to attend University of Mississippi

1963 SCLC and Alabama Christian Movement for Human Rights attempt to desegregate Birmingham's public facilities and open civil service jobs*

King writes "Letter from Birmingham City Jail"

Eugene "Bull" Connor, Birmingham's police commissioner, jails more than 600 adults and children and orders attacks on civil rights marchers in response to Birmingham Children's Crusade*

Mississippi NAACP leader Medgar Evers killed*

March on Washington for Jobs and Freedom*

Paul Robeson: A Cold War Civil Rights Warrior

On June 12, 1956, a weary Paul Robeson took a seat before the House Un-American Activities Committee (HUAC). Robeson, a prominent civil rights activist, had been subpoenaed to testify two weeks earlier, but his doctors had claimed he was too ill. Actually, Robeson was depressed. Throughout the 1930s and during World War II, he, like so many other African Americans, had been an outspoken critic of the United States, speaking in favor of the Double V campaign and the rights of trade unions and against colonialism and imperialism. But now, in the context of the Cold War with the Soviet Union, his remarks were denounced by Blacks and whites alike. A speech he made at a 1949 peace conference in Paris, which declared that Blacks would not make war on the Soviet Union, had ignited massive controversy. Blacklisted at home and prevented from going abroad when the government revoked his passport in 1950, a dispirited Robeson had reason to be distressed.

He remained defiant, however, in the face of his House interrogation. When asked, "Are you now a member of the Communist Party?" Robeson replied, "I am not being tried for whether I am a Communist. I am being tried for fighting for the rights of my people, who are still second class citizens in this U.S. of America." During his testimony, Robeson repeated his claim that Blacks would not take up arms against the Soviet Union. When this drew scoffs, he reiterated that the 900 million colored people of the world would not go to war in defense of Western imperialism.[1]

Robeson's activist sentiments were born many years before the Cold War. Although he graduated from Columbia Law School in 1923, he turned to acting and concert singing when racial discrimination forced him out of a New York law firm. His wide travels allowed him to experience different cultures and political systems, and he was especially taken with the Soviet Union: "When I first entered the Soviet Union I said to myself, 'I am a human being. I don't have to worry about my color.'"[2] He reminded people that Communists had defended the Scottsboro Boys. For Robeson, the Congress of Industrial Organizations (CIO) held the key to economic justice, and he was mindful that Communists had helped bring Blacks into that labor organization. Robeson was also a longtime Pan-Africanist, believing that the fate of all Blacks in the Western Hemisphere was linked to that of Black Africa, and in 1937, he helped found the International Committee on African Affairs, which served as a clearinghouse to disseminate accurate information about Africa to uninformed Americans. He also fought against racism and lynching, which led him to found the American Crusade against Lynching in 1946.

Robeson's experiences offer insight into the challenges African Americans faced in the postwar era. Though critical of their country during World War II, Blacks had served loyally on the battlefield and in war industries. Despite attempts to prove their disloyalty, even government operatives had been forced to admit that America, not its Black citizens, needed to change. Robeson's hearing before

HUAC evidenced a significant shift. During the war, Black people had demanded that the government remain true to the ideals expressed in the Four Freedoms. Now, America demanded that Blacks prove their commitment to those freedoms by denouncing communism; the Soviet Union and its leader, Joseph Stalin; and any activities undertaken by Communists in the United States and abroad.

Many African Americans would find this difficult to do. Stalin was unquestionably a tyrant, and even though Robeson refused to denounce him, most other Blacks did. But rank-and-file Communists and other left-leaning activists had been active in the Black freedom struggle. Many had been instrumental in the fight for jobs and Black workers' rights. Moreover, anticommunism gave segregationists a lethal weapon in their resistance to the Black freedom struggle. Robeson's enemies, for example, not only harmed his acting and singing career but also stifled his activism against racial injustice. Like Robeson, other African Americans remained defiant as they maneuvered in the new postwar environment. But the international movement for both civil and economic rights that emerged during World War II would be irrevocably altered by the climate of fear. Those who spoke against America's inequalities were branded Communists and punished.

The anti-Communist hysteria both helped and hindered African Americans' struggle for freedom. It helped by enabling Blacks to spotlight how few rights they had, demonstrating the contrast between American ideals and practice. For this tactic to work, however, the movement had to focus on demonstrable inequalities — segregation and disfranchisement — which could be altered by legislation and litigation. Less visible injustices — such as the systemic prejudices that drove housing and employment discrimination — had to be de-emphasized. The first phase of the postwar freedom struggle, therefore, used nonviolent direct-action protest — boycotts, sit-ins, Freedom Rides, and marches — to fight legalized discrimination. This new strategy was accompanied by new leaders and new organizations. Although the strategy was successful on many fronts, the persistence of virulent white resistance and the continued inequities caused many to question the movement's direction.

Please note that this chapter includes primary sources by Black writers and speakers that use the N-word, which we have chosen to reprint in this textbook to accurately reflect these speakers' original intent as well as the time period, culture, and racism discussed in each source. We recognize that this word has a long history as a derogatory and deeply hurtful expression when used by white people toward Black people. Black speakers' and writers' choice to use this word relates not only to that history but to a larger cultural tradition in which the N-word can take on different meanings, emphasize shared experience, and be repurposed as a term of endearment within Black communities. This chapter also includes primary sources by white writers and speakers that use the N-word, which we have chosen not to reprint in full here. We have replaced the term without hindering understanding of these sources. Be mindful of context, both historical and contemporary, as you read and discuss this chapter.

Content note: This chapter includes a photograph of the body of Emmett Till, a Black teenager who was lynched by two white men in 1955.

Anticommunism and the Postwar Black Freedom Struggle

What enduring forms of segregation and discrimination in daily life did African Americans face in the years after World War II?

How did anti-Communism in the United States impact civil rights organizations' strategies?

Robeson was not the first African American to be investigated by HUAC. Beginning in 1947, many well-known civil rights activists, including W. E. B. Du Bois, Mary McLeod Bethune, Adam Clayton Powell Jr., and Langston Hughes, were investigated or called on to prove that their activism was unconnected to Communist activities in the United States. This period — known as the second Red scare or the McCarthy era, after Wisconsin senator Joseph McCarthy, perhaps the most outspoken anti-Communist in the nation — wreaked havoc on the Black freedom struggle. The fear it generated forced civil rights and labor organizations to purge many of their most earnest and productive leaders and ultimately forced those organizations to shift direction and modify their goals.

AP® skills

Applying Disciplinary Knowledge: FDR's Four Freedoms are freedom of speech, freedom of religion, freedom from fear, and freedom from wanting economic opportunity. As you read this chapter, consider how these are reflected in several civil rights organization platforms.

African Americans, the Cold War, and President Truman's Loyalty Program

Ironically, it was Harry S. Truman, the same president who desegregated the armed services, who undermined the progress being made for economic and political justice. In March 1947, soon after he appointed the first President's Committee on Civil Rights, Truman issued an executive order establishing a **loyalty program** to confirm the loyalty of federal employees. Passed by Congress the following August and expanded in the McCarran Internal Security Act of 1950 — an act so extreme that even Truman vetoed it, unsuccessfully — the program established loyalty review boards in every department and agency of the executive branch. It also allowed the federal government to use any means necessary to investigate any person or organization, and it allowed the government to regulate, fine, imprison, and/or deport anyone deemed disloyal. Disloyalty was defined broadly as belonging to or being in sympathy with a "foreign or domestic organization, association, movement, or group or combination of persons, designated by the Attorney General as totalitarian, fascist, communist, or subversive."[3]

loyalty program The program instituted by President Harry Truman in 1947 requiring federal employees to swear that they were not Communists or Communist affiliates. Many unions and several civil rights organizations adopted similar programs thereafter.

The rationale for the order was the perceived threat of Communist infiltration of government agencies. In the years following World War II, tension mounted between the Soviet Union and its former allies as Moscow extended its influence throughout eastern Europe and the Middle East. U.S. leaders feared that communism would spread in America the way it had in Poland, Czechoslovakia, Hungary, East Germany, and Greece. To protect itself, the United States joined Britain, France, Canada, and

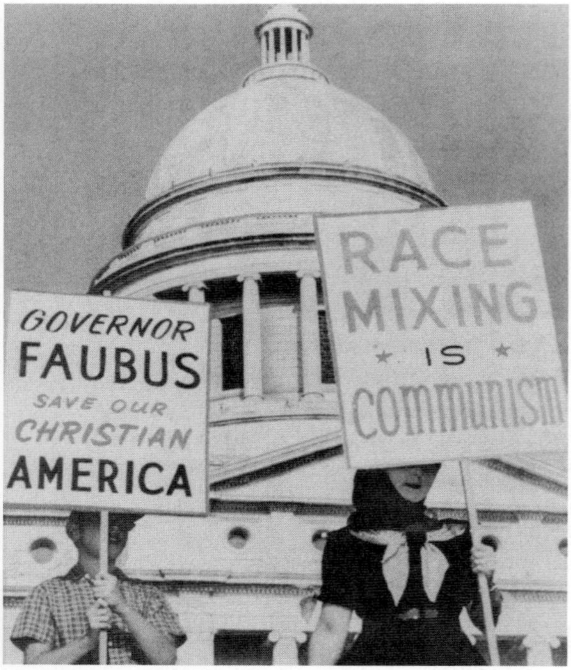

Using Communist Fears to Oppose Civil Rights
Segregationists used America's fear of communism to oppose African American civil rights. Here demonstrators who opposed the integration of Arkansas public schools equate integration with interracial marriage, a long-standing fear of many white Americans. **What fear did segregationists use as a strategy to oppose civil rights? Why was it effective?** *Everett Collection/AGE Fotostock.*

ACTIVITY ▸ Revisit Your Prediction

In the AP® Unit Warmup (p. U4-E), you made a prediction about this image. **What do you think Americans' perspective on issues such as segregation were in the mid-twentieth century? What clues from the image support your response? Support or revise your original prediction using evidence from this chapter.**

eight other nations in the North Atlantic Treaty Organization (NATO), a peacetime military pact signed in 1949 that promised mutual aid in the event of an armed attack. At home, leaders cautioned Americans to beware of subversives who wanted to destroy the country from within. During the "hot" war with Germany and Japan, the enemy was visible, and its military and weaponry could be defended against and attacked. But this new "cold" war with the Soviet Union was as much a battle to win the hearts and minds of Americans as it was a fight to gain strategic geographic advantage in the world. Every American citizen needed to be vigilant lest the new forces of evil steal government secrets, undermine America's productivity, and eventually destroy American democracy and subject American citizens to the kind of totalitarianism the Soviet Union was spreading. In actuality, few Communists infiltrated American institutions, but at midcentury, the threat seemed very real.

The loyalty program and subsequent anti-Communist hysteria made it very difficult to conduct a movement for Black political and economic justice. Racists and political conservatives fought hard for their right to discriminate — a right they believed was protected by the Constitution and America's free-enterprise system, which championed the rights of private property owners. Both Communists and socialists, however, were against private property, believing that the few owners of stores, companies, and land exploited the masses of workers. Communists thought that a state-directed economy was superior to a free market economy because the state would protect everyone, and the inequality between owners and workers would disappear. The Black freedom struggle involved not only challenging property owners' right to discriminate but also fighting for equal employment, education, health care, and housing at a time when programs that addressed equal opportunity could be interpreted as communistic or socialistic attempts at leveling. Worse yet, support for such programs could be taken as advocacy for state interference in private enterprise.

For activists who had spent a lifetime fighting for civil rights and economic justice, adjusting to the new reality was difficult. When W. E. B. Du Bois was called before Congress to demonstrate his loyalty in 1949, the scholar and longtime activist publicly pondered how a country that "hate[s] niggers and darkies propose[s] to control a world full of colored people."[4] Comments like these had been unwelcome during the war, but Black people who had made them were nevertheless protected under the First Amendment. The loyalty program signaled a change. When in 1950 Du Bois became chairman of the Peace Information Center, an organization that advocated general disarmament, the U.S. State Department indicted him as "an unregistered agent" of a foreign power. Though acquitted of the charges, Du Bois, like Robeson, had his passport revoked for eight years.[5] Other activists were deported, and cultural critics like Langston Hughes were subjected to humiliating appearances before HUAC. In 1954, even Ralph Bunche, the first Black person to hold a high-level position in the State Department and the first to win the Nobel Peace Prize, for his role in Middle East peace negotiations between Arab and Jewish people, was forced to appear before a civil service loyalty board. His twelve-hour, two-day grilling made it clear that tough times were ahead for civil rights advocates.[6]

African American protests that racism, not communism or socialism, posed the real threat to American democracy garnered little sympathy. In fact, many white liberals — people who, though not Communists or socialists, nevertheless believed that Blacks were unjustly treated and needed government help to remedy discrimination — joined racists in calling for African Americans to demonstrate their loyalty by ending their protests. This was evident as early as 1947, when the NAACP filed "An Appeal to the World," a petition to the United Nations, protesting the treatment of African Americans. The petition denounced American discrimination as indefensible and barbaric. It stated, "It is not Russia that threatens the United States so much as Mississippi. . . . internal injustice done to one's brothers is far more dangerous than the aggression of strangers from abroad." Boldly outlining America's shortcomings, the petition declared that "the disfranchisement of the American Negro makes the functioning of all democracy in the nation difficult and as democracy fails to function in the leading democracy in the world, it fails the world." Well-known white liberals, including Eleanor Roosevelt, refused to support the petition and, in fact, refused to allow the American delegation, or any nation at the UN, to even broach the subject of African American civil rights.[7]

Red-baited
Accused of being a Communist. Red-baiting was used to discredit individuals during the Red scare beginning in 1947 in order to undermine their politics.

This kind of sentiment spread rapidly across America. In Santa Monica, California, a well-organized protest against discriminatory hiring practices at Sears, Roebuck had to be called off when its leader was effectively **Red-baited**, or accused of being a Communist.[8] The director of the Chicago Housing Authority, Elizabeth Wood, was repeatedly charged with "communistic connections" for her efforts to desegregate public housing.[9] On the entertainment front, Hazel Scott, the first Black entertainer to host a television show, joined Robeson as a blacklisted artist. Her crimes: she had opposed segregated baseball; she had supported the election of Communist New York City councilman Ben Davis; and during the war, when the Soviet Union and United States were allies, she had entertained Soviet as well as American troops. Red-baiting also snared Judge Hubert T. Delany of New York, who was not reappointed because of his unequivocal support of Black civil rights. "I'm sick of hearing about the rights Russians don't have," Delany said. "I'm concerned about the rights we don't have right here in this country."[10]

The Cold War also brought new challenges for labor unions, whose worker advocacy was branded as communistic. The conservative turn of the CIO was a setback for Black activists. During the war, many of its unions had adopted civil rights agendas and had been leaders in the quest for equal employment opportunities, fair housing, and equal political representation for Blacks. In 1947, however, business owners and management took advantage of the Cold War climate and lobbied in favor of inserting loyalty oaths into the Taft–Hartley Bill then making its way through Congress. Passed later that year, the Taft–Hartley Act, which mandated that union officers sign affidavits of non-Communist affiliation, weakened the bargaining power of unions. Rather than resist the loyalty requirements, the CIO purged members and whole unions that had been associated with behavior that could be labeled socialistic or communistic. The effect was to abandon the African American struggle for economic justice as well.

AP® skills
Applying Disciplinary Knowledge: What was the primary effect of the Taft-Hartley Act?

Nationwide, this had devastating consequences for Black workers. In New York City, the CIO ousted the United Public Workers of America, one of the most integrated unions (by race and sex) and one that had persistently fought to create a federal Fair Employment Practices Commission. When loyalty requirements destroyed Local 22 of the Food, Tobacco, Agricultural, and Allied Workers of America, located in Winston-Salem, North Carolina, they destroyed the organization that had revitalized the NAACP, registered thousands of voters, and spearheaded the election of the first Black alderman since the turn of the century. Black members of the National Maritime Workers Union were similarly hard hit. Sailors and longshoremen had joined the union as a way to improve working conditions, raise wages, and eradicate racial barriers to promotion. As they had in other CIO unions, Communists and left-wing radicals had helped maritime workers to achieve these goals. During the Red scare, Blacks paid a price for this success, as an estimated 80 percent of those labeled "security risks" were Black and from 50 to 70 percent of the fired maritime workers were Black or foreign born; thus a generation of Black labor activists was effectively purged from the nation's docks.[11]

Loyalty Programs Force New Strategies

Black civil rights organizations were also put on the defensive, and they were forced to adopt new strategies to survive in the changed political climate. Shortly after Truman issued his 1947 loyalty order, the U.S. attorney general presented a list of seventy-eight "subversive" organizations. Nine of them were civil rights organizations, including the National Negro Congress, the Negro Labor Victory Committee, the United Negro and Allied Veterans of America, the Southern Negro Youth Congress, and Robeson's organization, the Council on African Affairs.

AP® skills

Applying Disciplinary Knowledge: How did the loyalty oathes lead to changes in civil rights organizations' strategies?

To escape the Communist label and resulting Red-baiting, some Black organizations, such as the NAACP, followed the CIO's lead and took it upon themselves to purge Communists and left-leaning radicals. Chastened by the rejection of its antiracist petition to the United Nations, the NAACP turned its back on W. E. B. Du Bois when he was accused of being a Communist. In 1950, NAACP leaders dismissed him from his post as director of special research projects and did not help him during his trial. Robeson was similarly denounced as someone who had abandoned his people for a foreign cause. To prove its membership's Americanism and stave off suspicions that the Communist Party was, as one liberal accuser described the situation, "sinking its tentacles into the NAACP,"[12] the NAACP at its 1950 national convention passed its own loyalty resolution. It called for an investigation of the "ideological composition and trends of the membership," instructing its board "to take the necessary action to suspend and reorganize, or lift the charter and expel any branch . . . coming under Communist . . . domination."[13]

In initiating their own anti-Communist programs, the NAACP and other civil rights organizations gambled that they could turn Cold War politics to their advantage. If America was in fact freer than the Soviet Union, they dared America to demonstrate it. If America cared more about colonial subjects in Asia and Africa, they dared America to show it. If America wanted to showcase its democracy, they challenged America to reverse its discriminatory policies. In short, they dared America to change or risk being shamed by the gross inconsistency between its rhetoric of freedom and its practice of giving Black people second-class citizenship.

It was a risky business, with benefits and drawbacks. Civil rights groups that adopted this tactic ensured their survival, were able to use the political climate as an effective tool, and made strides in dismantling the visible signs of segregation and enabling Black citizens to vote. But other rights had to be de-emphasized as a result. Issues associated with economic justice, such as inequities in employment, housing, and education, were more difficult to establish than disfranchisement, for example, which had ample evidence to support it and could be more readily addressed by law. Moreover, those seeking to prove these other types of discrimination, which presumed

de facto segregation
Racial separation that occurs in practice — as a result of housing patterns or social custom, for example — but is not based on law. Though this kind of segregation is caused by particular practices, its causes are less visible than the causes of de jure segregation and often appear to be the result of unintentional or natural circumstances.

to challenge the rights of employers and property owners, opened themselves up to accusations of communism. Thus, although they had not been eliminated, issues that had their roots in systemic racism, or the less visible **de facto segregation**, had to take a backseat to integration and suffrage.

Some of the strengths and weaknesses of this strategy were revealed during the election of 1948, when former vice president Henry Wallace and President Harry Truman vied for Democratic votes. Wallace, Roosevelt's third-term vice president (1941–1945), ran for president on a third-party ticket. As the standard-bearer of the Progressive Party, Wallace opposed the federal loyalty program and Truman's policy of making the Soviet Union America's enemy. He correctly predicted that reactionaries would use anticommunism to reinforce racial inequalities and economic injustices. Wallace called for the elimination of racism "from our unions, our business organizations, our educational institutions and our employment practices."[14] Believing that America had to lead the world by demonstrating its commitment to the common person, Wallace favored aggressive government policies like those initiated during the New Deal to bring about equal access and opportunity for all Americans.

Although Truman did not think Wallace could beat him on a third-party ticket, he did worry that Wallace would take enough votes away from him to allow the Republican candidate, Thomas Dewey, to win. To counter that possibility, Truman and his supporters inserted a civil rights plank into the Democratic Party platform that endorsed the findings of the President's Committee on Civil Rights. While Truman went on record as supporting antilynching legislation, desegregation of the armed forces, legislation to prevent discrimination in voter registration, and abolition of the poll tax, he stopped short when it came to measures that endorsed fair housing, employment, and education. Despite these shortcomings, African Americans and many civil rights organizations saw the inclusion of the civil rights plank in the party's platform as a victory. Southern segregationists, however, balked at any concession to African American rights. Foreshadowing their eventual move out of the Democratic Party, they bolted from the Democratic National Convention and ran their own segregationist candidate for president, Senator Strom Thurmond of South Carolina, under the newly formed States' Rights Party, also known as the Dixiecrats. Although Wallace's programs were more expansive than Truman's, Wallace had no chance of winning, and across the country, his candidacy was greeted with placards reading "Send Wallace Back to Russia." In Truman, civil rights advocates at least had someone who could take action; with Wallace, they faced more blacklists and censures.

The 1948 election seemed to validate the decision to support Truman over Wallace, especially when, just before the election, Truman issued his order to desegregate the armed services. Truman won two-thirds of the Black vote, with Black support in California, Illinois, and Ohio ensuring his election.

For African Americans, then, the die was cast. They would adopt more moderate platforms and keep more radical possibilities at arm's length. Although civil rights organizations did not abandon issues of economic justice, their leaders reasoned that the anti-Communist climate made it easier to dismantle segregation and fight for voting rights than to restructure employment. It was a gamble, but African Americans had a century of determined struggle for justice on their side.

The Transformation of the Southern Civil Rights Movement

What was the rationale for the *Brown v. Board of Education* decision to overturn "separate but equal"?

What were the essential methods of the major civil rights organizations?

Remarkably, although anticommunism shook the Black freedom movement to its core, it did not destroy the movement. While African Americans lost ground in their push for jobs and housing, they mounted an assault against legalized segregation and disfranchisement, or **de jure segregation**, which kept Blacks vulnerable to daily insults, substandard education, and a pervasive lack of political representation.

de jure segregation Racial separation mandated by law.

Many factors played into African Americans' dogged persistence. First, ordinary people's expectations had risen in the wake of World War II. Many had decided that the war was the point of no return, and they were not going to accept second-class citizenship anymore. New, effective leaders also emerged, especially Martin Luther King Jr., who appealed to both Black and white Americans by expressing African American aspirations in the Cold War language of freedom and democracy. The church assumed a new role during this period and facilitated the movement by espousing a philosophy of nonviolence. Finally, America's racial injustice proved an embarrassment on the international stage, and Black leaders were able to capitalize on this shame to pressure a reluctant federal government for support.

AP® skills

Applying Disciplinary Knowledge: How did policies in southern states contribute to expansion of the Civil Rights movement?

Brown v. Board of Education of Topeka (1954) A landmark U.S. Supreme Court case that overturned *Plessy v. Ferguson* (1896) by declaring that segregated public schools were inherently unequal.

Triumphs and Tragedies in the Early Years, 1951–1956

When the NAACP turned its attention to the fight against segregation, it had a foundation to build on. The U.S. Supreme Court had already declared segregation on interstate transportation illegal, and the Congress of Racial Equality (CORE) had already sent interracial teams through the South on a mission prefiguring the Freedom Rides of 1961. In 1951, the NAACP combined five legal cases against educational segregation into one class action suit known generally as ***Brown v. Board of Education of Topeka***. Although this U.S. Supreme Court case took aim at Black children's generally substandard education, it was designed to strike at the entire system of segregation. NAACP lawyers Thurgood Marshall, George E. C. Hayes, and James Nabrit argued that because segregation violated the equal protection clause of the Fourteenth Amendment, the 1896 *Plessy v. Ferguson* decision that established segregation was unconstitutional. (See Appendix for excerpts from both *Plessy v. Ferguson* and *Brown v. Board of Education of Topeka*.)

AP® exam tip

Be sure you can explain how major civil rights organizations, including the National Association for the Advancement of Colored People (NAACP) and the Congress for Racial Equality (CORE), united African Americans with different experiences and perspectives through a common desire to end racial discrimination and inequality.

AP® exam tip

Make sure you can explain how the language from the *Plessy v. Ferguson* decision contributed to the strategy used by segregationists in the mid-twentieth century.

While the Court did not strike down the entire 1896 decision, it did rule that segregation solely on the basis of race violated Black children's Fourteenth Amendment rights. In the Court's unanimous May 1954 decision, Chief Justice Earl Warren argued that separate facilities, even when identical, were inherently unequal because Black children who were siphoned off to separate facilities suffered a psychological impairment that could stay with them the rest of their lives.

Though not the first Supreme Court decision against segregation, *Brown* galvanized Black America more than earlier Court rulings did. Robert Williams, a young North Carolina marine, compared his feelings after *Brown* to what he imagined enslaved people felt when they heard about the Emancipation Proclamation: "Elation took hold of me so strongly that I found it very difficult to refrain from yielding to an urge of jubilation. . . . I was sure that this was the beginning of a new era of American democracy."[15]

AP® exam tip

You can use the historical context in this section to support and expand upon your understanding of the AP® course's required sources for Topic 3.5: Disenfranchisement and Jim Crow Laws.

That jubilation was short-lived, however. A year later, news of the murder of the Reverend George Lee, a grocery store owner and NAACP fieldworker in Belzoni, Mississippi, shook Black America. Lee was shot at close range while driving after trying to vote. Then came the news that Lamar Smith had been shot in broad daylight, after voting and before witnesses, in front of the Brookhaven, Mississippi, courthouse. The most shocking news of all came when fourteen-year-old Emmett Till's bloated, mutilated body was pulled from the Tallahatchie River in Mississippi on August 31, 1955.

All of these murders seemed to make a mockery of the *Brown* decision, but Till's left an imprint unlike any other. A Chicago teenager who had gone to Mississippi to visit his cousin, Till was murdered by half-brothers Roy Bryant and J. W. Milam, because, they claimed, he had grabbed Bryant's wife, Carolyn, with the intention of raping her. Mamie Till Bradley, Till's mother, was beside herself with grief. Determined to wring something meaningful from her son's senseless murder, she made the fateful decision to hold an open-coffin funeral and let the world view his grotesquely battered body. She wanted Americans to do something.

The murder and condition of Till's body enraged Blacks and whites alike, but in many white quarters throughout the nation, the idea that extra-legal justice was necessary to constrain Black men's lust for white women still held. Despite the outrage expressed by the more than 50,000 people who filed past Till's coffin, and the countless others who viewed pictures of the body in the *Chicago Defender* and the Black weekly magazine *Jet*; and despite the eyewitness testimony of Till's uncle, who testified that Milam and Bryant took Till from his home before the murder, a jury of twelve white men acquitted the brothers after less than seventy-five minutes of deliberation. Milam and Bryant were so confident that they had carried out the will of white America that a few months later, they bragged about the beating and murder to a *Look* magazine reporter. Said Milam: "As long as I live and can do anything about it, n*****s are gonna stay in their place." Obviously thinking about the recent *Brown* decision, he continued, "They ain't gonna go to school with my kids. And when a n***** gets close to mentioning sex with a white woman, He's tired o' livin."[16] Though the brothers

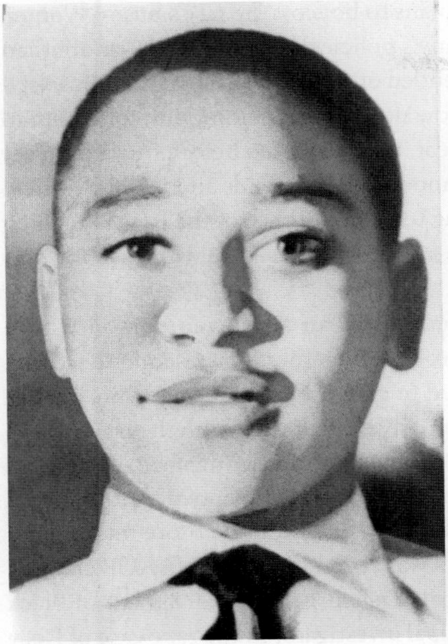
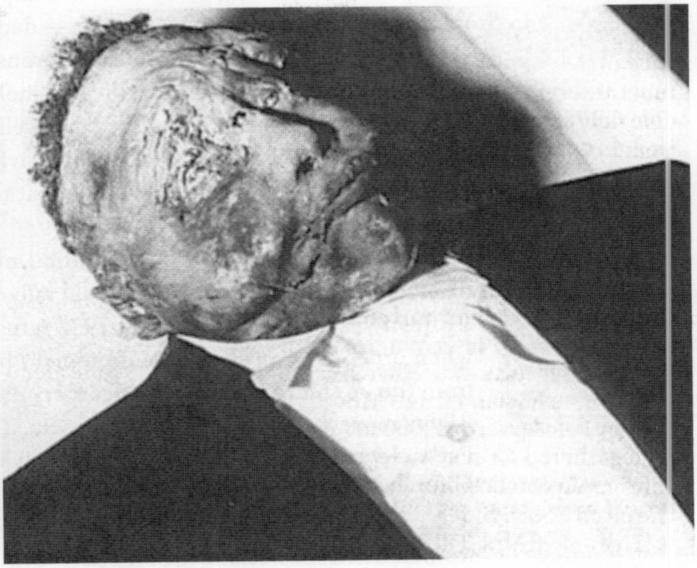

Emmett Till
On August 21, 1955, fourteen-year-old Emmett Till arrived in Mississippi from Chicago to visit his cousin. Less than two weeks later, his grief-stricken mother unlocked his wooden casket to view his bloated, mutilated body. Her decision to hold an open-coffin funeral so that the world could see what two murderers (who were subsequently acquitted) had done to her son sparked protests that led to the modern Civil Rights movement. ■ **Who is the intended audience for this image, and why is that significant? What message did Mamie Till-Mobley convey in deciding to hold an open-coffin funeral?** *Till in 1954: Courtesy Everett Collection; Till in 1955: Courtesy of the* Chicago Defender.

bragged about defending Carolyn Bryant's honor, Carolyn said nothing for over half a century. In 2008, she told historian Timothy Tyson that she had lied on the witness stand. Of her testimony that Till had grabbed her around the waist and uttered obscenities, she confessed "That part's not true." "Nothing that boy did could ever justify what happened to him."[17]

The truth was decades too late. Over fifty years earlier, the entire tragedy had moved people, especially young Blacks of Till's generation, into action. The author Anne Moody, then a fifteen-year-old Mississippian, dated her hatred of whites and Blacks to the Till murder. She hated whites who killed Blacks, and she hated Blacks, particularly Black men, "for not standing up and doing something about the murders."[18] (See AP® Working with Sources: We Are Not Afraid, pp. 581–87.)

Till's death, and especially the showing of the pictures of his mutilated body, was one of a few watershed events to shake America. Already in Montgomery, Alabama, the Women's Political Council, a Black middle-class women's organization under the leadership of Jo Ann Robinson, was making plans to boycott the city's buses. Women were particularly bothered by the bus company's policies, because they — more than men, who customarily traveled by car — depended on public transportation. Bus drivers sometimes did not stop for Black patrons or, after taking their money, told them to exit the front door and reenter through the rear, then departed before they could get back on. Such treatment threatened the livelihoods of Black maids and washerwomen, who relied on the buses to get to work. Having to sit in the back of the bus was galling enough, but being forced to give up a seat to a white person if the white section was full was even more humiliating.

AP® skills

Applying Disciplinary Knowledge: What strategies did the Women's Political Council use to fight bus companies' racist policies?

All the Women's Political Council needed was an aggrieved person whom Montgomery's Black population could rally around. First there was Claudette Colvin, a fifteen-year-old, who in March 1955 refused to give up her seat to a white person when ordered to do so by a Montgomery bus driver. Although Colvin was dragged from the bus and arrested by police, hers did not become the iconic face of the Civil Rights movement that was about to begin. That honor fell to forty-two-year-old Rosa Parks, whom Montgomery's civil rights leaders considered to be more mature and more representative of the city's Blacks. Parks was secretary of her NAACP chapter. A decade earlier, she had led a national campaign against the sexual assault of Black women when she became the NAACP's principal investigator in the rape case of Recy Taylor, a Black mother who had been kidnapped and assaulted by six white men. As an anti-rape crusader, Parks subsequently helped form the Committee for Equal Justice. Having been trained in social justice advocacy at the Highlander Folk School, a leadership training school in Tennessee, Parks was much more than the "sweet and reticent old woman, whose tired feet caused her to defy Jim Crow on Montgomery's city buses."[19] On December 1, 1955, when she was forced from a Montgomery bus after refusing to relinquish her seat, the Women's Political Council joined forces with other civil rights organizations to launch the planned boycott.

Montgomery bus boycott (1955–1956) A thirteen-month boycott begun on December 1, 1955, when Rosa Parks refused to give up her seat to a white person on an Alabama bus. The boycott resulted in significant economic losses for the bus company.

The **Montgomery bus boycott** lasted nearly thirteen months. Black locals traveled on foot or via makeshift taxis and carpool networks set up by a new organization, the Montgomery Improvement Association. The city's attempts to shut down these resources did not get Blacks back on the buses; neither did the verbal and physical assaults directed at walkers by belligerent whites. Blacks walked even after their churches and homes were bombed and crosses were burned on their properties. The boycott forced the bus company to lay off drivers, cut its operations, and raise fares, but the company still would not change its policies. Its fierce resistance convinced the Montgomery Improvement Association that more pressure was needed. In February 1956, attorney Fred Gray filed the federal district court case *Browder v. Gayle* on behalf of four plaintiffs, one of whom was Claudette Colvin. The court declared segregated buses illegal under the equal protection clause of the Fourteenth Amendment, and the boycott ended. On December 21, 1956, 381 days after the boycott began, African Americans boarded Montgomery's buses — and sat wherever they wanted to.

The *Brown* decision, Emmett Till's death, and especially the Montgomery bus boycott turned the Black civil rights struggle in a new direction and established some of its fundamentals. One was the importance of national attention. Once publicized, local issues became part of a national movement for a democracy that could withstand the criticism of the totalitarian Soviet Union. National attention also created bonds between hitherto separate Black communities. Across the nation, Black people in churches, beauty shops, unions, and fraternal and social organizations took up collections for the Montgomery boycott. Most sent money, and others sent shoes and warm clothes. Pacifist groups such as the Fellowship of Reconciliation and the Quakers took up collections, as did Jewish groups, which contributed money and lawyers to the NAACP. News coverage in the *New York Times* and *New York Herald Tribune* turned the local boycott into a national and international event. As the actions of local Black people were broadcast across the country, others, both Black and white, came to their assistance.

AP® skills

Applying Disciplinary Knowledge: Why was national media coverage essential to the success of the Civil Rights movement?

New Leadership for a New Movement

The emergence of the church as the guiding force in the Black freedom struggle was signaled when the sanctuary of the Holt Street Baptist Church became the nerve center of the Montgomery bus boycott. The preeminent leader of the boycott, the Reverend Martin Luther King Jr., also became the iconic figure of the entire freedom struggle. On the first night of the boycott, he wedded religion to the movement when he said, "We believe in the Christian religion. We believe in the teachings of Jesus. The only weapon that we have in our hands this evening is the weapon of protest."[20]

The bus boycott, like so much of the movement that followed in its wake, depended on Black women as foot soldiers, organizers, and fundraisers. But with the centrality of the church came Black patriarchal authority. King became president of the Montgomery Improvement Association, and the Reverend Ralph Abernathy became vice president. Five of the nine officers of the Montgomery Improvement Association were ministers, and despite the important roles played by the Women's Political Council, Rosa Parks, and the four female plaintiffs in *Browder v. Gayle*, it followed that the boycott, like the Black church, would put men in the most visible formal leadership roles. Reflecting on this gender imbalance, Thelma Glass of the Women's Political Council seemed resigned: "It looks like . . . a male-dominated world. . . . Somehow the male comes up and gets the attention. Others seem to just respect male leadership more. I think the men have always had the edge."[21] With some important exceptions, Glass's perception would hold. The Black struggle was publicly led by men but would not have been possible without the work done by women.

The choice of one man in particular, Martin Luther King Jr., was more fateful than anyone could have known. Fresh from Boston, where he had received his doctorate in theology, King was reluctant to take on the leadership role thrust upon him because he had been in Montgomery for only a little over a year before the boycott began. However, older freedom fighters saw King's newness and relative youth as pluses. At twenty-six, King, like Abernathy, brought a new kind of energy. It was an energy born of his belief that World War II had given Black Americans a new sense of self-respect and that suffering not only was redemptive but also could be used as a powerful weapon of coercion against southern segregationists. King infused the passive resistance tactics of Mohandas Gandhi, leader of the movement for Indian independence, with the New Testament theology of Christian love to lead what another minister, the Reverend Fred Shuttlesworth, called "the fight between light and darkness, right and wrong, good and evil, fair play and tyranny."[22] Though he was not against armed self-defense, he believed that political goals were best achieved by nonviolent, "socially organized masses on the march." In his mind, aggressive violence posed "incalculable perils," but disobeying laws, registering to vote, and boycotting Jim Crow establishments would, he thought, ultimately prevail against white terrorism.[23]

AP® exam tip

Make sure you can describe King's approach to achieving the political goals of the Civil Rights movement.

King's ideas about nonviolence would ultimately be challenged, but on the eve of the boycott, his speech tying together passive resistance, Christianity, anticommunism, and Black patriotism was nothing short of magnificent. First, he defended himself against the inevitable charges of communism by proclaiming protest to be an American tradition. "This is the glory of our democracy," he declared. "If we were incarcerated behind the iron curtains of a Communistic nation we couldn't do this. If we were trapped in the dungeon of a totalitarian regime we couldn't do this." Instead, while denouncing the anti-Americanism of racists, he declared Blacks to be patriots: "There will be nobody among us who will stand up and defy the Constitution of this nation." Finally, he wrapped himself and the bus boycott in both the American and Christian traditions: "If we are wrong, then the Supreme Court of this nation is wrong. . . . The Constitution of the United States is wrong. . . . God Almighty is wrong. If we are wrong, Jesus of Nazareth was merely a utopian dreamer and never came down to earth."[24]

The Watershed Years of the Southern Movement

AP® exam tip

Be sure you can explain how major civil rights organizations, including the Southern Christian Leadership Conference (SCLC), united African Americans with different experiences and perspectives through a common desire to end racial discrimination and inequality.

The years from 1957 to 1963 were watershed years. As the world watched, African Americans and their white allies mounted a multipronged attack that eventually triumphed over segregation and disfranchisement. One of the first tasks was to harness the energy generated by the successful Montgomery bus boycott. On January 10, 1957, the Southern Christian Leadership Conference (SCLC), a church-based organization, was founded in Atlanta. King became its first president. The church had not always taken the lead in the Black freedom struggle; in fact, most ministers were fearful of white reprisals and advised their impatient congregations to go slowly. But many saw great potential in an organization that took advantage of the tremendous networks of Black churches, which would be able to withstand Red-baiting and accusations of communistic atheism better than unions or civil rights organizations. The SCLC became the "political arm of the black church."[25] Voting rights became the SCLC's number-one goal.[26]

AP® skills

Applying Disciplinary Knowledge: Why might the SCLC's primary focus have been on the right to vote?

Demonstrators Kneeling in Prayer in Albany, Georgia, 1962
Albany, Georgia, was the scene of one of the first nonviolent direct-action protest movements conducted by civil rights organizations. The Albany protests, which lasted over a year, aimed to register Blacks to vote and to desegregate schools and public places. The city's notorious police chief, Laurie Pritchett, jailed hundreds of demonstrators, including women and children. The demonstrations achieved no immediate change in Albany's racial structure, but a year after they ended, all segregation statutes were eliminated from Albany's books, and the city's Black voters mobilized as a force to be reckoned with. The demonstration pictured here, in which men, women, and children kneel in prayer on an Albany sidewalk, is characteristic of the nonviolent direct-action protests that took place throughout the South. **What actions are captured in this image? How would you use this image to support an explanation of the protest methods of the Civil Rights movement's major organizations?** *Bettmann/Getty Images.*

Another task was to solidify nonviolence as the strategic tactic of choice while also not relinquishing the Black tradition of self-defense. Although boycotts, marches, sit-ins, and voter registration drives were calculated to expose the often hidden terrorism of whites who brought bats, batons, attack dogs, fire hoses, and guns to confrontations with Black demonstrators, local African Americans always understood nonviolence to be a tactic rather than a way of life. "All our parents had guns in the house," noted Joyce Ladner, a civil rights worker at this time, "and they were not just for hunting rabbits and squirrels, but out of self-defense."[27] While national civil rights leaders and organizations were the most steadfast defenders of the philosophy and tactic of nonviolence — and depended on it to get Americans to side with civil rights demonstrators — local Blacks never saw a contradiction between nonviolence and the use of firearms. The fact that neither local law enforcement nor the federal government would offer protection to demonstrators convinced local activists that they had to provide for their own self-defense, especially after the cameras and reporters had left the site of a demonstration. As put by Charles E. Cobb, a Student Nonviolent Coordinating Committee (SNCC) field secretary from 1962 to 1967, in his book *This Nonviolent Stuff'll Get You Killed: How Guns Made the Civil Rights Movement Possible*, "because nonviolence worked so well as a tactic for effecting change and was demonstrably improving their lives, some Black people chose to use weapons to defend the nonviolent Freedom Movement."[28] And they needed them because segregationists declared war on all who fought for change, regardless of age, gender, race, or religion. They bombed the home of the Reverend Ralph Abernathy, a founder of the SCLC, the first night the group convened. His wife and child managed to escape, but while he was on the phone talking to them, other churches in Montgomery were bombed, as was the home of Robert S. Graetz, a supportive white Lutheran minister.

AP® skills

Applying Disciplinary Knowledge: What role did Black children play in the Civil Rights movement? What role did gender play in their participation and the treatment they received?

If churches were not exempt from the wrath of segregationists, neither were Black children. Although the 1954 *Brown* decision had made segregation illegal, there was no directive on how to desegregate schools. The U.S. Supreme Court itself did not set a timetable but rather vaguely instructed schools to desegregate "with all deliberate speed." In practice, this meant that throughout the South, Black schoolchildren bore the burden of school integration. These children were disproportionately female, sent forth by their parents and communities not because they provoked less violence from whites — far from it — but because their upbringing enabled them to navigate sustained social hostility better than males, who were more prominent in the desegregation of lunch counters, public transportation, and parks. In some places, especially in the Upper South (Maryland, Delaware, West Virginia, and Washington, D.C.), these girls met little resistance. But even in these areas, most Black students continued to attend segregated schools. Some school districts, such as that in Prince Edward County, Virginia, closed their schools rather than integrate. In other places, Black children who showed up for school faced violence and anger.

AP® exam tip

Be prepared to explain how different groups responded to school integration as a result of the *Brown v. Board of Education* decision.

AP® exam tip

Be sure you can describe how, following the Supreme Court's ruling in *Brown v. Board of Education*, students such as the "Little Rock Nine" attempted to integrate schools throughout the South despite continued resistance.

In September 1957, when the federal district court ordered the whites-only Central High School in Little Rock, Arkansas, to admit nine Black students — six girls and three boys — the new enrollees confronted screaming, cursing, and threatening white men, women, and children. Governor Orval Faubus also attempted to block the students, ordering the Arkansas National Guard to surround the school. When fifteen-year-old Elizabeth Eckford arrived at Central High on September 4, she was met by angry crowds shouting, "Lynch her! Lynch her! . . . Let's take care of that n*****." When she tried to follow white students into the school, guards raised their bayonets to block her. (See AP® Working with Sources: We Are Not Afraid, pp. 581–87.)

Eckford and the other students could barely count on help from Republican president Dwight D. Eisenhower, who, though sworn to uphold the laws of the

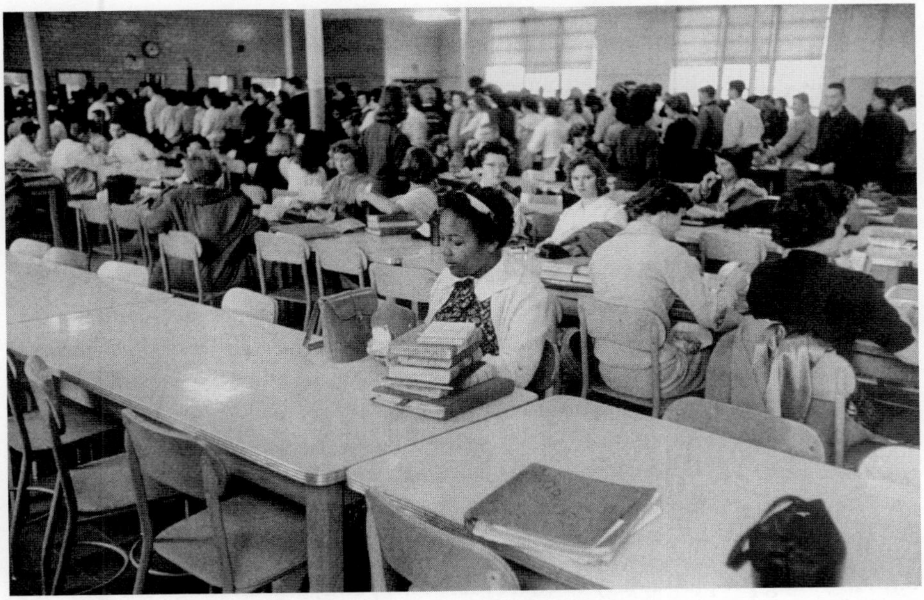

The Burden of Desegregation

Black children who integrated public schools often faced social ostracism. More Black girls than boys were on the frontlines of school desegregation battles. Here a Black student sits alone as the white students around her study, interact socially, and stare at her. **What does this image convey about the immediate effects of the *Brown* decision on Black students?** *Ed Clark/Getty Images.*

country and enforce the Constitution, personally opposed federally imposed integration. Eisenhower, reluctant to interfere with the South's customs, had denounced *Brown* as a measure that "set back progress in the South at least fifteen years."[29] Only after international headlines made Little Rock a national embarrassment, and after it was clear that the Soviet Union was using the incident to demonstrate the contradictions between American practice and the nation's professed democratic ideals, did Eisenhower act. He not only called out the army but also federalized the Arkansas National Guard, ordering both to protect the **Little Rock Nine**, as these brave pioneers became known. In a speech to the country, Eisenhower linked anticommunism to civil rights, and in the process he demonstrated the potential efficacy of the new civil rights strategy: "At a time when we face grave situations abroad because of the hatred that Communism bears toward a system of government based on human rights, it would be difficult to exaggerate the harm that is being done to the prestige and influence, and indeed to the safety, of our nation and the world."[30] Eisenhower's successor, John F. Kennedy, who was elected in 1960, repeatedly made similar statements.

On February 1, 1960, four young Black men from the historically Black North Carolina Agricultural and Technical College challenged the segregation ordinances in Greensboro, North Carolina, by sitting down at a Woolworth's lunch counter and

Little Rock Nine
The nine Black students who, in 1957, tested *Brown v. Board of Education of Topeka* (1954) by enrolling in Little Rock Central High School in Little Rock, Arkansas.

AP® exam tip

You can use the historical context in this section to support and expand upon your understanding of the AP® course's required sources for Topic 4.6: Major Civil Rights Organizations and Topic 4.7: Black Women's Leadership and Grassroots Organizing in the Civil Rights movement.

Greensboro Four
The four Black college students who, by sitting down at a segregated lunch counter in Greensboro, North Carolina, and requesting service in February 1960, initiated the nationwide sit-in movement.

requesting service. Later known as the **Greensboro Four**, the men were denied service, but they returned every day with more Black and white supporters, despite being bullied, spat on, and jailed and having ketchup emptied on their heads and cigarette butts ground into their skin. Black and white students from colleges across the nation soon staged similar protests, sitting in at a host of segregated lunch counters, beaches, churches, libraries, movie theaters, and skating rinks. That month saw fifty-four sit-ins in at least nine states and fifteen cities. In every instance, well-disciplined, peaceful demonstrators were met with fierce attacks by whites, who, try as they might, could not stop the students. "We had the confidence . . . of a Mack truck," said Franklin McCain, one of the Greensboro Four.[31] Protesters sometimes prayed or sang together, which not only distracted them from the chaos and danger of their situation, but also served to emphasize the contrast between their peaceful tactics and the violence being perpetrated against them.

Like the Black church, students — especially Black students — were an untapped source of energy, and it was important for activists to organize them. The ideal person to do this was Ella Baker. The first full-time staff member of the SCLC and later its interim director, Baker left that organization in 1960, after having grown disenchanted with King's top-down leadership style and the SCLC's male-centeredness. She had faith in young people's ability to chart their own paths, and although she lent all of her talent to help students organize the Student Nonviolent Coordinating Committee (SNCC) (pronounced "snick") in April 1960, she did not try to impose an agenda on them. She challenged adults to listen to their children, who, she said, "are asking us to forget our laziness and doubt and fear and follow our dedication to the truth to the bitter end."[32] SNCC debated everything. After deliberating over whether to focus on desegregation or voting rights, SNCC decided to do both. Similarly, after debating the role of white supporters in the movement, the organization decided that the "movement should not be considered one for Negroes but one for people who consider this a movement against injustice. This would include members of all races."[33]

AP® exam tip
Be sure you can explain how major civil rights organizations, including the Student Nonviolent Coordinating Committee (SNCC), united African Americans with different experiences and perspectives through a common desire to end racial discrimination and inequality.

In the spring of 1961, CORE showed how effective interracial student activism could be. Just as the U.S. Supreme Court had ordered school desegregation in 1954 without mandating how to achieve it, in a series of cases dating from 1946, the Court had ordered an end to segregation on interstate transportation and other facilities but had not provided for enforcement.[34] To force the issue, CORE organized interracial teams of activists to ride together on buses traveling from Washington, D.C., to New Orleans in what came to be called the **Freedom Rides** (Map 14.1). Along the way, the Freedom Riders also planned to integrate bus terminal facilities, including restrooms, lunch counters, and waiting rooms. The first group made it only as far as Alabama. Outside Anniston, one bus was firebombed, and in Anniston and Birmingham, mobs attacked the Freedom Riders. Interviewed on television from his hospital bed, rider James Zwerg told the world, "We will continue the Freedom Ride. . . . We'll take hitting, we'll take beating. We're willing to accept death."[35]

Freedom Rides
An organized effort in 1961 to desegregate interstate travel by having white and Black students ride buses through the South and use "whites only" facilities.

AP® exam tip
Be prepared to describe how local branches of major civil rights organizations launched a national movement built on the shared methods of nonviolent, direct, and racially inclusive protest and grassroots efforts.

Although President Kennedy announced that he had directed the Interstate Commerce Commission (ICC) to outlaw segregation in facilities under its jurisdiction, the

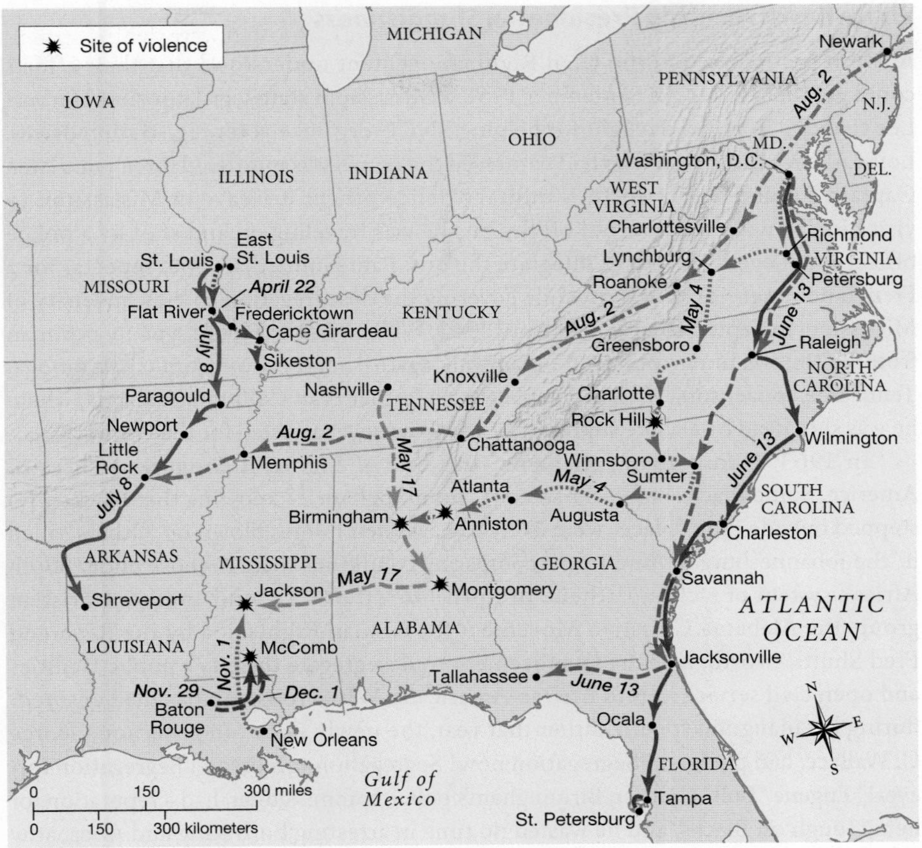

MAP 14.1 The Routes of the Freedom Rides, 1961

In the spring of 1961, the Congress of Racial Equality (CORE) organized interracial groups to ride south together by bus, integrating buses and bus terminal facilities along the way. As the activists entered the South, they were confronted by white mobs and deadly weapons, such as firebombs, and could not rely on protection from unsympathetic local officials. This map illustrates the origins and destinations of the rides, which cities the Freedom Riders passed through, and the places where violence occurred. ■ **Which Freedom Ride routes saw the most violence? Why were the violent acts accepted by many political authorities?**

Freedom Rides continued through November, when the segregation ban took effect. Hundreds of students rode buses from the North to Mississippi, where they were corralled in local jails; some were sent to the infamous Parchman Farm prison, where inmates were treated like enslaved people and subjected to unrestrained brutality. The ICC ban was evidence to many that nonviolent protest worked. Others, however, were not so sure.

White Resistance and Presidential Sluggishness

All who participated in the Civil Rights movement understood that their efforts could get them killed. In September 1961, a Mississippi state legislator shot Herbert Lee to death in broad daylight for helping SNCC organize voter registration drives. Louis Allen, a Black man who had witnessed the crime, was murdered three years later. Captain Roman Ducksworth, a military police officer on leave in Mississippi to visit his sick wife, was ordered off the bus he was traveling on and shot by a police officer for allegedly trying to integrate the bus. Paul Guihard, a white reporter for a French news service, was shot while covering the desegregation of the University of Mississippi in September 1962. In April 1963, William Lewis Moore, a white postman from Baltimore, undertook a one-man walk against segregation from Chattanooga, Tennessee, to Jackson, Mississippi. He got no farther than Collbran, Alabama, where he was shot dead by a white supremacist who was never arrested for the crime.

AP® skills

Applying Disciplinary Knowledge: Why was Birmingham considered one of the most dangerous cities in the 1960s?

In 1963, Birmingham, Alabama, was one of the most dangerous cities in America. Some Blacks had nicknamed it "Bombingham,"[36] knowing that Blacks who stepped outside their "place" were likely to have their homes blown up. Others called it "the Johannesburg of America,"[37] comparing conditions there to those under South Africa's system of racial apartheid. In April 1963, the SCLC and another Christian group, the Alabama Christian Movement for Human Rights, led by the Reverend Fred Shuttlesworth, launched a movement to desegregate the city's public facilities and open civil service jobs to African Americans. White resistance seemed ensured: during his inaugural speech earlier that year, the newly sworn-in governor, George C. Wallace, had pledged, "Segregation now! Segregation tomorrow! Segregation forever!" Eugene "Bull" Connor, Birmingham's police commissioner, had a reputation for being tough on Blacks, and he wasted no time in arresting both King and Abernathy shortly after the SCLC arrived in Birmingham.

Despite the predictability of white resistance, no one was prepared for the hostility that rained down on the activists, whose number included elementary and high school children. On May 2, Connor imprisoned more than 600 adults and children. The following day, he turned fire hoses on marchers, set attack dogs on them, and ordered police to beat them back with billy clubs. With the U.S. Information Agency reporting that the Soviet Union had "stepped up its propaganda on Birmingham . . . devoting about one-fifth of its radio output to the subject," President Kennedy was forced to act. He dispatched the assistant attorney general of the United States, Burke Marshall, to help civil rights demonstrators, city officials, and local business people work out an agreement that desegregated public accommodations and addressed employment issues.[38]

Like Eisenhower, Kennedy moved cautiously and slowly in civil rights matters. He and his brother Robert, the U.S. attorney general, favored negotiated mediation behind closed doors over direct-action demonstrations. Rather than protect the federal rights of the civil rights protesters, the president expressed anger at their actions.

Only reluctantly did he send troops to Oxford, Mississippi, in October 1962 to quell the deadly riots that ensued after James Meredith, a Black student, won the right in court to attend the previously segregated University of Mississippi. Kennedy's inaction stemmed in part from Cold War concerns: engaged in talks with Soviet premier Nikita Khrushchev about human rights in Soviet spheres, Kennedy did not want to have to explain embarrassing human rights violations at home. The attacks on civil rights activists were "exactly the kind of thing the Communists used to make the United States look bad around the world," he told his civil rights adviser.[39] In addition, most white supremacists were Democrats, and until 1964, when they joined the Republican Party, Democrats, including Kennedy, tried hard not to offend them.

The president's inaction weighed heavily on civil rights leaders' minds. King's frustration was clear in his poignant "Letter from Birmingham City Jail," which he wrote while imprisoned during the 1963 Birmingham demonstrations. In it, King chastised white moderates, whom he felt were more obstructionist than "the White Citizen's Counciler or the Ku Klux Klanner." The white moderate, King argued, was "more devoted to 'order' than to justice." The moderate perennially counseled Black people to "wait" and "paternalistically" felt that he could "set the timetable for another man's freedom." King argued that Blacks had waited for more than 340 years for constitutional rights that were their birthright and warned that if the repressed frustrations of Black people did not come out in nonviolent ways, they would "come out in ominous expressions of violence." "This is not a threat," he wrote. "It is a fact of history."

AP® skills

Applying Disciplinary Knowledge: What was King's argument about the white moderate in "Letter from Birmingham Jail"? How does that argument relate to President Kennedy's stance on the Civil Rights movement?

The 1963 Birmingham demonstrations energized the Civil Rights movement. National and international coverage sparked sympathy marches across the country, and negative publicity threatened to cripple Birmingham's businesses. The U.S. assistant attorney general was able to negotiate an agreement that ended segregation in the city and promised to open more jobs to Blacks. But even these modest gains did not sit well with some segregationists. They bombed the home of A. D. King, Martin Luther King Jr.'s brother, and the motel where they thought Martin was staying. As some outraged African Americans finally abandoned nonviolence and poured into the streets, throwing rocks and bottles, the nation held its breath.

Here was the violence, "the fact of history" King had predicted. It had been brewing for some time, and it spoke to the efficacy of nonviolent resistance. Nine years had passed since the landmark *Brown* decision, and the movement was taking a psychological toll on organizers and activists. Segregation still held fast, and Blacks in the South still could not vote or hold office despite the national and international attention that nonviolent direct-action demonstrations drew. They still could not get decent jobs or live where they wanted to. They were still the targets of relentless white violence, and the perpetrators of that violence continued to escape even the slightest reprimand from federal and state governments, neither of which provided protection against the white murderers and mobs. Although many demonstrators expressed a sense of self-respect at having put their lives on the line for such an important cause, others

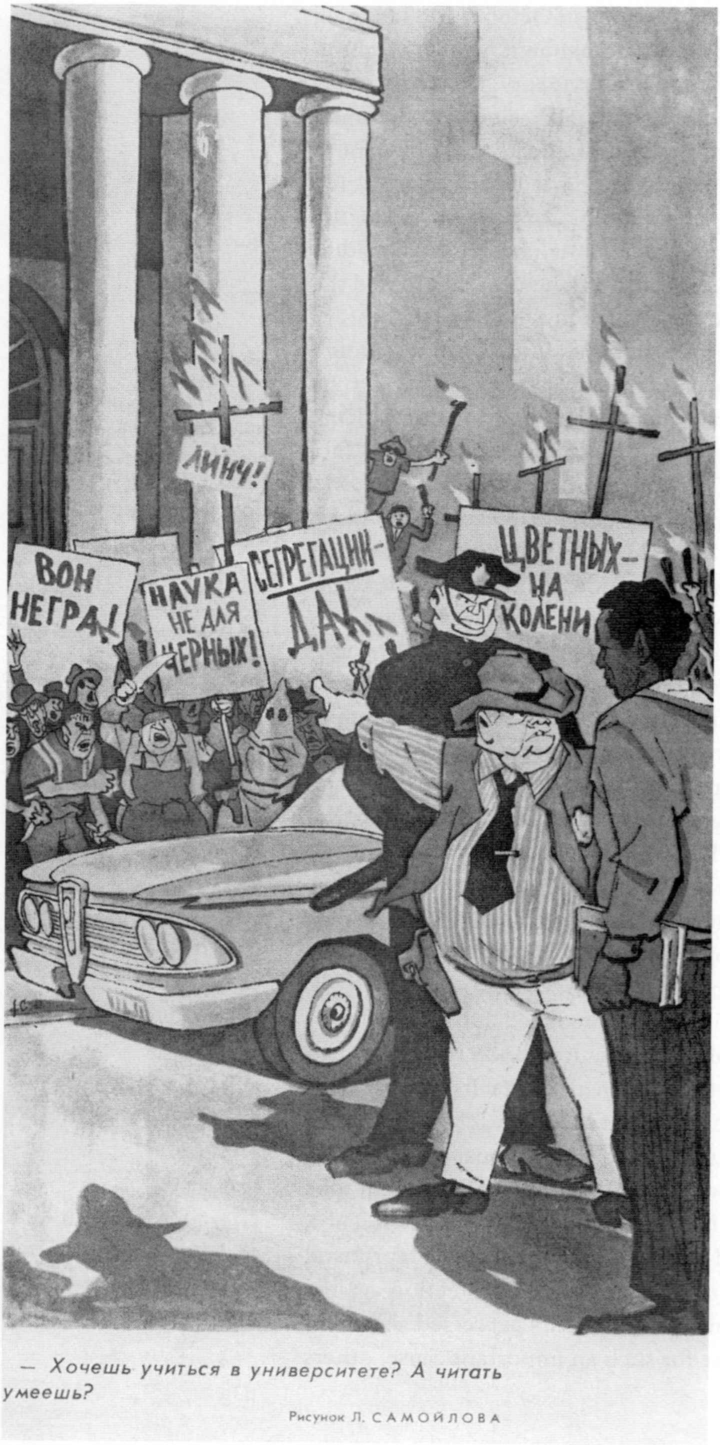

American Racism Depicted in the International Press
Presidents Dwight D. Eisenhower and John F. Kennedy feared the impact of the negative publicity generated by American racism. Convincing the world that America's system of government was superior to the Soviet Union's was hard when Black Americans were being attacked and murdered for demanding their rights. In this cartoon, published in the Soviet magazine *Krokodil*, a policeman prevents a Black student from entering a university. The signs in the background read "N***** Go Away," "Lynch Him," "We Want Segregation," and "Put the Colored on Their Knees." **What is the intended message of this cartoon? How does it undermine the idea that the U.S. system of government was superior to that of the Soviet Union?** *© Bettmann/Getty Images.*

found the constant danger, the uncertainty about their future, and the steady demand for a high level of physical energy draining. Many began to suffer from what is now recognized as post-traumatic stress disorder. "I was totally washed out, burned out," one student activist recalled.[40]

Moreover, the "non-threat" cited by King was fast becoming a reality. When King wrote from Birmingham, the nation was only one year away from a series of racially motivated revolts that would erupt in Harlem, Chicago, Philadelphia, and Jersey City. But throughout the 1950s and early '60s, community activists and supporters had created loosely organized units of self-defense. Robert Williams, the former marine who had been so exhilarated by *Brown* in 1954, became so disenchanted by government inaction that in the late 1950s, he turned his local NAACP chapter into an armed paramilitary group and vowed to "meet lynching with lynching."[41] "Nowhere in the annals of history does the record show a people delivered from bondage by patience alone," Williams wrote.[42] The national leaders of the NAACP denounced him, and the government forced him into exile in Cuba. But there were many more like Williams who, seeing that the government provided no security, took matters into their own hands. Everywhere local people armed themselves. Many, like Medgar Evers, were killed despite the precautions they took to be armed and have bodyguards, but others, like Daisy Bates and Fannie Lou Hamer, carried guns for self-defense. In 1956, after his house was bombed, even King applied for a gun permit, which was denied. Said Mississippi activist John Salter in 1994, "I'm alive today because of the Second Amendment and the natural right to keep and bear arms. . . . The knowledge that I had these weapons and was willing to use them kept enemies at bay."[43] In 1964, not long after King's "non-threat," the **Deacons for Defense and Justice** was organized in Louisiana to protect Black people against increased Ku Klux Klan activity. Although national leaders and organizations needed the aura that nonviolent passive resistance provided, local direct-action crusaders needed, sought, and appreciated the protection provided by the Deacons for Defense and Justice.

AP® exam tip

It is essential to be able to articulate how nonviolent forms of civil disobedience — including marches, sit-ins, litigation, economic boycotts, and the use of mass media — were often met with violence, which sometimes precipitated a response of self-defense.

AP® skills

Applying Disciplinary Knowledge: Why did some Black Americans view the provisions of the Second Amendment as a means to protect themselves and their communities?

Deacons for Defense and Justice
An armed grassroots organization formed in Louisiana in 1964 to protect Black people against increased Ku Klux Klan activity.

Civil Rights: A National Movement

What were the long-term effects of housing discrimination on African Americans in the second half of the twentieth century?

How did nonviolent resistance strategies mobilize the Civil Rights movement?

Although the most dramatic confrontations between civil rights workers and violent whites occurred in the South, Black northerners and westerners — many of whom were recent migrants from the South — also fought persistently against discrimination in all facets of life. Their struggle was different, but not because the North and West were more egalitarian. These regions were, in fact, more segregated than the South.[44] Inequality in the North and West, however, grew from systemic, or institutional, practices rather than legal mandates, making it in some ways more difficult to rectify than southern inequality. In August 1963, when the March on Washington for Jobs and Freedom brought Black and white citizens to the National Mall in Washington, D.C., people from all over the country gathered in support not just of southern Blacks, but of civil rights across the nation.

Racism and Inequality in the North and West

Beaches, parks, public swimming pools, skating rinks, theaters, and restaurants in the North and West did not usually post "Whites Only" signs, but in the 1950s they were, nevertheless, only for white people. In Los Angeles, for example, most restaurants did not serve Blacks. In Pasadena, California, Blacks were not allowed to attend citywide dances.[45] In Cleveland, Blacks could not go to the Skateland roller rink, and in Cincinnati, the Coney Island amusement park was off-limits. In downtown St. Louis, Blacks found the major department stores — Woolworth's and Sears, Roebuck — the Greyhound bus terminal, and the Fox Theatre inaccessible. In New Jersey, African Americans could not swim in the pool at Palisades Amusement Park. Across the country, recent Black migrants as well as longtime residents wondered whether they had gained much by living outside the South. Los Angeles civil rights worker Don Wheeldin recalled, "There were limits to what [Blacks] could do with what they made because they couldn't buy houses anywhere, and they couldn't enjoy themselves, in terms of theaters and other things.... They couldn't use that money for purposes of themselves or their families."[46]

Despite the hardships, Blacks throughout the country fought against discrimination and unequal treatment. The Louisiana migrant Andrew Murray and his friends staged a sit-in at the Witch's Stand drive-in restaurant in Los Angeles, and Wheeldin and his friends integrated the dances in Pasadena.[47] Across the North and West, local branches of CORE and the NAACP staged boycotts, sit-ins, stand-ins, and picket lines to desegregate public accommodations, private department stores, and recreation facilities. By the early 1960s, they had made substantial gains in these areas.

However, with housing, school desegregation, and fair hiring practices, white resistance proved that racism was a national problem, not just a southern problem. The housing picture was particularly bleak. The postwar era witnessed a phenomenal housing boom underwritten by the federal government, as the Federal Housing Administration (FHA) and the Veterans Administration (VA) issued low-interest loans with minimal down payments. However, the VA, and subsequently the FHA, would issue loans to Blacks only if they moved into Black neighborhoods. Moreover, although in *Shelley v. Kraemer* (1948) the U.S. Supreme Court had ruled against **restrictive covenants** — clauses in deeds that prohibited an owner from selling to a person or family of a particular racial or religious group — the FHA proved unwilling to challenge racist real estate practices. In some areas, it actually recommended or required restrictive covenants and would not guarantee government-secured loans without them. In other areas, such as Chicago, the FHA even refused to insure

restrictive covenants
Discriminatory clauses in deeds that prohibited owners from selling their property to a person or family of a particular racial or religious group.

mortgages in Black areas, thereby forcing Blacks to buy homes "on contract" from shady speculators who sold homes at exploitative prices. If a family missed a payment, the speculator who owned the home would evict them and resell it to another unsuspecting family and pocket the first family's down payment and monthly installments.[48]

Real estate companies compounded the problem by redlining (denying loans to an area inhabited by racial minorities), steering (directing minority buyers solely to homes in minority neighborhoods), and blockbusting (playing on white fears to encourage whites to sell their homes at low prices to real estate companies, which could resell them to minorities at higher prices).[49] Both the government and real estate companies turned Black people into pariahs, whom most feared would bring mayhem and drive down home values. When combined with the billions of dollars the government invested in building a highway system linking suburbs to urban areas, these practices allowed the government and real estate companies to pin Blacks in inner cities while they built white suburbs and financed white flight to them.

AP® skills

Applying Disciplinary Knowledge: Explain how blockbusting is different from redlining.

This was the case all over America. The *Los Angeles Sentinel*, a Black newspaper, reported in 1947 that "banks won't lend money and title companies won't guarantee titles [to Blacks] in what they regard as white communities even when no valid restrictions exist." A white resident of Hawthorne, California, claimed to represent the feeling of "99% of the people" when he argued that Blacks "should be placed in their own all-Negro communities . . . with their own churches, their own schools and recreational facilities." That, he said, "would certainly be one of the finest things that could happen to this region."[50]

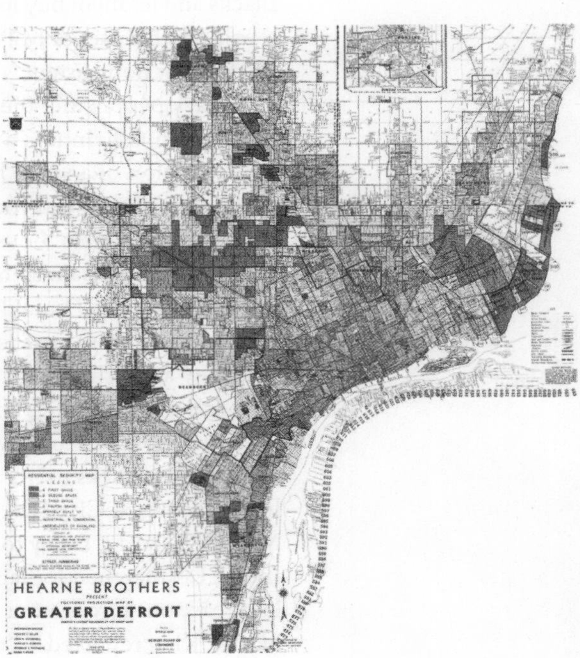

Redlining Map

Real estate agents used maps created by the U.S. government's Home Owners Loan Corporation to keep African Americans corralled in the inner city. Areas where racial minorities lived were shaded red (hence the term redlining) and designated off-limits for government-guaranteed bank loans, while areas furthest away from red areas were considered safe investments. People who lived in red areas could not secure loans to move elsewhere or make improvements on their property. Maps like this one for Detroit were replicated for large and small cities throughout the United States. **What do this map and caption reveal about the causes and effects of discrimination in housing and real estate faced by many Black Americans in the United States?** *University of Richmond Digital Scholarship Lab.*

Many whites tried to make that happen. The developer William Levitt built thousands of mass-produced homes in what became known as Levittowns in Pennsylvania, New York, and New Jersey, but his settlements were only for "members of the Caucasian Race."[51] As in the South, whites used intimidation and violence to keep Blacks out of places they considered their own. In 1959, in Pacoima, California, the Holmes family returned home one day to find their driveway spattered with paint, their windows broken by rocks, and a spray-painted sign that read "Black Cancer here. Don't let it spread!" Another Black family in California had a twelve-foot cross burned on the lot adjacent to their home. The citizens' group that put it there included a policeman, members of the chamber of commerce, the president of the local Kiwanis club, and a local real estate agent.[52] Just as southerners had formed White Citizens' Councils to resist Black advances, white homeowners in Detroit formed more than 190 associations designed to prevent Blacks from moving into their neighborhoods. In 1955, the family of Easby Wilson bought a home in one of Detroit's white neighborhoods, but before the Wilsons moved in, they found the walls and floors ruined, the drains stopped up, water damage from running faucets, and black paint everywhere. They moved in despite the warnings but were continually harassed with threatening phone calls; snakes thrown in their basement, rock-throwing incidents, and mobs of up to four hundred people who yelled, jeered, and shouted obscenities.

Across the country, the National Urban League, the NAACP, and other civil rights groups called for fair housing policies. They fought for city ordinances to outlaw real estate practices that preyed on white fears, pressured the FHA to issue loans to Blacks and let them buy foreclosed homes in white areas, and lobbied state agencies to revoke the licenses of real estate agents who steered, redlined, or blockbusted. Success was slow or nonexistent.

Black people met the same resistance even when they tried to move into public housing. In Cincinnati, a proposal to build an integrated housing project triggered the formation of a white homeowners' association that asked white residents in the surrounding area, "Do you want N*****s in your backyard?"[53] In Detroit, despite the fact that most public housing had white residents, white associations linked it negatively to both socialized housing and the presence of Blacks. In Chicago's Trumbull Park community, Donald and Betty Howard were greeted by more than fifty white teenagers shouting racial epithets and throwing stones and bricks. During the decade that they and other Black families lived in the mostly white public housing project, they endured bombings and physical attacks and were barely able to leave their homes without a police escort. When the head of the Chicago Housing Authority defended the rights of Blacks to live in Trumbull Park, she was fired. In 1955, civil rights groups held marches at City Hall to protest years of violence at Trumbull Park and met with Mayor Richard J. Daley to protest police failure to stop the violence.[54] In 1966, when the SCLC marched for fair housing in a neighboring community, white citizens' violent reactions forced even Martin Luther King Jr. to retreat. "I've never seen anything like it," King reported. "I've been in many demonstrations all across the South, but I can say that I have never seen — even in Mississippi and Alabama — mobs as hostile and as hate-filled as I've seen in Chicago."[55]

Police not only failed to stop the violence but contributed to it. To most African Americans, white police forces in the North and West seemed no better than the Bull Connors of the South. In New York City in 1950, when two white police officers shot and killed an unarmed Black Korean War veteran named John Derrick, the outspoken Harlem congressman Adam Clayton Powell Jr., one of only two Black congressmen (the other was Chicagoan William Levi Dawson), labeled it a lynching. "We don't call them that, but we do have lynchings right here in the north," Powell said. In 1952, New York City police beat a man and his wife, Jacob and Geneva Jackson, and a friend with whom they were driving, so badly that they needed hospitalization. In light of evidence that the police department had negotiated an agreement with U.S. Justice Department officials making the police exempt from prosecutions involving African Americans, outraged civil rights groups lobbied, unsuccessfully, for a civilian complaint review board. The depth of the problem they were up against was revealed when New York City police commissioner George P. Monaghan told the FBI that civil rights laws did not apply up north, only "south of the Mason Dixon line."[56]

AP® skills

Applying Disciplinary Knowledge: How did the police contribute to the opposition of social and economic rights?

This attitude prevailed throughout the North and West. Black people who migrated to these areas to find freedom instead found white authorities who were determined to restrict their movement. When asked in the 1950s about accusations of racial profiling, Los Angeles police chief William Parker said, "Any time that a person is in a place other than his place of residence or where he is conducting business, . . . it might be a cause for inquiry."[57] In Los Angeles, as elsewhere, police made race-based inquiries. When Blacks protested harassment and vicious police beatings, the police chief expressed sympathy — for the police. An early 1950s survey of residents of Watts, a Black neighborhood in Los Angeles, revealed that nearly half of them had been harassed, lined up on the sidewalk, frisked for no apparent reason, or slapped and kicked by the police.[58]

Farther north, in Oakland, California, police harassment was equally blatant. The Black migrant community had grown exponentially, and whites depended on police to keep it contained. In 1957, Oakland police established the Associated Agencies, an elaborate surveillance operation to control Black youths. It connected the city's schools, social service agencies, and recreational programs to the police and the dreaded California Youth Authority, a statewide incarceration and detention center, so that those deemed potential delinquents could be identified and contained. Try as they might, the Urban League, the NAACP, and CORE could not change this prevailing culture.

Fighting Back: The Snail's Pace of Change

One way to counter police brutality was to change the political climate of urban centers. This began to happen in the 1950s, as African Americans continued to migrate out of the South. In the North and West, Black people could vote and develop political alliances that yielded influence unavailable to them in the South. In cities where Blacks held the balance of power, they leveraged it for political offices and political power by voting as a bloc. Change, however, was slow — much too slow for many.

> **AP® skills**
>
> **Applying Disciplinary Knowledge:** Describe the political participation and activism of Black people in New York during the 1950s.

Events in New York City illustrate this well. In 1950, the year after American Labor Party candidate Ewart Guinier marshaled 38 percent of the vote in a losing battle for Manhattan borough president, Blacks were able to pressure the Democratic Party to nominate a Black candidate, Harold Stevens, to New York City's highest court. Stevens won that election, and two years later, Black leaders used the threat of a third-party candidate to force the Democratic Party to nominate Julius Archibald, who became New York's first Black state senator. He was one of about fifty Blacks elected to office across the nation in 1952. Further maneuvering and grassroots organizing between 1953 and 1954 resulted in the election of two more African Americans, including the first Black woman, Bessie Buchanan, to the New York State Assembly. Remarkably, the 1953 contest for Manhattan borough president devolved into a contest between five Black candidates.

In New York City and elsewhere, Black candidates ran on platforms that included calls for full employment, an end to police brutality and housing discrimination, and more schools, hospitals, and libraries in Black areas.[59] In Los Angeles, for example, with the help of white allies, Black elected officials were able to lobby successfully for a state Fair Employment Practices Commission in 1958 to address job discrimination, and a state fair housing act in 1963 that prohibited racial discrimination by real estate

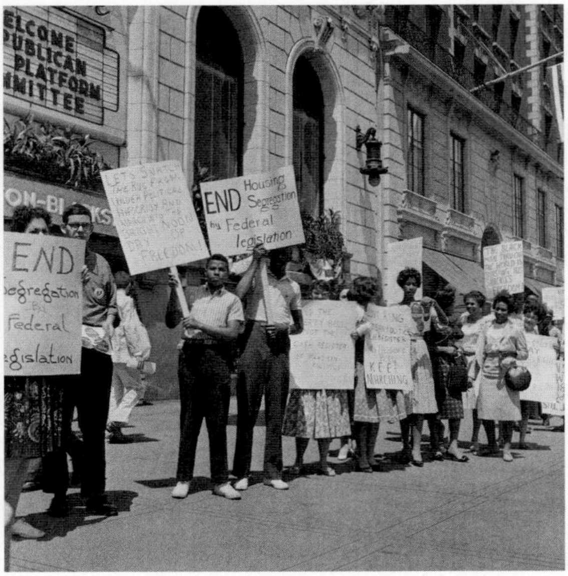

Protesting Housing Segregation in Chicago
Although northern and western states did not have signs designating the separation of "coloreds" and "whites," segregation was a national phenomenon, and African Americans protested nationwide. Here Chicagoans demonstrate against housing practices that kept Blacks from living where they chose. **Cities that were largely populated by Black Americans relocating from the South instituted de facto segregation policies. What impact did those policies and practices have on economic opportunities for Black people?** *Bettmann/Getty Images.*

brokers. At the community level, Black city council members improved neighborhood street lighting and other basic city services.[60]

Though impressive for the times, Black political advances proceeded at a snail's pace. An "intense struggle for small gains" was the way one activist remembered "progress" in New York City, where Blacks accounted for more than 1 million of the 14 million residents. In 1954, only 10 of 189 city judges were Black; the state supreme court was all white; only 1 of 58 state senators and 5 of 150 state assembly members were Black; and there was only 1 African American on the 25-member city council and 1 in the 43-member congressional delegation.[61] Like victories in the fight for equal access to jobs, education, housing, and other basic human rights, the few steps forward in gaining political office fueled expectations of more reforms, which, to the frustration of most African Americans, hardly ever materialized.

As they observed the sit-ins, marches, and demonstrations in the South, Blacks in the North and West had reason to believe that changes in their regions were occurring even more slowly. Schools, for example, were not desegregating. In St. Louis, Kansas City, Cleveland, Los Angeles, Chicago, Boston, New York, and Milwaukee, civil rights activists encountered intransigent public officials and hostile whites determined to keep Blacks from receiving the same education offered to whites.

Progress in employment also was slow. In an effort to end discriminatory practices in the labor movement, corporate personnel offices, and the larger institutional structure of the North and West, the NAACP and CORE targeted the employment practices of Bank of America, Bell Telephone, Western Electric, and the building and construction trades in cities such as Philadelphia, New York, San Francisco, and Newark. They also launched protests against Sheraton hotels; Howard Johnson's restaurants; Safeway; Sears, Roebuck; beer manufacturers; dealerships selling cars made by Mercury and Chrysler; and commercial advertising companies. Gains were so minimal that many wondered whether there was really any meaningful difference between the North and West and the South. Los Angeles "wasn't that much different from Oklahoma," remembered one disappointed migrant. "In Oklahoma, you knew. You was raised up that way and you didn't expect anything else. But out here, it was supposed to be different."[62]

By the time African Americans in the North and West saw pictures of the 1963 Birmingham demonstrations, they had begun to doubt the effectiveness of nonviolent direct-action protests and were beginning to look for other solutions. An idea about Black power was beginning to take hold. It inclined toward more militancy rather than continued passive resistance, and it expressed an urgency that could not abide patience.

President Kennedy seemed to sense this new mood and took action. In 1963, he followed up on his commitment to the Birmingham settlement with support for a new civil rights bill. Then, when Alabama governor George C. Wallace stood in a University of Alabama doorway to block two Black students from entering, Kennedy federalized the Alabama National Guard and ordered guardsmen to protect the students. On June 11, 1963, he went on national television to reiterate his support for Black civil and voting rights and for desegregation. In a stirring speech, he proclaimed that the nation would not be free until all citizens were free. "Who among us would be content with the counsels of patience and delay?" he asked. Sensing the explosive state of affairs, Kennedy proclaimed that racism was "not a sectional issue"; rather, "the fires of frustration and discord are burning in every city, North and South."[63] African Americans were pleased with Kennedy's speech. Finally, he seemed to move away from segregationists and join their side.

AP® skills

Applying Disciplinary Knowledge: Why did violence against Black Americans escalate even as the Civil Rights movement won supporters and achieved more of its goals?

The mood did not change in Mississippi, however. Within a few hours of the president's speech, Mississippi NAACP leader Medgar Evers was ambushed and shot dead in his driveway in Jackson.

The March on Washington and the Aftermath

March on Washington for Jobs and Freedom (1963)
A gathering of more than 250,000 Americans on August 28, 1963, to protest discrimination in all facets of American life. Martin Luther King Jr. delivered his "I Have a Dream" speech during the event.

On August 28, 1963, more than 250,000 Black and white Americans gathered on the National Mall for the historic **March on Washington for Jobs and Freedom**. It marked the culmination of nonviolent direct-action efforts to end segregation in every segment of American life and achieve economic justice for Black Americans. Although the march was peaceful, President Kennedy had readied National Guard units in case of violence. The juxtaposition of peaceful demonstrators and riot-ready troopers was in many ways symbolic of the tensions that prevailed during the latter part of 1963. In retrospect, the march proved to be one of the last gasps of what historians now call the "classic" Civil Rights movement — that part of the postwar freedom struggle when nonviolent direct action was most potent and effective.

A huge march on Washington seemed to be the right move for civil rights organizations in 1963. President Kennedy, embarrassed internationally by the racial violence in Birmingham and fearful of more violence, seemed ready to support the demands of marchers. Moreover, since progress on Black rights was moving so slowly and Blacks were more insistent on change, the time seemed right to pressure Congress to support Kennedy's civil rights bill. Just as A. Philip Randolph had organized the March on Washington Movement during World War II to force President Franklin Roosevelt's hand, civil rights activists in 1963 believed that the Cold War presented a similar opportunity to press for Black rights.

Organizing such a march was no small matter, not least because of the tensions that had been building within the movement itself. Each civil rights organization had its own perspective on the march, and each wanted the march organized in its own way. But it was A. Philip Randolph who conceived of the march, and Bayard Rustin, a longtime adviser of Martin Luther King Jr., who organized it. As a union organizer, Randolph had always believed that political advancement was useless without economic gains, but to get King's participation, the march had to emphasize civil rights. Once it was decided that the march would be about civil rights *and* jobs and King was brought on board, a decision had to be made about the use of civil disobedience. King wanted the gathering to include sit-ins and marches at the Capitol and the White House, but Roy Wilkins and Whitney Young, the respective heads of the NAACP and Urban League, vetoed this idea. More conservative than King and the SCLC, Wilkins and Young did not want to embarrass Kennedy or endanger the passage of the new bill. They also considered the SCLC and other new civil rights organizations to be Johnny-come-latelies and resented King's prominence. This decision outraged the younger, more radical SNCC members, who wanted to apply the utmost pressure on Washington and regarded the compromise as a sellout. They did, however, accept the leadership role of Rustin, which Wilkins rejected. Wilkins feared that Rustin's leftist past and homosexuality would be used to smear the march.[64]

A compromise was reached here, too, but male leaders incurred the wrath of Black women when not one woman was invited to participate in the planning of the march or to give a major speech. Pauli Murray, a civil rights lawyer and member of the newly created (1961) President's Commission on the Status of Women, expressed the anger of many women when she complained to Randolph that " 'tokenism' is as offensive when applied to women as when applied to Negroes."[65] She had not devoted the greater part of her adult life to civil rights advocacy to condone any policy that was not inclusive.

AP® skills

Applying Disciplinary Knowledge: What were the compromises made for the March on Washington, D.C.?

Perhaps the greatest and most lasting controversy was over the degree of militancy that speakers could express. John Lewis, the chairman of SNCC, had written a speech seething with anger and outrage. He denounced the civil rights bill as too little and too late because it did not protect Blacks against police brutality or help them to vote. At Randolph's request, Lewis toned down his speech, leaving King to give the most memorable and inspiring presentation to the hundreds of thousands who waited on the Mall, across the nation, and around the world.

AP® exam tip

You can use the historical context in this section to support and expand upon your understanding of John Lewis's speech, "The Revolution Is at Hand," which is one of the AP® course's required sources for Topic 4.6: Major Civil Rights Organizations.

Though not as scathing as Lewis's original speech, King's speech majestically made some of the same points. King cautioned the nation against returning to business as usual, noting that Black people were just beginning to fight for their rights. "It would be fatal for the nation to overlook the urgency of the moment and to underestimate the determination of the Negro," he said. There would be "neither rest nor tranquility in America until the Negro is granted his citizenship rights," King warned, and "the whirlwinds of revolt will continue to shake the foundations of our nation until . . . justice emerges." Mindful of the housing problems Blacks faced, King told his audience that Blacks would not be content "as long as the Negro's basic mobility is from a smaller ghetto to a larger one." Linking the southern and northern struggles, he added that there would be no satisfaction "as long as a Negro in Mississippi cannot vote and a Negro in New York believes he has nothing for which to vote."

Martin Luther King Jr. at the March on Washington for Jobs and Freedom, 1963
The major television networks (CBS, ABC, and NBC) sent more than five hundred camera operators, technicians, and correspondents to cover the March on Washington. All three networks led their evening newscasts with the march, and it appeared on the front page of every major newspaper the following day. This iconic photograph captures the dignity, strength, and massiveness of the march, which, despite the dedication and work of hundreds of people, would forever be associated with Martin Luther King Jr. and his "I Have a Dream" speech. **What aspects of this photo rebut the depiction of U.S. society in the Soviet cartoon on page 551? How might this photo also be viewed as evidence to support that depiction?** *Hulton-Deutsch Collection/Corbis/Getty Images.*

Although Lewis had paid lip service in his original speech to nonviolence, King, as he so often did, emphasized it because it was one of his core Christian beliefs. "Unearned suffering is redemptive," he proclaimed as he cautioned against meeting violence with violence. He paid homage to those who had come "fresh from narrow cells . . . from areas where your quest for freedom left you battered by the storms of persecution and staggered by the winds of police brutality." African Americans had to meet "physical force with soul force," reject bitterness and hatred, and embrace whites who had "come to realize that their destiny is tied up with our destiny . . . [and] that

The Bombing of the Sixteenth Street Baptist Church
In the aftermath of the March on Washington for Jobs and Freedom, these four girls were killed when the Sixteenth Street Baptist Church in Birmingham, Alabama, was bombed. In the top row are (left) Denise McNair, age eleven, and (right) Carole Robertson, age fourteen. In the bottom row are (left) Addie Mae Collins, age fourteen, and (right) Cynthia Wesley, age fourteen. When Cynthia's friend Carolyn McKinstry found out that the girls had been killed, she recalled, "I was sick inside; I was afraid. And then I was just numb. . . . I always had the sense of being protected. Now, all of a sudden, I wasn't."[69] **What does this tragedy suggest about the responses to the nonviolent tactics of civil rights activists? How did those responses affect perspectives on self-defense within the movement's major organizations?** *Associated Press/AP Images.*

AP® skills

Applying Disciplinary Knowledge: Why would King's views about economic inequality be omitted from this speech? What connections present-day inequalities do you see in his words?

their freedom is inextricably bound to our freedom." His voice reached a crescendo as he sketched out his dream and hopes for his children, for Black people, and for America. One line in particular stood out: "I have a dream that my four little children will one day live in a nation where they will not be judged by the color of their skin but by the content of their character."[66]

The March on Washington had worldwide impact. Some American citizens in Paris signed a petition supporting the march. Sympathy marches and demonstrations were held in Jamaica, Ghana, Burundi, Amsterdam, Tel Aviv, Oslo, and Munich. Newspapers across Africa and Europe and in India heralded the march with headlines that cast both aspersions and praise on America. The *Ghanaian Times* criticized the United States, claiming that American racism "casts much slur on Western civilization." But Rotterdam's *Algemeen Dagblad* praised America, asking readers to "imagine what would have happened had such a demonstration been planned in East Berlin."[67]

On September 15, just as the State Department was about to play up and capitalize on the latter sentiment, a bomb exploded in Birmingham's Sixteenth Street Baptist Church, which had been the organizing center of the city's civil rights demonstrations. The shock waves from the bomb shook world opinion and rocked the Civil Rights movement. Both King and Lewis had stressed nonviolence in their speeches, but a violent reaction could not be contained after news spread that the bomb had killed four Black girls, ranging in age from eleven to fourteen, during Sunday school. Black anger erupted into Birmingham's city streets, and during the disturbances, two Black male teenagers were shot and killed by police. The fires of African American outrage were further fanned by FBI director J. Edgar Hoover's decision to block the prosecution of the three white men implicated in the bombing. It was the twenty-first bombing in Birmingham in eight years; none of these crimes had been solved. Black people wanted justice, and in its absence, many resolved to fight back.

CONCLUSION

The Evolution of the Black American Freedom Struggle

The struggle for freedom changed substantially between 1945 and 1963. African Americans emerged from World War II determined, as defense worker Margaret Wright had said, not to "go back to what they were doing before."[68] A consequence of that determination was the Civil Rights movement — a nationwide crusade to get America to live up to its ideal of being a land of opportunity for everyone. The struggle was significantly affected, however, by the Cold War and the anti-Communist hysteria that accompanied it. To avoid being branded as Communists, African

Americans had to convince the world that America, not Blacks, had violated the American ideal.

Blacks and their white allies used nonviolent direct-action protests to this end. They sat in at segregated facilities, integrated segregated buses, marched in protest, and tried to register to vote. In doing so, they successfully exposed to the nation and the rest of the world the brutality and injustice that Blacks faced in every region of the country. However, nonviolent direct action took its toll on the freedom fighters. To be effective, it had to provoke the intense hostility and extreme, often deadly, violence used to subordinate Blacks. This meant that countless demonstrators had to endure untold traumas to their person and psyche and suppress the inclination to publicly defend themselves. These tactics also forced activists to de-emphasize economic issues, such as employment and housing discrimination, and tackle only the problems that could be proved and addressed through legal methods.

AP® skills

Applying Disciplinary Knowledge: How do the methods and strategies of civil rights activists and their demands for political, economic, and social justice relate to those of the abolition movement in the 1800s?

The March on Washington for Jobs and Freedom proved to be a watershed event. It was the highlight of the nonviolent, interracial phase of the classic Civil Rights movement, which had been effective in broadcasting American racism and embarrassing the nation to the point of forcing Presidents Eisenhower and Kennedy to do something. But that something seemed to be not nearly enough.

After a decade of lackluster commitment from the federal government and unremitting, terroristic resistance from both white citizens and local authorities, many freedom fighters — those who had come of age in the movement as well as new recruits — were ready for a change. Their search for new leaders, new tactics, and new ideologies brought about another transformation in the Black freedom struggle, as the philosophy of Black power and the quest to address long-ignored economic injustices came to the fore.

CHAPTER 14 REVIEW ▸ PRACTICING AP® SKILLS

AP® ESSENTIAL VOCABULARY AND SOURCES

** Essential terms and required sources from the AP® Course are marked with an asterisk.*

loyalty program p. 547
Red-baited p. 550
de facto segregation* p. 552
de jure segregation* p. 553
Brown v. Board of Education of Topeka (1954)* p. 553
Montgomery bus boycott (1955–1956)* p. 556
Little Rock Nine* p. 561
Greensboro Four p. 562
Freedom Rides* p. 562
Deacons for Defense and Justice p. 567
restrictive covenants p. 568
March on Washington for Jobs and Freedom (1963)* p. 574

APPLYING DISCIPLINARY KNOWLEDGE: ESSENTIAL QUESTIONS

1. What impact did the Cold War have on the Black freedom movement? How did Black organizations adapt to postwar changes? What were the outcomes, both negative and positive, for the movement and its direction?
2. Given the triumphs and tragedies of the southern movement's early years, how would you assess the strategy of nonviolent direct-action protest? How effective was it? What were its benefits and drawbacks?
3. How would you compare the degrees and types of segregation and institutional racism that characterized the South, North, and West in this era? In what ways was progress in the North and West even slower than that in the South?
4. How was the 1963 March on Washington for Jobs and Freedom both the height of the classic Civil Rights movement and an indicator of the tensions that had been building within it?

SUGGESTED REFERENCES

Anticommunism and the Postwar Black Freedom Struggle

Borstelmann, Thomas. *The Cold War and the Color Line: American Race Relations in the Global Arena*. Cambridge: Harvard University Press, 2001.

Duberman, Martin B. *Paul Robeson: A Biography*. New York: New Press, 1989.

Dudziak, Mary L. *Cold War Civil Rights: Race and the Image of American Democracy*. Princeton: Princeton University Press, 2000.

Korstad, Robert Rodgers. *Civil Rights Unionism: Tobacco Workers and the Struggle for Democracy in the Mid-Twentieth-Century South*. Chapel Hill: University of North Carolina Press, 2003.

Sullivan, Patricia. *Lift Every Voice: The NAACP and the Making of the Civil Rights Movement*. New York: New Press, 2009.

The Transformation of the Southern Civil Rights Movement

Carson, Clayborne. *In Struggle: SNCC and the Black Awakening of the 1960s*. Cambridge: Harvard University Press, 1981.

Carson, Clayborne, David J. Garrow, Gerald Gill, Vincent Harding, and Darlene Clark Hine, eds. *The Eyes on the Prize Civil Rights Reader: Documents, Speeches, and Firsthand Accounts from the Black Freedom Struggle*. New York: Viking, 1991.

Cobb, Charles E., Jr. *This Nonviolent Stuff'll Get You Killed: How Guns Made the Civil Rights Movement Possible*. New York: Basic Books, 2014.

Devlin, Rachel. *A Girl Stands at the Door: The Generation of Young Women who Desegregated America's Schools*. New York: Basic Book, 2018.

Fleming, Cynthia Griggs. *Soon We Will Not Cry: The Liberation of Ruby Doris Smith Robinson*. New York: Rowman & Littlefield, 1998.

Johnson, Nicolas J. "Firearms and the Black Community: An Assessment of the Modern Orthodoxy," *Connecticut Law Review: Commentary: Gun Control Policy and the Second Amendment* 45 (2013): 1545.

McGuire, Danielle L. *At the Dark End of the Street: Black Women, Rape, and Resistance: A New History of the Civil Rights Movement from Rosa Parks to the Rise of Black Power*. New York: Vintage Books, 2010.

Ransby, Barbara. *Ella Baker and the Black Freedom Movement: A Radical Democratic Vision*. Chapel Hill: University of North Carolina Press, 2003.

Robnett, Belinda. *How Long? How Long? African-American Women in the Struggle for Civil Rights*. New York: Oxford University Press, 1997.

Tyson, Timothy B. *The Blood of Emmett Till*. New York: Simon & Schuster, 2017.

Umoja, Akinyele Omowale. *We Will Shoot Back: Armed Resistance in the Mississippi Freedom Movement*. New York: New York University Press, 2013.

Civil Rights: A National Movement

Anderson, Jervis. *Bayard Rustin: Troubles I've Seen: A Biography*. New York: HarperCollins, 1997.

Biondi, Martha. *To Stand and Fight: The Struggle for Civil Rights in Postwar New York City*. Cambridge: Harvard University Press, 2003.

Jones, William P. *The March on Washington: Jobs, Freedom, and the Forgotten History of Civil Rights*. New York: Norton, 2013.

Lipsitz, George. *The Possessive Investment in Whiteness: How White People Profit from Identity Politics*. Philadelphia: Temple University Press, 1998.

Purnell, Brian, and Jeanne Theoharis, eds., with Komozi Woodard. *The Strange Career of the Jim Crow North: Segregation and Struggle outside of the South*. New York: New York University Press, 2019.

Sides, Josh. *L.A. City Limits: African American Los Angeles from the Great Depression to the Present*. Berkeley: University of California Press, 2003.

Sugrue, Thomas J. *Sweet Land of Liberty: The Forgotten Struggle for Civil Rights in the North*. New York: Random House, 2008.

Tyson, Timothy. *Radio Free Dixie: Robert F. Williams and the Roots of Black Power*. Chapel Hill: University of North Carolina Press, 1999.

We Are Not Afraid

The signature song of the early Civil Rights movement — the song sung before, during, and after meetings, demonstrations, and sit-ins — was titled "We Shall Overcome." Some have called it African Americans' gift to the world because freedom fighters around the globe have adopted it as their anthem.[70] One verse of the song, "We are not afraid," is very telling. It was one thing for African Americans to proclaim "We're not going to take it anymore," but quite another for them to conquer the paralyzing fear and feelings of hopelessness that white terrorism and violence were designed to provoke. For African Americans to overcome the tribulations of second-class citizenship, they first had to overcome their own fear.

This was far easier said than done in an era when lynchings, beatings, and bombings increased and were sanctioned by local and national law enforcement agencies. African Americans could not call on the police or the FBI for protection, for these organizations were often aligned with the perpetrators of terror. So, too, were the National Guard forces mustered by segregationist governors.

The following documents deal with terror and fear. They are firsthand accounts of movement activists' early encounters with violent racism. Recorded later in life, they tell us a good deal about how terrorism functions as a means of control and why young people were in the vanguard of the freedom movement.

key point

These firsthand accounts of civil rights activists show their early experiences of violent racism. They reveal how terrorism functions as a means of control and why young people were leaders in the Black freedom movement in this era.

AP® argumentation

DBQ Practice: Explain how African American youth galvanized the Civil Rights movement in the 1950s and 1960s. Use at least three of the documents to support your response.

DOCUMENT 1 Anne Moody | *Coming of Age in Mississippi*, 1968

Author ANNE MOODY (1940–2015), named Essie Mae Moody at birth, grew up in Mississippi. While attending Tougaloo College, she became active in the Civil Rights movement, participating in lunch counter sit-ins and voter registration drives. Her autobiography, *Coming of Age in Mississippi*, is a poignant account of rural Mississippi poverty and the way racism functioned to oppress African Americans.

Breaking it Down As you read this excerpt, consider how all-consuming white terrorism was. What kind of person did one have to be to not be paralyzed by it?

Not only did I enter high school with a new name, but also with a completely new insight into the life of Negroes in Mississippi. I was now working for one of the meanest white women in town, and a week before school started Emmett Till was killed.

Up until his death, I had heard of Negroes found floating in a river or dead somewhere with their bodies riddled with bullets. But I didn't know the mystery behind these killings then. I remember once when I was only seven I heard Mama and one of my aunts talking about some Negro who had been beaten to death. "Just like them low-down skunks killed him they will do the same to us," Mama had said. When

I asked her who killed the man and why, she said, "An Evil Spirit killed him. You gotta be a good girl or it will kill you too." So since I was seven, I had lived in fear of that "Evil Spirit." It took me eight years to learn what that spirit was. . . .

[Anne arrived home after hearing some fellow students discussing Till's murder.]

"Mama, did you hear about that fourteen-year-old Negro boy who was killed a little over a week ago by some white men?" I asked her.

"Where did you hear that?" she said angrily.

"Boy, everybody really thinks I am dumb or deaf or something. I heard Eddie them talking about it this evening coming from school."

"Eddie them better watch how they go around here talking. These white folks git a hold of it they gonna be in trouble," she said.

"What are they gonna be in trouble about, Mama? People got a right to talk, ain't they?"

"You go on to work before you is late. And don't you let on like you know nothing about that boy being killed before Miss Burke them. Just do your work like you don't know nothing," she said. "That boy's a lot better off in heaven than he is here," she continued, and then started singing again.

On my way to Mrs. Burke's that evening, Mama's words kept running through my mind. "Just do your work like you don't know nothing." . . .

[Anne went to work at the Burkes' home, where she served dinner and cleaned up the kitchen.]

When they had finished and gone into the living room as usual to watch TV, Mrs. Burke called me to eat. I took a clean plate out of the cabinet and sat down. Just as I was putting the first forkful of food in my mouth, Mrs. Burke entered the kitchen.

"Essie, did you hear about that fourteen-year-old boy who was killed in Greenwood?" she asked me, sitting down in one of the chairs opposite me.

"No, I didn't hear that," I answered, almost choking on the food.

"Do you know why he was killed?" she asked and I didn't answer.

"He was killed because he got out of his place with a white woman. A boy from Mississippi would have known better than that. This boy was from Chicago. Negroes up North have no respect for people. They think they can get away with anything. He just came to Mississippi and put a whole lot of notions in the boys' heads here and stirred up a lot of trouble," she said passionately.

"How old are you, Essie?" she asked me after a pause.

"Fourteen. I will soon be fifteen though," I said.

"See, that boy was just fourteen too. It's a shame he had to die so soon." She was so red in the face, she looked as if she was on fire.

When she left the kitchen I sat there with my mouth open and my food untouched. I couldn't have eaten now if I were starving. "Just do your work like you don't know nothing" ran through my mind again and I began washing the dishes.

I went home shaking like a leaf on a tree. For the first time out of all her trying, Mrs. Burke had made me feel like rotten garbage. Many times she had tried to instill fear within me and subdue me and had given up. But when she talked about Emmett Till there was something in her voice that sent chills and fear all over me.

Before Emmett Till's murder, I had known the fear of hunger, hell, and the Devil. But now there was a new fear known to me — the fear of being killed just because I was black. This was the worst of my fears. I knew once I got food, the fear of starving to death would leave. I also was told that if I were a good girl, I wouldn't have to fear the Devil or hell. But I didn't know what one had to do or not do as a Negro not to be killed. Probably just being a Negro period was enough, I thought.

Source: "Chapter 10" from COMING OF AGE IN MISSISSIPPI by Anne Moody,

DOCUMENT 2 Cleveland Sellers | *The River of No Return*, 1973

CLEVELAND SELLERS (b. 1944) was born and raised in Denmark, South Carolina, where he organized lunch counter sit-ins in 1961. While a student at Howard University, he became a member of the Student Nonviolent Coordinating Committee (SNCC) and worked with that organization on voter registration in Mississippi.

Breaking it Down Like Anne Moody, Sellers was deeply affected by Emmett Till's murder. As a young male, how might his concerns have been different from Moody's? How were they the same?

The adults, my parents included, were always afraid that we young people would take white racism too lightly. They were always urging us to "be careful." They realized that we were different from them, less afraid.

Although we did not possess the same amount of fear as our parents, we did understand what white racism was and what it could do. We learned these things from a number of sources, the most important one being the grapevine: an informal, black communications network connecting state to state, town to town, group to group and person to person.

Some of the most important pieces of information passed along the grapevine were accounts of atrocities. They contained valuable survival tips for those wise enough to heed them. I can remember hearing and reflecting on such accounts from the time I was a very young boy. They almost invariably dealt with situations where black people, usually black men, were brutalized by whites. . . .

The atrocity that affected me the most was Emmett Till's lynching. . . .

. . . Blacks across the country were outraged, but powerless to do anything.

Emmett Till was only three years older than me and I identified with him. I tried to put myself in his place and imagine what he was thinking when those white men took him from his home that night. I wondered how I would have handled the situation. I read and reread the newspaper and magazine accounts. I couldn't get over the fact that the men who were accused of killing him had not been punished at all.

There was something about the cold-blooded callousness of Emmett Till's lynching that touched everyone in the community. We had all heard atrocity accounts before, but there was something special about this one. For weeks after it happened, people continued to discuss it. It was impossible to go into a barber shop or corner grocery without hearing someone deploring Emmett Till's lynching.

We even discussed it in school. Our teachers were just as upset as we were. They did not try to distort the truth by telling us that Emmett Till's murder was an isolated event that could only have taken place in Mississippi or Alabama. Although they did not come right out and say it, we understood that our teachers held the South's racist legal system in the same low regard as we did. That's one of the good things about an all-black school. We were free to discuss many events that would have been taboo in an integrated school.

SOURCE: Excerpt from pp. 12–15 from *The River of No Return* by Cleveland L. Sellers, Robert L. Terrell.

DOCUMENT 3 Elizabeth Eckford | *The First Day: Little Rock*, 1957

Children and teenagers were in the vanguard of the Civil Rights movement. Coming of age in a new era, and with less life experience than their parents and grandparents, they had shallower reservoirs of fear. The desegregation of schools, in particular, fell squarely on the shoulders of girls. When judges and lawyers argued that desegregation led to "amalgamation" and "miscegenation," they

more often than not blamed it on the Black girls' promiscuity, which led to teenage pregnancy. Thinking back on the violence that visited girls who integrated schools, Ernest Green, one of the Little Rock Nine, remembered that "The girls got it the most. . . . People took their femininity as a weakness and attempted to take advantage of that."[71] ELIZABETH ECKFORD (b. 1941) was one of the Little Rock Nine who desegregated Little Rock Central High School in Arkansas in 1957. On the morning of the first day of school, the other eight Black students gathered with parents and civil rights workers at a designated place, but Eckford did not know that she was not to go directly to the school. There she encountered an angry white mob.

Note: This document includes the N-word, which we have chosen to reprint in this textbook to accurately reflect Eckford's original intent as well as the time period, culture, and racism discussed in the document. We recognize that this word has a long history as a derogatory and deeply hurtful expression when used by white people toward Black people, as it is in the context of this document. Be mindful of context, both Eckford's and yours, as you read and discuss this document.

Breaking it Down The extreme actions and dehumanizing words captured by Eckford in this passage illustrate segregationists' violent racism. How does she respond internally and externally to the mob that awaits her at school?

Before I left home Mother called us into the living room. She said we should have a word of prayer. Then I caught the bus and got off a block from the school. I saw a large crowd of people standing across the street from the soldiers guarding Central. As I walked on, the crowd suddenly got very quiet. Superintendent [Virgil] Blossom told us to enter by the front door. I looked at all the people and thought, "Maybe I will be safer if I walk down the block to the front entrance behind the guards."

At the corner I tried to pass through the long line of guards around the school so as to enter the grounds behind them. One of the guards pointed across the street. So I pointed in the same direction and asked whether he meant for me to cross the street and walk down. He nodded "yes." So, I walked across the street conscious of the crowd that stood there, but they moved away from me.

For a moment all I could hear was the shuffling of their feet. Then someone shouted, "Here she comes, get ready!" I moved away from the crowd on the sidewalk and into the street. If the mob came at me I could then cross back over so the guards could protect me.

The crowd moved in closer and then began to follow me, calling me names. I still wasn't afraid. Just a little bit nervous. Then my knees started to shake all of a sudden and I wondered whether I could make it to the center entrance a block away. It was the longest block I ever walked in my whole life.

Even so, I still wasn't too scared because all the time I kept thinking that the guards would protect me.

When I got in front of the school, I went up to a guard again. But this time he just looked straight ahead and didn't move to let me pass him. I didn't know what to do. Then I looked and saw that the path leading to the front entrance was a little further ahead. So I walked until I was right in front of the path to the front door.

I stood looking at the school — it looked so big! Just then the guards let some white students through.

The crowd was quiet. I guess they were waiting to see what was going to happen. When I was able to steady my knees, I walked up to the guard who had let the white students in. He too didn't move. When I tried to squeeze past him, he raised his bayonet and then the other guards moved in and they raised their bayonets.

They glared at me with a mean look and I was very frightened and didn't know what to do. I turned around and the crowd came toward me.

They moved closer and closer. Somebody started yelling, "Lynch her! Lynch her!"

I tried to see a friendly face somewhere in the mob — someone who maybe would help. I looked into the face of an old woman and it seemed a kind face, but when I looked at her again she spat on me.

They came closer, shouting, "No nigger bitch is going to get in our school! Get out of here!"

I turned back to the guards but their faces told me I wouldn't get any help from them. Then I looked down the block and saw a bench at the bus stop. I thought, "If I can only get there I will be safe." I don't know why the bench seemed a safe place to me, but I started walking toward it. I tried to close my mind to what they were shouting, and kept saying to myself, "If I can only make it to the bench I will be safe."

When I finally got there, I don't think I could have gone another step. I sat down and the mob crowded up and began shouting all over again. Someone hollered, "Drag her over to this tree! Let's take care of that nigger." Just then a white man sat down beside me, put his arm around me and patted my shoulder. He raised my chin and said, "Don't let them see you cry."

SOURCE: Daisy Bates, excerpts from The Long Shadow of Little Rock, pp. 73-75. Copyright © 1962, 1986 by Daisy Bates. Reprinted with the permission of The Permissions Company, Inc., on behalf of the University of Arkansas Press, www.uapress.com.

DOCUMENT 4 *Images of Protest and Terror*

As the following photographs demonstrate, the violence of the Civil Rights movement was very real, and the terror palpable. Somehow, demonstrators who were mostly teenagers and young adults found the strength and the will to carry out nonviolent protests despite the fire hoses, attack dogs, bombs, and mean-spirited hecklers. Every demonstration, be it a march, freedom ride, sit-in, pray-in, or voter registration drive, brought the possibility of death. Many participated in protests for over ten years.

Breaking it Down The expression that a picture can speak a thousand words is evident in this section. As you analyze these photos, note the expressions of the people wherever they are visible. Take notice of their body language, their clothing, and the setting of the image. What does each image convey about the methods of the civil rights protesters and the response they received? How do you think the protesters managed their fear?

John R. Salter, Joan Trumpauer, and Anne Moody sit in at Woolworth's in Jackson, Mississippi, 1963. *Bettmann/Getty Images.*

Freedom Riders beside their burned bus, 1961. *Bettmann/Getty Images.*

Birmingham demonstrators being sprayed with fire hoses, 1963. *Bill Hudson/Associated Press/AP Images.*

Elizabeth Eckford walking toward Little Rock Central High School, 1957. *Bettmann/Getty Images.*

PRACTICING AP® SKILLS

1. **AP® Comparison.** Describe the feelings that Anne Moody and Cleveland Sellers had to overcome. How did they respond to the pervasiveness of fear in their respective communities? How did Emmett Till's murder affect each of them? How would you have felt, and what would you have done in their environment?
2. **AP® Causation.** In the first two documents, the local Black community — the "grapevine," as Cleveland Sellers calls it — plays an important role. How did the grapevine function in each of these situations? Why was it so vital?
3. **AP® Continuity and Change.** In the 1950s and '60s, television was the latest and most revolutionary technology, much like the Internet is today. Every evening, Americans viewed scenes like the ones in this AP® Working with Sources collection on the nightly news. Imagine what coverage of the Civil Rights movement would look like in our current media climate, with the plethora of television news outlets, news blogs, and social networking websites now available. How do you think these images and accounts would be portrayed today?
4. **Connecting to AP® Themes.** Describe the act of resilience of Elizabeth Eckford. Where and to what extent do you see the activism of the 1960s in the activism of the present day?
5. **Class Discussion: Evidence-Based Argument.** Terrorism, as a means of controlling by fear, had long been used to keep African Americans subordinate to whites. It seems not to have worked on the authors of these documents, who grew up to be activists, or on the demonstrators in the photographs. What clues can you find in the written accounts and in the photographs to suggest how these individuals were able to conquer their fear?

Individual Student Project:
Topic Selection

Like all AP® courses, AP® African American Studies asks you to demonstrate your grasp of disciplinary knowledge in multiple ways. So far, AP® Skills Workshops have covered how to approach the multiple-choice, short-answer, and document-based questions you'll encounter on exam day. In addition to these more traditional assessment components, you will also have a chance to convey your understanding of African American Studies through an independent research project to be completed before exam day. This project will explore a topic of your choice, allowing you to tailor your exploration of African American Studies to your personal interests.

Over the course of the project, you will:

1. Select a topic
2. Articulate a central research question
3. Select four relevant, credible sources
4. Construct a claim
5. Curate evidence in support of your claim
6. Investigate at least two ways the sources relate to one another
7. Prepare for a presentation and an oral defense
8. Respond to a project validation question on exam day

In this first workshop, we'll focus on the first two steps. We'll walk through how to reflect on prior knowledge to uncover areas of interest, and we'll then clarify how to express your curiosity through a formal research question.

It's wise to devote time to topic selection because the most successful projects tend to be based on topics of high interest to the researcher. The more excited you are to explore your topic, the more likely you'll be to engage in high-quality research and critical analysis.

Selecting a Research Topic

Let's begin the brainstorming process! We can start by reflecting on the topics covered in class, with the goal of identifying two that stand out as especially engaging. Next, we can identify one additional topic that was not covered in this course but that sparks curiosity. Our initial exploration of these topics can be structured using a table like the following:

Topic ideas	What do you already know about the topic?	Why did you include this topic in your top three?
Favorite topic from course: Jazz music	• Jazz began in Southern Black communities. • The Great Migration helped jazz spread and evolve. • Jazz musicians created innovative styles during the New Negro Movement/the Harlem Renaissance. • Charles Mingus brought Black musical traditions into his protest songs. • Jazz influenced the development of hip-hop music.	I listen to a lot of jazz, and I've always wanted to learn more about the musical influences that shaped my favorite musicians.

Topic ideas	What do you already know about the topic?	Why did you include this topic in your top three?
Runner-up topic from course: Natural hair movement	• Natural hairstyles include cornrows, afros, box braids, Bantu knots, etc. • The Black Is Beautiful movement celebrated Afrocentric styles. • People like Kathleen Cleaver expressed pride in Black beauty. • The Grandassa models wore natural hairstyles to their fashion shows. • California's CROWN Act prohibits discrimination based on hair style or texture.	I liked learning about natural hair as it connects to Afrocentricity of the 1960s and 1970s, but I don't know much about how the natural hair movement evolved between then and now.
Topic beyond course curriculum: Negro baseball leagues	• Black athletes formed their own baseball leagues after the Civil War. • Jackie Robinson played for the Brooklyn Dodgers starting in 1947. • In 2024, MLB updated its records to include statistics from Negro leagues.	I want to learn more about how and why players from the Negro leagues integrated into Major League Baseball.

When brainstorming topics, try to come up with options that are complex enough to explore in-depth but specific enough to avoid becoming overwhelmed. For instance, "Sojourner Truth" would be too broad of a topic — four sources would not be nearly enough to become an expert on her entire life — while "Sojourner Truth's siblings" would likely be too narrow — there isn't much information out there about how their lives unfolded.

If you find it difficult to pick a topic, it can be useful to read through a list of options as a starting point. Consider the suggestions to follow. Which of these topics is most intriguing to you? Why? How would you revise the topics that appeal to you most to ensure they have an appropriate level of specificity? Do any related topics come to mind?

1. Colorism
2. Ballroom culture
3. Black experiences in health care
4. Black crafting collectives
5. Mass incarceration
6. Redlining in the twenty-first century
7. Black agricultural workers
8. Reasons to capitalize the word "Black"
9. The Chicago Renaissance
10. The War on Drugs
11. Black filmmakers
12. Vietnam and the Black community
13. Up-and-coming Black leaders
14. Black cuisine
15. Black children's books

Remember, you'll ultimately be presenting an argument, not a book report, so if you spot a topic that you already have an opinion on, that could be a promising place to start.

Drafting a Research Question

Once you have chosen a topic, there's one more step before research can begin: clarifying the purpose of your investigation. Without a clear purpose, research can feel like a slog. You might struggle to stay focused, and you won't be able to tell if your search is on the right track. To ensure your research process is as efficient and engaging as possible, you'll want to articulate a specific research question that will structure and guide your work.

Remember, you'll ultimately need to present a *claim* that goes beyond a statement of fact or a summary of your sources. So, think of a question whose answer is arguable; make sure you can imagine two contrasting ways your question could be answered, depending on what your research ends up revealing. To see what we mean, consider the difference between the following research questions:

Example 1	What was the Songhai empire?
Example 2	What was the most important reason for the decline of the Songhai empire?

While both questions focus on the topic of the Songhai empire, the first question wouldn't give your research enough structure. Any source you read about the Songhai empire could theoretically be relevant; you might soon become overwhelmed. Further, the first question doesn't really leave room for multiple perspectives; it's essentially asking for a definition of a concept historians already agree on.

In contrast, the second question would help target your research. It would help you search using more specific language than "Songhai empire"—you could add in search terms like "decline," "fall," or "collapse." Plus, the question could be answered in multiple ways. Some people might argue that rivalries between local rulers caused the empire to fall, while others might say the Moroccan invasion was more impactful. You'd need to do more research to determine which perspective is better supported by the available evidence.

If you already have strong opinions on your topic, you might feel pulled to write your research question in a way that leaves room for only one answer: yours. As tempting as that may be, challenge yourself to write a question that welcomes other points of view. Not only will the research process be more interesting if you consider multiple perspectives, but also the argument you develop will be more nuanced and, therefore, more convincing.

recap

Selecting a Research Topic and Drafting a Research Question

- To select a research topic, reflect on topics covered in class, and then consider if there are any topics you *wish* had been covered. Try to come up with options that are complex enough to explore in depth but specific enough to avoid becoming overwhelmed.
- A research question will make your research process more efficient. Make sure your question is specific enough to guide your research, and ensure that it could be answered in multiple ways.

Activity ▸ Selecting a Research Topic and Drafting a Research Question

Fill out a table like the one to follow.

Topic ideas	What do you already know about the topic? Provide 3–5 details.	Why did you include this topic in your top three?
Favorite topic from course:		
Runner-up topic from course:		
Topic beyond course curriculum:		
Topic Selection:		
What questions do you have about your topic?	1. 2. 3.	
What are some search terms you could use to locate information?	1. 2. 3. 4. 5.	
Research Question:		

Multiple-Choice Questions

Questions 1–2 refer to the following.

The racial discrimination required by Southern state legal codes represented one pole in a growing debate between two visions of sovereignty and human rights. Traditionalists adhered to a doctrine of local authority in managing social relations and maintaining order. This doctrine took the form of defending states' rights to manage their own internal affairs. It also bolstered national sovereignty against inquiries or incursions from international organizations. The second vision embodied the opposite view: that in the wake of the Holocaust, the international community could no longer fully trust any local sovereignty to protect its own citizens. Innocent people should no longer be allowed to suffer and die owing to the sheer misfortune of which government they happened to live under. Instead, standards for human rights needed to be made globally applicable. The United Nations embodied elements of each of these visions, with clauses in its charter declaring both the common rights of all people against discrimination and the sovereignty of nations over life within their borders. In the early post-war years, the U.S. government cited the latter clause in rejecting requests for an international investigation of American racial discrimination — a position shared by European colonial powers and South Africa. A few years later, white Southerners used precisely the same arguments in making their own case against federal investigations of Southern racial practices.

SOURCE: Thomas Borstelmann, *The Cold War and the Color Line: American Race Relations in the Global Arena*, 2009

1. Which of the following factors best explains Borstelmann's assertion about the United Nations?

(A) After World War II, many expected the United Nations to intervene when governments — even ones as powerful as that of the United States — failed to protect the citizens' rights.

(B) The United Nations was a collection of countries that gathered together to address the atrocities of the events leading up to World War II.

(C) Although the United Nations was founded on principles similar to those espoused in the Declaration of Independence, the United States had become less involved in the work of the United Nations due to the racial violence in southern states.

(D) The United Nations is expected to act on the best interest of countries within areas that were colonized.

2. Which of the following best describes the NAACP's 1947 petition to the United Nations entitled "An Appeal to the World"?

(A) The petition ended up stopping the hostile demonstrations of segregationists who were using the fear of communism to challenge the integration of schools and other public places.

(B) The petition was intended to persuade the United Nations to address the racist policies of the U.S. government that allowed violence to take place against Black Americans in many parts of the United States.

(C) The petition was intended to request help from the United Nations on behalf of Black American activists falsely accused of being communists or being an affiliate of the Communist Party.

(D) The petition was intended to bolster support for increased interaction between the United States and the Soviet Union while also calling out Black Americans who were supporters of the Soviet Union.

Short-Answer Question

The thirty owners who signed the agreement held title to forty-seven parcels, including the particular parcel involved in this case. At the time the agreement was signed, five of the parcels in the district were owned by Negroes. One of those had been occupied by Negro families since 1882, nearly thirty years before the restrictive agreement was executed . . .

In June, 1934, one Ferguson and his wife, who then owned the property located in the city of Detroit which is involved in this case, executed a contract providing in part:

'This property shall not be used or occupied by any person or persons except those of the Caucasian race.' . . .

[T]he Civil Rights Act of 1866, which was enacted by Congress while the Fourteenth Amendment was also under consideration,[1] provides:

'All citizens of the United States shall have the same right, in every State and Territory, as is enjoyed by white citizens thereof to inherit, purchase, lease, sell, hold, and convey real and personal property.'

SOURCE: *Shelley v. Kraemer*, Supreme Court ruling, 1948

[1]In *Oyama v. California*, 332 U. S. 633, 640 (1948), the section of the Civil Rights Act herein considered is described as the federal statute, 'enacted before the Fourteenth Amendment but vindicated by it.' The Civil Rights Act of 1866 was reenacted in § 18 of the Act of May 31, 1870, subsequent to the adoption of the Fourteenth Amendment. 16 Stat. 144.

1. Using the excerpt, answer A, B, C, and D.

(A) Describe the role of the federal government's allowance of racial covenants.

(B) Describe the rationale used to decide the outcome of the case.

(C) Explain why the Shelleys, the petitioners, used the Fourteenth Amendment to argue their case.

(D) Explain the outcome of the case and the impact it had on middle-class Black Americans.

CHAPTER **15**

Multiple Meanings of Freedom: The Movement Broadens

1961–1976

CHAPTER TIMELINE

Events specific to African American history are in purple. General U.S. history events are in black. Events from the AP® Course Framework are marked with an asterisk.

1961	Afro-American Association founded in Oakland, California
1962	Revolutionary Action Movement (RAM) founded in Ohio
	Cambridge Nonviolent Action Committee founded in Maryland*
1963	President John F. Kennedy assassinated; Vice President Lyndon Johnson becomes president
1964	Malcolm X breaks with Nation of Islam*
	Mississippi Freedom Democratic Party (MFDP) founded*
	Council of Federated Organizations (COFO) conducts Mississippi Freedom Summer Project*
	Three civil rights workers disappear in Mississippi in June; found murdered in August*
	Civil Rights Act*
	Malcolm X attends Cairo Conference of Organization of African Unity
	In New York City, Harlem and Bedford-Stuyvesant neighborhoods erupt in violence
	Economic Opportunity Act
	Martin Luther King Jr. wins Nobel Peace Prize
	Johnson reelected president
1965–1970	Height of American involvement in Vietnam War
1965	Malcolm X assassinated*
	Moynihan Report published
1965	Marchers attacked by Alabama police on Bloody Sunday
	Johnson increases number of U.S. troops in Vietnam
	Students for a Democratic Society (SDS) lead march against Vietnam War in Washington, D.C.
	Voting Rights Act*
	Violence erupts in Watts, Black neighborhood in Los Angeles
1966	Floyd McKissick assumes leadership of CORE
	Stokely Carmichael makes speech extolling Black power
	Huey Newton and Bobby Seale found Black Panther Party for Self-Defense (BPPSD) in Oakland*
1967	Heavyweight boxing champion Muhammad Ali convicted of draft evasion*
	Violence erupts in Detroit
	Welfare activists organize National Welfare Rights Organization
	King announces Poor People's Campaign
1968	King assassinated; U.S. cities erupt in violence
	Dodge Revolutionary Union Movement conducts strikes
1971	*Griggs v. Duke Power Co.* eliminates some barriers to Black employment
1973	Paris Peace Accords end Vietnam War

Please note that this chapter includes primary sources by Black writers and speakers that use the N-word, which we have chosen to reprint in this textbook to accurately reflect these speakers' original intent as well as the time period, culture, and racism discussed in each source. We recognize that this word has a long history as a derogatory and deeply hurtful expression when used by white people toward Black people. Black speakers' and writers' choice to use this word relates not only to that history but to a larger cultural tradition in which the N-word can take on different meanings, emphasize shared experience, and be repurposed as a term of endearment within Black communities. Be mindful of context, both historical and contemporary, as you read and discuss this chapter.

Stokely Carmichael and the Meaning of Black Power

"Wasteland, terra incognita . . . nothing, nada, squat."[1] That is how SNCC organizer Stokely Carmichael described Lowndes County, Alabama, in 1965. Situated between Selma and Montgomery, Lowndes seemed the most unlikely birthplace of the first Black Panther Party. The county was overwhelmingly rural, with about eighty white families owning 90 percent of the land, and although Blacks numbered 12,000 of the 15,000 inhabitants — 80 percent of the population — all of them were impoverished, and none of them could vote. The largest town in the county, Fort Deposit, was a Ku Klux Klan stronghold, and in Hayneville, the county seat, juries refused to convict the confessed murderers of Viola Liuzzo and Jonathan Daniels, two white civil rights workers who in separate incidents were killed for their work on behalf of Black civil and voting rights. In Lowndes County, Blacks lived in fear.[2] According to John Hulett, the man who would help Carmichael turn Black sharecroppers into an effective political force, before SNCC arrived, young Black men often ran and hid in the bushes if they saw car headlights on the road at night. Hulett said, "They thought the sheriff was coming by and maybe would do something to them."[3]

As bad as life was in this county, Carmichael thought he could "turn a negative into a positive."[4] Hidden behind the apparent Black subservience was a history of militancy. In the 1930s, for example, there had been a Black sharecroppers' union in the county that had a tradition of armed self-defense. In fact, most of the older Black people in the county carried guns to protect themselves and their families. "You turn the other cheek, and you'll get handed half of what you're sitting on," said one local leader who had met stiff white resistance when he had tried to register to vote.[5] Carmichael also liked the fact that although the two counties bordering Lowndes had been the scenes of well-publicized civil rights marches and violent reprisals, Lowndes was, as Carmichael described it, virgin territory. No organizations were vying for attention or loyalty. SNCC could apply its grassroots tactics of quietly meeting with families and community leaders, helping them organize and lead their own rebellion.

Carmichael planned to use a new independent Black political party as the vehicle for change. At first he met stiff resistance from both Blacks and whites. Most Blacks wanted access to the Democratic Party. Proponents of a separate party, however, said that Black people needed more than simple party membership. "What would it profit a man to have the vote and not be able to control it?" asked Courtland Cox, a SNCC strategist. "When you have a situation where the community is 80 percent black, why complain about police brutality when you can be the sheriff yourself? Why complain about substandard education when you could be the Board of Education? Why complain about the courthouse when you could move to take it over yourself? . . . Why protest when you can exercise power?"[6] As the idea evolved, locals grew excited about having a party that truly represented the county majority. Hulett described the party's chosen symbol, a black panther, as "an animal that when it is pressured it moves back until it is cornered, then it comes out fighting for life or death." Blacks in Lowndes thought they had been pushed long enough. They formed the Lowndes County Freedom Organization (LCFO) and resolved, as Hulett put it, to "come out and take over."[7]

For their part, white Democrats fired African American workers who tried to vote, forced them off white-owned land, and shot at Blacks who sought refuge in the tent city that SNCC set up for those who found themselves homeless as a result of these and other measures. In one particularly vicious incident, the sheriff arrested Carmichael and other civil rights workers who had come to help Blacks register to vote, only to release them to a lynch mob that shot and killed one white man, Jonathan Daniels, and left another, Father Richard Morrisroe, a priest, with a bullet in his back. Undeterred, Blacks continued to register, and the party sustained itself in the primary. It became the representative party of Blacks in Lowndes. Five years later, the same people who had ducked into the bushes when the white sheriff passed used their vote to make John Hulett the sheriff and another Black man, Charles Smith, the county commissioner.[8]

The tactics used in Lowndes represented an alternative to the nonviolent direct-action protest strategy used by mainstream civil rights organizations such as CORE and the SCLC. Lowndes showed what could happen when Black people controlled their own communities from an independent base of Black political strength. Carmichael observed, "They oppress us because we are black and we are going to use that blackness to get out of the trick bag they put us in."[9] Moreover, the lynch mob's pursuit of Daniels and Morrisroe convinced some Black organizers that the dangerous work of grassroots organizing did not need to be made more dangerous by the presence of white volunteers.

The 1960s and '70s were turbulent years. There were assassinations, urban rebellions, and a foreign war. The freedom struggle, though a cause of some of this turbulence, was also affected by it. Throughout this period, Blacks sought new approaches for realizing economic justice and political liberty. As time wore on and white resistance persisted, African Americans became more comfortable with a Black power strategy, which made Blacks less dependent on white acceptance and participation. Although this strategy still exposed Blacks to white retaliatory violence, it instilled race pride and self-respect and demonstrated new ways of using Black political power.

The Emergence of Black Power

How did civil rights activism in the mid-twentieth century lead to federal legislative achievements?

How did Black freedom movement strategies transition from civil rights to Black power?

The philosophy of Black power was not entirely new; it only seemed new because of the context of Black/white confrontation in which it emerged in the 1960s. Black people had been practicing self-help for some time. For most of the first half of the century, African Americans had resisted white dominance by turning inward and building Black America. The myriad institutions — the banks; mutual aid societies; hospitals; schools; professional, fraternal, and sororal societies; Black newspapers; the NACW, NAACP, Urban League, UNIA, and the Brotherhood of Sleeping Car Porters — all grew from the Black power idea that Black people had to depend on themselves to survive and that Blacks had, within their own communities, the wherewithal to prosper. Black music, literature, and art had nourished Black America while it affirmed Black culture. Moreover, white terrorism had fostered a tradition of self-defense.

AP® exam tip

Make sure you can describe the origin of the Black Power movement and explain the extent to which you think it fulfilled its goals.

In the context of the turbulent '60s, self-help transformed into Black power. In World War II, Blacks had fought both at home and abroad for freedom of speech and religion and freedom from want and fear (the Four Freedoms). Both at home and abroad, they had given their lives for economic advancement and social security (the Atlantic Charter). But after ten years of direct-action campaigns to integrate public schools and facilities, they had only scratched the surface of the larger problems of widespread unemployment and underemployment, economic injustice, and police brutality. After ten years of boycotts, demonstrations, sit-ins, and Freedom Rides, African Americans still felt like a colonized people who, as evidenced by the treatment of men such as Ralph Bunche, Paul Robeson, and W. E. B. Du Bois, were hardly free to speak their mind in the nation that was supposedly the freest on earth. In the mid-1960s, therefore, Black people went back to the drawing board and refitted self-help for a new generation — one unwilling to wait for white people to have a change of heart about Black freedom.

Expanding the Struggle beyond Civil Rights

The events of the early 1960s provided the right context for Black power to flourish. The emergence of forty new nation-states between 1945 and 1960 in the former colonial world had a dramatic effect on Black consciousness. No longer were whites, even liberal whites, the sole point of reference, or even the only possible allies of American Blacks. The Black writer James Baldwin made this point as early as 1960, when he identified what he called a "new mood" among African Americans. "The American Negro," he proclaimed, "can no longer, nor will he ever again be controlled by white

America's image of him. This fact has everything to do with the rise of Africa in world affairs."[10]

At home, a tumultuous start to the decade also fostered new ways of thinking. The bombing in Birmingham and the subsequent violent street uprisings during which two Black teenagers were killed were harbingers of the tragedies to come. Two months later, on Friday, November 22, 1963, President John F. Kennedy was assassinated. The entire nation went into mourning. African Americans were particularly aggrieved. Kennedy's support of Black civil rights had been halting, but the direct-action civil rights campaign had convinced him of the necessity of the civil rights bill that was stalled in Congress. Blacks were not confident that the new president, former vice president Lyndon Johnson, would see things the same way. During his twelve years as a senator from Texas, he had obstructed the passage and enforcement of civil rights laws. Spirits rose when Johnson announced, before a joint session of Congress, that "no memorial or eulogy could more eloquently honor President Kennedy's memory than the earliest possible passage of the civil rights bill for which he fought."[11] Johnson then proceeded to use all of his considerable influence to break a record-setting 534-hour filibuster in the Senate and get the bill passed in early July the following year.

Civil Rights Act of 1964
A law prohibiting discrimination in places of public accommodation, outlawing bias in federally funded programs, authorizing the U.S. Justice Department to initiate desegregation lawsuits, and providing technical and financial aid to communities desegregating their schools. President Lyndon Johnson used his considerable influence to break a record-setting 534-hour filibuster in the Senate.

Title VII
The most contentious part of the Civil Rights Act of 1964, it banned discrimination in employment on the basis of race, color, religion, sex, or national origin and created the Equal Employment Opportunity Commission to investigate and litigate cases of job discrimination.

The **Civil Rights Act of 1964** was the most important and extensive civil rights law passed in the United States since Reconstruction. It prohibited discrimination in places of public accommodation, outlawed bias in federally funded programs, authorized the U.S. Justice Department to initiate desegregation lawsuits, and provided technical and financial aid to communities desegregating their schools. The most contentious part of the act, and one that would prove the most far-reaching, was **Title VII**. It banned discrimination in employment on the basis of race, color, religion, sex, or national origin and created the Equal Employment Opportunity Commission (EEOC) to investigate and litigate cases of job discrimination. (See Appendix: Civil Rights Act of 1964 for highlights of this legislation.)

As significant as the act was, however, many agreed with John Lewis's earlier assessment that the bill did not address police brutality or voting rights. It did nothing to curb the violence directed at Black people, and it did not address the Justice Department's finding that in the eighteen-month period from January 1958 to June 1960, some 34 percent of all reported victims of police brutality were Black.[12] Furthermore, the act did nothing to protect Black voting rights, and with the Black unemployment rate double that of whites, the long and cumbersome legal process the law established to bring about equity in employment opportunities was not promising. The compromises civil rights organizations had made in the 1950s to silence anti-Communist critics had paid some dividends, but there had been no economic or political justice for African Americans. Moreover, segregation was still alive and well. By 1964, the systematic exclusion of Blacks from favorable housing areas was so complete that in both northern and southern cities, Black were the most isolated of all ethnic minorities. The failure of the Civil Rights Act to address these

AP® skills

Applying Disciplinary Knowledge: Why was the Civil Rights Act of 1964 both a success and a failure? Make a T-chart to gather evidence for each viewpoint.

issues fueled new, more militant ideas about America's problems and how Black people should respond.[13]

Early Black Power Organizations

Radical organizations approached the Black freedom struggle differently from mainstream organizations such as the NAACP and SCLC. They were not all the same, but they shared three important ideas. One was that more aggressive measures were needed to tackle the problems Black Americans faced. Another was that Blacks had, within their own communities, the resources to effect change. The third was that African Americans needed to be proud to be Black.

AP® skills

Applying Disciplinary Knowledge: What ideas were shared by the "old and new" civil rights organizations?

The Cambridge Nonviolent Action Committee (CNAC) is a case in point. Founded in 1962, under the direction of local leader Gloria Richardson, a forty-year-old Howard University graduate, the organization's initial aim of desegregating public facilities progressed to issues of unemployment and incarceration. Like Carmichael in Lowndes, Richardson realized that the African Americans in Cambridge, Maryland, could mobilize to vote out the local state senator who kept them impoverished by blocking new industries and unionized labor. Although unsuccessful in unseating the senator, Richardson's mobilization of poor and working-class Black people led to a protest movement that lasted over two years. They demonstrated to desegregate the public schools, to hire African Americans in the city government, to build public housing, to initiate job training, and to protest the lengthy detention of two juvenile demonstrators.

The demonstrations were in many ways traditional — sit-ins, boycotts, picketing, and marches — until whites fought these measures and organized anti-integration confrontations, including assaults, in Black neighborhoods. Over the objections of the NAACP and CORE, Cambridge Blacks abandoned nonviolence and fought back. In June 1963, several white-owned businesses were burned, and during the weeks of retaliatory violence, ten white men were shot. Richardson herself allegedly carried a gun. The National Guard was brought in, and Attorney General Robert Kennedy attempted to broker the peace. When an agreement was reached that put desegregation to a vote, Richardson and the CNAC again departed from conventional civil rights strategy. She urged Blacks *not* to vote, arguing, and "A first-class citizen does not beg for freedom. A first-class citizen does not plead to the white power structure to give him something that the whites have no power to give or take away, Human rights are human rights, not white rights."[14] The demonstrations did not lead to desegregation; that was accomplished by the 1964 Civil Rights Act. But they did lead to the opening of a few city jobs to African Americans, a job training program, and the release of the juvenile demonstrators. More important, Richardson and the CNAC demonstrated new strategies for confronting white resistance and expanding the objectives of the freedom struggle.

AP® skills

Applying Disciplinary Knowledge: What did Gloria Richardson mean by "human rights" and not white rights? How can the actions of the CNAC be viewed as a success?

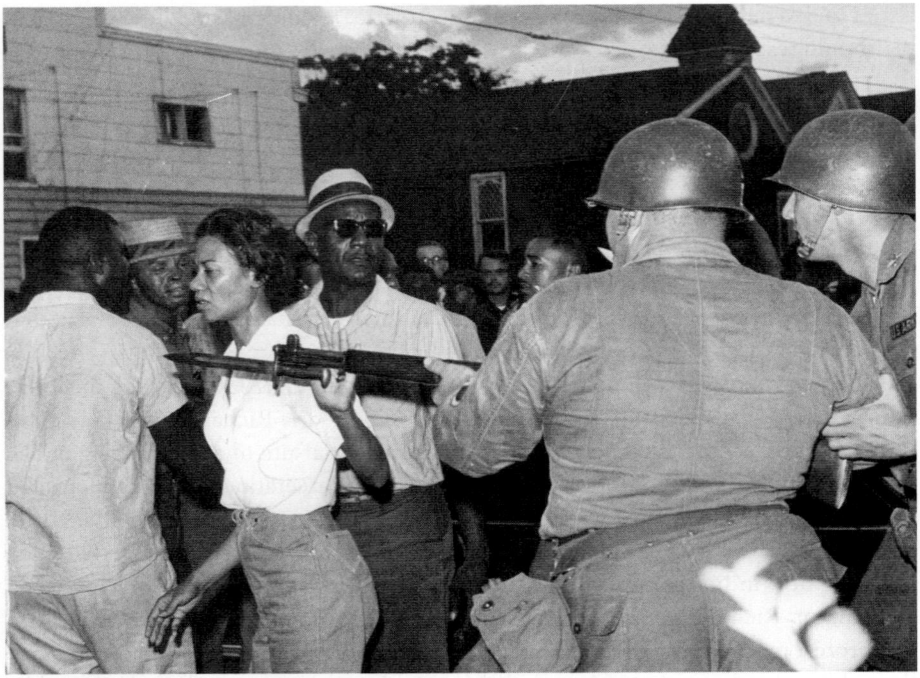

AP® source ***Gloria Richardson Leads a Demonstration in 1963***

Showing courage and defiance in the face of a bayonet-wielding National Guardsman, Gloria Richardson, leader of Maryland's Cambridge Nonviolent Action Committee, leads a demonstration for jobs, housing, and desegregation in 1963. **Describe the effectiveness of Richardson's actions. Use the image to support your answer.** *Associated Press/AP Images.*

Something similar was happening in Ohio, where a student group called the Revolutionary Action Movement (RAM) was forging new paths. Founded in 1962 by Maxwell Stanford, RAM was greatly influenced by Robert Williams, the activist denounced by the NAACP for his support of armed self-defense. Members of RAM supported the national liberation movements in Africa, Asia, and Latin America, connecting their own plight to those of colonial subjects abroad by arguing that police patrols turned Black communities into "occupied zones" or "internal colonies." They saw themselves as being engaged in an anticolonial war with the American nation-state and believed their first duty was to defend themselves and monitor police activity in their neighborhoods. RAM developed a twelve-point program calling for independent Black schools, national Black student organizations, rifle clubs, a guerrilla army made up of young people and the unemployed, and Black farmer cooperatives that fostered economic self-sufficiency. RAM's philosophy, termed **Black nationalism**, was founded on the idea that Black people constituted a nation within a nation, where survival depended on the exercise of power — Black power.[15]

Black nationalism
A diffuse ideology founded on the idea that Black people constituted a nation within a nation. It fostered Black pride and encouraged Black people to control the economy of their communities.

In Oakland, California, young Black college students were also searching for alternative strategies. Founded in 1961 by Donald Warden, the Afro-American Association laid the intellectual groundwork for the Black Power movement. The group's members, who had met as students at the University of California, Berkeley, emphasized the importance of Africa and decolonization movements to the African American freedom struggle. Other groups developed strategies that were politically focused. At the March on Washington for Jobs and Freedom, the activist William Worthy distributed leaflets announcing the Freedom Now Party, an independent Black political party. Although it never cohered as a national organization, the Freedom Now Party showed modest strength in local and state elections, especially in Michigan. These new organizations were joined by established groups that abandoned the moderate philosophy of nonviolence. For example, when Floyd McKissick assumed the leadership of CORE in 1966, he announced that CORE was "tired of condemning our own people when they start to fight back. . . . There is no possible return to non-violence."[16]

A variety of periodicals began to disseminate new ideas about Blacks being a proud people, a nation within a nation that needed to exercise more control over its economic well-being and to be more militant in the exercise of political power. These publications included *Soulbook, Liberator, Negro Digest, Freedomways,* and the Nation of Islam newspaper *Muhammad Speaks.*[17]

Black music, paintings, plays, and novels reified the message. In what would become known as the **Black Arts movement**, defined by one of its founders as the "spiritual sister of the Black Power Concept,"[18] artists, like their predecessors of the Harlem Renaissance, used their art to project the beauty and power of Black culture. Echoing the varying philosophies of the Black freedom movement, black artists of the 1960s and '70s were not of one mind about what Black art should be, but they had in common a notion that Black art was (or should be) different from white art, with unique roots, characteristics, and goals. How this idea was interpreted depended on the artist and his or her medium, politics, and influences. Like everything else about being Black during this period, art was contested, and artists were challenged to find their place on the continuum.

Black Arts movement
The cultural side of Black power, in which Black musicians, artists, dancers, playwrights, and novelists in the 1960s and 1970s used their talent to demonstrate Black pride and nationhood.

AP® exam tip

You will need to be able to explain how the Black Arts movement (BAM) influenced Black culture in the 1960s and 1970s.

One thing that was not often contested among Black power activists and Black nationalists was a common philosophy on gender. Black power became synonymous with the liberation of Black men from the emasculating effects of racism. One of activists' most enduring criticisms of nonviolent direct action was that real men did not allow *their* women to be brutalized by white segregationists. White men, activists argued, had for centuries kept the Black man unemployed or underemployed in order to control the Black family and keep Black men from protecting Black women. Whites had caricatured Black men as effeminate in order to deprive the Black male of his manhood, thereby keeping the race subservient. Black activists argued that the race would be free only when Black men were free to assume their full patriarchal rights. When the militant Floyd McKissick assumed the leadership of CORE, he said, "The year 1966 shall be remembered as the year we left our imposed status as Negroes and became Black men." Stokely Carmichael had a similar outlook. He predicted a race war in which Blacks would "stand on our feet and die like men. . . . If that's our only act of manhood, then Goddamnit we're going to die."[19]

Women had not been able to use all of their talents and play leadership roles in the direct-action phase of the movement, and the pressure on women to accept secondary roles became more pronounced as Black nationalist ideas took hold. Although it was Jo Ann Robinson who mobilized the Montgomery bus boycott; Daisy Bates who spearheaded the integration of Little Rock's Central High School; Ella Baker who became the first full-time staff member of the SCLC, and later its interim director, and who helped to found SNCC; Fannie Lou Hamer who was the principal organizer of and spokesperson for the Mississippi Freedom Democratic Party; and Black girls who led the desegregation of schools, in most Black power organizations, women were bombarded with demands to stop competing with men for jobs and to stay home and have babies "for the revolution." More often than not, they were expected to do menial chores such as make coffee and clean up after the men. If they objected, they were accused of allying with whites or emasculating Black men. As the activist Angela Davis noted, the late 1960s and early '70s were "a period in which one of the unfortunate hallmarks of some nationalist groups was their determination to push women into the background. The brothers opposing us leaned heavily on the male supremacist trends which were winding their way through the movement."[20]

Malcolm X

The most eloquent and influential proponent of Black power, including its gender politics, was Malcolm X. He had long maintained that the civil rights struggle needed a new and broader interpretation, and his was Black nationalism. He expanded the civil rights struggle to the level of human rights and argued that as a nation within a nation, Black Americans could take their cause to the United Nations, where Africans, Asians, and all people of color could weigh in on their side. Attending the 1964 Cairo Conference of the Organization of African Unity, which brought together the heads of the newly independent African nations, Malcolm told a reporter that he sought "to remind the African heads of state that there are 22 million of us in America who are also of African descent, and to remind them also that we are the victims of America's colonialism or American imperialism, and that our problem is not an American problem, it's a human problem. It's not a Negro problem, it's a problem of humanity. It's not a problem of civil rights, but a problem of human rights."[21] Malcolm X's Black nationalism was an outgrowth of his Muslim religion. As a minister in the nonpolitical Nation of Islam, Malcolm adhered strictly to the group's principles of economic uplift, puritan values, and race pride. Harkening back to the ideas and practice of self-help that had been the cornerstone of Black community development since the turn of the century, Malcolm X preached that if Black people pooled their resources; built their own hospitals, schools, and factories; and made their own neighborhoods good places to live,

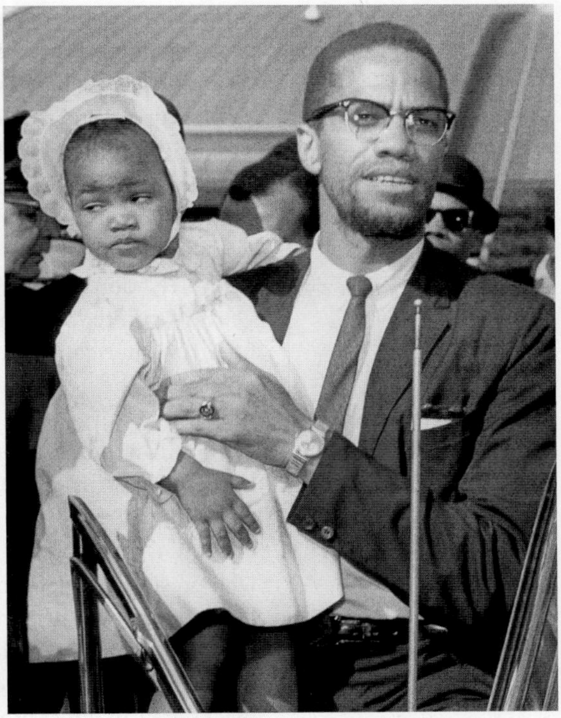

Malcolm X
Shown here with his young daughter Ilyasah, Malcolm X emerged as Black power's most influential advocate. Combining a philosophy of Black nationalism with his role as a minister in the Nation of Islam, Malcolm portrayed the freedom struggle as an issue of human rights and encouraged the use of revolutionary tactics. In 1964, he broke with the Nation of Islam and created the secular Organization of Afro-American Unity to address Black economic issues and encourage Black participation in mainstream politics. Less than a year later, members of the Nation of Islam assassinated Malcolm as he addressed his new organization. **How did Malcolm X inspire many to adopt the ideology of Black nationalism?** © *TopFoto/The Image Works.*

they wouldn't have to integrate white establishments. This could happen only if Black people learned to love themselves, protect themselves, and build their own economic system.

Articulating the gendered foundation of Black nationalism, Malcolm X believed that "while a man must at all times respect his woman, at the same time he needs to understand that he must control her if he expects to get her respect." He noted in his autobiography that women are "by their nature . . . fragile and weak" and "attracted to the male in whom they see strength."[22] In Malcolm's formulation of Black power, the strength and protection provided to Black women by Black men would be the foundation of Black families and communities — indeed, the Black nation.

AP® exam tip
Make sure you can explain the role gender played in the rise of Black nationalism, "Black Is Beautiful," and the Black Arts movement.

Malcolm's insistence that "Black is beautiful" had special significance for Black women, who had long been negatively impacted by white standards of feminine beauty, but it resonated with people regardless of their gender. He counseled Blacks to embrace themselves as Black people and not as "Negroes," a word that he believed whites had invented to separate Blacks from their African and Asian brothers. The word *Negro* made Black people hate themselves, he argued, because it was associated with slavery and docility. Malcolm agreed with the Black nationalist George Grant, who in 1926 argued for the voluntary embrace of the word *Black* as a way to "dispel the fallacious ideas of white purity, white beauty, and white superiority."[23]

AP® exam tip
Make sure you can explain how the ideas of Malcolm X reflect the influence of Marcus Garvey.

Malcolm X's ideas stood in contrast to Martin Luther King Jr.'s philosophy of nonviolence and strategy of direct-action protest. Malcolm derided civil rights leaders as sellouts who were handpicked by white liberals to keep Blacks in check. Black people needed land, power, and freedom, not desegregation, he argued. Desegregation did not address police brutality, substandard education, poverty, and unemployment, and from his perspective, African Americans would get nowhere by loving their oppressors. "Revolution," he said, "is never based on begging somebody for an integrated cup of coffee. Revolutions are never fought by turning the other cheek. . . . And revolutions are never waged singing 'We Shall Overcome.' " Instead, he argued, "Revolutions are based upon bloodshed. . . . Revolutions overturn systems."[24]

Early in 1964, Malcolm X moved to make his revolutionary vision a reality. He broke his ties with Elijah Muhammad, the leader of the Nation of Islam, and resigned his ministry. For some time, he had chafed under the organization's restriction against political activity and Elijah Muhammad's seeming jealousy of his national renown. He was also disturbed by rumors regarding Elijah Muhammad's indiscretions with women and the Nation of Islam's finances. Concerned that differences over religion were preventing a united front against white racism, he established the secular Organization of Afro-American Unity (OAAU), modeled on the Organization of African Unity created by the newly independent African states. Malcolm planned to use the organization not only to build independent Black institutions that would address Black economic issues, but also to support Black participation in mainstream politics and to represent African Americans on the world stage, particularly at the United Nations.

AP® skills

Applying Disciplinary Knowledge: Read the required source for Topic 4.9, "The Ballot or the Bullet," and explain Malcolm X's perspective on how to achieve equal rights. How does this speech reveal the evolution in Malcolm X's philosophy?

Neither Malcolm X nor the organization survived long enough to put this plan into effect. On February 21, 1965, Malcolm was assassinated by Nation of Islam members who presumably were angered by his very public defection. But Malcolm's ideas spread like wildfire even after his death. Members of SNCC and CORE who had heard him speak circulated his philosophies. His ideas and tactics were debated and compared with those of King and other prominent civil rights leaders. Their acceptance among Blacks grew in direct proportion to the growth of white resistance to Black equality.[25]

The Struggle Transforms

How did nonviolent resistance strategies mobilize civil rights activists in the Mississippi Freedom Summer Project?

How did the Black Panther Party pursue political, economic, and social reforms in the twentieth century?

AP® skills

Applying Disciplinary Knowledge: Explain the causes and effects of the transition from the Civil Rights movement to the Black Power movement.

At the end of 1963, Black power and nonviolent political protest coexisted within the Black freedom struggle. After 1965, however, the philosophies of Black power and Black nationalism became the dominant ideology. How and why that happened had to do with the intransigence of racism and the deepening determination of African Americans to resist its effects. It also had to do with some unpopular decisions and public missteps made by prominent civil rights leaders.

Black Power and Mississippi Politics

Mississippi Freedom Summer Project
A massive education and voter registration campaign conducted in the summer of 1964.

Black power ideas were floating around Mississippi in the summer of 1964 when the Council of Federated Organizations (COFO), a coalition of civil rights groups, conducted its **Mississippi Freedom Summer Project**, a massive education and voter registration campaign. During June, July, and August, more than a thousand volunteers descended on Mississippi. They founded freedom schools that taught Black youngsters, teenagers, and adults voter literacy and political organization skills. In alliance with local Black leaders, they canvassed Blacks and got them to register to vote. Although Blacks made up 45 percent of Mississippi's population, only 5 percent of voting-age Blacks voted. Their votes would prove pivotal in the upcoming presidential election.

It did not take much to convince Black Mississippians — 86 percent of whom lived below the poverty line — that their impoverishment was directly related to their disfranchisement. They had demonstrated their voting strength in November 1963, when they had participated in a mock vote held by civil rights organizations. Unable to cast a vote in the official election, nearly 100,000 Blacks had voted for the Freedom Ballot, a campaign designed to demonstrate Blacks' voting strength and desire to participate in Mississippi politics. In August 1964, Mississippi Blacks planned to take a separate delegation to the Democratic National Convention in Atlantic City, New Jersey, to challenge the party's all-white segregationist slate.

A tragedy during Freedom Summer highlighted Black southerners' plight and caused many Blacks to question the value of integrated civil rights activism. In early June, three civil rights workers — James Chaney, a native Black Mississippian, and Andrew Goodman and Michael Schwerner, two white northerners — disappeared in Mississippi. They were found murdered in early August. The media attention that began after their initial disappearance, and the arrival of about 150 FBI agents and more than 200 members of the U.S. navy to search for the missing men, brought more to light than the murders. To many Blacks, it seemed that America's leaders only became interested in Black people's plight when white deaths were involved. As John Lewis observed, "It is a shame that national concern is aroused only after two white boys are missing."[26]

AP® skills

Applying Disciplinary Knowledge: Why were Black people motivated to vote? What was John Lewis's perspective on national concern about the disfranchisement of Black people?

Although African Americans appreciated the work and sacrifices of the white volunteers who made up three-quarters of the Freedom Summer workers, many began to wonder whether they did more harm than good. Their middle-class background and education kept them removed from the daily realities most southern Blacks faced. For some Blacks, especially those attuned to Black power rhetoric, the presence of whites of greater wealth and superior education seemed to reinforce traditional patterns of racial dependence. Moreover, many understood that the presence of white women increased the wrath of segregationists, who were already convinced that the Civil Rights movement was a cover for interracial sexual relationships between Black men and white women. The activist Fannie Lou Hamer, who carried a gun for self-defense, summed up the feeling that Black men would be scapegoated when she warned, "If some whites laid hands on one of those young girls, every Negro man in Ruleville would be in trouble. That kind of trouble kills people in Mississippi."[27]

Despite these apprehensions, however, some Blacks had misgivings about a Blacks-only movement. As Hamer argued, "If we're trying to break down this barrier of segregation, we can't segregate ourselves." Like veteran civil rights worker Bob Moses, who argued that whites working alongside Blacks changed the calculus

Fannie Lou Hamer and the Mississippi Freedom Democratic Party
With the assistance of SNCC and COFO, Mississippi Blacks established the Mississippi Freedom Democratic Party (MFDP) in 1964. Fannie Lou Hamer was elected vice chair of the party's sixty-eight delegates, who planned to challenge their state's all-white segregationist delegation at the Democratic National Convention that summer. During the convention, however, national Black civil rights leaders and white liberals compromised with Mississippi Democratic Party delegates, and the MFDP was offered only two at-large seats on the convention floor, preventing their official participation in the convention. Here Hamer, standing at center, is surrounded by other notable civil rights activists, including (from left) Emory Harris, Stokely Carmichael (wearing a straw hat), Sam Block, Eleanor Holmes Norton, and Ella Baker. **How does this photograph demonstrate Black women's leadership in organizing for the Black Freedom movement?** *© George Ballis/Take Stock/The Image Works.*

ACTIVITY ▸ Revisit Your Prediction

In the AP® Unit Warmup (p. U4-E), you made a prediction about this image. **What does this photo suggest about the roles Black women played in the Civil Rights movement? Support or revise your original prediction using evidence from this chapter.**

from Blacks against whites to "a question of rational people against irrational people," Hamer believed that whites had been in the movement from the beginning and had an important role to play.[28] Hamer's own accomplishments, including a food and clothing drive she had run under SNCC's auspices and an unsuccessful run for a seat in Congress, had been facilitated by interracial efforts. Experience had also taught her that middle-class Blacks could harm the Black freedom movement as much as, if not more than, whites.

Hamer's experience with the **Mississippi Freedom Democratic Party (MFDP)** made her suspicious of both white liberals and middle-class Blacks. Black and white locals, aided by SNCC and COFO, had established the independent, nondiscriminatory political party on April 26, 1964, to represent Black Mississippians. Hamer was elected vice chair of the sixty-eight-person delegation that the party planned to send to the Democratic National Convention in August. During Freedom Summer, the Blacks and whites organizing the party caucuses, county assemblies, and convention that were necessary to send MFDP delegates to the national convention faced unrelenting terror. Hamer knew that people had died and lost jobs and homes for the cause; Hamer herself had lost the sight in one eye during a near-fatal beating in a Mississippi jail. But she and other activists persevered because the last thing she and other Black Mississippians wanted was for the white liberals who controlled the Democratic convention to seat the delegation that had been elected by the all-white Mississippi Democratic Party. That all-white segregationist delegation had no intention of backing Lyndon Johnson, whose support of the Civil Rights Act had antagonized them, and they were even more hostile toward the liberal Hubert Humphrey, Johnson's pick for vice president.

Mississippi Freedom Democratic Party (MFDP) An independent, nondiscriminatory political party established to represent Black Mississippians at the 1964 Democratic National Convention.

But during the convention, after intense negotiation and political wrangling, national Black civil rights leaders — along with Johnson, Humphrey, liberal white members of Congress, and other white liberals such as Walter Reuther, head of the United Auto Workers — compromised with and even appeased the segregationist delegates. The MFDP was offered only two at-large seats on the floor of the convention, which would not allow them to participate officially. The MFDP, as well as the SNCC staff that had supported them, rejected what they considered a "back of the bus" offer. Hamer agreed with Bob Moses, who argued that the MFDP belonged to "Mississippi and its own hopes and desires" — not to white liberals, or even to Martin Luther King Jr. and the other Black civil rights leaders who characterized Hamer and other MFDP leaders as wrongheaded and ignorant.[29]

Hamer and her supporters came away from the Democratic National Convention empty-handed, but much more was lost than the right of the MFDP to represent Black Mississippians. Those who backed the compromise might have thought they were being politically astute. King, for example, thought that any concession from the Democrats was better than nothing, and many liberals wanted to spare Johnson the political embarrassment of having southern white Democrats bolt from the convention. But the compromise left the strategy of nonviolent political protest impotent. According to Hamer, "We followed all the laws that the white people themselves made. . . . But we learned the hard way that even though we had all the laws and all the righteousness on our side — that white man is not going to give up his power to us."[30]

Exhausted after a summer of dodging white terrorists, John Lewis considered the MFDP defeat a turning point in the Civil Rights movement. "We had played by the rules, done everything we were supposed to do, had played the game exactly

AP® skills

Applying Disciplinary Knowledge: What point is Hamer making with her statement on this page? Why did Bob Moses suggest Blacks should "set up our own government"?

as required, had arrived at the doorstep and found the door slammed in our face," he argued.[31] Many felt that white liberals had double-crossed Blacks, and even Bob Moses, who had long endorsed an integrated movement, left Atlantic City vowing, according to Lewis, that he would never again speak to a white man. Like Hamer, who concluded that power was something "we have to take for ourselves,"[32] Moses suggested that Blacks should "set up our own [state] government . . . [and] declare the other one no good. And say the federal government should recognize us."[33] To say the least, Black power scored a victory at the 1964 Democratic National Convention.

Bloody Encounters

A month before the convention, Black power had also emerged victorious on the streets of New York. While search teams scoured the Mississippi countryside for the three missing civil rights workers, two Black New York City communities, Harlem and Bedford-Stuyvesant, erupted in violence in response to the fatal shooting of James Powell, a slightly built fifteen-year-old Black boy. "Is Harlem Mississippi?" one organization asked, issuing a call for "100 skilled revolutionaries who are ready to die."[34] African Americans threw bricks and bottles at police, looted white-owned stores, broke windows, set fires with Molotov cocktails, and booed the civil rights leaders who called for calm. In subsequent years, most cities saw similar unrest and violence. Conservatives blamed Communists, as well as Black criminality and backwardness. Social scientists blamed overcrowded and deteriorating housing, poor heath, dilapidated schools, and police brutality. Black nationalists blamed white power and Black powerlessness, which they vowed to change.[35]

The events following the summer of 1964 worked to the advantage of Black power advocates. Lyndon Johnson won the November election but without the support of southern Democrats. Their defection to the Republican Party candidate, archconservative Barry Goldwater, proved to many that Johnson had needlessly humiliated, and sacrificed the support of, the MFDP. Then, in 1965, Martin Luther King Jr. made a series of decisions that further destabilized the nonviolent direct-action sector of the Black freedom struggle.

The first occurred in March, in Selma, Alabama, where SNCC organizer Jimmie Lee Jackson had been shot and killed while protecting his mother from a police attack. Although doing so went against the organization's grassroots organizing tactics, SNCC answered King's call to participate in a protest march from Selma to Montgomery that both commemorated Jackson and supported voting rights. President Johnson and Attorney General Nicholas Katzenbach urged King to call off the march, concerned that the publicity it would generate would adversely affect the voting rights bill that was proceeding slowly through Congress. King conceded and was nowhere in sight on March 7, a day that subsequently became known as **Bloody Sunday**. Led by SNCC head John Lewis, marchers were met at the Edmund Pettus Bridge by local police and Alabama state troopers armed with billy clubs and tear gas. The marchers stopped and

Bloody Sunday (1965)
A confrontation on March 7, 1965, between Black voting rights advocates and Alabama state troopers on the Edmund Pettus Bridge in Selma, Alabama.

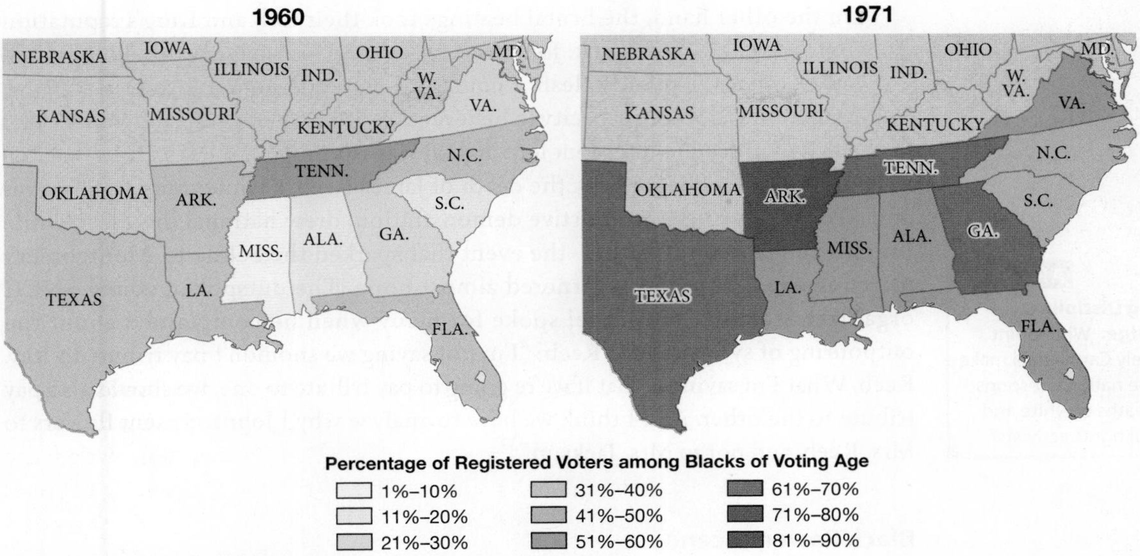

MAP 15.1 The Impact of the Voting Rights Act of 1965

Among its other provisions, the Voting Rights Act prohibited the literacy requirements and poll taxes that southern states had frequently used to prevent Blacks from voting. The act also sent federal election examiners to the South to enable Blacks to register and vote safely. As indicated in this map, Black voter registration skyrocketed as a result of the legislation. **Based on the information in this map, how effective were King's actions?**

knelt in prayer, which seemed only to gall the officers, who charged and clubbed their way forward, beating Lewis unconscious.

The marchers retreated but reassembled three days later, again at King's urging. Once again, however, King disappointed them. This time, although he led the march, when he got to the bridge, he stopped, knelt in prayer, and then asked the marchers to retreat. Angered by what they perceived as weakness on King's part, the marchers reluctantly turned back, ironically singing "Ain't Gonna Let Nobody Turn Me 'Round."[36]

King's compromises proved to be a double-edged sword. On one hand, the vicious police and trooper attacks proved that Black people needed a voting rights act if only to have a voice in electing those who held policing power, and King's concessions enabled President Johnson to push the measure through Congress by August. The 1965 **Voting Rights Act** prohibited states from imposing literacy requirements and poll taxes and sent federal election examiners south to protect Blacks' rights to register and vote. The impact was indisputable. Between 1964 and 1969, the percentage of Blacks registered to vote in Alabama increased from 19.3 percent to 61.3 percent. The percentage of registered Black voters in Georgia increased by 33 percent, and in Mississippi it increased by a spectacular 60 percent (Map 15.1).

AP® exam tip

Be sure you can explain how faith and music inspired African Americans to combat continued discrimination during the Civil Rights movement.

Voting Rights Act (1965)
An act outlawing literacy requirements and poll taxes and sending federal election examiners south to protect Blacks' rights to register and vote.

On the other hand, the brutal beatings took their toll, and King's reputation and strategy suffered a setback. John Lewis, who had his skull fractured on Bloody Sunday, noted, "We're only flesh. I could understand people not wanting to be beaten anymore. . . . Black capacity to believe [that a white person] would really open his heart, open his life to nonviolent appeal was running out." African Americans were also left to reflect on why the death of James Reeb, a white minister who was attacked shortly after the abortive demonstration, drew national publicity, while Jimmie Lee Jackson's death — the event that sparked the Selma-to-Montgomery march in the first place — garnered almost none. The outspoken young SNCC organizer Stokely Carmichael spoke for many when he complained about the outpouring of sympathy for Reeb: "I'm not saying we shouldn't pay tribute to Rev. Reeb. What I'm saying is that if we're going to pay tribute to one, we should also pay tribute to the other. And I think we have to analyze why [Johnson] sent flowers to Mrs. Reeb, and not to Mrs. Jackson."[37]

AP® skills

Applying Disciplinary Knowledge: What point did Stokely Carmichael make about the national response to the deaths of white and Black civil rights activists?

Black Power Ascends

Martin Luther King Jr. won the Nobel Peace Prize in 1964, but nonviolent, interracial protest was fast becoming a thing of the past. By the end of the Alabama demonstrations, even the moderate head of SNCC, James Forman, was proclaiming that "if we can't sit at the table of democracy, then we'll knock the fucking legs off."[38] Increasingly, activists believed that political work of the kind Carmichael was doing in Lowndes County paid more dividends than marches and beatings. Malcolm X's Black nationalism resonated more deeply with them, as did the tactics of a new group of militants called the Deacons for Defense and Justice, an armed group that organized in Mississippi and Louisiana in 1964 to protect Black people against increased Ku Klux Klan activity. Throughout 1965–1967, SNCC and CORE activists debated whether the Black freedom struggle was better off with Blacks-only organizations, and increasingly there were calls for whites to leave Black organizations and organize their own groups to support Black causes. In 1967, SNCC passed a resolution expelling whites. By that time, the leadership of SNCC had passed from the moderate John Lewis to the Black power advocate Stokely Carmichael. Similarly, the leadership of CORE had passed from the moderate James Farmer to the militant community organizer Floyd McKissick.

AP® skills

Applying Disciplinary Knowledge: What effect did Meredith's death have on the Civil Rights movement?

McKissick was present in June 1966 when Carmichael made his memorable public pronouncements on Black power. That summer, James Meredith — the student who had integrated the University of Mississippi — announced that he would march alone from Memphis to Jackson in what he called a "march against fear." Two days into the march, Meredith was shot in the neck, back, and legs by an avowed racist named Aubrey James Norvell. Civil rights leaders, including King, and Black power advocates alike rushed to continue the march in Meredith's honor, but they marched with different mindsets. For King, who by now was leading the old guard, the march offered proponents an unexpected opportunity to argue for new civil rights legislation and to force the government to accept responsibility for the safety of civil rights workers. Black power advocates, however, saw it as an opportunity to broadcast the perspective that Black people had to be more assertive.

To insiders, the split was apparent. When marching civil rights workers shouted "Freedom," Black nationalists shouted "Uhuru," the Swahili word for freedom. Black power marchers welcomed the protection of the Deacons for Defense and Justice, while civil rights workers only reluctantly accepted their support. And on the night of June 16, 1966, when Carmichael stood up and made public this advancing trend in African American thought, Black power advocates cheered what civil rights workers bemoaned. "This is the twenty-seventh time that I've been arrested," said the just-released Carmichael. "I ain't going to jail no more." He proclaimed, "The only way we gonna stop them white men from whuppin' us is to take over. What we gonna start saying now is Black Power." To Carmichael's resounding question "What do we want?" came the enthusiastic reply, "Black Power!"[39]

Four months later, two students at Merritt College in Oakland, California, responded to this cry. Huey Newton and Bobby Seale had been working with the Soul Students Advisory Council, a student organization that successfully lobbied the California State Board of Education to establish a Black studies department at Merritt College and to make Black studies credits transferable from junior to senior colleges. The council also was pressing for the appointment of a Black president at Merritt. In 1966, Seale and Newton broke with the council, believing that its emphasis on the glorification of Black culture and an African past — what Newton and Seale called *reactionary nationalism* — would not liberate Black people. They moved off campus and began organizing the poor people who lived in the area surrounding the campus. Seale and Newton then created the Black Panther Party for Self-Defense (BPPSD), with resistance to police repression its central mission. Clad in black leather jackets and black berets, the Black Panthers projected a hypermasculine identity meant to reclaim a "manhood" that, they argued, white America had robbed them of for centuries. To resist police harassment and brutality, they carried unconcealed weapons and adopted the policy of following and monitoring the police.

Although chapters of the Black Panther Party emerged in numerous cities — including Chicago; Indianapolis; Detroit; Des Moines; Paterson, New Jersey; and Wichita, Kansas — Oakland's BPPSD was the most influential. Its "Ten Point Program" encapsulated many of the principles that Black power and Black nationalism had, by the mid-1960s, come to represent.[40] Included among them were self-determination for Black people, full employment, decent housing and education, an end to police brutality, and exemption from military service.

The emergence of the Oakland Black Panthers revealed not only the divide between Black nationalists and civil rights activists but also the many different expressions of Black power. Although it was technically legal to carry unconcealed weapons in California until 1966, other Black power groups thought the Oakland patrols a suicidal tactic that would provoke government retaliation, and they rejected it.

The Black Panthers
Bobby Seale (left) and Huey Newton (right) created the Black Panther Party for Self-Defense (BPPSD) in Oakland, California, in 1966. Panthers made themselves recognizable by wearing black leather jackets and black berets, and they carried loaded, unconcealed weapons while patrolling Black neighborhoods and monitoring the activities of local police. Their revolutionary philosophy motivated many activists and signaled a shift in the Black freedom movement. For many activists, the Panthers also symbolized a reclamation of Black manhood. **Why was the attire of the Black Panther Party symbolic?** *Science History Images/Alamy Stock Photo.*

When the Soul Students Advisory Council, the Revolutionary Action Movement, and the Republic of New Africa — all of which advocated some form of Black power — objected to Seale and Newton's approach, their leaders were ridiculed by Seale and Newton followers as "intellectuals" whose Black separatism and glorification of Africa obscured the structural inequalities hidden behind American racism.[41]

This emphasis on structural inequalities allowed the Panthers to work with radical groups that prioritized class, regardless of race, which in practical terms permitted their alliance with white organizations. Structural inequality was important to all Black power organizations, but cultural nationalists believed that Black powerlessness was rooted in a deficient culture that kept African Americans estranged from Africa. Stokely Carmichael, who was convinced that the Black freedom struggle had to be international in scope and exclusively Black, argued, "We are an African people with an African ideology."[42] Maulana Karenga, organizer of a Los Angeles group called US — as opposed to "THEM" — promoted cultural reconstruction through *Kawaida*, a "total way of life" based on African principles. US members adopted Swahili names, dressed in traditional West African clothes, and engaged in African rituals. Karenga and US invented and first observed Kwanzaa, an African American holiday that celebrates the Seven Principles of Nguzo Saba, a Black value system stressing unity, self-determination, self-love, and cooperative economics.

AP® exam tip

Make sure you can compare the strategies used by the Black Panther Party, and their effects, to those of other organizations.

Differences between cultural naturalists and structuralists deepened divisions and made the entire freedom movement vulnerable to external attacks. While the Panthers called SNCC members and other Black power organizations "armchair revolutionaries" or, worse, "pork chop revolutionaries," most Black power activists derided civil rights activists as "sellouts," "chumps," "Oreos" (denoting persons who were Black on the outside but white on the inside), and "Uncle Tom Negroes" (an epithet drawn from the antebellum novel *Uncle Tom's Cabin*, denoting Black men who behaved subserviently toward whites). The word *Negro* itself became a derisive reference to a Black person who slavishly embraced white culture. Black power activists adopted the terms *Black* and *Afro* or *African American* to demonstrate their love of self and race and to symbolize their psychological emancipation from white oppressors.

Ultimately, the many expressions of Black militancy, especially carrying weapons, increased police harassment. Law enforcement officials were also incensed by the epithets used by militants to describe the police and members of America's political hierarchy. Made popular by the Black Panthers' newspaper, the term *pig* — described as "a low natured beast that has no regard for law, justice, or the rights of the people; a creature that bites the hand that feeds it; a foul depraved traducer, usually found masquerading as the victim of an unprovoked attack"[43] — was adopted by most left-wing radical groups of the era. Police retaliated by tearing down Black power posters and stepping up their harassment of activists. Search and seizure of activists' cars and homes became a regular activity. Panthers and other Black militants were arrested on flimsy charges and were even killed by local police and the FBI. (See AP® Working with Sources: Black Power: Expression and Repression, pp. 623–33.)

Economic Justice and Affirmative Action

How did grassroots organizing beyond the South advance the goals of the Civil Rights movement?

Black power was not the only response to the slow pace of change. Civil rights activists also adopted a new approach — or, more properly, returned to tried-and-true strategies for attaining economic and political justice. They did not endorse self-defense or the displays of militancy that were the hallmarks of the most radical Black power organizations. Instead, they worked through established institutions and, in the process, focused the nation's attention on a new concept called **affirmative action**, a set of ideas and programs aimed at compensating African Americans for past discrimination by giving them preferential treatment in hiring and school admissions.

affirmative action
A set of ideas and programs aimed at compensating African Americans for past discrimination by giving them preferential treatment in hiring and school admissions.

Politics and the Fight for Jobs

Lyndon Johnson and his administration deplored the Black freedom movement's turn to Black nationalism. From their perspective, progress on civil rights had been unprecedented. Johnson believed that his dedication to racial change and his effort to reduce the national poverty rate through what he called the War on Poverty were making a difference. Although he had known that the Civil Rights Act of 1964 would alienate southern Democrats and push them into the Republican Party, he had nevertheless forced the bill through Congress. Similar calculations were involved when he signed the Voting Rights Act in 1965. But Johnson also agreed with Martin Luther King Jr., who had, since Birmingham, urged "some compensatory consideration for the handicaps" Blacks had "inherited from the past."[44]

With this argument, King demonstrated that he, like the Black nationalists, was familiar with the dire economic state of Black America and that he was not content with the slow pace of change. Like most other civil rights leaders, he had de-emphasized economic concerns to minimize Cold War accusations of communism. He had never abandoned the goal of economic equality, however, and he traced urban violence directly to the economic disabilities racism produced. "We must get better jobs in order to help our children to better education and housing, and in order to enjoy some of the entertainment and eating facilities that are now open to us," King told the SCLC in 1962. Other leaders agreed. "Economics is part of our struggle," said activist Bayard Rustin. James Farmer of CORE concurred: "It will be a hollow victory, indeed, if we win the important rights to spend our money in places of public accommodation, on buses, or what have you, without also winning the even more vital right to earn money."[45]

AP® exam tip

Make sure you can describe your observations of data patterns and explain how they relate to political, social, and/or economic outcomes. Try comparing the data on Black unemployment on this page to the required AP® course source for Topic 4.15 (Economic Growth and Black Political Representation): Charts from "The Black Middle Class Needs Political Attention, Too," Brookings Institution Report by Andre M. Perry and Carl Romer, 2020. You can take this a step further by making comparisons to the data shared in images from W. E. B. Du Bois's exhibit at the 1900 Paris Exposition, which are optional AP® course sources for Topic 3.12 (Photography and Social Change).

When it came to earning money, African Americans had clearly fallen behind. Despite gains brought about by civil rights activism, Black unemployment was at the recession level of 10.2 percent, compared with the white rate of 4.9 percent. For Black male breadwinners, unemployment in 1963 was three times higher than it was for whites. On average, employed Blacks earned only 55 percent of what whites earned. The income gap between Black and white women had almost closed, but this was because Black women worked in greater numbers and for longer hours than white women. Among the young, Black teenagers suffered joblessness at twice the rate of white teenagers.[46]

The issue was rendered more intractable by most whites' belief that their advantage resulted from their natural superiority to Blacks. Surveys showed that even as they admitted that "their own employers do not open up certain types of jobs" to Blacks, most whites maintained that "companies give Negroes a good break [in hiring]." Similarly, most white employers, even those who hired Blacks, consistently maintained that "Negroes were not suited for any but production jobs."[47]

While liberals and conservatives differed in their views on economic injustice, their opinions had similar impact. Conservatives were apt to believe in Black incapacity. As one Milwaukee man editorialized in a conservative magazine, Blacks "make themselves the way they are by being lazy, uneducated, sick, [and] undependable. . . . They cannot or *will not* compete."[48] Liberals were more likely to admit that Blacks were profoundly wronged, but they nevertheless were apt to resist government action to redress those wrongs if it meant eliminating white privilege. For African Americans, then, the distinction between liberal and conservative was fast becoming irrelevant.

Urban Dilemmas: Deindustrialization, Globalization, and White Flight

At the same time that record numbers of Blacks were migrating out of the South in search of more secure, higher-paying work, deindustrialization — the decline of manufacturing, especially in the auto, steel, and consumer goods industries — was decreasing the number of jobs, especially in the unskilled and semiskilled industrial sector. Detroit lost 140,000 manufacturing jobs between 1947 and 1963, and New York lost 70,000 garment industry jobs. Chicago's meatpacking industry shrank, and longshoreman, shipbuilding, and warehouse jobs in port cities such as Oakland, Newark, Philadelphia, and Baltimore disappeared as fewer ships were built and the use of industrial shipping containers reduced the need for large numbers of dockworkers.[49] In one of the most bitter ironies of African American history, unskilled southern Blacks were moving north and west to escape insecure, low-paying, non-union jobs at the very time that northern and western companies were moving south and overseas in search of non-unionized, cheap labor and to suburbs in search of highly skilled professional labor.

Thus Black people arrived in northern and western cities just as these cities were declining. The first generation of Black migrants found the education in urban schools to be better than that in the schools they had left behind. However, as companies relocated, whites, with the help of federally subsidized low-interest loans that were denied to Blacks, left cities for racially exclusive suburban neighborhoods. This phenomenon, generally termed **white flight**, left education in Black neighborhoods just as separate and unequal in the North and West as it was in the South. Moreover, since redlining prevented investment in predominantly Black neighborhoods, these areas declined and became sites of urban decay. Suburban shopping malls thrived at the expense of downtown urban areas, and the highways that facilitated whites' travel to and from the cities in which they no longer lived often destroyed the Black neighborhoods that they cut through. Urban renewal projects designed to reinvigorate decaying cities had much the same effect. New York destroyed Manhattan's San Juan Hill, a Black and Puerto Rican neighborhood, to make way for the Lincoln Center for the Performing Arts, which housed the Metropolitan Opera. Philadelphia bulldozed its Black Bottom neighborhood to make way for a science and research center attached to the University of Pennsylvania. Chicago's Bronzeville neighborhood was cut off on one side by an expressway and on the other side by high-rise public housing.[50]

white flight
The movement of whites out of urban areas to racially exclusive suburbs, facilitated by federal highway construction, federally subsidized low-interest loans, and discrimination against Blacks.

Long a source of Black/white competition, public housing presented special problems for African Americans. When whites moved out of the city, making public housing more accessible to Blacks, it only added to the isolating concentration of Black poverty. Public housing was usually built in already impoverished Black neighborhoods or on marginal land, such as garbage dumps or toxic wetlands. Chicago's Robert Taylor Homes and Stateway Gardens, Boston's Columbia Point, and Philadelphia's Passyunk Homes were all built on sites that developers could use for nothing else.[51]

Discrimination in employment and housing helped highlight the idea of institutional racism that would inform activists' attempts to tackle economic injustice and mass incarceration. In the 1950s and early '60s, racism was still thought of as something practiced by individuals or mandated by law. Later in the decade, the idea that institutions

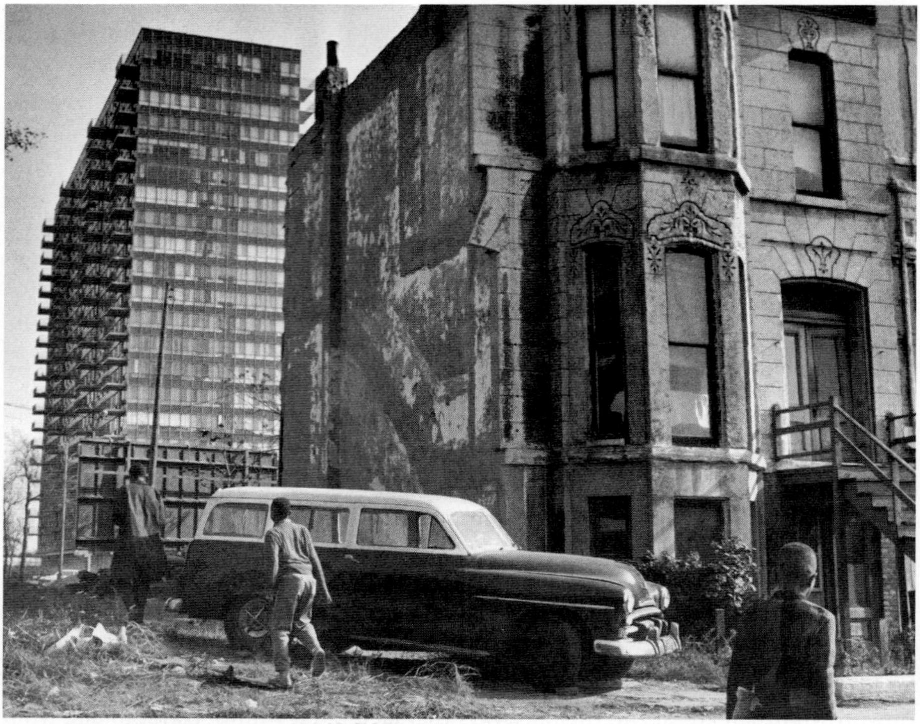

The Urban Crisis
Deindustrialization triggered the decline of many northern and western cities, which lost thousands of jobs just as African American migrants poured in seeking work. As jobs disappeared and white flight expanded the developing suburbs, the infrastructure of these cities began to decay. Urban renewal projects — many of which, ironically, focused on the development of public housing — often exacerbated these problems, decimating Black neighborhoods. Redlining by banks and government agencies caused further decline. In this 1963 photograph, a major public housing complex under construction in Chicago is visible behind tenements of the sort it has displaced. The residents of the new building would have higher incomes than the residents of the older homes. **How does this image illustrate the immediate effects of the urban crisis? What might be the potential long-term effects of the urban crisis?** *Charles E. Knoblock/Associated Press/AP Images.*

could and did operate as unfairly as individuals began to sink in. By this logic, corporations, unions, and governments developed policies and made decisions on the accepted premise that Blacks were inferior to whites. Housing discrimination — from the banks that granted mortgages and redlined, to the real estate industry that busted blocks, to the homeowner associations that monitored sales — was based on the same premise. Once activists understood that institutions both caused and reinforced racism, they began to argue that the legal and criminal justice systems were discriminatory because the systems themselves grew from customs steeped in centuries of racism.

Tackling Economic Injustice

Laws that promoted Black civil and voting rights could not and did not change the institutional racism that handicapped Blacks in the workforce, real estate market, and legal system. "Freedom is not enough," President Johnson said in a 1965 commencement speech at Howard University. In what was to become part of the philosophical foundation of the policy of affirmative action, Johnson declared, "You do not wipe away the scars of centuries by saying: Now you are free to go where you want, and do as you desire, and choose the leaders you please. You do not take a person who, for years, has been hobbled by chains and liberate him, bring him up to the starting line of a race and then say, 'you are free to compete with all the others,' and still justly believe that you have been completely fair."[52] In 1964, as part of his War on Poverty, Johnson signed the **Economic Opportunity Act**. It established the Job Corps, to create employment opportunities for the poor; Head Start, to give poor children a preschool education; the Neighborhood Youth Corps, to give inner-city youths summer jobs; and Volunteers in Service to America (VISTA), to give advantaged young people a chance to serve the less advantaged in the United States.

Economic Opportunity Act (1964)
Part of President Lyndon Johnson's War on Poverty, this act established the Job Corps, Head Start, the Neighborhood Youth Corps, and Volunteers in Service to America (VISTA).

More important for Black employment was Title VII of the 1964 Civil Rights Act, which banned employers and unions from practicing race and gender discrimination. When opponents could not beat back Johnson's support for the measure, they weakened the act by limiting the funding and abilities of the Equal Employment Opportunity Commission (EEOC), the agency charged with investigating discrimination. In particular, opponents would not allow plaintiffs to use the low number of minorities in a particular job as evidence of discrimination; neither could a group receive preferential treatment to redress the imbalance. Opponents' efforts, however, did not prevent African Americans from using the new law. From 9,000 cases in the EEOC's first year of operation, the caseload grew to 77,000 by 1975.[53]

With the help of the Office of Federal Contract Compliance (another Johnson agency), the NAACP, and the NAACP Legal Defense and Educational Fund, Black workers turned the weakened legislation to their advantage. In the process, they built a body of case law covering issues such as seniority lists that locked Blacks out of good jobs; discriminatory hiring and promotion procedures; biased recruiting; segregated unions; and the use of exclusionary testing and job requirements unrelated to job performance. Many cases ended unsuccessfully, especially in the northern construction trades, where Black workers met with stiff resistance from whites, who engaged in hate strikes and persistently excluded Blacks from apprenticeship programs. Whites took to calling the new policies "reverse racism." Some industries gave way, however. Blacks in the South successfully accessed jobs in the textile industry, where Black women especially benefited. According to a textile worker named Corine Cannon, work allowed Black women "to be full-fledged citizens."[54]

AP® skills

Applying Disciplinary Knowledge: You can create a T-chart to trace the goals and outcomes of the NAACP's strategy to lessen economic injustice.

The impact of Title VII extended beyond the actual number of cases won or lost. Along with the War on Poverty programs, the law breathed new life into strategies combating poverty that the Cold War had forced civil rights groups to put on hold.

In Chicago in 1966, for example, King's SCLC established Operation Breadbasket, which aimed to increase both Black employment in urban businesses and the number of Black-owned businesses. Sounding very much like his Black power counterparts, King explained that "the fundamental premise of Breadbasket is a simple one: Negroes . . . need not patronize a business which denies them jobs or advancement or plain courtesy."[55] Breadbasket won jobs by boycotting Country Delight dairy products and the A&P supermarket in Chicago. But King's ideas went beyond boycotts. Along with leaders such as A. Philip Randolph, Bayard Rustin, Whitney Young, and John Lewis, he argued for "a massive program by the government of special compensatory measures." Black civil rights leaders were virtually unanimous in supporting what they called the "Freedom Budget," or a "practical, step-by-step plan for wiping out poverty in America during the next ten years" by creating federally funded jobs at a cost of $180 billion.[56]

Proponents of compensatory programs challenged the prevailing notion that property rights gave employers the right to discriminate, that unions could promote and fire on the basis of seniority rules, and that equality and color blindness were the proper basis on which to hire workers. Instead, they insisted on affirmative action — preferential treatment for Blacks through the use of numerical hiring goals — arguing that white Americans had received preferential treatment for three hundred years on the basis of their color. According to Whitney Young, head of the National Urban League, "Indemnification means realistic reparations for past injuries and wrongs. . . . Industry must employ Negroes because they are Negroes."[57] Likewise, A. Philip Randolph argued that urban chaos could be avoided only by "mak[ing] work available for those in the ghettos."[58]

Griggs v. Duke Power Co. (1971)
A U.S. Supreme Court ruling which held that IQ tests, high school diplomas, and other requirements that were not necessary for the performance of a job were by their very nature discriminatory and had to be eliminated.

Griggs v. Duke Power Co. (1971) eliminated some of the barriers that kept Blacks from being employed. The case was filed in 1966 by the NAACP on behalf of Willie Griggs and thirteen other Black janitors whose North Carolina employer required workers to take IQ tests or present high school diplomas in order to advance to better-paying positions. These requirements disproportionately disadvantaged African Americans. Moreover, white workers who had been hired before the institution of the requirements were found to perform their jobs capably, making it clear that meeting such requirements did not predict job performance. The U.S. Supreme Court's unanimous decision declared that tests and other requirements unnecessary for the performance of a job were, by their very nature, discriminatory. Under the ruling, if employers could not demonstrate a business necessity for employment requirements, they had to eliminate the requirements. (See Appendix: *Griggs v. Duke Power Co.* for the text of this ruling.)

For many civil rights advocates, this victory was as important as the *Brown* decision in 1954. Previously, it had been almost impossible to prove that a company discriminated intentionally, and plaintiffs often did not have the financial resources to pursue cases. With *Griggs*, the burden of proof shifted to the employer, as the Court finally recognized that where minorities were concerned, seemingly neutral policies could be discriminatory. As more cases were settled under *Griggs*, it became increasingly customary for companies to set numerical hiring and promotion goals for minorities — something conservative members of Congress had explicitly omitted from the original Title VII legislation. These cases made a difference in the number of Blacks hired. By the second half of the 1970s, economists and social scientists concluded that affirmative action had, in fact, helped Black employment. "Direct pressure," concluded one economist, "does make a difference."[59]

War, Radicalism, and Turbulence

What effects did the Vietnam War have on Black communities at home and on Black men drafted into military service?

How did Muhammad Ali contest discrimination and advocate for racial equality?

By the mid-1960s, the Black freedom struggle had completely changed from what it had been just ten years earlier. Direct-action protest for civil rights had almost run its course, and Black power was fast supplanting nonviolent civil disobedience as the philosophy of choice. Economic justice was back on the front burner, and both civil rights and Black power groups were addressing issues of unemployment, housing, and poverty. Moreover, the movement had grown less interracial. Years of white resistance had bred Black suspicion and anger; for their part, whites were put off by Black power ideas, and poor whites looked suspiciously at affirmative action.[60] Black nationalists, meanwhile, donned African clothing, wore natural hairstyles, and heeded Black soul singer James Brown's commandment to "say it loud — I'm Black and I'm proud."

With the Vietnam War as the backdrop, these conditions made for an atmosphere that was divisive and explosive. Street protests by both antiwar and Black activists provoked counterdemonstrations and calls from conservatives for law and order. The assassination of Martin Luther King Jr. only deepened the nation's strife.

The Vietnam War and Black Opposition

Like Presidents Eisenhower and Kennedy, Lyndon Johnson judged the Southeast Asian nation of Vietnam central to U.S. interests in the Cold War. He believed that if Vietnam fell to the Communists, the rest of Southeast Asia would follow, imperiling democracy and American interests in the region. By 1965, the forces of the Communist and nationalist leader Ho Chi Minh controlled North Vietnam. Determined to keep South Vietnam out of the hands of the Communists, Johnson increased the number of U.S. troops already sent there by his predecessors. By the end of 1966, there were more than 385,000 U.S. combat troops in Vietnam, 15 percent of whom were African American. As the number of troops increased, so did the casualties. By the end of 1966, 6,378 Americans had been killed, and more than 35,393 had been wounded. Over the next two years, these numbers continued to rise.[61] As they did, African Americans' initial support for the war waned, and opposition intensified.

AP® skills

Applying Disciplinary Knowledge: How did African Americans' attitudes toward the Vietnam War shift? What were the primary causes of that shift?

There were many reasons for this shift in attitudes. First, Blacks were drafted and inducted into the service in disproportionate numbers. Although African Americans made up only 12 percent of the population in 1966, they made up 13.4 percent of military inductees. Between 1965 and 1970 — the height of U.S. involvement in Vietnam — this number rose to 14.3 percent; in 1967 and 1970, it was more than 16 percent.

Black leaders placed the blame squarely on institutional racism. Middle- and upper-class whites had an advantage, since the draft exempted students, professionals, and skilled workers. African Americans were also underrepresented on local draft boards, which played an important role in determining who would be accepted into the service. Blacks accounted for only 1.3 percent of board membership in 1966, and in most deep South states, which had large Black populations, there were no Black board members at all. Even when the number of Black board members increased, white board members so outnumbered them as to make their presence inconsequential. Furthermore, Blacks did not have the necessary personal connections to get medical deferments or even to be placed in the National Guard to avoid service in Vietnam.[62]

Second, although conditions in the armed services had improved since World War II, Blacks still faced relentless discrimination, and it often got them killed. The complaints were familiar: Blacks were seldom recommended for promotion; reports about them were biased; they got the most dangerous combat assignments; they were court-martialed and imprisoned at disproportionate rates; they had higher rates of dishonorable discharges than whites; and Black education was so deficient that unlike many whites who scored high on military tests, and were thus qualified for technical and specialty training, Blacks qualified mostly for service, supply, and combat training. For many, the proof of racism was in the casualty figures. In 1965, African Americans made up 25 percent of all U.S. soldiers killed in Vietnam. (See By the Numbers: African Americans in the Vietnam War.) Only after these numbers raised alarms did the Pentagon reduce the proportion of Blacks in combat units, which in turn reduced the number of Black deaths. The switch to airpower in the later years of the war also reduced the number. Still, as a white sergeant summed up the situation to a Black private, "If you're white, you're all right, but if you're soul, there ain't no hope."[63]

The Vietnam War inequities plagued even Blacks as renowned as Muhammad Ali, who had become the heavyweight boxing champion of the world in 1964. As a member of the Nation of Islam, Ali resisted the draft on moral grounds. In his application for conscientious objector status in 1966, he claimed that, as a Muslim, he could not participate in any war but a holy war. After more than a year of legal battles, Ali was convicted in 1967 of draft evasion, sentenced to five years in prison, and fined $10,000. Although the U.S. Supreme Court overturned his conviction in June 1971, by that time Ali had been stripped of his heavyweight title at the height of his career.[64]

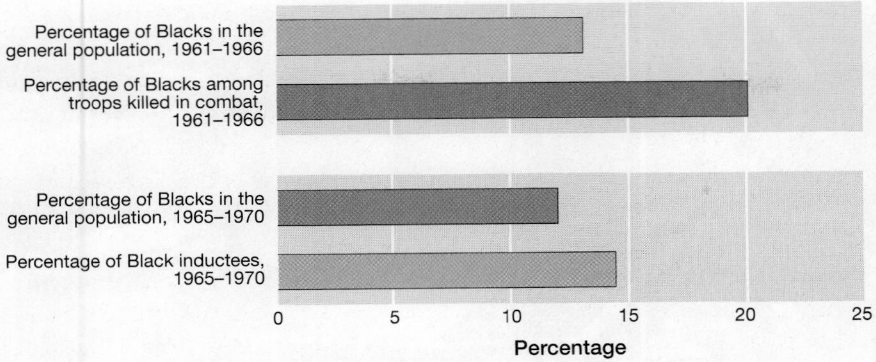

BY THE NUMBERS **African Americans in the Vietnam War**

As the averages in this figure indicate, Blacks were drafted — and died — in numbers disproportionate to their representation in the population. The draft exempted students, professionals, and skilled workers, giving middle- and upper-class whites a distinct advantage. African Americans also enjoyed little or no representation on the local draft boards that helped determine who would serve. The disproportionately high numbers of Black casualties led the Pentagon to reduce the number of Blacks in combat units. **How did civilian disfranchisement and discrimination within the military impact the data shown in this graph?**

ACTIVITY ▸ **Revisit Your Prediction**

In the AP® Unit Warmup (p. U4-F), you made a prediction about this image. **What conclusions can you draw from this graph about the conditions under which African Americans served during the Vietnam War? Support or revise your original prediction using evidence from this chapter.**

Ali became a hero to many Black Americans who opposed the war. They joined a growing and increasingly vocal antiwar effort. Like many other Americans, they balked at the anti-Communist arguments advanced by the Johnson administration, arguing that Vietnam did not pose an imminent threat to national security — and certainly not enough of a threat to justify the war's heavy casualties. The disproportionately high numbers of Black draftees and deaths fueled Black antiwar sentiment, as did Black nationalist arguments that Blacks should not fight other nonwhite people, especially those who were also fighting for liberation. "Why should black folks fight a war against yellow folks so that white folks can keep a land they stole from red folks?" asked Stokely Carmichael. He added, "Ain't no Vietcong ever called me nigger."[65] Most Black power groups agreed with Carmichael. Drawing connections between what they called America's capitalist imperial aggression abroad and its oppression of minorities at home, the Black Panthers, SNCC, CORE, and a new group called the National Black Anti-War Anti-Draft Union helped lead the country's militant antiwar movement from its very beginning.[66]

AP® skills

Applying Disciplinary Knowledge: What was the outcome of Muhammad Ali's protest of the Vietnam War? What fueled the antiwar sentiments many Black people held? What was a concern for Black people who supported, or remained silent about, participation in the war?

Others, including most civil rights leaders, took a less confrontational, more cautious approach. Future secretary of state Colin Powell, for example, believed that

Black Power and the Vietnam War
In this 1968 photo, U.S. marine artillerymen pose next to their howitzer with a "Black Power Is Number One" banner and a Black power salute. African Americans were drafted and inducted in disproportionate numbers throughout the Vietnam War; they accounted for disproportionate numbers of the war's casualties and faced discrimination of all kinds during their service. As the war dragged on, civil rights leaders, including Martin Luther King Jr., became more outspoken in their opposition to the conflict. **What conclusions about the soldiers' perspectives can be drawn from this image? What message does it send to audiences back home?** *Johner/Associated Press/AP Images.*

Blacks had to be involved in all national events, including those that were unpopular. Even though his father-in-law had had to arm himself to protect his home from segregationists during the Birmingham protests, Powell served two tours of duty in Vietnam and, like most civil rights leaders, believed that Blacks had to fight on both fronts. Leaders of the NAACP, Urban League, and SCLC had the added worry of offending their most powerful ally, President Johnson, and therefore either supported the war or stayed silent.

However, as the draft drained Black communities of their young men, and as money for the War on Poverty was reallocated to the war in Vietnam, civil rights leaders became more vocally antiwar. This was the case with Martin Luther King Jr., whose antiwar rhetoric sounded increasingly like that of Black nationalists. Initially, King had quietly expressed concern that America was spending nearly $500,000 to kill each enemy soldier but only $35 to feed each poor American.[67] But in 1967, in a public speech at Riverside Church in New York City, King spoke out passionately against the war, calling it an "enemy of the poor," both Black and white. He claimed that young Black men should not have to fight in Southeast Asia to guarantee liberties they could not find in southwest Georgia or East Harlem. Comparing U.S. actions in Vietnam to Hitler's genocide of Jewish people during World War II, King urged America to cease its bombing of Vietnamese families and villages. He also criticized capitalism, arguing for a new focus on people instead of things. "All over the globe," King pronounced, "men are revolting against old systems of exploitation and oppression, and . . . new systems of justice and equality are being born. . . . We in the West must support these revolutions."[68] America, King argued, had to once again become a force for revolutionary change. The best way to do that was to end the Vietnam War and take up an international war on poverty.

Later that year, King followed up his words with the announcement of the **Poor People's Campaign**. King's SCLC aimed to bring fifteen hundred protesters to Washington, D.C., in 1968 to lobby Congress and other government agencies for an "economic bill of rights." Specifically, the campaign requested a $30 billion antipoverty package that included a commitment to full employment, a guaranteed annual income measure, and increased construction of low-income housing. In what sounded like treason to President Johnson, King proclaimed that the poor people's movement had to "address itself to the question of restructuring the whole of American society." He announced that protest activities in Washington were to be supported by simultaneous demonstrations throughout the country.[69]

Poor People's Campaign A movement spearheaded in 1967–1968 by Martin Luther King Jr. and the Southern Christian Leadership Conference (SCLC) demanding a $30 billion antipoverty package from the U.S. government. The desired package would include a commitment to full employment, a guaranteed annual income measure, and increased construction of low-income housing.

AP® skills

Applying Disciplinary Knowledge: What were the demands of the Poor People's Campaign? What objectives did it seek to achieve?

Urban Radicalism

Johnson had more than King to be concerned about. By the time King came out against the Vietnam War in 1967, the intensity of the Black freedom struggle had been ratcheted up several notches. As radical as King had become, he remained more moderate than many Black power activists. In Detroit, Black workers in the Dodge, Ford, and Chrysler plants organized to prevent union and management discrimination. In 1968, the Dodge Revolutionary Union Movement conducted a series of unofficial strikes, one of which prevented the production of three thousand cars.[70] On another front were the welfare reformers. Beginning in 1964, local welfare groups in twenty-five cities, inspired by Johnson's War on Poverty, marched on statehouses and clashed with police in protest against the administration of the government-sponsored Aid to Families with Dependent Children program. As part of a nationwide, grassroots poor people's movement, welfare rights activists, most of whom were Black women, challenged eligibility requirements and insisted on better clothing and food allowances, job training programs for women, and subsidized day care. They also demanded to be employed as welfare agents, since they knew best what welfare recipients needed. In 1967, under the leadership of former welfare recipient Johnnie Tillmon and college professor George Wiley, welfare activists organized the National Welfare Rights Organization. Under its aegis, welfare recipients lobbied legislators, picketed and leafleted public offices, initiated legal suits, demanded that the government guarantee an annual income, and insisted that welfare was a right.[71]

Community Action Programs (CAPs)
Programs initiated and financed by President Lyndon Johnson's War on Poverty that directed antipoverty agencies to involve poor people in solving the problems of their own communities.

Many of the protests carried out by welfare activists were done through local **Community Action Programs (CAPs)** — programs that Johnson's War on Poverty legislation made possible by directing antipoverty agencies to recruit poor people to help solve inner-city problems. According to the logic behind the programs, community members had special insight into these problems and should participate in finding solutions. In Pittsburgh, for example, the government funded seven community offices to provide job training, child care, social services, Head Start classes, housing services, welfare consultants, legal services, and health care.[72]

AP® skills

Applying Disciplinary Knowledge: Why were CAPs ineffective?

The problem with CAPs was that they fed Black radicalism while failing to address racism and deindustrialization, the underlying causes of Black poverty. CAPs thus aroused everyone's ire. Poor people were angered by the government's failure to invest in job creation and restructure the real estate industry. City officials were angry because government-funded welfare consultants were fomenting protests that brought the wrath of recipients down on them. Community organizers were heartened by the government's newfound confidence in the power of "the people," and Black nationalists hailed the unexpected endorsement of their ideology. But when government-sponsored Black organizations ran anti–police brutality campaigns (as they did in New York City), or when they marched against grocery stores that overcharged Blacks for mediocre goods (as they did in Los Angeles), city officials, conservatives, and urban policymakers balked at Johnson's War on Poverty and accused him of inviting race and class warfare.[73]

This was no small accusation, because cities of all sizes were erupting in violence. Some called the violence "riots" to connote spontaneous, undisciplined hoodlum activity. Others called the uprisings "rebellions," signifying conscious and deliberate political action. By any name, the violence that erupted in 300 cities contributed to the radicalism and turbulence that characterized America in the second half of the 1960s. In the Watts section of Los Angeles in 1965, 34 people died and $35 million worth of property was destroyed. In Detroit in 1967, 43 people were killed, 2,000 were wounded, and 5,000 saw their homes destroyed by fire. On February 8, 1968, the **Orangeburg Massacre** occurred near the campus of the historically Black South Carolina State College when police were called to quell the violence that erupted after Blacks were refused admittance to a "whites only" bowling alley. The incident was subsequently called a massacre because 3 unarmed students were killed, and another 28 students were injured; nearly all of the victims were shot in the back or side by police. All told, the urban violence of the 1960s left 250 people dead, 10,000 seriously injured, and 60,000 arrested. Fire destroyed entire neighborhoods, leaving countless Blacks homeless.[74]

Orangeburg Massacre
An incident that occurred on February 8, 1968, in Orangeburg, South Carolina, near the campus of the historically Black South Carolina State College. Police were called to quell the violence that erupted after Blacks were refused admittance to a "whites only" bowling alley. This incident is called a massacre because twenty-eight students were injured, and three unarmed students were killed when they were shot in the back or side by police.

Subsequent studies showed that participants in the violence were mostly young, northern-born Black men who were better educated than their contemporaries but had been confined to low-end jobs or were unemployed. Although most were not formal members of a radical group, they nevertheless expressed race pride and saw their burning and looting as revolutionary — and as the first step to Black unity. Said one participant in recollection of the 1967 Plainfield, New Jersey, uprising, "Since the riot, we're not niggers anymore. We're Black men . . . and are working together and respecting the neighborhood."[75]

Both Blacks and whites struggled to make sense of the tumult. Most whites blamed the violence on Black power ideology.[76] The cries heard from the street to "get whitey" or "burn, baby, burn" scared and angered many. They did not see any potential political rationale behind burning and looting, which would not end poverty, eliminate unemployment, or stop police brutality. They had little understanding of the institutional racism — the redlining, the police harassment, the high-rise public housing ghettos — that kept Blacks penned in inner cities with few opportunities. One political scientist called the violence "outbreaks of animal spirits and of stealing by slum dwellers."[77] From the perspective of many whites, the riots, far from provoking a condemnation of police brutality, proved the necessity of police crackdowns on Black youths and the imperative of imposing law and order.

Although Blacks also abhorred the violence, their opinions were more varied. Many moderate civil rights leaders and organizations, including the NAACP, National Baptist Convention, National Council of Negro Women, and Prince Hall Masons, denounced the violence and the Black nationalists they believed fomented it. Calling it "black group suicide," they accused Black power leaders of being no better than white segregationists.[78] Floyd McKissick, the new leader of CORE, disagreed, claiming that Black people were finally fighting back. "The cup is running over in the ghetto," he argued. "It is inevitable that violence will occur."[79] Although he did not endorse the violence, Martin Luther King Jr. agreed with McKissick, arguing that "every single outbreak" had been caused by "gross unemployment, particularly among young people." He urged President Johnson to set up an agency "that shall provide a job to every person who needs work, young and old, white and Negro."[80] Still others agreed with Adam Clayton Powell Jr., the Black congressman from Harlem, who repudiated revolutionary violence while supporting self-defense and the need for Blacks to demand a "share of political jobs and appointments . . . equal to their proportion in the electorate."[81]

Opinions within the government also varied. The controversial **Moynihan Report**, written primarily by Assistant Secretary of Labor Daniel Patrick Moynihan, faulted the Black family. According to the report, which was published in 1965, Black family life was a "tangle of pathology" that poorly prepared blacks, especially Black men, for useful citizenship. In 1968, Johnson's National Advisory Commission on Civil Disorders, known as the **Kerner Commission**, found that the violence could be traced to job discrimination and institutional racism rather than to Black power ideology or a particular organization.

Despite these official studies, the government agreed with the police: the violence was unlawful and had to be stamped out. The militancy of Black nationalism and the boldness of Black power organizations made them natural targets of the nation's ire.

Moynihan Report
The controversial 1965 report written primarily by Assistant Secretary of Labor Daniel Patrick Moynihan that labeled the Black family dysfunctional and set off a storm of protest within Black America.

Kerner Commission
Officially, the National Advisory Commission on Civil Disorders. In 1968, it found that the violence plaguing inner cities could be traced to job discrimination and institutional racism rather than to Black power ideology or a particular organization.

AP® skills

Applying Disciplinary Knowledge: Explain the difference between the conclusions of the Moynihan Report and those of the Kerner Commission.

The government thus undertook a massive campaign against radical organizations. The FBI took advantage of its substantial power to disrupt, confuse, undermine, and eliminate radicals and their organizations, using extreme methods that were often both illegal and unconstitutional. At the top of the FBI's list were the Black Panthers and the Revolutionary Action Movement, the two organizations most critical of the government's police power. But even the markedly more moderate King was targeted as someone who had to be stopped.

No one knows whether the FBI was involved in the murder of Martin Luther King Jr., but on April 4, 1968, exactly one year after King publicly positioned himself against the Vietnam War, an assassin's bullet ended his life as he stood on the balcony of a Memphis hotel. True to his renewed focus on economic justice, King had gone to Memphis to help a predominantly Black sanitation workers' union gain recognition from the city. Upon news of the murder of this nonviolent icon, more than one hundred cities erupted in riots. Yet again, people died, and millions of dollars' worth of property was destroyed.

CONCLUSION

Progress, Challenges, and Change

AP® skills

Applying Disciplinary Knowledge: What concepts, developments, and processes discussed in this chapter best support the claim that the civil rights era was a second Reconstruction?

King's death marked the end of an era that many historians have called the second Reconstruction because of the progress made by African Americans to achieve all the citizenship rights that were not conferred, or that were conferred and then denied, during the period following the end of slavery. Activists in this era successfully struck down legal Jim Crow and achieved voting rights. Despite great obstacles and sometimes deadly opposition, they pried open the American workplace and forged new tactics and philosophies. In blazing their own path and demanding rights, African Americans provided a model for women, LGBTQ+ Americans, Latino Americans, and Indigenous Americans to do the same. But with their struggle came sacrifice. Many leaders lost their lives, and many more lost their spirit. As a whole, the movement lost its sense of unity, which gave way as different strategies emerged to tackle the problems of American racism.

At the end of the 1960s, some civil rights supporters, especially white liberals, blamed Black power for fracturing the postwar freedom struggle, but others, especially Black Americans, disagreed. Most African Americans celebrated Black power for the pride it instilled and for engendering intolerance of stereotypical representations of Blackness. Black power linked African American struggles to nationalist struggles throughout the world, and it linked African Americans to Black people in other countries. The problems faced by African Americans, many argued, were caused by whites' unwillingness to share the benefits of an ever-shrinking deindustrialized economy and by a government willing to spend billions of dollars to fight national liberation both at home and abroad.

Although the birthday of Martin Luther King Jr. would subsequently become a national holiday, and he would go down in American history as one of the nation's great freedom fighters, on the day of King's funeral, Lester Maddox, the governor of King's home state of Georgia, called him an "enemy of the country" and refused to close state offices in his honor.[82] Symbolic of the times, too, were the 120 state troopers in riot gear positioned at the entrances to the Georgia capitol to prevent the kinds of riots that erupted in Washington, D.C., and other cities.[83] As King's body was carried through the streets of Atlanta, few people understood how pivotal the 1960s legislation, court decisions, and race pride would be to Black America's future. Most just wondered, "Where do we go from here?"

CHAPTER 15 REVIEW ▸ PRACTICING AP® SKILLS

AP® ESSENTIAL VOCABULARY AND SOURCES

**Essential terms and required sources from the AP® Course are marked with an asterisk.*

Civil Rights Act of 1964* p. 592
Title VII p. 592
Gloria Richardson, Leads a Demonstration in 1963* (Image of Gloria Richardson confronted by Maryland National Guardsmen During Cambridge Protest, 1963) p. 594
Black nationalism* p. 594
Black Arts movement* p. 595
Mississippi Freedom Summer Project* p. 598
Mississippi Freedom Democratic Party (MFDP)* p. 601
Bloody Sunday (1965) p. 602
Voting Rights Act (1965)* p. 603
affirmative action p. 607
white flight p. 609
Economic Opportunity Act (1964) p. 611
Griggs v. Duke Power Co. (1971) p. 612
Poor People's Campaign p. 617
Community Action Programs (CAPs) p. 618
Orangeburg Massacre p. 618
Moynihan Report p. 619
Kerner Commission p. 619

APPLYING DISCIPLINARY KNOWLEDGE: ESSENTIAL QUESTIONS

1. What conditions fostered the blossoming of the Black Power movement? How was it similar to and different from earlier self-help initiatives?
2. How did the various Black power organizations and leaders help shape the Black power ideology? What philosophies and attitudes did they promote?
3. Describe the various strains of Black power that developed. How were these philosophies similar to and different from one another? In what ways did they all belong in the category "Black power"?
4. How did structural changes in the American economy affect African Americans and the different ideologies that they supported?
5. When the Oakland BPPSD first initiated the practice of carrying guns for self-defense, they were within their rights as California citizens. Yet the image of Black men carrying guns for self-protection did not garner the same sympathetic responses accorded to many other Second Amendment supporters. Why?
6. What challenges did Black activists confront in their fight for economic justice? What were their most significant victories in this struggle?
7. How did the conditions of the Vietnam War prompt civil rights activists to become more vocally antiwar?
8. Sometimes the urban violence of the 1960s is described as "riots," and sometimes the word "rebellions" is used. What is implied in each designation, and what accounts for the different perspectives?

SUGGESTED REFERENCES

The Emergence of Black Power

Carmichael, Stokely. *Ready for Revolution: The Life and Struggles of Stokely Carmichael (Kwame Ture)*. With Ekwueme Michael Thelwell. New York: Scribner, 2003.

Giddings, Paula. *When and Where I Enter: The Impact of Black Women on Race and Sex in America*. New York: Bantam, 1984.

Griffin, Farah Jasmine. " 'Ironies of the Saint': Malcolm X, Black Women, and the Price of Protection." In *Sisters in the Struggle: African American Women in the Civil Rights–Black Power Movement*, edited by Bettye Collier-Thomas and V. P. Franklin (pp. 214–29). New York: New York University Press, 2001.

Jeffries, Hasan Kwame. *Bloody Lowndes: Civil Rights and Black Power in Alabama's Black Belt*. New York: New York University Press, 2009.

Joseph, Peniel E. *Waiting 'Til the Midnight Hour: A Narrative History of Black Power in America*. New York: Henry Holt, 2006.

Malcolm X, with the assistance of Alex Haley. *The Autobiography of Malcolm X*. New York: Ballantine, 1992.

Millner, Sandra Y. "Recasting Civil Rights Leadership: Gloria Richardson and the Cambridge Movement." *Journal of Black Studies* 26, no. 6 (1996): 668–87.

Murch, Donna Jean. *Living for the City: Migration, Education, and the Rise of the Black Panther Party in Oakland, California*. Chapel Hill: University of North Carolina Press, 2010.

Levy, Peter B. *Civil War on Race Street: The Civil Rights Movement in Cambridge, Maryland*. Gainesville: University of Florida Press, 2003.

Singh, Nikhil Pal. *Black Is a Country: Race and the Unfinished Struggle for Democracy*. Cambridge: Harvard University Press, 2004.

Sugrue, Thomas J. *Sweet Land of Liberty: The Forgotten Struggle for Civil Rights in the North*. New York: Random House, 2008.

The Struggle Transforms

Abu-Lughod, Janet L. *Race, Space, and Riots in Chicago, New York, and Los Angeles*. New York: Oxford University Press, 2007.

Branch, Taylor. *At Canaan's Edge: America in the King Years, 1965–68*. New York: Simon & Schuster, 2006.

Carson, Clayborne. *In Struggle: SNCC and the Black Awakening of the 1960s*. Cambridge: Harvard University Press, 1981.

Lee, Chana Kai. *For Freedom's Sake: The Life of Fannie Lou Hamer*. Urbana: University of Illinois Press, 1999.

Lewis, John, with Michael D'Orso. *Walking with the Wind: A Memoir of the Movement*. New York: Simon & Schuster, 1998.

Miller, Jeanne-Marie A. "Review of *We Walk the Way of the New World*, by Don L. Lee." *Journal of Negro History* 56, no. 2 (April 1971): 153–55.

Payne, Charles M. *I've Got the Light of Freedom: The Organizing Tradition and the Mississippi Freedom Struggle*. Berkeley: University of California Press, 2007.

Self, Robert O. "The Black Panther Party and the Long Civil Rights Era." In *In Search of the Black Panther Party: New Perspectives on a Revolutionary Movement*, edited by Jama Lazerow and Yohuru Williams (pp. 15–55). Durham: Duke University Press, 2006.

Economic Justice and Affirmative Action

Anderson, Terry H. *The Pursuit of Fairness: A History of Affirmative Action*. New York: Oxford University Press, 2004.

Graham, Hugh Davis. *Collision Course: The Strange Convergence of Affirmative Action and Immigration Policy in America*. New York: Oxford University Press, 2002.

Katznelson, Ira. *When Affirmative Action Was White: An Untold History of Racial Inequality in Twentieth-Century America*. New York: Norton, 2005.

MacLean, Nancy. *Freedom Is Not Enough: The Opening of the American Workplace*. Cambridge: Harvard University Press, 2006.

Massey, Douglas S., and Nancy A. Denton. *American Apartheid: Segregation and the Making of the Underclass*. Cambridge: Harvard University Press, 1993.

War, Radicalism, and Turbulence

Blackstock, Nelson. *COINTELPRO: The FBI's Secret War on Political Freedom*. New York: Pathfinder, 1988.

Churchill, Ward, and Jim Vander Wall. *Agents of Repression: The FBI's Secret Wars against the Black Panther Party and the American Indian Movement*, 2nd ed. Cambridge, MA: South End Press, 2002.

Glaberman, Martin. "Survey: Detroit." *International Socialism* no. 36 (April/May 1969): 8–9.

Terry, Wallace. *Bloods: Black Veterans of the Vietnam War: An Oral History*. New York: Random House, 1984.

Westheider, James E. *The African American Experience in Vietnam: Brothers in Arms*. Lanham, MD: Rowman & Littlefield, 2008.

______. *Fighting on Two Fronts: African Americans and the Vietnam War*. New York: New York University Press, 1997.

Black Power: Expression and Repression

Black power was not just one thing. It was at once a political, social, and economic philosophy. It was a frame of reference — a new way of being for Black people and a new way of thinking. It was a consciousness. This "new mood," as James Baldwin referred to it, was as infectious as it was exhilarating, for at its core it presumed Black control over Black psyches, something that white domination had for centuries prevented and systematically crushed.

The way that Black power married culture to politics is arguably what made the philosophy so intimidating to white America. It was not just the many political manifestations of Black power (which were so numerous as to prevent organizing around a single agenda) that were so threatening but the "Black is beautiful" cultural concept at its root. The celebration of Africa and Africanness, of dark skin, of Black dance, music, and art, prompted African Americans to abandon the term *Negro* and self-identify as Black or African American — identifiers that earlier in the century would have been deemed derisive and understood as insults. Like proponents of the Black Arts movement, Black power activists maintained that African Americans' politics, economics, and artistic expression had to work to reverse the internalized feelings of inferiority wrought by the experience of slavery and Jim Crow oppression. They believed that no civil rights laws would liberate American Blacks if they did not psychologically accept the idea that Black was truly beautiful. Activists, writers, musicians, visual artists, poets, playwrights, and actors were all enlisted in the project to make African Americans' views of themselves, their history, and their culture more positive.

The following documents taken from the Black Power movement do not represent the full scope of the movement or the resistance to it, but they demonstrate the "new mood" and the government's repressive response. As you read and examine these written and visual documents, think about the relationship between art and politics and how Black power drove change. Think also about why Black power provoked such a malicious governmental reaction.

key point

Black power was a political, social, and economic philosophy that came to prominence in the 1960s and 1970s. The connection the movement drew between culture and politics frightened many white Americans. These documents do not capture the full scope of the Black Power movement, but they illustrate key aspects of it and the government response to it.

AP® argumentation

DBQ Practice: Explain how the Black Power movement connected culture and politics during the 1960s and 1970s. Use at least three of the documents to support your response.

DOCUMENT 1 Nina Simone | *Mississippi Goddam*, 1963

The murder of four Black girls in the 1963 bombing of Birmingham's Sixteenth Street Baptist Church left most Black Americans reeling. Coming less than a month after the awe-inspiring March on Washington, it convinced many that nonviolent passive resistance was a losing strategy against armed, bomb-throwing racists. NINA SIMONE (1933–2003) was among the dejected. A singer who, up until the bombing, sang mostly jazz, blues, gospel, and classical music, Simone composed the song "Mississippi Goddam" after learning of the children's deaths. It came to her, she said, in a "rush of fury, hatred and

determination."[84] Almost three years before Stokely Carmichael made his militant public pronouncement on Black power and Bobby Seale and Huey Newton founded the Oakland Black Panther Party for Self-Defense, Nina Simone wrote this song, which she recorded and performed through the 1970s. It became one of the anthems of the Black freedom struggle. Set to a frenetic beat, the opening lyrics speak to the urgency of the moment.

Breaking it Down As you read the following lyrics and examine the photo of Nina Simone, think about the image she projected and how it differed from that projected by Black men during this era. How might this singer, who was popular in Europe and Africa, have influenced foreign opinions about American race relations?

Alabama's gotten me so upset
Tennessee made me lose my rest
And everybody knows about Mississippi
Goddam

Can't you see it
Can't you feel it
It's all in the air
I can't stand the pressure much longer
Somebody say a prayer

Hound dogs on my trail
School children sitting in jail
Black cat cross my path
I think every day's gonna be my last

Lord have mercy on this land of mine
We all gonna get it in due time
I don't belong here
I don't belong there
I've even stopped believing in prayer

Don't tell me
I tell you
Me and my people just about due
I've been there so I know
They keep on saying "Go slow!"

But that's just the trouble
"do it slow"
Washing the windows
"do it slow"
Picking the cotton
"do it slow"
You're just plain rotten
"do it slow"

You're too damn lazy
"do it slow"
The thinking's crazy
"do it slow"
Where am I going
What am I doing
I don't know
I don't know

Just try to do your very best
Stand up be counted with all the rest
For everybody knows about Mississippi
Goddam

I bet you thought I was kiddin' — didn't you?

Picket lines, school boycotts
They try to say it's a communist plot
All I want is equality
for my sister, my brother, my people, and me

Yes you lied to me all these years
You told me to wash and clean my ears
And talk real fine just like a lady
And you'd stop calling me Sister Sadie

Oh but this whole country is full of lies
You're all gonna die and die like flies
I don't trust you any more
You keep on saying "Go slow!"
"Go slow!"

But that's just the trouble
"do it slow"
Desegregation
"do it slow"
Mass participation
"do it slow"
Reunification
"do it slow"
Do things gradually
"do it slow"
But bring more tragedy

"do it slow"
Why don't you see it
Why don't you feel it
I don't know
I don't know

You don't have to live next to me
Just give me my equality

Everybody knows about Mississippi
Everybody knows about Alabama
Everybody knows about Mississippi Goddam

David Redfern/Getty Images.

DOCUMENT 2 Loïs Mailou Jones | *Ubi Girl from Tai Region*, 1972

For artists like Larry Neal, an essayist and, with LeRoi Jones (later Amiri Baraka), cofounder of the Black Arts Repertory Theatre/School in 1965, Black power involved no less than the reordering of Western aesthetics. Neal argued that Black art should be underpinned by Black aesthetics, "a separate symbolism, mythology, critique, and iconology." He called for "the destruction of the white thing, the destruction of white ideas, and white ways of looking at the world." Black artists had to provide a "new aesthetic . . . mostly predicated on an Ethics which asks the question: whose vision of the world is finally more meaningful, ours or the white oppressors'?"[85] To this end, many artists experimented with various materials, making art with African American hair, food, and other ephemera, and, in a move inspired by African independence movements,

they incorporated African art and artifacts into their work. This synthesis signaled both a desire to seek influences outside the European cultural canon and a feeling of kinship with other Black arts and artists. Consider *Ubi Girl from Tai Region*, a painting by LOÏS MAILOU JONES (1905–1998).

Breaking it Down What aspects of this painting exemplify the goals and message of the Black Arts movement? To what end does Jones use African-inspired elements? What is the spirit of the painting? What political or philosophical message does it contain?

Acrylic on canvas, 43¾ x 60 in. Museum of Fine Arts, Boston. The Hayden Collection, Charles Henry Hayden Fund. Courtesy Loïs Mailou Jones Pierre-Noël Trust.

DOCUMENT 3 Faith Ringgold | *The Flag Is Bleeding, 1967*

While the impetus to make Black beautiful inspired most Black Arts movement artists, for others, such as Ron (later Maulana) Karenga, Black art had to do more. Karenga founded the Black nationalist organization US and created Kwanzaa, a Black holiday established in 1966 as a celebration of Black survival and achievement. For Karenga, the real purpose of Black art was to "reflect and support the Black Revolution." Black art, he noted in 1968, should be like the poems of LeRoi Jones (later Amiri Baraka), a founder of the Black Arts movement, whose writings and cultural critiques often generated great controversy. It had to "expose the enemy," "praise the people," and be like the "poems that kill and shoot guns and 'wrassle cops into alleys taking their weapons, leaving them dead with tongues pulled out and sent to Ireland.'"[86]

Breaking it Down How effectively does the painting *The Flag Is Bleeding* by Faith Ringgold (b. 1930) achieve the goals of the Black Arts movement? Consider how Black nationalism influenced the messages artists were trying to convey in the 1960s. What political statement is the artist making with her piece? Whose blood is she depicting? What about this image might disturb white Americans? How might the FBI interpret it?

Series: American People #18, 72 x 96 in., oil on canvas. © 2019 Faith Ringgold / Artists Rights Society (ARS), New York, Courtesy ACA Galleries, New York.

* * *

Given the catalytic nature of Black power, it was predictable that it would generate opposition. What was not so predictable was that Black liberation opponents would have the help of the FBI. The agency's involvement came to light in the 1970s, when citizens, congressional oversight committees, and some of the FBI's own agents revealed many of its illegal activities. Top-secret documents, some of which were stolen by the Citizens' Commission to Investigate the FBI and others that came to light during lawsuits filed against the FBI, showed that the bureau had been involved in anti-Black repression as far back as the 1920s, when it helped orchestrate the deportation of Marcus Garvey. The documents also showed that J. Edgar Hoover, head of the FBI, had opened a file on Martin Luther King Jr. in 1958 and had infiltrated the SCLC in 1960, and that by October 1962 he was planting disinformational "news stories" concerning the SCLC's alleged Communist connections. Other documents revealed that on August 25, 1967, Hoover initiated anti-Black operations under the FBI's COINTELPRO (Counterintelligence Program). COINTELPRO launched systematic covert actions — infiltration, psychological warfare, legal harassment, and violence — not only against the Black liberation movement but also against the American Indian Movement (AIM), the Puerto Rican independence movement, and the antiwar and student movements of the 1960s. In other words, the agency became a danger to the very democracy it was supposed to protect.

The bureau used a variety of tactics against Black power organizations. Its agents forged accusatory and insulting letters and sent them to organization members to incite feuds and prevent alliances. It also printed and distributed ridiculing pamphlets and cartoons and attributed them to a particular organization or person. The FBI made efforts to pit Black and Jewish people against one another and to get Black street gangs to attack Black political activists. It also was not above withholding or planting evidence to ensure the conviction and imprisonment of Black activists. These efforts were massive. In 1967, at least 1,246 FBI agents received racial intelligence assignments each month. By 1968, the number was 1,678.

The documents that follow unveil some of the FBI's covert activities. As you read them, consider how the FBI influenced white and Black America's opinion of Black power.

DOCUMENT 4 *COINTELPRO Targets Black Organizations, 1967*

This 1967 FBI memo initiated COINTELPRO efforts against what it called "black nationalist, hate-type organizations." The memo explains the purpose of this new program and directs twenty-three FBI field offices to recruit informants, continually monitor a range of groups, and look for counterintelligence opportunities to discredit them. It singles out organizations such as SNCC, CORE, the SCLC, and the Revolutionary Action Movement for special attention and identifies individuals such as SNCC leader Stokely Carmichael (1941–1998) for particular surveillance.

Breaking it Down Why might the FBI have considered Black organizations as particular threats?

The purpose of this new counterintelligence endeavor is to expose, disrupt, misdirect, discredit, or otherwise neutralize the activities of black nationalist, hate-type organizations and groupings, their leadership, spokesmen, membership, and supporters, and to counter their propensity for violence and civil disorder. The activities of all such groups of intelligence interest to this

Bureau must be followed on a continuous basis so we will be in a position to promptly take advantage of all opportunities for counterintelligence and to inspire action in instances where circumstances warrant. The pernicious background of such groups, their duplicity, and devious maneuvers must be exposed to public scrutiny where such publicity will have a neutralizing effect. Efforts of the various groups to consolidate their forces or to recruit new or youthful adherents must be frustrated. No opportunity should be missed to exploit through counterintelligence techniques the organizational and personal conflicts of the leaderships of the groups and where possible an effort should be made to capitalize upon existing conflicts between competing black nationalist organizations. . . .

Many individuals currently active in black nationalist organizations have backgrounds of immorality, subversive activity, and criminal records. Through your investigation of key agitators, you should endeavor to establish their unsavory backgrounds. Be alert to determine evidence of misappropriation of funds or other types of personal misconduct on the part of militant nationalist leaders so any practical or warranted counterintelligence may be instituted.

Intensified attention under this program should be afforded to the activities of such groups as the Student Nonviolent Coordinating Committee, the Southern Christian Leadership Conference, Revolutionary Action Movement, the Deacons for Defense and Justice, Congress of Racial Equality, and the Nation of Islam. Particular emphasis should be given to extremists who direct the activities and policies of revolutionary or militant groups such as Stokely Carmichael, H. "Rap" Brown,° Elijah Muhammad, and Maxwell Stanford.

°Activist who served as chairman of SNCC from 1967 to 1968 and in 1968 as the Minister of Justice of the Black Panthers.

SOURCE: Memorandum from FBI Director to 23 Field Offices, August 25, 1967.

DOCUMENT 5 *FBI Uses Fake Letters to Divide the Chicago Black Panthers and the Blackstone Rangers, 1969*

In this 1969 memo, the FBI authorized sending a fake anonymous letter to Jeff Fort (b. 1947), leader of the Chicago street gang the Blackstone Rangers, to stir up trouble between the Rangers and the Panthers and to thwart the Panthers' efforts to get the Rangers involved in constructive community work.

Breaking it Down Why would the FBI be opposed to the Panthers' anti-gang activity? What objective(s) do these letters seek to achieve?

Authority is granted to mail anonymous letter to Jeff Fort, as suggested in [previous letter from an FBI agent], in care of the First Presbyterian Church, 6401 South Kimbark, Chicago, Illinois.

Utilize a commercially purchased envelope for this letter and insure that the mailing is not traced to the source. . . .

"Brother Jeff:

"I've spent some time with some Panther friends on the west side lately and I know what's been going on. The brothers that run the Panthers blame you for blocking their thing and there's supposed to be a hit out for you. I'm not a Panther, or a Ranger, just black. From what I see these Panthers are out for themselves not black people. I think you ought to know what their up to, I know what I'd do if I was you. You might hear from me again."

"A black brother you don't know"

SOURCE: Memorandum from Special Agent in Charge, Chicago, to Director, January 30, 1969.

DOCUMENT 6 *"Special Payment" Request and Floor Plan of Fred Hampton's Apartment, 1969*

On November 19, 1969, FBI informant William O'Neal gave local police a detailed inventory of arms and explosives allegedly kept in Chicago Black Panther Party leader Fred Hampton's apartment. He included a floor plan of the apartment. On December 4, police used this information in a raid that killed Hampton and fellow Panther Mark Clark. In this excerpt from a December 11 memo, the Chicago FBI agent in charge praises the vital information supplied by O'Neal and asks for a "special payment" for the unnamed informant.

Breaking it Down What do these sources demonstrate about the relationship between the U.S. government and groups such as the Black Panthers? What do they reveal about the FBI's methods in responding to such groups?

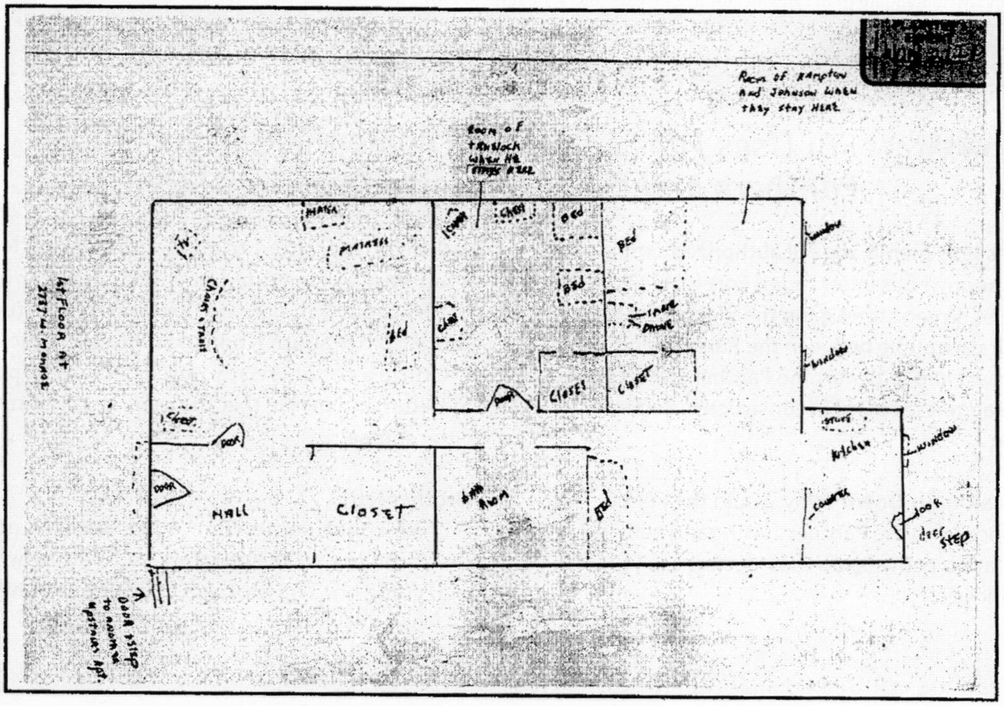

Information set forth in Chicago letter and letterhead memorandum of 11/21/69, reflects legally purchased firearms in the possession of the Black Panther Party (BPP) were stored at 2337 West Monroe Street, Chicago. A detailed inventory of the weapons and also a detailed floor plan of the apartment were furnished to local authorities. In addition, the identities of BPP members utilizing the apartment at the above address were furnished. This information was not available from any other source and subsequently proved to be of tremendous value in that it subsequently saved injury and possible death to police officers participating in a raid at the address on the morning of 12/4/69. The raid was based on the information furnished by informant. During the resistance by the BPP members at the time of the raid, the Chairman of the Illinois Chapter, BPP, FRED HAMPTON, was killed and a BPP leader from Peoria, Illinois, was also killed. A quantity of weapons and ammunition were recovered.

It is felt that this information is of considerable value in consideration of a special payment for informant requested in re Chicago letter.

SOURCE: Memorandum from Special Agent in Charge, Chicago, to Roy Martin Mitchell, December 11, 1969.

DOCUMENT 7 *Tangible Results, 1969*

In this chilling excerpt from a 1969 memo, the FBI takes credit for the decline of the Black Panther Party's Breakfast Program for impoverished children in San Diego and proudly touts what it calls "tangible results" of its attempts to incite violence and "a high degree of unrest" in the city.

Breaking it Down Why would the FBI want to disrupt positive efforts of groups such as the Black Panthers?

Tangible Results

The BPP Breakfast Program appears to be floundering in San Diego due to a lack of public support and unfavorable publicity concerning it. It is noted that it has presently been temporarily suspended. . . .

Shootings, beatings, and a high degree of unrest continues [*sic*] to prevail in the ghetto area of southeast San Diego. Although no specific counterintelligence action can be credited with contributing to this over-all situation, it is felt that a substantial amount of the unrest is directly attributable to this program.

In view of the recent killing of BPP member SYLVESTER BELL,° a new cartoon is being considered in the hopes that it will assist in the continuance of the rift between BPP and US.°

°Sylvester Bell was a Black Panther who was shot to death in 1969 by members of the US organization. The investigation of Bell's murder traced his death to COINTELPRO tactics that created unrest between the Panthers and US.

°Maulana Karenga founded the black nationalist organization US in 1965. Unlike the Panthers, which focused on structural racism, US espoused a form of cultural nationalism that prioritized black people's African past and southern traditions.

SOURCE: FBI memorandum, fragment, August 20, 1969.

DOCUMENT 8 *Church Committee Report, 1976*

In 1975, after a series of revelations suggesting that U.S. intelligence agencies had been conducting illegal operations, the Senate created the Church Committee — named after its chairman, Idaho senator Frank Church (1924–1984) — to investigate suspected abuses of power. Among the agencies investigated were the FBI, CIA, National Security Agency, and IRS. The following year, the committee issued a series of fourteen reports on its findings, which concluded that intelligence forces had conducted concerted domestic espionage that violated the rights of U.S. citizens. The committee's recommendations were debated in Congress, and some, though not all, were eventually carried out. One tangible legacy of the committee's report was the creation of the Senate Select Committee on Intelligence to act as an oversight body for intelligence services.

Breaking it Down What purpose does it serve to list observations before stating the report's conclusions?

IV. Conclusions and Recommendations

A. Conclusions

The findings which have emerged from our investigation convince us that the Government's domestic intelligence policies and practices require fundamental reform. We have attempted to set out the basic facts; now it is time for Congress to turn its attention to legislating restraints upon intelligence activities which may endanger the constitutional rights of Americans.

The Committee's fundamental conclusion is that intelligence activities have undermined the constitutional rights of citizens and that they have done so primarily because checks and balances designed by the framers of the Constitution to assure accountability have not been applied.

Before examining that conclusion, we make the following observations.

— While nearly all of our findings focus on excesses and things that went wrong, we do not question the need for lawful domestic intelligence. We recognize that certain intelligence activities serve perfectly proper and clearly necessary ends of government. Surely, catching spies and stopping crime, including acts of terrorism, is essential to insure "domestic tranquility" and to "provide for the common defense." Therefore, the power of government to conduct *proper* domestic intelligence activities under effective restraints and controls must be preserved.

— We are aware that the few earlier efforts to limit domestic intelligence activities have proven ineffectual. This pattern reinforces the need for statutory restraints coupled with much more effective oversight from all branches of the Government.

— The crescendo of improper intelligence activity in the latter part of the 1960s and the early 1970s shows what we must watch out for: In time of crisis, the Government will exercise its power to conduct domestic intelligence activities to the fullest extent. The distinction between legal dissent and criminal conduct is easily forgotten. Our job is to recommend means to help ensure that the distinction will always be observed.

— In an era where the technological capability of Government relentlessly increases, we must be wary about the drift toward "big brother government." The potential for abuse is awesome and requires special attention to fashioning restraints which not only cure past problems but anticipate and prevent the future misuse of technology. . . .

. . . Based upon our full record, and the findings which we have set forth . . . above, the Committee concludes that:

Domestic Intelligence Activity Has Threatened and Undermined The Constitutional Rights of Americans to Free Speech, Association and Privacy. It Has Done So Primarily Because The Constitutional System for Checking Abuse of Power Has Not Been Applied.

Our findings and the detailed reports which supplement this volume set forth a massive record of intelligence abuses over the years. Through a vast network of informants and through the uncontrolled or illegal use of intrusive techniques — ranging from simple theft to sophisticated electronic surveillance — the Government has collected, and then used improperly, huge amounts of information about the private lives, political beliefs and associations of numerous Americans.

SOURCE: United States Senate, *Final Report of the Select Committee to Study Governmental Operations with Respect to Intelligence Activities*, book 2, *Intelligence Activities and the Rights of Americans* (Washington, DC: Government Printing Office, 1976), 289, 290.

PRACTICING AP® SKILLS

1. **AP® Contextualization.** Nina Simone wrote "Mississippi Goddam" in 1963. What is significant about the timing? Why is it important that we note her gender?
2. **AP® Continuity and Change.** To what extent does the FBI's counterintelligence and surveillance of Black power activists bear any resemblance to the counterterrorist activities undertaken by the federal government since the September 11, 2001, attack on the World Trade Center in New York? What general concerns, if any, should the American public have about government surveillance of activists deemed "un-American"?
3. **AP® Comparison.** Black power activists insisted that Black history be taught at every educational level. How is their advocacy for Black history related to the politics and art of the Black Power movement?
4. **Connecting to AP® Themes.** What political concepts are made manifest in the art source collection? How do those concepts connect to the four themes of the AP® course?
5. **Class Discussion: Evidence-Based Argument.** To what extent was Black power a threat to national security? Did Black nationalists' activities warrant the crackdown undertaken by the FBI? Which documents support your response to both questions the most, and why?

Individual Student Project:
Source Selection

Having completed the AP® Skills Workshop for Chapter 14 (p. SW14-A), you've already selected a topic of interest and written a research question to guide your investigation. In this workshop, we will focus on the research process itself. We'll cover how to find sources appropriate to your research question, how to evaluate them for credibility, and how to complete the Selected Source Template for this course.

Examining the AP® Rubric

The rubric that will be used to assess your individual student project states:

Row A (2 points)

- One point is awarded for the completion of the source type, citation, and summary for four sources in the Selected Sources Template.
  - *At minimum, each citation must include:*
    - *Title or type*
    - *Date*
  - *Citations should also include, if available and applicable:*
    - *Title of the publication within which the source is contained (e.g., book, journal, website)*
    - *Author*
  - *Each of the four selected sources must be an actual primary or secondary source, not an encyclopedia (e.g., Wikipedia) article.*
- A second point is awarded for the completion of the "Description of the relevance to project topic" for four sources in the Selected Sources Template.

We'll walk through how these principles can guide your research methods and your evaluation of each source.

Finding and Evaluating Sources

The rubric for the project makes clear you'll ultimately need to select four credible sources relevant to your research topic. They could be primary or secondary written texts, but they could also be artwork, literature, data, music lyrics, performances, oral histories, or speeches.

Given how many sources are available on the internet, you'll want to home in on the most promising options as efficiently as possible. If your research topic expands on content covered in this textbook, you might consider consulting the Suggested References section that closes each chapter. School and public libraries are valuable resources as well; you can describe your research question to a librarian, request assistance locating relevant sources, and enjoy a place to focus with fewer distractions. Of course, having completed the AP® Skills Workshop for Chapter 14 (p. SW14-A), you should also have a list of key terms to include in a search on credible databases such as

Internet Archive, Library of Congress, or JSTOR. It will be more efficient to search using these key words rather than typing out your full research question.

Depending on the search functionality of the database or search engine you use, you can likely use the following tips to further target an internet search:

- **Quotation marks around a phrase** will return results containing that exact phrase.
- **An en dash in front of a word** will exclude results containing that word.
- **AND between two words** will return results containing both words.
- **OR between two words** will return results containing either of the words.

Once you've found sources that look promising, you can evaluate any written sources based on their credibility and relevance. To assess a source's credibility, you can ask yourself the following questions:

1. Is the writer or creator of the source respected in the subject area?
2. Does the publisher of the source have any financial or political ties that might introduce bias?
3. Does the source provide citations for outside information?
4. If the source includes quantitative data, how recently was it published?

If you're unsure whether a source is credible, you might consult a teacher, a librarian, or another trusted mentor to help you decide. Remember, even the most persuasive sources may be misleading; it's important to select options whose reliability and validity you can trust.

Relevance really comes down to how well a source provides an answer to your research question. Having engaged with a source, you can ask yourself:

1. Can I tell how the writer or creator of the source would answer the research question?
2. Does the information contained in the source help clarify my understanding of my research topic?
3. If I were to exclude this source from my research, would I miss out on important information?

Sources may be quite relevant to your project even if they aren't journal articles or other explicitly academic resources. The most useful sources will be those that speak to you and motivate you to explore your research question more deeply.

Having considered a wide range of potential research materials, you can use the principles of credibility and relevance to narrow down your options to the four most promising sources. These will be the ones you carry into the Suggested Sources Template in your Student Workbook.

recap

Selecting Sources

To assess a source's credibility, you can ask yourself the following questions:

1. Is the writer or creator of the source respected in the subject area?
2. Does the publisher of the source have any financial or political ties that might introduce bias?
3. Does the source provide citations for outside information?
4. If the source includes quantitative data, how recently was it published?

To assess a source's relevance, you can ask yourself the following questions:

1. Can I tell how the writer or creator of the source would answer the research question?
2. Does the information contained in the source help clarify my understanding of my research topic?
3. If I were to exclude this source from my research, would I miss out on important information?

Activity ▸ Selecting Sources

Fill out the Selected Sources Template in your Student Workbook.

Source #:	Source Type:
Citation: At minimum, each citation must include the source's title or type, the date, and, if available and applicable, the title of the publication within which the source is contained and the author.	
Brief summary or description:	
Description of the relevance to project topic:	

Then, answer the following questions to prepare for your oral defense:

1. Select one of the sources you used and explain why you chose this source to include in your project.
2. Identify the source that most deepened your understanding of your topic and explain in what way it added depth to your understanding of your topic.
3. Explain how excluding one of your sources would have weakened your argument.
4. Explain how you determined that one of your sources is reliable.
5. Identify which of your sources is the most persuasive and explain why it is so persuasive.
6. Identify the source that was most important to your research topic and explain its importance.
7. Explain why the four sources you selected, compared to other sources you considered but did not select, are the best for supporting your argument.
8. Describe the most important source of information you found while conducting your research and explain why it was important to your research process.
9. Describe which of the various perspectives you explored was most difficult for you to incorporate into your project and explain why this was the case.

Multiple-Choice Questions

Questions 1–2 refer to the following.

AP® source ***Gloria Richardson, Leader of Maryland's Cambridge Nonviolent Action Committee, 1963***

Associated Press/AP Images.

1. Which statement best describes Richardson's interaction with the authority figures in the image?

(A) Gloria Richardson is leaving a protest in Cambridge, Maryland, per the request of the police.

(B) Gloria Richardson is leading a nonviolent demonstration for jobs, housing, and desegregation in Cambridge, Maryland, while dealing with local police.

(C) Gloria Richardson is leading the Cambridge Nonviolent Action Committee during a public demonstration as a leader in the organization.

(D) Gloria Richardson is defying National Guardsman while leading a demonstration for jobs, housing, and desegregation.

2. Which of the following statements best explains why Gloria Richardson's approach to social justice was unique in the 1960s?

(A) Gloria Richardson led demonstrations to advocate for civil rights for African Americans in the 1960s.

(B) Gloria Richardson was not successful in her attempt to remove the local state senator from office.

(C) Gloria Richardson and other members of her organization used new strategies for confronting white resistance, such as carrying firearms for personal protection.

(D) To confront white resistance to integration and access to opportunities, Gloria Richardson would organize events that had a low turnout.

Short-Answer Question

1. Answer A, B, C, and D.

(A) The artists, writers, musicians, and dramatists who participated in the Black Arts movement of the 1960s and 1970s were not of one mind about what Black art could or should be. Nevertheless, they did have a common objective. Describe the primary objective of the Black Arts movement.

(B) Using a specific example of a work of art associated with the Black Arts movement, explain how this work of art reflects the overarching values or ideals of the movement.

(C) Explain how the Black Arts movement complemented or conflicted with activism of the Civil Rights movement.

(D) Using a specific example of a work of art associated with the Black Arts movement, explain how the Black Arts movement allowed Black and non-Black audiences alike to understand the emotional toll caused by racial discrimination.

CHAPTER 16

Racial Progress in an Era of Backlash and Change

1965–2000

CHAPTER TIMELINE

Events specific to African American history are in purple. General U.S. history events are in black. Events from the AP® Course Framework are marked with an asterisk.

1965	Immigration and Nationality Act of 1965
	Voting Rights Act
	Law Enforcement Assistance Act
1965–1975	The Black Arts movement (BAM) galvanizes work of Black artists, writers, musicians, and dramatists who envision art as a political tool to achieve Black liberation*
1967	National Welfare Rights Organization founded
1968	Fair Housing Act*
	Shirley Chisholm elected to Congress*
	Richard Nixon elected president
1968	Tommie Smith and John Carlos raise clenched fists during XIX Summer Olympics*
1969	Black Panthers begin "survival programs"*
	Nixon implements southern strategy
1970s	Stagflation intensifies competition in job market
1970	Student protesters are shot at Kent State and Jackson State
1971	Congressional Black Caucus founded*
	Milliken v. Bradley school ruling ignites massive white backlash
1970s	Afrofuturism emerges*
1971	*Soul Train* is created*
1972	Chisholm runs for president*
	Angela Davis acquitted of charges of aiding prison inmates in escaping from California courtroom
	Title IX outlaws discrimination in educational institutions receiving federal funding
1973	Black Panthers run for office in California
	Rockefeller drug laws instituted in New York
	OPEC oil crisis
1974	Supreme Court overturns lower courts' rulings in *Milliken v. Bradley*
	Nixon resigns due to Watergate scandal; Gerald Ford succeeds him as president
	Boston erupts in violence over busing
***Mid-1970s**	Rap music emerges on New York City streets
1976	Jimmy Carter elected president
1977	Lionel Wilson elected first Black mayor of Oakland
	"The Combahee River Collective Statement" published*
1978	*Regents of the University of California v. Bakke* deals blow to affirmative action
1979	*United Steelworkers of America v. Weber* upholds affirmative action
1980	Ronald Reagan elected president
	Refugee Act of 1980 loosens restrictions on those fleeing from conflict areas
1980	Writer Alice Walker coins the term *womanist**
1982	Reagan declares War on Drugs
1984	Reagan reelected president
	Comprehensive Crime Control Act of 1984 heightens surveillance and drug penalties
1985	Crack cocaine appears in inner-city neighborhoods
1987	*McCleskey v. Kemp* holds racial bias to be inevitable in criminal justice
1988	George H. W. Bush elected president
1990	U.S. Immigration Act of 1990 increases the number of immigrants coming from underrepresented nations
	Scholar Kimberlé Crenshaw introduces the term *intersectionality**
1991	Los Angeles police officers' beating of Rodney King caught on videotape
	Anita Hill accuses Supreme Court nominee Clarence Thomas of sexual harassment
1992	Los Angeles erupts in riots following acquittal of police in Rodney King case
	Bill Clinton elected president
	Physician, engineer, and NASA astronaut Mae Jemison becomes the first African American woman to travel to space*
1995	O. J. Simpson trial
	Million Man March in Washington, D.C.
1996	Personal Responsibility and Work Opportunity Reconciliation Act
	Clinton reelected president
1997	Million Woman March in Philadelphia

Contextualizing African American Stories

Shirley Chisholm: The First of Many Firsts

Sometime in the 1940s, Stanley Steingut, the district leader of Brooklyn's Democratic Party, gave a speech at Brooklyn College. Sophomore Shirley Anita St. Hill was in the audience. Though born in America, St. Hill had received her early education in Barbados, the birthplace of her Bajan mother, who, along with her Guyanese father, had sent St. Hill to Barbados at the age of three to live with her maternal grandmother, aunt, and uncle. Years later, Shirley Chisholm (she married Conrad Chisholm in 1949) credited Steingut's remarks as being the impetus for her career in politics. What she remembered about his speech was that although he had applauded Blacks for fighting for their rights, Steingut also had said that Blacks would have to accept "one basic truth" regardless of whether they "want to or not": "Black people cannot get ahead unless they have white people." Chisholm's response? "That's what you think."[1]

Chisholm received her master's degree in early childhood education from Columbia University Teachers College in 1952 and might have stayed in that traditionally female profession had not the state assemblyman for her district in New York vacated his seat. Her landslide victory in 1964 sent her to Albany as the state representative from the mostly poor, Black, and West Indian Bedford-Stuyvesant neighborhood of Brooklyn. Her first few years in politics were frustrating; of the fifty bills she sponsored, only eight passed. One of the eight was a measure establishing the SEEK (Search for Education, Elevation, and Knowledge) program, which provided college funding for disadvantaged youths. Another secured unemployment insurance for domestics and day care providers, and another enabled tenured schoolteachers who took maternity leave to keep their tenure on return to service.

Although her constituents appreciated her efforts, politics in the 1960s was still very much a male domain, and men of all stripes let the outspoken Chisholm know that she was not welcome. A founder of the National Organization for Women (NOW) and an early supporter of the National Black Feminist Organization, Chisholm always maintained that she met more resistance from men than from whites. "Men. White men, black men, Puerto Rican — men. They gave me a hard time," she remembered.[2] Her male colleagues feared her independence and the fact that she refused to be beholden to any political machine. "What they said," she noted, "was always that I was 'hard to handle.'"[3]

The 1968 election that sent Chisholm, instead of veteran civil rights worker James Farmer, to Congress also demonstrated the steadfast support she received from local women, both Black and white. During the election, Farmer played on Black men's fears of domineering women, portraying Chisholm as "a bossy female, a would-be matriarch."[4]

That year, however, Chisholm was elected to Congress. With help from women in PTAs, social groups, and civic clubs, Chisholm beat Farmer handily. As she later wrote, women "stay put, raise their families — and register to vote in

Shirley Chisholm
On January 25, 1972, Shirley Chisholm announced her run for the presidency, becoming the first Black major-party candidate for that office. **How did Chisholm's political career reflect a new era in African American history?** *Don Hogan Charles/Archive Photos/Getty Images.*

greater numbers." They "are always organizing for something."[5]

Women stayed devoted to Chisholm, and she did not disappoint them. While in Congress, she authored a bill to finance child care facilities that passed both houses. President Richard Nixon, who rode into office in 1968 on a conservative wave, vetoed it. She also helped push through a bill that gave domestic workers the right to earn a minimum wage. Her staff, composed almost entirely of women, half of whom were Black, helped her work on a number of bills that financed education, social services, and health care.

Chisolm's presidential candidacy, like her presence in Congress, unsettled many. She met resistance from native-born African Americans — who, she recalled, often derided West Indians as "monkeys," complaining that they were "taking over everything"[6] — and even from women. The National Women's Political Caucus, which did not immediately endorse Chisholm — instead hoping to influence the Democratic platform by promising a bloc vote to candidate George McGovern — characterized her candidacy as a "quixotic joke."[7] Black men, Chisholm recalled, felt that "in this first serious effort of Blacks for high political office, it would be better if it were a man."[8] Still, she was applauded when she proclaimed, "I am not the candidate of black America, although I am black and proud; I am not the candidate of the women's movement of this country, although

I am a woman and I'm equally proud of that. I am the candidate of the people of America. And my presence before you now symbolizes a new era in American political history."[9]

Chisholm did not win the Democratic Party nomination, but her candidacy, political career, and politics marked the beginning of a new era. In the early 1970s, America was rocked not only by the Black freedom movement but also by the freedom movements of Hispanics and Latinos, American Indians, women, and the lesbian, gay, bisexual, transgender, and queer (LGBTQ+) community. The anti–Vietnam War movement and the sexual revolution, which was changing relationships between men and women, also were in full swing. Meanwhile, deindustrialization and inflation made for a worsening economy. Chisholm's politics and candidacy symbolized all this change, proving that by virtue of the 1965 Voting Rights Act, Black power could be translated into electoral victories. Chisholm represented the aspirations of Black women, who insisted that their distinct issues were also race issues. As a Black American of West Indian descent, she also symbolized the increasing diversity of African America and the tensions that such diversity provoked. Finally, the reaction to her liberal politics reflected the tenor of the times, which were marked by a conservative backlash and a "law and order" agenda that would continue to repress the Black freedom movement.

Please note that this chapter includes primary sources by Black writers and speakers that use the N-word, which we have chosen to reprint in this textbook to accurately reflect these speakers' original intent as well as the time period, culture, and racism discussed in each source. We recognize that this word has a long history as a derogatory and deeply hurtful expression when used by white people toward Black people. Black speakers' and writers' choice to use this word relates not only to that history but to a larger cultural tradition in which the N-word can take on different meanings, emphasize shared experience, and be repurposed as a term of endearment within Black communities. This chapter also includes primary sources by white writers and speakers that use the N-word, which we have chosen not to reprint in full here. We have replaced the term without hindering understanding of these sources. Be mindful of context, both historical and contemporary, as you read and discuss this chapter.

Opposition to the Black Freedom Movement

Why did the FBI wage a campaign against the Black Panthers as a threat to national security, and what were the results?

Opposition to the Black freedom movement began at the movement's inception, but it reached its high point with the election of Republican president Richard Nixon in 1968. The ascendancy of the Republicans, the political party that had opposed the Civil Rights Act of 1964 and the Voting Rights Act of 1965, was a blow to African Americans. Nixon and subsequent Republican presidents legitimized and strengthened the massive political power behind white resistance, changing everything from the language of discrimination to the politics of racism. In doing so, they transformed the very nature of the Republican Party and reshaped the Black struggle for racial equality.

The Emergence of the New Right

The year 1964 marked the climax of a process that had been in the making since 1948. By that time, President Harry Truman's desegregation of the armed forces after World War II and Democratic support of the Civil Rights Acts of 1957 and 1964 (the former of which was a weak bill committing the federal government to support Black voting rights) had delivered southern Democrats to the Republican Party. William Rusher, publisher and editor of the conservative *National Review*, argued that Democrats had "run with the hares down South on the race issue, while riding with the hounds up North — nominating loudly integrationist presidential candidates while calmly raking in, on locally segregationist platforms, 95 percent of all Senate and House seats . . . south of the Mason–Dixon line."[10] Republicans felt they could exploit this divide by giving segregationist Democrats and other conservatives a permanent home in the Republican Party. But they had to repackage themselves. In 1964, when Republican presidential candidate Barry Goldwater had argued that it was unconstitutional to require states to desegregate public facilities, he had come across as an extremist and a racist. After 1964, conservatives remade themselves in the image of the American mainstream.

One of their first moves was to tone down their rhetoric on race. By the late 1960s and early '70s, most white Americans accepted token integration and rejected the ideologies of organizations such as the Ku Klux Klan. Blatant bigotry was unattractive, and Republicans now reasoned that they could garner more support if they targeted issues of social conservatism — law and order, and the drawbacks of a meddling federal government — rather than focus overtly on race.

New Right
An ideology introduced in the late 1960s meant to broaden the conservative base of the Republican Party. Proponents added the politics of law and order and a meritocratic color-blind ideal to an ideology that had previously been centered on anticommunism, limited government, and racialism.

The birth of what became known as the **New Right** can be traced to Richard M. Nixon's 1968 campaign for the presidency. Against the backdrop of urban riots, gun-toting Black Panthers, and protests to end the Vietnam War and obtain various rights, Nixon ran on a platform of "law and order"; against the independent party bid of rabid segregationist George Wallace, Nixon ran on a platform of tolerance. He promised to speak for the "silent majority," which he defined as "the great majority of Americans, the forgotten Americans, the non-shouters, the non-demonstrators . . . those who do not break the law, people who pay their taxes and go to work, who send their children to school, who go to their churches . . . people who love this country."[11] To African Americans, however, Nixon's "silent majority" was code for the white majority.

AP® skills

Applying Disciplinary Knowledge: Define the New Right and summarize their political platform.

Law and Order, the Southern Strategy, and Anti–Affirmative Action

southern strategy
Policies adopted by President Richard Nixon in 1969 aimed at moving southern whites, who were traditionally Democrats, into the Republican Party.

Once in office, Nixon implemented what he called the **southern strategy** — policies aimed at moving southern whites and northern conservatives into the

Republican Party. He placed staunch conservatives at the head of the Departments of Commerce and Health, Education, and Welfare. His head of the Office of Economic Opportunity, one of the agencies charged with implementing affirmative action, eliminated ten regional offices and scores of antipoverty programs before a federal court ruled the actions illegal. His attorney general, John Mitchell, opposed an extension of the 1965 Voting Rights Act, which was due to expire in 1970. To drive a wedge between Black and white laborers, Nixon supported equity in the hiring of Black construction workers on projects that received federal funding and then cut federal construction by 75 percent.[12] Nixon also came out against school desegregation, opposing Johnson administration guidelines that would have terminated federal funding to segregated schools. When the Supreme Court rebuffed his efforts, voting unanimously in favor of strategically busing students to integrate school systems, Nixon began the process — which subsequent Republicans would complete — of moving the federal judicial system to the right.

AP® skills

Applying Disciplinary Knowledge: How did Nixon use the southern strategy to dismantle the advances toward racial equality made during the Civil Rights movement?

Moreover, Nixon gave the FBI the green light to target and destroy the Black Panthers and other Black nationalist organizations. In 1969, deeply affected by government infiltration, the Panthers — now a nationwide organization with numerous chapters and substantial membership — expelled hundreds of members to "weed out provocateurs and agents." The tactics of the FBI and local police also led to interorganizational violence and several government-sanctioned assassinations. In 1969, for example, members of the Black nationalist organization US had a shoot-out with the rival Los Angeles Panthers on the UCLA campus, killing Panthers John Huggins and Alprentice "Bunchy" Carter. Subsequent documents revealed that the FBI had manipulated antagonism between the two groups, pushing them to the point of violence.[13]

The sensational trials of African Americans during the period heightened tensions among Blacks and convinced whites of the need for law and order. In 1968, the trial of Huey Newton for allegedly murdering a policeman infuriated law enforcement, as Black and white radicals joined forces to present Newton as a victim of political and police persecution. While the two thousand Black and white demonstrators outside the courthouse thought it a travesty that Newton received a prison sentence of two to fifteen years, most Americans thought it a tragedy that the sentence was so light. Similar sentiments were aroused when Bobby Seale was charged with inciting a riot during the 1968 Democratic National Convention in Chicago, and then again in 1970 when he was charged with murdering a Panther suspected of being a government informant. In 1972, Black Panther and UCLA philosophy professor Angela Davis was tried for aiding the escape of several prison inmates from a California courtroom — an incident during which a judge was killed and a prosecutor and a juror were wounded. Although she was acquitted, the trial enraged many whites. With her signature Afro hairdo, she became an iconic image of Black radicalism's challenge to America's racism.

AP® skills

Applying Disciplinary Knowledge: Describe Nixon's interpretation of the Black Panther Party. What was his solution to what he saw as the problems plaguing urban America?

From the White House point of view, Davis and the Panthers were examples of Black criminality, and like the Johnson administration before it, the Nixon administration singled out inner-city Black male youths as the culprits responsible for urban problems. Nixon's chief of staff recalls the president saying, "You have to face the fact that the whole problem is really the blacks. . . . The key is to devise a system that recognizes this while not appearing to."[14] While withdrawing social service funds, eliminating poverty agencies, and failing to address fundamental structural problems, Nixon turned the law enforcement, judicial, and prison systems into weapons in the War on Crime. He increased the number of police that patrolled Black communities and supplied them with military-grade equipment; he continued the policy, started under Johnson, of allowing police to arrest citizens without a warrant and detain anyone (particularly narcotics addicts) who looked like they *might* commit a crime or present a public danger. Judges and prosecutors now had to abide by mandatory minimum sentencing, which turned even the most trivial nonviolent crime into a crime punishable with prison time. In anticipation of having to incarcerate hundreds of thousands of Blacks between the ages of fifteen and twenty-four, Nixon devised a ten-year "Long Range Master Plan" for the construction of new prisons. As projected, the percentage of African Americans in prisons swelled. In Philadelphia, for example, the percentage of Black prisoners in the county jails increased from 50 percent in 1970 to 95 percent in 1974. African Americans represented less than 10 percent of Pennsylvania's population but accounted for more than 62 percent of inmates in the state's jails.[15]

Nixon's tough actions extended to Black and white student activists. On May 4, 1970, at Kent State University, four students were killed by National Guardsmen who had been called to the campus to quell demonstrations that erupted after Nixon expanded the Vietnam War by invading Cambodia. Eleven days later, in Jackson, Mississippi, local police killed two Black students and wounded twelve others during demonstrations at the historically Black Jackson State University. Students on the campus were outraged by the war in Vietnam, the Kent State shootings, and local racial issues that pitted Black students against white locals. Although the President's Commission on Campus Unrest, established in the wake of the two incidents, judged the tactics of the guard and the police as extreme and unjustified, no one was convicted of a crime in either case.

Nixon supporters also attacked affirmative action. In the mid-1960s, civil rights leaders and President Lyndon Johnson had argued that government jobs and antipoverty programs were compensatory measures needed to reverse past discrimination. Conservatives opposed affirmative action from the beginning, and Nixon's presidency provided the support they needed for a successful attack. So did the postindustrial economic downturn, which by the 1970s was devastating both Black and white communities. During this decade, factories closed, and commercial enterprises abandoned cities. Every major northeastern and midwestern city lost jobs. Philadelphia, for example, lost 150,000 jobs — one-sixth of its employment base.[16] High inflation, high unemployment, and stagnant economic growth, collectively termed "stagflation," made for intense competition in the job market. Affirmative action became a scapegoat.

Opponents of compensatory programs argued that the special college and professional admissions programs that aimed to increase the enrollment of minorities and women placed unqualified people in positions that rightfully belonged to the more meritorious. "Merit alone must govern," one critic wrote.[17] When Blacks and women pointed to real discrimination in the workplace and argued that race- and gender-based criteria redressed centuries of inequalities, the New Right argued that compensatory measures were un-American because they squelched equal opportunity and deprived individuals of due process of law. These measures, opponents said, were actually "reverse discrimination." In their rhetoric, antipoverty programs became taxpayer "handouts" for the undeserving, and race- and gender-based criteria for contracts, jobs, and education rewarded, as one opponent put it, "the dumb, lazy, and unambitious at the expense of the smart, talented, and ambitious."[18] These "reverse discrimination" and "color-blind" arguments were effective precisely because they employed the same rationale as affirmative action itself — that America was and should be a land of opportunity for everyone.

Such rhetoric appealed to many whites, who believed that affirmative action threatened their jobs and income. White workers in the construction trades often walked off the job when Black workers were hired under affirmative action guidelines. They hazed new Black journeymen and often refused to teach Black apprentices at all.[19] And they were angered when affirmative action also altered the time-honored system of seniority, which in practice gave the most secure and best-paying jobs to white workers, many of whom had been hired when discrimination barred Black workers from anything but janitorial work. Although a substantial number of labor leaders had allied with Blacks during the civil rights struggle, union support shifted politically in this harsher economic climate. Many white autoworkers responded by supporting segregationist George Wallace, the independent presidential candidate who charged that the government favored Blacks over whites. By and large, those who did not support Wallace withdrew their support from the Democratic candidate, George McGovern, a proponent of affirmative action, and gave their votes to Nixon. Thus the Black-labor alliance, which had already been strained by the CIO's McCarthy-era purging, was further jeopardized.[20]

The Reagan Era

Richard Nixon resigned his presidency in 1974 as a result of the Watergate scandal, a break-in at the Democratic National Committee headquarters that his administration attempted to cover up. But his law-and-order campaign and anti–affirmative action arguments gathered steam under Presidents Ford, Carter, and then Reagan. Republican Ronald Reagan launched his presidential campaign in Philadelphia, Mississippi, where three civil rights workers were murdered in 1964. There he announced his conservative agenda, saying pointedly, "I believe in states' rights," and arguing that discrimination was a "myth." According to one of Reagan's favorite conservative theorists, George Gilder, if discrimination had ever existed in the United States, it had "already been effectively abolished," and if anything, there now was "discrimination in favor of

AP® skills

Applying Disciplinary Knowledge: To what extent were Nixon's and Reagan's racial political theories similar?

blacks," a "racial spoils system" that was "odious" to "principle."[21] In coded language, Reagan demonized Black women by popularizing the myth of the "welfare queen," an irresponsible, sexually promiscuous Black woman who lived comfortably, even extravagantly, on the taxpayers' dime. He frequently used the fictitious example of a Chicago woman who "has 80 names, 30 addresses, 12 Social Security cards, and is collecting veterans' benefits on four non-existing deceased husbands."[22]

Reagan was elected in 1980 with the support of the white working class, a traditional Democratic Party constituency that had been turning Republican since Nixon. Once he became president, Reagan acted on the principle that welfare actually caused poverty by making recipients dependent and lazy. He cut child nutrition and job training programs — programs that both the white and Black poor depended on. He also axed the Comprehensive Employment and Training Act (CETA), a program initiated by his predecessor, Jimmy Carter, that had provided more than 300,000 jobs for poor people. Ten percent of welfare recipients were cast adrift, and an additional 300,000 families had their welfare assistance reduced. Determined to please conservatives, Reagan filled the Civil Rights Commission and the Equal Employment Opportunity Commission (EEOC) with people opposed to civil rights and slashed the budgets of both the EEOC and the Office of Federal Contract Compliance. He encouraged school boards to resist court-ordered **busing** — transporting both Black and white children to schools in different neighborhoods in order to promote integration — and he ordered his attorney general to fight affirmative action in the courts.

busing
A strategy to promote integration by transporting Black children to predominantly white schools and white children to predominantly Black schools.

One of Reagan's more onerous moves was his 1982 declaration that turned the War on Crime into the War on Drugs. With the support of liberal Democratic members of Congress who feared appearing soft on crime, Reagan passed punitive antidrug laws that allowed for imprisoning many first-time offenders and that disproportionately affected African Americans.[23] Under the **Comprehensive Crime Control Act of 1984**, the Justice Department and the Department of Defense joined forces so that the navy, coast guard, air force, and army could provide information, helicopters, surveillance, and forces to help apprehend offenders. The act reinforced judges' rights to detain defendants deemed a "danger to the community," and it also mandated five years in prison for a crime committed with a firearm. It included a new provision that allowed local law enforcement to keep 90 percent of the cash and property it seized from drug dealers, which augmented the budgets of local law enforcement and provided increased incentive to surveil law-abiding African Americans. Reagan's policies so ballooned the number of inmates — from 204,000 in 1976 to 400,000 in 1984 — that the nation turned to private industry, or prisons for profit, to house prisoners.

Comprehensive Crime Control Act (1984)
A major revision of the U.S. criminal code that included provisions increasing drug penalties and that incentivized law enforcement to cooperate with the Department of Defense to increase their surveillance of African American communities.

AP® skills

Applying Disciplinary Knowledge: Define the Comprehensive Crime Control Act of 1984. How did it affect the carceral system in the United States?

Reagan's Anti-Drug Abuse Act of 1988 imposed a mandatory minimum sentence of five years for anyone convicted of first-time possession of one-fifth of an ounce of crack cocaine. Modeled after the Rockefeller Drug Laws passed in New York in 1973, which made possession of four ounces of any narcotic a crime that carried a mandatory prison sentence of fifteen years to life — about the same sentence as for second-degree

BY THE NUMBERS Incarceration Rates for Blacks and Whites, 1974–2001

This figure shows the percent of the adult population of the United States ever incarcerated in state or federal prison, by race and gender. It illustrates that Black people are incarcerated at higher rates than are white people. **Describe the impact of Reagan's war on crime and drugs. What specific elements of his legal policies contributed to the data shown in this graph?**

DATA SOURCE: Bureau of Justice Statistics Special Report, Prevalence of Imprisonment in the U.S. Population, 1974–2001, Table 5.

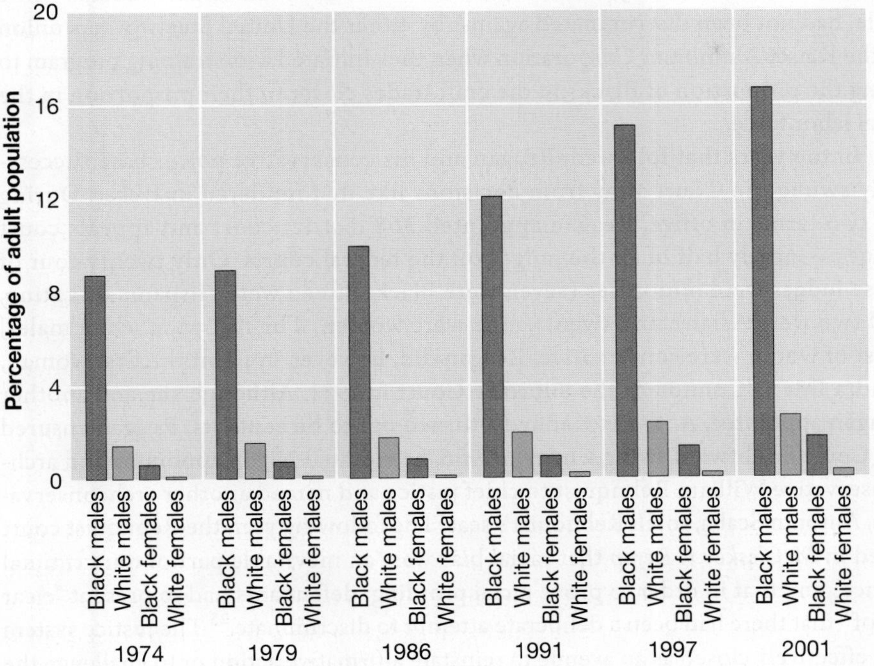

murder — Reagan's new laws seemed targeted to hurt minorities. The mandatory minimum penalty for *trafficking* 500 grams of powder cocaine (over 1.5 lbs.), a more expensive drug used by more whites than Blacks, was five years. The mere *possession* of only 5 grams of crack (one-fifth of an ounce) garnered the same penalty.[24] Also, the explosion of arrests of African Americans led people to believe that the joblessness, low-performing schools, deficient health care facilities, and decrepit housing present in Black neighborhoods were results of drug use.

The effect of Reagan's War on Drugs was felt almost immediately. In New York State, for example, 886 people were incarcerated for drug offenses in 1980. Of these individuals, 32 percent were white, 38 percent were Black, and 29 percent were Hispanic or Latino. In 1992, the year in which the state reported the highest number of incarcerations for drug offenses, only 5 percent of those incarcerated were white, while 50 percent were Black and 44 percent were Hispanic or Latino.

Reagan secured his War on Drugs and anti–affirmative action agenda by turning the judicial branch to the right. By the time he took office, the U.S. Supreme Court

AP® skills

Applying Disciplinary Knowledge: What were the primary effects of Reagan's Anti-Drug Abuse Act? How did it influence public perception of drug use among African Americans?

Regents of the University of California v. Bakke (1978)
A U.S. Supreme Court decision ruling that the university's medical school at Davis had discriminated against Allan Bakke, a white male, when it took race into account in determining admissions.

United Steelworkers of America v. Weber (1979)
A U.S. Supreme Court case considered a victory for affirmative action. The Court ruled that Brian Weber, a white male, had not been discriminated against by either the United Steelworkers union or the Kaiser Aluminum Corporation when they initiated a job training program to bring the proportion of Blacks in the craft trades closer to their proportion in the local labor force.

AP® skills

Applying Disciplinary Knowledge: How did both court cases discussed on this page the debate over affirmative action?

had rendered two contradictory decisions on affirmative action. In ***Regents of the University of California v. Bakke*** (1978), the Court ruled that the university's medical school at Davis had discriminated against Allan Bakke, a white male, when it took race into account in determining admissions. (See Appendix: *Regents of the University of California v. Bakke* for the text of this ruling.) In ***United Steelworkers of America v. Weber*** (1979), however, the Court declared that Brian Weber, a white male, had not been discriminated against by either the United Steelworkers union or the Kaiser Aluminum Corporation when they initiated a job training program to bring the proportion of Blacks in the craft trades closer to their proportion in the local labor force.

In the years that followed, Reagan and his conservative power base successfully swung the Court away from decisions like that rendered in *Weber*. During his two terms in office, Reagan appointed 368 district court and appeals court judges — nearly half of all the judges on the federal courts. Only twenty-four of these judges were minorities (seven were Black, fifteen were Hispanic or Latino, and two were Asian), and twenty-nine were women. The rest were white males, most of whom were conservative. Reagan did, however, appoint the first woman, Sandra Day O'Connor, to the Supreme Court in 1981. Although she and another Reagan appointee, Anthony Kennedy, turned out to be centrists, Reagan ensured the Court's rightward swing when, in 1986, he elevated Nixon appointee and archconservative William Rehnquist to chief justice and named another archconservative, Antonin Scalia, to fill Rehnquist's seat. The following year, the Rehnquist court ruled in *McCleskey v. Kemp* that racial bias was "an inevitable part of our criminal justice" and that in order to prove racial profiling, defendants had to present "clear proof" that there had been a deliberate attempt to discriminate.[25] The justice system was effectively closed as an avenue to reinstate affirmative action or to challenge the mass incarceration of African Americans.

The Persistence of the Black Freedom Struggle

How did the concept of "interlocking systems of oppression" apply to all waves of Black feminism?

How has economic growth in Black communities been hindered and promoted in the second half of the twentieth century?

The assault on the national Black power movement and the conservative backlash did not destroy the African American freedom struggle. It did, however, force African Americans to pursue equality on a more local level and to seek more diverse leadership. This shift was evident in the decline of the Black Panther Party and the new emphasis on local politics, the emergence of women's issues, and the local nature of the conflicts that occurred over open housing, school desegregation and community control, and neighborhood economic development.

The Transformation of the Black Panthers

The Black Panthers and other Black power groups succumbed to law enforcement's assault on their organizations. With their leaders dead, in jail, or on the run, these organizations turned their programs inward, toward their communities, and refocused on providing African Americans with social services and establishing community control of Black neighborhoods.

Late in 1969, the Panthers began what they called "survival programs." Across the country, chapters established breakfast programs for children, health clinics, clothing drives, and schools. In doing so, they reconnected with local churches, where they often conducted their community service programs. Huey Newton acknowledged the new relationship in 1971: "We will work with the church to establish a community which will satisfy most of our needs so that we can live and operate as a group."[26] Accordingly, the Oakland Black Panthers held their first breakfast program at St. Augustine's Episcopal Church.

Community service programs also served as a conduit to women's organizations that worked both within and outside the church. Until this turn toward community survival, the Panthers, like other Black power organizations, had been male-oriented and sexist. Women such as Kathleen Cleaver, wife of Panther leader Eldridge Cleaver, and Angela Davis, who wanted their opinions and leadership recognized, had to either act as "masculine" as possible or appear nonthreatening to the men with whom they worked. The survival programs, however, needed community women, and so, like Shirley Chisholm in her first congressional campaign, the Panthers turned to them for help. The Panthers announced their new direction with ads in their newspaper: "The Black Panther Party is calling on all mothers, and others who want to work with this revolutionary program of making sure that our young . . . ha[ve] full stomach[s] before going to school. . . . Mothers, welfare recipients, grandmothers, guardians and others who are trying to raise children . . . LET'S DO IT NOW!"[27]

The Panthers also focused on schooling. "Why should it be that a school in East Oakland . . . should have a public school . . . [that is] poorly equipped and poorly cared for with little or no funding for extra programming? And a school in the same city, in the hills, run by the same school district would have all kinds of additional programming and funding?" they asked. The Panthers addressed this issue by setting up "liberation schools" for children ages four through eleven in cities across the country. These schools fed children breakfast and lunch and offered a first-rate education that included Black history and culture classes. In Oakland, the Intercommunal Youth Institute was established in 1971 under the direction of Ericka Huggins. Later renamed the Oakland Community School, it employed accredited instructors in math, science, social science, Spanish, environmental studies, physical education, and fine arts. With a motto that revealed its focus on "learning *how* to think, not *what* to think," the school represented Blacks' efforts to control education in their communities.[28]

Similarly, the Panthers' turn toward electoral politics represented African American efforts to take political control of their communities across the country.

AP® exam tip

Be prepared to explain how the Black Panther Party pursued political, economic, and social reforms in the twentieth century.

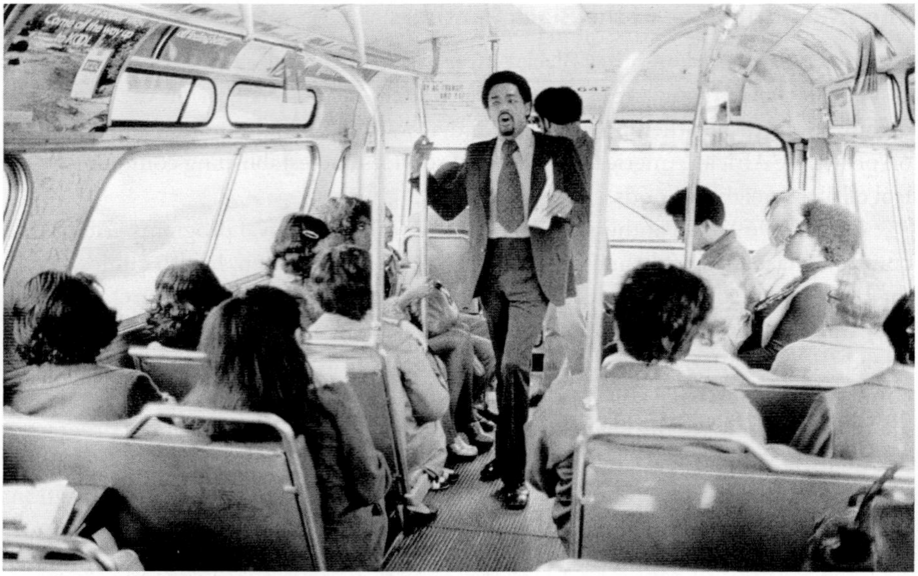

Bobby Seale Campaigning

In May 1973, Black Panther Bobby Seale ran for mayor of Oakland, California. Seale and fellow Black Panther Elaine Brown, who ran for city council, sought to increase taxes on the wealthy and put the money collected toward improvements in education, transportation, street lighting, and crime fighting. They worked to mobilize young people and the Black poor and middle class, encouraging them to take control of their communities. Here Seale is addressing riders on a city bus. **Compare and contrast the image of Bobby Seale here with the image of Seale on page 592. What similarities and differences do you see in his attire? Using what you learned in chapters 15 and 16, evaluate the extent to which the message, goals, and strategies of the Black Panther Party had changed by 1973.** *Associated Press/AP Images.*

In May 1973, Bobby Seale turned in his leather jacket and black beret for a dark business suit and white shirt and announced that he was running for mayor of Oakland. Alongside him was the Panthers' new minister of information, Elaine Brown, who announced that she was running for city council. On a platform that included promises to increase taxes on the rich and use the additional revenue to improve education, transportation, street lighting, and crime fighting, Seale and Brown mobilized the Black poor and middle class, as well as Black and white students, into a new voting bloc to demonstrate that "voting unity . . . is Power of the People: the only means to begin implementing community control."[29] Although neither candidate won, Seale received enough votes to force a runoff election. In the process, the Panthers returned to the tactic used by the Lowndes County Freedom Organization in Alabama back in 1965. In winning 40 percent of the vote, Seale and the Panthers registered enough voters to make a difference in other municipal elections, most notably those for Oakland's antipoverty agencies. Four years later, the Panthers' efforts paid big dividends when Lionel Wilson was elected Oakland's first Black mayor.

Black Women Find Their Voice

As Black America refocused on local issues in the late 1960s and '70s, Black women emerged from the shadow of their male counterparts. Shirley Chisholm led the way in politics; also noteworthy was Barbara Jordan, who served as a Texas state senator from 1966 to 1972 and was elected to Congress in 1972. Black women authors such as Toni Morrison, Maya Angelou, Ntozake Shange, Toni Cade Bambara, Alice Walker, bell hooks, and Michele Wallace used novels, plays, poetry, and literary criticism to articulate Black women's perspectives on just about everything. Black women had persistently argued that sexual exploitation, reproductive rights, equal pay for equal work, and quality child care were issues that affected all Blacks. They had marched, organized, and been imprisoned and beaten during the Black freedom struggle, but it was only in the late 1960s and 1970s that they were able to make their needs, ideas, and feelings fully known.

AP® exam tip

Be prepared to describe how Black writers represented interlocking systems of oppression in their work.

Poor Black women especially needed help. With so many men ensnared in the criminal justice system, too many were raising children without the financial support or presence of a man. These women typically had to rely on Aid to Families with Dependent Children, commonly known as welfare, to survive. As a result, they were forced to endure various indignities, including "midnight raids," in which caseworkers would barge into clients' homes in the middle of the night to search for evidence of a male presence, and welfare office interviews in which clients would be asked humiliating questions such as "When did you get pregnant? Who got you pregnant? How many men did you go with before you got pregnant?"[30] Conservatives even went so far as to call for mandatory sterilization of women on welfare, egged on by politicians such as Louisiana senator Russell Long, who referred to welfare rights leaders as "brood mares."[31] Even though the overwhelming majority of women on welfare were white, by the 1960s, the stereotypical welfare recipient was a lazy, irresponsible, and immoral Black woman.

Alternately treated like children or criminals, and virtually ignored by civil rights and Black power organizations, poor, Black, single women began organizing as early as 1962 into local welfare rights organizations. They brought these groups together into the National Welfare Rights Organization (NWRO) in 1967. They fought national and local laws prohibiting welfare recipients from having a male presence in the home and challenged the constitutionality of midnight raids. They supported women's right to reproductive freedom, which to them meant the right to have children and not be forced to undergo chemical or surgical sterilization. They also fought against forced work programs and supported job training for skilled work — work that paid enough for Black mothers to be able to afford quality child care. But because they believed that a skilled job did not exist for every worker, they pressed for a guaranteed annual income based on need that would include cost-of-living increases.

AP® skills

Applying Disciplinary Knowledge: How did the perspective of female welfare rights advocates differ from members of the Civil Rights and Black Power movements?

Female welfare rights advocates were different from civil rights and Black power advocates in that they identified their issues not just as Black issues but as class and women's issues. They understood that their race, class, and gender intersected and reinforced one another. They were poor not just because they were female or because they were Black but because they were both female *and* Black. They understood that white welfare recipients were not automatically stereotyped. For Black women, their race intersected with their gender and class to determine the treatment meted out to them. Johnnie Tillmon, the chair of the NWRO, described it this way: "I'm a woman, I'm a Black woman. I'm a poor woman. I'm a fat woman. I'm a middle-aged woman. And I'm on welfare. In this country, if you're any one of those things — poor, Black, fat, female, middle-aged, on welfare — you count less as a human being. If you're all those things, you don't count at all."[32]

Due to internal conflicts, the NWRO folded in 1975, but local welfare rights organizations and other Black women's groups continued to articulate Black women's experiences at the intersection of race, class, and gender. The Third World Women's Alliance, for example, began when a group of women within SNCC challenged the sexism of that organization. When these women split from SNCC in 1969, one of the first issues they addressed was the 1965 Moynihan Report, the government document blaming Black women for the decline of the Black family. In addition, in establishing solidarity with Asian, Puerto Rican, Indigenous, and Mexican American women — other women of color — members demonstrated the interrelatedness of women's rights and international liberation struggles.[33]

AP® exam tip

You will need to be able to explain how the Black feminist movement of the twentieth century drew inspiration from earlier Black women's activism.

Other Black feminist groups were established in the late 1960s and early '70s. The National Black Feminist Organization, the National Alliance of Black Feminists, the Combahee River Collective, and Black Women Organized for Action all emerged in response to the Black freedom movement, which they felt excluded them, and the new women's rights movement, which likewise neglected their particular issues. Over and over, they reiterated the concept of double jeopardy — "the phenomenon of being Black and female, in a country that is *both* racist and sexist."[34] They argued that all black people had to fight on several fronts simultaneously, and they challenged white feminists to make racism and classism women's issues.

Black feminists tackled negative images of Black women in popular culture, protesting, for example, a television show called *That's My Mama,* which featured a heavyset Black woman as a domineering mother. According to Sandra Flowers of the National Black Feminist Organization's Atlanta chapter, the show "repopularized the concept of the devious . . . black woman . . . not by implication, and not indirectly, but actively and by design."[35] Black feminists also addressed domestic violence, women's health care and reproductive rights, day care, welfare, the exploitation of women workers worldwide, and prisoners' rights.

More than any other Black constituency, Black feminists tackled the issue of Black heterosexism and homophobia. Although the Black Panthers had allied with gays and lesbians as part of their political program to topple capitalism, feminists dealt with lesbianism on a daily basis — not only because some of the founders of Black feminist organizations were lesbians, but also because one of the ideological tenets of Black feminism was that all women did not experience their gender the same way. Just as race determined how Black and white women approached their womanhood, so too did sexuality. Black feminists were not always successful in eliminating bias against lesbians, but to their credit, they introduced into the Black public discussion a topic that would persist into the next century. The Third World Women's Alliance put it this way: "Whether homosexuality is societal or genetic, it exists in the third world community. The oppression and dehumanizing ostracism that homosexuals face must be rejected and their right to exist as dignified human beings must be defended."[36]

The Fight for Education

Women took the lead in the fight for quality education for their children. In cities of all sizes, African American children received a substandard education. Black children's achievement levels were consistently lower than those of white children. Their dropout rates were higher, their schools were dilapidated and increasingly patrolled by police, their textbooks were out of date, and their often demoralized teachers were more concerned with maintaining order than with teaching. In cities as large as Chicago, New York, Detroit, and Denver, and as small as Plainfield, New Jersey, and Stamford, Connecticut, Black mothers mobilized to improve the quality of their children's education. They fought for integration via busing, mostly because they believed it was the best way to address the problem quickly. White children went to well-funded, well-equipped schools that were often underpopulated. Black mothers, such as those who organized Chicago's Truth Squad or Englewood, New Jersey's Englewood Movement, sought to place these "neighborhood schools" within the reach of Black children. NAACP lawyers supported them, arguing that there was no difference between school segregation that occurred as a result of a legal mandate (de jure segregation) and that which occurred as a result of state-sanctioned real estate discrimination (de facto segregation). Both types of segregation resulted in Black deprivation.[37]

AP® skills

Applying Disciplinary Knowledge: What obstacles did African American children face in public schools in the 1970s?

Black education advocates met with stiff resistance from whites, also mostly mothers, who greeted Black children with racial epithets. In Plainfield, after a 1964 state order to desegregate schools, Black students found the words "n***** steps" and "n***** entrance" painted on parts of Plainfield High School. In 1971, a U.S. district court mandated in *Milliken v. Bradley* that Detroit's public schools be merged with those in the surrounding suburbs; hundreds of thousands of whites organized against the decision. They rejected the district judge's finding that federal, state, and local governments had combined with private organizations to keep housing, and thereby schools, segregated. White parents claimed reverse discrimination, insisting that their right to send their children to their neighborhood schools was being violated. "Why ship the kids someplace else when we got a school right here?" one white mother asked. Whites claimed that Blacks attended segregated schools out of choice, not because of a racist real estate market that kept Blacks and whites segregated.[38]

White resistance forced African Americans to reconsider busing. Not only did conservatives, who had initiated the program, withdraw support, but by the 1970s, whites who could do so had either moved to suburban areas that were beyond the reach of desegregation orders or sent their children to private schools. Instead of focusing on busing, Black mothers demanded that more state and federal funding be directed toward Black schools so that per capita spending on Black and white students would be the same. They also wanted special programs to bring Black students up to par with whites. And they demanded more control of their schools, hoping to hold principals and teachers more accountable to the community and therefore more sensitive, respectful, responsive, and concerned about Black youths.[39]

These efforts also met with white resistance. Whites argued that their property taxes paid for their children's education and that they were not responsible for segregated housing. In addition, they believed that federal tax dollars should be distributed equally. Without extra money, however, schools in Black areas could not afford the special programs that Black students needed.

Community Control and Urban Ethnic Conflict

White resistance to school integration and affirmative action convinced many African Americans that their progress hinged on their ability to procure city, state, and federal resources and to dictate what happened in their communities while protecting the gains of the freedom movement. However, their efforts only increased tensions between Blacks and other ethnic and racial groups that felt the same way.

One explosive issue was community control of schools. In 1967, the New York legislature made school funding contingent on local control of education. When Blacks gained control of the school board in the Harlem and Ocean Hill–Brownsville sections of New York City, they fired or threatened to fire white principals and teachers. The powerful United Federation of Teachers (UFT), which was predominantly Jewish American, opposed advocates of community control. Tens of thousands of the city's teachers went on strike in the fall of 1968, prompting members of the Black community to cry racism, while some in the Jewish community made allegations of antisemitism against community control proponents. Still others, including both Black and Jewish people, condemned the firing of teachers and saw the issue as a dispute over labor rights and class. In the end, the city assumed control of the hiring and placement of teachers, but the traditional alliance of Black and Jewish people, a relationship forged during the freedom movement, had been sorely tested.

In New York and elsewhere, the problem was not so much one of governance as one of resources.[40] Deindustrialization, globalization, and white flight had diminished urban tax bases, making public resources scarce; those who could not or would not move were left to fight among themselves — and fight they did. In 1974, Boston erupted in violence after a judge ordered the city to implement a busing program to desegregate its schools. In South Boston, a predominantly Irish American working-class neighborhood, angry white mobs shut down high schools, pelted buses with bricks and stones, and besieged city council meetings.[41] It had been twenty years since

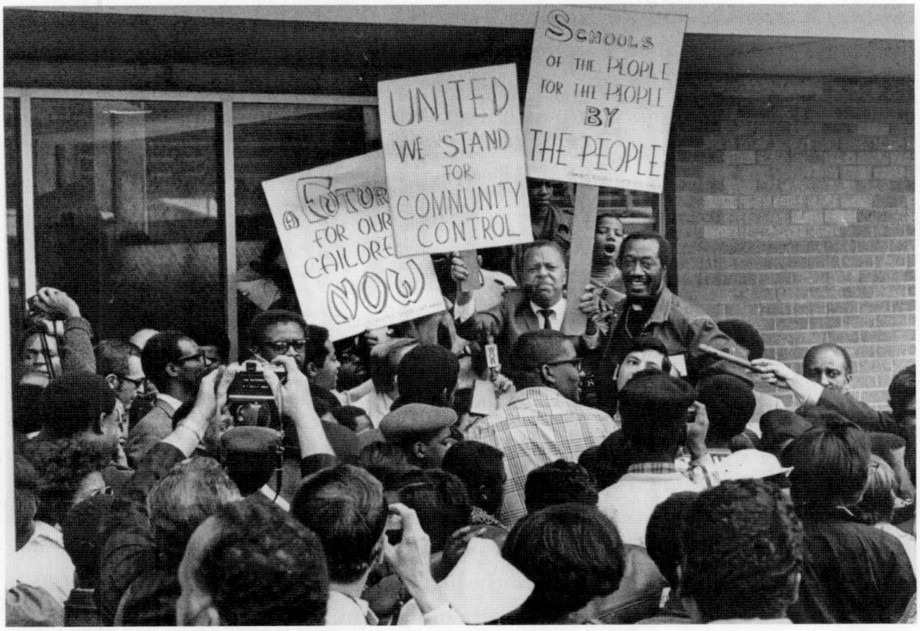

Ocean Hill–Brownsville Parents Rally

In the late 1960s, community control of schools emerged as a viable alternative to desegregation of schools, which was opposed by both Blacks and whites. Here, Ocean Hill–Brownsville residents register their support for parental control over the teachers and resources designated to educate their children. **Use the image to summarize the goals of attendants at the Ocean Hill–Brownsville Parent Rally. How did their goals reflect the objectives of the Black Power movement? How did their demands compare to those of the Black Campus Movement of the late 1960s?**

Patrick A. Burns/© The New York Times/Redux Pictures.

the U.S. Supreme Court had outlawed segregated schools, but the South Boston riots proved just how intractable the issue was. In addition to pitting Blacks against white ethnic groups, the fight over desegregation showed how much class mattered. Those who could escape the city for quality schools in the suburbs avoided the issue completely. This was especially so after the Supreme Court overturned *Milliken v. Bradley* in 1974. Freed from the prospect of city/suburban school mergers, the affluent left the poor and middle classes to compete for shrinking city resources. By the late 1970s, middle-class Blacks also were escaping the cities.

> **AP® skills**
>
> **Applying Disciplinary Knowledge:** Why did tensions emerge between African Americans and other ethnic groups over funds for state and federal funds for education?

African Americans felt pressure to compete with other ethnic groups in order to keep what gains they had and to progress further. For example, the NAACP initially opposed extending coverage of the 1965 Voting Rights Act to "language minorities," including Latinos. The fear was that the addition of language provisions would undercut the central focus on Blacks and also jeopardize extension of the act. Although in 1975 Congress mandated that voting materials had to be provided for different language groups, many Blacks felt that the Voting Rights Act was theirs exclusively

AP® exam tip

Be sure you can explain how the Voting Rights Act of 1965 impacted the growth of Black political representation in American politics in the late twentieth century.

because African Americans had fought for its passage. They protectively thought, "What are you doing fooling around with our act?"[42] Many also coveted the money that governments allocated for bilingual education, arguing that African American children needed just as much help with English as immigrants. Their advocacy peaked in the 1990s, as educators in California pushed to get the state to recognize Ebonics, a kind of Black dialect, as a language spoken in African American homes. The strategy behind the argument was to persuade legislators that Black children needed enhanced instruction in Standard English in the hope that the state would then direct a portion of the bilingual education funds toward programs for African Americans. The effort failed miserably, however, as politicians and even some Black leaders perceived Ebonics advocates as endorsing the dialect rather than trying to eliminate it.[43]

As demonstrated by the clashes over voting rights and bilingual education, African Americans were increasingly at odds with Latinos and other immigrant groups who, following passage of the Immigration and Nationality Act of 1965, entered the country in greater numbers than they had in previous years. In both New York and California, relations between Blacks and the Koreans who owned many of the shops in their neighborhoods were hostile. A 1992 survey found that Korean shopkeepers in New York City viewed their Black customers, when compared to whites, as violent and dishonest. Most believed Blacks were more criminally oriented and less intelligent than whites. Almost half thought Blacks were lazy, and few believed Blacks were poor because of racial discrimination. By contrast, this same survey revealed that most Blacks felt Koreans were dishonest, disrespectful, and violent in their dealings with Blacks. They believed that Korean shopkeepers charged high prices for low-quality goods and that Koreans were concerned only about profits and added nothing of value to their communities. In Los Angeles, the distrust between Blacks and Koreans manifested itself during the 1980s in the murders of nineteen Korean merchants, nearly all of which were committed by African Americans.[44] Tensions in the city came to a head in 1991 when Latasha Harlins, a fifteen-year-old Black girl, was shot in the back of the head by Korean store owner Soon Ja Du. Though Du was convicted of voluntary manslaughter, an offense that carries a maximum prison sentence of sixteen years, she was only fined and sentenced to probation and community service. Harlins's murder was one of the events that precipitated the 1992 Los Angeles riots, during which Du's store was burned, along with many other Korean establishments.

Black Political Gains

Ultimately, the control of resources was a question of political economics and electoral politics. The battle to control the allocation of tax dollars was waged on every political front, from school boards, antipoverty commissions, and city councils to mayoral offices, state legislatures, and congressional chambers. African American candidates fared best in places where Blacks constituted a majority, and where they did not, they joined with new immigrants, white liberals, and some working-class whites to forge political alliances. Starting in 1971, the **Congressional Black Caucus** helped get Black candidates elected. Founded by Shirley Chisholm, the only Black woman in Congress, and twelve Black congressmen, the Congressional Black Caucus supported Black candidates in local races; lobbied for reforms in job training, health care, welfare, and social service programs; and attempted to fashion a national strategy to increase Black political power.

Congressional Black Caucus
An organization of Black representatives that became an official presence in Congress in 1971. It supported Black candidates, lobbied for social reforms, and attempted to fashion a national strategy to increase Black political power.

Black political efforts paid dividends. In 1970, there were only 1,469 Black-elected elected officials in the United States; by 2006, the number had increased six-fold, to 9,040.[45] In 1964, there were only 4 African Americans in Congress; by 1968, there were 10, the highest number since Reconstruction, and by 1972, that number had increased to 15. Similar developments occurred on the local level. In 1970, there were only 2 African American mayors of big cities — Carl Stokes in Cleveland and Richard Hatcher in Gary, Indiana. In 1973, Tom Bradley and Maynard Jackson were elected mayor in Los Angeles and Atlanta, respectively. By 2001, there were 47 African American mayors in cities with populations greater than 50,000, and only about half of those cities had Black majorities.[46] It is important to note that the largest annual increase in the percentage of Black elected officials between 1969 and 2000 occurred in 1971, indicating that the impact of the Black freedom movement on Black electoral participation and representation was immediate.[47]

AP® skills

Applying Disciplinary Knowledge: What was the Congressional Black Caucus? What political goals did it pursue during this era?

African Americans also continued to have an impact on presidential elections. Blacks voted overwhelmingly Democratic in the last three decades of the twentieth century and, as part of the Democratic Party base, helped elect Jimmy Carter and Bill Clinton. In 1984 and 1988, Jesse Jackson, an African American civil rights worker who had worked closely with Martin Luther King Jr., won several hundred Democratic Party delegates. In 1988, he captured close to seven million votes after winning seven primaries and four caucuses. Jackson's candidacy proved that white Americans would vote for a Black man if he had the right message and could build coalitions. In 1988, Jackson brought together rural farmers, Black and white urban workers, women, and environmentalists in the Rainbow Coalition with a populist message that condemned big business for exporting jobs and Reagan policies that gave tax breaks to the rich.[48]

AP® exam tip

On the AP® Exam, you may be asked to describe the major advances in Black federal political leadership in the late twentieth century.

Electoral gain was one thing, but economic power was another. As with education, political leaders had no magic wand that would make resources materialize out of thin air. Economic progress, therefore, was steady but halting. With more African Americans holding political office, however, Blacks had more access to government employment. It is no accident that the largest gains in white-collar employment among Blacks came in personnel offices that dealt with local, state, and federal agencies, especially those that enforced antidiscrimination laws.[49] Blacks made progress in other areas of the labor market as well. The U.S. Supreme Court's ruling in ***Griggs v. Duke Power Co.*** (1971) enabled African Americans to put Title VII, the antidiscrimination clause of the 1964 Civil Rights Act, to work for them. (See Appendix: *Griggs v. Duke Power Co.* for the text of this ruling.) In 1972, Congress passed Title IX of the Education Amendments of 1972, which outlawed discrimination in educational institutions

Griggs v. Duke Power Co. (1971)
A U.S. Supreme Court ruling which held that IQ tests, high school diplomas, and other requirements that were not necessary for the performance of a job were by their very nature discriminatory and had to be eliminated.

receiving federal funding. A subsequent amendment made it unlawful to discriminate against personnel in academic institutions. These laws helped achieve what Black electoral power alone could not: putting Black people to work so that they had the ability to help themselves.

The Expansion of the Black Middle Class

AP® exam tip

Be sure you can explain how the Black middle class changed over the course of the twentieth century.

The Black middle class transformed considerably in the late 1960s and throughout the 1970s and 1980s. In the years before midcentury, the Black middle and upper classes comprised Blacks who served their own communities. They were morticians, barbers, beauticians, and owners of restaurants, stores, and clubs. Black middle-class professionals, from teachers to doctors, also served a community that was almost exclusively Black. The Black freedom movement, however, changed the very nature of Black America (and, by extension, the rest of America) by opening up jobs that had previously been closed to Blacks. In 1963, when the Ford Motor Company was asked to list its white-collar jobs for which Blacks were welcome to apply, it mentioned valets, porters, security guards, messengers, barbers, mail clerks, and telephone operators — a list that by its narrowness explained the urgency and militancy of the struggle for jobs and education.[50] By 1980, things had changed dramatically. Nationwide, the number of Black professional and managerial workers had tripled, and the number of Black sales and clerical workers — about half of whom were women — had increased fivefold. Between 1970 and 1980 alone, the number of Black college students doubled, increasing from 522,000 to more than 1 million. These gains were accompanied by an increase in Black earnings relative to those of whites. The emergence of a substantial Black middle class was a hallmark of the Black struggle for economic and political justice — despite the fact that a Black middle-class family was more likely than its white counterpart to depend on the income of both spouses, an indication of the fragility of its status.[51]

Fair Housing Act (1968)
A law prohibiting discrimination based on race, color, religion, or national origin in the sale or rental of housing and making the practices of blockbusting, steering, and redlining illegal. Subsequent amendments prohibited discrimination based on sex, familial status, and disability.

That fragility could also be seen in housing. In 1968, Congress passed another civil rights act. Title VIII of this act, known as the **Fair Housing Act**, prohibited discrimination based on race, color, sex, religion, and national origin in the sale or rental of housing. It also made the practices of blockbusting, steering, and redlining illegal. As initially passed, however, the act excluded 80 percent of the nation's housing stock, reflecting the conservative backlash that was already underway. (A subsequent 1968 Supreme Court ruling brought all of the nation's housing under the act.) In addition, the act gave no government agency the power to identify and root out discrimination, in effect ensuring that if desegregation occurred at all, it would occur not because the government had provided strong enforcement mechanisms but because victims, on a case-by-case basis, bore the costs of investigation and prosecution. As one political scientist noted, "What Congress did was hatch a beautiful bird without wings to fly."[52]

In practice, despite the tireless efforts of churches, civil rights organizations, and numerous open-housing groups to desegregate white suburbs, the same

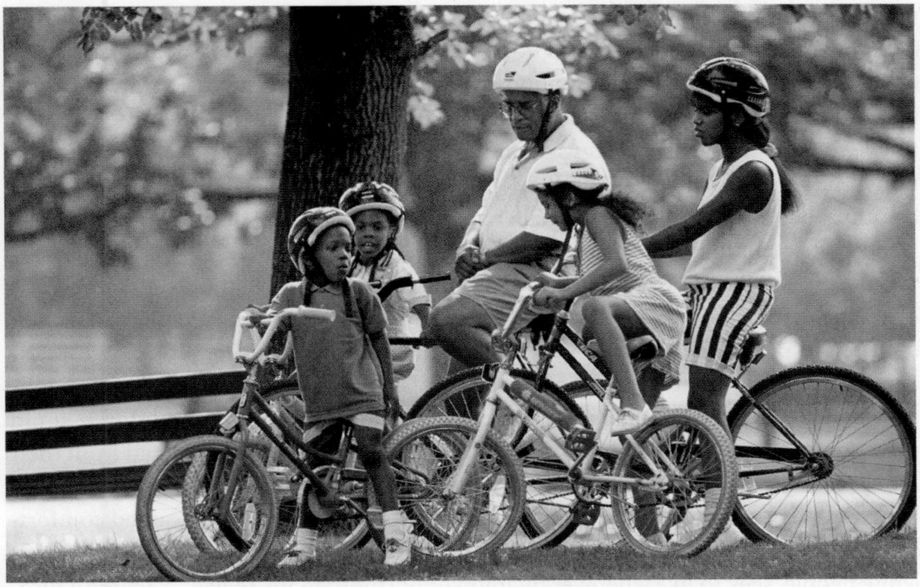

The Black Middle Class
African Americans' ability to move to the suburbs was hindered by the discriminatory policies of private banks and real estate agencies and others in the mortgage industry, and of federal agencies such as the Federal Housing Authority and the Veterans Administration. Blacks who accomplished the move were able to experience a lifestyle that had been common to that of middle-class whites for decades. **What details from this image suggest the quality of life members of the Black middle class were able to enjoy in the second half of the twentieth century?** *© Hub Willson/ClassicStock/The Image Works.*

discriminatory housing policies used in the 1950s and '60s by private homeowners, real estate agents, mortgage brokers, and FHA and VA administrators continued to be used for the remainder of the twentieth century. Increasingly, class-based bias was used to keep Blacks out of white suburbs. Some towns were rezoned so that affordable housing was disallowed or only the very wealthy could afford to move in. Towns were helped by a series of Supreme Court rulings that made such rezoning legal. In 1977, for example, the Court ruled that Arlington Heights, a suburb of Chicago, did not violate the Constitution by prohibiting a church-sponsored apartment development. In this blow to open housing, the Court ruled that even though Arlington Heights's refusal to rezone for the apartments might have discriminatory effects, the plaintiff had not demonstrated that the town's intent was discriminatory. Only regulations clearly designed "with racially discriminatory intent," the Court held, violated the Constitution. Since, as a federal appeals court warned, "clever men may easily conceal their motivation," legal reliance on racist intent provided ample cover for race bias.[53]

AP® exam tip
Be sure you can explain the long-term effects of discriminatory housing policies and practices on the Black community.

Many African Americans argued that the Black middle class ought to stay in Black neighborhoods to uplift and empower them. Some opponents of open housing asked why Blacks should have to beg whites for acceptance. According to one preacher, Blacks were "coming to realize that even though they must fight for 'open occupancy' or the right to live any place they choose, once this right is secured for cultural, political and economic reasons it is desirable that the great majority of Black men choose to live together in separate Negro communities." For other opponents, it was a question of black power politics. One Black politician noted, "If they [Blacks] disperse the communities, they'll only create smaller ghettos subservient to the white middle class. If they [the communities] remain intact, they'll have some power."[54]

AP® skills

Applying Disciplinary Knowledge: How did Black middle class families face similar racial housing discrimination as Black families prior to the passage of the Fair Housing Act of 1968?

These arguments were not lost on members of the Black middle class. But like other Americans, they wanted quiet residential neighborhoods, safe places for their children to play, supermarkets where the food was fresh, modern homes with new appliances, streets that were cleaned on a regular basis, responsive fire departments, police protection against crime, and, above all, schools where their children could get a quality education. When asked what she and her neighbors expected from their move from New York City to Long Island, one Black woman said that they "wanted backyards and front yards, they wanted a garage for themselves, they wanted comfortable spaces." The Harlem businessman Percy Sutton explained, "Black people, just as white people, seek to live wherever their job opportunities are, to live . . . where educational opportunities are, so they are seeking to move into the suburbs."[55]

African Americans moved, but within the limits set by white resistance. Sometimes Black inner-city neighborhoods simply expanded outward past city limits. Kept out of white areas that were distant from the city, Blacks were forced to stay in older inner-ring areas that were just beyond city boundaries. Residents of these inner-ring suburbs usually had the same problems as their inner-city counterparts — inferior municipal services, unresponsive political leaders, poor schools, high crime rates, and high property taxes. Blacks who moved to integrated suburbs usually found that the suburb remained integrated for only a short time. Once a Black family moved in, real estate agents scared or steered white families away, leading to racial turnover in as little as a year. Once turnover occurred, municipal services declined, reproducing patterns of racial segregation and neighborhood deterioration. A few suburbs, such as Oak Park, Illinois, had open-housing committees that valued integration and worked to prevent resegregation. Blacks who moved to these suburbs enjoyed the kind of life they had imagined. So, too, did those who lived in all-Black, upscale, upper-middle-class communities. Generally, however, African Americans did not reap the same gains as whites when they moved to the suburbs. The few who moved to predominantly white suburbs — a phenomenon that occurred with greater frequency toward the end of the century — paid for their benefits with greater social isolation.[56]

By the year 2000, one-third of all African Americans lived in suburbs. In the last two decades of the twentieth century, as many moved there as had moved in the first seventy years.[57] That most Black suburbanites lived in Black suburbs and that most African Americans still lived mostly in all-Black neighborhoods, city or otherwise, testified to the persistence of racism and the resistance to integration.

And yet the fact that the fight for equality continued in the face of overwhelming white power is testimony to the strength of African Americans' commitment to full inclusion in American society.

The Different Faces of Black America

How has the African American population grown and become more diverse since 2000?

What African American political cultural movements of the 1960s and 1970s influenced the emergence of hip-hop and the elements that define hip-hop culture?

In 1998, the Harvard University professor Henry Louis Gates Jr. hosted an episode of the PBS series *Frontline* titled "The Two Nations of Black America." At issue was the question of class, or, more specifically, the emergence of a Black America that was possibly more divided by class than it was united by race. Gates, a distinguished African American scholar, put the question front and center in an essay he wrote in conjunction with the program: "How have we reached this point, where we have both the largest black middle class and the largest black underclass in our history?"[58]

One of the many points brought to light by "The Two Nations of Black America" was the fact that by 1990, a new generation of African Americans had emerged that reflected all of the advances and setbacks of the past forty years. Although most African Americans still had a profound sense that what happened to them as a group affected them as individuals — what political scientists call "linked fate"[59] — more Blacks than ever before approached life first as individuals and only secondarily as African Americans.

African America was also marked by gender, ethnic, sexual, and generational diversity. By the end of the twentieth century, Black immigrants from other parts of the world were changing the meaning of African American culture, and a new generation of young African Americans were spurning their parents' way of thinking and were remaking Blackness.

The Class Divide

African Americans had never been a monolithic people. Nevertheless, by 1998, class differences had become a more defining feature of this group. Although there was debate over the precise percentage of Blacks in each class, it was accepted as fact that one portion of Black America had advanced into the middle and upper classes, while another was mired in poverty.

The use of the term *underclass* to describe the impoverished was new in the 1990s. It referenced a whole set of conditions, ranging from the factual conditions of poverty, such as unemployment and low income, to the culture of poverty that these conditions gave rise to. Some preferred the term *truly disadvantaged* over *underclass*. Both terms, however, referred almost exclusively to African Americans who, for any number of reasons, were trapped in declining cities, unable to find employment in the new postindustrial economy that demanded skills they did not possess and could not obtain.[60]

AP® skills

Applying Disciplinary Knowledge: What specific challenges did many disadvantaged African Americans face in the 1990s? What were the primary causes of these challenges?

As a group, African Americans had the highest rate of poverty in the nation. More than one-third lived in poverty, and the unemployment rate for young Black males reached 50 percent in the 1990s. (See By the Numbers: Incarceration and Unemployment Rates for Blacks and Whites, 1974–1997, p. 643.) The firearm homicide rate for Black males was two to four times higher than that for any other socioeconomic census group, accounting for 42 percent of all young Black male deaths. And although African Americans made up only 11.4 percent of the total U.S. population, African American males accounted for almost 31 percent of all prison inmates. By 1990, there were more Black males between the ages of eighteen and twenty-two in jail than in college. With so many men in prison, two-thirds of Black women of marriageable age were left unmarried. By 1990, half of all African American children lived in single-parent, female-headed households, and almost 50 percent of them were born into poverty.[61]

The use of heroin and phencyclidine (PCP, or angel dust) in the 1960s and '70s and crack cocaine in American cities during the 1980s were both causes and effects of the devastation these statistics represent. Caught in a downward spiral of unemployment and poverty, many urban Blacks turned to these highly addictive, inexpensive drugs in an attempt to escape their hopelessness.[62] Others used the drug trade as a source of employment. As one scholar of the Los Angeles drug trade explained, many African Americans, particularly young men, were excluded from both the service and high-tech industries that developed in the postindustrial era. Unable to find blue-collar work in the new economy — the kind of work that had fueled migration and sustained Black families during World War II — African Americans found the drug trade, especially involving crack, an attractive alternative to the abject poverty they otherwise faced.[63] And yet this trade increased Black-on-Black crime. In poor and working-class Black neighborhoods, assaults, robberies, rapes, and homicides spiked, as did the gang violence that accompanied the competition for drug markets.

When law-abiding Black citizens begged their municipal and national governments to wipe out the drug corners, crack houses, gangs, and gun violence, they got tougher no-tolerance laws, but they also got more aggressive policing. In many cities, police adopted military-like operations that gave officers the prerogative to clear corners, establish roadblocks, make undercover purchases, seize property, and condemn apartments. Police stopped, searched, and verbally abused the law-abiding along with the criminals. To the miseries of failing schools, no jobs, and dilapidated houses, poor and working-class Blacks could add unrelenting police harassment.[64]

Black people were also disproportionately harmed by the AIDS epidemic and the government's response to the crisis. Under President Reagan, little government funding was directed toward researching and fighting the disease. By 1990, HIV/AIDS was the sixth leading cause of death for African Americans, and it was fast becoming the leading cause of death for African American women between the ages of twenty-five and thirty-four.[65] Although the number of Americans who died from AIDS declined toward the end of the century, Blacks failed to benefit from new treatments in the same proportion as whites because they lacked the resources to pay for the more expensive drugs and because they were, as one historian put it, "invisible as objects of public concern."[66] At the end of 2006, there were an estimated 1.1 million people living with HIV in the United States, of which almost half (46 percent) were African American.

AP® skills

Applying Disciplinary Knowledge: How were African Americans impacted by the AIDS epidemic? To what extent did the federal government effectively address the crisis?

Although Democrat Bill Clinton, who held office from 1993 to 2001, was popular among African Americans, his policies did not narrow the gap between the Black poor and the middle and working classes. Unlike Reagan, Clinton lent his support to health and education programs to help the disadvantaged. His support for the earned income tax credit, an increased minimum wage, and funding for civil rights enforcement benefited all working Blacks. His 1997 race initiative, which involved colleges and universities, cities, and states in a national dialogue on the issue of race, earned him Black support. Yet his appointments, 14 percent of which went to Blacks, immediately impacted only the Black middle and upper classes.

Clinton's fear of a conservative backlash made him careful not to appear too sympathetic to the Black poor. This was illustrated by the case of Lani Guinier, a Black woman whom Clinton nominated as a candidate for assistant attorney general for civil rights. When conservatives characterized her opinion on cumulative voting and proportionate interest representation (European-style voting that ensures that minorities are always represented) as a "quota" voting system and labeled her a "quota queen," Clinton withdrew the nomination.

The administration's priorities were confirmed when Clinton signed the 1996 Personal Responsibility and Work Opportunity Reconciliation Act, ending sixty years of guaranteed federal aid to the country's poorest citizens. Although the act replaced the much-maligned Aid to Families with Dependent Children, federal aid to the poor was frozen at 1996 levels, and in 2003, the House voted to continue the freeze through 2008. America's poor families could receive aid for only two consecutive years and for five years total. States received bonuses for sharply cutting their public assistance rolls and could be penalized if they did not force recipients to work a minimum of twenty hours a week.[67]

A sign of the times was the lack of outrage in response to this act and to Clinton's crime bills, which increased the number of private prisons, the number of police on the street, and the number of crimes punishable by death. By the mid-1990s, the disproportionate number of imprisoned African Americans made it apparent that the police treated Blacks and whites differently and that punitive policing in place of jobs, job training, good schools, and adequate housing was a failed policy. Yet few social service agencies lobbied on behalf of welfare recipients, and the Congressional Black Caucus offered only minimal resistance to Clinton's crime bills.[68]

AP® skills

Applying Disciplinary Knowledge: Summarize Clinton's crime bills. How did they affect African Americans in particular?

On the local level, the Black poor and the Black middle class were estranged from one another. A study done of Washington, D.C., neighborhoods showed the difference.

While Blacks in a poor area complained about racial profiling — "Me and my friends are out there and we're being stopped for no good reason, and it doesn't happen once, it happens repeatedly, and we're sick and tired of it" — Blacks in a middle-class neighborhood praised the job done by the police: "I just want to thank you for all the hard work you do day in and day out, and the police really never get enough credit."[69] By the end of the century, middle-class Blacks were likely to think of the poor as race traitors, an opinion expressed by comedian Bill Cosby when he in 2004 publicly proclaimed that "the lower economic and lower middle economic people are [not] holding their end in this deal. In the neighborhood that most of us grew up in, parenting is not going on."[70] Said eleven years before his credibility plummeted because of his arrest on charges of sexual assault (and subsequent conviction), Cosby's comments were applauded by much of middle-class Black America. At that time, he was admired for articulating what many thought but were reluctant to say.

Hip-Hop, Violence, and the Emergence of a New Generation

rap music
A type of music developed in the early to mid-1970s critiquing poverty, police surveillance, drug addiction, Black-on-Black crime, and unemployment.

AP® exam tip

Be sure you can describe the cultural and societal developments that influenced hip-hop and hip-hop culture.

The withdrawal of government support for Black equality, the hostility and equivocation of national and local leaders who were former allies of the Black freedom struggle, and the staggering poverty and disruption of Black inner-city neighborhoods affected African Americans in a variety of ways. One of the most profound developments was the emergence of the hip-hop counterculture and **rap music** among younger African Americans. Originating on the streets of Harlem and the South Bronx in the early to mid-1970s, rap music began as pure showmanship at block parties, recreation centers, and parks, where disc jockeys, or DJs (also called emcees), competed with one another by layering in beats at the turntable, rhyming while friends battled it out on the break-dancing floor. Very quickly, however, the music emerged as a way for young people to deal with the violence and poverty of their neighborhoods. On one hand, young DJs used rap lyrics to critique poverty, police surveillance, drug addiction, Black-on-Black crime, and unemployment. On the other hand, stage competitions often replaced gang rivalries. Rap music allowed for the expression and release of frustrations, and as an industry, it also functioned as an avenue to escape the poverty that produced it. Rap artists such as Notorious B.I.G. and Tupac Shakur became millionaires seemingly overnight, and Black record labels such as Death Row Records were similarly successful. But as hip-hop moved into the mainstream, it became, in the minds of older Black and white Americans, a symbol of everything that was wrong with the underclass, and that thinking had a negative effect on all of Black America.

Some of the animosity stemmed from discomfort with lyrics that offered explicit descriptions of ghetto life, were graphically sexual and violent, and denigrated women while glorifying "gangstas." More discomfort grew from the unabashed use of profanity and the word *nigga,* which hip-hop artists claimed defanged the historically pejorative reference to Black people. Even greater anxiety arose when rap music was

Still from the Movie* Beat Street, *1984
The movie *Beat Street* featured break-dancing contests and a new DJ technique subsequently labeled turntablism (whereby the DJ simultaneously plays two records on separate turntables and mixes them by holding and scratching them in a particular sequence). The film introduced to America and the rest of the world the fantastically athletic and rhythmic moves that would forever marry hip-hop and break dancing to the young. Here a lead character demonstrates one of the vigorous moves that are the hallmark of break dancing. ■ **How does this photo capture the culture of Black urban communities? How did hip-hop artists carry on the tradition of West African griots you learned about in Unit 1?**

embraced wholeheartedly by white and Black youths who rejected America's mainstream middle-class culture.

Like Black nationalists before them, rappers targeted the police, who again were likened to an occupying army. From the time of the 1970s' block parties, the police, armed with the new drug laws, had gone after artists for their appropriation of public spaces. As rappers' lyrics became more incendiary and violence accompanied rap concerts, the opinion that rap not only expressed but also caused violence was reinforced.[71] When one act, N.W.A. (Niggaz with Attitude), penned an anthem unapologetically titled "Fuck tha Police," the FBI issued a warning to the group.[72] The drive-by shootings that killed Tupac Shakur and Notorious B.I.G. in 1996 and 1997, respectively, convinced both white and Black Americans of the danger of hip-hop.

AP® exam tip

Be sure you can explain how African American political and cultural movements of the 1960s and 1970s influenced the emergence of hip-hop.

White Americans had difficulty disassociating the violence and antisocial behavior of hip-hop from other violent events that occurred in the 1990s. In 1991, the public repeatedly viewed a bystander's videotape of the arrest of a Black man named Rodney King by white Los Angeles police officers. It showed King lying on the ground while police beat him with batons. Although the officers argued that King's violent resistance required the use of force, many, including most African Americans, saw it as police brutality and proof of the general mistreatment of Blacks by law enforcement. When the assault case against the officers was moved out of racially diverse Los Angeles to the predominantly white suburb of Simi Valley and a mostly white jury returned a not guilty verdict in 1992, Los Angeles, still simmering over the murder of Latasha Harlins, erupted in riots that left 55 people dead and 2,300 injured. The verdict also ignited violence in Atlanta, Birmingham, Chicago, and Seattle. Underlying the violence were the poverty and unemployment caused by the postindustrial economy. But for African Americans, the whole King incident, from arrest through trial, symbolized the continuation of the unmitigated extralegal justice that followed Blacks, particularly Black men, wherever they went.

For this reason, a majority of African Americans sided with former football superstar O. J. Simpson in 1994 when he was arrested for killing his white ex-wife, Nicole Brown Simpson, and her white friend Ronald Goldman. After nine months of sensational televised hearings that featured the best defense lawyers money could buy, and a defense that effectively put the Los Angeles Police Department and the criminal justice system on trial for racism, Simpson was acquitted in 1995 by a mostly Black and female jury. As evidence of just how far apart Blacks and whites were on issues of race, Blacks overwhelmingly approved of the verdict, while most whites thought Simpson was guilty.[73]

Gender and Sexuality

Other changes in Black America could be seen in the Clarence Thomas Supreme Court hearings. President George H. W. Bush's 1991 nomination of the Black jurist to replace the venerable Thurgood Marshall highlighted the emergence of a relatively small but significant population of Black conservatives. Marshall, the first African American to serve on the U.S. Supreme Court, had earned his liberal credentials arguing civil rights cases, most notably *Brown v. Board of Education of Topeka* (1954). By contrast, Thomas had opposed affirmative action as a federal judge and as head of the Equal Employment Opportunity Commission (EEOC). Thomas's record on race earned him the rebuke of leading civil rights organizations, and his conservative credentials made him anathema to pro-choice women, who correctly predicted that Thomas would add his weight to the growing antiabortion contingent on the Supreme Court.

Women grew even more opposed to Thomas after the African American law professor Anita Hill testified before the Senate that Thomas had sexually harassed her when she worked for him at the EEOC. The vicious Senate battle that ensued, after which Thomas was narrowly approved by a vote of 52 to 48, reverberated throughout

Clarence Thomas and Anita Hill
In 1991, President George H. W. Bush's nomination of the conservative Black jurist Clarence Thomas to the U.S. Supreme Court was challenged when the African American law professor Anita Hill testified before the Senate that Thomas had sexually harassed her when she worked for him at the EEOC. The televised hearings that followed revealed fissures in the Black community that set liberals against conservatives and men against women as they chose sides in the very public debate. Hill's accusations also brought the issues of sexism and sexual harassment firmly to the fore, a significant and lasting development for women of all races. **To what extent can the concept of intersectionality help to better explain the events surrounding, and the significance of, the Anita Hill and Clarence Thomas case?** *Thomas: Doug Mills/Associated Press/AP Images; Hill: © Mark Reinstein/The Image Works.*

Black America. Not only did Black liberals oppose Black conservatives, but Black people, regardless of gender, also found themselves in an unprecedented public debate about the significance of sexual harassment — indeed, sexism in general — in Black America. The televised Senate hearings, which featured the testimony of the most educated and privileged African Americans, also revealed the depth of the class divisions in Black America. Never before had the schisms been so deep and so public.

In addition to the ideological, gender, and class differences exposed during the hearings, African Americans were torn between debating Thomas's record and presenting a united racial front. When Hill and her supporters were accused of racial treason, they retorted that Thomas's supporters had committed racial suicide by supporting a nominee opposed to affirmative action. Black men accused Black women of emasculating Thomas, and Black women returned with the charge of sexism. So intense was the dispute that some African Americans saw the conflagration as the end of racial solidarity. Nobel laureate Toni Morrison noted, "In matters of race and

AP® skills

Applying Disciplinary Knowledge: How did the reaction to the Clarence Thomas and Anita Hill case demonstrate the ideological and gender differences that had emerged within the African American community in the 1990s?

gender, it is now possible and necessary, as it seemed never to have been before, to speak about these matters without the barriers, the silences, the embarrassing gaps in discourse. . . . The time for undiscriminating racial unity has passed."[74]

Several years later, African Americans did what Morrison suggested. In October 1995, African American men gathered on the National Mall in Washington, D.C., for the **Million Man March**. Depending on who was reporting, from 400,000 to 2 million Black men were present to address America's criminalization of Black men and what Black men needed to do to improve themselves and their communities. Women were specifically asked not to attend. At the march, Black men pledged to atone for their neglect and abuse of Black women, families, and communities. They vowed to dedicate their lives to spiritual, moral, mental, social, political, and economic improvement. Two years later, in October 1997, African American women gathered on the Benjamin Franklin Parkway in Philadelphia for the **Million Woman March**. They called for "Repentance, Restoration, and Resurrection": repentance for the pain Black women caused one another, and restoration and resurrection of the bonds of family and community in African American life. Though organized in the name of racial unity, these marches, which ironically found Black people addressing their gender issues in separate forums, reflected the divisions in Black America that had intensified since the late 1960s.

Million Man March (1995)
A gathering of mostly African American men on the National Mall in Washington, D.C. The men gathered to affirm their commitment to Black women, children, and communities and to dedicate their lives to improving themselves and their communities.

Million Woman March (1997)
A gathering of mostly African American women on the Benjamin Franklin Parkway in Philadelphia. The women came together to affirm their commitment to one another and to the Black family and community.

That the Black LGBTQ+ community insisted on representation in these marches also showed how much Black America had changed since 1963, when civil rights activist Bayard Rustin had had to hide the fact that he was gay for fear of hurting the Black cause. In the 1990s, Black LGBTQ+ people openly protested the heterosexual construction of Black identity. They marched to counter the idea that sexual difference was inherently abnormal, undesirable, shameful, and "un-Black." As one gay marcher observed, the Million Man March offered a "unique opportunity to empower black gay men and lesbians and black gay youth" by providing "positive images of open, courageous, proud and diverse black gay people."[75]

Ethnic Diversity

Nothing more clearly illustrates Black America's diversity at the end of the twentieth century than the different ethnic groups that defined themselves as Black. Black immigration increased exponentially as a result of a series of policy changes: the Immigration and Nationality Act of 1965, which abolished a quota system established in 1924 that had limited immigration by country of origin; the Refugee Act of 1980, which loosened restrictions on those fleeing from conflict areas; and the Immigration Act of 1990, which increased the number of immigrants coming from underrepresented nations. In 2016, the Pew Research Center reported that there were 3.8 million Black immigrants in the United States, more than four times the number in 1980, with most Black immigrants, especially those from Africa, arriving after 2000.[76] With immigrants composing 10 percent of the Black population, scholars were quick to note that the United States is the only place in the world where all of Africa's children — native-born Africans, Afro-Caribbeans, Afro-Latinos, Afro-Europeans, and African Americans — are represented in significant numbers (Map 16.1).

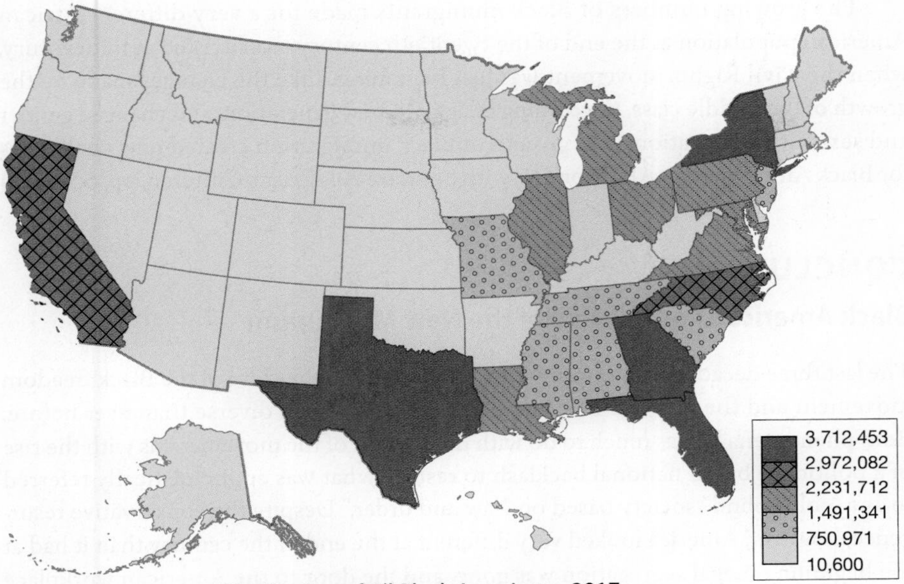

Distribution of All Black Americans, 2017

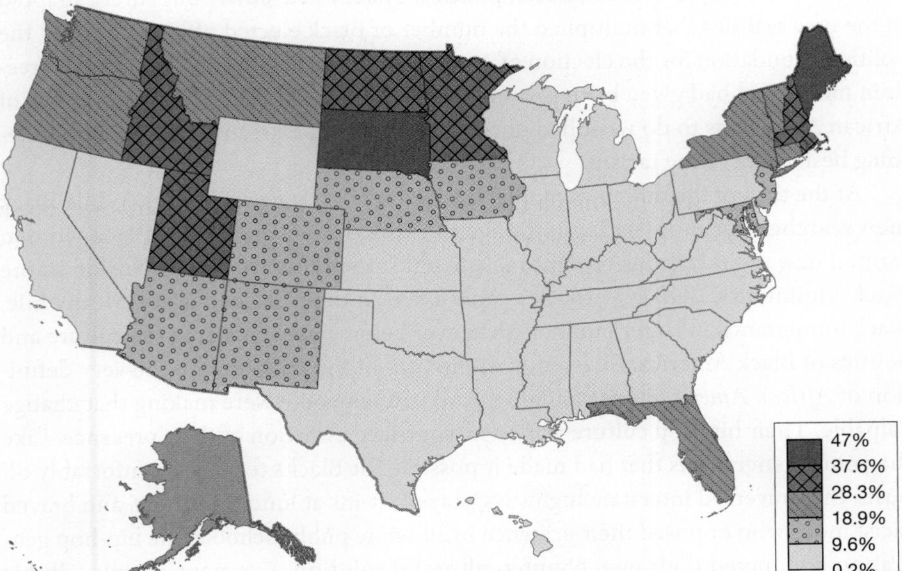

Foreign-Born Blacks as a Percentage of the Black Population, 2017

MAP 16.1 All Black Americans and Foreign-Born Blacks by State, 2017

Black immigrants are settling in areas of the country that traditionally have had low percentages of African Americans. **Why do you think these areas are attractive to them, and how might these new immigrants change the politics and culture of these regions?** DATA SOURCE: U.S. Census Bureau, "Place of Birth (Black or African American Alone) in the United States American Community Survey 1-Year Estimates," 2017, https://censusreporter.org/data/table/?table=B06004B&geo_ids=01000US,040%7C01000US,020%7C01000US&primary_geo_id=01000US.

The growing numbers of Black immigrants made for a very different African American population at the end of the twentieth century than existed at midcentury, when the Civil Rights movement was just beginning. Like the changes made by the growth of the middle class, the coming of age of a new generation, and changed gender and sexuality expectations, the growth of Black immigration created new challenges for Black America. (See AP® Working with Sources: All Africa's Children, pp. 669–75.)

CONCLUSION

Black Americans on the Eve of the New Millennium

The last three decades of the twentieth century marked the close of the Black freedom movement and the rise of a Black America that was more diverse than ever before. Both phenomena had as much to do with the success of the movement as with the rise of a politically based national backlash to restore what was euphemistically referred to as a "color-blind" society based on "law and order." Despite the conservative resurgence, however, America looked very different at the end of the century than it had at the beginning. Legal segregation was gone, and the door to the American workplace had been pried open. The American political system had slowly but surely adapted to the new realities that multiplied the number of Black elected officials and laid the political foundation for the election of America's first Black president. The Black freedom movement had given birth to a substantial middle class and allowed millions of African Americans to do what had once been only a pipe dream: to prioritize something besides surviving racism.

At the turn of the millennium, Black America faced new challenges. While Black men searched for more satisfying ways to express their manhood, Black women formed new organizations to fight racism and sexism. Insisting on inclusion in the Black community, LGBTQ+ Black people asserted their Black identity. Meanwhile, Black immigrants, in larger numbers than ever before, were changing the culture and politics of Black America. In essence, at the turn of the millennium, the very definition of *African American* was changing. And young people were making that change palpable. Their hip-hop culture was an in-your-face assertion of their presence. Like the young generations that had made it possible for Blacks to travel comfortably on buses that traversed interstate highways, staged sit-ins at lunch counters, and braved racist mobs who opposed their presence in all-white public schools, the hip-hop generation conducted their own countercultural revolution. For many people, all this change was welcome, a just reward for more than a century of struggle. For others, it was foreboding, for it seemed to signal the end of a unified Black America.

In 1903, the historian and activist W. E. B. Du Bois prophetically proclaimed that the problem of the twentieth century was "the problem of the color-line."[77] He probably would have been overjoyed, yet troubled, on the eve of the twenty-first century. For even though the visible lines of apartheid had disappeared, invisible markers — such as high rates of imprisonment, segregated housing and schooling, employment discrimination, and the criminalization of Black spaces — remained. At the beginning of the new century, Black America could look back on the previous century and see progress against racism. Looking ahead to continued progress in the future, however, was a bit more challenging.

CHAPTER 16 REVIEW ▸ PRACTICING AP® SKILLS

AP® ESSENTIAL VOCABULARY AND SOURCES

** Essential terms and required sources from the AP® Course are marked with an asterisk.*

New Right p. 638

southern strategy p. 638

busing p. 642

Comprehensive Crime Control Act of 1984 p. 642

Regents of the University of California v. Bakke (1978) p. 644

United Steelworkers of America v. Weber (1979) p. 644

Congressional Black Caucus* p. 653

Griggs v. Duke Power Co. (1971) p. 653

Fair Housing Act (1968)* p. 654

rap music* p. 660

Million Man March (1995) p. 664

Million Woman March (1997) p. 664

APPLYING DISCIPLINARY KNOWLEDGE: ESSENTIAL QUESTIONS

1. Describe the tactics of Richard Nixon and the New Right. What strategies did they pursue in their opposition to the Black freedom movement and affirmative action?
2. How did Ronald Reagan build on Nixon's policies?
3. What new tactics did Black activists adopt to counter the New Right? How successful were they?
4. What roles did Black women play in the evolving Black freedom struggle? Why were their efforts so significant?
5. How did the fight for jobs and resources affect political alliances in the post–civil rights era?
6. Describe the many divisions that came to characterize Black America in the decades following the civil rights and Black power movements. In what ways did these changes undermine racial unity? In what ways did they enhance solidarity?
7. How did the War on Crime and the War on Drugs contribute to the mass incarceration of African Americans?

SUGGESTED REFERENCES

Opposition to the Black Freedom Movement

Black, Earl, and Merle Black. *The Rise of Southern Republicans*. Cambridge: Belknap Press of Harvard University Press, 2002.

Diamond, Sara. *Roads to Dominion: Right-Wing Movements and Political Power in the United States*. New York: Guilford Press, 1995.

Ferguson, Thomas, and Joel Rogers, eds. *The Hidden Election: Politics and Economics in the 1980 Presidential Campaign*. New York: Pantheon, 1981.

———. *Right Turn: The Decline of the Democrats and the Future of American Politics*. New York: Hill and Wang, 1986.

Guinier, Lani, and Gerald Torres. *The Miner's Canary: Enlisting Race, Resisting Power, Transforming Democracy*. Cambridge: Harvard University Press, 2002.

Hancock, Ange-Marie. *The Politics of Disgust: The Public Identity of the Welfare Queen*. New York: New York University Press, 2004.

Hinton, Elizabeth. *From the War on Poverty to the War on Crime*. Cambridge: Harvard University Press, 2016.

MacLean, Nancy. *Freedom Is Not Enough: The Opening of the American Workplace*. Cambridge: Harvard University Press, 2006.

McGirr, Lisa. *Suburban Warriors: The Origins of the New American Right*. Princeton: Princeton University Press, 2001.

The Persistence of the Black Freedom Struggle

Bositis, David A. *Black Elected Officials: A Statistical Summary*. Washington, DC: Joint Center for Political and Economic Studies, 1998–2009.

Dawson, Michael C. *Behind the Mule: Race and Class in African-American Politics*. Princeton: Princeton University Press, 1994.

Formisano, Ronald P. *Boston against Busing: Race, Class, and Ethnicity in the 1960s and 1970s*, 2nd rev. ed. Chapel Hill: University of North Carolina Press, 2004.

Goldberg, David, and Trevor Griffey, eds. *Black Power at Work: Community Control, Affirmative Action, and the Construction Industry*. Ithaca: ILR Press/Cornell University Press, 2010.

Hero, Rodney E., and Robert R. Preuhs. *Black-Latino Relations in U.S. National Politics: Beyond Conflict or Cooperation*. New York: Cambridge University Press, 2013.

Horne, Gerald. *Fire This Time: The Watts Uprising and the 1960s*. New York: Da Capo Press, 1997.

Massey, Douglas S., and Nancy A. Denton. *American Apartheid: Segregation and the Making of the Underclass*. Cambridge: Harvard University Press, 1993.

Murch, Donna Jean. *Living for the City: Migration, Education, and the Rise of the Black Panther Party in Oakland, California*. Chapel Hill: University of North Carolina Press, 2010.

Orleck, Annelise. *Storming Caesar's Palace: How Black Mothers Fought Their Own War on Poverty*. Boston: Beacon Press, 2005.

Podair, Jerald E. *The Strike That Changed New York: Blacks, Whites, and the Ocean Hill–Brownsville Crisis*. New Haven: Yale University Press, 2008.

Springer, Kimberly. *Living for the Revolution: Black Feminist Organizations, 1968–1980*. Durham: Duke University Press, 2005.

Stevenson, Brenda. *The Contested Murder of Latasha Harlins: Justice, Gender, and the Origins of the LA Riots*. New York: Oxford University Press, 2013.

Sugrue, Thomas J. *Sweet Land of Liberty: The Forgotten Struggle for Civil Rights in the North*. New York: Random House, 2008.

White, Deborah Gray. *Too Heavy a Load: Black Women in Defense of Themselves, 1894–1994*. New York: Norton, 1999.

Wiese, Andrew. *Places of Their Own: African American Suburbanization in the Twentieth Century*. Chicago: University of Chicago Press, 2004.

The Different Faces of Black America

Alexander, Michelle. *The New Jim Crow: Mass Incarceration in the Age of Colorblindness*. New York: New Press, 2010.

Capps, Randy, Kristan McCabe, and Michael Fix, "Diverse Streams: Black African Migration to the United States," Migration Policy Institute, 2012, http://www.migrationpolicy.org.

Chisholm, Shirley. *The Good Fight*. New York: Harper & Row, 1973.

———. *Unbought and Unbossed*. Boston: Houghton Mifflin, 1970.

Collins, Patricia Hill. *Black Sexual Politics: African Americans, Gender, and the New Racism*. New York: Routledge, 2004.

Foner, Nancy. *Islands in the City: West Indian Migration to New York*. Berkeley: University of California Press, 2001.

Forman, James, Jr. *Locking Up Our Own: Crime and Punishment in Black America*. New York: Farrar, Straus & Giroux, 2017.

Forman, Murray, and Mark Anthony Neal, eds. *That's the Joint: The Hip-Hop Studies Reader*. New York: Routledge, 2004.

Giddings, Paula. *When and Where I Enter: The Impact of Black Women on Race and Sex in America*. New York: Bantam, 1984.

Greer, Christina M. *Black Ethnics: Race Immigration, and the Pursuit of the American Dream* Oxford: Oxford University Press, 2013.

Johnson, E. Patrick, and Mae G. Henderson, eds. *Black Queer Studies: A Critical Anthology*. Durham: Duke University Press, 2005.

Kasinitz, Phillip, John Mollenkoff, Mary C. Waters, and Jennifer Holdaway, *Inheriting the City: The Children of Immigrants Come of Age*. New York: Russell Sage Foundation, 2008.

Lusane, Clarence. *Pipe Dream Blues: Racism and the War on Drugs*. Boston: South End Press, 1991.

Morrison, Toni, ed. *Race-ing Justice, En-Gendering Power: Essays on Anita Hill, Clarence Thomas, and the Construction of Social Reality*. New York: Pantheon, 1992.

Murakawa, Naomi. *The First Civil Right: How Liberals Built Prison America*. New York: Oxford University Press, 2014.

Smith, Candis Watts. *Black Mosaic: The Politics of Black Pan-Ethnic Diversity*. New York: New York University Press, 2014.

Waters, Mary C. *Black Identities: West Indian Immigrant Dreams and American Realities*. Cambridge: Harvard University Press, 1999.

Wilson, William Julius. *The Truly Disadvantaged: The Inner City, the Underclass, and Public Policy*. Chicago: University of Chicago Press, 1987.

Womack, Ytasha L. *Post Black: How a New Generation Is Redefining African American Identity*. Chicago: Lawrence Hill, 2010.

All Africa's Children

The year 1965 was game-changing for African Americans. In June, President Johnson addressed the graduating class of Howard University, one of the oldest and most prestigious HBCUs (Historically Black Colleges and Universities) in the country, and he expressed his support for policies that would subsequently become known as affirmative action. Slavery, Jim Crow, racial violence, and persistent discrimination had so disadvantaged African Americans, Johnson proclaimed, that special programs were needed to give Blacks the same opportunities that white Americans enjoyed. Two months later, Johnson signed the Voting Rights Act into law, and the impact was almost immediate. As the numbers of Black voters increased, so did Black influence in all levels of government.

How African Americans experienced both affirmative action and the Voting Rights Act would be affected by another government action in 1965: the passage in October of the Immigration and Naturalization Act. In fact, when one scholar later put all these developments together — affirmative action and the voting rights and immigration acts — he said these policies were on a "collision course"[78] that could ultimately nullify their individual achievements. Why? What was evident at the end of the twentieth century was not always apparent in 1965 or the decade or so after that. If affirmative action was meant to rectify the inequality caused by centuries of systemic discrimination, what would happen when millions of new Black and brown immigrants experienced racism? Would they also be covered by affirmative action laws and programs, or was affirmative action only for native-born Blacks? And as immigrants naturalized and became Americans, would they identify with native-born Blacks and embrace the same civil rights issues? Would immigrants from Black-majority societies understand how American racism worked? Would they empathize with native-born Blacks, or would they be swayed by arguments that cast American Blacks as undeserving? Would they even vote the same way, or would their political coalitions differ from coalitions forged by the survivors of America's racial terrorism?

Culture caused other potential collisions. Like African Americans in the Great Migration, Caribbean and African people moved from their homes with the hope of a better life for themselves and their children. But America's historic racial divide dictated that Black and brown immigrants assimilate into America's lowest caste, something they resented and resisted. At the same time, some native-born Blacks insisted that Black American identity was rooted in slavery and discrimination in the United States. In 1965, Black people proclaimed, "I'm Black and I'm Proud." By the twenty-first century, the question on a lot of minds was "Who is Black?" Were Nigerian Americans, Jamaican Americans, Somali Americans, and the like also African Americans? These same immigrants also wondered what would become of their children if they somehow became more African American than Nigerian, Jamaican, or Somali. To complicate matters further, there were as many differences among immigrant groups as existed between the Black immigrants and the American born. Would they, could they, all get along?

The following documents demonstrate these concerns in varying ways. They speak to the changing culture, politics, and economics of African America. Ultimately, they address the very definition of the "Black community" in the twenty-first century.

key point

The year 1965 was pivotal: President Johnson voiced his support for affirmative action programs as well as signed the Voting Rights Act and the Immigration and Naturalization Act into law. As a result, new doors to political and economic opportunities opened for African Americans and immigrants of African descent.

AP® argumentation

DBQ Practice: Explain how the political and cultural changes of the 1960s shaped Black experiences during the late twentieth century. Use at least three of the documents to support your response.

DOCUMENT 1

A Statistical Look at Foreign-Born Blacks in the United States, 1980–2016

For most of African America's four-hundred-year history, the designation Black (or colored, Negro, Afro, or African American) was assigned to dark-skinned people who had a heritage of slavery and/or discrimination in this country. America's dichotomous racial system, which was established by the laws governing slavery, determined that anyone with "one drop" of Black blood was Black. However, the influx of millions of Black people from other parts of the world has complicated this understanding of Black identity. In 1965, there were only 125,000 foreign-born Blacks in this country. The number increased to 816,000 in 1980, and by 2016, the number of Black foreign-born immigrants had quadrupled, to 4.2 million, with immigration from Africa outpacing that from the Caribbean. As of 2016, immigrants made up 10 percent of the Black population. In some states, foreign-born Blacks account for a larger proportion than native born. (See Map 16.1, p. 665.) Examine the following data with an eye to the kind of changes precipitated by the influx of these "new Blacks."

Breaking it Down What statistical changes can you see in the Black immigrant population in the United States from 1980 to 2016? What countries were most represented among Black immigrants? Although numbers can be interpreted many ways, what do they suggest about the changing understanding of Blackness in America? Are these "new Blacks" African American?[79]

Black Immigrants Compared to Other Groups, 2013

	Foreign-born Blacks	U.S.-born Blacks	All immigrants	U.S. population
Total population (in thousands)	3,793	39,892	41,341	316,129
Median age (in years)	42	29	43	37
Median household income	$43,800	33,500	48,000	52,000
College degree earners (adults 25 and older)	26%	19	28	30
Poverty	20%	28	19	16
Home ownership	40%	42	51	64
Currently married (adults 18 and older)	48%	28	60	50

Note: U.S.-born and foreign-born Blacks include single-race Blacks and mixed-race Blacks, regardless of Hispanic or Latino origin.

SOURCE: *A Rising Share of the U.S. Black Population Is Foreign Born.* Pew Research Center tabulations of the 2013 American Community Survey (1% IPUMS). For unauthorized status, Pew Research Center estimates based on the 2012 augmented American Community Survey. Pew Research Center, Washington, DC, April 9, 2015, https://www.pewsocialtrends.org/2015/04/09/a-rising-share-of-the-u-s-black-population-is-foreign-born/.

The U.S. Black Immigrant Population, 1980–2016

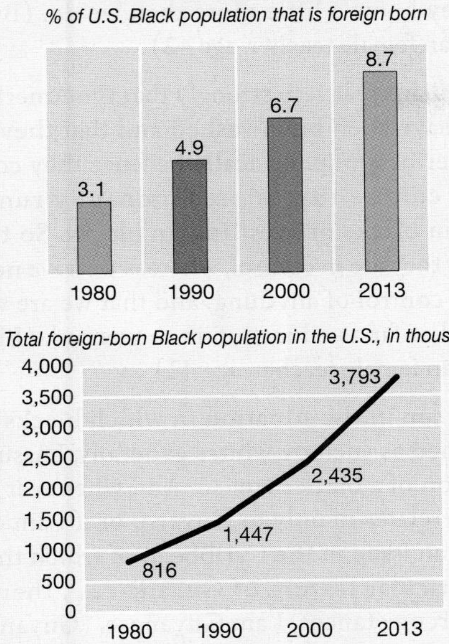

Note: In 2000 and later, foreign-born Blacks include single-race Blacks and mixed-race Blacks, regardless of Hispanic or Latino origin. Prior to 2000, Blacks include only single-race Blacks regardless of Hispanic or Latino origin since a mixed-race option was not available.

SOURCE: *A Rising Share of the U.S. Black Population Is Foreign Born.* Pew Research Center tabulations of the 2016 American Community Survey (1% IPUMS) and the 1980, 1990, and 2000 censuses (5% IPUMS). Pew Research Center, Washington, DC, April 9, 2015, https://www.pewsocialtrends.org/2015/04/09/a-rising-share-of-the-u-s-black-population-is-foreign-born/.

Birth Countries of Black Immigrants in the United States, 2013

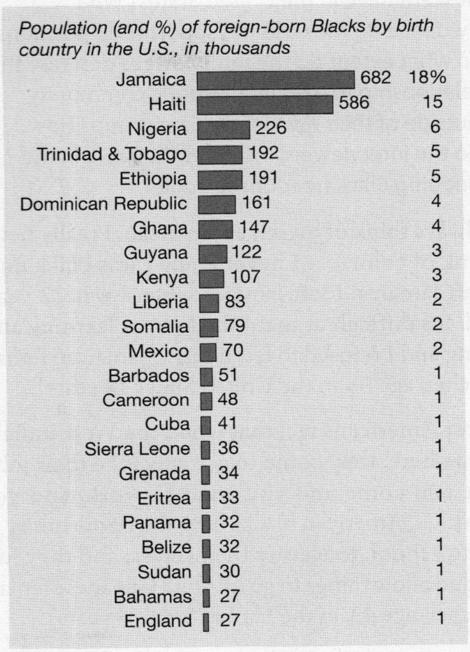

SOURCE: *A Rising Share of the U.S. Black Population Is Foreign Born.* Pew Research Center tabulations of the 2013 American Community Survey (1% IPUMS). Pew Research Center, Washington, DC, April 9, 2015, https://www.pewsocialtrends.org/2015/04/09/a-rising-share-of-the-u-s-black-population-is-foreign-born/.

DOCUMENT 2 Can We All Get Along? Interviews with Immigrants and Native-Born Blacks

Forced to live and play together and to forge a meaningful existence in a country that refused to integrate them into its fabric, Black Americans developed their own institutions and neighborhoods, music, and culture; their own style, aesthetic, and food; their own ways of knowing. With the entry of the millions of Blacks with their own unique histories, aesthetics, religions, and ways of knowing, things are changing. Like it or not, these foreigners have to become Black Americans, a process that involves navigating both American racism and native-born Black culture. Neither native-born nor immigrant Blacks were or are quite prepared for the encounter. The following excerpts from interviews conducted by scholars reveal the intricacies of the process of assimilation. As you read them, keep in mind the data from the previous section and the kinds of choices both immigrant and American Blacks have to make.

Breaking it Down How do the interviewees describe the opportunities people of African descent have in the United States? What evidence do they use to support their positions? To what extent do the interviewees describe their relationship to a larger diasporic community outside of their own immediate group? How do the interviewees interpret their role in the ongoing Black freedom struggle?

I always think of myself as Jamaican. I really never think of color. . . . I never knew I was black until I left Jamaica. I left Jamaica when I was 22 years old. It's difficult at that time to start learning anything and I refused to learn that. (Jamaican female teacher, age 51, in the United States 18 years)

Most Americans feel that when the West Indians come here, they come to actually take their jobs, but you come and you want to work, and you work. . . . American blacks have the opportunity to go to school, to elevate themselves, and they just sit and allow things to go idle by. (Guyanese female teacher, age 43, in the United States 4 years)

I love American blacks, most of them. But I find that, I guess because of their slavery experience and the problems after that, there is a total difference with American blacks as against West Indians. For example, I grew up seeing blacks in charge; that was my experience so I expect to be in charge. That's my frame of reference. American blacks because of what was done to them, they don't see it quite like that. . . . They see themselves as inferior. . . . (Jamaican female teacher, age 37, in the United States 10 years)

Q: What about West Indians, any characteristics that come to mind?
A: . . . When I see them, to me they are just black. When they speak to me, then I know they are West Indian, but I don't see that as a major difference between us. That camaraderie is still there, if there's two of us in the room, we know we better watch each other's backs. (Black American male teacher, age 41)

Q: What about West Indians, are there any images of them that come to mind?
A: I think of arrogance, somewhat abrupt, loud. It certainly does not pertain to all of them, but those that I have been around. They do tend to think that they know a little more than we do. (Black American female teacher, age 42)

West Indians feel very strongly that the American blacks have been brainwashed and that they are the superior group. Basically because they come from a culture that is predominantly run by Jamaican blacks or West Indian blacks. So they feel that they are in control, whereas we have never been in control of anything, and that we are very wasteful as far as education is concerned. (Black American female teacher, age 42)

When I am in the situation in which blacks are threatened as such by whites generally, I assume a position of a black man. . . . And whenever the conflict relates mainly to Guyana, or if I am discussing an issue in the Caribbean of which there is a particular feature of Guyana . . . , then in those circumstances, I am Guyanese. (Guyanese male teacher, age 36, in the United States 2 years)

I can say "hey mon," you know, . . . I can go into that dialect and with that accent walk into a West Indian club and be West Indian. I can also walk into a bar and be American. . . . But I can never stop being black. (Grenadian male teacher, age 46, in the United States 26 years)

Q: How do you think your children will identify?
A: Black American. 'Cause they're gonna be raised in a black American society and most people will ask them where they're from, they're gonna have to say America 'cause that is where they were really brought up. (Trinidadian female, age 17, in the United States 5 years)

Until some qualifier that makes a Black immigrant more known as a Black immigrant is exposed, you're going to be looked at as a Black person. And I think that if that's the case, we should work together. . . . I mean, if we're going to be treated as a group, we might as well act as one. (Joshua, an African American from Dallas, Texas)

We can see throughout history, you know, when people band together, people are able to promote a certain agenda. . . . From the outside looking in, you guys are the same. And in that way, people are going to treat you the same. And in that sense, your experiences are going to be similar. So you might as well promote that agenda. (Ahmad, a second-generation Eritrean immigrant)

SOURCES: First nine quotes: *Black Identities: West Indian Immigrant Dreams and American Realities* by Mary C. Waters, Cambridge, Mass.: Harvard University Press. Copyright © 1999 by the Russell Sage Foundation. Last two quotes: Candis Watts Smith, *Black Mosaic: The Politics of Black Pan-Ethnic Diversity*, New York: New York University Press, 2014.

DOCUMENT 3 Douglass S. Massey, Margarita Mooney, Kimberly C. Torres, and Camille Z. Charles | *Black Immigrants and Black Natives Attending Selective Colleges and Universities in the United States, 2007*

In 2004, African American Harvard law professor Lani Guinier provocatively indicted universities, both public and private, for valuing diversity over affirmative action. She claimed that "the children of African and West Indian immigrants who come from majority Black countries and who arrived in the United States after 1965" disproportionately benefited from college admissions programs. These students, she claimed, tested well because "they retain a national identity free of America's racial caste system and enjoy material and cultural advantages." Colleges preferred these students because they did not "internalize the stigma of race," which ultimately was at the root of native-born students' low test scores and because these students had educated parents and were not generally trapped in depressed inner-city schools.[80] Guinier's comments were a prompt for a study whose conclusion, which is backed by thorough statistical analysis, is presented here.

Breaking it Down Consider the nature of this document: How is it both a primary source and a secondary source? How is it similar to or different from other documents you have examined? What does the document tell us about the twenty-first-century African American community and about the difference between affirmative action and diversity? How does this evidence from this source validate or challenge the arguments made in Document 1? How does this source provide evidence of the existence of both a diverse and collective experience among both Black native and immigrant groups in the United States?

In recent years, observers have increasingly recognized the overrepresentation of the children of immigrants among African Americans attending selective colleges and universities in the United States, and this fact has become the focus of a vigorous debate about the purposes of affirmative action in higher education and whether blacks of immigrant origins are appropriate beneficiaries. The debate so far, however, has transpired largely in the absence of information about the phenomenon, and in this article we have drawn upon data from the National Longitudinal Survey of Freshmen to provide an empirical foundation for future discussions.

The NLSF surveyed the cohort of freshmen entering 28 selective colleges and universities in the fall of 1999. . . . In general, we found the overrepresentation of immigrants to be greater in private than in public institutions and within more rather than less selective schools. . . . Within the Ivy League, perhaps the most exclusive segment of American higher education, students of immigrant origin made up 41 percent of entering black freshmen.

Given that first- and second-generation immigrants make up just 13 percent of the African American population, the overrepresentation of immigrant origins is substantial within all segments of elite academia. Nonetheless, data from the NLSF suggest relatively few and generally modest differences in the social origins between black students of immigrant and native origins. In terms of most indicators — income, wealth, parental employment, parental child-rearing practices, peer support, perceptions of social distance, academic preparation, and academic achievement — the two groups are virtually identical. Demographically, students of immigrant origin are . . . somewhat more likely to come from two-parent families.

Perhaps, the most critical difference, however, is that black immigrant fathers were far more likely to have graduated from college and to hold advanced degrees than native fathers. Possibly as a result of this difference, immigrant children were more likely to attend private school, and in this setting they experienced a lower exposure to violence than the children of native blacks and modestly more exposure to members of other groups. Black immigrant students were more likely to have grown up within integrated neighborhoods and thus to have more nonblack friends and to have emerged from high school with a low susceptibility to peer influence. . . .

Although the NLSF data do not permit a direct assessment of the mechanism by which immigrant-origin students came to be overrepresented at elite colleges and universities, the fact that most indicators of socioeconomic status, social preparation, psychological readiness, and especially academic preparation are identical for immigrants and natives suggests that immigrant origins per se are not favored in the admissions process but, for whatever reason, children from immigrant families have come to exhibit the set of traits and characteristics valued by admissions committees, both those that are readily observable (grade point average, quality of high school, and advanced placement courses taken) and those that are more difficult to observe directly (self-esteem, self-efficacy, and social distance from whites).

The fact that immigrant parents are much better educated than native parents is consistent with an immigrant population that is highly selected for human capital and the drive to attain it, traits that are passed on to children to put them into a superior position for admission to a selective college or university. Once on campus, however, immigrant- and native-origin African Americans perform roughly at the same academic level. . . . Evidence of the high motivation and determination of immigrant-origin black students is that the process of college grade achievement appears to be considerably more arduous for them relative to their native counterparts. Once on campus, the advantages of high parental education appear to be erased, as immigrant blacks are less able than natives to translate parental education into high grades and are less able to convert advanced placement courses and self-confidence into academic achievement.

Ultimately, the data we have presented cannot answer the question of whether the children of black immigrants are worthy beneficiaries of affirmative action, for the answer rests largely on a moral judgment about whether the policy is a form of restitution for past racial injustice or a mechanism to ensure that selective schools continue to reflect the racial and ethnic diversity of a nation that is being transformed by immigration. All we can say is that, with several notable exceptions, black immigrants and natives display similar traits and characteristics and, more important, evince equal levels of academic preparation. Whatever processes are operating on college campuses to depress black academic performance below that of whites with similar characteristics, they function for immigrants as well as natives.

SOURCE: From "Black Immigrants and Black Natives Attending Selective Colleges and Universities in the United States" by Douglas S. Massey, Margarita Mooney, Kimberly C. Torres, and Camille Z. Charles (*American Journal of Education*, Volume 113, Issue 2, pp. 243–271). © 2007 by The University of Chicago. Reproduced by permission of the publisher.

DOCUMENT 4 *The Meeting of Cultures*

African America now looks like a South Carolinian in New York, a Guyanese in Brooklyn, a Somali in Tennessee, a Mississippian in Chicago, a Nigerian in Houston, a Haitian in Miami, and an Ethiopian in Minnesota. In the United States, all of Africa's people are slowly blending their cultures. Time will

tell whether American racism will do what it has in the past: forge a Black community and an identity around the idea of freedom. However, the following pictures demonstrate what is happening on a day-to-day level. Photo 1 is a mural for a restaurant in Brooklyn, New York, home to a very large Caribbean population. Photo 2 shows a typical hair braiding salon that could be anywhere in the United States.

Breaking it Down As you examine photo 1, consider the role food and eating play in preserving and extending one's cultural identity. What messages are conveyed by the advertisement? What does photo 2 say about the meeting of cultures? How do both of these images, taken together, illustrate how Black immigration to the United States has shaped and influenced the Black community?

Courtesy Kim D. Butler.

Frances Roberts/Alamy Stock Photo.

PRACTICING AP® SKILLS

1. **AP® Continuity and Change.** To what extent did the conditions around Black immigration in the United States change or follow a similar pattern in the 1920s and in the period following the signing of the Immigration and Naturalization Act of 1965? What evidence from the documents supports your response?
2. **AP® Causation.** Describe the reason for different educational outcomes among the children of native Blacks and Black immigrants before college. Do these outcomes exist at the university level? Why or why not?
3. **AP® Comparison.** Compare the experience of Black immigrants in the United States in the 1920s and the 1960s.
4. **Connecting to AP® Themes.** How did the migratory patterns of people of the diaspora influence the diversity of the Black American community after 1965?
5. **Class Discussion.** Discuss the degree to which Black immigrant groups are able to fully assimilate into the Black American community. To what extent are they able to maintain their cultural identity and be recognized as a member of their immigrant group?

Individual Student Project: *Evidence-Based Argument*

In the AP® Skills Workshop for Chapter 15 (p. SW15-A), we walked through how to select credible sources that are relevant to your research topic. First, we went over how key terms and reliable databases help to make an internet search more targeted and therefore more efficient. Then, we discussed how to evaluate potential sources and decide which four options provide the most comprehensive, nuanced window into a research topic.

Now that you've explored various perspectives, it's time to bring in your own opinion on your research topic. The individual student project is more than a summary of existing sources. You won't just be recapping the sources you've selected; you'll be explaining how evidence from those sources supports your own arguable **claim**. In other words, the individual research project is your chance to make an evidence-based argument. In this workshop, we'll cover how to consider, explain, and integrate several sources into a cohesive and compelling argument.

Examining the AP® Rubric

The rubric that will be used to assess your individual student project states:

- **Row B (1 point):** One point is awarded for an argument or claim that serves as the anchor for the presentation. *Students must include in their presentation their main argument or claim developed from careful study of the four selected sources. The argument or claim should serve as the anchor for the presentation and synthesize the sources and/or perspectives conveyed in the sources. The argument or claim should be more than a declarative statement of fact and must move beyond summary of individual sources.*
- **Row C (4 points):** One point is awarded for accurate evidence from each of the four sources that are discussed in the presentation. *Students must reference each source by name and must describe a specific detail or piece of evidence from each source, and how it relates to their overarching argument or claim.*
- **Row D (2 points):** One point is awarded for an explanation of one point of comparison (similarity or difference) between two of the selected sources. The comparison must be relevant to the project topic. A second point is awarded for an explanation of a second point of comparison (similarity or difference) between two of the selected sources. *Both points of comparison may be situated in the same two sources; however, each comparison must be distinct and unrelated. Both comparisons must be relevant to the project topic.*

We can put these guidelines together to articulate that a successful individual student project will include an arguable claim supported by four pieces of evidence, and will consider at least two points of comparison.

Constructing a Claim

As you learned in the AP® Skills Workshop on Document-Based Questions: Thesis Statements (p. SW7-A), a claim is an assertion that requires a defense — it has to state a position with which some people might disagree. You already know that a statement of fact isn't a claim because it can be easily verified as true or false.

Similarly, now that we're considering an in-depth evidence-based argument, we'll add that a summary of sources isn't a claim because you need to assert *your own* arguable opinion. An effective claim for your individual student project will directly answer your research question and assert an arguable position. As the rubric highlights, this claim must anchor your presentation and tie together all four of the sources.

Let's use the following sample research question to review how to craft a strong claim:

How influential was the Black Power movement in the long term?

We can imagine we've already used this research question to guide us to four credible, relevant sources, and we've briefly summarized these sources in a Selected Sources Template. Now would be a good time to pause, review that completed template, and then complete the following steps.

1. **Try out one possible position.** Put your metaphorical blinders on and imagine you've encountered only Source 1. How would you answer your research question drawing only on information from that source?
2. **Try out a few other positions.** Repeat Step 1, but with Sources 2–4.
3. **Check your gut reaction.** Review the four potential answers you drafted in Steps 1 and 2. Which answer stands out to you as the most convincing response to your research question?
4. **Add nuance to your position.** How can you revise the answer you selected in Step 3 so that it takes information from all sources into account?
5. **Add finishing touches.** What tweaks can you make to feel fully confident in your answer to the research question?

These steps should help clarify a position in response to any research question. It's important to make sure that position is an arguable claim. Take a look at the following two claims, and consider which one would provide a stronger anchor for an evidence-based argument:

Claim 1	The Black Power movement has been influential in American history.
Claim 2	The Black Power movement directly influenced grassroots political organizing of the modern day.

You may recognize that the first claim isn't really a claim at all; it's a statement of fact. After all, if the Black Power movement hadn't been influential, you wouldn't be learning about it in this AP® African American Studies course! In contrast, the second claim is specific, and some people might disagree with it. For instance, detractors could argue that the impact of the Black Power movement only extended a few years beyond its period of greatest popularity. In order to make the second assertion convincing, you'd need to provide evidence and persuasive commentary. That means it's truly an arguable claim.

When it comes time to answer your own research question using the five steps we've suggested, you'll need to revise your answer until it's an arguable claim that goes beyond a statement of fact or a summary of sources.

Gathering Evidence

In order to be convincing, a claim must be backed up by relevant **evidence** from credible sources. Now that you've crafted your claim, it's time to go back to each source and pull out the piece of evidence that best supports your claim. Look for evidence that's specific, verifiable, and easy to understand even outside of the source material's context.

Be sure as well that you're able to articulate how each piece of evidence strengthens your claim — this **commentary** is your opportunity to make your personal perspective clear. Imagine you've never read any of your sources and you've only gotten to see each piece of evidence out of context. What logical explanations would help tie all evidence to your overarching claim?

You can use a graphic organizer like the following to keep your evidence and commentary organized:

Claim:		
Evidence from source	Explanation of how evidence supports your claim	Source title

Explaining Comparisons

As noted earlier in this workshop, successful individual student projects consider two points of comparison between selected sources. By putting sources in conversation with one another, you'll add nuance to your argument and demonstrate your ability to synthesize multiple perspectives. The following sentence templates can help prompt the process of comparison:

Differences: Whereas Source __ suggests that ______, Source __ suggests that ______.

Similarities: Source __ suggests that ______. Similarly, Source __ suggests that ______.

Persuasiveness: Source __ is more convincing than Source __ because ______.

Credibility: Source __ is more reliable than Source __ because ______.

Synthesis: Because I have explored both Source __ and Source __, I now understand ______.

When it comes time to give your presentation, acknowledging commonalities and distinctions between your selected sources will help your audience understand how you progressed from exploring each source to synthesizing them into a cohesive argument.

recap

Building an Evidence-Based Argument

- To find your own position on your research topic, it can be helpful to follow the steps below:
  1. **Try out one possible position.** Put your metaphorical blinders on and imagine you've encountered only Source 1. How would you answer your research question drawing only on information from that source?
  2. **Try out a few other positions.** Repeat Step 1, but with Sources 2–4.
  3. **Check your gut reaction.** Review the four potential answers you drafted in Steps 1 and 2. Which answer stands out to you as the most convincing response to your research question?
  4. **Add nuance to your position.** How can you revise the answer you selected in Step 3 so that it takes information from all sources into account?
  5. **Add finishing touches.** What tweaks can you make to feel fully confident in your answer to the research question?
- You'll need to back up your claim with evidence that's specific, verifiable, and easy to understand even outside of the source material's context. Be sure you're able to articulate how each piece of evidence strengthens your claim.
- Explore similarities and differences between sources to add nuance to your argument and demonstrate your ability to synthesize multiple perspectives.

Activity ▸ Building an Evidence-Based Argument

Review your Selected Sources Template and then take the following steps to articulate an answer to your research question:

1. **Try out one possible position.** Put your metaphorical blinders on and imagine you've encountered only Source 1. How would you answer your research question drawing only on information from that source?
2. **Try out a few other positions.** Repeat Step 1, but with Sources 2–4.
3. **Check your gut reaction.** Review the four potential answers you drafted in Steps 1 and 2. Which answer stands out to you as the most convincing response to your research question?
4. **Add nuance to your position.** How can you revise the answer you selected in Step 3 so that it takes information from all sources into account?
5. **Add finishing touches.** What tweaks can you make to feel fully confident in your answer to the research question?

Does your answer to your research question state an arguable position in the form of a clear claim? If it does not, revise your answer until you're satisfied it goes beyond a statement of fact or a summary of sources. Then, collect the strongest piece of evidence from each source using a graphic organizer like the one below:

Claim:		
Evidence from source	Explanation of how evidence supports your claim	Source title

Finally, answer the following questions to prepare for your oral defense:

1. Explain how two of your sources provide different perspectives on an aspect of your topic.
2. Explain how two of your sources provide similar perspectives on an aspect of your topic.
3. Explain why one of your sources is more convincing than another.
4. Explain why one of your sources is more reliable than another.

5. Explain how a combination of two of your sources strengthened your argument.
6. Explain how a combination of two of your sources added depth or insight to your understanding of your topic.
7. Describe any lack of agreement or contradictory information you found as you did your research. Explain what this lack of agreement or contradiction revealed about your topic.

Multiple-Choice Questions

Questions 1–2 refer to the following.

Chisholm: I stand before you today as a candidate for the Democratic nomination for the presidency of the United States of America. I am not the candidate of black America, although I am black and proud. I am not the candidate of the women's movement of this country, although I am a woman and I'm equally proud of that. I am not the candidate of any political policies or fatcats or special interests. I stand here now, without endorsements from many big name politicians or celebrities or any other kind of prop, I do not intend to offer you the tired clichés that have too long been an accepted part of our political life. I am the candidate of the people of America. . . .

Reporter: You represent a trend for more women and specifically black women to get involved with politics and go after elected office in this country.

Chisholm: Yes I specifically recommend, do I recommend a trend for more women and specifically black women to enter into politics. . . . Yes I definitely am feeling and recognizing that as a result of over 20 years in political life, only emerging 8 years ago publicly, there is a great need for more women in the political arena. I happen to believe that there's certain aspects of legislation that probably would be given much more attention if we had more women's voices in the halls of the legislatures on the city, state, and national level. And I will — legislation that pertains to daycare centers, education, social services, mental services — the kind of legislation that has to do with the conservation and preservation of the most important resources that any nation has, and that is its human resources.

Source: Shirley Chisholm, *Presidential Announcement Speech*, 1972

1. Which of the following broader contextual trends best explains Chisholm's political ambition and perspective on Black political participation in the 1970s?

(A) By 1971, the disparity between Black and white federal political representation had been eliminated.

(B) Throughout the nineteenth century, Black women became increasingly disillusioned with politics and community leadership after being silenced or sidelined when bringing up the need for both racial and gender equality.

(C) At the time of Chisholm's campaign, the majority of Black Americans in the South were still unable to vote due to the prevalence of racial violence and discriminatory local voting requirements.

(D) Between 1970 and 2006, the number of Black elected officials in the United States would increase by sixfold.

2. Chisholm's organizational efforts most directly led to which of the following?

(A) The acceptance of Black Republicans and other Black Independents

(B) The establishment of the Congressional Black Caucus

(C) The ratification of the Equal Rights Amendment

(D) The election of the first Black president of the United States

Short-Answer Question

***Members of the Combahee River Collective*, 1980**

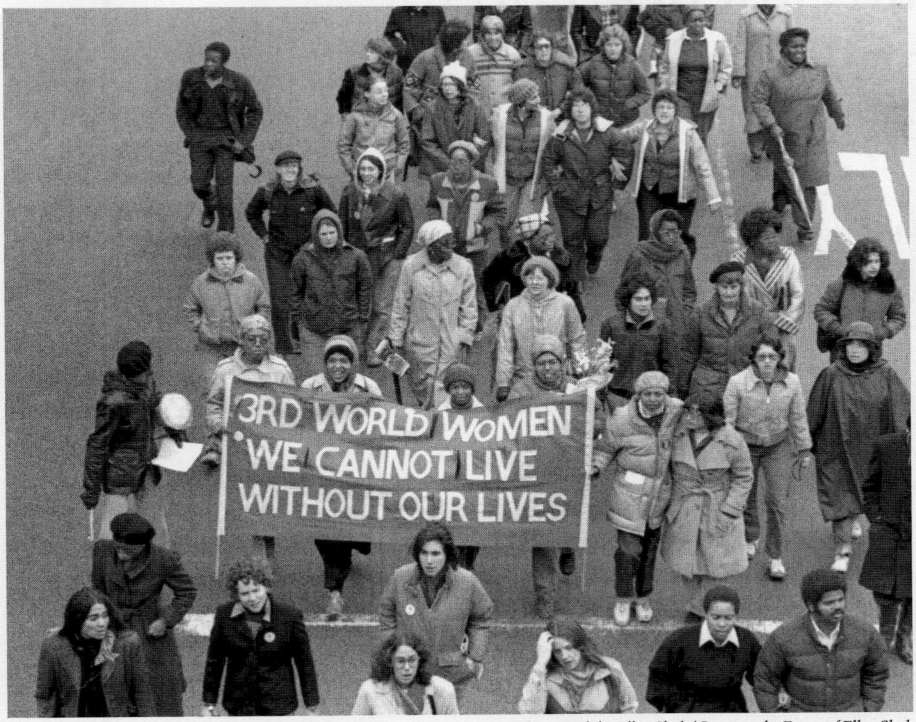

Photograph by Ellen Shub/Courtesy the Estate of Ellen Shub

1. Using the image, answer A, B, C, and D.

(A) Describe how the banner in the image reflects the central philosophy of intersectionality or intersectional feminism.

(B) Using one specific example, explain how the Black feminist movement of the twentieth century drew inspiration from eighteenth- or nineteenth-century Black women's activism.

(C) Explain how the objectives or focus of Black women's feminist organizations changed by the twentieth century.

(D) Using one specific example, explain how the idea of intersectionality became central to Black feminism during the twentieth century.

CHAPTER **17**

African Americans in the Twenty-First Century

2000–Present

CHAPTER TIMELINE

Events specific to African American history are in purple. General U.S. history events are in black. Events from the AP® Course Framework are marked with an asterisk.

2000 George W. Bush elected president

2001 *Freestyle* exhibition debuts post-Black art in Harlem

Colin Powell becomes first Black secretary of state, serving under President George W. Bush*

Al Qaeda terrorists crash hijacked planes into World Trade Center, Pentagon, and field in Pennsylvania

Afghanistan War begins

2003–2011 Iraq War

2004 Bill Cosby delivers Pound Cake speech

Bush reelected president

Barack Obama elected to U.S. Senate

2005 Condoleezza Rice becomes the first Black woman to become secretary of state*

Hurricane Katrina devastates Gulf coast

2006 Democrats retake control of Congress

Six Black teenagers charged with attempted murder in Jena Six case

2008 Obama delivers historic speech on race, "A More Perfect Union"

Global financial crisis begins

Obama elected first African American president*

2009 American Recovery and Reinvestment Act (ARRA)

Henry Louis Gates Jr. arrested at his home in Cambridge, Massachusetts

Obama wins Nobel Peace Prize

2010 Obama signs health care reform bill

Republicans gain seats in U.S. Senate, win majority of seats in House of Representatives

2011 Osama bin Laden killed by U.S. forces

Obama certifies that LGBTQ+ people can serve openly in military

2012 Black teenager Trayvon Martin fatally shot by George Zimmerman in Sanford, Florida

Obama issues executive order preventing deportation of some young immigrants

Obama reelected president

2013 #BlackLivesMatter founded after acquittal of George Zimmerman*

Shelby County v. Holder voids key section of the Voting Rights Act

2014 Obama launches My Brother's Keeper

Eric Garner dies after being choked by New York police officer Daniel Pantaleo

Black teenager Michael Brown fatally shot by Ferguson, Missouri, police officer Darren Wilson

2015 Supreme Court legalizes same-sex marriage nationwide

2016 Obama establishes diplomatic relations with Cuba

Colin Kaepernick and other NFL players began kneeling during the playing of the national anthem*

Hillary Clinton becomes the first woman to be nominated by a major party for president

Fisher v. University of Texas upholds consideration of race in college admissions

Donald Trump elected president

Husted v. A. Philip Randolph Institute allows states to use voter inactivity as a trigger to clear voting rolls

Trump v. Hawaii upholds presidential order denying entry visas to people from several Muslim-majority countries

Democrats win House majority

2019 African Americans commemorate the 400th year of their arrival in America

2020–2024 Coronavirus kills over 1,200,000 Americans; African Americans suffer disproportionately

2020 A national and global protest movement against racism sparked by police killing of George Floyd

Joseph Biden elected president

Kamala Harris becomes first African American vice president

2023 Supreme Court strikes down affirmative action programs in college admissions

2024 Kamala Harris is the first African American woman to become the Democratic Party nominee for President

Donald Trump reelected president

Barack Hussein Obama, America's Forty-Fourth President

By the time Barack Obama left his high-paying job at a Manhattan consulting firm to become a community organizer, the national civil rights and Black power movements of the 1960s and early '70s were a fading memory. It was 1983, and although the future president was unsure about what a community organizer did, he was certain that change needed to occur on the local level. With few exceptions, those around him greeted his aspirations with disappointment and skepticism. Ike, a Black security guard who worked in Obama's office building, advised, "Organizing? . . . Why you wanna do something like that? . . . Forget about this organizing business and do something that's gonna make you some money. . . . Young man like you, got a nice voice — hell, you could be one a them announcers on TV. Or sales. . . . That's what we need, see. Not more folks running around here, all rhymes and jive. You can't help folks that ain't gonna make it nohow, and they won't appreciate you trying. Folks that wanna make it, they gonna find a way to do it on they own."[1]

Ike's blunt but well-meaning advice grew from his having seen the workplace open for Black people. Jobs that had once been the exclusive reserve of white men were, by the mid-1980s, available to minorities and women. Millions of people of color were in higher occupational categories than they had been twenty years earlier.[2] The better-off Black working and middle classes had narrowed the gap in earnings that had once existed between college-educated Blacks and whites. There were advances in politics as well: in 1965, there were only about 100 Black elected officials in the nation. Ten years later, there were 3,500. As Blacks became the mayors of major cities, African Americans gained greater access to municipal services and employment opportunities. The number of Black businesses likewise increased. In 1960, Black-owned businesses numbered approximately 32,000; by 1977, that number had grown to 231,000. Given all the opportunities that seemed to be opening up, Ike had good reason to advise the aspiring young Obama to shoot for the moon.

Obama was mindful of these gains, but he thought they could be sustained only by people committed to organizing the poor at the grassroots level. In 1985, his commitment took him to Altgeld Gardens, a public housing project on Chicago's South Side, where 5,300 African Americans eked out an existence amid an abandoned steel mill, a toxic landfill, and a rancid sewage plant. Altgeld Gardens presented the kinds of problems Obama wanted to address. By the 1980s, it had been abandoned not only by whites who had left the city for the suburbs but also by Blacks who had left the inner city for the inner suburbs.

Like many other urban centers, Chicago had sworn in its first Black mayor, Harold Washington, two years before Obama arrived. Washington, however, faced the same problems as other inner-city mayors. Chicago had lost a good portion of its middle- and upper-class residents, as well as its industrial plants.

Consequently, its tax base had shrunk, leaving Washington with limited resources to address the poverty, homelessness, single-parent households, crime, drug addiction, and deteriorating health conditions that plagued the city's poor. Even if the mostly female residents of Altgeld Gardens could get Washington's attention — a big if — it was unlikely that the mayor could fix even a small part of this ailing South Side community.

Obama worked among the residents of Altgeld Gardens for three years before deciding that he would be more effective with a law degree. After graduating from Harvard Law School in 1991 and beginning a political career, he lost his 2000 bid for the U.S. House of Representatives to the Democratic incumbent, Bobby Rush, a former Black Panther who beat Obama decisively in an election nicknamed "the Black Panther against the professor." The election epitomized the tensions in Black America at the turn of the millennium. Generational tensions were clear as Rush, by that time part of the old guard, defended his turf against the younger newcomer, who had the kind of education that most people of Rush's generation could only dream of. Class and ethnic tensions also surfaced, as did the perennial issue of race, which in 2000 presented itself differently than it had in the past. Obama, a lecturer at the University of Chicago who lived

A Young Barack Obama with His Grandparents
Obama, of biracial descent, was born in Hawaii and raised mostly by his maternal grandparents, Stanley and Madelyn Dunham. His Ivy League education, political acumen, and charismatic personality identified him as someone who transcended race even before he became the first Black president of the United States in 2009. **Use the image to explain how Barack Obama reflected the growing diversity of the Black community after 1965.** *Obama Press Office/UPI/Newscom.*

in the posh Hyde Park section of the South Side, connected with his district's white constituency but failed to do so with the Black working-class residents of the predominantly Black community. His biracial half Kenyan heritage prompted the question, "Is Obama really Black? Is he Black enough?" These questions reverberated throughout millennial elections in places where a new, well-educated Black leadership class was emerging. They reflected the new reality of Black Americans — a reality that was representative of both the advances that had occurred and the divisiveness that flowed from them.

The choices Obama had available to him, the dilemmas he faced, the world he knew — these were familiar to turn-of-the-twenty-first-century African Americans. It was a period marked by the expansion of a middle class that could take advantage of the opportunities Ike, the security guard, had alluded to. Yet this period was also marked by widespread surveillance that gave rise to the highest incarceration rates Black America had ever experienced, and the ascendance of a generation that venerated individualism and diversity as it rejected the unity and communalism of the civil rights and Black power movements. Sadly, for all of the optimism generated by the election of the first Black president, many viewed the election of Obama's successor, Donald J. Trump, as a continuation of the backlash that had marked the Republican administrations of the post–freedom struggle era. In sum, this period reflected the hope that fueled Obama's successful run for president in 2008 but also the enduring racism that continued to haunt Black freedom.

Please note that this chapter includes primary sources by Black writers and speakers that use the N-word, which we have chosen to reprint in this textbook to accurately reflect these speakers' original intent as well as the time period, culture, and racism discussed in each source. We recognize that this word has a long history as a derogatory and deeply hurtful expression when used by white people toward Black people. Black speakers' and writers' choice to use this word relates not only to that history but to a larger cultural tradition in which the N-word can take on different meanings, emphasize shared experience, and be repurposed as a term of endearment within Black communities. Be mindful of context, both historical and contemporary, as you read and discuss this chapter.

The State of Black America

How has the African American population grown and become more diverse since 2000?

What social, educational, and community-building roles have religion and faith played in African American communities?

In October 2007, *Washington Post* reporter and columnist Eugene Robinson wrote an op-ed piece proclaiming that "if there ever was a monolithic 'black America' — absolutely and uniformly deprived and aggrieved, with invariant values and attitudes — there certainly isn't one now." Robinson, an African American, called for "a new language, a new vocabulary and syntax" because, he claimed, " 'black America' is an increasingly meaningless concept."[3] One month later, the Pew Research Center, an independent, nonpartisan public opinion research organization, found that 37 percent of African Americans agreed with Robinson, believing that "because of the diversity within their community, blacks can no longer be thought of as a single race."[4] The sentiment reflected the fact that African Americans were entering the new century with a diversity that challenged their age-old sense of themselves as a nation within a nation. More secure about their freedom, they were more willing to think and speak publicly about their nonracial identities and to question the need for racial solidarity.[5] Although the election of Donald Trump in 2016 rekindled for many the feeling of African Americans as a "community," bound by a heritage of oppression and united by their need for self-defense (a development we discuss later in the chapter), at the turn of the new century, a growing number of Black people were beginning to construct new ideas about racial belonging.

The Black "Community"

By the beginning of the twenty-first century, Black America had come to be characterized by class, gender, sexuality, and generational diversity. There was, however, another way to characterize differences in Black America: namely, by the way various groups related to American institutions. Similar in many respects to the twentieth-century categories delineating the middle and working classes and the underclass or truly disadvantaged, this new categorization spoke also to Black America's perception of racial progress and its sense of racial and national belonging.[6]

AP® skills

Applying Disciplinary Knowledg: What disparities emerged between the Black and white middle class in the twenty-first century?

Middle- and working-class African Americans entered the new century better situated economically than previous generations but well below the economic well-being of whites and Asian Americans. In 2006, for example, the Black median household income was just 61 percent of the white median household income, and in 2018, the National Urban League calculated the equality index — the relative status of Blacks versus whites in American society — at 72.5 percent, meaning that Blacks' income was only 72.5 percent of whites' income.[7] Home ownership for Blacks reached an all-time high in 2004, with nearly 50 percent of Blacks owning their own homes. But in the fourteen years after that, home ownership dropped to 42.9 percent; meanwhile, the white home ownership rate was 73 percent.[8] Nevertheless, by 2010, one-fourth of Black adults worked in management or professional jobs, and this figure grew to 31 percent by 2018. College enrollments of African Americans were encouraging for the first ten years of the new century, increasing by 73 percent during that time (from 1.5 million to 2.7 million students). But between 2010 and 2017, Black enrollment decreased by 19 percent (from 2.7 million to 2.2 million students). During that time white enrollment declined as well.[9]

Overall, the Black middle class was fragile. The wealth gap told the story. In 2016, the median wealth for Black families — including home ownership, stocks, bonds, and other forms — was $17,600, compared with white families' median wealth of $171,000. Put another way, the median white family had 41 times more wealth than the median Black family. The inequality did not escape middle-class African Americans. In his book *The Rage of a Privileged Class: Why Are Middle-Class Blacks Angry? Why Should America Care?*, journalist Ellis Cose described the anger provoked by the **Black tax**: the understanding that Blacks had to work twice as hard as whites to achieve the same outcomes and were held responsible for the negative actions of other Blacks. The strategy and consciousness of color blindness — the idea that race never enters into decisions affecting advancement — infuriated Blacks who, every day, experienced racism that impacted their happiness and determined their life chances. By pronouncing the death of racism, whites had effectively silenced Black protest and made any criticism of racist job relations hazardous to Blacks' employment, promotion, and interactions with coworkers. Middle-class African Americans also felt that they were always held to a higher standard when a job or a bank loan was at stake, and they chafed and grew rageful when they saw whites with less talent, less ability, and less intelligence soar ahead of them in rank, salary, and status.[10]

Black tax
A colloquial reference to the extra work African Americans must do to achieve the same goals as whites. Many also use the term to indicate that Black people, regardless of individual achievements, are held responsible for the behavior of Black people collectively.

AP® skills
Applying Disciplinary Knowledge: Define the "Black tax." Can you provide any historical evidence from previous chapters to support this concept?

While middle-class Blacks fumed over the extra hurdles they had to surmount, poor Blacks felt the full brunt of racism. Living at or below the poverty line, which in the year 2000 was about $8,000 in annual income for one person and roughly $17,000 for a family of four, about one-quarter of the African American population felt abandoned. "They really don't care too much," said a welfare recipient when asked what she thought Congress felt about women on welfare.[11] With almost half (48 percent) of all Black families single-parent, female-headed households, an astonishingly large proportion of those below the poverty line were women and children. Although the unemployment rate for African Americans dropped from a high of 15.4 percent in 2010 to 6.8 percent in 2019, poor Blacks found it difficult to find stable employment for reasons ranging from educational attainment to child care. Without stable employment, there was no way for these lower-class Blacks to live the American dream of home ownership. The victims of the most intense police surveillance, poor Blacks attended the worst schools in the nation, lived in the most dilapidated housing, had the least access to hospitals, were the most likely victims of crimes, and were the most likely to be exposed to the illicit drug and sex trade economy. Many felt unworthy. Describing how poverty generated feelings of shame in many in the Black community, a mother of an incarcerated teenager lamented, "We hate ourselves. . . . We have been programmed that it's something that's wrong with us."[12]

AP® skills
Applying Disciplinary Knowledge: Describe the obstacles faced by members of the poor Black community. What evidence from previous chapters helps explain the extent to which those problems are a continuation of historic issues?

A few Blacks, called the "Transcendent" by Eugene Robinson, managed to escape racial identification altogether. Although wealth was not their only asset — education and talent were important, too — the color green influenced their lives more than their brown skin did. Oprah Winfrey belonged in this group, as did sports stars such as Tiger Woods and LeBron James, entertainment giants like Beyoncé and Jay-Z, actors such as Samuel L. Jackson and Kerry Washington, media moguls such as Robert L. Johnson of Black Entertainment Television and Shonda Rhimes of Shondaland, and CEOs such as Ursula M. Burns at the international telecom company VEON and Robert F. Smith, founder of Vista Equity Partners. More numerous than at any other time in history, this group, having achieved fame, prosperity, and power, were not just Black Americans who had done well; they were quintessentially American and recognized as such at home and abroad.[13]

Black immigrants, on the other hand, struggled to understand what it meant to be American. The Census Bureau projects that by 2060, 16.5 percent of U.S. Blacks (not including afro-Latinos) will be immigrants,[14] and scholars have discerned that while those individuals may very well hold on to their *ethnic* identity, they will develop a *racial* consciousness like that of African Americans.[15] Racism is the reason. Coming from Black majority societies, Black immigrants are unaccustomed to being judged first by their color and only secondarily by their accomplishments.[16] The families of Mulugeta Seraw (Ethiopian), Abner Louima (Haitian), and Amadou Diallo (Guinean) learned hard lessons in American racism. Seraw was bludgeoned to death in Portland, Oregon, by a group of white skinheads; Louima was sodomized by New York policemen; and, though unarmed, Diallo was shot forty-one times by police as he reached for his wallet. All three deaths involved white men acting on their perceived ideas about Black people (rather than about immigrants). Racism, therefore, is forging a new Black community because, as noted by political scientist Candis Watts Smith, "Black immigrants' racial identity tends to be more salient when policies affect them due to their racial group membership, and this identity is mobilized in instances when there is a sense of racial threat."[17]

Similar conclusions have been suggested regarding biracials who have a Black parent and a white parent. According to the 2000 census, the first census that let respondents self-identify as belonging to more than one race, 785,000 people — or about 11 percent — claimed to be half Black and half white. The number of biracials was actually estimated to be larger than that because, historically, a person with any "Black blood" was defined as Black, and biracials — especially those with discernible Black pigmentation or features — typically checked only the "black" box on the census. By 2015, so many Blacks were checking more than one racial box that the 15-year span saw a 238 percent increase in Blacks with multiracial heritage, amounting to 2.7 million people who identified as Black/white multiracials. Not only does this suggest that the one-drop rule has changed to mean one more race in a multiple-race identity, but the fact that so many more Blacks checked more than one box suggests that African Americans no longer feel bound by the one-drop rule — the white-legislated definition of Blackness declared unconstitutional in 1967.[18] An overwhelming majority of Black/white biracials — 71 percent — choose to call themselves multiracial,[19] and even though they choose not to call themselves Black, 61 percent of white/Black biracials feel that they are seen as Black. Being seen as Black, they tend to identify as Black, [20] particularly if they are in the Black middle class. They understand that Black people do not always accept them and often ask "are you really one of us?"[21] Still, at least for the foreseeable future, African Americans can count on most Black/white biracials to feel politically and even culturally part of the Black community.[22]

Solidarity, Culture, and the Meaning of Blackness

The changes in the state of Black America have rattled its expectation of solidarity. Throughout most of the twentieth century, Black unity could be counted on to challenge the economic and political injustices caused by racism. But twenty-first-century diversity has the potential to undermine this staple of Black self-defense. For example, in the twentieth century, the Black upper class (known as the "talented tenth") was depended on to speak for — indeed, represent — the race. In the early twenty-first century, the best-educated, wealthiest, and most prominent African Americans could not be counted on to do that. For most of the twentieth century, even when Black men and women saw issues differently, they marched together. By the end of the century, however, they found themselves marching separately.

The disruption of unity is suggested by the passionate discussion of "Blackness" and who is "Black." In the twentieth century, Black people debated what they wanted to be *called* — colored, Negro, Afro-American, African American, Black — but not who was actually Black. Black/white multiracials, Black immigrants, and Transcendents have complicated the meaning of Blackness in the twenty-first century. When the professional golfer Tiger Woods called himself a "Cablinasian" in recognition of his white, Black, American Indian, and Asian ancestry, he set off a firestorm of debate. Some argued that Woods was not Black but biracial. Others believed that he had earned his Black credentials because he had experienced racism, with one commentator arguing that "before he [Woods] was famous, there were golf clubs in the U.S. that wouldn't let him play." And there were many who were outright angry about his Transcendent status. As one user of an online forum commented, "F him if he doesn't want to be considered black. When his fame has ended and white people turn on him, because he no longer benefits them, he'll want to be black."[23] Similar issues emerged during Barack Obama's 2008 presidential campaign, with many believing that Obama's midwestern white mother and Kenyan father made him something other than African American. In 2006, the novelist and columnist Stanley Crouch proclaimed that Obama was not "black like me" because he "did not — does not — share a heritage with the majority of black Americans, who are descendants of plantation slaves."[24] According to Debra Dickerson, the author of *The End of Blackness*, "'Black,' in our political and social reality, means those descended from West African slaves," and that did not include Obama.[25]

AP® skills

Applying Disciplinary Knowledge: What were the primary causes of increased division within the Black community in the twenty-first century?

AP® skills

Applying Disciplinary Knowledge: What are "transcendants"? How were Black people able to become members of this group? To what extent are they similar to Du Bois's concept of the Talented Tenth?

Although there was never a time in African American history when it could be said that "all Black people think alike," during the first ten years of the twenty-first century, researchers found racial unity on important issues to be on the decline. To be sure, compared to whites, Black people on average felt that they experienced more discrimination and that the criminal justice system was unfair to Blacks. More Blacks than whites said that poor schools, high dropout rates, unwed motherhood, and poor housing were real problems in their communities. Yet in 2007 and 2010, slightly more than half of all Black people believed that "blacks who cannot get ahead in this country are mainly responsible for their own situation." Only about one-third (34 percent)

Rashid Johnson,* China Gates, *2008

Post-Black art such as Rashid Johnson's *China Gates*, a freestanding steel sculpture, is not immediately recognizable as "Black art." Artists of this genre emphasize the diversity of the Black experience and the individuality of the artist, and the art they produce is often conceptual and enigmatic in nature. They depart from the tradition of the Black Arts movement in that they feel they do not have to directly represent Black people as a group. **How does Rashid Johnson's post-Black art compare with art from the Black Arts movement and the Harlem Renaissance?** *Rashid Johnson,* China Gates, *2008. Steel, brass, shea butter, and incense. 66 × 48 × 18 in. (67.64 × 121.92 × 45.72 cm.). Inv# RJ 09.54. Courtesy of David Kordansky Gallery, Los Angeles, California.*

blamed racial discrimination as the reason Blacks did not advance. This was an astounding change from 1994, when a majority felt that racial discrimination held Blacks back. Economics and generation made the difference. More affluent and better-educated African Americans were not only less concerned about job discrimination, unwed motherhood, and crime, but, along with younger Blacks, they were also more likely to believe that Blacks and whites had a lot in common and that the Black middle class and poor were growing apart. This, too, had changed over time. In 1986, there was less divergence between the Black poor and middle class on these issues.[26]

These changes were reflected in Black culture. The Black Arts movement of the 1960s and '70s had been founded on the ideas that black art had to mirror the Black experience, advance the politics of freedom, and boost the psychological morale of African Americans, and it emphasized the notion that Black and white art were fundamentally different. The *Freestyle* exhibition, which debuted at the Studio Museum in Harlem in 2001, announced a new direction for Black art. According to Thelma Golden, the museum's chief curator, the exhibition embodied a new **post-Black** art in that it "was characterized by artists who were adamant about not being labeled as 'black' artists, though their work was steeped, in fact deeply interested, in redefining complex notions of blackness."[27] As explained by Golden and some of the exhibition's artists, Blackness had new meaning in the twenty-first century. There were so many ways to be Black that "Black" had lost its meaning as a signifier of identity. Ironically, the unifying force of this exhibition was "individuality," which gave birth to the title *Freestyle*. Like the improvisational musician who "finds the groove and goes all out in a relentless and unbridled expression of the self," Golden believed that Black artists and Black people needed to free themselves from old ideas about Blackness and be whoever they could and wanted to be.[28]

post-Black
A controversial term differentiating Black identity at the end of the twentieth century from that during other periods in American history. Not to be confused with *post-racial*, this term emphasizes the individuality and diversity of Black Americans.

Throughout the first decade of the twenty-first century, the idea of post-Blackness stirred up intense debate among artists, writers, social critics, and scholars. Many agreed with Golden and sided with art historian Michael Harris, who argued that "an African American artist needs a cultural rootedness as a foundation."[29] But the Harvard scholar Henry Louis Gates Jr. doubted the utility of such a foundation. There were "forty million ways" to be Black, he argued. The writer and cultural critic Touré concurs: "There is no dogmatically narrow, authentic Blackness because the possibilities for Black identity are infinite."[30]

Diversity in Politics and Religion

That Black people in the early 2000s did not speak with one voice was evident in the political realm. A small minority of African Americans self-identified as conservatives, believing that Blacks who had not advanced should blame it on their own inability to compete, deficient values, and victimization mentality. They endorsed the belief that affirmative action was harmful because its beneficiaries could never be fully confident that their success stemmed from their talent and because affirmative action engendered backlash. Conservatives felt that the single parenthood and crime in Black communities could be traced to social welfare programs that fostered a debilitating dependency and irresponsible behavior. Welfare is "a license not to develop," argued the prominent Black conservative Shelby Steele in 2001. Steele felt that welfare "all but mandated inner-city inertia, . . . destroyed the normal human relationship to work and family, and . . . turned the values of hard work, sacrifice, and delayed gratification into a fool's game."[31]

AP® skills

Applying Disciplinary Knowledge: Identify and explain what Black conservatives believed were the main causes for the problems afflicting the Black community in the twenty-first century.

Although the number of African Americans who self-identified as conservative was small, a much larger number of Blacks held conservative opinions on a wide variety of issues. Again, welfare is a good example. When researchers asked Americans whether they agreed with the statement "Many people today think they can get ahead without working hard and making sacrifices," there were only modest differences between whites and African Americans; 61 percent of whites and 56 percent of African Americans agreed. When researchers presented the statement "Poor people have become too dependent on government assistance programs," the responses from Blacks and whites again differed only slightly. Blacks still believed that affirmative action programs were necessary, but a majority agreed with Shelby Steele, who advocated self-help and argued that "a group is no stronger than its individuals; when individuals transform themselves they transform the group; the freer the individual, the stronger the group; social responsibility begins in individual responsibility."[32] Ike, the security guard who encouraged Barack Obama, put it differently: "Folks that wanna make it, they gonna find a way to do it on they own."[33]

Black diversity also spawned new attitudes about Black leadership. For most of the twentieth century, when a Black leader spoke for the race, he or she spoke for most Black people. As journalist Eugene Robinson wrote, "What was good for poor people was good for black people, since so many black people were poor. Conversely, what was good for rich people was bad for black people, since so few black people were rich."

Similarly, "what was good for the established order was bad for black people, who didn't belong to the Establishment."[34] In the twenty-first century, a variety of leaders emerged to represent different segments of Black America and the American population in general, and fewer "race men and women" — Blacks who dedicated their lives to working for and representing African Americans — took up the cause of civil rights. According to National Football League Hall of Famer Lynn Swann, who in 2006 ran for governor of Pennsylvania on the Republican ticket, "We as African-Americans are as diversified as any group. . . . I don't think we have real freedom unless we have real choices." "It's a new day and a new way," said Charles Steele, head of the Southern Christian Leadership Conference from 2004 to 2009, touting the veteran civil rights organization's new slogan.[35]

AP® skills

Applying Disciplinary Knowledge: Describe and compare the Black political leaders of the 1970s and those of the 2000s, and the communities they represented. What evidence from this and previous chapters helps explain points of similarity and difference?

The new day and new way gave rise to a new kind of Black politician and a politics that reified Black diversity. Mayors such as Cory Booker of Newark, New Jersey, and Adrian Fenty of Washington, D.C., and members of Congress such as Harold Ford of Tennessee and Artur Davis of Alabama were heirs to privileges that the civil rights generation fought for and won. Unlike the politicians of the 1970s and '80s, who emerged out of the civil rights struggle and served a constituency that was overwhelmingly African American, early twenty-first-century Black politicians represented diverse communities. Like Barack Obama, whose Hyde Park district was 35 percent white when he first ran for Congress, new Black politicians had to appeal to a wider constituency and also satisfy the demands of the business people and financiers who backed them. "We're not trying to integrate lunch counters so much," said Michigan state senator Bert Johnson during his 2012 bid to unseat civil rights worker and founding Congressional Black Caucus member John Conyers Jr.[36] Some, like Booker, minimized the differences between the old guard and the new guard. "It's just a different set of challenges," said Booker. He added, "Our community needs everyone. We need not start separating a people and talking about disconnects. We need a full team on the field."[37] Others were not so sure. When asked about the relevance of people such as the Reverend Jesse Jackson — the veteran head of the Chicago-based Rainbow PUSH (People United to Serve Humanity) Coalition who was trained and mentored by Martin Luther King Jr. — a young African American minister suggested that younger Blacks in the twenty-first century face different problems and need their own set of leaders: "The reality is most of our traditional civil rights leaders don't have a clue about the hip-hop community. It's not a part of their understanding."[38]

Black church
A term often used to indicate the centrality of Black religious congregations in African American life. Traditionally, the church served as an educational, social, and civil rights center as well as a place of worship. This does not, however, indicate that all Black people attend the same church or belong to the same denomination.

The new generation of African Americans also had a different understanding of the **Black church**. In its size and theology, the twenty-first-century Black megachurch was different from the denominationally based neighborhood congregations of the twentieth century. Since most Black churches have traditionally been congregational, or not bound to follow the dictates of an overarching governing body, there has always been great diversity in and among Black congregations. But in general, the 1950s saw most Black churches prioritize issues of social justice. Pastors such as Martin Luther King Jr. and Ralph Abernathy preached the gospel but also became

T. D. Jakes
The Reverend T. D. Jakes is pastor of the 30,000-member nondenominational Potter's House in Dallas, Texas. As head of TDJ Enterprises, Jakes produces television and radio shows, films, and music that appeal to all Americans. Unapologetic about his wealth and lavish lifestyle, he resembles a corporate CEO as much as a Pentecostal preacher of the past. **Using details from this image and from this chapter, explain the evolution of the role of the Black church and its religious leaders in the twenty-first century.** *John Bazemore/Associated Press/AP Images.*

leaders of the civil rights struggle. Churches such as the Holt Street Baptist Church, where the Montgomery bus boycott was organized, or St. Augustine's Episcopal Church, where the Oakland Black Panthers operated their breakfast program, were both places of worship and centers of cooperative social justice movements. The new Black megachurch departed from the social justice model. Like the *Freestyle* art exhibition that premiered post-Black art, most Black megachurches encouraged individual internal reflection and promoted an individualistic theology of self-empowerment. In addition, unlike old-guard churches that served people who lived relatively close by, megachurch congregations number upward of two thousand members. Though grounded in the African American emotional and musical heritage, especially the Pentecostal tradition, they are often nondenominational, led by pastors with college and advanced degrees, and located in suburbs inaccessible by public transportation.[39]

Changes were also under way in the relatively small community of African American Muslims (about 2 percent of all Blacks). Before the 1960s, most Black Muslims were members of the Nation of Islam. But when their leader, Elijah Muhammad, died in 1975, his son Warith Deen Muhammad assumed leadership and moved toward more traditional Islam. By the turn of the century, only 3 percent of Black Muslims identified as members of the Nation of Islam, most of them identifying with the Sunni faith. In the new century, the number of Black Muslims grew with the arrival of African immigrants, but American-born black Muslims remained outliers. Like Christian churches, each mosque has a dominant ethnic group, and since native-born Blacks and immigrant Blacks tend to live and build mosques in separate communities, there has been little cross-cultural organization, even in the face of the hostility all Muslims have faced since 9/11. In addition, Black American Muslims orient their faith toward their experience in the United States, which is very different from the immigrant experience of Africa, South Asia, or the Middle East.

AP® exam tip

Be sure you can describe ways in which the African American population has become more religiously diverse since 2000.

Thus the new century found Black America facing new challenges. Black people were relating to the nation, to themselves, and to one another differently. There was a new culture, a new politics, a new religious life, and new theologies. As the first decade of this new century progressed, these changes would play out not in a vacuum, but on a transformative stage filled with both tragedy and joy.

Trying Times

How was economic growth in Black communities both hindered and promoted in the second half of the twentieth century?

The first years of the new millennium were trying ones in many ways. Black Americans had to work through their issues with diversity while responding to a nation that had, since the Black freedom struggle, moved consistently to the right. Just how difficult this would be was suggested by a 2001 U.S. Civil Rights Commission investigation which found that officials in Florida had effectively disfranchised large numbers of traditionally Democratic African American voters, thus giving George W. Bush a victory in the 2000 presidential election.

African Americans also had to reconcile racial loyalty with diverse Black leadership. Black officeholders, like their white counterparts, could be corrupt and ineffective. They could champion the causes of the Black middle class over the lower classes, or they could bypass racial issues altogether and prioritize their individual needs or the needs of their political party. With no movement and fewer leaders to champion the cause of civil rights, African Americans had to navigate the early twenty-first-century terrain without race men and women to guide them. The continued rise of the carceral state, the wars in Afghanistan and Iraq, and the disaster in the aftermath of Hurricane Katrina showed how bumpy the terrain had become.

The Carceral State, or "the New Jim Crow"

African Americans watched the rightward turn of the judicial system with dismay. Each election that brought a Republican president to the helm brought fears that the accomplishments of the freedom struggle would be transformed, if not actually undone, by a judicial system that endorsed the conservative ideas of reverse discrimination and color blindness. African Americans, especially those of the middle and working classes, focused their attention on affirmative action cases, where the Supreme Court increasingly narrowed the circumstances under which racial preferences could be used. When it came to college admissions, the Court generally allowed schools to consider an applicant's race in order to promote diversity in its student body while disallowing specific racial quotas. This was the decision in *Fisher v. University of Texas* (2016), where Abigail Fisher, a white woman, sued the University of Texas on the grounds that she had been unfairly denied admission on the basis of her race. Although the Court ruled against Fisher, the decision was a blow to affirmative action because the Court viewed the goal of considering race to be educational diversity rather than the original intention of compensating African Americans for past discrimination.

While the judicial system weakened affirmative action, it escalated the imprisonment of African Americans. Since the official beginning of the War on Drugs in the 1980s, the number of people incarcerated for drug offenses in the United States skyrocketed from 40,900 in 1980 to 452,964 in 2017.[40] Although the number of imprisoned Blacks peaked in 2007, when there were 592,900 Black inmates, and the number has been declining since then, Blacks are still 3.6 times more likely to be incarcerated than whites.[41] (See By the Numbers: Black Male Incarceration Rates, 2000–2017.) Despite documented reports in 2000 that "white students use cocaine at seven times the rate of black students, use crack cocaine at eight times the rate of black students, and use heroin at seven times the rate of black students" and that whites between the ages of twelve and seventeen were "more than a third more likely to have sold illegal drugs than African American youth," Black juveniles were punished more severely than white juveniles. Although the majority of illegal drug users and dealers nationwide were white, three-fourths of all people imprisoned for drug offenses were Black

AP® skills

Applying Disciplinary Knowledge: Summarize the *Fisher v. University of Texas* (2016) case. How did this ruling signal a change in the support of affirmative action since the Johnson administration?

BY THE NUMBERS Black and White Prison Population, 2000–2017

Though the number of imprisoned African Americans rose steadily in the first years of the twenty-first century, fewer Blacks have been imprisoned since 2007, and the gap between imprisonment rates for Blacks and whites has narrowed. Experts cite the effectiveness of African American protests against the unfairness of the criminal justice system, as well as the increase in the number of whites imprisoned for drugs, as reasons for the change. Still, African Americans are incarcerated at a rate that is 3.6 times that of whites. **Use both the image and information from the chapter to describe the disparity that occurred between Black and White incarceration from 2001 to 2017. What are its primary causes, and what were its effects on the Black community?**

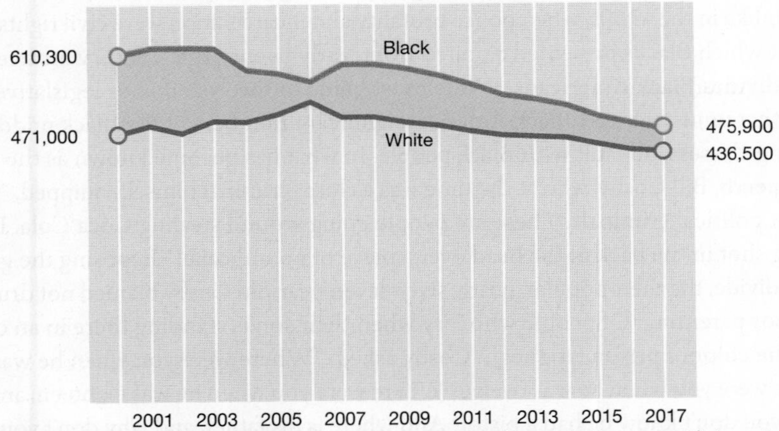

DATA SOURCE: Bureau of Justice Statistics. Data for 2000–2006: *Prisoners in 2010* (published February 9, 2012), Appendix Table 12; Data for 2007–2017: *Prisoners in 2017*, Table 3 (published April 2019).

or Latino. Young Black offenders were more likely to be transferred to adult courts and to receive longer sentences. Whereas white juveniles were more likely to be sentenced to serve time in jails, small local lockups that could be easily visited by family and friends, Blacks were more likely to be sent to prisons, large facilities far from home.[42]

These disproportionate incarceration rates can be traced, in general, back to the "law and order" agenda that both Democrats and Republicans adopted in the wake of the Black freedom movement. Although the second decade of the twenty-first century witnessed a decline in Black incarceration rates, the effects of these "zero tolerance" measures on African Americans were, and continue to be, devastating. One scholar has called the mass incarceration of Black "the new Jim Crow" because, like legal segregation, it is a system of racialized social control that maintains the racial hierarchy and "locks a huge percentage of the African American community out of the mainstream society and economy."[43] Others use the term **carceral state** to indicate the extensive surveillance and penalties employed to restrict the movement of Black people and control their behavior.

carceral state
The extensive surveillance and criminalization of public spaces that result in restricted mobility and control of people's behavior.

AP® skills

Applying Disciplinary Knowledge: Define "the new Jim Crow." How does this concept relate to the crime bills of the late twentieth century?

Incarcerated Blacks have no social mobility, not just because they are locked behind bars but also because once they have served their time and are released, they are burdened with continued punishment. Those convicted on felony drug charges, even for minor infractions, are barred by law from public housing, discriminated against by private landlords, ineligible for food stamps, and forced to disclose their felony status on employment applications. They are denied licenses for a wide range of professions, subject to regular surveillance by police and parole personnel, and denied basic citizenship rights such as voting or serving on juries. Making the analogy to Jim Crow lynching, one felon said, "They don't have to call you a nigger anymore. They just say you're a felon. . . . Today's lynching is a felony charge. Today's lynching is incarceration. Today's lynch mobs are professionals. They have a badge; they have a law degree. A felony is a modern way of saying, 'I'm going to hang you up and burn you.' "[44]

Unlike in the 1960s, when police brutality and incarceration were civil rights issues against which Blacks presented a united front, early twenty-first-century incarceration often divides Black Americans. While most bemoan the systemic or legislative inequities that unjustly target Black America, significant numbers of the Black middle and working classes find fault with Black people. In what has become known as the **Pound Cake speech**, Bill Cosby, who at the time was a closet criminal himself, quipped, "These are not political criminals. These are people going around stealing Coca Cola. People getting shot in the back of the head over a piece of pound cake!" Exposing the generational divide, the then-popular, nearly sixty-seven-year-old Cosby blamed not drug laws but poor parenting. Of people who "cry when their son is standing there in an orange suit [the color of prison fatigues]," Cosby asked, "Where were you when he was two? Where were you when he was twelve? Where were you when he was eighteen, and how come you don't know he had a pistol? And where is his father, and why don't you know where he is? And why doesn't the father show up to talk to this boy?"[45]

Pound Cake speech (2004)
A widely debated speech in which the Black comedian Bill Cosby castigated lower-class Blacks for their behavior.

Although many Blacks endorsed Cosby's perspective, large numbers cried foul in 2002, when DNA proved that the five Black youths who had been convicted of the rape and beating of a white female in the infamous 1989 Central Park Jogger case were actually innocent of the crime that had sent them to prison for anywhere from six to thirteen years. Critics lambasted law enforcement officials for their relentlessly long interrogations, which manipulated the youths into confessing to a crime they did not commit and for which the prosecutors had no physical evidence. They also criticized the press for describing the youths' behavior as "wilding," which resurrected the historic stereotype of the Black man as a violent predator. When a serial rapist confessed to the crime and it was revealed that law enforcement not only had reason to suspect him at the time of the crime but did not test his DNA until years later, many saw the case as yet another way to cripple Black males. In fact, one scholar found that beginning in 1992, three years after the incident, almost every state had passed laws to make it easier to try to sentence youths in the adult criminal justice system.[46]

The treatment of six Black teenagers in Jena, Louisiana, convinced African Americans that these laws were, in fact, aimed at them. In the **Jena Six case**, Black youths were indicted as adults on a charge of attempted murder after a schoolyard fight in December 2006 left a white teen, Justin Barker, with bruises and a mild concussion. Earlier in the school year, three white students at Jena High School had been found guilty of hanging nooses from a tree they wanted reserved for whites only; the school principal recommended suspension, but the school board overruled him, claiming the nooses were just a childish prank. Although the attempted murder charges were dropped after a nationwide outcry, the case exposed the differential punishment often meted out to Blacks and whites. What was unfair, said Charles Ogletree, a Black Harvard law professor who testified before Congress on the matter, is that the white students who hung nooses committed a hate crime, as defined by federal and Louisiana statutes, but neither the federal nor the state government chose to prosecute the white students because they were juveniles. By contrast, the Black juveniles were indicted for attempted murder and subject to up to twenty years in prison for what some believed was no more than a schoolyard fight. Ogletree asked, "Why is it that one set of conduct which violates the law was prosecuted and another set was handled within the school system? It's a disparity, it's based on race, and it's hard to justify under these circumstances."[47]

Jena Six case (2006)
The arrest and indictment as adults of six Black teenagers in Jena, Louisiana, for attempted murder after a schoolyard fight sent a white youth to the hospital.

9/11 and the Wars in Afghanistan and Iraq

On the morning of September 11, 2001, the twin towers of the World Trade Center in New York were attacked by Al Qaeda terrorists, who piloted two hijacked planes into the skyscrapers. Before the shock of that attack could sink in, hijackers flew another plane into the Pentagon in Washington, D.C. Yet another hijacked airliner crashed in a field in Pennsylvania when some passengers attempted to regain control of the plane. Americans watched in horror as the twin towers collapsed and people in New York and Washington ran for their lives. Close to three thousand people were killed in the attacks. President George W. Bush and Congress declared a war on terror, first invading Afghanistan, which was thought to be harboring Al Qaeda leaders such as Osama bin Laden, and then, two years later, invading Iraq, whose leader, Saddam Hussein, was thought to have weapons of mass destruction.

Like all other Americans, Blacks were saddened and outraged by the 9/11 attacks, but while they supported the war on terror and the war in Afghanistan, an overwhelming majority of Blacks opposed the war in Iraq. One poll showed a 40 percent differential between Black and white support for the Iraq War, although white support for the war eventually dwindled.[48] That the African American secretary of state, the four-star general Colin Powell, and the African American national security adviser, Condoleezza Rice, supported the war was proof that Blacks were getting used to expressing a diversity of political opinion.

AP® skills

Applying Disciplinary Knowledge: Describe Black support of the war in Iraq. How did the division over the war compare to African American support for wars in the past?

Reflecting African American opposition to the war, Black enrollment in America's now all-volunteer army fell from 23 percent in 2001 to 12.4 percent in 2006. Having previously enrolled in the military in larger numbers than their proportion in the general population because poor schooling and discrimination limited their opportunities, African Americans were loath to fight a war that appeared to benefit the exclusionary military defense industry and oil companies. As one Black soldier put it, "This is not a black people's war. This is not a poor people's war. This is an oilman's war."[49]

Hurricane Katrina

When the winds of Hurricane Katrina roared through the Gulf coast states of Mississippi, Alabama, and Louisiana in the early morning of Monday, August 29, 2005, Black Americans came to believe that the White House had forsaken them. Katrina devastated the Gulf coast states, but the historic below-sea-level city of New Orleans sustained the most damage when levees broke and pumps failed. By the time the hurricane departed, more than 85 percent of New Orleans was under water that was, in some places, twenty feet deep. Although both the mayor of the city, African American Ray Nagin, and white Louisiana governor Kathleen Blanco issued evacuation orders and established emergency procedures days before Katrina hit, upward of two thousand people lost their lives, and many more had to be rescued with boats and helicopters. (The number of deaths has never been confirmed. Estimates run as high as four thousand and as low as one thousand.) Countless people lost all their earthly possessions.

Although whites, Blacks, and Latinos were all victims of the storm, Katrina put the issue of racism front and center. In part this was because most of the people who were stranded for days with no food, clean water, or police or fire protection were Black and poor. Without cars, money, or out-of-town friends, they could not escape the hurricane. Ordinarily these people were invisible, but Katrina exposed their poverty. When significant federal and state aid failed to arrive in a timely fashion, many took it as a

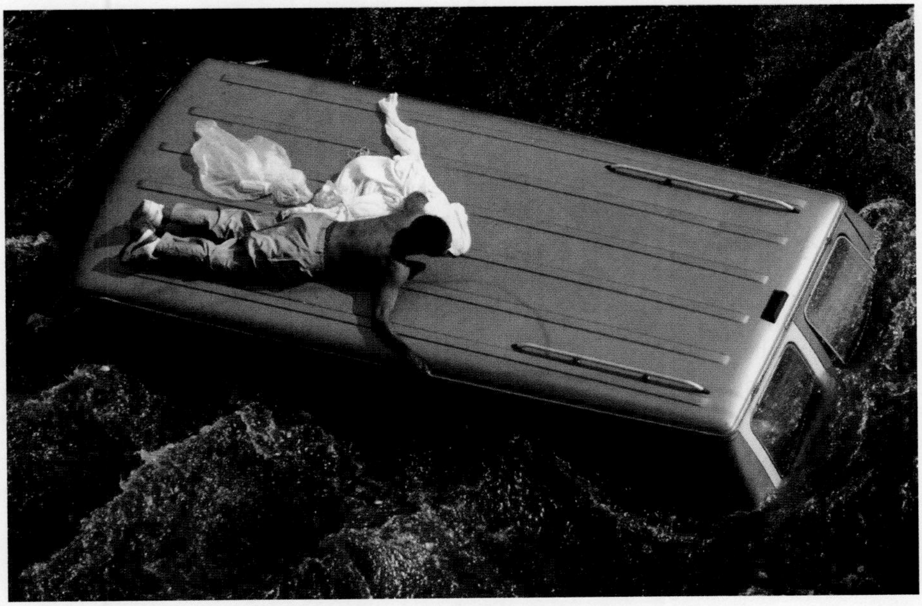

Man Clinging to a Vehicle after Hurricane Katrina
Hurricane Katrina wreaked havoc on the Gulf coast region and caused terrible human suffering. Many New Orleans residents barely escaped the rushing waters, and some who did left their homes with only the clothes on their backs. Those who survived faced additional hardships in the days and weeks following the crisis. They had to find shelter and food and keep themselves and their families, friends, and neighbors safe. Images like this one shocked the nation. **What effect might an image like this have on the national understanding of not only the destruction of Katrina but the hidden ongoing suffering of the Black community?** *Robert T. Galbraith/Reuters/Newscom.*

sign of the nation's neglect of and insensitivity to poor Blacks. African American political leaders charged that the response would have been far quicker had the hurricane hit a predominantly white city such as Palm Beach or Boca Raton, Florida. The rap artist Kanye West said what many African Americans believed: "George Bush doesn't care about Black people." When whites in Algiers Point, an upland area that had escaped the brunt of the storm and was designated an official evacuation zone, barricaded the neighborhood and shot at Blacks trying to take refuge there, many wondered why the perpetrators were not arrested for their actions.

The finger-pointing that occurred after the hurricane raised more questions than it answered. Some blamed Mayor Nagin for not evacuating the city earlier, not anticipating the problems poor people would have in evacuating, and not using city funds to strengthen the levees. He and others blamed the federal government and the Army Corps of Engineers for the poor design and maintenance of the levees. The government, they argued, had been slow to respond, and when it did, the response was ineffectual and led by incompetent officials. Others blamed the wars

AP® skills

Applying Disciplinary Knowledge: What impact did Hurricane Katrina have on the Black community of New Orleans? How did the federal and state response to Hurricane Katrina reveal deep-seated racial and economic challenges faced by Black people?

in Iraq and Afghanistan. Funds for strengthening the levees had been diverted to the war, as had high-water vehicles, Humvees, generators, and refuelers that could have been used to aid Katrina's victims. The Katrina relief effort needed human power, but 35 percent of the Louisiana National Guard and 40 percent of the Mississippi National Guard were serving in Iraq. So were Louisiana's 256th Infantry Brigade and Mississippi's 155th Armored Brigade, both of which included engineering and support battalions that specialized in disaster relief.

On the issue of Katrina, Blacks and whites were as far apart as they had been almost fifteen years earlier, when America's racial pulse had been taken by the Rodney King beating and the O. J. Simpson murder trial verdict. When polled about whether race had affected the government's response (or lack thereof), whites generally proclaimed that race did not matter, while Blacks believed it was the only thing that mattered.[50] Almost a year and a half after the hurricane, the levees had not been rebuilt, and neighborhoods, including the predominantly Black Ninth Ward, were still in shambles. Although tourist areas were up and running, victims of the storm were still living in cheaply built government trailers that were revealed to emit toxic levels of formaldehyde gas, and no one person had been appointed to oversee the recovery operation. Again, Blacks felt that race figured in the process, and whites felt that it did not.

Census estimates from 2018 seem to support Blacks. Compared to the year 2000, about 92,245 fewer African Americans and 8,631 fewer whites lived in New Orleans. The city has become more diverse: Its Latino population has increased from 3 percent to 6 percent and there are more Asian Americans. But the Lower Ninth Ward, the part of the city that experienced the worst flooding, has less than half the population it had prior to Katrina.[51] Said one displaced mother who was forced to relocate to Houston, "I wish I could go back, but I know it's impossible. . . . My whole life has been rooted up and I have been put somewhere else, somewhere I didn't ask to be at."[52]

Change Comes to America

What were the major advances in Black federal political leadership from 2000 to 2012?

Barack Obama's nomination for president in 2008 symbolized change on many levels. It was not just that, for the first time in history, a Black man would run on a major party ticket for the highest office in the land on a platform that made "change" its signature slogan. Obama was a self-identified African American who had no Black ancestor born on American soil and who in previous centuries might have been advantaged by his biracial heritage but would never have been perceived as transcending race. For all the doubts and anxiety raised by what some called post-Blackness, here was a sign that the changes that had occurred in the era following the Black freedom movement might have a positive outcome. Here was a change that Americans of all races were being asked to endorse.

AP® skills

Applying Disciplinary Knowledge: What kind of political change did the election of Barack Obama signal?

Obama's Forerunners, Campaign, and Victory

Barack Obama was not the first Black presidential candidate to be taken seriously. Congressperson Shirley Chisholm saw herself as a pathfinder when she launched her campaign for the Democratic Party nomination for president in 1972. Many Blacks ran for president on lesser-known third- and fourth-party tickets, and Jesse Jackson made serious runs for the Democratic Party nomination in 1984 and 1988. Other African Americans also blazed the trail for Obama. General Colin Powell, a Republican, served as national security adviser under President Ronald Reagan before becoming the first — and so far the only — African American chair of the Joint Chiefs of Staff. In 2001, appointed by President George W. Bush, he became the first African American to serve as U.S. secretary of state. Four years later, he was succeeded by another African American, Condoleezza Rice, who was only the second woman (after Madeleine Albright) to be appointed to the post. Like Powell, Rice had previously served as national security adviser, another first for African American women.

A combination of factors made it possible for Obama to win the 2008 election, not the least of which was his compelling personal story. Born in 1961 to a white mother from Kansas and a Black father from Kenya, he was raised in Hawaii mostly by his white grandparents, although he also spent some years in Indonesia with his mother and her second husband. Only in America, he would later proclaim, could such improbable circumstances not prevent one from becoming president of the United States.

AP® exam tip

Be prepared to explain how the Voting Rights Act of 1965 impacted the growth of Black political representation in American politics in the late twentieth and twenty-first centuries.

Obama's personal story embodied his campaign theme of "change." On the eve of the election, the nation was bogged down in two wars, with no victory in sight. Bush's economic policies of tax cuts, deficit spending to finance the wars, and deregulation of the financial markets blew up in America's face in the summer and fall of 2008. Banks folded, the credit market froze, and industry laid off workers. All Americans suffered in what became the worst financial disaster since the Great Depression of the 1930s. African Americans were disproportionately hurt by mortgage foreclosures, losing a reported $71 billion to $122 billion in housing assets.[53] Obama promised to end the war in Iraq and to rescue the American middle class. These and other ideas resonated with many Americans, including most Blacks.

Still, Obama's road to the White House was not easy. His principal rival was New York senator Hillary Clinton, the former first lady and wife of former president Bill Clinton, who was very popular with African Americans. Obama's early win in the Iowa caucuses established him as a serious contender, but over the next two months, Obama and Clinton traded primary victories. In March, the Obama campaign suffered a setback when *ABC News* aired inflammatory remarks made by Obama's pastor, the Reverend Jeremiah Wright, including Wright's contention that the 9/11 attacks proved that "America's chickens are coming home to roost."[54] As his polling numbers slipped, Obama took the opportunity to speak publicly about race, a subject he had to that point avoided addressing directly.

Colin Powell and Condoleezza Rice
The Republican Party was the first party to give African Americans top leadership positions in the executive branch. General Colin Powell and Condoleezza Rice both served as national security adviser before going on to become secretary of state. The highest-ranking Black executive branch appointees in history, these two politicians helped blaze the trail for Barack Obama. **What does this image communicate about Black political gains in the early twenty-first century? To what extent did two high-ranking officials in the Republican Party help pave the way for the election of a Black president from the Democratic Party?** *Stephen Jaffe/AFP/Getty Images.*

In his speech at the National Constitution Center in March 2008, Obama put the issue front and center. (See Appendix: "A More Perfect Union" for a transcript of this speech.) He explained how the history of slavery contradicted the principles outlined in the U.S. Constitution and noted that slavery's end, and the end of Jim Crow, was made possible by the Constitution, which promised liberty and justice for all. He lauded America's quest for a "more perfect union" and pledged to continue to bring the nation's promise closer to reality. But he challenged all races to focus on mutual understanding and a path to unity. White Americans needed to realize that Black Americans did not simply imagine injustice: they did, in fact, experience discrimination that resulted in widespread poverty, high incarceration rates, disruption of the family, and inferior schools and health care. But he also told Black Americans that they did not have a lock on suffering. White Americans, too, were hurting: Black and white Americans, he said, could either focus on the things that divided them or find the things that united them. He urged Americans of all races to go forward, united in their dedication to create the most perfect union possible.

When Hillary Clinton conceded the Democratic nomination on June 7, Obama turned his full attention to his Republican rival, Senator John McCain, who chose little-known Alaska governor Sarah Palin as his running mate. Palin immediately went on the attack, calling into question Obama's patriotism and background, saying on more than one occasion that Obama is "not like us" — language many pundits identified as thinly veiled racism.[55]

AP® skills

Applying Disciplinary Knowledge: Describe the obstacles Barack Obama faced during his presidential campaign. Can you identify other examples in American history where Black people have faced similar challenges?

In the last months of the campaign, the economy weighed heavily on voters' minds. In the fall of 2008, news sources reported that the economy was in its worst shape since the Great Depression. Nevertheless, after the collapse of Lehman Brothers, a giant financial services firm, McCain announced that "the fundamentals of our economy are strong."[56] McCain's position on the economy was one reason the Republican former secretary of state Colin Powell endorsed Obama. McCain "didn't have a complete grasp of the economic problems," Powell said.[57]

On November 4, 2008, Obama won the election, early and big. He took several states that had previously been staunchly Republican, including the southern states Virginia and North Carolina, and lost by only a small margin in Georgia. He won the swing states of Florida, Ohio, and Pennsylvania, as well as the entire Northeast, by a comfortable margin and captured the Great Lakes states of Michigan, Wisconsin, and Minnesota by double digits. By 11 p.m. on election night, news organizations had declared Obama the winner. When all the votes were tallied, he was victorious in the electoral college by a margin of 365 to 173 and had received more than eight million more popular votes than McCain. Most African Americans were especially jubilant. Oprah Winfrey, an early supporter of Obama, wept as she stood in Chicago's Grant Park to witness his victory speech. "It feels like hope won. It feels like there's a shift in consciousness. It feels like something really big and bold has happened here," she exclaimed.[58]

The New Obama Administration

Through the inauguration and the first one hundred days of the Obama administration, the president's approval ratings reached 82 percent, according to the *Los Angeles Times*. At age forty-seven, Obama was the fifth-youngest president to take office, and reporters could hardly resist drawing comparisons with John F. Kennedy, who was only forty-three upon his inauguration. Both men were strikingly handsome, and each was married to an attractive, stylish wife. After Kennedy was assassinated, his administration was often referred to as Camelot, an allusion to its idealism, and with Obama's election, there were references to a "Black Camelot." Similarly, the Princeton- and Harvard-educated Michelle Obama was compared favorably with her counterpart, Jacqueline Kennedy. And the public seemed pleased that Obama, like Kennedy, brought young children to the White House. When Malia and Sasha posed with their parents for a White House family photo, they composed a portrait few could have imagined would ever carry the caption "First Family."

In keeping with Obama's campaign pledge to roll back many Bush-era policies, the new administration outlawed the torture of prisoners detained in the war on terror, lifted restrictions on federal funding for stem cell research, and ended the ban on federal grants to international groups that provide abortion services or counseling. Obama also was true to his promises regarding the wars in Afghanistan and Iraq. On October 21, 2011, he announced the end of the Iraq War, and by the end of the year, most American troops had returned home. Obama also ordered Operation Neptune Spear, which successfully located and murdered Osama bin Laden, the Al Qaeda leader behind the 9/11 attacks. Obama began the withdrawal of troops from Afghanistan in 2011 as well, at one point affirming plans to complete the drawdown of troops by the end of 2014, but in 2015, he announced that U.S. troops would remain in Afghanistan until at least 2017. Obama's early efforts to replace American armed intervention abroad with diplomacy earned him the 2009 Nobel Peace Prize. When asked whether Obama deserved the prize so early in his tenure as president, the Nobel Committee cited the hope that he had inspired around the world and the deep changes occurring because of his promise to reduce nuclear weapons and ease U.S. tensions with Muslim nations.[59]

American Recovery and Reinvestment Act (ARRA) (2009)
A measure intended to boost the economy that included tax incentives, expansion of unemployment benefits, aid to low-income workers and retirees, and money for infrastructure improvements.

Of the legislation enacted in Obama's first one hundred days, perhaps the most controversial was the **American Recovery and Reinvestment Act (ARRA)**. Passed on February 13, 2009, the $787 billion stimulus package was intended to bolster the faltering economy and included tax incentives, expansion of unemployment benefits, aid to low-income workers and retirees, and money for infrastructure improvements. The vote was largely partisan, with no Republican support for the legislation in the House and only three moderate Republicans voting for it in the Senate. Reacting to the immense price tag, conservatives across the country organized protests against what they termed Obama's "obesity" spending. The protests increased in March and April, when Obama directed the U.S. Department of the Treasury to make loans to General Motors and Chrysler, allowing those companies to restructure so they would not close down and throw hundreds of thousands of people out of work. Over the following months, and especially when Obama and congressional Democrats introduced plans to revamp health care in July, opposition to government spending coalesced into the Tea Party movement, a loose affiliation of national and local groups. Sarah Palin reemerged as the unofficial leader of the movement, which over the summer of 2009 disrupted town hall meetings convened nationwide to inform the public about the proposed health care reform bill.

After a long and divisive battle, the two bills comprising Obama's health care program passed Congress in March 2010. Supporters of the Patient Protection and Affordable Care Act and the Health Care and Education Reconciliation Act praised

Obama Family Portrait, 2015
One of the things that made Barack Obama appealing to Americans, especially African Americans, was the traditional image his family projected. Before Barack became president, Michelle Obama had been a working mom, and the two of them had had to balance the pressures of work and home life while raising well-adjusted children and paying back student loans. Given how social scientists and policymakers had pathologized African American family life, Blacks took particular delight in celebrating this two-parent family with visibly dark skin. **What does this portrait reveal about Black political leaders during the early twenty-first century? What does it signal about the experience of the Black middle class during this time?** *Pete Souza/The White House/SIPA/Newscom.*

the provisions, which, broadly summarized, guaranteed medical coverage to everyone, including the poor, and prevented insurance companies from raising premiums on the sick, denying claims based on preexisting conditions, or establishing coverage caps. The Tea Party derisively labeled the legislation "Obamacare" and vowed to repeal it. They and other opponents charged that the provisions related to government subsidies to help the poor purchase insurance would swell the federal budget and give the government license to interfere in what ought to be a private concern. They also argued that the provision requiring everyone to purchase insurance violated Americans' right to freedom of choice and was unconstitutional. In June 2012, the Supreme Court ruled against Obama's opponents. In a five-to-four decision that upheld the new health care law, the Supreme Court ruled that the government's power to tax gave it the power to require everyone to purchase health insurance.

AP® skills

Applying Disciplinary Knowledge: What bills and policies did Obama support during his first term? What caused the backlash that followed?

Some Tea Party supporters objected as much to Obama himself as to his policies, sponsoring websites questioning his U.S. citizenship and displaying placards with patently racist language and images at rallies. Former president Jimmy Carter spoke out against the extreme rhetoric, saying that "when a radical fringe element of demonstrators and others begin to attack the president of the United States as an animal or as a reincarnation of Adolf Hitler or when they wave signs in the air that said we should have buried Obama with Kennedy, those kinds of things are beyond the bounds."[60] Carter drew fire from Republican leaders, whom he also took to task for not condemning the attacks as racist and dangerous. A sign of the diversity of opinion that now characterized Black America was the response that came from Michael Steele, who had become the first African American head of the Republican National Committee in early 2009. "President Carter is flat-out wrong," he said. "This isn't about race. It is about policy."[61]

Racism Confronts Obama in His First Term

post-racial
A controversial term used to indicate that racism no longer inhibits the life chances of people of color in America. Not to be confused with *post-Black*, this term is often used by conservative Blacks and whites.

Ironically, although America had its first Black president, race as a policy issue became off-limits. For many Americans, Obama's election signaled the end of race as a problem. The country, they argued, had entered a **post-racial** era, in which Martin Luther King Jr.'s dream of people being judged by the content of their character rather than the color of their skin was finally a reality. Those who pointed to the disparity between white and Black incomes, education, wealth, and incarceration were called unpatriotic and accused of being divisive. Saying that America had entered a new age, Sarah Palin asked, "Isn't it time we put aside the divisive politics of the past once and for all and celebrate the fact that neither race nor gender is any longer a barrier to achieving success in America — even in achieving the highest office in the land?"[62]

AP® skills

Applying Disciplinary Knowledge: What does *post-racial* mean? Using the information from this chapter about economic, social, and political developments of the early 2000s, evaluate the extent to which Black Americans lived in a post-racial society.

During his campaign, Obama gave the memorable speech on race that was celebrated as the most significant in years, but during his administration, he had to walk a fine line. When he spoke his mind about racial disparity, he was accused of being a Black partisan, unrepresentative of all Americans. When he did not address racial issues, either in speeches or in policy initiatives, he was criticized for being so transcendent as to have forgotten how hard it was to be Black in America.

Obama's comments regarding two racially charged incidents show just how difficult the issue was for him. In July 2009, the Harvard professor Henry Louis Gates Jr. was arrested at his home in Cambridge, Massachusetts, for disorderly conduct. Police had arrived at the professor's residence after receiving calls that someone was burglarizing the home. It turned out that the reported "burglar" was Gates himself, trying to unjam his front door, but the police demanded proof that Gates was the owner of the house and that he was who he claimed to be. After Gates showed police his driver's license and Harvard identification, an altercation ensued. Gates was angry at what he took to be an incident of **racial profiling** — the use of race, rather than specific evidence, to determine how a person should be treated.

racial profiling
Using race, rather than specific evidence, to determine how a person should be treated.

Obama's impromptu comments about the incident, made at the end of a news conference on health care reform, intensified a debate that had been passionate from the start. Not having witnessed the event personally, Obama at first hesitated to answer a question about the role race might have played in Gates's arrest. Yet he did note the "long history in this country of African Americans and Latinos being stopped by law enforcement disproportionately." After joking that he would get shot if he tried to unjam the door to his home, the White House, Obama said that the "police acted stupidly" when there was already proof that Gates was in his own house.[63]

The firestorm of criticism that followed Obama's comments forced him to make the incident a "teachable moment." In order to demonstrate that he did not, as critics maintained, hate white people or wish to undermine the police, Obama invited Gates and James Crowley, the arresting officer, to the White House, where he and Vice President Joe Biden sat down with them to work out their differences in what was colloquially called the "beer summit." If the incident proved anything, it was that race still mattered in America, and the post-racial ideal had not yet been achieved.

In 2012, the Trayvon Martin case similarly demonstrated the dilemma that race posed for Obama and the nation. On February 26, Martin, a Black teenager in Sanford, Florida, who was on his way home from buying candy and an iced tea, was shot and killed by a neighborhood watch volunteer named George Zimmerman. Interracial protests erupted nationwide when Zimmerman was not arrested for the killing. Critics of the police claimed that Martin had been a victim of racial profiling. When Obama was asked about the case, he said, "If I had a son, he'd look like Trayvon, and I think they [his parents] are right to expect that all of us as Americans are going to take this with the seriousness it deserves and that we're going to get to the bottom of exactly what happened."[64] Republican presidential hopeful Newt Gingrich called Obama's comments "disgraceful" and "appalling."[65] Although Obama's aides reiterated the president's feeling that the incident was a tragedy for the country, the controversy nevertheless illustrated how difficult the subject of race was for a Black president governing a country that many believed no longer had to grapple with race.

AP® skills

Applying Disciplinary Knowledge: To what degree was Obama free to speak on race issues as president? Use evidence from this chapter to support your position.

The 2012 Election

In the midterm elections of 2010, Democrats lost six seats in the U.S. Senate and sixty-three seats in the House of Representatives. The big winners were the Tea Party candidates. In 2012, after months of debates, Mitt Romney, former Massachusetts governor and cofounder of the investment firm Bain Capital, emerged as the Republican presidential candidate. He chose Wisconsin congressperson and Tea Party favorite Paul Ryan as his running mate. The Romney/Ryan ticket advocated tax cuts that would reduce taxes for corporations and wealthy Americans; across-the-board deregulation; increased military spending; and dramatic cuts in federal spending for programs like Medicaid, subsidies for low-income housing, food stamps, and financial aid for college students. In their focus on entitlement programs, Republicans also argued that President Obama and the Democrats fostered government dependency and opposed individual responsibility.

AP® skills

Applying Disciplinary Knowledge: Based on the policies and bills Obama championed during his presidency, describe where his administration and second presidential campaign platform fell on the spectrum of Black "old" and "new" guard politicians discussed on page 690.

For his part, Obama championed the middle class and Democratic principles. In campaign speeches, he argued that America could not afford to return to the policies that had resulted in the worst economic downturn since the Great Depression. Deregulation of corporations and banking had hurt the middle class, as had a Republican tax policy that benefited the extremely wealthy. Obama and his vice president, Joe Biden, touted their health care program, their bailout of the automobile industry, their opposition to shipping jobs abroad, their commitment to manufacturing jobs — especially clean energy jobs — and their support for a woman's right to equal pay for equal work as well as abortion rights. Democrats also lauded Obama's support of same-sex marriage, something he announced just months before the election. (Three years later, in *Obergefell v. Hodges*, the Supreme Court ruled that the Fourteenth Amendment requires states to recognize and issue licenses for same-sex marriages.) Another change that came late in the election cycle had to do with the nation's immigration policy. Throughout his first years in office, Obama had called on Congress to pass the Democratic-backed DREAM Act, a legislative proposal to give immigrants who had entered the country before the age of sixteen and who had been here for five years a path to citizenship. As the 2012 election approached, Obama, who had come under criticism for deporting close to 400,000 illegal immigrants annually since he became president, used his executive power to sign into law a measure that allowed this same cohort to remain in the United States and work without fear of deportation for at least two years.

As both candidates crisscrossed the nation, delivering their platforms to voters, campaign financing and voter fraud emerged as issues. In some states, Republican lawmakers tried to institute measures limiting early voting periods, requiring government-issued photo IDs at the polls, and excluding felons from the voter rolls. Advocates of these laws insisted that such measures bolstered the integrity of the voting process, but voting rights activists believed that they disproportionately impacted African American, Latino, young, disabled, elderly, and homeless voters, for whom, for example, photo IDs were not always easily attainable. As the election drew nearer, many of the restrictive voting laws were struck down in the courts.

The race was not as close as predicted. African Americans, Asians, LGBTQ+ people, Latinos, women, and young people voted in record numbers for Obama, who emerged victorious with a nearly five-million-vote margin over Romney in the popular vote and an electoral college victory of 332 to 206. Obama's victory made him only the fourth Democratic president — Woodrow Wilson, Franklin D. Roosevelt, and Bill Clinton were the others — to be elected to a second term since the beginning of the twentieth century. Foreshadowing things to come was the election-eve flurry of tweets that came from Donald Trump, the then star of the popular television show *The Apprentice*. At 12:33 a.m. he tweeted: "This election is a total sham and a travesty. We are not a democracy!" As millions of Americans celebrated the reelection of the nation's first African American president, Trump tweeted: "Our country is now in serious and unprecedented trouble . . . like never before."[66]

Moving Forward

What were the major advances in Black federal political leadership from 2012 to 2016?

From the outset, Republicans made it clear that they would be no more cooperative during Obama's second term than they had been during his first. Gridlock came to characterize relations between the White House and Congress, especially after the 2014 midterm elections gave Republicans a majority in both the Senate and the House of Representatives. Nevertheless, Obama used his victory as a mandate to do as his campaign slogan had promised: press "forward." The president worked with Congress when possible; otherwise, he used the powers of the executive branch to push his agenda. The Democratic losses in the midterm elections paradoxically seemed to embolden Obama, as he continued to use executive orders to bypass a defiant Congress in both foreign and domestic policy. And despite congressional complaint — and to the approval of African Americans — Obama became more vocal about race and racism in America.

Obama's Second Term

Both in foreign policy and in domestic policy, Obama undertook new initiatives while maintaining focus on old problems. The war in Afghanistan, for example, still waged. During his 2012 campaign, Obama had pledged to bring the war to a close by the end of 2014, and he reaffirmed this promise in his 2013 State of the Union address. However, the spread of Al Qaeda and the rise of a new terrorist group — the Islamic State, or ISIS — forced the Obama administration to rethink those plans, and in October 2015, Obama announced that around five thousand U.S. troops would remain in Afghanistan until after his term ended in 2017. Changes in policy toward Iran and Cuba marked Obama's new initiatives. In July 2015, the Obama administration announced a deal with Iran in which the economic sanctions that had been imposed and enhanced since 1979 would be withdrawn in exchange for Iran agreeing to severe restrictions on its nuclear weapons program. On another front, Obama used his executive powers to reestablish diplomatic relations with Cuba. Reasoning that America would exert a more positive influence on these nations through open contact than it would through isolating punitive measures, Obama said, "The progress that we mark today is yet another demonstration that we don't have to be imprisoned by the past."[67]

On the domestic front, two Supreme Court decisions greatly impacted African Americans. In *Shelby v. Holder* (2013), the Court struck down the heart of the 1965 Voting Rights Act when it declared that states and counties with a previous history of discrimination did not need federal approval to change voting laws. Despite Attorney General Eric Holder's argument that federal oversight had ensured minority voting rights, the Court held that because the laws that defined what was and was not discriminatory had not been updated, it was impossible to determine whether voting municipalities were in fact violating the law. Clarence Thomas, the only African American justice, voted with the majority in the five-to-four decision. The ruling effectively killed the Voting Rights Act; Congress could pass legislation explicitly delineating discriminatory behavior, but it is unlikely to do so as long as Republicans control the Senate. Without federal oversight, states are freer to pass voter ID laws and other measures that have been shown to hinder minority voting.

African Americans fared better in the Supreme Court's June 2015 decision in *King v. Burwell*, upholding Obamacare. In the first five years immediately following enactment of the health care legislation in 2010, congressional Republicans held more than fifty votes attempting to weaken or repeal the Patient Protection and Affordable Care Act, which provides federal subsidies to millions who would otherwise be unable to afford medical insurance. The *King* decision resolved a dispute over language in the bill that allowed federal coverage in state plans. It was the second major defeat on this issue for the Court's conservative contingent, which again included Justice Thomas. Speaking of his administration's victory in the case, Obama predicted that "the Affordable Care Act is here to stay"[68] — a statement that expressed more optimism than fact since the president's signature domestic achievement continues to face challenges in both Congress and the Supreme Court.

Nevertheless, the decision boded well for Obama's relationship with African Americans, many of whom were critical of the president for failing to explicitly address Black issues, despite his receiving 96 percent of the African American vote in 2008 and 93 percent of it in 2012. In his second term, Obama gave more public attention to racial inequality. One fact he emphasized was that the Affordable Care Act enabled more African Americans than ever before to obtain medical insurance. According to the Office of the Assistant Secretary for Planning and Evaluation, during Obama's second term, the uninsured rate among Blacks declined from 22.4 percent to 12.1 percent, and an additional 2.6 million adults gained coverage.[69]

Obama also turned his attention to the criminal justice system. In 2013, Attorney General Eric Holder directed the Justice Department to drop the federal mandatory minimum sentencing requirements that had sent so many African Americans to jail for long periods of time for minor drug offenses. The policy change decriminalized some drug offenses and allowed judges and prosecutors to be more lenient in punishing others. In addition, Obama commuted the sentences of ninety inmates who had been sent to prison in the 1980s for drug offenses that he believed did not merit the long sentences mandated by the drug laws of that era. To underscore his commitment to criminal justice reform, Obama toured the El Reno federal prison in Oklahoma in July 2015 and met with inmates there. This dramatic move made him the first sitting president to visit a penitentiary. In another first, Obama appointed Loretta Lynch to the position of U.S. attorney general after Eric Holder, the first African American to hold that position, stepped down. The appointment, which came after Senate Republicans had blocked the nomination for five months, made Lynch the first African American woman to serve in that role.

Refusing to capitulate to truculent Republicans in the House and Senate, Obama went before the NAACP at its annual convention in July 2015 and called on Congress to pass laws reducing mandatory sentencing and preventing employers from asking job applicants about their criminal history. He also announced that he had asked the attorney general to conduct a review of the use of solitary confinement in federal prisons. This request was a response to the suicide of Kalief Browder a month earlier. Browder was sixteen when he was arrested for stealing a backpack in the spring of 2010. Unable to raise the $3,000 bail, Browder awaited trial in prison for three years, spending much of that time in solitary confinement. Although the charges were ultimately dismissed, the ordeal took a toll on Browder. "I'm not all right. I'm messed up," he told a journalist in the fall of 2014, nine months before he took his life.[70]

My Brother's Keeper (MBK), a $200 million initiative launched by the Obama administration in February 2014, was designed to help young men like Browder. In a White House report on the economic costs of keeping Black boys undereducated, jobless, and exposed to the criminal justice system, Obama outlined the MBK program, which works to get business, church, and civic leaders engaged in establishing and financing mentoring programs for boys and young men of color. My Brother's Keeper aims to ensure that, among other things, boys learn how to read by third grade; graduate from high school and receive education and training beyond that; become gainfully employed; and stay safe from violent crime. In practice, MBK involves private businesses like the National Basketball Association, the Citi Foundation, and the College Board in projects that break down stereotypes and develop career readiness skills.

> **AP® skills**
>
> **Applying Disciplinary Knowledge:** To what extent was the Obama administration able to further the goals of the Black freedom struggle? What setbacks occurred during his presidency?

Despite Obama's insistence that he would do more if he had a cooperative Congress, critics complained that Obama's approach was not extensive enough. Many wanted sweeping legislation to reform the criminal justice system; others wanted a comprehensive jobs program. They pointed to the Black unemployment rate, which remained significantly higher than for whites through the ups and downs of the recovery. Obama also took a lot of criticism for not including girls within the scope of the My Brother's Keeper initiative. Law professor Kimberlé Williams Crenshaw spoke for many Black women when she argued that Obama's focus on males amounted to "an abandonment of women of color, who have been among his most loyal supporters." Crenshaw pointed out that Black girls grew up in the same impoverished households, attended the same underfunded schools, and were just as exposed to violence as Black boys, and they were more likely than other females to be victims of sex trafficking and domestic violence. And Black women's income, argued Crenshaw, was less than that of either white or Black men.[71] Although many shared Crenshaw's frustration over the exclusion of Black females from My Brother's Keeper, others noted that the program fell short of making the kind of institutional changes that would alter the racism that structured education and employment in America.

While critics debated the merits of Obama's initiatives, Obama himself became more vocal about racism. In July 2013, a few days after George Zimmerman was acquitted of murder charges in the death of Trayvon Martin, Obama addressed the American people as a Black man in America. Speaking for and about African Americans, he told the nation that, before he became a senator, he had been racially profiled while shopping and knew what it felt like to have people fearfully lock their car doors as he walked down the street. He asked white Americans to consider the context of Black peer violence and to understand that African Americans were not dismissive of it. He also asked them to consider whether Trayvon Martin had the right to defend himself against a threatening, armed assailant. Making it clear that America had not entered a post-racial era, Obama called for programs to help Black male youth (the genesis of My Brother's Keeper), and he called on Attorney General Eric Holder to review federal incarceration guidelines (the genesis of Holder's changes to federal minimum sentencing requirements).

AP® skills

Applying Disciplinary Knowledge: Compare and contrast Obama's public remarks and stance on racism and race relations in the United States during his first and second terms.

Obama made more impassioned remarks on race in his eulogy for the Reverend Clementa Pinckney, a pastor and state senator who was killed along with eight other African Americans after Dylann Roof opened fire at a Bible study inside the Emanuel AME Church in Charleston, South Carolina, on June 2015. A white supremacist, Roof reportedly made racist statements before and during the attack, and he had previously set up a website on which he posted a photo of himself holding a Confederate flag. At Pinckney's funeral, Obama once again spoke not just as the nation's president but as an African American. He talked about the Black church and how it had historically nourished African Americans and the American principles of liberty and equality. He argued for the removal of the Confederate flag from the state capitol of South Carolina and asserted that the flag was not just a symbol of a proud southern heritage but a painful reminder of slavery and Jim Crow. And he urged Americans to recognize that racism did not manifest only in racial slurs but also in the "impulse to call Johnny back for a job interview but not Jamal," a reference to job discrimination. Obama called on people to roll up their sleeves and do the hard work of eradicating racism.[72]

African Americans in the Shadow of Ferguson

The way police patrol African American neighborhoods directly relates to the issue of mass incarceration. An inordinate number of African Americans are imprisoned for minor offenses because they are more likely than whites to be arrested. Many urban police departments have adopted the **broken windows theory** of policing, which holds that if minor crimes are kept to a minimum, then major crimes are unlikely to occur. This approach has manifested itself in **"stop and frisk"** programs, in which citizens are stopped and patted down for weapons and other contraband. According to the New York Civil Liberties Union, in New York City, where police must record all stop-and-frisk encounters, pedestrians were stopped by the police 685,724 times in 2011, and 88 percent of those stopped were completely innocent. Moreover, 56 percent of those stopped were Black, 29 percent were Latino, and only 11 percent were white.

African American complaints that broken windows practices and stop-and-frisk policies resulted in police harassment and civil rights violations sparked a debate that led to the reduction of such stops in New York and other cities, but concerns arose over another, more distressing phenomenon: the number of African Americans killed each year by police officers. When eighteen-year-old Michael Brown was killed in August 2014 by a policeman in Ferguson, Missouri, protest against the shooting energized a movement begun after George Zimmerman was acquitted of killing Trayvon Martin. **#BlackLivesMatter**, the movement's moniker, compelled the nation to take a candid look at the number of African Americans murdered by police each year. (See AP® Working with Sources: #BlackLivesMatter, pp. 717–32.) Although local police departments were woefully negligent in keeping officer shooting statistics, the numbers that were available were startling, as were the individual cases that made it onto nightly news broadcasts. For example, a *Washington Post* study revealed that in the first five months of 2015, 385 people were shot and killed by police nationwide, and Blacks were killed at three times the rate of whites.

When investigators from the Department of Justice and other agencies and organizations looked behind the violence in Ferguson, they found much that was disturbing but not atypical. Ferguson had once been 80 percent white, but when Black families moved to Ferguson, whites fled. In 2014, Ferguson's population was 69 percent Black, but the mayor and police chief were both white, as were five of six city council members (though in April 2015 two African Americans were elected to the Ferguson City Council, including its first African American woman). Blacks were not represented on the city's school board because few owned enough property to induce them to establish political roots. Of the fifty-three officers in the Ferguson Police Department, only three were Black; on the other hand, according to statistics kept by the state attorney general's office, Blacks accounted for 86 percent of traffic stops in the city and 93 percent of the arrests resulting from those stops. Economic indicators were equally startling. In the St. Louis metro area, which includes Ferguson, the unemployment rate for young African American men between the ages of sixteen and twenty-four was 47 percent in 2012, compared to 16 percent for young white men; the poverty rate

broken windows theory
A criminology theory that holds that if small crimes are left unaddressed, bigger, more serious crimes are sure to follow. For example, if the windows of a building are not repaired, vandals will break more windows, and soon the building itself will be burglarized. Cities that adopt the broken windows method of policing closely monitor behavior such as loitering and public alcohol and drug consumption in order to prevent crimes like larceny and murder.

"stop and frisk"
Otherwise known as a "Terry stop"—after a 1968 Supreme Court decision that upheld the constitutionality of such stops—stop and frisk is the practice by which police detain and search anyone who appears to be engaged in suspicious activity. While some Blacks and police argue that stop-and-frisk laws, which are used in tandem with broken windows policing, are necessary to keep a community and the police safe, most Blacks and Latinos complain that stop and frisk amounts to police harassment of mostly innocent people. They believe that people of color are more likely than whites to be detained and patted down, which they say is unfair.

#BlackLivesMatter
The hashtag for a national movement that protests all the ways that racism destroys Black lives, including the state-sanctioned killing of Black people by the police and the mass incarceration of people of African descent.

AP® skills

Applying Disciplinary Knowledge: What are the causes and goals of the #BlackLivesMatter movement? How does it fit into the context of the Black freedom movement?

between 2007 and 2012 was consistently two to three times higher for Blacks than for whites. According to a Brookings Institution study, "As dramatic as the growth in economic disadvantage has been in this community, Ferguson is not alone."[73] That Blacks living in suburban neighborhoods outside of a hundred other large metropolitan areas experience some of the same economic disadvantages as Blacks in Ferguson was demonstrable proof that, despite the two-time victory of Barack Obama, America had not yet become post-racial.

Backlash, Again: African Americans in the Age of Trump

What did Trump's election mean for the political advancements Black people had made since the twentieth century?

To what extent was Trump's administration a continuation of late twentieth-century and early twenty-first century Republican administrations?

Running on a platform aimed at undoing the policies of the Obama administration, Republican Donald Trump defeated Democrat Hillary Clinton on November 8, 2016, and became the forty-fifth president of the United States. Clinton, the first female nominee of a major party, made history when she was nominated and subsequently won the popular vote by close to three million votes. But Trump's electoral college victory sealed the day for the Republicans, who also won both houses of Congress. And because the Republican-controlled Senate had refused to consider Obama's nominee during the president's last year in office, a new Supreme Court appointment was also in Republican hands. While it is too soon to know the full import of the Trump presidency for African American history, many have experienced it as a backlash against the Obama years.

Making America Great Again

The *USA Today* headline "Trump's Victory Leaves Black Community Reeling" was an understatement.[74] Throughout Obama's presidency, Trump had been a leading supporter of the birther movement, which falsely claimed that Obama was an illegitimate president because he was not born in the United States (a constitutional requirement for the office). Trump also questioned the legitimacy of Obama's college and law school credentials, saying, "How does a bad student go to Columbia and then to Harvard?" When candidate Trump promised to "make America great again," most Black people, including the late Nobel Laureate Toni Morrison, interpreted it to mean that he was going to "make America white again."[75] White supremacists shared that interpretation. David Duke, former Imperial Wizard of the KKK, applauded Trump's election, claiming "our people have played a HUGE role in electing Trump!" Larry Davis, the founder and director of the Center on Race and Social Problems at the University of Pittsburgh, compared Trump's election to the end of the Reconstruction era, when the

Oval Office Meeting, 2016

In the week following his election victory, Trump met Obama face-to-face for the first time at the White House for a transition meeting. Trump disparaged Obama throughout his presidency and spent several years promoting the false claim that Obama was not born in the United States. During the 2016 campaign, Obama had attacked Trump's judgment, motivations, and fitness for office. Nonetheless, the meeting was reported to be cordial. **To what extent was the transition from Obama to Trump a continuity with previous major political shifts during and after the Reconstruction era and the Civil Rights movement? Identify the causes and explain the effects of this transition.**

Jim Watson/AFP/Getty Images.

federal troops that had protected newly freed Blacks from whites were withdrawn: "I try to put myself in their place and what it must have been like to know that the group that was looking after you is no longer looking after you. It's stunning for the country."[76]

In his first year in office, Trump signed legislation, issued executive orders, and rescinded rules that undid 130 Obama-era initiatives.[77] He intentionally appointed cabinet officials whose ideas and policy orientation were opposed to those of the Obama administration, and during his first year in office, there were twenty-two unsuccessful attempts to kill or revise the Affordable Care Act, Obama's signature health care legislation. At the same time, Trump was able to leave a conservative imprint on the federal courts that will extend well beyond his presidency: he appointed three Supreme Court justices — Neil Gorsuch, Brett Kavanaugh, and Amy Coney Barrett — about one in four of the nation's federal appeals court judges, and one in seven of its district judges. In total, roughly 5 percent of the federal judges Trump appointed during his term were Black; about 65 percent were white men who were generally more conservative than those they replaced.[78]

AP® skills

Applying Disciplinary Knowledge: What major policies were carried out during Trump's presidential term? To what degree did these policies mirror the political backlash to the Civil Rights movement that occurred in the 1970s and 1980s?

Commentators such as Van Jones, a former adviser to Obama, theorized that the voter turn to Trump was not just a backlash against liberalism but a racially tinged "white-lash" against the Black and brown leadership Obama represented.[79] They pointed to Trump's policies and statements targeting and denigrating people of color as evidence of this view. Just weeks after being sworn in, Trump issued an executive order banning the entry of citizens from Iraq, Syria, Iran, Libya, Somalia, Sudan, and Yemen. Though courts initially blocked the order, the Supreme Court ruled in *Trump v. Hawaii* that the ban on five of these Muslim-majority countries was permissible. Justified as an antiterrorism measure, the singling out of Muslims generated fear in Muslim communities, particularly those that are Black. In November 2016, when Trump visited Minneapolis and claimed that some Somali immigrants were "joining Isis and spreading their extremist views all over our country and all over the world," he

A Clash in Charlottesville

Opinion polls show that Americans across all racial and ethnic classes detect a more toxic racial climate where racist or racially insensitive views are increasingly expressed. At the "Unite the Right" rally held in Charlottesville, Virginia, on August 12, 2017, white nationalists who carried Nazi signs and Confederate flags and who chanted "Blood and soil!," "Jews will not replace us!," and "White lives matter!" were confronted by their opponents. When a white nationalist drove his car into a crowd of pedestrians, killing one woman and injuring nineteen others, President Trump's comment that there was an "egregious display of hatred, bigotry and violence on many sides . . ." disturbed many American citizens. **To what degree was the Unite the Right rally a continuation of or departure from racial violence that has occurred in U.S. history? Use both the image and information from this chapter to support your response.** *Evelyn Hockstein/The Washington Post via Getty Images.*

emboldened anti-Muslim radicals.[80] In St. Cloud, Minnesota, where the mosque had been regularly vandalized, Somalis established their own neighborhood patrol because they did not think that the police took their safety seriously. Across the nation, Black Muslim women have borne the brunt of the hostility because their hijab makes them easily identifiable as Muslim. "As a Black woman, I'm scared of the police because I see people that look like me killed simply for being Black. As a Muslim woman, I'm scared of being attacked and killed; Do they notice I'm a Muslim because of my hijab and my Blackness because of my melanin?" said Ahlaam Ibraahim, a Somali-American student at the University of Washington.[81]

Beyond the travel ban, other aspects of Trump's policies were experienced by many people of color as a racist endorsement of white nationalism.[82] They point to his focus on building a border wall and his rhetoric around Mexican migrants, most famously the statement, "They're bringing drugs. They're bringing crime. They're rapists." Said 60-year-old Niyonu Spann on the morning after the election, "Trump was masterful in tapping in on a perception that people of color are causing working-class people's pain," she said. "So whether it's in the package of immigration, or in the package of black lazy folks, or the package of Mexicans, that scapegoat, he's able to tap in on that."[83] Trump's directives on the treatment of Mexican and Central American asylum seekers, especially his border policy of separating asylum applicants from their children and housing them in pens within warehouse facilities, provoked outrage. Leveling his gaze beyond the southern border, Trump has called Haiti, El Salvador, and African nations "shithole countries," and he has said that "all Haitians have AIDS," and Nigerian immigrants would never "go back to their huts."[84]

AP® exam tip

Be sure you can explain how Black athletes in the twenty-first century contested discrimination and advocated for racial equality.

During his time in office, Trump responded with angry rhetoric to African American citizens who spoke out on racial injustice. When quarterback Colin Kaepernick protested police shootings of unarmed Blacks by kneeling during the national anthem, Trump advised National Football League owners to instruct coaches to "Get that son of a bitch off the field right now"[85] and told Kaepernick that "he should find a country that works better for him."[86] When four Democratic congresswomen criticized his immigration policies, Trump said that these women, "who originally came from countries whose governments are a complete and total catastrophe, the worst, most corrupt and inept anywhere in the world," should "go back and help fix the totally broken and crime infested places from which they came."[87] These progressive House members — Ayanna Pressley (Massachusetts), Rashida Tlaib (Michigan), Alexandria Ocasio-Cortez (New York), and Ilhan Omar (Minnesota) — are all women of color and all are citizens of the United States; Pressley, Tlaib, and Ocasio-Cortez were born here. When Trump failed to stop supporters from chanting "Send her back," in reference to these four members of Congress, many were reminded of how the slur "go back to where you came from" has historically been used to demean people thought to be outsiders. Said one Atlanta woman, " 'Go back to where you came from' and all its variants are words people of color hear and swallow all the time. It's hard to pinpoint a specific time because the sting of alienation never subsides."[88]

The Trump administration's push for more stringent voter photo ID laws has been interpreted as an attempt to suppress minority voting. Indeed, one such law was blocked by a Texas federal district judge, who ruled that the law "perpetuates the selection of types of ID most likely to be possessed by Anglo voters and, disproportionately, not possessed by Hispanics and African-Americans."[89] Political scientists who have shown that voter fraud is overstated and that voter ID laws do indeed suppress minority voting have likened the voter ID laws to measures like poll taxes, literacy tests, residency requirements, and at-large elections that were used by the white majority for decades to deny Blacks their civic rights. When added to other measures, such as shortened early voting periods, repeal of same-day voter registration, reduced polling hours, a decrease in poll locations, and increased restrictions on voting by felons, some observers found parallels to the Jim Crow era.

AP® skills

Applying Disciplinary Knowledge: How did the Trump administration's policies weaken the 1965 Voting Rights Act?

Renewed Solidarity and Grassroots Organizing

It was not long into the Trump presidency before Black America's instinctive self-defense mechanisms kicked into gear. Indeed, as hate crimes rose,[90] many Americans across all racial and ethnic groups detected a toxic racial climate in which it became more common for people to express racist or racially insensitive views.[91] The climate of the Trump administration may have led Black Americans to focus more on race than they had twelve years previously. In contrast to the 63 percent of Black Americans who in 2007 felt that what happened to other Black people affected them, in 2019, 73 percent felt their fate was linked to other Blacks. Moreover, in 2007, only 30 percent of African Americans thought that discrimination held Blacks back, with a majority saying that they could advance through hard work and sacrifice. In 2019, opinion was just the opposite: only 30 percent thought that race did not make a difference in how Blacks advanced, while 68 percent thought discrimination held Blacks back.[92] In addition, there is evidence that the threat Black immigrants face has led many of them to identify more closely with African Americans. According to Hind Makki, a Sudanese American interfaith and antiracism educator, older-generation immigrants have begun to embrace an African American identity. In the Minneapolis community she works with, she has noticed "a shift of feeling and claiming Blackness as a cultural, political, and religious identity, and a shift away from the Middle Eastern/Arab identity."[93]

#SayHerName
The hashtag for a social justice movement that calls attention to the invisibility of Black women's experience with police brutality and anti-Black violence.

Besides rekindling Black cohesiveness, the Trump administration ignited political activism, especially among Black women. Black women created the hashtags #BlackLivesMatter in 2013 and **#SayHerName** in 2014. Both of these movements have sparked reforms in the police and criminal justice systems. (See AP® Working with Sources: #BlackLivesMatter, pp. 717–32.) Black women have also been central in the #MeToo movement, which put the issue of sexual assault front and center. In 2017, Alyssa Milano's call for women to tweet "me too" if they had been sexually assaulted or harassed sparked a response from millions of women. But the phrase had actually been coined in 2006 by Tarana Burke, an African American woman who began raising awareness while working with Black girls who were survivors of sexual assault. The publicity garnered by Milano, in contrast to that which had greeted Burke, brought to light the different ways Black women are slighted or generally ignored. As a leader in the reinvigorated movement, Burke and other Black women take pride in the fact that the silence about sexual violence against all women has been broken, and a bona fide movement against sexual predators was launched.

AP® exam tip

Be sure you can describe the major advances in federal political leadership among Black women in the late twentieth and early twenty-first centuries.

Black women also made some headway in formal politics. In 2018, more than four hundred Black women ran for political offices at the local, state, and federal levels. In 2019, Black representation in Congress reached a historical peak of fifty-five; twenty-two of these representatives were women. An important fact to note is that many won in predominantly white districts while not shying away from racial issues. Lucy McBath won in a mostly white Georgia district after focusing her campaign on the death of her son at the hands of a white man who fired into a car of teenagers after complaining about their music. Lauren Underwood defeated a four-term Republican incumbent in a mostly white Chicago suburb, and Minnesotan Ilhan Omar became one of two Muslim American women in Congress. Among other firsts were the election of Ayanna Pressley and Jajana Hayes as the first Black congresswomen from Massachusetts and Connecticut, respectively; the election of Lori Lightfoot as Chicago's first openly lesbian Black mayor; and the candidacy of Kamala Harris for the Democratic nomination for president of the United States. The near victory of Democrat Stacey Abrams for the governorship of the deep South state of Georgia was also historic; Abrams lost her bid to become the first Black female governor in the United States by a slim 1.4 percent margin. Her opponent, the Georgia secretary of state, oversaw an aggressive effort to purge voter rolls before the election; in addition, polling places were closed in nearly 200 poor and minority neighborhoods.[94] Abrams responded by becoming a nationally recognized crusader against voter suppression.

The Squad Puts America First
Representative Ayanna Pressley makes remarks at a July 2019 press conference as Representatives Rashida Tlaib, Ilhan Omar, and Alexandria Ocasio-Cortez stand by her side. The four first-term congresswomen, nicknamed the "squad," were responding to derogatory remarks by President Trump. Pressley said, "This is a disruptive distraction from the issues of care, concern and consequence to the American people. Our squad is big. Our squad includes any person committed to building a more equitable and just world." **How does this image reveal the growing diversity among twenty-first-century political leadership? What other contemporary examples of coalition-building among women of color can you think of?** *Mike Theiler/Reuters/Newscom.*

As the country approached the 2020 presidential election, Black solidarity seemed to take on life-and-death meaning. In response to the Covid-19 pandemic that left over one hundred thousand Americans dead as the summer began, many states shut down all businesses that were not considered essential. As they shut their doors, many Black Americans, overrepresented in service industry jobs, lost their employment. Even worse, Blacks died in disproportionate numbers because so many did not have access to adequate health care, and their jobs did not privilege them to shelter at home or distance themselves from those who had the disease. Then in the spring, three murders of unarmed Black people hit the news. In February, Ahmaud Arbery, a Black man out for a jog, was murdered by two white vigilantes. In March, Breonna Taylor, a Louisville emergency medical service technician, was shot by police who entered the wrong apartment in search of drugs. In May, George Floyd was killed by police officers who pinned his neck and back to the ground while they squeezed the life out of him. Disgust at the actions of the police rose as Americans viewed the video footage of the Arbery and Floyd murders and the seeming reluctance of the police and prosecutors to make arrests in any of the cases. With a unity that had not been seen in years, African Americans marched together against police brutality. As an unsupportive president watched, African Americans were joined in their protests by white, Latino, and Asian Americans. To many participants and observers, a new day in American race relations seemed to have arrived.

CONCLUSION

The Persistence of the Color Line

African Americans began the twenty-first century with new opportunities, the fruits of the midcentury freedom movement. The workplace had been integrated, as had higher education — not nearly to the extent Black people desired, but enough to make a difference in the ways significant numbers of African Americans related to the nation and their racial community. Race mattered, but so did gender, sexuality, class, and ethnicity. At the beginning of the twenty-first century, Blacks could and did take advantage of the many different ways of being Black.

But beneath the surface of all of Black America's progress lurks a harsh reality. The color line, which W. E. B. Du Bois said was the problem of the twentieth century, is alive and well in the twenty-first century. America has not moved into a post-racial or color-blind era. The color line was evident during the Hurricane Katrina disaster, and the mass incarceration of African Americans tells the same story. The police still kill Black people at higher rates than anyone else, and poverty, surveillance, and discrimination still circumscribe Black lives in incomparable ways.

For sure, Obama brought both real and symbolic change, and the national and worldwide jubilation witnessed upon his election demonstrated the hope that he brought to America and the rest of the world. But the irony of being the first Black president in an age proclaimed by many to be color-blind is obvious: for many, his color was and is the most defining feature of his presidency. The election of his successor, Donald Trump, and his administration's subsequent policies, underscored the persistence of the color line.

The year 2019 marked the four hundredth anniversary of the arrival of African captives in America; it also marked the beginning of the African American struggle for freedom and the codependent nature of that struggle with the nation that made liberty its founding principle. In 2020, a deadly pandemic and a multiracial protest movement against police brutality echoed throughout the country and the world. Many Americans were hungry for change. In November 2020, Joseph Biden was elected president, and Kamala Harris became the first Black and Asian woman to serve as vice president. Although much about American politics remained polarized, this achievement represented progress and hope for many Black Americans, especially Black women.

On July 21, 2024, President Biden announced to the country that he would not seek reelection, endorsing Vice President Kamala Harris as the Democratic nominee. Within hours of his announcement, endorsements quickly followed upon a wave of political excitement. Within a week of Biden's announcement, Kamala Harris, daughter of an Indian mother and Jamaican father, graduate of Howard University, and member of Alpha Kappa Alpha Sorority, had received over 200 million dollars in campaign donations. At the Democratic National Convention, Harris made history as the first Black and Asian woman to be the Democratic nominee for President of the United States. And yet, many systemic issues that disproportionately affect Black Americans persisted. The same month Harris made history as a presidential nominee, Sonya Massey, a thirty-six-year-old unarmed Black woman in Illinois who many believe was suffering from a mental health crisis, called police to her home because she was afraid there was an intruder. The responding officer, who had a history of misconduct, shot her three times in the face. Her death was quickly ruled a homicide. Ultimately, Harris's bid for the presidency was unsuccessful. In November 2024, Donald Trump was elected to a second term, winning a majority of both the electoral college and the popular vote.

Long ago, Frederick Douglass, a fugitive from slavery and a freedom fighter, tied the liberty and freedom of Black people to America's fate. He claimed that "the destiny of the colored man is bound up with that of the white people of this country. . . . *We are here,* and here we are likely to be. . . . We shall neither die out, nor be driven out; but shall go with this people, either as a testimony against them, or as an evidence in their favor throughout their generations."[95] The twenty-first century has brought changes that Douglass could hardly have predicted. Yet the verdict is still out on which testimony about America and its Black citizens will ultimately prevail.

CHAPTER 17 REVIEW ▸ PRACTICING AP® SKILLS

AP® ESSENTIAL VOCABULARY AND SOURCES

**Essential terms and required sources from the AP® Course are marked with an asterisk.*

Black tax p. 681
post-Black p. 684
Black church p. 686
carceral state p. 690
Pound Cake speech (2004) p. 690
Jena Six case (2006) p. 691
American Recovery and Reinvestment Act (ARRA) (2009) p. 698
post-racial p. 700
racial profiling p. 701
broken windows theory p. 707
"stop and frisk" p. 707
#BlackLivesMatter p. 707
#SayHerName p. 712

APPLYING DISCIPLINARY KNOWLEDGE: ESSENTIAL QUESTIONS

1. How would you describe the differences that had come to characterize Black America by the first decade of the twenty-first century? How were those differences made manifest in politics, culture, and religion?
2. How did the challenges of the new century — the rise of the carceral state, the war in Iraq, Hurricane Katrina — reveal the changes that had taken place in post–civil rights Black America?
3. In what ways was the Obama presidency — and the president himself — emblematic of the changing times?
4. What is meant by a post-racial era? Has the nation entered such a period? What evidence can you provide for your argument?
5. What, if anything, does the election and presidency of Donald Trump say about the African American fight for equality in America?
6. Do the disproportionate number of African American deaths from COVID-19, and the deaths of Ahmaud Arbery, Breonna Taylor, and George Floyd provide evidence of structural racism? Explain.

SUGGESTED REFERENCES

The State of Black America

Dickerson, Debra J. *The End of Blackness: Returning the Souls of Black Folk to Their Rightful Owners*. New York: Pantheon, 2004.

Golden, Thelma. *Freestyle: The Studio Museum in Harlem* [Exhibition catalog]. New York: Studio Museum in Harlem, 2001.

Hancock, Ange-Marie. *The Politics of Disgust: The Public Identity of the Welfare Queen*. New York: New York University Press, 2004.

Johnson, Charles. "The End of the Black American Narrative." *American Scholar* 77, no. 3 (Summer 2008): 32–42.

Moore, Sharon E., ed. "African American Megachurches and Community Empowerment: Fostering Life in Dry Places." *Journal of African American Studies* 15, no. 2 (June 2011).

Obama, Barack. *Dreams from My Father: A Story of Race and Inheritance*. New York: Random House, 1995.

Robinson, Eugene. *Disintegration: The Splintering of Black America*. New York: Doubleday, 2010.

Touré. *Who's Afraid of Post-Blackness? What It Means to Be Black Now*. New York: Free Press, 2011.

Trying Times

Alexander, Michelle. *The New Jim Crow: Mass Incarceration in the Age of Colorblindness*. New York: New Press, 2010.

Latty, Yvonne. *We Were There: Voices of African American Veterans, from World War II to the War in Iraq*. New York: Amistad, 2004.

Manza, Jeff, and Christopher Uggen. *Locked Out: Felon Disenfranchisement and American Democracy*. New York: Oxford University Press, 2006.

Marable, Manning, and Kristen Clarke, eds. *Seeking Higher Ground: The Hurricane Katrina Crisis, Race, and Public Policy Reader*. New York: Palgrave Macmillan, 2008.

Phillips, Kimberly. *War! What Is It Good For? Black Freedom Struggles and the U.S. Military from World War II to Iraq*. Chapel Hill: University of North Carolina Press, 2012.

Thompson, Heather Ann. "Why Mass Incarceration Matters: Rethinking Crisis, Decline, and Transformation in Postwar American History." *Journal of American History* 97, no. 3 (December 2010): 703–34.

Wailoo, Keith, Karen M. O'Neill, Jeffrey Dowd, and Roland Anglin, eds. *Katrina's Imprint: Race and Vulnerability in America*. New Brunswick: Rutgers University Press, 2010.

Change Comes to America

Bonilla-Silva, Eduardo. *Racism without Racists: Color-Blind Racism and the Persistence of Racial Inequality in the United States*, 2nd ed. Lanham, MD: Rowman & Littlefield, 2006.

Lusane, Clarence. *Pipe Dream Blues: Racism and the War on Drugs*. Boston: South End Press, 1991.

———. *Race in the Global Era: African Americans at the Millennium*. Boston: South End Press, 1997.

Ogletree, Charles. *The Presumption of Guilt: The Arrest of Henry Louis Gates Jr. and Race, Class, and Crime in America*. New York: Palgrave Macmillan, 2010.

Sugrue, Thomas J. *Not Even Past: Barack Obama and the Burden of Race*. Princeton: Princeton University Press, 2010.

Wise, Tim. *Colorblind: The Rise of Post-Racial Politics and the Retreat from Racial Equity*. San Francisco: City Lights, 2010.

Moving Forward

Ransby, Barbara. *Making All Black Lives Matter: Reimaging Freedom in the 21st Century*. Oakland: University of California Press, 2018.

Ritchie, Andrea. *Invisible No More: Police Violence Against Black Women and Women of Color*. Boston: Beacon Press, 2017.

#BlackLivesMatter

It took eight minutes and forty-six seconds for Officer Derek Chauvin and his three accomplices to kill George Floyd, a Black Minneapolis security guard whose last words on May 25, 2020, were "I can't breathe." Caught on camera by onlookers who pleaded with Chauvin to take his knee off Floyd's neck, the video sparked weeks of protest demonstrations. This outrage came during the global coronavirus pandemic. By the time of Floyd's death, it was clear that the illness that had claimed over one hundred thousand American lives and put millions out of work harmed African Americans disproportionately. Floyd's murder deepened the anger and anxiety the virus had provoked, feelings that were exacerbated by news that prosecutors had failed to arrest two white vigilantes in Georgia who had been caught on video fatally shooting Ahmaud Arbery as he jogged in a white neighborhood, and that no charges were brought against police in the killing of Breonna Taylor, an emergency room technician, during a drug raid on the wrong apartment in Louisville, Kentucky. As they had done in 2014 when Michael Brown was killed in Ferguson and Eric Garner was killed in New York, African Americans took to the streets shouting "Black Lives Matter." This time, however, they were joined by Latino, Asian, and white Americans—and by demonstrators around the world. This time the chant became a global chorus: "Black Lives Matter."

This worldwide solidarity came eight years after three Black women had cofounded the hashtag #BlackLivesMatter. In February 2012, Alicia Garza, Patrisse Cullors, and Opal Tometi launched the online movement in response to the killing of Trayvon Martin, a seventeen-year-old Black teenager, by George Zimmerman, a neighborhood watch volunteer in Sanford, Florida. The hashtag protested anti-Black violence in all of its forms, not only police brutality but also racially motivated vigilante attacks and mass incarceration.[96] After the 2014 deaths of Michael Brown and Eric Garner, the #BlackLivesMatter call to action moved beyond social media and into the streets.

The movement grew quickly. It resonated with those who remembered the police action taken against Blacks marching for integration and voting rights in the 1960s; others remembered how police authorities harassed young, Black urban migrants, how they collaborated with the FBI's COINTELPRO to kill Black Panthers and destroy Black nationalism, and how city after city rejected calls for civilian review boards.

Turning to the modern day, protesters rallied around an ever-growing list of examples of police brutality against young African Americans. One research agency reported that 336 Blacks were shot and killed by police in 2015 alone.[97] A 2019 study found that a Black man was 2.5 times more likely than a white man to be killed by the police during his lifetime.[98]

One of the most publicized cases, which was eerily similar to George Floyd's killing, occurred in Staten Island, New York, in July 2014. In a violent encounter captured by several bystanders on their phones, police officer Daniel Pantaleo held forty-three-year-old Eric Garner around his neck and did not release him despite Garner's pleas of "I can't breathe." Garner was pronounced dead an hour after the incident, and the coroner subsequently ruled the death a homicide. Though the New York City Police Department officially prohibits chokeholds, a grand jury failed to indict Pantaleo. Similarly, though the coroner ruled Floyd's death a homicide, it took days before Chauvin and the three other officers involved were arrested and charged. In both cases, #BlackLivesMatter pointed to the failure to arrest and indict police as indications not only of the racism of individual police, but also as evidence of a systemically racist police and justice system.

Previous investigations by the Department of Justice (DOJ) and by various organizations concurred. Investigation of the police department and court system in Ferguson, for example, revealed that, although 69 percent of Ferguson's population was Black, almost 90 percent of the documented uses of force by police officers were against African Americans, and in every police canine bite incident, the person bitten was Black. The report also showed how the police and the courts worked together to use traffic arrests and the imprisonment of African Americans to raise revenue for the city, often in violation of the Fourth and Fourteenth Amendments.[99] Studies of the Minneapolis police reveal similar patterns of systemic bias. Although African Americans compose only 20 percent of the city's population, they suffer 60 percent of the forceful arrests made by police. According to their own records, since 2015, Minneapolis police have used force against Black people at seven times the rate of whites.[100]

key point

The murder of George Floyd by Minneapolis policemen in 2020 brought global attention to a problem that had plagued the Black community for decades. Although Black people and organizations have tried to shine light on police brutality and racial profiling since the end of Reconstruction, the murder of George Floyd led to increased support for social justice campaigns like #BlackLivesMatter and #SayHerName. These resulted in national debates about institutional racism and led to some local police reform. At the same time, increased calls for reform also resulted in stalwart support for the police and a rejection of the assertion that police departments were operating within a biased system.

In the wake of the Floyd protests, #BlackLivesMatter and other organizations have demanded different approaches to policing. In some cases, local and state governments have responded. For example, after two weeks of protests, the state of New York passed a law which outlawed chokeholds, allowed the release of police disciplinary records, and put the prosecutions of police in the hands of a special prosecutor. Other states and municipalities are considering laws that make body cams mandatory, demilitarize the police, and eliminate no-knock warrants. Some #BlackLivesMatter advocates argue that policing needs to be totally rethought and that money targeted for law enforcement should be redirected to social service agencies that target specific community problems. They argue that tens of millions of dollars were spent on body cams and retraining after Michael Brown's murder, all to no avail.[101] "Why," asks #BlackLivesMatter cofounder Patrisse Cullers, "is law enforcement the first responders for a mental health crisis? Why are they the first responders for domestic violence issues? Why are they the first responders for homelessness?" If police departments were defunded, Cullers argues, there would be more money available to invest in the things that have been proven to increase safety—like schools, hospitals, housing, and food. Disinvesting in the police would mean "reducing the ability of law enforcement to have resources that harm our communities."[102]

The following documents and photographs relate to law enforcement and to the #BlackLivesMatter movement. As you review them, consider the different points of view that are represented.

AP® argumentation

DBQ Practice: Evaluate the extent to which racial violence and systemic racism have shaped African Americans' experiences during the twenty-first century. Use at least three of the documents to support your response.

DOCUMENT 1 Alicia Garza | *A Herstory of the #BlackLivesMatter Movement*, 2014

Although #BlackLivesMatter was created by ALICIA GARZA (b. 1981), PATRISSE CULLORS (b. 1984), and OPAL TOMETI (b. 1984) after George Zimmerman was acquitted of murder charges in the death of Trayvon Martin, it moved to the streets and became a protest movement only after eighteen-year-old Michael Brown was killed in Ferguson, Missouri. While it coalesced and gathered steam around the issues of police shootings and Black incarceration, it was founded with the broad intention of calling attention to institutional racism and state violence against Black people — not only Black men but also Black women, as well as queer, trans, disabled, and poor Black people. The creators of #BlackLivesMatter are careful to note that they believe that all lives matter, but their focus on Blacks has to do with America's long history of oppression in which Blacks were excluded from Thomas Jefferson's dictum that "all men are created equal."

> **Breaking it Down** How did the Black Lives Matter movement start? How does Garza characterize the movement, and to what extent does she believe the movement has maintained its initial meaning and purpose? What is Garza's sense of the movement's place in history?

I created #BlackLivesMatter with Patrisse Cullors and Opal Tometi, two of my sisters, as a call to action for Black people after 17-year-old Trayvon Martin was posthumously placed on trial for his own murder and the killer, George Zimmerman, was not held accountable for the crime he committed. It was a response to the anti-Black racism that permeates our society and also, unfortunately, our movements.

Black Lives Matter is an ideological and political intervention in a world where Black lives are systematically and intentionally targeted for demise. It is an affirmation of Black folks' contributions to this society, our humanity, and our resilience in the face of deadly oppression.

We were humbled when cultural workers, artists, designers, and techies offered their labor and love to expand #BlackLivesMatter beyond a social media hashtag. Opal, Patrisse, and I created the infrastructure for this movement project — moving the hashtag from social media to the streets. Our team grew through a very successful Black Lives Matter ride, led and designed by Patrisse Cullors and Darnell L. Moore, organized to support the movement that is growing in St. Louis, MO, after 18-year-old Mike Brown was killed at the hands of Ferguson Police Officer Darren Wilson. We've hosted national conference calls focused on issues of critical importance to Black people working hard for the liberation of our people. We've connected people across the country working to end the various forms of injustice impacting our people. We've created space for the celebration and humanization of Black lives.

THE THEFT OF BLACK QUEER WOMEN'S WORK

As people took the #BlackLivesMatter demand into the streets, mainstream media and corporations also took up the call; #BlackLivesMatter appeared in an episode of *Law & Order: SVU* in a mash up containing the Paula Deen racism scandal and the tragedy of the murder of Trayvon Martin.

Suddenly, we began to come across varied adaptations of our work — all lives matter, brown lives matter, migrant lives matter, women's lives matter, and on and on. While imitation is said to be the highest form of flattery, I was surprised when an organization called to ask if they could use "Black Lives Matter" in one of their campaigns. We agreed to it, with the caveat that a) as a team, we preferred that we not use the meme to celebrate the imprisonment of any individual and b) that it was important to us they acknowledged the genesis of #BlackLivesMatter. I was surprised when they did exactly the opposite and then justified their actions by saying they hadn't used the "exact" slogan and, therefore, they deemed it okay to take our work, use it as their own, fail to credit where it came from, and then use it to applaud incarceration.

I was surprised when a community institution wrote asking us to provide materials and action steps for an art show they were curating, entitled "Our Lives Matter." When questioned about who was involved and why they felt the need to change the very specific call and demand around Black lives to "our lives," I was told the artists decided it needed to be more inclusive of all people of color. I was even more surprised when, in the promotion of their event, one of the artists conducted an interview that completely erased the origins of their work — rooted in the labor and love of queer Black women.

When you design an event/campaign/et cetera based on the work of queer Black women, don't invite them to participate in shaping it, but ask them to provide materials and ideas for next steps for said event, that is racism in practice. It's also hetero-patriarchal. Straight men, unintentionally or intentionally, have taken the work of queer Black women and erased our contributions. Perhaps if we were the charismatic Black men many are rallying around these days, it would have been a different story, but being Black queer women in this society (and apparently within these movements) tends to equal invisibility and non-relevancy.

We completely expect those who benefit directly and improperly from White supremacy to try and erase our existence. We fight that every day. But when it happens amongst our allies, we are baffled, we are saddened, and we are enraged. And it's time to have the political conversation about why that's not okay.

We are grateful to our allies who have stepped up to the call that Black lives matter, and taken it as an opportunity to not just stand in solidarity with us, but to investigate the ways in which anti-Black racism is perpetuated in their own communities. We are also grateful to those allies who were willing to engage in critical dialogue with us about this unfortunate and problematic dynamic. And for those who we have not yet had the opportunity to engage with around the adaptations of the Black Lives Matter call, please consider the following points.

BROADENING THE CONVERSATION TO INCLUDE BLACK LIFE

Black Lives Matter is a unique contribution that goes beyond extrajudicial killings of Black people by police and vigilantes. It goes beyond the narrow nationalism that can be prevalent within some Black communities, which merely call on Black people to love Black, live Black, and buy Black, keeping straight cis Black men in the front of the movement while our sisters, queer and trans and disabled folk take up roles in the background or not at all. Black Lives Matter affirms the lives of Black queer and trans folks, disabled folks, Black-undocumented folks, folks with records, women, and all Black lives along the gender spectrum. It centers those that have been marginalized within Black liberation movements. It is a tactic to (re)build the Black liberation movement.

When we say Black Lives Matter, we are talking about the ways in which Black people are deprived of our basic human rights and dignity. It is an acknowledgment [that] Black poverty and genocide is state violence. It is an acknowledgment that 1 million Black people are locked in cages in this country — one half of all people in prisons or jails — [that] is an act of state violence. It is an acknowledgment that Black women continue to bear the burden of a relentless assault on our children and our families and that assault is an act of state violence. Black queer and trans folks bearing a unique burden in a hetero-patriarchal society that disposes of us like garbage and simultaneously fetishizes us and profits off of us is state violence; the fact that 500,000 Black people in the US are undocumented immigrants and relegated to the shadows is state violence; the fact that Black girls are used as negotiating chips during times of conflict and war is state violence; Black folks living with disabilities and different abilities [bearing] the burden of state-sponsored

Darwinian experiments that attempt to squeeze us into boxes of normality defined by White supremacy is state violence. And the fact that the lives of Black people — not ALL people — exist within these conditions [a] is consequence of state violence.

When Black people get free, everybody gets free.

#BlackLivesMatter doesn't mean your life isn't important — it means that Black lives, which are seen as without value within White supremacy, are important to your liberation. Given the disproportionate impact state violence has on Black lives, we understand that when Black people in this country get free, the benefits will be wide reaching and transformative for society as a whole. When we are able to end hyper-criminalization and sexualization of Black people and end the poverty, control, and surveillance of Black people, every single person in this world has a better shot at getting and staying free. When Black people get free, everybody gets free. This is why we call on Black people and our allies to take up the call that Black lives matter. We're not saying Black lives are more important than other lives, or that other lives are not criminalized and oppressed in various ways. We remain in active solidarity with all oppressed people who are fighting for their liberation and we know that our destinies are intertwined.

And, to keep it real — it is appropriate and necessary to have strategy and action centered around Blackness without other non-Black communities of color, or White folks for that matter, needing to find a place and a way to center themselves within it. It is appropriate and necessary for us to acknowledge the critical role that Black lives and struggles for Black liberation have played in inspiring and anchoring, through practice and theory, social movements for the liberation of all people. The women's movement, the Chicano liberation movement, queer movements, and many more have adopted the strategies, tactics, and theory of the Black liberation movement. And if we are committed to a world where all lives matter, we are called to support the very movement that inspired and activated so many more. That means supporting and acknowledging Black lives.

Progressive movements in the United States have made some unfortunate errors when they push for unity at the expense of really understanding the concrete differences in context, experience, and oppression. In other words, some want unity without struggle. As people who have our minds stayed on freedom, we can learn to fight anti-Black racism by examining the ways in which we participate in it, even unintentionally, instead of the worn out and sloppy practice of drawing lazy parallels of unity between peoples with vastly different experiences and histories.

When we deploy "All Lives Matter" as to correct an intervention specifically created to address anti-blackness, we lose the ways in which the state apparatus has built a program of genocide and repression mostly on the backs of Black people — beginning with the theft of millions of people for free labor — and then adapted it to control, murder, and profit off of other communities of color and immigrant communities. We perpetuate a level of White supremacist domination by reproducing a tired trope that we are all the same, rather than acknowledging that non-Black oppressed people in this country are both impacted by racism and domination, and, simultaneously, BENEFIT from anti-Black racism.

When you drop "Black" from the equation of whose lives matter, and then fail to acknowledge it came from somewhere, you further a legacy of erasing Black lives and Black contributions from our movement legacy. And consider whether or not when dropping the Black you are, intentionally or unintentionally, erasing Black folks from the conversation or homogenizing very different experiences. The legacy and prevalence of anti-Black racism and hetero-patriarchy is a lynch pin holding together this unsustainable economy. And that's not an accidental analogy.

In 2014, hetero-patriarchy and anti-Black racism within our movement is real and felt. It's killing us and it's killing our potential to build power for transformative social change. When you adopt the work of queer women of color, don't name or recognize it, and promote it as if it has no history of its own such actions are problematic. When I use

Assata's* powerful demand in my organizing work, I always begin by sharing where it comes from, sharing about Assata's significance to the Black Liberation Movement, what its political purpose and message is, and why it's important in our context.

When you adopt Black Lives Matter and transform it into something else (if you feel you really need to do that — see above for the arguments not to), it's appropriate politically to credit the lineage from which your adapted work derived. It's important that we work together to build and acknowledge the legacy of Black contributions to the struggle for human rights. If you adapt Black Lives Matter, use the opportunity to talk about its inception and political framing. Lift up Black lives as an opportunity to connect struggles across race, class, gender, nationality, sexuality, and disability.

And, perhaps more importantly, when Black people cry out in defense of our lives, which are uniquely, systematically, and savagely targeted by the state, we are asking you, our family, to stand with us in affirming Black lives. Not just all lives. Black lives. Please do not change the conversation by talking about how your life matters, too. It does, but we need less watered down unity and more active solidarities with us, Black people, unwaveringly, in defense of our humanity. Our collective futures depend on it.

*Black Nationalist Assata Shakur was a member of the Black Panther Party before joining the Black Liberation Army. She escaped to Cuba after being convicted of murdering a New Jersey state trooper.

Source: Alicia Garza (October 7, 2014), "A Herstory of the #BlackLivesMatter Movement." The Feminist Wire. Used with permission.

DOCUMENT 2 #SayHerName

Although the Black Lives Matter movement was founded by three Black women, Black women's encounters with the police have been largely ignored. Yet in 1996, five years after the nation viewed the vicious beating of Rodney King on video, Sandra Antor was pulled over and brutalized by a South Carolina state trooper in an incident also captured on video. Just weeks after Eric Garner was choked to death in 2014, Rosann Miller was placed in a chokehold by a New York City police officer despite the fact that she was seven months pregnant. Like Freddie Gray, who died in 2015 while in Baltimore police custody, Alesia Thomas died from the beating she received from a Los Angeles police officer in 2012, and Sandra Bland, who was pulled over for failing to signal, died while in the custody of Texas police. And two months before the murder of George Floyd of Minneapolis in May 2020, Breonna Taylor of Louisville, Kentucky, was murdered by police. She was shot eight times after being awoken by police executing a no-knock drug warrant. The list of Black women profiled, beaten, sexually assaulted, and killed by law enforcement officials is long, but while Black men have been centered in public conversation about police brutality, Black women have been conspicuously overlooked.

In 2015, the African American Policy Forum (AAPF) established the Say Her Name movement (and #SayHerName hashtag) to call attention to the invisibility of Black women's encounters with police brutality and anti-Black violence. In a report titled "Say Her Name: Resisting Police Brutality Against Black Women," the AAPF notes that the social justice movement in the United States has theorized and developed a clear framework to understand how Black boys and men are systematically criminalized but the same has not been done for Black women and girls. When their experiences are the same as those of Black men, Black women are ignored, and when their experiences are distinctly informed by race, gender, gender identity, and sexual orientation, they still remain invisible. Say Her Name highlights police violence against Black women to help the media and the public understand that racial profiling by the police affects Black people, regardless of gender. For example, the report notes that in New

York City, a jurisdiction with the most extensive data collection on police stops, "the rate of disparities in stops, frisks, and arrest are identical for Black men and Black women. However, the media, researchers, and advocates tend to focus only on how profiling impacts Black men."[103] The AAPF insists that we develop an understanding of the way that gender and sexuality affect anti-Black state-sanctioned violence.

The following is a photo of a protest held by the Oklahoma City Artist for Justice, an organization founded by two Black women, who organized against Daniel Holtzclaw, a police officer who stood trial and was convicted in 2015 of multiple charges, including rape, sexual battery, and forcible oral sodomy. During the trial, thirteen Black women accused and testified against Holtzclaw, who was eventually found guilty and sentenced to 263 years in prison. The Oklahoma City case hardly made national news. Why do you think it was underreported? How do cases like this underscore AAFP's point?

Breaking it Down Analyze the messages on the protest signs. What are some the issues plaguing Black women in the twenty-first century? To what extent are these issues unique or have been a constant problem facing Black women throughout America history?

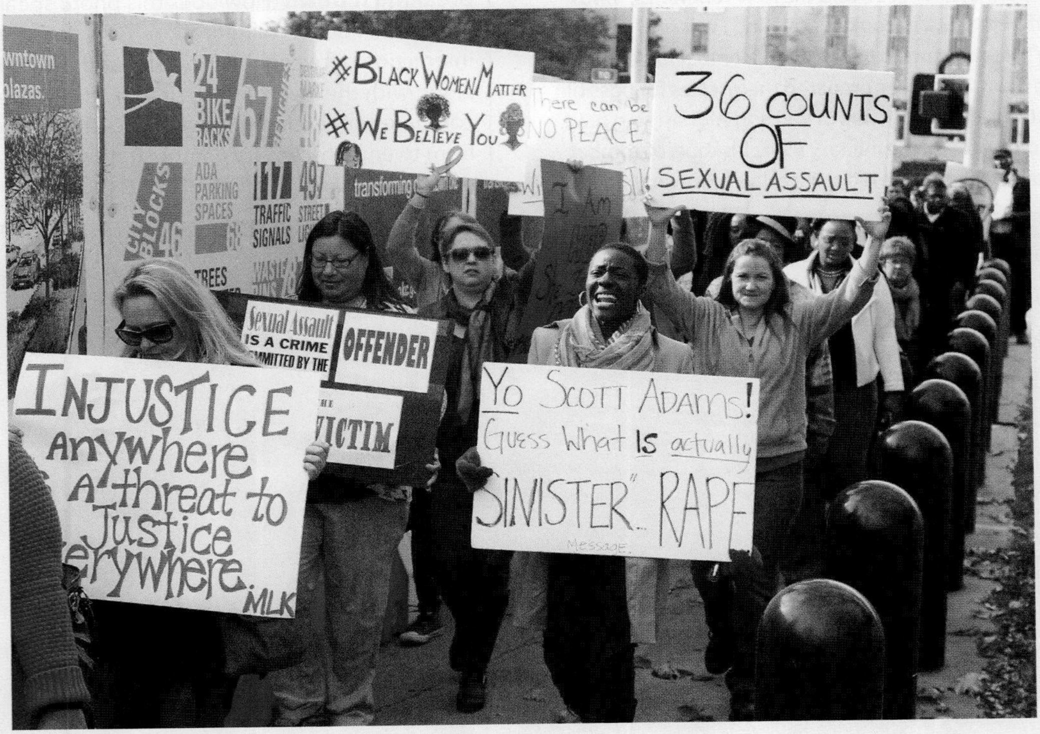

Sue Ogrocki/Associated Press/AP Images.

DOCUMENT 3 Citizen–Police Confrontation in Ferguson

Demonstrators who gathered in Ferguson, Missouri, on August 11, 2014, to protest Michael Brown's killing were confronted by police who wore Kevlar vests, helmets, and camouflage and who, armed with pistols, shotguns, and automatic rifles, used rubber bullets and tear gas to disperse the protesters.[104] The show of such overwhelming force against citizens exercising their First Amendment right to free speech and protest prompted many to question how and why a relatively small city like Ferguson had acquired weapons normally found on the battlefields of Iraq and Afghanistan.

Researchers traced the militarization of police departments back to Ronald Reagan's War on Drugs, when federal money and military equipment began to flow into state and local law enforcement agencies. The Pentagon regularly gave millions of dollars in firepower to local law enforcement agencies around the country, which they used in setting up special weapons and tactics (SWAT) teams for narcotics enforcement. In 1997 alone, the Pentagon handed over more than 1.2 million pieces of military equipment to local police departments. A retired police chief in New Haven, Connecticut, told the *New York Times*, "I was offered tanks, bazookas, anything I wanted."[105] After 9/11, federal funding for tools of combat increased, as towns and cities prepared themselves for possible attack; and as the wars in Iraq and Afghanistan have wound down, the military's surplus tools of combat have been transferred to local law enforcement. It is not uncommon for small towns like Ferguson to use these weapons of war to carry out community policing.

Critics of police militarization argue that communities are not war zones and that police should be trained to protect citizens and their right to be presumed innocent until proven guilty. Police, they argue, are not soldiers trained to kill the enemy. Supporters of militarization, however, argue that communities must be prepared, even for something that may never happen. Moreover, they say, the equipment keeps police safe and allows them to keep up with criminals, who are arming themselves more heavily.[106]

Breaking it Down How does this photo speak to the issue of police militarization? How does the interaction between the protester and the police, along with the level of force used by the police, compare with exchanges you have learned about from twentieth-century demonstrations?

Jeff Roberson/Associated Press/AP Images.

DOCUMENT 4 *"We Can't Breathe"*: 2014, 2020

Eric Garner was choked to death by Officer Daniel Pantaleo on July 17, 2014. Protest erupted immediately, but it reached fever pitch when a Long Island grand jury failed to indict Pantaleo, even though the coroner had ruled the death a homicide. George Floyd was choked to death on May 25, 2020, by Officer Derek Chauvin while two other Minneapolis officers pinned his back and legs to the ground and a fourth held off distressed bystanders. Only after nine days of protest were the charges against Chauvin upgraded and the other three officers arrested. The following images show the December 4, 2014, cover of the *Daily News*, a popular New York tabloid, and a photo of a protest march following Floyd's death.

Breaking it Down What words or phrases are used to grab the reader's attention in the newspaper? What comparisons can you draw between the importance of the media and the power of images during the Civil Rights movement and the Black Lives Matter movement?

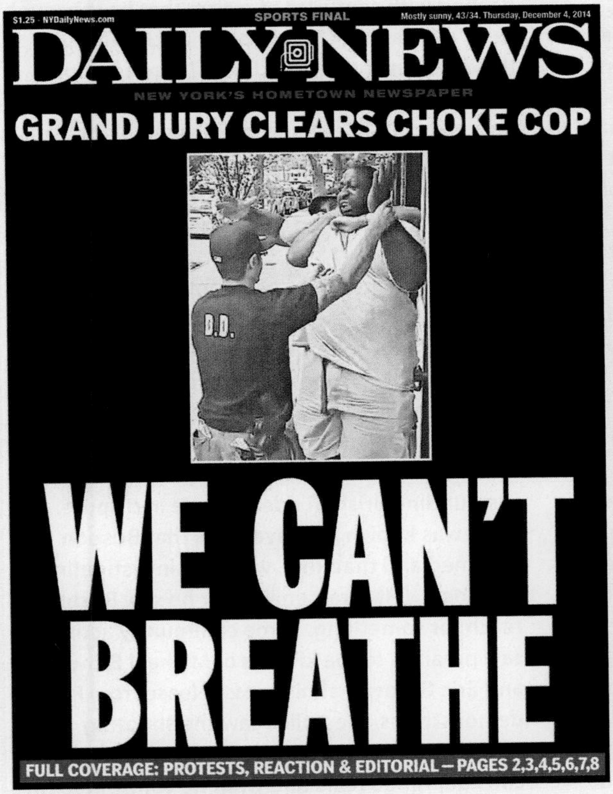

$1.25 · NYDailyNews.com SPORTS FINAL Mostly sunny, 43/34. Thursday, December 4, 2014

DAILY NEWS

NEW YORK'S HOMETOWN NEWSPAPER

GRAND JURY CLEARS CHOKE COP

WE CAN'T BREATHE

FULL COVERAGE: PROTESTS, REACTION & EDITORIAL — PAGES 2,3,4,5,6,7,8

New York Daily News Archive/Getty Images.

ANGELA WEISS/Getty Images.

DOCUMENT 5 *The Police See It Differently*

George Floyd's killing has renewed inquiries into police militarization and has also led to scrutiny of general community policing, particularly police use of firearms. In the wake of statistics that reveal the high number of African Americans killed in civilian–police encounters and criticism that police departments are inherently racist, the police have pushed back against their portrayal as gun-toting vigilantes. They argue that a high number of police shootings occur in Black neighborhoods because that is where the most crimes occur, and their presence in these neighborhoods is needed and *requested* by residents who daily are the victims of Black crime. Their priority is the safety of both themselves and the citizens they protect; race, they maintain, is irrelevant. They argue that they are the first line of defense against society's social, economic, and psychological problems—problems that they have no part in creating. They express regret that some suspects are harmed in their custody, but suspects, they say, always complain that the police are hurting them when they are handcuffed or otherwise detained because they do not want to go to the police station or jail. Guns are everywhere, police argue, and officers need to be skeptical and vigilant in doing their job, lest they be victims of gun crimes.[107]

In making their rebuttal, law enforcement officials point to police shot in the line of duty. The December 2014 murder of Wenjian Liu and Rafael Ramos, two minority police officers in New York City, by Ismaaiyl Brinsley, a Black man with a history of mental illness, provided proof of the dangers cops face every day. Brinsley was seeking revenge for the deaths of Michael Brown and Eric Garner and shot Liu and Ramos as they sat in full uniform in their patrol car; they were killed for no reason other than that they were police officers. Law enforcement officials argue that the danger they face, day in and day out, goes unrecognized and unappreciated, not only by the minority communities they serve but also by city, state, and federal officials, who, they say, too often side with antipolice activists. Indeed, at the funeral of Officer Ramos, many of the thousands of police officers who had come from around the country to pay their respects turned their backs on New York City mayor Bill de Blasio because they believed he did not support the New York City Police Department. Earlier in the month, after the grand jury's decision not to issue an indictment in the death of Eric Garner but before Liu and Ramos were killed, de Blasio had told the press that he and his Black wife had for years schooled their biracial son on "how to take special care in any encounters he has with the police officers who are there to protect him." The mayor also stated that "we are dealing with centuries of racism that have brought us to this day. . . . One chapter has closed with the decision of this grand jury. There are more chapters to come."[108] From the point of view of the police, de Blasio seemed to side with Black leaders such as the National Action Network's Reverend Al Sharpton, whose antipolice rhetoric, they believed, contributed to the murder of Officers Liu and Ramos.

The following two documents reflect police sentiment. The first is a press release issued by the Phoenix Law Enforcement Association (PLEA) after Rumain Brisbon, a thirty-four-year-old Black man, was shot and killed by Mark Rine, a white police officer, on December 2, 2014. At the time of this press release, the events surrounding Brisbon's death were in dispute. What was known, however, was that Brisbon was unarmed and that Rine, who was investigating a drug deal, felt threatened after he saw Brisbon reach for something. Some community activists saw parallels to the killings of Michael Brown and Eric Garner. As this press release from PLEA demonstrates, the police saw the shooting differently. As you read PLEA's side of things, consider Rine's fears and what he confronted on December 2. Does race appear to have been a factor in Brisbon's killing?

The second document is a letter written to President Obama and Attorney General Eric Holder by Thomas J. Nee, president of both the Boston Police Patrolmen's Association and the National Association of Police Organizations, after the funeral of Patrolman Rafael Ramos. Like PLEA's press release, the letter expresses the sentiment common among law enforcement officials that police officers risk their lives daily, and lack of support from the nation's top officials makes their work even riskier. Do you agree with Nee?

Breaking it Down How do the authors describe the character of police officers and the hardships associated with their occupational duties and responsibilities to the community? Explain how the authors depict those individuals killed in conflicts with the police. What are the authors' opinions of movements like #BlackLivesMatter and #SayHerName? What role do the authors believe the government should play in the tensions between the police and the Black community?

Phoenix Law Enforcement Association

The Professional Association of Phoenix Police Officers since 1975

Date: December 15, 2014
To: All Valley Media
Subject: Recent Phoenix Police Officer Involved Shooting

The recent officer involved shooting that occurred on December 2, 2014, involving Phoenix Officer Mark Rine and criminal suspect Rumain Brisbon that occurred at an apartment complex near 25th Avenue and Greenway Road was an unfortunate incident that did not have to end the way it did.

The Phoenix Law Enforcement Association believes it is important for the media and public to view this case from a perspective of examining the facts rather than emotion devoid of fact. It is important for the media and public to understand a few things about this incident:

First, it is truly unfortunate when anyone, be it citizen or officer, is injured or killed as a result of a police contact. Contrary to what many may believe, our officers do not relish the thought of conflict with the citizens we serve.

Officer Rine is an exemplary, decorated employee with seven years of police service. The incident on December 2nd was the first shooting incident he has been involved in.

Officer Rine did not start his shift on December 2nd with the intent of shooting someone, let alone with the intent of targeting someone because of their race. Officer Rine initiated contact with Rumain Brisbon after he [Brisbon] and the vehicle he was in had been previously identified to him by two different citizens in the span of approximately 10–15 minutes as possibly being involved in the sale of drugs. The first citizen even provided a license plate number which matched the description of the vehicle Brisbon was in.

It was only after the second citizen pointed out Brisbon's vehicle and identified Brisbon as a person selling drugs from the vehicle that Officer Rine attempted to surveil Brisbon and his vehicle until backup officers could arrive to render assistance. Prior to arrival of backup, Mr. Brisbon exited the vehicle and began walking towards nearby apartments. Officer Rine had a decision to make and elected to make contact with Mr. Brisbon before he could get inside an apartment.

Mr. Brisbon failed to follow instructions given him by a uniformed sworn peace officer and acted in a threatening manner by reaching for an object concealed in his waistband. In the ensuing altercation, Officer Rine, while attempting to physically detain Mr. Brisbon, believed him to be in possession of a concealed handgun. Mr. Brisbon's continued refusal to submit to lawful authority, obey verbal commands, and let go of the object in his waistband while fighting with Officer Rine ultimately culminated in him being shot.

The media has already published details of the backgrounds of Officer Rine and Rumain Brisbon. Suffice it to say that Mr. Brisbon is no stranger to police contact and the legal and prison systems. Mr. Brisbon had the choice to live that evening. Mr. Brisbon knew he was engaged in illegal activity and likely knew he would stand a good chance of returning to prison if arrested. It was Mr. Brisbon who elected to disobey repeated commands, run from the police, fight with police, resist any efforts to detain him, and engage in further behavior leading the officer to believe he was armed. Had Rumain Brisbon simply submitted to lawful authority there would have been no arguments, no physical altercation, and most importantly, the situation would not have escalated to the point where lethal force would have been needed to control the situation.

Some in the media and in the community have expressed concerns that Mr. Brisbon was ultimately found to be unarmed after the shooting. There are certain fallacies that need to be exposed here.

- Any time a police officer is involved in a close-quarter physical fight with a suspect there is always a weapon available — the officer's. Suspects who engage in fights with officers are often successful in gaining control of the officer's gun. This scenario is a very real concern for everyone in law enforcement and justifiably so, as every year in America, police officers are killed by suspects who gain control of their side arms. This is why the rule of thumb, on the wear of body armor, is that it be able to stop the caliber of the handgun carried by the officer.
- Police officers are trained to always keep in the back of their minds that persons they come in contact with are possibly armed. This is not to say officers pull guns on everyone they come in contact with, but that they are extra vigilant and look for tell-tale cues and indicators that could spell danger. These cues can include things such as conspicuous ignoring, failure to follow verbal commands, sudden or furtive movements, intentionally turning away, putting hands in pockets or the front or rear waistband, belligerent attitude and profane language, and squaring off in a fighting stance, many of which are often a prelude to a fight.
- **"They shot an unarmed person!"** There are numerous accounts from across the nation where police officers have justifiably shot unarmed subjects and not been prosecuted or faced internal discipline from their departments. Police use of force is judged based on Supreme Court case law, relevant state statutes governing the justification for use of deadly force, and police department policies. Most states, including Arizona, have statutes that allow police officers to use lethal force as long as they can reasonably articulate fear of imminent serious injury or death to themselves or another. The law does not require an officer to see a handgun or a muzzle flash before shooting. The law looks at whether or not a reasonable officer on scene would have believed the suspect to be armed and would have perceived a lethal threat given the totality of the circumstances.
- **"Why didn't the officer use a Taser?"** Tasers, while effective in many instances, are not a cure-all. They are a less lethal force option and are applied only in certain scenarios. Phoenix officers are generally trained not to deploy a Taser unless lethal backup is available. Officers involved in lethal force encounters, particularly in a one-on-one setting, are not trained to respond with lesser force options such as a Taser, pepper spray, baton, or fist strikes.
- **Police are only 50% of the equation.** The vast majority of police contacts are concluded

peacefully and without harm because citizens comply and yield to lawful authority. They follow directions, keep their hands in plain view, don't engage in argumentative or abusive language, and don't attempt to make furtive moves or elude officers. The place to butt heads and engage in disagreement is not in the street but in the legal arena of a courtroom.

As a final note, the Phoenix Law Enforcement Association is always open to improving how we do business and how we interact with all segments of the community we serve. It is our belief that we should always strive to have open dialogue and communication.

However, issues confronting the community at large cannot be constructively addressed when self-anointed "civil rights leaders" such as the Reverend Jared Maupin are out in public trying their best to turn Phoenix into another Ferguson. At a recent protest filmed by ABC News 15, Maupin was heard making the following statements:

- "Just remember that a lot of these officers are ni - - er killers."
- "The PPD tried to make Rumain look like a ni - - er criminal."
- "The officers themselves were ni - - er killers."
- In another statement Maupin states: "and if all of us showed up on 24th Street and Camelback and pointed out every two-bit cracker in an Escalade and said there were drug dealers . . ." Referring to white people with the racist label of "two-bit crackers."

The Phoenix Law Enforcement Association has tried in the past to have constructive dialog with Reverend Maupin. We can no longer have a relationship with a person that spews unfounded, hate-filled, racist statements such as the ones enumerated above. Our members pay a heavy price to serve the community and baseless allegations such as these only serve to further inflame and aggravate an already tense situation.

As far as the Phoenix Law Enforcement Association is concerned, our first obligation is the care of the members of our organization. We protect those who protect the citizens, and we will not tolerate individuals or groups who attack our Officers in the furtherance of their own selfish agendas.

SOURCE: Phoenix Law Enforcement Association, "Recent Phoenix Police Officer Involved Shooting," news release, December 15, 2014. Used with permission.

National Association of Police Organizations, Inc.

Representing America's Finest

December 29, 2014

The President
The White House
1600 Pennsylvania Avenue, N.W.
Washington, D.C. 20500

The Attorney General
United States Department of Justice
Constitution Avenue and Tenth Street, N.W.
Washington, D.C. 20530

Dear Mr. President and Mr. Attorney General,

American police officers are, quite literally, bleeding to death. In the entirely predictable fulfillment of well-publicized threats, killers are stalking and murdering our officers. They are cloaking themselves in the rhetoric of protest and "justice." But their very public actions are those of violence and bloodshed. American officers are not just "putting their lives on the line," they are dying.

Rightly or wrongly, these violent killers are reading the inaction of your administration as a tacit concession that their goals have merit. They hear your words of sympathy for violent protestors as conferring legitimacy upon their cause. The firebrands and provocateurs among them are only too willing to fill the void left by your absence of condemnation of their crimes and riots with chants of "What do we want? Dead cops! When do we want them? Now!" And now, completely predictably, the continued lack of any meaningful response whatsoever by your administration has allowed an atmosphere of hatred against police officers to grow, to fester and to finally burst forth in murderous gunfire, hatchet attacks and vehicular run-downs of officers across our nation. The mere fact that you permit the likes of Al Sharpton to sit by your side and have a place in the White House is a clear shot across the bow of the law enforcement community.

The time for standing by and offering weak platitudes about peaceful protest has passed. These are no peaceful protests and they never were. Both "Burn this bitch down!" and "What do we want? Dead cops!" have proved to be open notices of exactly what was going to be done. Some 750,000 sworn officers go to work each day, risking their own safety to uphold our freedoms and constitutional liberty, yet the violent anarchists have made it dangerous merely to wear our uniforms in public.

Unless and until you reverse course and *take action* against these killers and the violent and lawless mobs that support them, unless and until you are just as swift in effectively protecting our police as you have proved to be in doubting them, here will be more officers killed. Both of you men have attended many of our group's meetings and have always pledged your strong support for law enforcement. Now more than ever our men and women in uniform need that support to be shown in a very open way. As Vice President Biden put it at Officer Ramos's funeral this weekend, "When an assassin's bullet targeted two officers, it targeted this city and it touched the soul of the entire nation." Our nation and our nation's police need your public support. More than that, they deserve it.

Sincerely,
Thomas J. Nee

SOURCE: Thomas J. Nee, letter to President Barack Obama and Attorney General Eric Holder, 29 December 2014, National Association of Police Organizations, Inc., www.napo.org.

DOCUMENT 6 Philonise Floyd | *Testimony Before the House Judiciary Committee Hearing on "Policing Practices and Law Enforcement Accountability," 2020*

On June 10th, 2020, at the peak of that summer's #BlackLivesMatter protests, the U.S. House of Representatives held a hearing on the issues of racial profiling and police brutality. The hearing accompanied the unveiling of the George Floyd Justice in Policing Act, named in honor of the Black man murdered by a white police officer two weeks prior. Democrats leading the hearing called on George Floyd's younger brother PHILONISE FLOYD (b. 1981) as a key witness attesting to the importance of police reforms like a ban on chokeholds and greater consequences for police misconduct. The following document is an excerpt from his testimony, given as the opening statement to the hearing. After the hearing, the George Floyd Justice in Policing Act passed the Democratic-controlled House of Representatives but stalled in the Republican-controlled Senate. Democratic

Representative Sheila Jackson Lee (Texas) reintroduced the bill in May 2024, just before the fourth anniversary of Floyd's death. At the time of this writing, the bill had not advanced to a vote.

> **Breaking it Down** Some scholars argue that "the personal is political." What do you think this means? As you read Philonise Floyd's statement, pay attention to the ways he connects personal tragedy to a political movement. What is Philonise calling upon Congress to do?

Thank you for the invitation to be here today to talk about my big brother, George. . . .

[M]aybe by speaking with you today, I can help make sure that his death isn't in vain. To make sure that he is more than another face on a T-shirt. More than another name on a list that won't stop growing. . . .

I'm tired of the pain I'm feeling now and I'm tired of the pain I feel every time another black person is killed for no reason. I'm here today to ask you to make it stop. Stop the pain. Stop us from being tired. George's calls for help were ignored. Please listen to the call I'm making to you now, to the calls of our family, and to the calls ringing out in the streets across the world. People of all backgrounds, genders and race have come together to demand change. Honor them, honor George, and make the necessary changes that make law enforcement the solution — and not the problem. Hold them accountable when they do something wrong. Teach them what it means to treat people with empathy and respect. Teach them what necessary force is. Teach them that deadly force should be used rarely and only when life is at risk.

George wasn't hurting anyone that day. He didn't deserve to die over twenty dollars. I am asking you, is that what a black man's life is worth? Twenty dollars? This is 2020. Enough is enough. The people marching in the streets are telling you enough is enough. Be the leaders that this country, this world, needs. Do the right thing.

The people elected you to speak for them, to make positive change. George's name means something. You have the opportunity here to make your names mean something, too.

If his death ends up changing the world for the better. . . . Then he died as he lived. It is on you to make sure his death isn't in vain. . . .

PRACTICING AP® SKILLS

1. **AP® Contextualization.** Explain how Black women leaders in the twenty-first century have furthered the goals of civil rights. What examples of this can be found in these documents?
2. **AP® Continuity and Change.** Describe the discrimination faced by both the founders of the twenty-first century Black Lives Matter movement and the twentieth-century Combahee River Collective. To what extent has bias within civil rights movements changed over time?
3. **AP® Comparison.** Compare the Phoenix Law Enforcement Association and the National Association of Police Organizations, Inc. perspective on policing with the viewpoints of supporters of the 1970s Law and Order initiative and 1980s Comprehensive Crime Control Act.
4. **Connecting to AP® Themes.** How has police brutality in the twenty-first century given rise to various forms of resistance and resilience within Black communities in the United States?
5. **Class Discussion.** To what extent has the United States evolved into a post-racial society in the twenty-first century? What evidence from these documents supports your position? What evidence from these documents might be used to counter your position, and how would you rebut or refute that counterargument?

Individual Student Project:
Presentation and Oral Defense

So far, the AP® Skills Workshops on the individual student project have guided you through the process to choose a research topic; select four credible, relevant sources; construct a claim; and curate and analyze evidence in support of that claim. Ideally, you've developed a deep understanding of your research topic informed by a variety of perspectives. It's now time to convey that expertise to your teacher and your classmates through a live presentation and an oral defense. This workshop is designed to increase your familiarity with presentation expectations and build up your confidence before project presentation day.

Examining the AP Rubric

As covered in previous AP® Skills Workshops, the rubric that will be used to assess your Individual Student Project states:

- **Row A (2 points):** One point is awarded for the completion of the source type, citation, and summary for four sources in the Selected Sources Template. A second point is awarded for the completion of the "Description of the relevance to project topic" for four sources in the Selected Sources Template.
- **Row B (1 point):** One point is awarded for an argument or claim that serves as the anchor for the presentation.
- **Row C (4 points):** One point is awarded for accurate evidence from each of the four sources that are discussed in the presentation.
- **Row D (2 points):** One point is awarded for an explanation of one point of comparison (similarity or difference) between two of the selected sources. The comparison must be relevant to the project topic. A second point is awarded for an explanation of a second point of comparison (similarity or difference) between two of the selected sources. *Both points of comparison may be situated in the same two sources; however, each comparison must be distinct and unrelated. Both comparisons must be relevant to the project topic.*

Essentially, you can earn up to two points by filling out the Selected Sources Template, and up to seven additional points by completing a successful presentation. The oral defense and exam day validation account for the remaining five points:

- **Row E (3 points):** One point is awarded for each sufficient response to three oral defense questions. *The Project Manual will include a list of questions from which the teacher may select. The teacher should share this list with students in advance to help them prepare for their defense.*
- **Exam Day Validation (2 points):** During the AP® Exam's free-response section, students will be asked a question about their individual project. *This question will be similar to one of the sample project oral defense questions, but students will respond in writing to this question on the exam.*

These guidelines make clear how important effective preparation for the presentation and oral defense will be; the majority of the fourteen available points are earned on presentation day. Not to worry, though — by the end of this workshop, you'll be well prepared to confidently complete these key components of your Individual Student Project.

Planning Your Presentation

It may be a relief to hear you won't need to improvise your presentation. Like most public speakers, you're allowed (and, in fact, encouraged) to plan out your remarks in advance. You'll have only five minutes to present your argument, so we recommend outlining your presentation using time guidelines like the following:

- **30 seconds:** Introduce your research topic and state your claim.
- **30 seconds:** Preview the sources you selected.
- **3 minutes, 30 seconds:** Present four pieces of evidence, explain how each piece supports your claim, and draw two comparisons.
- **30 seconds:** Wrap up your presentation, perhaps by explaining the significance of your topic within the field of African American Studies.

When deciding on the order in which to present your evidence, it can be helpful to group sources whose perspectives are clearly similar or different. For instance, if Source 1 and Source 2 both support a certain conclusion, it will be useful to discuss them together. After discussing Source 1, you can move to Source 2 with a phrase such as, "Like Source 1, Source 2 supports the idea that . . ." On the other hand, imagine that Source 3 is a counterargument that contrasts with Source 1. You can introduce this dissenting source with a phrase such as, "Unlike Source 1, Source 3 offers evidence that . . ." You might also find it helpful to identify the source that you find most compelling with a phrase like, "Source 4 provides the strongest evidence to support my claim because . . ."

Once you've completed a presentation outline, make sure to rehearse out loud to confirm how long each section will *actually* take. If you struggle to stay on track, you can use a physical or virtual stopwatch to keep track of how much time passes as you speak. We also recommend inviting friends or family members to watch you practice and to give feedback on your presentation approach. These dress rehearsals will help you practice speaking at a pace and volume that's sustainable for you and comprehensible by an audience.

Preparing for the Oral Defense

Following your live presentation, you'll have three minutes to answer three questions about your project out loud. Fortunately, these questions simply ask you to reflect on the project steps you've already completed. And, if you completed the activities from the previous two AP® Skills Workshops, you've actually brainstormed answers to the majority of the questions that could be asked:

Strategic Selection of Sources

1. Select one of the sources you used and explain why you chose this source to include in your project.
2. Identify the source that most deepened your understanding of your topic and explain in what way it added depth to your understanding of your topic.
3. Explain how excluding one of your sources would have weakened your argument.
4. Explain how you determined that one of your sources is reliable.
5. Identify which of your sources is the most persuasive and explain why it is so persuasive.
6. Identify the source that was most important to your research topic and explain its importance.
7. Explain why the four sources you selected, compared to other sources you considered but did not select, are the best for supporting your argument.
8. Describe the most important source of information you found while conducting your research, and explain why it was important to your research process.
9. Describe which of the various perspectives you explored was most difficult for you to incorporate into your project, and explain why this was the case.

Comparison of Sources

1. Explain how two of your sources provide different perspectives on an aspect of your topic.
2. Explain how two of your sources provide similar perspectives on an aspect of your topic.
3. Explain why one of your sources is more convincing than another.
4. Explain why one of your sources is more reliable than another.
5. Explain how a combination of two of your sources strengthened your argument.
6. Explain how a combination of two of your sources added depth or insight to your understanding of your topic.
7. Describe any lack of agreement or contradictory information you found as you did your research. Explain what this lack of agreement or contradiction revealed about your topic.

Other Questions

1. Describe one piece of information you learned from a source you used in your project that was not included in your classroom instruction.
2. Describe one piece of information you learned from a source you used in your project that adds to information you learned in your classroom instruction.
3. Explain how the research you conducted connects to a topic from the course in ways that you did not know or expect until after you had completed your research.
4. Explain how the research you conducted revealed additional questions or insights about your topic.
5. Explain why you were initially interested in this topic and how well your research aligned with what you expected to learn about your topic.

The questions asked during your oral defense aren't meant to be trick questions. Your evaluator(s) will simply use your responses to confirm you performed high-quality research, discovered connections between your sources, and reflected on your project's significance within and beyond the AP® African American Studies course.

To prepare for a successful oral defense, practice answering each question in front of a mirror or an audience under a strict one-minute time limit. Keep your answers as clear and as succinct as possible. On exam day, you'll also have to respond in writing to one of the oral defense questions. So, in the days prior to the exam, you'll want to make sure you're still comfortable articulating answers to each of the questions.

Setting Yourself Up for Success

It's natural to be nervous before your presentation. Keep in mind, however, that you chose your research topic because it's interesting and exciting! Enthusiasm is infectious — if you bring passion for your project topic, your audience is much more likely to find your presentation engaging. Review the following tips if you could use an additional confidence boost:

- **Plan ahead to prevent anxiety.** If public speaking makes you nervous, don't hesitate to speak with your teacher ahead of time so you can do some troubleshooting together. Perhaps your teacher could connect you to a peer who'd be a good practice partner, or arrange for you to present toward the end of the class period once your nerves settle out. Next, in the days before your presentation, try to find time for an activity that brings you joy and gives you a sense of accomplishment. Keep that feeling of confidence fresh in your mind so you can tap into it during your presentation. Then, the night before your presentation, do your best to get a good night's sleep so you can be as alert and attentive as possible. Finally, if you're a perfectionist who worries about making mistakes, remember, the rubric doesn't *subtract* points from your score; it gives evaluators opportunities to award you points. As long as your presentation includes all of the components defined in the rubric, you will earn full points.
- **Prepare for distractions.** No matter how much you've practiced your presentation, on presentation day you may encounter unexpected circumstances that throw off the talking points you've rehearsed. That's why we recommend bringing a physical copy of your presentation outline with you and keeping it nearby or in hand while you present. In the case of technical issues, interruptions, or surprises like unexpected audience members, you can pause, find the place where you left off in your outline, and take a deep breath before continuing.
- **Project confidence.** No matter how you feel on the inside, do your best to communicate confidently. Stand up straight, and try to breathe smoothly. Be sure that you project your voice. What you have to say is important, and people in the back of the room should be able to hear you. Avoid filler words like "um" or "like" to the best of your ability. Finally, remind yourself that you're the expert on your presentation topic and will almost certainly know more about it than anyone else in the room.

Following your presentation, make sure to congratulate yourself for bringing your best effort to a college-level research project. Take a moment to reflect on your progress from the beginning of the school year and consider how you'd like to apply your new skills!

recap

Preparing for Presentation Day

Give yourself the best chance of success by:

- Preparing a thorough outline to bring with you on presentation day
- Rehearsing your presentation out loud in front of a mirror and then for friends and family
- Practicing your responses to each oral defense question under a one-minute time limit
- Boost your confidence by communicating your needs to your teacher, preparing for distractions, and prioritizing public speaking skills like projection and grounded body language

Activity ▸ Preparing for Presentation Day

To prepare for presentation day, draft an outline like the one to follow:

Task	Notes
30 seconds: Introduce your research topic and state your claim.	**Topic:** **Claim:**
30 seconds: Preview the sources you selected.	**Source 1:** **Source 2:** **Source 3:** **Source 4:**

3 minutes, 30 seconds: Present four pieces of evidence, explain how each piece supports your claim, and draw two comparisons.	1. **Connection to claim:** **Transition to next source:** 2. **Connection to claim:** **Transition to next source:** 3. **Connection to claim:** **Transition to next source:** 4. **Connection to claim:**
30 seconds: Wrap up your presentation.	**Significance of topic within African American Studies:**

Multiple-Choice Questions

Questions 1–2 refer to the following.

Pete Souza, *Official Portrait of President Barack Obama in the Oval Office*, 2012

Library of Congress, Prints & Photographs Division, Reproduction number LC-DIG-ppbd-00603 (original digital file)

1. Which of the following historical developments is most directly responsible for the historical situation depicted in the image?

(A) The federal enforcement of the Civil Rights Act of 1964

(B) The political compromises that produced the Equal Employment Act of 1972

(C) The protections offered under the Voting Rights Act of 1965

(D) The access to Black middle-class status by the Fair Housing Act of 1968

2. The degree of growth in Black political representation in the early 2000s mirrored which of the following historical developments from previous centuries?

(A) Black abolitionists running for local office in the North before the Civil War (1815–1861)

(B) First-generation Black college graduates holding local school board positions during the nadir (1878–1940s)

(C) Newly emancipated freedmen serving in state and federal political positions during Reconstruction (1865–1877)

(D) SNCC members occupying municipal political positions during the Black freedom struggle (1940s–1970s)

Short-Answer Question

"When you design an event/campaign/et cetera based on the work of queer Black women, don't invite them to participate in shaping it, but ask them to provide materials and ideas for next steps for said event, that is racism in practice. It's also hetero-patriarchal. Straight men, unintentionally or intentionally, have taken the work of queer Black women and erased our contributions. Perhaps if we were the charismatic Black men many are rallying around these days, it would have been a different story, but being Black queer women in this society (and apparently within these movements) tends to equal invisibility and non-relevancy. We completely expect those who benefit directly and improperly from White supremacy to try and erase our existence. We fight that every day. But when it happens amongst our allies, we are baffled, we are saddened, and we are enraged. And it's time to have the political conversation about why that's not okay. . . . It's important that we work together to build and acknowledge the legacy of Black contributions to the struggle for human rights. If you adapt Black Lives Matter, use the opportunity to talk about its inception and political framing. Lift up Black lives as an opportunity to connect struggles across race, class, gender, nationality, sexuality, and disability."

SOURCE: Alicia Garza, "A Herstory of the #BlackLivesMatter Movement," 2014

1. Using the excerpt, answer A, B, C, and D.

(A) Describe the broader context of Garza's speech.

(B) Using one specific example, explain how Garza's experience and perspective compared to the experience and perspective of the women of the Combahee River Collective.

(C) Using one specific example, explain how gender discrimination faced by Black women within the movement for racial equality in the twenty-first century compared to gender discrimination faced by Black women within the movement for racial equality in the mid-nineteenth century.

(D) Explain how one Black woman activist brought attention to interlocking systems of oppression.

Multiple-Choice Questions

Questions 1–3 refer to the following.

African American Population of the United States, 1790–2020

Year	Black Population	Percentage of Total Population	Number of Enslaved People	Percentage of Blacks Who Were Enslaved
1790	757,208	19.3	697,681	92
1800	1,002,037	18.9	893,602	89
1810	1,377,808	19.0	1,191,362	86
1820	1,771,656	18.4	1,538,022	87
1830	2,328,642	18.1	2,009,043	86
1840	2,873,648	16.1	2,487,355	87
1850	3,638,808	15.7	3,204,287	88
1860	4,441,830	14.1	3,953,731	89
1870	4,880,009	12.7	—	—
1880	6,580,793	13.1	—	—
1890	7,488,788	11.9	—	—
1900	8,833,994	11.6	—	—
1910	9,827,763	10.7	—	—
1920	10,463,131	9.9	—	—
1930	11,891,143	9.7	—	—
1940	12,865,518	9.8	—	—
1950	15,044,937	10.0	—	—
1960	18,871,931	10.6	—	—
1970	22,580,289	11.1	—	—
1980	26,482,349	11.8	—	—
1990	29,986,060	12.0	—	—
2000	34,658,190	12.3	—	—
2010	38,929,319	12.6	—	—
2020	46,936,733	14.2	—	—

SOURCE: *U.S. Census Bureau, Historical Statistics of the United States, Colonial Times to 1970* (1975); *Statistical Abstract of the United States*, 2010; 2020 Census Demographic Profile.

1. Which of the following best describes why the percentage of Black Americans making up the total U.S. population declined in the 1870s?

(A) Due to an influx of white European immigrants into the United States after the Civil War, there was a relative decline in the population of African Americans.

(B) Due to the ratification of the Thirteenth, Fourteenth, and Fifteenth Amendments, many Black Americans emigrated to Canada and Mexico.

(C) Due to the failure of the federal government to enforce the Fourteenth Amendment, lynchings took the lives of many African Americans.

(D) Due to the Supreme Court decision *Plessy v. Ferguson*, the population of Black Americans declined.

2. Which of the following best explains the decline in African Americans' percentage of total population from 1920 to 1940?

(A) Many Black Americans who joined the military decided to remain in Europe after World War I.

(B) The United States and other Western democracies were dealing with a global economic crisis historically known as the Great Depression, which had a devastating impact on rural and Black Americans.

(C) The United States supported the formation of the American Colonization Society, which worked to create a new homeland for displaced Black Americans in Africa.

(D) Many Black Americans died from the global influenza pandemic in the 1920s, and their population numbers did not fully recover until the 1950s.

3. Which of the following claims is best supported by the evidence displayed in the chart?

(A) From 1790 to 2010, the percentage of the total population represented by Black Americans has steadily declined.

(B) From 1790 to 1870, the total population of Black Americans declined as demand for enslaved labor diminished.

(C) From 1790 to 2010, the percentage of the total population represented by Black Americans experienced a slow but steady downtrend followed by a slow but steady uptrend, reflecting the resilience of Black American culture.

(D) From 1870 to 2010, the total population of Black Americans has stopped growing due to increased emigration to countries outside the United States.

Questions 4–6 refer to the following.

Dorothea Lange, *Negro sharecropper's son goes up and down the long rows worming tobacco*, Wake County, North Carolina, July 1939

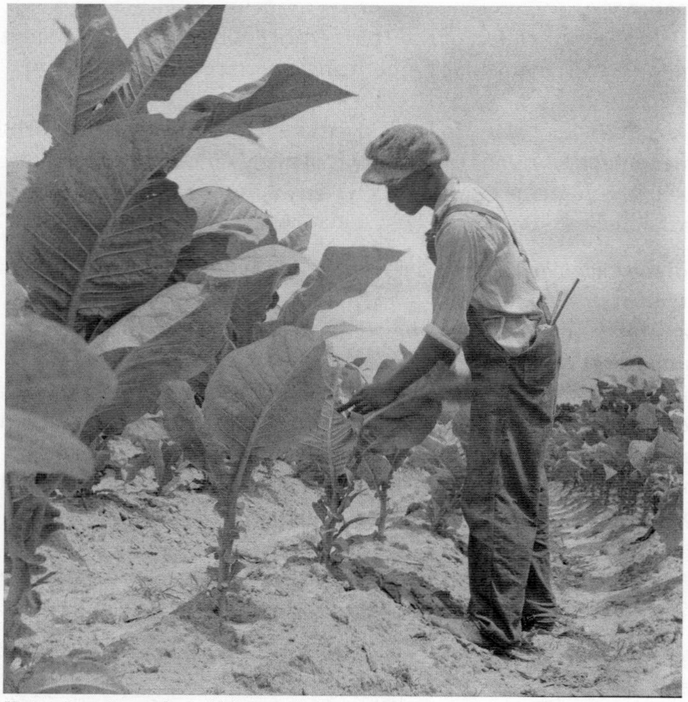

Heritage Image Partnership Ltd/Alamy Stock Photo

4. Which of the following best describes the economic circumstances of Black Americans in the early 1900s as reflected in the image?

(A) Due to the Great Migration, many affluent African Americans relocated and established new institutions of higher education.

(B) Many African Americans took the advice of Booker T. Washington and worked as farmhands rather than pursue manufacturing jobs.

(C) Many African Americans in the South had to work as sharecroppers, often for the same families who had enslaved them or their family members.

(D) After Reconstruction, most African Americans pushed for the establishment of colleges and universities in the South as a way to escape the physical difficulty of agricultural labor.

5. Which of the following best describes the employment options available to Black Americans in the early 1900s?

(A) In addition to sharecropping, Black Americans were encouraged and allowed to pursue any form of work.

(B) In addition to sharecropping, Black Americans could often find low-wage union jobs performing manual labor.

(C) In addition to sharecropping, Black Americans often took jobs in factories, domestic labor, or joined the military.

(D) In addition to sharecropping, Black Americans could also work in the entertainment industry or pursue higher education at colleges and universities.

6. Which of the following statements best reflects the work experiences of Black women in the North during the early 1900s?

(A) Black women in the North were often subject to forced labor under the convict leasing system.

(B) Black women in the North often were forced to work as domestic laborers, often enduring discrimination and inhumane treatment.

(C) Black women in the North were often able to find lucrative employment in factories as the end of Reconstruction in the South led to an industrial boom in the North.

(D) Black women in the North worked primarily as laundry workers and successfully staged protests to address the inequalities they experienced.

Questions 7–9 refer to the following.

Flag outside of the headquarters of the National Association for the Advancement of Colored People (NAACP), New York City, 1936

MPI/Getty Images

7. Which of the following statements best explains why the NAACP stopped displaying the flag seen in the image?

(A) The flag was removed after the owners of the building where the NAACP had its headquarters threatened to evict the NAACP from its office space.

(B) The flag was removed as a sign of successful protest after the federal government agreed to investigate the widespread use of lynching in the South to intimidate and terrorize Black citizens.

(C) The flag was removed after the NAACP decided to change tactics from public protests to legal challenges, using the court system to fight racial injustice.

(D) The flag was removed after the federal government agreed to the NAACP's demands to make lynching a federal hate crime with stiffer criminal penalties.

8. Which of the following best reflects a shift in policy that resulted from NAACP activism?

(A) The ratification of the Fourteenth and Fifteenth Amendments, ensuring the rights of citizenship for all freedpeople and outlawing discrimination of voting rights based on race

(B) The issuance of Executive Order 8802 by President Roosevelt, ending racial discrimination in defense industries and creating the Fair Employment Practices Commission (FEPC) to ensure compliance

(C) The decision by prominent news outlets like the *New York Tribune* and the *Atlanta Constitution* coverage to cover lynching as a problem in the United States

(D) Activism by the NAACP did not result in any meaningful policy changes in the United States during the twentieth century.

9. Which of the following events is most similar to the lynchings that caused the NAACP to display the flag in the image?

(A) The rise of exploitation of Black urban communities due to discriminatory housing policies

(B) The decrease in employment opportunities for Black Americans during the Great Depression

(C) The revocation of tax cuts for Black college students who attended historically Black colleges and universities

(D) The proliferation of racial violence incited by white supremacists in the summer of 1919, also known as the "Red Summer"

Questions 10–12 refer to the following.

SOURCE 1

Captain Charity Adams, the first African American Women's Army Corps (WACs) officer, leading her company at the Fort Des Moines Training Center in Iowa, 1942

National Archives and Records Administration, Still Pictures Record Section, NARA-531334/111-SC-238651

SOURCE 2

Red, white, and blue linen handkerchief promoting the "Double V" campaign during World War II

Collection of the Smithsonian National Museum of African American History and Culture

10. Which of the following best describes the context out of which the "Double Victory" campaign emerged?

(A) Black men and women were often discriminated against at home despite their patriotic sacrifices during World War II.

(B) Black women were often denied the opportunity to serve in the U.S. military, prompting a push to raise awareness about this form of inequality.

(C) Black women who enlisted in the military were often relegated to menial labor despite being trained to perform more advanced duties in support of the war.

(D) The discriminatory administration of the GI Bill after World War II deepened the economic inequality suffered by Black Americans, prompting many to push for an end to system or institutionalized racism.

11. Which of the following best explains the connection between the experiences of Black women in the military like Frances Thorpe and the "Double Victory" campaign?

(A) Black women were faced with the same discriminatory practices within the navy, which is one of the reasons why only two Black women were able to obtain an officer's rank during World War II.

(B) An estimated 500 Black women who served in the army as nurses during World War II were initially allowed only to care for Black soldiers, but with few Black men in combat and non-Black casualties rising, the army reversed this policy.

(C) The Roosevelt administration's initial decision to bar Black men from joining the navy was so distasteful that only a few Black women volunteered even after Roosevelt lifted the ban.

(D) Since millions of Black women experienced discrimination due to the federal government's failure to enforce the Fourteenth Amendment, many did not volunteer to serve in the military during World War II.

12. Which of the following best reflects the ideals of the "Double Victory" campaign, as expressed by James G. Thompson's letter in the *Pittsburgh Courier* in 1942?

(A) Black Americans ought to be united in their struggle for equality.

(B) Black Americans should commit to a dual victory: defeating fascists abroad and defeating racists at home.

(C) Black Americans had to accept the slow pace of change regarding the end of racist discrimination.

(D) Black Americans should feel proud that their contributions to the war effort were making a major difference in Europe.

Questions 13–15 refer to the following.

American record producer Berry Gordy Jr., founder of the Motown record label, with his sister Esther Gordy Edwards, an executive at Motown, United Kingdom, October 10, 1964

Evening Standard/Getty Images

13. Which of the following best explains the relationship between Black musicians and activism in the 1960s?

(A) In the 1960s, Black musicians had relatively small audiences, so when their music addressed the problem of racism, it had little impact.

(B) In the 1960s, Black musicians had increasingly large audiences, so their songs brought awareness to problems of racism as well as the other experiences of Black Americans.

(C) In the 1960s, Black musicians did not focus on activism and instead focused on breaking barriers by creating their own businesses.

(D) In the 1960s, Black musicians shied away from incorporating the musical styles and expressions associated with African heritage, hoping to create a more commercially successful product.

14. Which of the following historical contexts most fed the evolution of Black American music in the 1960s?

(A) Historically, American music companies engaged in discriminatory practices against Black musicians, from refusing to produce their music to refusing them fair compensation.

(B) Historically, Black Americans found strength and solidarity in musical performance, from the singing of songs during the era of enslavement, to the singing of spirituals at protests during the civil rights era.

(C) World War II exposed Black soldiers to musical traditions in Europe and Asia, which the soldiers brought back home.

(D) Due to enslavement, none of the musical traditions of Africa survived to influence Black musicians in the United States, so the evolution of Black music was driven purely by exposure to other American cultures.

15. Which statement best describes how Black American musicians employed African musical and performative traditions?

(A) The song "Inner City Blues" by Marvin Gaye, produced by Motown Records, employed bongo drums, an instrument associated with the once-enslaved Bantu people in Cuba.

(B) Black American musicians rarely used African musical and performative traditions because they were afraid it would make their music less appealing to the commercial mainstream.

(C) Several hit songs by the Supremes that were produced by Motown Records — "Where Did Our Love Go," "Baby Love," "Back in My Arms Again," and "Come See about Me" — were all love songs, tapping the African tradition of songs about love and romantic desire.

(D) Black American musicians exclusively used African musical and performative traditions because they had no interest in appealing to the commercial mainstream.

Short-Answer Questions

1. Using the image, answer A, B, C, and D.

Poster for concert to aid sit-ins and Martin Luther King's legal defense, 1960

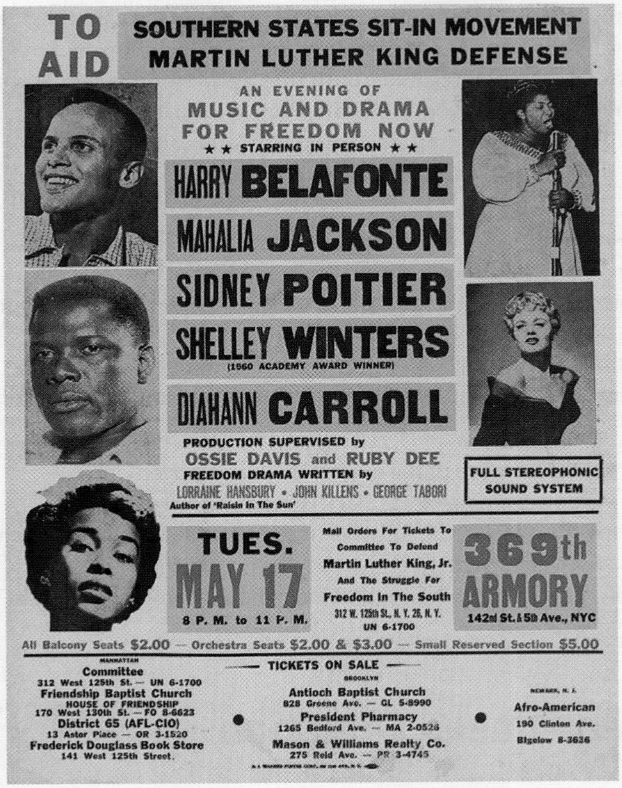

Collection of the Smithsonian National Museum of African American History and Culture

(A) Describe the broader historical context relevant to the poster.
(B) Describe the poster's connection to the Civil Rights movement.
(C) Describe the outcome of sit-ins like the one promoted by the poster.
(D) Explain how the poser used the power of celebrities to advance the Civil Rights movement.

2. Using the excerpt, answer A, B, C, and D.

"To those who have said, 'Be patient and wait,' we have long said that we cannot be patient. We do not want our freedom gradually, but we want to be free now! We are tired. We are tired of being beaten by policemen. We are tired of seeing our people locked up in jail over and over again. And then you holler, 'Be patient.' How long can we be patient? We want our freedom and we want it now. . . . I appeal to all of you to get into this great revolution that is sweeping this nation. Get in and stay in the streets of every city until true freedom comes. . . . We must get in this revolution and complete the revolution. . . .

They're talking about slow down and stop. We will not stop. . . . If we do not get meaningful legislation out of this Congress, the time will come when we will not confine our marching to Washington. We will march through the South; through the streets of Jackson, through the streets of Danville, through the streets of Cambridge, through the streets of Birmingham. But we will march with the spirit of love and with the spirit of dignity that we have shown here today. By the force of our demands, our determination, and our numbers, we shall splinter the segregated South into a thousand pieces and put them together in the image of God and democracy. We must say: 'Wake up America! Wake up!' For we cannot stop, and we will not and cannot be patient."

SOURCE: John Lewis, chair of the Student Nonviolent Coordinating Committee (SNCC), Speech at the March on Washington, 1963

(A) Describe the broader historical context that led to the March on Washington.
(B) Describe one way in which John Lewis's speech at the March on Washington reflects the activism of another civil rights activist from the same time period.
(C) Describe the outcome of the March on Washington.
(D) Explain how Lewis's speech reflects the principles of nonviolent resistance.

3. **Answer A, B, C, and D.**
(A) Describe the purpose of the Black Is Beautiful movement.
(B) Describe one example of the Black Is Beautiful movement.
(C) Describe the relationship between the Black Is Beautiful movement and another social movement in the twentieth or twenty-first century.
(D) Explain how the Black Is Beautiful movement relates to the Black Campus movement.

Document-Based Question

1. **Explain how Black political ideologies have evolved or remained consistent from the 1960s to the present.**

In your response you should do the following:

- **Respond to the prompt with a defensible thesis or claim that establishes a line of reasoning.**
- **Describe a broader historical or disciplinary context relevant to the topic of the prompt.**
- **Support an argument in response to the prompt using at least three of the sources.**
- **Use at least one additional piece of specific evidence (beyond the evidence found in the sources) relevant to your argument.**
- **For at least two sources, explain how or why the perspective, purpose, context, and/or audience for each source is relevant to your argument.**
- **Reference or cite the sources you use in your argument. You can reference or cite the source letter, title, or author.**

SOURCE A

The Voting Rights Act of 1965, signed into law on August 6, 1965, by President Lyndon Johnson

About the source: Although the Fifteenth Amendment, ratified in 1870, banned voting discrimination, southern states still adopted discriminatory voting practices after Reconstruction ended to disfranchise African Americans, including literacy tests and poll taxes as a prerequisite to voting. This act marked the first time this amendment was fully enforced, nearly a century later.

> AN ACT To enforce the fifteenth amendment to the Constitution of the United States, and for other purposes.
>
> Be it enacted by the Senate and House of Representatives of the United States of America in Congress assembled, That this Act shall be known as the "Voting Rights Act of 1965."
>
> SEC. 2. No voting qualification or prerequisite to voting, or standard, practice, or procedure shall be imposed or applied by any State or political subdivision to deny or abridge the right of any citizen of the United States to vote on account of race or color. . . .
>
> SEC. 4. (a) To assure that the right of citizens of the United States to vote is not denied or abridged on account of race or color, no citizen shall be denied the right to vote in any Federal, State, or local election because of his failure to comply with any test or device in any State. . . .
>
> (c) The phrase "test or device" shall mean any requirement that a person as a prerequisite for voting or registration for voting (1) demonstrate the ability to read, write, understand, or interpret any matter, (2) demonstrate any educational achievement or his knowledge of any particular subject, (3) possess good moral character, or (4) prove his qualifications by the voucher of registered voters or members of any other class. . . .
>
> SEC. 10. (a) The Congress finds that the requirement of the payment of a poll tax as a precondition to voting (i) precludes persons of limited means from voting or imposes unreasonable financial hardship upon such persons as a precondition to their exercise of the franchise, (ii) does not bear a reasonable relationship to any legitimate State interest in the conduct of elections, and (iii) in some areas has the purpose or effect of denying persons the right to vote because of race or color. Upon the basis of these findings, Congress declares that the constitutional right of citizens to vote is denied or abridged in some areas by the requirement of the payment of a poll tax as a precondition to voting.

SOURCE B

AP® source **Protest photographs: (1) Fred Ward, photograph of Gloria Richardson, leader of Maryland's Cambridge Nonviolent Action Committee at a demonstration for jobs, housing, and desegregation, 1963; (2) Timothy A. Clary, photograph of a vigil for George Floyd and demonstration against police brutality at the Cathedral Church of St. John the Divine in New York, 2020**

Associated Press/AP Images

TIMOTHY A. CLARY/Getty Images

SOURCE C

Pew Research Center, *Black Americans' views on political strategies, leadership and allyship for achieving equality*, 2022

Majorities of Black adults say voting and supporting Black businesses are effective ways to move toward equality

% of Black adults who say each of the following are extremely/very effective tactics for helping Black people move toward equality in the U.S.

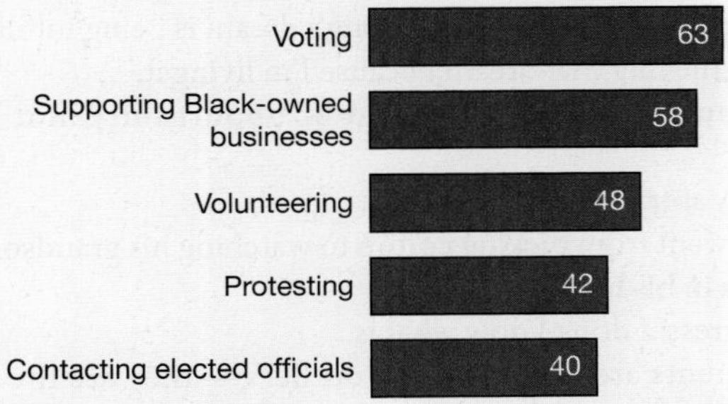

Note: Black adults include those who say their race is Black alone and non-Hispanic. Black and at least one other race and non-Hispanic, or Black and Hispanic.

Source: Survey of U.S. adults conducted Oct. 4-17, 2021.

"Black Americans Have a Clear Vision for Reducing Racism but Little Hope It Will Happen"

PEW RESEARCH CENTER

Nearly four-in-ten Black adults say Black Lives Matter has done the most to help Black people in recent years

% of Black adults who say ____ has done the most to help Black people in the U.S. in recent years

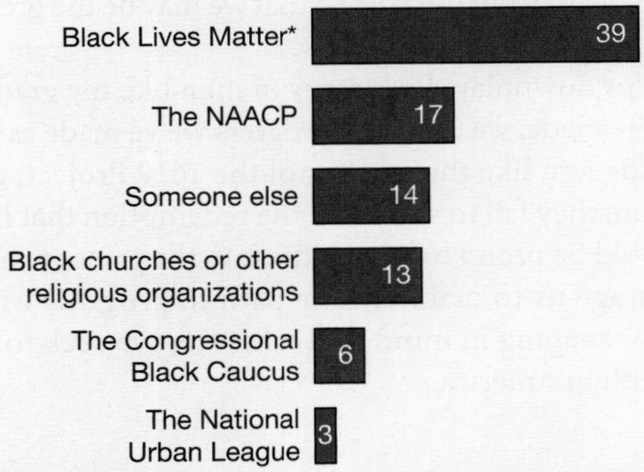

*Survey question did not specify whether "Black Lives Matter" was the name of an organization or a broader movement.

Note: Black adults include those who say their race is Black alone and non-Hispanic. Black and at least one other race and non-Hispanic, or Black and Hispanic. Share of respondents who didn't offer a response not shown.

Source: Survey of U.S. adults conducted Oct. 4-17, 2021.

"Black Americans Have a Clear Vision for Reducing Racism but Little Hope It Will Happen"

PEW RESEARCH CENTER

SOURCE D

Senator Tim Scott (R-SC), "Dr. King Would Be Proud of America's Progress," ***New York Post*** **op-ed, August 28, 2023**

Instead of resigning himself to the idea we were hopeless, [Martin Luther King Jr.] had hope that America would meet the challenge.

King believed then what some doubt now — that if you have faith in God, faith in each other and faith in our nation's future, all things are possible.

America is meeting the challenge, and King's dream is being fulfilled.

I know we are achieving that dream because I'm living it.

I am living proof America is the land of opportunity, not a land of oppression.

This isn't just my story. It's all our stories.

My grandfather went from picking cotton to watching his grandson pick out his seat in Congress in his lifetime.

If that's not progress, I don't know what is.

These achievements are no longer the outliers — they are the stories of millions of Americans.

Yesterday, stories like ours were the exceptions. Today, they can be the rule for anyone willing to work hard for his or her piece of the American dream.

Unfortunately, the radical left is seeking to first deny and then reverse our progress in achieving King's dream. . . .

To say there isn't work to be done would not be an argument made in good faith.

But that's what the pursuit of maintaining the American Dream is all about. . . .

We can't cancel our history, no matter how painful it may have been.

Instead, we should learn from our past so that we may be the great protectors of our future.

When we ignore or downplay the history of men like my granddaddy and the progress his family made, we erase the progress we've made as a nation.

While those on the left, like the authors of the 1619 Project, dwell on our original sin as a nation, they fail to showcase the redemption that has followed.

I believe King would be proud to bear witness to the gains we have made.

He would encourage us to maintain the path to progress with the same hopeful optimism — keeping in mind that whatever we seek to achieve can only be done with faith in America.

SOURCE E

House Representative Ayanna Pressley (D-MA, 7th District), "Keeping the Promise of Democracy: Remarks at the 54th Annual Martin Luther King Jr. Memorial Breakfast," Boston, Massachusetts, January 15, 2024

I don't have to tell any of you that we need . . . young truth tellers, especially right now, when there are so called leaders among us who deny election results, assert the Civil War was not about slavery, and ignorant enough to affirm that the enslavement of Africans was a workforce development program.

[Martin Luther King Jr.] understood that education is not merely about acquiring knowledge but also about fostering the kind of thinking that empowers individuals to challenge injustice, question the status quo, and to build a better future.

It's why he put his body on the line alongside so many of you, time and again in the fight to desegregate our schools, both as a means to dismantle institutionalized racism and to ensure that every Black child [has] equal access to a quality education and the opportunities that come with it.

He understood clearly the role of education in the broader fight for our liberation.

Today's movement work remains intersectional as do the attacks, at every level, from our far-right and imbalanced Supreme Court dismantling affirmative action, to state legislatures across our country threatening to ban books, which affirm our lived experience, honor Black brilliance and confront white supremacy, to the coordinated, national assault on DEI programs, from the boardroom to the classroom, and a rise in the same political violence that took Dr. King.

Throughout this weekend of national observance, excerpts from King's speeches will be weaponized, even perverted, to justify legislated white supremacy.

When the truth of the matter is that the real Reverend Dr. Martin Luther King Jr. was a proud and unapologetic Black man, a prophetic preacher, and radical dreamer with a bold vision and desire for revolutionary change, who affirmed in word and deed, despite the selective amnesia of many, that Black Lives Matter.

NOTES

Part I: Multiple-Choice

Questions 1–5 refer to the following.

"The central reality of Plessy was that discrimination on Louisiana's trains would be legal under the following circumstances: namely, when the separate services and facilities offered Black and white passengers by race were substantially equal.... As had been the case with the Founding Fathers vis-à-vis slavery a century earlier, these justices could have decided otherwise. They could have said the Constitution meant something other than what it did specifically and plainly say. Instead they chose.... to decide on the basis of the document's exact words. They could have foreseen that services and facilities for African Americans neither would nor could ever in fact be equal."

SOURCE: Jerrold M. Packard, *American Nightmare: The History of Jim Crow*, 2003

1. Which of the following best describes the author's central claim in this excerpt?
(A) The *Plessy v. Ferguson* case had long-lasting consequences.
(B) The Founding Fathers did not take strong stances on issues of race.
(C) The Founding Fathers intended for a literal interpretation of the Constitution.
(D) The eventual consequences of the *Plessy v. Ferguson* ruling were obvious and could have been avoided by the Supreme Court.

2. Which of the following statements would the author of the excerpt most likely agree with?
(A) Strong resentment against the federal government during Reconstruction made the rise of Jim Crow inevitable.
(B) The Founding Fathers were clear on their support for gradual equality before the law.
(C) Weak federal support for equity and civil rights paved the way for the formation of a Jim Crow South.
(D) The concept of "separate but equal" could have worked in the South if it were not for former Confederates who refused to respect the authority of the Supreme Court.

3. The period surrounding the *Plessy v. Ferguson* court case is commonly referred to as which of the following?
(A) The nadir
(B) The Harlem Renaissance
(C) The Second Middle Passage
(D) The Great Migration

4. Which of the following strategies in the 1950s eventually led to the overturn of *Plessy v. Ferguson*?
(A) Nonviolent civil disobedience and pursuit of federal legislation making segregation illegal
(B) Ratification of a new constitutional amendment specifically outlawing segregation
(C) The emigration of Black Americans to Liberia in the 1950s
(D) International sanctions from countries condemning segregationist policies in the United States

5. Which of the following statements best describes the impact of *Plessy v. Ferguson*?
   (A) Its widespread impact was felt in the South only.
   (B) Its ruling applied to hospitals, transportation, schools, and cemeteries.
   (C) It excluded Black Americans from society and left them without businesses or organizations to meet their needs.
   (D) It was left unchallenged until the 1950s.

Questions 6–8 refer to the following.

Africa's Diverse Geography

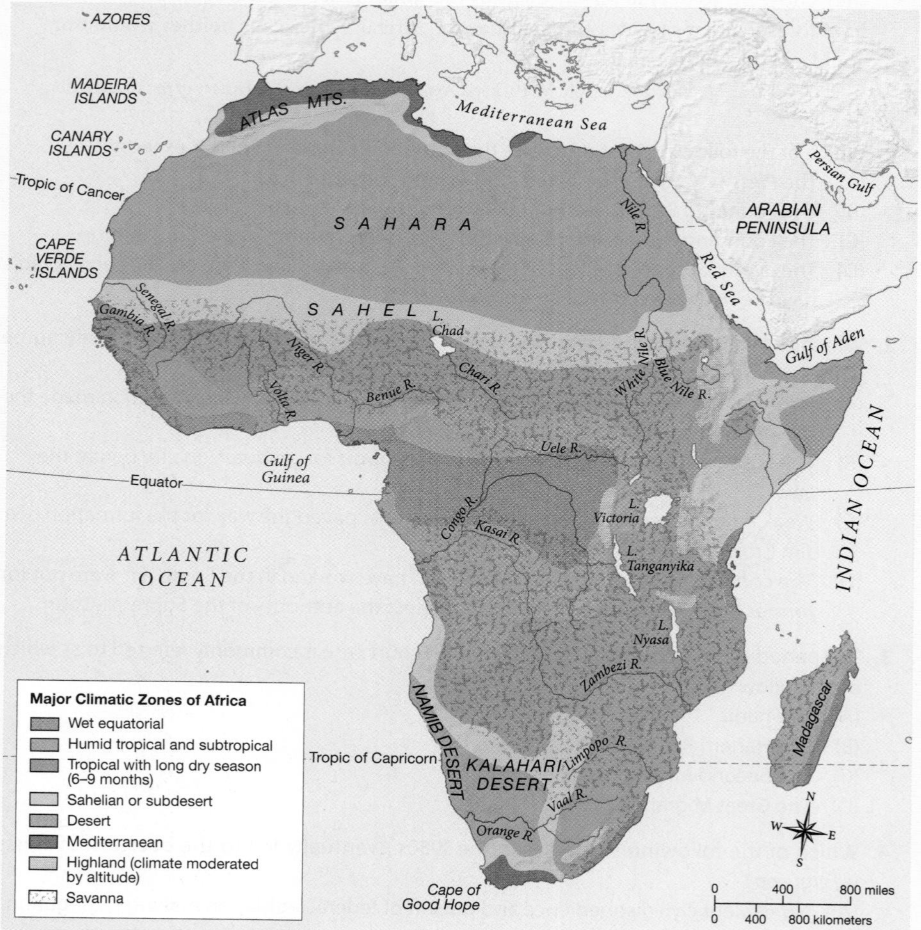

6. Which of the following best describes the relationship of African geography to the rise of ancient and medieval African civilizations?

(A) The diversity of African geography resulted in few large or complex ancient and medieval African societies.

(B) The large desert and dense equatorial climates cut off trade within the continent, leaving societies in northern and central Africa isolated and without global trading partners.

(C) The diversity of African geography offered many resources to ancient and medieval African societies, including clay, iron, navigable rivers, and fertile farmland.

(D) The diversity of African geography produced only one major resource, iron, limiting the growth of ancient and medieval African societies.

7. Which of the following best describes how access to water influenced African civilizations?

(A) Inland waterways such as the Niger, Congo, Nile, and Zambezi Rivers allowed ancient African societies to develop lucrative trade networks within Africa.

(B) The flooding of Africa's rivers provided its ancient civilizations with agricultural productivity that was the primary driver of their growth.

(C) Africa's long coastlines, from the Atlantic and Indian Oceans to the Mediterranean and Red Seas, gave rise to the global trading networks that primarily drove the growth of ancient societies.

(D) Africa's coastlines and many internal rivers supplied both global and African trade networks, and river floodplains supplied some societies with fertile agricultural lands.

8. Which of the following best describes the geographic features of the continent of Africa that influenced the Bantu migration?

(A) The poor farmland in West Africa led to a food shortage that drove the Bantu people to migrate east and south.

(B) The drying of the grasslands along the southern Sahara plus a rise in population likely pushed the Bantu people to migrate east and south.

(C) The impassibility of the Great Rift Valley cut off Bantu migration along the Swahili Coast.

(D) The density of trees in the Congo River basin forced the Bantu people to choose different routes, causing them to migrate in more directions.

Questions 9–11 refer to the following.

"While driving in a chaise from Portsmouth to Deep-river, I picked up on the road a jaded looking negro, who proved to be a very intelligent and good-natured fellow. His account of the lumber business, and of the life of the lumbermen in the swamps, in answer to my questions, was clear and precise, and was afterwards verified by information obtained from his master. He told me that his name was Joseph, that he belonged to a church in one of the inland counties, and that he was hired out by the trustees of the church to his present master. He expressed entire contentment with his lot, but showed great unwillingness to be sold to go on to a plantation. He liked to 'mind himself,' as he did in the swamps. The Dismal Swamps are noted places of refuge for runaway negroes.... Children were born, bred, lived and died here.... There were people in the swamps still, he thought, that were the children of runaways, and who had been runaways themselves all their lives. What a life it must be; born outlaws; educated self-stealers; trained from infancy to be constantly in dread of the approach of a white man as a thing more fearful than wild-cats or serpents, or even starvation.... Joseph said that they had huts in 'back places,' hidden by bushes, and difficult of access; he had, apparently, been himself quite intimate with them. When the shingle negroes employed them, he told me, they made them get up logs for them, and would give them enough to eat, and some clothes, and perhaps two dollars a month in money. But some, when they owed them money, would betray them, instead of paying them. I asked if they were ever shot. 'Oh, yes,' he said, when the hunters saw a runaway, if he tried to get from them, they would call out to him, that if he did not stop they would shoot, and if he did not, they would shoot, and sometimes kill him. 'But some on 'em would rather be shot than be took, sir,' he added, simply."

SOURCE: Frederick Law Olmsted, *A Journey in the Seaboard Slave States; With Remarks on Their Economy*, 1856

9. Which of the following claims is best supported by the text?

(A) Life in the swamps posed challenges but was preferred by Black people over enslavement.
(B) Self-emancipated people did not settle for long in the swamps.
(C) Encampments of most self-emancipated people in the swamp were economically self-sufficient.
(D) Security and protection were not issues for self-emancipated people in the camps.

10. Which of the following broader historical contexts best helps to explain Olmsted's account?

(A) Maroon settlements tended to be established outside of major port cities, creating employment opportunities for those who settled there.
(B) Fort Mose had attracted self-emancipated people from all over the South and led to an increased presence of maroons in southeastern swamps.
(C) Maroon communities emerged throughout the diaspora and consisted of self-emancipated people and those born free in the community.
(D) The Fugitive Slave Act of 1850 increased self-emancipated people's fear of capture and return to slavery.

11. Which of the following best describes the purpose of Olmsted's account of self-emancipated settlements?

(A) To advocate for the military eradication of the people in the settlements so that they could defend themselves against enslavers
(B) To provide a better look into the conditions of the settlements and the determination of self-emancipated people
(C) To encourage abolitionists to provide financial and moral support for the settlements
(D) To further the proslavery argument that Black people were better taken care of in slavery than in freedom

Questions 12–13 refer to the following.

"Often, Africa was denied a deep history ... while everything African was considered inferior to the people, inventions, and ideas from outside the continent.... Not surprisingly, past African achievements such as Great Zimbabwe ... were appropriated and accorded outside origins.... Predictably, African resistance was bound to bubble as various peoples on the continent fought for self-determination from colonial rule.... In the ensuing struggle, the deep and recent histories of Africa provided ideological undercurrents that underwrote the struggle for independence across the continent.... African nationalist leaders ... saw the value of the past in mobilising African people to achieve self-rule.... As a consequence, the fight for African political, economic, and intellectual independence became inextricably linked to reclaiming the African past and embedded inheritances.... The Négritude movement ... emphasised the African origins and nature of Egypt and Nubia as a testament to the fact that the continent had a glorious and deep history, full of achievement across all walks of life, including the arts, the sciences and technology. For its part, Great Zimbabwe [wall] provided inspiration to the liberation struggle in Southern Rhodesia and beyond.... Inevitably, the site gave its name to the independent nation called Zimbabwe in 1980 ... After various forms of independence struggles, both violent and non-violent, African countries from the 1950s onwards — one by one — started to gain political independence, such that by the dawn of the 21st century virtually all but one had gained 'notional' self-rule."

SOURCE: Shadreck Chirikure, *Great Zimbabwe: Reclaiming a 'Confiscated' Past*, 2021

12. Based on the excerpt, ancient and medieval African societies matter to modern Black communities because those societies

(A) produced significant works of art, such as the terracotta sculptures of the Nok people and the Malian epic poem, the *Epic of Sundiata*.

(B) represent a history that was cut off by enslavement and colonialism, and restoring that history has empowered the present-day communities of the Black diaspora.

(C) controlled lucrative global trade networks, as evidenced by the discovery of porcelain and Arab coins at Great Zimbabwe.

(D) represent anthropologically important opportunities to study the history of human language and culture, such as the impact of the Bantu migration on the spread of languages.

13. Which of the following best describes the function of the Great Zimbabwe wall, also known as the Great Enclosure, to the medieval kingdom of Zimbabwe?

(A) To host dignitaries who traveled to see the majestic structure

(B) To protect people from potential danger as well as provide shelter from natural elements

(C) To provide a site for religious and administrative activities, with the conical tower most likely serving as a granary

(D) To host traveling merchants and ensure their wares against theft

Questions 14–17 refer to the following.

Redlining Map, Detroit

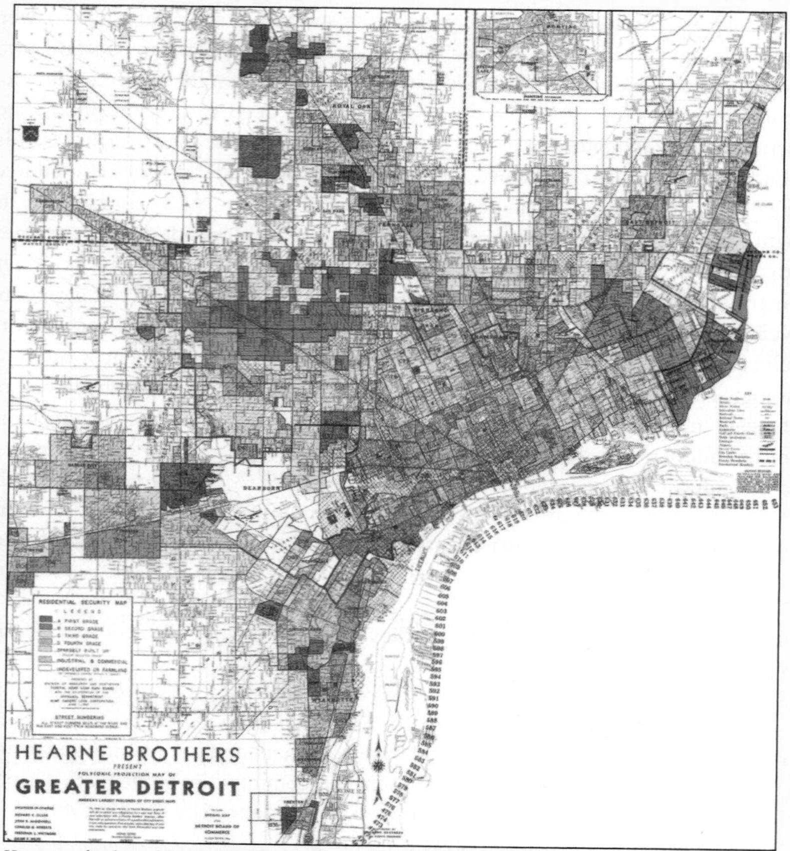

University of Richmond Digital Scholarship Lab.

14. Which of the following best describes the process of redlining as depicted in the map?

(A) Black residential areas often lacked sufficient infrastructure for public transportation, slowing economic development and raising the costs of getting to work for Black laborers.

(B) Mortgage lenders withheld mortgages from Black Americans and other people of color within a defined geographical area under the pretense of "hazardous" financial risk those homeowners posed.

(C) After acquiring property in predominantly white neighborhoods, Black Americans were often subject to acts of racist violence and intimidation.

(D) Before Black Americans could even acquire property in predominantly white neighborhoods, white supremacists often used racial terrorism to discourage such purchases.

15. How did redlining contribute to the formation of "black belts," or urban neighborhoods where large concentrations of Black Americans lived, in many American cities?

(A) Redlining offered tax incentives and economic bonuses to Black Americans for living in specific neighborhoods.

(B) Redlining harshly penalized Black Americans with fines and higher taxes for moving into neighborhoods.

(C) Redlining was not a significant factor in the formation of "black belts" in American cities.

(D) Redlining entailed denying Black Americans loans for the purchase of homes in majority white neighborhoods.

16. Which of the following statements best describes the relationship between redlining and the racial wealth gap?

(A) After redlining was banned in 1968, there was a swift and massive decline in the racial wealth gap.

(B) Neighborhoods that were once redlined are still undervalued, which has led to less funding for public schools and slowed economic development.

(C) Many Black entrepreneurs were denied loans to start their own businesses, resulting in a disproportionately small number of Black startup enterprises.

(D) The wealth gap between white and Black households actually narrowed because of redlining.

17. Which statement best describes a significant effect of redlining in Chicago?

(A) In court cases such as *Shelley v. Kraemer* (1948), the U.S. Supreme Court ruled against restrictive covenants.

(B) Continued poverty and limited access to quality education and healthcare in some Black Chicago neighborhoods today reflect the long-term effects of redlining.

(C) During the height of redlining, the Federal Housing Authority in Chicago refused to insure mortgages in Black areas, which forced Black Chicagoans to buy homes at exploitative rates.

(D) At the time when redlining was openly supported by the federal government, many people were evicted from their homes for missing a payment.

Questions 18–22 refer to the following.

"From the beginning of my coming to stay in Egypt I heard talk of the arrival of this sultan Musa on his Pilgrimage and found the Cairenes [the people of Cairo] eager to recount what they had seem of the Africans' prodigal spending.... Then he forwarded to the royal treasury many loads of unworked native gold and other valuables. I tried to persuade him to go up to the Citadel to meet the sultan, but he refused persistently saying: 'I came for the Pilgrimage and nothing else. I do not wish to mix anything else with my Pilgrimage.' He had begun to use this argument but I realized that the audience was repugnant to him because he would be obliged to kiss the ground and the sultan's hand. I continue to cajole him and he continued to make excuses but the sultan's protocol demanded that I should bring him into the royal presence, so I kept on at him till he agreed.

[Mansa Musa] flooded Cairo with his benefactions. He left no court emir nor holder of a royal office without the gift of a load of gold. The Cairenes made incalculable profits out of him and his suite in buying and selling and giving and taking. They exchanged gold until they depressed its value in Egypt and caused its price to fall....

Gold was at a high price in Egypt until they came in that year.... from that time its value fell and it cheapened in price and has remained cheap till now.... This has been the state of affairs for about twelve years until this day by reason of the large amount of gold which they brought into Egypt and spent there."

SOURCE: Al-Umari, historian, description of Mansa Musa's 1324 visit to Cairo, c. 1337–1338

18. Which of the following best describes how Al-Umari viewed Mansa Musa?

(A) Al-Umari emphasizes Mansa Musa's dedication to Islam, highlighting his pilgrimage and the mosques he built.

(B) Al-Umari emphasizes Mansa Musa's international renown, showcasing how Mansa Musa impressed the Egyptian rulers.

(C) Al-Umari emphasizes Mansa Musa's generosity, showcasing how he freely distributed gold during his pilgrimage to Mecca.

(D) Al-Umari emphasizes Mansa Musa's eagerness to return home, focusing on his dispute with hostile Egyptian rulers.

19. Which of the following conclusions can be most reasonably drawn from the evidence in the excerpt?

(A) Under Mansa Musa's rule, the Mali empire was unable to obtain the wealth or influence of Egypt.

(B) Under Mansa Musa's rule, the Mali empire remained isolated and self-contained as a way to consolidate power.

(C) Under Mansa Musa's rule, the Mali empire resisted the growing influence of the Islamic religion.

(D) Under Mansa Musa's rule, the Mali empire gained famed outside its borders as an empire of great wealth.

20. According to the excerpt, the long-term impact of Mansa Musa's pilgrimage to Egypt was to

(A) demonstrate the wealth and power of the Mali empire.

(B) celebrate Mansa Musa's faith and devotion to Islam.

(C) disrupt the economy of Egypt by distributing so much gold.

(D) secure an alliance with Egypt that would help protect the Mali empire.

21. Which of the following best describes how Al-Umari's account and others like it affected perceptions of Mansa Musa throughout the world?

(A) Because such accounts focused only on Mansa Musa's wealth, they had little effect on his global reputation.

(B) Because such accounts provided proof of Mansa Musa's wealth, he soon became the target of those abroad who wished to seize that wealth by force.

(C) Because such accounts testified to Mansa Musa's economic prowess, he was soon visited by foreign emissaries seeking advice on how to build a prosperous kingdom.

(D) Because such accounts demonstrated Mansa Musa's great wealth, many foreign leaders and merchants sought to establish trade with Mansa Musa.

22. Which of the following factors most directly contributed to the wealth and fame of the Mali empire?
(A) Mansa Musa's successful pilgrimage to Mecca
(B) Sonni Ali's military prowess and ability to exploit trans-Saharan trade routes
(C) Sundiata's skills as a military leader and strategist, as chronicled in the *Epic of Sundiata*
(D) Mali's location, which gave it access to trans-Saharan trade routes, salt, gold, and rich agricultural lands

Questions 23–27 refer to the following.

"Central and South America must be our future homes. Our oppressors will not want us to go there. They will move heaven and earth to prevent us — they will talk about us getting our rights, and offer us a territory here, and all that. It is of no use. They have pressed us to the last retreat — the die is cast — the Rubicon must be crossed — go we will, in defiance of all the slave-power in the Union. And we shall not go there, to be idle — passive spectators to an invasion of South American rights. No — go when we will, and where we may, we shall hold ourselves amenable to defend and protect the country that embraces us. We are fully able to defend ourselves, once concentrated, against any odds — and by the help of God, we will do it. We do not go, without counting the cost, cost what it may; all that it may cost, it is worth to be free.... We have advised an emigration to Central and South America, and even to Mexico and the West Indies, to those who prefer either of the last named places, all of which are free countries, Brazil being the only real slave-holding State in South America — there being nominal slavery in Dutch Guiana, Peru, Buenos Ayres, Paraguay, and Uraguay, in all of which places colored people have equality in social, civil, political, and religious privileges; Brazil making it punishable with death to import slaves into the empire.... We love our country, dearly love her, but she don't love us — she despises us, and bids us begone, driving us from her embraces; but we shall not go where she desires us; but when we do go, whatever love we have for her, we shall love the country none the less that receives us as her adopted children. Every people should be the originators of their own designs, the projector of their own schemes, and creators of the events that lead to their destiny — the consummation of their desires. Situated as we are, in the United States, many, and almost insurmountable obstacles present themselves. We are four-and-a-half millions in numbers, free and bond; six hundred thousand free, and three-and-a-half millions bond."

AP® source Martin Delany, *The Condition, Elevation, Emigration, and Destiny of the Colored People of the United States*, 1852

23. Which of the following best describes Delany's central claim?
(A) Black people can find opportunities in America if they organize and hold steadfast to hope.
(B) Black people are more patriotic than any other group in the United States.
(C) Black people's contributions to the United States are the reason for the United States' success.
(D) Black people will be allowed to flourish and enjoy full equality only if they move abroad.

24. The excerpt best reflects which of the following nineteenth-century historical developments?

(A) Amplified calls for a revolution similar to the Haitian Revolution

(B) A mass exodus of Black Americans to the British colony of Sierra Leone in West Africa

(C) A rise in Black nationalism among Black Americans

(D) Significant political influence of a growing free Black community

25. Which of the following historical figures would most likely have disagreed with Delany's central argument regarding Black emigration?

(A) Frederick Douglass

(B) Paul Cuffee

(C) Marcus Garvey

(D) Henry Highland Garnet

26. Which of the following best describes Delany's purpose in writing this passage?

(A) To highlight the lack of opportunities Black Americans have in the United States

(B) To convince more Black Americans to consider resettling in countries where they would have better opportunities for self-determination

(C) To provide support for and change the image and reputation of the American Colonization Society

(D) To remind Black northerners of their duty to support efforts to free enslaved Black Americans in the South

27. Which of the following historical events best supports Delany's claim?

(A) The passage of the 1850 Fugitive Slave Act

(B) The repeal of the 1808 Act Prohibiting the Importation of Slaves

(C) The abolition of the slave trade in the District of Columbia

(D) The repeal of the gag rule in 1844

Questions 28–32 refer to the following.

Illustration of a "mtepe" Swahili ship, 1327

Heritage Images/Getty Images.

28. Which of the following best describes the global impact that trade from the Swahili coast had on the rest of the world?

(A) Trade along the Swahili coast facilitated an immense exchange of culture, linking Africa's interior to Arab, Persian, Indian, and Chinese trading communities.

(B) Trade along the Swahili coast linked African merchants with Chinese and Indian traders, enriching all.

(C) Trade along the Swahili coast increased the exchange of spices like cloves and cinnamon.

(D) Trade along the Swahili coast increased the exchange of gold, greatly enriching African gold merchants.

29. Which of the following best describes the geographic features that contributed to the success of the Swahili city-states?

(A) The natural harbors along the coast of the Swahili city-states allowed for safe anchorage, facilitating trade by sea.

(B) The strategic location near the Indian Ocean as well as the natural harbors and monsoon winds contributed to the success of the Swahili city-states.

(C) The availability of cowrie shells on Indian Ocean islands to use as currency facilitated trade across Africa.

(D) The shared language and Islamic religion of the Swahili city-states increased economic cooperation.

30. Which of the following best describes the cultural factors that allowed trade along the Swahili coast to thrive?

(A) A tradition of weak rulers allowed for a more democratic economic collaboration between the many trading communities along the Swahili coast.

(B) A tradition of entrepreneurialism persisted along the Swahili coast, encouraging even farmers and laborers to participate in overseas trading in the hopes of becoming rich.

(C) A tradition of shared religion (Islam) and shared language (Swahili, a Bantu lingua franca) promoted collaboration among the many trading communities.

(D) The coastline linked Africa's interior with Arab, Persian, Indian, and Chinese trading communities, which allowed for the exchange of porcelain, cowry shells, and glass beads.

31. Which of the following best explains why the city-states along the Swahili coast declined?

(A) The success of trade along the Swahili coast led to the invasion of the Portuguese, who later established settlements to control trade in the Indian Ocean.

(B) The success of trade along the Swahili coast led to increased competition from Arab and Indian traders, who ultimately obtained economic dominance in the region.

(C) The Swahili coast city-states declined in power when European merchants found a more direct trade route to Asia.

(D) The Swahili coast city-states declined in power due to internal division and infighting.

32. Which statement best explains how the conversion to Islam influenced the political structures along the Swahili trade coast?

(A) After converting to Islam, Swahili merchants saw little change to their culture or political structure.

(B) After converting to Islam, Swahili merchants gained cultural influence among and strong political ties to merchants of the Arabian Peninsula, where Islam originated.

(C) Despite converting to Islam, merchants along the Swahili Coast still retained a distinctive political structure, forbidding the construction of mosques in prime locations.

(D) After converting to Islam, Swahili merchants swept east, converting the majority of southern and western Africa into a single Islamic merchant republic.

Questions 33–36 refer to the following.

Nettie Hunt on the steps of the U.S. Supreme Court, explaining the meaning of the Supreme Court's ruling in the* Brown v. Board of Education *case to her daughter, Nikie, 1954

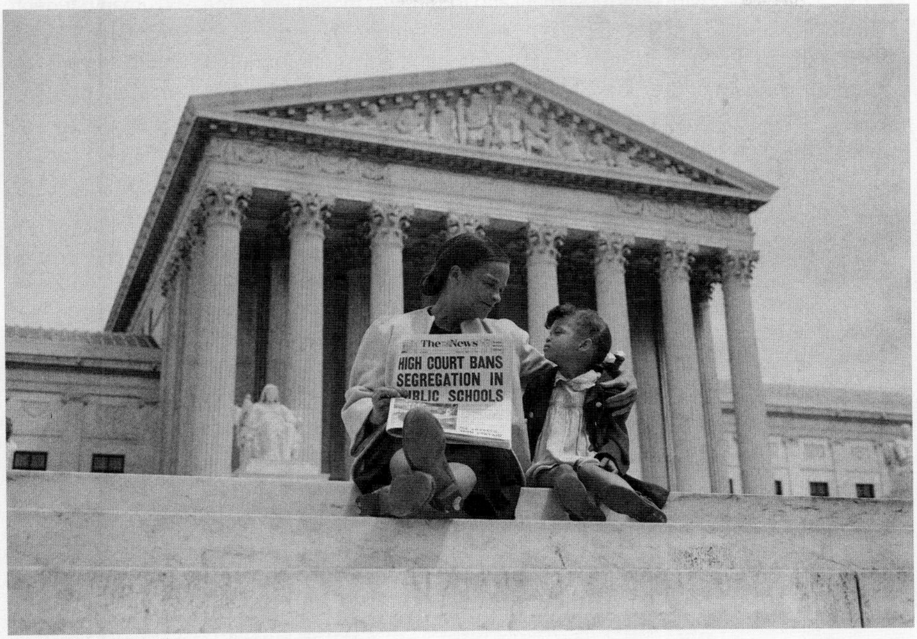

UPI/Bettmann/Getty Images.

33. Which statement best describes an indirect impact of the 1954 *Brown v. Board of Education* decision that outlawed racial segregation in public schools?

(A) Many state legislators issued policies that ensured the immediate implementation of the decision.

(B) Many Black teachers and school administrators in the South were forced out of their roles.

(C) Schools in rural communities were given additional resources from city taxes.

(D) States revised their standards for educating students in grades K-12.

34. Which of the following best explains the Supreme Court's rationale in the *Brown v. Board of Education* ruling?

(A) According to the Fourteenth Amendment, there is no federal mandate regarding the quality of and access to education, so schools could use their own timeline to desegregate.

(B) Social experiences within the United States would benefit from the gradual end of segregated public facilities.

(C) As long as an educational facility met the same standards as facilities for other school-age children between the ages of five and sixteen, discriminatory statutes did not violate the Fourteenth Amendment.

(D) States that use race to determine who has access to school facilities are in violation of the equal protection clause of the Fourteenth Amendment.

35. Which of the following best describes the relationship between the Black Studies movement and the impact of the *Brown v. Board of Education* ruling?

(A) The ruling in *Brown v. Board of Education* led to adoption of the Higher Education Act of 1965, which contributed to the rise of the Black Studies movement.

(B) During the Civil Rights movement and the antiwar movement of the 1960s, many students demanded access to an improved quality of education that was still being denied.

(C) Although the case banned racial segregation in public schools, it actually slowed the growth of the Black Studies movement by reducing the number of schools that served only Black students.

(D) Although the case outlawed racially segregated schools, schools were still free to offer low-quality or biased educational content to Black children, and this is what gave rise to the Black Studies movement.

36. Which of the following best describes the social impact of the *Brown v. Board of Education* ruling?

(A) Many Black parents felt relief and elation that their children would be able to attend an integrated school.

(B) Black American families were able to keep their children in schools located within their communities.

(C) Given that property taxes were used to fund schools, Black families would have to raise funds to support their children's travels to newly integrated schools while dealing with frequent racial slurs and discriminatory treatment.

(D) Although the ruling ended racism and discrimination in schools, neither white nor Black Americans fully embraced integration.

Questions 37–40 refer to the following.

Wilberforce University, Xenia, Ohio

Library of Congress, Prints & Photographs Division, [LC-DIG-pga-03979].

37. Which of the following describes the historical significance of the institution depicted in the image?

(A) It was the first Historically Black University established and run by Black Americans.

(B) It was founded by Booker T. Washington and based upon his industrial education model.

(C) It was the first institution of higher learning to be staffed by volunteer white educators from the North during Reconstruction.

(D) It was destroyed during the Red Summer and became a symbol of white resistance during the early twentieth century.

38. Which of the following explains how institutions similar to the one depicted in the image came to be established in the late nineteenth and early twentieth centuries?

(A) The establishment of historically Black colleges and universities was a key component of the Republicans' Radical Reconstruction Plan.

(B) The federal government required states to open land-grant colleges to all races or establish separate Black colleges.

(C) The NAACP pooled their money together and fundraised to provide institutions for higher learning for Black people throughout the South.

(D) Land set aside by Special Field Order No. 15 was earmarked for the future locations of Black colleges.

39. Which of the following impacts did institutions similar to the one depicted in the image have on the Black community?

(A) They indirectly created a permanent class of industrial workers.

(B) They allowed many Black people to rise out of poverty and become leaders in all sectors of society.

(C) They slowed the process of school integration.

(D) They refused to admit Caribbean and Black Puerto Rican students, leaving those groups with few opportunities for higher education within the United States.

40. Which of the following best describes the impact of the rise of Black Greek-letter organizations (BGLOs) that emerged at HBCUs and predominantly white institutions?

(A) BGLOs promoted the assimilation of Black Americans into mainstream white society.

(B) BGLOs provided Black Americans with spaces to support one another in the areas of self-improvement, educational excellence, leadership, and lifelong community service.

(C) BGLOs primarily allowed Black Americans in higher education to finance the construction of schools in struggling Black neighborhoods.

(D) BGLOs became an important wing of the Black Power movement in the 1960s and 1970s.

Questions 41–45 refer to the following.

SOURCE 1

FiveThirtyEight, *The number of women serving in Congress since 1917*, 2021

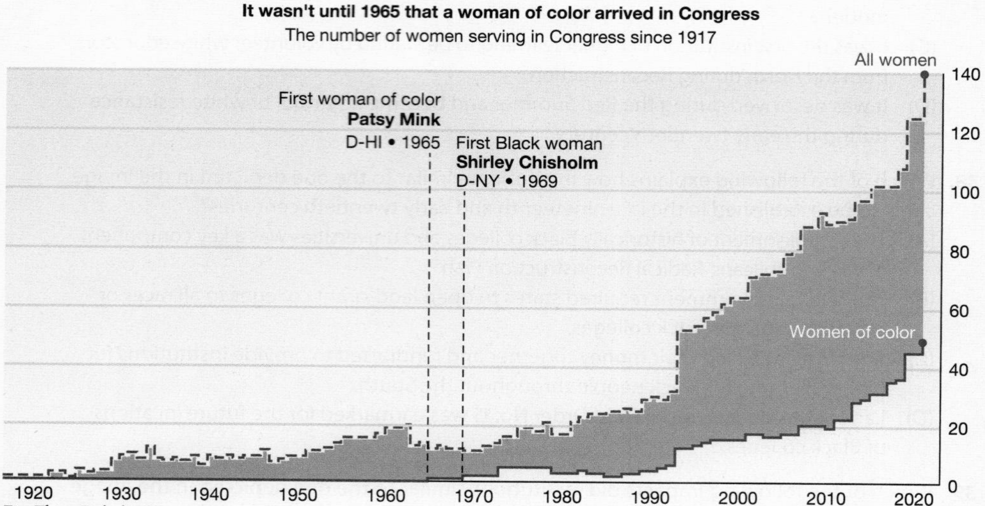

Five Thirty Eight/ABC.

SOURCE 2

Pew Research Center, *Women of Color Represent 25 States, Three Territories and D.C. in 118th Congress*, 2023

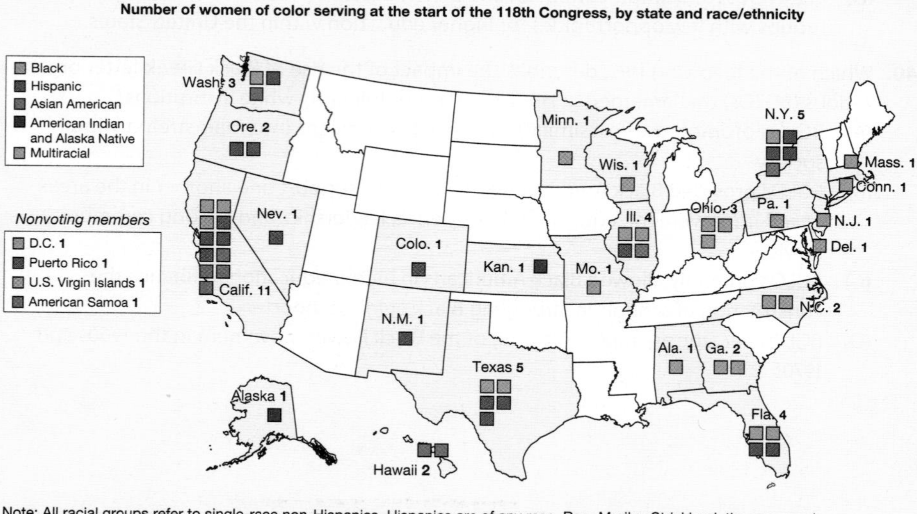

Note: All racial groups refer to single-race non-Hispanics. Hispanics are of any race. Rep. Marilyn Strickland, the one member who has more than one racial or ethnic identity for the above groups, is counted only once, as multiracial. Portuguese lawmakers are not counted with the Hispanic members. Figures are current as of Feb. 16, 2023.
Source: U.S. House and Senate historical records.

PEW RESEARCH CENTER

22 states have ever elected a Black woman to Congress, Pew Research Center, Washington, D.C. February 16, 2023. https://www.pewresearch.org/shortreads/2023/02/16/22-states- have-ever-elected-ablack-woman-to-congress/

41. Which of the following best describes the purpose of Source 2?
(A) To highlight the multiracial and women representatives serving in Congress in 2023.
(B) The first woman of color was not elected to Congress until 1965.
(C) Women have been seeking political opportunities since the adoption of the U.S. Constitution.
(D) Both sources demonstrate the progress the United States has made with political representation.

42. Which of the following historical events best explains the gains in political representation made by women of color that are shown in the sources?
(A) Due to the ratification of the Fifteenth Amendment, more people of color were able to gain political power.
(B) With the adoption of the Nineteenth Amendment, women were able to register to vote.
(C) The creation of the Equal Employment Opportunity Commission (EEOC) investigated and litigated cases of discrimination within the United States.
(D) The ratification of the Voting Rights Act of 1965 enabled the opportunity to vote without discrimination.

43. Which of the following most directly led to the election of Representatives Mink and Chisholm, as depicted in the first chart?
(A) At the conclusion of Reconstruction, many Black men sought the opportunity to vote but were denied due to local and state laws such as the poll tax and literacy tests.
(B) The Million Woman March in 1997 led directly to the election of the first women representatives of color.
(C) The Montgomery bus boycott from 1955 to 1956, spearheaded by female activist Rosa Parks, led directly to the election of the first women representatives of color.
(D) Voter registration campaigns like the 1964 Mississippi Freedom Summer Project led directly to the election of the first women representatives of color.

44. Which of the following conclusions does Source 1 best support?
(A) Over time, Black American women have increasingly gained political opportunities.
(B) Over time, Black American women have become less involved in the right to vote in the United States.
(C) Had there been greater awareness about the issues of discrimination in the United States during the early twentieth century, Black women could have had more political opportunities.
(D) Despite the massive gains in the United States, only one woman has ever been elected to federal office.

45. Which of the following best describes the difference between Source 1 and Source 2?
(A) Source 1 shows the slow growth of multiracial representation in the United States over time, while Source 2 shows the geographic distribution of multiracial representatives in the United States currently.
(B) Source 1 shows how many people have sought political office since the conclusion of the Civil War, and Source 2 shows how many women currently hold congressional office.
(C) Source 1 demonstrates the slow progress toward political freedom, while Source 2 demonstrates that that progress has been fully achieved as of 2023.
(D) Source 1 highlights the growth of multiracial representation in various federal offices across the United States, while Source 2 highlights the decline of multiracial representation.

Questions 46–48 refer to the following.

LAWS OF VIRGINIA,
ACT XIII.

Edit. 1733 and 1752.

Negro womens children to serve according to the condition of the mother. (a)

Purvis 111.
Children to be bond or free, according to the condit'n of their mother.

Double fines for fornication with a negro.

WHEREAS some doubts have arisen whether children got by any Englishman upon a negro woman should be slave or [free], *Be it therefore enacted and declared by this present grand assembly,* that all children borne in this country [shall be] held bond or free only according to the condition of the mother, And that if any christian shall commit [fornication] with a negro man or woman, [he or she so] offending shall pay double the [fines] imposed by the former act.

AP® source *The Statutes at Large; Being a Collection of All the Laws of Virginia from the First Session of the Legislature, in the Year 1619*

46. Which of the following court cases contributed to the law described in the excerpt?
(A) The case of Dred Scott, who sued his owner for his freedom after living in free territory
(B) The case of Sojourner Truth, who sued her owner to regain custody of her son
(C) The case of Elizabeth Key, who sued her enslaver for her freedom based on her heritage
(D) The case of Harriet Jacob, who sued her enslaver for her freedom and custody of her children based upon the children's father's position in politics

47. Which of the following resulted from the adoption of the Laws of Virginia Act XII?
(A) The number of white men fathering children with enslaved women dropped dramatically.
(B) More Black women petitioned for the freedom of their children in the courts.
(C) Black Americans' claims to their children were increasingly invalidated.
(D) Phenotype became a greater factor in determining the free or enslaved status of children born to enslaved children.

48. Which of the following best explains the historical significance of Laws of Virginia Act XII?
(A) It shows that interracial relationships occurred in the South and were initially accepted.
(B) It shows that the colonial governments were intent on protecting enslaved women from sexual assault.
(C) It shows that the colonies had a robust legal system.
(D) It shows how slavery in North America was defined as an inherited status linked to racial identity.

Questions 49–51 refer to the following.

History of the Haitian Revolution, 1815

Révolte générale des Nègres. Massacre des Blancs.
SAINT-DOMINGUE,
OU
HISTOIRE
DE SES RÉVOLUTIONS;
CONTENANT
Le récit effroyable des divisions, des troubles, des ravages, des meurtres, des incendies, des dévastations et des massacres qui eurent lieu dans cette île, depuis 1789 jusqu'à la perte de la colonie.
A PARIS,
Chez TIGER, Imprimeur-Libraire; rue du Petit-Pont St-Jacques, n. 10.
Au Pilier littéraire.

Schomberg Center, NYPL/Art Resource, NY.

49. Which of the following does the image best reflect?

(A) White fears of the outbreak of and spread of slave rebellions
(B) Vulnerability of nineteenth-century American architecture to city fires
(C) British defeat of the French army and the invasion of Haiti
(D) Racial diversity of the colony of Haiti

50. Depictions similar to that illustrated in the image contributed to which of the following?

(A) The relaxation and revision of slave codes in the United States
(B) The French decision to sell Montreal to the United States
(C) An influx of plantation owners from Haiti to the United States
(D) The American establishment of the African colony of Liberia

51. Which of the following best describes the historical significance of the Haitian Revolution?

(A) It had an enduring impact on Black political thinking.
(B) It was the first slave rebellion to take place in the Americas since the beginning of the transatlantic slave trade.
(C) It stoked fears of retribution among enslaved Black Americans and decreased the occurrence of slave rebellions.
(D) It became one of the wealthiest and prosperous countries in the Western Hemisphere after Haiti won its independence.

Questions 52–54 refer to the following.

"Philadelphia."

"[12th, 4th mo., 1778] — Whereas, Absalom Jones and Richard Allen, two men of the African race, who, for their religious life and conversation have obtained a good report among men, these persons, from a love to the people of their complexion whom they beheld with sorrow, because of their irreligious and uncivilized state, often communed together upon this painful and important subject in order to form some kind of religious society, but there being too few to be found under the like concern, and those who were, differed in their religious sentiments; with these circumstances they labored for some time, till it was proposed, after a serious communication of sentiments, that a society should be formed, without regard to religious tenets, provided, the persons lived an orderly and sober life, in order to support one another in sickness, and for the benefit of their widows and fatherless children."

ARTICLES.

"[17th, 5th mo., 1787]—We, the free Africans and their descendants, of the City of Philadelphia, in the State of Pennsylvania, or elsewhere, do unanimously agree, for the benefit of each other, to advance one shilling in silver Pennsylvania currency a month; and after one year's subscription from the date hereof, then to hand forth to the needy of this Society, if any should require, the sum of three shillings and nine pence per week of the said money: provided, this necessity is not brought on them by their own imprudence."

SOURCE: "Preamble of the Free African Society, 1787," *Annals of the First African Church, in the United States of America*, 1862

52. Which of the following best describes the purpose of the Free African Society?
(A) To raise money for the cause of abolition
(B) To establish a fraternity for Black Christian clergymen
(C) To provide aid for free Black people in need
(D) To help the Underground Railroad stay in operation

53. Which of the following organizations had the most in common with the Free African Society?
(A) Universal Negro Improvement Association
(B) National Negro Business League
(C) New York African Society for Mutual Relief
(D) African Colonization Society

54. Which of the following statements about free Black societies in the North does the image best support?
(A) Free Black people in the North built community through institutions.
(B) Free Black people in the North were for the most part economically helpless because of lack of economic opportunities.
(C) Free Black people fought to be fully integrated into white religious organizations.
(D) Free Black people in the North were too small in number to establish social organizations.

Questions 55–56 refer to the following.

Elijah Muhammad Addressing Black Muslims at Convention, 1966

Bettmann/Getty Images.

55. Which statement best describes why the Nation of Islam gained influence within the Black community?
(A) Its leaders promoted the idea of Black nationalism, pride in their African ancestry, and demanded immediate racial equality rather than adopting a more gradual approach.
(B) Its leaders presented themselves as moderates who were willing to work with white institutions and leaders in order to achieve a gradual transition from the era of segregation to an era of quality.
(C) Its leaders were mostly apolitical and spread a message that Black Americans should ignore the violence against civil rights protesters during the 1950s and 1960s.
(D) Its leaders organized events that celebrated Black culture and the African Diaspora.

56. Which statement best describes how Malcolm X influenced the Black Power movement?
(A) Malcolm X promoted a message of toleration, compromise, and nonviolence, influencing the Black Power movement to adopt the same values.
(B) Malcolm X promoted the message that Black Americans should share their experiences and express their feelings through art, which the Black Power movement later adopted.
(C) Malcolm X promoted a message of prayer and religious obligation over civil rights protest, which the Black Power movement also adopted.
(D) Malcolm X promoted a message of self-defense and self-determination for Black Americans, ideas which the Black Power movement adopted.

Questions 57–60 refer to the following.

"The Color Line Still Exists — In this Case," *Harper's Weekly v. 23,* 1879

About the Source: Uncle Sam is writing the following on a wall: "Eddikashun qualifukashun. The Black man orter be eddikated afore he kin vote with US Wites, signed Mr. Solid South." (Education qualification. The Black man ought to be educated before he can vote with us whites, signed Mr. Solid South.)

Library of Congress, Prints & Photographs Division, [LC-USZ62-83004].

57. This image was intended to highlight which of the following?

(A) Economic policies in the South that limited Black people to jobs in agriculture

(B) Discriminatory laws being passed in the South with the intent of disenfranchising Black Americans

(C) Racist caricature used to depict Black people in nineteenth-century art

(D) Lack of educational opportunities for Black people in the South

58. Which of the following policies contributed to the historical situation depicted in the cartoon?

(A) Unpaid apprenticeships

(B) Vagrancy laws

(C) Crop liens

(D) Grandfather clauses

59. Which of the following best describes a result of the historical situation depicted in the image?

(A) Congress required southern states to offer public education after the Civil War for both white and Black citizens.

(B) Congress sought to protect the voting rights of Black Americans by strengthening federal oversight measures under the Civil Rights Act of 1875.

(C) The Republican Party gained more political support in the South and maintained control over southern state legislatures.

(D) Southern state legislatures became dominated by former Confederates and left Black Americans without effective political representation.

60. Which of the following historical events would most directly prevent subsequent practices similar to those depicted in the image?

(A) *Davis v. County of School Board* (1954)

(B) The Civil Rights Act of 1964

(C) The Voting Rights Act of 1965

(D) *Brown v. Board of Education* (1954)

Part II: Free-Response

Short-Answer Questions

1. Using the image, answer A, B, C, and D.

AP® source **James Van Der Zee, *Couple in Raccoon Coats*, 1932**

James Van Der Zee Archive, The Metropolitan Museum of Art; Gift of Donna Van Der Zee, 2021.

(A) Describe the historical context of the image.

(B) Describe one major difference between the manner in which Black people were portrayed in the image by this photographer, and how Black people were portrayed in images by mainstream white photographers of the era.

(C) Describe the contributions of one other Black artist or writer associated with the artistic movement represented by the image and its photographer.

(D) Explain how the attitudes and political and social perspectives of Black people had changed by 1932.

2. Using the excerpt, answer A, B, C, and D.

"By the end of the decade, white conservative Democrats had honed a potent formula to destroy all of these coalitions — create a moral panic, cry rape. The race riot in Wilmington, North Carolina, in 1898 provides one of the more explicit demonstrations of this technique. There a coalition of white Populists and Black Republicans had won control of many state and local offices in the mid-1890s. A white opposition formed, led by men born and/or reared largely in the postwar era — the counterpart ironically of the New Negroes. This particular group of "new men" was determined to win by violence and fraud what they had lost in fair elections. Seizing upon then novel techniques of political mobilization and propaganda, they launched a campaign to demonize Black men and drive them from public life, much like the metaphorical figure central to the disenfranchisement campaign two years later — the incubus, a winged demon alleged to have sexually violated white women while they slept. Thrust beyond the boundaries of human sympathy, Blacks were effectively served upon for the remorseless slaughter that followed a few days after election day: three hundred dead by one estimate, many more wounded, and fourteen hundred forced into exile."

SOURCE: Thomas C. Holt, *Children of Fire: A History of African Americans*, 2010

(A) Describe the broader historical context of the period Holt examines.

(B) Describe one piece of evidence Holt provides in the text to support his claim about white political strategy and racial violence during the nineteenth century.

(C) Describe one historical event from the early twentieth century that supports Holt's claim.

(D) Explain how Black people challenged the discriminatory practice described by Holt.

3. Answer A, B, C, and D.

(A) Describe the contributions of Black Americans to American music in the late nineteenth to the early twentieth century.

(B) Describe one way in which Black American musical traditions changed by the early 1930s.

(C) Describe one way in which Black American musical traditions remained the same by the early 1930s.

(D) Explain how one historical event influenced African American musical traditions in the early twentieth century.

Document-Based Question

1. Explain how Afrofuturism explores new possibilities for representing Black experiences in the intersections of spaces that both shape and reflect culture and identity, such as art, music, film, fashion, literature, and architecture.

In your response you should do the following:

- **Respond to the prompt with a defensible thesis or claim that establishes a line of reasoning.**
- **Describe a broader historical or disciplinary context relevant to the topic of the prompt.**
- **Support an argument in response to the prompt using at least three of the sources.**
- **Use at least one additional piece of specific evidence (beyond the evidence found in the sources) relevant to your argument.**
- **For at least two sources, explain how or why the perspective, purpose, context, and/or audience for each source is relevant to your argument.**
- **Reference or cite the sources you use in your argument. You can reference or cite the source letter, title, or author.**

SOURCE A

Ytasha L. Womack, *Afrofuturism: The World of Black Sci-Fi and Fantasy Culture*, 2013

Afrofuturism is an intersection of imagination, technology, the future, and liberation. "I generally define Afrofuturism as a way of imagining possible futures through a black cultural lens," says Ingrid LaFleur, an art curator and Afrofuturist....

Whether through literature, visual arts, music, or grassroots organizing, Afrofuturists redefine culture and notions of blackness for today and the future. Both an artistic aesthetic and a framework for critical theory, Afrofuturism combines elements of science fiction, historical fiction, speculative fiction, and magic realism with non-Western beliefs. In some cases, it's a total reenvisioning of the past and speculation about the future rife with cultural critiques.

Take William Hayashi's self-published novel *Discovery: Volume 1 of the Darkside Trilogy*. The story follows the discovery of rumored black American separatists whose disgust with racial disparity led them to create a society on the moon long before Neil Armstrong's arrival. The story is a commentary on separatist theory, race, and politics that inverts the nationalistic themes of the early space race....

[T]he creativity born from rooting black culture in sci-fi and fantasy is an exciting evolution.

This blossoming culture is unique. Unlike previous eras, today's artists can wield the power of digital media ... to tell their stories, share their stories, and connect with audiences inexpensively — a gift from the sci-fi gods, so to speak, that was unthinkable at the turn of the century....

While technology empowers creators, this intrigue with sci-fi and fantasy itself inverts conventional thinking about black identity and holds the imagination supreme. Black identity does not have to be a negotiation with awful stereotypes, a dystopian view of the race (remember those black-man-as-endangered-species stories or the constant "Why are black women single?" reports?), an abysmal sense of powerlessness, or a reckoning of hardened realities. Fatalism is not a synonym for blackness.

SOURCE B

N. K. Jemisin, Introduction, *How Long 'til Black Future Month*, 2019

How Long 'til Black Future Month takes its name from an essay that I wrote in 2013. It's ... a meditation on how hard it's been for me to love science fiction and fantasy as a black woman. How much I've had to fight my own internalized racism in addition to that radiating from the fiction and the business. How terrifying it's been to realize no one thinks my people have a future. And how gratifying to finally accept myself and begin spinning the futures I want to see.

SOURCE C

Tomi Adeyemi, *Children of Virtue and Vengeance* (novel), 2019 (280 words)

My fingers tense as I grab my helmet, preparing for what I might cause. Revealing my transformation is far from the smart move....

I take one last breath. My white streak tumbles free when my helmet hits the ground.

"She's one of them!"

"The queen is a tîtán!"[1]

Gasps ripple through the crowd. A handful of maji[2] push toward the front....

I am the only one who can bring [the nation of] Orïsha together. I am the queen who can keep all of these people safe.

"I wanted to hide my truth," I shout. "My apprehension about what I've become. But the return of magic and the birth of the tîtáns are living proof that we are finally returning to the Orïsha the gods have always wanted for us! We're so full of hatred and fear, we've forgotten what blessings these abilities are. For centuries these powers have been the source of our strife, but the gods ordained us with magic so the people of Orïsha could thrive!" . . .

"Think of how Grounders could farm our land. How teams of Tiders could cut the work of fishermen in half," I say. "Welders could erect new cities in days. Healers[3] could ensure those we love don't perish from wounds or sickness!" . . .

I paint each dissenter a picture with my words, seeing my dreams almost as clearly as the mural carved into the ceiling above.

"Under my rule, this will be a land where even the poorest villagers are fed, housed, and clothed. A kingdom where everyone is protected, where everyone is accepted! The divisions of the past are over!" I extend my hands and lift my voice. "A new Orïsha is on the horizon!"

---

[1]People who can perform blood magic without having to use spells. They can be recognized by a white streak in their hair. — Eds.

[2]People with magical abilities who can be recognized by their completely white hair. — Eds.

[3]Tiders, Welders, and Healers are all different clans of maji who possess different magical abilities. — Eds.

SOURCE D

Afrofuturistic Art: (1) Georgia Nakima (Garden of Journey), *Salt Water* (mural, 35 x 110 feet), George C. Arnold Building, Providence, Rhode Island, 2021; (2) Hew Locke, *Ambassador 4* (sculpture, 162 x 50 x 137cm plus flag), In the Black Fantastic Exhibition at the Hayward Gallery, London, UK, 2022

Jonathan Wiggs/Boston Globe/Getty Images.

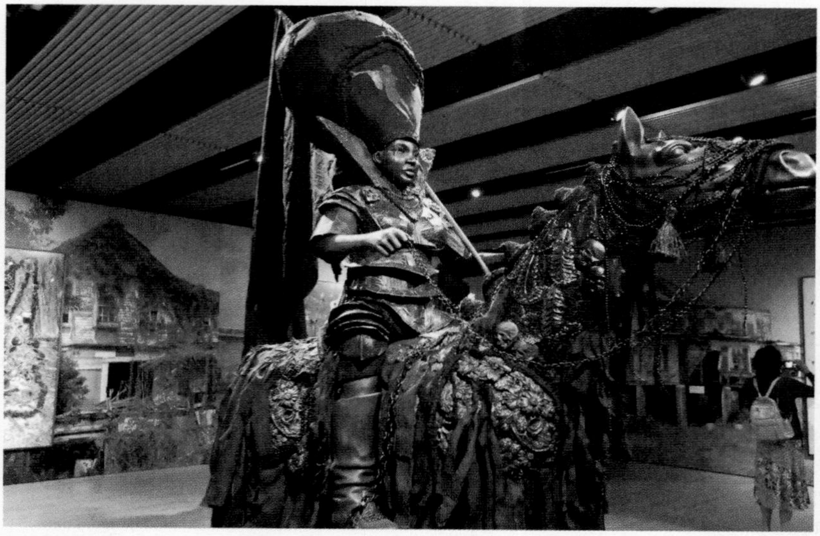

Andrew Lalchan/Alamy Stock Photo.

SOURCE E

Christina Sharpe, "Notes 244–245," *Ordinary Notes*, 2023

Note 244

[A]fter an onstage conversation called "The Work of Words" between Dionne Brand, David Chariandy, and me, a young Black woman in the audience stood up and asked the most beautiful question.

> Fern Ramoutar: *"Hi. I want to return to a quote that you made, Dr. Sharpe, about how the weather is the total climate, and it is anti-Black. That just struck me because I think to be born Black is to know that weather intimately But the effect, whether intentional or not, of the work of your words, of all of your words, is to change the weather and to expand my capacity and, I think, the capacity of many black women ... to expand our capacity for survival.... [M]y question is, What is the weather that you're working towards? ... What is the world you're working towards and what does freedom look like to each of you?"*

The room gasped and momentarily we fell silent with awe and gratitude at the sound this young woman had brought into the room. It was a question that she was the answer to.

Note 245

There is a deep and long tradition of Black arts ranging across continents and archipelagos attendant on the modern and its legacies of transatlantic slavery, colonialism, and racial capitalism. Black artists across form and those whose only form is their lives are engaged in the knowledges produced by those legacies and contemporaneous tragedies. They have always performed, thought, lived, enacted a desire for freedom — they have always fought for and made spaces, imagined ways when there was no way. Every movement for Black liberation, every era of Black struggle, has been accompanied by its singers, its dancers, its poets, its storytellers, its musicians, its artists — its theorists of the possible world, its theorists of the imagined world.

The Declaration of Independence

IN CONGRESS, JULY 4, 1776, THE UNANIMOUS DECLARATION OF THE THIRTEEN UNITED STATES OF AMERICA

When in the Course of human events, it becomes necessary for one people to dissolve the political bands which have connected them with another, and to assume among the Powers of the earth, the separate and equal station to which the Laws of Nature and of Nature's God entitle them, a decent respect to the opinions of mankind requires that they should declare the causes which impel them to the separation.

We hold these truths to be self-evident, that all men are created equal, that they are endowed by their Creator with certain unalienable rights, that among these are Life, Liberty, and the pursuit of Happiness. That to secure these rights, Governments are instituted among Men, deriving their just powers from the consent of the governed. That whenever any Form of Government becomes destructive of these ends, it is the Right of the People to alter or to abolish it, and to institute new Government, laying its foundation on such principles and organizing its powers in such form, as to them shall seem most likely to effect their Safety and Happiness. Prudence, indeed, will dictate that Governments long established should not be changed for light and transient causes; and accordingly all experience hath shown, that mankind are more disposed to suffer, while evils are sufferable, than to right themselves by abolishing the forms to which they are accustomed. But when a long train of abuses and usurpations, pursuing invariably the same Object evinces a design to reduce them under absolute Despotism, it is their right, it is their duty, to throw off such Government, and to provide new Guards for their future security. —Such has been the patient sufferance of these Colonies; and such is now the necessity which constrains them to alter their former Systems of Government. The history of the present King of Great Britain is a history of repeated injuries and usurpations, all having in direct object the establishment of an absolute Tyranny over these States. To prove this, let Facts be submitted to a candid world.

He has refused his Assent to Laws, the most wholesome and necessary for the public good.

He has forbidden his Governors to pass Laws of immediate and pressing importance, unless suspended in their operation till his Assent should be obtained; and, when so suspended, he has utterly neglected to attend to them.

He has refused to pass other Laws for the accommodation of large districts of people, unless those people would relinquish the right of Representation in the Legislature, a right inestimable to them and formidable to tyrants only.

He has called together legislative bodies at places unusual, uncomfortable, and distant from the depository of their public Records, for the sole purpose of fatiguing them into compliance with his measures.

He has dissolved Representative Houses repeatedly, for opposing with manly firmness his invasions on the rights of the people.

He has refused for a long time, after such dissolutions, to cause others to be elected; whereby the Legislative powers, incapable of Annihilation, have returned to the People at large for their exercise; the State remaining in the meantime exposed to all the dangers of invasion from without and convulsions within.

He has endeavored to prevent the population of these States; for that purpose obstructing the Laws of Naturalization of Foreigners; refusing to pass others to encourage their migrations hither, and raising the conditions of new Appropriations of Lands.

He has obstructed the Administration of Justice, by refusing his Assent to Laws for establishing Judiciary powers.

He has made Judges dependent on his Will alone, for the tenure of their offices, and the amount and payment of their salaries.

He has erected a multitude of New Offices, and sent hither swarms of Officers to harass our People, and eat out their substance.

He has kept among us, in times of peace, Standing Armies without the Consent of our legislature.

He has combined with others to subject us to a jurisdiction foreign to our constitution, and unacknowledged by our laws; giving his Assent to their Acts of pretended Legislation:

For quartering large bodies of armed troops among us:

For protecting them, by a mock Trial, from Punishment for any Murders which they should commit on the Inhabitants of these States:

For cutting off our Trade with all parts of the world:

For imposing taxes on us without our Consent:

For depriving us, in many cases, of the benefits of Trial by jury:

For transporting us beyond Seas to be tried for pretended offences:

For abolishing the free System of English Laws in a neighboring Province, establishing therein an Arbitrary government, and enlarging its Boundaries so as to render it at once an example and fit instrument for introducing the same absolute rule into these Colonies:

For taking away our Charters, abolishing our most valuable Laws, and altering fundamentally the Forms of our Governments:

For suspending our own Legislatures, and declaring themselves invested with Power to legislate for us in all cases whatsoever.

He has abdicated Government here, by declaring us out of his Protection and waging War against us.

He has plundered our seas, ravaged our Coasts, burnt our towns, and destroyed the lives of our people.

He is at this time transporting large armies of foreign mercenaries to compleat the works of death, desolation, and tyranny, already begun with circumstances of Cruelty & perfidy scarcely paralleled in the most barbarous ages, and totally unworthy the Head of a civilized nation.

He has constrained our fellow Citizens taken Captive on the high Seas to bear Arms against their Country, to become the executioners of their friends and Brethren, or to fall themselves by their Hands.

He has excited domestic insurrections amongst us, and has endeavored to bring on the inhabitants of our frontiers, the merciless Indian Savages, whose known rule of warfare, is an undistinguished destruction of all ages, sexes, and conditions.

In every stage of these Oppressions We have Petitioned for Redress in the most humble terms: Our repeated Petitions have been answered only by repeated injury. A Prince, whose character is thus marked by every act which may define a Tyrant, is unfit to be the ruler of a free people.

Nor have We been wanting in attention to our British brethren. We have warned them from time to time of attempts by their legislature to extend an unwarrantable jurisdiction over us. We have reminded them of the circumstances of our emigration and settlement here. We have appealed to their native justice and magnanimity, and we have conjured them by the ties of our common kindred to disavow these usurpations, which would inevitably interrupt our connections and correspondence. They too have been deaf to the voice of justice and of consanguinity. We must, therefore, acquiesce in the necessity, which denounces our Separation, and hold them, as we hold the rest of mankind, Enemies in War, in Peace Friends.

We, therefore, the Representatives of the United States of America, in General Congress, Assembled, appealing to the Supreme Judge of the world for the rectitude of our intentions, do, in the Name, and by Authority of the good People of these Colonies, solemnly publish and declare, That these United Colonies are, and of Right ought to be FREE AND INDEPENDENT STATES; that they are Absolved from all Allegiance to the British Crown, and that all political connection between them and the State of Great Britain, is and ought to be totally dissolved; and that as Free and Independent States, they have full Power to levy War, conclude Peace, contract Alliances, establish Commerce, and to do all other Acts and Things which Independent States may of right do. And for the support of this Declaration, with a firm reliance on the Protection of Divine Providence, we mutually pledge to each other our Lives, our Fortunes, and our sacred Honor.

John Hancock

Button Gwinnett
Lyman Hall
Geo. Walton
Wm. Hooper
Joseph Hewes
John Penn
Edward Rutledge
Thos. Heyward, Junr.
Thomas Lynch, Junr.
Arthur Middleton
Samuel Chase
Wm. Paca
Thos. Stone
Charles Carroll of Carrollton

George Wythe
Richard Henry Lee
Th. Jefferson
Benja. Harrison
Thos. Nelson, Jr.
Francis Lightfoot Lee
Carter Braxton
Robt. Morris
Benjamin Rush
Benja. Franklin
John Morton
Geo. Clymer
Jas. Smith
Geo. Taylor

James Wilson
Geo. Ross
Caesar Rodney
Geo. Read
Thos. M'Kean
Wm. Floyd
Phil. Livingston
Frans. Lewis
Lewis Morris
Richd. Stockton
John Witherspoon
Fras. Hopkinson
John Hart
Abra. Clark

Josiah Bartlett
Wm. Whipple
Matthew Thornton
Saml. Adams
John Adams
Robt. Treat Paine
Elbridge Gerry
Step. Hopkins
William Ellery
Roger Sherman
Sam'el Huntington
Wm. Williams
Oliver Wolcott

AP® source

The Constitution of the United States of America

AGREED TO BY PHILADELPHIA CONVENTION, SEPTEMBER 17, 1787
IMPLEMENTED MARCH 4, 1789

We the People of the United States, in Order to form a more perfect Union, establish Justice, insure domestic Tranquility, provide for the common defence, promote the general Welfare, and secure the Blessings of Liberty to ourselves and our Posterity, do ordain and establish this Constitution for the United States of America.

ARTICLE I

SECTION 1. All legislative Powers herein granted shall be vested in a Congress of the United States, which shall consist of a Senate and a House of Representatives.

SECTION 2. The House of Representatives shall be composed of Members chosen every second Year by the People of the several States, and the Electors in each State shall have the Qualifications requisite for Electors of the most numerous Branch of the State Legislature.

No Person shall be a Representative who shall not have attained to the Age of twenty-five Years, and been seven Years a Citizen of the United States, and who shall not, when elected, be an Inhabitant of that State in which he shall be chosen.

Representatives and direct Taxes shall be apportioned among the several States which may be included within this Union, according to their respective Numbers, *which shall be determined by adding to the whole Number of free Persons, including those bound to Service for a Term of Years, and excluding Indians not taxed, three fifths of all other Persons.*[1]

The actual Enumeration shall be made within three Years after the first Meeting of the Congress of the United States, and within every subsequent Term of ten Years, in such Manner as they shall by Law direct. The Number of Representatives shall not exceed one for every thirty Thousand, but each State shall have at Least one Representative; and *until such enumeration shall be made, the State of New Hampshire shall be entitled to chuse three, Massachusetts eight, Rhode Island and Providence Plantations one, Connecticut five, New-York six, New Jersey four, Pennsylvania eight, Delaware one, Maryland six, Virginia ten, North Carolina five, South Carolina five, and Georgia three.*

Note: The Constitution became effective March 4, 1789. Provisions in italics are no longer relevant or have been changed by constitutional amendment. Copy highlighted in yellow pertains to African Americans.

1. Changed by Section 2 of the Fourteenth Amendment.

When vacancies happen in the Representation from any State, the Executive Authority thereof shall issue Writs of Election to fill such Vacancies.

The House of Representatives shall chuse their Speaker and other Officers; and shall have the sole Power of Impeachment.

Section 3. The Senate of the United States shall be composed of two Senators from each State, *chosen by the Legislature thereof,*[2] for six Years; and each Senator shall have one Vote.

Immediately after they shall be assembled in Consequence of the first Election, they shall be divided as equally as may be into three Classes. The Seats of the Senators of the first Class shall be vacated at the Expiration of the second Year, of the second Class at the Expiration of the fourth Year, and of the third Class at the Expiration of the sixth Year, so that one-third may be chosen every second Year; and if Vacancies happen by Resignation, or otherwise, during the Recess of the Legislature of any State, the Executive thereof may make temporary Appointments until the next Meeting of the Legislature, which shall then fill such Vacancies.[3]

No person shall be a Senator who shall not have attained to the Age of thirty Years, and been nine Years a Citizen of the United States, and who shall not, when elected, be an Inhabitant of that State for which he shall be chosen.

The Vice President of the United States shall be President of the Senate, but shall have no Vote, unless they be equally divided.

The Senate shall chuse their other Officers, and also a President pro tempore, in the absence of the Vice President, or when he shall exercise the Office of President of the United States.

The Senate shall have the sole Power to try all Impeachments. When sitting for that Purpose, they shall be on Oath or Affirmation. When the President of the United States is tried, the Chief Justice shall preside: And no Person shall be convicted without the Concurrence of two thirds of the Members present.

Judgment in Cases of Impeachment shall not extend further than to removal from Office, and disqualification to hold and enjoy any Office of honor, Trust or Profit under the United States: but the Party convicted shall nevertheless be liable and subject to Indictment, Trial, Judgment and Punishment, according to Law.

Section 4. The Times, Places and Manner of holding Elections for Senators and Representatives, shall be prescribed in each State by the Legislature thereof; but the Congress may at any time by Law make or alter such Regulations, except as to the Places of Chusing Senators.

The Congress shall assemble at least once in every Year, and such Meeting *shall be on the first Monday in December, unless they shall by Law appoint a different Day.*[4]

Section 5. Each House shall be the Judge of the Elections, Returns and Qualifications of its own Members, and a Majority of each shall constitute a Quorum to do Business; but a smaller number may adjourn from day to day, and may be authorized to compel the Attendance of absent Members, in such Manner, and under such Penalties, as each House may provide.

Each House may determine the Rules of its Proceedings, punish its Members for disorderly Behavior, and, with the Concurrence of two thirds, expel a Member.

Each House shall keep a Journal of its Proceedings, and from time to time publish the same, excepting such Parts as may in their Judgment require Secrecy; and the Yeas and Nays of the Members of either House on any question shall, at the Desire of one-fifth of those Present, be entered on the Journal.

Neither House, during the Session of Congress, shall, without the Consent of the other, adjourn for more than three days, nor to any other Place than that in which the two Houses shall be sitting.

Section 6. The Senators and Representatives shall receive a Compensation for their Services, to be ascertained by Law, and paid out of the Treasury of the United States. They shall in all Cases, except Treason, Felony and Breach of the Peace, be privileged from Arrest during their Attendance at the Session of their respective Houses, and in going to and returning from the same; and for any Speech or Debate in either House, they shall not be questioned in any other Place.

No Senator or Representative shall, during the Time for which he was elected, be appointed to any

2. Changed by Section 1 of the Seventeenth Amendment.
3. Changed by Clause 2 of the Seventeenth Amendment.
4. Changed by Section 2 of the Twentieth Amendment.

civil Office under the Authority of the United States, which shall have been created, or the Emoluments whereof shall have been increased, during such time; and no Person holding any Office under the United States, shall be a Member of either House during his Continuance in Office.

Section 7. All Bills for raising Revenue shall originate in the House of Representatives; but the Senate may propose or concur with Amendments as on other Bills.

Every Bill which shall have passed the House of Representatives and the Senate, shall, before it becomes a Law, be presented to the President of the United States; If he approve he shall sign it, but if not he shall return it, with his Objections to that House in which it shall have originated, who shall enter the Objections at large on their Journal, and proceed to reconsider it. If after such Reconsideration two thirds of that House shall agree to pass the Bill, it shall be sent, together with the Objections, to the other House, by which it shall likewise be reconsidered, and if approved by two thirds of that House, it shall become a Law. But in all such Cases the Votes of both Houses shall be determined by Yeas and Nays, and the Names of the Persons voting for and against the Bill shall be entered on the Journal of each House respectively. If any Bill shall not be returned by the President within ten Days (Sundays excepted) after it shall have been presented to him, the Same shall be a Law, in like Manner as if he had signed it, unless the Congress by their Adjournment prevent its Return, in which Case it shall not be a Law.

Every Order, Resolution, or Vote to which the Concurrence of the Senate and the House of Representatives may be necessary (except on a question of Adjournment) shall be presented to the President of the United States; and before the Same shall take Effect, shall be approved by him, or being disapproved by him, shall be repassed by two thirds of the Senate and House of Representatives, according to the Rules and Limitations prescribed in the Case of a Bill.

Section 8. The Congress shall have Power to lay and collect Taxes, Duties, Imposts and Excises, to pay the Debts and provide for the common Defence and general Welfare of the United States; but all Duties, Imposts and Excises shall be uniform throughout the United States;

To borrow money on the credit of the United States;

To regulate Commerce with foreign Nations, and among the several States, and with the Indian Tribes;

To establish an uniform Rule of Naturalization, and uniform Laws on the subject of Bankruptcies throughout the United States;

To coin Money, regulate the Value thereof, and of foreign Coin, and fix the Standard of Weights and Measures;

To provide for the Punishment of counterfeiting the Securities and current Coin of the United States;

To establish Post Offices and post Roads;

To promote the Progress of Science and useful Arts, by securing for limited Times to Authors and Inventors the exclusive Right to their respective Writings and Discoveries;

To constitute Tribunals inferior to the supreme Court;

To define and punish Piracies and Felonies committed on the high Seas, and Offenses against the Law of Nations;

To declare War, grant Letters of Marque and Reprisal, and make Rules concerning Captures on Land and Water;

To raise and support Armies, but no Appropriation of Money to that Use shall be for a longer Term than two Years;

To provide and maintain a Navy;

To make Rules for the Government and Regulation of the land and naval Forces;

To provide for calling forth the Militia to execute the Laws of the Union, suppress Insurrections and repel Invasions;

To provide for organizing, arming, and disciplining the Militia, and for governing such Part of them as may be employed in the Service of the United States, reserving to the States respectively, the Appointment of the Officers, and the Authority of training the Militia according to the discipline prescribed by Congress;

To exercise exclusive Legislation in all Cases whatsoever, over such District (not exceeding ten Miles square) as may, by Cession of particular States, and the acceptance of Congress, become the Seat of Government of the United States, and to exercise like Authority over all Places purchased by the Consent of the Legislature of the State in which the Same shall be, for the Erection of Forts, Magazines, Arsenals, dock-Yards, and other needful Buildings; — And

To make all Laws which shall be necessary and proper for carrying into Execution the foregoing Powers, and all other Powers vested by this Constitution in the Government of the United States, or in any Department or Officer thereof.

SECTION 9. *The Migration or Importation of such Persons as any of the States now existing shall think proper to admit, shall not be prohibited by the Congress prior to the Year one thousand eight hundred and eight but a tax or duty may be imposed on such Importation, not exceeding ten dollars for each Person.*

The privilege of the Writ of Habeas Corpus shall not be suspended, unless when in Cases of Rebellion or Invasion the public Safety may require it.

No Bill of Attainder or ex post facto Law shall be passed.

No capitation, or other direct, Tax shall be laid, unless in Proportion to the Census or Enumeration herein before directed to be taken.[5]

No Tax or Duty shall be laid on Articles exported from any State.

No Preference shall be given by any Regulation of Commerce or Revenue to the Ports of one State over those of another: nor shall Vessels bound to, or from, one State, be obliged to enter, clear, or pay Duties in another.

No Money shall be drawn from the Treasury, but in Consequence of Appropriations made by law; and a regular Statement and Account of the Receipts and Expenditures of all public Money shall be published from time to time.

No Title of Nobility shall be granted by the United States: And no Person holding any Office of Profit or Trust under them, shall, without the Consent of the Congress, accept of any present, Emolument, Office, or Title, of any kind whatever, from any King, Prince, or foreign State.

SECTION 10. No State shall enter into any Treaty, Alliance, or Confederation; grant Letters of Marque and Reprisal; coin Money; emit Bills of Credit; make any Thing but gold and silver Coin a Tender in Payment of Debts; pass any Bill of Attainder, ex post facto Law, or Law impairing the Obligation of Contracts, or grant any Title of Nobility.

No State shall, without the Consent of the Congress, lay any Imposts or Duties on Imports or Exports, except what may be absolutely necessary for executing its inspection Laws: and the net Produce of all Duties and Imposts, laid by any State on Imports or Exports, shall be for the Use of the Treasury of the United States; and all such Laws shall be subject to the Revision and Control of the Congress.

No State shall, without the Consent of the Congress, lay any duty of Tonnage, keep Troops, or Ships of War in time of Peace, enter into any Agreement or Compact with another State, or with a foreign Power, or engage in War, unless actually invaded, or in such imminent Danger as will not admit of delay.

ARTICLE II

SECTION 1. The executive Power shall be vested in a President of the United States of America. He shall hold his Office during the Term of four Years, and, together with the Vice President, chosen for the same Term, be elected, as follows:

Each State shall appoint, in such Manner as the Legislature thereof may direct, a Number of Electors, equal to the whole Number of Senators and Representatives to which the State may be entitled in the Congress; but no Senator or Representative, or Person holding an Office of Trust or Profit under the United States, shall be appointed an Elector.

The Electors shall meet in their respective States, and vote by Ballot for two Persons, of whom one at least shall not be an Inhabitant of the same State with themselves. And they shall make a List of all the Persons voted for, and of the Number of Votes for each; which List they shall sign and certify, and transmit sealed to the Seat of the Government of the United States, directed to the President of the Senate. The President of the Senate shall, in the Presence of the Senate and House of Representatives, open all the Certificates, and the Votes shall then be counted. The Person having the greatest Number of Votes shall be the President, if such Number be a Majority of the whole Number of Electors appointed; and if there be more than one who have such Majority, and have an equal Number of Votes, then the House of Representatives

5. Changed by the Sixteenth Amendment.

shall immediately chuse by Ballot one of them for President; and if no Person have a Majority, then from the five highest on the List the said House shall in like Manner chuse the President. But in chusing the President, the Votes shall be taken by States, the Representation from each State having one Vote; a quorum for this Purpose shall consist of a Member or Members from two thirds of the States, and a Majority of all the States shall be necessary to a Choice. In every Case, after the Choice of the President, the Person having the greatest Number of Votes of the Electors shall be the Vice President. But if there should remain two or more who have equal Votes, the Senate shall chuse from them by Ballot the Vice President.[6]

The Congress may determine the Time of chusing the Electors, and the Day on which they shall give their Votes; which Day shall be the same throughout the United States.

No Person except a natural born Citizen, or a Citizen of the United States, at the time of the Adoption of this Constitution, shall be eligible to the Office of President; neither shall any Person be eligible to that Office who shall not have attained to the Age of thirty five Years, and been fourteen Years a Resident within the United States.

In Case of the Removal of the President from Office, or of his Death, Resignation, or Inability to discharge the Powers and Duties of the said Office, the same shall devolve on the Vice President, *and the Congress may by Law provide for the Case of Removal, Death, Resignation, or Inability, both of the President and Vice President, declaring what Officer shall then act as President, and such Officer shall act accordingly, until the Disability be removed, or a President shall be elected.*[7]

The President shall, at stated Times, receive for his Services a Compensation, which shall neither be increased nor diminished during the Period for which he shall have been elected, and he shall not receive within that Period any other Emolument from the United States, or any of them.

Before he enter on the Execution of his Office, he shall take the following Oath or Affirmation: — "I do solemnly swear (or affirm) that I will faithfully execute the Office of President of the United States, and will to the best of my Ability, preserve, protect and defend the Constitution of the United States."

Section 2. The President shall be Commander in Chief of the Army and Navy of the United States, and of the Militia of the several States, when called into the actual Service of the United States; he may require the Opinion, in writing, of the principal Officer in each of the executive Departments, upon any Subject relating to the Duties of their respective Offices, and he shall have Power to Grant Reprieves and Pardons for Offences against the United States, except in Cases of Impeachment.

He shall have Power, by and with the Advice and Consent of the Senate, to make Treaties, provided two thirds of the Senators present concur; and he shall nominate, and by and with the Advice and Consent of the Senate, shall appoint Ambassadors, other public Ministers and Consuls, Judges of the supreme Court, and all other Officers of the United States, whose Appointments are not herein otherwise provided for, and which shall be established by Law: but the Congress may by Law vest the Appointment of such inferior Officers, as they think proper, in the President alone, in the Courts of Law, or in the Heads of Departments.

The President shall have Power to fill up all Vacancies that may happen during the Recess of the Senate, by granting Commissions which shall expire at the End of their next Session.

Section 3. He shall from time to time give to the Congress Information of the State of the Union, and recommend to their Consideration such Measures as he shall judge necessary and expedient; he may, on extraordinary Occasions, convene both Houses, or either of them, and in Case of Disagreement between them, with Respect to the Time of Adjournment, he may adjourn them to such Time as he shall think proper; he shall receive Ambassadors and other public Ministers; he shall take Care that the Laws be faithfully executed, and shall Commission all the Officers of the United States.

Section 4. The President, Vice President and all civil Officers of the United States, shall be removed from Office on Impeachment for, and Conviction of, Treason, Bribery, or other high Crimes and Misdemeanors.

---

6. Superseded by the Twelfth Amendment.
7. Modified by the Twenty-Fifth Amendment.

ARTICLE III

SECTION 1. The judicial Power of the United States, shall be vested in one supreme Court, and in such inferior Courts as the Congress may from time to time ordain and establish. The Judges, both of the supreme and inferior Courts, shall hold their Offices during good Behaviour, and shall, at stated Times, receive for their Services a Compensation, which shall not be diminished during their Continuance in Office.

SECTION 2. The judicial Power shall extend to all Cases, in Law and Equity, arising under this Constitution, the Laws of the United States, and Treaties made, or which shall be made, under their Authority; — to all Cases affecting Ambassadors, other public Ministers and Consuls; — to all Cases of admiralty and maritime Jurisdiction; — to Controversies to which the United States shall be a Party; — to Controversies between two or more States; — *between a State and Citizens of another State*;[8] — between Citizens of different States; — between Citizens of the same State claiming Lands under Grants of different States, and between a State, or the Citizens thereof, and foreign States, Citizens or Subjects.

In all Cases affecting Ambassadors, other public Ministers and Consuls, and those in which a State shall be Party, the supreme Court shall have original Jurisdiction. In all the other Cases before mentioned, the supreme Court shall have appellate Jurisdiction, both as to Law and Fact, with such Exceptions, and under such Regulations as the Congress shall make.

The trial of all Crimes, except in Cases of Impeachment, shall be by Jury; and such Trial shall be held in the State where said Crimes shall have been committed; but when not committed within any State, the Trial shall be at such Place or Places as the Congress may by Law have directed.

SECTION 3. Treason against the United States, shall consist only in levying War against them, or in adhering to their Enemies, giving them Aid and Comfort. No Person shall be convicted of Treason unless on the Testimony of two Witnesses to the same overt Act, or on Confession in open Court.

The Congress shall have Power to declare the Punishment of Treason, but no Attainder of Treason shall work Corruption of Blood, or Forfeiture except during the Life of the Person attainted.

ARTICLE IV

SECTION 1. Full Faith and Credit shall be given in each State to the public Acts, Records, and judicial Proceedings of every other State. And the Congress may by general Laws prescribe the Manner in which such Acts, Records, and Proceedings shall be proved, and the Effect thereof.

SECTION 2. The Citizens of each State shall be entitled to all Privileges and Immunities of Citizens in the several States.

A Person charged in any State with Treason, Felony, or other Crime, who shall flee from Justice, and be found in another State, shall on demand of the executive Authority of the State from which he fled, be delivered up, to be removed to the State having Jurisdiction of the Crime.

No Person held to Service or Labour in one State, under the Laws thereof, escaping into another, shall, in Consequence of any Law or Regulation therein, be discharged from such Service or Labour, but shall be delivered up on Claim of the Party to whom such Service or Labour may be due.[9]

SECTION 3. New States may be admitted by the Congress into this Union; but no new State shall be formed or erected within the Jurisdiction of any other State; nor any State be formed by the Junction of two or more States, or parts of States, without the Consent of the Legislatures of the States concerned as well as of the Congress.

The Congress shall have Power to dispose of and make all needful Rules and Regulations respecting the Territory or other Property belonging to the United States; and nothing in this Constitution shall be so construed as to Prejudice any Claims of the United States, or of any particular State.

SECTION 4. The United States shall guarantee to every State in this Union a Republican Form of Government, and shall protect each of them against Invasion; and on Application of the Legislature, or of the Executive (when the Legislature cannot be convened) against domestic Violence.

8. Restricted by the Eleventh Amendment.

9. Superseded by the Thirteenth Amendment.

ARTICLE V

The Congress, whenever two thirds of both Houses shall deem it necessary, shall propose Amendments to this Constitution, or, on the Application of the Legislatures of two thirds of the several States, shall call a Convention for proposing Amendments, which, in either Case, shall be valid to all Intents and Purposes, as Part of this Constitution, when ratified by the Legislatures of three fourths of the several States, or by Conventions in three fourths thereof, as the one or the other Mode of Ratification may be proposed by the Congress; Provided that no Amendment which may be made prior to the Year One thousand eight hundred and eight shall in any Manner affect the first and fourth Clauses in the Ninth Section of the first Article; and that no State, without its Consent, shall be deprived of its equal Suffrage in the Senate.

ARTICLE VI

All Debts contracted and Engagements entered into, before the Adoption of this Constitution, shall be as valid against the United States under this Constitution, as under the Confederation.

This Constitution, and the Laws of the United States which shall be made in Pursuance thereof; and all Treaties made, or which shall be made, under the Authority of the United States, shall be the supreme Law of the Land; and the Judges in every State shall be bound thereby, any Thing in the Constitution or Laws of any State to the Contrary notwithstanding.

The Senators and Representatives before mentioned, and the Members of the several State Legislatures, and all executive and judicial Officers, both of the United States and of the several States, shall be bound by Oath or Affirmation, to support this Constitution; but no religious Test shall ever be required as a Qualification to any Office or public Trust under the United States.

ARTICLE VII

The Ratification of the Conventions of nine States shall be sufficient for the Establishment of this Constitution between the States so ratifying the Same.

Done in Convention by the Unanimous Consent of the States present the Seventeenth Day of September in the Year of our Lord one thousand seven hundred and Eighty seven and of the Independence of the United States of America the Twelfth. In Witness whereof We have hereunto subscribed our Names.

Go. Washington
President and deputy from Virginia

New Hampshire
John Langdon
Nicholas Gilman

Massachusetts
Nathaniel Gorham
Rufus King

Connecticut
Wm. Saml. Johnson
Roger Sherman

New York
Alexander Hamilton

New Jersey
Wil. Livingston
David Brearley
Wm. Paterson
Jona. Dayton

Pennsylvania
B. Franklin
Thomas Mifflin
Robt. Morris
Geo. Clymer
Thos. FitzSimons
Jared Ingersoll
James Wilson
Gouv. Morris

Delaware
Geo. Read
Gunning Bedford jun
John Dickinson
Richard Bassett
Jaco. Broom

Maryland
James McHenry
Dan. of St. Thos. Jenifer
Danl. Carroll

Virginia
John Blair
James Madison, Jr.

North Carolina
Wm. Blount
Richd. Dobbs Spaight
Hu Williamson

South Carolina
J. Rutledge
Charles Cotesworth Pinckney
Charles Pinckney
Pierce Butler

Georgia
William Few
Abr. Baldwin

AMENDMENT I [1791][1]

Congress shall make no law respecting an establishment of religion, or prohibiting the free exercise thereof; or abridging the freedom of speech, or of the press; or the right of the people peaceably to assemble, and to petition the government for a redress of grievances.

AMENDMENT II [1791]

A well-regulated militia being necessary to the security of a free State, the right of the people to keep and bear arms shall not be infringed.

AMENDMENT III [1791]

No soldier shall, in time of peace, be quartered in any house without the consent of the owner, nor in time of war, but in a manner to be prescribed by law.

AMENDMENT IV [1791]

The right of the people to be secure in their persons, houses, papers, and effects, against unreasonable searches and seizures, shall not be violated, and no warrants shall issue but upon probable cause, supported by oath or affirmation, and particularly describing the place to be searched, and the persons or things to be seized.

AMENDMENT V [1791]

No person shall be held to answer for a capital, or otherwise infamous crime, unless on a presentment or indictment of a grand jury, except in cases arising in the land or naval forces, or in the militia, when in actual service in time of war or public danger; nor shall any person be subject for the same offence to be twice put in jeopardy of life or limb; nor shall be compelled in any criminal case to be a witness against himself, nor be deprived of life, liberty, or property, without due process of law; nor shall private property be taken for public use without just compensation.

AMENDMENT VI [1791]

In all criminal prosecutions, the accused shall enjoy the right to a speedy and public trial, by an impartial jury of the State and district wherein the crime shall have been committed, which district shall have been previously ascertained by law, and to be informed of the nature and cause of the accusation; to be confronted with the witnesses against him; to have compulsory process for obtaining witnesses in his favor, and to have the assistance of counsel for his defence.

AMENDMENT VII [1791]

In suits at common law, where the value in controversy shall exceed twenty dollars, the right of trial by jury shall be preserved, and no fact tried by a jury shall be otherwise reexamined in any court of the United States, than according to the rules of the common law.

AMENDMENT VIII [1791]

Excessive bail shall not be required, nor excessive fines imposed, nor cruel and unusual punishments inflicted.

AMENDMENT IX [1791]

The enumeration in the Constitution, of certain rights, shall not be construed to deny or disparage others retained by the people.

AMENDMENT X [1791]

The powers not delegated to the United States by the Constitution, nor prohibited by it to the States, are reserved to the States respectively, or to the people.

AMENDMENT XI [1798]

The judicial power of the United States shall not be construed to extend to any suit in law or equity, commenced or prosecuted against one of the United States by citizens of another State, or by citizens or subjects of any foreign state.

AMENDMENT XII [1804]

The electors shall meet in their respective States, and vote by ballot for President and Vice-President, one of whom, at least, shall not be an inhabitant of the same State with themselves; they shall name in their ballots the person voted for as President, and in distinct ballots

1. The date in brackets indicates when the amendment was ratified.

the person voted for as Vice-President, and they shall make distinct lists of all persons voted for as President, and of all persons voted for as Vice-President, and of the number of votes for each, which lists they shall sign and certify, and transmit sealed to the seat of government of the United States, directed to the President of the Senate; — the President of the Senate shall, in the presence of the Senate and House of Representatives, open all the certificates and the votes shall then be counted; — the person having the greatest number of votes for President shall be the President, if such number be a majority of the whole number of electors appointed; and if no person have such majority, then from the persons having the highest numbers not exceeding three on the list of those voted for as President, the House of Representatives shall choose immediately, by ballot, the President. But in choosing the President, the votes shall be taken by States, the representation from each State having one vote; a quorum for this purpose shall consist of a member or members from two-thirds of the States, and a majority of all the States shall be necessary to a choice. And if the House of Representatives shall not choose a President whenever the right of choice shall devolve upon them, before *the fourth day of March* next following, then the Vice-President shall act as President, as in the case of the death or other constitutional disability of the President.[2]

The person having the greatest number of votes as Vice-President shall be the Vice-President, if such number be a majority of the whole number of electors appointed; and if no person have a majority, then from the two highest numbers on the list the Senate shall choose the Vice-President; a quorum for the purpose shall consist of two-thirds of the whole number of Senators, and a majority of the whole number shall be necessary to a choice. But no person constitutionally ineligible to the office of President shall be eligible to that of Vice-President of the United States.

AMENDMENT XIII [1865]

SECTION 1. Neither slavery nor involuntary servitude, except as a punishment for crime whereof the party shall have been duly convicted, shall exist within the United States, or any place subject to their jurisdiction.

SECTION 2. Congress shall have power to enforce this article by appropriate legislation.

AMENDMENT XIV [1868]

SECTION 1. All persons born or naturalized in the United States, and subject to the jurisdiction thereof, are citizens of the United States and of the State wherein they reside. No State shall make or enforce any law which shall abridge the privileges or immunities of citizens of the United States; nor shall any State deprive any person of life, liberty, or property, without due process of law; nor deny to any person within its jurisdiction the equal protection of the laws.

SECTION 2. Representatives shall be appointed among the several States according to their respective numbers, counting the whole number of persons in each State, excluding Indians not taxed. But when the right to vote at any election for the choice of electors for President and Vice-President of the United States, Representatives in Congress, the executive and judicial officers of a State, or the members of the legislature thereof, is denied to any of the male inhabitants of such State, being twenty-one years of age and citizens of the United States, or in any way abridged, except for participation in rebellion, or other crime, the basis of representation therein shall be reduced in the proportion which the number of such male citizens shall bear to the whole number of male citizens twenty-one years of age in such State.

SECTION 3. No person shall be a Senator or Representative in Congress, or Elector of President and Vice-President, or hold any office, civil or military, under the United States, or under any State, who, having previously taken an oath, as a member of Congress, or as an officer of the United States, or as a member of any State legislature, or as an executive or judicial officer of any State, to support the Constitution of the United States, shall have engaged in insurrection or rebellion against the same, or given aid or comfort to the enemies thereof. Congress may, by a vote of two-thirds of each house, remove such disability.

SECTION 4. The validity of the public debt of the United States, authorized by law, including debts incurred for payment of pensions and bounties for services in suppressing insurrection or rebellion, shall not be questioned. But neither the United States nor any State shall assume or pay any debt or obligation incurred in aid of insurrection or rebellion against the

2. Superseded by Section 3 of the Twentieth Amendment.

United States, or any claim for the loss or emancipation of any slave; but all such debts, obligations, and claims shall be held illegal and void.

Section 5. The Congress shall have power to enforce, by appropriate legislation, the provisions of this article.

AMENDMENT XV [1870]

Section 1. The right of citizens of the United States to vote shall not be denied or abridged by the United States or by any State on account of race, color, or previous condition of servitude.

Section 2. The Congress shall have power to enforce this article by appropriate legislation.

AMENDMENT XVI [1913]

The Congress shall have power to lay and collect taxes on incomes, from whatever source derived, without apportionment among the several States, and without regard to any census or enumeration.

AMENDMENT XVII [1913]

Section 1. The Senate of the United States shall be composed of two Senators from each State, elected by the people thereof, for six years; and each Senator shall have one vote. The electors in each State shall have the qualifications requisite for electors of [voters for] the most numerous branch of the State legislatures.

Section 2. When vacancies happen in the representation of any State in the Senate, the executive authority of such State shall issue writs of election to fill such vacancies: Provided, that the Legislature of any State may empower the executive thereof to make temporary appointments until the people fill the vacancies by election as the Legislature may direct.

Section 3. This amendment shall not be so construed as to affect the election or term of any Senator chosen before it becomes valid as part of the Constitution.

AMENDMENT XVIII [1919; Repealed 1933 by Amendment XXI]

Section 1. After one year from the ratification of this article the manufacture, sale, or transportation of intoxicating liquors within, the importation thereof into, or the exportation thereof from the United States and all territory subject to the jurisdiction thereof, for beverage purposes, is hereby prohibited.

Section 2. The Congress and the several States shall have concurrent power to enforce this article by appropriate legislation.

Section 3. This article shall be inoperative unless it shall have been ratified as an amendment to the Constitution by the legislatures of the several States, as provided by the Constitution, within seven years from the date of the submission thereof to the States by the Congress.

AMENDMENT XIX [1920]

Section 1. The right of citizens of the United States to vote shall not be denied or abridged by the United States or by any State on account of sex.

Section 2. Congress shall have the power to enforce this article by appropriate legislation.

AMENDMENT XX [1933]

Section 1. The terms of the President and Vice-President shall end at noon on the twentieth day of January, and the terms of Senators and Representatives at noon on the third day of January, of the years in which such terms would have ended if this article had not been ratified; and the terms of their successors shall then begin.

Section 2. The Congress shall assemble at least once in every year, and such meeting shall begin at noon on the third day of January, unless they shall by law appoint a different day.

Section 3. If, at the time fixed for the beginning of the term of the President, the President-elect shall have died, the Vice-President-elect shall become President. If a President shall not have been chosen before the time fixed for the beginning of his term, or if the President-elect shall have failed to qualify, then the Vice-President-elect shall act as President until a President shall have qualified; and the Congress may by law provide for the case wherein neither a President-elect nor a Vice-President-elect shall have qualified, declaring who shall then act as President, or the manner in which one who is to act shall be selected, and such person shall act accordingly until a President or Vice-President shall have qualified.

Section 4. The Congress may by law provide for the case of the death of any of the persons from whom the House of Representatives may choose a President whenever the right of choice shall have devolved upon them, and for the case of the death of any of the persons from whom the Senate may choose a Vice-President whenever the right of choice shall have devolved upon them.

SECTION 5. Sections 1 and 2 shall take effect on the 15th day of October following the ratification of this article.

SECTION 6. This article shall be inoperative unless it shall have been ratified as an amendment to the Constitution by the Legislatures of three-fourths of the several States within seven years from the date of its submission.

AMENDMENT XXI [1933]

SECTION 1. The eighteenth article of amendment to the Constitution of the United States is hereby repealed.

SECTION 2. The transportation or importation into any State, Territory, or Possession of the United States for delivery or use therein of intoxicating liquors, in violation of the laws thereof, is hereby prohibited.

SECTION 3. This article shall be inoperative unless it shall have been ratified as an amendment to the Constitution by conventions in the several States, as provided in the Constitution, within seven years from the date of the submission thereof to the States by the Congress.

AMENDMENT XXII [1951]

SECTION 1. No person shall be elected to the office of the President more than twice, and no person who has held the office of President, or acted as President, for more than two years of a term to which some other person was elected President shall be elected to the office of President more than once. But this article shall not apply to any person holding the office of President when this Article was proposed by the Congress, and shall not prevent any person who may be holding the office of President, or acting as President, during the term within which this Article becomes operative from holding the office of President or acting as President during the remainder of such term.

SECTION 2. This article shall be inoperative unless it shall have been ratified as an amendment to the Constitution by the legislatures of three-fourths of the several States within seven years from the date of its submission to the States by the Congress.

AMENDMENT XXIII [1961]

SECTION 1. The District constituting the seat of Government of the United States shall appoint in such manner as the Congress may direct: A number of electors of President and Vice-President equal to the whole number of Senators and Representatives in Congress to which the District would be entitled if it were a State, but in no event more than the least populous State; they shall be in addition to those appointed by the States, but they shall be considered for the purposes of the election of President and Vice-President, to be electors appointed by a State; and they shall meet in the District and perform such duties as provided by the twelfth article of amendment.

SECTION 2. The Congress shall have the power to enforce this article by appropriate legislation.

AMENDMENT XXIV [1964]

SECTION 1. The right of citizens of the United States to vote in any primary or other election for President or Vice-President, for electors for President or Vice-President, or for Senator or Representative in Congress, shall not be denied or abridged by the United States or any State by reason of failure to pay any poll tax or other tax.

SECTION 2. The Congress shall have the power to enforce this article by appropriate legislation.

AMENDMENT XXV [1967]

SECTION 1. In case of the removal of the President from office or of his death or resignation, the Vice-President shall become President.

SECTION 2. Whenever there is a vacancy in the office of the Vice-President, the President shall nominate a Vice-President who shall take office upon confirmation by a majority vote of both Houses of Congress.

SECTION 3. Whenever the President transmits to the President pro tempore of the Senate and the Speaker of the House of Representatives his written declaration that he is unable to discharge the powers and duties of his office, and until he transmits to them a written declaration to the contrary, such powers and duties shall be discharged by the Vice-President as Acting President.

SECTION 4. Whenever the Vice-President and a majority of either the principal officers of the executive departments or of such other body as Congress may by law provide, transmit to the President pro tempore of the Senate and the Speaker of the House of Representatives their written declaration that the President is unable to discharge the powers and duties of his office, the Vice-President shall immediately assume the powers and duties of the office as Acting President.

Thereafter, when the President transmits to the President pro tempore of the Senate and the Speaker of the House of Representatives his written declaration that no inability exists, he shall resume the powers and duties of his office unless the Vice-President and a majority of either the principal officers of the executive department[s] or of such other body as Congress may by law provide, transmit within four days to the President pro tempore of the Senate and the Speaker of the House of Representatives their written declaration that the President is unable to discharge the powers and duties of his office. Thereupon Congress shall decide the issue, assembling within forty-eight hours for that purpose if not in session. If the Congress, within twenty-one days after receipt of the latter written declaration, or, if Congress is not in session, within twenty-one days after Congress is required to assemble, determines by two-thirds vote of both Houses that the President is unable to discharge the powers and duties of his office, the Vice-President shall continue to discharge the same as Acting President; otherwise, the President shall resume the powers and duties of his office.

AMENDMENT XXVI [1971]

Section 1. The right of citizens of the United States, who are eighteen years of age or older, to vote shall not be denied or abridged by the United States or by any State on account of age.

Section 2. The Congress shall have power to enforce this article by appropriate legislation.

AMENDMENT XXVII [1992]

No law, varying the compensation for the services of the Senators and Representatives, shall take effect, until an election of Representatives shall have intervened.

Selected Legislative Acts

The following pieces of legislation touched on myriad aspects of African American life: unjust employment practices, discrimination in public facilities, and Black voter disfranchisement. From opening new work and educational opportunities to spurring Black voter participation, these acts had profound consequences for African Americans. The brief excerpts that follow provide some of the key provisions of the acts. As you read them, consider the specific impact these words had on the lives of African Americans — both individually and as a group.

The Civil Rights Act of 1875

The Civil Rights Act of 1875, introduced by Senator Charles Sumner and passed after his death, stipulated that all individuals were to receive equal treatment in public facilities — such as hotels, trains, and places of public amusement — regardless of race. The act made discrimination in such facilities a criminal offense and established monetary damages for those who were victims of discrimination. The law was not well enforced, however. It was finally struck down altogether in the 1883 *Civil Rights Cases*, in which the Supreme Court ruled that Congress lacked the authority to outlaw discriminatory practices by private individuals and businesses.

Whereas it is essential to just government we recognize the equality of all men before the law, and hold that it is the duty of government in its dealings with the people to mete out equal and exact justice to all, of whatever nativity, race, color, or persuasion, religious or political; and it being the appropriate object of legislation to enact great fundamental principles into law: Therefore,

Be it enacted, That all persons within the jurisdiction of the United States shall be entitled to the full and equal enjoyment of the accommodations, advantages, facilities, and privileges of inns, public conveyances on land or water, theaters, and other places of public amusement; subject only to the conditions and limitations established by law, and applicable alike to citizens of every race and color, regardless of any previous condition of servitude.

Section 2. That any person who shall violate the foregoing section . . . shall, for every offense, forfeit and pay the sum of five hundred dollars to the person aggrieved thereby, to be recovered in an action of debt, with full costs; and shall also, for every such offense, be deemed guilty of a misdemeanor, and, upon conviction thereof, shall be fined not less than five hundred nor more than one thousand dollars, or shall be imprisoned not less than thirty days nor more than one year. . . .

Section 3. That the district and circuit courts of the United States shall have . . . cognizance of all crimes and offenses against, and violations of, the provisions of this act; and actions for the penalty given by the preceding section may be prosecuted in the territorial, district, or circuit courts of the United States wherever the defendant may be found, without regard to the other party; and the district attorneys, marshals, and deputy marshals of the United States, and commissioners appointed by the circuit and territorial courts of the United States . . . are hereby specially authorized and required to institute proceedings against every person who shall violate the provisions of this act, and cause him to be arrested and imprisoned or bailed, as the case may be, for trial before such court of the United States, or territorial court, as by law has cognizance of the offense, except in respect of the right of action accruing to the person aggrieved; and such district attorneys shall cause such proceedings to be prosecuted to their termination as in other cases . . . and any district attorney who shall willfully fail to institute and prosecute the proceedings herein required, shall, for every such offense, forfeit and pay the sum of five hundred dollars to the person aggrieved thereby, to be recovered by an action of debt, with full costs, and shall, on conviction thereof, be deemed guilty of a misdemeanor, and be fined not less than one thousand nor more than five thousand dollars. . . .

Section 4. That no citizen possessing all other qualifications which are or may be prescribed by law shall be disqualified for service as grand or petit juror in any court of the United States, or of any State, on account of race, color, or previous condition of servitude; and any officer or other person charged with any duty in the selection or summoning of jurors who shall exclude or fail to summon any citizen for the cause aforesaid shall, on conviction thereof, be deemed guilty of a misdemeanor, and be fined not more than five thousand dollars.

The Civil Rights Act of 1964

The Civil Rights Act of 1964 was a watershed for both African Americans and women. It prohibited discrimination on the basis of race, color, religion, sex, or national origin in employment and voting practices, federally assisted programs, public education, and places of public accommodation; authorized the Justice Department to institute desegregation suits; and provided technical and financial aid to assist communities in the desegregation of their schools. The act's fundamental Title VII, which dealt with discrimination in the workplace, established the Equal Employment Opportunity Commission to investigate cases of job discrimination.

AN ACT

To enforce the constitutional right to vote, to confer jurisdiction upon the district courts of the United States to provide injunctive relief against discrimination in public accommodations, to authorize the Attorney General to institute suits to protect constitutional rights in public facilities and public education, to extend the Commission on Civil Rights, to prevent discrimination in federally assisted programs, to establish a Commission on Equal Employment Opportunity, and for other purposes. . . .

TITLE I — VOTING RIGHTS

. . .

"(2) No person acting under color of law shall —

"(A) in determining whether any individual is qualified under State law or laws to vote in any Federal election, apply any standard, practice, or procedure different from the standards, practices, or procedures applied under such law or laws to other individuals . . . who have been found by State officials to be qualified to vote;

"(B) deny the right of any individual to vote in any Federal election because of an error or omission on any record or paper relating to any application, registration, or other act requisite to voting, if such error or omission is not material in determining whether such individual is qualified under State law to vote in such election; or

"(C) employ any literacy test as a qualification for voting in any Federal election unless (i) such test is administered to each individual and is conducted wholly in writing, and (ii) a certified copy of the test and of the answers given by the individual is furnished to him within twenty-five days of the submission of his request...."

TITLE II — INJUNCTIVE RELIEF AGAINST DISCRIMINATION IN PLACES OF PUBLIC ACCOMMODATION

... (a) All persons shall be entitled to the full and equal enjoyment of the goods, services, facilities, and privileges, advantages, and accommodations of any place of public accommodation, as defined in this section, without discrimination or segregation on the ground of race, color, religion, or national origin.

(b) Each of the following establishments which serves the public is a place of public accommodation within the meaning of this title if its operations affect commerce, or if discrimination or segregation by it is supported by State action:

(1) any inn, hotel, motel, or other establishment which provides lodging to transient guests, other than an establishment located within a building which contains not more than five rooms for rent or hire and which is actually occupied by the proprietor of such establishment as his residence;

(2) any restaurant, cafeteria, lunchroom, lunch counter, soda fountain, or other facility principally engaged in selling food for consumption on the premises....

(3) any motion picture house, theater, concert hall, sports arena, stadium or other place of exhibition or entertainment; and

(4) any establishment (A)(i) which is physically located within the premises of any establishment otherwise covered by this subsection, or (ii) within the premises of which is physically located any such covered establishment, and (B) which holds itself out as serving patrons of such covered establishment....

(d) Discrimination or segregation by an establishment is supported by State action within the meaning of this title if such discrimination or segregation (1) is carried on under color of any law, statute, ordinance, or regulation; or (2) is carried on under color of any custom or usage required or enforced by officials of the State or political subdivision thereof; or (3) is required by action of the State or political subdivision thereof.

(e) The provisions of this title shall not apply to a private club or other establishment not in fact open to the public, except to the extent that the facilities of such establishment are made available to the customers or patrons of an establishment within the scope of subsection (b)....

TITLE III — DESEGREGATION OF PUBLIC FACILITIES

SECTION 301. (a) Whenever the Attorney General receives a complaint in writing signed by an individual to the effect that he is being deprived of or threatened with the loss of his right to the equal protection of the laws, on account of his race, color, religion, or national origin ... the Attorney General is authorized to institute for or in the name of the United States a civil action in any appropriate district court of the United States against such parties and for such relief as may be appropriate....

TITLE IV — DESEGREGATION OF PUBLIC EDUCATION ...

Survey and Report of Educational Opportunities

SECTION 402. The Commissioner shall conduct a survey and make a report to the President and the Congress, within two years of the enactment of this title, concerning the lack of availability of equal educational opportunities for individuals by reason of race, color, religion, or national origin in public educational institutions at all levels in the United States, its territories and possessions, and the District of Columbia.

Technical Assistance

SECTION 403. The Commissioner is authorized, upon the application of any school board, State, municipality, school district, or other governmental unit legally responsible for operating a public school or schools, to render technical assistance to such applicant in the preparation, adoption, and implementation of plans for the desegregation of public schools. Such technical assistance may, among other activities, include making available to such agencies information regarding effective methods of coping with special educational problems occasioned by desegregation, and making available to such agencies personnel of the Office of Education or other persons specially equipped to advise and assist them in coping with such problems. . . .

TITLE V — COMMISSION ON CIVIL RIGHTS . . .

SECTION 104. (a) The Commission shall —

"(1) investigate allegations . . . that certain citizens of the United States are being deprived of their right to vote and have that vote counted by reason of their color, race, religion, or national origin; . . .

"(2) study and collect information concerning legal developments constituting a denial of equal protection of the laws under the Constitution because of race, color, religion or national origin or in the administration of justice;

"(3) appraise the laws and policies of the Federal Government with respect to denials of equal protection of the laws under the Constitution because of race, color, religion or national origin or in the administration of justice;

"(4) serve as a national clearinghouse for information in respect to denials of equal protection of the laws because of race, color, religion or national origin, including but not limited to the fields of voting, education, housing, employment, the use of public facilities, and transportation, or in the administration of justice;

"(5) investigate allegations . . . that citizens of the United States are unlawfully being accorded or denied the right to vote, or to have their votes properly counted, in any election. . . ."

TITLE VI — NONDISCRIMINATION IN FEDERALLY ASSISTED PROGRAMS

SECTION 601. No person in the United States shall, on the ground of race, color, or national origin, be excluded from participation in, be denied the benefits of, or be subjected to discrimination under any program or activity receiving Federal financial assistance. . . .

TITLE VII — EQUAL EMPLOYMENT OPPORTUNITY . . .

Discrimination Because of Race, Color, Religion, Sex, or National Origin

SECTION 703. (a) It shall be an unlawful employment practice for an employer —

(1) to fail or refuse to hire or to discharge any individual, or otherwise to discriminate against any individual with respect to his compensation, terms, conditions, or privileges of employment, because of such individual's race, color, religion, sex, or national origin; or

(2) to limit, segregate, or classify his employees in any way which would deprive or tend to deprive any individual of employment opportunities or otherwise adversely affect his status as an employee, because of such individual's race, color, religion, sex, or national origin.

(b) It shall be an unlawful employment practice for an employment agency to fail or refuse to refer for employment, or otherwise to discriminate against, any individual because of his race, color, religion, sex, or national origin, or to classify or refer for employment any individual on the basis of his race, color, religion, sex, or national origin.

(c) It shall be an unlawful employment practice for a labor organization —

(1) to exclude or to expel from its membership, or otherwise to discriminate against, any individual because of his race, color, religion, sex, or national origin;

(2) to limit, segregate, or classify its membership, or to classify or fail or refuse to refer for employment any individual, in any way which would deprive or tend to deprive any individual of employment opportunities, or would limit such employment opportunities or otherwise adversely affect his status as an employee or as an applicant for employment, because of such individual's race, color, religion, sex, or national origin; or

(3) to cause or attempt to cause an employer to discriminate against an individual in violation of this section.

(d) It shall be an unlawful employment practice for any employer, labor organization, or joint labor-management committee controlling apprenticeship or other training or retraining, including on-the-job training programs to discriminate against any individual because of his race, color, religion, sex, or national origin in admission to, or employment in, any program established to provide apprenticeship or other training.

(e) Notwithstanding any other provision of this title, (1) it shall not be an unlawful employment practice for an employer to hire and employ employees, for an employment agency to classify, or refer for employment any individual, for a labor organization to classify its membership or to classify or refer for employment any individual, or for an employer, labor organization, or joint labor-management committee controlling apprenticeship or other training or retraining programs to admit or employ any individual in any such program, on the basis of his religion, sex, or national origin in those certain instances where religion, sex, or national origin is a bona fide occupational qualification reasonably necessary to the normal operation of that particular business or enterprise, and (2) it shall not be an unlawful employment practice for a school, college, university, or other educational institution or institution of learning to hire and employ employees of a particular religion if such school, college, university, or other educational institution or institution of learning is, in whole or in substantial part, owned, supported, controlled, or managed by a particular religion or by a particular religious corporation, association, or society, or if the curriculum of such school, college, university, or other educational institution or institution of learning is directed toward the propagation of a particular religion. . . .

Equal Employment Opportunity Commission

SECTION 705. (a) There is hereby created a Commission to be known as the Equal Employment Opportunity Commission, which shall be composed of five members, not more than three of whom shall be members of the same political party, who shall be appointed by the President by and with the advice and consent of the Senate. . . .

(g) The Commission shall have power —

(1) to cooperate with and, with their consent, utilize regional, State, local, and other agencies, both public and private, and individuals;

(2) to pay to witnesses whose depositions are taken or who are summoned before the Commission or any of its agents the same witness and mileage fees as are paid to witnesses in the courts of the United States;

(3) to furnish to persons subject to this title such technical assistance as they may request to further their compliance with this title or an order issued thereunder;

(4) upon the request of (i) any employer, whose employees or some of them, or (ii) any labor organization, whose members or some of them, refuse or threaten to refuse to cooperate in effectuating the provisions of this title, to assist in such effectuation by conciliation or such other remedial action as is provided by this title;

(5) to make such technical studies as are appropriate to effectuate the purposes and policies of this title and to make the results of such studies available to the public;

(6) to refer matters to the Attorney General with recommendations for intervention in a civil action brought by an aggrieved party under section 706, or for the institution of a civil action by the Attorney General under section 707, and to advise, consult, and assist the Attorney General on such matters. . . .

TITLE VIII — REGISTRATION AND VOTING STATISTICS

SECTION 801. The Secretary of Commerce shall promptly conduct a survey to compile registration and voting statistics in such geographic areas as may be recommended by the Commission on Civil Rights.

The Voting Rights Act of 1965

The 1965 Voting Rights Act eliminated the practices responsible for the widespread disfranchisement of Blacks in the South, such as poll taxes and literacy tests. It also established a strict system of enforcement, providing federal oversight for the administration of elections — particularly in states that had consistently engaged in discriminatory voting practices. The impact of the act was tremendous: Blacks registered in droves, and Black voter participation skyrocketed throughout the South.

SECTION 2. No voting qualification or prerequisite to voting, or standard, practice, or procedure shall be imposed or applied by any State or political subdivision to deny or abridge the right of any citizen of the United States to vote on account of race or color.

SECTION 3. (a) Whenever the Attorney General institutes a proceeding under any statute to enforce the guarantees of the fifteenth amendment in any State or political subdivision the court shall authorize the appointment of Federal examiners by the United States Civil Service Commission . . . to serve for such period of time and for such political subdivisions as the court shall determine is appropriate to enforce the guarantees of the fifteenth amendment. . . .

(b) If in a proceeding instituted by the Attorney General under any statute to enforce the guarantees of the fifteenth amendment in any State or political subdivision the court finds that a test or device has been used for the purpose or with the effect of denying or abridging the right of any citizen of the United States to vote on account of race or color, it shall suspend the use of tests and devices in such State or political subdivisions as the court shall determine is appropriate and for such period as it deems necessary. . . .

SECTION 4. (a) To assure that the right of citizens of the United States to vote is not denied or abridged on account of race or color, no citizen shall be denied the right to vote in any Federal, State, or local election because of his failure to comply with any test or device in any State. . . .

SECTION 7. (a) The examiners for each political subdivision shall, at such places as the Civil Service Commission shall by regulation designate, examine applicants concerning their qualifications for voting. An application to an examiner shall be in such form as the Commission may require and shall contain allegations that the applicant is not otherwise registered to vote.

(b) Any person whom the examiner finds, in accordance with instructions received under section 9(b), to have the qualifications prescribed by State law not inconsistent with the Constitution and laws of the United States shall promptly be placed on a list of eligible voters. . . . The examiner shall certify and transmit such list, and any supplements as appropriate, at least once a month, to the offices of the appropriate election officials, with copies to the Attorney General and the attorney general of the State, and any such lists and supplements thereto transmitted during the month shall be available for public inspection on the last business day of the month and, in any event, not later than the forty-fifth day prior to any election. The appropriate State or local election official shall place such names on the official voting list. Any person whose name appears on the examiner's list shall be entitled and allowed to vote in the election district of his residence unless and until the appropriate election officials shall have been notified that such person has been removed from such list. . . .

(c) The examiner shall issue to each person whose name appears on such a list a certificate evidencing his eligibility to vote. . . .

SECTION 8. Whenever an examiner is serving under this Act in any political subdivision, the Civil Service Commission may assign, at the request of the Attorney General, one or more persons, who may be officers of the United States, (1) to enter and attend at any place for holding an election in such subdivision for the purpose of observing whether persons who are entitled to vote are being permitted to vote, and (2) to enter and attend at any place for tabulating the votes cast at any election held in such subdivision for the purpose of observing whether votes cast by persons entitled to vote are being properly tabulated. . . .

SECTION 9. (a) Any challenge to a listing on an eligibility list prepared by an examiner shall be heard and determined by a hearing officer appointed by and responsible to the Civil Service Commission and under such rules as the Commission shall by regulation prescribe. . . .

SECTION 10. (a) The Congress finds that the requirement of the payment of a poll tax as a precondition to voting (i) precludes persons of limited means from voting or imposes unreasonable financial hardship upon such persons as a precondition to their exercise of the franchise, (ii) does not bear a reasonable relationship to any legitimate State interest in the conduct of elections, and (iii) in some areas has the purpose or effect of denying persons the right to vote because of race or color. Upon the basis of these findings, Congress declares that the constitutional right of citizens to vote is denied or abridged in some areas by the requirement of the payment of a poll tax as a precondition to voting. . . .

SECTION 11. (a) No person acting under color of law shall fail or refuse to permit any person to vote who is entitled to vote under any provision of this Act or is otherwise qualified to vote, or willfully fail or refuse to tabulate, count, and report such person's vote.

Selected Supreme Court Decisions

The cases that follow were landmarks in African American legal history, bringing about both immediate and long-term change and establishing vital precedents for future cases. Grappling with issues as diverse as the right of Congress to limit slavery, the citizenship status of enslaved people, the permissibility of state-sanctioned segregation, discrimination in the workplace, and the constitutionality of affirmative action, these cases exerted a tremendous impact on both Black citizens and the nation as a whole. The following brief excerpts have been carefully selected from the full opinions of the U.S. Supreme Court. As you read them, consider how they are reflective of the specific historical and social contexts in which they were written.

AP® source *Dred Scott v. Sandford* [1857]

In 1846, the Missouri enslaved couple Dred and Harriet Scott sued for their freedom, claiming that their temporary residence with their enslaver on free soil had rendered them free. Eleven years later, in *Dred Scott v. Sandford*, the Supreme Court ruled that the Scotts were to remain enslaved. In its decision, the Court harked back to the original intent of the writers of the Declaration of Independence and the U.S. Constitution, arguing that this was of paramount importance in interpreting the meaning of those documents for enslaved people and others of African descent. The Court argued that neither Scott nor any other person of African descent was entitled to U.S. citizenship, and thus they could not legitimately bring suit in court. Further, the Court asserted that enslaved people were property and emphasized that Congress lacked the authority to deny enslavers their property. With this decision, the Court made it clear that Congress could not prevent enslavement anywhere, rendering all laws that forbade slavery in the territories — including the Missouri Compromise of 1820 — unconstitutional.

The question is simply this: Can a negro whose ancestors were imported into this country, and sold as slaves, become a member of the political community formed and brought into existence by the Constitution of the United States, and as such become entitled to all the rights and privileges and immunities guaranteed to the citizen? One of which rights is the privilege of suing in a court of the United States in the cases specified in the Constitution. . . .

In the opinion of the court, the legislation and histories of the times, and the language used in the Declaration of Independence, show, that neither the class of persons who had been imported as slaves, nor their descendants, whether they had become free or not, were then acknowledged as a part of the people, nor intended to be included in the general words used in that memorable instrument.

It is difficult at this day to realize the state of public opinion in relation to that unfortunate race, which prevailed in the civilized and enlightened portions of the world at the time of the Declaration of Independence, and when the Constitution of the United States was framed and adopted. But the public history of every European nation displays it in a manner too plain to be mistaken.

They had for more than a century before been regarded as beings of an inferior order, and altogether unfit to associate with the white race, either in social or political relations; and so far inferior, that they had no rights which the white man was bound to respect; and that the negro might justly and lawfully be reduced to slavery for his benefit. He was bought and sold, and treated as an ordinary article of merchandise and traffic, whenever a profit could be made by it. This opinion was at that time fixed and universal in the civilized portion of the white race. It was regarded as an axiom in morals as well as in politics, which no one thought of disputing. . . .

The language of the Declaration of Independence . . . would seem to embrace the whole human family, and if [these words] were used in a similar instrument at this day would be so understood. But it is too clear for dispute, that the enslaved African race were not intended to be included, and formed no part of the people who framed and adopted this declaration. . . .

. . . The right of property in a slave is distinctly and expressly affirmed in the Constitution. . . .

Upon these considerations, it is the opinion of the court that the act of Congress which prohibited a citizen from holding and owning property of this kind in the territory of the United States north of the line therein mentioned, is not warranted by the Constitution, and is therefore void; and that neither Dred Scott himself, nor any of his family, were made free by being carried into this territory; even if they had been carried there by the owner, with the intention of becoming a permanent resident.

AP® source *Plessy v. Ferguson* [1896]

In this landmark case, a shoemaker named Homer Plessy, who was seven-eighths white, argued that he had been denied equal protection under the Fourteenth Amendment when a Louisiana train conductor forced him to ride in the "colored car" rather than in the first-class car for which he had purchased a ticket. Plessy was arrested and charged with violating Louisiana's Separate Car Act. The Court found the act to be constitutional, arguing that separate facilities did not violate one's right to equal protection under the laws or imply the inferiority of Blacks. In protecting local custom and state-sanctioned discrimination and establishing the legal doctrine of separate but equal, the decision effectively legitimized and legalized Jim Crow, paving the way for new and ever more sweeping laws. In 1954, the Court would take up the issue once again in *Brown v. Board of Education of Topeka*, this time with a very different outcome.

A statute which implies merely a legal distinction between the white and colored races — a distinction which is founded in the color of the two races, and which must always exist so long as white men are distinguished from the other race by color — has no tendency to destroy the legal equality of the two races, or re-establish a state of involuntary servitude. . . .

. . . The object of the [fourteenth] amendment was undoubtedly to enforce the absolute equality of the two races before the law, but, in the nature of things, it could not have been intended to abolish distinctions based upon color, or to enforce social, as distinguished from political, equality, or a commingling of the two races upon terms unsatisfactory to either. Laws permitting, and even requiring, their separation, in places where they are liable to be brought into contact, do not necessarily imply the inferiority of either race to the other, and have been generally, if not universally, recognized as within the competency of the state legislatures in the exercise of their police power. . . .

We consider the underlying fallacy of the plaintiff's argument to consist in the assumption that the enforced separation of the two races stamps the colored race with a badge of inferiority. If this be so, it is not by reason of anything found in the act, but solely because the colored race chooses to put that construction upon it. The argument necessarily assumes that if, as has been more than once the case, and is not unlikely to be so again, the colored race should become the dominant power in the state legislature, and should enact a law in precisely similar terms, it would thereby relegate the white race to an inferior position. We imagine that the white race, at least, would not acquiesce in this assumption. The argument also assumes that social prejudices may be overcome by legislation, and that equal rights cannot be secured to the negro except by an enforced commingling of the two races. We cannot accept this proposition. If the two races are to meet upon terms of social equality, it must be the result of natural affinities, a mutual appreciation of each other's merits, and a voluntary consent of individuals. . . . Legislation is powerless to eradicate racial instincts, or to abolish distinctions based upon physical differences, and the attempt to do so can only result in accentuating the difficulties of the present situation. If the civil and political rights of both races be equal, one cannot be inferior to the other civilly or politically.

AP® source *Brown v. Board of Education of Topeka* [1954]

In the 1954 *Brown v. Board of Education of Topeka* decision, the Supreme Court unanimously declared the establishment of separate public schools for Black and white children unconstitutional, thereby reversing its 1896 ruling in *Plessy v. Ferguson*. While the case dealt specifically with education, it was designed to have larger repercussions for the system of segregation as a whole. The NAACP lawyer Thurgood Marshall, who served as lead counsel on the case — and later became the first African American Supreme Court justice — argued successfully that segregation violated the equal protection clause of the Fourteenth Amendment, rendering *Plessy v. Ferguson* unconstitutional. The Court did not strike down the entire 1896 decision, but it did rule that race-based segregated facilities were inherently unequal in their psychological effects on Black children.

Today, education is perhaps the most important function of state and local governments. . . . It is the very foundation of good citizenship. Today it is a principal instrument in awakening the child to cultural values, in preparing him for later professional training, and in helping him to adjust normally to his environment. In these days, it is doubtful that any child may reasonably be expected to succeed in life if he is denied the opportunity of an education. Such an opportunity, where the state has undertaken to provide it, is a right which must be made available to all on equal terms.

We come then to the question presented: Does segregation of children in public schools solely on the basis of race, even though the physical facilities and other "tangible" factors may be equal, deprive the children of the minority group of equal educational opportunities? We believe that it does. . . .

. . . To separate them from others of similar age and qualifications solely because of their race generates a feeling of inferiority as to their status in the community that may affect their hearts and minds in a way unlikely ever to be undone. The effect of this separation on their educational opportunities was well stated by a finding . . . by a court which nevertheless felt compelled to rule against the Negro plaintiffs:

["]Segregation of white and colored children in public schools has a detrimental effect upon the colored children. The impact is greater when it has the sanction of the law, for the policy of separating the races is usually interpreted as denoting the inferiority of the negro group. A sense of inferiority affects the motivation of a child to learn. Segregation with the sanction of law, therefore, has a tendency to [retard] the educational and mental development of negro children and to deprive them of some of the benefits they would receive in a racial[ly] integrated school system.["]

Whatever may have been the extent of psychological knowledge at the time of *Plessy v. Ferguson*, this finding is amply supported by modern authority. Any language in *Plessy v. Ferguson* contrary to this finding is rejected.

We conclude that, in the field of public education, the doctrine of "separate but equal" has no place. Separate educational facilities are inherently unequal. Therefore, we hold that the plaintiffs and others similarly situated for whom the actions have been brought are, by reason of the segregation complained of, deprived of the equal protection of the laws guaranteed by the Fourteenth Amendment.

Griggs v. Duke Power Co. [1971]

In *Griggs v. Duke Power Co.*, an employment discrimination case, the Supreme Court decided unanimously that under Title VII of the Civil Rights Act of 1964, intelligence and other tests that did not measure one's ability to perform a job were discriminatory. The NAACP filed the case on behalf of Willie Griggs and thirteen other Black janitors whose employer had begun to require IQ tests or high school diplomas as prerequisites for promotion. These requirements affected African Americans disproportionately, and the able performance of workers hired before the institution of the requirements made it clear that the tests were unnecessary to perform the work. In its verdict, the Court placed the burden of proof on the employer: unless intelligence or other tests were "demonstrably a reasonable measure of job performance," employers could not require them under Title VII.

The objective of Congress in the enactment of Title VII is plain from the language of the statute. It was to achieve equality of employment opportunities and remove barriers that have operated in the past to favor an identifiable group of white employees over other employees. Under the Act, practices, procedures, or tests neutral on their face, and even neutral in terms of intent, cannot be maintained if they operate to "freeze" the *status quo* of prior discriminatory employment practices.

The Court of Appeals' opinion, and the partial dissent, agreed that, on the record in the present case, "whites register far better on the Company's alternative requirements" than Negroes. . . . This consequence would appear to be directly traceable to race. Basic intelligence must have the means of articulation to manifest itself fairly in a testing process. Because they are Negroes, petitioners have long received inferior education in segregated schools. . . . Congress did not intend by Title VII, however, to guarantee a job to every person regardless of qualifications. In short, the Act does not command that any person be hired simply because he was formerly the subject of discrimination, or because he is a member of a minority group. Discriminatory preference for any group, minority or majority, is precisely and only what Congress has proscribed. What is required by Congress is the removal of artificial, arbitrary, and unnecessary barriers to employment when the barriers operate invidiously to discriminate on the basis of racial or other impermissible classification.

. . . The Act proscribes not only overt discrimination, but also practices that are fair in form, but discriminatory in operation. The touchstone is business necessity. If an employment practice which operates to exclude Negroes cannot be shown to be related to job performance, the practice is prohibited. . . .

The Court of Appeals held that the Company had adopted the diploma and test requirements without any "intention to discriminate against Negro employees." . . . We do not suggest that either the District Court or the Court of Appeals erred in examining the employer's intent; but good intent or absence of discriminatory intent does not redeem employment procedures or testing mechanisms that operate as "built-in headwinds" for minority groups and are unrelated to measuring job capability. . . .

Nothing in the Act precludes the use of testing or measuring procedures; obviously they are useful. What Congress has forbidden is giving these devices and mechanisms controlling force unless they are demonstrably a reasonable measure of job performance. Congress has not commanded that the less qualified be preferred over the better qualified simply because of minority origins. Far from disparaging job qualifications as such, Congress has made such qualifications the controlling factor, so that race, religion, nationality, and sex become irrelevant. What Congress has commanded is that any tests used must measure the person for the job, and not the person in the abstract.

Regents of the University of California v. Bakke [1978]

In this case, the Supreme Court ruled that the medical school of the University of California, Davis, had discriminated against Allan Bakke, a white prospective student, when it denied him admission. Bakke believed he was the victim of reverse discrimination. The school maintained an admissions quota, overseen by a special committee, in which sixteen out of one hundred seats in each entering class were reserved for racial minorities. The justices were divided over the case. Ultimately, in a 5–4 decision, the Court argued that a system of racial "quotas" was unconstitutional, whereas a more flexible policy of affirmative action — with educational diversity as its goal — could, under some circumstances, be constitutional. The Court believed that the medical school's system did not meet the requirements for constitutionality and thus ordered Bakke's admission.

Racial and ethnic classifications of any sort are inherently suspect and call for the most exacting judicial scrutiny. While the goal of achieving a diverse student body is sufficiently compelling to justify consideration of race in admissions decisions under some circumstances, petitioner's special admissions program, which forecloses consideration to persons like respondent, is unnecessary to the achievement of this compelling goal, and therefore invalid under the Equal Protection Clause. . . .

The concept of "discrimination," like the phrase "equal protection of the laws," is susceptible of varying interpretations, for as Mr. Justice Holmes declared, "[a] word is not a crystal, transparent and unchanged, it is the skin of a living thought and may vary greatly in color and content according to the circumstances and the time in which it is used." . . .

. . . The parties fight a sharp preliminary action over the proper characterization of the special admissions program. Petitioner prefers to view it as establishing a "goal" of minority representation in the Medical School. Respondent, echoing the courts below, labels it a racial quota.

This semantic distinction is beside the point: The special admissions program is undeniably a classification based on race and ethnic background. To the extent that there existed a pool of at least minimally qualified minority applicants to fill the 16 special admissions seats, white applicants could compete only for 84 seats in the entering class, rather than the 100 open to minority applicants. Whether this limitation is described as a quota or a goal, it is a line drawn on the basis of race and ethnic status.

Selected Documents

These documents, penned by two of history's most influential African Americans, are revealing of the state of Black America at key points in the nation's history. In each document, the author lays out the circumstances as he sees them and provides his thoughts on how best to address the situation. As you read these documents, consider how they would have been received by their audiences and what they have to tell us about the evolution of race relations in the nineteenth and twenty-first centuries.

AP® source Booker T. Washington, *The Atlanta Compromise Speech* [1895]

When Booker T. Washington delivered the following speech at the Cotton States and International Exposition in Atlanta, he managed to speak to multiple audiences. Washington urged that Blacks remain in the South, start at the bottom, and advance within the confines of the prevailing system. White employers, he argued, should do their part by recognizing Blacks' contributions and hiring them rather than foreign laborers. Washington's emphasis on Black self-help and economic uplift as the keys to race advancement provided a hopeful message for many Blacks. Whites, however, focused on Washington's accommodationism and acceptance of the racial status quo, drawing encouragement from his admonition that Blacks should struggle for their own economic prosperity rather than agitate for social equality.

Mr. President and Gentlemen of the Board of Directors and Citizens.

One-third of the population of the South is of the Negro race. No enterprise seeking the material, civil, or moral welfare of this section can disregard this element of our population and reach the highest success. I but convey to you, Mr. President and Directors, the sentiment of the masses of my race when I say that in no way have the value and manhood of the American Negro been more fittingly and generously recognized than by the managers of this magnificent Exposition at every stage of its progress. It is a recognition that will do more to cement the friendship of the two races than any occurrence since the dawn of our freedom.

Not only this, but the opportunity here afforded will awaken among us a new era of industrial progress. Ignorant and inexperienced, it is not strange that in the first years of our new life we began at the top instead of at the bottom; that a seat in Congress or the state legislature was more sought than real estate or industrial skill; that the political convention or stump speaking had more attractions than starting a dairy farm or truck garden.

SOURCE: Booker T. Washington, *Up from Slavery: An Autobiography* (New York: Doubleday, Page, 1907), 218–25.

A ship lost at sea for many days suddenly sighted a friendly vessel. From the mast of the unfortunate vessel was seen a signal, "Water, water; we die of thirst!" The answer from the friendly vessel at once came back, "Cast down your bucket where you are." A second time the signal, "Water, water; send us water!" ran up from the distressed vessel, and was answered, "Cast down your bucket where you are." And a third and fourth signal for water was answered, "Cast down your bucket where you are." The captain of the distressed vessel, at last heeding the injunction, cast down his bucket, and it came up full of fresh, sparkling water from the mouth of the Amazon River. To those of my race who depend on bettering their condition in a foreign land or who underestimate the importance of cultivating friendly relations with the Southern white man, who is their next-door neighbor, I would say: "Cast down your bucket where you are" — cast it down in making friends in every manly way of the people of all races by whom we are surrounded.

Cast it down in agriculture, mechanics, in commerce, in domestic service, and in the professions. And in this connection it is well to bear in mind that whatever other sins the South may be called to bear, when it comes to business, pure and simple, it is in the South that the Negro is given a man's chance in the commercial world, and in nothing is this Exposition more eloquent than in emphasizing this chance. Our greatest danger is that in the great leap from slavery to freedom we may overlook the fact that the masses of us are to live by the productions of our hands, and fail to keep in mind that we shall prosper in proportion as we learn to dignify and glorify common labour and put brains and skill into the common occupations of life; shall prosper in proportion as we learn to draw the line between the superficial and the substantial, the ornamental gewgaws of life and the useful. No race can prosper till it learns that there is as much dignity in tilling a field as in writing a poem. It is at the bottom of life we must begin, and not at the top. Nor should we permit our grievances to overshadow our opportunities.

To those of the white race who look to the incoming of those of foreign birth and strange tongue and habits for the prosperity of the South, were I permitted I would repeat what I say to my own race, "Cast down your bucket where you are." Cast it down among the eight millions of Negroes whose habits you know, whose fidelity and love you have tested in days when to have proved treacherous meant the ruin of your firesides. Cast down your bucket among these people who have, without strikes and labour wars, tilled your fields, cleared your forests, builded your railroads and cities, and brought forth treasures from the bowels of the earth, and helped make possible this magnificent representation of the progress of the South. Casting down your bucket among my people, helping and encouraging them as you are doing on these grounds, and to education of head, hand, and heart, you will find that they will buy your surplus land, make blossom the waste places in your fields, and run your factories. While doing this, you can be sure in the future, as in the past, that you and your families will be surrounded by the most patient, faithful, law-abiding, and unresentful people that the world has seen. As we have proved our loyalty to you in the past, in nursing your children, watching by the sick-bed of your mothers and fathers, and often following them with tear-dimmed eyes to their graves, so in the future, in our humble way, we shall stand by you with a devotion that no foreigner can approach, ready to lay down our lives, if need be, in defence of yours, interlacing our industrial, commercial, civil, and religious life with yours in a way that shall make the interests of both races one. In all things that are purely social we can be as separate as the fingers, yet one as the hand in all things essential to mutual progress.

There is no defence or security for any of us except in the highest intelligence and development of all. If anywhere there are efforts tending to curtail the fullest growth of the Negro, let these efforts be turned into stimulating, encouraging, and making him the most useful and intelligent citizen. Effort or means so invested will pay a thousand per cent interest. These efforts will be twice blessed — "blessing him that gives and him that takes."

There is no escape through law of man or God from the inevitable: —

The laws of changeless justice bind
Oppressor with oppressed;
And close as sin and suffering joined
We march to fate abreast.

Nearly sixteen millions of hands will aid you in pulling the load upward, or they will pull against you the load downward. We shall constitute one-third and more of the ignorance and crime of the South, or one-third its intelligence and progress; we shall contribute one-third to the business and industrial prosperity of the South, or we shall prove a veritable body of death, stagnating, depressing, retarding every effort to advance the body politic.

Gentlemen of the Exposition, as we present to you our humble effort at an exhibition of our progress, you must not expect overmuch. Starting thirty years ago with ownership here and there in a few quilts and pumpkins and chickens (gathered from miscellaneous sources), remember the path that has led from these to the inventions and production of agricultural implements, buggies, steam-engines, newspapers, books, statuary, carving, paintings, the management of drug-stores and banks, has not been trodden without contact with thorns and thistles. While we take pride in what we exhibit as a result of our independent efforts, we do not for a moment forget that our part in this exhibition would fall far short of your expectations but for the constant help that has come to our educational life, not only from the Southern states, but especially from Northern philanthropists, who have made their gifts a constant stream of blessing and encouragement.

The wisest among my race understand that the agitation of questions of social equality is the extremest folly, and that progress in the enjoyment of all the privileges that will come to us must be the result of severe and constant struggle rather than of artificial forcing. No race that has anything to contribute to the markets of the world is long in any degree ostracized. It is important and right that all privileges of the law be ours, but it is vastly more important that we be prepared for the exercise of these privileges. The opportunity to earn a dollar in a factory just now is worth infinitely more than the opportunity to spend a dollar in an opera-house.

In conclusion, may I repeat that nothing in thirty years has given us more hope and encouragement, and drawn us so near to you of the white race, as this opportunity offered by the Exposition; and here bending, as it were, over the altar that represents the results of the struggles of your race and mine, both starting practically empty-handed three decades ago, I pledge that in your effort to work out the great and intricate problem which God has laid at the doors of the South, you shall have at all times the patient, sympathetic help of my race; only let this be constantly in mind, that, while from representations in these buildings of the product of field, of forest, of mine, of factory, letters, and art, much good will come, yet far above and beyond material benefits will be that higher good, that, let us pray God, will come, in a blotting out of sectional differences and racial animosities and suspicions, in a determination to administer absolute justice, in a willing obedience among all classes to the mandates of law. This, this, coupled with our material prosperity, will bring into our beloved South a new heaven and a new earth.

Barack Obama, *A More Perfect Union* [2008]

In March 2008, during the presidential primaries, presidential hopeful Senator Barack Obama delivered the following speech. He addressed the issue of race head-on, partially in response to public concern over controversial statements made by his former pastor, the Reverend Jeremiah Wright. Quoting the preamble of the Constitution, Obama laid out the lingering problems and divisions that characterized Black and white America. Americans could either focus on divisiveness, he said, or they could move forward by addressing their shared concerns in a unified way. This, Obama argued, would be the first step toward improving the American lot and creating as perfect a union as possible.

"We the people, in order to form a more perfect union."

Two hundred and twenty-one years ago, in a hall that still stands across the street, a group of men gathered and, with these simple words, launched America's improbable experiment in democracy. Farmers and scholars; statesmen and patriots who had traveled across an ocean to escape tyranny and persecution finally made real their declaration of independence at a Philadelphia convention that lasted through the spring of 1787.

The document they produced was eventually signed but ultimately unfinished. It was stained by this nation's original sin of slavery, a question that divided the colonies and brought the convention to a stalemate until the founders chose to allow the slave trade to continue for at least twenty more years, and to leave any final resolution to future generations.

Of course, the answer to the slavery question was already embedded within our Constitution — a Constitution that had at its very core the ideal of equal citizenship under the law; a Constitution that promised its people liberty, and justice, and a union that could be and should be perfected over time.

And yet words on a parchment would not be enough to deliver slaves from bondage, or provide men and women of every color and creed their full rights and obligations as citizens of the United States. What would be needed were Americans in successive generations who were willing to do their part — through protests and struggle, on the streets and in the courts, through a civil war and civil disobedience and always at great risk — to narrow that gap between the promise of our ideals and the reality of their time.

This was one of the tasks we set forth at the beginning of this campaign — to continue the long march of those who came before us, a march for a more just, more equal, more free, more caring and more prosperous America. I chose to run for the presidency at this moment in history because I believe deeply that we cannot solve the challenges of our time unless we solve them together — unless we perfect our union by understanding that we may have different stories, but we hold common hopes; that we may not look the same and we may not have come from the same place, but we all want to move in the same direction — towards a better future for our children and our grandchildren.

This belief comes from my unyielding faith in the decency and generosity of the American people. But it also comes from my own American story.

I am the son of a black man from Kenya and a white woman from Kansas. I was raised with the help of a white grandfather who survived a Depression to serve in Patton's Army during World War II and a white grandmother who worked on a bomber assembly line at Fort Leavenworth while he was overseas. I've gone to some of the best schools in America and lived in one of the world's poorest nations. I am married to a black American who carries within her the blood of slaves and slaveowners — an inheritance we pass on to our two precious daughters. I have brothers, sisters, nieces, nephews, uncles and cousins, of every race and every hue, scattered across three continents, and for as long as I live, I will never forget that in no other country on Earth is my story even possible.

It's a story that hasn't made me the most conventional candidate. But it is a story that has seared into my genetic makeup the idea that this nation is more than the sum of its parts — that out of many, we are truly one.

Throughout the first year of this campaign, against all predictions to the contrary, we saw how hungry the American people were for this message of unity. Despite the temptation to view my candidacy through a purely racial lens, we won commanding victories in states with some of the whitest populations in the country. In South Carolina, where the Confederate Flag still flies, we built a powerful coalition of African Americans and white Americans.

This is not to say that race has not been an issue in the campaign. At various stages in the campaign, some commentators have deemed me either "too black" or "not black enough." We saw racial tensions bubble to the surface during the week before the South Carolina primary. The press has scoured every exit poll for the latest evidence of racial polarization, not just in terms of white and black, but black and brown as well.

And yet, it has only been in the last couple of weeks that the discussion of race in this campaign has taken a particularly divisive turn.

On one end of the spectrum, we've heard the implication that my candidacy is somehow an exercise in affirmative action; that it's based solely on the desire of wide-eyed liberals to purchase racial reconciliation on the cheap. On the other end, we've heard my former pastor, Reverend Jeremiah Wright, use incendiary language to express views that have the potential not only to widen the racial divide, but views that denigrate both the greatness and the goodness of our nation; that rightly offend white and black alike.

I have already condemned, in unequivocal terms, the statements of Reverend Wright that have caused such controversy. For some, nagging questions remain. Did I know him to be an occasionally fierce critic of American domestic and foreign policy? Of course. Did I ever hear him make remarks that could be considered controversial while I sat in church? Yes. Did I strongly disagree with many of his political views? Absolutely — just as I'm sure many of you have heard remarks from your pastors, priests, or rabbis with which you strongly disagreed.

But the remarks that have caused this recent firestorm weren't simply controversial. They weren't simply a religious leader's effort to speak out against perceived injustice. Instead, they expressed a profoundly distorted view of this country — a view that sees white racism as endemic, and that elevates what is wrong with America above all that we know is right with America; a view that sees the conflicts in the Middle East as rooted primarily in the actions of stalwart allies like Israel, instead of emanating from the perverse and hateful ideologies of radical Islam.

As such, Reverend Wright's comments were not only wrong but divisive, divisive at a time when we need unity; racially charged at a time when we need to come together to solve a set of monumental problems — two wars, a terrorist threat, a falling economy, a chronic health care crisis and potentially devastating climate change; problems that are neither black or white or Latino or Asian, but rather problems that confront us all.

Given my background, my politics, and my professed values and ideals, there will no doubt be those for whom my statements of condemnation are not enough. Why associate myself with Reverend Wright in the first place, they may ask? Why not join another church? And I confess that if all that I knew of Reverend Wright were the snippets of those sermons that have run in an endless loop on the television and YouTube, or if Trinity United Church of Christ conformed to the caricatures being peddled by some commentators, there is no doubt that I would react in much the same way.

But the truth is, that isn't all that I know of the man. The man I met more than twenty years ago is a man who helped introduce me to my Christian faith, a man who spoke to me about our obligations to love one another; to care for the sick and lift up the poor. He is a man who served his country as a U.S. Marine; who has studied and lectured at some of the finest universities and seminaries in the country, and who for over thirty years led a church that serves the community by doing God's work here on Earth — by housing the homeless, ministering to the needy, providing day care services and scholarships and prison ministries, and reaching out to those suffering from HIV/AIDS.

In my first book, *Dreams from My Father*, I described the experience of my first service at Trinity:

"People began to shout, to rise from their seats and clap and cry out, a forceful wind carrying the reverend's voice up into the rafters. . . . And in that single note — hope! — I heard something else; at the foot of that cross, inside the thousands of churches across the city, I imagined the stories of ordinary black people merging with the stories of David and Goliath, Moses and Pharaoh, the Christians in the lion's den, Ezekiel's field of dry bones. Those stories — of survival, and freedom, and hope — became our story, my story; the blood that had spilled was our blood, the tears our tears; until this black church, on this bright day, seemed once more a vessel carrying the story of a people into future generations and into a larger world. Our trials and triumphs became at once unique and universal, black and more than black; in chronicling our journey, the stories and songs gave us a means to reclaim memories that we didn't need to feel shame about . . . memories that all people might study and cherish — and with which we could start to rebuild."

That has been my experience at Trinity. Like other predominantly black churches across the country, Trinity embodies the black community in its entirety — the doctor and the welfare mom, the model student and the former gang-banger. Like other black churches, Trinity's services are full of raucous laughter and sometimes bawdy humor. They are full of dancing, clapping, screaming and shouting that may seem jarring to the untrained ear. The church contains in full the kindness and cruelty, the fierce intelligence and the shocking ignorance, the struggles and successes, the love and yes, the bitterness and bias that make up the black experience in America.

And this helps explain, perhaps, my relationship with Reverend Wright. As imperfect as he may be, he has been like family to me. He strengthened my faith, officiated my wedding, and baptized my children. Not once in my conversations with him have I heard him talk about any ethnic group in derogatory terms, or treat whites with whom he interacted with anything but courtesy and respect. He contains within him the contradictions — the good and the bad — of the community that he has served diligently for so many years.

I can no more disown him than I can disown the black community. I can no more disown him than I can my white grandmother — a woman who helped raise me, a woman who sacrificed again and again for me, a woman who loves me as much as she loves anything in this world, but a woman who once confessed her fear of black men who passed by her on the street, and who on more than one occasion has uttered racial or ethnic stereotypes that made me cringe.

These people are a part of me. And they are a part of America, this country that I love.

Some will see this as an attempt to justify or excuse comments that are simply inexcusable. I can assure you it is not. I suppose the politically safe thing would be to move on from this episode and just hope that it fades into the woodwork. We can dismiss Reverend Wright as a crank or a demagogue, just as some have dismissed Geraldine Ferraro, in the aftermath of her recent statements, as harboring some deep-seated racial bias.

But race is an issue that I believe this nation cannot afford to ignore right now. We would be making the same mistake that Reverend Wright made in his offending sermons about America — to simplify and stereotype and amplify the negative to the point that it distorts reality.

The fact is that the comments that have been made and the issues that have surfaced over the last few weeks reflect the complexities of race in this country that we've never really worked through — a part of our union that we have yet to perfect. And if we walk away now, if we simply retreat into our respective corners, we will never be able to come together and solve challenges like health care, or education, or the need to find good jobs for every American.

Understanding this reality requires a reminder of how we arrived at this point. As William Faulkner once wrote, "The past isn't dead and buried. In fact, it isn't even past." We do not need to recite here the history of racial injustice in this country. But we do need to remind ourselves that so many of the disparities that exist in the African American community today can be directly traced to inequalities passed on from an earlier generation that suffered under the brutal legacy of slavery and Jim Crow.

Segregated schools were, and are, inferior schools; we still haven't fixed them, fifty years after *Brown v. Board of Education*, and the inferior education they provided, then and now, helps explain the pervasive achievement gap between today's black and white students.

Legalized discrimination — where blacks were prevented, often through violence, from owning property, or loans were not granted to African American business owners, or black homeowners could not access FHA mortgages, or blacks were excluded from unions, or the police force, or fire departments — meant that black families could not amass any meaningful wealth to bequeath to future generations. That history helps explain the wealth and income gap between black and white, and the concentrated pockets of poverty that persist in so many of today's urban and rural communities.

A lack of economic opportunity among black men, and the shame and frustration that came from not being able to provide for one's family, contributed to the erosion of black families — a problem that welfare policies for many years may have worsened. And the lack of basic services in so many urban black neighborhoods — parks for kids to play in, police walking the beat, regular garbage pick-up and building code enforcement — all helped create a cycle of violence, blight and neglect that continues to haunt us.

This is the reality in which Reverend Wright and other African Americans of his generation grew up. They came of age in the late fifties and early sixties, a time when segregation was still the law of the land and opportunity was systematically constricted. What's remarkable is not how many failed in the face of discrimination, but rather how many men and women overcame the odds; how many were able to make a way out of no way for those like me who would come after them.

But for all those who scratched and clawed their way to get a piece of the American Dream, there were many who didn't make it — those who were ultimately defeated, in one way or another, by discrimination. That legacy of defeat was passed on to future generations — those young men and increasingly young women who we see standing on street corners or languishing in our prisons, without hope or prospects for the future. Even for those blacks who did make it, questions of race, and racism, continue to define their worldview in fundamental ways. For the men and women of Reverend Wright's generation, the memories of humiliation and doubt and fear have not gone away; nor has the anger and the bitterness of those years. That anger may not get expressed in public, in front of white co-workers or white friends. But it does find voice in the barbershop or around the kitchen table. At times, that anger is exploited by politicians, to gin up votes along racial lines, or to make up for a politician's own failings.

And occasionally it finds voice in the church on Sunday morning, in the pulpit and in the pews. The fact that so many people are surprised to hear that anger in some of Reverend Wright's sermons simply reminds us of the old truism that the most segregated hour in American life occurs on Sunday morning. That anger is not always productive; indeed, all too often it distracts attention from solving real problems; it keeps us from squarely facing our own complicity in our condition, and prevents the African American community from forging the alliances it needs to bring about real change. But the anger is real; it is powerful; and to simply wish it away, to condemn it without understanding its roots, only serves to widen the chasm of misunderstanding that exists between the races.

In fact, a similar anger exists within segments of the white community. Most working- and middle-class white Americans don't feel that they have been particularly privileged by their race. Their experience is the immigrant experience — as far as they're concerned, no one's handed them anything, they've built it from scratch. They've worked hard all their lives, many times only to see their jobs shipped overseas or their pension dumped after a lifetime of labor. They are anxious about their futures, and feel their dreams slipping away; in an era of stagnant wages and global competition, opportunity comes to be seen as a zero sum game, in which your dreams come at my expense. So when they are told to bus their children to a school across town; when they hear that an African American is getting an advantage in landing a good job or a spot in a good college because of an injustice that they themselves never committed; when they're told that their fears about crime in urban neighborhoods are somehow prejudiced, resentment builds over time.

Like the anger within the black community, these resentments aren't always expressed in polite company. But they have helped shape the political landscape for at least a generation. Anger over welfare and affirmative action helped forge the Reagan Coalition. Politicians routinely exploited fears of crime for their own electoral ends. Talk show hosts and conservative commentators built entire careers unmasking bogus claims of racism while dismissing legitimate discussions of racial injustice and inequality as mere political correctness or reverse racism.

Just as black anger often proved counterproductive, so have these white resentments distracted attention from the real culprits of the middle class squeeze — a corporate culture rife with inside dealing, questionable accounting practices, and short-term greed; a Washington dominated by lobbyists and special interests; economic policies that favor the few over the many. And yet, to wish away the resentments of white Americans, to label them as misguided or even racist, without recognizing they are grounded in legitimate concerns — this too widens the racial divide, and blocks the path to understanding.

This is where we are right now. It's a racial stalemate we've been stuck in for years. Contrary to the claims of some of my critics, black and white, I have never been so naive as to believe that we can get beyond our racial divisions in a single election cycle, or with a single candidacy — particularly a candidacy as imperfect as my own.

But I have asserted a firm conviction — a conviction rooted in my faith in God and my faith in the American people — that working together we can move beyond some of our old racial wounds, and that in fact we have no choice if we are to continue on the path of a more perfect union.

For the African American community, that path means embracing the burdens of our past without becoming victims of our past. It means continuing to insist on a full measure of justice in every aspect of American life. But it also means binding our particular grievances — for better health care, and better schools, and better jobs — to the larger aspirations of all Americans — the white woman struggling to break the glass ceiling, the white man who's been laid off, the immigrant trying to feed his family. And it means taking full responsibility for own lives — by demanding more from our fathers, and spending more time with our children, and reading to them, and teaching them that while they may face challenges and discrimination in their own lives, they must never succumb to despair or cynicism; they must always believe that they can write their own destiny.

Ironically, this quintessentially American — and yes, conservative — notion of self-help found frequent expression in Reverend Wright's sermons. But what my former pastor too often failed to understand is that embarking on a program of self-help also requires a belief that society can change.

The profound mistake of Reverend Wright's sermons is not that he spoke about racism in our society. It's that he spoke as if our society was static; as if no progress has been made; as if this country — a country that has made it possible for one of his own members to run for the highest office in the land and build a coalition of white and black; Latino and Asian, rich and poor, young and old — is still irrevocably bound to a tragic past. But what we know — what we have seen — is that America can change. That is [the] true genius of this nation. What we have already achieved gives us hope — the audacity to hope — for what we can and must achieve tomorrow.

In the white community, the path to a more perfect union means acknowledging that what ails the African American community does not just exist in the minds of black people; that the legacy of discrimination — and current incidents of discrimination, while less overt than in the past — are real and must be addressed. Not just with words, but with deeds — by investing in our schools and our communities; by enforcing our civil rights laws and ensuring fairness in our criminal justice system; by providing this generation with ladders of opportunity that were unavailable for previous generations. It requires all Americans to realize that your dreams do not have to come at the expense of my dreams; that investing in the health, welfare, and education of black and brown and white children will ultimately help all of America prosper.

In the end, then, what is called for is nothing more, and nothing less, than what all the world's great religions demand — that we do unto others as we would have them do unto us. Let us be our brother's keeper, Scripture tells us. Let us be our sister's keeper. Let us find that common stake we all have in one another, and let our politics reflect that spirit as well.

For we have a choice in this country. We can accept a politics that breeds division, and conflict, and cynicism. We can tackle race only as spectacle — as we did in the OJ trial — or in the wake of tragedy, as we did in the aftermath of Katrina — or as fodder for the nightly news. We can play Reverend Wright's sermons on every channel, every day and talk about them from now until the election, and make the only question in this campaign whether or not the American people think that I somehow believe or sympathize with his most offensive words. We can pounce on some gaffe by a Hillary supporter as evidence that she's playing the race card, or we can speculate on whether white men will all flock to John McCain in the general election regardless of his policies.

We can do that.

But if we do, I can tell you that in the next election, we'll be talking about some other distraction. And then another one. And then another one. And nothing will change.

That is one option. Or, at this moment, in this election, we can come together and say, "Not this time." This time we want to talk about the crumbling schools that are stealing the future of black children and white children and Asian children and Hispanic children and Native American children. This time we want to reject the cynicism that tells us that these kids can't learn; that those kids who don't look like us are somebody else's problem. The children of America are not those kids, they are our kids, and we will not let them fall behind in a 21st century economy. Not this time.

This time we want to talk about how the lines in the Emergency Room are filled with whites and blacks and Hispanics who do not have health care; who don't have the power on their own to overcome the special interests in Washington, but who can take them on if we do it together.

This time we want to talk about the shuttered mills that once provided a decent life for men and women of every race, and the homes for sale that once belonged to Americans from every religion, every region, every walk of life. This time we want to talk about the fact that the real problem is not that someone who doesn't look like you might take your job; it's that the corporation you work for will ship it overseas for nothing more than a profit.

This time we want to talk about the men and women of every color and creed who serve together, and fight together, and bleed together under the same proud flag. We want to talk about how to bring them home from a war that never should've been authorized and never should've been waged, and we want to talk about how we'll show our patriotism by caring for them, and their families, and giving them the benefits they have earned.

I would not be running for President if I didn't believe with all my heart that this is what the vast majority of Americans want for this country. This union may never be perfect, but generation after generation has shown that it can always be perfected. And today, whenever I find myself feeling doubtful or cynical about this possibility, what gives me the most hope is the next generation — the young people whose attitudes and beliefs and openness to change have already made history in this election.

There is one story in particular that I'd like to leave you with today — a story I told when I had the great honor of speaking on Dr. King's birthday at his home church, Ebenezer Baptist, in Atlanta.

There is a young, twenty-three-year-old white woman named Ashley Baia who organized for our campaign in Florence, South Carolina. She had been working to organize a mostly African American community since the beginning of this campaign, and one day she was at a roundtable discussion where everyone went around telling their story and why they were there.

And Ashley said that when she was nine years old, her mother got cancer. And because she had to miss days of work, she was let go and lost her health care. They had to file for bankruptcy, and that's when Ashley decided that she had to do something to help her mom.

She knew that food was one of their most expensive costs, and so Ashley convinced her mother that what she really liked and really wanted to eat more than anything else was mustard and relish sandwiches. Because that was the cheapest way to eat.

She did this for a year until her mom got better, and she told everyone at the roundtable that the reason she joined our campaign was so that she could help the millions of other children in the country who want and need to help their parents too.

Now Ashley might have made a different choice. Perhaps somebody told her along the way that the source of her mother's problems were blacks who were on welfare and too lazy to work, or Hispanics who were coming into the country illegally. But she didn't. She sought out allies in her fight against injustice.

Anyway, Ashley finishes her story and then goes around the room and asks everyone else why they're supporting the campaign. They all have different stories and reasons. Many bring up a specific issue. And finally they come to this elderly black man who's been sitting there quietly the entire time. And Ashley asks him why he's there. And he does not bring up a specific issue. He does not say health care or the economy. He does not say education or the war. He does not say that he was there because of Barack Obama. He simply says to everyone in the room, "I am here because of Ashley."

"I'm here because of Ashley." By itself, that single moment of recognition between that young white girl and that old black man is not enough. It is not enough to give health care to the sick, or jobs to the jobless, or education to our children.

But it is where we start. It is where our union grows stronger. And as so many generations have come to realize over the course of the two hundred and twenty-one years since a band of patriots signed that document in Philadelphia, that is where the perfection begins.

APPENDIX: Tables and Charts

African American Population of the United States, 1790–2010

Year	Black Population	Percentage of Total Population	Number of Enslaved People	Percentage of Blacks Who Were Enslaved
1790	757,208	19.3	697,681	92
1800	1,002,037	18.9	893,602	89
1810	1,377,808	19.0	1,191,362	86
1820	1,771,656	18.4	1,538,022	87
1830	2,328,642	18.1	2,009,043	86
1840	2,873,648	16.1	2,487,355	87
1850	3,638,808	15.7	3,204,287	88
1860	4,441,830	14.1	3,953,731	89
1870	4,880,009	12.7	—	—
1880	6,580,793	13.1	—	—
1890	7,488,788	11.9	—	—
1900	8,833,994	11.6	—	—
1910	9,827,763	10.7	—	—
1920	10,463,131	9.9	—	—
1930	11,891,143	9.7	—	—
1940	12,865,518	9.8	—	—
1950	15,044,937	10.0	—	—
1960	18,871,931	10.6	—	—
1970	22,580,289	11.1	—	—
1980	26,482,349	11.8	—	—
1990	29,986,060	12.0	—	—
2000	34,658,190	12.3	—	—
2010	38,929,319	12.6	—	—
2020	46,936,733	14.2	—	—

SOURCES: U.S. Census Bureau, *Historical Statistics of the United States, Colonial Times to 1970* (1975); *Statistical Abstract of the United States*, 2010; 2020 Census Demographic Profile

Historically Black Colleges and Universities, 1865–Present

College/University and Location	Year Founded	Principal Funding Source
Alabama A&M University, Normal, Alabama	1875	Alabama
Alabama State University, Montgomery, Alabama	1867	Alabama
Albany State University, Albany, Georgia	1903	Georgia
Alcorn State University, Lorman, Mississippi	1871	Mississippi
Allen University, Columbia, South Carolina*	1870	African Methodist Episcopal
Arkansas Baptist College, Little Rock, Arkansas	1884	Baptist
Barber-Scotia College, Concord, North Carolina	1867	Presbyterian
Benedict College, Columbia, South Carolina*	1870	Baptist
Bennett College, Greensboro, North Carolina*	1873	United Methodist
Bethune-Cookman College, Daytona Beach, Florida*	1904	United Methodist
Bluefield State College, Bluefield, West Virginia	1895	West Virginia
Bowie State University, Bowie, Maryland	1865	Maryland
Central State University, Wilberforce, Ohio	1887	Ohio
Cheyney University, Cheyney, Pennsylvania	1837	Quaker
Claflin College, Orangeburg, South Carolina*	1869	United Methodist
Clark Atlanta University, Atlanta, Georgia*	1988	United Methodist
Concordia College, Selma, Alabama	1922	Lutheran
Coppin State University, Baltimore, Maryland	1900	Maryland
Delaware State University, Dover, Delaware	1891	Delaware
Dillard University, New Orleans, Louisiana*	1869	United Church of Christ and United Methodist
Edward Waters College, Jacksonville, Florida*	1866	African Methodist Episcopal
Elizabeth City State University, Elizabeth City, North Carolina	1891	North Carolina
Fayetteville State University, Fayetteville, North Carolina	1867	North Carolina
Fisk University, Nashville, Tennessee*	1866	United Church of Christ
Florida A&M University, Tallahassee, Florida	1887	Florida
Florida Memorial College, Miami, Florida*	1879	Baptist Church
Fort Valley State College, Fort Valley, Georgia	1895	Georgia
Grambling State University, Grambling, Louisiana	1901	Louisiana
Hampton University, Hampton, Virginia	1868	American Missionary Association and Freedmen's Bureau
Harris-Stowe State College, St. Louis, Missouri	1857	Missouri
Howard University, Washington, D.C.	1867	Federal
Huston-Tillotson University, Austin, Texas*	1877	United Church of Christ
Jackson State University, Jackson, Mississippi	1877	Mississippi

* United Negro College Fund member college

Continued

Continued

College/University and Location	Year Founded	Principal Funding Source
Jarvis Christian College, Hawkins, Texas*	1913	Christian Church (Disciples of Christ)
Johnson C. Smith University, Charlotte, North Carolina*	1867	Presbyterian Church
Kentucky State University, Frankfort, Kentucky	1886	Kentucky
Knoxville College, Knoxville, Tennessee	1875	Presbyterian Church
Lane College, Jackson, Tennessee*	1882	Christian Methodist Episcopal Church
Langston University, Langston, Oklahoma	1897	Oklahoma
LeMoyne-Owen College, Memphis, Tennessee*	1871	United Church of Christ
Lincoln University, Jefferson City, Missouri	1866	Missouri
Lincoln University, Lincoln, Pennsylvania	1854	Pennsylvania
Livingstone College, Salisbury, North Carolina*	1879	African Methodist Episcopal Zion
Miles College, Birmingham, Alabama*	1908	Christian Methodist Episcopal
Mississippi Valley State University, Itta Bena, Mississippi	1946	Mississippi
Morehouse College, Atlanta, Georgia*	1867	Baptist
Morgan State University, Baltimore, Maryland	1867	Maryland
Morris Brown College, Atlanta, Georgia	1881	African Methodist Episcopal
Morris College, Sumter, South Carolina*	1908	Baptist
Norfolk State University, Norfolk, Virginia	1935	Virginia
North Carolina A&T State University, Greensboro, North Carolina	1892	North Carolina
North Carolina Central University, Durham, North Carolina	1909	North Carolina
Oakwood College, Huntsville, Alabama*	1896	Seventh-day Adventist
Paine College, Augusta, Georgia*	1882	United Methodist Church and Christian Methodist Episcopal
Paul Quinn College, Dallas, Texas	1872	African Methodist Episcopal
Philander Smith College, Little Rock, Arkansas*	1877	United Methodist
Prairie View A&M University, Prairie View, Texas	1878	Texas
Rust College, Holly Springs, Mississippi*	1866	United Methodist
Saint Augustine's University, Raleigh, North Carolina*	1867	Episcopal
Saint Paul's College, Lawrenceville, Virginia	1888	Episcopal
Savannah State University, Savannah, Georgia	1890	Georgia
Selma University, Selma, Alabama	1878	Baptist
Shaw University, Raleigh, North Carolina*	1865	American Baptist Home Mission Society and Freedmen's Bureau
Simmons College, Louisville, Kentucky	1879	Baptist
South Carolina State University, Orangeburg, South Carolina	1896	South Carolina

* United Negro College Fund member college

Continued

Continued

College/University and Location	Year Founded	Principal Funding Source
Southern University and A&M College, Baton Rouge, Louisiana	1880	Louisiana
Southern University at New Orleans, New Orleans, Louisiana	1956	Louisiana
Southwestern Christian College, Terrell, Texas	1949	Church of Christ
Spelman College, Atlanta, Georgia*	1881	Presbyterian
Stillman College, Tuscaloosa, Alabama*	1876	Presbyterian
Talladega College, Talladega, Alabama*	1867	United Church of Christ
Tennessee State University, Nashville, Tennessee	1912	Tennessee
Texas College, Tyler, Texas*	1894	Christian Methodist Episcopal
Texas Southern University, Houston, Texas	1947	Texas
Tougaloo College, Tougaloo, Mississippi*	1869	United Church of Christ
Tuskegee University, Tuskegee, Alabama*	1881	Alabama
University of Arkansas at Pine Bluff, Pine Bluff, Arkansas	1873	Arkansas
University of Maryland Eastern Shore, Princess Anne, Maryland	1886	Maryland
University of the District of Columbia, Washington, D.C.	1977	D.C./Federal
University of the Virgin Islands, St. Thomas, United States Virgin Islands	1962	U.S. Virgin Islands
Virginia State University, Petersburg, Virginia	1882	Virginia
Virginia Union University, Richmond, Virginia*	1865	Baptist
Virginia University of Lynchburg, Lynchburg, Virginia	1886	Baptist
Voorhees College, Denmark, South Carolina*	1897	Episcopal
West Virginia State University, Institute, West Virginia	1891	West Virginia
Wilberforce University, Wilberforce, Ohio*	1856	Methodist Episcopal
Wiley College, Marshall, Texas*	1873	Methodist Episcopal
Winston-Salem State University, Winston-Salem, North Carolina	1892	North Carolina
Xavier University of Louisiana, New Orleans, Louisiana*	1925	Catholic

* United Negro College Fund member college

Glossary/Glosario

This Glossary of Key Terms contains definitions of words and ideas that are central to your understanding of the material covered in this textbook. Each term in the Glossary is in **boldface** in the text where it is first defined.

GLOSSARY	GLOSARIO
#BlackLivesMatter: The hashtag for a national movement that protests all the ways that racism destroys Black lives, including the state-sanctioned killing of Black people by the police and the mass incarceration of people of African descent.	**#BlackLivesMatter:** El hashtag de un movimiento nacional que protesta contra todas las formas en que el racismo destruye vidas negras, incluidos los asesinatos de personas negras a manos de la policía, sancionados por el Estado, y el encarcelamiento masivo de afrodescendientes.
#SayHerName: The hashtag for a social justice movement that calls attention to the invisibility of Black women's experience with police brutality and anti-Black violence.	**#SayHerName:** El hashtag de un movimiento de justicia social que llama la atención sobre la invisibilidad de la experiencia de las mujeres negras con la brutalidad policial y la violencia contra los negros.
A	
abolitionist movement: A loose coalition of organizations with Black and white members that worked in various ways to end slavery immediately.	**movimiento abolicionista:** Coalición informal de organizaciones con miembros negros y blancos que trabajaron de diversas formas para acabar de inmediato con la esclavitud.
abroad marriages: Marriages between enslaved people who belonged to different enslavers and lived on different plantations.	**matrimonios en el extranjero:** Matrimonios entre personas esclavizadas que pertenecían a diferentes esclavizadores y vivían en diferentes plantaciones.
accommodationism: A strategy, popularized by Booker T. Washington, for achieving Black progress through vocational/industrial training and an acceptance of the racial status quo, including segregation.	**acomodación:** Estrategia, popularizada por Booker T. Washington, para lograr el progreso negro mediante la formación profesional/industrial y la aceptación del statu quo racial, incluida la segregación.
affirmative action: A set of ideas and programs aimed at compensating African Americans for past discrimination by giving them preferential treatment in hiring and school admissions.	**acción afirmativa:** Conjunto de ideas y programas destinados a compensar a los afroamericanos por la discriminación del pasado dándoles un trato preferente en la contratación y la admisión escolar.
Allies: The nations that fought against the Axis powers in World War II. Among the Allies were the United States, Canada, France, Great Britain, Mexico, and the Soviet Union.	**Aliados:** Las naciones que lucharon contra las potencias del Eje en la Segunda Guerra Mundial. Entre los Aliados estaban Estados Unidos, Canadá, Francia, Gran Bretaña, México y la Unión Soviética.
American Missionary Association: A Protestant missionary organization resulting from the merger of Black and white missionary societies in 1846 to promote abolition and Black education.	**Asociación Misionera Estadounidense:** Organización misionera protestante que resultó de la fusión de sociedades misioneras blancas y negras en 1846 para promover la abolición y la educación de los negros.
American Recovery and Reinvestment Act (ARRA) (2009): A measure intended to boost the economy that included tax incentives, expansion of unemployment benefits, aid to low-income workers and retirees, and money for infrastructure improvements.	**Ley de Reinversión y Recuperación de Estados Unidos (ARRA) (2009):** Medida destinada a impulsar la economía que incluía incentivos fiscales, ampliación de las prestaciones por desempleo, ayudas a los trabajadores con rentas bajas y a los jubilados y dinero para mejorar las infraestructuras.

***Amistad* case:** An 1839 slave insurrection aboard the *Amistad*, a Spanish ship, in international waters near Cuba. The case became a widely publicized abolitionist cause and ultimately reached the U.S. Supreme Court, which freed the rebels in 1841.	**Caso *Amistad*:** Insurrección de esclavos en 1839 a bordo de *La Amistad*, un barco español, en aguas internacionales cerca de Cuba. El caso se convirtió en una causa abolicionista ampliamente difundida y finalmente llegó al Tribunal Supremo de EE. UU., que liberó a los rebeldes en 1841.
argument: A persuasive discourse resulting in a coherent and considered movement from a claim to a conclusion.	**argumento:** Discurso persuasivo que resulta en una transición coherente y considerada de una afirmación a una conclusión.
***asiento*:** A contract or trade agreement created by the Spanish crown.	***asiento*:** Contrato o acuerdo comercial creado por la corona española.
Atlanta Compromise speech (1895): Booker T. Washington's classic statement of racial conciliation and accommodationism.	**Discurso del Compromiso de Atlanta** (1895): La clásica declaración de Booker T. Washington sobre la conciliación y la acomodación raciales.
Atlantic Charter (1941): A document signed by President Franklin Roosevelt and British prime minister Winston Churchill in August 1941. Among other things, it declared that all people had the right to economic advancement, to social security, and to choose their own form of government.	**Carta del Atlántico** (1941): Documento firmado por el presidente Franklin Roosevelt y el primer ministro británico Winston Churchill en agosto de 1941. Entre otras cosas, declaraba que todas las personas tenían derecho al progreso económico, a la seguridad social y a elegir su propia forma de gobierno.
audience: The listener, viewer, or reader of a text. It has both shared and individual beliefs, values, needs, and backgrounds. Most texts are likely to have multiple audiences.	**público:** Oyente, espectador o lector de un texto. Tiene creencias, valores, necesidades y antecedentes compartidos e individuales. La mayoría de los textos pueden dirigirse a diferentes públicos.
Axis powers: The nations that fought against the United States and the other Allies in World War II. The principal Axis powers were Germany, Italy, and Japan.	**Potencias del Eje:** Las naciones que lucharon contra Estados Unidos y los demás Aliados en la Segunda Guerra Mundial. Las principales potencias del Eje eran Alemania, Italia y Japón.

B

barracoons: Barracks or sheds where some enslaved people were confined before boarding slave ships during the second leg of the three-part journey to the Americas.	***barracoons*:** Barracones o cobertizos donde se confinaba a personas esclavizadas antes de embarcar en los barcos negreros durante la segunda etapa del viaje en tres partes a las Américas.
bilboes: Iron hand and leg cuffs used to shackle enslaved people.	**bilboes:** Esposas de hierro para manos y piernas utilizadas para encadenar a las personas esclavizadas.
Black Arts movement: The cultural side of Black power, in which Black musicians, artists, dancers, playwrights, and novelists in the 1960s and 1970s used their talent to demonstrate Black pride and nationhood.	**Movimiento de las Artes Negras:** La vertiente cultural del Poder negro, en la que músicos, artistas, bailarines, dramaturgos y novelistas negros de los años 60 y 70 utilizaban su talento para demostrar el orgullo y la nacionalidad negros.
Black Cabinet: The informal name of the Federal Council on Negro Affairs, a group of Black New Deal political advisers organized by Mary McLeod Bethune in 1937.	**Gabinete negro:** Nombre informal del Consejo Federal de Asuntos Negros, un grupo de asesores políticos negros del New Deal organizado por Mary McLeod Bethune en 1937.
Black Campus movement: Protests from 1965 to 1972 at roughly 1,000 colleges nationwide to advocate for the establishment of Black Studies courses.	**Movimiento Campus Negro:** Protestas de 1965 a 1972 en unas 1,000 universidades de todo el país para defender la creación de cursos de Estudios Negros.

Black church: A term often used to indicate the centrality of Black religious congregations in African American life. Traditionally, the church served as an educational, social, and civil rights center as well as a place of worship. This does not, however, indicate that all Black people attend the same church or belong to the same denomination.	**Iglesia negra:** Término utilizado con frecuencia para indicar la centralidad de las congregaciones religiosas negras en la vida afroamericana. Tradicionalmente, la iglesia servía como centro educativo, social y de derechos civiles, además de como lugar de culto. Sin embargo, esto no indica que todos los negros acudan a la misma iglesia o pertenezcan a la misma confesión.
black codes: Laws regulating the labor and behavior of freedpeople passed by southern states in the immediate aftermath of emancipation. These laws were overturned by the Civil Rights Act of 1866.	**códigos negros:** Leyes que regulan el trabajo y el comportamiento de los libertos aprobadas por los estados del sur inmediatamente después de la emancipación. Estas leyes fueron anuladas por la Ley de Derechos Civiles de 1866.
Black convention movement: A series of national, regional, and local conventions, starting in 1830, where Black leaders addressed the concerns of free and enslaved Blacks.	**Movimiento de la Convención Negra:** Serie de convenciones nacionales, regionales y locales, que comenzaron en 1830, en las que los líderes negros abordaron las preocupaciones de los negros libres y esclavizados.
Black History Month: A celebration of African American history and culture that began in 1926 as Negro History Week, established by Carter G. Woodson. It became Black History Month in 1976.	**Mes de la Historia Negra:** Celebración de la historia y la cultura afroamericanas que comenzó en 1926 como la Semana de la Historia Negra, establecida por Carter G. Woodson. En 1976 se convirtió en el Mes de la Historia Negra.
black laws: Laws adopted in some midwestern states requiring all free Black residents to supply legal proof of their free status and post a cash bond of up to $1,000 to guarantee their good behavior.	**leyes negras:** Leyes adoptadas en algunos estados del medio oeste que exigían a todos los residentes negros libres que aportaran una prueba legal de su condición de libres y depositaran una fianza en metálico de hasta 1,000 dólares para garantizar su buena conducta.
Black nationalism: A diffuse ideology founded on the idea that Black people constituted a nation within a nation. It fostered Black pride and encouraged Black people to control the economy of their communities.	**nacionalismo negro:** Ideología difusa fundada en la idea de que los negros constituían una nación dentro de una nación. Fomentó el orgullo negro y animó a los negros a controlar la economía de sus comunidades.
Black Reconstruction: The revolutionary political period from 1867 to 1877 when, for the first time ever, Black men actively participated in the mainstream politics of the reconstructed southern states and, in turn, transformed the nation's political life.	**Reconstrucción negra:** El revolucionario periodo político de 1867 a 1877 en el que, por primera vez en la historia, los hombres negros participaron activamente en la política dominante de los estados sureños reconstruidos y, a su vez, transformaron la vida política de la nación.
Black settlement houses: Urban institutions created by progressive women reformers to house migrant women and help them adjust to urban life.	**Casas de asentamiento negras:** Instituciones urbanas creadas por reformadoras progresistas para alojar a mujeres inmigrantes y ayudarlas a adaptarse a la vida urbana.
Black tax: A colloquial reference to the extra work African Americans must do to achieve the same goals as whites. Many also use the term to indicate that Black people, regardless of individual achievements, are held responsible for the behavior of Black people collectively.	**impuesto negro:** Referencia coloquial al trabajo adicional que deben hacer los afroamericanos para conseguir los mismos objetivos que los blancos. Muchos también utilizan el término para indicar que los negros, independientemente de sus logros individuales, son considerados responsables del comportamiento de los negros colectivamente.
Bloody Sunday (1965): A confrontation on March 7, 1965, between Black voting rights advocates and Alabama state troopers on the Edmund Pettus Bridge in Selma, Alabama.	**Domingo sangriento** (1965): Enfrentamiento del 7 de marzo de 1965 entre defensores negros del derecho al voto y policías del estado de Alabama en el puente Edmund Pettus de Selma, Alabama.

Bobalition: A rendition of the word *abolition*, based on what whites heard as a mispronunciation by Blacks. It was used on broadsides and in newspapers to mock free Black celebrations of abolition.	**bobalición:** Una interpretación de la palabra *abolición*, basada en lo que los blancos oían como una mala pronunciación de los negros. Se utilizó en folletos y periódicos para burlarse de las celebraciones de los negros libres por la abolición.
***bozales*:** A term used by the Spanish for recently imported African captives.	***bozales*:** Término utilizado por los españoles para designar a los cautivos africanos recién importados.
broken windows theory: A criminology theory that holds that if small crimes are left unaddressed, bigger, more serious crimes are sure to follow. For example, if the windows of a building are not repaired, vandals will break more windows, and soon the building itself will be burglarized. Cities that adopt the broken windows method of policing closely monitor behavior such as loitering and public alcohol and drug consumption in order to prevent crimes like larceny and murder.	**teoría de las ventanas rotas:** Teoría criminológica que sostiene que si no se abordan los pequeños delitos, seguramente se cometerán delitos mayores y más graves. Por ejemplo, si no se reparan las ventanas de un edificio, los vándalos romperán más ventanas, y pronto el propio edificio será asaltado. Las ciudades que adoptan el método policial de las ventanas rotas vigilan de cerca comportamientos como el vagabundeo y el consumo público de alcohol y drogas, para prevenir delitos como el hurto y el asesinato.
Brotherhood of Sleeping Car Porters and Maids: The union formed in 1925 to represent the rights of low-paid Black railroad workers.	**Hermandad de Maleteros y Mucamas de Coches Cama:** El sindicato se formó en 1925 para representar los derechos de los trabajadores ferroviarios negros mal pagados.
***Brown v. Board of Education of Topeka* (1954):** A landmark U.S. Supreme Court case that overturned *Plessy v. Ferguson* (1896) by declaring that segregated public schools were inherently unequal.	***Brown contra el Consejo de Educación de Topeka* (1954):** Caso histórico del Tribunal Supremo de EE. UU. que anuló el caso *Plessy contra Ferguson* (1896) al declarar que las escuelas públicas segregadas eran intrínsecamente desiguales.
buffalo soldiers: Black soldiers who served in U.S. army units in the West.	**soldados búfalo:** Soldados negros que prestaron servicio en unidades del ejército estadounidense en el Oeste.
busing: A strategy to promote integration by transporting Black children to predominantly white schools and white children to predominantly Black schools.	***busing*:** Estrategia para promover la integración transportando a los niños negros a escuelas predominantemente blancas y a los niños blancos a escuelas predominantemente negras.

C

carceral state: The extensive surveillance and criminalization of public spaces that result in restricted mobility and control of people's behavior.	**estado carcelario:** La exhaustiva vigilancia y criminalización de los espacios públicos que dan lugar a una movilidad restringida y al control de la conducta de las personas.
carracks/caravels: Small sailing ships used by the Portuguese to explore Africa and the Atlantic world. Lightweight, fast, and easy to maneuver, they generally had two or three masts.	**carracas/caravelas:** Pequeños veleros utilizados por los portugueses para explorar África y el mundo atlántico. Ligeros, rápidos y fáciles de maniobrar, generalmente tenían dos o tres mástiles.
cash crops: Readily salable crops grown for commercial sale and export rather than for local use.	**cultivos comerciales:** Cultivos fácilmente vendibles destinados a la venta comercial y a la exportación más que al consumo local.
chain migration: A migration pattern in which initial migrants prepare the way for family members and friends to follow, creating migrant clusters from specific locales in their new settings.	**migración en cadena:** Patrón migratorio en el que los emigrantes iniciales preparan el camino para que les sigan sus familiares y amigos, creando grupos de emigrantes de localidades específicas en sus nuevos entornos.
chattel slavery: A system by which enslaved people were considered portable property and denied all rights or legal authority over themselves or their children.	**esclavitud de bienes muebles:** Sistema por el cual las personas esclavizadas eran consideradas bienes muebles y se les negaba todo derecho o autoridad legal sobre sí mismas o sobre sus hijos.

Chicago Renaissance: A rich and wide-ranging Black arts movement of the 1930s and 1940s reflecting the cultural worlds of Black Chicago.	**Renacimiento de Chicago:** Un rico y amplio movimiento artístico negro de las décadas de 1930 y 1940 que refleja los mundos culturales del Chicago negro.
civil disobedience: The refusal to obey a law that one believes is unjust.	**desobediencia civil:** La negativa a obedecer una ley que uno considera injusta.
Civil Rights Act of 1866: An act defining U.S. citizenship and protecting the civil rights of freedpeople.	**Ley de Derechos Civiles de 1866:** Ley que define la ciudadanía estadounidense y protege los derechos civiles de los libertos.
Civil Rights Act of 1875: An act requiring equal treatment regardless of race in public accommodations and on public conveyances.	**Ley de Derechos Civiles de 1875:** Ley que exige la igualdad de trato independientemente de la raza en los alojamientos públicos y en los transportes públicos.
Civil Rights Act of 1964: A law prohibiting discrimination in places of public accommodation, outlawing bias in federally funded programs, authorizing the U.S. Justice Department to initiate desegregation lawsuits, and providing technical and financial aid to communities desegregating their schools. President Lyndon Johnson used his considerable influence to break a record-setting 534-hour filibuster in the Senate.	**Ley de Derechos Civiles de 1964:** Ley que prohíbe la discriminación en los lugares de alojamiento público, proscribe los prejuicios en los programas financiados con fondos federales, autoriza al Departamento de Justicia de EE. UU. a iniciar procesos judiciales de desegregación y proporciona ayuda técnica y económica a comunidades que desegregan sus escuelas. El presidente Lyndon Johnson utilizó su considerable influencia para romper un filibustero de 534 horas en el Senado, lo que supuso un récord.
Civil Rights Cases (1883): A U.S. Supreme Court ruling that overturned the Civil Rights Act of 1875.	***Casos de Derechos Civiles*** (1883): Sentencia del Tribunal Supremo de EE. UU. que anuló la Ley de Derechos Civiles de 1875.
claim: Also called an assertion or proposition, a claim states the argument's main idea or position. A claim differs from a topic or subject in that a claim has to be arguable.	**afirmación:** También llamada aseveración o proposición, establece la idea o postura principal de un argumento. Una afirmación se diferencia de un tema o sujeto en que tiene que ser debatible.
Code Noir: The slave code used in France's colonies in the Americas.	**Code Noir:** El código de los esclavos utilizado en las colonias francesas de las Américas.
coffle: A group of animals, prisoners, or slaves enslaved people chained together in a line.	**cáfila:** Grupo de animales, prisioneros o personas esclavizadas encadenados en fila.
colonization: The action of appropriating a place or domain for one's own use. In the context of nineteenth-century emigrationism, colonization refers to the idea that Blacks should be sent back to Africa or moved to another territory outside the United States.	**colonización:** Acción de apropiarse de un lugar o dominio para uso propio. En el contexto del emigracionismo del siglo XIX, la colonización se refiere a la idea de que los negros deberían ser devueltos a África o trasladados a otro territorio fuera de Estados Unidos.
Colored Farmers' Alliance (CFA): A late-nineteenth-century organization comprised of African American farmers and farm workers, which fought for farmers' rights.	**Alianza de Agricultores de Color (CFA):** Organización de finales del siglo XIX formada por agricultores y trabajadores agrícolas afroamericanos, que luchaba por los derechos de los agricultores.
Community Action Programs (CAPs): Programs initiated and financed by President Lyndon Johnson's War on Poverty that directed antipoverty agencies to involve poor people in solving the problems of their own communities.	**Programas de Acción Comunitaria (PAC):** Programas iniciados y financiados por la Guerra contra la Pobreza del presidente Lyndon Johnson, que ordenaban a los organismos de lucha contra la pobreza implicar a los pobres en la resolución de los problemas de sus propias comunidades.

Comprehensive Crime Control Act (1984): A major revision of the U.S. criminal code that included provisions increasing drug penalties and that incentivized law enforcement to cooperate with the Department of Defense to increase their surveillance of African American communities.	**Ley Integral de Lucha contra la Delincuencia** (1984): Importante revisión del código penal estadounidense que incluía disposiciones que aumentaban las penas por drogas y que incentivaban a las fuerzas del orden a cooperar con el Departamento de Defensa para aumentar su vigilancia de las comunidades afroamericanas.
Compromise of 1850: A compromise aimed at reducing sectional tensions by admitting California as a free state; permitting the question of slavery to be settled by popular sovereignty in New Mexico and Utah Territories; abolishing the slave trade in the District of Columbia; resolving the Texas debt issue; and enacting a new fugitive slave law.	**Compromiso de 1850:** Compromiso destinado a reducir las tensiones seccionales admitiendo a California como estado libre; permitiendo que la cuestión de la esclavitud fuera resuelta por la soberanía popular en los Territorios de Nuevo México y Utah; aboliendo el comercio de esclavos en el Distrito de Columbia; resolviendo la cuestión de la deuda de Texas y promulgando una nueva ley sobre los esclavos fugitivos.
concept: In the AP® African American Studies course, a concept is a person, place, theory, or theme.	**concepto:** En el curso de AP® African American Studies, un concepto es una persona, lugar, teoría o tema.
context: The circumstances, atmosphere, attitudes, and events surrounding a text.	**contexto:** Circunstancias, atmósfera, actitudes y eventos que rodean a un texto.
Confederate States of America: The eleven southern states that seceded from the United States in 1860 and 1861, precipitating the Civil War.	**Estados Confederados de América:** Los once estados sureños que se separaron de Estados Unidos en 1860 y 1861, precipitando la Guerra Civil.
Congress of Industrial Organizations (CIO): An association of unions based on industry rather than skill. African Americans joined CIO unions in record numbers during World War II.	**Congreso de Organizaciones Industriales (CIO):** Asociación de sindicatos basada en la laboriosidad y no en la aptitud. Los afroamericanos se afiliaron a los sindicatos del CIO en cifras récord durante la Segunda Guerra Mundial.
Congressional Black Caucus: An organization of Black representatives that became an official presence in Congress in 1971. It supported Black candidates, lobbied for social reforms, and attempted to fashion a national strategy to increase Black political power.	**Caucus Negro del Congreso:** Organización de representantes negros que se convirtió en presencia oficial en el Congreso en 1971. Apoyó a candidatos negros, presionó en favor de reformas sociales e intentó diseñar una estrategia nacional para aumentar el poder político de los negros.
conjure: Traditional African folk magic in which people called conjurers draw on the powers of the spirit world to influence human affairs.	**conjuro:** Magia popular tradicional africana en la que personas llamadas prestidigitadores recurren a los poderes del mundo de los espíritus para influir en los asuntos humanos.
contraband: A freedom seeker pursuing protection behind Union lines. This designation recognized enslaved people's status as human property and paved the way for their emancipation.	**esclavo fugitivo:** Un buscador de la libertad que busca protección tras las líneas de la Unión. Esta designación reconoció a las personas esclavizadas su condición de propiedad humana y allanó el camino para su emancipación.
convict lease: A penal system in which convict labor is hired out to landowners or businesses to generate income for the state.	**arrendamiento de convictos:** Sistema penal en el que la mano de obra de los presos se contrata a terratenientes o empresas para generar ingresos para el Estado.
country marks: Facial scars indicating particular African origins.	**marcas de origen:** Cicatrices faciales que indican orígenes africanos particulares.
creole: A language that originated as a combination of other languages; the term *creole* can also refer to people who are racially or culturally mixed.	**criollo:** Lengua que se originó como combinación de otras lenguas; el término *criollo* también puede referirse a las personas de raza o cultura mixta.

***Creole* insurrection:** An 1841 slave insurrection aboard the *Creole*, a ship carrying 135 enslaved people from Hampton Roads, Virginia, to New Orleans, Louisiana.	**Insurrección del *Creole*:** Insurrección de esclavos en 1841 a bordo del *Creole*, un barco que transportaba 135 personas esclavizadas desde Hampton Roads, Virginia, a Nueva Orleans, Luisiana.
crop lien: An agricultural system in which a farmer borrows against his anticipated crop for the seed and supplies he needs and settles his debt after the crop is harvested.	**embargo de cultivos:** Sistema agrícola en el que el agricultor pide prestado contra su cosecha prevista para obtener las semillas y los suministros que necesita y salda su deuda después de la cosecha.

D

de facto segregation: Racial separation that occurs in practice — as a result of housing patterns or social custom, for example — but is not based on law. Though this kind of segregation is caused by particular practices, its causes are less visible than the causes of de jure segregation and often appear to be the result of unintentional or natural circumstances.	**segregación de hecho:** Separación racial que se produce en la práctica (como resultado de patrones de vivienda o costumbres sociales, por ejemplo) pero que no está basada en la ley. Aunque este tipo de segregación se debe a prácticas concretas, sus causas son menos visibles que las de la segregación de derecho y suele deberse a circunstancias involuntarias o naturales.
de jure segregation: Racial separation mandated by law.	**segregación de iure:** Separación racial obligatoria por ley.
Deacons for Defense and Justice: An armed grassroots organization formed in Louisiana in 1964 to protect Black people against increased Ku Klux Klan activity.	**Diáconos por la Defensa y la Justicia:** Organización armada popular formada en Luisiana en 1964 para proteger a la población negra contra el aumento de la actividad del Ku Klux Klan.
debt peonage: A system of forced labor requiring servitude in exchange for payment of one's debts. This system trapped thousands of Black agricultural workers in the South in conditions not unlike those of slavery.	**servidumbre por deudas:** Sistema de trabajo forzado que exige servidumbre a cambio del pago de las deudas. Este sistema retuvo a miles de trabajadores agrícolas negros del Sur en condiciones no muy diferentes a las de la esclavitud.
development: In the AP® African American Studies course, a development is an event; a political, social, or cultural movement; or a time period — essentially, anything important that happens.	**desarrollo:** En el curso de AP® African American Studies, un desarrollo es un evento; un movimiento político, social o cultural; o un período de tiempo — esencialmente, cualquier cosa importante que sucede.
diaspora: The dispersion of a people from their homeland. Applied to Africans, this term usually describes the mass movement of Africans and their descendants to the Americas during the slave trade.	**diáspora:** La dispersión de un pueblo de su patria. Aplicado a los africanos, este término suele describir el traslado masivo de africanos y sus descendientes a las Américas durante la trata de esclavos.
Dismal Swamp: A coastal plain on Virginia's southeastern border that became a refuge for runaway freedom seekers in 1730.	**Dismal Swamp:** Llanura costera en la frontera sureste de Virginia que se convirtió en refugio de buscadores de libertad en 1730.
"Don't Buy Where You Can't Work" boycotts: Grassroots campaigns during the 1930s that fought for the hiring of Blacks at white-owned stores in Black communities.	**Boicots de No compres donde no puedas trabajar:** Campañas populares durante la década de 1930 que lucharon por la contratación de negros en tiendas de propiedad blanca en comunidades negras.
Double V campaign: Nickname for the "Double Victory" campaign, a World War II strategy committing African Americans to fight for liberty both at home and abroad.	**Campaña Doble V:** Sobrenombre de la campaña "Doble Victoria", una estrategia de la Segunda Guerra Mundial que comprometía a los afroamericanos a luchar por la libertad tanto en casa como en el extranjero.

Dred Scott v. Sandford (1857): A controversial U.S. Supreme Court decision ruling that Scott, an enslaved man, was not entitled to sue in the Missouri courts and was not free even though he had been taken into a free territory; that no person of African descent could be a citizen; that enslaved people were property; and that Congress had no authority to regulate slavery in the territories.	***Dred Scott contra Sandford*** (1857): Decisión controvertida del Tribunal Supremo de EE. UU. que dictaminó que Scott, un hombre esclavizado, no tenía derecho a demandar en los tribunales de Misuri y no era libre aunque hubiera sido llevado a un territorio libre; que ninguna persona de ascendencia africana podía ser ciudadana; que las personas esclavizadas eran propiedad; y que el Congreso no tenía autoridad para regular la esclavitud en los territorios.
driver: An enslaved person assigned to oversee the work of other enslaved people.	**capataz:** Persona esclavizada encargada de supervisar el trabajo de otras personas esclavizadas.
dynasty: A family of royal rulers.	**dinastía:** Familia de gobernantes reales.
E	
Economic Opportunity Act (1964): Part of President Lyndon Johnson's War on Poverty, this act established the Job Corps, Head Start, the Neighborhood Youth Corps, and Volunteers in Service to America (VISTA).	**Ley de Oportunidades Económicas** (1964): Como parte de la Guerra contra la Pobreza del presidente Lyndon Johnson, esta ley estableció el Cuerpo Laboral, Head Start, el Cuerpo Juvenil de Vecindario y Voluntarios al Servicio de Estados Unidos (VISTA).
Elmina Castle: A fortress in present-day Ghana, built by the Portuguese as a trading post in 1482 and used as a major slave trading center by the Dutch from 1637 to 1814.	**Castillo de Elmina:** Fortaleza de la actual Ghana, construida por los portugueses como puesto comercial en 1482 y utilizada como importante centro de comercio de esclavos por los holandeses desde 1637 hasta 1814.
Emancipation Proclamation (1863): A presidential proclamation, issued by Abraham Lincoln, freeing all enslaved people under Confederate control and authorizing the use of Black troops in the Civil War.	**Proclamación de la Emancipación** (1863): Proclamación presidencial, emitida por Abraham Lincoln, por la que se liberaba a todas las personas esclavizadas bajo control confederado y se autorizaba el uso de tropas negras en la Guerra Civil.
***encomienda*:** A labor system used by the Spanish in their colonization of the Americas. Under this system, the crown granted colonists control over a specified number of Indigenous Americans from whom they could extract labor.	***encomienda*:** Sistema de trabajo utilizado por los españoles en su colonización de las Américas. Según este sistema, la corona concedía a los colonos el control sobre un número determinado de indígenas americanos de los que podían extraer mano de obra.
evidence: Support for a claim or argument.	**evidencia:** Respaldo de una afirmación o argumento.
Executive Order 8802 (1941): President Franklin Roosevelt's response to the March on Washington Movement. It banned racial discrimination in defense industries and created the Fair Employment Practices Commission (FEPC).	**Decreto 8802** (1941): Respuesta del presidente Franklin Roosevelt al Movimiento de la Marcha sobre Washington. Prohibió la discriminación racial en las industrias de defensa y creó la Comisión de Prácticas Laborales Justas (FEPC).
Executive Order 9981 (1948): Issued by President Harry Truman, this order called for "equality of treatment and opportunity for all persons in the armed services without regard to race, color, religion, or national origin."	**Decreto 9981** (1948): Emitida por el presidente Harry Truman, esta orden pedía "igualdad de trato y de oportunidades para todas las personas en los servicios armados sin distinción de raza, color, religión u origen nacional".
Exodusters: The name given to the more than 6,000 Blacks from Texas, Louisiana, and Mississippi who migrated to Kansas and were able to settle on land that became theirs.	***Exodusters*:** Nombre dado a los más de 6,000 negros de Texas, Luisiana y Misisipi que emigraron a Kansas y pudieron establecerse en tierras que pasaron a ser suyas.

F

Fair Housing Act (1968): A law prohibiting discrimination based on race, color, religion, or national origin in the sale or rental of housing and making the practices of blockbusting, steering, and redlining illegal. Subsequent amendments prohibited discrimination based on sex, familial status, and disability.	**Ley de Vivienda Justa** (1968): Ley que prohíbe la discriminación por motivos de raza, color, religión u origen nacional en la venta o alquiler de viviendas, y que declara ilegales las prácticas de *blockbusting, steering* y *redlining*. Enmiendas posteriores prohibieron la discriminación por razón de sexo, estado civil y discapacidad.
fictive kin: People regarded as family even though they were not related by blood or marriage.	**parentesco ficticio:** Personas consideradas como familiares aunque no estuvieran emparentadas por sangre o matrimonio.
Fifteenth Amendment (ratified 1870): The constitutional amendment that enfranchised Black men.	**Decimoquinta Enmienda** (ratificada en 1870): La enmienda constitucional que otorgó el derecho de voto a los hombres negros.
First Confiscation Act (1861): A congressional act authorizing the confiscation of Confederate property, including enslaved people employed in the rebellion, who were then considered free.	**Primera Ley de Confiscación** (1861): Ley del Congreso que autorizaba la confiscación de bienes confederados, incluidos los esclavos empleados en la rebelión, que entonces se consideraban libres.
Force Acts (1870, 1871): Two laws providing federal protection of Blacks' civil rights in the face of white terroristic activities.	**Leyes de Fuerza** (1870, 1871): Dos leyes que proporcionan protección federal a los derechos civiles de los negros frente a las actividades terroristas de los blancos.
Fort Mose: The first free Black town within the present-day borders of the United States, located within what is now Florida and founded by Blacks who had escaped enslavement in the Carolina colony.	**Fuerte Mose:** La primera ciudad negra libre dentro de las fronteras actuales de Estados Unidos, situada en lo que hoy es Florida y fundada por negros que habían escapado de la esclavitud en la colonia de Carolina.
Four Freedoms: The four essential human rights that, in January 1941, President Franklin Roosevelt proclaimed people everywhere ought to have: freedom of speech and religion, and freedom from want and fear.	**Cuatro Libertades:** Los cuatro derechos humanos esenciales que, en enero de 1941, el presidente Franklin Roosevelt proclamó que debían tener todas las personas: libertad de expresión y de religión, y libertad frente a la miseria y el miedo.
Fourteenth Amendment (ratified 1868): The constitutional amendment that defined U.S. citizenship to include Blacks and guaranteed citizens due process and equal protection of the law.	**Decimocuarta Enmienda** (ratificada en 1868): La enmienda constitucional que definió la ciudadanía estadounidense para incluir a los negros y garantizó a los ciudadanos el debido proceso y la igualdad de protección de la ley.
Freedmen's Bureau (1865–1872): A federal agency created during Reconstruction to aid freedpeople in their transition to freedom.	**Oficina de Hombres Libres** (1865–1872): Organismo federal creado durante la Reconstrucción para ayudar a los libertos en su transición a la libertad.
Freedom Rides: An organized effort in 1961 to desegregate interstate travel by having white and Black students ride buses through the South and use "whites only" facilities.	**Viajes de la Libertad:** Iniciativa organizada en 1961 para eliminar la segregación en los viajes interestatales haciendo que estudiantes blancos y negros viajaran en autobús por el Sur y utilizaran instalaciones que eran "solo para blancos".
freedom suits: Legal actions by which enslaved people sought to achieve freedom in British and American courts.	**demandas por libertad:** Acciones legales mediante las cuales las personas esclavizadas intentaban conseguir la libertad en los tribunales británicos y estadounidenses.

Fugitive Slave Act (1850): Part of the Compromise of 1850, this law strengthened federal authority over freedom seekers.	**Ley de Esclavos Fugitivos** (1850): Como parte del Compromiso de 1850, esta ley reforzó la autoridad federal sobre los buscadores de libertad.
fugitive slave clause: A constitutional clause permitting enslavers of any state to retrieve freedom seekers they had previously enslaved from any other state.	**cláusula de los esclavos fugitivos:** Cláusula constitucional que permite a los esclavizadores de cualquier estado recuperar en otro estado a los buscadores de libertad que previamente habían esclavizado.
G	
Gabriel's rebellion: An abortive slave revolt plot that took place in Richmond, Virginia, in 1800. It was led by an enslaved man known as Prosser's Gabriel.	**Rebelión de Gabriel:** Complot frustrado de revuelta de esclavos que tuvo lugar en Richmond, Virginia, en 1800. Fue dirigido por un hombre esclavizado conocido como Gabriel de Prosser.
gag rule: A series of congressional resolutions passed by the House of Representatives between 1836 and 1840 that tabled, without discussion, petitions regarding slavery; the gag rule was instituted to silence dissent over slavery. It was repealed in 1844.	**ley mordaza:** Serie de resoluciones del Congreso aprobadas por la Cámara de Representantes entre 1836 y 1840 que presentaba, sin debate, peticiones relativas a la esclavitud; la ley mordaza se instituyó para silenciar la disidencia sobre la esclavitud. Fue derogada en 1844.
GI Bill (1944): The popular name of the Servicemen's Readjustment Act, which provided returning soldiers with educational benefits, low-interest home loans, and unemployment benefits. African Americans were disproportionately denied these benefits.	**Ley GI** (1944): El nombre popular de la Ley de Reajuste de los Militares, que proporcionaba prestaciones educativas, préstamos hipotecarios a bajo interés y subsidios de desempleo a los soldados que regresaban. A los afroamericanos se les negaron estas prestaciones de forma desproporcionada.
gospel music: A popular and influential musical genre that achieved prominence in the 1930s and continues to evolve. Gospel marries Black sacred music with popular Black musical forms.	**música gospel:** Género musical popular e influyente que alcanzó prominencia en la década de 1930 y sigue evolucionando. El gospel une la música sacra negra con las formas musicales negras populares.
Great Awakening: A multidenominational series of evangelical revivals that took place in North America between the 1730s and the 1780s.	**El Gran Despertar:** Serie multiconfesional de avivamientos evangélicos que tuvieron lugar en América del Norte entre las décadas de 1730 y 1780.
Great Migration: The migration of 1.5 million African Americans from the South to the metropolises of the North in the years from 1915 to 1940.	**La Gran Migración:** La migración de 1.5 millones de afroamericanos del Sur a las metrópolis del Norte entre 1915 y 1940.
Greensboro Four: The four Black college students who, by sitting down at a segregated lunch counter in Greensboro, North Carolina, and requesting service in February 1960, initiated the nationwide sit-in movement.	**Los Cuatro de Greensboro:** Los cuatro estudiantes universitarios negros que, al sentarse en una cafetería segregada de Greensboro, Carolina del Norte, y solicitar servicio en febrero de 1960, iniciaron el movimiento nacional de sentadas.
Griggs v. Duke Power Co. (1971): A U.S. Supreme Court ruling which held that IQ tests, high school diplomas, and other requirements that were not necessary for the performance of a job were by their very nature discriminatory and had to be eliminated.	***Griggs contra Duke Power Co.*** (1971): Sentencia del Tribunal Supremo de EE. UU. que sostenía que los tests de inteligencia, los títulos de bachillerato y otros requisitos que no eran necesarios para el desempeño de un trabajo eran, por su propia naturaleza, discriminatorios y debían eliminarse.

griot: Prestigious historians, storytellers, and musicians who maintained and shared a community's history, traditions, and cultural practices.	**griot:** Historiadores, narradores y músicos prestigiosos que mantenían y compartían la historia, las tradiciones y las prácticas culturales de una comunidad.
Guanches: The aboriginal inhabitants of the Canary Islands.	**guanches:** Los habitantes aborígenes de las Islas Canarias.
Gullah: A creole language composed of a blend of West African languages and English.	**gullah:** Lengua criolla compuesta por una mezcla de lenguas de África Occidental y el inglés.

H

habeas corpus: A feature of English common law that protects prisoners from being detained without trial. Translated literally, the Latin phrase means "you should have the body."	**habeas corpus:** Característica del derecho consuetudinario inglés que protege a los presos de ser detenidos sin juicio previo. Traducida literalmente, la frase latina significa "debes tener el cuerpo".
Haitian Revolution (1791–1804): A rebellion against slavery and colonialism in the French colony of Saint Domingue that led to the establishment of an independent country with Black rule.	**Revolución Haitiana** (1791–1804): Rebelión contra la esclavitud y el colonialismo en la colonia francesa de Saint Domingue que condujo al establecimiento de un país independiente con gobierno negro.
half-freedom: A status allotted primarily to people enslaved by the Dutch who helped defend New Netherland against American Indian attacks. Half-freedom liberated enslaved adults but not their children.	**semilibertad:** Estatus asignado principalmente a las personas esclavizadas por los neerlandeses que ayudaron a defender Nuevos Países Bajos de los ataques de los indios americanos. La semilibertad liberaba a los adultos esclavizados, pero no a sus hijos.
Harlem Renaissance: The New Negro arts movement, a flourishing of African American art and culture rooted in Harlem in the 1920s.	**Renacimiento de Harlem:** El movimiento artístico New Negro, un florecimiento del arte y la cultura afroamericanos arraigado en Harlem en la década de 1920.
Hell Fighters: The 369th Infantry Regiment, formed from the Fifteenth New York National Guard in Harlem, one of the most highly decorated fighting units of World War I.	**Combatientes del Infierno:** El 369º Regimiento de Infantería, formado a partir de la Decimoquinta Guardia Nacional de Nueva York en Harlem, una de las unidades de combate más condecoradas de la Primera Guerra Mundial.
hiring out: The practice of enslavers contracting out those they enslaved to work for other employers.	**alquiler:** La práctica de los esclavizadores de alquilar a quienes esclavizaban para que trabajaran para otros empleadores.
historically Black colleges and universities: Separate institutions of higher learning for African Americans. Most of them were founded in the post-emancipation era.	**universidades históricamente negras:** Instituciones de enseñanza superior separadas para los afroamericanos. La mayoría se fundaron en la época posterior a la emancipación.
hominins: Members of the primate group that includes the species *Homo sapiens.*	**homínidos:** Miembros del grupo de los primates que incluye a la especie *Homo sapiens.*
human rights: Rights that apply universally to all people, regardless of nation, history, and culture.	**derechos humanos:** Derechos que se aplican universalmente a todas las personas, independientemente de su nación, historia y cultura.
hunter-gatherers: People kept on the move by their method of subsistence, which involves following game and tracking down plant foods as they ripen.	**cazadores-recolectores:** Personas que se desplazan continuamente en virtud de su método de subsistencia, que consiste en seguir animales a los que cazan y rastrear alimentos vegetales conforme maduran.

I

ideology: A system of ideas and beliefs.	**ideología:** un sistema de ideas y creencias.
imperialism: The late-nineteenth-century European and U.S. extension of political and economic power over nations in Africa, Asia, and the Americas.	**imperialismo:** La extensión a finales del siglo XIX del poder político y económico europeo y estadounidense sobre naciones de África, Asia y América.
indentured servants: White laborers who came to the English North American colonies under contract to work for a specified amount of time, usually four to seven years.	**sirvientes contratados:** Obreros blancos que llegaban a las colonias inglesas de América del Norte con un contrato para trabajar durante un tiempo determinado, normalmente de cuatro a siete años.
Indian Removal Act (1830): An act signed into law by President Andrew Jackson that forced American Indians living east of the Mississippi River to relocate to Indian Territory (present-day Oklahoma).	**Ley de Traslado Forzoso de los Indios** (1830): Ley promulgada por el presidente Andrew Jackson que obligaba a los indios americanos que vivían al este del río Misisipi a trasladarse al Territorio Indio (actual Oklahoma).
institutionalized racism (also known as **systemic racism**): Discrimination practiced by corporations and governments.	**racismo institucionalizado** (también conocido como **racismo sistémico**): Discriminación practicada por las empresas y los gobiernos.
interdisciplinary: Incorporating multiple academic disciplines, including history, art, music, literature, science and technology, religion, and politics.	**interdisciplinar:** Que incorpora múltiples disciplinas académicas, como historia, arte, música, literatura, ciencia y tecnología, religión y política.
invisible church: A term used to describe groups of enslaved African Americans who met in secret for Christian worship.	**iglesia invisible:** Término utilizado para describir a los grupos de afroamericanos esclavizados que se reunían en secreto para el culto cristiano.

J

Jena Six case (2006): The arrest and indictment as adults of six Black teenagers in Jena, Louisiana, for attempted murder after a schoolyard fight sent a white youth to the hospital.	**Caso de los Seis de Jena** (2006): La detención y acusación como adultos de seis adolescentes negros en Jena, Luisiana, por intento de asesinato tras una pelea en el patio de la escuela por la que un joven blanco terminó en el hospital.
Jim Crow: A system of laws and customs that enforced segregation, the spatial and physical separation of the races.	**Jim Crow:** Sistema de leyes y costumbres que imponía la segregación, o separación espacial y física de las razas.
John Brown's raid (1859): An unsuccessful attempt by the white abolitionist John Brown to seize the federal arsenal at Harpers Ferry, Virginia, and incite a slave insurrection.	**Incursión de John Brown** (1859): Intento infructuoso del abolicionista blanco John Brown de apoderarse del arsenal federal de Harpers Ferry, Virginia, e incitar una insurrección de esclavos.
Juneteenth: The June 19 holiday that celebrates the effective end of slavery in the United States.	**Juneteenth:** La fiesta del 19 de junio que celebra el fin efectivo de la esclavitud en Estados Unidos.

K

Kansas-Nebraska Act (1854): A law that allowed the residents of Kansas and Nebraska Territories to decide whether slavery should be allowed.	**Ley Kansas-Nebraska** (1854): Ley que permitía a los residentes de los Territorios de Kansas y Nebraska decidir si debía permitirse la esclavitud.
Kerner Commission: Officially, the National Advisory Commission on Civil Disorders. In 1968, it found that the violence plaguing inner cities could be traced to job discrimination and institutional racism rather than to Black power ideology or a particular organization.	**Comisión Kerner:** Oficialmente, la Comisión Consultiva Nacional de Desórdenes Civiles. En 1968, descubrió que la violencia que asolaba los centros urbanos podía atribuirse a la discriminación laboral y al racismo institucional, más que a la ideología del poder negro o a una organización concreta.

kinship: Political alliances with other African communities that did not include blood ties.	**hermandades:** Alianzas políticas con otras comunidades africanas que no incluían lazos de sangre.
L	
***ladinos*:** Latinized Blacks who were born or raised in Spain, Portugal, or these nations' Atlantic or American colonies and who spoke fluent Spanish or Portuguese, worked as intermediaries, and were essential in European colonization of the Americas.	***ladinos*:** Negros latinizados nacidos o criados en España, Portugal o las colonias atlánticas o americanas de estas naciones que hablaban español o portugués con fluidez. Trabajaron como intermediarios y fueron esenciales en la colonización europea de las Américas.
line of reasoning: The connections between the claims in the writer's argument and the evidence presented to support them.	**línea de razonamiento:** Conexiones entre las afirmaciones presentadas en el argumento del escritor y la evidencia presentada para respaldarlas.
Little Rock Nine: The nine Black students who, in 1957, tested *Brown v. Board of Education of Topeka* (1954) by enrolling in Little Rock Central High School in Little Rock, Arkansas.	**Los Nueve de Little Rock:** Los nueve estudiantes negros que, en 1957, pusieron a prueba el caso *Brown contra el Consejo de Educación de Topeka* (1954) matriculándose en el Little Rock Central High School de Little Rock, Arkansas.
living out: The practice of allowing enslaved people who were hired out in urban areas to keep part of their wages to pay for their rented lodgings.	**vivir afuera:** Práctica que permitía a las personas esclavizadas que eran contratadas en zonas urbanas quedarse con parte de su salario para pagar el alojamiento alquilado.
Lord Dunmore's Proclamation (1775): A document issued by Virginia's royal governor John Murray, the Earl of Dunmore, in November 1775, offering freedom to those enslaved by "rebel" colonists if they joined his forces.	**Proclamación de Lord Dunmore** (1775): Documento emitido por el gobernador real de Virginia, John Murray, conde de Dunmore, en noviembre de 1775, en el que ofrecía la libertad a los esclavizados por los colonos "rebeldes" si se unían a sus fuerzas.
Louisiana Purchase (1803): The federal government's purchase of Louisiana from France, which doubled the size of the United States and fostered the spread of slavery.	**Compra de Luisiana** (1803): La compra de Luisiana a Francia por el gobierno federal, que duplicó el tamaño de Estados Unidos y fomentó la expansión de la esclavitud.
loyalists: Colonists who remained loyal to Britain during the American Revolution.	**leales:** Colonos que permanecieron leales a Gran Bretaña durante la Revolución Americana.
loyalty program: The program instituted by President Harry Truman in 1947 requiring federal employees to swear that they were not Communists or Communist affiliates. Many unions and several civil rights organizations adopted similar programs thereafter.	**programa de lealtad:** Programa instituido por el presidente Harry Truman en 1947 por el que se exigía a los empleados federales que juraran que no eran comunistas ni afiliados comunistas. Muchos sindicatos y varias organizaciones de derechos civiles adoptaron posteriormente programas similares.
lying out: A form of resistance in which enslaved people hid near their home plantations, often to escape undesirable work assignments or abusive treatment by their enslavers.	**tumbada:** Forma de resistencia en la que las personas esclavizadas se escondían cerca de sus plantaciones de origen, a menudo para escapar de asignaciones de trabajo indeseables o del trato abusivo de sus esclavizadores.
lynching: The public murder, by a lawless mob, of an individual alleged to have committed a crime or a breach of social custom.	**linchamiento:** Asesinato público, por una turba sin ley, de un individuo que presuntamente ha cometido un delito o una infracción de las costumbres sociales.

M	
mandatory sentencing laws: Laws that require a judge to impose a specified sentence regardless of the circumstances of a crime.	**leyes de condena obligatoria:** Leyes que obligan a un juez a imponer una condena determinada independientemente de las circunstancias de un delito.
manumission: A legal process that enslavers could initiate to grant freedom to an enslaved person.	**manumisión:** Proceso legal que los esclavizadores podían iniciar para conceder la libertad a una persona esclavizada.
March on Washington for Jobs and Freedom (1963): A gathering of more than 250,000 Americans on August 28, 1963, to protest discrimination in all facets of American life. Martin Luther King Jr. delivered his "I Have a Dream" speech during the event.	**Marcha sobre Washington por el Trabajo y la Libertad** (1963)**:** Reunión de más de 250,000 estadounidenses el 28 de agosto de 1963 para protestar contra la discriminación en todas las facetas de la vida estadounidense. Martin Luther King Jr. pronunció su discurso "Tengo un sueño" durante el acto.
March on Washington Movement (1941): A. Philip Randolph's call for 50,000 to 100,000 Black Americans to gather in Washington, D.C., on July 1, 1941, to demand equal opportunity for Blacks in defense industries and the armed services.	**Movimiento Marcha sobre Washington** (1941): Llamamiento de A. Philip Randolph para que entre 50,000 y 100,000 negros estadounidenses se reunieran en Washington, D.C., el 1 de julio de 1941, para exigir igualdad de oportunidades para los negros en las industrias de defensa y en las fuerzas armadas.
maroons: Members of freedom-seeking communities; also known as cimarrons, from the Spanish *cimarrón*.	**cimarrones:** Miembros de comunidades que buscaban la libertad.
matrilineal succession: The practice of passing property and/or leadership from generation to generation from mother to daughter.	**sucesión matrilineal:** La práctica de pasar la propiedad y/o el liderazgo de generación en generación, de madre a hija.
Middle Passage: Second part of the three-part journey to the Americas in the transatlantic slave trade in which slave ships transported enslaved people from the West African coast to slave ports in the Americas.	**Pasaje del medio:** Segunda parte del viaje en tres partes a las Américas en la trata transatlántica de esclavos, en la que los barcos negreros transportaban a personas esclavizadas desde la costa occidental africana hasta los puertos negreros de las Américas.
Million Man March (1995): A gathering of mostly African American men on the National Mall in Washington, D.C. The men gathered to affirm their commitment to Black women, children, and communities and to dedicate their lives to improving themselves and their communities.	**Marcha del Millón de Hombres** (1995): Reunión de hombres, en su mayoría afroamericanos, en el National Mall de Washington D.C. Los hombres se reunieron para afirmar su compromiso con las mujeres, los niños y las comunidades negras y para dedicar sus vidas a mejorarse a sí mismos y a sus comunidades.
Million Woman March (1997): A gathering of mostly African American women on the Benjamin Franklin Parkway in Philadelphia. The women came together to affirm their commitment to one another and to the Black family and community.	**Marcha del Millón de Mujeres** (1997): Reunión de mujeres, en su mayoría afroamericanas, en el Benjamin Franklin Parkway de Filadelfia. Las mujeres se reunieron para afirmar su compromiso mutuo y con la familia y la comunidad negras.
Mississippi Freedom Democratic Party (MFDP): An independent, nondiscriminatory political party established to represent Black Mississippians at the 1964 Democratic National Convention.	**Partido Democrático de la Libertad de Misisipi (MFDP):** Partido político independiente y no discriminatorio creado para representar a los negros de Misisipi en la Convención Nacional Demócrata de 1964.

Mississippi Freedom Summer Project: A massive education and voter registration campaign conducted in the summer of 1964.	**Proyecto del Verano de la Libertad de Misisipi:** Campaña masiva de educación y registro de votantes llevada a cabo en el verano de 1964.
Missouri Compromise (1820): An agreement balancing the admission of Missouri as a slave state with the admission of Maine as a free state and prohibiting slavery north of latitude 36°30′ in any state except Missouri.	**Compromiso de Misuri** (1820): Acuerdo que equilibra la admisión de Misuri como estado esclavista con la admisión de Maine como estado libre y que prohíbe la esclavitud al norte de la latitud 36°30′ en todo estado excepto Misuri.
Montgomery bus boycott (1955–1956): A thirteen-month boycott begun on December 1, 1955, when Rosa Parks refused to give up her seat to a white person on an Alabama bus. The boycott resulted in significant economic losses for the bus company.	**Boicot a los autobuses de Montgomery** (1955–1956): Boicot de trece meses que comenzó el 1.º de diciembre de 1955, cuando Rosa Parks se negó a ceder su asiento a una persona blanca en un autobús de Alabama. El boicot ocasionó importantes pérdidas económicas a la empresa de autobuses.
moral suasion: A primary strategy in the abolitionist movement that relied on vigorous appeals to the nation's moral and Christian conscience.	**persuasión moral:** Estrategia primaria en el movimiento abolicionista que se basaba en vigorosos llamamientos a la conciencia moral y cristiana de la nación.
Morgan v. Virginia (1946): A U.S. Supreme Court ruling that declared illegal the practice of making Blacks sit in the back of the bus behind whites in interstate bus travel.	***Morgan contra Virginia*** (1946): Sentencia del Tribunal Supremo de EE. UU. que declaró ilegal la práctica de hacer que los negros se sentaran en la parte trasera del autobús detrás de los blancos en los viajes interestatales en autobús.
Moynihan Report: The controversial 1965 report written primarily by Assistant Secretary of Labor Daniel Patrick Moynihan that labeled the Black family dysfunctional and set off a storm of protest within Black America.	**Informe Moynihan:** El controvertido informe de 1965, redactado principalmente por el Subsecretario de Trabajo Daniel Patrick Moynihan, que calificó a la familia negra de disfuncional y desencadenó una tormenta de protestas entre la población negra de Estados Unidos.
mulatto: A person with mixed white and African ancestry.	**mulato:** Persona con ascendencia mixta blanca y africana.
mutual aid society: An organization or voluntary association in which members agreed to assist one another in securing benefits such as insurance.	**sociedad de ayuda mutua:** Organización o asociación voluntaria en la que los miembros acuerdan ayudarse mutuamente para obtener prestaciones, como seguros.

N

National Association for the Advancement of Colored People (NAACP): Founded in 1909, the leading advocacy group for Black civil rights up to the present.	**Asociación Nacional para el Progreso de las Personas de Color (NAACP):** Fundada en 1909, el principal grupo de defensa de los derechos civiles de los negros hasta la actualidad.
National Association of Colored Women (NACW): A federation of Black women's clubs founded in 1896 to promote the interrelated uplift of Black women and Black people.	**Asociación Nacional de Mujeres de Color (NACW):** Federación de clubes de mujeres negras fundada en 1896 para promover la elevación interrelacionada de las mujeres y los negros.
National Equal Rights League: An organization established by Black leaders in 1864 to promote emancipation, legal equality, and Black male suffrage.	**Liga Nacional por la Igualdad de Derechos:** Organización creada por dirigentes negros en 1864 para promover la emancipación, la igualdad jurídica y el sufragio masculino negro.
National Negro Congress: An umbrella organization of Black organizations whose first national meeting in 1936 expressed a commitment to radical politics and militant labor organization and activism.	**Congreso Nacional Negro:** Organización que agrupa organizaciones negras cuya primera reunión nacional en 1936 expresó un compromiso con la política radical y la organización y el activismo laboral militante.

National Urban League (NUL): An organization founded in the early twentieth century dedicated to assisting Black migrants from the South and to advancing the concerns of urban Blacks.	**Liga Urbana Nacional (NUL):** Organización fundada a principios del siglo XX dedicada a ayudar a los emigrantes negros del Sur y a promover los intereses de los negros urbanos.
Naturalization Act of 1790: The nation's first immigration law, which instituted a two-year residency requirement for immigrants who wished to become U.S. citizens and limited naturalization to free white people.	**Ley de Naturalización de 1790:** La primera ley de inmigración de la nación, que instituyó un requisito de residencia de dos años para los inmigrantes que desearan convertirse en ciudadanos estadounidenses y limitó la naturalización a los blancos libres.
Nazism: A racist totalitarian ideology proclaiming certain non-Jewish Germans to be a superior race destined to rule the world.	**nazismo:** Ideología racista totalitaria que proclamaba que ciertos alemanes no judíos eran una raza superior destinada a dominar el mundo.
Negrismo: Movement that emerged in the Spanish-speaking Caribbean that celebrated African contributions to Latin American art, music, and literature.	**negrismo:** Movimiento surgido en el Caribe hispanohablante que celebraba las aportaciones africanas al arte, la música y la literatura latinoamericanos.
Négritude: A cultural movement launched in the 1930s that called for a common identity among Africans dispersed throughout the world, supported decolonization and the liberation of African and African-descended peoples, and generally favored Marxism.	**négritude:** Movimiento cultural iniciado en la década de 1930 que reivindicaba una identidad común entre los africanos dispersos por todo el mundo, apoyaba la descolonización y la liberación de los pueblos africanos y afrodescendientes y, en general, estaba a favor del marxismo.
Negro Election Day: An annual New England celebration in which Black communities elected their own kings and governors in elaborate ceremonies that included royal processions, political parades, and inaugural parties.	**Día de las Elecciones Negras:** Celebración anual de Nueva Inglaterra en la que las comunidades negras elegían a sus propios reyes y gobernadores en elaboradas ceremonias que incluían procesiones reales, desfiles políticos y fiestas inaugurales.
New Lights: Protestant ministers who, during the Great Awakening, challenged traditional religious practices by delivering emotional sermons that urged listeners to repent and find salvation in Christ.	**Nuevas luces:** Ministros protestantes que, durante el Gran Despertar, desafiaron las prácticas religiosas tradicionales pronunciando emotivos sermones que instaban a los oyentes a arrepentirse y encontrar la salvación en Cristo.
New Negro: A term used increasingly after World War I to describe a growing assertiveness animating African Americans, especially those associated with Marcus Garvey's Universal Negro Improvement Association and the Harlem Renaissance.	**Nuevo Negro:** Término utilizado cada vez más después de la Primera Guerra Mundial para describir una creciente asertividad que animaba a los afroamericanos, especialmente a los asociados a la Asociación Universal de Desarrollo Negro de Marcus Garvey y al Renacimiento de Harlem.
New Right: An ideology introduced in the late 1960s meant to broaden the conservative base of the Republican Party. Proponents added the politics of law and order and a meritocratic color-blind ideal to an ideology that had previously been centered on anticommunism, limited government, and racialism.	**nueva derecha:** Ideología introducida a finales de los años 60 con la intención de ampliar la base conservadora del Partido Republicano. Sus defensores añadieron la política de la ley y el orden y un ideal meritocrático daltónico a una ideología que anteriormente se había centrado en el anticomunismo, el gobierno limitado y el racialismo.
New York City draft riots (1863): Anti-Black riots sparked by white working-class opposition to the Union's military draft.	**Disturbios por la conscripción en Nueva York** (1863): Disturbios contra los negros provocados por la oposición de la clase obrera blanca al servicio militar obligatorio de la Unión.

Niagara movement (1905): A militant protest organization committed to revitalizing a national Black civil rights agenda in opposition to Booker T. Washington's accommodationist program.	**Movimiento del Niágara** (1905): Organización militante de protesta comprometida con la revitalización de un programa nacional de derechos civiles de los negros en oposición al programa acomodacionista de Booker T. Washington.
North Star: A star, also known as Polaris, that always points north and was used by freedom seekers to navigate their way to freedom.	**Estrella del Norte:** Estrella, también conocida como Polaris, que siempre apunta al norte y que los buscadores de libertad usaban para orientarse en su camino hacia la libertad.
Northwest Ordinance (1787): An act of the Confederation Congress organizing the region known as the Old Northwest, which included U.S. territories north of the Ohio River and east of the Mississippi River. Slavery was banned in these territories.	**Ordenanza del Noroeste** (1787): Ley del Congreso de la Confederación por la que se organizaba la región conocida como el Viejo Noroeste, que incluía los territorios estadounidenses que están al norte del río Ohio y al este del río Misisipi. La esclavitud estaba prohibida en estos territorios.

O

oba: A royal title in the ancient kingdom of Benin.	**oba:** Título real del antiguo reino de Benín.
Orangeburg Massacre: An incident that occurred on February 8, 1968, in Orangeburg, South Carolina, near the campus of the historically Black South Carolina State College. Police were called to quell the violence that erupted after Blacks were refused admittance to a "whites only" bowling alley. This incident is called a massacre because twenty-eight students were injured, and three unarmed students were killed when they were shot in the back or side by police.	**Masacre de Orangeburg:** Incidente ocurrido el 8 de febrero de 1968 en Orangeburg, Carolina del Sur, cerca del campus de la universidad históricamente negra South Carolina State College. Se llamó a la policía para sofocar la violencia que estalló después de que se negara a los negros la entrada a una bolera "solo para blancos". Este incidente se denomina masacre porque veintiocho estudiantes resultaron heridos y tres estudiantes desarmados murieron al recibir disparos de la policía por la espalda o por el costado.

P

Pan-African Congress (1900): An international meeting in London to address the welfare of Africans around the world and to argue for an end to European colonization of Africa.	**Congreso Panafricano** (1900): Reunión internacional en Londres para abordar el bienestar de los africanos de todo el mundo y defender el fin de la colonización europea de África.
Pan-Africanism: A global political movement committed to African self-determination and the end of European domination of the African continent.	**Panafricanismo:** Movimiento político mundial comprometido con la autodeterminación africana y el fin de la dominación europea del continente africano.
***partus sequitur ventrem*:** A seventeenth-century law defining a child's legal status based on the legal status of the mother.	***partus sequitur ventrem*:** Ley del siglo XVII que define el estatuto jurídico de un niño en función del estatuto jurídico de la madre.
patrilineal succession: The practice of passing property and/or leadership from generation to generation from father to son.	**sucesión patrilineal:** La práctica de pasar la propiedad y/o el liderazgo de generación en generación, de padre a hijo.
Pentecostalism: A religious movement that emphasizes a personal and life-changing experience of grace and promotes the belief that the presence of the Holy Spirit is manifested by speaking in tongues.	**pentecostalismo:** Movimiento religioso que hace hincapié en una experiencia personal y transformadora de la gracia y promueve la creencia de que la presencia del Espíritu Santo se manifiesta al hablar en lenguas.
personal liberty laws: A series of state laws in the North aimed at preventing the return of freedom seekers to the South.	**leyes de libertad personal:** Serie de leyes estatales del Norte destinadas a impedir el regreso de los buscadores de libertad al Sur.

perspective: A writer's view of a topic, based on that writer's background, interests, and expertise. Writers may hold the same position on a topic yet have different perspectives on it.	**perspectiva:** Punto de vista de un escritor sobre un tema, que se basa en sus orígenes, intereses y experiencia. Los escritores pueden tener posturas semejantes sobre un tema y, al mismo tiempo, perspectivas diferentes al respecto.
pharaoh: An Egyptian ruler during the period of empire, recognized as the ultimate source of power.	**faraón:** Gobernante egipcio durante el periodo del imperio, reconocido como la suprema fuente de poder.
Plessy v. Ferguson (1896): A U.S. Supreme Court decision upholding the constitutionality of state laws mandating racial segregation in public facilities.	***Plessy contra Ferguson*** (1896): Decisión del Tribunal Supremo de EE. UU. que confirma la constitucionalidad de las leyes estatales que obligan a la segregación racial en los establecimientos públicos.
political action: A primary strategy in the abolitionist movement that relied on working through political channels to force changes in the law and political practices.	**acción política:** Estrategia primaria del movimiento abolicionista que se basaba en trabajar a través de canales políticos para forzar cambios en la ley y en las prácticas políticas.
Poor People's Campaign: A movement spearheaded in 1967–1968 by Martin Luther King Jr. and the Southern Christian Leadership Conference (SCLC) demanding a $30 billion antipoverty package from the U.S. government. The desired package would include a commitment to full employment, a guaranteed annual income measure, and increased construction of low-income housing.	**Campaña de los Pobres:** Movimiento encabezado en 1967–1968 por Martin Luther King Jr. y la Conferencia de Liderazgo Cristiano del Sur (SCLC), que exigía al gobierno estadounidense un paquete de medidas contra la pobreza por valor de 30,000 millones de dólares. El paquete deseado incluiría un compromiso con el pleno empleo, una medida de ingresos anuales garantizados y un aumento de la construcción de viviendas para personas con bajos ingresos.
popular sovereignty: An approach to resolving the question of whether to allow slavery in new states by letting residents of the territories decide.	**soberanía popular:** Planteamiento para resolver la cuestión de si se debía permitir la esclavitud en los nuevos estados dejando que decidieran los residentes de los territorios.
Port Royal Experiment: An attempt by government officials and civilian volunteers to assist Sea Island enslaved people, who had been abandoned by their enslavers, in their transition to freedom.	**Experimento Port Royal:** Intento de funcionarios gubernamentales y voluntarios civiles de ayudar a los esclavizados de Sea Island, que habían sido abandonados por sus esclavizadores, en su transición a la libertad.
post-Black: A controversial term differentiating Black identity at the end of the twentieth century from that during other periods in American history. Not to be confused with *post-racial*, this term emphasizes the individuality and diversity of Black Americans.	**post-negro:** Término controvertido que diferencia la identidad negra de finales del siglo XX de la de otros periodos de la historia estadounidense. No confundir con *post-racial*, este término hace hincapié en la individualidad y la diversidad de los negros estadounidenses.
post-racial: A controversial term used to indicate that racism no longer inhibits the life chances of people of color in America. Not to be confused with *post-Black*, this term is often used by conservative Blacks and whites.	**post-racial:** Término controvertido utilizado para indicar que el racismo ya no inhibe las oportunidades vitales de las personas de color en Estados Unidos. No confundir con *post-negro*, este término lo utilizan a menudo los negros y blancos conservadores.
Pound Cake speech (2004): A widely debated speech in which the Black comedian Bill Cosby castigated lower-class Blacks for their behavior.	**Discurso de Pound Cake** (2004): Discurso ampliamente debatido en el que el cómico negro Bill Cosby fustigó a los negros de clase baja por su comportamiento.
preliminary Emancipation Proclamation (1862): A presidential proclamation giving the Confederacy one hundred days to cease the rebellion. If it did not all its entire enslaved population would be freed.	**Proclamación de Emancipación preliminar** (1862): Proclamación presidencial que concedía a la Confederación cien días para cesar la rebelión. Si no lo hacía, toda su población esclavizada sería liberada.

primary source: A text created during a specific time period from the past.	**fuente principal:** Texto creado durante una época específica del pasado.
process: In the AP® African American Studies course, a process is two or more related developments. The developments might cause, contrast with, or have commonalities with one another.	**proceso:** En el curso de AP® African American Studies, un proceso consiste en dos o más desarrollos relacionados. Los desarrollos pueden causarse, contrastar o tener puntos en común entre sí.
Proclamation of Amnesty and Reconstruction (1863): Lincoln's proposal for the reorganization and readmission into the Union of the defeated Confederate states.	**Proclamación de Amnistía y Reconstrucción** (1863): Propuesta de Lincoln para la reorganización y readmisión en la Unión de los estados confederados derrotados.
progressivism: A wide-ranging reform movement that sought to eliminate corruption, bring efficiency to American political and economic life, and improve society.	**progresismo:** Amplio movimiento reformista que pretendía eliminar la corrupción, aportar eficacia a la vida política y económica estadounidense y mejorar la sociedad.
purpose: The goal the writer or speaker of a text wants to achieve.	**propósito:** Meta que el escritor u orador de un texto quiere lograr.
Q	
Quaker: A member of the Religious Society of Friends, a pacifist Protestant sect known for its commitment to social justice.	**cuáquero:** Miembro de la Sociedad Religiosa de los Amigos, secta protestante pacifista conocida por su compromiso con la justicia social.
R	
racial profiling: Using race, rather than specific evidence, to determine how a person should be treated.	**perfilado racial:** Utilizar la raza, en lugar de pruebas concretas, para determinar cómo debe tratarse a una persona.
rap music: A type of music developed in the early to mid-1970s critiquing poverty, police surveillance, drug addiction, Black-on-Black crime, and unemployment.	**música rap:** Tipo de música desarrollada a principios y mediados de los años 70 que critica la pobreza, la vigilancia policial, la drogadicción, la delincuencia entre negros y el desempleo.
Reconstruction Act of 1867 (first): An act dividing the South into military districts and requiring the former Confederate states to write new constitutions at conventions with delegates elected by universal male suffrage.	**Ley de Reconstrucción de 1867 (primera):** Ley que dividía el Sur en distritos militares y obligaba a los antiguos estados confederados a redactar nuevas constituciones en convenciones con delegados elegidos por sufragio universal masculino.
Red-baited: Accused of being a Communist. Red-baiting was used to discredit individuals during the Red scare beginning in 1947 in order to undermine their politics.	**Difamado como comunista:** Acusado de comunista. Se difamaba a personas como comunistas para desacreditarlas durante el Terror Rojo, a partir de 1947, con el fin de socavar su política.
Red Summer (1919): The summer of 1919, in the aftermath of World War I, during which a series of more than two dozen race riots, many in northern cities, took place.	**Verano Rojo** (1919): El verano de 1919, tras la Primera Guerra Mundial, durante el cual se produjo una serie de más de dos docenas de disturbios raciales, muchos en ciudades del norte.
Regents of the University of California v. Bakke (1978): A U.S. Supreme Court decision ruling that the university's medical school at Davis had discriminated against Allan Bakke, a white male, when it took race into account in determining admissions.	***Regentes de la Universidad de California contra Bakke*** (1978): Sentencia del Tribunal Supremo de EE. UU. que dictaminó que la facultad de medicina de la universidad de Davis había discriminado a Allan Bakke, varón blanco, al tener en cuenta la raza a la hora de determinar las admisiones.
restrictive covenants: Discriminatory clauses in deeds that prohibited owners from selling their property to a person or family of a particular racial or religious group.	**pactos restrictivos:** Cláusulas discriminatorias en escrituras que prohibían a los propietarios vender su propiedad a una persona o familia de un determinado grupo racial o religioso.

ring shout: A religious ritual developed by enslaved people in the West Indies and North America that involved forming a circle and shuffling counter-clockwise while singing and praying.	**anillo de gritos:** Ritual religioso desarrollado por los esclavos de las Indias Occidentales y América del Norte que consistía en formar un círculo y girar en sentido contrario a las agujas del reloj mientras cantaban y rezaban.
S	
Sahel: A stretch of semi-arid land that cuts across the African continent, dividing the Sahara desert to its north from the savannah (grasslands) to its south.	**Sahel:** Extensión de tierra semiárida que atraviesa el continente africano y divide el desierto del Sahara al norte y la sabana (praderas) al sur.
scientific racism: Pseudoscientific yet powerful notions of white superiority endorsed by most of the academic and scientific establishment until well into the twentieth century.	**racismo científico:** Nociones pseudocientíficas pero poderosas de la superioridad blanca respaldadas por la mayor parte del establishment académico y científico hasta bien entrado el siglo XX.
Scottsboro Boys case (1931): A highly publicized series of trials of Black youths in Scottsboro, Alabama, who were falsely accused of rape and successfully defended by lawyers paid for by the Communist Party.	**caso de los chicos de Scottsboro** (1931): Serie muy publicitada de juicios de jóvenes negros en Scottsboro, Alabama, que fueron falsamente acusados de violación y defendidos con éxito por abogados pagados por el Partido Comunista.
secondary source: A text that provides an account of the past after the fact.	**fuente secundaria:** Texto que ofrece un relato del pasado después de los hechos.
Second Confiscation Act (1862): A congressional act declaring freedom for all enslaved people employed in the rebellion and for freedom seekers able to make it to Union-controlled territory.	**Segunda Ley de Confiscación** (1862): Ley del Congreso que declaraba la libertad para todos los esclavizados empleados en la rebelión y para los buscadores de la libertad que pudieran llegar a territorio controlado por la Unión.
Second Great Awakening: A Christian revival movement that took place during the first half of the nineteenth century.	**Segundo Gran Despertar:** Movimiento de avivamiento cristiano que tuvo lugar durante la primera mitad del siglo XIX.
separate but equal: The legal doctrine established in *Plessy v. Ferguson* (1896) stating that as long as they were deemed equal to those of whites, separate (Jim Crow) facilities and accommodations for Blacks did not violate the Fourteenth Amendment's equal protection clause.	**separados pero iguales:** La doctrina legal establecida en el caso *Plessy contra Ferguson* (1896), según la cual, siempre que se consideraran iguales a las de los blancos, las instalaciones y alojamientos separados (Jim Crow) para los negros no violaban la cláusula de igual protección de la Decimocuarta Enmienda.
sharecropping: An agricultural system that emerged during Reconstruction in which a landowner contracts with a farmer to work a parcel of land in return for a share of the crop.	**aparcería:** Sistema agrícola surgido durante la Reconstrucción en el que un terrateniente contrata a un agricultor para que trabaje una parcela de tierra a cambio de una parte de la cosecha.
silent march (1917): A mass march orchestrated by the NAACP down New York City's Fifth Avenue on July 28, 1917, to protest the horrific East St. Louis, Illinois, race riot of July 2.	**marcha silenciosa** (1917): Marcha multitudinaria orquestada por la NAACP por la Quinta Avenida de Nueva York el 28 de julio de 1917, en protesta por los terribles disturbios raciales del 2 de julio en East St.
Slaughterhouse Cases (1873): A U.S. Supreme Court ruling limiting the authority of the Fourteenth Amendment. The ruling expanded the scope of state-level citizenship at the expense of U.S. citizenship.	***Casos de los mataderos*** (1873): Sentencia del Tribunal Supremo de EE. UU. que limitaba la autoridad de la Decimocuarta Enmienda. La sentencia amplió el alcance de la ciudadanía a nivel estatal a expensas de la ciudadanía estadounidense.

Social Darwinism: The idea that the evolutionary notion of the survival of the fittest applies to society and the economy, used to justify white domination of both.	**Darwinismo social:** La idea de que la noción evolutiva de la supervivencia del más apto se aplica a la sociedad y a la economía, utilizada para justificar la dominación blanca de ambas.
soldiers without swords: The name given to African American journalists because of their relentless reporting of the injustices Blacks suffered during World War II.	**soldados sin espadas:** Nombre dado a los periodistas afroamericanos por sus implacables reportajes sobre las injusticias que sufrieron los negros durante la Segunda Guerra Mundial.
Somerset case (1772): A British legal case that freed an enslaved American named James Somerset and inspired other enslaved people to sue for their freedom.	**Caso Somerset** (1772): Caso legal británico que liberó a un estadounidense esclavizado llamado James Somerset e inspiró a otras personas esclavizadas a demandar su libertad.
Southern Negro Youth Congress: A radical southern-based youth organization that promoted the interrelated concerns of Black youth and their people framed around four core commitments: jobs, education, health, and citizenship.	**Congreso de la Juventud Negra del Sur:** Organización juvenil radical con sede en el Sur que promovía las preocupaciones interrelacionadas de la juventud negra y su pueblo enmarcadas en torno a cuatro compromisos fundamentales: empleo, educación, salud y ciudadanía.
southern strategy: (1) An unsuccessful British military plan, adopted in late 1778, that was designed to defeat the patriots by recapturing the American South. (2) Policies adopted by President Richard Nixon in 1969 aimed at moving southern whites, who were traditionally Democrats, into the Republican Party.	**estrategia del Sur:** (1) Plan militar británico fracasado, adoptado a finales de 1778, que pretendía derrotar a los patriotas reconquistando el Sur de EE. UU. (2) Políticas adoptadas por el presidente Richard Nixon en 1969, destinadas a que los blancos del sur, tradicionalmente demócratas, se pasaran al Partido Republicano.
Special Field Order 15 (1865): A military order by Union general William T. Sherman that granted freedpeople the right to land that had been abandoned by Confederate plantation owners.	**Orden Especial de Campo 15** (1865): Orden militar del general de la Unión William T. Sherman que concedía a los libertos el derecho a las tierras abandonadas por los propietarios de plantaciones confederados.
Stono rebellion (1739): A slave rebellion that took place near South Carolina's Stono River in 1739. It was led by enslaved people who hoped to find freedom in Spanish Florida. The rebels killed about twenty whites before they were captured and subdued.	**Rebelión de Stono** (1739): Rebelión de esclavos que tuvo lugar cerca del río Stono, en Carolina del Sur, en 1739. Estaba dirigida por personas esclavizadas que esperaban encontrar la libertad en la Florida española. Los rebeldes mataron a unos veinte blancos antes de ser capturados y sometidos.
"stop and frisk": Otherwise known as a "Terry stop" — after a 1968 Supreme Court decision that upheld the constitutionality of such stops — stop and frisk is the practice by which police detain and search anyone who appears to be engaged in suspicious activity. While some Blacks and police argue that stop-and-frisk laws, which are used in tandem with broken windows policing, are necessary to keep a community and the police safe, most Blacks and Latinos complain that stop and frisk amounts to police harassment of mostly innocent people. They believe that people of color are more likely than whites to be detained and patted down, which they say is unfair.	**"parar y cachear":** También conocida como "parada Terry" -por una decisión del Tribunal Supremo de 1968 que confirmó la constitucionalidad de dichas paradas-, la parada y cacheo es la práctica mediante la cual la policía detiene y registra a cualquier persona que parezca estar realizando una actividad sospechosa. Mientras que algunos negros y policías sostienen que las leyes de "parar y cachear", que se utilizan junto con la vigilancia policial de "ventanas rotas", son necesarias para mantener la seguridad de la comunidad y de la policía, la mayoría de los negros y latinos se quejan de que "parar y cachear" equivale a acosar policialmente a personas en su mayoría inocentes. Creen que las personas de color tienen más probabilidades que los blancos de ser detenidos y cacheados, lo que consideran injusto.
syncretic: The combination of different religious beliefs and traditions.	**sincrético:** La combinación de diferentes creencias y tradiciones religiosas.

systemic racism (also known as **institutionalized racism**): Discrimination practiced by corporations and governments.	**racismo sistémico** (también conocido como **racismo institucionalizado**): Discriminación practicada por las empresas y los gobiernos.
T	
Taino Indians: One of the Indigenous peoples of the Caribbean.	**indios taínos:** Uno de los pueblos indígenas del Caribe.
task system: A system of enslaved labor in which enslaved workers were assigned daily tasks and permitted to work unsupervised as long as they completed their tasks.	**sistema de tareas:** Sistema de trabajo en régimen de esclavitud en el que a los trabajadores esclavizados se les asignaban tareas diarias y se les permitía trabajar sin supervisión siempre que completaran sus tareas.
text: While this term generally refers to the written word, in the humanities it has come to mean any cultural product that can be "read" — meaning not just consumed and comprehended but also investigated. This includes fiction, nonfiction, poetry, political cartoons, fine art, photography, performances, fashion, cultural trends, and much more.	**texto:** Si bien este término generalmente se refiere a la palabra escrita, en las humanidades significa cualquier producto cultural que puede ser "leído", es decir que no solo puede ser consumido y comprendido, sino investigado. Incluye ficción, no ficción, poesía, cartones políticos, artes plásticas, fotografía, obras, moda, tendencias culturales y mucho más.
thesis statement: The articulation of the main argument in an argumentative piece of writing. Usually a single sentence, it often previews or sets the stage for the central claims the writer will make.	**enunciado de tesis:** Afirmación principal que plantea un escritor en cualquier texto de escritura argumentativa y que se escribe en una oración.
Thirteenth Amendment (ratified 1865): The constitutional amendment that formally abolished slavery.	**Decimotercera Enmienda** (1865): La enmienda constitucional que abolió formalmente la esclavitud.
Three-Fifths Compromise: A compromise between the northern and southern states, reached during the Constitutional Convention, establishing that three-fifths of each state's enslaved population would be counted in determining federal taxes and representation in the House of Representatives.	**Compromiso de los Tres Quintos:** Un compromiso entre los estados del Norte y del Sur, alcanzado durante la Convención Constitucional, por el que se establecía que se contabilizarían las tres quintas partes de la población esclavizada de cada estado a la hora de determinar los impuestos federales y la representación en la Cámara de Representantes.
tight packing: Crowding the human cargo carried on slave ships to maximize profits. By contrast, "loose packing" involved carrying fewer enslaved people in better conditions in an effort to keep mortality rates low.	**embalaje hermético:** Hacinamiento de la carga humana transportada en barcos negreros para maximizar los beneficios. Por el contrario, el "embalaje suelto" consistía en transportar a menos personas esclavizadas en mejores condiciones, en un esfuerzo por mantener bajas las tasas de mortalidad.
Title VII: The most contentious part of the Civil Rights Act of 1964, it banned discrimination in employment on the basis of race, color, religion, sex, or national origin and created the Equal Employment Opportunity Commission to investigate and litigate cases of job discrimination.	**Título VII:** La parte más polémica de la Ley de Derechos Civiles de 1964, que prohibía la discriminación en el empleo por motivos de raza, color, religión, sexo u origen nacional y creó la Comisión de Igualdad de Oportunidades en el Empleo para investigar y litigar los casos de discriminación laboral.
topic sentence: A sentence that states the main point of a paragraph, usually the first sentence.	**oración temática:** Oración que establece el punto principal de un párrafo, generalmente la primera oración.
transitions: Words that signify a change in thought while keeping writing cohesive. Common transition words include therefore, because of this, and for instance.	**transiciones:** Palabras que significan un cambio en el pensamiento mientras mantienen, a la vez, la cohesión de la escritura. Algunas palabras comunes de transición son: por lo tanto, debido a esto y por ejemplo.

trans-Saharan trade: Trade that connected Berber-speaking merchants of North Africa with West African merchants of the Sahel.	**comercio transahariano:** Comercio que conectaba a los mercaderes de habla bereber del norte de África con los mercaderes de África Occidental del Sahel.
triangle trade: The trade system that propelled the transatlantic slave trade, in which European merchants exchanged manufactured goods for enslaved Africans, whom they shipped to the Americas to exchange for New World commodities, which they then shipped back to European markets.	**comercio triangular:** Sistema comercial que impulsó la trata transatlántica de esclavos, en la que los mercaderes europeos intercambiaban productos manufacturados por africanos esclavizados, a los que enviaban a las Américas para intercambiarlos por mercancías del Nuevo Mundo, que luego enviaban de vuelta a los mercados europeos.
truant: An enslaved person who ran away for a limited period of time to visit loved ones; attend religious meetings or other social events; or escape punishment, abusive treatment, or undesirable work assignments.	**ausente sin permiso:** Persona esclavizada que huía durante un periodo de tiempo limitado para visitar a sus seres queridos, asistir a reuniones religiosas u otros actos sociales, o escapar de castigos, tratos abusivos o tareas laborales indeseables.
Tuskegee Airmen: Black pilots trained by the Army Air Corps at Tuskegee Institute during World War II. The pilots earned distinction despite efforts to disband and malign them.	**Aviadores de Tuskegee:** Pilotos negros entrenados por el Cuerpo Aéreo del Ejército en el Instituto Tuskegee durante la Segunda Guerra Mundial. Los pilotos se ganaron la distinción a pesar de los esfuerzos por disolverlos y difamarlos.
Tuskegee Syphilis Study: A federally funded study in collaboration with Tuskegee Institute of the long-term consequences of untreated syphilis, now infamous for the horrific and unethical treatment of its subjects, mostly local, poor, and illiterate Black male sharecroppers.	**Estudio sobre la sífilis de Tuskegee:** Un estudio financiado por el gobierno federal en colaboración con el Instituto Tuskegee sobre las consecuencias a largo plazo de la sífilis no tratada, hoy tristemente célebre por el trato horrible y poco ético que dispensaba a sus sujetos, en su mayoría aparceros negros locales, pobres y analfabetos.

U

Uncle Tom's Cabin **(1852):** A best-selling novel by Harriet Beecher Stowe that portrayed the horrors of slavery, boosted the abolitionist cause, and angered the proslavery South.	***La cabaña del tío Tom*** **(1852):** Novela exitosa de Harriet Beecher Stowe que retrató los horrores de la esclavitud, impulsó la causa abolicionista y enfureció al Sur proesclavista.
Underground Railroad: A network of antislavery activists who helped freedom seekers escape to the North and Canada.	**Ferrocarril subterráneo:** Red de activistas antiesclavistas que ayudaron a los buscadores de libertad a escapar al Norte y a Canadá.
Union League: An organization founded in 1862 to promote the Republican Party. During Reconstruction, the league recruited freedpeople into the party and advanced their political education.	**Liga de la Unión:** Organización fundada en 1862 para promover el Partido Republicano. Durante la Reconstrucción, la Liga reclutó a libertos para el partido y fomentó su educación política.
United Steelworkers of America v. Weber **(1979):** A U.S. Supreme Court case considered a victory for affirmative action. The Court ruled that Brian Weber, a white male, had not been discriminated against by either the United Steelworkers union or the Kaiser Aluminum Corporation when they initiated a job training program to bring the proportion of Blacks in the craft trades closer to their proportion in the local labor force.	***United Steelworkers of America contra Weber*** **(1979):** Caso del Tribunal Supremo de EE. UU. considerado una victoria de la discriminación positiva. El Tribunal dictaminó que Brian Weber, varón blanco, no había sido discriminado ni por el sindicato United Steelworkers ni por la Kaiser Aluminum Corporation cuando iniciaron un programa de formación laboral para acercar la proporción de negros en los oficios artesanos a su proporción en la población activa local.
Universal Negro Improvement Association (UNIA): The global organization founded by Marcus Garvey in Jamaica in 1914 that promoted race pride, racial unity, Black separatism, and African redemption.	**Asociación Universal para la Mejora de los Negros (UNIA):** La organización mundial fundada por Marcus Garvey en Jamaica en 1914 que promovía el orgullo racial, la unidad racial, el separatismo negro y la redención africana.

uplift: The idea that racial progress demands autonomous Black efforts; especially seen as the responsibility of the more fortunate of the race to help lift up the less fortunate.	**elevación:** La idea de que el progreso racial exige esfuerzos autónomos de los negros; se considera especialmente que es responsabilidad de los más afortunados de la raza ayudar a levantar a los menos afortunados.
U.S. Colored Troops: The official designation for the division of Black units that joined the U.S. army beginning in 1863.	**tropas de color de EE. UU:** Designación oficial de la división de unidades negras que se unieron al ejército estadounidense a partir de 1863.
V	
vigilance committees: Groups led by free Blacks and their allies in the North to assist freedom seekers.	**comités de vigilancia:** Grupos dirigidos por negros libres y sus aliados en el Norte para ayudar a los buscadores de libertad.
Voting Rights Act (1965): An act outlawing literacy requirements and poll taxes and sending federal election examiners south to protect Blacks' rights to register and vote.	**Ley del Derecho al Voto** (1965): Ley que prohibía los requisitos de alfabetización y los impuestos electorales y enviaba examinadores electorales federales al Sur para proteger los derechos de los negros a registrarse y votar.
W	
Wade–Davis Bill (1864): A congressional proposal for the reorganization and readmission into the Union of the defeated Confederate states. Lincoln refused to sign the bill.	**Proyecto de ley Wade-Davis** (1864): Propuesta del Congreso para la reorganización y readmisión en la Unión de los estados confederados derrotados. Lincoln se negó a firmar la ley.
white flight: The movement of whites out of urban areas to racially exclusive suburbs, facilitated by federal highway construction, federally subsidized low-interest loans, and discrimination against Blacks.	**huida blanca:** El desplazamiento de los blancos de las zonas urbanas a suburbios racialmente exclusivos, facilitado por la construcción de autopistas federales, los préstamos a bajo interés subvencionados por el gobierno federal y la discriminación contra los negros.
white primary: A state primary election in the Democratic Party–controlled South in which the party functioned as a private club that determined its own membership and was thus able to exclude Blacks. This practice was outlawed by *Smith v. Allwright* in 1944.	**primarias blancas:** Elecciones primarias estatales en el Sur, controladas por el Partido Demócrata, en las que el partido funcionaba como un club privado que determinaba su propia afiliación y, por tanto, podía excluir a los negros. Esta práctica fue prohibida por *Smith contra Allwright* en 1944.
Wilmington Insurrection (1898): A race riot in Wilmington, North Carolina, that restored white political power in the city and signaled the end of biracial politics in the city and state.	**Insurrección de Wilmington** (1898): Motín racial en Wilmington, Carolina del Norte, que restauró el poder político blanco en la ciudad y señaló el fin de la política birracial en la ciudad y el estado.
Wilmot Proviso (1846): A controversial congressional proposal that sought to prohibit slavery in the new territories gained as a result of the Mexican-American War. Although it did not pass the Senate, it sparked angry debate between the North and South.	**Proviso Wilmot** (1846): Controvertida propuesta del Congreso que pretendía prohibir la esclavitud en los nuevos territorios ganados como resultado de la guerra mexicano-estadounidense. Aunque no fue aprobada por el Senado, provocó un airado debate entre el Norte y el Sur.
Z	
zoot suit riots: World War II riots in Los Angeles that pitted white sailors and civilians against African American as well as Hispanic and Latino men. So called because of the Blacks' and Latinos' broad felt hats, pegged trousers, and gold chains, which were popularly referred to as zoot suits.	**disturbios de los trajes zoot:** Disturbios de la Segunda Guerra Mundial en Los Ángeles que enfrentaron a marineros y civiles blancos con hombres afroamericanos, así como hispanos y latinos. Llamados así por los amplios sombreros de fieltro, los pantalones de pinzas y las cadenas de oro de los negros y latinos, a los que popularmente se denominaba trajes zoot.

Notes and Text Credits

Introduction: The Study of African American History

1. W. E. B. Du Bois, *The Souls of Black Folk: Essays and Sketches* (Chicago: A. C. McClurg, 1903), 11.
2. W. E. B. Du Bois, "The Conservation of Races," in *W. E. B. Du Bois: A Reader*, ed. David Levering Lewis (New York: Henry Holt, 1995), 25.
3. W. E. B. Du Bois, *Black Reconstruction in America, 1860–1880* (1935; repr., New York: Free Press, 1998), 721.
4. Ibid., 714.

Chapter 1: African Origins

1. Countée Cullen, "Heritage," *The Survey* (March 1, 1925), 674.
2. Phillis Wheatley, "On Being Brought from Africa to America," *Poems on Various Subjects, Religious and Moral* (1773).
3. John Russwurm, "The Mutability of Human Affairs," *Freedom's Journal* (April 4, 1827).
4. John Iliffe, *Africans: The History of a Continent*, 3rd ed. (Cambridge: Cambridge University Press, 2017), 1.
5. Georg Wilhelm Friedrich Hegel, *The Philosophy of History*, trans. J. Sibree, M.A. (New York: Wiley Book Co., 1900), 99.
6. Quoted in David Conrad, *Empires of Medieval West Africa*, 26.
7. Al-Bakri, *The Book of Routes and Realms*, cited in Levitzion and Hopkins, *Corpus of Early Arabic Sources for West African History* (Cambridge: Cambridge University Press, 1981), 79–81.
8. John Hunwick, ed., "Leo Africanus," *Timbuktu and the Songhay Empire. Al-Sa'Di's Ta'Rikh Al-Sudan Down to 1613 and Other Contemporary Documents*, 281.
9. Martin A. Klein, "The Slave Trade and Decentralized Societies," *The Journal of African History* 42, no. 1 (2001).
10. John S. Mbiti, *African Religions and Philosophy* (New York: Praeger, 1969), 108.
11. Orlando Patterson, *Slavery and Social Death: A Comparative Study* (Cambridge: Harvard University Press, 2007).
12. Olaudah Equiano, *The Interesting Narrative of the Life of Olaudah Equiano* (London: Author, 1789), 26–27, http://docsouth.unc.edu/neh/equiano1/equiano1.html.

Chapter 2: From Africa to America

1. Gomes Eannes de Azurara, *The Chronicle of the Discovery and Conquest of Guinea* (c. 1453), trans. C. Raymond Beazley and Edgar Prestage, in *Documents Illustrative of the History of the Slave Trade to America*, ed. Elizabeth Donnan (Washington, DC: Carnegie Institution, 1930), 1:28.
2. Luis de Camões, *Os Lusíadas*, quoted in Luis Madureira, "The Accident of America: Marginal Notes on the European Conquest of the World," *CR: The New Centennial Review* 2, no. 1 (2002): 145.
3. Matthew Restall, "Black Conquistadors: Armed Africans in Early Spanish America," *Americas* 57, no. 2 (October 2000): 176.
4. *Dum Diversas*, as summarized in the bull *Romanus Pontifex* (January 8, 1455), translated and reprinted in *European Treaties Bearing on the History of the United States and Its Dependencies to 1648*, ed. Frances Gardiner Davenport (Washington, DC: Carnegie Institution, 1917), 23.
5. Quoted in George Sanderlin, trans. and ed., *Bartolomé de Las Casas: A Selection of His Writings* (New York: Knopf, 1971), 81.
6. Quoted in Lawrence Clayton, "Bartolomé de las Casas and the African Slave Trade," *History Compass* 7, no. 6 (September 2009): 1528.
7. Olaudah Equiano, *The Interesting Narrative of the Life of Olaudah Equiano, or Gustavus Vassa, the African* (London: printed for the author, 1789), 49, 51.
8. Samuel Ajayi Crowther, "Narrative of the Events in the Life of a Liberated Negro," *The Missionary Register* (London: Seeley, Jackson, & Halliday, 1837), 436.
9. John Barbot, "A Description of the Coasts of North and South-Guinea," in *A Collection of Voyages and Travels*, ed. Awnsham Churchill and John Churchill (London: J. Walthoe, 1732), 5:326.
10. Quoted in Stephanie E. Smallwood, *Saltwater Slavery: A Middle Passage from Africa to American Diaspora* (Cambridge: Harvard University Press, 2007), 119.
11. Equiano, *Interesting Narrative*, 70, 76.
12. Mahommah Gardo Baquaqua and Samuel Moore, *Biography of Mahommah G. Baquaqua, a Native of Zoogoo, in the Interior of Africa* (Detroit: Geo. E. Pomeroy, 1854), 41.
13. Quoted in Michael A. Gomez, *Exchanging Our Country Marks: The Transformation of African Identities in the Colonial and Antebellum South* (Chapel Hill: University of North Carolina Press, 1998), 158.
14. Marcus Rediker, *The Slave Ship: A Human History* (New York: Viking, 2007), 63.
15. Herbert S. Klein, Stanley L. Engerman, Robin Haines, and Ralph Shlomowitz, "Transoceanic Mortality: The Slave Trade in Comparative Perspective," *William and Mary Quarterly* 58, no. 1 (2001): 93–118.
16. Thomas Clarkson, *The History of the Rise, Progress, and Accomplishment of the Abolition of the African Slave-Trade by the British Parliament* (London: R. Taylor, 1808), 197.
17. Alexander Falconbridge, *An Account of the Slave Trade on the Coast of Africa* (London: J. Phillips, 1788), 23.
18. Ibid., 24–25.
19. John Newton, *Thoughts upon the African Slave Trade* (1788), in *The Works of Reverend John Newton* (New York: J. Seymour, 1811), 6:532.
20. John Newton, *Journal of a Slave Trader*, ed. Bernard Martin and Mark Spurrell (London: Epworth Press, 1962), 75.

21. Ottobah Cugoano, *Narrative of the Enslavement of Ottobah Cugoano, a Native of Africa; Published by Himself, in the Year 1787*, reprinted in Thomas Fisher, "The Negro's Memorial, or, Abolitionist's Catechism; by an Abolitionist" (London: printed for the author, 1825), 124.
22. Thomas Phillips, *A Journal of a Voyage Made in the* Hannibal *of London, Ann. 1693, 1694*, in *A Collection of Voyages and Travels*, ed. Awnsham Churchill and John Churchill (London: J. Walthoe, 1732), 6:235.
23. Captain Thomas Snelgrave, quoted in Hugh Thomas, *The Slave Trade: The Story of the Atlantic Slave Trade, 1440–1870* (New York: Simon & Schuster, 1999), 427.
24. Barbot, "Coasts of North and South-Guinea," 272.
25. Neta Crawford, *Argument and Change in World Politics* (Cambridge: Cambridge University Press, 2002), 64.
26. Smallwood, *Saltwater Slavery*, 152.
27. Rediker, *Slave Ship*, 5.
28. Vincent Carretta, *Equiano, the African: Biography of a Self-Made Man* (Athens: University of Georgia Press, 2005).

Chapter 3: Slavery in North America

1. John Rolfe, "A Letter to Sir Edwin Sandys, January 1619/20," in *The Records of the Virginia Company of London*, ed. Susan Myra Kingsbury (Washington, DC: Government Printing Office, 1933), 3:243.
2. Tim Hawshaw, *The Birth of Black America: The First African Americans and the Pursuit of Freedom at Jamestown* (New York: Carroll and Graf, 2007), 69.
3. John Thornton, "The African Experience of the '20. and Odd Negroes' Arriving in Virginia in 1619," *William and Mary Quarterly* 55, no. 3 (1998): 421–24.
4. Raphael Holinshed, William Harrison, and others, *Holinshed's Chronicles of England, Scotland, and Ireland* (1587; repr., London: J. Johnson, 1807), 1:275.
5. Quoted in Anthony S. Parent Jr., *Foul Means: The Formation of a Slave Society in Virginia, 1660–1740* (Chapel Hill: University of North Carolina Press, 2003), 16.
6. Meeting minutes, July 9, 1640, in *Minutes of the Council and General Court of Colonial Virginia* (Richmond, VA: Colonial Press, 1924), 466.
7. William Waller Hening, ed., *The Statutes at Large; Being a Collection of All the Laws of Virginia* (Richmond, VA: Samuel Pleasants, 1810), 2:170.
8. Ibid, 3: 87.
9. Ibid, 2: 260.
10. *Virginia Gazette* (Williamsburg), November 2, 1739.
11. "Bacon's 'Manifesto,'" *Virginia Magazine of History and Biography* 1 (1893), quoted in Warren Billings, ed., *The Old Dominion in the Seventeenth Century: A Documentary History of Virginia, 1606–1689* (Chapel Hill: University of North Carolina Press, 1975), 277–79.
12. William Byrd to John Perceval, Earl of Egmont, July 12, 1736, in *Documents Illustrative of the History of the Slave Trade to America*, ed. Elizabeth Donnan (Washington, DC: Carnegie Institution, 1930), 4:131–32.
13. Olaudah Equiano, *The Interesting Narrative of the Life of Olaudah Equiano, or Gustavus Vassa, the African* (London: printed for the author, 1789), 90.
14. Ira Berlin, *Many Thousands Gone: The First Two Centuries of Slavery in North America* (Cambridge: Harvard University Press, 1998), 111.
15. John Brickell, *The Natural History of North-Carolina* (1737), quoted in Parent, *Foul Means*, 161.
16. Quoted in Daniel Littlefield, *Rice and Slaves: Ethnicity and the Slave Trade in Colonial South Carolina* (Baton Rouge: LSU Press, 1981), 100.
17. Advertisement, *Charleston Evening Gazette*, July 11, 1785, quoted in Judith Ann Carney, *Black Rice: The African Origins of Rice Cultivation in the Americas* (Cambridge: Harvard University Press, 2001), 90.
18. Gideon Johnston, "Instructions of the Clergy of South Carolina Given to Mr. Johnston" (1713), in *Carolina Chronicle: The Papers of Commissary Gideon Johnston, 1707–1716*, ed. Frank J. Klingberg, University of California Publications, vol. 35 (Berkeley: University of California Press, 1946), 123, 124.
19. Henry Melchior Muhlenberg, *The Journals of Henry Melchior Muhlenberg*, trans. Theodore G. Tappert and John W. Doberstein (Philadelphia: Muhlenberg Press, 1942), 1:58.
20. Quoted in Albert J. Raboteau, *Slave Religion: The "Invisible Institution" in the Antebellum South* (New York: Oxford University Press, 1978), 122.
21. Francis Le Jau, *The Carolina Chronicle of Dr. Francis Le Jau, 1706–1717* (Berkeley: University of California Press, 1980).
22. "The Massachusetts Body of Liberties" (1641), reprinted in Charles W. Eliot, ed., *American Historical Documents, 1000–1904*, The Harvard Classics (New York: P. F. Collier & Son, 1910), 43:79.
23. Samuel Sewall, *Diary of Samuel Sewall*, June 19, 1700, Collections of the Massachusetts Historical Society, vol. 6 (Boston: Published by the Society, 1878), 16.
24. Samuel Sewall, *The Selling of Joseph: A Memorial* (Boston: Bartholomew Green and John Allen, 1700), 3, 1.
25. John Saffin, *A Brief and Candid Answer to a Late Printed Sheet, Entitled, The Selling of Joseph*, 1701. Reprinted in George Henry Moore, *Notes on the History of Slavery in Massachusetts* (New York: D. Appleton & Co., 1866), 256.
26. Cotton Mather, *The Negro Christianized. An Essay to Excite and Assist That Good Work, the Instruction of Negro-Servants in Christianity* (1706), ed. Paul Royster, Electronic Texts in American Studies, paper 28, UNL DigitalCommons@ University of Nebraska-Lincoln, 16, 20, http://digitalcommons.unl.edu/cgi/viewcontent.cgi?article=1028&context=etas.
27. Quoted in William Dillon Piersen, *Black Yankees: The Development of an Afro-American Subculture in Eighteenth-Century New England* (Amherst: University of Massachusetts Press, 1988), 5.
28. *Connecticut Courant*, February 23, 1733.

29. Quoted in Wendy Warren, "'Thrown Upon the World': Valuing Infants in the Eighteenth-Century North American Slave Market," *Slavery and Abolition* 39, no. 4 (2018): 624.
30. Quoted in Thelma Wills Foote, *Black and White Manhattan: The History of Racial Formation in Colonial New York City* (New York: Oxford University Press, 2004), 36.
31. "Freedoms and Exemptions Granted by the Board of the Nineteen of the Incorporated West India Company, to All Patroons, Masters or Private Persons Who Will Plant Colonies in New Netherland" (1630), in *Documents Relative to the Colonial History of the State of New-York*, ed. Edmund B. O'Callaghan (Albany: Weed, Parsons and Company, 1858), 2:557.
32. Foote, *Black and White Manhattan*, 39.
33. See, for example, "Draft of Instructions for Robert Hunter, Governor of New-York" (1709), in *Documents Relative to the Colonial History of the State of New-York*, ed. Edmund B. O'Callaghan (Albany: Weed, Parsons and Company, 1855), 5:136.
34. *New-York Weekly Journal*, June 21, 1742.
35. William Penn, quoted in Samuel McPherson Janney, *The Life of William Penn; With Selections from His Correspondence and Auto-biography* (Philadelphia: Hogan, Perkins and Company, 1852), 422.
36. The Germantown Protest (1688), quoted in David Brion Davis, "Slavery and Emancipation in Western Culture," in *Slavery and Freedom in American History and Memory*, Gilder Lehrman Center for the Study of Slavery, Resistance, and Abolition, Yale University, http://www.yale.edu/glc/aces/germantown.htm.
37. Nicolas de la Salle to the French Ministry of the Colonies, Fort Louis, 29 August 1709, trans. and quoted in Gwendolyn Midlo Hall, *Africans in Colonial Louisiana: The Development of Afro-Creole Culture in the Eighteenth Century* (Baton Rouge: LSU Press, 1995), 57.
38. William Finch, a British merchant who visited Sierra Leone in 1607, quoted in Alexander Peter Kup, *A History of Sierra Leone, 1400–1787* (New York: Cambridge University Press, 1961), 160.
39. Quoted in Jane Landers, *Black Society in Spanish Florida* (Urbana: University of Illinois Press, 1999), 25.
40. Quoted in Patrick Riordan, "Finding Freedom in Florida: Native Peoples, African Americans, and Colonists, 1670–1816," *Florida Historical Quarterly* 75, no. 1 (1996): 30–31.
41. Patrick Telfair, Douglass Hugh Anderson, and others. "A True and Historical Narrative of the Colony of Georgia in America, &c." (1740), in *Collections of the Georgia Historical Society*, Volume II (Savannah: Georgia Historical Society, 1842), 166.
42. Salzburger Petition 91739, quoted in James Van Horn Melton, "From Alpine Miner to Low-Country Yeoman: The Transatlantic Worlds of a Georgia Salzburger, 1693–1761," *Past and Present* 201, no. 1 (2008): 125.
43. Johann Martin Bolzius, quoted in Melton, "From Alpine Miner," 126, 127.
44. "Protest of the Salzburgers," in Charles Colcock Jones Jr., *The History of Georgia* (Boston: Houghton, Mifflin, 1883), 1:307.
45. "Statements Made in the Introduction to the Report on General Oglethorpe's Expedition to St. Augustine" (1741), in *Historical Collections of South Carolina*, ed. Bartholomew Rivers Carroll (New York: Harper & Bros., 1836), 2:359.
46. "Report of the Committee Appointed to Enquire into the Causes of the Disappointment of Success in the Late Expedition against St. Augustine" (1741), in *Stono: Documenting and Interpreting a Southern Slave Revolt*, ed. Mark Michael Smith (Columbia: University of South Carolina Press, 2005), 28.
47. Joseph Brevard, *An Alphabetical Digest of the Public Statute Law of South-Carolina* (Charleston: John Hoff, 1816), 229, 231.
48. William Bull to the Royal Council, October 5, 1739, South Carolina Department of Archives and History, Columbia.
49. Quoted in Parent, *Foul Means*, 155, 153, 154.
50. "The Massachusetts Body of Liberties" (1641), reprinted in Charles W. Eliot, ed., *American Historical Documents, 1000–1904*, The Harvard Classics (New York: P. F. Collier & Son, 1910), 43:84.

Chapter 4: African Americans in the Age of Revolution

1. Daniel Horsmanden, *The New York Conspiracy, or a History of the Negro Plot, with the Journal of the Proceedings against the Conspirators at New-York in the Years 1741–2* (New York: Southwick and Pelsue, 1810), 181.
2. Ibid., 28, 155, 160, 161.
3. Quoted in Jill Lepore, *New York Burning: Liberty, Slavery, and Conspiracy in Eighteenth-Century Manhattan* (New York: Knopf, 2005), 50, 51.
4. Leopold S. Launitz-Schurer Jr., "Slave Resistance in Colonial New York: An Interpretation of Daniel Horsmanden's New York Conspiracy," *Phylon* 41, no. 2 (1980): 137–52.
5. Marcus Rediker, "A Motley Crew of Rebels: Sailors, Slaves, and the Coming of the American Revolution," in *The Transforming Hand of Revolution: Reconsidering the American Revolution as a Social Movement*, ed. Ronald Hoffman and Peter J. Albert (Charlottesville: University Press of Virginia, 1995), 155.
6. Quoted in Thelma Wills Foote, *Black and White Manhattan: The History of Racial Formation in Colonial New York City* (New York: Oxford University Press, 2004), 46.
7. Quoted in Gary B. Nash and Jean R. Soderlund, *Freedom by Degrees: Emancipation in Pennsylvania and Its Aftermath* (New York: Oxford University Press, 1991), xii.
8. Leslie M. Harris, *In the Shadow of Slavery: African Americans in New York City, 1626–1863* (Chicago: University of Chicago Press, 2003), 47.
9. Quoted in Philip D. Morgan, *Slave Counterpoint: Black Culture in the Eighteenth-Century Chesapeake and Lowcountry* (Chapel Hill: University of North Carolina Press, 1998), 490.
10. Quoted in William Dillon Piersen, *Black Yankees: The Development of an Afro-American Subculture in Eighteenth-Century New England* (Amherst: University of Massachusetts Press, 1988), 121.

11. Quoted ibid., 77.
12. Quoted in Morgan, *Slave Counterpoint*, 572.
13. Morgan, *Slave Counterpoint*, 567.
14. Quoted in Thomas S. Kidd, *The Great Awakening: The Roots of Evangelical Christianity in Colonial America* (New Haven: Yale University Press, 2007), 215–16.
15. Charles Chauncy, *Seasonable Thoughts on the State of Religion in New-England* (Boston: Rogers and Fowle, 1743), 226.
16. Mukhtar Ali Isani, "Phillis Wheatley in London: An Unpublished Letter to David Wooster," *American Literature* 51, no. 2 (1979): 257.
17. James Albert Ukawsaw Gronniosaw, *A Narrative of the Most Remarkable Particulars in the Life of James Albert Ukawsaw Gronniosaw, An African Prince, as Related by Himself* (Bath: Printed by W. Gye, 1770), 12.
18. Quoted in Timothy L. Hall, *American Religious Leaders* (New York: *Facts on File*, 2003), 137.
19. Quoted in Stephen J. Stein, "George Whitefield on Slavery: Some New Evidence," *Church History* 42, no. 2 (1973): 243–56.
20. George Whitefield, *The Works of the Reverend George Whitefield, M.A.* (London: printed for Edward and Charles Dilly, 1771), 4:38.
21. Quoted in Allan Gallay, "The Origins of Slaveholders' Paternalism: George Whitefield, the Bryan Family, and the Great Awakening in the South," *Journal of Southern History* 53, no. 3 (1987): 386.
22. "Davies' Account of the Negroes" (1756), reprinted in William Henry Foote, *Sketches of Virginia, Historical and Biographical* (Philadelphia: W. S. Martien, 1850), 290.
23. Albert J. Raboteau, *Slave Religion: The "Invisible Institution" in the Antebellum South* (New York: Oxford University Press, 2004).
24. John Marrant, *A Narrative of the Lord's Wonderful Dealings with John Marrant, a Black, (Now Going to Preach the Gospel in Nova-Scotia) Born in New-York, in North-America* (London: R. Hawes, 1785), 30–33.
25. James Otis, *The Rights of the British Colonists, Asserted and Proved* (1761), reprinted in *Pamphlets of the American Revolution, 1750–1776*, ed. Bernard Bailyn (Cambridge: Harvard University Press, 1965), 444.
26. Quoted in Patricia Bradley, *Slavery, Propaganda, and the American Revolution* (Jackson: University Press of Mississippi, 1999), 3.
27. John Locke, *The Second Treatise of Civil Government* (1689; repr., Amherst, NY: Prometheus Books, 1986), 54.
28. Quoted in Sylvia R. Frey, *Water from the Rock: Black Resistance in a Revolutionary Age* (Princeton: Princeton University Press, 1993), 15.
29. Quoted in John Wood Sweet, *Bodies Politic: Negotiating Race in the American North, 1730–1830* (Philadelphia: University of Pennsylvania Press, 2006), 253.
30. Phillis Wheatley, *The Collected Works of Phillis Wheatley*, John Shields, ed. (New York: Oxford University Press, 1988), 73, 74, 177.
31. John Adams, *The Works of John Adams, Second President of the United States: With a Life of the Author, Notes and Illustrations* (Boston: Charles C. Little and James Brown, 1850), 2:200.
32. "Felix" [Holbrook], "The humble PETITION of Many Slaves" in *A Documentary History of the Negro People in the United States*, ed. Herbert Aptheker (New York: Citadel Press, 1951), 6.
33. *Virginia Gazette* (Williamsburg, VA), June 30, 1774.
34. Quoted in Aptheker, *A Documentary History of the Negro People in the United States*, 7, 8.
35. Quoted in David McCullough, *John Adams* (New York: Simon & Schuster, 2008), 67.
36. The quote is from a poem by John Boyle O'Reilly that appears on the Crispus Attucks Memorial on Boston Common.
37. George T. Downing to William Cooper Nell, 3 March 1860, in *William Cooper Nell, Nineteenth-Century African American Abolitionist, Historian, Integrationist: Selected Writings from 1832–1874*, ed. Dorothy Porter Wesley and Constance Porter Uzelac (Baltimore: Black Classic Press, 2002), 581.
38. Ruth Bogin, "'The Battle of Lexington': A Patriotic Ballad by Lemuel Haynes," *William and Mary Quarterly*, 3rd ser., 42, no. 4 (1985): 501, 503.
39. Quoted in Michael Stephenson, *Patriot Battles: How the War of Independence Was Fought* (New York: HarperCollins, 2008), 184.
40. Benjamin Quarles, *The Negro in the American Revolution* (Chapel Hill: University of North Carolina Press, 1996), 10–11.
41. Margaret Elizabeth May, *Brookline in the Revolution*, Publications of the Brookline Historical Publication Society, 1st ser., no. 3 (Brookline, MA: Riverdale Press, 1897), 30.
42. Ruth Bogin, "'Liberty Further Extended': A 1776 Antislavery Manuscript by Lemuel Haynes," *William and Mary Quarterly*, 3rd ser., 40, no. 1 (1983): 92.
43. Boyrereau Brinch, *The Blind African Slave, or Memoirs of Boyrereau Brinch* (St. Albans, VT: Harry Whitney, 1810), 156.
44. Quoted in Sidney Kaplan and Emma Nogrady Kaplan, *The Black Presence in the Era of the American Revolution* (Amherst: University of Massachusetts Press, 1989), 254.
45. Quoted in Robin Blackburn, *The Overthrow of Colonial Slavery, 1776–1848* (New York: Verso, 1988), 112–13.
46. Quoted in Simon Schama, *Rough Crossings: The Slaves, the British, and the American Revolution* (New York: Harper-Collins, 2007), 123.
47. Quoted in Peter A. Dorsey, *Common Bondage: Slavery as Metaphor in Revolutionary America* (Knoxville: University of Tennessee Press, 2009): 131.
48. "Memoirs of the Life of Boston King, a Black Preacher," *Methodist Magazine*, April 1798, 15.
49. Schama, *Rough Crossings*, 127.
50. Quoted in Henry Wiencek, *An Imperfect God: George Washington, His Slaves, and the Creation of America* (New York: Macmillan, 2004), 248.

51. Quoted in Catharine Maria Sedgwick, "Slavery in New England," *Bentley's Miscellany* 34 (1853), 424.
52. Jeremiah Asher, *Incidents in the Life of the Reverend J. Asher* (1850; repr., Freeport, NY: Books for Libraries Press, 1971), 18.
53. "Petition for Freedom to the Massachusetts Council and the House of Representatives" (January 1777), in *Collections of the Massachusetts Historical Society*, 5th ser. (Boston: The Massachusetts Historical Society, 1877), 3:436.

Chapter 5: Slavery and Freedom in the New Republic

1. Benjamin Banneker to Thomas Jefferson, 19 August 1791, reprinted in John H. B. Latrobe, "Memoir of Benjamin Banneker," *African Repository, and Colonial Journal* 21 (November 1845): 330.
2. Ibid.
3. Jefferson to Benjamin Banneker, 30 August 1791, in *The Works of Thomas Jefferson*, ed. Paul Leicester Ford, vol. 6 (New York: G. P. Putnam's Sons, 1904), 309–10.
4. Thomas Jefferson, *Notes on the State of Virginia* (London: printed for John Stockdale, 1787), 239.
5. Thomas Jefferson to Joel Barlow, 8 October 1809, in *The Works of Thomas Jefferson*, ed. Paul Leicester Ford, vol. 11 (New York: G. P. Putnam's Sons, 1905), 121.
6. James Madison, speech, Constitutional Convention, June 1787, in *The Debates in the Several State Conventions on the Adoption of the Federal Constitution*, ed. Jonathan Elliott (New York: Lippincott, 1876), 5:162.
7. Quoted in Ira Berlin, *Generations of Captivity: A History of African-American Slaves* (Cambridge: Belknap Press of Harvard University Press, 2003), 151.
8. Charles Ball, *Fifty Years in Chains; or, The Life of an American Slave* (New York: H. Dayton, 1859), 29.
9. Ibid., 430.
10. Quoted in Thomas J. Fleming, *The Louisiana Purchase* (Hoboken, NJ: John Wiley and Sons, 2003), 110.
11. Quoted in Seth Rockman, *Scraping By: Wage Labor, Slavery, and Survival in Early Baltimore* (Baltimore: Johns Hopkins University Press, 2008), 36.
12. "Proceedings of the Virginia Legislature on the Subject of African Colonization," *African Repository, and Colonial Journal* 8, no. 4 (June 1832): 104.
13. Douglas R. Egerton, *Gabriel's Rebellion: The Virginia Slave Conspiracies of 1800 and 1802* (Chapel Hill: University of North Carolina Press, 1993), 164.
14. Quoted in Ira Berlin, *Slaves without Masters: The Free Negro in the Antebellum South* (New York: New Press, 2007), 89.
15. Revisors of the Laws, Virginia, *Draughts of Such Bills as Have Been Prepared by the Revisors of the Laws* (Richmond, VA: Ritchie, Trueheart & Du-Val, and Shepherd & Pollard, 1817), 263.
16. Berlin, *Slaves without Masters*, 147.
17. Sojourner Truth, *Narrative of Sojourner Truth*, ed. Olive Gilbert (Boston: printed for the author, 1850), 39.
18. Ibid., 43.
19. "Preamble of the Free African Society," in William Douglass, *Annals of the First African Church, in the United States of America, Now Styled the African Episcopal Church of St. Thomas, Philadelphia* (Philadelphia: King & Baird, 1862), 15.
20. Quoted in Richard Newman, *Freedom's Prophet: Bishop Richard Allen, the AME Church, and the Black Founding Fathers* (New York: New York University Press, 2008), 64.
21. Ibid., 67.
22. Jarena Lee, *Religious Experience and Journal of Mrs. Jarena Lee, Giving an Account of her Call to Preach the Gospel* (Philadelphia: Printed and published for the author, 1849).
23. Hosea Easton, *A Treatise on the Intellectual Character, and Civil and Political Condition of the Colored People of the U. States* (Boston: Isaac Knapp, 1837), 41, 43.
24. New York Manumission Society, *An Address to the Parents and Guardians of the Children Belonging to the New York African Free School, by the Trustees of the Institution* (New York: Samuel Wood and Sons, 1818), 20–21.
25. Quoted in Charles C. Andrews, *The History of the New-York African Free-Schools* (New York: Mahlon Day, 1830), 132.
26. *New York Evening Post*, September 22, 1826.
27. Quoted in *Proceedings of the One Hundredth Anniversary of the Granting of Warrant 459 to African Lodge, at Boston* (Boston: Franklin Press, 1885), 15.
28. *Annals of the Congress of the United States*, 4th Cong., 2nd sess. [March 1795–March 1797] (Washington, DC: Gales and Seaton, 1849), 6:2015–18.
29. Absalom Jones and Richard Allen, *A Narrative of the Proceedings of the Black People, During the Late Awful Calamity in Philadelphia, in the Year 1793: And a Refutation of Some Censures, Thrown upon Them in Some Late Publications* (Philadelphia: printed for the authors by William W. Woodward, 1794), 25.
30. Militia Act of 1792, May 8, 1792, United States Congress, *United States Statutes at Large*, v.1 Public Acts of the Second Congress, First Session, Chapter 33, https://www.loc.gov/law/help/statutes-at-large/2nd-congress/session-1/c2s1ch33.pdf.
31. Gerald T. Altoff, *Amongst My Best Men: African-Americans and the War of 1812* (Put-in-Bay, OH: Perry Group, 1996), 23, 36, 40.
32. Prince Hall and African Lodge No. 1, "Petition for Repatriation to Africa" (1787), in *The African American Experience: Black History and Culture through Speeches, Letters, Editorials, Poems, Songs, and Stories*, ed. Kai Wright (New York: Black Dog, 2009), 101.
33. Paul Cuffe to Nathan G. M. Senter, 1 March 1814, in *Captain Paul Cuffe's Logs and Letters, 1808–1817: A Black Quaker's "Voice from within the Veil,"* ed. Rosalind Cobb Wiggins (Washington, DC: Howard University Press, 1996), 276.
34. Quoted in Julie Winch, *A Gentleman of Color: The Life of James Forten* (New York: Oxford University Press, 2002), 188.
35. Prince Hall and African Lodge No. 1, "Petition for Repatriation to Africa," 101.

36. Resolution of Assembled Free Blacks, Bethel AME Church, Philadelphia, January 15, 1817, reprinted in William Lloyd Garrison, *Thoughts on African Colonization*, Part II (Boston: Garrison and Knapp, 1832), 9–10.
37. James Forten to Paul Cuffe, 25 January 1817, Cuffe Papers, quoted in Winch, *A Gentleman of Color*, 191.
38. American Convention for Promoting the Abolition of Slavery and Improving the Condition of the African Race, *Minutes of the Proceedings of a Special Meeting of the Fifteenth American Convention for Promoting the Abolition of Slavery and Improving the Condition of the African Race, Assembled at Philadelphia on the Tenth Day of December, 1818* (Philadelphia: printed for the convention by Hall & Atkinson, 1818), 70.

Chapter 6: Black Life in the Slave South

1. William Wells Brown, *Narrative of William W. Brown, a Fugitive Slave. Written by Himself*, 2nd ed. (Boston: Anti-Slavery Office, 1848), 15.
2. Ibid., 20.
3. Ibid., 44, 61.
4. Thomas Jefferson to John Holmes, 22 April 1820, in *Thomas Jefferson: Writings*, ed. Merrill D. Peterson (New York: Library of America, 1984), 1433–35.
5. Lyman Abbott, *Reminiscences* (New York: Houghton Mifflin, 1915), 102.
6. Interview with Charity Bowery, in *Slave Testimony: Two Centuries of Letters, Speeches, Interviews, and Autobiographies*, ed. John W. Blassingame (Baton Rouge: LSU Press, 1977), 265.
7. William Johnson, quoted in Benjamin Drew, ed., *Refugees from Slavery* (Mineola, NY: Dover, 2004), 19.
8. Interview with Carrie E. Davis, in *The WPA Oklahoma Slave Narratives*, ed. T. Lindsay Baker and Julie P. Baker (Norman: University of Oklahoma Press, 1996), 102.
9. Robert James Turnbull [Brutus], *The Crisis: or, Essays on the Usurpations of the Federal Government*, no. 26 (Charleston, SC: A. E. Miller, 1827), 133.
10. Quoted in Douglas R. Egerton, *He Shall Go Out Free: The Lives of Denmark Vesey* (Madison, WI: Madison House, 1999), 198.
11. Thomas Wentworth Higginson, "Denmark Vesey," *Atlantic*, June 1861, 735.
12. David Walker, *Walker's Appeal, in Four Articles; Together with a Preamble, to the Coloured Citizens of the World, but in Particular, and Very Expressly, to Those of the United States of America, Written in Boston, State of Massachusetts, September 28, 1829*, rev. ed (Boston: published by the author, 1830), 5.
13. Ibid., 41.
14. Quoted ibid., 63.
15. Ibid., 19–20, 35.
16. William Lloyd Garrison, "Walker's Appeal," *Liberator*, January 8, 1831, 1; William Lloyd Garrison, "Walker's Pamphlet," *Liberator*, January 29, 1831, 4.
17. Nat Turner, *The Confessions of Nat Turner, the Leader of the Late Insurrection in Southampton, Va.* (Baltimore: Thomas R. Gray, 1831), 10, 11.
18. Both quoted in Kenneth S. Greenberg, ed., *Nat Turner: A Slave Rebellion in History and Memory* (New York: Oxford University Press, 2003), 154, 156.
19. Interview with May Satterfield, in *Weevils in the Wheat: Interviews with Virginia Ex-Slaves*, ed. Charles L. Perdue Jr., Thomas E. Barden, and Robert K. Phillips (Charlottesville: University of Virginia Press, 1976), 244–45; Rosa Barnwell, quoted in Blassingame, *Slave Testimony*, 698; Louisa Gause, quoted in Federal Writers' Project, *Slave Narratives: A Folk History of Slavery in the United States from Interviews with Former Slaves*, vol. 14, *South Carolina Narratives*, part 2 (Washington, DC: 1941), 110.
20. *Cozzins v. Whitacker* (1833), quoted in Ariela Gross, "Pandora's Box: Slave Character on Trial in the Antebellum Deep South," *Yale Journal of Law & the Humanities* 7, no. 2 (1995): 308; James Stirling, *Letters from the Slave States* (London: John W. Parker and Son, 1857), quoted in Robert Vaughan, "Epilogue on Books — English Literature," *British Quarterly Review* 26 (July and October 1857): 517.
21. Frederick Douglass, *Narrative of the Life of Frederick Douglass, an American Slave, Written by Himself* (Boston: Anti-Slavery Office, 1845), 63, 71, 73.
22. *John v. State*, 16 GA 203 (1854).
23. Quoted in Sally E. Hadden, *Slave Patrols: Law and Violence in Virginia and the Carolinas* (Cambridge: Harvard University Press, 2001), 120.
24. Solomon Northup, *Twelve Years a Slave: Narrative of Solomon Northup, a Citizen of New-York, Kidnapped in Washington City in 1841, and Rescued in 1853* (Auburn, NY: Derby and Miller, 1853), 230.
25. Quoted in Deborah Gray White, *Ar'n't I a Woman? Female Slaves in the Plantation South*, rev. ed. (New York: Norton, 1999), 72.
26. Interview with Anna Morgan, in *The American Slave: A Composite Autobiography, North Carolina and South Carolina Narratives*, ed. George P. Rawick, suppl., 1st ser., vol. 11, part 1 (Westport, CT: Greenwood Press, 1978), 149.
27. Interview with Wes Brady, in *The American Slave: A Composite Autobiography, Texas Narratives*, ed. George P. Rawick, suppl., 2nd ser., vol. 2, part 1 (Westport, CT: Greenwood Press, 1979), 401.
28. Interview with Mose Hursey, in *The American Slave: A Composite Autobiography, Texas Narratives*, ed. George P. Rawick, suppl., 2nd ser., vol. 4, part 2 (Westport, CT: Greenwood Press, 1979), 170–71.
29. Frederick Douglass, *My Bondage and My Freedom* (New York: Miller, Orton & Mulligan, 1855), 35.
30. Quoted in Richard Follett, "Heat, Sex, and Sugar: Pregnancy and Childbearing in the Slave Quarters," *Journal of Family History* 28 (October 2003): 528.
31. White, *Ar'n't I a Woman?*, 112.

32. Paul D. Escott, *Slavery Remembered* (Chapel Hill: University of North Carolina Press, 1979), 43.
33. William Goodell, *The American Slave Code in Theory and Practice* (New York: American and Foreign Anti-Slavery Society, 1853), 105.
34. Quoted in Rebecca J. Fraser, *Courtship and Love among the Enslaved in North Carolina* (Jackson: University Press of Mississippi, 2007), 89.
35. Quoted in Thomas E. Will, "Weddings on Contested Grounds: Slave Marriage in the Antebellum South," *Historian* 62, no. 1 (1999): 111.
36. Ibid., 110.
37. Interview with Louisa Everett, in *Far More Terrible for Women: Personal Accounts of Women in Slavery*, ed. Patrick Neal Minges (Winston-Salem, NC: John F. Blair, 2006), 16–17.
38. Quoted in White, *Ar'n't I a Woman?*, 102.
39. Harriet Ann Jacobs, *Incidents in the Life of a Slave Girl* (Boston: printed for the author, 1861), 58.
40. Quoted in Edward D. C. Campbell Jr. and Kim S. Rice, *Before Freedom Came: African-American Life in the Antebellum South* (Charlottesville: University of Virginia Press, 1997), 62.
41. Emily West, "The Debate on the Strength of Slave Families: South Carolina and the Importance of Cross-Plantation Marriages," *Journal of American Studies* 33, no. 2 (1999): 225.
42. Interview with Millie Barbie, in *The American Slave: A Composite Autobiography, South Carolina Narratives*, ed. George P. Rawick, vol. 2, part 1 (Westport, CT: Greenwood Press, 1973), 39.
43. Henry Bibb, *Narrative of the Life and Adventures of Henry Bibb, an American Slave, Written by Himself* (New York: published by the author, 1849), 42.
44. Ibid., 43, 44.
45. Interview with Julia Woodberry, in *The American Slave: A Composite Autobiography, South Carolina Narratives*, ed. George P. Rawick, 1st ser., vol. 3, part 4 (Westport, CT: Greenwood Press, 1972), 95–96.
46. Quoted in Ira Berlin, *The Making of African America: The Four Great Migrations* (New York: Penguin, 2010), 119.
47. This phrase is drawn from the title of Ira Berlin's *Generations of Captivity: A History of African-American Slaves* (Cambridge: Belknap Press of Harvard University Press, 2004).
48. Anthony G. Barthelemy, ed., *Collected Black Women's Narratives* (New York: Oxford University Press, 1990), xlvii.

Chapter 7: The Northern Black Freedom Struggle and the Coming of the Civil War

1. *North Star*, March 23, 1849, quoted in Jane Rhodes, *Mary Ann Shadd Cary: The Black Press and Protest in the Nineteenth Century* (Bloomington: Indiana University Press, 1998), 21.
2. *Frederick Douglass' Paper*, November 9, 1855, quoted ibid., 109.
3. Alexis de Tocqueville, *Democracy in America*, ed. Phillips Bradley (New York: Knopf, 1945), 1:359–60.
4. Quoted in Patrick Rael, *Black Identity and Black Protest in the Antebellum North* (Chapel Hill: University of North Carolina Press, 2002), 262.
5. George Wilson Pierson, *Tocqueville and Beaumont in America* (New York: Oxford University Press, 1938), 565.
6. James O. Horton and Lois E. Horton, *Black Bostonians: Family Life and Community Struggle in the Antebellum North* (New York: Holmes & Meier, 1979), 2; Ira Berlin, *Slaves without Masters: The Free Negro in the Antebellum South* (New York: New Press, 2007), 176.
7. George Foster, "Philadelphia in Slices" (1848–1849), quoted in Leonard P. Curry, *The Free Black in Urban America, 1800–1850: The Shadow of the Dream* (Chicago: University of Chicago Press, 1986), 49; George Foster, "New York in Slices" (1849), quoted ibid., 78.
8. Julie Winch, *A Gentleman of Color: The Life of James Forten* (New York: Oxford University Press, 2003), 84–85.
9. Leslie M. Alexander, *African or American? Black Identity and Political Activism in New York City, 1784–1861* (Urbana: University of Illinois Press, 2008), 158.
10. Martin R. Delany, *The Condition, Elevation, Emigration, and Destiny of the Colored People of the United States* (1852; repr., New York: Arno Press, 1969), 45–46.
11. *Minutes and Proceedings of the Second Annual Convention, for the Improvement of the Free People of Color in These United States* (Philadelphia: published by order of the convention, 1832), 34.
12. *Proceedings of the National Convention of Colored People and Their Friends, Held in Troy, N.Y., on the 6th, 7th, 8th, and 9th October, 1847*, quoted in Leon Litwack, *North of Slavery: The Negro in the Free States, 1790–1860* (Chicago: University of Chicago Press, 1961), 135.
13. *Maria W. Stewart, America's First Black Woman Political Writer: Essays and Speeches*, ed. Marilyn Richardson (Bloomington: Indiana University Press, 1987), 21, 35, 59–60.
14. Ibid., 46.
15. Lewis Woodson [Augustine], "Moral Work for Colored Men," *Colored American*, August 12, 1837.
16. Howard H. Bell, "The American Moral Reform Society, 1836–1841," *Journal of Negro Education* 27, no. 1 (Winter 1958): 34–40; *Minutes and Proceedings of the First Annual Meeting of the American Moral Reform Society* (1837), quoted in Litwack, *North of Slavery*, 238.
17. *Report of the Proceedings of the Colored National Convention, Held at Cleveland, Ohio, on Wednesday, September 6, 1848* (Rochester, NY: John Dick, 1848), 18.
18. *Freedom's Journal*, March 16, 1827.
19. Quoted in Ronald L. F. Davis and B. J. Krekorian, "The Black Press in Antebellum America," *Slavery in America*, http://www.slaveryinamerica.org/history/hs_es_press.htm.
20. *Frederick Douglass' Paper*, March 9, 1855, quoted in Benjamin Quarles, *Black Abolitionists* (New York: Oxford University Press, 1969), 86.

21. Despite several early positive reviews, Jacobs's text languished in obscurity, its authenticity questioned, until Jean Fagan Yellin convincingly demonstrated its authenticity in the 1980s. Jean Fagan Yellin, *Harriet Jacobs: A Life* (New York: Basic Civitas Books, 2004).
22. Quoted in Nell Irvin Painter, *Sojourner Truth: A Life, a Symbol* (New York: Norton, 1996), 160.
23. Quoted ibid., 125.
24. Ibid.
25. "Legal Rights Vindicated," *Frederick Douglass' Paper*, March 2, 1855. Cited in Elizabeth Stordeur Pryor, *Colored Travelers: Mobility and the Fight for Citizenship before the Civil War* (Chapel Hill: University of North Carolina Press, 2016), 98.
26. Charles Sumner, *Argument . . . against the Constitutionality of Separate Colored Schools, in the Case of Sarah C. Roberts vs. the City of Boston. Before the Supreme Court of Mass., Dec. 4, 1849*, quoted in Litwack, *North of Slavery*, 147.
27. Quoted in Quarles, *Black Abolitionists*, 23.
28. Winch, *A Gentleman of Color*, 241–42.
29. Lois E. Horton, "Kidnapping and Resistance: Antislavery Direct Action in the 1850s," in *Passages to Freedom: The Underground Railroad in History and Memory*, ed. David W. Blight (Washington, DC: Smithsonian Books, 2004), 166.
30. Quoted in Milton C. Sernett, "Jermain Wesley Loguen," in *African American Lives*, ed. Henry Louis Gates Jr. and Evelyn Brooks Higginbotham (New York: Oxford University Press, 2004), 542.
31. This information is drawn largely from Sarah H. Bradford's nineteenth-century biography *Harriet Tubman: The Moses of Her People* (New York: printed for the author by G. R. Lockwood and Son, 1886). Recently, however, scholars have challenged several aspects of this text. For an overview of the debate, see Milton Sernett, *Harriet Tubman: Myth, Memory, and History* (Durham, NC: Duke University Press, 2007), 55–66.
32. Quoted in Quarles, *Black Abolitionists*, 212.
33. Taney, C. J., Opinion of the Court, *Scott v. Sandford* 60 U.S. 393 (1857).
34. All quoted in Quarles, *Black Abolitionists*, 231.
35. Martin R. Delany, *Official Report of the Niger Valley Exploring Party*, in *Search for a Place: Black Separatism and Africa*, ed. Howard H. Bell (1861; repr., Ann Arbor: University of Michigan Press, 1969), 35.
36. Quoted in Quarles, *Black Abolitionists*, 231.
37. Quoted ibid., 240, 241.
38. Quoted in David S. Reynolds, *John Brown, Abolitionist: The Man Who Killed Slavery, Sparked the Civil War, and Seeded Civil Rights* (New York: Knopf, 2005), 395.
39. "The Destiny of Colored Americans," *North Star*, November 16, 1849.

Chapter 8: Freedom Rising: The Civil War

1. *New York Times*, October 3, 1862.
2. South Carolina Ordinance of Secession, December 20, 1860, in *Documents of American History*, ed. Henry Steele Commager and Milton Cantor (Englewood Cliffs, NJ: Prentice Hall, 1988), 1:372; Declaration of the Immediate Causes Which Induce and Justify the Secession of South Carolina from the Federal Union, December 24, 1860, in ibid., 1:372–74.
3. Abraham Lincoln, First Inaugural Address, March 4, 1861, in ibid., 385–88.
4. Quoted in Roy C. Basler, ed., *The Collected Works of Abraham Lincoln* (New Brunswick: Rutgers University Press, 1953), 4:331–32.
5. Letter from Hannibal Guards to General James S. Negley, *Pittsburgh Gazette*, April 18, 1861, quoted in James M. McPherson, *The Negro's Civil War: How American Negroes Felt and Acted during the War for the Union* (New York: Pantheon, 1965), 19–20.
6. Benjamin Quarles, *The Negro in the Civil War* (Boston: Little, Brown, 1953), 28.
7. Peter H. Clark, *The Black Brigade of Cincinnati* (Cincinnati, 1864), 4–5.
8. Quoted in Basler, *Collected Works of Abraham Lincoln*, 5:423.
9. James M. McPherson, *Battle Cry of Freedom: The Civil War Era* (New York: Oxford University Press, 1988), 563.
10. *Anglo-African Magazine*, April 20–27, 1861.
11. *Douglass' Monthly*, May 1861, 45–52.
12. Quoted in Basler, *Collected Works of Abraham Lincoln*, 5:388–89.
13. Quoted in Willie Lee Rose, *Rehearsal for Reconstruction: The Port Royal Experiment* (Indianapolis: Bobbs-Merrill, 1964), xiii.
14. Second Confiscation Act, July 17, 1862, Freedmen and Southern Society Project, http://www.history.umd.edu/Freedmen/conact2.htm.
15. Ira Berlin et al., eds., *Freedom: A Documentary History of Emancipation, 1861–1867*, 1st ser., vol. 1, *The Destruction of Slavery* (New York: Cambridge University Press, 1985), 103–14, 187–99.
16. Henry M. Turner, *The Negro in Slavery, War and Peace* (Philadelphia: A.M.E. Book Concern, 1913), 6–7.
17. Charlotte Forten, "Life on the Sea Islands," *Atlantic Monthly*, June 1864, 4.
18. Interview with Felix Haywood, in *The American Slave: A Composite Autobiography, Texas Narratives*, ed. George P. Rawick, 2nd ser., vol. 4, part 2 (Westport, CT: Greenwood Press, 1972–1973), 131.
19. *Liberator*, May 22, 1863.
20. *Douglass' Monthly*, August 1863. Douglass said this in an address to a meeting for the promotion of colored enlistments on July 6, 1863.
21. William Wells Brown, *The Negro in the American Rebellion* (Boston: Lee and Shepard, 1867), 172.
22. Charles A. Dana, *Recollections of the Civil War* (New York: D. Appleton, 1899), 86.
23. McPherson, *Battle Cry of Freedom*, 634.
24. Quoted ibid., 638.
25. Lewis Douglass to Amelia Loguen, 20 July 1863, quoted in McPherson, *The Negro's Civil War*, 190–91.

26. *New York Tribune*, September 8, 1865.
27. Abraham Lincoln, Gettysburg Address, November 19, 1863, in Commager and Cantor, *Documents of American History*, 1:428–29.
28. Resolutions of the Illinois State Legislature, January 7, 1863, in ibid., 1:421–22. See also New Jersey Peace Resolutions, March 18, 1863, in ibid., 1:427–28, and McPherson, *Battle Cry of Freedom*, 595–96.
29. *Christian Recorder*, July 25, 1863, quoted in McPherson, *The Negro's Civil War*, 74.
30. J. W. C. Pennington, "The Position and Duties of the Colored People," cited in Philip S. Foner and Robert James Branham, eds., *Lift Every Voice: African American Oratory, 1787–1900* (Tuscaloosa: University of Alabama Press, 1998), 397–407.
31. Abraham Lincoln, Proclamation of Amnesty and Reconstruction, December 8, 1863, in Commager and Cantor, *Documents of American History*, 1:429–31.
32. Elizabeth Botume, *First Days amongst the Contrabands* (New York: Lee and Shepard, 1893; repr., New York: Arno Press, 1968), 15.
33. *Second Annual Report of the Freedmen and Soldiers Relief Association (Late Contraband Relief Association), Organized August 12, 1862*, quoted in McPherson, *The Negro's Civil War*, 139.
34. Abraham Lincoln, Second Inaugural Address, March 4, 1865, in Commager and Cantor, *Documents of American History*, 1:442–43.
35. For information on the Freedmen's Bureau, see Mary Farmer-Kaiser, *Freedwomen and the Freedmen's Bureau: Race, Gender, and Public Policy in the Age of Emancipation* (New York: Fordham University Press, 2010).
36. Interview with Richard Carruthers, in *The American Slave: A Composite Autobiography, Texas Narratives*, ed. George P. Rawick, vol. 4, part 1 (Westport, CT: Greenwood Press, 1972–1973), 200; Haywood interview, in ibid., 133; interview with Virginia woman, in Virginia Writers Project, *The Negro in Virginia* (New York: Hastings House, 1940), 210.
37. Interview with a former Mississippi slave, in *The American Slave: A Composite Autobiography, Oklahoma and Mississippi Narratives*, ed. George P. Rawick, vol. 7 (Westport, CT: Greenwood Press, 1971), 94; interview with a former South Carolina slave, in *The American Slave: A Composite Autobiography, South Carolina Narratives*, ed. George P. Rawick, vols. 2–3 (Westport, CT: Greenwood Press, 1972), 54.
38. Interview with Aleck Trimble, in *The American Slave: A Composite Autobiography, Texas Narratives*, ed. George P. Rawick, vol. 5, part 4 (Westport, CT: Greenwood Press, 1972), 109; Texas woman, quoted in Edward D. C. Campbell Jr., with Kym S. Rice, eds., *Before Freedom Came: African-American Life in the Antebellum South* (Charlottesville: University of Virginia Press, 1991), xiii.
39. Thomas Morris Chester, *Black Civil War Correspondent: His Dispatches from the Virginia Front*, ed. R. J. M. Blackett (Baton Rouge: LSU Press, 1989), 46. See also Hugh Davis, *"We Will Be Satisfied with Nothing Less": The African American Struggle for Equal Rights in the North during Reconstruction* (Ithaca: Cornell University Press, 2011), 17–26.
40. Quoted in John Hope Franklin, "The Emancipation Proclamation: An Act of Justice," *Prologue* 25, no. 2 (Summer 1993): 3.
41. Davis, *"We Will Be Satisfied,"* 11–12.
42. Quoted in Basler, *Collected Works of Abraham Lincoln*, 5:370–75.
43. William Kloss and Doreen Bolger, *Art in the White House: A Nation's Pride*, 2nd ed. (Washington, DC: White House Historical Association, 2008), 158–59, 302–3.
44. Kirk Savage, *Standing Soldiers, Kneeling Slaves: Race, War, and Monument in Nineteenth-Century America* (Princeton: Princeton University Press, 1997), 90.
45. Aaron Lloyd, "Statue of Limitations: Why Does D.C. Celebrate Emancipation in Front of a Statue That Celebrates 19th-Century Racism?" *Washington City Paper*, April 28, 2000; John W. Cromwell, quoted in Freeman H. M. Murray, *Emancipation and the Freed in American Sculpture: A Study in Interpretation* (Washington, DC: published by the author, 1916), 199.

Chapter 9: Reconstruction: The Making and Unmaking of a Revolution

1. Jourdon Anderson to Colonel P. H. Anderson, 7 August 1865, quoted in Leon F. Litwack, *Been in the Storm So Long: The Aftermath of Slavery* (New York: Knopf, 1979), 333–35.
2. Quoted ibid., 230.
3. Provost Marshal at Sedalia, Missouri, to the Superintendent of the Organization of Missouri Black Troops, 21 March 1864, in *Freedom: A Documentary History of Emancipation, 1861–1867*, ed. Ira Berlin et al., 1st ser., vol. 1, *The Destruction of Slavery* (New York: Cambridge University Press, 1985), 481–82.
4. Litwack, *Been in the Storm So Long*, 230.
5. Ibid., 229.
6. Tera Hunter, *To 'Joy My Freedom: Southern Black Women's Lives and Labors after the Civil War* (Cambridge: Harvard University Press, 1997), 39.
7. Quoted in Henry L. Swint, ed., *Dear Ones at Home: Letters from Contraband Camps* (Nashville: Vanderbilt University Press, 1966), 242–43.
8. Interview, in *The American Slave: A Composite Autobiography, North Carolina Narratives*, ed. George P. Rawick, vol. 14, part 1 (Westport, CT: Greenwood Press, 1972–1973), 248–52.
9. Interview, in *The American Slave: A Composite Autobiography, Unwritten History of Slavery*, ed. George P. Rawick, vol. 18 (Westport, CT: Greenwood Press, 1972), 124.
10. Interview, in *The American Slave: A Composite Autobiography, Arkansas Narratives*, ed. George P. Rawick, vol. 8, part 2 (Westport, CT: Greenwood Press, 1972), 52.
11. Matthew Gilbert, "Colored Churches: An Experiment," quoted in William E. Montgomery, *Under Their Own Vine and Fig Tree: The African-American Church in the South, 1865–1900* (Baton Rouge: LSU Press, 1993), 54.

12. C. Eric Lincoln and Lawrence H. Mamiya, *The Black Church in the African American Experience* (Durham: Duke University Press, 1990), 25, 66.
13. Leslie A. Schwalm, *Emancipation's Diaspora: Race and Reconstruction in the Upper Midwest* (Chapel Hill: University of North Carolina Press, 2009), 144.
14. Quoted in Carter G. Woodson, *The History of the Negro Church* (Washington, DC: Associated Publishers, 1921), 225.
15. Quoted in Reginald F. Hildebrand, *The Times Were Strange and Stirring: Methodist Preachers and the Crisis of Emancipation* (Durham: Duke University Press, 1995), 65.
16. Quoted in Steven Hahn et al., eds., *Freedom: A Documentary History of Emancipation, 1861–1867*, 3rd ser., vol. 1, *Land and Labor, 1865* (Chapel Hill: University of North Carolina Press, 2008), 396.
17. Quoted in Manuel Gottlieb, "The Land Question in Georgia during Reconstruction," *Science & Society* 3, no. 3 (1939): 364.
18. Quoted in Hahn, *Freedom*, 51–52.
19. Quoted in Litwack, *Been in the Storm So Long*, 366.
20. Cited in Henry Lewis Gates Jr. and Nellie Y. McKay, *The Norton Anthology of African Literature* (New York: Norton), 418–419.
21. *The 2003 National Assessment of Adult Literacy*, Institute of Education Sciences, National Center for Education Statistics, U.S. Department of Education.
22. Quoted in Adam Fairclough, *A Class of Their Own: Black Teachers in the Segregated South* (Cambridge: Belknap Press of Harvard University Press, 2007), 42.
23. Quoted in Clarence E. Walker, *A Rock in a Weary Land: The African Methodist Episcopal Church during the Civil War and Reconstruction* (Baton Rouge: LSU Press, 1982), 51.
24. Quoted in Fairclough, *A Class of Their Own*, 69.
25. Quoted in "Fisk's Storied Past," Fisk University, http://www.fisk.edu/AboutFisk/HistoryOfFisk.aspx.
26. Quoted in "History," Hampton University, http://www.hamptonu.edu/about/history.cfm.
27. *Louisianian*, May 10, 1879, quoted in James D. Anderson, *The Education of Blacks in the South, 1860–1935* (Chapel Hill: University of North Carolina Press, 1988), 64.
28. Samuel Thomas to O. O. Howard, 6 September 1865, quoted in Eric Foner, *Reconstruction: America's Unfinished Revolution, 1863–1877* (New York: Harper & Row, 1988), 150.
29. W. E. B. Du Bois, *Black Reconstruction in America: An Essay toward a History of the Part Which Black Folk Played in the Attempt to Reconstruct Democracy in America, 1860–1880* (1935; repr., New York: Atheneum, 1970), 708. See also W. E. B. Du Bois, "Reconstruction and Its Benefits," *American Historical Review* 15, no. 4 (July 1910): 781–99.
30. Eric Foner, *Freedom's Lawmakers: A Directory of Black Officeholders during Reconstruction*, rev. ed. (Baton Rouge: LSU Press, 1993), xi. This book includes entries for the 1,500 officials for whom Foner found documentation. The number of black officeholders cited in the text includes those for whom documentation was lacking.
31. Eric Foner, *The Second Founding: How the Civil War and Reconstruction Remade the Constitution* (New York: Norton, 2019), xx.
32. Quoted in James M. McPherson, *Ordeal by Fire: The Civil War and Reconstruction* (New York: Knopf, 1982), 536.
33. Emanuel Fortune, quoted in Foner, *Reconstruction*, 426; Jack Dupree story, cited ibid., 426.
34. *Christian Recorder*, November 8, 1883, quoted in Henry M. Turner, "The Barbarous Decision of the Supreme Court," in *Respect Black: The Writings and Speeches of Henry McNeal Turner*, ed. Edwin Redkey (New York: Arno Press, 1971), 60.
35. Schwalm, *Emancipation's Diaspora*, 46.
36. Quoted in Quintard Taylor, *In Search of the Racial Frontier: African Americans in the American West, 1528–1990* (New York: Norton, 1998), 164.
37. Quoted in Nell Irvin Painter, *Exodusters: Black Migration to Kansas after Reconstruction* (New York: Knopf, 1977), 158.
38. *Nicodemus Western Cyclone*, March 24, 1887, quoted in Taylor, *In Search of the Racial Frontier*, 140.
39. "Go to Kansas": History and Culture, Nicodemus National Historic Site, National Park Service, http://www.nps.gov/nico/index.htm.
40. Quoted in Painter, *Exodusters*, 4.
41. Taylor, *In Search of the Racial Frontier*, 138.
42. "Caroline Le Count," Pennsylvania Civil War 150, http://www.pacivilwar150.com/people/africanamericans/Story.aspx?id=1.
43. Quoted in Hugh Davis, *"We Will Be Satisfied with Nothing Less": The African American Struggle for Equal Rights in the North during Reconstruction* (Ithaca: Cornell University Press, 2011), 78.
44. Davis, *"We Will Be Satisfied,"* 95.
45. Foner, *Reconstruction*, 448.
46. Frances Ellen Watkins Harper, "We Are All Bound Up Together," speech, Eleventh National Women's Rights Convention, New York, May 1866, http://www.blackpast.org/?q=1866-frances-ellen-watkins-harper-we-are-all-bound-together-0. In this speech, Harper describes her humiliation at not being allowed to ride Philadelphia's streetcars.
47. Frederick Douglass, *Proceedings of the Republican National Convention, Held at Cincinnati, Ohio . . . June 14, 15, and 16, 1876*, http://quod.lib.umich.edu/cgi/t/text/text-idx?c=moa&cc=moa&q1=republican%20national%20convention&view=text&rgn=main&idno=AEW7097.0001.001.
48. Quoted in August Meier, *Negro Thought in America, 1880–1915: Racial Ideologies in the Age of Booker T. Washington* (Ann Arbor: University of Michigan Press, 1963), 69.

Chapter 10: Black Life and Culture during the Nadir

1. Ida B. Wells, *Crusade for Justice: The Autobiography of Ida B. Wells*, ed. Alfreda Duster (Chicago: University of Chicago Press, 1970), 19.

2. Ibid., 19.
3. Mia Bay, *To Tell the Truth Freely: The Life of Ida B. Wells* (New York: Hill and Wang, 2009), 76, 79.
4. Quoted in *Plessy v. Ferguson: A Brief History with Documents*, ed. Brook Thomas (Boston: Bedford/St. Martin's, 1997), 41.
5. *Plessy v. Ferguson*, 163 U.S. 537 (1896), 3, 7.
6. Quoted in Phillips Verner Bradford and Harvey Blume, *Ota Benga: The Pygmy in the Zoo* (New York: St. Martin's Press, 1992), 183.
7. Quoted in Christopher Waldrep, ed., *Lynching in America: A History in Documents* (New York: New York University Press, 2006), 186.
8. Ray Stannard Baker, *Following the Color Line: American Negro Citizenship in the Progressive Era* (1908; repr., New York: Harper & Row, 1964), 175–76.
9. Wells, *Crusade for Justice*, 47–52; Bay, *To Tell the Truth Freely*, 82–85.
10. The pamphlet, titled *The Reason Why the Colored American Is Not in the World's Columbian Exposition*, is available online at http://digital.library.upenn.edu/women/wells/exposition/exposition.html. See also Bay, *To Tell the Truth Freely*, 151–68.
11. Quoted in Bay, *To Tell the Truth Freely*, 222.
12. Evelyn Brooks Higginbotham, *Righteous Discontent: The Women's Movement in the Black Baptist Church*, 1880–1920 (Cambridge: Harvard University Press, 1993), 186–87.
13. Fannie Barrier Williams, "The Club Movement among Colored Women of America" (1904), in Jane Dailey, *The Age of Jim Crow* (New York: Norton, 2009), 106, 107. On uplift generally, see Kevin K. Gaines, *Uplifting the Race: Black Leadership, Politics, and Culture in the Twentieth Century* (Chapel Hill: University of North Carolina Press, 1996).
14. Bay, *To Tell the Truth Freely*, 48–49.
15. Martha Robb Montgomery, quoted in Neil R. McMillen, *Dark Journey: Black Mississippians in the Age of Jim Crow* (Urbana: University of Illinois Press, 1989), 129.
16. Quoted in Leon Litwack, *Trouble in Mind: Black Southerners in the Age of Jim Crow* (New York: Knopf, 1998), 126.
17. Quoted in Charles L. Perdue Jr., Thomas E. Barden, and Robert K. Phillips, eds., *Weevils in the Wheat: Interviews with Virginia Ex-slaves* (Charlottesville: University of Virginia Press, 1976), 53.
18. Quoted in W. E. B. Du Bois, *The Souls of Black Folk*, in *Three Negro Classics* (1903; repr., New York: Avon, 1965), 312.
19. W. E. B. Du Bois, "The Economic Revolution in the South," in *The Negro in the South: His Economic Progress in Relation to His Moral and Religious Development* (1907; repr., New York: Citadel Press, 1970), 99, 100.
20. *Souvenir Views: Negro Enterprises and Residences, Richmond, Va.* (Richmond: D. A. Ferguson, 1907), available online at American Memory, Library of Congress.
21. *Richmond Planet*, April 8, 1905.
22. *Richmond Planet*, July 16, 1910.
23. Quoted in Geoffrey C. Ward, *Unforgivable Blackness: The Rise and Fall of Jack Johnson* (New York: Vintage, 2006), 235.
24. W. E. B. Du Bois, "The Upbuilding of Black Durham: The Success of the Negroes and Their Value to a Tolerant and Helpful Southern City," *World's Work*, January 1912.
25. Quoted in Karen Sotiropoulos, *Staging Race: Black Performers in Turn of the Century America* (Cambridge: Harvard University Press, 2006), 42.
26. John Rosamond Johnson and James Weldon Johnson, "Lift Every Voice and Sing," in *Negro Year Book: An Annual Encyclopedia of the Negro*, 1918–1919, ed. Monroe N. Work (Tuskegee Institute, AL: Negro Year Book Publishing Company, 1919).
27. William Christopher Handy, *Father of the Blues: An Autobiography*, ed. Arna Bontemps (1955; repr., New York: Da Capo Press, 1991), 75.
28. Wells, *Crusade for Justice*, 53.
29. Quoted in Willard B. Gatewood Jr., comp., *"Smoked Yankees" and the Struggle for Empire: Letters from Negro Soldiers, 1898–1902* (Fayetteville: University of Arkansas Press, 1987), 28. See also "Black Americans in the U.S. Military from the American Revolution to the Korean War: The Spanish American War and the Philippine Insurgency," New York State Military Museum and Veterans Research Center, New York State Division of Military and Naval Affairs, http://dmna.ny.gov/historic/articles/blacksMilitary/BlacksMilitarySpanAm.htm.
30. Quoted in Willard B. Gatewood Jr., *Black Americans and the White Man's Burden, 1898–1903* (Urbana: University of Illinois Press, 1975), 212.
31. Quoted in Marcy Sacks, *Before Harlem: The Black Experience in New York City before World War I* (Philadelphia: University of Pennsylvania Press, 2006), 19–20.
32. Booker T. Washington, *Up from Slavery: An Autobiography*, ed. William L. Andrews (New York: Norton, 1996), 99–100, 101.
33. W. E. B. Du Bois, *The Souls of Black Folk*, ed. David W. Blight and Robert Gooding-Williams (Boston: Bedford/St. Martin's, 1997), 67, 68, 72.
34. W. E. B. Du Bois, "To the Nations of the World," in *W. E. B. Du Bois: A Reader*, ed. David Levering Lewis (New York: Henry Holt, 1995), 639.
35. "Declaration of Principles," in *Black Protest Thought in the Twentieth Century*, ed. August Meier, Elliott Rudwick, and Francis L. Broderick, 2nd ed. (Indianapolis: Bobbs-Merrill, 1971), 62.
36. *Clyatt v. United States*, 197 U.S. 207 (1905).
37. See, for example, Douglas A. Blackmon, *Slavery by Another Name: The Re-enslavement of Black Americans from the Civil War to World War II* (New York: Anchor Books, 2009).
38. "The Lynching at Urbana," *New York Times*, June 6, 1897.

Chapter 11: The New Negro Comes of Age

1. "Additional Letters of Negro Migrants of 1916–1918," comp. Emmett J. Scott, *Journal of Negro History* 4, no. 4 (October 1919): 447.
2. "Letters of Negro Migrants of 1916–1918," comp. Emmett J. Scott, *Journal of Negro History* 4, no. 3 (July 1919): 318.

3. Ibid., 295.
4. Ibid., 319.
5. Ibid., 298.
6. James Grossman, "Chicago and the 'Great Migration,'" *Migration*, Illinois Periodicals Online (IPO) Project, Northern Illinois University Libraries, http://www.lib.niu.edu/1996/iht329633.html.
7. Quoted in Eric Arnesen, "Introduction: The Great American Protest," in *Black Protest and the Great Migration: A Brief History with Documents* (Boston: Bedford/St. Martin's, 2003), 11.
8. Quoted in James R. Grossman, Land of Hope: *Chicago, Black Southerners, and the Great Migration* (Chicago: University of Chicago Press, 1989), 157.
9. Chicago Commission on Race Relations, *The Negro in Chicago: A Study of Race Relations and a Race Riot* (Chicago: University of Chicago Press, 1922), 122.
10. Quoted in Davarian L. Baldwin, *Chicago's New Negroes: Modernity, the Great Migration, and Black Urban Life* (Chapel Hill: University of North Carolina Press, 2007), 64.
11. "Close Ranks," *Crisis 16*, no. 3 (July 1918): 111.
12. Quoted in Arnesen, *Black Protest and the Great Migration*, 20–21.
13. Ibid., 86.
14. Walter White, "Chicago and Its Eight Reasons," *Crisis* 18, no. 6 (1919): 297.
15. Claude McKay, "If We Must Die," in *The Norton Anthology of African American Literature*, ed. Henry Louis Gates Jr. and Nellie Y. McKay (New York: Norton, 1997), 984.
16. A. Philip Randolph and Chandler Owen, "The New Negro — What Is He?" *Messenger* 2 (August 1920): 73–74, in Jeffrey B. Ferguson, *The Harlem Renaissance: A Brief History with Documents* (Boston: Bedford/St. Martin's, 2008), 40–41.
17. James Weldon Johnson, *Black Manhattan* (New York: Knopf, 1930), in Ferguson, *The Harlem Renaissance*, 46, 54.
18. Arthur A. Schomburg, "The Negro Digs Up His Past" (1925), in Gates and McKay, *The Norton Anthology of African American Literature*, 937.
19. Quoted in Claude McKay, *Harlem: Negro Metropolis* (New York: Dutton, 1940), 154, cited in E. David Cronon, ed., *Great Lives Observed: Marcus Garvey* (Englewood Cliffs, NJ: Prentice Hall, 1973), 5.
20. Lawrence W. Levine, "Marcus Garvey and the Politics of Revitalization," in *Black Leaders of the Twentieth Century*, ed. John Hope Franklin and August Meier (Urbana: University of Illinois Press, 1982), 121.
21. Cited in A. Jacques Garvey, *Garvey and Garveyism* (Kingston, Jamaica: United Printers, 1963), 50.
22. W. E. B. Du Bois, "Opinion of W. E. B. Du Bois," *Crisis* 28, no. 1 (May 1924): 8.
23. Alain Locke, "Harlem," *Survey Graphic* 6 (March 1925), reprinted in Ferguson, *The Harlem Renaissance*, 79.
24. Ibid., 80.
25. W. E. B. Du Bois, "Criteria of Negro Art" (1926), in Ferguson, *The Harlem Renaissance*, 167.
26. Langston Hughes, "The Negro Artist and the Racial Mountain" (1926), in Ferguson, *The Harlem Renaissance*, 149, 154.
27. David Levering Lewis, ed., *The Portable Harlem Renaissance Reader* (New York: Viking, 1994), xliii.

Chapter 12: Catastrophe, Recovery, and Renewal

1. Harvard Sitkoff, *A New Deal for Blacks: The Emergence of Civil Rights as a National Issue: The Depression Decade* (New York: Oxford University Press, 2008), 39.
2. "The Patriot and the Partisan," *Pittsburgh Courier*, September 17, 1932.
3. Richard Wright, "Blueprint for Negro Writing," in Jeffrey B. Ferguson, *The Harlem Renaissance: A Brief History with Documents* (Boston: Bedford, 2007), 172, 175.
4. Quoted in Lawrence W. Levine, *Black Culture and Black Consciousness: Afro-American Folk Thought from Slavery to Freedom* (New York: Oxford University Press, 1977), 434.

Chapter 13: Fighting for a Double Victory in the World War II Era

1. Quoted in Yvonne Latty, *We Were There: Voices of African American Veterans, from World War II to the War in Iraq* (New York: Amistad, 2004), 40.
2. Ibid., 41.
3. Quoted in Michael Keith Honey, *Black Workers Remember: An Oral History of Segregation, Unionism, and the Freedom Struggle* (Berkeley: University of California Press, 1999), 101.
4. Ibid., 105.
5. Quoted in Robert B. Edgerton, *Hidden Heroism: Black Soldiers in America's Wars* (Boulder, CO: Westview Press, 2001), 128.
6. Both quoted in Bernard C. Nalty, *Strength for the Fight: A History of Black Americans in the Military* (New York: Free Press, 1986), 139.
7. All quoted in Jack D. Foner, *Blacks and the Military in American History* (New York: Praeger, 1974), 133–38.
8. Ibid., 141.
9. Quoted in Marc Gallicchio, *The African American Encounter with Japan and China: Black Internationalism in Asia, 1895–1945* (Chapel Hill: University of North Carolina Press, 2000), 119.
10. Ibid., 118.
11. Gallicchio, *The African American Encounter*, 122–38.
12. Quoted ibid., 116–17.
13. Foner, *Blacks and the Military*, 148–54.
14. Quoted in Latty, *We Were There*, 20.
15. Nalty, *Strength for the Fight*, 191–92.
16. Edgerton, *Hidden Heroism*, 135–38.
17. Foner, *Blacks and the Military*, 149.
18. Patricia Sullivan, *Days of Hope: Race and Democracy in the New Deal Era* (Chapel Hill: University of North Carolina Press, 1996), 136.
19. Quoted in Foner, *Blacks and the Military*, 154.
20. Quoted in Sullivan, *Days of Hope*, 137.

21. Harvard Sitkoff, "Racial Militancy and Interracial Violence in the Second World War," *Journal of American History* 58, no. 3 (1971): 668–69.
22. Edgerton, *Hidden Heroism*, 134.
23. Foner, *Blacks and the Military*, 157–59.
24. Joanna Bourke, *An Intimate History of Killing: Face-to-Face Killing in Twentieth-Century Warfare* (New York: Basic Books, 1999), 119.
25. Quoted in Edgerton, *Hidden Heroism*, 163.
26. Quoted in Vincent Harding, Robin D. G. Kelley, and Earl Lewis, *We Changed the World: African Americans, 1945–1970* (New York: Oxford University Press, 1997), 28.
27. Ronald Takaki, *Double Victory: A Multicultural History of America in World War II* (Boston: Little, Brown, 2000), 40.
28. Charles D. Chamberlain, *Victory at Home: Manpower and Race in the American South during World War II* (Athens: University of Georgia Press, 2003), 26, 56.
29. Chamberlain, *Victory at Home*, 62, 80–81.
30. Takaki, *Double Victory*, 42–43.
31. Chamberlain, *Victory at Home*, 63–67.
32. Quoted in Donna Jean Murch, *Living for the City: Migration, Education, and the Rise of the Black Panther Party in Oakland, California* (Chapel Hill: University of North Carolina Press, 2010), 15–16.
33. Quintard Taylor, "African American Men in the American West, 1528–1990," *Annals of the American Academy of Political and Social Science* 569 (May 2000): 111–12.
34. Chamberlain, *Victory at Home*, 85–86.
35. Quoted in Takaki, *Double Victory*, 45.
36. Ibid., 45–46.
37. Sitkoff, "Racial Militancy and Interracial Violence," 671.
38. Marilynn Johnson, "Gender, Race, and Rumors," *Gender and History* 10, no. 2 (1998): 256–60.
39. Quoted in Harriet Sigerman, ed., *The Columbia Documentary History of American Women since 1941* (New York: Columbia University Press, 2003), 36.
40. Quoted in Chamberlain, *Victory at Home*, 124.
41. Ibid., 122–23.
42. Sullivan, *Days of Hope*, 162.
43. Quoted in Takaki, *Double Victory*, 51.
44. Nicholson Baker, *Human Smoke: The Beginnings of World War II, the End of Civilization* (New York: Simon & Schuster, 2008), 343.
45. *Crisis* 50, no. 1 (January 1943): 8.
46. Takaki, *Double Victory*, 51.
47. Chamberlain, *Victory at Home*, 138–39.
48. Ibid., 110–14.
49. Quoted in Nancy MacLean, *Freedom Is Not Enough: The Opening of the American Workplace* (Cambridge: Harvard University Press, 2006), 25.
50. Richard M. Dalfiume, "The 'Forgotten Years' of the Negro Revolution," *Journal of American History* 55, no. 1 (1968): 100.
51. *The Black Press: Soldiers without Swords* (South Burlington, VT: California Newsreel, 1998), DVD.
52. Quoted in Steven F. Lawson, *Black Ballots: Voting Rights in the South, 1944–1969* (Lanham, MD: Lexington Books, 1999), 130.
53. Quoted in Harding, Kelley, and Lewis, *We Changed the World*, 26–27.
54. Quoted in Robert Korstad and Nelson Lichtenstein, "Opportunities Found and Lost: Labor, Radicals, and the Early Civil Rights Movement," *Journal of American History* 75, no. 3 (1988): 793.
55. Quoted in Sullivan, *Days of Hope*, 119.
56. Quoted in Patricia Sullivan, "Movement Building during the World War II Era: The NAACP's Legal Insurgency in the South," in *Fog of War: The Second World War and the Civil Rights Movement*, ed. Kevin M. Kruse and Stephen Tuck (New York: Oxford University Press, 2012), 75.
57. Sullivan, *Days of Hope*, 170.
58. Quoted in Takaki, *Double Victory*, 50.
59. Sullivan, *Days of Hope*, 218–19.
60. Darlene Clark Hine, *Black Women in White: Racial Conflict and Cooperation in the Nursing Profession, 1890–1950* (Bloomington: Indiana University Press, 1989), 183–86.
61. Sandra M. Bolzenius, *Glory in Their Spirit: How Four Black Women Took on the Army During World War II* (Urbana: University of Illinois Press, 2018), 3–4, 155.
62. Both quoted in Nalty, *Strength for the Fight*, 242.
63. Karen Brodkin Sacks, "How Did Jews Become White Folks?" in *Race*, ed. Steven Gregory and Roger Sanjek (New Brunswick: Rutgers University Press, 1994), 89–99.
64. Associated Press, "House Committee Urges Army Quit Use of 'Blue' Discharges," *Sarasota Herald Tribune*, January 30, 1946.
65. Hilary Herbold, "Never a Level Playing Field: Blacks and the GI Bill," *Journal of Blacks in Higher Education* 6 (Winter 1994–1995): 104–8.
66. Ira Katznelson, *When Affirmative Action Was White: An Untold History of Racial Inequality in Twentieth-Century America* (New York: Norton, 2005), 113–41.
67. James H. Jones, *Bad Blood: The Tuskegee Syphilis Experiment* (New York: Free Press, 1981), 179.
68. U.S. Army War College, "The Army War College Studies Black Soldiers," HERB: Resources for Teachers, American Social History Project/Center for Media and Learning, accessed August 22, 2015, http://herb.ashp.cuny.edu/items/show/808.
69. "Who Were They?" Tuskegee Airmen National Historical Museum, accessed August 22, 2015, http://www.tuskegeemuseum.org/who-were-they/.

Chapter 14: The Early Civil Rights Movement

1. Martin B. Duberman, *Paul Robeson: A Biography* (New York: New Press, 1989), 440–41.
2. Quoted in Roberta Yancy Dent, ed., *Paul Robeson Tributes and Selected Writings* (New York: Paul Robeson Archives, 1976), 65.
3. Quoted in Legal Information Institute of Cornell University Law School at www.law.cornell.edu, CFR, Title 5, Chapter V, Part 1501, Section 1501.8.
4. Quoted in Nikhil Pal Singh, *Black Is a Country: Race and the Unfinished Struggle for Democracy* (Cambridge: Harvard University Press, 2004), 163.

5. Singh, *Black Is a Country*, 164.
6. Robert Harris, "Ralph Bunche and Afro-American Participation in Decolonization," in *The African American Voice in U.S. Foreign Policy since World War II*, ed. Michael Krenn (New York: Garland, 1998), 163–80.
7. Mary L. Dudziak, *Cold War Civil Rights: Race and the Image of American Democracy* (Princeton: Princeton University Press, 2000), 44–45.
8. Josh Sides, *L.A. City Limits: African American Los Angeles from the Great Depression to the Present* (Berkeley: University of California Press, 2003), 147.
9. Singh, *Black Is a Country*, 165.
10. Quoted in Martha Biondi, *To Stand and Fight: The Struggle for Civil Rights in Postwar New York City* (Cambridge: Harvard University Press, 2003), 179.
11. Biondi, *To Stand and Fight*, 151.
12. Quoted in Patricia Sullivan, *Lift Every Voice: The NAACP and the Making of the Civil Rights Movement* (New York: New Press, 2009), 349.
13. Quoted in Biondi, *To Stand and Fight*, 167.
14. Quoted in Patricia Sullivan, *Days of Hope: Race and Democracy in the New Deal Era* (Chapel Hill: University of North Carolina Press, 1996), 227.
15. Quoted in Vincent Harding, Robin D. G. Kelley, and Earl Lewis, *We Changed the World: African Americans, 1945–1970* (New York: Oxford University Press, 1997), 36.
16. Quoted in William Bradford Huie, "The Shocking Story of Approved Killing in Mississippi," *Look* 20 (January 24, 1956): 46–48.
17. Quoted in Timothy Tyson, *The Blood of Emmett Till* (New York: Simon & Schuster, 2017), 6–7.
18. Anne Moody, *Coming of Age in Mississippi* (New York: Dell, 1968), 129.
19. Danielle L. McGuire, *At the Dark End of the Street: Black Women, Rape, and Resistance: A New History of the Civil Rights Movement from Rosa Parks to the Rise of Black Power* (New York: Vintage Books, 2010), xvii.
20. Quoted in Clayborne Carson et al., eds., *The Eyes on the Prize Civil Rights Reader: Documents, Speeches, and Firsthand Accounts from the Black Freedom Struggle* (New York: Viking, 1991), 49.
21. Quoted in Belinda Robnett, *How Long? How Long? African-American Women in the Struggle for Civil Rights* (New York: Oxford University Press, 1997), 59.
22. Quoted in Chappell, *A Stone of Hope*, 88.
23. Nicholas J. Johnson, "Firearms and the Black Community: An Assessment of the Modern Orthodoxy," *Connecticut Law Review: Commentary: Gun Control Policy and the Second Amendment* 45 (2013): 1545.
24. Quoted in Carson et al., *Eyes on the Prize Civil Rights Reader*, 49–50.
25. Aldon Morris, quoted in Barbara Ransby, *Ella Baker and the Black Freedom Movement: A Radical Democratic Vision* (Chapel Hill: University of North Carolina Press, 2003), 175.
26. Ibid., 175–77.
27. Quoted in Cynthia Griggs Fleming, *Soon We Will Not Cry: The Liberation of Ruby Doris Smith Robinson* (New York: Rowman & Littlefield, 1998), 112
28. Charles E. Cobb Jr., *This Nonviolent Stuff'll Get You Killed: How Guns Made the Civil Rights Movement Possible* (New York: Basic Books, 2014), 2.
29. Quoted in Harding, Kelley, and Lewis, *We Changed the World*, 67.
30. Quoted in Mary L. Dudziak, *Cold War Civil Rights: Race and the Image of American Democracy* (Princeton: Princeton University Press, 2000), 133.
31. Interview with Franklin McCain, in Howell Raines, *My Soul Is Rested: The Story of the Civil Rights Movement in the Deep South* (New York: Penguin Books, 1983), 75–82.
32. Quoted in Harding, Kelley, and Lewis, *We Changed the World*, 96.
33. Ibid., 97.
34. Abraham L. Davis and Barbara Luck Graham, *The Supreme Court, Race, and Civil Rights* (Thousand Oaks, CA: Sage, 1995), 81–83.
35. Quoted in Dudziak, *Cold War Civil Rights*, 157–58.
36. Harding, Kelley, and Lewis, *We Changed the World*, 121.
37. Thomas Borstelmann, *The Cold War and the Color Line: American Race Relations in the Global Arena* (Cambridge: Harvard University Press, 2001), 160.
38. Dudziak, *Cold War Civil Rights*, 169–71.
39. Quoted ibid., 158–59.
40. Quoted in Cynthia Griggs Fleming, *Soon We Will Not Cry: The Liberation of Ruby Doris Smith Robinson* (New York: Rowman & Littlefield, 1998), 67.
41. Quoted in Harding, Kelley, and Lewis, *We Changed the World*, 72.
42. Quoted in Timothy Tyson, *Radio Free Dixie: Robert F. Williams and the Roots of Black Power* (Chapel Hill: University of North Carolina Press, 1999), 215.
43. Quoted in Cobb, *This Nonviolent Stuff'll Get You Killed*, 5.
44. Biondi, *To Stand and Fight*, 223.
45. Sides, *L.A. City Limits*, 133.
46. Quoted in Sides, *L.A. City Limits*, 132.
47. Sides, *L.A. City Limits*, 133.
48. Beryl Satter, *Family Properties: How the Struggle over Race and Real Estate Transformed Chicago and Urban America* (New York: Metropolitan, 2009), 36–64.
49. George Lipsitz, *The Possessive Investment in Whiteness: How White People Profit from Identity Politics* (Philadelphia: Temple University Press, 1998), 26.
50. Both quoted in Sides, *L.A. City Limits*, 106.
51. Quoted in Biondi, *To Stand and Fight*, 230.
52. Sides, *L.A. City Limits*, 105–7.
53. Joe William Trotter Jr., *River Jordan: African American Urban Life in the Ohio Valley* (Lexington: University Press of Kentucky, 1998), 157.
54. Arnold Hirsch, "Massive Resistance in the Urban North: Trumbull Park, Chicago, 1953–1966," *Journal of American History* 82, no. 2 (September 1995): 522–50.

55. Quoted in Philip A. Klinkner and Rogers M. Smith, *The Unsteady March: The Rise and Decline of Racial Equality in America* (Chicago: University of Chicago Press, 2002), 280.
56. Both quoted in Biondi, *To Stand and Fight*, 193, 204.
57. Quoted in Sides, *L.A. City Limits*, 135.
58. Sides, *L.A. City Limits*, 136.
59. Biondi, *To Stand and Fight*, 208–22.
60. Sides, *L.A. City Limits*, 151–58.
61. Biondi, *To Stand and Fight*, 218–19.
62. Quoted in Sides, *L.A. City Limits*, 200.
63. Quoted in Lance Hill, *The Deacons for Defense: Armed Resistance and the Civil Rights Movement* (Chapel Hill: University of North Carolina Press, 2004), 263.
64. Jervis Anderson, *Bayard Rustin: Troubles I've Seen: A Biography* (New York: HarperCollins, 1997), 239–59.
65. Quoted in Sarah Azaransky, *The Dream Is Freedom: Pauli Murray and American Democratic Faith* (New York: Oxford University Press, 2011), 62.
66. All quoted in Peter Levy, *Let Freedom Ring: A Documentary History of the Modern Civil Rights Movement* (Westport, CT: Praeger, 1992), 123.
67. Both quoted in Dudziak, *Cold War Civil Rights*, 194, 197–200.
68. Ronald Takaki, *Double Victory: A Multicultural History of America in World War II* (Boston: Little, Brown, 2000), 50.
69. Quoted in Charles E. Cobb Jr., *On the Road to Freedom: A Guided Tour of the Civil Rights Trail* (Chapel Hill: Algonquin Books, 2008), 257.
70. For two versions of this song, see "We Shall Overcome," on *Voices of the Civil Rights Movement: Black American Freedom Songs, 1960–1966*, Smithsonian Folkways Recordings SF 40084, 1997, compact disc.
71. Rachel Devlin, *A Girl Stands at the Door: The Generation of Young Women who Desegregated America's Schools* (New York: Basic Book, 2018), xxii.

Chapter 15: Multiple Meanings of Freedom: The Movement Broadens

1. Stokely Carmichael, *Ready for Revolution: The Life and Struggles of Stokely Carmichael (Kwame Ture)*, with Ekwueme Michael Thelwell (New York: Scribner, 2003), 457.
2. Charles E. Cobb, *On the Road to Freedom: A Guided Tour of the Civil Rights Trail* (Chapel Hill: Algonquin Books, 2008), 241–45.
3. Quoted in Carmichael, *Ready for Revolution*, 461–62.
4. Ibid., 458.
5. Quoted in Clayborne Carson, *In Struggle: SNCC and the Black Awakening of the 1960s* (Cambridge: Harvard University Press, 1981), 164.
6. Quoted in Hasan Kwame Jeffries, *Bloody Lowndes: Civil Rights and Black Power in Alabama's Black Belt* (New York: New York University Press, 2009), 149.
7. Quoted in Carson, *In Struggle*, 166.
8. Carmichael, *Ready for Revolution*, 457–83.
9. Quoted in Jeffries, *Bloody Lowndes*, 180.
10. Quoted in Nikhil Pal Singh, *Black Is a Country: Race and the Unfinished Struggle for Democracy* (Cambridge: Harvard University Press, 2004), 184–85.
11. Quoted in Vincent Harding, Robin D. G. Kelley, and Earl Lewis, *We Changed the World: African Americans, 1945–1970* (New York: Oxford University Press, 1997), 131–32.
12. Mary Frances Berry and John W. Blassingame, *Long Memory: The Black Experience in America* (New York: Oxford University Press, 1982), 242.
13. Douglas S. Massey and Nancy A. Denton, *American Apartheid: Segregation and the Making of the Underclass* (Cambridge: Harvard University Press, 1993), 42–57.
14. Peter B. Levy, *Civil War on Race Street: The Civil Rights Movement in Cambridge, Maryland.* (Gainesville: University of Florida Press, 2003), 97. See also "*Gloria Hayes Richardson oral history interview conducted by Joseph Mosnier in New York, New York, 2011-07-19*," July 19, 2011, https://www.loc.gov/item/afc2010039_crhp0035/.
15. Thomas J. Sugrue, *Sweet Land of Liberty: The Forgotten Struggle for Civil Rights in the North* (New York: Random House, 2008), 318–23.
16. Quoted ibid., 340–41. In these pages, also note Stokely Carmichael's statement about the amorphous and uncongealed nature of black radicalism. According to Carmichael, in the North, it had "no clear, solid center . . . no single accepted community of leadership and resistance you could identify" (340). It is impossible, and would be inaccurate, to impose more order on the philosophy and nature of black radicalism than actually existed.
17. Peniel E. Joseph, *Waiting 'til the Midnight Hour: A Narrative History of Black Power in America* (New York: Henry Holt, 2006), 53.
18. Larry Neal, "The Black Arts Movement," in *Within the Circle: An Anthology of African American Literary Criticism from the Harlem Renaissance to the Present*, ed. Angelyn Mitchell (Durham: Duke University Press, 1994), 184.
19. Both quoted in Paula Giddings, *When and Where I Enter: The Impact of Black Women on Race and Sex in America* (New York: Bantam, 1984), 315.
20. Ibid., 317–24.
21. "Malcolm X: A Problem of Human Rights," interview, YouTube, July 1964, http://www.youtube.com/watch?v=mzjn11OGBK8.
22. Malcolm X, *The Autobiography of Malcolm X*, with the assistance of Alex Haley (New York: Ballantine, 1992), 91, 226.
23. Berry and Blassingame, *Long Memory*, 110–12, 394.
24. Quoted ibid., 417.
25. Harding, Kelley, and Lewis, *We Changed the World*, 145.
26. Quoted in Carson, *In Struggle*, 113–15.
27. Quoted in Chana Kai Lee, *For Freedom's Sake: The Life of Fannie Lou Hamer* (Urbana: University of Illinois Press, 1999), 75.
28. Both quoted in Carson, *In Struggle*, 99.

29. Quoted in Lee, *For Freedom's Sake*, 85–102.
30. Ibid., 100.
31. John Lewis, *Walking with the Wind: A Memoir of the Movement*, with Michael D'Orso (New York: Simon & Schuster, 1998), 291.
32. Quoted in Lee, *For Freedom's Sake*, 100.
33. Quoted in Carson, *In Struggle*, 128.
34. Both quoted in Joseph, *Waiting 'til the Midnight Hour*, 110.
35. Janet L. Abu-Lughod, *Race, Space, and Riots in Chicago, New York, and Los Angeles* (New York: Oxford University Press, 2007), 159–94.
36. Carson, *In Struggle*, 158–61.
37. Both quoted ibid., 161.
38. Quoted ibid., 160.
39. Quoted in Joseph, *Waiting 'til the Midnight Hour*, 142.
40. Robert O. Self, "The Black Panther Party and the Long Civil Rights Era," in *In Search of the Black Panther Party: New Perspectives on a Revolutionary Movement*, ed. Jama Lazerow and Yohuru Williams (Durham: Duke University Press, 2006), 36–38; Sugrue, *Sweet Land of Liberty*, 342–43.
41. Joseph, *Waiting 'til the Midnight Hour*, 207–14.
42. Quoted ibid., 225.
43. U.S. Congress, House Comm. on Internal Security, *Gun-Barrel Politics: The Black Panther Party, 1966–1971*, rep., 92d Cong., 1st sess. (Washington, DC: Government Printing Office, 1971), 43.
44. Quoted in Nancy MacLean, *Freedom Is Not Enough: The Opening of the American Workplace* (Cambridge: Harvard University Press, 2006), 55.
45. All quoted ibid., 38, 39, 52–53.
46. Sugrue, *Sweet Land of Liberty*, 256.
47. Quoted in MacLean, *Freedom Is Not Enough*, 54–55.
48. Ibid., 54–55, 62.
49. Sugrue, *Sweet Land of Liberty*, 257–58.
50. Ibid., 259–60.
51. Ibid., 261.
52. Quoted in Ira Katznelson, *When Affirmative Action Was White: An Untold History of Racial Inequality in Twentieth-Century America* (New York: Norton, 2005), 175.
53. MacLean, *Freedom Is Not Enough*, 70–71, 76.
54. Ibid., 88, 95–103.
55. Quoted in Chester Higgins, "We Can Change Course of U.S.," *Jet*, July 1967, 23.
56. Both quoted in MacLean, *Freedom Is Not Enough*, 104–5.
57. Quoted in Sugrue, *Sweet Land of Liberty*, 273.
58. Quoted in MacLean, *Freedom Is Not Enough*, 106.
59. Ibid., 109–10.
60. Ibid., 242–43.
61. James E. Westheider, *The African American Experience in Vietnam: Brothers in Arms* (Lanham, MD: Rowman & Littlefield, 2008), 21.
62. Ibid., 23–36.
63. Ibid., 25–36, 39–62.
64. Ibid., 30–32.
65. Quoted ibid., 25.
66. Westheider, *The African American Experience in Vietnam*, 64–65.
67. Harding, Kelley, and Lewis, *We Changed the World*, 155.
68. Martin Luther King Jr., *I Have a Dream: Writings and Speeches That Changed the World*, ed. James Melvin Washington (New York: HarperSanFrancisco, 1992), 138, 149.
69. MacLean, *Freedom Is Not Enough*, 340.
70. Martin Glaberman, "Survey: Detroit," *International Socialism*, no. 36 (April/May 1969): 8–9.
71. Sugrue, *Sweet Land of Liberty*, 384–91.
72. Ibid., 371.
73. Ibid., 367–74.
74. Harding, Kelley, and Lewis, *We Changed the World*, 147–48.
75. Quoted in Sugrue, *Sweet Land of Liberty*, 346–47.
76. Sugrue, *Sweet Land of Liberty*, 346.
77. Quoted ibid., 349.
78. Sugrue, *Sweet Land of Liberty*, 338–39.
79. Quoted ibid., 340.
80. Quoted in MacLean, *Freedom Is Not Enough*, 106.
81. Quoted in Sugrue, *Sweet Land of Liberty*, 340.
82. B. Marybeth Gasman with Louise W. Sullivan, *The Morehouse Mystique: Becoming a Doctor at the Nation's Newest African American Medical School* (Baltimore, MD: The Johns Hopkins University Press, 2012), 5.
83. Rebecca Burns, *Burial for a King: Martin Luther King Jr.'s Funeral and the Week That Transformed Atlanta and Rocked the Nation* (New York: Scribner, 2011), 137.
84. Quoted in Ruth Feldstein, *How It Feels to Be Free: Black Women Entertainers and the Civil Rights Movement* (Oxford: Oxford University Press, 2013), 84, 84–112.
85. Neal, "The Black Arts Movement," 184, 186.
86. Quoted in Jerry Gafio Watts, *Amiri Baraka: The Politics and Art of a Black Intellectual* (New York: New York University Press, 2001), 194.

Chapter 16: Racial Progress in an Era of Backlash and Change

1. "Shirley Chisholm: Men in My Political Career," interview, YouTube video, 4:01, posted by "visionaryproject," April 26, 2010, http://www.youtube.com/watch?v=Hubaho0vX2U&feature=related.
2. Ibid.
3. Shirley Chisholm, *Unbought and Unbossed* (Boston: Houghton Mifflin, 1970), 67.
4. Ibid., 74.
5. Ibid., 75.
6. Ibid., 76.
7. Quoted in Paula Giddings, *When and Where I Enter: The Impact of Black Women on Race and Sex in America* (New York: Bantam, 1984), 337–38.
8. Quoted ibid., 339.
9. "Chisholm '72 Unbought & Unbossed Women Make Movies Clip," YouTube video, 3:09, from the documentary film *Chisholm '72 — Unbought and Unbossed* by Shola Lynch,

posted by Women Make Movies, January 22, 2010, http://www.youtube.com/watch?v=vU0jtxf7-vo.

10. Quoted in Sara Diamond, *Roads to Dominion: Right-Wing Movements and Political Power in the United States* (New York: Guilford Press, 1995), 63.
11. Quoted in William H. Chafe, *The Unfinished Journey: America since World War II*, 5th ed. (New York: Oxford University Press, 2003), 364.
12. Nancy MacLean, *Freedom Is Not Enough: The Opening of the American Workplace* (Cambridge: Harvard University Press, 2006), 100.
13. Peniel E. Joseph, *Waiting 'til the Midnight Hour: A Narrative History of Black Power in America* (New York: Henry Holt, 2006), 242.
14. Elizabeth Hinton, *From the War on Poverty to the War on Crime* (Cambridge: Harvard University Press, 2016), 142.
15. Hinton, *From the War on Poverty to the War on Crime*, 173–74.
16. Thomas J. Sugrue, *Sweet Land of Liberty: The Forgotten Struggle for Civil Rights in the North* (New York: Random House, 2008), 518.
17. Quoted in MacLean, *Freedom Is Not Enough*, 208.
18. Ibid., 233.
19. David Goldberg and Trevor Griffey, eds., *Black Power at Work: Community Control, Affirmative Action, and the Construction Industry* (Ithaca: ILR Press/Cornell University Press, 2010), 135.
20. Kevin Boyle, *The UAW and the Heyday of American Liberalism, 1945–1968* (Ithaca: Cornell University Press, 1998), 252–53.
21. MacLean, *Freedom Is Not Enough*, 303–4.
22. Quoted in Sugrue, *Sweet Land of Liberty*, 518–19.
23. Michelle Alexander, *The New Jim Crow: Mass Incarceration in the Age of Colorblindness* (New York: New Press, 2010), 40–57.
24. Alexander, *The New Jim Crow: Mass Incarceration in the Age of Colorblindness*, 109.
25. *McCleskey v. Kemp*, U.S. 279 (1987), 481.
26. Quoted in Donna Jean Murch, *Living for the City: Migration, Education, and the Rise of the Black Panther Party in Oakland, California* (Chapel Hill: University of North Carolina Press, 2010), 173.
27. Ibid., 172.
28. Ibid., 178, 181–83.
29. Ibid., 203.
30. Annelise Orleck, *Storming Caesar's Palace: How Black Mothers Fought Their Own War on Poverty* (Boston: Beacon Press, 2005), 107.
31. Quoted in Deborah Gray White, *Too Heavy a Load: Black Women in Defense of Themselves, 1894–1994* (New York: Norton, 1999), 235.
32. Quoted ibid., 234.
33. Kimberly Springer, *Living for the Revolution: Black Feminist Organizations, 1968–1980* (Durham: Duke University Press, 2005), 47–50.
34. Ibid., 186.
35. Quoted in White, *Too Heavy a Load*, 245.
36. Quoted in Springer, *Living for the Revolution*, 132–33.
37. Sugrue, *Sweet Land of Liberty*, 449–92.
38. Ibid., 465–83.
39. Ibid., 464.
40. Ibid., 476.
41. Ibid., 488.
42. Ari Berman, "The Lost Promise of the Voting Rights Act," *Atlantic*, August 5, 2015, http://www.theatlantic.com/politics/archive/2015/08/give-us-the-ballot-expanding-the-voting-rights-act/399128/.
43. DeBray "Fly Benzo" Carpenter, "Bilingual Education as It Relates to African-Americans: The Ebonics Debate," *San Francisco Bay View*, March 9, 2012.
44. Brenda Stevenson, *The Contested Murder of Latasha Harlins: Justice, Gender, and the Origins of the LA Riots* (New York: Oxford University Press, 2013), 75–77.
45. David A. Bositis, *Black Elected Officials: A Statistical Summary* (Washington, DC: Joint Center for Political and Economic Studies, 1998–2009), 5.
46. Ibid., 26.
47. Ibid., 17.
48. See Frank Clemente, ed., *Keep Hope Alive: Jesse Jackson's 1988 Presidential Campaign* (Boston: South End Press, 1989).
49. Sugrue, *Sweet Land of Liberty*, 537.
50. Ibid.
51. Andrew Wiese, *Places of Their Own: African American Suburbanization in the Twentieth Century* (Chicago: University of Chicago Press, 2004), 2, 124–25, 217–18, 259, 285.
52. Quoted in Douglas S. Massey and Nancy A. Denton, *American Apartheid: Segregation and the Making of the Underclass* (Cambridge: Harvard University Press, 1993), 195–96.
53. Both quoted in Wiese, *Places of Their Own*, 228.
54. Both quoted in Sugrue, *Sweet Land of Liberty*, 425.
55. Both quoted in Wiese, *Places of Their Own*, 231.
56. Wiese, *Places of Their Own*, 254.
57. Ibid., 255.
58. Henry Louis Gates Jr., "Are We Better Off?" *Frontline*, PBS.org, 1998, http://www.pbs.org/wgbh/pages/frontline/shows/race/etc/gates.html.
59. Michael C. Dawson, *Behind the Mule: Race and Class in African-American Politics* (Princeton: Princeton University Press, 1994), 80–84.
60. See William Julius Wilson, *The Truly Disadvantaged: The Inner City, the Underclass, and Public Policy* (Chicago: University of Chicago Press, 1987), 6–8, 112–18.
61. Patricia Hill Collins, *Black Sexual Politics: African Americans, Gender, and the New Racism* (New York: Routledge, 2004), 80–81.
62. Clarence Lusane, *Pipe Dream Blues: Racism and the War on Drugs* (Boston: South End Press, 1991), 22–25, 44–47, 62–63.

63. Mark Anthony Neal, "Postindustrial Soul: Black Popular Music at the Crossroads," in *That's the Joint: The Hip-Hop Studies Reader*, ed. Murray Forman and Mark Anthony Neal (New York: Routledge, 2004), 368.
64. Elizabeth Hinton, *From the War on Poverty to the War on Crime* (Cambridge: Harvard University Press, 2016), 307–332.
65. Clarence Lusane, *Pipe Dream Blues: Racism and the War on Drugs* (Boston: South End Press, 1991), 56.
66. Chafe, *The Unfinished Journey*, 522.
67. Orleck, *Storming Caesar's Palace*, 305.
68. Naomi Murakawa, *The First Civil Right: How Liberals Built Prison America* (New York: Oxford University Press, 2014), 143–147.
69. James Forman Jr., *Locking Up Our Own: Crime and Punishment in Black America* (New York: Farrar, Straus & Giroux, 2017), 210.
70. "Dr. Bill Cosby Speaks at the 50th Anniversary Commemoration of the *Brown vs. Topeka Board of Education* Supreme Court Decision," May 17, 2004, transcript, Eight Cities Media and Publications, http://www.eightcitiesmap.com/transcript_bc.htm.
71. Michael Eric Dyson, "The Culture of Hip-Hop," in Forman and Neal, *That's the Joint*, 62.
72. Neal, "Postindustrial Soul," 378.
73. Chafe, *The Unfinished Journey*, 518–19.
74. Toni Morrison, "Introduction: Friday on the Potomac," in *Race-ing Justice, En-Gendering Power: Essays on Anita Hill, Clarence Thomas, and the Construction of Social Reality*, ed. Toni Morrison (New York: Pantheon, 1992), xxx.
75. Quoted in Darren Lenard Hutchinson, "'Claiming' and 'Speaking' Who We Are: Black Gays and Lesbians, Racial Politics, and the Million Man March," in *Black Men on Race, Gender, and Sexuality: A Critical Reader*, ed. Devon W. Carbado (New York: New York University Press, 1999), 28.
76. Monica Anderson, "A Rising Share of the U.S. Black Population Is Foreign Born: 9 Percent Are Immigrants; and While Most Are from the Caribbean, African Dive Recent Growth," Pew Research Center, April 9, 2015, https://www.pewsocialtrends.org/2015/04/09/a-rising-share-of-the-u-s-black-population-is-foreign-born/.
77. W. E. Burghardt Du Bois, *The Souls of Black Folk: Essays and Sketches* (Chicago: A. C. McClurg, 1907), vii.
78. Hugh Davis Graham, *Collision Course: The Strange Convergence of Affirmative Action and Immigration Policy in America* (Oxford: Oxford University Press, 2002).
79. Candis Watts Smith, *Black Mosaic: The Politics of Black Pan-Ethnic Diversity* (New York: New York University Press, 2014), 8–10; Christina M. Greer, *Black Ethnics: Race Immigration, and the Pursuit of the American Dream* (Oxford: Oxford University Press, 2013), 39–44.
80. Lani Guinier, "Our Preference for the Privileged," *The Boston Globe*, July 9, 2004.

Chapter 17: African Americans in the Twenty-First Century

1. Quoted in Barack Obama, *Dreams from My Father: A Story of Race and Inheritance* (New York: Random House, 1995), 135–36.
2. Nancy MacLean, *Freedom Is Not Enough: The Opening of the American Workplace* (Cambridge: Harvard University Press, 2006), 317–18.
3. Eugene Robinson, "Which Black America?" *Washington Post*, October 9, 2007.
4. Pew Research Center, "Blacks See Growing Values Gap between Poor and Middle Class: Optimism about Black Progress Declines," November 13, 2007, https://www.pewsocialtrends.org/2007/11/13/blacks-see-growing-values-gap-between-poor-and-middle-class/.
5. Juliana Menasce Horowitz, Anna Brown, and Kiana Cox, "Race in America 2019: *Public Has Negative Views of the Country's Racial Progress; More Than Half Say Trump Has Made Race Relations Worse*." Pew Research Center, April 9, 2019, https://www.pewsocialtrends.org/2019/04/09/race-in-america-2019/.
6. This discussion parallels Eugene Robinson's exploration of black diversity in *Disintegration: The Splintering of Black America* (New York: Doubleday, 2010). He describes four categories of difference: Mainstream, Abandoned, Transcendent, and Emergent.
7. Pew Research Center, "Blacks See Growing Values Gap," 4; National Urban League, "Save Our Cities: Powering the Digital Revolution, The State of Black America, 2018," http://www.ncbw-qcmc.org/uploads/1/0/2/9/102980742/nul-soba2018-executive_summary.pdf.
8. Sean Veal and Jonathan Spader, "Rebounds in Homeownership Have Not Reduced the Gap for Black Homeowners." July 10, 2019, Joint Center for Housing Studies of Harvard University, https://www.jchs.harvard.edu/blog/rebounds-in-homeownership-have-not-reduced-the-gap-for-black-homeowners/.
9. "Labor Force Characteristics by Race and Ethnicity, 2017," Report 1076, Bureau of Labor Statistics, August 2018, https://www.bls.gov/opub/reports/race-and-ethnicity/2017/home.htm.
10. Ellis Cose, *The Rage of a Privileged Class: Why Are Middle-Class Blacks Angry? Why Should America Care?* (New York: HarperCollins, 1993), 6–8.
11. Quoted in Ange-Marie Hancock, *The Politics of Disgust: The Public Identity of the Welfare Queen* (New York: New York University Press, 2004), 121.
12. Quoted in Michelle Alexander, *The New Jim Crow: Mass Incarceration in the Age of Colorblindness* (New York: New Press, 2010), 163.
13. Robinson, *Disintegration*, 139–62.
14. Monica Anderson, "A Rising Share of the U.S. Black Population Is Foreign Born: *9 Percent Are Immigrants; and While Most Are from the Caribbean, Africans Drive Recent Growth*," Pew Research Center, April 9, 2015, https://www

.pewsocialtrends.org/2015/04/09/a-rising-share-of-the-u-s-black-population-is-foreign-born/.

15. Candis Watts Smith, *Black Mosaic: The Politics of Black Pan-Ethnic Diversity* (New York: New York University Press, 2014), 156. See also Christina M. Greer, *Black Ethnics: Race Immigration, and the Pursuit of the American Dream* (Oxford: Oxford University Press, 2013), 139.
16. Lisa Jean Francois, "How I Learned That Being West Indian Didn't Make Me Better than African Americans," *BGLH Marketplace*, January 18, 2016, https://bglh-marketplace.com/2016/01/how-i-learned-that-being-west-indian-didnt-make-me-better-than-african-americans/.
17. Smith, 156.
18. Lauren Davenport, *Politics beyond Black and White: Biracial Identity and Attitudes in America* (Cambridge, UK: Cambridge University Press, 2018), 35; Rhea M. Perkins, "Life in Duality: Biracial Identity Development," *Race, Gender & Class* 21, no. 1–2 (2014): 211–19.
19. Davenport, 49; Kim Parker et al., "Multiracial in America: Proud, Diverse, and Growing in Numbers," Pew Research Center, June 11, 2015, https://www.pewsocialtrends.org/2015/06/11/multiracial-in-america/.
20. Davenport, 166–69.
21. Ibid., 125–128.
22. Davenport, 166–68; Perkins, 211–19.
23. Michael A. Fletcher, "Tiger Woods Says He's 'Cablinasian,' But the Police Only Saw Black," May 30, 2017, *The Undefeated*, https://theundefeated.com/features/tiger-woods-dui-arrest-police-only-saw-black/.
24. Stanley Crouch, "What Obama Isn't: Black Like Me on Race," *New York Daily News*, November 2, 2006, http://www.nydailynews.com/archives/opinions/obama-isn-black-race-article-1.585922.
25. Debra J. Dickerson, "Colorblind," *Salon*, January 22, 2007, http://www.salon.com/2007/01/22/obama_161/.
26. Pew Research Center, "Blacks See Growing Values Gap," 19–29; Pew Research Center, "Blacks Upbeat about Black Progress, Prospects: A Year after Obama's Election," January 12, 2010, 5, https://www.pewsocialtrends.org/2010/01/12/blacks-upbeat-about-black-progress-prospects/.
27. Thelma Golden, introduction to *Freestyle: The Studio Museum in Harlem*, exhibition catalog (New York: Studio Museum in Harlem, 2001), 14.
28. Ibid., 15.
29. Catherine Fox, "National Black Arts Festival: Role of Race in Black Art Debated," *Atlanta Journal Constitution*, July 25, 2003, 4F.
30. Touré, *Who's Afraid of Post-Blackness? What It Means to Be Black Now* (New York: Free Press, 2011), 5.
31. Shelby Steele, "The Double Bind of Race and Guilt," *Hoover Digest*, no. 1 (2001).
32. Shelby Steele, "The Age of White Guilt: And the Disappearance of the Black Individual," *Harper's Magazine*, November 2002, 34.
33. Quoted in Obama, *Dreams from My Father*, 135–36.
34. Robinson, *Disintegration*, 229.
35. Both quoted in Joy Bennett Kinnon, "Election 2006: The New Black Power," *Ebony*, November 2006, 166.
36. Quoted in Norman Merchant, "New Generation Challenging Old Guard Blacks in Congress," *Washington Times*, May 14, 2012.
37. Quoted in Ed Gordon, "Cory Booker Wins Newark's 'Street Fight,'" *News and Notes*, NPR, June 2, 2006, https://www.npr.org/templates/story/story.php?storyId=5446231.
38. Quoted in Sylvester Monroe, "Does the Rev. Jesse Jackson Still Matter?" *Ebony*, November 2006, 176.
39. For an extensive review of the black megachurch, see Sharon E. Moore, ed., "African American Megachurches and Community Empowerment: Fostering Life in Dry Places," *Journal of African American Studies* 15, no. 2 (June 2011).
40. The Sentencing Project, "Criminal Justice Facts," https://www.sentencingproject.org/criminal-justice-facts/.
41. John Gramlich, "The Gap between the Number of Blacks and Whites in Prison Is Shrinking," Pew Research Center, April 30, 2019; Chantel de Silva, "Racial Gap in U.S. Jails Narrows as White Incarceration Rates Rise and Black Imprisonment Declines, Study Says," *Newsweek*, February 27, 2018.
42. Heather Ann Thompson, "Why Mass Incarceration Matters: Rethinking Crisis, Decline, and Transformation in Postwar American History," *Journal of American History* 97, no. 3 (December 2010): 707–14.
43. Alexander, *The New Jim Crow*, 12–13.
44. Quoted ibid., 159.
45. "Dr. Bill Cosby Speaks at the 50th Anniversary Commemoration of the *Brown vs. Topeka Board of Education* Supreme Court Decision," May 17, 2004, Eight Cities Media and Publications, http://www.eightcitiesmap.com/transcript_bc.htm.
46. Natalie Byfield, *Savage Portrayals: Race, Media, & the Central Park Jogger Story* (Philadelphia: Temple University Press, 2014), 184.
47. Quoted in Neal Conan, "Congress Questions 'Jena 6' Lawyers," *Talk of the Nation*, NPR, October 16, 2007, https://www.npr.org/transcripts/15340680?storyId=15340680.
48. Derrick Z. Jackson, "Blacks Have Good Cause to Oppose War in Iraq," *Boston Globe*, February 26, 2003.
49. Quoted in Derrick Z. Jackson, "For African-Americans, Folly of This War Hits Home," *Boston Globe*, May 9, 2007.
50. Stephen Zunes, "Hurricane Katrina and the War in Iraq," CommonDreams.org, September 3, 2005.
51. "Neighborhood Change Rates: Growth continues through 2018" Aug 23, 2018, The Data Center, Independent Analysis for Informed Decisions in Southeast Louisiana https://www.datacenterresearch.org/about-us/; "Who Lives in New Orleans and Metro Parishes Now?" October 10, 2019; The Data Center, Independent

Analysis for Informed Decisions in Southeast Louisiana, https://www.datacenterresearch.org/data-resources/who-lives-in-new-orleans-now/.

52. Laura Bliss, "10 Years Later, There's So Much We Don't Know about Where Katrina Survivors Ended Up," Citylab.com, August 25, 2015, https://www.citylab.com/equity/2015/08/10-years-later-theres-still-a-lot-we-dont-know-about-where-katrina-survivors-ended-up/401216/.
53. Christina Kasica, "Subprime Crisis Causing Huge Loss of African-American Wealth," *San Francisco Bay View*, January 23, 2008, https://sfbayview.com/2008/01/subprime-mortgage-crisis-causing-greatest-loss-of-african-american-wealth-in-modern-u-s-history/.
54. Quoted in Brian Ross and Rehab el-Buri, "Obama's Pastor: God Damn America, U.S. to Blame for 9/11," *ABC News*, March 13, 2008.
55. See, for example, Douglass K. Daniel, "AP: Palin's Ayers Attack 'Racially Tinged,'" *Huffington Post*, October 5, 2008, https://straighttalkexpresswatch.wordpress.com/tag/palin-racially-tinged/.
56. Quoted in John Bentley, "McCain Says Taxpayers Should Not Bail Out Wall Street, Criticizes Obama for 'Nasty' Campaign," CBSNews.com, September 15, 2008, https://www.cbsnews.com/news/mccain-says-taxpayers-should-not-bail-out-wall-street-criticizes-obama-for-nasty-campaign/.
57. Quoted in Tom Brokaw, "Meet the Press," NBC, October 19, 2008, http://www.nbcnews.com/id/27266223/ns/meet_the_press/t/meet-press-transcript-oct/#.XiDBglNKhuU.
58. Quoted in Kate Stroup, "Oprah on Obama's Election: 'It Feels Like Hope Won,'" *People*, November 5, 2008.
59. "Obama Wins Nobel Peace Prize," *Huffington Post*, October 9, 2009.
60. Quoted in "Carter Again Cites Racism as Factor in Obama's Treatment," CNN.com, September 15, 2009, https://www.cnn.com/2009/POLITICS/09/15/carter.obama/index.html.
61. Ibid.
62. "The Charge of Racism: It's Time to Bury the Divisive Politics of the Past," Sarah Palin's Facebook page, July 13, 2010, https://www.facebook.com/notes/sarah-palin/the-charge-of-racism-its-time-to-bury-the-divisive-politics-of-the-past/408166998434/.
63. The White House, Office of the Press Secretary, News Conference By The President, East Room, July 22, 2009 https://obamawhitehouse.archives.gov/realitycheck/the_press_office/News-Conference-by-the-President-July-22-2009.
64. David A. Graham, "Quote of the Day: Obama: 'If I Had a Son, He'd Look Like Trayvon'" *The Atlantic*, March 23, 2012, https://www.theatlantic.com/politics/archive/2012/03/quote-of-the-day-obama-if-i-had-a-son-hed-look-like-trayvon/254971/.
65. Newt Gingrich, interview by Sean Hannity, *The Sean Hannity Show*, YouTube video, March 23, 2012, http://www.youtube.com/watch?v5Oa_pb6dXqK4.
66. Adam Kelsey, "Donald Trump's 2012 Election Tweetstorm Resurfaces as Popular and Electoral Vote Appear Divided," *ABCNews*, November 9, 2016, https://abcnews.go.com/Politics/donald-trumps-2012-election-tweetstorm-resurfaces-popular-electoral/story?id=43431536.
67. The White House, Office of the Press Secretary, "Statement by the President on the Re-Establishment of Diplomatic Relations with Cuba," July 1, 2015, https://www.whitehouse.gov/the-press-office/2015/07/01/statement-president-re-establishment-diplomatic-relations-cuba.
68. See Ariane de Vogue and Jeremy Diamond, "Supreme Court Saves Obamacare," CNN.com, June 25, 2015, http://www.cnn.com/2015/06/25/politics/supreme-court-ruling-obamacare/.
69. The source is: "Health Insurance Coverage and the Affordable Care Act, 9/22/2015," Office of the Assistant Secretary for Planning and Evaluation, https://aspe.hhs.gov/basic-report/health-insurance-coverage-and-affordable-care-act-september-2015.
70. Jennifer Gonnerman, "Before the Law," *New Yorker*, October 6, 2014, http://www.newyorker.com/magazine/2014/10/06/before-the-law.
71. Kimberlé Williams Crenshaw, "The Girls Obama Forgot," *New York Times*, July 29, 2014.
72. "Remarks by the President in Eulogy for the Honorable Reverend Clementa Pinckney," whitehouse.gov, June 26, 2015, https://www.whitehouse.gov/the-press-office/2015/06/26/remarks-president-eulogy-honorable-reverend-clementa-pinckney.
73. Elizabeth Kneebone, "Ferguson, Mo. Emblematic of Growing Suburban Poverty," *The Avenue/Rethinking Metropolitan America*, Brookings Institution, August 15, 2014, http://www.brookings.edu/blogs/the-avenue/posts/2014/08/15-ferguson-suburban-poverty.
74. Aamer Madhani, "Trump's Victory Leaves Black Community Reeling," *USA Today*, November 10, 2016.
75. Toni Morrison, "Making America White Again," *The New Yorker*, November 14, 2016, https://www.newyorker.com/magazine/2016/11/21/making-america-white-again.
76. Quoted in Madhani, "Trump's Victory Leaves Black Community Reeling."
77. Juliet Eilperin and Darla Cameron, "How Trump Is Rolling Back Obama's Legacy," *The Washington Post*, March 24, 2017, updated January 20, 2018.
78. Carrie Johnson, "Trump's Impact on Federal Courts: Judicial Nominees by the Numbers," NPR, August 5, 2019, https://www.npr.org/2019/08/05/747013608/trumps-impact-on-federal-courts-judicial-nominees-by-the-numbers.
79. Madhani, "Trump's Victory Leaves Black Community Reeling."
80. Quoted in Akinyi Ochieng, "Black Muslims Face Double Jeopardy, Anxiety in the Heartland," NPR, February 25, 2017, https://www.npr.org/sections/codeswitch/2017/02/25/516468604/black-muslims-face-double-jeopardy-anxiety-in-the-heartland.

81. Quoted ibid.
82. Jayashri Srikantiah and Shirin Sinnar, "White Nationalism as Immigration Policy," *Stanford Law Review*, March 2019, https://www.stanfordlawreview.org/online/white-nationalism-as-immigration-policy/.
83. Quoted in Jesse Washington, "African-Americans See Painful Truths in Trump Victory," *The Undefeated*, November 10, 2016, https://theundefeated.com/features/african-americans-see-painful-truths-in-trump-victory/.
84. Quoted in Srikantiah and Sinnar, "White Nationalism as Immigration Policy."
85. Quoted in Bryan Armen Graham, "Donald Trump Blasts NFL Anthem Protesters: 'Get That Son of a Bitch Off the Field,'" *The Guardian*, September 23, 2017, https://www.theguardian.com/sport/2017/sep/22/donald-trump-nfl-national-anthem-protests.
86. Quoted in Sean Sullivan, "Trump Slams Colin Kaepernick: 'Maybe He Should Find a Country That Works Better for Him,'" *The Washington Post*, August 29, 2016.
87. Quoted in "Felicia Sonmez and Mike DeBonis, "Trump Tells Four Liberal Congresswomen to 'Go Back' to Their Countries, Prompting Pelosi to Defend Them," *The Washington Post*, July 14, 2019.
88. Quoted in Maya Eliahou, "'Go Back to Where You Came From': Our Readers Recall Racist Taunts from Their Lives," *Los Angeles Times*, July 15, 2019.
89. Quoted in Ariane de Vogue and Steve Almasy, "New Texas Voter ID Law Discriminates, Federal Judge Rules," CNN, August 23, 2017, https://www.cnn.com/2017/08/23/politics/texas-voter-id-ruling/index.html.
90. Griffin Sims Edwards and Stephen Rushin, "The Effect of President Trump's Election on Hate Crimes," Social Science Research Network, January 14, 2018, https:/ssrn.com/abstract=3102652.
91. Juliana Menasce Horowitz, Anna Brown, and Kiana Cox, "Race in America 2019: Public Has Negative Views of the Country's Racial Progress; More Than Half Say Trump Has Made Race Relations Worse," Pew Research Center, April 9, 2019, https://www.pewsocialtrends.org/2019/04/09/race-in-america-2019/.
92. https://abcnews.go.com/Politics/donald-trumps-2012-election-tweetstorm-resurfaces-popular-electoral/story?id=43431536. Ibid. See also Pew Research Center, "Blacks See Growing Values Gap."
93. Quoted in Akinyi Ochieng, "Black Muslims Face Double Jeopardy, Anxiety in the Heartland."
94. Glenn Kessler, "Fact Checker: Did Racially Motivated Voter Suppression Thwart Stacey Abrams?" *The Washington Post*, October 30, 2019.
95. Quoted in Derrick Bell, *Faces at the Bottom of the Well: The Permanence of Racism* (New York: Basic Books, 1992), 40.
96. Black Lives Matter, "About the Black Lives Matter Network," http://blacklivesmatter.com/about/.
97. Mapping Police Violence, home page, last modified January 1, 2016, http://mappingpoliceviolence.org.
98. Quoted in Lynn Peeples, "What the data say about police shootings," *Nature*, September 4, 2019: Edwards, F., Lee, H. & Esposito, M. *Proc. Natl Acad. Sci. USA* 116, 16793–16798 (2019).
99. U.S. Department of Justice, Civil Rights Division, *Investigation of the Ferguson Police Department*, March 4, 2015, https://www.justice.gov/sites/default/files/opa/press-releases/attachments/2015/03/04/ferguson_police_department_report.pdf.
100. Richard A. Oppel Jr. and Lazaro Gamio, "Minneapolis Police Use Force Against Black People at 7 Times the Rate of Whites," *New York Times*, June 3, 2020.
101. Shaila Dewan and Mike Baker, "Rage and Promises Followed Ferguson, but Little Changed," *New York Times*, June 13, 2020.
102. "Defunding the Police Can Achieve 'Real Accountability and Justice,' Black Lives Matter Co-Founder Says," https://www.wbur.org/hereandnow/2020/06/03/black-lives-matter-co-founder. Accessed June 13, 2020.
103. African American Policy Forum, Center for Intersectionality and Social Policy Studies, "Say Her Name: Resisting Brutality Against Black Women," 2015, https://aapf.org/sayhernamereport.
104. Alex Kane, "Not Just Ferguson: 11 Eye-Opening Facts about America's Militarized Police Forces," Moyers & Company, August 13, 2014, http://billmoyers.com/2014/08/13/not-just-ferguson-11-eye-opening-facts-about-americas-militarized-police-forces/14.
105. Quoted in Alexander, *The New Jim Crow*, 72–73.
106. Matt Apuzzo, "War Gear Flows to Police Departments," *New York Times*, June 8, 2014.
107. Ira Glass, "547: Cops See It Differently, Part One," *This American Life*, podcast audio, February 6, 2015, https://www.thisamericanlife.org/547/cops-see-it-differently-part-one; Ira Glass, "548: Cops See It Differently, Part Two," *This American Life*, podcast audio, February 13, 2015, https://www.thisamericanlife.org/548/cops-see-it-differently-part-two.
108. Erin Durkin, "De Blasio Talks of Worries for Son Dante after Grand Jury Declines to Indict Cop in Eric Garner Death," *New York Daily News*, December 3, 2014.

Text Credits

Daisy Bates. Excerpts from *The Long Shadow of Little Rock*, pp. 73–75. Copyright © 1962, 1986 by Daisy Bates. Reprinted with the permission of The Permissions Company, Inc., on behalf of the University of Arkansas Press, www.uapress.com.

Ruth Bogin. "'Liberty Further Extended': A 1776 Antislavery Manuscript by Lemuel Haynes." *William and Mary Quarterly*, 3rd ser., vol. 40, no. 1 (1983): 94–96. Reprinted by permission of the Omohundro Institute of Early American History and Culture.

W. E. B. Du Bois. "Negro Editors on Communism: A Symposium of the American Negro Press." Copyright © Crisis Publishing Co. Used with permission. Bedford/St. Martin's wishes to thank Crisis Publishing Co., Inc., the publisher of the magazine of the National Association of the Advancement of Colored People, for the use of this material first published in the April and May 1932 issue of *Crisis Magazine.*

Alicia Garza. "A Herstory of the #BlackLivesMatter Movement." *The Feminist Wire* (October 7, 2014). Used with permission.

Harold Head. Excerpt from "English/Modern African Thought and Literature." Black Studies curriculum, S.F. State college archives, Spring 1968. Used with permission.

John Lewis, chair of the Student Nonviolent Coordinating Committee (SNCC). Speech at the March on Washington, 1963.

Douglas S. Massey, Margarita Mooney, Kimberly C. Torres, and Camille Z. Charles. From "Black Immigrants and Black Natives Attending Selective Colleges and Universities in the United States," *American Journal of Education*, vol. 113, no. 2 (2007): 243–71. Copyright © 2007 by The University of Chicago. Reproduced by permission of the publisher.

Anne Moody. Excerpts from Chapter 10 of *Coming of Age in Mississippi*, copyright © 1968 by Anne Moody. Used by permission of Doubleday, an imprint of the Knopf Doubleday Publishing Group, a division of Penguin Random House LLC. All rights reserved.

National Public Radio. Excerpt from NPR® news report titled "A Tuskegee Airman's Harrowing WWII Tale" was originally broadcast on NPR's News & Notes on November 10, 2006, and is used with the permission of NPR. Copyright © 2006 National Public Radio, Inc. Any unauthorized duplication is strictly prohibited.

Phoenix Law Enforcement Association. "Recent Phoenix Police Officer Involved Shooting," news release, December 15, 2014. Used with permission.

Senator Tim Scott (R-SC). Excerpt from "Dr. King Would Be Proud of America's Progress," *New York Post* op-ed, August 28, 2023. Used with permission.

Cleveland L. Sellers and Robert L. Terrell. From *The River of No Return*. Copyright © 1973 by Cleveland Sellers and Robert Terrell. Used by permission of HarperCollins Publishers.

Nina Simone. "Mississippi Goddam." Words and music by Nina Simone. Copyright © 1964 (renewed) WC Music Corp. All rights reserved. Used by permission of Alfred Music.

Mary C. Waters. *Black Identities: West Indian Immigrant Dreams and American Realities*. Cambridge, Mass.: Harvard University Press, copyright © 1999 by the Russell Sage Foundation. Used by permission. All rights reserved.

Index

Aaron, Hank, 526
Abbott, Lyman, 216
Abbott, Robert, 435
Abernathy, Ralph, 557–58, 686
Abolitionists and abolitionism. *See also* Emancipation; *specific Antislavery entries*
Amistad case and, 224
Black freedom struggle and, 263
Civil War and, 296
converts among whites, 263, 271
in 1840s and 1850s, 251–52
female abolitionists and, 270
lecturers and, 266–67
Liberty Party and, 270, 273, 278
moral suasion and, 269
in North, 147–48, 164
in Oregon Territory, 273
political action and, 269
Revolution and northern slavery, 164
Walker on, 221
Abortion rights, 702
Abrams, Stacey, 712
Abroad marriage, 236
Abyssinian Baptist Church, 479
Accommodationism
of Booker T. Washington, 405, 410
W. E. B. Du Bois as critic of, 410
"Account of the Slave Trade on the Coast of Africa, An" (Falconbridge), 69–70*(d)*
Acculturation, in Chesapeake region, 126
ACS. *See* American Colonization Society
"Act for Regulating of Slaves in New Jersey, An," 112–13
Act for the Gradual Abolition of Slavery (Pennsylvania), 181
Activism. *See also* Civil rights movement
by Adam Clayton Powell Jr., 478
affirmative action and, 608
anti-Communist hysteria and, 546
Black, 190, 262, 265–69
by Black women, 439
after Civil War, 321
by 1860, 252
by free Blacks, 197–203
in 1960s and 1970s, 591, 598–607
Nixon actions against, 638
political, 388–89
Adam (enslaved man), freedom struggles of, 90
Adams, Eliza, 238
Adams, Henry, migration promoted by, 363
Adams, John, 132
Adams, John Quincy, 224
Adams-Onís Treaty (1821), 215
Addams, Jane, 414, 435
"Address of the Colored State Convention to the People of Iowa in Behalf of Their Enfranchisement, 1868" (Clark), 376–77
"Address to the Slaves of the United States of America, An" (Garnet), 288–89
Adeline Brown v. State (1865), 346
Administration of Justice Act, 137
Adventurers, English, 77
Affirmative action, 607, 613
Black American debate on, 685
Nixon and, 638
opponents of, 611
Thomas, Clarence, and, 662
Affordable Care Act, 698, 704, 709
Afghanistan, 687
Black support for war in, 691–92
Obama troop withdrawal from, 698, 703
Africa. *See also* Black(s); Colonization; Slave trade
African American arts inspired by, 626*(v)*
African American colonization of, 192–94
African American culture and, 122–23
ancient societies of, 8–15, 9*(m)*
celebration of, 623
climate of, 4, 5*(m)*
countries of, 4
cultural geography of, 6
as "Dark Continent," 3
Du Bois on colonization of, 412
enslaved people from, 122
facial markings from, 88
geography of, 5*(m)*
humankind origins in, 6
hunter-gatherers in, 7
landscape of, 4–6
livestock in, 7, 8*(i)*
map of, 5*(m)*
mobility and migration in, 6–7
newly independent nations of, 58
peoples of, 6–8
population of enslaved people from, 58–60
Portuguese and, 37
religions of, 4
religious traditions from, 88
size of, 4
slave trade and, 41–43, 46
social identity of, 26
soils of, 4
"Africa for Africans" idea, of Garvey, 452
African American Policy Forum (AAPF), 722–23
African American Soldiers Storm Fort Wagner, 309*(i)*
African Americans, 615*(c)*. *See also* Black(s); Black men; Black women; Enslaved people; Interracial relationships
African origins of, 43–45
Africans as, 76
AIDS treatments and, 658–59
American Revolution and, 120, 131–50, 136*(i)*, 164
ancestral origins of, 3–4
in Battle of New Orleans, 192
Black immigrants and, 682
British taxation and, 131
in Civil War battles, 310–11, 312*(m)*
class divide among, 657–60
Cold War, loyalty program, and, 547–51
competence and equality after Civil War, 354
culture of, 122–26, 684
as distinct people, 264
election impacts of, 653
end to federal protections for rights of, 383
families separated and, 170–71
GI Bill and, 528–29
in Great Depression, 473–75
identification with Jewish people, 506
John F. Kennedy assassination and, 592
law enforcement and, 707–8
lifestyle in eighteenth-century North America, 121–31
migration by, 430–34, 433*(m)*, 513–16, 514*(m)*
Muslims, 687
police killings of, 706
population in United States (1790–2010), A-33
in public schools, 188
in South, 121
spread of population, 433*(m)*
Trump and, 708–13
Tuskegee experiments and, 534–43
in United States (1770 and 1800), 149*(m)*
use of term, 607, 664
in Vietnam War, 613–17
in Virginia, 75–76
visual arts of, 455
voting by, 192
in War of 1812, 191–92
white marriages with, 92
World War I and, 440–43
World War II and, 506–9, 513–20
African Brigade, Louisiana Native Guards as, 310–11
African Episcopal Church of St. Thomas, 186
African Meeting House (Boston), 186
African Methodist Episcopal (AME) Church, 185. *See also* Bethel AME Church
destruction of, 219
in South, 341
Vesey and, 219
African Methodist Episcopal Zion (AME Zion) Church, 341
African Orthodox Church, 452
African Society (Boston), 184
African Society for Mutual Relief (New York), 184
African Times and Orient Review, 450
African Union Meeting House (Providence), 186
African Union Society (Providence), 184, 186

Africans
as African Americans, 76
arrivals in Americas, 43–45, 84–85
in New England, 89–93
supplies of, 81
value as enslaved laborers, 81
Africanus, 22
Afro, use of term, 607
Afro-American Association, 595
Afro-Christianity, 131
Agassiz, Louis, 253
Agency (purposeful action), constraint and, 419–27
Agrarian protest movements, in South and Midwest, 389
Agricultural Adjustment Administration, 476
Agriculture. *See also* Farming; Plantation agriculture
Black labor in, 513–14
enslaved people in, 54, 86, 96, 122, 209–10
in Louisiana, 99
in Maryland, 176
in slave South (1860), 210*(m)*
teaching of techniques, 233
Ahmose I, 11
Aid to Families with Dependent Children, 617, 647, 659
AIDS epidemic, 658–59
Aircraft industry, 515
Akan people, 59, 60
Aksum, 9, 12–13
Al Qaeda
Obama policy toward, 703
September 11, 2001 attacks and, 691–92, 698
Alabama. *See also* Birmingham, Alabama; Wallace, George C
Black voters in, 602
integration of University of, 573
National Guard federalization in, 574
riots in (1943), 517
Selma to Montgomery march in, 602
slavery in, 168, 215
University of, 573–74
Alabama Christian Movement for Human Rights, 564
Alabama Sharecroppers Union (ASU), 482
Albany, Georgia, demonstrators in, 559*(i)*
Albright, Madeleine, 695
Alcorn Agricultural and Mechanical College (Alcorn A&M), 348
Alexander the Great, 8–9, 12
al-Hamawi, Yaqut, 17
Ali, Duse Muhammad, 450, 614
Allegheny Institute, 261
Allen, Louis, 564
Allen, Richard, 184–86, 189, 191, 263
Black church and, 184–85, 189
colonization and, 194
resolutions about colonization opposition and, 201
Alliances, Black-Jewish, 650
Allies
in World War I, 439
in World War II, 505, 520, 531
Almanac (Banneker), 163, 164*(i)*
"Along the Color Line" (Du Bois), 425*(d)*
Al-Sahili, Abu Ishaq Ibrahim, 21
Altgeld Gardens public housing project (Chicago), 677
Alton, Illinois, race riot in, 255
Aluminum Ore company, Black workers in, 441
AMA. *See* American Missionary Association
Amadioha, 23
AME Church. *See* African Methodist Episcopal (AME) Church
AME Zion Church. *See* African Methodist Episcopal Zion (AME Zion) Church
Amendments, A-10–A-14
Fifteenth, 358–59, 366–67, 370, A-12
Fourteenth. *See* Fourteenth Amendment
Nineteenth, A-12
Tallmadge, 212
Thirteenth, 320, 323, 370, 420, A-11
Twenty-fourth, A-13
America(s). *See also* Slave trade
African identities in, 60
Africans in, 41–45, 60
enslavement of Indigenous peoples in, 41–43
French colonies in, 100–101
slave trade in, 41–43
American and Foreign Anti-Slavery Society (AFAS), 270
American Anti-Slavery Society, 269–70
American Civil Liberties Union (ACLU), 471
American Colonization Society (ACS), 193–94, 407
migration to Liberia sponsored by, 221, 253, 282
American Crusade against Lynching, 545
American Equal Rights Association
"Debate, A: Negro Male Suffrage Equal Rights Association *vs.* Woman Suffrage," 371–74
Sojourner Truth at, 370–71
women and Blacks in, 367, 370
American Federation of Labor (AFL), 480
Black organizing and, 519
Blacks excluded from, 400
American Football League, 526
American Freedmen's Union Commission, schools and, 348
American Indian
Bacon's Rebellion and, 83
in Chesapeake, 80
conversion to Christianity, 43
as enslaved labor, 99
New England enslavement of, 90
removal of, 212–15, 362
as slave catchers, 89, 170
westward expansion and, 272–73
American Indian Movement, COINTELPRO and, 628
American Missionary Association (AMA)
assistance to formerly enslaved people by, 302
formation of, 272
school sponsored by, 343
American Moral Reform Society, 262
American Negro Academy, 408
American Negro Theatre (ANT), 526
American Nurses Association, color bar eliminated in, 526
American Recovery and Reinvestment Act (ARRA), 698
American Red Cross, separation of Black and white blood by, 507
American Revolution
African Americans and, 120, 131–42, 136*(i)*
chances for freedom after, 147–50
enslaved people's freedom and, 120, 147–50, 164
enslaved soldiers in, 134–35
events leading to, 131–34
free Black life after, 183–94
opening of, 133
outcomes of, 146–50
status of slavery after, 166–67
American Society for Colonizing the Free People of Color of the United States, 193
American Sociological Association, 447–48
American Woman Suffrage Association, 367
Amherst College, 484
Amistad case, 224
Amos 'n' Andy Show, 480
Amsterdam News (newspaper), 453
Ancient societies, of Africa, 8–15, 9*(m)*
Aksum, 12–13
Bantu, 13–15
Egypt, 8–12
Kush, 12–13
Nok, 13–15
Nubia, 12–13
overview of, 8–9
Anderson, Jourdan and Mandy, 337–38
Anderson, Major, at Fort Sumter, 297
Anderson, Marian, 492, 492*(i)*
Anderson, P. H., 337
Angelou, Maya, 647
Anglican Church, missionaries from, 87
Anglo-Saxons, scientific racism and, 387
Angola
description of, 14
slave trade and, 46, 75
Anna Lucasta (Yordan), 527
Anne (Queen of England), 92
Annexation, of Texas, 209, 215
Anslinger, Henry, 489
Antebellum era, 286
reform in, 262
enslaved communities in, 239
Anthony, Susan B., 367, 370, 372–74, 372*(d)*, 374, 374*(d)*
Anthropology
on "primitives" and Anglo-Saxons, 387
slavery justified by, 253
Antiabortion justices, 662
Anti-Black riots. *See also* Race riots
in Civil War, 314
Anti-Catholicism, of Know-Nothings, 256
Anticolonization campaign, 194
Anticommunism
Black freedom struggle and, 546
civil rights and, 561
after World War II, 547–53
Anti-Lynching Bill (Dyer), 419

Antilynching campaign, of Wells, 393
Antimiscegenation laws, 81, 387
Antipoverty programs
Community Action Programs and, 618
Poor People's Campaign and, 617
Antislavery movement
emancipation as focus of, 221
Pennsylvania organizations and, 182
Antislavery petitions
in Congress, 224
in Georgia, 104
Antislavery political parties, 270
Antiwar movement, during Vietnam War, 615
Antor, Sandra, 722
AP® Exam Practice
Chapter 1: African Origins (Beginnings to ca. 1600 C.E.), EP1-A–EP1-B
Chapter 2: From Africa to America (1441–1808), EP2-A–EP2-B
Chapter 3: Slavery in North America (1619–1740), EP3-A–EP3-B
Chapter 4: African Americans in the Age of Revolution (1741–1783), EP4-A–EP4-B
Chapter 5: Slavery and Freedom in the New Republic (1775–1820), EP5-A–EP5-B
Chapter 6: Black Life in the Slave South (1820–1860), EP6-A–EP6-B
Chapter 7: The Northern Black Freedom Struggle and the Coming of the Civil War (1830–1860), EP7-A–EP7-B
Chapter 8: Freedom Rising: The Civil War (1861–1865), EP8-A–EP8-B
Chapter 9: Reconstruction: The Making and Unmaking of a Revolution (1865–1877), EP9-A–EP9-B
Chapter 10: Black Life and Culture during the Nadir (1877–1915), EP10-A–EP10-B
Chapter 11: The New Negro Comes of Age (1915–1930), EP11-A–EP11-B
Chapter 12: Catastrophe, Recovery, and Renewal (1930–1942), EP12-A–EP12-B
Chapter 13: Fighting for a Double Victory in the World War II Era (1938–1950), EP13-A–EP13-B
Chapter 14: The Early Civil Rights Movement (1945–1963), EP14-A–EP14-B
Chapter 15: Multiple Meanings of Freedom: The Movement Broadens (1961–1976), EP15-A–EP15-B
Chapter 16: Racial Progress in an Era of Backlash and Change (1965–2000), EP16-A–EP16-B
Chapter 17: African Americans in the Twenty-First Century (2000–Present), EP17-A–EP17-B
Practice Exam, PE-1–PE-28
Unit 1: Origins of the African Diaspora, U1EP-A–U1EP-N
Unit 2: Freedom, Enslavement, and Resistance, U2EP-A–U2EP-L
Unit 3: The Practice of Freedom, U3EP-A–U3EP-L
Unit 4: Movements and Debates, U4EP-A–U4EP-P
AP® Skill Workshops
Chapter 1: Visual Texts: Active Reading, SW1-A–SW1-L
Chapter 2: Written Texts: Active Reading, SW2-A–SW2-J
Chapter 3: Sourcing Visual or Written Primary Sources, SW3-A–SW3-D
Chapter 4: Short-Answer Questions, SW4-A–SW4-G
Chapter 5: Document-Based Questions: Prompts, SW5-A–SW5-C
Chapter 6: Document-Based Questions: Skillful Skimming, SW6-A–SW6-F
Chapter 7: Document-Based Questions: Thesis Statements, SW7-A–SW7-G
Chapter 8: Document-Based Questions: Introductions, SW8-A–SW8-C
Chapter 9: Document-Based Questions: Evidence, SW9-A–SW9-H
Chapter 10: Document-Based Questions Commentary, SW10-A–SW10-J
Chapter 11: Document-Based Questions: Conclusions, SW11-A–SW11-C
Chapter 12: Multiple-Choice Questions with Paired Stimuli, SW12-A–SW12-H
Chapter 13: Responding to Short-Answer Questions without Stimuli, SW13-A–SW13-E
Chapter 14: Individual Student Project: Topic Selection, SW14-A–SW14-D
Chapter 15: Individual Student Project: Source Selection, SW15-A–SW15-D
Chapter 16: Individual Student Project: Evidence-Based Argument, SW16-A–SW16-F
Chapter 17: Individual Student Project: Presentation and Oral Defense, SW17-A–SW17-F
AP® Unit Introductions
Unit 1: Origins of the African Diaspora, U1-A–U1-F
Unit 2: Freedom, Enslavement, and Resistance, U2-A–U2-F
Unit 3: The Practice of Freedom, U3-A–U3-F
Unit 4: Movements and Debates, U4-A–U4-F
AP® Working with Sources collections
Chapter 1: Imagining Africa, 31–35
Chapter 2: Firsthand Accounts of the Slave Trade, 63–73
Chapter 3: Making Slaves, 108–17
Chapter 4: Black Freedom Fighters, 153–61
Chapter 5: Free Black Activism, 197–205
Chapter 6: Testimony of Enslaved People, 242–49
Chapter 7: Forging an African American Nation—Enslaved and Free, North and South, 286–93
Chapter 8: Wartime and Emancipation, 325–35
Chapter 9: The Vote, 370–79
Chapter 10: Agency and Constraint, 419–27
Chapter 11: The Harlem/New Negro Renaissance, 460–69
Chapter 12: Communist Radicalism and Everyday Realities, 495–501
Chapter 13: African Americans and the Tuskegee Experiments, 534–43
Chapter 14: We Are Not Afraid, 581–87
Chapter 15: Black Power: Expression and Repression, 623–33
Chapter 16: All Africa's Children, 669–75
Chapter 17: #BlackLivesMatter, 717–31
Apaches, Geronimo at World's Fair, 386
Apartheid, 564
Appomattox Court House, Lee's surrender at, 318
Apprentices, 346
Arabian Peninsula, 13
Arbery, Ahmaud, 713, 717
Archibald, Julius, 572
Argall, Samuel, 77
Arkansas, 174*(m)*
cotton in, 215
school desegregation in, 560, 583–84
slavery in, 168, 174
Arlington Heights, Illinois, 655
Armed forces. *See* Military; *specific battles and wars; specific wars*
Armistead, James, 144
Armstrong, Louis "Satchmo," 457, 486
Armstrong, Samuel Chapman, 350, 409
Army Air Corps, NAACP lawsuit against, 507
Army Corps of Engineers, Hurricane Katrina and, 693
Army of Northern Virginia, 301
Army of the Potomac, 311
Art(s). *See also* Black Arts Movement; Literature
Chicago Renaissance, 486–88
Harlem Renaissance and, 453–57
New Negro arts movement and, 453
post-Black, 684
as propaganda, 446, 455
Articles of Constitution. *See* Constitution (U.S.)
Artisans, enslaved people trained by, 122
Ashmun Institute, 261
Asia, World War II in, 505
Asians, racism against, 387
Asiento system, 46
Associated Agencies (Oakland), 571
Associated Negro Press, 520
Association for the Study of Negro Life and History, 448
Atlanta Compromise speech (Washington), 410, A-24–A-26
Atlanta Life Insurance Company, 475
Atlantic Charter (1941), 506, 520
Atlantic Ocean region, slave trade in, 40
Atomic bombs, in World War II, 531
Attorney general
Lynch as, 704
"subversive" organizations, 551
Attucks, Crispus, 134–35
Attucks Guards, 298
Auctions, of enslaved people, 37, 97*(i)*, 217, 218*(i)*
Australia, Black loyalists in, 146

Australopithecus afarensis, 6, 7*(i)*
Autobiography, of Jarena Lee, 266
Automobile industry, government loans to, 698, 702
Avery, Charles, 261
Aviators, Black, in World War II, 512, 539–40, 539–40*(v)*
AWOL soldiers, in World War II, 512
Axis powers, in World War II, 505, 508
Axum, 13
Azores, 39
Azusa Street Revival (Los Angeles), 436

Bacchus (enslaved man), 134
Back to Africa Movement
  of Garvey, 452
  in 19th century, 408
Backcountry, white migration to (1790–1820), 169
Bacon, Nathaniel, and Bacon's Rebellion, 83
Bahamas, Black loyalists in, 146
Bailey v. Alabama, 420, 425
Baker, Ella, 474, 596, 600*(i)*
Baker, Frank, 301
Baker, George, 479
Baker, Josephine, 455
Baker, Ray Stannard
  on lynching, 390
  on National Negro Committee, 414
Bakke case (1978), 644
Bakri, Al, 18
Baldwin, James, 512, 592
Balkan region, forced labor from, 40
Ball, Charles, 172
Ball, Thomas, *Emancipation (Freedmen's Memorial),* 334–35*(v)*
Baltimore
  Federal occupation of, 298
  slavery and free Blacks in, 175–76
Baltimore Afro-American, 507, 520
Bambara, Toni Cade, 647
Bambara enslaved people, 100
Banjo Lesson, The (Tanner), 404, 404*(i)*
Banks, 397
Banks, Ernie, 526
Banneker, Benjamin, 163–64
  Almanac of, 163, 164*(i)*
  letter to Thomas Jefferson, 163–65
Bantu, 13–15
Bantu expansion, 9, 14
Bantu-speaking people, 9
Baptists
  Black, 126, 186, 229
  churches in Richmond and, 398
  revivals and, 223
  in South, 341
Baquaqua, Mahommah G., 54
Baraka, Amiri (LeRoi Jones), 520, 625–26*(v)*
Barbadoes, James G., 269
Barbados
  enslaved people's disembarkation in, 60
  enslaved labor in, 88
  immigrants from, 408
Barbie, Millie, 236
Barbot, James Jr., 52
  "General Observations on the Management of Slaves," 67–69
Barbot, John, 58
Barkley, Alben, 522
Barnett, Ferdinand L., 414
Barnett, Ida B. Wells. *See* Wells-Barnett, Ida B
Barnwell, Rosa, 225
Barracoons (barracks), life in, 50, 52
Barrett, Amy Coney , 709
Barrett, Janie Porter, 399
Bartering, 479
Bas du Fleuve, 101
Baseball
  desegregation of, 526
  racism in, 490
Basketball, desegregation of, 526
Bates, Evelyn, 513, 517
  in World War II, 503–4
Bates, Ruby, 471
Battles. *See specific battles and wars*
Baumfree, Isabella. *See* Truth, Sojourner
Bear Creek settlement, 146
Beat Street (film), 661*(i)*
Beaumont, Texas, race riot in (1943), 517
Bebop, 528
Bectom, John, 235
Bedford-Stuyvesant, race riot in, 602
Beliefs. *See* Ideology; Religion
Benevolent societies, 435
Benezet, Anthony, 182
Benga, Ota, 386
Benguela, 75
Benin, 25–27, 46
Bennett, Gwendolyn, 455
Berbers, 16, 18
Berkeley, California, Afro-American Association and, 595
Berkeley, William, 83
Bethel AME Church (Philadelphia), 185, 185*(i)*, 260, 263. *See also* African Methodist Episcopal (AME) Church
Bethune, Mary McLeod, 477*(i)*
  HUAC and, 547
  in NACW, 398
Bethune-Cookman College, 477*(i)*
Bett, Mum, 147, 148*(i)*
Beyoncé, 681
Bibb, Henry, 217, 236, 266
Bibb, James, 236
Bibb, Mary Frances, 237
Biden, Joe, 702, 714
Bilbo, Theodore, 521
Bilboes (iron cuffs), 55
Bilingual education, 652
Bin Laden, Osama, 692, 698
Biracials, 682
Biram, 25
Birmingham, Alabama
  Civil Rights movement in, 564–67
  Sixteenth Street Baptist Church bombing in, 576*(i)*, 578
  veteran killed in, 443
Birth of a Nation (film), 414
Birther movement, 708
Birthrate, enslaved people, 92, 126
Black(s). *See also* African Americans; Enslaved people; Free Blacks
  African- *vs.* American-born, 123
  alliances with Jewish people, 650
  American Revolution's results and, 148
  in Baptist churches, 126
  biracial children and, 682
  caricatures of, 292–93*(v)*
  churches of, 185
  conversions by, 131
  distribution of (1680), 78*(m)*
  as elected officials, 653
  enslaved population, 148
  ethnic groups defined as, 664
  in Ferguson, Missouri, 707–8
  free, 175–76
  as freedom fighters, 153–61
  GI Bill and, 528–29
  health care insurance among, 704
  institutions of, 166
  leadership by, 685
  as loyalists, 138–43, 144–47, 145*(i)*
  in Massachusetts, 133
  in military, 613–14, 692
  in militias, 191
  myth of corrupt Black voters and, 388
  as patriots, 134–38, 136*(i)*, 142–43, 145*(i)*
  protesting the killing of unarmed Black men, 723–24*(v)*
  responsibility for own uplift, 368
  revival meetings and, 130
  as Revolutionary soldiers, 134–35, 141–42
  rights denied to, 278
  as runaway servants, 80
  schools for, 186, 260
  as soldiers, 134–35
  as southern patriots, 138
  study of, as "primitives," 387
  support for Revolution by, 132–33
  unemployment of, 705
  use of term, 88, 597, 607
  voting rights for, 255, 352, 356, 366–67
  white attacks on, after Civil War, 359–60
Black activism. *See* Activism
Black Arts Movement, 595
  post-Black art and, 684, 684*(i)*
Black Arts Repertory Theatre/School, 626*(v)*
Black belt
  in Chicago, 437
  in South, 361*(m)*
Black Brigade, 141
Black Cabinet, 478
"Black Camelot," 697
Black church(es), 342*(i)*, 479, 686–87. *See also* Church(es); Religion
Black codes. *See also* Black laws; Slave codes
  after Civil War, 346
  Code Noir (Louisiana), 100, 116*(v)*
Black convention movement, 263–65

Black culture. *See* Culture
Black Entertainment Television, 681
Black Folk, Then and Now (Du Bois), 448
Black freedom movement
  Black middle and upper classes and, 653
  by mid-1960s, 613
  opposition to, 637–44
  persistence of, 644–57
Black History Month (February), 449, 449*(i)*
Black identity. *See* Identity
"Black Immigrants and Black Natives Attending Selective Colleges and Universities in the United States" (Massey, Mooney, Torres, and Charles), 673–74
"Black is beautiful," 623
"Black Land," 10
Black laws. *See also* Slave codes
  in Illinois, 253
  in Indiana, 253
  in Missouri, 253
  in Ohio, 181, 253
  in Wisconsin, 253
Black life, sociological studies of, 447
Black Manhattan (James Weldon Johnson), 448
Black men, 689*(c)*. *See also* African Americans; Black(s); Black women
  incarceration rates for, 643*(i)*, 689
Black Metropolis:... (Drake and Cayton), 447
Black middle class. *See* Middle class (Black)
Black Muslims, 687. *See also* Nation of Islam
Black nationalism, 594, 604–5, 613, 619
  Blyden and, 408
  after Civil War, 363
  Delany and, 281–82
  economic, 452
  Garvey and, 450
  Lyndon B. Johnson on, 607
  of Malcolm X, 596–98, 597*(i)*
  militancy of, 619
Black Panther Party, 589, 605–7, 606*(i)*
  Breakfast Program of, 631*(d)*, 645
  FBI fake letters about, 629–30
  Nixon, FBI, and, 639
  in politics, 645
  transformation of, 644–45
  Vietnam War and, 615
  women and, 645
Black power, 591, 604–7, 623–33, 625–26*(i)*, 630*(v)*
  early organizations for, 593–96
  emergence of, 591–98
  FBI and, 628–31
  Mississippi politics and, 598–602
  in New York, 602–3
  Vietnam War and, 615, 616*(i)*
  violence and, 619
Black pride, 594–95
Black Reconstruction, 350, 354–58, 357*(m)*
  Du Bois on, 354–55
  education during, 366–67
  equal rights in state constitutions during, 383
  politics and, 350
Black Reconstruction (Du Bois), 448
Black Seminoles, 214–15, 214*(i)*
"Black Shirts," 473
Black Star Line steamship company, 452
Black studies, 429–30
Black tax, 681
Black teachers. *See* Teachers
Black Thunder (Bontemps), 486
Black uplift, 259, 261, 264
Black women. *See also* Million Woman March (1997); Woman suffrage; Women
  as attorney general, 704
  on Black woman suffrage, 370
  childbearing by, 230
  education and, 261
  elite, 287, 393
  in freedom's first generation, 393–96, 396*(i)*
  as national security adviser and secretary of state, 695
  roles of, 647–49
  in teaching, 261
  as widows, 256, 259
  at work during Civil War, 326
Black Women Organized for Action, 648
Blackface, in minstrel shows, 292–93*(v)*
Black-labor alliance, 641
Blacklist, in entertainment industry, 550
#BlackLivesMatter, 707, 717–18
  "Herstory of the #BlackLivesMatter Movement, A" (Garza), 719–22
Blackness, 165, 683–85
Black-on-Black crime, 658
Blackstone Rangers, FBI and, 629–30
Blake, Eubie, 455
Blanco, Kathleen, 692
Bland, Ann, 516*(i)*
Bland, Sandra, 722
"Bleeding Kansas," 278
Blockbusting, in housing, 569
Blood, separation of Black and white, 507
Bloody Sunday (1965), 602
"Blue" discharges, in World War II, 530
"Blueprint for Negro Writing" (Wright), 486
Blues music
  in Harlem Renaissance, 456–57
  popularization of, 402
Blues music, ring shouts and, 232
Blyden, Edward, 408, 412
Boas, Franz, 429
Bobalition, 191
"Bobalition" (*Life in Philadelphia* cartoon, Clay), 203–4*(v)*
Body of Liberties (Massachusetts), chattel slavery sanctioned in, 90
Bolden, Charles "Buddy," 403
Boley, Oklahoma, 405
Boll weevil, 432
Bolzius, Johann Martin, 103–4
Bombings, in Chicago, 437
Bonaparte, Napoleon, 173
Bond requirement, for free Blacks in North, 181
Bondmen and bondwomen, 106
Bontemps, Arna, 486
Booker, Archie, 395
Booker, Cory, 686
Booth, John Wilkes, 318
Border states
  in Civil War, 298
  emancipation and, 300
  slavery protected in, 302
Boston
  African Meeting House in, 186
  African Society in, 186
  busing in, 650
  enslaved people in, 90, 122
  "Nigger Hill" in, 258
  public schools in, 188
  resistance to Fugitive Slave Act in, 276
  school integration in, 268
  Walker, David, in, 221
Boston Guardian (newspaper), 410
Boston Massacre (1770), 135
Boston Port Act, 137
Boston Riot (1903), 410
Boston Tea Party (1773), 136
Boston Vigilance Committee, 276
Botswana, 7
Botume, Elizabeth, 316
Bowdoin College, 33*(d)*
Bowery, Charity, 217
Bowser, Mary Elizabeth, 316
Boxing
  integration of, 526
  Johnson, Jack, and, 400
  racism in, 491
Boycotts
  of British goods, 132, 137
  of Chicago World's Fair (1893), 392
  of Montgomery buses, 556–57
  by Urban League, 447
  of Virginia Passenger and Power Company streetcars, 400
Boys, in My Brother's Keeper initiative, 705
Bozales (African-born enslaved people), 45
Braddock, Jim, 491
Bradley, Mamie Till, 554
Bradley, Tom, 653
Brady, Wes, 231
Brain capacity, Morton on, 253
Brief and Candid Answer to a Late Printed Sheet, Entitled, The Selling of Joseph (Saffin), 91
Brinch, Boyrereau, 138
Brinsley, Ismaaiyl, 726
Brisbon, Rumain, 726–28
Britain. *See* England (Britain)
British Anti-Lynching Committee, 392
British North America
  distribution of Blacks and whites in (1680), 78*(m)*
  enslaved people in, 121
Broken windows theory, 707
"Bronx Slave Market, The," 474
Brooklyn Dodgers, desegregation of baseball by, 526
Brooks, Preston S., 278
Broomstick ceremonies, 124*(i)*, 340
Brotherhood of Sleeping Car Porters and Maids, 480, 506
Browder, Kalief, 705

Browder v. Gayle (1956), 556, 557
Brown, Elaine, politics and, 646, 646(*i*)
Brown, Everett, 490
Brown, Henry "Box," 228, 229(*i*), 266
Brown, James, 613
Brown, John
  murder of proslavery settlers by, 278
  slave insurrection and, 282
Brown, Michael, 707, 718
  revenge for, 726
Brown, Sterling, 453
Brown, William Wells
  on African American militia, 310
  background of, 205–8
  Clotel, 266
  mother of, 205, 234
  narratives by, 242, 266
  as successful fugitive, 227
"Brown Bomber, The," 491
Brown Fellowship Society (Charleston), 184
Brown v. Board of Education of Topeka (1954), 485, 553, 662, A-22
Browne, William Washington, 398
Brownsville, Texas, Twenty-Fifth Infantry Regiment in, 407
Bruce, Blanche K., 356
Bryan, Hugh and Jonathan, 129
Bryan, William Jennings, 389
Bryant, Roy, 554
Buchanan, Bessie, 572
Buchanan v. Warley (1917), 447
Buffalo soldiers, after Civil War, 362
Bull Run, battle at, 298
Bunche, Ralph, 483, 549
Bunker Hill, Battle of, 137
Bure, 18–19
Burgoyne, John, patriot defeat at Saratoga and, 142
Burke, Edmund, 145
Burke, Tarana, 712
Burkina Faso, 19, 23–24
Burnham, Dorothy, 484
Burnham, Lewis, 484
Burns, Anthony, 276, 277(*i*)
Burns, Tommy, 400
Burns, Ursula M., 682
Bus boycott, in Montgomery, Alabama, 556–57
Bush, George H. W., 662, 663(*i*)
Bush, George W
  Colin Powell and, 695
  September 11, 2001 attacks and, 692
Bush, George W., 2000 election and, 688
Business
  Black, 258, 474, 677
  slave trade as, 40
Busing
  in Boston, 650
  for integration, 639, 642, 649
  Reagan and, 642
Butler, Andrew P., 278
Butler, Benjamin F
  freedom seekers and, 301, 304, 322
  U.S. Colored Troops and, 307
Butler School for Negro Children, 347, 350
Buxtun, Peter, 534
Byrd, William, 83
Byzantine Empire, 17

Cabin in the Sky (film), 526
Cabinet, during Reconstruction, 353
Cain, Richard, 344, 348
Cairo Conference, of Organization of African Unity, 596
Cakewalk (dance), 401
Caldwell, Elias, 221
California
  as free state, 273
  race riots in, 517
  schools for Black children in, 366
  University of California (Berkeley), 595
Call to the Unconverted (Baxter), 129
Cambodia, invasion of, 640
Cambridge Nonviolent Action Committee, 593
Cameroon, 14
Camp fever, 142
Campbell, Robert, 281
"Can We All Get Along? Interviews with Immigrants and Native-Born Blacks," 671–73
Canada
  African Americans in, 251–52, 255, 281
  Black loyalists in, 146
Canary Islands, 40
Cane (Toomer), 453
Cannibalism, African fears of, 54
Cannon, Corinne, 611
Cape Bojador, 39
Cape Coast Castle, 52–53
Cape Verde Islands, 39–40
CAPs. *See* Community Action Programs
Captives, enslaved African, 49–53
Caravels, 39–40
Carceral state, 688–91
  use of term, 690
Caribbean region
  in American Revolution, 143
  enslaved people from, 122
  immigrants from, 408
  Middle Passage to, 55
Carlton, William Tolman, 327, 332
  Watch Meeting-Dec. 31st-Waiting for the Hour, 333(*v*)
Carmichael, Stokely, 589–90, 600(*i*), 604–5
  Black power and, 604–5
  FBI and, 628(*d*)
  on international Black freedom struggle, 606
  on Vietnam War, 615
Carnegie, Andrew, Tuskegee Institute funding from, 409
Carnera, Primo, 491
Carolina(s), 85–89. *See also* North Carolina; South Carolina
  freedom seekers to Spanish Florida from, 101
  loyalists in, 144
  plantations in, 86
  rice cultivation in, 86
Carpetbaggers, 354
Carracks (ships), 39
Carruthers, Richard, 319
Carter, Alprentice "Bunchy," 639
Carter, Jimmy, 642, 653, 698
Cary, Mary Ann Shadd, 251–52, 272, 281
  "Woman's Right to Vote, Early 1870s," 374–75
Case law, for employment issues, 611
Cash crops, 105. *See also* Cotton
  in Jamestown, 77
  slavery for, 209
Castles, slave, 46, 52
Catawba Indians, 105, 147
Catholic Church
  African slavery and, 43
  in Kongo, 104
  in Spanish Florida, 101
Catto, Octavius, 311, 321, 365–66
Cavalry, post-Civil War Blacks in, 361–62
Cayton, Horace R., 447
Center on Race and Social Problems, 708
Central High School, Little Rock
  desegregation of, 560, 583–85
Central powers, in World War I, 439
Ceremonies. *See also* Marriage
  of Black funerals, 125
  of Negro Election Day, 123
Césaire, Aimé, 488
CFA. *See* Colored Farmers' Alliance
"Chain Gang," 426–27(*v*)
Chain gangs, 420, 426–27(*v*)
Chain migration pattern, 432
Chains
  enslaved people being marched in, 50, 51(*i*)
Chaney, James, 599
Charles, Camille Z., "Black Immigrants and Black Natives Attending Selective Colleges and Universities in the United States," 673–74
Charles II (England), 93
Charles II (Spain), 101
Charleston
  Brown Fellowship Society of, 184
  in Revolution, 143
  slave trade in, 175
  Vesey's rebellion in, 218–20
Chattel slavery, 80, 82. *See also* Slavery
Chauncey, Isaac, 192
Chauvin, Derek, 717–18, 725
Cherokee Indians
  removal of, 212, 214
  Trail of Tears and, 214
Chesapeake Marine Railway and Dry Dock Company, 364
Chesapeake region, 84(*c*)
  Black and white populations in, 83–85
  decline of enslaved labor in, 168
  Dutch slave trade in, 81
  enslaved people in religious revivals and, 130
  enslaved population in, 121
  free Blacks in, 143

slave trade in, 125
slavery in, 77, 79–80, 79(*i*), 83–85
tobacco in, 77, 79
Chesnutt, Charles, 404
Chester, Thomas Morris, 311, 321
Chicago
Black businesses in, 437
Black medicine and hospitals in, 437
Black migration to, 432–33
Black women in, 439
Chicago Defender and, 432
civil rights activists in, 571
Commission on Race Relations in, 446
Democratic National Convention in (1968), 639
gospel music in, 436
housing in, 437, 568–69, 570
migration to, 432–35, 515
New Negro arts movement in, 453
Obama in, 677
Operation Breadbasket in, 612
public housing in, 570
race riots in, 442–43, 446, 517
storefront churches in, 436
strikes in, 437
urban renewal in, 609, 610(*i*)
Chicago Defender (newspaper), 520
Great Migration and, 430, 432
Till photos in, 554
World War I and, 440
Chicago Housing Authority, 550, 570
Chicago Renaissance, 486–88
Chicago School, 446
Chicago World's Fair (1893)
Black boycott of, 392
Chickasaw Indians, 105, 212
"Chiefs of Indigo," 25
Childbearing
by enslaved women, 234
women's workloads and, 233
Children
education for free Blacks, 188
enslaved, 215
flight from Confederate control, 316
in Middle Passage, 57
slave raids for, 50
status of enslaved women's children, 80, 182
Childs, Lyn, 516
China Gates (Johnson), 684(*i*)
Chinese Exclusion Act (1882), 387
Chisholm, Shirley, 635–36, 637(*i*), 647
Congressional Black Caucus and, 653
as presidential candidate, 635
Choctaw Indians, 212
Christiana Resistance, 276
Christianity. *See also* Church(es); Great Awakening; Religion; Revivals
abolitionist movement and, 271–72
of African Americans, 13
Civil Rights movement and, 557–58
conversion of American Indians to, 43
Crusades and, 39
freedoms of African converts to, 109
Great Awakening and, 126–29
as justification for slavery, 230–32
in Kongo, 104
pagan beliefs *vs.*, 88
slavery and, 81, 101, 130
Christianization, of contrabands, 302
Chrysler, government loans to, 698
Church(es). *See also* Religion
Black, 185, 185(*i*), 189
bombings of, 560
in Chicago, 436
Civil Rights movement and, 553
after emancipation, 341–44, 342(*i*)
enslaved people's attendance at, 231
folk religion and, 343
in Great Awakening, 126
in Great Depression, 478–80
independent, 259
institutions stimulated by, 343
invisible, 231
in Richmond, 398
Church, Frank, abuses of power investigated by, 632–33
"Church Committee Report," 632–33
Churchill, Winston, Atlantic Charter and (1941), 506
Cincinnati
Black high school in, 261
Blacks in, during Civil War, 299–300
race riots in, 255
CIO. *See* Congress of Industrial Organizations
CIO Political Action Committee, 522, 523(*i*)
Cities. *See also* Urban areas; *specific locations*
all-Black, 363–65
Black communities in New South, 397–401
educational quality in, 649–50
free Blacks in northern, 183
Great Migration and, 430, 435–39
migration to, 609
racial diversity in, 257
violence in, 619
Citizens' Commission to Investigate the FBI, 628
Citizenship
denied to African Americans, 281
Dred Scott decision and, 281, 321
Fourteenth Amendment and, 352, 360
for free Blacks, 181
struggle in World War II, 520–31
after World War II, 522
Civil disobedience. *See also* Black power
by aiding freedom seekers, 276
against segregated railroads, 384
World War II and, 520
Civil rights. *See also* Nonviolent protest; Voting and voting rights
anticommunism and, 561
attorney general's list of "subversive" organizations and, 551
for Blacks, 192, 278
Du Bois on, 405
in 1870s, 358–60
Fourteenth Amendment and, 352
Griggs decision and, 612
in 1948 election, 552
organizing for, 483–85
post-Civil War struggle for, 365–67
Robeson and, 545–46
Supreme Court undermining of, 360
Civil Rights Act
of 1866, 352
of 1869, 383
of 1875, 358, 383, A-14–A-15
of 1957, 638
of 1964, 592–93, 607, 611, 637, A-15–A-18
of 1968, 654
Civil Rights Cases (1883), 360, 383
Civil rights laws, 571
Civil Rights movement. *See also* Black nationalism; Black power; Nonviolent protest
in Birmingham, Alabama, 564–67
Black power and, 591
expansion of, 591–93
fracturing of, 620
leadership of, 557–62
Montgomery bus boycott and, 556–57
as national movement, 567–78
protests in, 585–87(*v*)
in South, 553–67
students in, 561–65
violence in, 554–56, 555(*v*), 560–64, 567, 586(*i*)
Civil rights organizations, 552
Civil War, 308(*c*). *See also* Reconstruction
Black migration during, 430
Black military service in, 295–96, 298–99, 307–10, 312(*m*), 322, 339
Black patriotism in, 299
Black women during, 316, 326
border states in, 300
causes of, 295–96
coming of (1861–1862), 296–304
families separated during, 339
free Blacks before, 252–62
military in, 297
northern freedom seekers in, 295–96
opportunities and dilemmas in, 326
Civilian Conservation Corps (CCC), 476
Civilization, 386
Clark, A., "Address of the Colored State Convention to the People of Iowa in Behalf of Their Enfranchisement, 1868," 376–77
Clark, Laura, 238
Clarke, George, 119
Clarke, Lewis Garrard, "Questions and Answers about Slavery," 243–44
Clash in Charlottesville, A, 710(*i*)
Class
among African Americans, 657–60
diversity based on, 680
of elite Black southern women, 393
female welfare rights and, 647
Clay, Edward Williams, "Bobalition" (*Life in Philadelphia* cartoon), 203–4(*v*)

Clay, Henry
African colonization and, 193
Missouri Compromise and, 212
Cleaver, Eldridge, 645
Cleaver, Kathleen, 645
Clerical workers, Black, 654
Clinton, Bill
African American support for, 653, 659
Clinton, Henry, 143
Clinton, Hillary
Trump and, 708
2008 election and, 697
2016 election and, 708
Clotel (Brown), 266
Clotel (Jefferson's alleged daughter), 266
Clothing, homespun, 169
Clyatt v. United States (1905), 420
Coasts
slave coast, 53–55, 56*(i)*, 57*(i)*
West African, 39, 46
Cocaine
Black and white use of, 688
crack, 658
Code Noir ("Black Code"), 100, 116*(v)*
Codes of law. *See also* Black codes; Slave codes
in New England, 111*(d)*
in Virginia, 224
"Codification of Slavery and Race in Seventeenth-Century Virginia," 110–11
Coffles
enslaved people being marched in, 50, 51*(i)*
enslaved people's forced migration in, 215
Coggeshall, Jane, "Petition for Freedom, 1785," 197–98
COINTELPRO (Counterintelligence Program, FBI), Black freedom movement and, 628–29, 717
Cold War
labor unions during, 550
Red scare during, 547–53
Cole, Bob, 402
Collective action, by rural Black women, 395
Colleges and universities
historically Black, 343, 348, 531, 561, 669, A-34–A-36
liberal arts curriculum at, 348, 350
teacher training at, 348
Collins, Addie Mae, 576*(i)*
Colman, Benjamin, 127
Colonel's Dream, The (Chesnutt), 404
Colonies and colonization
in Africa, 192–94
African Americans and, 596
British, after American Revolution, 146
Carolinas as, 85–89
in Chesapeake region, 77
enslaved Africans sent to, 42
enslaved and free Blacks in, 121–23
French, 172
Georgia as, 103–4
nation-states in, 591
resolutions opposing, 201
slave trade and, 60
white supremacy in, 386–87
Colonization
in Africa, 412
in Liberia, 363
opposition to, 264
Walker on, 221
white northerners on, 253
Colonization bill, in Virginia, 224
Colonization Council (Kansas), 363
Color. *See* Skin color
Colorado, 174*(m)*
Color-blind arguments, 641
Colored American (newspaper), 262
Colored Farmers' Alliance (CFA), 389
Colored Ladies of Baltimore, 299*(i)*
Colored National Labor Union, 365
Colored Orphan Asylum (New York City), 259, 313
Colored Rule in a Reconstructed(?) State, 1874 (Nast), 378*(v)*
Colored Troops under General Wild, Liberating Slaves in North Carolina, 319*(i)*
Colvin, Claudette, 556
Combahee River Collective, 648
"Coming of Age in Mississippi" (Moody), 581–82*(d)*
Commercial farms, 211
Commission on Race Relations (Chicago), 446
Committee for Industrial Organization (CIO), 519
Committee for Preventing Irregular Conduct Among Free Negroes, 189
Common man, era of, 254
Common school movement, 261
Communal belief systems, of the enslaved, 88
Communism. *See also* Communist Party of the United States
radicalism, 495–96
Red scare after World War I and, 443
Red scare after World War II and, 547–53
Communist Party of the United States (CPUSA)
African Americans and, 495
radicalism of, 495–96
Robeson and, 545
Scottsboro Boys case and, 481–83
Communities
African American, 123, 238, 256–59
church networks in, 343
of enslaved people on plantations, 88
of free Blacks, 184–87
in Great Depression, 479–80
in New South cities, 397–401
northern Black urban, 437
school control by, 650
Community Action Programs (CAPs), War on Poverty and, 618
Community service programs, Black Panthers and, 645
Company of the West Indies (France), 99, 100
Compensation, for emancipation from slavery, 300
Compensatory programs, 612
opponents of, 640–41
Comprehensive Crime Control Act of 1984, 642
Comprehensive Employment and Training Act (CETA), 642
Compromise of 1850, 272
Concord, battle at, 137
Concubinage, 28
Condition, Elevation, Emigration, and Destiny of the Colored People of the United States, The (Delany), 281
Confederate flag, in South Carolina, 706
Confederate States of America. *See also* South
Black migration from, 360–65
Black Union soldiers and, 310
creation of, 297
emancipation and, 305–6
and emancipation of the enslaved after Civil War, 318–19
enslaved labor for army of, 314–15
Fifteenth Amendment and, 366–67
flag of, 299*(i)*
as independent nation, 298
Jim Crow in, 384–85, 385*(m)*
lands to freedpeople from, 318
Lincoln's attitude toward, 318
military districts in, 354
military of, 297
Reconstruction for, 317–18, 350–60
refugee freedom seekers and, 301–2, 303*(i)*
state governments dissolved in, 354
Confederate White House, Black spy in, 316
Congo River, 14
Congress (U.S.). *See also* Radical Republicans; Reconstruction
African Americans in, 653, 712
antilynching bills in, 419–20
De Priest in, 438
on debt peonage, 419–20
gag rule against antislavery petitions in, 224
Obama and, 703, 705
post-emancipation Blacks in, 355*(i)*
Congress of Industrial Organizations (CIO), 480, 518, 523*(i)*
during Red scare, 550
Congress of Racial Equality (CORE), 520, 553, 595
Black power and, 604
Black violence and, 619
employment discrimination protests by, 571
Freedom Rides and, 563*(m)*
interracial student activism and, 590
Vietnam War and, 615
Congressional Black Caucus, 653, 659
Congressional Medal of Honor, 362
Congressional Reconstruction, 351–53, 357*(m)*
Conjure, power of, 126
Connecticut, 92
Connor, Eugene "Bull," 544, 564
emancipation in, 181
slavery in, 90
Conquistadors, Black, 43, 44*(i)*

Conscription. *See also* Military draft
into British Royal Navy, 191
Conservatives and conservatism. *See also* New Right
Black, 685
in early twenty-first century, 688
on economic injustice, 608
Constitution (ship), 192
Constitution (U.S.), A-1–A-3
amendments to, A-10–A-14
as antislavery document, 270
during Reconstruction, 354
slavery in, 165–68, 272
on state discrimination, 181
Constitutional Convention, 166–68, 354
Constitutional Union Party, 283
Continental army, Black soldiers in, 138, 143
Continental Congress
First, 137
Second, 137
Contraband
Army of the Potomac and, 311
enslaved people as, 301, 302, 303(*i*), 322
in Hampton, Virginia, 346–47
Contraband Relief Association, 316
Contracts, labor, 345
Conventions
Black, 263–65, 321
women's rights (Seneca Falls), 271
Conversion
of American Indians, 43
by Black lay preachers, 131
of enslaved people, 101, 130
Convict lease system, 346
Conyers, John Jr., 686
Cook, Will Marion, 401
Cooke, Marvel, 474
Cooper, Anna Julia, 394, 412
Cooper, Charles "Chuck," 526
Cooperative action, in Richmond, 397–401
Cooperative economic enterprises, Black, 263
Copley, John Singleton, *Death of Major Peirson, The*, 159, 160(*v*)
CORE. *See* Congress of Racial Equality
Cornish, Samuel, 33(*d*), 264, 272
Cornwallis, Charles, 144
Coronavirus pandemic, 676, 713, 717
Corrupt voters, myth of Black, 388
Cortés, Hernán, 43, 44(*i*)
Cortor, Eldzier, 486
Cosby, Bill, 660
Pound Cake speech by, 690
Cotton and cotton industry, 170(*c*)
boll weevil and, 432
enslaved families and, 237(*v*)
enslaved laborers' processing of, 171(*i*)
expansion of plantation agriculture and, 208–9
frontiers of slavery and, 168–72, 195
growth of, 215
in Louisiana Purchase, 174
overproduction in, 473
slavery and, 209–11, 210(*m*)
Cotton Club, 457
Cotton gin, 168, 171(*i*)
Cotton States and International Exposition (Atlanta, 1895), 409
Council of Federated Organizations (COFO), 598
Council on African Affairs, 551
Country marks (facial scars), 88
Countryside. *See* Rural areas
Courts. *See also* Juries; Supreme Court (U.S.)
Black testifying in, 321
discrimination ended by, 268
Kansas-Nebraska Act and, 278
Reagan and, 644
rightward turn of, 670
Covert actions, by FBI, 628(*d*)
Covert resistance, 239
Covid-19. *See* Coronavirus pandemic
Cowboys, Blacks as, 406
Cox, Courtland, 589
Crack cocaine, 658
Craft, Ellen and William, 228
Crandall, Prudence, 260
Crania Americana (Morton), 253
Craniology, 253
Creek Indians
forced migration of, 212
in Oklahoma, 363
Crenshaw, Kimberlé Williams, 706
Creole communication, 85
Creole insurrection, 225
Criminal justice, Obama reform of, 705
Criminal surety laws, 420
Criminality, Blacks accused of, 254
Criminalization, of African Americans, 664
Crisis, The (journal), 414, 425, 426, 439
Du Bois and, 484
Harlem Renaissance and, 453
Crittenden, John J., 297
Croix de Guerre, for Black regiments (World War I), 440
Crop(s). *See also* Cash crops; Sharecropping
enslaved workers for, 209
in Middle Atlantic colonies, 96
in New England, 89
sugarcane as, 40
Crop lien system, 346
Crouch, Stanley, 683
Crowley, James, 701
Crowther, Samuel Ajayi, 50
Crummell, Alexander, 408, 412
Crusades, 39
Cuba
enslaved Africans in, 43
Obama policy toward, 703
Cuffe (Cuffee), Paul, 193
Cugoano, Ottobah, 58
Cullen, Countee, 3, 34(*d*), 453
Cullors, Patrisse, 717, 719(*d*)
Cultural activism, 489
Culture, 485–92. *See also* Art(s); Harlem Renaissance; Religion
African American, 122–26, 526
African Americans in France and, 440–41
Black Arts Movement and, 453, 454(*m*)
Blackness and, 683–85
blended African and American, 126
creation of African American, 122–26, 124(*i*)
expressions of, 401–4
Hurston on, 429–30
popular images of Black women in, 648
racial stereotypes in, 490–92
Currer (Jefferson's alleged mistress), 266
Curriculum, at Hampton Institute, 348–50

"Daddy Grace," 479
Daley, Richard J., violence against Blacks and, 570
Damas, Léon, 488
Dana, Charles, 311
Dance. *See also* Minstrel shows
in Chicago Renaissance, 485
in Harlem Renaissance, 455
"Negroes Jitterbugging in a Juke Joint on Saturday Afternoon, Clarksdale, Mississippi Delta, 1939" (Wolcott), 500–501, 501(*i*)
"Dancing the slaves," on slave ships, 57, 57(*i*)
Daniels, Jonathan, 589–90
Darrow, Clarence, 496
Darwin, Charles
natural selection and, 387
Social Darwinism and, 387
Daughters of the American Revolution, 492
Daura, 25
Davies, Samuel, 130
Davis, Angela, 596, 639, 645
Davis, Artur, 686
Davis, Ben (NYC councilman), 550
Davis, Benjamin O. Jr., 535
Davis, Benjamin O. Sr., 507
Davis, Elizabeth Lindsay, 435
Davis, Hugh, 109
Davis, Jefferson. *See also* Confederate States of America
election of, 297
emancipation and, 318
Davis, John P., 477, 483
Davis, Larry, 708
Davis, Miles, 528
Davis, Pauline W., 372, 373(*d*)
Dawson, William Levi, 571
"Days of Slavery, The" (Reynolds), 246–48, 247(*i*)
Daytona Normal and Industrial Institute for Negro Girls, 398
De Bieuw, Edward, 233
De Blasio, Bill, 726
De facto segregation, 437, 552
De jure segregation, 437, 553
De la Silva, Juan, 119
De Large, Robert C., 355(*i*)
De Priest, Oscar, 438, 478
De Tocqueville, Alexis, 253
De Verger, Jean Baptiste Antoine, *Soldiers in Uniform*, 157, 158(*v*)

Deacons for Defense and Justice, 604
Death. *See* Mortality
Death of Major Peirson, The (Copley), 153, 159, 160(*v*)
Death Row Records, 660
"Debate, A: Negro Male Suffrage Equal Rights Association *vs.* Woman Suffrage" (American Equal Rights Association), 371–74
Debt
in crop lien system, 346
imprisonment for, 420
Debt peonage, 396, 420, 423–25
Declaration of Independence (1776), 137, 139, A-1–A-3
equality in, 137
slavery and, 163
DeCuir, Josephine, 383
Defense industries
Blacks in, 518
racial discrimination in, 507
Deindustrialization, 610(*i*), 618
Delany, Hubert T., 550
Delany, Martin R., 412
on Black self-help, 259
Condition, Elevation, Emigration, and Destiny of the Colored People of the United State, The, 281
family in Canada, 281
novels by, 266
in U.S. Colored Troops, 308
Delaware, 93, 94, 320
Democracy
fight for in World War II, 522
limits of, 165–66
Democratic National Committee, Watergate and, 641
Democratic National Convention
in 1944, 522
in 1964, 599, 601–2
in 1968, 639
Democratic Party
African Americans in, 477–78, 653, 688
as all-white party after Civil War, 358
Chisholm as candidate of, 635
in 1860, 283
in 1948 election, 552
as private club, 388
proslavery interests of, 278
racism during Civil War, 313
in South, 388
Democratic Party, 1864 election and, 317–18
"Democratic Party Broadside" (1866), 353(*v*)
Democratic Republic of the Congo, 14
Demonstrations. *See also* Protests
in Albany, Georgia, 559(*i*)
in Ferguson, Missouri, 717
at Kent State and Jackson State, 640
Denmark, slave trade and, 60
Deportations, by Obama, 702
Depression (economic). *See also* Great Depression (1930s); Recession
in 1870s, 360
Great Migration to North and, 432
Depression (emotional), among captives, 58
Derrick, John, 571
Desegregation. *See also* Integration; Racial segregation
in Birmingham, 564
of lunch counters, 561–62
of military, 528–31
Nixon on, 638–39
in North, 321
of Philadelphia public conveyances, 365–66
of schools, 554, 560, 571
of sports, 526
of University of Mississippi, 564
white resistance and, 649
Detroit
Black auto workers in, 515
housing in, 570
migration to, 513–14
public housing in, 570
race riots in, 516–17, 618
school segregation in, 649
strikes in, 517, 518, 618
Dewey, Thomas, 552
Diallo, Amadou, 682
Diaspora, in slave trade, 60
Diasporic, 3
Dickerson, Debra, 683
Dinkinesh, 6
Discrimination. *See also* Civil Rights Act; Racial discrimination; Racial segregation
in academic institutions, 653–54
Constitution on state laws, 181
in educational institutions receiving federal funding, 653–54
in employment, 572, 592
Fair Housing Act and, 654
in housing, 609
institutional racism and, 609
in military, 691
Reagan on, 641–41
in World War II military, 509–13
Disease
AIDS epidemic and, 658–59
Black hospitals and, 343
during Middle Passage, 56(*i*), 58–60
Old World in Americas, 42
Disfranchisement, political activism and, 388–89
Dismal Swamp, 85
Dissent. *See also* Demonstrations; Protests; Revolts and rebellions
African American in World War II, 508
enslaved people and, 217–25
District of Columbia Emancipation Act, 301
Diversity
of Black America, 664, 679–80
of Black leadership, 688
in cities, 257
in politics and religion, 685–88
in twenty-first century, 683–84
Division of Negro Affairs, National Youth Administration, 506
Dixiecrat Party, 552
Dixon, Paul, 515
Djenne, 19
Djibouti, 13
DJs
rap music and, 660
turntablism and, 661(*i*)
Dodge Revolutionary Union Movement, 617
Dodson, Ben and Betty, reuniting of, 339
Dolly, Quamino (enslaved person), 143
Domestic slave trade, 209, 215–17, 216(*m*)
Domestic Workers' Union, 480
Dominican missionaries, critique of mistreatment of native peoples, 43
"Don't Buy Where You Can't Work" boycotts, 479–80
Dorsey, Thomas, 487
Double Victory campaign, in and after World War II, 504, 510(*i*), 513, 520, 528
Douglas, Aaron, 455
Douglas, H. Ford, 281
Douglas, Stephen A., 278
Douglass, Charles, 309(*i*)
Douglass, Frederick, 286
American Equal Rights Association and, 367, 370, 371–74
Black military recruitment and, 307–8
on Black voting rights, 352
on Brown, John, 282
on codependent relationship of Blacks and whites, 715
Contraband Relief Association and, 316
desegregation of streetcars and, 383
on destiny of colored man, 284
on *Dred Scott* decision, 281–82
Emancipation Proclamation celebrated by, 322
on escape by Henry "Box" Brown, 229(*i*)
as a formerly enslaved person, 226–27
Freedman's Savings and Trust Company and, 360
on *Freedmen's Memorial*, 334–35
at Fugitive Slave Law Convention, 271(*v*)
Garrison and, 269–71
grandmother of, 233
lectures by, 265, 266
My Bondage and My Freedom, 266
Narrative of the Life of Frederick Douglass, an American Slave, 266
National Convention of Colored Men and, 321
North Star (newspaper) of, 265, 271(*d*)
novels by, 242, 265–66
portrait of, 265(*i*)
at Republican National Convention (1876), 368
in Republican Party, 279
at Seneca Falls convention, 271
on slavery and Civil War, 265, 300
sons of, 309, 309(*i*), 311
as a successful freedom seeker, 227
Wells and, 381, 392
"What to the Slave Is the Fourth of July?," 290–91
Douglass, Grace, 270
Douglass, Lewis, 309(*i*), 407

Douglass, Sarah Mapps, 261, 270, 286
  "To Make the Slaves' Cause Our Own," 287*(d)*
Draft. *See* Military draft
Draft riots, in New York City (1863), 313
Drake, Francis, 77
Drake, St. Clair, 447
DREAM Act, 702
Dred Scott v. Sandford (1857), A-20–A-21
  citizenship and, 281, 321
  Douglass on, 281
  impact of decision, 281
  portrait of plaintiffs, 280*(v)*
  reversal of, 352
Drew, Charles, 507
Driver (Black overseer), 83
Drug use
  imprisonment for, 688
  war on drugs and, 642–43
Du Bois, W. E. B. *See also Crisis, The* (journal)
  "Along the Color Line," 425*(d)*
  Black Folk, Then and Now, 448
  on Black Reconstruction, 354–55
  Black Reconstruction by, 448
  on civil and political rights, 405
  on color line, 666
  communism and, 547
  Crisis, The (journal) and, 414, 425, 426, 484
  on Durham, North Carolina, 401
  emergence of, 410–16
  "From the South" (Letter to the Editor), 426*(d)*
  Garvey and, 455
  on group economy in Black urban communities, 397
  Harlem Renaissance and, 455
  NAACP and, 414
  "Negro Editors on Communism: A Symposium of the American Negro Press, 1932," 496–97
  Philadelphia Negro, The, and, 446
  portrait of, 411*(i)*
  Red scare and, 547
  "Upbuilding of Black Durham, The," 401
  Washington and, 412
  on World War I, 439–40
Ducksworth, Roman, 564
Duke, David, 708
Dum Diversas (papal bull), 43
Dumont, John, 182
Dunbar, Paul Laurence, 403
  "Haunted Oak, The," 403
  "We Wear the Mask," 404
Dunham, Katherine, 487–88, 487*(i)*
Dunham, Stanley and Madelyn, 677*(i)*
Dunmore, Earl of, 139–44
Dupree, Jack, 359
Durham, North Carolina, Black progress in, 401
Dutch. *See also* New Amsterdam; New Netherland
  in Middle Atlantic colonies, 93–96
  slave trade and, 46, 60, 76, 81
Dutch West India Company, 95
Duties, on enslaved Africans, 122–23
Dwight, Ed, 219*(v)*
Dyer, Leonidas, 419
Dyer Anti-Lynching Bill, 419, 447
Dynasties, 10

East Africa, 9
East St. Louis, Illinois, race riot in (1917), 442, 442*(i)*
Eastern Europe, communism in, 548
Eastern Woodlands Indians, 79
Easton, Hosea, 188
  Treatise on the Intellectual Character, and Civil and Political Condition of the Colored People of the U. States, A, 266
Ebonics, 652
Eckford, Elizabeth, 560, 584*(v)*
  "First Day, The: Little Rock," 583–85*(d)*
Economic bill of rights, 617
Economic nationalism, of Garvey, 452
Economic Opportunity Act (1964), 611
Economy
  Black freedom struggle and, 613
  Black power in, 654
  Great Depression effects on, 473–75
  injustice in, 611–13
  in New England, 89
  Obama and, 698
  organizing for opportunity in, 517–20
  panic of 1873 and, 360
  politics, jobs, and, 607–13
  regional differences in, 209–11
  slave, 168
  in South, 209–10
  2008 election and, 696, 697
  after World War I, 443
Edmund Pettus Bridge, 602
Edo, 25–26
Education. *See also* Colleges and universities; Schools
  Bill Clinton and, 660
  Brown decision and, 554, 560
  after Civil War, 366–67
  for enslaved people, 129
  equal, 650
  forbidden to Blacks, 221
  for free Blacks, 187–90, 260–61
  for freedpeople, 346–50
  GI Bill and, 530
  passage through generations, 232
  religious, 232
  for Richmond Blacks, 398
Education Amendments (1972), Title IX of, 653
Edwards, Jonathan, 129
EEOC. *See* Equal Employment Opportunity Commission
Efik-Ibibio language, 126
Egalitarianism
  of Great Awakening, 131, 148
  after Revolution, 191
Egypt, 3, 8–12
  dynasties of, 10
  literacy in, 12
  Middle Kingdom of, 10
  military in, 12
  New Kingdom of, 11, 13
  Old Kingdom of, 10, 12
  pharaohs of, 10–11, 11*(i)*
  pyramid complex in, 10, 12
  religion in, 11
  taxation in, 12
"Eight box law" (South Carolina), 388
Eighteenth Dynasty, 11
Eisenhower, Dwight D
  on international image of Black Americans, 566*(i)*
  school desegregation and, 560–61
El Salvador, 710
Elders, schooling by, 232
Election(s)
  African American impacts on, 653
  of 1860, 272, 296
  of 1864, 317–18, 351
  of 1876, 382
  of 1896, 389
  of 1932, 475
  of 1948, 552
  of 1964, 598–602
  of 1968, 635
  of 1972, 637*(i)*, 647
  of 1980, 642
  of 1984, 653, 695
  of 1988, 653, 695
  of 2000, 688
  of 2008, 679, 695–97
  of 2012, 702–3
Election officials, Black, 653
Elite Black women
  attitudes and experiences of, 287
  lifestyle of, 393
Ellington, Duke, 457
Elliott, Robert Brown, 355*(i)*
Ellis, Harold, 408
Ellison, Ralph, 486
Elmina Castle, 46, 53
Emancipation. *See also* Abolitionists and abolitionism; Freedpeople; Formerly enslaved people; Gradual emancipation
  churches and community after, 341–44, 342*(i)*
  in District of Columbia, 301
  education after, 346–50
  gradual, 181
  land and labor after, 344–46
  Lincoln on, 301
  meaning of, 334*(v)*, 335*(v)*
  national state-sponsored, 320–21
  in North after Louisiana Purchase, 180–83
  in North after Revolution, 164–67
  political revolution after, 350–60
  social revolution after, 338–50
  as war goal, 312–13
Emancipation (Freedmen's Memorial, Ball), 335*(v)*
Emancipation Day, parade in Richmond, 399*(i)*, 400

Emancipation Oak, school at, 306, 347
Emancipation Proclamation (1863), 305–7, 313, 322, 331–32
Emanuel AME Church (Charleston, South Carolina), 706
Emigration. *See also* Migration
  to Canada, 251, 252, 255, 281
  payment for relocation and, 300–301
Emperor Jones, The, 489
Empires
  slavery and, 172–75
  white supremacy in, 386–87
Employment. *See also* Labor unions; Unemployment
  discrimination in, 572, 592
  for educated Blacks, 188
  of free Blacks, 187–90
  in northern cities, 435–36
Employment Service, U.S., 515
Encomienda system, 42
End of Blackness, The (Dickerson), 683
England (Britain). *See also* British North America; Enslaved people; Slavery
  American Revolution and, 131–46
  antislavery movement in, 133
  Middle Atlantic colonies and, 93
  New Netherland and, 95
  Oregon Treaty with, 273
  slave trade and, 46, 60, 81, 145
  slavery and, 76
  slavery in middle colonies of, 96–98
  Somerset case and, 133
  southern strategy in American Revolution, 143–44
Englewood Movement (New Jersey), 649
English language
  enslaved people's uses of, 85
  Gullah and, 126
English North America. *See* British North America
Enlightenment, American Revolution and, 131
Enslaved people. *See also* Abolitionists and abolitionism; Black(s); Emancipation; Families; Formerly enslaved people; Freedom seekers; Marriage; Religion; Slavery
  accused of killing whites, 227
  African in Americas, 43–45
  in American Revolution, 136*(i)*, 138–43
  assemblages of, 179
  in Boston, 90
  Brown insurrection and, 282
  capture and confinement of, 49–53
  in Carolinas, 85–89
  in Chesapeake region, 79*(i)*, 80
  childbearing by, 230
  confiscation of Confederate, 301
  constraints on congregating by, 130
  conversion of, 101, 130
  cotton processing by, 171*(i)*
  decreased demand for, 169
  defection from Confederacy, 295–96
  desirability by age, 91
  education for, 129
  emancipation forced by, 322
  emancipation in North, 180–83
  enslaved families in Georgia, 237*(v)*
  enslavers yielding to demands in Civil War, 315
  family breakups by sales, 172
  former, 304
  former, as Revolutionary soldiers, 137
  free Blacks and, 121–23
  freedom for (1865), 313
  freedom petitions by, 134
  imprinting of, 52
  infant mortality among, 233
  literacy and, 130, 232–33
  loyalists after Revolution, 146
  in Maryland, 176–77
  in Middle Passage, 50–60
  in Missouri, 302
  mulatto, 85
  mutinies by, 56
  in New Amsterdam, 95*(i)*
  "new Negroes" as, 82, 84
  in New Netherland, 93–96
  origins and destinations of, 47*(m)*
  out-of-state sales of, 182
  as plantation workers, 304
  population of, 167, 175–77, 208
  pre-Revolution escapes by, 132
  punishment of, 243*(v)*
  Seminole, 213–14
  servants and, 83
  shipments of, 216
  in St. Augustine, 76–77, 101, 102*(i)*
  state taxation, representation, and, 167
  supply from Africa, 122
  testimony of, 241–48
  transforming African captives into, 110–11
Enslaved labor
  for agriculture, 54
  for cotton production, 169
  northern dependence on, 122
  in South, 208
  trade in, 40–43
Enslavers
  anthropological justifications of slavery and, 253
  insecurity of, 225
  sex and power of, 82*(i)*
Entertainment and entertainment industry. *See also* Films
  Black, 401–4
Epic of Sundiata, 18–19
Episcopal church, African American, 186
Equal Employment Opportunity Commission (EEOC), 592, 611, 642, 662
Equal rights. *See also* Rights
  post-Civil War struggle for, 365–67
  in southern state constitutions, 383
Equal School Rights Committee (Boston), 268
"Equal Voting Rights" (Truth), 370–71
Equality
  abolitionism and, 268
  in Declaration of Independence, 137
  educational, 650
  Equal rights. *See* Rights
  post-Civil War struggle for, 365–67
  in public accommodations, 358
  social, 446
Equality index, in 2018, 680
Equiano, Olaudah, 50, 54–55, 56*(i)*, 85
  "Interesting Narrative of the Life of Olaudah Equiano, or Gustavus Vassa, the African, The," 63–66
Eritrea, 13
"Escaping Slavery via the Underground Railroad," 292*(v)*
Establishment, Black people and, 686
Ethiopia, 3, 6, 13
Ethiopian Manifesto, The (Young), 266
Ethiopian Orthodox Church, 13
Ethiopian Regiment, of Dunmore, 140
Ethnic groups, 88, 664
Europe
  immigration from, 209
  transatlantic slave trade and, 39, 60
  West African separation from, 39
  in World War II, 505
Europe, James Reese, 441
Evangelicalism, 129
Evans, Walker, 495
Everett, Louisa, 235
Evers, Medgar, 574
"Evil Injustice of Colonization, The" (Wears), 328–29*(d)*
Executive Orders
  8802 (1941), 507, 518
  9981 (1948), 530
  Truman's loyalty program and, 547
Exodusters, 363, 405
Expansion. *See also* Exploration; Westward expansion
  Black communities in era of, 256–59
  of slavery, 83–85, 208–17
  westward, 272–74
Exploration
  of Mississippi River region, 99
  by Portugal, 39–40
Exports, of enslaved Africans, 45
Exposition Universelle. *See* World's Fair, in Paris (1900)
Ezana, King, 13

Facsimile of the Catalan Atlas Showing the King of Mali Holding a Gold Nugget, 20*(i)*
Factories, Black women in, 504, 516
Fair Employment Practices Commission (FEPC), 507, 519
  Red scare and, 550
Fair housing. *See* Housing
Fair Housing Act (1968), 654
Fair Labor Standards Act, 476

Falconbridge, Alexander, "Account of the Slave Trade on the Coast of Africa, An," 69–70*(d)*
Families
African American, 680
of Black loyalists, 146
Black violence and, 619
cotton industry and, 237*(v)*
enslaved people's names and, 340
fictive kin and, 238
of freedom seekers, 230
growth of enslaved families, 122
marriage and, 339–40
migration of, 362, 363
of Obama, 699*(i)*
reuniting after emancipation, 339–41
scattering along cotton frontier, 170–71
separation of, 92, 215
size in North, 256
in slave trade, 55–57
Farm Security Administration (FSA), 495
Farmer, James, 604, 608
Farmers' Alliance, 389
Farming. *See also* Agriculture
in Carolinas, 86
in Chesapeake region, 84
men in, 395
in Middle Atlantic colonies, 96
moral virtue of, 263
in North, 210
women in, 395
"Father Divine," 479
"Father of Negro History," Woodson as, 449, 449*(i)*
Fathers. *See* Men
Faubus, Orval, 560
FBI
African Americans and, 508
Black Panther Party and, 629–30, 630*(v)*, 639
Black power and, 628–31
"Church Committee Report" and, 632–33
King targeted by, 620
Nixon and, 639
N. W. A. and, 661
"FBI Uses Fake Letters to Divide the Chicago Black Panthers and Blackstone Rangers," 629–30
Federal Bureau of Investigation. *See* FBI
Federal Council on Negro Affairs, 478
Federal Emergency Relief Administration (FERA), 476
Federal Housing Administration (FHA), 476, 568–69
Federal Theatre Project, 487
Federal Writers' Project, 242, 246
Felix (enslaved man), 134
Fellowship of Reconciliation, 557
Female Literary Society of Philadelphia, 287
Female-headed households, 681
Females. *See* Black women; Feminists; Women
Feminists, 367
Black, 648
white and Black, 367
Fenty, Adrian, 686
FEPC. *See* Fair Employment Practices Commission
Ferguson, Missouri, Brown killing in, 707, 717, 719
Fetchit, Stepin, 490
FHA. *See* Federal Housing Administration
Fictive kin, 238, 341
Field hands, gender-based segregation of, 233
Fifteenth Amendment (1869)
protection of, 358–59
voting rights for men in, 356, 370
whites on, 356
women's rights and, 366–67
Fifty-Fourth Massachusetts Volunteer Infantry Regiment, 309, 309*(i)*, 311
Films, Black actors in, 526
Finances
of Black women, 395
of Fisk University, 349
Finley, Robert, 193
Fire!! (magazine), 455
First Confiscation Act (1861), 302
First Continental Congress (1774), 137
"First Day, The: Little Rock" (Eckford), 583–85*(d)*
First Great Awakening. *See* Great Awakening
First Louisiana, 310
First South Carolina Volunteers (Thirty-Third U.S. Colored Troops), 307
First Vote, The (Waud), 375–76*(v)*
First World War. *See* World War I
Fisher, Abigail, 688
Fisher v. University of Texas, 688
Fisk Jubilee Singers, 349, 349*(i)*
Fisk University
Douglas, Aaron, at, 455
liberal arts curriculum at, 348
scholars at, 448
Fitzgerald, Ella, 489
Five Civilized Tribes, 212–15
Five Points district (New York), 257, 258*(i)*
Flag Is Bleeding, The (Ringgold), 627*(v)*
Flipper, Henry O., 362
Floods, Great Migration and, 432
Florida
Black society in, 101–2
freedpeople in, 346
slavery in, 76, 98–99, 101–2, 102*(i)*, 215
Spanish cession to United States, 215
U.S. control of, 168
Florida, 2000 election and, 688
"Florida Negro, The," 485
Florida War Training Center, 515
Flowers, Sandra, 648
Floyd, George, 676, 713, 717–18, 722, 725, 726*(v)*
Floyd, Philonise, 730–31
Fodio, Usman dan, 25
Folk culture
newly freed families and, 341
women and religion in, 343
Folk religion, women in, 343
Food, Tobacco, Agricultural, and Allied Workers of America, 550
Football, desegregation of, 526
For My People (Wright), 486
Force Acts (1870, 1871), 359
Forced labor
in frontier settlements, 98–101
from Russia and Balkans, 40
Forced migration, of African Americans, 193
Ford, Harold, 686
"Foreword to *The New Negro*, 1925" (Locke), 461–63*(d)*
Forman, James, 604
Formerly enslaved people. *See also* Emancipation; Freedpeople
in Black convention movement, 264
landownership and, 344
Fort Bragg, 511
Fort Devens strike, 528
Fort George, 119
Fort Mose, 102
Fort Sumter, 297, 300
Fort Wagner, 309*(i)*, 311, 330
Forten, Charlotte, 347
on Emancipation Proclamation, 307
as teacher of the formerly enslaved, 303, 347
Forten, James, 258, 262, 269, 303
"Letters from a Man of Colour," 200–201
Fortress Monroe, freedom seekers in, 301–2, 303*(i)*
Fortune, Emanuel, 359
Fortune, T. Thomas, 391–92, 412
Foster, Andrew "Rube," 490
Four Freedoms, 506
Fourteenth Amendment (1866), A-11–A-12
bus segregation and, 556
citizenship and, 352, 360
civil rights and, 352
debt peonage and, 420
Plessy v. Ferguson and, 384, 553
protection of, 360
suffrage and, 370
France
Black soldiers in World War I and, 440–41
Haitian Revolution and, 172, 173*(i)*
Louisiana and, 99–101
Louisiana Purchase and, 173–74
Natchez uprising against, 100
slave trade and, 60, 76
sugar colonies of, 99
Franklin, Benjamin
in antislavery organization, 182
on slavery, 122
Fraternal orders, Black, 186
Frazier, E. Franklin, 447
Frederick Douglass' Paper, 265, 268
Free African Society (Philadelphia), 184, 186
Free Blacks, 257*(c)*, 186–87
activism by, 197–203
American Colonization Society and, 221
after American Revolution, 147–50
in Baltimore, 175–76
in Cincinnati, 255
citizenship and, 181
during Civil War, 298–99, 326
communities of, 184–87

Free Blacks (*Continued*)
education for, 187–90, 260–61
enslaved and, 121–23
employment of, 187–90
after Gabriel's rebellion, 179
lifestyle after Revolution, 184–87
in Lower South, 147
in North and South, 143, 165
in northern cities, 256–59
northern communities of, 122, 256–59
in Ohio, 181
organizations of, 185(*i*)
"Petition for Freedom, 1785," 197–98
"Petition to Congress on the Fugitive Slave Act," 198–99
prejudice against, 191
in South, 122, 147–49, 195
in South Carolina, 220–21
southern slavery and, 150
as southern workers, 175–76
in Upper South, 147–49
Vesey as, 218–20
Virginia restrictions on, 224
in War of 1812, 191
"Washington's Runaway Slave, 1845," 202–3
Free education. *See also* Education
forbidden to Blacks, 221
Free labor. *See also* Labor
in North, 209
Free produce movement, 270
Free states
California as, 273
from Louisiana Purchase, 180
Maine as, 212
Freedman's Savings and Trust Company, 360
Freedmen. *See* Freedpeople
Freedmen's Bureau (1865)
Blacks in Republican Party and, 356
cartoon, 353(*v*)
establishment of, 318
Medical Division of, 343
post-emancipation labor contracts and, 344–45
reauthorization of, 351
schools and, 348, 399
Freedmen's Friend Society, 316
Freedmen's Memorial (Ball), 335(*v*)
Freedom(s). *See also* Emancipation; Rights
after American Revolution, 147–50
during American Revolution, 137, 138–43
for Black loyalists, 140, 142, 144–47
for Blacks, 122–23, 262–72, 313
chances for, after American Revolution, 120
before Civil War, 252–62
enslaved people's petitions for, 134
enslaved people's purchase of, 92
first generation after, 393–404
legislation for, 181
religious path to, 128–29
"Freedom Budget," 612
Freedom fighters, Black, 153–61
Freedom Now Party, 595
Freedom Rides and Riders, 562–63
routes of (1961), 563(*m*)
Freedom seekers. *See also* Fugitives from slavery
American-born Blacks as, 85
British regiment of, 138
in Carolinas, 88, 101
in Civil War, 304
in Florida, 101, 102(*i*)
Fugitive Slave Act (1850) and, 274
fugitive slave crisis and, 274–78
guidance for, 228
in Louisiana, 101
North Star as guide to, 228
Seminole protection of, 214
successful, 227–28
support for, 226
Tubman as, 226
Underground Railroad and, 229
Union use in Civil War, 295–96
women as, 230
Freedom suits, 132–33, 148(*i*)
Freedom's Journal, 33(*d*), 221, 265
Freedpeople. *See also* Emancipation; Freedmen's Bureau
Black women's support of, 316
in Civil War period, 301–4
education for, 346–50
after emancipation, 338–50
government abandonment of, 360
public land for, 344
in Republican Party, 356
Freeman, Elizabeth. *See* Bett, Mum
Free-Soil Party, 270, 278. *See also* Liberty Party
Freestyle art exhibit (2001), 684, 687
Frelinghuysen, Theodore, 128–29
Frémont, John C., 279, 302, 317, 351
French Revolution (1789), Haitian Revolution after, 173
French Royal Africa Company, 52
"From the South" (Letter to the Editor), 426(*d*)
Frontier settlements
enslavement in, 121
forced labor in, 98–101
Fugitive slave(s). *See* Freedom seekers
Fugitives from slavery. *See* Freedom seekers
Fugitive Slave Act
of 1793, 166, 198–99
of 1850, 254(*i*), 274–75, 276
Fugitive slave clause, 166
Fugitive Slave Law Convention, 271(*v*)
Funerals
Black, 125, 437
cultural importance of, 220

Gabon, 14
Gabriel's rebellion (1800), 175, 177–80
Gag rule, against antislavery petitions in Congress, 224
Gaines, Lloyd, 484
Gambia, 19, 40
Gandhi, Mohandas, King and, 558
Gao, 19
Garner, Eric, 717, 722, 725(*v*)
revenge for, 726
Garnet, Henry Highland, 286
"Address to the Slaves of the United States of America, An," 288–89
American and Foreign Anti-Slavery Society and, 270
in American Missionary Association, 272
Black military recruitment and, 307
call for rebellion by, 264
Contraband Relief Association and, 316
on emigration, 282, 408
on Smalls escape, 295
Garrido, Juan, 43–44, 44(*i*)
Garrison, William Lloyd
on colonization, 222
on constitutional incorporation of Blacks, 358
Douglass and, 265, 269–71
moral suasion and, 269
on slavery, 269
Garvey, Amy Jacques, 450
Garvey, Marcus
Black Star Line steamship company and, 452
Garveyites and, 451, 451(*i*)
UNIA and, 449–52
Garza, Alicia, 719(*d*)
"Herstory of the #BlackLivesMatter Movement, A," 719–22
Gates, Henry Louis Jr., 657
arrest of, 698
on cultural rootedness in Black arts, 685
Gause, Louisa, 225
Ge'ez, 13
Gender. *See also* Men; Women
African American agency and, 420
Black feminists and, 648
Black nationalism and, 596
diversity based on, 680
equality of enslaved people, 233
segregation during Middle Passage, 58
sexuality and, 662–64
tasks by, 233
Gender roles, in post-emancipation families, 339, 341
"General Observations on the Management of Slaves" (Barbot), 67–69
Generations, social diversity based on, 680
Georgia
Black loyalists in, 144
Black voters in, 603
Blacks during American Revolution and, 138
cotton boom and slavery in, 169
enslaved population in, 103, 121
freedom seekers in, 89, 132
loyalists in, 144
slavery in, 98, 103–4
Georgia Negro peon, A, "New Slavery in the South, The," 423–25
German prisoners of war, and discrimination against Black soldiers, 511
Germany, surrender in 1945, 531

Geronimo, displayed at World's Fair, 386
Gettysburg, battle at, 311
Gettysburg Address, 312
Ghana, 15–19, 22
  slave trading posts in, 46
GI Bill (1944), 528–31
Gibson, Althea, 526
Gibson, Josh, 491
Gilbert, Matthew, 341
Gilder, George, 641
Gillespie, Dizzy, 528
Gingrich, Newt, 701
Girls, in My Brother's Keeper initiative, 705
Giza, 12
Glass, Thelma, 557
Gliddon, George Robins, 253
Gobir, 25
Gold, 17–18
Gold Bug, The (musical), 401
Gold Coast
  Akan captives from, 59
  enslaved Africans from, 46
Golden, Thelma, 684
Goldman, Ronald, 662
Goldwater, Barry, 602, 638
Gone with the Wind, 490
Goodman, Andrew, 599
Gordon, James H., 386
Gorsuch, Edward, 276
Gorsuch, Neil, 709
Gospel music, 232, 436, 486–87
Government
  Blacks in, after Civil War, 356
  racial separation by, 387
  state emancipation and, 320–21
  support for Black equality, 660
Grace, Charles Emmanuel, 479
Gracia Real de Santa Teresa de Mose, 102
Gradual emancipation
  free laborers in North and, 209
  Missouri border of, 212
  in North, 181
Graetz, Robert S., 560
Granada, 21
Grandfather clauses
  in Oklahoma, 414
  for voting, 388
Grant, George, 597
Grant, Ulysses S., 311
Gray, Freddie, 556, 722
Great Awakening
  egalitarianism of, 131, 148
  of the enslaved, 126–31
  manumission and, 147
  Second, 223
Great Depression (1930s)
  African Americans in, 457, 473–75
  Black collective action in, 480–81
  causes of, 473
  churches during, 478–80
  Communist Party's appeal during, 481–83
  community during, 479–80
  economic crisis in, 473–75
  Harlem Renaissance and, 457
  insurance companies in, 475
  interracial unionism in, 480–81
  joblessness in, 473–75
  medical care in, 475
  stock market crash, 473
  World War II and, 513
Great Gbara Assembly, 19
Great Migration
  Black opposition to, 434
  1910–1929, 430–34, 433(*m*)
  to northern cities, 433(*i*), 435–39
  resources pooled for travel during, 432
Great Mississippi Flood of 1927, 473
Great War. *See* World War I
Greeley, Horace, 301
Green, Alfred M., 326
  Let Us . . . Take Up the Sword, 327–28(*d*)
Green, Joe, 443
Greensboro Four, 562
Griggs v. Duke Power Co. (1971), 612, 653, A-22–A-23
Grimké, Angelina, 271(*v*)
Griot, 18
Gronniosaw, James Albert Ukawsaw, 128–29
Guadalupe Hidalgo, Treaty of, 273
Guadeloupe, 99
  enslaved Africans in, 43–44
  indigo from, 100
Guam, 386
Guanches, 40
Guihard, Paul, 564
Guinea-Bissau, 19, 46
Guinier, Lani, 659, 673
Guinn v. United States (1915), 414
Gullah language, 126

Habeas corpus, 133
Hadar, 6
Hair Culturists Union of America, 439
Haiti, 710
  emigration promoted to, 282
  freedpeople's relocation to, 301
Haitian Revolution (1791–1804), 173, 173(*i*)
Hakluyt, Richard, 77
Half-freedom, in New Netherland, 93–96
Hall, Felix, 511
Hall, Prince, 190
Hall v. DeCuir, 383
Hamburg Massacre, 359
Hamer, Fannie Lou, 599–602, 600(*i*)
Hampton, Fred, 630–31, 630(*v*)
Hampton Institute
  curriculum at, 348–50
  Washington at, 409
Hampton University, 306
Handy, William Christopher "W. C.," 402, 441
Harassment, by police, 571
Hardin, Lil, 486
Harlem
  arts in, 453–57, 454(*m*)
  foreign-born Blacks in, 408
  Johnson, James Weldon, on, 448
  New Negro and, 446
  race riot in (1964), 602
  riot in (1935), 483
"Harlem: Mecca of the New Negro," Locke and, 453
Harlem Renaissance, 453–57, 454(*m*), 460–68, 485–86
Harlins, Latasha, 652, 662
Harper, Frances Ellen Watkins
  on Brown's raid, 282
  desegregation of streetcars and, 365
  as feminist, 367, 371, 374, 374(*d*)
  "Learning to Read," 347
  literary works by, 266, 347(*i*)
  at NACW meeting, 393
  Poems on Miscellaneous Subjects, 266, 347(*i*)
  portrait of, 347(*i*)
Harpers Ferry, Brown insurrection at, 282
Harper's Weekly
  Colored Rule in a Reconstructed(?) State, 1874 (Nast), 378(*v*)
  First Vote, The (Waud), 375–76(*v*)
Harris, Abram, 483
Harris, Kamala, 714
Harris, Michael, 685
Hartwell family, migration to Kansas by, 362
Hastie, William H., 478, 507, 512
  "Resignation Memo and Response," 541–43
Hatcher, Richard, 653
Hate strikes, in 1960s, 611
"Haunted Oak, The" (Dunbar), 403
Hausaland, 25
Hawaii, Pearl Harbor bombing in, 505
Hayden, Palmer, 488
Hayes, George E. C., *Brown* decision and, 554
Hayes, Jajana, 712
Hayes, Rutherford B., 360
Haymarket bombing (Chicago, 1886), 365
Haynes, Lemuel, 137, 153
  "Liberty Further Extended," 155–57
Haywood, Felix, 307, 319
Head Start, 611
Health Care and Education Reconciliation Act, 698
Health programs
  Clinton, Bill, and, 659
  Obama and, 698
Hedgeman, Anna Arnold, 473
Hegel, 6
Hell Fighters regiment, in World War I, 440
Hemp, 209, 210(*m*)
Henry the Navigator (Portugal), 39
Heritability. *See* Inheritance
Herndon, Angelo, 481–82, 495
  "You Cannot Kill the Working Class, 1934," 498–99
Herodotus, 10
Heroin use, Black and white use of, 688
"Herstory of the #BlackLivesMatter Movement, A" (Garza), 719–22

Hieroglyphic writing, 9
Higginson, Thomas Wentworth, 307
Higher education. *See* Colleges and universities; Education
Hijab, 710
Hill, Abram, 526
Hill, Anita, 662, 663*(i)*
Hill, Fanny Christina, 516, 517
Hill, T. Arnold, 446, 478, 506
Hill, W. R., 362
Hip-hop culture, 660–62
Hippodrome Theater, 401
Hiring-out system, 177, 178*(i)*
Hiroshima, atomic bombing of, 531
Hispanics. *See* Latinos
Hispaniola
  African workers in, 43
  Spaniards in, 42
Historically Black colleges and universities, 343, 348, 531, 561, 669, A-34–A-36
Hitler, Adolf, 491, 491*(i)*
  Jewish people and, 506
  World War II and, 505–6
Ho Chi Minh, 613
Hoard, Rosina, 395
Holder, Eric, 704–6
Holiday, Billie, 489
Holidays, King's birthday as, 620
Holidays, Negro Election Day as, 123
Holiness movement, 436
Holland. *See* Dutch
Holly, James Theodore, 282
Holt Street Baptist Church, 557, 687
Holtzclaw, Daniel, 723
Home fronts, 312–22, 513–20
Home Owners Loan Corporation (HOLC), 476
Home rule, 358
Homespun clothing, cotton and, 168
Homestead Act (1862), Black migration and, 362
Homicides, among Black men, 658
Hominins, 6
Homo sapiens, 4, 6
Homophobia, Black feminists and, 648
Homosexuality. *See* LGBTQ+ people
"Honoring African American History with a Kente Cloth Stole," 35*(d)*
hooks, bell, 647
Hoover, Herbert, 476
Hoover, J. Edgar
  King and, 628
  Sixteenth Street Baptist Church bombing and, 578
Hopkins, Esek, *Sally's* log and, 70–72*(i)*
Horne, Lena, 491, 526
Horse, John (Black Seminole), 214*(i)*, 215
Horsmanden, Daniel, 121
Horton, Robert, 432
Horus, 12
Hospitals, Black, 343, 437
Hour of Emancipation, The. *See Watch Meeting-Dec. 31st-Waiting for the Hour* (Carlton)
House of Representatives
  Blacks in, 355*(i)*, 356
  slave states and, 167, 212
House Un-American Activities Committee (HUAC), 545–46
Households, female-headed and single-parent, 681
Households, in Black urban communities, 256
Housing. *See also* Residential segregation
  Black home ownership and, 680
  in Chicago, 437, 568–69
  discrimination in, 609
  Fair Housing Act and, 653
  GI Bill and, 530
  in Los Angeles, 571
  in 1960s, 568
  in northern cities, 435–36
  public, 609
  segregation in, 592
  after World War I, 443
Houston, Charles Hamilton, 484, 506
Houston, Texas, race riot in (1919), 443
Houston Works Progress Administration, 515
Howard, Donald and Betty, 570
Howard University, 483
Howard University Law School, 484
Howe, Julia Ward, 372
HUAC. *See* House Un-American Activities Committee
Huggins, Ericka, 645
Huggins, John, 639
Hughes, Langston, 453, 455, 464–65*(d)*, 488
  HUAC and, 547, 549
Hulett, John, 589–90
Hull, Isaac, 192
Hull House, 435
Human rights, Malcolm X on, 596
Human zoos, at Paris World's Fair (1900), 386
Humanitarian aid, by Black women in Civil War, 316
Humphrey, Hubert, 601
Hunter, David, 304, 307, 322
Hunter-gatherers, 7
Hurricane Katrina, 692–94
  photographs of, 693*(i)*
Hurricane Plantation, 232*(i)*
Hursey, Mose, 231
Hurston, Zora Neale, 429–30, 455, 485–86
Hussein, Saddam, 692
Hyksos, 11

"I Have a Dream" speech (King), 576*(i)*, 578
Iberian Peninsula, 39
Ibraahim, Ahlaam, 710
Ice age, 8
ID laws, for voting, 704
Identity
  of African Americans, 121
  Black, 264
  Harlem Renaissance and, 457
  LGBTQ+, 664
  in New World, 60
Ideology, of white supremacy, 386–87
"If We Must Die" (McKay), 443
Igbo people (Africa), 50, 60
Igboland, 24
Ike (security guard), 677, 685
Iliffe, John, 6
Illegal immigrants, Obama policy toward, 702
Illinois
  repeal of law fining African Americans, 321
  schools for Black children in, 366
  slavery banned in, 181
Illiteracy, decrease in, 348
Immigrants and immigration, 671–73
  Black, 408, 664, 682
  European, 209
  quotas on, 664
  undocumented, 702
  white, in New Netherland, 93
  after World War I, 444
Immigration and Nationality Act (1965), 652, 664
Impeachment, of Andrew Johnson, 353
Imperialism, white supremacy and, 386–87
Imports, enslaved people, 100, 121
Imprisonment, 689*(c)*
  of Blacks, 254, 689
  for debt, 420
  for drug use, 689
In re Turner (1867), 346
Inauguration
  of Lincoln (first), 297
  of Lincoln (second), 318
Incarceration. *See* Imprisonment
Incidents in the Life of a Slave Girl (Jacobs), 266
Income, 680
Indentured servants, 80
  from Georgia, 103
  gradual emancipation and, 181
Independence
  of Haiti, 173
  road to Revolution and, 131–34
  slave rebellions and, 132
  for Texas, 215
Independent Black churches, 259
Independent Order of St. Luke, 398
Indian policy, in Virginia, 83
Indian Removal Act (1830), 213–14
Indian Territory
  Black migrants in, 363
  slavery in, 212–15
Indian wars, Black regiments in, 362–63
Indiana
  schools for Black children in, 366
  slavery banned in, 181
Indigenous peoples, enslavement of, 41–43
Indigo, in Louisiana, 100
Industrialization
  slavery, cotton, and, 209–11, 210*(m)*
  South and, 208
Industry. *See also* Labor
  Black labor in, 515–16
  enslaved labor in South, 209–10
  in World War II, 503–4

Infants
care of enslaved, 234
mortality of enslaved, 233
Inheritance, of enslaved status, 80, 81
Inner-ring suburbs, 656
Institute for Colored Youth (Philadelphia), 261, 287, 365
Institutional racism, 609, 614
Institutions, Black, 166
Insurance, health care, 698
Insurance companies, 475
Insurrections. *See also* Revolts and rebellions
fears of, 138
Integration. *See also* Civil Rights movement; Desegregation; Racial segregation
acceptance of, 638
Brown decision and, 554
busing for, 639, 650
Freedom Rides and, 562–63
Garvey's condemnation of, 453
of labor unions, 519
of military in World War II, 509
of Revolutionary troops, 138
of suburbs, 656
Intercommunal Youth Institute (Oakland), 645
"Interesting Narrative of the Life of Olaudah Equiano, or Gustavus Vassa, the African, The" (Equiano), 63–66
Intermarriage. *See also* Interracial relationships; Miscegenation
as crime, 81
International Brotherhood of Boilermakers (IBB), 519
International Committee on African Affairs (1937), 545
International Labor Defense (ILD), 471, 482*(i)*, 498
International Migration Society, 408
International relations, U.S. racism and, 553
Interracial civil rights movement, 599
Interracial labor unions, 437
demise of, 400
Interracial relationships
labor solidarity and, 365
marriage as, 81, 387
Wilmington Insurrection and, 389
Interracial unionism, 480–81
Interstate bus travel, segregation outlawed in, 525
Interstate commerce, segregation of, 383
Interstate Commerce Commission (ICC), segregation outlawed by, 562
"Interview with a Tuskegee Airman" (Jefferson), 539–40
Intolerable Acts, 137
Invisible church, 231
African Americans' Christianity as invisible institution, 130
Involuntary migrants. *See* Enslaved people
Iowa, 174*(m)*
Iran, Obama policy toward, 703
Iraq War, 688
Black opposition to, 692
end of, 698
Iron technology, 13, 16
ISIS (Islamic State), 703
Islam, 18–19
Ivory Coast, 19, 23

Jackson, Andrew
American Indian removal and, 214
and Blacks in War of 1812, 192
Jackson, Esther, 484
Jackson, Jacob and Geneva, 571
Jackson, James, 484
Jackson, Jesse
Obama, 2008 election, and, 695
as presidential candidate, 653
relevance of, 686
Jackson, Jimmie Lee, 602
Jackson, Luther Porter, 522
Jackson, Maynard, 653
Jackson, Samuel L., 681
Jackson State University, violence at, 640
Jackson Ward (Richmond), churches in, 398
Jacobs, Harriet, 236, 383
Incidents in the Life of a Slave Girl, 266
Jakes, T. D., 687*(i)*
Jamaica
Black loyalists in, 146
immigrants from, 408
maroons in, 119
James, Joseph, 519
James, LeBron, 681
James I (England), 77
James II (Duke of York, England), 96
Jamestown
Bacon's Rebellion and, 83
enslaved people transported to, 75
as North America's first permanent settlement, 77
Japan
Black admiration of, 508
Pearl Harbor bombing by, 505
surrender in, 531
Japanese Americans, discrimination against, 508
Jasper, John, 398
Jay, John, 182
Jay-Z, 681
Jazz, 528
in Europe, 441
in Harlem Renaissance, 457
popularization of, 402–3
Jefferson, Alexander, "Interview with a Tuskegee Airman," 539–40
Jefferson, Thomas
Banneker's letter to, 163–64
Gabriel's rebellion and, 179
Louisiana Purchase and, 173–74
slavery and, 163–64
Jeffries, Jim, 400
Jena Six case, 691
Jennings, Elizabeth, 268, 383
Jet magazine, Till photos in, 554
Jewish people
African American identification with, 506
alliances with Blacks, 650
Civil Rights movement and, 557
school control and, 650
after World War I, 444
World War II and, 506
Jim Crow
in armed forces, 407
in former Confederate states, 384–85, 385*(m)*
Great Migration and, 432
men and women under, 393–96
new Jim Crow and, 690
Obama on, 696
racial etiquette of, 384–85
segregation and, 384–85
in unions, 519
during World War II, 511
"Jim Crow" (character), 286, 292–93*(v)*
Job(s). *See also* Economy; Employment; Labor; Occupations
Black men in, 256, 263
Black unemployment and, 608
opened for Blacks, 654, 677
politics and, 607–8
Job Corps, 611
Joblessness, 473–75
John Brown's raid (1859), 282
John v. State (1854), 227
Johnson, Andrew
impeachment of, 353
land distribution and, 344
Radical Republicans and, 338
Reconstruction and, 351–53
Johnson, Andrew, 1864 election and, 318
Johnson, Charles S., 446–47, 453, 515
Johnson, George H., "Sphinx Builder Speaks, 1919, The," 34*(d)*
Johnson, Jack, 400
Johnson, James Weldon, 443, 447, 453, 463*(d)*
Lift Every Voice and Sing, 402, 488
NAACP and, 447
Johnson, John Rosamond, *Lift Every Voice and Sing,* 402, 463*(d)*
Johnson, Lyndon B., 669
on Black nationalism, 607
Black organizations in Vietnam War and, 615
civil rights and, 592, 602
social/economic programs of, 611
Vietnam War and, 613
Johnson, Lyndon B., 1964 election and, 602
Johnson, Rashid, *China Gates,* 684*(i)*
Johnson, Robert L., 681
Johnston, Gideon, 87–88
Joint-stock company, Virginia Company as, 77
Jones, Absalom, 184–86, 186*(i)*, 191
colonization and, 193
"Petition to Congress on the Fugitive Slave Act," 198–99
Jones, Elizabeth, 227
Jones, Eugene K., 447, 478

Jones, Gabriel, 134
Jones, John, 321
Jones, LeRoi (Amiri Baraka), 520, 625–26(*i*), 627(*v*)
Jones, Loïs Mailou, *Ubi Girl from Tai Region*, 625–26(*v*)
Jones, Van, 709
Joplin, Scott, 403
Jordan, Barbara, 647
Jos Plateau, 14(*i*)
Journal of Negro History, 448, 449(*i*)
Journey of Reconciliation, 525
Jubilee Singers, at Fisk University, 349, 349(*i*)
Judge, Ona, "Washington's Runaway Slave, 1845," 202–3
Judicial system. *See* Courts
"Jumping the broom[stick]" ceremonies, 124(*i*), 340
Juneteenth, 319
Juries, Blacks on, 254
Justice Department (DOJ), and police brutality, 592, 718
Juveniles, punishment of Black, 689

Kaepernick, Colin, 710
Kaiser Shipyards, Black women in, 516(*i*)
Kangaba, 18–19
Kano, 25
Kansas, 174(*m*)
  Exodusters in, 363
  migration to, 362, 364(*v*), 405
  slavery and, 278
Kansas City, civil rights demonstrations in, 573
Kansas-Nebraska Act (1854)
  free and slave states after, 279(*m*)
  Free-Soilers and, 279
  terms of, 278
Karenga, Ron (Maulana), 627(*v*)
Katrina (Hurricane). *See* Hurricane Katrina
Katsina, 25
Katzenbach, Nicholas, 602
Kavanaugh, Brett, 709
Keckley, Elizabeth, 316, 317(*i*)
Keita, Sundiata, 18–19
Kelly, Rogers, 514
Kemet, 10
Kennedy, Anthony, 644
Kennedy, John F
  assassination of, 592
  civil rights bill and, 573–74
  Civil Rights movement and, 562–63, 564
  on international image of Black Americans, 566(*i*)
  March on Washington and, 574
  Obama and, comparisons between, 697
Kent State University, 640
Kente cloth, 35(*d*)
Kentucky
  emancipation from slavery in, 320
  lynchings in, 422
  slavery in, 168
Kenya, 14
Kerner Commission, 619
Key, Elizabeth, 81
Khoikhoi, 7
Khoisan peoples, 7
King, A. D., 565
King, Boston, 146, 153
  "Memoirs of a Black Loyalist," 158–59
King, Edward, 329
King, Martin Luther Jr. *See also* Civil Rights movement
  antiwar movement and, 320
  assassination of, 613, 620
  Birmingham, Alabama, and, 562–67
  birthday as national holiday, 620
  on Black violence, 620
  on Chicago housing, 571
  economic concerns and, 607–8
  "I Have a Dream" speech, 576(*i*), 578
  "Letter from Birmingham City Jail," 565
  Malcolm X's ideas and, 597
  March against Fear and, 604
  March on Washington and, 574–75, 576(*i*), 578
  Montgomery bus boycott and, 557
  Nobel Peace Prize to, 604
  nonviolence of, 576, 578
  Operation Breadbasket and, 612
  as pastor and civil rights leader, 686
  SCLC and, 558
  Selma-Montgomery march and, 604
  Vietnam War and, 616(*i*)
King, Rodney, 662, 722
King v. Burwell, 704
Kinship. *See also* Families
  family structures and, 341
  fictive, 238
  in West Africa, 24–25
Kirinia, battle of, 19
KKK. *See* Ku Klux Klan
Kleinpeter, Joseph, 233
Knights of Labor, interracial labor solidarity in, 365
Knights of the White Camelia, 359
Know-Nothings, 256
Knox, Frank, 506
Kongo, 46, 75, 104
Koreans, Black relations with, 652
Ku Klux Klan (KKK)
  in Alabama, 589
  in *Birth of a Nation* (film), 414
  Black protection against, 604
  after Civil War, 358
  Garvey and, 452
  lynchings and, 419
  Trump's election and, 708
  during World War II, 522
Kumbi Saleh, 16–18
Kush, 9, 12–13
Kushites, 12–13
Kwanzaa, 606

La France maritime... (engraving), 57(*i*)
La Salle, Robert de, 99
Labor. *See also* Enslaved people; Enslaved labor(ers); Forced labor; Servants; Sharecropping; Whites
  African, in making of Americas, 60
  along cotton frontier, 169
  American Indians as, 99
  black code enforcement of, 346
  of Black men, 395
  of Black women, 395
  in Carolinas, 89
  of contrabands, 304
  contracts after emancipation, 344–45
  debt peonage and, 420, 423–25
  after emancipation, 338–39, 344–46
  encomienda system and, 42
  enslaved people, 45, 98
  fair wages for Blacks, 365
  hiring-out system for, 177, 178(*i*)
  interracial solidarity in, 365
  living-out system for, 177
  in Maryland, 175–76
  in Middle Atlantic colonies, 96–97
  segregation of, 513–14
  southern loss of, 513–14
Labor movement, discrimination in, 573
Labor unions
  all-Black "auxiliary," 519
  Blacks and, 365, 519, 523(*i*)
  Cold War and, 550
  discrimination in, 617
  interracialism in, 437
  Jim Crow in, 519
  Red scare and, 550
  in Richmond, 401
Ladies' Anti-Slavery Society of Rochester, New York, 290
Ladinos, 45
Lafayette, Marquis de, 144
"L'Ag 'Ya," 487
Lagos, Nigeria, 50
Land. *See also* Sharecropping
  American Indian, 212–15
  contraband purchase of, 304
  after emancipation, 344
  for freedpeople in Confederacy, 318
Land-Grant College Act (1890), 399
Land-grant institutions, for Blacks, 348
Landowners
  Black, 363
  cotton and, 169
  dependence on enslaved laborers, 122
Lange, Dorothea, 495
Langston, John Mercer, National Convention of Colored Men and, 321
Language minorities, 651
Languages
  of African American blended culture, 126
  Creole, 85
  enslaved people's uses of, 85
  Gullah as, 126

Las Casas, Bartolomé de, 43, 77
Latinos
  African Americans and, 651
  police stops of, 707
  racism against, 516
Laveau, Marie, 343
Law(s). *See also* Black codes; Slave codes; *specific laws*
  Black inferior status decreed in, 80
  civil rights, 571
  discrimination against Blacks in, 253–54
  legal status of enslaved women's children in, 80
"Law and order"
  Black incarceration rates and, 689
  Nixon on, 638–39
  Reagan war on drugs and, 688
Law enforcement
  African Americans and, 707–8
  Pentagon firepower to, 724(*v*)
Lawrence, Kansas, 278
Le Count, Caroline, 365–66
Leaders and leadership
  Black, 685, 688
  of Civil Rights movement, 557–62
Leaders and leadership, Black, 125, 191, 263–64
"Learning to Read" (Harper), 347
Lecturers, abolitionist, 266–67
Lee, Euel, 497
Lee, George, 554
Lee, Herbert, 564
Lee, Jarena, 266
Lee, Robert E
  on emancipation from slavery, 318
  at Gettysburg, 311
Lee, Russell
  "Negro Drinking at 'Colored' Water Cooler in Streetcar Terminal, Oklahoma City, Oklahoma, 1939," 499
Left wing (political), 452, 607
Leftwing (political), 550
Legal codes. *See* Codes of law
Legal Defense and Educational Fund (NAACP), 611
Legalization, of marriages between enslaved people, 340
Legislation, for Black freedom, 181
Leibowitz, Samuel, 471
Lesbian, gay, bisexual, transgender, queer (LGBTQ+) community, 664
  Black feminists and, 648
Let Us . . . Take Up the Sword (Green), 327–28(*d*)
"Letter from Birmingham City Jail" (King), 565
"Letter to the Editor," *From the South*, 426(*d*)
"Letter to the Reverend Samson Occom" (Wheatley), 155
"Letters from a Man of Colour" (Forten), 200–201
Levitt, William, and Levittowns, 570
Lewis, John (SNCC), 575, 592, 599, 602
  Bloody Sunday beating of, 602
  Carmichael and, 604
  compensatory employment and, 612
Lewis, John Solomon, 363
Lexington, battle at, 137
LGBTQ+ people, 620, 664, 666, 703
Liberal arts curriculum
  in colleges and universities, 348–50
  vocational curriculum *vs.*, 348–50
Liberals, on economic injustice, 608
"Liberation schools," 645
Liberator (newspaper), 269, 307
Liberia, 194
  Black migration to, 253, 282, 363, 407–8
  founding of, 221
"Liberties of Forreiners and Strangers," 111(*d*)
"Liberty Further Extended" (Haynes), 137, 155–57
Liberty Party
  abolitionism and, 270, 278
  Slave Power and, 272
Life expectancy
  of Black men *vs.* women, 256
  of Black women, 395
  for Blacks *vs.* whites, 256
Life in Philadelphia cartoons, "Bobalition" (Clay), 203–4(*v*)
Lifestyle
  of 18th-century Blacks in North America, 121–31
  of enslaved people in Carolina, 88
  moral virtue and, 263
  righteous, 263
  of southern Black women, 395
  of southern Blacks, 205–8
Lift Every Voice and Sing (Johnson and Johnson), 402, 488
"Lifting As We Climb" motto, of NACW, 394
Lightfoot, Lori, 712
Lincoln, Abraham, 344
  assassination of, 318
  1860 election of, 296
  1864 election and, 317–18
  Emancipation Proclamation and, 305–6, 331–32
  as Great Emancipator, 327, 334, 335(*v*)
  inaugural address of, 297
  land distribution and, 344
  as president, 272
  on slavery, 283, 300, 322
Lincoln, Mary Todd, Keckley, Elizabeth, and, 316
Lincoln Memorial concert, 491, 492(*i*)
Lincoln University, 261
Lineage, classification of race by, 387
Linguistic patterns. *See* Languages
Lion King, The, 18
Literacy
  after emancipation, 347
  of enslaved people, 130, 232
  in Egypt, 12
  forbidden to Blacks, 221
  increase in, 348
Literacy tests, for voting, 388
Literature
  Black, 266, 402
  Black heritage and, 429–30
  in Harlem Renaissance, 453
Little, Wilbur, 443
Little Rock, Arkansas, school desegregation in, 560–61, 583–85(*d*)
Little Rock Nine, 561, 584(*d*)
Liu, Wenjian, 726
Livestock, 7, 8(*i*)
Living Way (Black Baptist newspaper), 381
Living-out system, 177
Lobi-Dagarti, 23
Locke, Alain, 453, 455, 483
  "Foreword to *The New Negro*, 1925," 461–63(*d*)
Loguen, Jermain W., 271, 275
Lone Star Republic (Texas), 273–74
Long, Jefferson F., 355(*i*)
Long, Russell, 647
Lord Dunmore's Proclamation (1775), 139–41, 143
Los Angeles
  civil rights activists in, 572–73
  Pentecostalism in, 436
  race riot in, 516
  Rodney King riots in, 662
  Simpson case in, 662
  Watts neighborhood in, 571
  Watts riot in (1965), 618
Los Angeles Sentinel (newspaper), 569
Louima, Abner, 682
Louis, Joe, 491, 526
Louis XIV (France), 100
Louis XV (France), 99
Louisiana, 174(*m*). *See also* New Orleans
  Black voters in, 389
  civil rights act in (1869), 383
  emancipation from slavery in, 320
  slavery in, 76, 99–101, 168, 215
  sugar in, 210, 210(*m*)
  in United States, 168
Louisiana National Guard, Hurricane Katrina and, 694
Louisiana Native Guards, as African Brigade, 310
Louisiana Purchase (1803), 166, 173–74, 174(*m*)
  emancipation in North after, 180–83
  slavery prohibited in, 212
Louisiana Territory, slavery and, 273
Louisiana Weekly, 514
Louisianian (newspaper), 350
Louisville, New Orleans and Texas Railway v. Mississippi (1890), 383
"Louisville Flood, 1937, The" (Bourke-White), 500
Lovejoy, Elijah P., 255
Low-country Blacks, English language and, 89
Lower Egypt, 10, 13

Lower South. *See also* South
African American movement from Upper South, 215, 216(*m*)
auctions of the enslaved in, 217, 218(*i*)
conjure and other traditions in, 126
cotton in, 168
enslavement in, 124(*i*)
free Blacks in, 147
sales of surplus enslaved people from, 209
Lowndes County Freedom Organization (LCFO), 590, 646
Loyalists, 138
Black, 138–42, 139(*m*), 144–47, 145(*i*)
as refugees, 146
Loyalty programs, of Truman, 547, 551–53
Luanda, enslaved people from, 75
Lucy, 6, 7(*i*)
Lydia (enslaved woman), 227
Lying out, as resistance to slavery, 226
Lyles, Aubrey, 455
Lynch, Loretta, 705
Lynching, 390–92, 419
of Black soldier (1885), 362
after Civil War, 359
Dyer Anti-Lynching Bill and, 419, 447
Emmett Till, 583
felony charge as, 690
in Memphis, 391
of Mitchell, Charles, 421(*v*)
in New York City draft riots, 313
1940–1946, 524(*m*)
in 1946, 523
Wells's campaign against, 393
after World War I, 443
during World War II, 524(*m*)
Lynching of Charles Mitchell, The, 421(*v*)
Lyrics of Lowly Life (Dunbar), 404

Maat, 12
Macedonia, 12
Madagascar, 46
Maddox, Lester, 620
Madeira, 40
Madison, James
on slave insurrection, 138
on slavery and abolition, 164, 168
Maghan, Nare, 18
Magic, enslaved people's beliefs in, 88
Mail carriers, Blacks as, 321
Maine, as free state, 212
"Make America Great Again," 708–11
Makki, Hind, 712
Malcolm X, 596–98, 597(*i*)
assassination of, 597(*i*), 598
Maldives, 17
Mali, 18–22, 20(*m*)
Malinke-speaking peoples, 100
Mallory, Shepard, 301
Managerial workers, Black, 654
Mandinka people, 60
Manhattan
Black candidates in, 572
Dutch in, 94
Manifest Destiny, 273
Manly, Alexander, 389
Mann, John, 227
Mansa Musa, 19
Mansfield, Earl of, 133
Manufacturing, North and, 208, 210–11
Manumission
colonization and, 193
definition of, 28
laws discouraging, 123
in Maryland, 176
in Upper South, 147, 168
in Virginia, 180
in West Africa, 28
"Maple Leaf Rag" (Joplin), 403
March against Fear (1966), 604
March on Washington for Jobs and Freedom (1963), 568, 574–78, 576(*i*), 579
media coverage of, 579
March on Washington Movement (1941), 507
A. Philip Randolph and, 518
Marine Corps
Blacks restricted in, 191
in World War II, 510
Mariners, Portuguese, 39
Maroons, 89, 132
American Indian slave catchers and, 170
Francis Drake and, 77
in Jamaica, 119
in Louisiana, 101
Marrant, John, 130
Marriage
abroad, 236
antimiscegenation laws and, 81, 387
between Blacks and whites, 92
broomstick ceremonies and, 124(*i*), 340
choice of, 236
of enslaved people, 92, 234–38
imposed on enslaved people, 235
legalization of for enslaved people, 340
separating enslaved people and, 92
Marrow of Tradition, The (Chesnutt), 404
Marshall, Burke, 564
Marshall, Thurgood, 484
Brown v. Board of Education (1954) and, 553
replacement for, 662
Martin, Trayvon, 701, 719(*d*)
killing of, 707, 717, 730–32
Martinique, 99
indigo from, 100
Maryland
Adeline Brown v. State in, 346
Black population of, 84
emancipation from slavery in, 320
enslaved people in, 80, 122, 175–76
enslaved people in Baltimore, 175–76
evangelicalism in, 129
loyalty in Civil War, 300
white servitude in, 80
Masonic Lodge, Black, 123, 186
Massachusetts
abolition of slavery in, 164
Black population of, 122
Blacks on juries in, 254
freedom petitions in, 134
Free-Soilers and, 279
nullification of Fugitive Slave Law (1850) and, 274
slavery in, 89–93, 181
"Massachusetts Body of Liberties, The," 111(*d*)
Massachusetts Government Act, 137
Massachusetts Safety Committee, 137
Massachusetts Supreme Court, on slavery in Massachusetts, 147
Massey, Douglas S., "Black Immigrants and Black Natives Attending Selective Colleges and Universities in the United States," 673–74
Mather, Cotton, 91
Matrilineal, 24
Mauritania, 15, 18
Maybank, Burnet R., 512, 522
Mayors, Black, 653, 677
Mays, Willie, 526
McBath, Lucy, 712
McCabe, Edward P., 362
McCain, John, 697
McCarthy, Joseph, McCarthy era and, 547
McClellan, George B., 318
McCombs, Henry, 362
McCrummell, James, 269
McDaniel, Hattie, 490
McDowell, Calvin, 391
McGovern, George, 641
McKay, Claude, 453
"If We Must Die," 443
"Outcast, 1922," 34–35(*d*)
McKinley, William, 1896 election and, 389
McKissick, Floyd, 595–96, 604, 619
McNair, Denise, 576(*i*)
McQueen, Thelma "Butterfly," 490
Mecca, 19, 21
Mechanics Savings Bank (Richmond), 398
Medical Division, of Freedmen's Bureau, 343
Medical education, Douglass, Sarah Mapps, and, 261
Medical insurance, 704
Obamacare and, 698, 704
Medicine
AIDS treatment costs, 659
Black, in Chicago, 437
Black hospitals and, 343
Mediterranean region, sugarcane in, 40
Meeropol, Abel, 489
"Meeting of Cultures, The," 674(*d*), 674(*i*)
Megachurch, Black, 686–87, 687(*i*)
"Memoirs of a Black Loyalist" (King), 158–59
Memphis
entertainment in, 402
lynchings in, 391

Memphis Free Speech and Headlight (newspaper)
on lynchings, 391
Wells and, 381, 405
Men. *See also* Black men; Black women; Gender; Million Man March (1995)
in church leadership, 341
free Black employment and, 188
in Jim Crow era, 393–96
labor of, 395
in Middle Passage, 58
in newly freed families, 341
suffrage for, 370
unemployment of Blacks and, 608
voting rights for, 366–67, 370
work of, 233
Mendes da Cunha, Manuel, 75
Menéndez de Avilés, Pedro, 76
Menes, 10
Meredith, James, 565, 604
Messenger (socialist magazine), 440, 446
Methodists and Methodist Church
Allen and, 185
Black, 185, 229
revivals and, 223
Methodists and Methodist Church, in Chicago, 436
#MeToo, 712
Metropolitan Funeral Home Association (Chicago), 437
Mexican-American War (1846), slavery in West and, 273
Mexico
enslaved Africans in, 43
Texas slavery and, 273
Michigan, Black laborers in, 514
Middle Atlantic colonies
Dutch in, 93–96
English in, 96–98
slavery in, 93–98, 97*(i)*
Middle class (Black), 654–57, 679
Black poor and, 684
in early 20th century, 393
in early 21st century, 680
expansion of, 654–55
southern, 382–83, 401
Middle colonies (England), 96–98, 122
Middle Kingdom, 10
Middle Passage, 49–60, 56*(i)*, 63–70
conditions during, 50–53, 55–58
gender segregation during, 58
life in barracoons and, 50, 52
log of brig *Sally* from, 70–72*(v)*
mortality in, 52, 56*(i)*, 59
suicide in, 55, 58
survivors of, 75
Midsummer Night in Harlem, 488
Midwest
African American migration to, 513
commercial farms in, 211
Migrants (enslaved), fictive kin of, 238
Migration. *See also* Emigration; Enslaved people; Great Migration; Immigrants and immigration; Removal, of American Indians
of African Americans (1940–1970), 514*(m)*
of African Americans during World War II, 513
African colonization and, 193
by Black people, 430
to Chicago, 435–39
during and after Civil War, 362–65, 364*(v)*, 430
Du Bois on, 412
of enslaved people, forced, 169, 215, 216*(m)*
fair wages for, 365
of families, 362
free Blacks and, 256
to Liberia, 282, 407–8
to North, 430–39, 444
to northern and western cities, 609
from South, 405–7, 430–34, 433*(m)*
to West, 513, 515
of white enslavers with the people they enslaved, 169
Migration club, 432
Milam, J. W., 554
Milano, Alyssa, 712
Militancy
Black, 266, 589, 619
at March on Washington (1963), 575
Militarization, of local police, 726
Military, 308*(c)*. *See also specific battles and wars*
Black officers in, 362–63
Black service in Civil War, 298–99, 307–10, 312*(m)*, 322
Black soldiers in American Revolution, 137–38
Black women in World War II, 511
after Civil War, 362–63
Confederate, 297
decline of Blacks in, 692
desegregation of, 528–31
formerly enslaved people in, 306–7
in Hurricane Katrina, 693
Jim Crow in, 407
Union, 297, 305
Vietnam War and, 613–17
violence and discrimination in, 509–13
in World War I, 430, 440–41
in World War II, 503–4, 505–6
Military districts, in former Confederacy, 352
Military draft
of Blacks for Confederate army, 314
in Civil War, 313
in Vietnam War, 613–14
in World War I, 440
in World War II, 505–6, 509–10
Military Intelligence, African Americans and, 508
Militia
Black, in Louisiana, 100
Blacks in, 191, 298–99
Union, 297
Miller, Flournoy, 455
Miller, Rosann, 722
Milliken v. Bradley (1970), 649, 651
Milliken's Bend, battle at, 311
Million Man March (1995), 664
Million Woman March (1997), 664
Mills, Florence, 455
Milwaukee, civil rights activists in, 573
Ministers, Black, 686–87, 687*(i)*
Minkins, Shadrach (Frederick Wilkins), 276
Minnesota, 174*(m)*
Minorities
employment discrimination and, 612
language, 651
Minstrel shows, 292–93*(v)*
stereotypes from, 349*(i)*
Miscegenation
antimiscegenation laws and, 81, 387
interracial relationships and, 389
Miss Crandall's School for Young Ladies and Little Misses of Color, 260
Missionaries
abolitionist, 272
in Carolinas, 88
contrabands assisted by, 303
on mistreatment of native peoples, 43
Mississippi
Black power and politics in, 598–607
Black voting in, 388, 603
Evers killed in, 574
integration of University of Mississippi and, 564–65
labor of freedpeople in, 346
slavery in, 168
Mississippi Freedom Democratic Party (MFDP), 596, 600*(i)*, 601–2
Mississippi Freedom Summer Project (1964), 599
Mississippi National Guard, Hurricane Katrina and, 694
Mississippi River region
in Civil War, 310–11
cotton in, 168
exploration of, 99
slavery in, 99
sugar cultivation in, 173
Missouri, 174*(m)*
in Civil War, 297
congressional debates over, 219
cotton in, 215
emancipation from slavery in, 320
Kansas-Nebraska Act and, 279*(m)*
slavery in, 168, 174, 211–12, 273
Missouri Compromise
approval of, 211–12, 213*(m)*
Civil War and, 297
Kansas-Nebraska Act and, 280
popular sovereignty and, 272
Missouri ex rel. Gaines v. Canada, 484
Mitchell, Arthur, 478
Mitchell, Charles, 421*(v)*
Mitchell, John (Nixon attorney general), 639

Mitchell, John Jr., 398, 400
Mitchell, Margaret, 490
Mixed ballads, 402
Mohammad, 18
Momyer, William, 539
Monaghan, George P., 571
Monarchies, European, 39
Monk, Thelonious, 528
Monroe, James
  Gabriel's rebellion and, 179
  Louisiana Purchase and, 173–74
Montesinos, Antonio de, 43
Montgomery, Alabama
  bus boycott in, 557
  march from Selma to (1965), 602
Montgomery, Olen, 471, 482(*i*)
Montgomery Improvement Association, 556–57
Moody, Anne, 555
  "Coming of Age in Mississippi," 581–82(*d*)
Mooney, Margarita, "Black Immigrants and Black Natives Attending Selective Colleges and Universities in the United States," 673–74
"Moonshine Blues" (Rainey), 402
Moore, William Lewis, 564
Moral reform
  abolitionism and, 263
  Black self-help and, 259–62
Moral suasion, 266, 269
Moral virtues, 263
Morality
  of Black women, 393
  of slavery, 91
Moravian Baptism Ceremony, A, 127(*v*)
More Perfect Union, A, speech (Obama), 696, A-26–A-32
Morgan v. Virginia (1946), 525
Moring, Richard, 235
Morocco, 6, 17, 23
Morris, Gouverneur, 166
Morris, Robert, 268
Morrison, Toni, 647, 663–64, 708
Morrisroe, Richard, 590
Mortality
  of enslaved people, 88, 92
  in Louisiana, 99
  in Middle Passage, 52, 56(*i*), 59–60
  on slave ships, 59–60
Mortgages, in 1960s, 569
Morton, Jelly Roll, 403
Morton, Samuel G., 10, 253
Mortuary rites, West African, 59
Moses, Bob, 600, 602
Mosque, 687
Moss, Thomas, 391
Mossi kingdom, 25
Mothers. *See* Black women; Families; Women
Motley, Archibald, 486
Mott, Lucretia, 270–71
Movies. *See* Films
Moynihan, Daniel Patrick, 619
Moynihan Report and, 648
Muhammad, Askia al-Hajj, 22–23, 25
Muhammad, Elijah, 598, 687
Muhammad, Warith Deen, 687
Mulattoes, 81, 85
Mules and Men (Neale), 485
Mum Bett. *See* Bett, Mum
Murals, by Aaron Douglas, 455
Murray, Andrew, 568
Murray, Donald, 484
Murray, John (Earl of Dunmore). *See* Dunmore, Earl of
Murray, Pauli, 575
Murray, William (Earl of Mansfield). *See* Mansfield, Earl of
Musa, Mansa, 20(*i*), 21
"Muse Melley," 20(*i*)
Music
  African American, 348, 349(*i*), 402, 528
  blues, 402
  Chicago Renaissance, 486
  gospel, 436, 486–87
  in Harlem Renaissance, 455, 457
  jazz, 402–3
  rap, 660
  shout as, 231
  spirituals as, 231
Musical theater
  Black, 402
  Dunbar, Paul Laurence, and, 402
Muslims, 18–19, 22
  African American, 687
  Ali as, 614
  travel ban against, 709
"Mutability of Human Affairs, The," 33(*d*)
Mutiny, of enslaved people, 54, 56
Mutual aid societies, 184, 194
  in Black communities, 259
My Bondage and My Freedom (Douglass), 266
My Brother's Keeper, 705
Myers, Isaac, 364–65

NAACP (National Association for the Advancement of Colored People), 477
  on Black violence, 619
  Brown v. Board of Education and, 553
  Chicago race riot (1919) and, 443
  Chicagoans and, 440
  civil rights and, 414
  Communist Party and, 551
  criticisms of, 484
  Du Bois and, 414
  economic opportunity and, 519, 611
  employment discrimination protests by, 573, 612
  fair housing and, 447, 570
  Legal Defense and Educational Fund, 484
  on lynching, 419–20
  Silent March and, 442(*i*), 443
  Tuskegee Syphilis Study and, 535
  voting rights and, 522
Nabrit, James, *Brown* decision and, 553
Nagasaki, atomic bombing of, 531
Nagin, Ray, 692
Names, for formerly enslaved people, 340
Napoleon. *See* Bonaparte, Napoleon
Narmer, 10
"Narrative of Bethany Veney, a Slave Woman, 1889" (Veney), 244–46
Narrative of the Life of Frederick Douglass, an American Slave (Douglass), 266
Nast, Thomas, *Colored Rule in a Reconstructed(?) State, 1874*, 378–79, 378(*v*)
Nat Turner's rebellion, 217, 223–25
Natchez Indians, uprising by, 100
Nation of Islam (NOI), 687
  Malcolm X in, 596–98, 597(*i*)
National Advisory Commission on Civil Disorders (Kerner Commission), 619
National Afro-American Council (1898–1908), 412
National Afro-American League, 412
National Alliance of Black Feminists, 648
National Association for the Advancement of Colored People. *See* NAACP
National Association of Colored Graduate Nurses, 525
National Association of Colored Women (NACW), 347(*i*), 393–94, 398, 435, 478
National Association of Police Organizations, Inc., 727
National Baptist Convention, on Black violence, 619
National Basketball Association, desegregation of, 526
National Black Anti-War Anti-Draft Union, 615
National Black Feminist Organization, 648
National Convention of Colored Men, 321
National Council of Negro Women, 478, 619
National Equal Rights League, 321, 365, 368, 412
National Federation of Afro-American Women, 393
National Football League, 526
National Guard
  in Alabama, 571
  in Arkansas school integration, 561
  Hurricane Katrina and, 694
  at Kent State, 640
  World War I Hell Fighters in, 440
National Labor Relations Act, 476
National League of Colored Women, 393
National liberation movements, in former colonies, 594
National Negro Business League
  description of, 438
  formation of, 409
National Negro Committee, 414
National Negro Congress (Chicago, 1936), 479, 483, 551
National Negro Convention
  Buffalo (1843), 288
  Philadelphia (1855), 251, 263
National Negro Funeral Directors Association, 437

National Newspaper Publishers Association, 520
National Recovery Administration (NRA), 476
National Review, 638
National Union Party, 318
National Urban League
in Chicago, 435, 438, 446
equality index of (2018), 680
fair housing and, 570
labor opportunities and, 519, 612
Richmond welfare associations and, 399
National Welfare Rights Organization (NWRO), 618, 647
National Woman Suffrage Association, 367, 374
National Youth Administration, Division of Negro Affairs, 477, 506
Nationalism. *See also* Black nationalism
Black. *See* Black nationalism
white, 710
Nation-states, European, 39
Native Son (Wright), 486
Natural disasters, Great Migration and, 432
Natural rights, enslaved people's freedom as, 132
Natural selection, scientific racism and, 387
Naturalization, availability of, 181
Naturalization Act (1790), residence and racial requirements for citizenship, 181
Navy
in War of 1812, 191
in World War II, 511
Nazism, 506
racism and, 520
Ndongo, 75
Neal, Larry, 625*(v)*
Nebraska, 174*(m)*
slavery and, 279
Nee, Thomas J., letter to Obama and Holder by, 727, 730
Négritude, 488
Negro, use of term, 597, 607, 623
Negro Act (South Carolina), 105
Negro American League, 490–91, 526
Negro Dance Group, 487
"Negro districts," in northern cities, 430
"Negro Drinking at 'Colored' Water Cooler in Streetcar Terminal, Oklahoma City, Oklahoma, 1939" (Lee), 499
"Negro Editors on Communism: A Symposium of the American Negro Press, 1932" (Du Bois), 496–97
Negro Election Day, 123
Negro Factories Corporation, 452
Negro Family in Chicago, The (Frazier), 447
Negro History Bulletin, 449
Negro History Week, 449, 449*(i)*
Negro in Chicago, The: A Study of Race Relations and a Race Riot (Charles S. Johnson), 446
Negro in Our History, The (Woodson), 449
"Negro jobs," 612
Negro Labor Victory Committee, 551
Negro league baseball, 526
Negro National Anthem, 402
Negro National League, 490
"Negro problem"
after Civil War, 359
Du Bois on, 412
"Negro Villages," at Paris World's Fair, 386
Negro World newspaper, UNIA and, 450
"Negroes Jitterbugging in a Juke Joint on Saturday Afternoon, Clarksdale, Mississippi Delta, 1939" (Wolcott), 500–501, 501*(i)*
Neighborhood Youth Corps, 611
Neighborhoods
Black, 257–58, 438
in Chicago, 438
white flight, urban renewal, and, 609
Nell, William Cooper, 266
Netherlands. *See* Dutch; New Amsterdam; New Netherland
New Amsterdam, 94
"New consciousness," after World War II, 525
New Deal. *See also* Great Depression
Black culture in, 485
inequality in, 475–77
racial discrimination in, 476
Roosevelt and, 475–77
New England
enslaved people in, 89–93, 105
integration of Revolutionary troops in, 138
legal code in, 111*(d)*
Negro Election Day in, 123
New England Confederation, slavery recognized in, 90
New Hampshire, enslaved people in, 164, 181
New Haven colony, slavery in, 90
New Jersey, 94, 96
Black Brigade and, 141
enslaved people in, 94
emancipation in, 181
regulating of enslavement in, 112–13
"New Jim Crow," 690
New Kingdom, 11, 13
New Lights, 126–27
New Mexico, 174*(m)*, 273
New Negro (1915–1940), 428–69, 486
arts movement by, 453
Harlem Renaissance and, 453–57
after World War I, 445–57
New Negro, The (Locke), 453
"New Negro" (new African arrivals), 82, 84
New Negro for a New Century, A (Washington and Williams), 446
New Netherland, 94–94
English and, 95
slavery in, 76, 93–96
New Orleans
Black employment in, 514
Hurricane Katrina and, 692–94
slave trade in, 175
Union capture of, 304
U.S. purchase of, 173
New Orleans, Battle of, 192
New Right, 638
"New Slavery in the South, The" (Georgia Negro peon), 423–25
New South. *See also* South
Black communities in cities of, 397–401
racist ideology of, 388
New World. *See* America(s)
New York (city)
African Society for Mutual Relief in, 184
Black politicians in, 572
Blacks in, 122
draft riots in (1863), 313
Five Points district in, 257, 258*(i)*
foreign-born Blacks in, 408
Korean views on Blacks in, 652
New Amsterdam as, 95*(i)*
political climate of, 572
public schools in, 189*(i)*
September 11, 2001 attack and, 691
slave plot of 1741 in, 119–20
stop and frisk in, 707
urban renewal in, 609
victory parade after World War I, 441
violence in, 572
New York (colony), 93, 96
enslavement in, 121
New York (state), emancipation in, 181
New York African Free School, 189–90, 189*(i)*, 261
New York Age (newspaper), 453
New York Manumission Society (NYMS), 182, 189, 189*(i)*
New York Public Library (Harlem), 455
New York Vigilance Committee, 275
Newspapers
American racism in international press, 566*(i)*
Black, 264–65, 381, 397, 398
Liberator as, 269
on Montgomery bus boycott, 557
Newton, Huey, 605, 606*(i)*, 639, 645
Newton, Isaac, 522
Newton, John, 57–58
Niagara movement
Du Bois and, 412
goals of, 412
Nicholas V (Pope), 42
Nicodemus, Kansas, Black migration to, 362, 364*(v)*
Nieu Amsterdam, 95*(i)*
Niger River, 19, 22, 24
Nigeria, 13–14, 24–25
"Nigger Hill" (Boston), 258
Night riders, 359
Nile River, 8, 10–12
Niles, W. J., 362
Nineteenth Amendment, woman suffrage in, 439
Ninety-Ninth Pursuit Squadron, 512
Ninety-Second Infantry, 503, 509
Ninth Ward. *See* Hurricane Katrina
Nixon, Richard
1968 election and, 638–39
resignation of, 641
southern strategy of, 638–39
Nkrumah, Kwame, 35*(d)*

Nobel Peace Prize
  to Bunche, 549
  to King, Martin Luther Jr., 604
  to Obama, 698
Nok, 13–15
Nok Sculpture, 14(*i*)
Nonviolent protest, 553, 578–79
  Malcolm X on, 597
  March on Washington and, 579
Nonwhites, regarded as primitives, 386
Nooitgedacht (Dutch slave ship), 59
Norfolk (Virginia) Journal and Guide, 520
Normal schools, 343
Norris, Clarence, 471, 482(*i*)
Norris v. Alabama, 481
North. *See also* Union (Civil War)
  abolition in, 147
  African American migration to, 513–14, 514(*m*)
  African colonization and, 253
  American Revolution, slavery, and, 144
  Black communities in, 256–57
  Black freedom struggle in, 131–38, 251–52
  desegregation after Civil War, 321
  differences from South, 209–11
  economy in, 208
  end of slavery in, 253
  enslaved population of, 122
  enslavement in (1770–1840), 183
  free Blacks in, 122–23, 144, 166, 183, 256–57
  free laborers in, 209
  fugitive slave crisis and, 276
  migration to, 430–39, 433(*m*)
  racism in, 568–71
  school segregation in, 413(*m*)
  voting rights in, 438
North Africa, 17
North America. *See also* America(s)
  African American life in18th century, 121–31
  slavery in English colonies, 76
North Atlantic Treaty Organization (NATO), 548
North Carolina. *See also* Carolina(s)
  emancipation from slavery in, 319(*i*)
  freedom seekers in, 89
North Carolina, Black and white Populists in, 389
North Carolina Agricultural and Technical College, 561
North Carolina Mutual Life, 475
North Dakota, 174(*m*)
North Star (newspaper), 265, 271
North Star, as guide to freedom seekers, 228
Northup, Solomon, 228
Northwest Ordinance (1787), 166, 167(*m*)
Northwest Territory, slavery prohibited in, 167(*m*)
Norvell, Aubrey James, 604
"Notice to Colored People," 254(*i*)
Notorious B.I.G., 662
Nott, Josiah Clark, 253
Nubia, 9, 12–13
Nubians, 12, 27
Nuclear family, 341
Nuclear weapons, in Iran, 704
Nurses, Black, in World War II, 511
Nursing, discrimination ended in military, 525
N.W.A. (Niggaz with Attitude), 661
NWRO. *See* National Welfare Rights Organization

Oak Park, Illinois, open-housing committees in, 656
Oakland, California
  Afro-American Association in, 595
  Black Panther Party in, 605, 606(*i*), 645
  police harassment in, 571
  schools in, 645
Oakland Community School, 645
Oba of Benin, with Attendants, The, 26(*i*)
Obama, Barack, 677–79, 678(*i*)
  administration of, 697–700
  birther movement, 708
  Black presidential candidate forerunners of, 695
  Blackness of, 683
  in Chicago, 677–78
  Congress and, 703
  constituency of, 686
  family of, 678(*i*), 695, 699(*i*)
  first term of, 700–701
  on Gates's arrest, 701
  health care program and, 698
  More Perfect Union, A, speech (Obama), 696, A-26–A-32
  racism against, 700–701
  second term of, 703–6
  on Trayvon Martin, 701
Obama, Barack, 2008 election and, 679, 683, 695–97
Obama, Barack, 2012 election and, 702–3
Obamacare, 698
  Court upholding of, 704
Obas, 26
Obergefell v. Hodges, 702
Oberlin College, 261
Ocasio-Cortez, Alexandria, 711, 713(*v*)
Occupations
  of enslaved people, 122
  for free Blacks, 187–90
Ocean Hill-Brownsville Parents Rally, 651(*i*)
O'Connor, Sandra Day, 644
Octoroons, 387
Office of Federal Contract Compliance, 611, 642
Office of War Information, on economic gains made by Blacks, 518
Officeholders
  Black in Kansas, 362
  Black post-emancipation, 356
Ogletree, Charles, 691
Ohio
  Attucks Guards of free Blacks in, 298
  black laws in, 181
Ohio River region, 166
Oklahoma, 174(*m*)
  American Indian removal to, 212
  Black towns in, 363
  grandfather clause in, 414
  migration to, 405
  slavery in, 174
Oklahoma City Artists for Justice, 723
Old Kingdom, 10, 12
Old Northwest, free territory in, 180
Old Plantation, The, 124(*i*)
Olivet Baptist Church (Chicago), 436
Omar, Ilhan, 711, 712, 713(*v*)
"On the Egyptians as Africans, 1827," 33(*d*)
O'Neal, Frederick, 526
One-drop rule, 387
O'Neill, Eugene, 489
Open-housing programs, 654
Operation Breadbasket, 611
Operation Neptune Spear, 698
Opportunity (journal), 447
  Harlem Renaissance and, 453
Orangeburg Massacre, 618
Oregon Territory, slavery abolished in, 273
Oregon Treaty (1846), 273
"Oreos," 606
Organization of African Unity, 598
  Cairo Conference of, 596
Organization of Afro-American Unity, 597(*i*), 598
Organizations. *See also* Labor unions
  Black, 123
  for economic opportunity, 517–20
  of free Blacks, 184–87, 185(*i*)
Orphanages, Black, 259
Osceola (Seminoles), 215
Osiris, 12
Otis, James Jr., 131, 134
Ottley, Roi, 478
Our Nig, or Sketches from the Life of a Free Black (Wilson), 266
"Outcast, 1922," 34–35(*d*)
Oval Office Meeting, 709(*i*)
Ovando, Nicols de, 42
Overseers
  Black, 86
  white, 84
Ovington, Mary White, 414
Owen, Chandler, 440, 446
Owens, Jesse, 491, 491(*i*)
Oyo County, Nigeria, 50

Pacifists, Civil Rights movement support from, 557
Packinghouses, in Chicago, 437
Pagan beliefs, *vs.* Christianity, 88
Paige, Satchel, 491
Paine, Thomas, in antislavery organization, 182
Painting. *See* Art(s)
Pale Faces, 359
Palin, Sarah, 697, 700
Pan-African Congress (1900), Du Bois at, 412
Pan-Africanism, 412, 450, 452, 488

Panic (financial), of 1873, 360
Pantaleo, Daniel, 725*(v)*
Papal bull
  on African enslavement, 43
  on converting American Indians, 43
Parchman Farm prison, 563
Parenthood. *See also* Families
  of enslaved people, 236
Paris, African Americans in, 455
Paris, Treaty of (1783), 146
Paris World's Fair (1900)
  African American achievements and, 412
  human zoos at, 386
Parker, Charlie, 528
Parker, William (Los Angeles police chief), 571
Parker, William and Eliza (freedom seekers), 276
Parks, Gordon, 477*(i)*, 495
Parks, Rosa, 556, 557
Parliament (England), taxation by, 131
Passive resistance, 567
Patient Protection and Affordable Care Act, 698, 704
Patrilineal, 24
Patriotism, of Blacks in Civil War, 298
Patriots (American Revolution), 139*(m)*
  Black, 134–38, 144
  slave trade and, 131
  white, 136
Patterson, Haywood, 471, 482*(i)*
Patterson, Robert P., 507
Paul, Thomas, 221
Paul III (Pope), 43
Pawns, 28
Peace Information Center, 549
Peace Mission movement, 480
Peace resolutions, during Civil War, 313
Peake, Mary S., 306, 347
Peale, Raphaelle, Jones, Absalom, portrait by, 186*(i)*
Pearl Harbor, Japanese bombing of, 505
Pearson v. Murray, 484
Penicillin, as syphilis treatment, 534
Penn, William, 97–98
Pennington, James W. C., 266, 272, 314
Pennsylvania, 93
  Blacks disfranchised in, 254
  emancipation in, 181
  Quakers in, 97–98
  September 11, 2001 plane crash in, 691
Pennsylvania Society for Promoting the Abolition of Slavery (PAS), 189
Pennsylvania Society for Promoting the Abolition of Slavery and for the Relief of Free Negroes Unlawfully Held in Bondage, 182
Pentagon, September 11, 2001 terrorist attack and, 691
Pentecostal, 389
Pentecostalism, 436
Peonage Abolition Act, 420
Peons
  Black, 420
  "New Slavery in the South, The," and, 423–25
People of color. *See also* African Americans; Black(s)
  Attucks as, 135
  as cowboys, 406
Pepper, Claude, 521
Perry, Lincoln, 490
Perry, Oliver Hazard, on African American sailors, 192
Personal liberty laws, 274
Personal Responsibility and Work Opportunity Reconciliation Act (1996), 659
Peru, enslaved Africans in, 43
"Petition of Belinda, 1782," 32–33*(d)*
Pew Research Center, on Black diversity, 680
Pharaoh and the Goddess, 11*(i)*
Pharaohs, 10–11, 11*(i)*
Philadelphia
  African American education in, 189
  Bethel AME Church in, 260, 263
  desegregation of public conveyances in, 365–66
  enslavement in, 122
  Free African Society in, 184, 186
  race riots in, 255, 517
  urban renewal in, 609
  in War of 1812, 192
Philadelphia Female Anti-Slavery Society, 270, 287
Philadelphia Negro, The (Du Bois), 446
Philadelphia Vigilance Committee, 276
Philippine Reservation, at St. Louis World's Fair, 386
Philippines, 386
Philipsburg Proclamation, 143–44
Phillis (ship), 31*(d)*
Phoenix Law Enforcement Association, Brisbon killing and, 727–29
Photographs
  of Black homesteaders, 364*(v)*
  of Civil War, 315*(v)*, 334*(v)*
  of slavery, 237*(v)*
Phyllis Wheatley Home (Chicago), 435
Piedmont, importation of enslaved people to, 122, 125
Pierce, Franklin, freedom seekers and, 278
Pierson, Abraham, 75
Pig, use of term, 607
Pilgrims, 89
Pilgrim's Progress, A (Bunyan), 129
Pilots. *See* Tuskegee Airmen
Pinckney, Clementa, 706
Pitcairn, John, 137
Pittsburgh Courier (newspaper), 478, 504, 508, 508*(i)*, 520
Plainfield, New Jersey, Black uprising in, 619
Plainfield High School, 649
Planet (Richmond newspaper), 398, 400
Plantation agriculture. *See also* Enslaved labor
  enslaved labor and, 84
  expansion of, 208
Plantation Burial, A, 232*(i)*
Plantation colonies
  Carolinas as, 86
  in South, 76
Plantation economy, cotton and, 168
Planter (Confederate steamer), 295
Planters and plantations
  cotton frontier and, 170
  enslaved people and land abandoned by, during Civil War, 304
  freedpeople as workers on, 304
  importation of enslaved people to, 121
  in Lower South, 215
  slavery and freedom outside plantation South, 175–83
  spread of slavery and, 150
Plessy, Homer, 384
Plessy v. Ferguson (1896), 384, 484, 553, A-21
Plymouth, slavery in, 90
"Poem to the Earl of Dartmouth, A" (Wheatley), 154
Poems on Miscellaneous Subjects (Harper), 266, 347*(i)*
Poems on Various Subjects, Religious and Moral (Wheatley), 128*(i)*
Poetry
  Claude McKay, 34–35*(d)*, 443, 453
  Countee Cullen, 3, 34, 453
  of Frances Ellen Watkins Harper, 347*(i)*
  Gwendolyn Bennett, 465*(d)*
  Gwendolyn Brooks, U4-C
  in Harlem Renaissance, 453
  of Paul Laurence Dunbar, 402
  of Phillis Wheatley, 128
Poindexter, James, 344
Police
  African Americans killed by, 706, 718
  anti-Black violence and, 571, 607
  Black violence and, 619
  and charges in killings of unarmed civilians, 723–24*(v)*
  on community policing policies, 726
  in Ferguson, Missouri, 707–8
  harassment by, 571
Police brutality, and Justice Department (DOJ), 592
Police militarization and, 726
Political action, in abolitionist movement, 269
Political activism. *See* Activism
Political parties, antislavery, 270
Political rights
  Du Bois on, 405
  Wells on, 405
Politics
  African Americans in, 439
  Black exclusion from, 254
  Blacks in, 571
  churches and, 344
  after Civil War, 355–57, 357*(m)*
  diversity in, 685–88
  jobs and, 607–8
  northern Black political struggle and, 279
  Panthers in, 645
  of Reconstruction, 350–60
  tax allocations and, 653

Politics of Respectability, 394
Polk, Oscar, 490
Poll taxes, 83, 388, 521–22
Poor People's Campaign (1967), 617
Poor people's movement, 617
Popular sovereignty, 274
Population, 257(*c*)
  African American (1790–2010), A-33
  African American (1860 and 1890), 361(*m*)
  of Blacks in Chicago, 438–39
  of Blacks in South, 432
  of enslaved people, 208
  of enslaved people in the North, 122
  of enslaved people in the South, 121, 175–76
  of free Blacks in North, 184
  on slave voyages from Africa, 59
  spread of African American, 433(*m*)
  of Taino people, 42–43
Populist Party, Black and white support for, 389
Port cities
  Africans in, 123
  free Blacks in, 184
Port Hudson, Battle of, 310
Port Royal Experiment, 304, 322
Portugal
  slave trade and, 39, 40, 54, 55, 60
  Treaty of Tordesillas and, 46
  West African exploration by, 39–40
Post-Black art, 684, 684(*i*)
Post-racial era, Obama in, 700–701, 708
Post-traumatic stress disorder, among student civil rights activists, 567
Potter's House, Dallas, Texas, 687(*i*)
Pound Cake speech (Cosby), 690
Poverty
  of African Americans, 658
  of Black women, 647
  female welfare rights and, 647
Powell, Adam Clayton Jr., 481, 571
  on Black violence, 619
  HUAC and, 547
Powell, Adam Clayton Sr., 481
Powell, Colin, 695, 696(*i*)
  on Black military participation, 615, 692
Powell, James, 602
Powell, Ozie, 471, 482(*i*)
Powell v. Alabama, 481
Powhatan, confederacy of, 79
Pregnancy, of enslaved women, 233–34
Prejudice
  African American responses to, 191
  against Black soldiers, 309
  decreasing by Black moral and intellectual improvement, 262
  against Japan, 508
  racial, 253
Preliminary Emancipation Proclamation (1862), 305
President's Commission on Campus Unrest, 640
President's Commission on the Status of Women, 575
President's Committee on Civil Rights, 524(*m*), 530
Pressley, Ayanna, 711, 712, 713(*v*)
Price, Victoria, 471
Prigg v. Pennsylvania, 274
Primary elections, white, 388
"Primitives," anthropological study of Blacks as, 387
Prince Hall Masonic Lodge, 186, 619
Prioleau, George, 406
Prison, 689(*c*). *See also* Imprisonment
  African American men in, 689
  Obama review of policies for, 705
Prison farms, 426
Prisoners of war
  Black, in Civil War, 310
  German, and discrimination against Black soldiers, 511
Pritchett, Laurie, 559(*i*)
"Private Hubbard Pryor, before and after Enlisting in the U.S. Colored Troops," 333–34(*v*)
Privateers, importation of enslaved people by, 75, 80
Prizefighting, integration of, 526
Proceedings of the American Equal Rights Association, "Debate, A: Negro Male Suffrage Equal Rights Association *vs.* Woman Suffrage," 371–74
Proclamation of Amnesty and Reconstruction (1863), 314
Production, cotton, 169
Professionals, Black, 654, 680
Progressive Democratic Party, 522
Progressivism, disfranchisement and, 388
Propaganda
  art as, 455
  in World War II, 508
Property
  enslaved people as, 274, 280, 301
  restoration of freedpeople, 314
  as voting requirement, 366
Prosser, Thomas, 177
Protestants and Protestantism
  evangelicalism and, 230
  in Georgia, 103
Protests. *See also* Demonstrations
  in Civil Rights movement, 585–87(*v*)
  against Civil War pay inequities, 310
  lunch counter sit-ins as, 562
  against Obama's economic policy, 698
  over Garner killing, 725(*v*)
  during pre-Revolution period, 132
  against race riots, 442, 442(*i*)
  against racial segregation, 383–84
  against separate but equal facilities, 383–84
  by welfare groups, 617
  against white racism, 190–91
Provident Hospital (Chicago), 437
Provincial Freeman (newspaper), 251
Pryor, Hubbard, 327, 334(*v*)
Public accommodations
  discrimination prohibited in, 592
  equality in, 358
  in World War II, 513–16
Public accommodations, equality in, 358
Public Health Service, Tuskegee Syphilis Study and, 534
Public housing, 570, 609
Public places, segregation of, 383
Public schools, 260–61
  for Black children, 189
  in New York, 189
Public transportation
  campaigns against segregated seating on, 368
  desegregation of, 383
  segregation of, 383
Public worship, restrictions on Black, 130
Publications, Black pride and, 595
Puerto Rico
  enslaved Africans in, 43
  imperialism and, 386
  independence movement in, 628
Punishment
  for drug use, 690
  of enslaved people, 243(*v*)
  of freedom seekers, 89
Puritans, 91
Purvis, Robert, 269, 281
Pyramid complex, 10, 12

Quadroons, 387
Quakers, 97–98
  abolitionist, 275
  antislavery attitudes of, 164(*i*), 182
  arrests of, 276
  Civil Rights movement and, 557
  Penn as, 97–98
  in Pennsylvania, 97–98
  on slavery, 97–98
Quartering Act, 137
"Questions and Answers about Slavery" (Clarke), 243–44
Quinn Chapel African Methodist Episcopal Church (Chicago), 436
Quota systems
  for immigrants, 664
  for voting, 659

Race
  classification of, 387
  debates over, 253
  hierarchic development of peoples by, 387
  Obama on, 697, 700
  Republican Party on, 638
  after Revolution, 190–91
  transcending of, 681
  writers and, 402
Race bombings, in Chicago, 437
"Race labels," recordings on, 457
Race pride, 619, 621
Race riots
  in Chicago (1919), 442–43, 446
  in Cincinnati, 255
  in Civil War, 313–14
  in Colfax, Louisiana (1873), 359

in Columbia, Tennessee (1946), 523
in Detroit, 516–17, 618
in East St. Louis, Illinois (1917), 442, 442*(i)*
1820–1849, 255
Hamburg Massacre as, 359
in Houston, 443
in Los Angeles (1992), 652
after Martin Luther King Jr. assassination, 621
in Monroe, Georgia (1946), 523
New York City draft riots and (1863), 313
in 1964, 602
in Red Summer (1919), 443
Rodney King and, 662
in Springfield, Illinois (1908), 414
in Watts (1965), 618
after World War I, 442–43
during World War II, 512, 516–17
zoot suit riots as, 516
Rachel (enslaved woman), childbearing by, 233
Racial discrimination. *See also* Discrimination
in armed forces, 407
Black advancement and (2007 and 2010), 683
court ending of, 268
in courts, 321
in defense industries, 508
in housing, 447
legal, 253
in New Deal, 476
in states, 352
Racial diversity. *See* Diversity
Racial prejudice. *See* Prejudice
Racial profiling, 701
Racial segregation. *See also* Racism
Black hospitals and, 344
Brown decision and, 553
in Chicago neighborhoods, 443
in churches, 187, 231
continued existence in 1960s, 592
de facto, 437, 552
de jure, 437, 553
in Detroit, 649
GI Bill and, 530
government regulation of, 387
lunch counter sit-ins and, 562
military service and, 440–41, 503–4, 509–10, 512, 528–29
of Montgomery buses, 556–57
in national professional organizations, 525
outlawed in interstate bus travel, 525
of public places, 383
residential, 437
of Richmond streetcars, 400
of schools, 348–49, 365–66, 382, 413*(m)*
in South, 383–85
Third Avenue Railroad (New York) and, 268
of transportation, 368, 383
types of, 649
in World War II, 522–23
Racial slavery, 77, 83
Racial stereotypes, 490–92
Racial unity, 259
Racial uplift ideology, of Du Bois, 410
Racial wealth gap, 477
Racism
American, in international press, 566*(i)*
of Democrats in Civil War, 313
disfranchisement and, 388–89
economic disabilities from, 608
Henry Wallace and, 552
Hurricane Katrina and, 692–94
institutional, 609, 614
international relations and, 553
John F. Kennedy on, 574
lynching and, 390–92
in minstrel shows, 292–93*(v)*
in North and West, 568–71
Obama on, 703
prejudice and, 253
protests against, 190–91
reverse, 611
Robeson and, 545–46
scientific, 387
segregation and, 383–85
toward Obama, 700–701
white supremacy and, 359, 386–87
in World War II, 508, 511–12
Radical Republicans
in Congress, 338
in 1864, 317
Reconstruction and, 350–53
Radicalism, Communist, 495–96
Radicals and radicalism. *See also* Communist Party of the United States (CPUSA)
Angela Davis and, 639
on Blacks in World War I, 440
CAPs and, 618
urban, 617–20
after World War I, 442–43
Radio, 490
Rage of a Privileged Class: Why Are Middle-Class Blacks Angry? Why Should America Care? (Cose), 681
Railroads
Great Migration via, 432, 433*(m)*
separate but equal accommodations on, 383
shipments of enslaved people on, 216
Rainbow Coalition, 653
Rainey, Joseph H., 355*(i)*
Rainey, Ma, 402, 457, 464*(d)*
RAM. *See* Revolutionary Action Movement
Ramesses II, 12
Ramos, Rafael, 726–27
Randolph, A. Philip, 478, 480, 481*(i)*, 483
on integration of armed services, 507
March on Washington movement and, 507, 518, 574–75
Messenger and, 440, 446
on World War I, 440
Rano, 25
Rap music, 660
Rape, 359
Blacks as targets for, 359
lynchings and, 391–92, 414, 421*(v)*
riots over rumors of, 516–17
Reading. *See also* Education; Literacy
education and, 348
Reagan, Ronald
AIDS epidemic and, 658
on discrimination, 641–42
war on drugs and, 642–43
welfare and, 642
Reagan, Ronald, 1980 election and, 642
Rebellions. *See* Revolts and rebellions
Recession, in 2008, 696
Reconstruction, 344–60. *See also* Black Reconstruction
Congressional, 350–53
defeat of, 358–60
education during, 346–50
land distribution during, 344–46
politics of, 350–60
second, 620
Reconstruction Acts (1867 and 1868), 352
Recruitment, of Black Civil War soldiers, 310
Red Record, A (Wells), 392
Red scare, 495–96
after World War I, 443
after World War II, 547–53
Red Summer (1919), 443
Red-baiting, 550
Redcoats (British), 134
Redemption, through Democratic Party, 358
Redlining, 476–77, 569
Reeb, James, 604
Reenslavement, Fugitive Slave Act (1850) and, 274–75
Reform. *See also* Moral reform
of criminal justice system, 705
religion and, 267
Refugees
Black loyalists as, 142, 146
enslaved people as, 301–4, 303*(i)*
from New Orleans plantations, 304
Regents of the University of California v. Bakke (1978), 644, A-23–A-24
Regiments, Black, in World War I, 440
Regionalism, labor and, 209
Regions
economies in, 209–11
variations in slavery by, 105–6
Registration. *See* Voting and voting rights
Rehnquist, William, 644
Religion. *See also* Church(es); Great Awakening; Revivals
abolitionist movement and, 272
African traditions of, 88
Civil Rights movement and, 557
conjurers and, 88, 126
diversity in, 686–88
after emancipation, 341–44, 342*(i)*
for enslaved people in Carolinas, 86–87
in Egypt, 11
Great Awakening and, 126–31
as justification for slavery, 230–32, 239
morality of slavery and, 91
reform and, 267

Religion (*Continued*)
restrictions on Virginia Blacks and, 223–25
spirituals and, 231
West African, 58, 88
Religious Society of Friends. *See* Quakers
Remembering Denmark Vesey, 219*(v)*
Remick, Christian, 136
"Reminiscences of My Life in Camp" (Taylor), 329–30
Remond, Sarah Parker, 268
Removal, of American Indians, 212–15
Renaissance
African American literature in 1820s–1850s, 266
Chicago Renaissance, 486–88
Harlem Renaissance, 453–57, 454*(m)*, 460–68, 485–86
Repeal Association (Illinois), 321
Representation
Black, 355*(i)*, 356
enslaved population and, 167
taxation and, 131
Reproduction, by enslaved people, 84, 150, 208, 233–34
Reproductive rights, 647
Republic of New Africa, 606
Republican National Committee, Steele and, 700
Republican Party, 637–44
African Americans in, 688
antislavery formation of, 279
Black advocation for equal rights and, 368
after Civil War, 356
freedpeople in, 356
in 1870s, 359
southern Democrats in, 638
Republican Party, 1864 election and, 317
Resettlement Administration (RA), 495
Residential segregation. *See* Housing
"Resignation Memo and Response" (Hastie), 541–43
"Resignation Memo and Response" (Stratemeyer), 541*(d)*
Resistance. *See also* Freedom seekers; Revolts and rebellions
Christiana, 276
covert, 239
disobedience and defiance as, 225–27
by landless freedpeople, 345
overt, 177
Resources, taxes for schools and, 650
Restrictive covenants, 568
Reuther, Walter, 601
Revels, Hiram R., 355*(i)*, 356
Revere, Paul, 135
Reverse discrimination, 641, 688
Reverse racism, 611
Revivals, 130
characteristics of, 130
enslaved people in, 130
in Second Great Awakening, 223–25
Revolts and rebellions. *See also* Protests; Resistance
Bacon's Rebellion, 83
by Brown, John, 282
calls for, 264
Constitution on aid to enslavers, 166
Gabriel's rebellion, 175, 177–80
New York slave plot of 1741 and, 119–20
prevention of, 89
slave mutiny and, 54, 56
on slave ships, 58
Stono rebellion, 104–5
by Turner, 217, 223–25
by Vesey, 218–20
Revolution. *See also* American Revolution
French, 173
in Haiti (1791–1804), 173, 173*(i)*
Malcolm X on, 597
Revolutionary Action Movement (RAM), 594, 606
FBI targeting of, 620
Revolutionary War. *See* American Revolution
Reynolds, Mary, 242, 246
"Days of Slavery, The," 246–48, 247*(i)*
Rezoning, for segregation, 655
Rhimes, Shonda, 681
Rhode Island
emancipation in, 181
enslaved people seeking freedom during Revolution and, 138
slavery in, 90
Rice
in Carolinas, 86, 87*(i)*
in Georgia, 103
enslaved laborers' production of, 209, 210*(m)*
in Louisiana, 100
Rice, Condoleezza, 692, 695, 696*(i)*
Rice, T. D. (Thomas Dartmouth) "Daddy," 292–93*(v)*
Richardson, Gloria, 593
Richmond, Virginia
Black community in, 397–401
as Confederate capital, 298
Gabriel's rebellion in, 175
slavery in, 175, 178–79
Richmond Colored Normal School (Armstrong High School), 398
Richmond Planet (newspaper), 34*(d)*, 398, 400
Rights. *See also* Equal rights
of African Americans, 382–83
denied to Blacks, 281
Du Bois on, 405, 412
Malcolm X on human rights, 596
for women, 268, 647
during World War II, 521–23
Rights of All, The (newspaper), 264
Rine, Mark, 726–28
Ring shout, 231
Ringgold, Faith, *Flag Is Bleeding, The*, 627*(v)*
Riots. *See* Race riots
"River of No Return, The" (Sellers), 583*(d)*
Rivers, Eunice, 535*(d)*
Roberson, Willie, 471, 482*(i)*
Roberts, Benjamin, 268
Roberts Temple Church of God in Christ, 437
Roberts v. City of Boston, 268
Robertson, Carole, 576*(i)*
Robeson, Paul, 489
blacklisting of, 550
HUAC and, 545, 546
Robinson, Bill (Bojangles), 401, 441, 455
Robinson, Eugene, 679–80, 681, 685
Robinson, Jackie, 526
Robinson, Jo Ann, 556, 596
Rock, John S
National Convention of Colored Men and, 321
Supreme Court and, 321
Rockefeller, John D., Tuskegee Institute funding from, 409
Rockefeller, Nelson, 642
Rockefeller drug laws (New York), 642
Rogers, J. A., 509
Romney, Mitt, 702
Roosevelt, Eleanor, 477, 492
Black voting rights and, 522
Roosevelt, Franklin D
Atlantic Charter and (1941), 506
Black women in military and, 511
Four Freedoms of, 506
New Deal and, 475–77
World War II and, 505–6
Roosevelt, Franklin D., 1932 election of, 475
Roosevelt, Theodore
Black soldiers discharged by, 407
Washington, Booker T., and, 410
Root doctors, 126
Rosenwald, Julius, Black education and, 409
Ross, Araminta 'Minty' (Harriet Tubman). *See* Tubman, Harriet
Royal African Company (England), 81, 96
Royal Navy
evacuation of Black loyalists by, 146
forcible conscription into, 191
Royall, Isaac, 32*(d)*
Royalty, in European nation-states, 39
Ruffin, Josephine St. Pierre, 393, 414
Ruffin, Thomas, 227
Ruggles, David, 275
Rural areas
Black men in, 395
Black women's labor in, 395, 396*(i)*
slavery in, 175
Rush, Bobby, 678
Rusher, William, 638
Russia, forced labor from, 40
Russwurm, John, 3, 264
"On the Egyptians as Africans, 1827," 33*(d)*
Rustin, Bayard, 574, 608
sexual orientation of, 664
Ryan, Paul, 702

Saffin, John, 91
Brief and Candid Answer to a Late Printed Sheet, Entitled, The Selling of Joseph, 91
Sahara desert, transatlantic trade and, 39
Sahel, 15

Sailors, African American, 191
Saint Domingue, 99
  Haitian Revolution in, 172, 173*(i)*
  indigo from, 100
Salem, Peter, 137
Sales, Blacks in, 654
Sally (brig), log of, 70–72*(v)*
Salt, 17
Salzburgers (German-speaking Protestants), 103
Samson (Black sailor), 143
San peoples, 7
Sankore Mosque, Timbuktu, Mali, 21*(i)*
São Tomé, 39–40
Saratoga, battle at, 142
Sarly, Jacob, 119
Savage, Augusta, 466*(d)*, 488
Savannah, in Revolution, 143
#SayHerName, 712, 722–23
Scalawags, 354
Scalia, Antonin, 644
Scat singing, 457
Schmeling, Max, 491, 526
Scholarship
  debates over race, 253
  on urban problems, 447
Schomburg, Arthur, 449, 453
Schomburg Center for Research in Black Culture, 449
Schools. *See also* Busing; Colleges and universities; Education
  Black, 186, 189
  for Black beauty methods training, 439
  Brown decision and, 553, 560–61
  busing and, 639, 642, 651
  community control of, 650
  curriculum in, 348–49
  desegregation of, 553, 560–61, 571
  after emancipation, 346–50
  for enslaved people, 129
  for free Blacks, 260–61
  Nixon on desegregation and, 638–39
  punishment for conduct in, 691
  segregation of, 260, 348–49, 365–66, 382
Schuyler, George, 508
Schwerner, Michael, 599
Scientific racism, 387
SCLC. *See* Southern Christian Leadership Conference
Scott, Dred and Harriet, 280*(v)*, 281, 286
Scott, Hazel, 550
Scottsboro Boys, 471–72, 481–83, 482*(i)*, 495, 545
Scripture. *See also* Religion
  stories from, 231
Sea Islands
  in Civil War, 316
  cotton from, 169
  freedpeople in, 303–4
  schools in, 347
Seale, Bobby, 605, 606*(i)*, 639
  politics and, 646, 646*(i)*
Secession, of South, 296–97
Second Cavalry Division, 512
Second Confiscation Act (1862), 304, 306
Second Continental Congress (1775), 137
Second Great Awakening
  enslaved people's religious ceremonies and, 231
  revivals during, 223
Second Reconstruction, 620
Second war of independence, War of 1812 as, 191
Second World War. *See* World War II
Secondary education, teacher training in, 261
Sectional conflict, 209, 213, 213*(m)*
Sectionalism, Lincoln's election and, 296
Securities and Exchange Commission (SEC), 475
Security risks, in Red scare, 550
Sedgwick, Theodore, 147, 148*(i)*
Segregation. *See* Racial segregation
Selassie, Haile, 488
Self-determination
  Delany on, 281
  Garvey and, 450–52
Self-governing villages, 24
Self-government, right to, 131
Self-help, 259–62, 685
Self-improvement
  of Black communities, 262
  in Kansas, 363
Self-improvement, in Kansas, 363
Self-purchase, in Virginia, 180
Self-reliance, Black self-determination and, 281
Sellers, Cleveland, "River of No Return, The," 583*(d)*
Selling of Joseph, The (Sewall), 91
Selma-to-Montgomery march (1965), 602
Seminole Indians
  Black Seminoles and, 214–15, 214*(i)*
  displacement of, 215
  slavery among, 213–14
Senate, Blacks in, 355*(i)*, 356
Seneca Falls, New York, women's rights convention in, 271
Seneca Village (New York City), 259
Senegal, 15, 19
  enslaved people from, 100
Senegal River, 17
Senegambia, 40, 46
  enslaved people from, 3, 100
Senghor, Léopold Sédar, 488
"Sentiments of the People of Color," 201
Separate but equal doctrine
  Plessy v. Ferguson and, 384
Separate Car Act (Louisiana, 1890), 384
Separatism, Black, 450, 606
September 11, 2001, terrorist attacks, 691
Seraw, Mulugeta, 682
Serfs, in England, 77
Servants
  enslaved people and, 83
  indentured, 80
  supplies of, 81
  white, 80, 83
Service trades, free Blacks in, 188
Servicemen's Readjustment Act (GI Bill), 530
Settlement(s). *See also* Liberia; Maroons; Sierra Leone
  in Africa, 282
  expansion of slavery and, 208–9
  of freedom seekers, 304
  in Jamestown, 77
Settlement houses, Black, 435
Seven Principles of Nguzo Saba, 606
'76 Association, 359
Sewall, Samuel, 91
  Selling of Joseph, The: A Memorial (1700), 91
Sex. *See also* Gender
  antimiscegenation laws and, 387
  enslaved marriages and, 235
  white enslavers' power and, 82*(i)*
Sex, Power, and Slavery in Virginia, 82*(i)*
Sex segregation, of field hands, 233
Sexism, 663*(i)*
Sexual harassment, 663*(i)*
Sexual violence. *See also* Rape
  enslavers' rape of enslaved women, 57–58
  on slave ships, 57
Sexuality, gender and, 649, 662–64
Seymour, William, 436
SFA. *See* Southern Farmers' Alliance
Shackles, 55, 56
Shadd, Mary Ann. *See* Cary, Mary Ann Shadd
Shadow of the Plantation (Charles Johnson), 448
Shahn, Ben, 495
Shakur, Tupac, 662
Shange, Ntozake, 647
Sharecroppers, Black laborers as, 515
Sharecropping, 345
Sharia law, 22–23
Sharp, Granville, 133, 193
Shaw, Robert Gould, 309, 309*(i)*, 311
Shelby v. Holder, 704
Shelley v. Kraemer, 568
Sherman, William Tecumseh
  on landownership, 344
  Special Field Order 15 and, 318
Sherman's Reserve, former Confederate land as, 344
Ships and shipping, 515. *See also* Slave ships
  Portuguese, 39
Shondaland, 681
"Shout" (ring shout), 231
Shuffle Along (musical), 455
Shuttlesworth, Fred, 564
Sierra Leone, Black Bostonians to, 193
Silent Majority, 638
Silent March (1917), 442, 442*(i)*
Simpson, Nicole Brown, 662
Simpson, O. J., 662
Single-parent households, 681
Singleton, Benjamin "Pap," 363
Sissle, Noble, 455
Sit-down strike, by CORE during World War II, 520

Sit-ins, 583(*v*)
at Woolworth lunch counters, 561–62
Sixteenth Street Baptist Church
Birmingham, bombing in, 576(*i*), 578
Sixth Mount Zion Baptist Church (Richmond), 398
Skills, teaching of, 232–33
Skin color, of Africans, 82
Skull measurements, as proof of racial inferiority, 253
Slaughterhouse Cases (1873), 360
Slave coast, Middle Passage and, 53–55, 56(*i*), 57(*i*)
Slave codes, 105. *See also* Black codes; Law(s)
from Barbados, 89
marriages of enslaved people and, 234
in South Carolina, 113–15
Slave markets. *See also* Auctions
in North, 97(*i*)
Slave patrols, in South, 180, 315
Slave Power
as conspiracy, 272, 281
South as, 168
Slave quarters, religious education in, 230–31
Slave raids, 40
Slave ships, 55–60, 70–72(*v*). *See also* Ships and shipping
conditions on, 55–58, 57(*v*)
Slave states. *See also* Confederate States of America
as border states, 298
creation of in 1812–1845, 215
after Lincoln's election, 283
from Louisiana Purchase, 173–74
Missouri as, 211–12
Texas as, 273
Slave trade. *See also* Mortality; Slave ships
African, 40–43, 49
in Atlantic region, 40
business of, 40
in Chesapeake region, 125
diaspora in, 60
domestic, 175, 208, 209, 215–17, 216(*m*)
Dutch, 81
end of, 193
English, 52, 60, 81, 145
enslaved population carried in, 43
Europe during, 39–41
families in, 57–58
in New England, 91
number of African exports, 46
Portuguese, 40–41
Revolutionary patriots and, 131
transatlantic, 38–49
trans-Saharan, 17
Slavery, 170(*c*). *See also* Abolitionists and abolitionism; Emancipation; Enslaved people; Free Blacks; Freedpeople
in Africa, 42
African American views of, 241–48
anthropological justifications of, 253
in backcountry, 169
Black challenges to, 217–25
Black petitions against, 134
Britain and, 145
in Carolinas, 85–89, 87(*i*)
Catholic Church sanction of, 43
chattel, 80, 82
in Chesapeake region, 77
Christianity and, 81
in Constitution, 166–68, 272
cotton and, 168–72, 209–11, 210(*m*)
debate over expansion of, 211–12
debt peonage and, 420, 423–25
empire and, 172–75
expansion of, 83–85, 122, 208–17
in Florida, 98, 101–2, 102(*i*)
Garrison on, 269
in Georgia, 98, 103–4
in Indian Territory, 212–15
inheritance of, 80, 81
legal status in Chesapeake, 80
Lincoln on, 300, 318, 322
in Louisiana, 76, 99–101
in Louisiana Purchase, 173–74, 174(*m*)
in Middle Atlantic colonies, 93–98
movement to freedom in South, 180
narratives about, 265–66
in New Jersey, 112–13
in New Netherland, 93–96
prohibited in Northwest Territory, 167(*m*)
protections of, 195
Quakers on, 97–98
question of, 272–83
racial, 77, 83
regional variations in, 105–6
Seminoles on, 213–14
status after Revolution, 166–68
Thirteenth Amendment and, 370
urban, 175–77
in West Africa, 27–28, 38
westward expansion and, 272–74
Slew, Jenny, freedom suit by, 133
Smalls, Robert, 295–96, 308, 354, 356
Smallwood, Stephanie, 59
Smith, Bessie, 456
Smith, Charles, 590
Smith, James McCune, 189, 259, 265
Smith, Lamar, 554
Smith, Luther, 509
Smith, Robert F., 682
Smith, Venture, 91
Smith v. Allwright (1944), 522
SNCC. *See* Student Nonviolent Coordinating Committee
Snipes, Macio, 523
So Joo Bautista (ship), 75
Social circles, of churches, 343
Social class. *See* Class
Social Darwinism, 387
Social equality, New Negro and, 446
Social media
#BlackLivesMatter on, 717–18
news spread by, 717–18
#SayHerName, 712, 722–23
Social Security, 475, 476
Society
African American after emancipation, 338–39
Black, in Spanish Florida, 101–2
changes brought by slavery, 122
European, 39
in Louisiana, 100
plan for post-Civil War, 314
Society for the Relief of Free Negroes Unlawfully Held in Bondage, 182
Society of Friends. *See* Quakers
Sociology, Chicago School of, 446
Sokoto Caliphate, 25
Soldiers (Black), 137, 308(*c*), 362–63. *See also* GI Bill; Military
after Civil War, 362–63
in Civil War, 298–99, 307–10, 312(*m*), 322
in Revolutionary era, 137–38, 141–42
in World War I, 420–41, 443
in World War II, 511
Soldiers in Uniform (de Verger), 153, 157, 158(*v*)
Soldiers without Swords, 520
Somalia, 13, 709
Somaliland, 13
Somerset, James, 133
Somerset case (1772), 133
Songhai, 22–23
Songs. *See* Music
Soninke, 16–17
Soon Ja Du, 652
Sossi, 19
Soul Students Advisory Council, 606
Souls of Black Folk, The (Du Bois), 412
Soumaoro, 18–19
South. *See also* Civil War; Confederate States of America; New South; Slavery; Southern strategy; *specific Confederate States of America entries*
African American families separated in, 170–71
African Americans in, 121, 194
agriculture in (1860), 210(*m*)
Black belt in, 361(*m*)
Black middle class in, 382–83
Black migration from, 430
Black patriots in, 138
Black political participation in, 357(*m*)
Black population of, 432
Black vote and, 521–22
Black workers in, 611
Blacks and whites in agrarian protests, 389
cash crops in, 209
Civil Rights movement in, 553–67
Democratic Party in, 358, 388
differences from North, 209–11
economy in, 168, 208–10
enslaved people liberated after American Revolution, 164
enslaved population in, 175–77
free Blacks in, 122, 147–49
fugitive slave crisis and, 276
Great Migration from, 405–7

immigration to, 209
lifestyle of Blacks in, 205–8
Lord Dunmore's Proclamation and, 139–41
movement from slavery to freedom in, 180
NAACP in, 446
opportunities outside of, 360–67
plantation colonies in, 76
racial segregation in, 383–85
recognition of marriages of enslaved people in, 234
representation in, 167
school desegregation in, 560
secession in Civil War, 296–97
as Slave Power, 168
slavery and freedom outside, 175–83
state constitutions during Reconstruction, 354–55
Walker's Appeal... in, 221
white political control of, 360
white rule restored in, 382–83
South Africa
Black loyalists in, 146
description of, 6
South Carolina. *See also* Carolina(s)
Blacks during American Revolution and, 138
Civil War and, 297
cotton boom and slavery in, 169
on education of enslaved people, 129
"eight box law" in, 388
enslaved population in, 13
freedom seekers in, 132
limits on enslaved people in, 220–21
Negro Act in, 105
secession by, 296–97
slave code in, 113–15
Vesey's rebellion in, 218–20
South Carolina State College, Orangeburg Massacre in, 618
South Dakota, 174*(m)*
South Side of Chicago, Black population of, 437
Southern Christian Leadership Conference (SCLC), 558–59, 564, 570, 575, 616
Charles Steele and, 686
FBI and, 628*(d)*
Southern Democrats
in 1964 election, 602
in Republican Party, 638
Southern Farmers' Alliance (SFA), 389
Southern Homestead Act (1866), 344
Southern Horrors: Lynch Law in All Its Phases (Wells), 391
Southern Negro Youth Congress, 479, 484, 551
Southern strategy
by British in American Revolution, 143–44
of Nixon, 638–39
Southern whites, political control of South by, 360
Souvenir Views: Negro Enterprises and Residences (1907), on Richmond Black residents, 397
Soviet Union
propaganda during Civil Rights movement, 564
Robeson and, 545–46
after World War II, 548
Spain
Atlantic trade and, 40
enslaved people in Florida and, 98–99
slave trade and, 42, 60
Treaty of Tordesillas and, 46
Spanish Florida. *See* Florida
Spanish-American War
Black soldiers in, 407
U.S. colonies after, 386
Special Field Order 15 (1865), 318
"Special Payment' Request and Floor Plan of Fred Hampton's Apartment," 630–31, 630*(v)*
Sphinx, 12
"Sphinx Builder Speaks, 1919, The," 34*(d)*
Spies, Black Revolutionary, 143
Spingarn Medal, 449
Spirituals, 231
Sports, integration of, 526–28
Spotswood, Alexander, 105
Springfield, Illinois, race riot in (1908), 414
Squad Puts American First, The, 713*(v)*
St. Augustine
enslaved people in, 76–77, 101, 102*(i)*
freedom seekers in, 101
St. Augustine's Episcopal Church, 686
St. Hill, Shirley Anita. *See* Chisholm, Shirley
St. Louis
civil rights activists in, 573
World's Fair at, 386
"St. Louis Blues" (Handy), 402, 441
St. Luke Herald (newspaper), 398, 400
Stagflation, 640
Stamp Act (1765), 132
Standard English, 652
Stanford, Maxwell, 594
Stanley, Sarah G., 348
Stanton, Edwin M., 353
Stanton, Elizabeth Cady, 271, 367, 370, 372–74, 374*(d)*
State v. Mann, 227
States (U.S.). *See also* Free states
Black disfranchisement in, 254–55
emancipation and, 300, 320
plan for reorganization of Confederacy, 314
process for reentry into Union, 352
racial discrimination in, 352
southern constitutions during Reconstruction, 354–55, 383
Supreme Court on voting laws in, 704
Texas as, 273
States' Rights (Dixiecrat) Party, 552
"Statistical Look at Foreign-Born Blacks in the United States, 1980–2016," 670–71
Staupers, Mabel, 525
Steele, Charles, 686
Steele, Michael, 700
Steele, Shelby, 685
Steering, in housing, 569
Stereotypes
from minstrel shows, 349*(i)*
racial, in culture, 490–92
Stevens, Harold, 572
Stevens, Thaddeus, 351
Stewart, Charles, 133
Stewart, Maria W., 261–62, 269
Stewart, William, 391
Still, William, 276, 282, 365
Underground Rail Road, The, 292*(v)*
Stimson, Henry L., 507, 512, 541
Stock market crash (1929). *See* Great Depression
Stockyards Labor Council, 437
Stokes, Carl, 653
Stone, Lucy, 367, 372, 373*(d)*
Stono rebellion, 104–5
"Stop and frisk" programs, 707–8
Stormy Weather (film), 526
Stowe, Harriet Beecher, 278
Stowers, Freddie, Congressional Medal of Honor to, 440
"Strange Fruit," 489
Stratemeyer, George E., "Resignation Memo and Response," 541–43
Streetcars, boycott of Richmond streetcars and, 400
Strikes
in Baltimore shipyards (1865), 364
by Black washerwomen, 395
Blacks hired as strikebreakers and, 364
in Chicago, 437
in Detroit, 517, 518, 618
hate (1960s), 611
Knights of Labor and, 364–65
Strong, Edward E., 484
Student(s). *See also* Education
in Civil Rights movement, 561–65
protests by, 640
Student Nonviolent Coordinating Committee (SNCC), 484, 562, 589, 604, 615
Sub-Saharan Africa, 14
Subsidies, for health care, 704
Suburbs
Blacks in, 656
desegregation efforts in, 656
inner-ring, 656
whites in, 569
"Subversive" organizations, U.S. attorney general's list of, 551
Suffering, King on, 558
Suffrage. *See* Voting and voting rights
Sugar and sugar industry
African labor for, 43
in Haiti, 173
in Louisiana and Texas, 210*(m)*
in Mississippi valley, 173
slavery in, 209–10
Sugar colonies
English, 145
French, 99
Sugarcane, 40
Suicide, in Middle Passage, 55, 58

Sumner, Charles, 279
beating of, 278
on Black citizenship, 321
civil rights bill introduced by, 358
death of, 359
Radical Republicans and, 351
on school segregation, 268
Sunday school, Black, 186
Supreme Court (U.S.)
Brown decision and, 554
on discriminatory job performance requirements, 612
on racial segregation in interstate commerce, 383
Reconstruction and, 351
school desegregation and, 554, 560
selected decisions of, A-20–A-24
on segregation in interstate bus travel, 525
southerners and, 168
Trump appointments to, 709
Voting Rights Act (1965) and, 704
woman on, 644
Survey Graphic (journal), Harlem issue of, 453
"Survival of the fittest," 387
"Survival programs," run by Black Panthers, 645
Sutton, Belinda, "Petition of Belinda, 1782," 32–33*(d)*
Sutton, Percy, 656
Swann, Lynn, 686
SWAT teams, 724*(v)*
Sweden, slavery and, 60, 94
Sweet, Ossian, 447
"Sweet Daddy Grace," 479
Syphilis experiment, at Tuskegee, 475, 534–38, 535–36*(v)*, 537*(v)*
Syria, 10

Taft, William Howard, Washington, Booker T., and, 410
Taft-Hartley Act (1947), 550
Taghaza, 17, 19
Taino Indians, 42–43
Talented Tenth
Black upper class as, 682
Du Bois on, 412
Tallmadge, James, 211–12
"Tangible Results" (FBI memo), 631*(d)*
Tanner, Henry Ossawa, *Banjo Lesson, The,* 404, 404*(i)*
Tanzania, 14
Taoudenni, 17
Tappan, Arthur and Lewis, 269–70
American and Foreign Anti-Slavery Society and, 270
Task system, 86
Taxation
allocation of, 653
Black tax and, 681
of Charleston free Blacks, 221
poll taxes, 388
representation and, 131
Three-Fifths Compromise and, 167
Taylor, Breonna, 713, 717, 722
Taylor, Susie King, 316, 326, 346
"Reminiscences of My Life in Camp," 329–30
Taylor, William Lee, 398
Tea Act (Britain), 136
Tea Party movement, 698, 702
Teachers
Black, 260–62, 398
contrabands assisted by, 302–3
elders as, 232
need for, 348–49
training of, 261, 348–49
white, of Black children, 261
white and Black, 348
Teenagers
Black unemployment and, 705–6
fictive kin of, 238
indicted as adults, 691
Television, images of Black women on, 648
Tell My Horse (Neale), 485
Ten Point Program (Black Panthers), 605
Tennessee
emancipation from slavery in, 320
slavery in, 168
Tennis, desegregation of, 526
Tenure of Office Act (1867), 352
Terrell, Mary Church, 393, 414
Territories, slavery in, 272–74, 301
Terrorism
ISIS and, 703
September 11, 2001, attacks and, 691–92
Testimonies, enslaved people, 241–48
Texas, 174*(m)*
emancipation from slavery in, 319
Mexican cession of, 273
slavery in, 174, 215, 273
That's My Mama (television program), 648
Theater, Blacks in, 402
Their Eyes Were Watching God (Hurston), 485
Third party, in 1948 election, 552
Third World Women's Alliance, 648–49
Thirteenth Amendment (1865)
debt peonage and, 420
slavery and, 320, 323, 370
Thirteen-Year-Old Sharecropper, 474*(i)*
Thirty Years of Lynching in the United States (NAACP), 419
Thirty-Third U.S. Colored Troops, 307
Thomas, Alesia, 722
Thomas, Clarence, 662–63, 663*(i)*, 704
Thomas (ship), slave revolt on, 58
Thompson, James G., Double V campaign and, 508*(i)*
Three-Fifths Compromise, 167, 211
368th Regiment, 440
369th Infantry Regiment (Hell Fighters), 440–41
371st Regiment, 440
Thurman, Wallace, 455
Thurmond, Strom, 552
Tight packing, on slave ships, 55
Tigrinya language, 13
Tigré language, 13
Tilden, Samuel, 360
Till, Emmett, 554–57, 555*(i)*, 581–82, 581–82*(d)*
Tillman, James, 503, 509
Tillmon, Johnnie, 617, 648
Timbuktu, 19, 21–22
Title II, of Civil Rights Act (1964), A-16
Title III, of Civil Rights Act (1964), A-16
Title IV, of Civil Rights Act (1964), A-16–A-17
Title V, of Civil Rights Act (1964), A-17
Title VII, of Civil Rights Act (1964), 592, 611, 613, 653, A-17–A-18
Title VIII, as Fair Housing Act, 653–54
Title IX, of Education Amendments (1972), 653
Titus (enslaved man), 140–41
Tlaib, Rashida, 711, 713*(v)*
"To Make the Slaves' Cause Our Own" (Douglass, Sarah Mapps), 287*(d)*
To Secure These Rights, 530
Tobacco
Black workers and, 397
in Chesapeake region, 84
in Louisiana, 100
production decline of, 168
slavery and, 209
in Upper South, 210*(m)*
in Virginia, 77, 79*(i)*, 80
Tometi, Opal, 717, 719*(d)*
Toomer, Jean, 453
Tordesillas, Treaty of, 46
Torres, Kimberly C., "Black Immigrants and Black Natives Attending Selective Colleges and Universities in the United States," 673–74
Touré, 684
Toussaint-Louverture, 173
Townsend, James, 301
Trade. *See also* Slave trade
in New England, 90
in New Netherland, 94
triangle, 46, 48*(m)*, 54
Trade unions, in Richmond, 400
Trades, at Hampton Institute, 348–50
Trading centers, for slave trade, 46
Trail of Tears, 214
Transatlantic slave trade, 38–49, 47*(m)*. *See also* Triangle trade
European, 39–40
Middle Passage and, 50–60
"Transcendent" Blacks, 681
Transportation. *See also* Public transportation
revolution in North, 211
shipments of enslaved people and, 216
Trans-Saharan trade, 15, 16*(m)*
Travis, Joseph, 223
Treaties. *See also specific treaties*
Portuguese-West African, 40
of Tordesillas, 46

Treatise on the Intellectual Character, and Civil and Political Condition of the Colored People of the U. States, A (Easton), 266
Trial by jury
for enslaved people in New England, 91
Virginia restrictions on, 224
Trials, of Newton, Huey, 639
Triangle trade, 46, 48*(m)*, 54
"Trickster tales," 385
Trimble, Aleck, 320
Troops. *See* Military
Trotter, William Monroe, 410–12
Truant, 226
True Reformers Bank (Richmond), 398
Truly disadvantaged, use of term, 658
Truman, Harry S
on anti-Black violence, 530
loyalty program of, 547, 551–53
Truman, Harry S., 1948 election and, 552
Trumbull Park, Chicago, Black housing in, 570
Trump, Donald J.
African Americans and, 708–13
birther movement and, 708
border wall and, 710
immigration and, 710
"Make America Great Again," 708–11
Obama and, 679, 708–9, 709*(i)*
Supreme Court justices appointed by, 709
travel ban by, 710
voter photo ID laws and, 711
Trump v. Hawaii, 709
Truth, Sojourner (Isabella Baumfree), 517
as abolitionist lecturer, 267–68
Contraband Relief Association and, 316
desegregation of streetcars and, 366
emancipation of, 181
"Equal Voting Rights," 370–71
as feminist, 367
portrait of, 267*(i)*
on women's rights, 268
Truth Squad (Chicago), 649
Tubman, Harriet (Araminta "Minty" Ross), 226, 226*(i)*
in Civil War, 316
desegregation of streetcars and, 365
at NACW meeting, 393
portrait of, 226*(i)*
as successful freedom seeker, 228
as Underground Railroad conductor, 276
unsuccessful escape attempt by, 226
Tucker, Tilghman, 232*(i)*
Tullahassee, Oklahoma, 363
Turner, Benjamin S., 355*(i)*
Turner, Henry M., 306, 360, 408, 412
Turner, In re, 346
Turner, Nat, 217, 224–25
Tuskegee Airmen, 509, 539–40*(v)*, 539–41
interview with, 539–40
Tuskegee Institute, 475, 534
curriculum at, 348
founding of, 408
funding of, 409
syphilis experiments at, 475, 534–38, 535–36*(v)*, 537*(v)*
Tuskegee Machine, 409, 412
Tuskegee Veterans Hospital, 475
Twelve Years a Slave (Northup), 228
Twenty-Fifth Infantry Regiment, in Brownsville, Texas, 407
Twenty-Fourth Infantry Regiment, 443
"Two Nations of Black America, The" (PBS program), 657
Types of Mankind, or Ethnological Researches (Nott and Gliddon), 253

Ubi Girl from Tai Region (Jones), 625–26*(v)*
Uganda, 14
"Uhuru" (freedom), 605
Uli, Mansa, 19
"Uncle Tom Negroes," 607
Uncle Tom's Cabin (Stowe), publication of, 278
Uncle Tom's Children (Wright), 486
Underclass, 657
Underground Rail Road, The (Still), 276, 292*(v)*
Underground Railroad
description of, 229, 275*(m)*, 276, 292*(v)*
"Understanding clauses," for voting, 388
Underwood, Lauren, 712
Unemployment
of African Americans, 473, 608, 681, 705–6
of whites, 681
UNIA. *See* Universal Negro Improvement Association
Union (Civil War), 308*(c)*
African American workers for, 315*(v)*
African Americans in military of, 295–96, 298–99, 305, 307–10, 312*(m)*, 323
armies of, 304
freedom seekers in, 295–96
Lincoln on, 301
policy on Black soldiers and freedom, 298–301
state reentry into, 352
Union, labor. *See* Labor unions
Union League, 356
Union Missionary Society, 272
Unionism, interracial, 480–81
United Automobile Workers (UAW)
Black members in Detroit, 519
Black workers and, 519
United Federation of Teachers (UFT), 650
United House of Prayer for All People, 479
United Nations, Malcolm X on African Americans at, 598
United Negro and Allied Veterans of America, 551
United Public Workers of America, 550
United Service Organizations (USO), Black women and, 511
United States
African Americans in (1770 and 1800), 149*(m)*
enslaved Africans in, 60
United States v. Reynolds (1914), 420
United Steelworkers of America v. Weber (1979), 644
Universal Negro Improvement Association (UNIA), 449–52
Universal suffrage. *See also* Voting and voting rights
male, in post-Civil War South, 354
for white males, 254
woman suffrage and, 370–75
Universities. *See* Colleges and universities
University of Pittsburgh, 708
University of Sankore, 21*(i)*, 23
Up from Slavery (Washington), 408, 450
"Upbuilding of Black Durham, The" (Du Bois), 401
Upland cotton, 169
Uplift
Black responsibility for, after Civil War, 368
as Du Bois's ideology, 410
free Black, 259, 261, 264
programs for, 394
Washington on, 416
Upper California, 273
Upper class, Black, 683
Upper Egypt, 10, 13
Upper South. *See also* South
African American movement to Lower South from, 215, 216*(m)*
crops in, 210*(m)*
manumission in, 147, 168
migration from, 175
Upper Volta River, 24
Uprisings. *See* Resistance; Revolts and rebellions
Urban areas. *See also* Cities
Black communities in, 397–401, 571–72
Black migration to, 609
crisis in, 610*(i)*
gender balance in Black communities, 256
radicalism in, 617
in South, 175, 397–401
white flight from, 609
Urban League. *See* National Urban League
Urban renewal, 609, 610*(i)*
Urban sociology, 446
U.S. Colored Troops
beginnings of, 307
disbanding of, 361
families and, 339
flag of, 299*(i)*
inequities faced by, 309–10
in major Civil War battles, 311
recruitment for, 309–10
USA Today, 709
Utah, 273

Vagrancy laws, after emancipation, 346
Van Wagenen, Maria and Isaac, 182
Vann, Robert L., 478
Variety Plantation, Louisiana, 233

Velázquez, Diego, 43
Veney, Bethany, "Narrative of Bethany Veney, a Slave Woman, 1889," 244–46
Vermont, abolition of slavery in, 164, 181
Vesey, Denmark, 218–20, 219(*v*)
Veterans
  Blacks disqualified from GI Bill after World War II, 530
  race riots after World War I and, 443
  after Revolution, 147–50
Veterans Administration (VA)
  GI Bill and, 530
  housing loans from, 568
Vicksburg, surrender of, 311
Vietnam War, 613–17
  Black power during, 615, 616(*i*)
  costs of, 615
"View Taken from Bain on the Coast of Guinea, . . . A," 41(*i*)
Vigilance committees, in North, 275
Vigilantes
  after Civil War, 358
  mob justice by, 419
Villard, Oswald Garrison, 414
Villenage (serfdom), 77
Violence. *See also* Punishment; Race riots
  against African Americans in World War II, 531
  anti-Black (1919), 443, 446
  Black families and, 619
  against Black soldiers, 362
  in cities, 618–19
  against Civil Rights movement activists, 554–56, 555(*v*), 560–64, 567, 586(*v*)
  by FBI, 639
  hip-hop culture and, 660–62
  in New York City, 571
  by police, 571, 618–19
  in World War II military, 509–13
Virginia. *See also* Piedmont
  Bacon's Rebellion in, 83
  Black patriots in, 138
  Black population of, 83
  chattel slavery in, 80
  Civil War and, 297, 298
  enslavement in, 80, 122, 177–80
  evangelicalism in, 129
  first African Americans in, 75–76
  Gabriel's rebellion in, 177–80
  government of, 83
  importation of enslaved people to, 75–76
  Jamestown colony in, 77
  legal code on Black religious observance, 224
  manumission for former soldiers in Revolutionary War, 147
  mulatto children in, 82(*i*)
  petitions for freedom in, 133–34
  slave revolts and, 105
  tobacco in, 79(*i*), 80
  white servitude in, 80
Virginia Company, 77
Virginia General Assembly, streetcar segregation mandated by, 400
Virginia Industrial School for Colored Girls, 399
Virginia legal code, on Black religious observance, 224
Virginia Normal and Collegiate (Industrial) Institute, 399
Virginia Passenger and Power Company, segregated streetcars of, 400
Virginia play, 205
Virginia State Federation of Colored Women's Clubs, 400
Virginia Union, 399
Vista Equity Partners, 682
Visual arts. *See also* Art(s)
  of Aaron Douglas, 455
Vocational education
  at Hampton Institute, 348–50
  liberal arts education *vs.,* 348–50
Vocational-industrial curriculum model, in colleges and universities, 348–50
Volunteers in Service to America (VISTA), 611
Voodoo, 343
Voter photo ID laws, 711
Voting and voting rights
  anti-Black rules for, 388–89
  Black post-emancipation, 352, 356
  for Blacks, 254–55, 590
  after Civil War, 354, 366–67
  Fourteenth Amendment and, 370
  grandfather clauses, 388, 521
  for men, 370
  myth of corrupt Black voter and, 388
  in 1948 election, 552
  in North, 438
  property requirements and, 366
  Republican requirements for (2012), 704
  as SCLC goal, 562
  Supreme Court change for states and, 704
  universal white male suffrage and, 254
  for women (and Black women), 367, 637
  in World War II, 521–23
Voting Rights Act (1965), 603, 608, 637, 639, 651, 704, A-18–A-19
  extension of, 639
  Republican opposition to, 639
  Supreme Court ruling and, 704

Wade-Davis Bill (1864), 317
Wages
  of Black teachers, 261
  for Black workers, 365
Wagner Act, 476, 480
Wald, Lillian, 414
Walker, Alice, 647
Walker, C. J. (Madame), 439
Walker, David, 218, 221–23, 261
  Walker's Appeal . . . to the Coloured Citizens of the World, 221, 222(*i*), 266
Walker, George, 401, 403(*i*)
Walker, Maggie L., 400
  as first Black woman bank president, 398
Walker, Margaret, 486
Walker, Quock, 147
Walker, William, 310
Walker Clubs, 439
Walker's Appeal . . . to the Coloured Citizens of the World (Walker), 221, 221(*i*), 266
Wallace, George C., 564, 573, 638, 641
Wallace, Henry, 552
Wallace, Michele, 647
Walls, Josiah T., 355(*i*)
War. *See specific battles and wars; specific wars*
War Department, on World War II racial violence, 512
War Manpower Commission, 519
War of 1812, Blacks in, 191–92
War of Jenkins's Ear, Fort Mose destroyed in, 102
War on drugs, 642–43, 689
War on Poverty, 607, 611, 616
  Community Action Programs and, 618
Ward, Herbert, 518
Ward, Jackson, 397, 398, 401
Warden, Donald, 595
Warren, Earl, *Brown* decision and, 554
Washington, Booker T., 408–10
  accommodationism of, 405, 410
  Atlanta Compromise speech by, 410, A-24–A-26
  Bailey v. Alabama and, 420
  on Black soldiers discharged by Roosevelt, Theodore, 407
  criticism of, 410
  Du Bois and, 412
  Garvey and, 450
  on New Negro, 446
  portrait of, 411(*i*)
  Tuskegee Institute and, 348
  on uplift, 416
  on vocational *vs.* liberal arts training, 348, 350
  wife of, 393
Washington, D.C
  desegregation of streetcars in, 366
  March on Washington for Jobs and Freedom (1963), 568, 574–78, 576(*i*)
  March on Washington Movement (1941) and, 507, 518
  New Negro arts movement in, 453
  September 11, 2001 attack and, 691
Washington, George, Black soldiers and, 138
Washington, Harold, 677–78
Washington, Kerry, 681
Washington, Madison, 224
Washington, Margaret Murray, 393
"Washington's Runaway Slave, 1845" (Judge), 202–3
Watch Meeting-Dec. 31st-Waiting for the Hour (Carlton), 333(*v*)
Watergate scandal, 641
Watkins, Frances Ellen. *See* Harper, Frances Ellen Watkins
Watkins, Lucille, on Jack Johnson, 400
Watts neighborhood (Los Angeles), 571
  riot in, 618

Waud, A. R., *First Vote, The,* 375–76*(v)*
WAVES. *See* Women Accepted for Volunteer Emergency Service
"We Can't Breathe": 2014, 2020, 725*(v)*
"We Shall Overcome" (song), 581
"We Wear the Mask" (Dunbar), 404
Weapons, for local law enforcement, 724*(v)*
Wears, Isaiah C., 326
  "Evil Injustice of Colonization, The," 328–29*(d)*
Weaver, Robert C., 477, 478
Webb, Chick, 489
Weber case, 644
Webster, Daniel, 225
Wedding of Enslaved People, A, 232*(i)*
Weddings. *See also* Marriage
  mass, 340
Weems, Charlie, 472, 482*(i)*
Welfare
  politics and, 685
  protests about, 617
  Reagan and, 642
  stereotypes of recipients, 648
  women on, 647
Welfare queen, Reagan on, 642
Wells-Barnett, Ida B., 439
  desegregation of streetcars and, 381
  lynching and, 381, 391–93
  in Memphis, 381, 397
  on migration, 405
  NACW and, 394
  Niagara movement and, 414
  on political equality, 405
  portrait of, 392*(i)*
Wesley, Cynthia, 576*(i)*
West
  Blacks in, 257, 361–63, 364*(v)*, 405–7, 515
  racism in, 568–71
  school segregation in, 413*(m)*
  slavery in, 181, 272–74
West, Kanye, 693
West Africa
  African American colonization in, 193
  African Americans from, 3
  Bantu-speaking people of, 9
  coastal region in, 46, 50, 53–55
  Delany on emigration to, 281
  domestication of plants in, 8
  enslaved people from, 46
  Europe separation from, 39
  Ghana, 15–18
  history of, 13
  iron-making in, 13
  kinship affiliations in, 24–25
  medieval empires of, 15–23, 16*(m)*
  peoples of, 13–14
  Portuguese exploration in, 39–40
  religions from, 58, 88
  in 16th century, 23–28
  slave raids in, 40
  slavery in, 27–28, 38
  trans-Saharan trade of, 15, 16*(m)*
  treaties with Portugal in, 40
West Asia, 11
West Coast
  African American migration to, 513
  Black population of, 515
  union policies on, 519
"West End Blues" (Armstrong), 457
West India Company (Dutch), 94, 95
West Indies
  Blacks from, 408
  British, 145
  sugar colonies in, 99, 145
West Point, Blacks in, 362
Westall, Richard, "View Taken from Bain . . . A," 41*(i)*
Western world, white supremacy in, 386
Westward expansion, slavery and, 172–75, 272–74
"What to the Slave Is the Fourth of July?" (Douglass), 290–91
Wheatley, John, 31*(d)*
Wheatley, Phillis, 3, 128–29, 128*(i)*, 153
  "Letter to the Reverend Samson Occom," 155
  "On Being Brought from Africa to America," 3, 31–32
  "Poem to the Earl of Dartmouth, A," 154
  support for American Revolution by, 132–33
Wheeldin, Don, 568
Whig Party
  antislavery wing of, 270
  end of, 278
White, George Henry, 389, 419, 439
White, George L., 349
White, Walter, 443, 453, 478, 492, 506
White Brotherhood, 359
White Citizens' Councils, 570
White flight, 609
White House, African American dressmaker in, 316
White Lion (Dutch warship), African cargo on, 75
White male suffrage, 254
"White man's burden," 386
White nationalism, 710
White primary, racist policies and, 388
White suburbs, desegregation of, 656
White supremacy, 254–55
  in Alabama, 589
  campaigns for, 386*(i)*
  ideologies of, 386–87
  reinforcement through Social Darwinism, 387
White women. *See* Whites; Women
Whitefield, George, 130
Whites. *See also* Blackface; Minstrel shows
  as abolitionists, 264, 272
  African American soldiers and, 440–41
  African colonization and, 193
  on African religious traditions, 123
  attitudes of supremacy, 255
  biracial people and, 682
  Black education and, 189
  Black marriages with, 92
  on Black workers, 608
  on Blackness, 165
  and Blacks in agrarian protests, 389
  Boston Massacre and, 136
  Chicago housing integration and, 439
  Civil Rights movement resistance by, 562–67
  competition for jobs with Blacks, 256
  desegregation and, 649
  on differences from Blacks, 685
  distribution of (1680), 78*(m)*
  emancipation and, 313
  enslaved people accused of killing, 227
  era of common man for, 254
  expelled from SNCC, 604
  former Confederate land for, 344
  in Harlem nightclubs, 456
  Hurricane Katrina and, 692–94
  in Louisiana, 99
  migration to backcountry, 169
  naturalization for, 181
  New York African Free School and, 189
  political control of South by, 360
  population increase of, 256
  in post-Civil War Democratic Party, 358
  racial hostility, 190–91
  as runaway servants, 80
  schools for, 261
  as servants, 80, 81
  in South, 281
  Tuskegee Institute funded by, 409
  in Virginia, 180
Whitney, Eli, 168
Widows, in Black communities, 256, 259
Wilberforce, William, Canadian community named after, 255
Wilberforce University, 261
Wilding, 691
Wiley, George, 618
Wilkins, Frederick (Shadrach Minkins), 276
Wilkins, Roy, 575
Williams, Bert, 401, 403*(i)*
Williams, Eugene, 472, 482*(i)*
Williams, Fannie Barrier, 439
  in NACW, 394
  New Negro and, 446
Williams, Henry Sylvester, 412, 488
Williams, Robert, 554, 567, 594
Williams, Rose, 236
Williams, Yancey, 507
Williams v. Mississippi, 389
Wilmington Insurrection
  in Chesnutt book, 404
  interracial relationships and, 389
Wilmot, David, 273
Wilmot Proviso, 273
Wilson, Darren, 719
Wilson, Harriet E., 266
Wilson, Lionel, 646
Wilson, Maggie, 440
Wilson, Woodrow, World War I and, 439
Windsor, Ontario, African Americans in, 251
Winfrey, Oprah, 681
Wisconsin, Fugitive Slave Law (1850) challenged by, 274

Wolcott, Marion Post, 495
  "Negroes Jitterbugging in a Juke Joint on Saturday Afternoon, Clarksdale, Mississippi Delta, 1939," 500–501, 501*(i)*
Wolof people, 60
Woman suffrage, 439
  Black rights and, 367, 370
  male support for, 271
  universal suffrage and, 370–75
Woman's Era (Black women's newspaper), 393
"Woman's Right to Vote, Early 1870s" (Cary), 374–75
Women. *See also* Black women; Gender
  in abolition movement, 271
  as activists, 439
  affirmative action and, 641
  in American Anti-Slavery Society, 271
  Black and white in World War II, 503–4
  Black Panthers and, 645
  campaigns against segregated seating by, 366
  childbearing by, 230
  in church leadership, 341–44
  in Civil Rights movement, 555–56
  in Civil War North relief societies, 316
  classification as workers, 233
  in defense industries, 515–16
  Fifteenth Amendment and, 367
  flight from Confederate control, 316
  as folk religion leaders, 343
  free Black employment and, 188
  in Haitian Revolution, 173*(i)*
  in Jim Crow era, 393–96
  jobs for Black, 654
  labor of, 395
  Malcolm X and, 596–97
  March on Washington (1963) and, 575
  #MeToo movement, 712
  in Middle Passage, 57
  National Association of Colored Women and, 435
  in newly freed families, 341–42
  #SayHerName movement, 712, 722–23
  sexual abuses of enslaved, 236
  support for, 233
  voting rights for, 439
  in war industries, 516*(i)*
  in World War II military, 511
Women Accepted for Volunteer Emergency Service (WAVES), 511
Women of color. *See also* Black women
  solidarity of, 648
Women's Army Corps (WAC)
  Black women in, 511
  in Fort Devens strike, 528
Women's Political Council, 556–57
Women's rights, Truth on, 268
Women's rights convention, in Seneca Falls, New York, 271
Wood, Elizabeth, 550
Woodberry, Julia, 238
Woods, Tiger, 681, 683
Woodson, Carter G., 448–49, 449*(i)*
Woodson, Lewis, 262
Woolworth's lunch counter protests, 561–62
Work. *See* Labor; Workers
Workday, of enslaved people, 88
Workers. *See also* Enslaved people; Labor; Labor unions; Slavery
  African Americans as, 315*(v)*
  Black, 313, 432, 681
  Black *vs.* white, 187–89
  Black women during Civil War, 326
  in cotton fields, 237*(v)*
  fair wages for, 365
  free Blacks as, 175
  Taft-Hartley Act and, 550
  women classified as, 233
Working class
  Black, in early 21st century, 680
  white, as Reagan supporters, 642
Works Progress Administration (WPA), 242, 246, 485, 488, 515
World Trade Center, September 11, 2001 attack on, 691
World War I
  African Americans and, 440–41
  Black radicals on, 440
  Black workers for northern industries during, 433
  Blacks in, 440–41
  Hell Fighters, 440
  New Negro after, 445–57
  race riots after, 443
  victory parade after, 441
World War II
  African American migration during, 513–14
  African American responses to, 506–9
  African Americans in, 503–4, 506–9
  Allied and Axis powers in, 505
  Black women in, 503–4
  citizenship rights struggle during, 520–31
  Civil Rights movement after, 553–54
  jobs in, 513–16
  race riots during, 512, 516–17
  as turning point, 525
  United States in, 505–6
  violence and discrimination in military during, 509–13
World's Fair
  in Chicago (1893), 392, 488
  in Paris (1900), 386, 412
  in St. Louis (1904), 386
Worthy, William, 595
WPA. *See* Works Progress Administration
Wright, Andy, 472, 482*(i)*
Wright, Jeremiah, 695
Wright, LeRoy, 472, 482*(i)*
Wright, Margaret, 525
Wright, Richard, 486
Writers. *See also* Literature
  Black, 403
  in Harlem Renaissance, 453

Yeardley, George, 75
Yordan, Philip, 527
Yorktown, Cornwallis at, 144
Yoruba, 25
"You Cannot Kill the Working Class, 1934" (Herndon), 498–99
Young, Robert Alexander, 266
Young, Whitney, 575

Zaria, 25
"Zero tolerance" policy, 690
Zimmerman, George, 701, 706–7, 719*(d)*, 730*(d)*
Zoning, for segregation, 655
Zoos. *See* Human zoos
Zoot suit riots, 516
Zwerg, James, 562